ENGINEERING GRAPHICS ESSENTIALS

WITH AUTOCAD 2027 INSTRUCTION

Kirstie Plantenberg
University of Detroit Mercy

SDC
PUBLICATIONS

SDC Publications
P.O. Box 1334
Mission, KS 66222
913-262-2664
www.SDCpublications.com
Publisher: Stephen Schroff

ISBN-13: 978-1-63057-814-5
ISBN-10: 1-63057-814-2

Printed and bound in the United States of America.

PREFACE

Engineering Graphics Essentials with AutoCAD® 2027 Instruction is specifically designed to be used in a 1 or 2 credit introduction to engineering graphics course. It covers the main topics of engineering graphics, including tolerancing and fasteners, and gives engineering students a basic understanding of how to create and read engineering drawings.

This text is designed to encourage students to interact with the instructor during lecture. It has many exercises that require student participation.

In this new edition, the subjects are broken up into a reading and a creating chapter. For example, Chapter 3 is Reading Orthographic Projection and Chapter 4 is Creating Orthographic Projections. This has been done to give instructors more flexibility on how and when they want to introduce the materials. You can decide to cover all the reading chapters and then go back and cover the creating materials. Or, you can go through the book in sequential order.

Instructor Resources

PowerPoint Lecture and Video Material

PowerPoint lecture and video materials accompany the *Engineering Graphics Essentials with AutoCAD Instruction* text. The presentations cover the entire book. For each chapter of the book, there is one PowerPoint lecture file to be used during lecture, and several videos. Students have access to all the videos. This allows you to run an online course very easily or have the students use the videos for review.

Solution Manual

A PDF solution manual file accompanies the *Engineering Graphics Essentials with AutoCAD Instruction* text. There are solutions to the questions and the end of the chapter problem sets.

Student Supplements

Your purchase of *Engineering Graphics Essentials with AutoCAD Instruction* includes access to a rich collection of online, independent learning materials. These supplements have been completely redesigned for this edition to provide a more interactive and effective learning experience. Presented in a modern video course interface, the material is now accessed online by redeeming the unique access code printed on the front cover of your book or provided with your eBook purchase. The new format is focused on clear, video-based instruction. The typical learning path for each chapter includes:

- **Video Lectures:** For each section of the textbook, the author provides a detailed video lecture, guiding you through the core concepts and examples.
- **Interactive Exercises:** Following each video, you can test your comprehension with an interactive quiz. These exercises are designed to help you master the material, and you can retake them as many times as you wish.

- **Supplemental Problem Solutions:** Additional problem solutions are provided to further support your learning and practice.
- **AutoCAD Tutorial files:** Some tutorials require a start file which are supplied.
- **AutoCAD Videos:** Tutorial videos are supplied to allow the student to complete the tutorials using the book or videos.

Within the online platform, you can easily navigate through all the content, allowing you to select the specific video or exercise you want to review at any time.

Have engineering graphics questions? Please e-mail Kirstie at: plantenk@gmail.com

Have an AutoCAD question? Please e-mail Summer at: rayesssummer@gmail.com

Found a mistake? Please e-mail a detailed description of the errata to: The publisher or plantenk@gmail.com

All e-mails should include
- Title of the book
- Edition of the book
- Page related to the question
- Problem related to the question

This book is dedicated to family.

TABLE OF CONTENTS

CHAPTER 1

INTRODUCTION TO ENGINEERING DRAWINGS

CHAPTER OUTLINE

CHAPTER SUMMARY

In this chapter you will learn the importance of engineering drawings, how they relate to design and manufacturing, and the general arrangement and placement of the components on a print. In addition, the information that is contained within the various blocks (e.g., title block) will be described.

1.1) DESIGN

Design is a strategic approach to problem solving. The design process may involve considerable research, thought, modeling, adjustments, and redesign. In the field of Engineering, the design process leads to the creation of a plan for the construction of an object or system. These plans define things such as the specifications, parameters, costs, processes, and constraints of the system. Designing often necessitates considering the aesthetics, functionality, economics, and sociopolitical aspects of the system. In mechanical engineering, the designed object is most likely a manufactured part or machine that performs a required function. In the field of electrical engineering, the design could be a computer algorithm or a circuit. In civil engineering, the design could be subdivision or bridge plans. No matter what kind of design is required, you will be required to communicate this design to someone. Your audience may vary from your classmates, instructor, boss, or potential investors.

1.2) COMMUNICATING A DESIGN

Why would you want to communicate your design? You want to develop your communication skills so that you can inspire, attract, and motivate people to respond to your design. Methods of design communications can be written or oral. Written communication could be in the form of reports, memos, or drawings. Design communication through drawings may be as simple as a sketch or as complex as a computer-generated technical drawing.

1.2.1) Sketching

A sketch is a quickly executed freehand drawing that is not intended to be a drawing used to manufacture a finished part. It is only used to express an idea. Sketching is a useful skill that may be used to quickly convey an idea in a design meeting or to have as a record of an idea for later use like the skateboard and wheelchair shown in Figure 1.2-1. Maybe you want to discuss a new shape for the skateboard's deck or how you would attach a retractable table to a wheelchair. It is much easier when you have a picture to aid in your description.

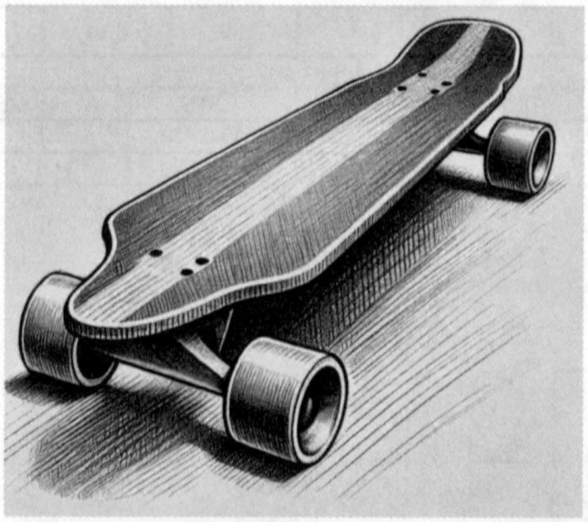 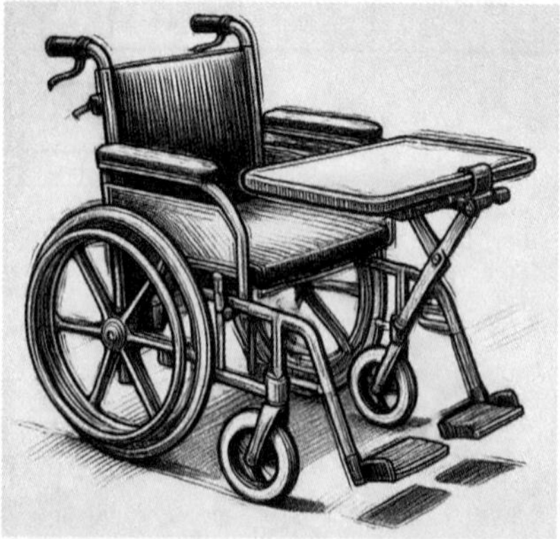

Figure 1.2-1: Hand sketches used to aid design idea communication

1.2.2) Technical Drawing

Technical drawing may be used as both a noun and a verb. **Technical drawing is the process of creating an engineering drawing.** *Technical drawing* is governed by a set of rules or standards that allow you to create an *engineering drawing* that is understandable and unambiguous.

A technical drawing is a drawing or a set of drawings that communicate an idea, design, schematic, or model. They are often used to show the look and function of an object or system. Each engineering field has its own type of technical drawings. For example, electrical engineers draw circuit schematics and circuit board layouts, civil engineers draw plans for bridges and road layouts, and mechanical engineers draw parts and assemblies that need to be manufactured. This book focuses on the technical drawings of parts and systems for manufacture. This is not to say that only students in a mechanical engineering curriculum will benefit from learning the skills necessary to read and create part drawings. It benefits everyone from the weekend carpenter who wants to draw plans for his/her new bookshelf to the electrical engineer who wants to analyze electrical component cooling using a CAE (i.e., computer aided engineering) program. Technical drawing teaches you how to visualize and see all sides of an object in your mind. Being able to visualize in your mind will help you in several aspects of critical thinking.

Engineering drawings, a type of technical drawing, are used to fully and clearly define all manufacturing requirements for an engineered part or system. It communicates all the needed information from the engineer who designed the part to the machinist who will make it. The process of producing an engineering drawing is often referred to as technical drawing or drafting. The person that generates the drawing may be called the designer or drafter. Before the advent of computers, copies of an engineering drawing were duplicated through the process of blueprinting. Therefore, engineering drawings are often referred to as prints. Figure 1.2-2 shows one example of an engineering drawing.

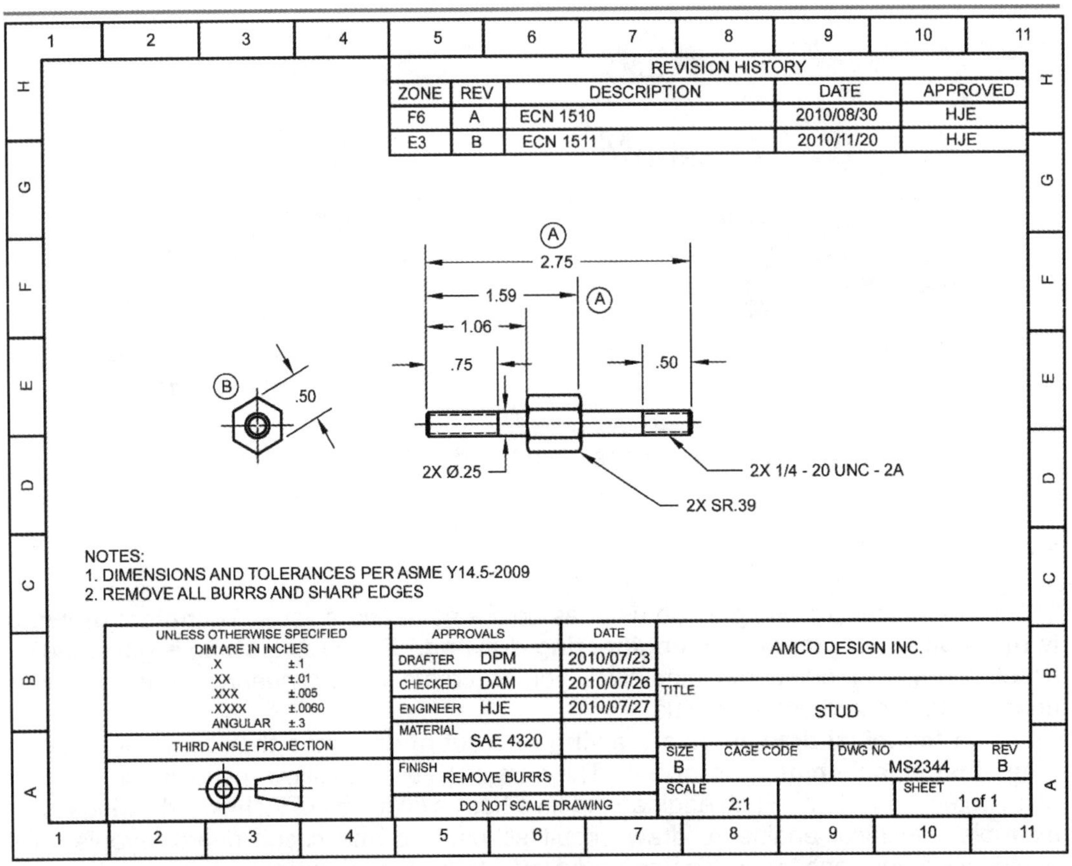

Figure 1.2-2: Engineering drawing example

1.2.3) Computer-Aided Drawing

Today, the mechanics of drafting have been automated through the use of **computer-aided drawing or design** (i.e., CAD) systems. Computer-aided drawing or design refers to computer software that allows an engineer to create drawings of their design ideas. There are two types of CAD systems used to create technical drawings. The first type allows you to draw two-dimensional drawings from scratch. The other types, and more prevalent today, are programs that start from a three-dimensional model and automatically create the two-dimensional drawing from the model. Communicating ideas is critical for developing the best possible solution and solid models allow you to show a three-dimensional version of your system instead of the traditional two-dimensional drawing. Many people are able to more quickly understand the idea if they are shown a three-dimensional representation of the design.

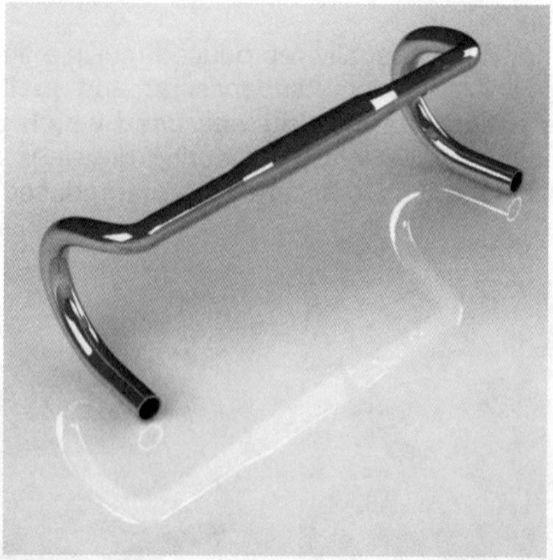

Figure 1.2-3: Three-dimensional CAD model of a dropdown bicycle handlebar

1.3) STANDARDS

An engineering drawing is a legal document because it communicates all the needed information about what is wanted to the people who will expend resources turning the idea into reality. Therefore, if the resulting product is wrong, the manufacturer is protected from liability as long as they have faithfully executed the instructions conveyed by the drawing. **Mistakes made by the designer during the drawing phase and manufacturers misreading prints are costly.** This is the biggest reason why the conventions and standards of engineering drawings have evolved over decades toward a very precise and unambiguous state.

In the pursuit of unambiguous communication, engineering drawings often follow certain national and international standards, such as ASME Y14.5M or a group of ISO standards. Standardization also aids with globalization. Standards allow people from different countries who speak different languages to share a common language of engineering drawing.

Standards define how to create an orthographic projection, apply dimensions, symbols use, perspectives, and layout conventions among many other things. This enables the drafter to communicate more concisely by using a commonly understood convention.

1.4) HISTORY OF TECHNICAL DRAWING

For centuries, all engineering drawings were done manually by using pencil and paper. This process took time, precision, and a certain degree of artistic ability. Since the advent of computers, an increasing number of engineering drawings are drawn within the virtual world of a computer-aided design or drawing (i.e., CAD) program. Currently, it is very hard to find any company that still practices manual drafting.

Some of the tools used in manual drafting include pencils, erasers, straightedges, T-square, French curves, triangles, rulers, protractor, compass, and drawing board. The English saying, "Go back to the drawing board.", means to rethink something altogether.

It was inspired by the literal act of discovering design errors and returning to a drawing board to revise the design.

An engineering drawing is usually reproduced multiple times. These copies are distributed to the shop floor, vendors, supervisors, and to the company archives. **Historically, a process called blueprinting was used which produced a copy that was blue in appearance.** This is why engineering drawings are still referred to as blueprints or simply prints. Drawings today are simply reproduced using a plotter, printer, or just shared virtually.

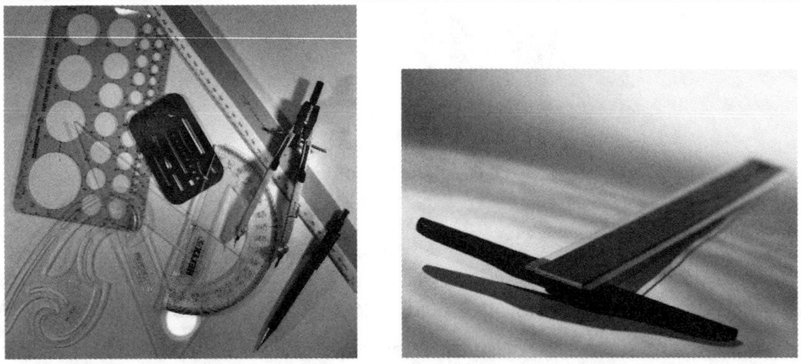

Figure 1.4-1: Drafting implements

1.5) MANUFACTURING

Engineering drawings provide an understanding of how a product will function and be manufactured. Historically, two-dimensional engineering drawings have served as the sole method of transferring information from design into a manufactured part. However, there are always challenges involved in trying to describe a 3D world in a 2D drawing. Many companies are realizing that two-dimensional drawings alone are not sufficient and often lead to design errors and higher manufacturing costs.[1] Recently, 3D solid modeling software have been developed that take the computer drawing or model information and produce a G-code, which is executed by a CNC (i.e., computer numerical control) machine. However, two-dimensional drawings still play an important role in the design process by providing tolerancing, annotations, parts lists and other information that is critical to manufacturing and quality control.[1]

Engineering drawings transform ideas into products and communicate information between engineering and manufacturing. **Engineering drawings give all the information needed to manufacture and inspect the part.**

1.6) ENGINEERING DRAWING FORMAT AND CONTENTS

The drawing format, arrangement, and organization of information within a drawing is controlled by ASME Y14.1 and Y14.1M. A drawing sheet's main elements are the drawing, various blocks, notes and zones as shown in Figure 1.6-1. However, there are other components that are optional and may be included on the drawing sheet. First and foremost, engineering drawings contain all the information needed to make the product. A drawing could be anything from a simple part print to a complex assembly drawing. Note that the drawing format may vary slightly depending on the drawing size and orientation.

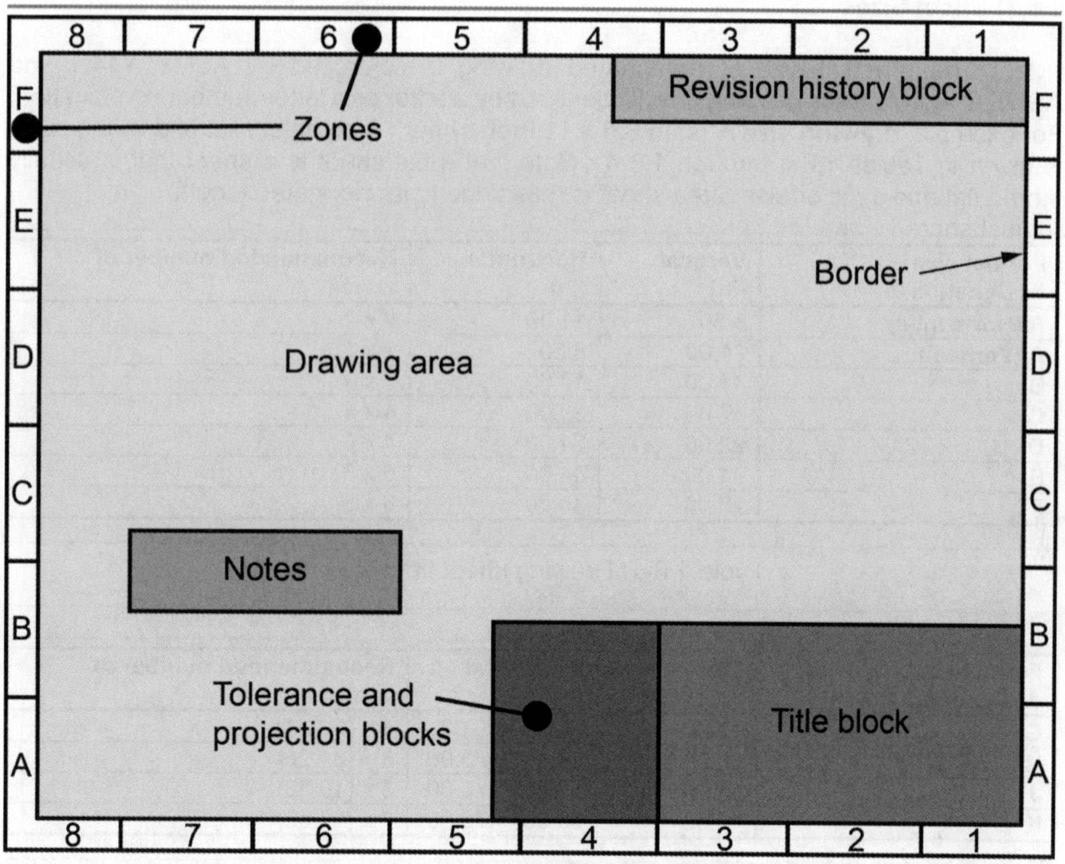

Figure 1.6-1: Engineering drawing format

1.6.1) Sheet Sizes

The physical size of the printed drawing is controlled by ASME Y14.1 and ASME Y14.1M. Each drawing size is identified by a letter or a letter number combination. For example, **drawing size A is an 8.5 x 11 inch sheet**. A complete list of drawing sizes is given in Tables 1.6-1 through 1.6-4. Note that a flat sheet is a sheet that is usually stored flat and a roll or elongated sheet is rolled due to its elongated length.

Format size designation	Vertical (in)	Horizontal (in)	Recommended number of zones
A (Horizontal)	8.50	11.00	2 x 2
A (Vertical)	11.00	8.50	2 x 2
B	11.00	17.00	2 x 4
C	17.00	22.00	4 x 4
D	22.00	34.00	4 x 8
E	34.00	44.00	8 x 8
F	28.00	40.00	6 x 8

Table 1.6-1: Drawing sheet flat sizes [2]

Format size designation	Vertical (in)	Horizontal (in)	Recommended number of zones
G	11.00	22.50 - 90.00	4 x (6 - 24)
H	28.00	44.00 - 143.00	8 x (8 - 26)
J	34.00	55.00 - 176.00	8 x (10.32)
K	40.00	55.00 - 176.00	8 x (10.32)

Table 1.6-2: Drawing sheet roll sizes [2]

Designation	Vertical (mm)	Horizontal (mm)	Recommended number of zones
A0	841	1189	16 x 24
A1	594	841	12 x 16
A2	420	594	8 x 12
A3	297	420	6 x 8
A4	297	210	6 x 4

Table 1.6-3: Basic sheet sizes (metric) [3]

Designation	Vertical (mm)	Horizontal (mm)	Recommended number of zones
A1.0	594	1189	12 x 24
A2.1	420	841	8 x 16
A2.0	420	1189	8 x 24
A3.2	297	594	6 x 12
A3.1	297	841	6 x 16
A3.0	297	1189	6 x 24

Table 1.6-4: Elongated sheet sizes (metric) [3]

1.6.2) Drawing

The most important part of a print is the drawing and the most important part of reading the print is the ability to visualize the part. The drawing area (see Figure 1.6-1) may contain an orthographic projection and a pictorial of the object as shown in Figure 1.6-2. The orthographic projection is a two-dimensional representation of a three-dimensional object. It usually contains three views (e.g., front view, top view, right side view) but it may contain more or less than three. The number of views needed is determined by the complexity of the part. A pictorial is a pseudo 3D drawing. Pictorials are very useful in helping the reader visualize the object.

Dimensions are an important part of the drawing that give the size, shape and finish of the part. Without the dimensions, the part would not be able to be manufactured. Dimensions communicate more than just the size of the part; they also give the manufacturing department an idea of the object's function and important surfaces.

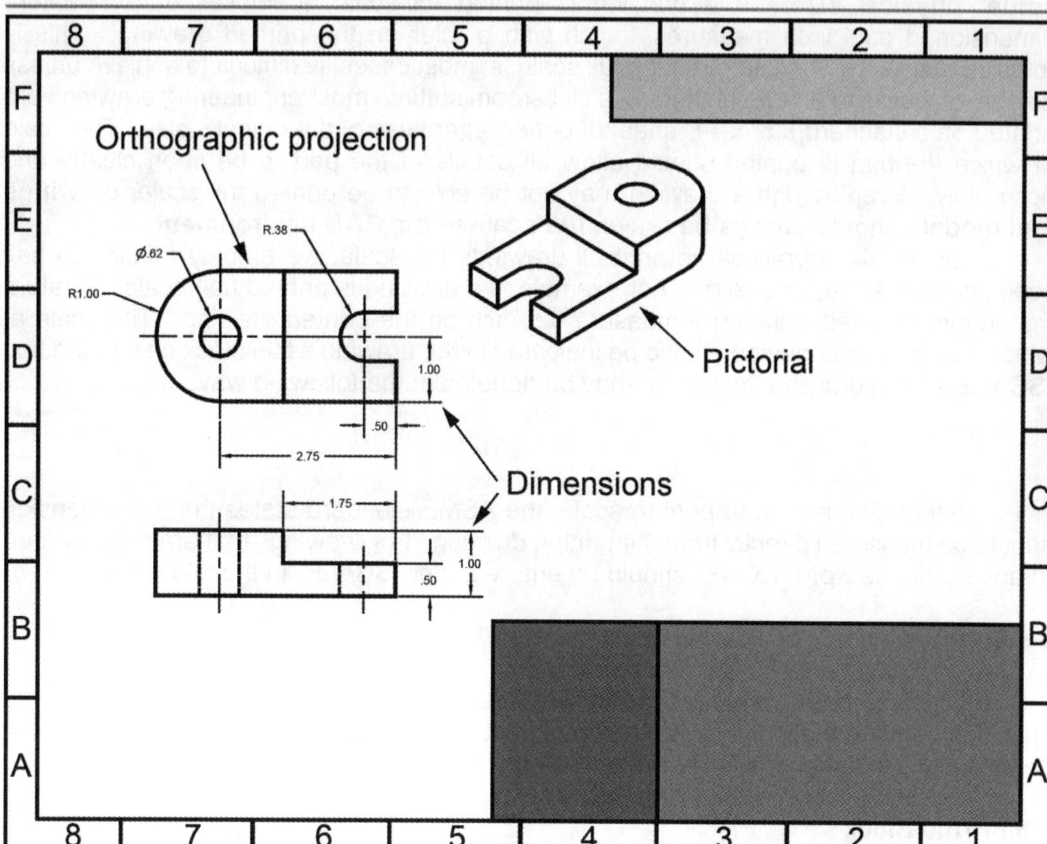

Figure 1.6-2: The drawing component of an engineering drawing

1.6.3) Zoning

The zone letters and numbers are located in the drawing margins outside the border. **The zone's letter-number combinations allow you to indicate a specific location on an engineering drawing.** Zones are similar to how cells are identified in a spread sheet application. For example, zone B6 is located where row B and column 6 intersect (see Figure 1.6-1). On inch drawings, zone sizes are equal, not less than 1 inch, and not more than 5.50 inches. On metric drawings, the zone size selected is equal on the horizontal and the vertical, except that the upper and far left zones may be an odd size to accommodate the size of the sheet.

1.6.4) Scale

The drawing scale expresses the ratio of the object's size as printed to its actual physical size. If a drawing is printed full-scale, it implies that a feature dimensioned as 1 inch measures 1 inch with a ruler on the printed drawing. This is referred to as a 1 to 1 scale. Printing full scale, in most cases, is difficult to achieve unless you have access to a large plotter. In a classroom setting, most engineering drawings are printed on a standard 8.5" x 11" sheet of paper regardless of the object's size. The scale at which the part is printed should allow all details of the part to be seen clearly and accurately. Even though a drawing may not be able to be printed full scale, **drawings and models should always be drawn full scale in the CAD environment.**

Since it is impractical to print all drawings full scale, we employ printing to half scale, quarter-scale, and so on. For example, if a drawing is printed half-scale, a feature that is dimensioned 1 inch will measure 0.5 inch on the printed drawing. The scale at which the drawing is printed should be indicated in the drawing's title block next to the text "SCALE". On a drawing, half-scale may be denoted in the following ways.

1/2 or 1:2 or 0.5

Although it is nice to print to scale, the ASME standard states that no dimension should be measured directly from the printed drawing. For drawings that are not prepared to any scale, the word "NONE" should be entered after "SCALE" in the title block.

1.6.5) Notes

Drawing notes provide information that clarifies a particular requirement or specifies new information necessary to manufacture the object correctly. This concept will be discussed in the chapters on dimensioning.

1.6.6) Title Block

Every engineering drawing should have both a border and a title block. The border defines the drawing area, and the title block gives pertinent information about the part or assembly being drawn. There are several different types of title blocks, but they all contain similar information. The information that is included depends on the drawing type, field of engineering, and viewing audience.

The title block is located in the lower right corner of the sheet as shown in Figure 1.6-1. The information common to all drawings is shown in Figure 1.6-3 where the identification letters refer to the following information. For a more complete explanation, see ASME Y14.100.

A. Company name and address.
B. Drawing title.
C. Drawing number.
D. Sheet revision. This block may be omitted when a revision history block is included.
E. This block may contain sub-blocks such as DRAFTER, CHECKER, and ENGINEER.
F. This block is used for approval by the design activity when different from the source preparing the drawing. This block may be necessary when a contractor-subcontractor condition exists.
G. Approval by an activity other than those described for blocks E and F.
H. Scale of the drawing sheet.
I. DAI (Design activity identification).
J. Drawing size.
K. Actual or estimated weight of the item.
L. Sheet number.

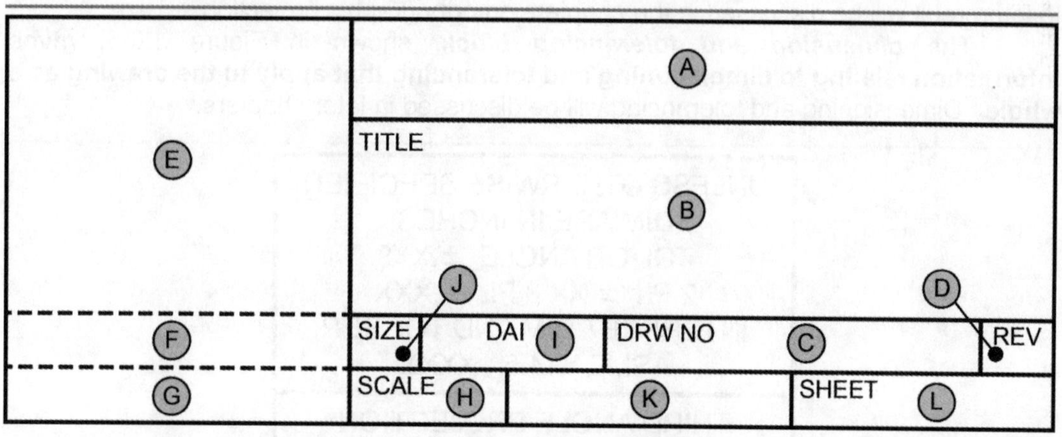

Figure 1.6-3: Title block contents

1.6.7) Revision History Block

The revision history block is used to record changes to the drawing and is located in the upper right corner of the drawing sheet as shown in Figure 1.6-1. The block is extended downward as required. Revisions are necessary when the part is redesigned. The information contained in the revision history block is shown in Figure 1.6-4 where the identification letters refer to the following information. For a more complete explanation, see ASME Y14.100.

A. Specifies the zone location of the revision.
B. The revision letter or number is found in this location.
C. Gives a short description of the change.
D. The revision date is given numerically in order of *year-month-day*. For example, the date, May 31, 2025, would be indicated as 2025-05-31 or 2025/05/31.
E. The initials of the person approving the change.

	REVISION HISTORY			
ZONE	REV	DESCRIPTION	DATE	APPROVED
(A)	(B)	(C)	(D)	(E)

Figure 1.6-4: Revision history block

1.6.8) Tolerance and Projection Blocks

The *tolerance* and *projection blocks* are located to the left of the title block as shown in Figure 1.6-1. **The *angle of projection block* shown in Figure 1.6-5 indicates the projection method that was used to create the drawing.** The two methods of projection are third angle projection and first angle projection. What projection is and how to interpret it will be discussed in the chapters on orthographic projection.

The *dimension and tolerancing block*, shown in Figure 1.6-5, **gives information relating to dimensioning and tolerancing that apply to the drawing as a whole.** Dimensioning and tolerancing will be discussed in later chapters.

UNLESS OTHERWISE SPECIFIED
DIM ARE IN INCHES
TOL ON ANGLE ±.XX°
2 PL ±.XX 3 PL ±.XXX
INTERPRET DIM AND TOL PER
ASME Y14.5 - XXXX

THIRD ANGLE PROJECTION

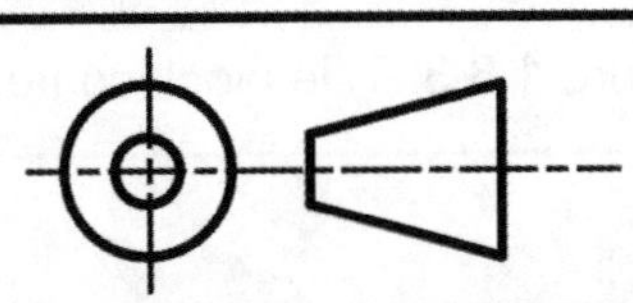

Figure 1.6-5: Tolerance and projection blocks

INTRODUCTION TO ENGINEERING DRAWINGS QUESTIONS – SET 1

Name: ______________________________________ Date: __________

Design and Technical Drawing

Q1-1) Design is a strategic approach to ____________________. (fill in the blank)

Q1-2) The process of creating an engineering drawing is called ______________.

Q1-3) A *technical drawing* is a drawing that may be used to communicate which of the following? (choose all that apply)

a) an idea.
b) a design.
c) information used to manufacture a part.
d) inspection specifications.

Q1-4) CAD stands for … (choose all that apply)

a) computer achieved drafting.
b) computer aided drawing.
c) computer aided design.
d) computer aided development.

Standards and Manufacturing

Q1-5) The two organizations that control the content of engineering drawings.

a) ASME
b) AMCE
c) ISO
d) EAU

Q1-6) Historically, engineering drawings are also called ___________.

a) copies
b) drafting
c) prints
d) details

Drawing Content and Format

Q1-7) The letters and numbers along the margins allowing you to specify a location on the drawing are called _____________.

a) referencing
b) zones
c) mapping
d) celling

Q1-8) This block gives information about the drawing such as *title, sheet size*, and *scale*.

a) Revision history block
b) Dimension and tolerance block
c) Angle of projection block
d) Title block
e) Note

Q1-9) This block gives information about the drawing's modifications.

a) Revision history block
b) Dimension and tolerance block
c) Angle of projection block
d) Title block
e) Note

Q1-10) This block gives information about general dimensions and tolerancing specifications.

a) Revision history block
b) Dimension and tolerance block
c) Angle of projection block
d) Title block
e) Note

INTRODUCTION TO ENGINEERING DRAWINGS QUESTIONS – SET 2

Name: ____ Date: _______________

Q1-11) Mistakes made in misreading a part print are not costly. (True, False)

Q1-12) *Engineering drawings* give all the information needed to ________________ and ________________ the part.

Q1-13) Engineering drawings have the following main areas.

a. Borders & Zones
b. ____________________
c. ____________________
d. Drawing

Q1-14) This block gives information about the drawing's projection method.

a) Revision history block
b) Dimension and tolerance block
c) Angle of projection block
d) Title block
e) Note

Q1-15) What is the size of an A sheet?

a) 8.50” x 11.00”
b) 11.00” x 17.00”
c) 17.00” x 22.00”
d) 22.00” x 34.00”

Q1-16) What is the size of an A4 sheet in mm?

a) 594 x 841
b) 420 x 594
c) 297 x 420
d) 297 x 210

Q1-17) The scale of a drawing is the ratio of the …

a) printed size of the part to its actual size.
b) actual size of the part to its printed size.
c) the part’s size to the sheet size.
d) sheet size to the part’s size.

Q1-18) What scale should a part or model be drawn in the CAD environment?

Q1-19) Standards are a set of ____________ that control how an engineering drawing is presented.

NOTES:

INTRODUCTION TO ENGINEERING DRAWINGS PROBLEMS

Name: ____ Date: ______________

P1-1) Identify the different content areas of an engineering drawing. Put your answers in the white boxes.

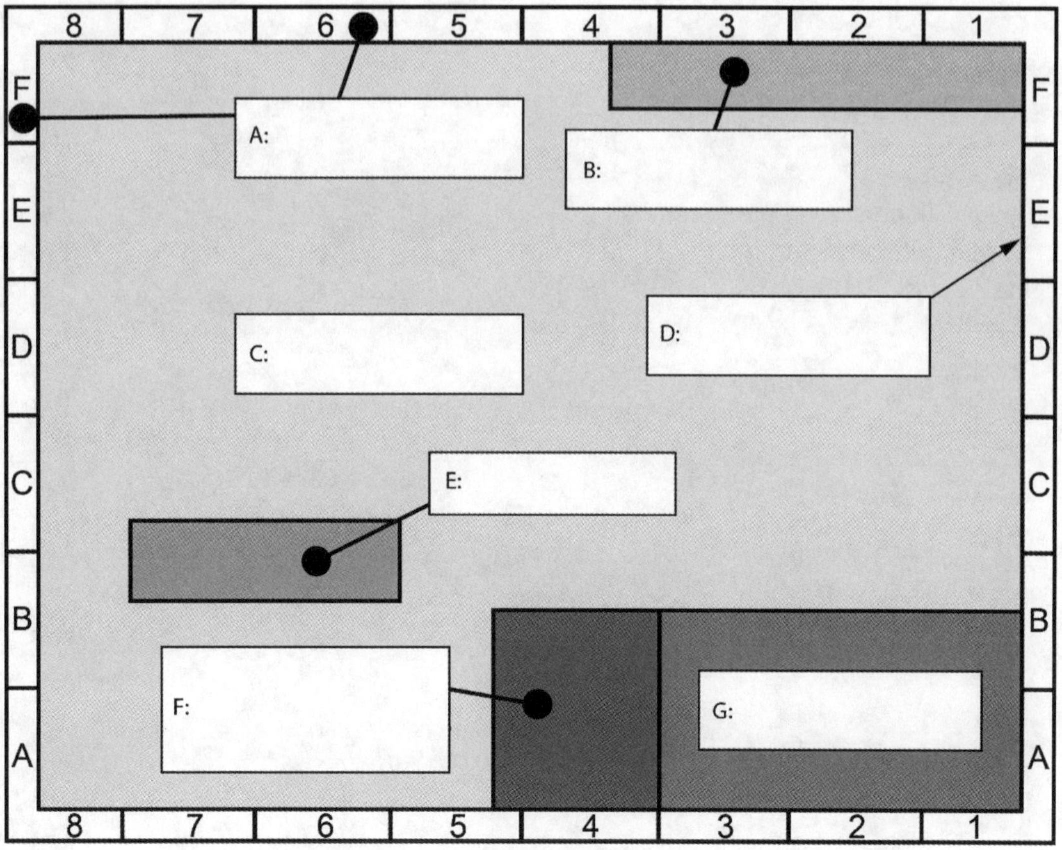

NOTES:

Name: ______________________________________ Date: ____________

P1-2) Given the print shown on the next page, fill in the following information.

Company name	
Print title	
Print number	
Print scale	
Sheet size	
Number of revisions	
Revision A zone location	
Number of sheets	
Material	
Projection method	
Finish requirements	
Approving drafter	
Approving checker	
Approving engineer	
Tolerance for a .XXX dimension	
Number of notes	

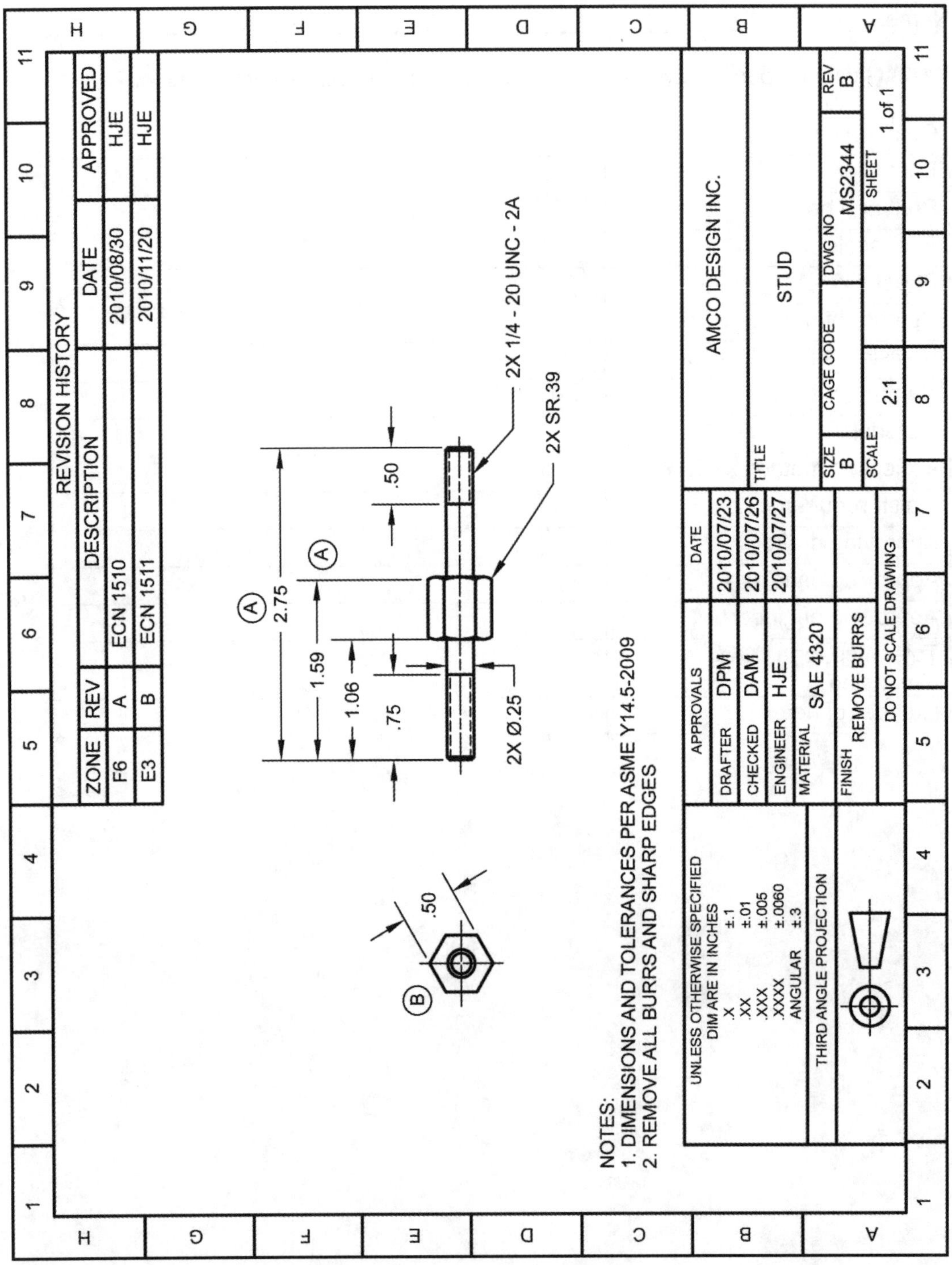
REVISION HISTORY
ZONE | REV | DESCRIPTION | DATE | APPROVED
F6 | A | ECN 1510 | 2010/08/30 | HJE
E3 | B | ECN 1511 | 2010/11/20 | HJE
2X 1/4 - 20 UNC - 2A
2X SR.39
2.75
1.59
1.06
.75
.50
2X Ø.25
A
B
.50
NOTES:
1. DIMENSIONS AND TOLERANCES PER ASME Y14.5-2009
2. REMOVE ALL BURRS AND SHARP EDGES
UNLESS OTHERWISE SPECIFIED
DIM ARE IN INCHES
.X ±.1
.XX ±.01
.XXX ±.005
.XXXX ±.0060
ANGULAR ±.3
THIRD ANGLE PROJECTION
APPROVALS
DATE
DRAFTER DPM 2010/07/23
CHECKED DAM 2010/07/26
ENGINEER HJE 2010/07/27
MATERIAL SAE 4320
FINISH REMOVE BURRS
DO NOT SCALE DRAWING
AMCO DESIGN INC.
TITLE STUD
SIZE B
CAGE CODE
DWG NO MS2344
REV B
SCALE 2:1
SHEET 1 of 1

Name: ______________________________ Date: ________________

P1-3) Given the print shown below, fill in the following information.

Company name	
Print title	
Print number	
Print scale	
Sheet size	
Number of revisions	
Revision A zone location	
Sheet number	
Number of sheets	
Material	
Projection method	
Finish requirements	
Approving drafter	
Approving checker	
Approving engineer	
Tolerance for a .XX dimension	

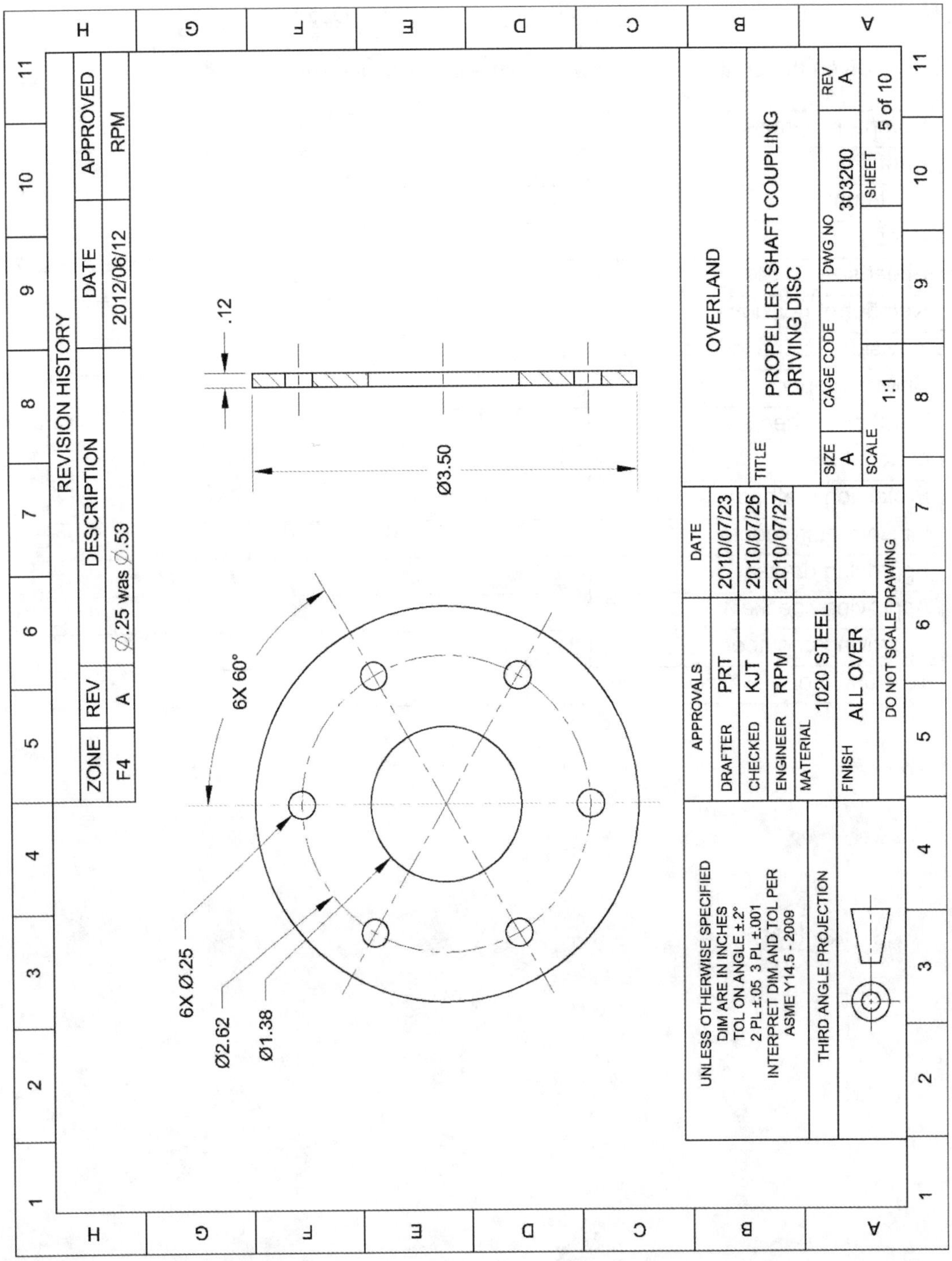
REVISION HISTORY
ZONE
REV
DESCRIPTION
DATE
APPROVED
F4
A
Ø.25 was Ø.53
2012/06/12
RPM
.12
Ø3.50
6X 60°
6X Ø.25
Ø2.62
Ø1.38
UNLESS OTHERWISE SPECIFIED
DIM ARE IN INCHES
TOL ON ANGLE ±.2°
2 PL ±.05 3 PL ±.001
INTERPRET DIM AND TOL PER
ASME Y14.5 - 2009
THIRD ANGLE PROJECTION
APPROVALS
DATE
DRAFTER
PRT
2010/07/23
CHECKED
KJT
2010/07/26
ENGINEER
RPM
2010/07/27
MATERIAL
1020 STEEL
FINISH
ALL OVER
DO NOT SCALE DRAWING
OVERLAND
TITLE
PROPELLER SHAFT COUPLING
DRIVING DISC
SIZE
A
CAGE CODE
DWG NO
303200
REV
A
SCALE
1:1
SHEET
5 of 10

Name: ______________________________ Date: ______________

P1-4) Using the ruler provided, determine the scale that should be indicated in the drawing title block for the following objects.

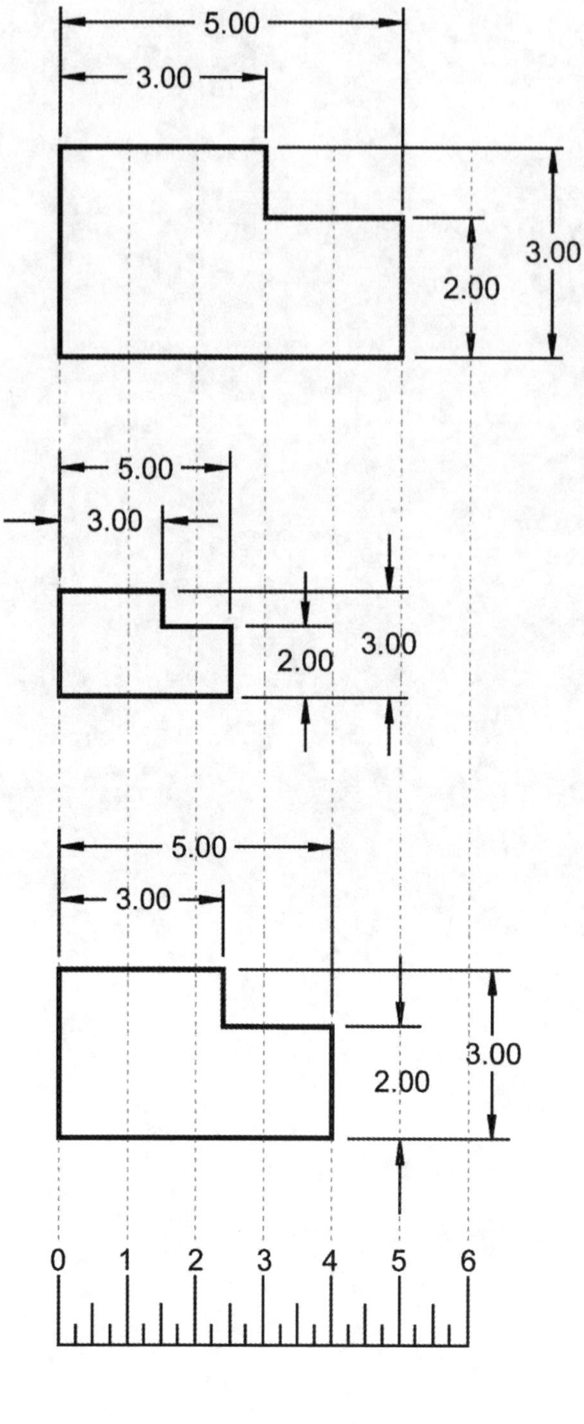

Scale =

Scale =

Scale =

NOTES:

CHAPTER 2

DRAWING IN AUTOCAD®

CHAPTER OUTLINE

CHAPTER SUMMARY

In this chapter you will learn how to navigate through and create drawings within AutoCAD's 2-D drawing workspace. Entities within the AutoCAD® environment are created within a coordinate framework. Objects such as Lines, Circles, Polygons, etc… are created using a set of defining coordinates points. Although this may sound complex, AutoCAD® makes creating professional looking engineering drawings very simple. By the end of this chapter, you will be able to create and edit complex geometries.

2.1) INTRODUCTION

AutoCAD® allows you to visualize, document and share a design idea in either a 2-D or 3-D environment. This chapter will focus on AutoCAD's 2-D drawing capabilities. AutoCAD® gives you the tools to create accurate and professional looking detailed and assembly drawings. Figure 2.1-1 shows a detailed drawing created in AutoCAD's 2-D drawing workspace.

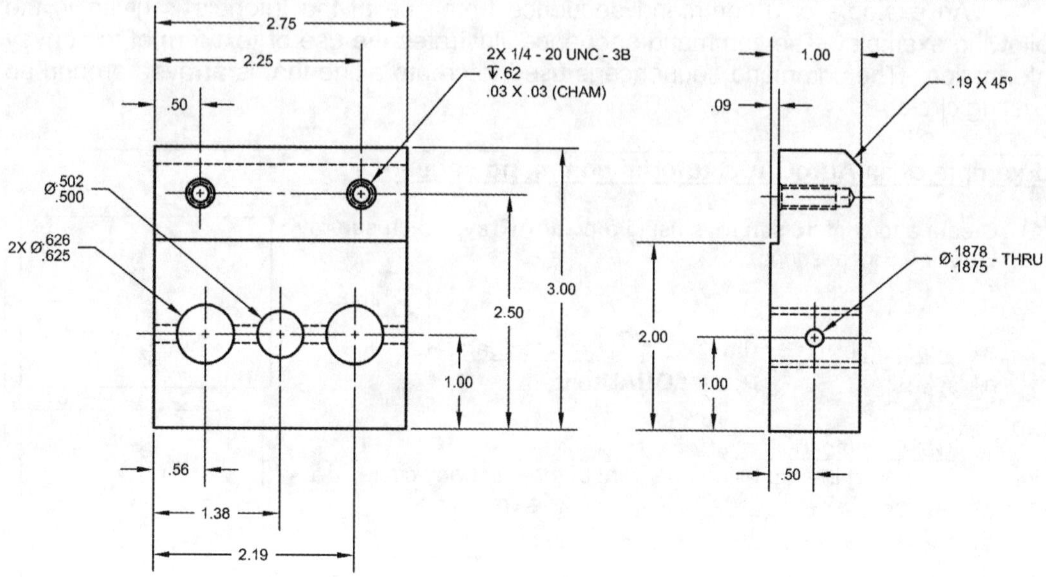

Figure 2.1-1: AutoCAD® drawing example

2.1.1) Navigating through the AutoCAD tutorials

The AutoCAD® tutorials presented in this book have specific objectives which are stated at the beginning. Each tutorial is designed to introduce the user to a particular feature of AutoCAD® or to a set of commands. As you will see, there are several ways to access AutoCAD's commands. For each command sequence, the tutorial will usually state one or two ways to access a command. This doesn't mean that you would not be able to access it in another way.

The format of each tutorial is consistent. For each step, a general statement of what is to be accomplished is given, followed by a command sequence that takes you step by step through the process. Within the tutorials the font, capitalization, and boldness of the text are used to convey information. The text format scheme used in each tutorial is as follows:

- Underlined text: Gives a location of where the command or options should be entered or selected.
- *Italic text:* Gives the name of a window, palette, ribbon, tab, or a field.
- **Bold text:** Text that should be typed in the *Command* window or into a field to access a command. Many AutoCAD commands may be entered in an abbreviated form. The "line" command may be accessed by typing the full word **LINE** or by just typing **L**. Therefore, when a command is written in full within a tutorial contained in this book, only the capitalized letters need to be typed. For example, if you see **ELlipse**, you may type the full word, but you only need to type **EL**.
- ***Bold italic text:*** Represents the name of a command, toggle, button, or icon that should be selected.
- **`Bold Courier font:`** Indicates a key on the keyboard that needs to be pressed.
- Normal text: Gives instructions.
- `Courier font:` Represents AutoCAD prompts within the *Command* window.

An example of a command sequence from one of the tutorials is given in the following example. The command sequence illustrates the use of text format to convey information. The command sequence is used to create a line that is arrayed around an existing circle.

Example of an AutoCAD® tutorial command sequence

1) Create a total of **16** sun rays using a polar **ARray**. Each sun ray **Line** is **0.5** inches long.

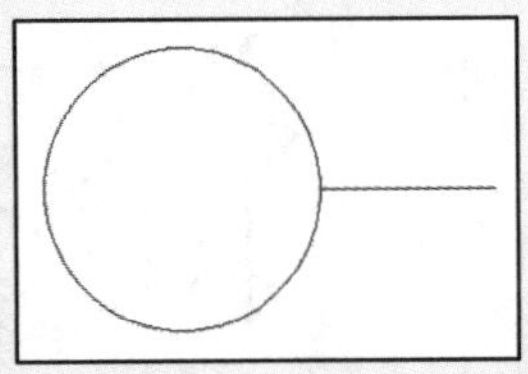

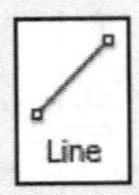

a) Command: **l** or **line** or *Draw* toolbar:

b) `Specify first point:` **QUADrant** or

Object Snap toolbar:
`or` Select the right-side quadrant of the sun body circle.

c) `Specify next point or [Undo]:` **@.5<0**

d) `Specify next point or [Undo]:` **`Enter`**

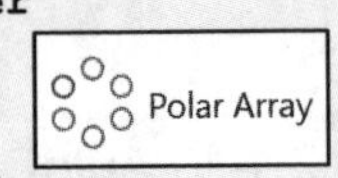

e) Command: **ARray** or *Modify* toolbar:

i. `Select objects:` Select the line.
ii. `Select objects:` **`Enter`**
iii. `Enter array type [Rectangular/PAth/POlar] <Rectangular>:` **PO**
iv. `Specify center point of array or [Base point/Axis of rotation]:` **cen**
v. `or` Select the center of the circle.
vi. `Select grip to edit array or [ASsociative/Base point/Items/Angle between /Fill angle/ROWs/Levels/ROTate items/eXit] <eXit>:` **F**
vii. `Specify the angle to fill (+=ccw, -=cw) or [EXpression] <360>:` **360**
viii. `Select grip to edit array or [ASsociative/Base point/Items/Angle between /Fill angle/ROWs/Levels/ROTate items/eXit] <eXit>:` **I**
ix. `Enter number of items in array or [Expression] <6>:` **16**
x. `Select grip to edit array or [ASsociative/Base point/Items/Angle between /Fill angle/ROWs/Levels/ROTate items/eXit] <eXit>:` **`Enter`**

2.2) AUTOCAD'S WORKSPACES AND USER INTERFACE

AutoCAD® has three predefined workspaces: *Drafting & Annotation*, *3D Basics* and *3D Modeling*. Each workspace allows for easy access to operations that are relevant to the current workspace.

AutoCAD's user interface is workspace dependent. We will focus on the *Drafting & Annotation* workspace in this book. The *Drafting & Annotation* workspace user interfaces are shown in Figure 2.2-1. The important areas of the interfaces are identified and will be discussed in the sections indicated.

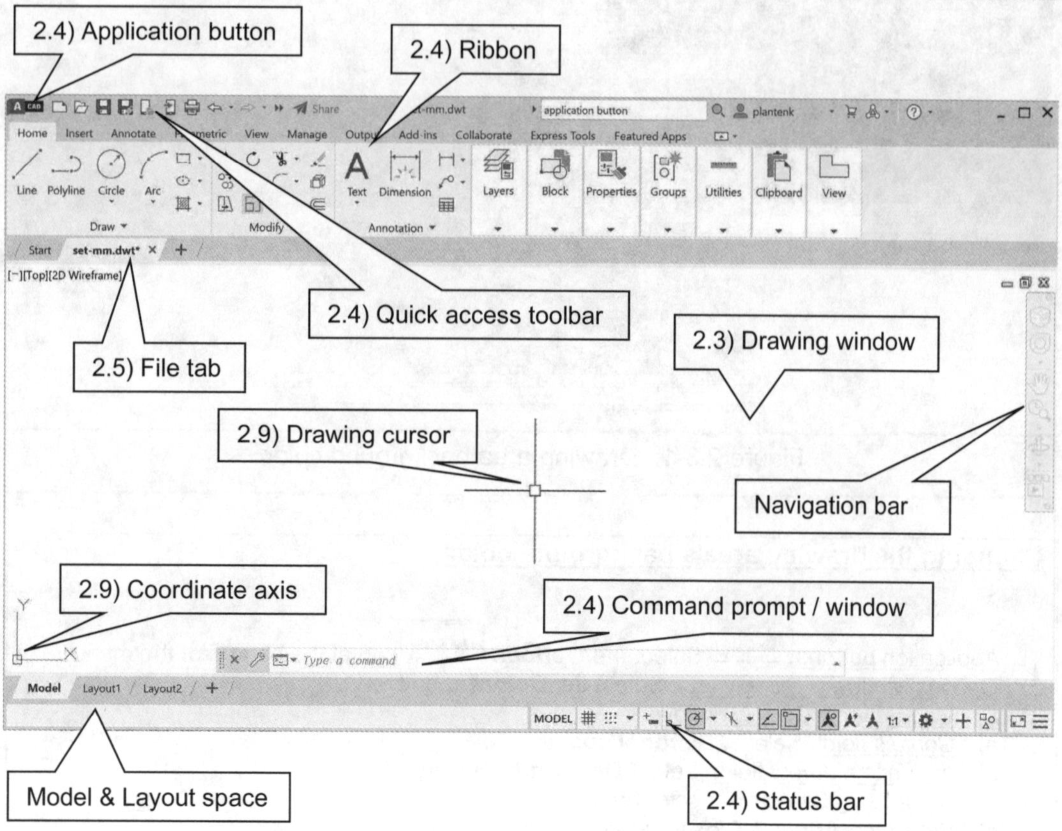

Figure 2.2-1: *Drafting & Annotation* workspace user interface

2.3) THE DRAWING AREA

The drawing area/window is the place where you create and view your drawing. The background color of the drawing window may be changed to suit the user's preference as shown in Figure 2.3-1.

The drawing area is as large as you need it to be. The usable drawing area does not just consist of the area that you can see. You can pan around the drawing area using the **Pan** command to reveal areas of your drawing that are out of view. You can also **Zoom** in and out to reveal more or less of the drawing area. Both the **Pan** and **Zoom** commands are located in the *Utilities* ribbon panel in the *Home* tab or the *Standard* toolbar. You can also pan and zoom by manipulating the mouse wheel.

- **Pan**: Hold down the mouse wheel and move the mouse.
- **Zoom**: Rotate the mouse wheel.
- **Zoom All**: Double click the mouse wheel.

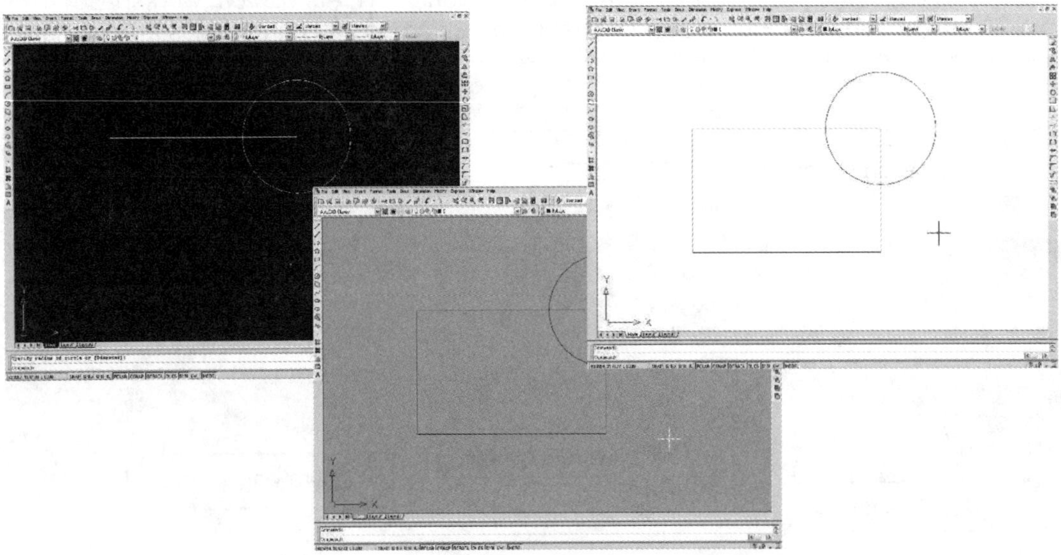

Figure 2.3-1: Drawing area background color

<u>Changing the drawing area's background color</u>

1) <u>Application button:</u>  Select the ***Options*** 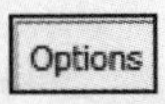 icon at the bottom of the menu.
2) <u>*Options* window – *Display* tab:</u> Select the ***Colors...*** button.
3) <u>*Drawing Window Colors* window:</u>
   a) <u>*Context* field</u>: Select ***2D model space***
   b) <u>*Interface element* field:</u> Select ***Uniform background***
   c) <u>*Color* field:</u> Select your color preference.
   d) Select the ***Apply & Close*** button.

Because the drawing area is so large, it is a good idea to indicate the region that you wish to use. This is your drawing size or limits. This is usually the area that will be printed. You can change your drawing size using the **LIMITS** command.

<u>Setting your drawing size</u>

1) <u>Command:</u> **limits**
2) `Specify lower left corner or [ON/OFF] <0.0000,0.0000>:` **`Enter`** (The lower left corner of your limits should always remain 0,0.)
3) `Specify upper right corner <420.0000,297.0000>:` **280,216** (This changes a Metric drawing area to the equivalent of an 11 x 8.5 sheet of paper.)

The units (i.e. inches, millimeters, feet) used to draw objects in the drawing area can be selected using the **UNits** command.

Setting your drawing units, precision and angle directions

1) Command: **UNits**
2) *Drawing Units* window: Use this window to set your units and precision.

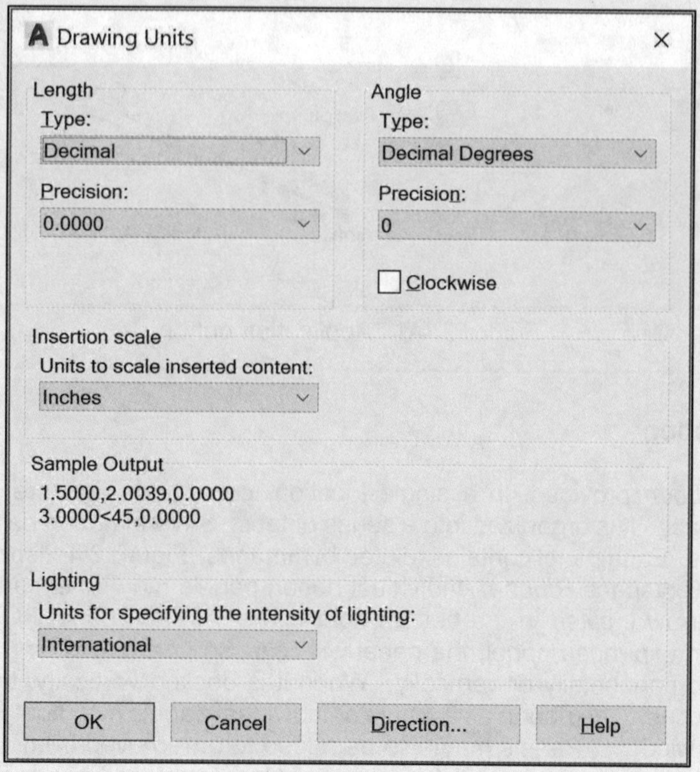

2.4) ACCESSING AUTOCAD COMMANDS

AutoCAD® allows its users to access commands in many different ways. One of which will no doubt become your favorite. The most common ways of accessing AutoCAD's commands within the *Drafting & Annotation* workspace are through the application button, ribbon, command window, shortcut menus, and status bar.

2.4.1) Application button

Menus are available through the *Application button* in the upper left corner of the drawing window. These menus contain the commands used to create, save, print and manage your drawing. Figure 2.4-1 shows the *Application button*. The *Search menu* (near the top) allows you to perform a keyword command search. The search even works for commands that are not directly accessible through the *Application button*. Note the location of the ***Options*** button at the bottom. This button will be referenced several times in the upcoming tutorials.

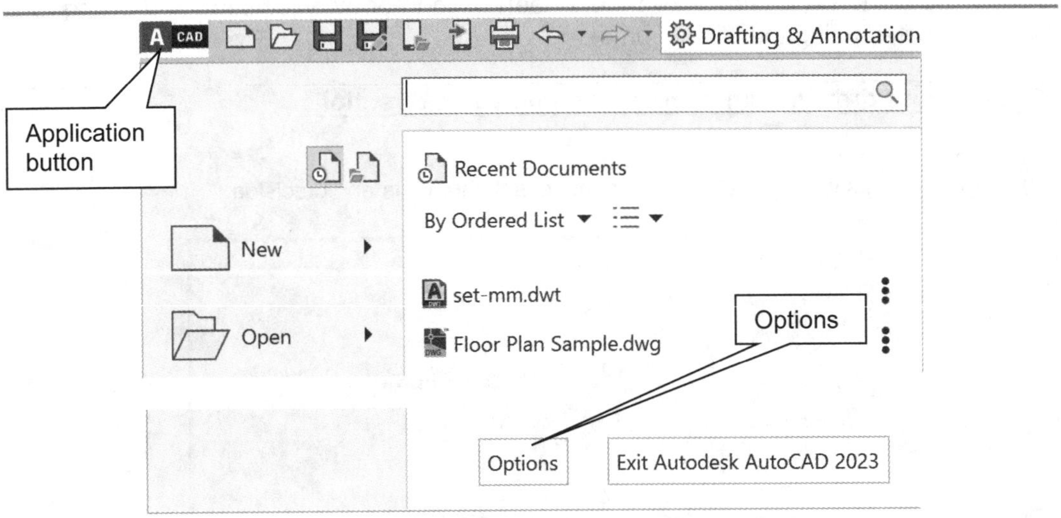

Figure 2.4-1: Application button

2.4.2) The ribbon

The *Ribbon* provides, in a single location, commands that are relevant to the current workspace. It is organized into a series of tabs. Several ribbon panels are located in each tab area. Each panel contains related commands. Figure 2.4-2 shows the *Drafting & Annotation* workspace *Ribbon*. Individual ribbon panels may be expanded by clicking on the black arrow located in the bottom right corner of each panel. Once the mouse moves off of an expanded panel, the panel will collapse unless it is pinned. The ribbon may be docked horizontally or vertically. When it is docked vertically, the text tabs are replaced with icons. The ribbon as a whole or individual panels may float freely anywhere in the drawing window. Panels may also be added to or removed from a specific ribbon tab. This requires accessing the CUI (Customize User Interface) manager.

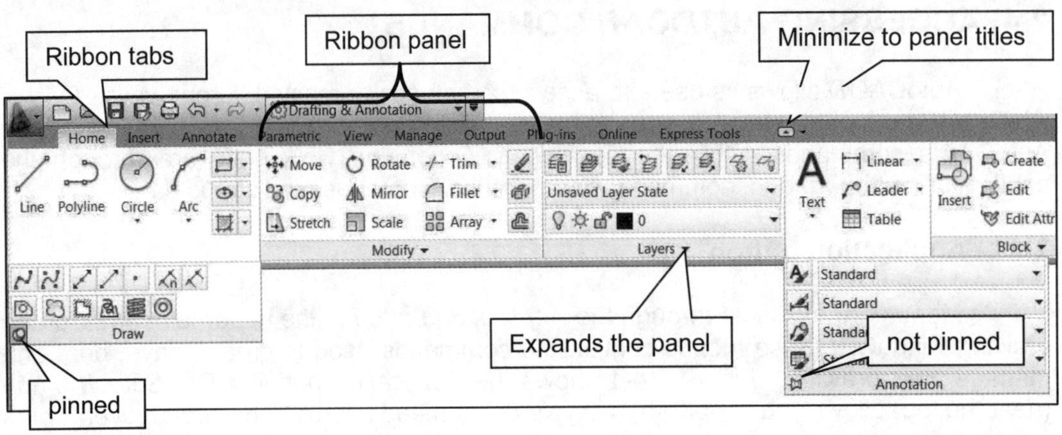

Figure 2.4-2: The Ribbon

Floating and docking ribbon panels

1) Floating: Click on a ribbon panel title and drag it to the drawing window.
2) Docking: Once the panel is floating, it may be moved, sent back to the ribbon, or the orientation may be changed.

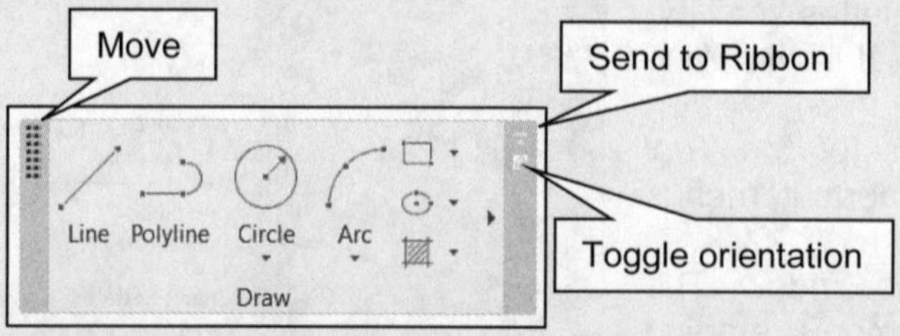

Floating panel when activated with cursor

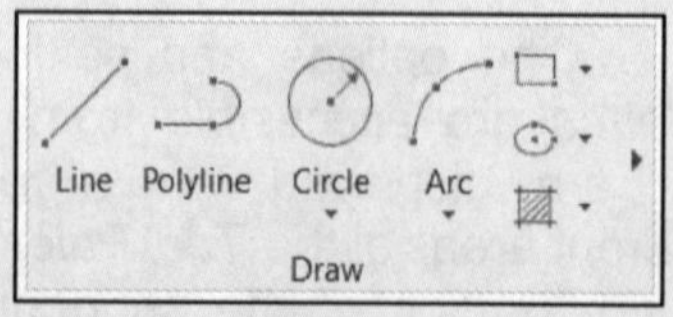

Floating panel when idle

Tooltips appear when your mouse hovers over an icon. For the first few seconds an abbreviated tooltip appears. If the mouse remains over the icon, an expanded tooltip will appear as shown in Figure 2.4-3. The tooltips help you navigate through the command steps if you are uncertain how to proceed. Tooltip appearance may be modified by accessing in the ***Display*** tab of the ***Options*** window (*Application button – Options - Display tab*).

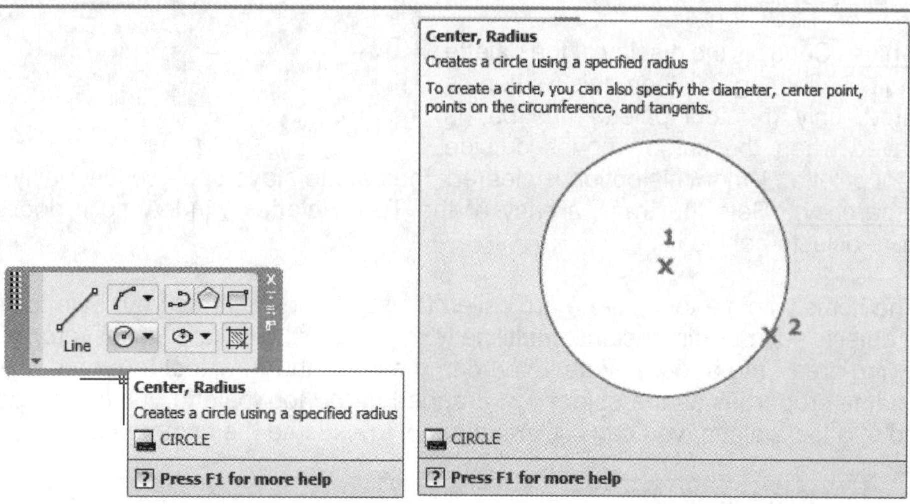

Figure 2.4-3: Tooltips

2.4.3) Tool palettes

Tool palettes are tabbed areas within the *Tool Palettes* window that provide an efficient method for organizing, sharing, and repeatedly using blocks, hatches, and your most frequently used commands. The Tool Palettes may be activated within the ***Palettes*** panel in the ***View*** tab.

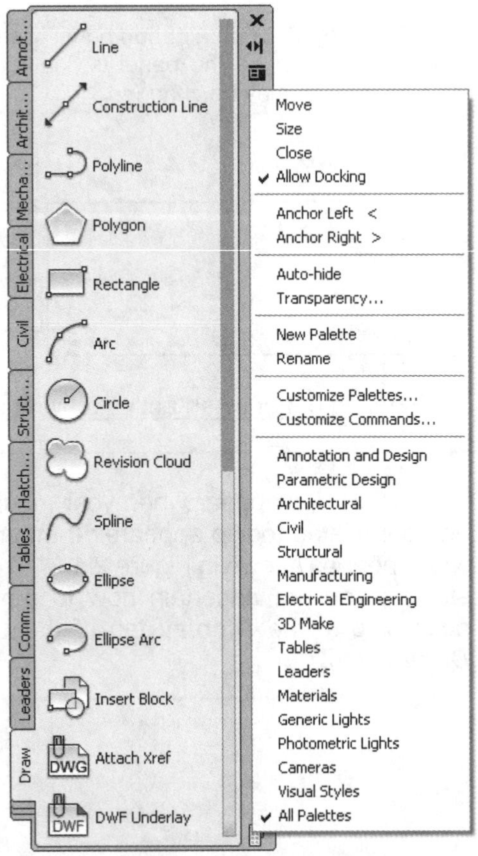

The options and settings for the *Tool Palettes* are accessible from shortcut menus that are displayed when you right-click in different areas of the *Tool Palettes* window. The bottom portion of the shortcut menu, starting with *Dynamic Blocks,* are subsets of all the palettes. Other settings include:

- Allow Docking: Toggles the ability to dock or anchor palette windows. If this option is selected, a window can be docked when you drag it over a docking area at the side of a drawing. Selecting this option also makes *Anchor Right* and *Anchor Left* available. Press the `Ctrl` key if you want to prevent docking as you move the *Tool Palettes* window.
- Auto-hide: Controls the display of the palette when it is floating. When this option is selected, only the tool palette title bar is displayed when the cursor moves outside the tool palette. When this option is cleared, the palette stays open continuously.
- Transparency: Sets the transparency of the Tool Palettes window so it does not obscure objects behind it.

The items within a tool palette are called tools. You can create your own tools by dragging objects such as dimensions, multiline text, polylines, blocks, hatches, etc… from your drawing area onto a tool palette. You can then use the new tool to create objects with the same properties as the object you dragged to the tool palette. Once you add a command to a tool palette, you can click on the tool to execute the command.

Adding a tool to a tool palette

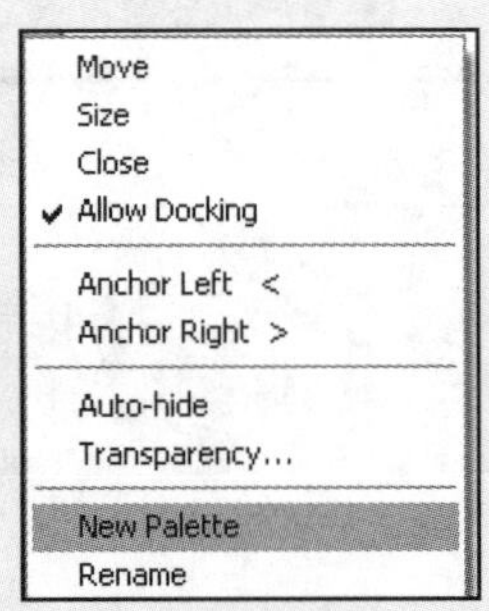

1) Place your cursor over the *Tool Palettes* window and click your right mouse button. A shortcut menu will appear.
2) Shortcut menu: Select ***New Palette***.
3) Name the new palette **My Palette**.
4) Drawing area: Select the object you wish to add to your palette.
5) Place your cursor over your object, right click your mouse button and drag the object to the *My Palette* area.
6) To create another object like the one used to create the tool, just click on the icon in the *My Palette* area.

2.4.4) Command prompt / window

The *Command* window (Figure 2.4-4) is the place where you can type in AutoCAD commands, enter coordinates, and select what type of information you wish to enter. This is also the place where AutoCAD prompts you and asks you questions. It is important to read the *Command* prompt when working with an unfamiliar command. The *Command* window, by default, is located at the bottom of the drawing area. However, it can be moved, resized, and closed to suit the user's need. If the Command window has been closed, you can type **`ctrl + 9`** to reopen it.

To enter a command using the keyboard, type the command name on the *Command* line and press **`Enter`** or the **`Spacebar`**. Commands entered at the *Command* line are not case sensitive and you do not have to move the mouse over the *Command* window before you type. When the *Dynamic Input* is switched on and is set to display dynamic prompts, the entered commands will appear near the cursor.

Most commands may be abbreviated, for example: Line = L, Circle = C, Move = M, and Copy = CO. Abbreviated command names are called command aliases and are defined in the acad.pgp file.

When you type a command, you will see a set of suggestions. To select one of these suggested commands, click on it with your mouse to activate the command. The system variable **Inputsearchdelay** controls the number of milliseconds to delay before the command line suggestion list is displayed. A finer level of control may be accessed through the *Input Search Options* window. This is opened by typing the command **Inputsearchoptions**.

The *Command* window shown in Figure 2.4-4 shows the process used to draw a circle. First, **C** is entered to activate the CIRCLE command. Second, AutoCAD prompts us to enter a center point or choose another option. A center point was chosen with the mouse. Third, AutoCAD prompts you for a radius or the option of a diameter. **D** was entered to indicate that a diameter is to be entered. Lastly, AutoCAD prompts you for the circle's diameter. The diameter is then entered.

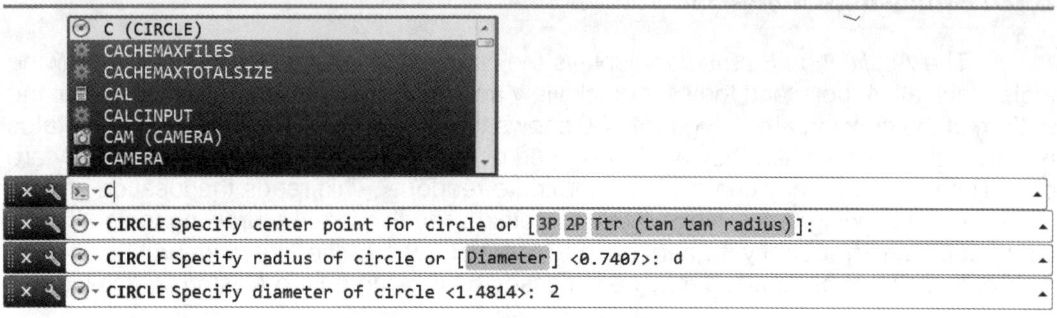

Figure 2.4-4: The *Command* window

A command may be repeated by pressing **`Enter`** or the **`Spacebar`**. A history of inputs may be shown by clicking on the black arrow on the right side of the command window. To find a command, you can type a letter on the command line and a list of commands starting with that letter will be shown (see Figure 2.4-4). To restart a recently used command, right click on the command line to access a shortcut menu.

2.4.5) Shortcut menus

Shortcut menus allow quick access to commands that are relevant to your current activity. You can display different shortcut menus when you right-click different areas of the screen and during a command. The shortcut menus shown in Figure 2.4-5 appear when you right click in the drawing window and during the LINE command.

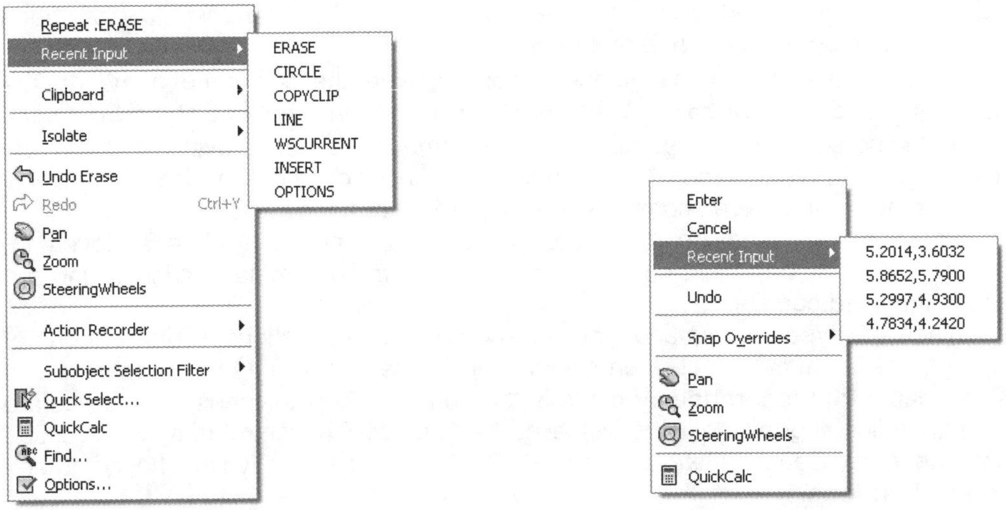

Drawing window shortcut menu LINE command shortcut menu

Figure 2.4-5: Shortcut menu examples

2.4.6) Application status bar

The *Application Status bar* displays the coordinate values of your cursor, drawing tools, navigation tools, and tools for quick view and annotation scaling. It is located at the bottom of the drawing area. Figure 2.4-6 shows the *Status Bar*. The buttons in the status bar are active or on when they are highlighted or light blue (they look gray when they are off). The status bar may contain the coordinate readout. This reads the location of your cursor in the drawing area. Next to the coordinate reading are the drawing tools. These commands are frequently turned on and off throughout the drawing process. The *Application Status bar* options may be accessed by clicking on the *Customization* icon.

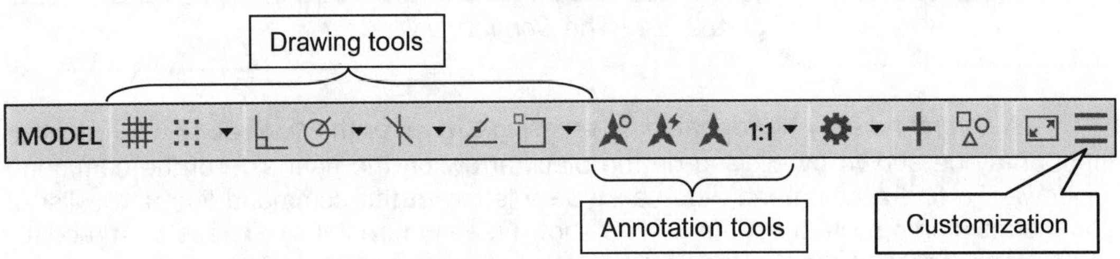

Figure 2.4-6: The *Status Bar*

2.4.7) Quick access toolbar

The *Quick Access* toolbar, displayed in the *Drafting & Annotation* workspace, is located at the very top of the drawing window next to the *Application* button. The *Quick Access* toolbar may be customized by adding or removing commands. This is done by right clicking on the toolbar and selecting ***Customize Quick Access toolbar...***, or selecting the arrow at the end of the toolbar. The *Quick Access* toolbar is shown in Figure 2.4-7.

Figure 2.4-7: The *Quick Access* toolbar

The *Quick Access* toolbar contains the following commands (reading left to right):

- QNew: Opens a new drawing.
- Open...: Opens an existing drawing. (Ctrl+O)
- Save: Saves the current drawing. (Ctrl+S)
- Save as: Allows you to save the current drawing under a different name. (Ctrl+Shift+S)
- Open from Web & Mobile: Allows you to open a file from the online cloud.
- Save to Web & Mobile: Allows you to save a file to the online cloud.
- Plot...: Plots or prints the current drawing. (Ctrl+P)
- Undo: Used to undo previous commands or actions.
- Redo: Used to redo commands that have been undone.

2.4.8) Touch screen

For those using a touch-enabled screen or interface, the system variable **TOUCHMODE** controls the display of the *Touch* panel on the ribbon. If TOUCHMODE is set to 0, then the *Touch* panel is not displayed on the ribbon. If it is set to 1, then the *Touch* panel is displayed on the ribbon. The system variable **MAXTOUCHES** indicates whether a digitizer or touch pad is in use.

2.5) STARTING, SAVING, AND OPENING DRAWINGS

2.5.1) Starting a new drawing

When starting a new drawing (QNEW ), you have a choice of either starting from the *Create New Drawing* window or the *Select Template* window. The *Create New Drawing* window allows you to set up a drawing to your preferences. You may set parameters such as the units (Imperial or Metric), the size of the drawing, and the degree of precision. The *Select Template* window allows you to choose from predefined templates. Figure 2.5-1 shows both startup windows. The **STARTUP** variable is used to choose what is displayed when the application is started, or which window will appear when you start a new drawing. It has 4 values that may be set (i.e. 0, 1, 2, and 3). However, for starting a new drawing, only 0 and 1 are of interest. If STARTUP = 0, then the *Select Template* window will appear. If STARTUP = 1, then the *Create New Drawing* window will appear.

Template drawings store all the settings for a drawing and may also include predefined layers, dimension styles, and views. Template drawings are distinguished from other drawing files by the .dwt file extension. Several template drawings are included in AutoCAD®. You can make additional template drawings by changing the extensions of drawing file names to .dwt.

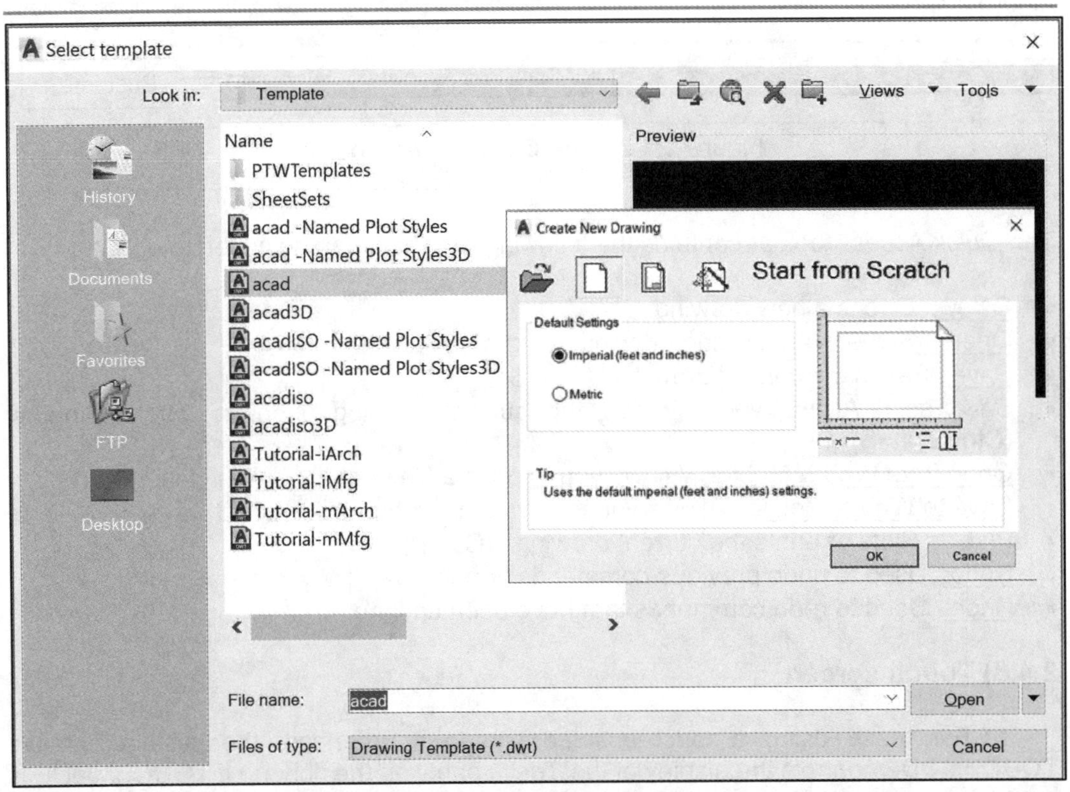

Figure 2.5-1: Startup window

Starting a new drawing using the *Create New Drawing* window

1) Command: **startup**
2) `Enter new value for STARTUP <0>:` **1**
3) *Quick Access* toolbar: [icon] or *Application* button: ***File – New...*** (`Ctrl+N`).
   The *Create New Drawing* window will appear.
4) *Create New Drawing* window: Activate the ***Start from Scratch*** button, activate either ***Imperial*** or ***Metric*** toggle, and then select ***OK***.

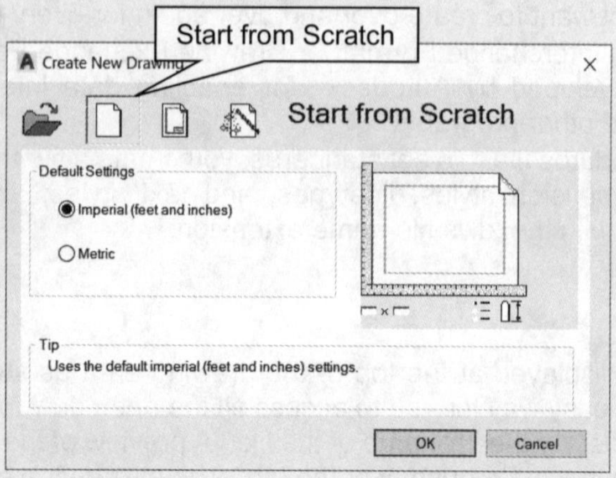

5) *Quick Access* toolbar: [icon]
6) *Create New Drawing* window:
   a) Activate the ***Use a Wizard*** button.
   b) *Select a Wizard* field: Select ***Advanced Setup*** and then ***OK***.

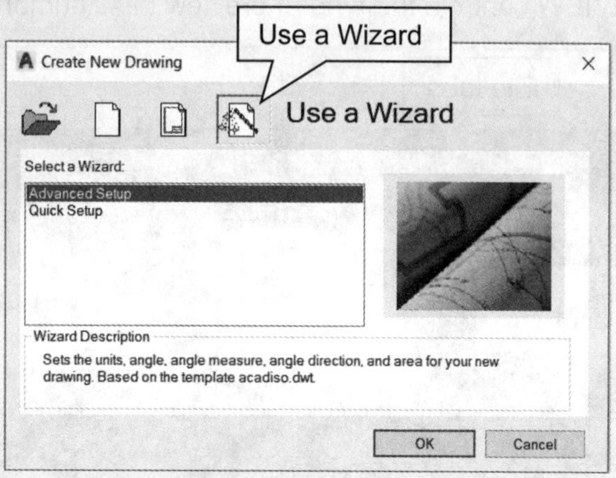

7) The wizard will take you through a setup which will allow you to choose your drawings units, angle, angle measure, angle direction and drawing area.

2.5.2) Saving and opening a drawing

When saving (or open) a drawing (***Application*** button - ***Save*** or ***Saveas*** or ***Open***), you have the option of saving (or opening) the following file types.

- **DWG** (DraWinG) is a binary file format used for storing two and three dimensional design data and metadata. Most of what you draw will be saved in this format.
- **DWT** is a template file. These files are used as a starting point when starting a new drawing. They may contain drawing preferences, settings, and title blocks that you do not want to create over and over again for every new drawing.
- **DXF** (Drawing Interchange Format, or Drawing Exchange Format) is a CAD data file format developed by Autodesk® for enabling data interoperability between AutoCAD® and other programs.
- **DWS** is a standards file. To set standards, you create a file that defines properties for layers, dimension styles, linetypes, and text styles, and you save it as a standards file with the .dws file name extension.

2.5.3) File tab

File tabs are displayed at the top of the drawing area as shown in Figure 2.5-2. They help provide an easy way for you to access all the open drawings in the application. The file tabs usually display the full name of the file. A preview of the file and all its spaces appears when you hover your mouse over the tab. The plus button on the right end of the file tabs displays the *Select Template* dialog box to create a new drawing. The following are the system variables that relate to the file tabs.

- **FILETAB** opens the file tabs.
- **FILETABCLOSE** closes the file tabs.
- **FILETABPREVIEW** controls the type of preview (1 = thumbnail, 0 = list).

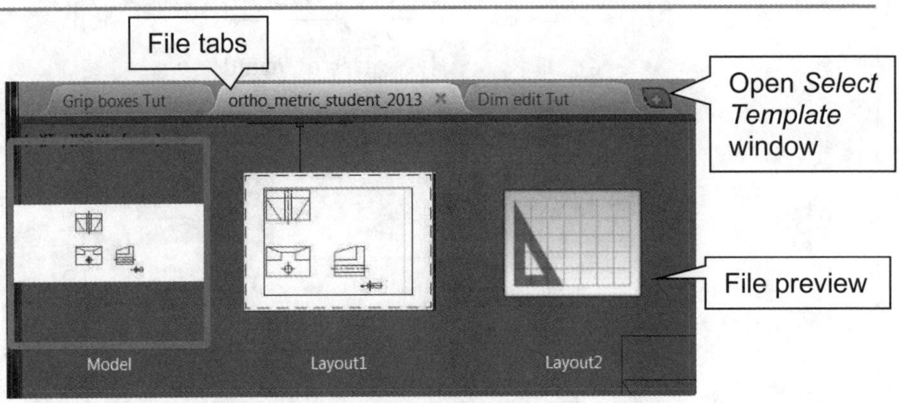

Figure 2.5-2: File tab preview

2.5.4) Saving and opening from the web or mobile device.

The ***Save to web & mobile***  and ***Open from web & mobile***  allow you to save and open drawings online from any remote location and from any device that has internet access. The first time you use either of these commands, AutoCAD will prompt you to install the ***Save to AutoCAD web & Mobile*** plugin. If you don't already have an account, the program will ask you to create one.

2.6) CUSTOMIZE USER INTERFACE (CUI)

The CUI allows you to adjust the user interface and drawing area to match the way you work. Many of these settings are available from shortcut menus and the *Options* window. Some workspace elements, such as the presence and location of ribbon panels, toolbars and palettes can be specified and saved using the *Customize User Interface* manager. However, you should not make major changes to the CUI if you are using a public access computer.

2.7) USER INTERFACE AND STARTUP TUTORIAL

The objective of this tutorial is to set up AutoCAD's user interface and start a new drawing. AutoCAD® allows you to set up an interface that suits the user. As you become more familiar with using AutoCAD®, you will develop an interface configuration that best suits you.

2.7.1) Setting up the user interface

1) View the *User Interface* video and read sections 2.1) to 2.6).

2) Start AutoCAD 2027®.

3) If a sign in window appears, sign in or create an account and enter the necessary information.

4) When you first launch AutoCAD® you may or may not enter a window that looks like what is shown in the following illustration. This will depend on whether you are using a personal copy or a school computer where the settings have already been adjusted. If you **don't see** this window perform the following steps.
   a) <u>Command:</u> **startup**
   b) `Enter new value for startup <1>:` **3**
   c) Close down AutoCAD® and restart the program.

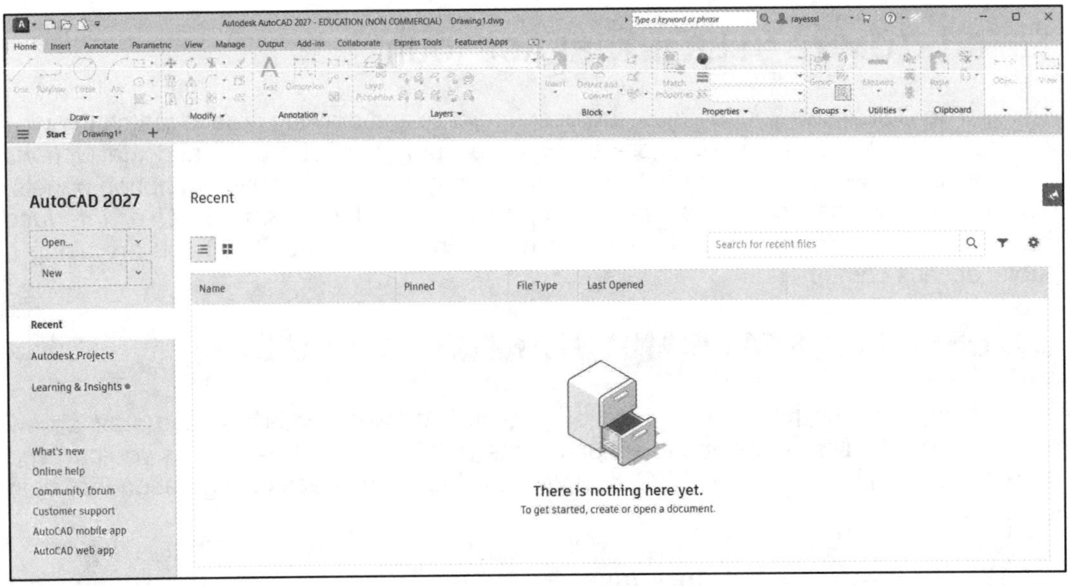

5) The above window is where you can access instructional videos and create an account which allows you to save, share and edit drawings online.

6) Select ***New*** 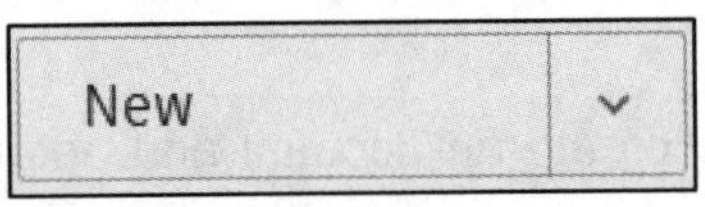

on the left located in the *Start* tab.

7) Activate the workspace selection menu.

   a) In the *Quick Access* toolbar (located at the top left of the program window), click on the ***Customize Quick Access Toolbar*** arrow  and select ***Workspace***. The *Workspace* pulldown menu will be added to the *Quick Access* toolbar.

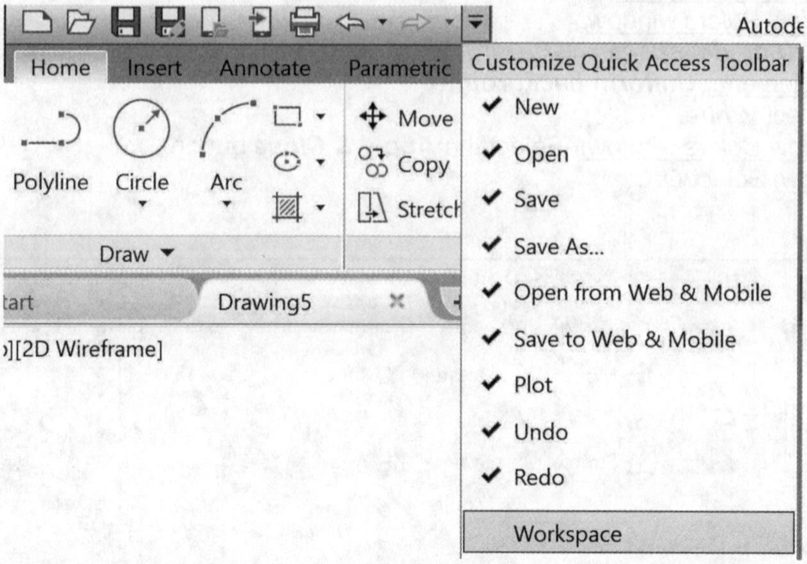

8) Select the ***Drafting & Annotation*** workspace (if not already selected).

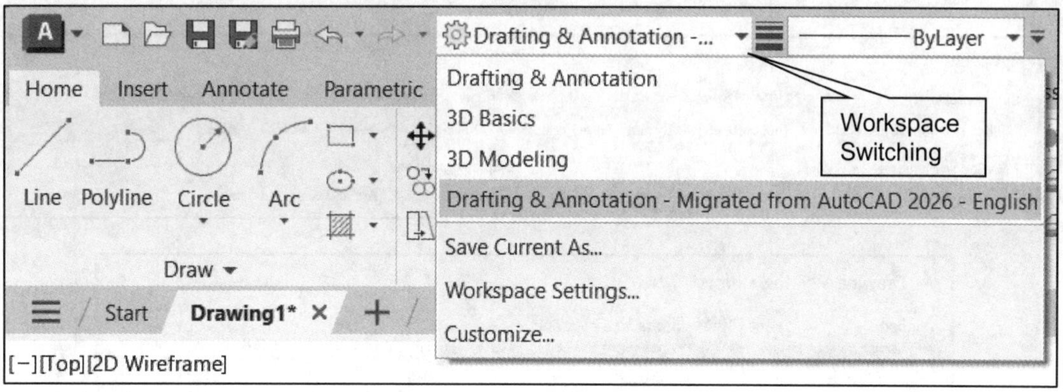

9) Change the color scheme of your workspace to white.

a) <u>*Application button:*</u> Select the ***Application***  button and then select the ***Options*** icon at the bottom of the menu.
b) <u>*Options* window – *Display* tab – *Color scheme* area:</u> Select the **Light** option.
c) <u>*Options* window – *Display* tab:</u> Select the ***Colors…*** button.
d) <u>*Drawing Window Colors* window:</u>
   i. <u>Context:</u> ***2D model space***
   ii. <u>Interface element:</u> ***Uniform background***
   iii. <u>Color:</u> Select ***White***.
e) <u>*Drawing Window Colors* window:</u> Select the ***Apply & Close*** button.
f) <u>*Options* window:</u> Select ***OK***.

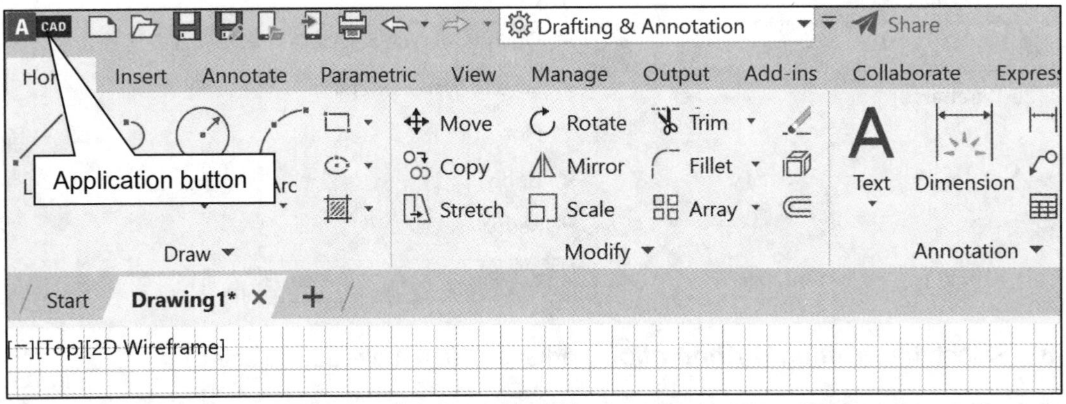

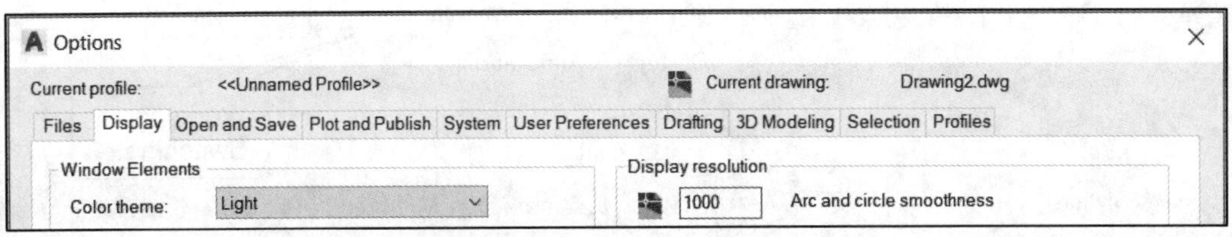

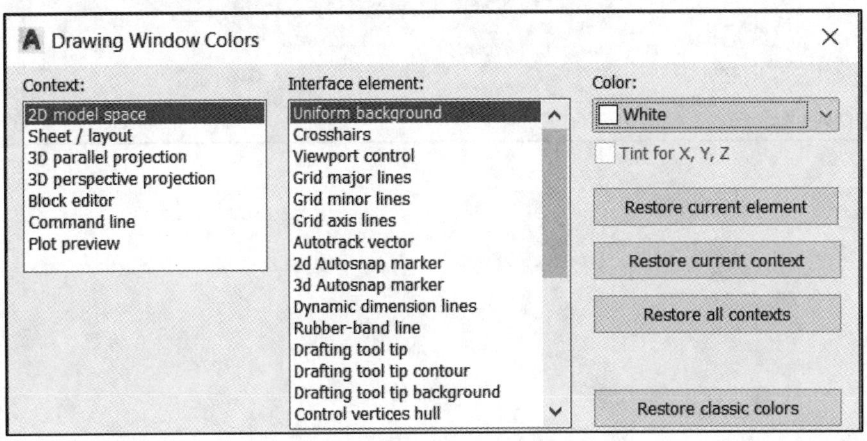

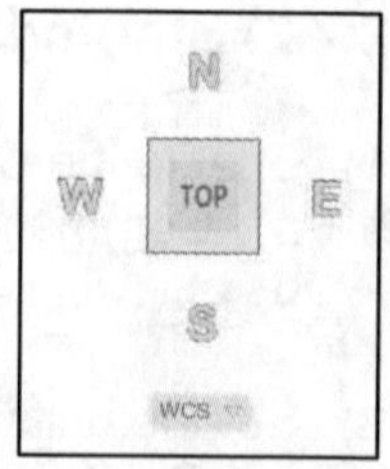

10) If you see the *View Cube* in the upper right of your drawing area, you may want to hide it. The *View Cube* is a navigation tool that allows you to switch between viewing directions. While this is very useful in 3D space, it is not very useful in 2D space.

a) Application button:  Select the ***Options*** icon at the bottom of the menu.
b) Options window – *3D Modeling* tab – *Display Tools in Viewport* area: Deactivate the ***2D Wireframe visual style*** check box.
c) *Options* window: Select ***OK***.

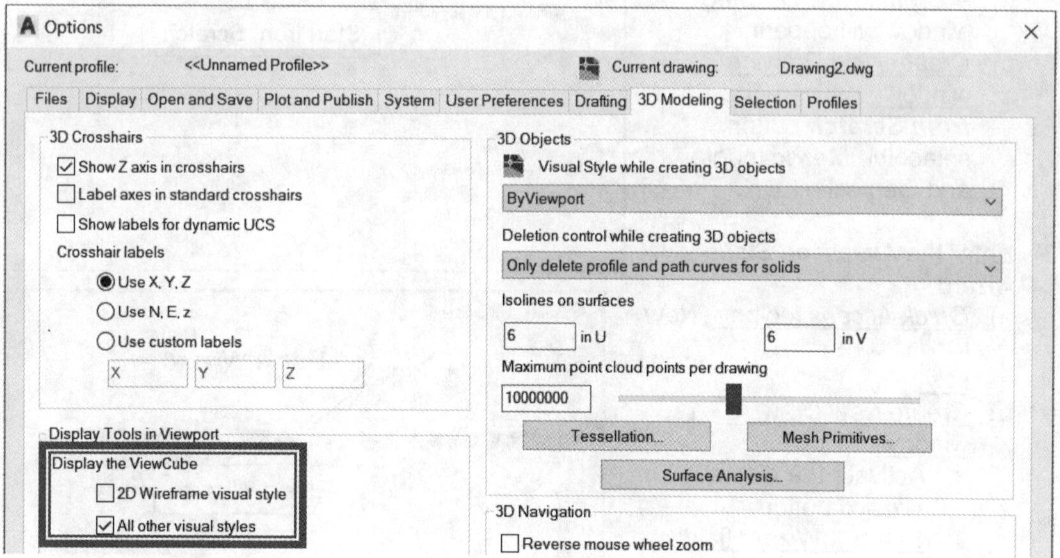

11) In the *Drawing Status bar*, deactivate the ***Grid*** 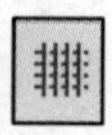 and ***Dynamic Input*** 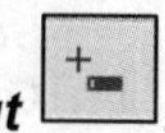. The *Drawing Status bar* is located at the bottom/right of the drawing area. The command icons should look gray and not highlighted blue after they are deactivated. If the *Dynamic Input* command is not shown, click on the ***Customization*** icon and add it to the *Status bar*.

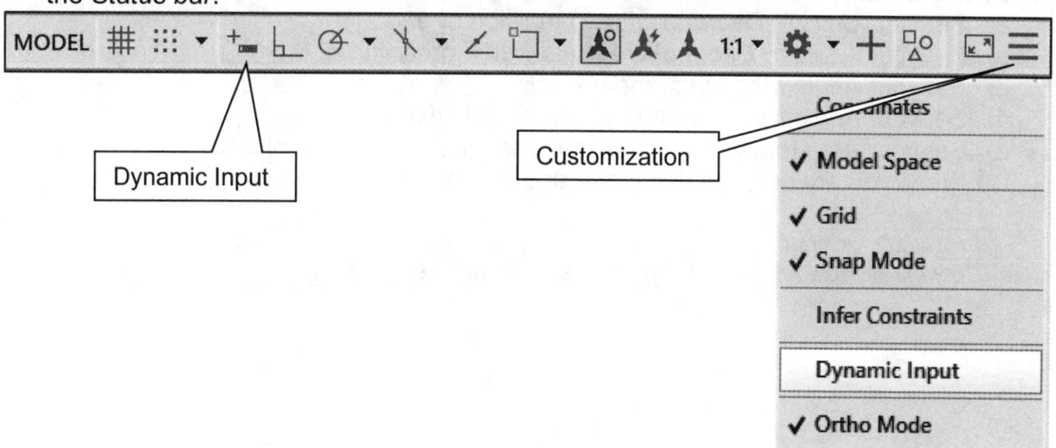

2.7.2) Starting a new drawing

1) Enable the *Create New Drawing* window.
   a) Command: **startup**
   b) `Enter new value for STARTUP <0>:` **1**

2) Set the units for your drawing.
   a) *Quick Access* toolbar: **New** 
   b) A *Create New Drawing* window will appear.
   c) *Create New Drawing* window: Activate the ***Start from Scratch*** button, select the ***Metric*** toggle and then select ***OK***.

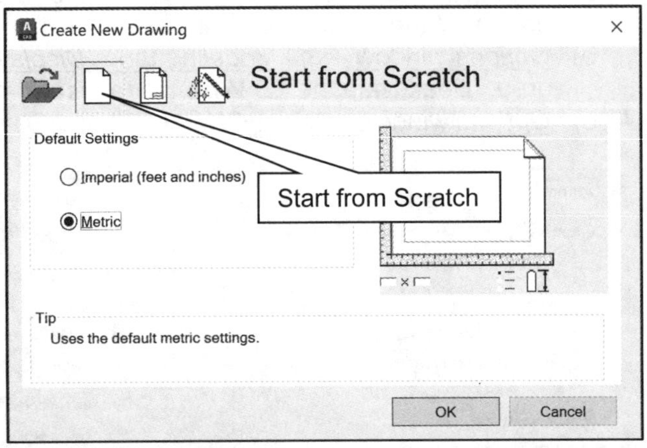

3) Enter the *Advanced Setup* wizard.
   a) *Quick Access* toolbar: **New** 
   b) *Create New Drawing* window:
      i. Activate the ***Use a Wizard*** button.
      ii. *Select a Wizard* field: Select ***Advanced Setup***.
      iii. ***OK***.

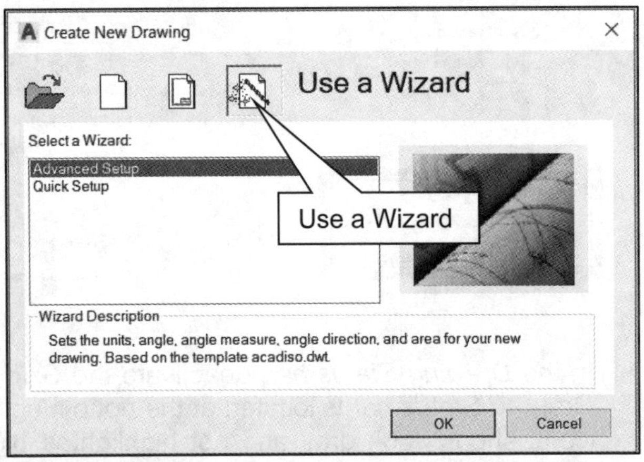

4) Step through the *Advanced Setup* wizard and set the following parameters.
   a) Set your *Units* to **Decimal** with a precision of ***0***.
   b) Set your *Angle* to **Decimal Degrees** with a precision of ***0***.
   c) Set your *Angle Measurement* to ***East***.
   d) Set your *Angle Direction* to ***Counter-Clockwise***.
   e) Set your *Area* to a width of **297** mm and a length (height) of **210** mm.
   f) When you are done setting your parameters, select ***Finish***.

> **Problem?** If your paper size is 12 x 9, you need to re-enter the *Create New Drawing* window and select *Metric* units. (Repeat steps 2 & 3)

5) Visualize your drawing area.
   a) Locate the *Navigation Bar* icon in the *View* Ribbon tab. Activate and deactivate the *Navigation* bar. The *Navigation* bar is located on the right side of the drawing area. Watch it appear and disappear as you click on the *Navigation bar* icon. End with the ***Navigation Bar*** **activated or showing**.

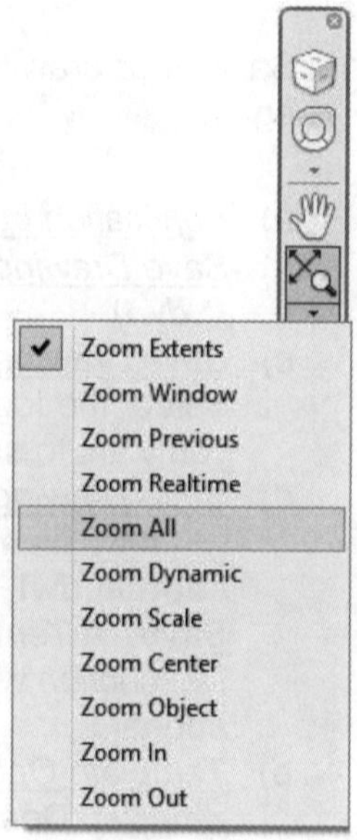

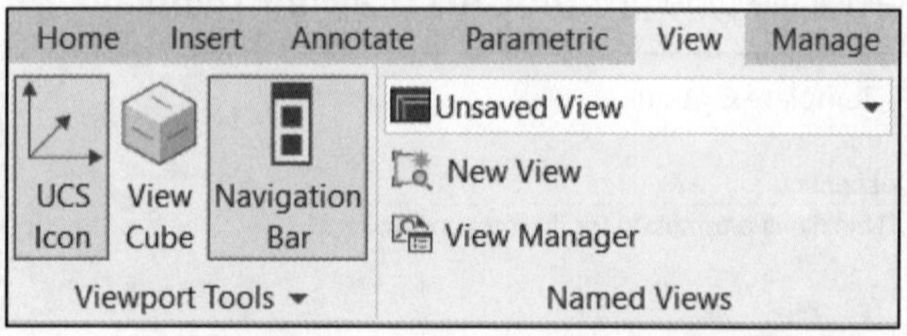

   b) <u>Navigation bar:</u> **Zoom All**. (You may also *Zoom Extents* by double clicking your mouse wheel.)
   c) <u>Command:</u> **grid**
   d) `Specify grid spacing(X) or ON/OFF/Snap/Major/aDaptive/ Limits/Follow/Aspect] <10>:` **5**
   e) Notice that your *Grid* icon in the *Drawing Status Bar* has become active.
   f) <u>Navigation bar:</u> **Zoom Realtime**
      i. Move your mouse to the center of the drawing area. Click and hold your left mouse button and move the mouse down until you can see the edges of your grid and then release your left mouse button.
      ii. **`Esc`** to exit the command.
   g) Zoom using the mouse.
      i. If your mouse has a wheel, take the cursor to the center of the drawing area and roll the wheel to zoom in and out.
   h) <u>Navigation bar:</u> **Pan**
      i. Move your mouse to the center of the drawing area. Click and hold your left mouse button and move the mouse around the drawing area. When you are done, release your left mouse button.
      ii. **`Esc`**
   i) Pan using the mouse.
      i. If your mouse has a wheel, take the cursor to the center of the drawing area, press and hold the wheel and move your mouse around to pan.
   j) **Zoom All**

6) Turn off your **GRID** .

2.7.3) Saving your drawing as a template

1) Save your drawing as an AutoCAD® drawing template that you will be able to use again.
   a) <u>*Application button:*</u>  

(`Ctrl+Shift+S`)
   b) <u>*Save Drawing As* window:</u> Select a file type of ***AutoCAD Drawing Template (*.dwt)***.
   c) <u>*Save Drawing As* window:</u> Select the location where you want to save the file.
   d) <u>*Save Drawing As* window:</u> Name your file **set-mm.dwt**, and select ***Save***. A *Template Description* window will appear.
   e) <u>*Template Options* window:</u> Describe your template file in the *Description* field, select your *Measurement* units and then select ***OK***.

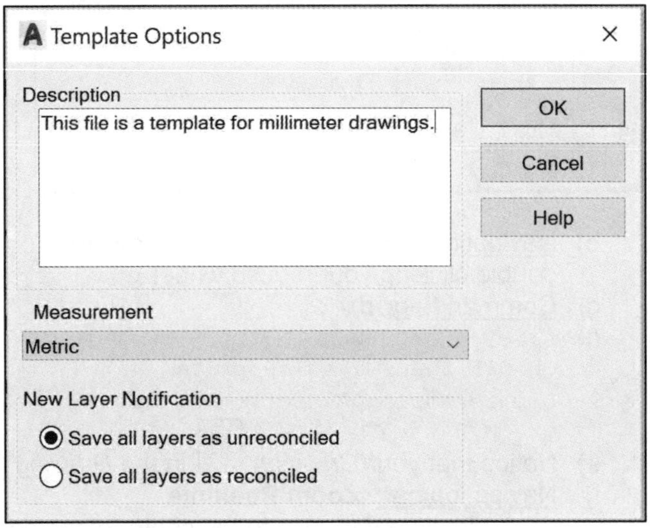

> **Note:** You may save your drawings and templates on your hard drive, portable memory device, or to the web using the *Save to Web & Mobile* command.

2.7.4) Checking your drawing parameters

1) Check your drawing units.
   a) <u>Command:</u> **un** or **units**
   b) <u>*Drawing Units* window:</u> Make sure that your units and precision are correct and then select ***OK***.

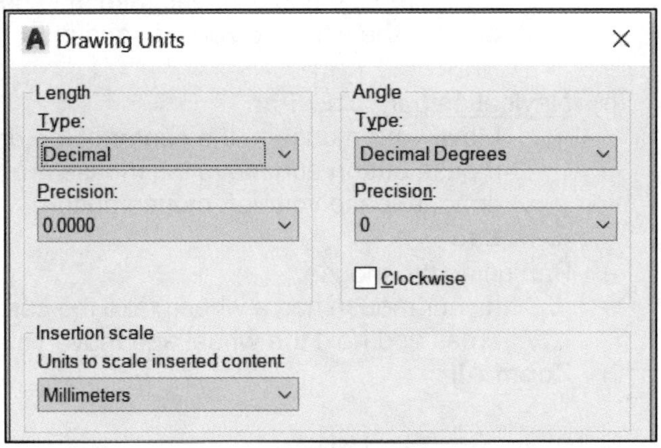

2) Check the size of your drawing.
   a) <u>Command:</u> **limits**
   b) `Specify lower left corner or [ON/OFF] <0,0>:` **`Enter`**
   c) `Specify upper right corner <297,210>:` **`Enter`** (If needed, you can change your drawing size by entering larger or smaller numbers in this area.)

3) <u>*Quick Access* toolbar:</u> ***Save As*** 

set-mm.dwt

Exercise 2.7-1: User interface and startup

Create and save a **set-inch.dwt** drawing template with the following drawing parameters.

- Start a new drawing and set your units to ***Imperial (feet and inches).***
- Select **OK** in the *Create New Drawing* window.
- Start a new drawing. Inch units should already be selected.
- Set up your drawing parameters.
  - Set your precision to **0.00**.
  - Set your drawing size to **11** by **8.5**.
- Use the command **UNITS** to check your settings.

2.8) COORDINATES

2.8.1) Cartesian and polar coordinates

Objects created in AutoCAD such as lines and circles are defined by coordinate points. The user may specifically state the defining coordinate points using the *Command* window or use the geometry of other objects to define the coordinate points. The two main coordinate systems used by AutoCAD are the Cartesian coordinate system (x,y) and the polar coordinate system (r,θ). Let's review both.

2.8.2) Cartesian coordinate system

The Cartesian coordinate system consists of three mutually perpendicular axes. The axes are labeled the x-axis, the y-axis and the z-axis as shown in Figure 2.8-1. The point where all the axes meet is called the origin. The origin is defined to be the zero location (0,0,0). The location of any point in space can be identified by an x position, a y position and a z position relative to the origin. Since this chapter only deals with AutoCAD's 2-D capabilities, a point in space will be defined by an x and y value. The z value will always remain zero.

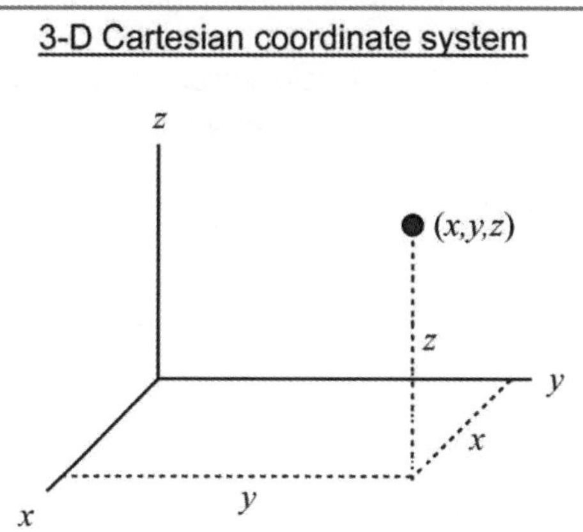

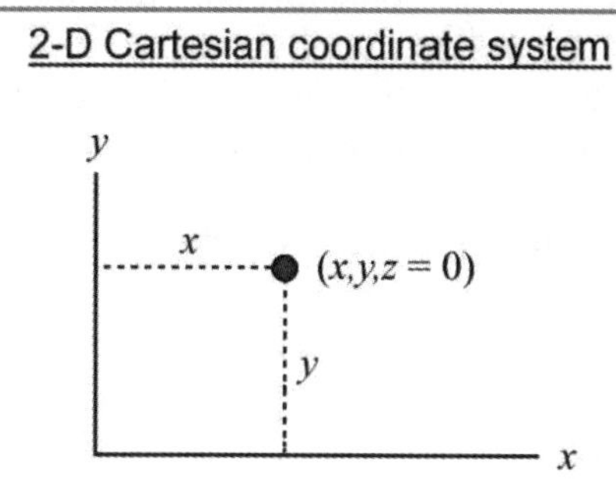

Figure 2.8-1: The Cartesian coordinate system

To illustrate the use of Cartesian coordinates in AutoCAD, let's look at the sequence of commands used to draw the line shown in Figure 2.8-2. As shown, the line lies in the x-y plane. It starts at the point $x = 2$ and $y = 1$. It ends at the point $x = 6$ and $y = 3$. The command sequence used to create this line in AutoCAD is:

- Command: **l** or **line**
- `LINE Specify first point:` **2,1**
- `Specify next point or [Undo]:` **6,3**
- `Specify next point or [Undo]:` Press **`Enter`** to end the LINE command.

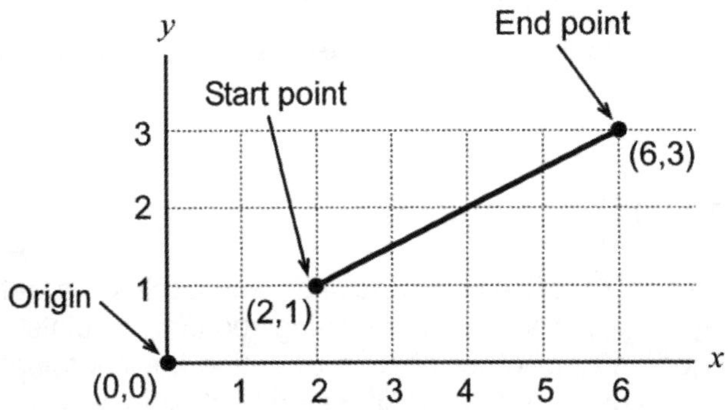

Figure 2.8-2: A line defined by Cartesian coordinate points

2.8.3) Polar Coordinates

The 2-D polar coordinate system consists of two mutually perpendicular axes. The axes are labeled the x-axis and the y-axis as shown in Figure 2.8-3. The point where the axes meet is called the origin. The origin is defined to be the zero location (0,0). The location of any point in space can be identified by the radial coordinate r and the angular coordinate θ. The radial coordinate is the shortest measured distance between the origin and the point under consideration, and the angular coordinate θ is the angle between the radial coordinate line and the x-axis.

The angular coordinate θ is measured positive counterclockwise starting at the positive x-axis. Therefore, if a point lies on the positive x-axis, its angular coordinate is zero. If a point lies on the y-axis, its angular coordinate is 90 degrees. The angular coordinate directions are illustrated in Figure 2.8-3.

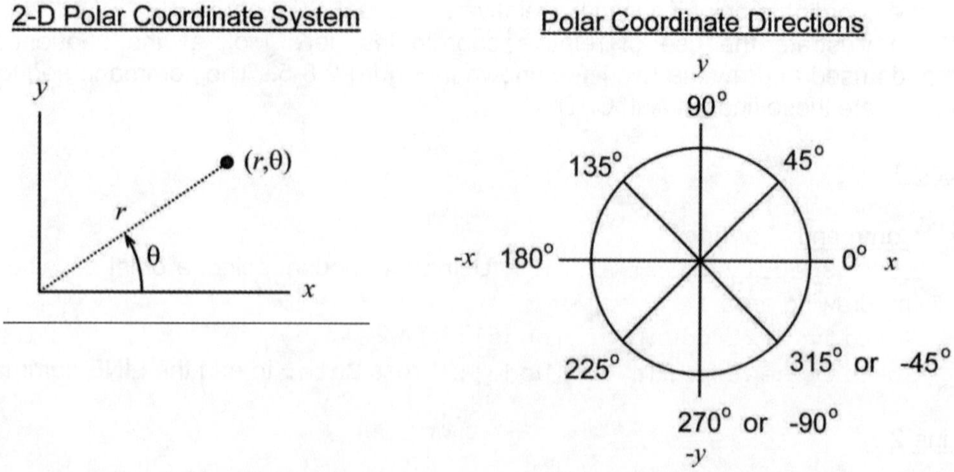

Figure 2.8-3: The polar coordinate system.

To illustrate the use of polar coordinates in AutoCAD®, let's look at the sequence of commands used to draw the line shown in Figure 2.8-4. As shown, the line lies in the *x-y* plane. It starts at the point r = 2.5 and θ = 60 degrees. It ends at the point r = 7 and θ = 10 degrees. The command sequence used to create this line in AutoCAD® is:

- <u>Command:</u> **l** or **line**
- `LINE Specify first point:` **2.5<60**
- `Specify next point or [Undo]:` **7<10**
- `Specify next point or [Undo]:` Press **`Enter`** to end the LINE command.

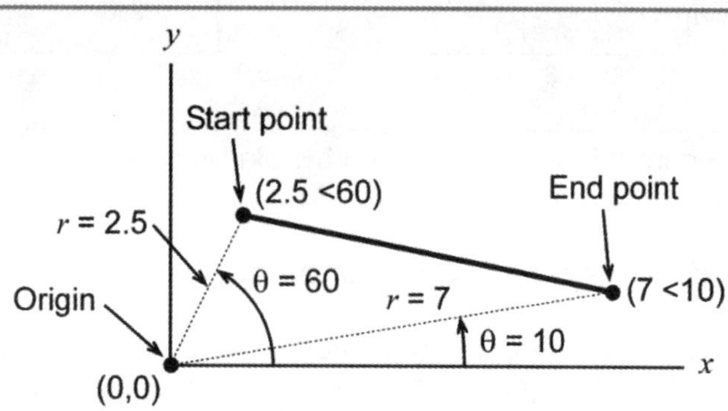

Figure 2.8-4: A line defined by polar coordinate points

2.8.4) Relative coordinates

Many times, the start point of a line is unknown or the length and angle of the line is known but not the coordinate for the end point. Therefore, AutoCAD® allows you to enter coordinate points that are relative to the last point entered and not relative to the origin. It is like making the last point entered a temporary origin. The symbol @ is placed before the coordinate point if it is to be relative to the last point entered.

To illustrate the use of relative coordinates, let's look at the sequence of commands used to draw the two lines shown in Figure 2.8-5. The command sequence used to create these lines in AutoCAD® is:

Line 1

- Command: **l** or **line**
- `LINE Specify first point:` Using the mouse, select a point anywhere in the drawing area.
- `Specify next point or [Undo]:` **@4,2**
- `Specify next point or [Undo]:` Press **`Enter`** to end the LINE command.

Line 2

- Command: **l** or **line**
- `LINE Specify first point:` **2,1**
- `Specify next point or [Undo]:` **@5<25**
- `Specify next point or [Undo]:` Press **`Enter`** to end the LINE command.

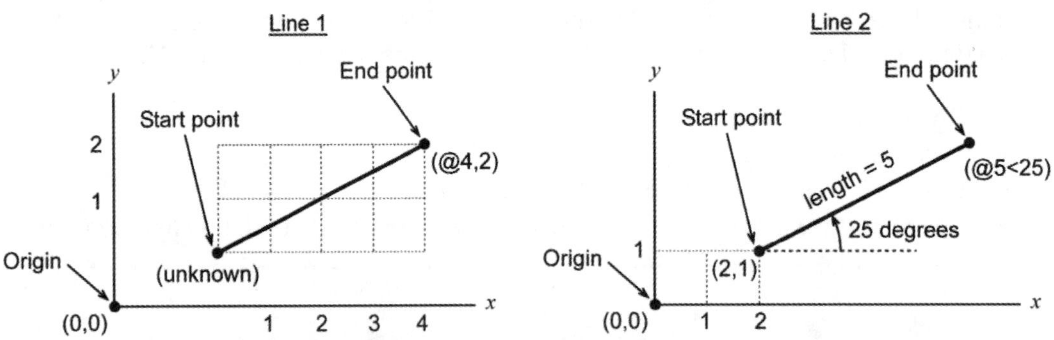

Figure 2.8-5: Lines defined by relative coordinates

2.8.5) World coordinate system (WCS) and user coordinate system (UCS)

AutoCAD® has two different coordinate systems: the *world coordinate system* (WCS), which is fixed and cannot be moved, and the *user coordinate system* (UCS), which is movable. The WCS origin is always located in the same place. When opening a new drawing, it is located in the bottom left corner of the drawing window. The UCS origin may be translated, and its axes rotated using the commands found in the *UCS* panel. The UCS is very useful when drawing objects that are relative to a point on an existing object. Figure 2.8-6 shows the coordinate axes for the WCS and a translated and rotated UCS. Notice that the WCS coordinate axes have a box at the origin and the UCS does not. Visually this is how you can tell them apart. The properties of the coordinate axes may be changed to suit the user's preferences.

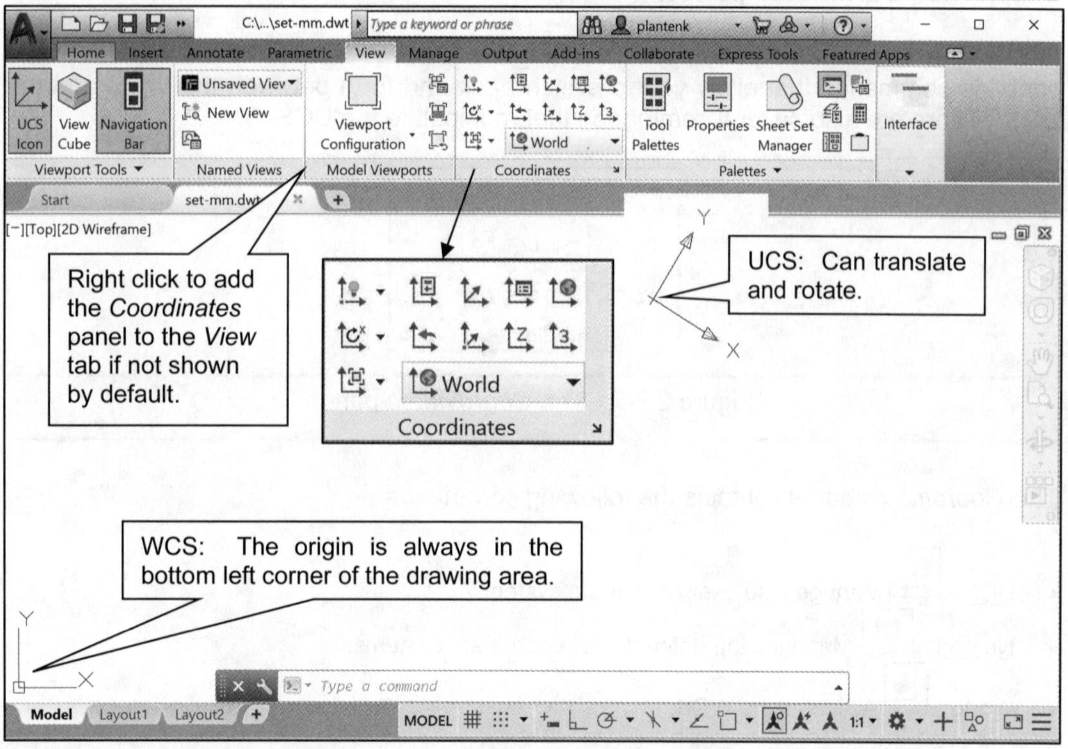

Figure 2.8-6: AutoCAD's coordinate axes

<u>Changing properties of the UCS icon</u>

1) *<u>View</u>* <u>tab -</u> *<u>Coordinates</u>* <u>panel:</u> (*UCS icon, Properties…*)
2) Within the *UCS Icon* window, you can change the UCS icon style, its size and its color.

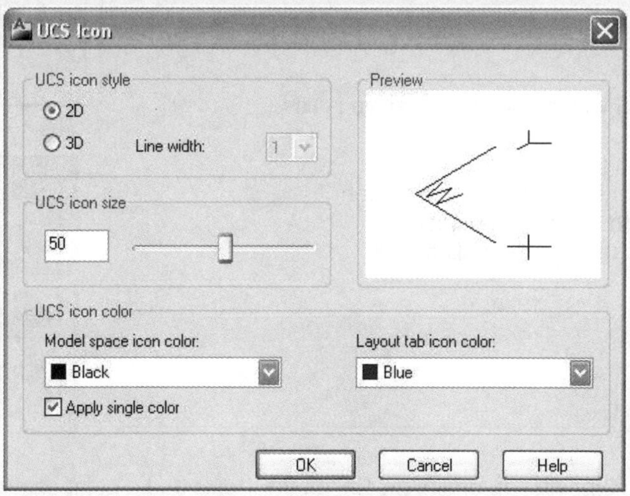

2.8.6) The coordinates panel

The *Coordinates* panel, shown in Figure 2.8-7, is located in the *View* tab and contains commands that allow you to switch back and forth between the WCS and the UCS. There are also several commands that manipulate the UCS.

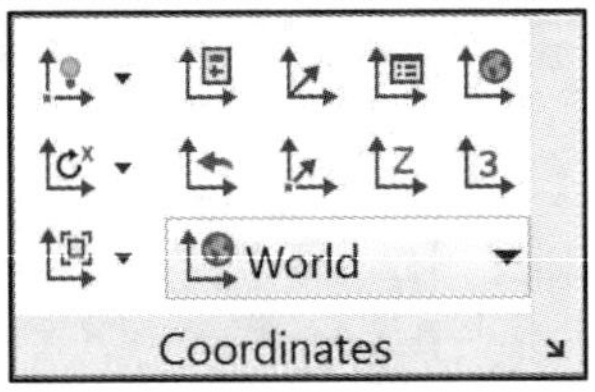

Figure 2.8-7: The *Coordinates* panel

The *Coordinates* panel contains the following commands:

- UCS:  Manages the user coordinate system.
- Named:  Manages the defined user coordinate systems.
- World:  Activates the WCS.
- Previous:  Restores the previous UCS.
- Origin: 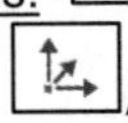 Allows you to change the origin of your UCS.
- Rotate pull-down: This command rotates the UCS coordinate system a specified number of degrees about the x, y or z-axis.

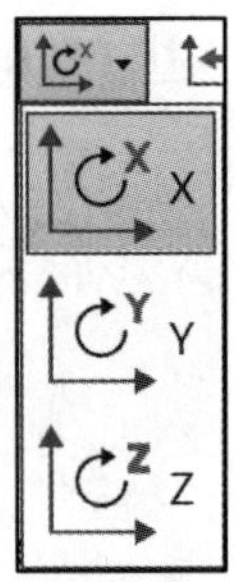

- Z Axis Vector:  Defines a UCS with a specified positive z-axis.
- Align pull-down: Allows you to align the UCS.
    - View: Aligns the xy-plane of the UCS with the screen.
    - Object: Aligns the UCS with a selected object.
    - Face: Aligns the UCS with the face of a 3D object.

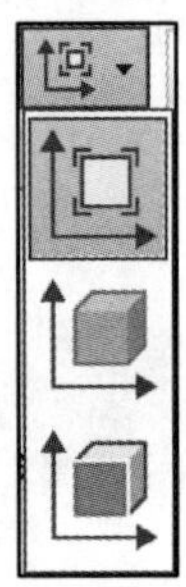

- 3 Point:  Defines a UCS using 3 points: an origin, a point on the x-axis and a point on the y-axis.

- Show UCS Icon at Origin: 

Displays the UCS icon at the origin only.
- Show UCS icon: 

Allows you to show the coordinate axis.
- Hide UCS icon: 

Allows you to hide the coordinate axis.
- UCS Icon Properties:  Allows you to change the look of the coordinate axis.

2.8.7) Coordinate position

The coordinate position of your cursor is displayed at the left of the *Status Bar*. It is not visible by default. You need to select **Coordinates** in the *Status Bar* **Customization**. It dynamically states the x, y and z position of your cursor. To turn the coordinate display on and off, just click on the area where the coordinate numbers are displayed. The command **COORDS** controls whether the coordinate display is on or off and whether it displays absolute x,y,z coordinates or relative r,θ,z coordinates during a command. Figure 2.8-8 shows the coordinate display for the cursor position in both the x,y,z coordinates and the r,θ,z coordinates.

- Coords = 0: The coordinate display is off.
- Coords = 1: The coordinate display is on and reads absolute x,y,z coordinates at all times.
- Coords = 2: The coordinate display is on and reads absolute x,y,z coordinates before a command and relative r,θ,z coordinates during the command.

x,y,z coordinate display

r,θ,z coordinate display

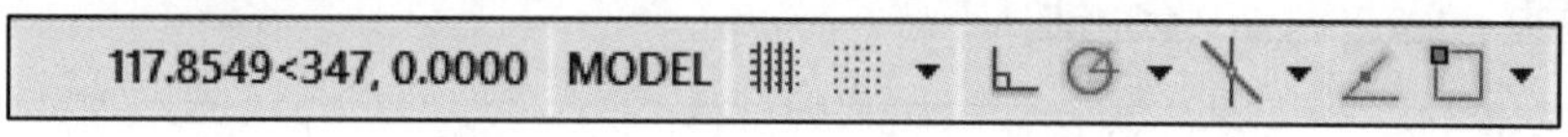

Figure: 2.8-8: Coordinate display

2.9) WCS/UCS COORDINATE SYSTEMS TUTORIAL

The objective of this tutorial is to familiarize the user with AutoCAD's coordinate systems. AutoCAD® has two different coordinate systems: the world coordinate system (WCS), which is fixed and cannot be moved, and the user coordinate system (UCS), which may be translated and rotated.

2.9.1) Coordinates

1) View the *UCS* video and read section 2.8).

2) Open your ***set-inch.dwt*** drawing template (created in Exercise 2.7-1).

   a) *Application button*: 

 (`Ctrl+O`)
   b) *Select File* window: Select the file type of ***AutoCAD Drawing Template (*.dwt)*** and then the location of the file (e.g. on your hard drive, online, etc…) and select the file ***set-inch.dwt***. Select ***Open*** after you have selected the file.

3) Save your template file as a drawing file named **WCS-UCS Coord Tut.dwg**.
   a) *Application button*: ***Save As…***
   b) *Save Drawing As* window:
      i. Select a file type of ***AutoCAD 2018 Drawing (*.dwg)***.
      ii. Name your file **WCS-UCS Coord Tut.dwg.**
      iii. Select a location for your file.
      iv. Select ***Save***.

4) 

 (**Zoom All**) - (`z Enter a Enter`)

5) Show your coordinate axis at the origin.

   a) *View* ribbon tab – *Coordinate* panel: 

   Problem? If your *Coordinate* panel is not shown, right click on one of the panel names, select ***Show panel*** and then select ***Coordinate***.

6) **Pan** 

 your drawing a little to the right and a little up and `Esc` to exit the command.

7) Activate your coordinate readout. Select ***Customize***  in the *Status Bar* and then ***Coordinates***. A coordinate readout will appear next to the *Status Bar*.

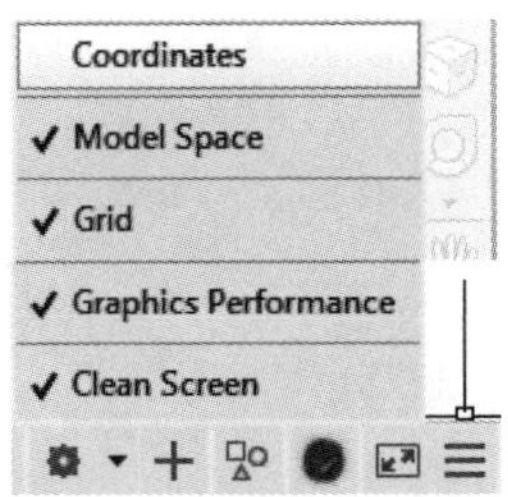

8) Move your cursor around the graphics screen and watch the coordinate display change as your cursor changes locations.

9) Find the origin. It should be located at the intersection of the coordinate axes.

10) Turn your coordinate readings off by clicking on the coordinate display reading.

11) Turn your coordinate display back on.

2.9.2) Change to the *user coordinate system* (UCS)

12) Change the location of your **UCS** (User Coordinate System) origin to the middle of your drawing area.

 a) *View* ribbon tab - *Coordinate* panel:  (UCS - ORIGIN)
 b) `UCS Specify new origin point <0, 0, 0>:` Click the left mouse button somewhere in the middle of the drawing window. (Notice that the coordinate axis moves to the new origin point and the `W` or box at the origin disappears.)

13) Find the origin.

14) Change back to the WCS (World Coordinate System).

 a) *View* ribbon tab - *Coordinate* panel: 

15) Change the appearance of the UCS.

 a) *View* ribbon tab - *Coordinate* panel:  (UCS icon, Properties…)
 b) *UCS Icon* window: Select the *UCS icon style* to be **3D** and change the coordinate axis line width to **3**.
 c) *UCS Icon* window: ***OK***

 d) *View* ribbon tab - *Coordinate* panel:  (UCS icon, Properties…)
 e) *UCS Icon* window: Select the *UCS icon style* to be **2D**.
 f) *UCS Icon* window: ***OK***

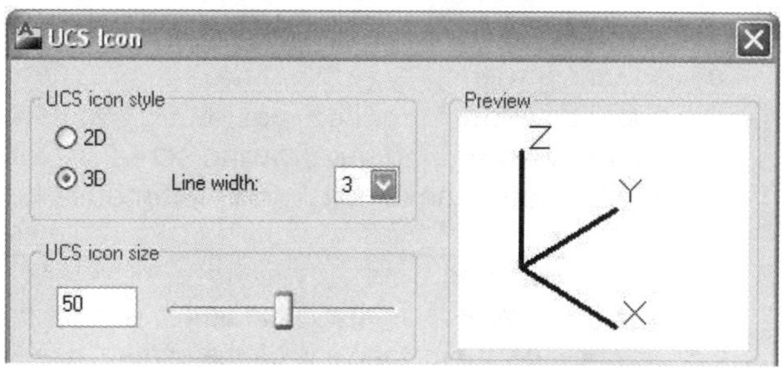

2.9.3) Coordinate display and drawing

1) Change the value or your **COORDS** system variable so that the coordinate display will read absolute *x, y, z* coordinates.
   a) Command: **coords**
   b) `Enter new value for COORDS <2>:` **1**

2) Draw a **Line**, but only enter the first point.
   a) Command: **l** or **line**
   b) `Specify first point:` Move your cursor to the center of your drawing area and click your left mouse button.
   c) `Specify next point or [Undo]:` Move your cursor around the drawing area and watch the coordinate display change. Notice that the coordinate position of your cursor is relative to the origin of the WCS. Press **Esc** when done.

> **Problem?** If you have coordinates attached to the line itself, deactivate the **dynamics input** in the *Status Bar.*

3) Change the value of your **COORDS** system variable to **2** so that the coordinate display will read relative polar coordinates (r, θ).

4) Draw a **Line**, but only enter the first point.
   a) Command: **l** or **line**
   b) `Specify first point:` Move your cursor to the center of your drawing area and click your left mouse button.
   c) `Specify next point or [Undo]:` Move your cursor around the drawing area and watch the coordinate display change. Notice that the coordinate position of your cursor is relative to the first point of the line. Press **Esc** when done.

2.9.4) Drawing using the UCS coordinate system

1) Draw a **RECtangle**, near the center of the graphics screen, which is 4 inches long and 3 inches high.
   a) Command: **rec** or **rectangle**
   b) `Specify first corner point or [Chamfer/Elevation/Fillet/ Thickness/Width]:` Select a point near the center of your drawing area.
   c) `Specify other corner point or [Area/Dimensions/Rotation]:` **d**
   d) `Specify length for rectangles <10.00>:` **4**
   e) `Specify width for rectangles <10.00>:` **3**
   f) `Specify other corner point or [Area/Dimensions/Rotation]:` Move your mouse around the drawing screen. Notice that the rectangle flips from one position to the next. Click your left mouse button to select a position.

> **Problem?**
> - If your rectangle is too small, you are probably in a metric drawing.
> - If your rectangle is off the screen, use **Pan** to bring it into view.

2) Turn your *Object Snap* on.

   a) Activate the ***OBJECT SNAP*** icon  in the *Drawing Status* bar. It should look highlighted.

3) Draw a **Circle** of radius 1 whose center is located at the geometric center of the rectangle.

   a) Change the origin of your **UCS** to the bottom left corner of the rectangle.

   b) <u>*View* ribbon tab - *Coordinate* panel:</u>  (UCS – ORIGIN)

   c) `UCS Specify new origin point <0, 0, 0>:` Move your cursor near the bottom left corner of the rectangle. As soon as a box appears locating the corner, click your left mouse button.

   a) <u>Command:</u> **c** or **circle**

   b) `CIRCLE Specify center point for circle or [3P/2P/Ttr (tan tan radius)]:` **2,1.5**

   c) `Specify radius of circle or [Diameter]:` **1**

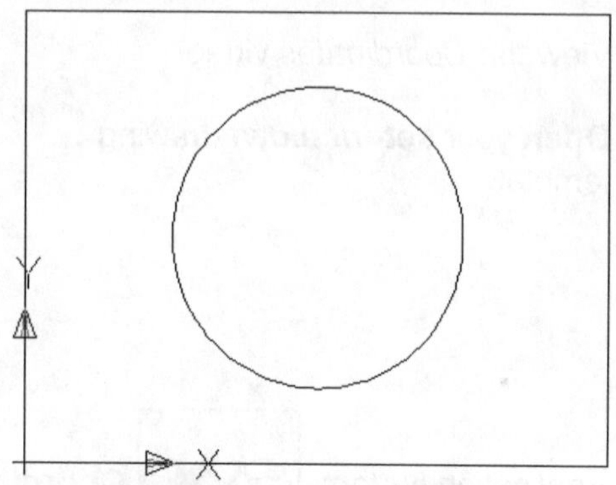

IMPORTANT! The UCS is used to reference existing geometry. The UCS allows us to position an object relative to a particular feature on an existing object.

4) **Save** your drawing.

2.10) DRAWING USING COORDINATES TUTORIAL

The objective of this tutorial is to familiarize the user with using both absolute and relative coordinates. You can enter the location and/or size of an object in AutoCAD by using either Cartesian (x,y) or polar coordinates ($r < \theta$). Both coordinate systems can be entered on an absolute basis (relative to the UCS or WCS origin) or a relative basis (relative to the last point entered). Relative coordinates are preceded by the symbol @.

> **IMPORTANT!:** If you make a mistake when drawing, type **u** or **undo**. This will undo the last point or command that you entered. The UNDO command may be used repeatedly to undo several mistakes.

2.10.1) Drawing a rectangle using Cartesian coordinates

We will be drawing the rectangle shown using lines defined by absolute and relative Cartesian coordinates.

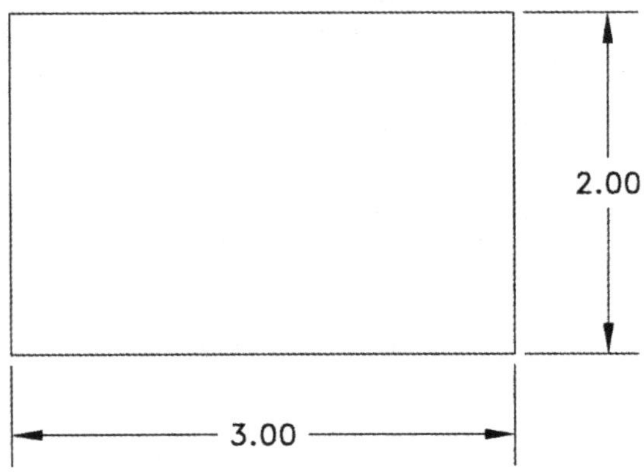

1) View the *Coordinates* video.

2) **Open** your ***set-inch.dwt*** drawing template.

3) <u>*Application button:*</u> 

Coordinate Tut – a.dwg

4) Turn everything off in your *Drawing Status Bar* at the bottom of the drawing area. They should look gray.

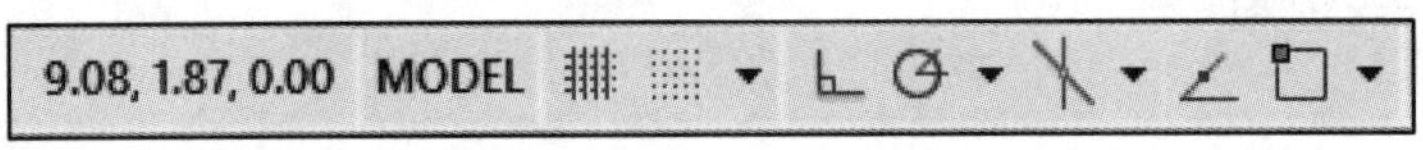

5) Turn your **GRID** on and set the grid spacing to be 1 inch by 1 inch.

> **How?**
> a) `Command:` **grid**
> b) `Specify grid spacing(X) or [ON/OFF/Snap/Major/aDaptive/Limits/Follow/ Aspect] <0.25>:` 1

> **Problem?**
> - If your grid is too dense, you are probably in a metric drawing.

6) **Zoom All**

7) Draw a 3 x 2 rectangle using absolute coordinates.
   a) Command: **l** or **line**
   b) `LINE Specify first point:` **2,2**
   c) `Specify next point or [Undo]:` **5,2**
   d) Follow the figure and enter the remaining points. **`Enter`** when done.

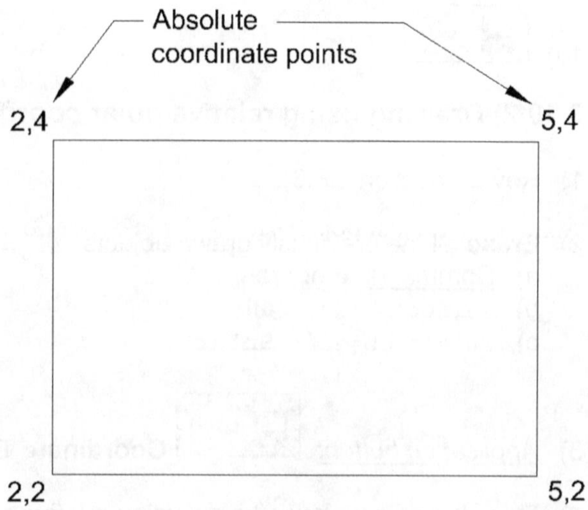

> **Note:** An **absolute coordinate** is measured from the WCS origin. The figure shows the actual coordinate points used to create the rectangle.

> **Problem?**
> - If your rectangle is too small, you are probably in a metric drawing.

8) Use the grid to confirm that the rectangle is 3 inches wide and 2 inches high.

9) Draw the same rectangle using relative coordinates.

> **Note:** A **relative coordinate** is measured from the last point drawn. The advantage of using relative coordinates is that you do not have to know where the original coordinate point is. We use the symbol @ to tell AutoCAD that we are entering a relative coordinate.

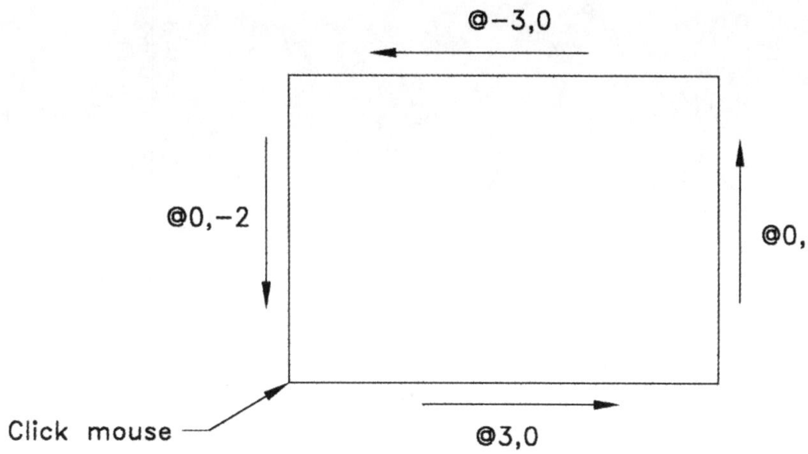

   a) Command: **l** or **line**
   b) `LINE Specify first point:` Select a point to the right of the first rectangle.
   c) `Specify next point or [Undo]:` **@3,0**
   d) Follow the figure and enter the remaining points. **`Enter`** when done.

10) 

2.10.2) Drawing using relative polar coordinates

1) Review section 2.8.3).

2) **Erase** all the previously drawn objects.
   a) <u>Command:</u> **e** or **erase**
   b) `Select object:` **all**
   c) `Select object:` **`Enter`**

3) <u>*Application button:*</u> 

Coordinate Tut – b.dwg

4) Draw the object shown below using relative polar coordinates.
   a) <u>Command:</u> **l** or **line**
   b) `Specify first point:` **3,2** (at "A") or choose any point near the bottom left corner of your drawing area.
   c) `Specify next point or [Undo]:` **@6<0** (to "B")
   d) `Specify next point or [Undo]:` **@5<90** (to "C")
   e) `Specify next point or [Close/Undo]:` **@3<180** (to "D")
   f) `Specify next point or [Close/Undo]:` **@4<270** (to "E")
   g) Follow the figure and enter the remaining points. **`Enter`** when done.

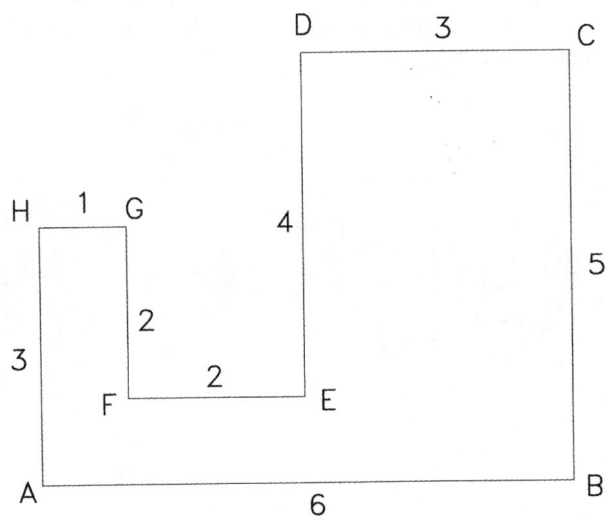

5) 

2.10.3) Drawing using both Cartesian and polar coordinates

1) **Erase** all previously drawn objects.

2) *Application button:* 

Coordinate Tut – c.dwg

3) Draw the object shown below using a combination of polar and Cartesian coordinates.
   a) Command: **l** or **line**
   b) `Specify first point:` **2,2** (at "A") or choose any point near the bottom left corner of your drawing area.
   c) `Specify next point or [Undo]:` **@3<90** (to "B")
   d) `Specify next point or [Undo]:` **@2,2** (to "C")
   e) Follow the figure and enter the remaining points. **`Enter`** when done.

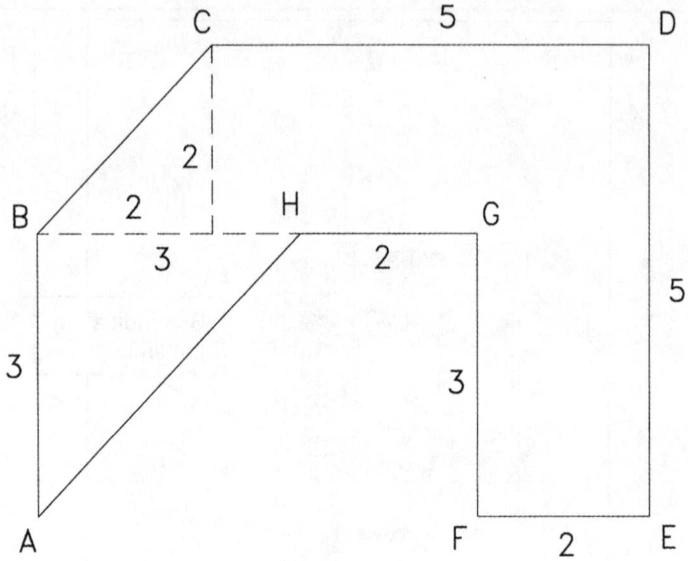

4) 

2.11) PRINTING

When you print or plot a drawing, you need to specify what region you would like to print. From within *Paper* space you usually print the *Layout*. However, in *Model* space, there are four different ways of selecting a region to print. The *Model* and *Paper* space will be discussed in "*Drawing Orthographic Projections in AutoCAD®*".

1. Display: Prints everything that you can see, at the moment, in the drawing area.
2. Extents: Prints the minimum area which will include everything that is drawn.
3. Limits: Prints the area that you have defined as your drawing size.
4. Window: Prints the area that you select using a window.

Figure 2.11-1 and 2.11-2 show a drawing and the printing results using the first three region selection methods. The line around the drawing's title block indicates the limits/drawing size.

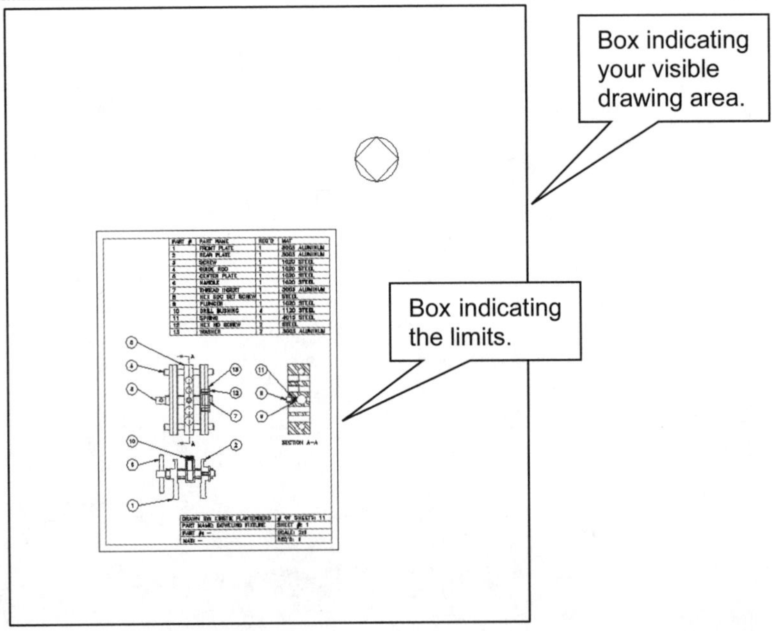

Figure 2.11-1: Drawing as displayed in AutoCAD®.

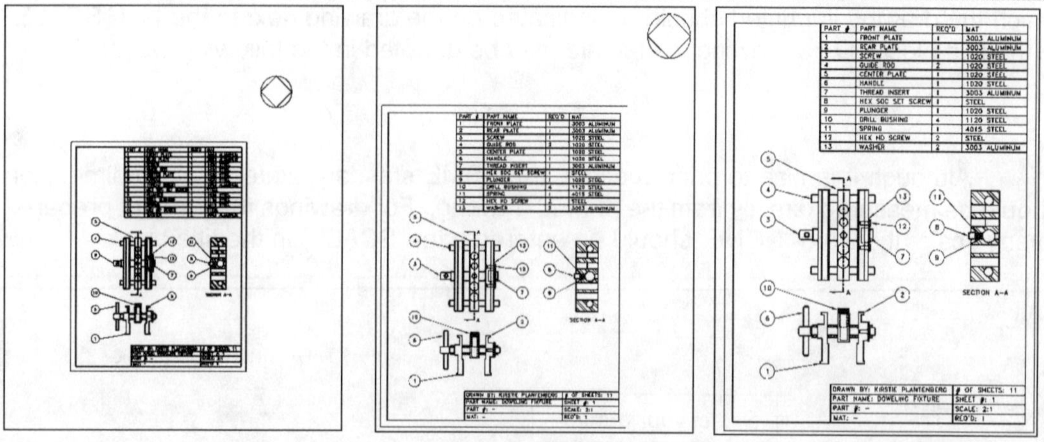

Printing the *Display* Printing the *Extent* Printing the *Limits*

Figure 2.11-2: Printing regions.

2.11.1) Page setup

Printing preferences for a particular drawing may be set in the *Page Setup - Model* window. These settings are drawing specific which means that they are stored in the drawing or template file and not in the program. To access the *Page Setup - Model* window select ***Application button – Print – Page Setup...*** and then click on the ***Modify...*** button. Figure 2.11-3 shows the *Page Setup - Model* window with the important features identified.

2.11.2) Plot

The *Plot – Model* window allows you to send your drawing to a printer or plotter. The default settings used to print your drawing are specified in the *Page Setup – Model* window. The *Plot – Model* window allows you to change some of these default settings without having to access the *Page Setup – Model* window again. To access the *Plot - Model* window select ***Application button - Print - Plot...***.

2.11.3) Printing to scale

Print scale expresses the ratio between the printed size of an object to its actual size. If a drawing is printed full-scale, it implies that a feature dimensioned as 1 inch measures 1 inch with a ruler on the printed drawing. This is referred to as a 1 to 1 scale. Printing full scale, in most cases, is difficult to achieve unless you have access to a large plotter. In a classroom setting, most engineering drawings are printed on a standard 8.5" x 11" sheet of paper regardless of the object's size. The scale at which the part is printed should allow all details of the part to be seen clearly and accurately. **Even though a drawing may not be able to be printed full scale, they should always be drawn full scale in the CAD environment.**

Since it is impractical to print all drawings full scale, we employ printing to half scale, quarter-scale and so on. For example, if a drawing is printed half-scale, a feature that is dimensioned 1 inch will measure 0.5 inch on the printed drawing. The scale at which the drawing is printed should be indicated on the drawing next to the text "SCALE" in the title block. On a drawing, half-scale may be denoted in the following ways.

1/2 or 1:2 or 0.5

Although it is nice to print to scale, the ASME standard states that no dimension should be measured directly from the printed drawing. For drawings that are not prepared to any scale, the word "NONE" should be entered after "SCALE" in the title block.

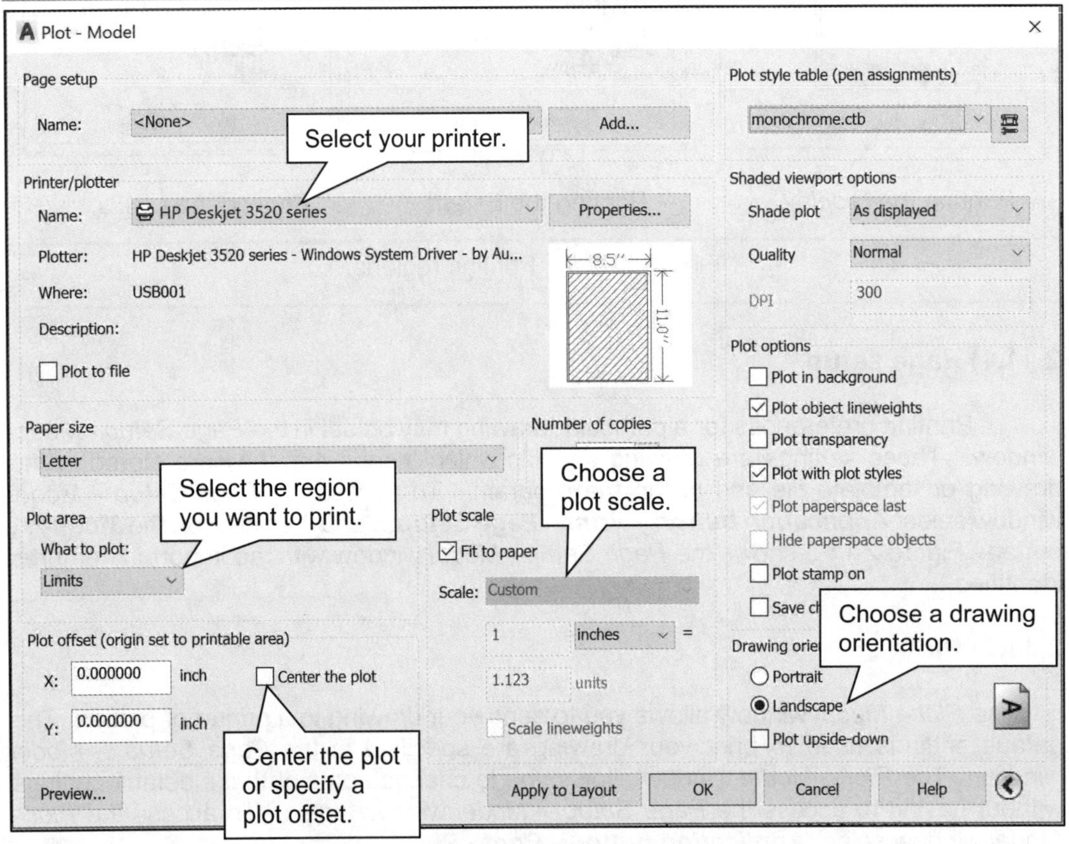

Figure 2.11-3: *Page Setup - Model* window

2.12) PRINTING TUTORIAL

The objective of this tutorial is to familiarize the user with different printing methods. We will set up a drawing that will be printed in three different ways: *limits*, *extents*, and *display*. These three methods may all give similar results or vastly different results depending on the drawing. We will also go through the steps used to print an object to scale.

2.12.1) Creating the drawing

1) Read section 2.11).

2) Open up your ***set-mm.dwt*** drawing template.

3) Check your paper size.

> **How?**
> a) Command: **limits**
> b) `Specify lower left corner or [ON/OFF] <0,0>:` **Enter**
> c) `Specify upper right corner <280,216>:` **Enter** (Your paper size should be **297** by **210**. If it is not, set it to this size now. If it is 12 x 9 or 11 x 8.5, you are in an *inch* drawing.)

4) 

Printing Tut.dwg

5) Turn your ***OBJECT SNAP*** 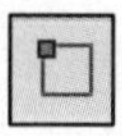 and your ***DYNAMIC INPUT***  off (*Drawing Status* bar).

6) Enter your **World coordinate system** .

> **Where?** *View* ribbon tab – *Coordinate* panel
> - If the *Coordinate* panel is not shown, right click on one of the panel names and activate it.

7) Draw a **RECtangle** whose lower left corner is located at (0, 0) and is 297 mm long by 210 mm high (width). (This rectangle indicates the edge of the paper or limits.)

> **How?**
> a) Command: **rec** or **rectangle**
> b) `Specify first corner point or [Chamfer/Elevation/Fillet/Thickness/Width]:` **0,0**
> c) `Specify other corner point or [Area/Dimensions/Rotation]:` **d**
> d) `Specify length for rectangles <10>:` **297**
> e) `Specify width for rectangles <10>:` **210**
> f) `Specify other corner point or [Area/Dimensions/Rotation]:` Select a point in the middle of your drawing area.

8) 

. (**Zoom All**)

9) Draw a **Circle** of radius **50**, and center located at **350,100**. (Don't worry, this circle will be off of your paper.)

> **How?**
> a) <u>Command:</u> **c** or **circle**
> b) `Specify center point for circle or [3P/2P/Ttr (tan tan radius)]:` **350,100**
> c) `Specify radius of circle or [Diameter]:` **50**

10) 

. (**Zoom All**) and 

2.12.2) Printing

1) <u>*Application button*:</u>  ***Print – Plot...***

2) <u>*Plot – Model* window:</u>
   a) Choose a printer.
   b) Activate the ***Fit to Paper*** toggle.
   c) Select ***Extents*** as your plot area.
   d) Activate the ***Center the plot*** toggle.
   e) Select the ***Preview...*** button. Take note of what is being printed and then hit **`Esc`** to exit the plot preview.
   f) Select ***Display*** as your plot area.
   g) Select the ***Preview...*** button. Take note of what is being printed and then hit **`Esc`** to exit the plot preview.
   h) Select ***Limits*** as your plot area.
   i) Select the ***Preview...*** button. Take note of what is being printed and then hit **`Esc`** to exit the plot preview.
   j) Select the ***Cancel*** button.

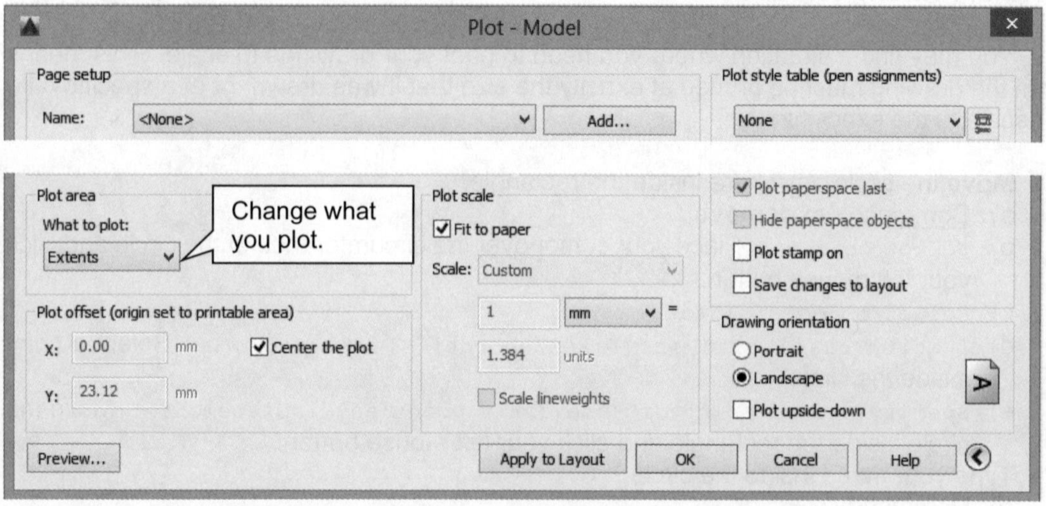

3) **Pan** 

the drawing so that the rectangle is in the center of the drawing area and the circle is slightly off the screen.

Where? *View* ribbon tab – *Navigate* panel or use your mouse wheel.

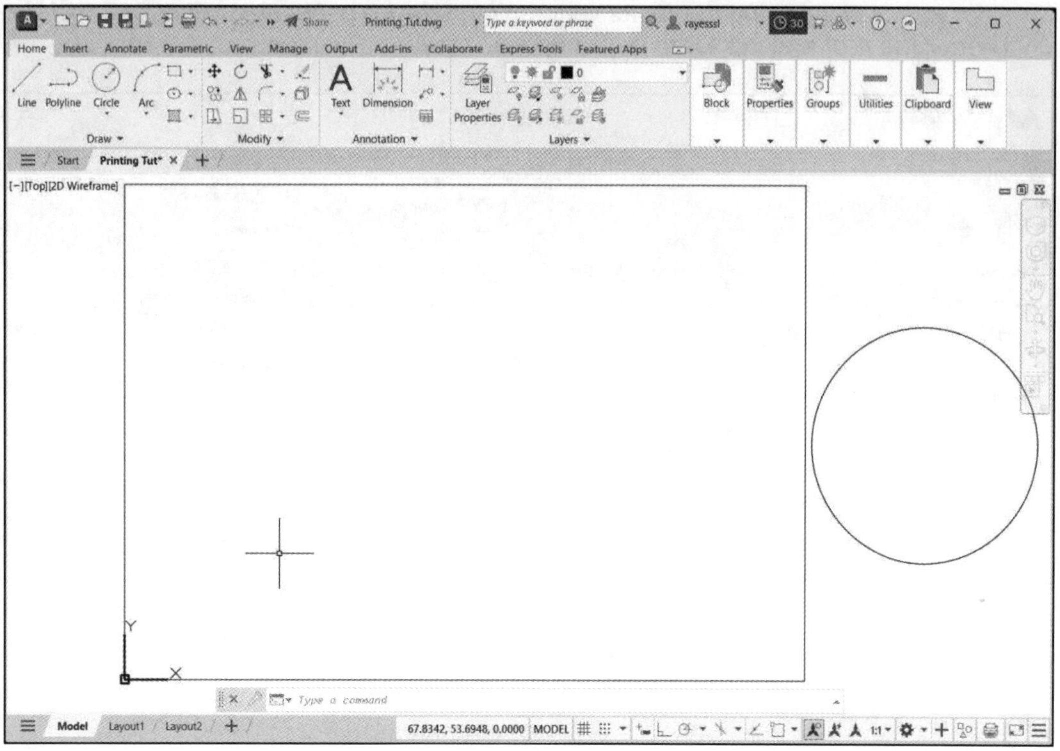

4) Repeat step 2). and notice that this time the display printing method gives a different result.

2.12.3) Printing to scale

You may find a situation where you need to print your drawings to scale. This means that the drawing must be printed at exactly the size that it was drawn, or at a specific ratio or scale to the exact size.

1) **Move** the circle anywhere inside the rectangle.
   a) Command: **m** or **move**
   b) `Select objects:` Place your cursor over the circumference of the circle and click your left mouse button.
   c) `Select objects:` **`Enter`**
   d) `Specify base point or [Displacement] <Displacement>:` Select a point inside the circle.
   e) `Specify second point or <use first point as displacement>:` Move the circle inside the rectangle and click your left mouse button.
2) Type your name inside the circle.
   a) Command: **text**
   b) `Specify start point of text or [Justify/Style]:` Select a point inside the circle.
   c) `Specify height <3>:` **3**
   d) `Specify rotation angle of text <0>:` **`Enter`**
   e) Type your name and hit **`Enter`** twice when you are done.

3) Print your drawing using ***Limits*** as your region, select a paper size of ***Letter 8.5x11in***, ***Center the plot*** and the ***Fit to paper*** option.

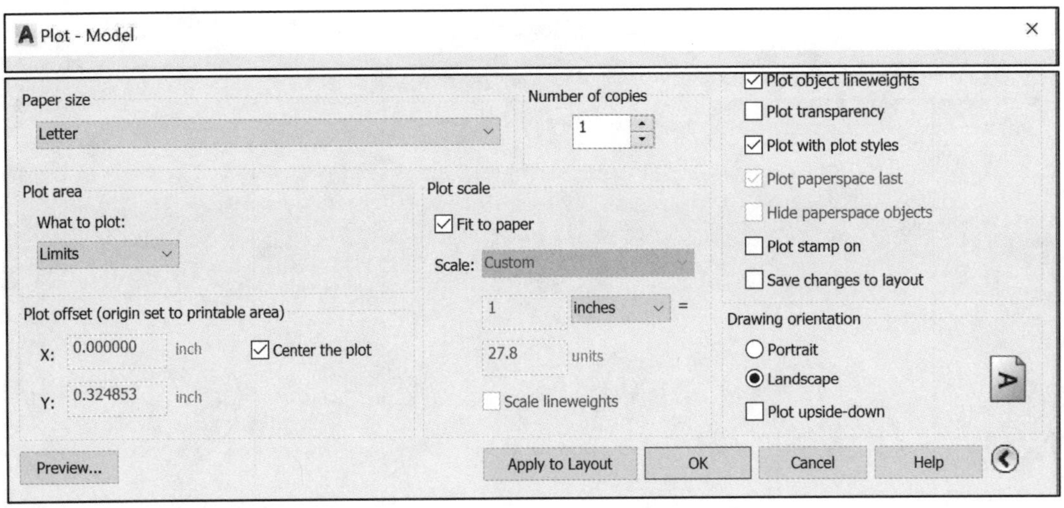

4) Print your drawing using ***Limits*** as your region, select a paper size of ***Letter 8.5x11in***, ***Center the plot*** and a ***1:1 scale***. Note that not all of the rectangle will be printed.

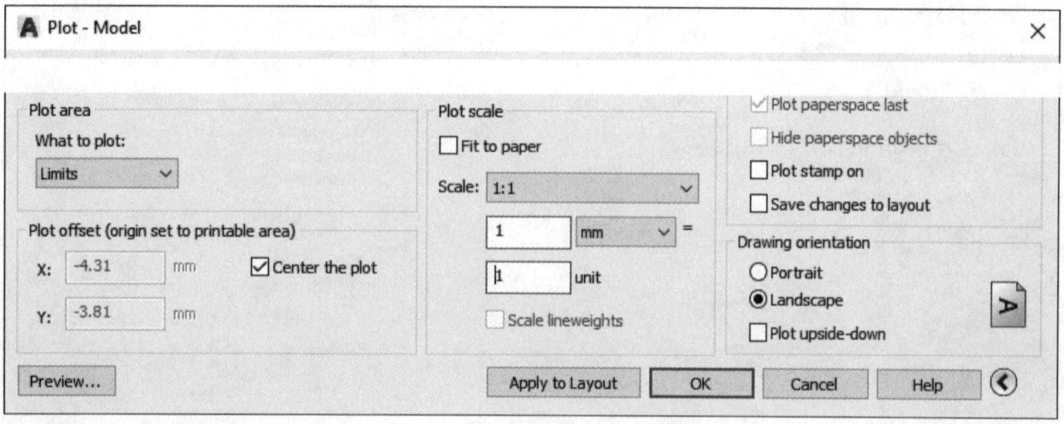

5) Measure both printed circles and indicate their measured diameters.

6) 

2.12.4) Printing to PDF

You may find a situation where you need to print your drawings to PDF or another format. AutoCAD allows you to do this using its export feature.

1) <u>Application button</u>: ***Export – PDF...***
   a) Select the file location.
   b) <u>File name:</u> Name the file.
   c) <u>Export:</u> ***Window*** (Select what you want to print)
   d) <u>Page Setup:</u> If you have already set up your page you can select ***Current***. If you have not set up your page use *Override* to set up your page.
   e) If you want to view your print, select the ***Open in viewer when done toggle***.

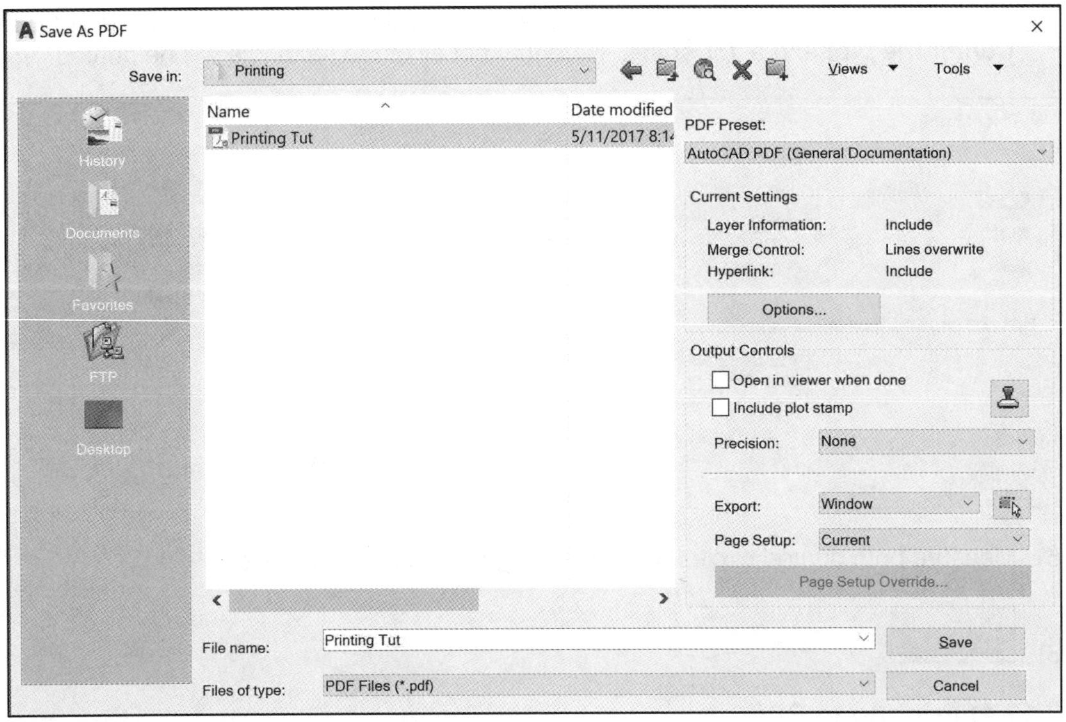

2) **Save** your drawing.

2.13) DRAW COMMANDS

The *Draw* panel (Figure 2.13-1) contains commands that allow you to draw standard geometries. The *Draw* commands can be used to create new objects such as lines and circles. Most AutoCAD® drawings are composed purely and simply from these basic components. A good understanding of the *Draw* commands is fundamental to the efficient use of AutoCAD®. To determine the name of the command associated with each icon in the *Draw* panel, place the cursor over each icon in turn and the associated command name will pop up and then in a few seconds an extended tooltip will appear.

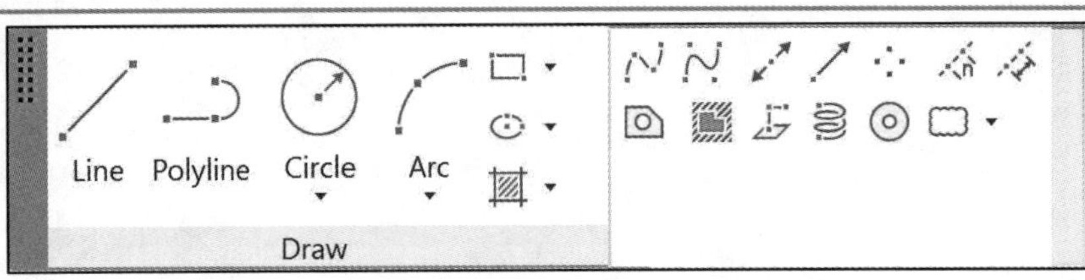

Figure 2.13-1: *Draw* panel

As is usual with AutoCAD®, the *Draw* commands can be accessed in one of several ways: typing the command in the *Command* window, from the *Draw* panel, and from the *Draw* tool palette.

2.13.1) Line

Lines are probably the most simple of AutoCAD's objects. Using the **LINE** command, a line can be drawn between any two points picked within the drawing area. A line drawn between two points is often called a vector. This terminology is used to describe the type of drawings that AutoCAD® creates. AutoCAD® drawings are generically referred to as "vector drawings." Vector drawings are extremely useful where precision is the most important criterion because they retain their accuracy irrespective of scale.

With the LINE command you can draw a simple line from one point to another, or you can continue picking points and AutoCAD® will draw a straight line between each picked point and the previous point. Each line segment drawn is a separate object and can be moved or erased as required. While the LINE command is active, you can un-enter the last point by using the **UNDO** option available in the *Command* window. You can also close a sequence of lines (connect the start and end point) using the **CLOSE** option.

The LINE command may be accessed in the following way.

- *Draw* panel: 

- *Command* window: **l** or **line**

2.13.2) Construction line

The construction line (**XLINE**) command creates a line of infinite length which passes through two picked points. Construction lines are very useful for creating construction frameworks or grids. Construction lines are not normally used as objects in finished drawings. Therefore, it is usual to draw all your construction lines on a separate layer which will be turned off or frozen prior to printing. Because of their nature, the ZOOM EXTENTS command ignores construction lines.

The construction line command may be accessed in the following way.

- *Draw* panel: 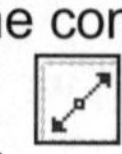
- *Command* window: **xl** or **xline**

Construction line options (`Specify a point or [Hor/Ver/Ang/Bisect/Offset]:`).

- Hor: Creates a horizontal construction line.
- Ver: Creates a vertical construction line.
- Ang: Creates a construction line at a specified angle.
- Bisect: Create a construction line that bisects an angle defined by 3 points.
- Offset: Creates a construction line that is offset from an existing line by a specified distance.

2.13.3) Ray

The **RAY** command creates a line starting at a point and going off to infinity through another specified point. The `through point:` prompt is repeated allowing you to create multiple rays. Because of their nature, the ZOOM EXTENTS command ignores rays.

The RAY command may be accessed in the following way.

- *Draw* panel: 
- *Command* window: **ray**

2.13.4) Polyline

Polylines (**PLINES**) differ from lines in that they are more complex objects. A single polyline can be composed of a number of straight-line or arc segments. Polylines can also be assigned line widths to make them appear solid. Figure 2.13-2 shows a number of polylines to give you an idea of the flexibility of this type of line. Because of their complexity, polylines use up more memory than the equivalent line. As it is desirable to keep file sizes as small as possible, it is a good idea to use LINEs rather than polylines unless you have a particular requirement.

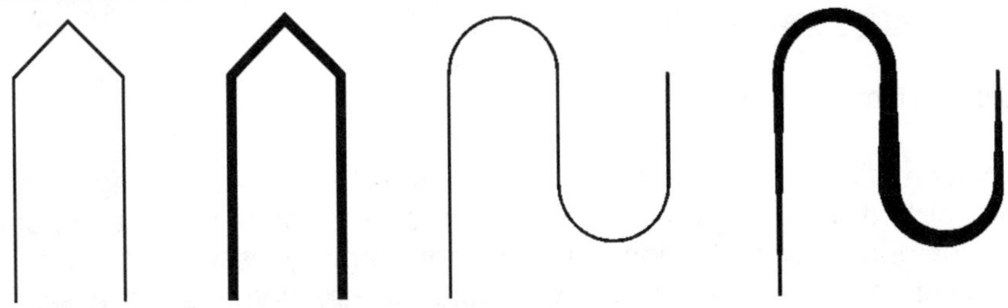

Figure 2.13-2: Polylines

The PLINE (polyline) command may be accessed in the following way.

- *Draw* panel: 
- *Command* window: **pl** or **pline**

Polyline LINE options (`Specify next point or [Arc/Halfwidth/Length/Undo/Width]:`).

- Halfwidth: Enables you to set the halfwidth of the start and end of the line.
- Length: Enables you to specify the length of the line.
- Undo: Removes the most recent segment added to the polyline.
- Width: Enables you to set the start and end widths of the line.

Polyline ARC options (`Specify endpoint of arc or [Angle/CEnter/CLose/Direction/Halfwidth/Line/Radius/Second pt/Undo/Width]:`).

- Angle: Enables you to specify the included angle of the arc segment.
- CEnter: Enables you to specify the center point of the arc.
- Direction: Enables you to specify the starting direction of the arc.
- Halfwidth: Enables you to set the halfwidth of the start and end of the arc.
- Radius: Enables you to specify the radius of the arc.
- Second pt: Enables you to specify the second point of a three point arc.
- Undo: Removes the most recent segment added to the polyline.
- Width: Enables you to set the start and end widths of the arc.

The **Undo** option is particularly useful. This allows you to unpick polyline vertices one at a time so that you can easily correct mistakes. Also, polylines may be edited after they are created using the command **PEDIT**.

2.13.5) Polygon

The **POLygon** command can be used to draw any regular polygon from 3 sides up to 1024 sides. This command requires four inputs from the user, the number of sides, a pick point for the center of the polygon, whether you want the polygon inscribed or circumscribed and then a pick point which determines both the radius of this imaginary circle and the orientation of the polygon. This command also allows you to define the polygon by entering the length of a side using the EDGE option.

The POLYGON command may be accessed in the following way.

- *Draw* panel: 
- *Command* window: **pol** or **polygon**

2.13.6) Rectangle

The **RECtangle** command is used to draw a rectangle whose sides are, by default, vertical and horizontal. However, you may draw a rectangle at a specified angle.

The RECTANGLE command may be accessed in the following way.

- *Draw* panel: 
- *Command* window: **rec** or **rectangle**

RECTANGLE options (`Specify first corner point or [Chamfer/Elevation/Fillet/Thickness/Width]:`).

- Chamfer: Creates a rectangle with chamfered corners.
- Elevation: Enables you to specify the elevation of the rectangle.
- Fillet: Creates a rectangle with filleted corners.
- Thickness: Enables you to specify the thickness of the rectangle.
- Width: Enables you to specify the line width of the rectangle.

RECTANGLE options after picking the first corner point (`Specify other corner point or [Area/Dimensions/Rotation]:`).

- Area: Enables you to specify the area and length of the rectangle.
- Dimension: Enables you to specify the length and width of the rectangle.
- Rotation: Enables you to specify the angle of the line that connects the first and second corner of the rectangle.

2.13.7) Arc

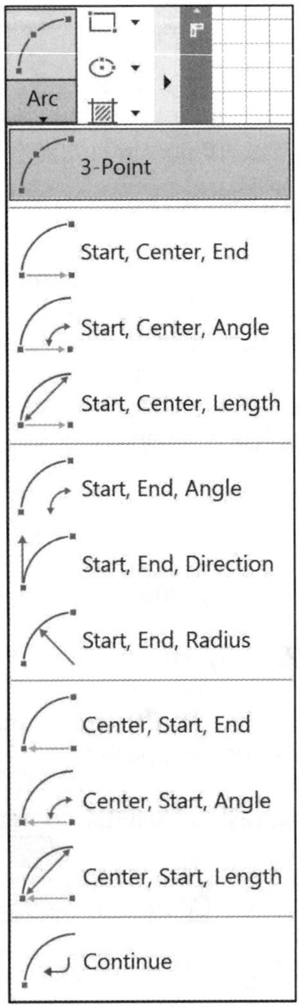

The **Arc** command allows you to draw an arc of a circle. There are numerous ways to define an arc; the default method uses three pick points, a start point, a second point and an end point. Using this method, the drawn arc will start at the first pick point, pass through the second point and end at the third point. Other ways of defining an arc can be accessed through the fly-out menu under the ARC icon.

Arcs, by default, travel in the counterclockwise direction. This default direction may be changed by holding down the `Ctrl` key as you drag.

The ARC command may be accessed in the following way.

- *Draw* panel: 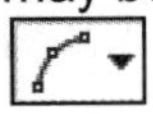
- Command window: **a** or **arc**

2.13.8) Circle

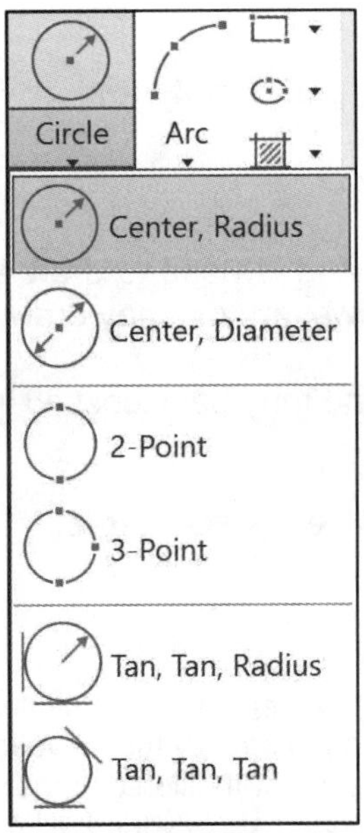

The **Circle** command is used to draw circles. There are a number of ways that you can define a circle. The default method is to pick the center point and then to either pick a second point on the circumference of the circle or to enter the circle's radius in the *Command* window. Other ways of defining a circle can be accessed through the fly-out menu under the CIRCLE icon.

The CIRCLE command may be accessed in the following way.

- *Draw* panel: 
- Command window: **c** or **circle**

2.13.9) Spline

A **SPLine** is a smooth curve that is fitted along a number of control points. Splines can be edited after they have been created using the **SPLINEDIT** command. Using this command, you can change the tolerance, add more control points, move control points and close a spline. However, if you just want to move spline control points, it is best to use the grips boxes.

You can create or edit splines using either *control vertices* or *fit points* (see Figure 2.13-3). The grip boxes are shown when you click on the spline. Creating a spline using *control vertices* has the advantage of fine control. The variables **CVSHOW** and **CVHIDE** control whether or not the control vertices are displayed. The options available within the spline command depend on the method used to create the spline.

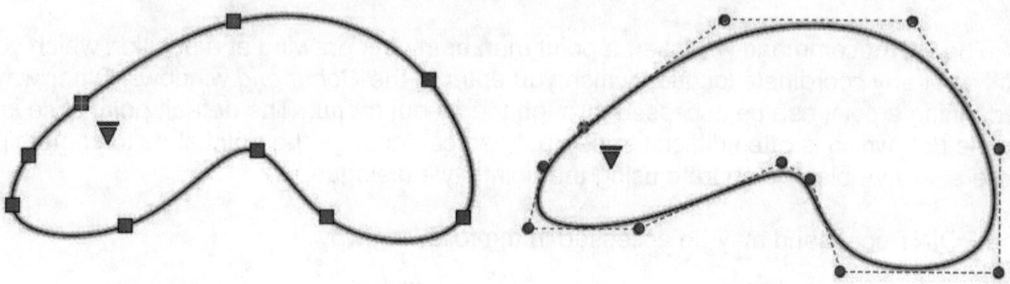

Spline Fit   Spline CV

Figure 2.13-3: Spline methods

The SPLINE fit command may be accessed in the following way.

- Draw panel:  (fit)  (CV)
- *Command* window: **spl** or **spline**

Spline Fit options (`Specify first point or [Method/Knots/Object]:`)

- Method: Allows you to choose between the *fit* and *control vertices* methods.
- Knots: Allows you to choose the knot parameterization (chord, square root or uniform).

Spline Fit options (`Enter next point or [start Tangency/toLerance]:`)

- start Tangency: Allows you to specify the tangency of the first curved segment.
- toLerance: Allows you to control how closely the spline conforms to the control points. A low tolerance value causes the spline to form close to the control points. A tolerance of 0 (zero) forces the spline to pass through the control points.

Spline Fit options (`Enter next point or [end Tangency/toLerance/Undo/Close]:`)

- end Tangency: Allows you to specify the tangency of the last curved segment.
- Undo: Removes the last point.
- Close: Closes the spline.

Spline CV options (`Specify first point or [Method/Degree/Object]:`)

- Degree: Allows you to specify the degree of the spline.

2.13.10) Ellipse

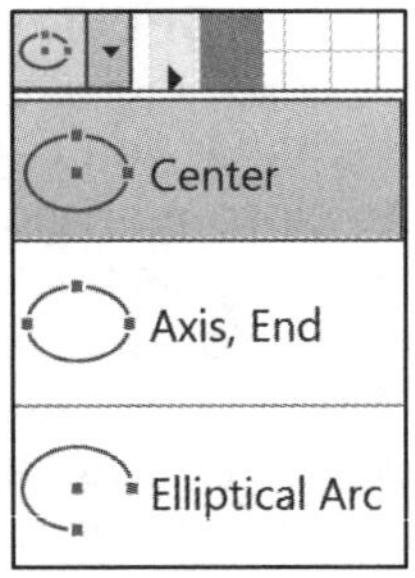

The **ELlipse** command gives you a number of different creation options. The default option is to pick the two end points of an axis and then a third point to define the eccentricity of the ellipse. Other ways of defining an ellipse can be accessed through the fly-out menu under the ELLIPSE icon.

The ELLIPSE command may be accessed in the following way.

- *Draw* panel: 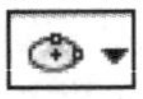
- Command window: **el** or **ellipse**

2.13.11) Point

The **POint** command will insert a point marker in your drawing at a position which you pick or at any coordinate location which you enter in the *Command* window. Other ways of defining a point can be accessed through the fly-out menu. The default point style is a simple dot, which is often difficult to see but you can change the point style to something more easily visible or elaborate using the point style dialogue box.

The POINT command may be accessed in the following way.

- *Draw* panel: 
- *Command* window: **po** or **point**

You can access the *Point Style* window with the command **DDPTYPE.** To change the point style, just pick the picture of the style you want and then click the *OK* button (see Figure 2.13-4). You may also change the point size (**PDSIZE**) in this window. You will need to use the **REGEN** (regenerate) command to update your existing points. Any new points created after the style has been set will automatically display in the new style.

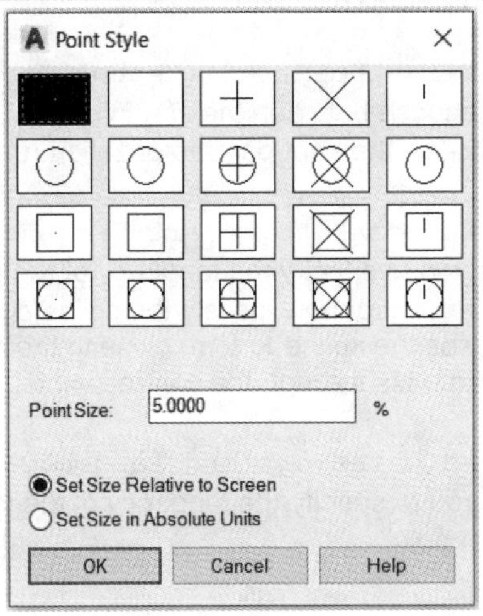

Figure 2.13-4: *Point Style* window

2.14) TEXT

Text may be added to any location of your drawing and is present in your drawing dimensions. AutoCAD's text is very flexible. It offers all of the standard Windows® fonts plus a few extra fonts. Various text commands and settings may be found in two locations. Text commands may be found in the *Annotation* panel in the *Home* tab and the *Text* panel in the *Annotate* tab shown in Figure 2.14-1.

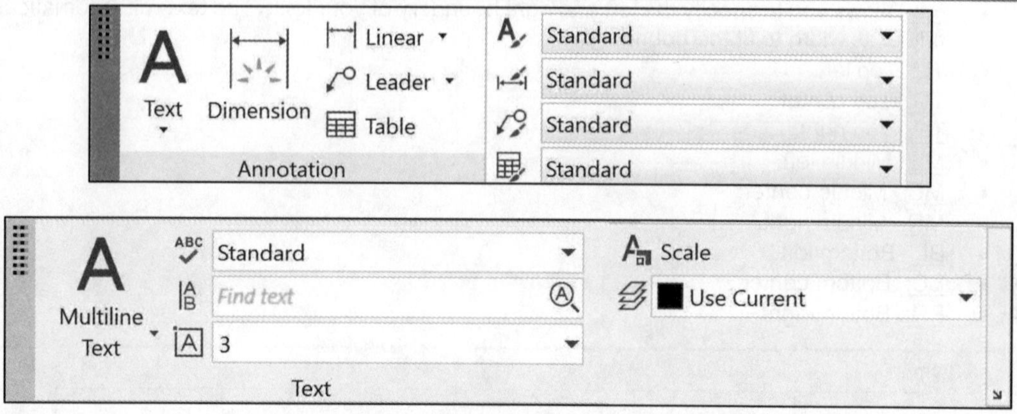

Figure 2.14-1: Annotation and Text panels

2.14.1) Style

The default text font and size may be set in the *Text Style* window. Many text styles may be created and saved under a style name. Properties such as the text direction and the text angle may also be set. The *Text Style* window shown in Figure 2.14-2 may be accessed by typing the command **STyle** or **ST**. Figure 2.14-2 also shows some examples of different text effects performed on an Arial font.

2.14.2) Single-line text

The **TEXT** command creates a single line of text. When creating text, you can click anywhere in a drawing to create a new text block. The advantage of using single line text is its wide variety of justification options. If TEXT was the last command entered, pressing **`Enter`** at the `Specify Start Point of Text:` prompt skips the prompts for height and rotation angle and enters the text directly underneath the previously entered text. The command **DDEDIT** may be used to edit existing text.

The TEXT command may be accessed in the following way.

- *Annotation* panel: 

- *Command* window: **text** or **dt** or **dtext**

JUSTIFY options (`Enter an option [Left/Center/Right/Align/Middle/Fit/TL/TC/TR/ML/MC/MR/BL/BC/BR]:`).

- Left: Justify left.
- Center: Allows you to specify the center of the text.
- Right: Justify right.
- Align: Allows you to specify the left and right boundary of your text. The text will automatically adjust its height to fit the boundary.
- Middle: Allows you to specify the middle of the text.
- Fit: Allows you to specify the left and right boundary of your text. The text will automatically adjust its width to fit the boundary.
- TL: Top left.
- TC: Top center.
- TR: Top right.
- ML: Middle left.
- MC: Middle center.
- MR: Middle right.
- BL: Bottom left.
- BC: Bottom center.
- BR: Bottom right.

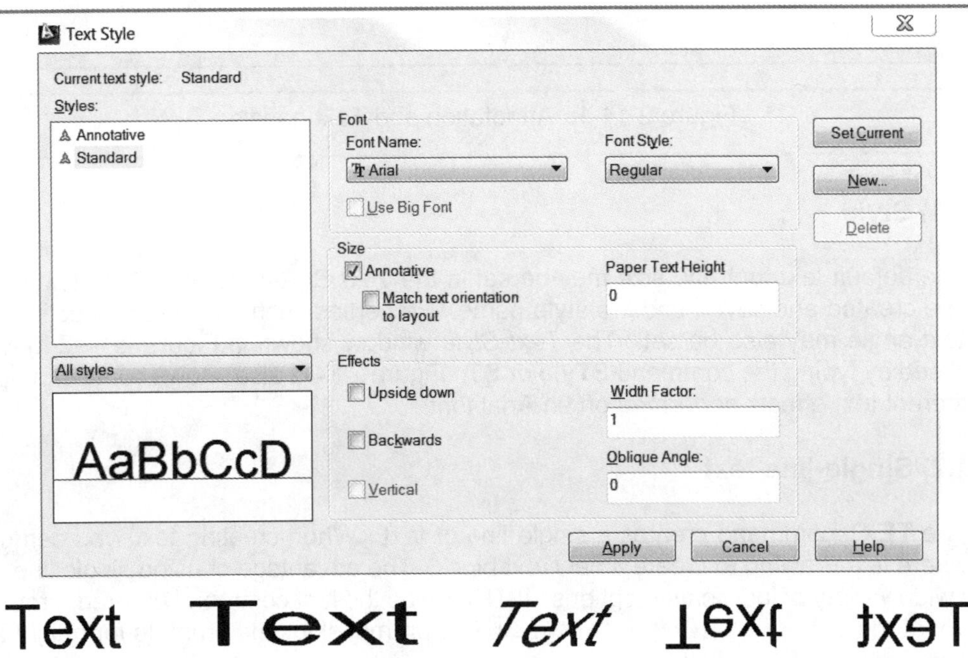

Figure: 2.14-2: *Text Style* window and text effects examples

2.14.3) Multi-lined text

Using the multi-lined text (**MText**) command activates an in-place text editor and adds a *Text Editor* tab to the ribbon. The *Text Editor* tab includes several different panels that allow you to change your text properties (i.e. font, size, justification). Figure 2.14-3 shows the *Text Editor* tab and in-place text editor. To edit multi-lined text, you can double click on the text or use the commands **DDEDIT** or **MTEDIT**. Also, the command

TEXTTOFRONT may be used to move text and dimensions in front of all other objects in the drawing.

The MTEXT command may be accessed in the following way.

- *Annotation* panel: 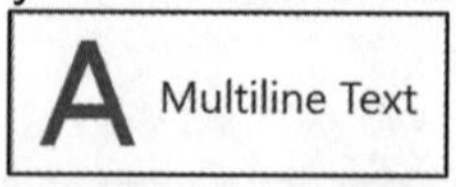

- *Command* window: **t** or **mt** or **mtext**

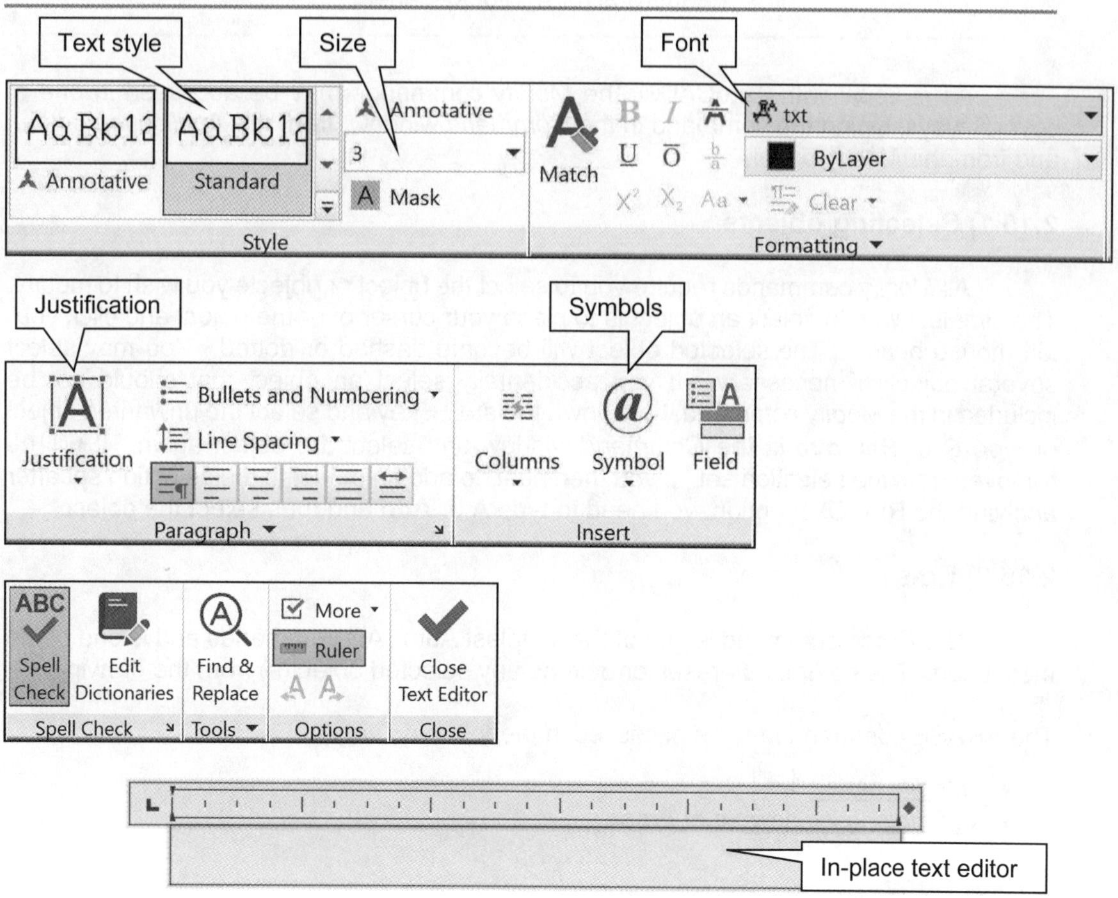

Figure 2.14-3: In place text editor.

2.15) MODIFY COMMANDS

AutoCAD® drawings are rarely completed simply by drawing lines, circles and other geometries available within the *Draw* commands. It is more than likely that you will need to modify these basic objects, in some way, to create the shape you need. The *Modify* panel (Figure 2.15-1) contains commands that allow you to change standard geometries. AutoCAD provides a wide range of *Modify* commands such as MOVE, COPY, ROTATE and MIRROR. As you can see, the command names are easily understandable. However, the way these commands work is not always obvious. It is very important to read the prompt displayed in the *Command* window while applying a *Modify* command.

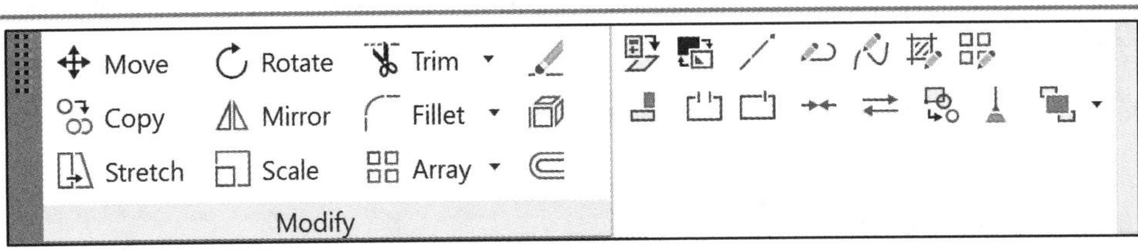

Figure 2.15-1: Modify panel

As is usual with AutoCAD®, the *Modify* commands may be accessed in one of several ways: typing the command in the *Command* window, from the *Application button*, and from the *Modify* panel.

2.15.1) Selecting objects

All *Modify* commands require you to select the object or objects you wish to modify. The simplest way to select an object is to place your cursor over the object and click your left mouse button. The selected object will become dashed or dotted. You may select several objects if necessary. If you accidentally select an object that should not be included in the *Modify* command, hold down the `Shift` key and select the unwanted object or type **R** or **Remove** in the *Command* window and select the object again. It will be removed from the selection set. If you then need to add an object to the selection set after applying the REMOVE option, you need to type **A** or **Add** and then select the object.

2.15.2) Erase

The **Erase** command is one of the simplest AutoCAD commands and is one of the most used. The command erases or deletes any selected object(s) from the drawing.

The ERASE command may be accessed in the following way.

- *Modify* panel: 
- *Command* window: **e** or **erase**

2.15.3) Copy

The **COpy** command can be used to create one or more duplicates of any object(s) which have been previously created.

The COPY command may be accessed in the following way.

- *Modify* panel: 

- *Command* window: **co** or **cp** or **copy**

<u>Copying an object(s)</u>

1) <u>Command:</u> **co** or **copy** or *<u>Modify</u>* <u>panel:</u> 

2) `Select objects:` Select an object that you want to copy.
3) `Select objects:` Select an object that you want to copy or hit **`Enter`** to stop selecting objects.
4) `Specify base point or [Displacement/mOde] <Displacement>:` **o**
5) `Enter a copy mode option [Single/Multiple] <Multiple>:` **m**
6) `Specify base point or [Displacement/mOde] <Displacement>:` Select a base point (see selecting base points).
7) `Specify second point or [Array] <use first point as displacement>:` Select a second base point.
8) `Specify second point or [Array/Exit/Undo] <Exit>:` To make another copy, select another second base point or hit **`Enter`** to exit.

<u>Selecting base points</u>

- <u>Copying an object(s) a specified distance:</u> The two base points are simply used to indicate the distance and direction of the copied object from the original object. The first *base point* does not have to be picked on or near the object, just select a point anywhere on the drawing area. The *second base point* is specified as a relative (@) coordinate. This relative coordinate gives the specified distance and direction.
- <u>Copying an object(s) to a specific location:</u> In this situation, the base points need to have a geometric relationship with the object and its subsequent final location. The first *base point* should be a geometric location on the object, and the *second base point* should be either a coordinate point or a geometric location on an existing object.

2.15.4) Mirror

The **MIrror** command allows you to mirror selected objects in your drawing by picking them and then defining the position of an imaginary mirror line using two points. To create perfectly horizontal or vertical mirror lines turn the ORTHO command on. Figure 2.15-2 shows examples of mirroring.

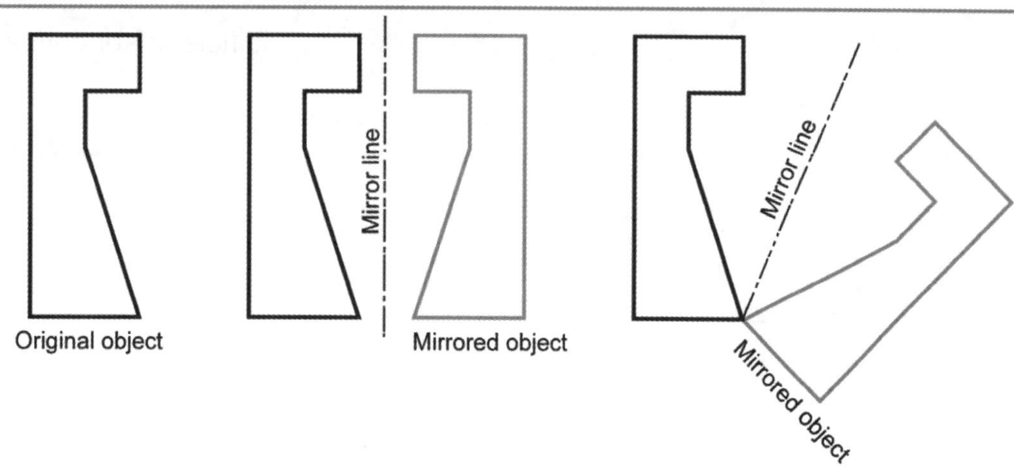

Figure 2.15-2: Mirroring an object

The MIRROR command may be accessed in the following way.

- *Modify* panel: Mirror
- *Command* window: **mi** or **mirror**

Mirroring an object(s)

1) Command: **mi** `or` **mirror** `or` *Modify* panel: Mirror
2) `Select objects:` Select an object that you want to mirror.
3) `Select objects:` Select an object that you want to mirror or hit **`Enter`** to stop selecting objects.
4) `Specify first point of mirror line:` Select a point
5) `Specify second point of mirror line:` Select a point
6) `Erase source objects? [Yes/No] <N>:` (Entering **Y** will erase your originally selected objects)

2.15.5) Offset

The **OFFSET** command creates a new object parallel to or concentric with a selected object. The new object is drawn at a user defined distance (the offset) from the original and in a direction chosen. The OFFSET command may only be used on one object or entity at a time. Figure 2.15-3 shows a rectangle being offset. This effect could not be obtained by offsetting a rectangle that was created using four lines.

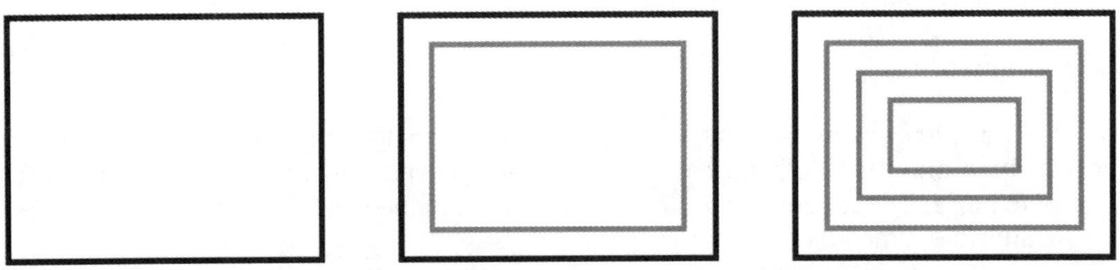

Figure 2.15-3: Offsetting a rectangle

The OFFSET command may be accessed in the following way.

- *Modify* panel: 
- *Command* window: **offset**

Offsetting an object

1) Command: **offset** or *Modify* panel: 
2) `Specify offset distance or [Through/Erase/Layer] <1.0000>:` Specify the distance to offset.
3) `Select object to offset or [Exit/Undo] <Exit>:` Select an object.
4) `Specify point on side to offset or [Exit/Multiple/Undo] <Exit>:` Select a point on either side of the object to specify the direction of offset. Select the option MULTIPLE if you want to perform multiple offsets. The offset will be relative to the last offset object.
5) `Select object to offset or [Exit/Undo] <Exit>:` Select another object to be offset by the distance specified above or hit **Enter** to exit the command.

2.15.6) Array

The **ARray** command makes multiple copies of selected objects in a rectangular pattern (columns and rows) or a polar (circular) pattern. Figure 2.15-4 shows an example of a rectangle and a polar array. The system variable **ARRAYTYPE** sets the type of array: Arraytype = 0 (rectangular), 1 (path array), 2 (Polar array).

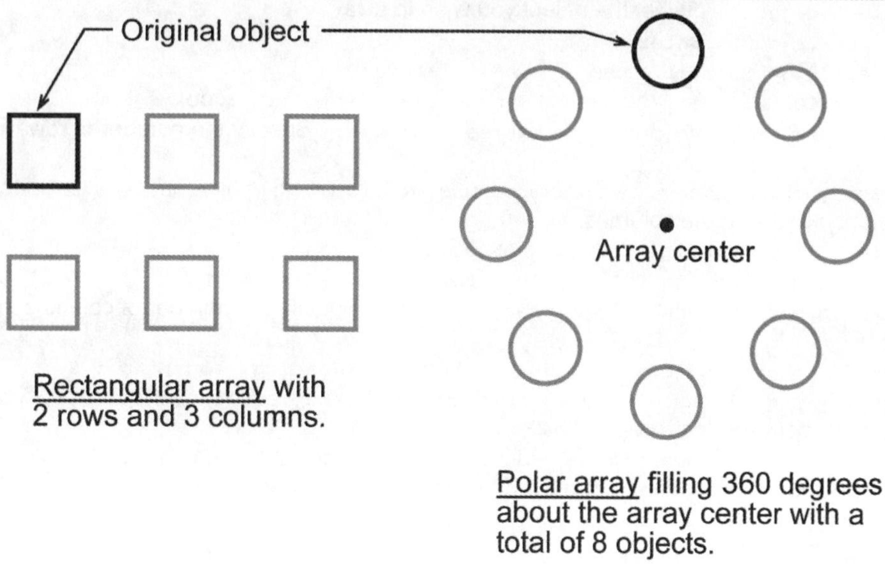

Figure 2.15-4: Rectangular and polar array

The ARRAY command may be accessed in the following way.

- *Modify* panel: 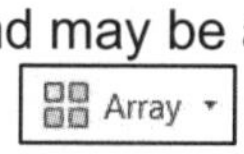
- *Command* window: **ar** or **array**

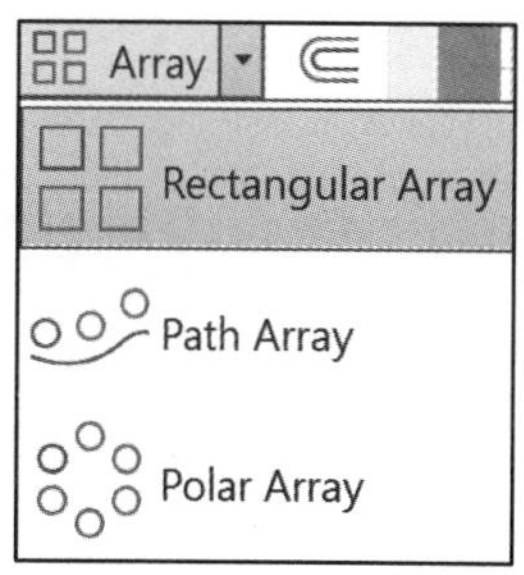

Creating an array

1) <u>Command:</u> **ar** or **array** or *<u>Modify</u>* <u>panel:</u> 

2) `Select objects:` Select the object you wish to array.
3) `Select objects:` **`Enter`**
4) `Select grip to edit array or [ASsociative/Base point/COUnt/Spacing/COLumns/Rows/Levels/eXit <eXit>:` Select array options or enter the options in the *Array Creation* tab.

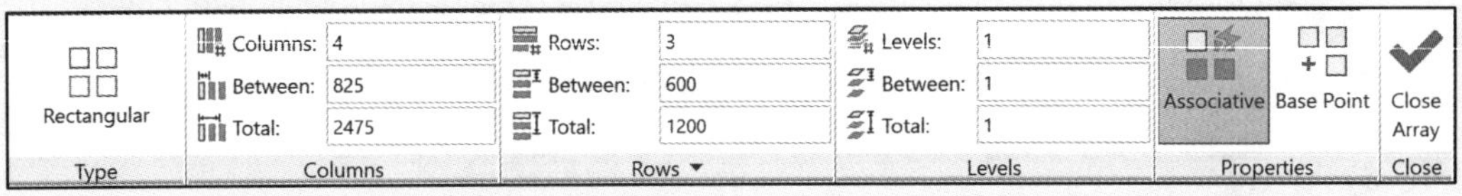

Creating a Rectangular array

1) <u>Command:</u> **arrayrect** or *<u>Modify</u>* <u>panel:</u> 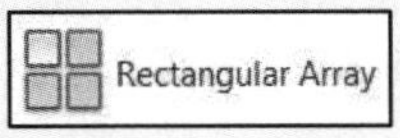

2) `Select objects:` Select the object you wish to array.
3) `Select objects:` **`Enter`**
4) `Select grip to edit array or [ASsociative/Base point/COUnt/Spacing/COLumns/Rows/Levels/eXit]<eXit>:` **col**
5) `Enter number of columns or [Expression] <4>:` Specify the number of rows in the array.
6) `Specify the distance between columns or [Total/Expression] <58>:` Specify the distance between the columns.
7) `Select grip to edit array or [ASsociative/Base point/COUnt/Spacing/COLumns/Rows/Levels/eXit]<eXit>:` **r**
8) `Enter number of rows or [Expression] <4>:` Specify the number of columns in the array.
9) `Specify opposite corner to space items or [Spacing] <Spacing>:` **s**
10) `Specify the distance between rows or [Total/Expression] <48>:` Specify the distance between the rows.
11) `Specify the incrementing elevation between rows or [Expression] <0>:` Specify the row elevation. For a 2D drawing, there is no need for elevation.
12) `Select grip to edit array or [ASsociative/Base point/COUnt/Spacing/COLumns/Rows/Levels/eXit]<eXit>:` **x**

Creating a Polar array

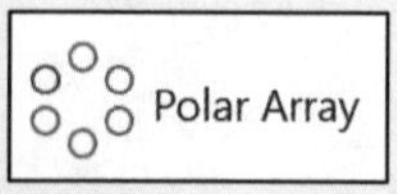

1) Command: **arraypolar** or *Modify* panel:
2) `Select objects:` Select the object you wish to array.
3) `Select objects:` **`Enter`**
4) `Specify center point of array or [Base point/Axis of rotation]:` Select the center point.
5) `Select grip to edit array or [ASsociative/Base point/Items/Angle between/Fill angle/ROWs/Levels/ROTate items/eXit] <eXit>:` **i**
6) `Enter number of items or [Expression] <3>:` Enter the number of items.
7) `Select grip to edit array or [ASsociative/Base point/Items/Angle between/Fill angle/ROWs/Levels/ROTate items/eXit] <eXit>:` **f**
8) `Specify the angle to fill (+=ccw, -=cw) or [EXpression] <360>:` Enter the angle to fill.
9) `Select grip to edit array or [ASsociative/Base point/Items/Angle between/Fill angle/ROWs/Levels/ROTate items/eXit] <eXit>:` **x**

Creating a Path array

1) Command: **arraypolar** or *Modify* panel:
2) `Select objects:` Select the object you wish to array.
3) `Select objects:` **`Enter`**
4) `Select path curve:` Select the curve that the array will follow
5) `Select grip to edit array or [ASsociative/Base point/Items/Angle between/Fill angle/ROWs/Levels/ROTate items/eXit] <eXit>:` **i**
6) `Specify the distance between items along the path or [Expression] <1>:` **10**
7) `Specify number of items or [Fill entire path/Expression] <29>:` 20
8) `Select grip to edit array or [ASsociative/Base point/Items/Angle between/Fill angle/ROWs/Levels/ROTate items/eXit] <eXit>:` **x**

Once an array has been created, it becomes a group of objects. That means that the individual objects that make up the array cannot be edited independently. The array as a whole may be modified by clicking on the group. After the array has been selected, an *Array Edit* panel will appear. The array parameters may be changed in this panel as shown in Figure 2.15-5. Alternatively, you may enter the command prompt editing options by using the ARRAYEDIT command. If you want to edit an individual array object, you may **`ctrl`**-click to Erase, Move, ROtate or SCale the selected object without affecting the array as a whole. Alternatively, you may EXPLODE the array and break it up into its individual objects.

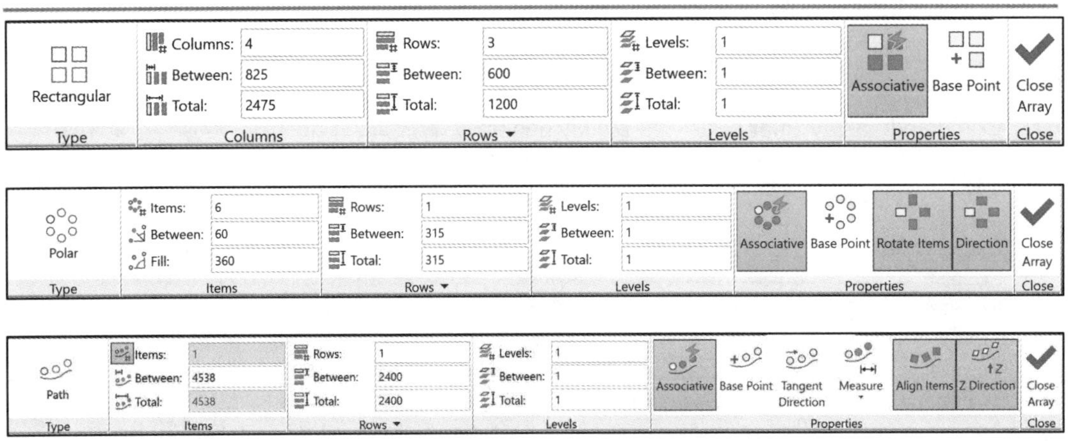

Figure 2.15-5: Array edit panel

2.15.7) Move

The **Move** command works in a similar way to the COPY command except that no copy is made; the selected object(s) is simply moved from one location to another.

The MOVE command may be accessed in the following way.

- *Modify* panel: Move
- *Command* window: **m** or **move**

Moving an object(s)

1) Command: **m** or **move** or *Modify* panel: Move
2) `Select objects:` Select an object that you want to move.
3) `Select objects:` Select an object that you want to move or hit **Enter** to stop selecting objects.
4) `Specify base point or [Displacement] <Displacement>:` Select a base point (see selecting base points).
5) `Specify second point or <use first point as displacement>:` Select a second base point.

Selecting base points

- Moving an object(s) a specified distance: The two base points are simply used to indicate the distance and direction of the final location from the original location. The first *base point* does not have to be picked on or near the object, just select a point anywhere on the drawing area. The *second base point* is specified as a relative (@) coordinate. This relative coordinate gives the specified distance and direction.
- Moving an object(s) to a specific location: In this situation, the base point needs to have a geometric relationship with the object and its subsequent final location. The first *base point* should be a geometric location on the object, and the *second base point* should be either a coordinate point or a geometric location on an existing object.

2.15.8) Rotate

The **ROtate** command allows an object or objects to be rotated about a point selected by the user. AutoCAD prompts for a second rotation point or an angle which can be typed in the *Command* window. Figure 2.15-6 shows examples of rotating.

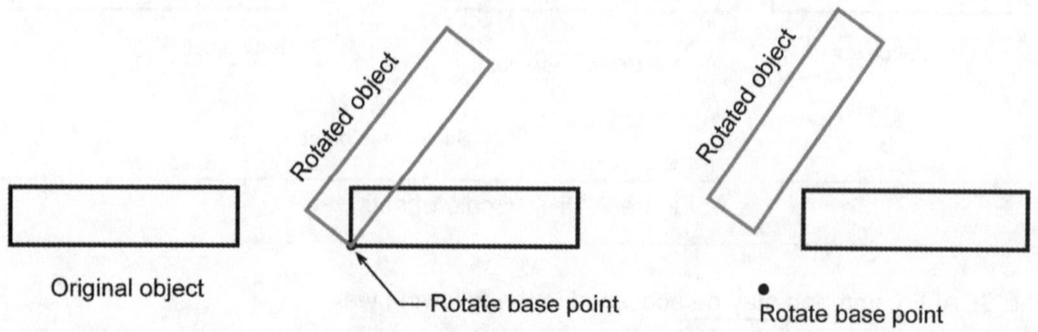

Figure 2.15-6: Rotate effects

The ROTATE command may be accessed in the following way.

- *Modify* panel: 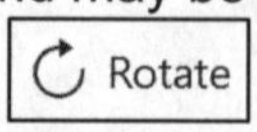

- *Command* window: **ro** or **rotate**

Rotating an object(s)

1) Command: **ro** or **rotate** or *Modify* panel: 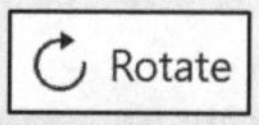

2) `Select objects:` Select an object that you want to rotate.
3) `Select objects:` Select an object that you want to rotate or hit **`Enter`** to stop selecting objects.
4) `Specify base point:` Select the point to rotate about.
5) `Specify rotation angle or [Copy/Reference] <0>:` Enter the angle of rotation or select the COPY option if you want to keep the original object.

2.15.9) Scale

The **SCale** command can be used to change the size of an object or group of objects. You are prompted for a base point about which the selection set will be scaled. Scaling can then be completed by picking a second point or by entering a scale factor. Figure 2.15-7 shows examples of scaling.

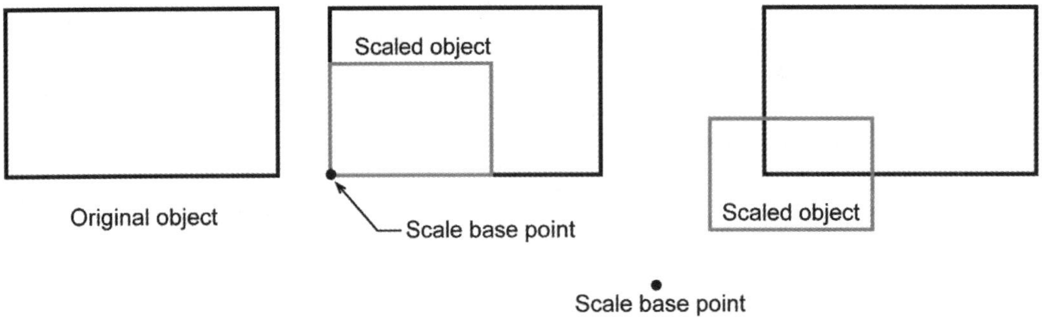

Figure 2.15-7: Scale effects

The SCALE command may be accessed in the following way.

- *Modify* panel: Scale
- *Command* window: **sc** or **scale**

Scaling an object(s)

1) Command: **sc** or **scale** or *Modify* panel: Scale
2) `Select objects:` Select an object that you want to scale.
3) `Select objects:` Select an object that you want to scale or hit **`Enter`** to stop selecting objects.
4) `Specify base point:` Select a scale reference point.
5) `Specify scale factor or [Copy/Reference] <1.000>:` Enter the scale factor or select the COPY option if you want to keep the original object.

2.15.10) Stretch

The **STRETCH** command can be used to move one or more vertices of an object while leaving the rest of the object unchanged. In Figure 2.15-8, a rectangle has been stretched by moving one vertex to create an irregular shape.

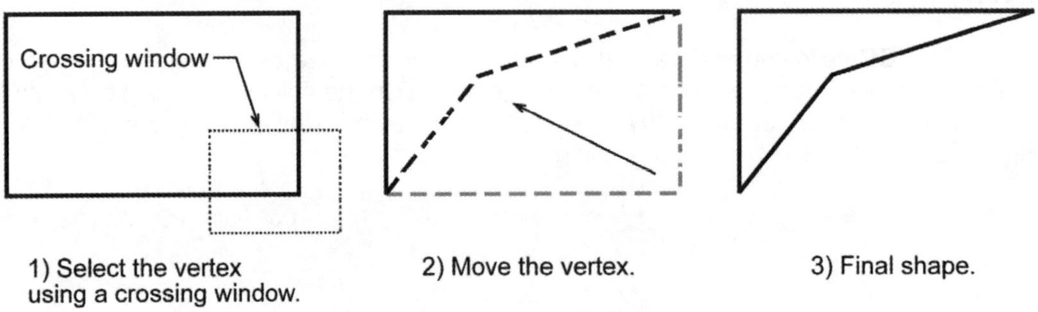

Figure 2.15-8: Using the STRETCH command

The STRETCH command may be accessed in the following way.

- *Modify* panel: 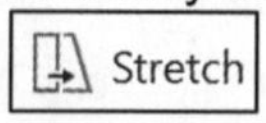

- *Command* window: **stretch**

Stretching a vertex

1) Command: **stretch** or *Modify* panel: 

2) `Select objects:` **c** (for crossing window)
3) `Specify first corner:` Select the first corner of the window.
4) `Specify opposite corner:` Select the opposite corner of the window.
5) `Select objects:` Press **`Enter`** or **`Space`** to discontinue selecting objects.
6) `Specify base point or [Displacement] <Displacement>:` Select the vertex to stretch.
7) `Specify second point or <use first point as displacement>:` Select the final position of the vertex or enter relative coordinates to specify the distance to move relative to its original position.

2.15.11) Lengthen

The **LENgthen** command is used to change the length of objects and the included angle of arcs. The LENgthen command maintains the current orientation of the object, unlike the STRETCH command. The LENgthen command allows you to specify the total length/angle of the object, or change the length by a percentage of the original length or by a specified amount (delta amount).

The LENgthen command may be accessed in the following way.

- *Modify* panel: 
- *Command* window: **len** or **lengthen**

2.15.12) Trim

The **TRim** command can be used to trim off part of an object. There are two modes that you can use to trim objects, *Quick mode* and *Standard mode*. In the ***Quick mode***, you can click on an object that you want to trim or click and drag (creating a fence line) to select several objects to trim. In the quick mode, AutoCAD will select what it believes are the correct cutting edges. In the ***Standard mode***, you must manually select the cutting edges first and then select what you want to trim. The **TRIMEXTENDMODE** system variable controls whether the **TRim** command defaults to *Quick* (TRIMEXTENDMODE = 1) or *Standard mode* (TRIMEXTENDMODE = 0).

In either mode, in order to trim an object, you must have a second object which forms the cutting edge. Cutting edges can be lines, xlines, rays, polylines, circles, arcs or ellipses. Blocks and text cannot be trimmed or used as cutting edges. At each trimming step you are given the option to UNDO the previous trim. This can be very useful if you inadvertently pick the wrong object. Figure 2.15-9 shows an example of trimming.

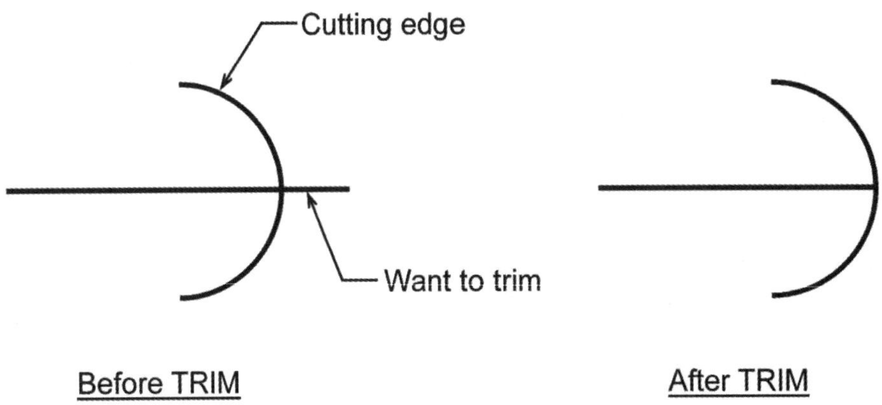

Figure 2.15-9: An example of trimming

The TRIM command may be accessed in the following way.

- *Modify* panel: 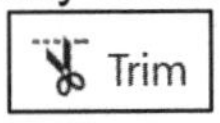

- *Command* window: **tr** or **trim**

2.15.13) Extend

The **EXtend** command extends a line, polyline or arc to meet an existing object (known as the boundary edge) as illustrated in Figure 2.15-10. There are two modes that you can use to extend objects, *Quick mode* and *Standard mode*. In the ***Quick mode***, you can click on an object that you want to extend or click and drag (creating a fence line) to select several objects to extend. In the quick mode, AutoCAD will select what it believes are the correct boundary edges. In the ***Standard mode***, you must manually select the boundary edges first and then select what you want to trim. The **TRIMEXTENDMODE** system variable controls whether the **EXtend** command defaults to *Quick* (TRIMEXTENDMODE = 1) or *Standard mode* (TRIMEXTENDMODE = 0).

You can tell AutoCAD which direction to extend the object by picking a point to one side or the other of the midpoint. If the object does not extend, it means that you are either picking the wrong end of the object or the object you are trying to extend will not meet the boundary edge. The solution is to either pick nearer the end you want to extend, move the boundary edge so that the extended object will intersect it, or use the EDGE option. The EDGE/EXTEND option will create an imaginary boundary for the object to intersect. Figure 2.15-10 shows an example extending an object.

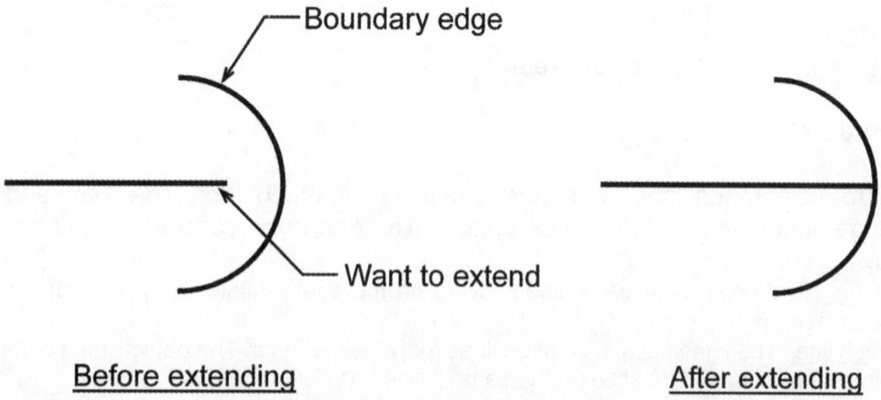

Figure 2.15-10: Extending an object

The EXTEND command may be accessed in the following way.

- *Modify* panel: 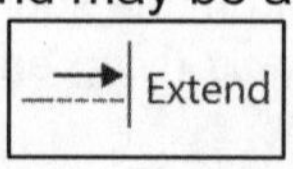

- *Command* window: **ex** or **extend**

2.15.14) Break

The **BReak** command enables you to break (remove part of) an object by defining two break points. In Figure 2.15-11, a corner of a rectangle has been removed using the BREAK command. The remaining lines are still part of one entity. By default, AutoCAD assumes that the point used to select the object is the first break point. However, you can use the FIRST POINT option to override this. If you need to break an object into two without removing any part of it, use the **BREAKATPOINT** command .

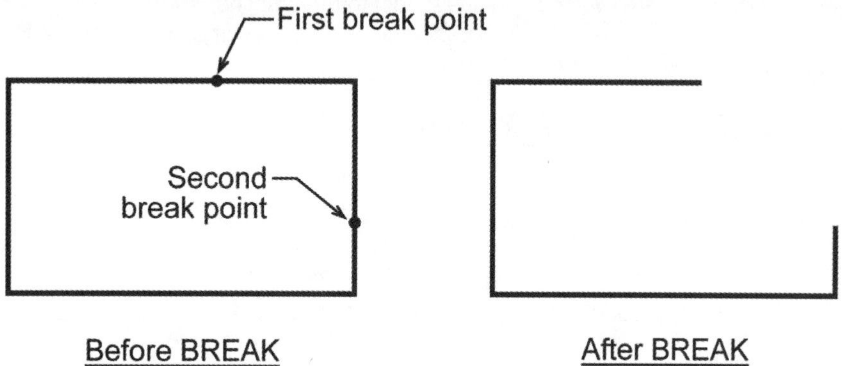

Figure 2.15-11: Breaking an object

The BREAK command may be accessed in the following way.

- *Modify* panel: 
- *Command* window: **br** or **break**

2.15.15) Join

The **Join** command joins two separate objects into one object. The command prompt will change depending on the source object. The restrictions of the JOIN command for the following source objects are:

- Line: The lines must be collinear (lying on the same infinite line), but can have gaps between them.
- Polyline: The joined objects can be lines, polylines, or arcs. The objects cannot have gaps between them and must lie on the same plane parallel to the UCS *xy* plane.
- Arc: The arcs must lie on the same imaginary circle, but can have gaps between them. The CLOSE option converts the source arc into a circle. The arcs are joined counterclockwise beginning from the source object.
- Elliptical Arc: The elliptical arcs must lie on the same ellipse, but can have gaps between them. The CLOSE option closes the source elliptical arc into a complete ellipse. The elliptical arcs are joined counterclockwise beginning from the source object.
- Spline: The spline or helix objects must be contiguous (lying end-to-end). The resulting object is a single spline.
- Helix: The helix must be contiguous (lying end-to-end). The resulting object is a single spline.

The JOIN command may be accessed in the following way.

- *Modify* panel: 
- *Command* window: **j** or **join**

Joining a line to a line

1) Command: **j** or **join** or *Modify* panel: 
2) `Select source object or multiple objects to join at once:` Select the first line.
3) `Select objects to join:` Select a line to join to the first line.
4) `Select objects to join:` Select a line to join or hit **`Enter`** or **`Space`** to end selection.
5) If the join was successful the prompt will read: `1 line joined to source.`

Joining an arc to create a complete circle

1) Command: **j** or **join** or *Modify* panel: 
2) `Select source object or multiple objects to join at once:` Select the arc.
3) `Select arc to join to source or [cLose]:` **close**
4) If the join was successful the prompt will read: `Arc converted to a circle.`

2.15.16) Chamfer

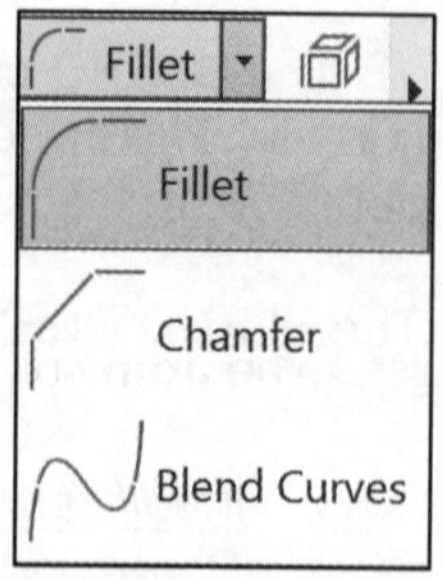

The **CHAmfer** command enables you to create a chamfer (an angled corner) between any two non-parallel lines or any two adjacent polyline segments. A chamfer is usually applied to intersecting lines. The lines do not have to intersect, but their separation cannot be more than the chamfer distance. The FILLET, CHAMFER and BLEND CURVES command reside in the same icon stack.

The CHAMFER command may be accessed in the following way.

- *Modify* panel: 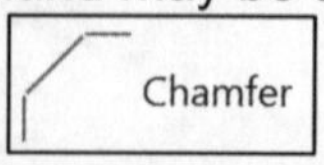

- *Command* window: **cha** or **chamfer**

CHAMFER options (`Select first line or [Undo/Polyline/Distance/Angle/Trim/mEthod/Multiple]:`).

- Undo: Enables you to undo the last chamfer while in the multiple mode.
- Polyline: Enables you to chamfer polylines.
- Distance: Enables you to specify two distances that defines the chamfer size.
- Angle: Enables you to specify an angle and a distance that defines the chamfer size.
- Trim: Enables you to specify whether you want the original line trimmed or not trimmed.
- mEthod: Controls whether a chamfer is created using two distances or a distance and an angle.
- Multiple: Allows you to create several chamfers within the same command.

2.15.17) Fillet

The **Fillet** command is a very useful tool which allows you to draw a tangent arc between two objects. The objects are usually intersecting. The objects do not have to intersect, but their separation cannot be more than the fillet radius. It's worth experimenting with this command. It can save you a lot of time and enables you to construct shapes which otherwise would be quite difficult.

The FILLET command may be accessed in the following way.

- *Modify* panel: 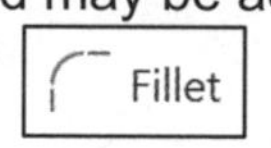

- *Command* window: **f** or **fillet**

FILLET options (`Select first object or [Undo/Polyline/Radius/Trim/Multiple]:`).

- Undo: Enables you to undo the last fillet while in the multiple mode.
- Polyline: Enables you to fillet polylines.
- Radius: Enables you to specify the radius of the fillet.
- Trim: Enables you to specify whether you want the original line trimmed or not trimmed.
- Multiple: Allows you to create several fillets within the same command.

2.15.18) Blend curves

The **BLEND curves** command creates a tangent or smooth spline between two open curves. The selected curves remain unchanged, and the shape of the connecting spline depends on the specified continuity.

The BLEND CURVES command may be accessed in the following way.

- *Modify* panel: 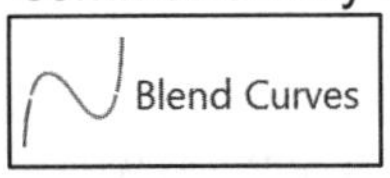

- *Command* window: **bl or blend**

2.15.19) Explode

The **EXPLODE** command is used to break apart single objects into their constituent parts. In other words, the command is used to return blocks, polylines, rectangles, etc... (which may be composed of a number of component objects) back to their individual component parts.

The EXPLODE command may be accessed in the following way.

- *Modify* panel: 
- *Command* window: **explode**

2.16) OBJECT SNAP COMMANDS

The *Object Snap* commands (Osnaps for short) are drawing aids which are used in conjunction with other commands to help you draw accurately. Osnaps allow you to snap to specific geometric locations on an existing object. For example, you can accurately pick the end point of a line or the center of a circle. Osnaps are so important that you cannot draw quickly or accurately without them. For this reason, you must develop a good understanding of what the Osnaps are and how they work.

The *Object Snap* panel shown in Figure 2.16-1 contains commands that allow you to snap to the geometry of an existing object. The *Object Snap* panel is not usually displayed by default, but you can add it through the CUI.

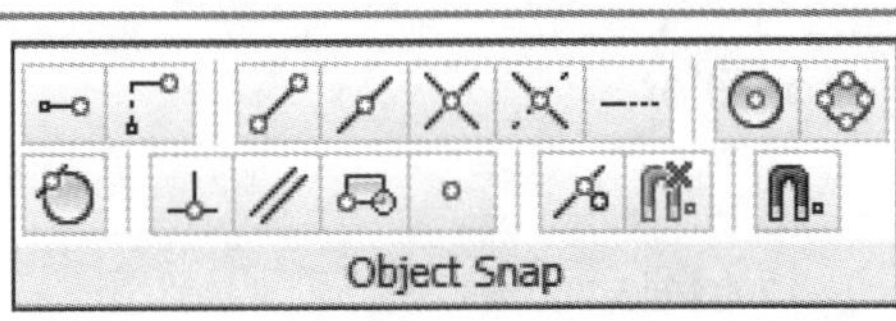

Figure 2.16-1: The *Object Snap* panel

When using Osnaps, you only need to pick a point which is near the desired point because AutoCAD automatically snaps to the location implied by the particular Osnap you are using. While drawing, notice that when you move the cursor close enough to an Osnap location, it is highlighted with an Osnap marker. Each Osnap has a different marker. Figure 2.16-2 shows examples of some of the different Osnap markers.

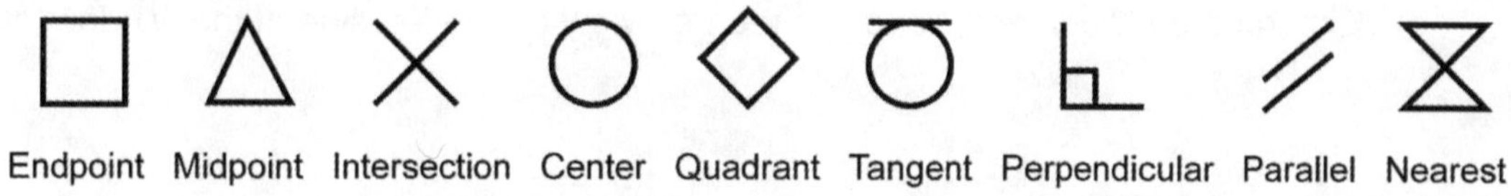

Figure 2.16-2: Object snap markers

Object snaps are so important that AutoCAD automatically detects an object's geometric locations while you are drawing. This automatic feature may be turned on and off in the *Status Bar* by clicking on the ***Object Snap*** 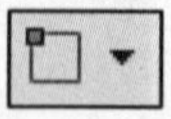 icon or by using the command **OSNAP**. To override an automatically chosen Osnap, you can select your preferred Osnap in the *Object Snap* panel or type the command in the *Command* window.

Adding the *Object Snap* panel to the *Home* tab

1. Command: **cui** or *Manage* tab – *Customization* panel:
2. *Customize User Interface* window: Expand the *Toolbars* in the tree view on the left side of the window.
   a) Scroll down until you see the *Object Snap* toolbar. Right click on *Object Snap* and select ***Copy to Ribbon Panels***.
   b) Select ***Yes*** in the *CUI Editor – Confirm Copy to Ribbon Panels Node* Window, if one appears.

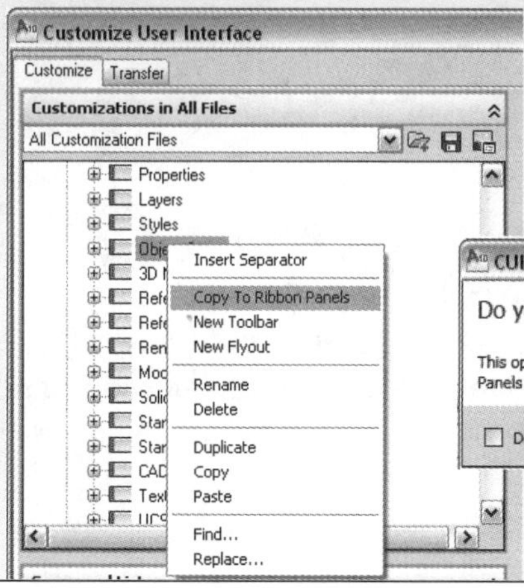

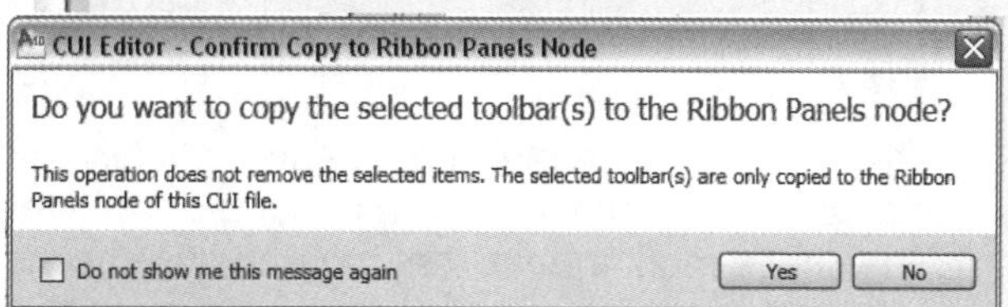

c) Expand the *Ribbon* and *Panels* in the tree view on the left side of the window.

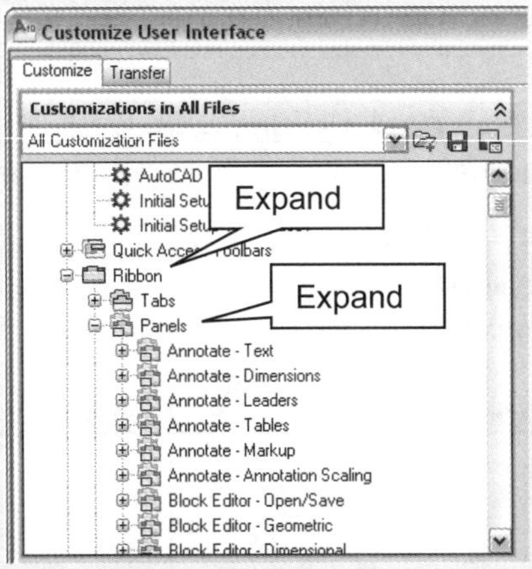

d) Find the *Object Snap* panel. It should be all the way at the bottom. Right click and select ***Copy***.
e) Within the *Tabs* root, right click on the *Home 2D* tab and select ***Paste***.
f) Select ***OK***.

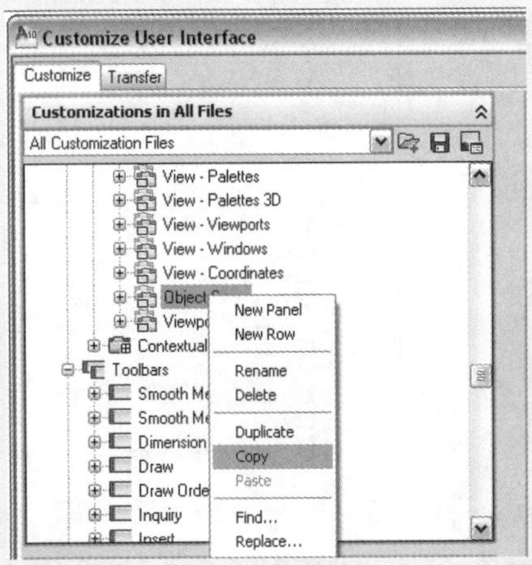

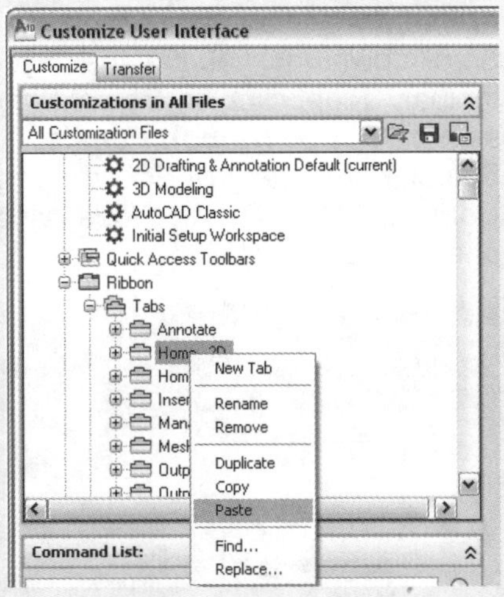

g) The *Object Snap* panel should automatically show up in the *Home* tab. You can hide or show panels by right clicking on an existing panel and selecting panel. The check mark means that the panel is showing.

2.16.1) Endpoint

The **ENDpoint** Osnap snaps to the end points of lines and arcs and to polyline vertices.

The ENDPOINT command may be accessed in the following way.

- *Object Snap* panel: 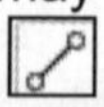
- *Command* window: **end** or **endpoint**

2.16.2) Midpoint

The **MIDpoint** Osnap snaps to the midpoint of a line, an arc and a polyline segment.

The MIDPOINT command may be accessed in the following way.

- *Object Snap* panel: 
- *Command* window: **mid** or **midpoint**

2.16.3) Intersection

The **INTersection** Osnap snaps to the physical intersection of any two drawn objects (i.e. where lines, arcs or circles cross each other) and to polyline vertices. However, this Osnap can also be used to snap to intersection points which do not physically exist. This feature is called the *Extended Intersection*. To use the extended intersection feature, you must pick two points to indicate which two objects should be used.

The INTERSECTION command may be accessed in the following way.

- *Object Snap* panel: 
- *Command* window: **int** or **intersection**

2.16.4) Apparent intersection

The Apparent Intersection (**APPINT**) Osnap snaps to the point where objects (on different planes) appear to intersect in the current view. For example, you may be looking at a drawing in plan view where two lines cross; however, since AutoCAD is a 3-dimensional drawing environment, the two lines may not physically intersect.

The Apparent Intersection (APPINT) command may be accessed in the following way.

- *Object Snap* panel: 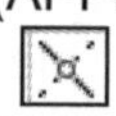
- *Command* window: **appint**

2.16.5) Extension

The **EXTension** Osnap enables you to snap to some point along the imaginary extension of a line, arc or polyline segment. To use this Osnap, you must hover the cursor over the end of the object. When the end is found, a small cross appears at the endpoint, and a dashed extension line is displayed from the endpoint to the cursor. The tool tip for the extension displays the relative polar coordinate of the current cursor position. This can be a useful guide for positioning your next point. In the case of the arc extension, the tool tip displays the distance along the arc. Once the extension is visible the distance from the endpoint may be entered. Figure 2.16-3 shows the extension snap in action.

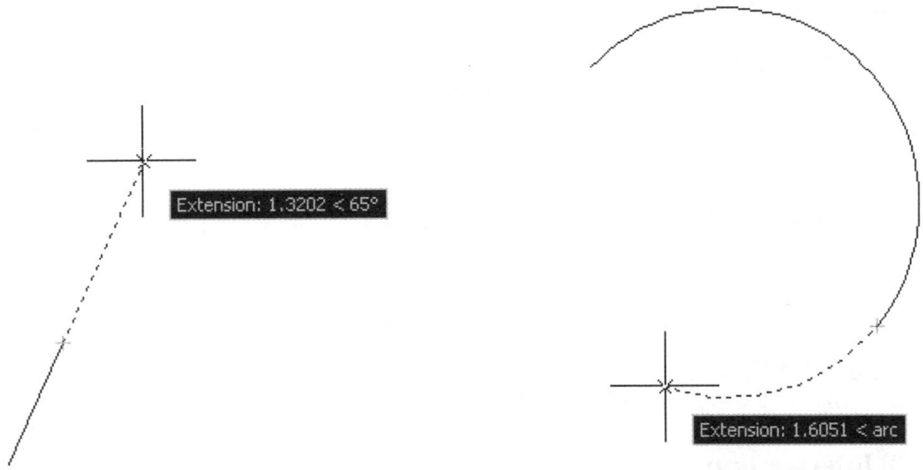

Figure 2.16-3: Extension snap

The EXTENSION command may be accessed in the following way.

- <u>*Object Snap* panel:</u> 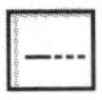
- <u>*Command* window:</u> **ext** or **extension**

2.16.6) Center

The **CENter** Osnap snaps to the center of a circle, arc or polyline arc segment. The cursor must pass over the circumference of the circle or the arc before the center can be found.

The CENTER command may be accessed in the following way.

- <u>*Object Snap* panel:</u> 
- <u>*Command* window:</u> **cen** or **center**

2.16.7) Quadrant

The **QUADrant** Osnap snaps to one of the four circle quadrant points located at north, south, east and west or 90, 270, 0 and 180 degrees respectively.

The QUADRANT command may be accessed in the following way.

- <u>*Object Snap* panel:</u> 
- <u>*Command* window:</u> **quad** or **quadrant**

2.16.8) Tangent

The **TANgent** Osnap snaps to a tangent point on a circle or arc. This Osnap works in two ways. For example, you can either draw a line from a point to the tangent point or you can draw a line between two tangent points. The second method does not give you a rubber band line to view when selecting the second point.

The TANGENT command may be accessed in the following way.

- *Object Snap* panel: 
- *Command* window: **tan** or **tangent**

2.16.9) Perpendicular

The **PERpendicular** Osnap snaps to a point which forms a 90 degree angle between the selected object and the object being drawn.

The PERPENDICULAR command may be accessed in the following way.

- *Object Snap* panel: 
- *Command* window: **per** or **perpendicular**

2.16.10) Parallel

The **PARallel** Osnap is used to draw a line parallel to any other line in your drawing.

The PARALLEL command may be accessed in the following way.

- *Object Snap* panel: 
- *Command* window: **par** or **parallel**

Drawing a line parallel to another line

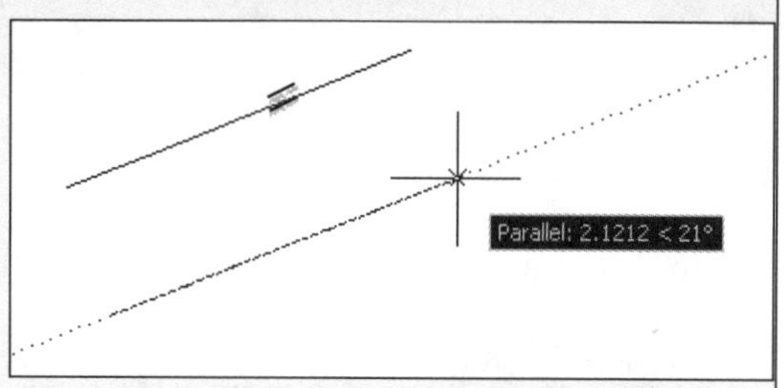

1) Command: **l** or 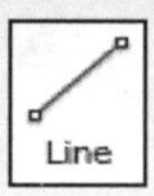

2) `Specify first point:` Select or enter your first point.
3) `Specify next point or [Undo]:` **par** or

   Object Snap panel: 

   `to` Move your cursor over the reference line. The parallel marker will appear. Move your cursor to a position that is approximately parallel to the reference line. A dashed line will appear that indicates you will create a line parallel to the reference line.

2.16.11) Nearest

The **NEARest** Osnap snaps onto an existing object. This Osnap is useful if you want to make sure that the point lies on an object but you don't necessarily mind exactly where it is located.

The NEAREST command may be accessed in the following way.

- *Object Snap* panel: 
- *Command* window: **nea** or **nearest**

2.16.12) Snap from

The SNAP **FROM** Osnap is a little more complicated than the other object snaps but it can be very useful. The SNAP FROM Osnap does not snap to an object, rather it snaps to a point at some distance or offset from an object snap location.

The SNAP FROM command may be accessed in the following way.

- *Object Snap* panel: 
- *Command* window: **from**

Using the SNAP FROM Osnap

The following command sequence creates a line that starts 1 unit away from the midpoint of an existing line.

1) Command: **l** or 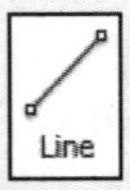

2) `Specify first point:` **from** or *Object Snap* panel: 
3) `Base point:` **mid** or *Object Snap* panel: 
`of` Select the midpoint of the reference line.
4) `<Offset>:` **1**
5) `Specify next point or [Undo]:` Select the second point.

2.16.13) Insert

The **INSert** Osnap snaps to the insertion point of a block, text or an image.

The INSERT command may be accessed in the following way.

- *Object Snap* panel: 
- *Command* window: **ins** or **insert**

2.16.14) Node

The **NODE** Osnap snaps to the center of a point, a dimension definition point or a dimension text origin. This Osnap can be useful if you have created a number of POINTS with the MEASURE OR DIVIDE commands.

The NODE command may be accessed in the following way.

- *Object Snap* panel:
- *Command* window: **node**

2.16.15) Geometric Center

The *Geometric Center* osnap snaps to the geometric center of a closed object (e.g. rectangle, polygon, closed spline). The *Geometric Center* snap is not accessible in the *Object Snap* panel, but can be automatically detected or access using the command **GCE**.

2.16.16) Object snaps settings

Individually picking or entering the *Object Snaps* commands can sometimes be a time-consuming process. With *Object Snap* set to on, AutoCAD will automatically snap to a geometric location of an object. The specific snaps that AutoCAD will detect can be set in the *Object Snap* tab of the *Drafting Settings* window (Figure 2.16-4). This can be accessed by selecting the ***Object Snap Settings*** icon, by right clicking on OSNAP in the *Status* bar and selecting **Settings...** or by entering **OSNAP** in the *Command* window. The snaps that have a check mark next to them will be automatically detected. You can set the *AutoSnap Markers Size* and *Aperture Size* by selecting the *Options…* button (Figure 2.16-5). The aperture size controls the size of the area around the current cursor position used to search for object snaps.

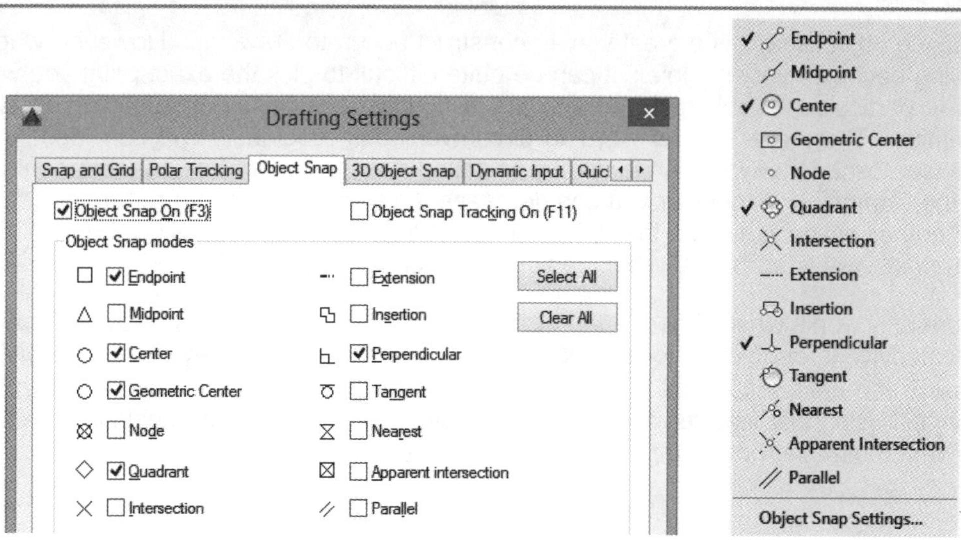

Figure 2.16-4: *Object Snap* settings

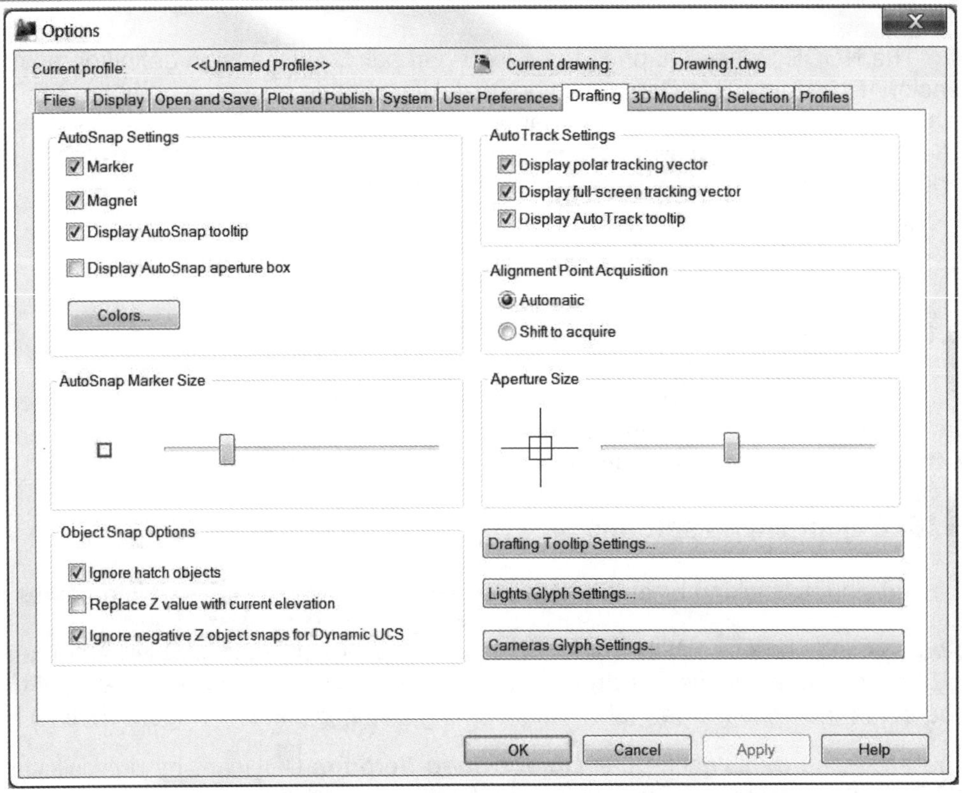

Figure 2.16-5: *Object Snap* options

2.16.17) Object snap cycling and aperture

Using object snaps is a great way to construct accurate drawings. However, when a drawing becomes very complex, it can be quite difficult to pick the exact point you want. This is particularly problematic if there are a number of possible snap points in close proximity. There are several ways to circumvent this problem. You can identify the particular Osnap that you wish to use by selecting it in the *Object Snap* panel or entering it in the *Command* window, or you can decrease the size of your aperture box.

Another option is to use the object snap cycling feature. This allows you to cycle through all valid snap points within the aperture area until you find the one you want. This feature only works when *Object Snap* 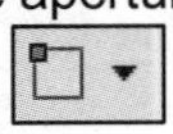 is turned on. Once a snap marker appears, you can cycle through other local snap points by pressing the **`Tab`** key. Each time **`Tab`** is pressed, the next snap point is highlighted along with the object or objects to which it belongs. Using this feature, you can be absolutely sure that you are selecting the point you want, no matter how complex the arrangement of objects.

2.17) WAGON TUTORIAL

The objective of this tutorial is to draw several different entities such as LINES, CIRCLES, POLYGONS, etc..., and use several different modifying commands such as MOVE and COPY.

AutoCAD® allows you to draw many predefined entities or shapes. Some entities can be defined in many different ways. For example, a circle can be defined by a center point coordinate and a radius, or by two tangent points and a radius. During each command, look at the command prompt and make note of the different options. Also, notice the commands enclosed in angled brackets < >. They are the default values or options and are selected by pressing the `Enter` or `Space` key.

2.17.1) Preparing to draw

1) View the *Modify*, *Move & Copy* and *Text* videos and read sections 2.13) to 2.16).

2) Open your ***set-inch.dwt*** template.

3) Set your default text font and size.
   - Command: **STyle**
   - *Text Style* window: Set your text *Font Name* to ***Arial***, check the ***Annotative*** toggle, and set your text *Height* to **0.12**, select ***Apply*** and then ***Close***.

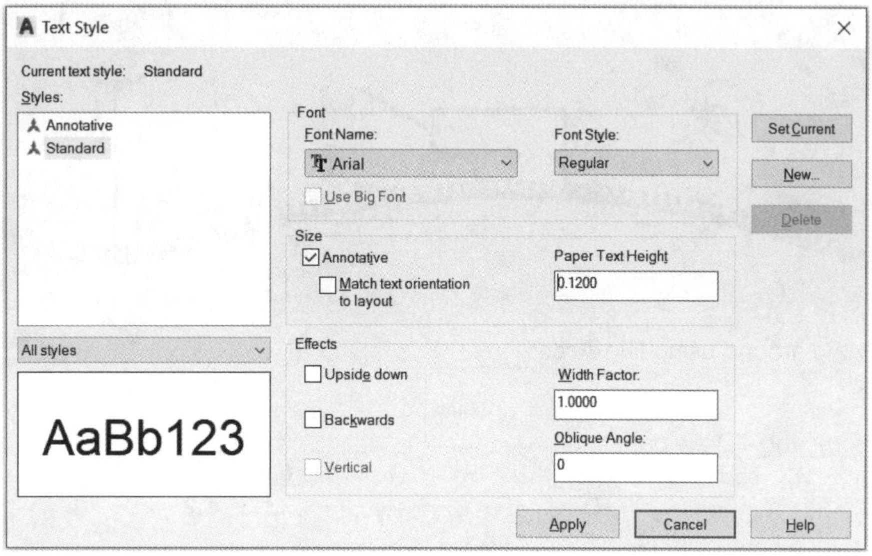

4) 

(You have just added features to your template file.)

5) 

Wagon Tut.dwg.

6) Activate a **GRID** that is **0.5** x 0.5.

7) 

(Zoom All).

8) Enter your **WCS**  (*View* tab - *Coordinates* panel) or (**UCS - W**).

9) Turn your ***Dynamic input*** off and your ***Object Snap*** off in the *Status* bar.

2.17.2) Drawing

You will be drawing the following scene.

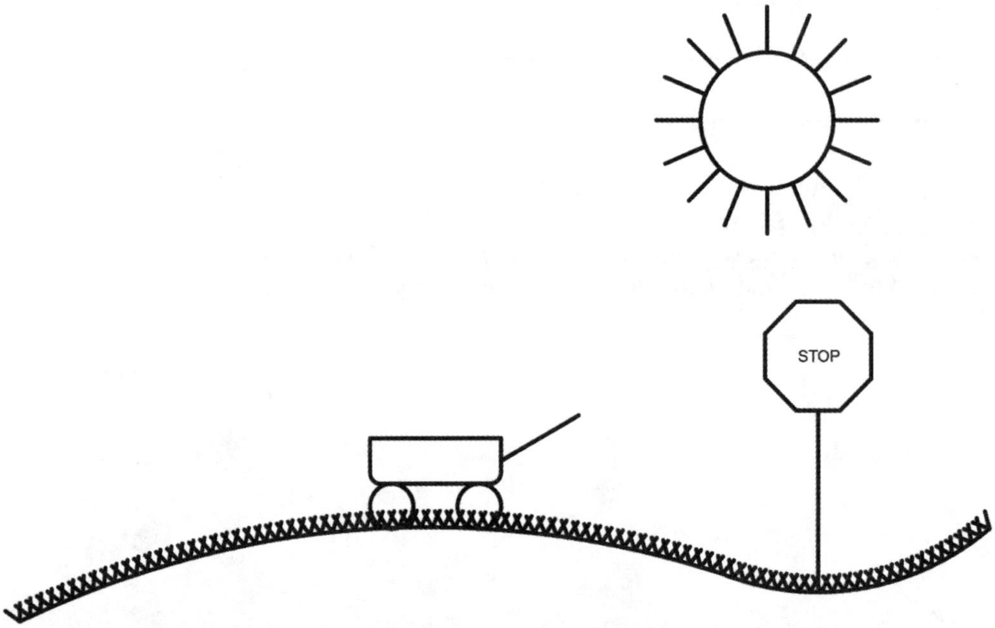

1) Draw the ground using two **Arcs**.

   a) <u>*Home* tab - *Draw* panel:</u> 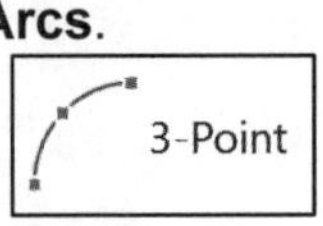

   b) `Specify start point of arc or [Center]:` **0,1**
   c) `Specify second point of arc or [Center/End]:` **4,2**
   d) `Specify end point of arc:` **8,1.5**
   e) <u>*Home* tab - Draw panel:</u> 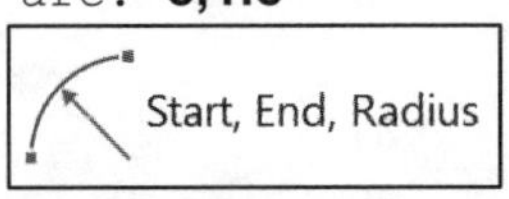

   f) `Specify start point of arc or [Center]:` **end**
   g) `of` Select the right end of the existing arc. (right side)
   h) `Specify end point of arc:` **11,2**
   i) `Specify center point of arc (hold Ctrl to switch direction):` **3**

Note: By selecting a specific type of arc from the pull-down menu, AutoCAD® automatically inputs the correct options.

2) **Join** the two arcs.
   a) `Command:` **j** or **join**
   b) `Select source object or multiple objects to join at once:` Select one of the arcs.
   c) `Select objects to join:` Select the other arc.
   d) `Select objects to join:` **`Enter`** (If the join was successful, it will say 2 objects converted to 1 polyline)

3) Add grass to your ground.
   a) Draw a **line** that is **0.2** units long at an angle of **145°** starting at the left **end** of the ground.
      i. `Command:` **l** or **line** 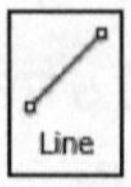

      ii. `Specify first point:` **end**
      iii. `of` Select the left end of the arc.
      iv. `Specify next point or [Undo]:` **@0.2<145**
      v. `Specify next point or [Undo]:` **`Enter`**
   b) Draw a **line** that is **0.2** units long at an angle of **90°** starting at the left **end** of the ground.
   c) **Array** the grass blade along the **path** of the ground.
      i. <u>*Home* tab – *Modify* panel</u> 

      ii. `Select objects:` Select the two lines that you just drew.
      iii. `Select objects:` **`Enter`**
      iv. `Select path curve:` Select the ground.
      v. `Select grip to edit array or [ASsociative/Method/Base point/Tangent direcction/Items/Rows/Levels/Align items/Z direction/eXit] <eXit>:` **i**
      vi. `Specify the distance between items along path or [Expression] <0.25>:` **0.1**
      vii. `Specify number of items or [Fill entire path/ Expression] <114>:` **f**
      viii. `Select grip to edit array or [ASsociative/Method/Base point/Tangent direcction/Items/Rows/Levels/Align items/Z direction/eXit] <eXit>:` **x**

4) Create the wagon wheels.
   a) Draw a **Circle** 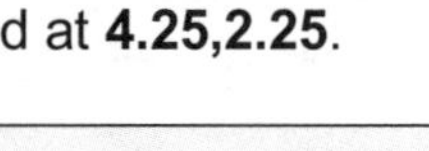

   that has a <u>diameter</u> of **0.5** inches and whose center is located at **4.25,2.25**.

How?
   ii. <u>Command:</u> **c** or **circle**
   iii. `Specify center point for circle or [3P/2P/Ttr (tan tan radius)]:` **4.25,2.25**
   iv. `Specify radius of circle or [Diameter] <1.00>:` **d**

v. `Specify diameter of circle <2.00>:` **0.5**

b) **COPY** the circle 1 inch to the right.

i. Command: **co** or **copy** or *Modify* panel: 
ii. `Select object:` Use the square cursor to select the circle with the mouse. Place the square on the border of the circle and click the left mouse button.
iii. `Select object:` **Enter**
iv. `Specify base point or [Displacement/mOde] <Displacement>:` **o**
v. `Enter copy mode option [Single/Multiple] <Multiple>:` **s**
vi. `Specify base point or [Displacement/mOde/Multiple ] <Displacement>:` Pick a point anywhere within the drawing area.
vii. `Specify second point or <use first point as displacement>:` **@1<0** (This moves the circle 1 inch to the right or at an angle of 0 degrees)

5) Create the body of the wagon by drawing a **1.5 x 0.5 RECtangle** 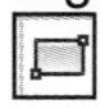 whose lower left corner starts at (**4,2.5**).

How?

a) Command: **rec** or **rectangle** or 
b) `Specify first corner point or [Chamfer/Elevation/Fillet/ Thickness/Width]:` **4,2.5**
c) `Specify other corner point or [Area/Dimensions/Rotation]:` **d**
d) `Specify length for rectangles <10.00>:` **1.5**
e) `Specify width for rectangles <10.00>:` **0.5**
f) `Specify other corner point or [Area/Dimensions/Rotation]:` Select a point above the two wheels.

6) Draw the handle of the wagon using a **Line** that is **1** inches long at a **30** degree angle and starts at the midpoint of the right side of the wagon.

a) Command: **line** or **l** or 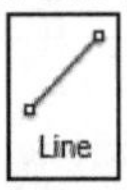
b) `LINE Specify first point:` **mid**
c) `of` Select the midpoint of the right side of the wagon.
d) `Specify next point or [Undo]:` **@1<30**
e) `Specify next point or [Undo]:` **Enter**

7) Round the corners of the wagon body using a **0.125** radius **FILLET**.

a) Command: **fillet** or *Home* tab - *Modify* Panel: 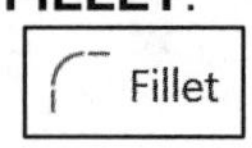
b) `Select first object or [Undo/Polyline/Radius/Trim/Multiple]:` **r**
c) `Specify fillet radius <0.00>:` **0.125**
d) `Select first object or [Undo/Polyline/Radius/Trim/Multiple]:` Select the bottom line of the wagon body and then select one of the vertical lines of the wagon body.
e) Hit the `Space` bar and then fillet the other bottom corner.

8) Create the sun body using a **Circle** of radius **0.75** and whose center is located at **8.5,6.5**.

9) Create the sun rays using a polar **ARray**. Each sun ray is **0.5** inches long.

a) Command: **l** or **line** or 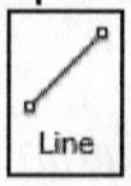

b) `Specify first point:` **quad**
c) `of` Select the right side quadrant of the sun body circle.
d) `Specify next point or [Undo]:` **@0.5<0**
e) `Specify next point or [Undo]:` **Enter**
f) *Home* tab - *Modify* panel: 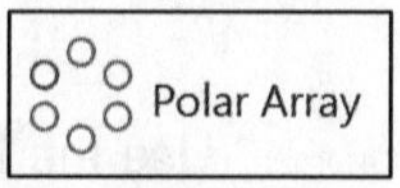

g) `Select objects:` Select the newly created line.
h) `Select objects:` **Enter**
i) `Specify center point of array or [Base point/Axis of rotation]:` **cen**
j) `of` Select the circumference of the sun.
k) `Select grip to edit array or [ASsociative/Base point/Items/Angle between/Fill angle/ROWs/Levels/ROTate items/eXit] <eXit>:` **i**
l) `Enter number of items in array or [Expression] <6>:` **16**
m) `Select grip to edit array or [ASsociative/Base point/Items/Angle between/Fill angle/ROWs/Levels/ROTate items/eXit] <eXit>:` **x**

10) Create the stop sign post using a **Line** that starts at the **QUADrant** of the second ground arc and is **2** inches long and travels vertically upward.

11) Create the stop sign using an octagon (**POLygon**) that is circumscribed in a circle of radius **0.75** at the top of the sign post.

a) Command: **pol** or **polygon** or *Home* tab - *Draw* panel: 
b) `Enter number of sides <4>:` **8**
c) `Specify center of polygon or [Edge]:` **ext** or **extension**
`of` Place your cursor over the top end of the sign post. Once AutoCAD locates the end, move your cursor up to create an extension line. Enter **0.6** in the *Command* window without losing the extension line.
d) `Enter an option [Inscribed in circle/Circumscribed about circle] <I>:` **c**
e) `Specify radius of circle:` **0.6**

12) Enter the word **STOP** in the middle of the stop sign using single line **text**.

a) Command: **text** or *Home* tab - *Annotation* panel: 

b) *Select Annotation Scale* Window: Select **OK**. Note: If you do not get this window, your text is not annotative. You need to fix this in the *Style Manager* window (*STYLE*).

c) `Specify start point of text or [Justify/Style]:` **j**

d) `Enter an option [Left/Center/Right/Align/Middle/Fit/TL/TC/TR/ML/MC/MR/BL/BC/BR]:` **m**

e) `Specify middle point of text:` Use the **EXTension** snap to locate a point **0.6** inches above the stop sign post like we did before.

f) `Specify rotation angle of text <0>:` **Enter**

g) Type the word **STOP** and hit **Enter** twice.

13) 

2.17.3) Using modify commands

For the following commands, you will need to select objects that contain more than one entity. The easiest way to do this is to use a window. When the command asks you to *select object*, you will draw a window around the entire object using the following steps. Click your left mouse button and release, drag the mouse so that the box encloses the entire object, and click the left mouse button again. If an entity was not selected, use the mouse to select the entities individually. If an entity was selected and you do not want it to be selected, type an **R** for *remove* and select the entity.

> **IMPORTANT!** While performing the following commands, READ THE COMMAND PROMPT to see what AutoCAD® is wanting.

1) 

Wagon Tut Modified.dwg

2) On your own, **Move** 

the sun directly to the left by **6** units and **SCALE** 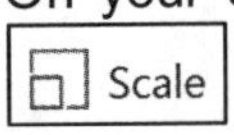

the sun by half using the center of the sun body as the base point. (See figure on the next page.)

3) On your own, **OFFSET**  the wagon body to the inside by **0.125** to produce a double line.

4) On your own, **MIrror** 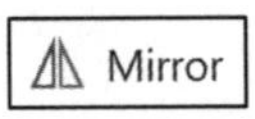

the entire wagon using the left vertical edge of the wagon as the mirror line. Delete the original wagon.

5) On your own, **ROtate** 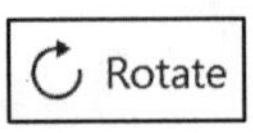

the stop sign **45** degrees using the bottom of the sign post as the base point.

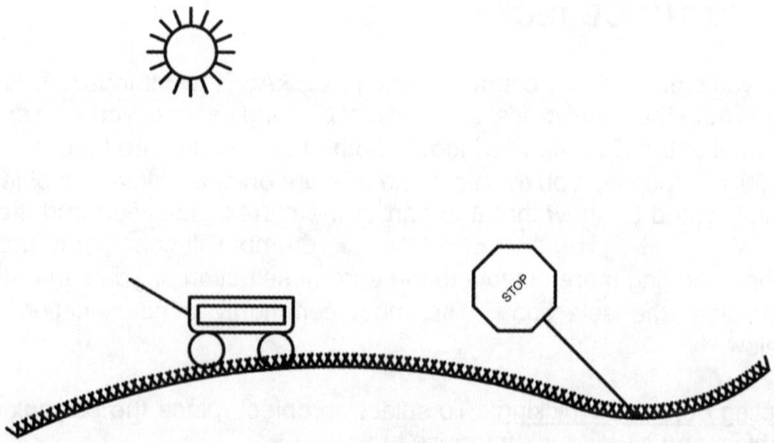

6) Print the completed drawings using ***Limits*** as your print area and the ***Scale to Fit*** option.

7) 

Exercise 2.17-1: Text Style

1) Open your **set-mm.dwt** template file. Set your text font to ***Arial***, text height to **3** mm and make the text ***Annotative***. Resave your file.

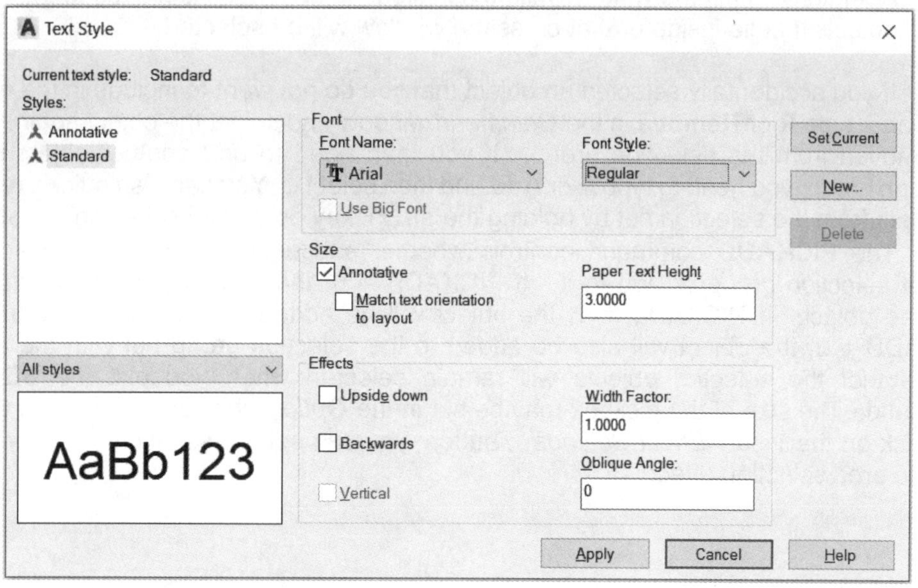

2.18) SELECTING OBJECTS

When you start a *Modify* command such as ERASE, two things happen. First, the cursor changes from the usual *crosshairs* to a *pickbox* and second, you will see the `Select objects:` prompt in the *Command* window. Both of these cues are there to let you know that AutoCAD® is expecting you to select one or more objects. When an object has been picked it is highlighted to show that it is part of the current selection and the *Command* window reports `1 found`. The `Select objects:` prompt will continue to appear so that you can continue adding more objects to the current selection or you can press **`Enter`** or **`Space`** to complete the selection. The most commonly used selection options are explained below.

- <u>Selecting objects by picking:</u> To select an object, place the *pickbox* over part of the object and click your left mouse button.
- <u>Window selection:</u> The WINDOW option is invoked by typing **W** in response to the `Select objects:` prompt or by clicking and releasing the left mouse button and then moving the mouse to the <u>right</u> and up or down. The WINDOW option allows you to define a rectangle using two points. Once the window is defined, all objects that lie entirely within the window will be selected.
- <u>Crossing window selection:</u> The CROSSING WINDOW option is invoked by typing **C** in response to the `Select objects:` prompt or by clicking and releasing the left mouse button and then moving the mouse to the <u>left</u> and up or down. Once the window is defined, all objects that lie inside or that cross the window will be selected.
- <u>Lasso window selection:</u> The LASSO WINDOW option is invoked by clicking and holding the left mouse button. If the mouse is moved to the <u>right</u>, only objects that lie entirely within the window will be selected. If the mouse is moved to the <u>left</u>, all objects that lie inside or that cross the window will be selected.

If you accidentally selected an object that you do not want to include in the modify command, type **R** or **Remove** in the *Command* window and select the object again. It will be removed from the selection group. If you then need to add another object to the selection group, you need to type **A** or **Add** and then select it. You can also quickly remove an object from the selection set by holding the **`Shift`** key down and selecting the object.

The **PICKADD** command controls whether subsequent selections replace the current selection group or add to it. If PICKADD = 0, then the object will replace the selected object. If PICKADD = 1, the object will be added to the selection group. If PICKADD = 2, the object will also be added to the selection group but with the added feature that the selected objects will remain selected when you exit the **SELECT** command. The size of the pickbox may be set in the *Options* window – *Selection* tab. If you click on the *Visual Effect Settings…* button, you can set the selection preview filters and the area selection effect.

2.19) OBJECT SELECTION TUTORIAL

AutoCAD® has a whole range of tools which are designed to help you select just the objects you need. This tutorial is designed to familiarize you with these selection options.

2.19.1) Selecting objects using the pickbox.

1) View the *Selection* video and read section 2.18).

2) Open your ***set-mm.dwt*** template file.

3) 

Selection Tut.dwg.

4) Get into your ***World Coordinate System***.

5) Draw a **Circle** of radius **20** mm whose center is located at **75,100**.

6) **ARray** the *Circle* using the following settings.

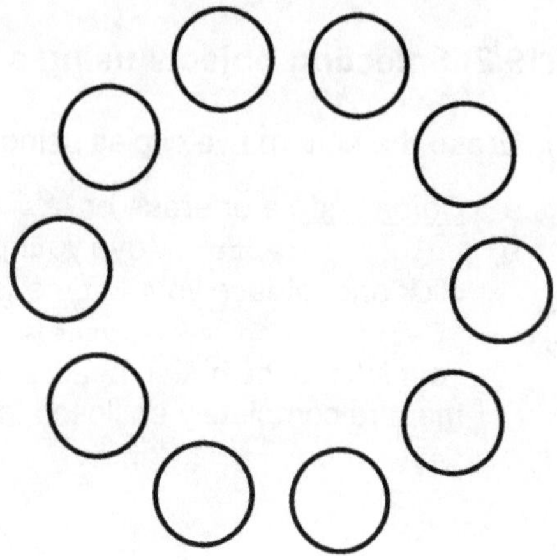

   a) ***Polar Array*** 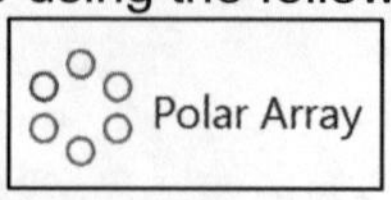

   b) Center point = **150,150**
   c) Total number of items = **10**
   d) Fill angle = **360**

7) **Zoom All**

8) **EXPLODE** the array group.
   a) <u>Command:</u> **explode** or

      <u>*Modify*</u> <u>Panel:</u> 
   b) `Select objects:` Select the array group.
   c) `Select objects:` **`Enter`**

9) 

10) Use the pickbox/ cursor to **Erase** objects.

   a) <u>Command:</u> **e** or **erase** or <u>*Modify*</u> <u>panel:</u> 
   b) `Select objects:` **all**
   c) `Select objects:` **r** (Note: This command allows you to remove an object from your selection set. You may also remove objects from the selection set by holding down the **`Shift`** key.)
   d) `Remove objects:` Select all but the left and right circles using the pickbox as shown in the next figure on the left.
   e) `Remove objects:` **a**

f) `Select objects:` Select the bottom two circles using the pickbox/ cursor as shown in the figure on the right.

g) `Select objects:` **Enter**

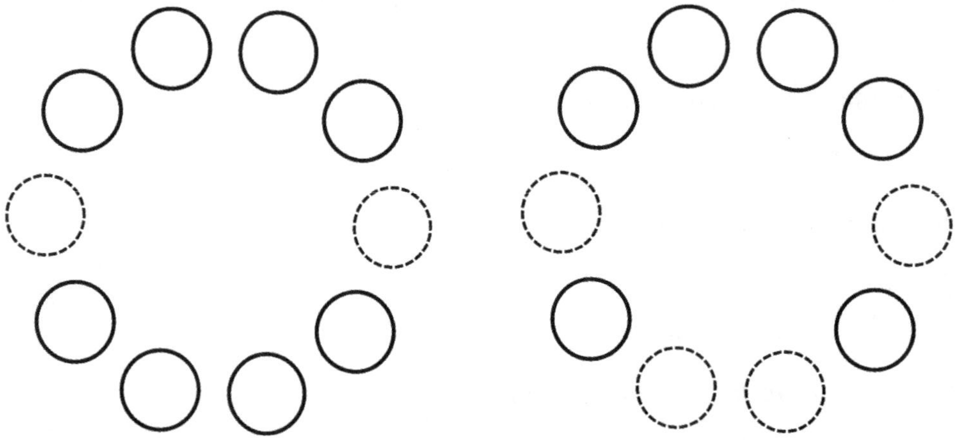

2.19.2) Selecting objects using a window

1) **Erase** the bottom two circles using a window.

   a) Command: **e** or **erase** or 

   b) `Select objects:` Move your pickbox to the approximate location of *Corner 1* and click and release your left mouse.

   c) `Specify opposite corner:` Move the mouse down and to the right and click your left mouse button again at the approximate location of *Corner 2*. (Only objects that are completely enclosed in the window will be selected.)

   d) `Select objects:` **Enter**

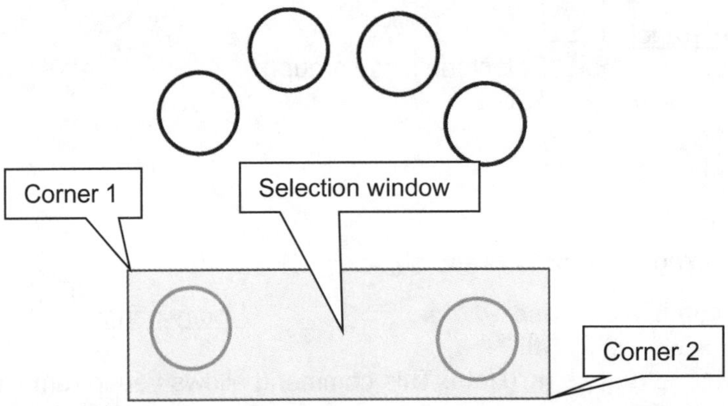

2) **Erase** the top four circles using the crossing window option.

   a) <u>Command:</u> **e** or **erase** or
   b) `Select objects:` Move your pickbox/ cursor to the approximate location of *Corner 1* and click and release your left mouse button.
   c) `Specify opposite corner:` Move the mouse down and to the left and click your left mouse button again at the approximate location of *Corner 2*. (Objects that are completely enclosed in or cross the window will be selected.)
   d) `Select objects:` **`Enter`**

> **Note:** Clicking left to right will create a standard window, and clicking right to left creates a crossing window.

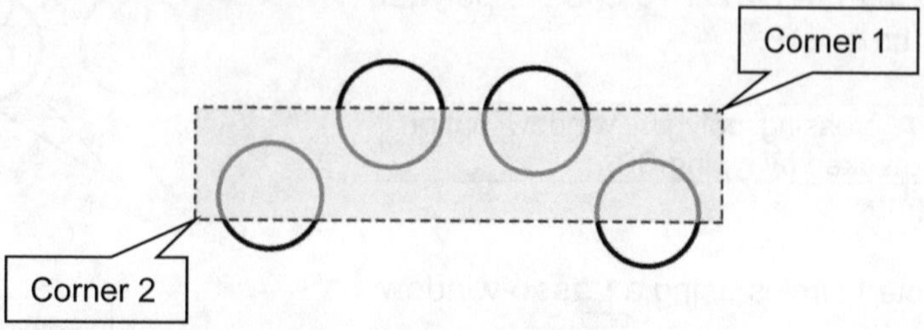

2.19.3) <u>Selecting objects using advanced techniques</u>

1) **Close** and <u>don't</u> save your drawing and reopen **Selection Tut.dwg**. This will give you your full array of circles back. If you forget to save or saved in between steps, you will need to draw the circle array again or use the UNDO command to get your circles back.

2) **Erase** selected circles using a **Fence** line.

   a) <u>Command:</u> **e** or **erase** or
   b) `Select objects:` **f**
   c) `Specify first fence point or pick/drag cursor:` Select a point near *Point 1*.
   d) `Specify next fence point or [Undo]:` Select a point near *Point 2*.
   e) `Specify next fence point or [Undo]:` Select a point near *Point 3*.
   f) `Specify next fence point or [Undo]:` Select a point near *Point 4*.

g) `Specify next fence point or [Undo]:` **Enter** (Note: All objects that cross the fence line are selected.)

h) `Select object:` **Enter**

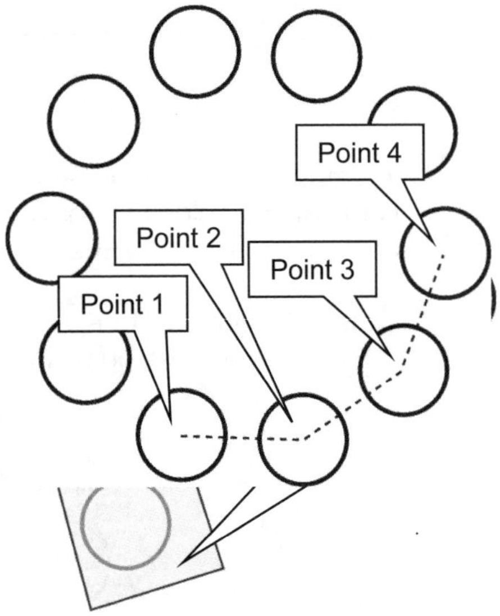

3) **Erase** selected circles using a **W**indow **P**olygon.

   a) <u>Command:</u> **e** or **erase** or

   b) `Select objects:` **wp**

   c) On your own, create the selection window shown. **IMPORTANT!** To end the polygon window hit `Enter`.

Note: A crossing polygon window option may be invoked by typing **CP**.

4) **Erase** selected circles using a **Lasso** window.

   a) <u>Command:</u> **e** or **erase** or

   b) `Select objects:` Click and hold your left mouse button while dragging your mouse to create the selection window shown.

Note: If you drag your mouse to the left, you will create a crossing window.

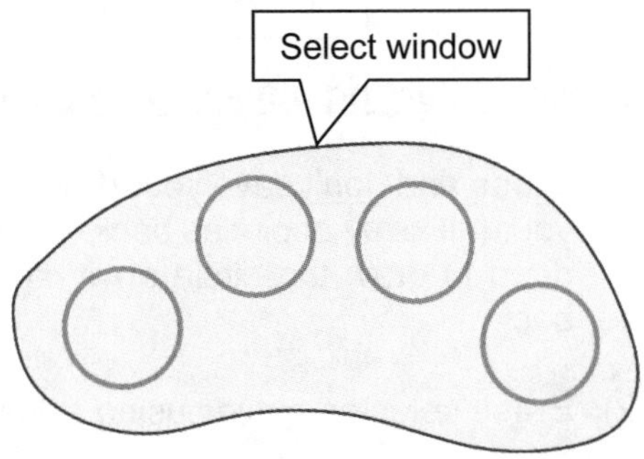

2.20) OBJECT SNAP TUTORIAL

The objective of this tutorial is to familiarize the reader with the OSNAP and TRIM commands. Object snaps automatically select specified geometric locations on an existing object such as the endpoint or the center. Osnaps help you draw accurately and quickly. In this tutorial we will be using the Automatic Object Snaps. Therefore, you will not have to type the OSNAP command in the *Command* window. For the most part, AutoCAD will automatically detect them

2.20.1) Drawing using osnaps

We will be drawing the following object.

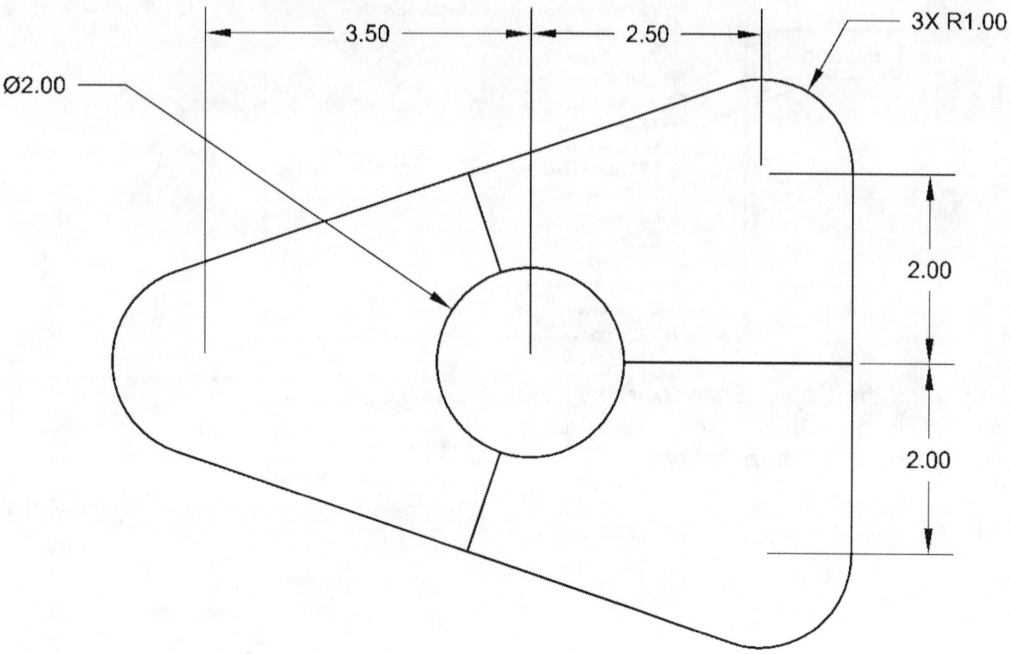

1) View the *Trim and Extend* and *Object Snaps* videos and review section 2.16).

2) 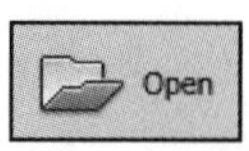

set-inch.dwt.

3) 

OSNAP Tut.dwg.

4) Add the *Object Snap* panel to the *Home* tab.

a) Command: **cui** or *Manage* tab – *Customization* panel: 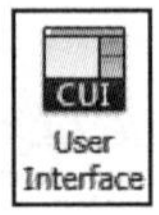

b) *Customize User Interface* window: Expand the *Toolbars* in the tree view on the left side of the window.

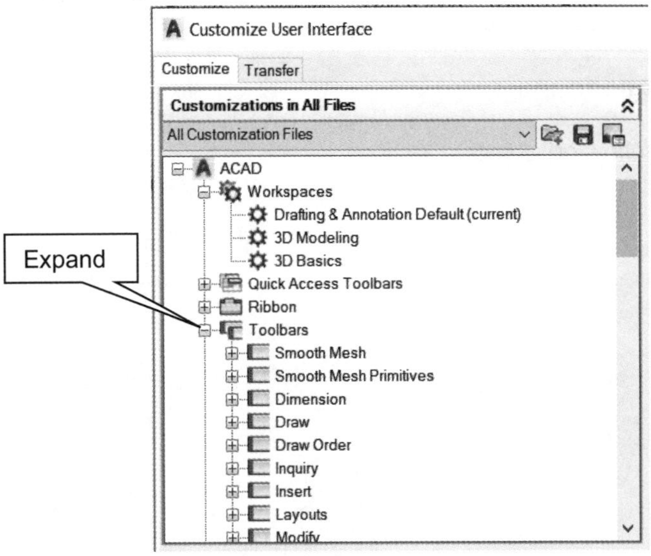

c) Find the *Object Snap* toolbar. Right click on *Object Snap* and select ***Copy to Ribbon Panels***.

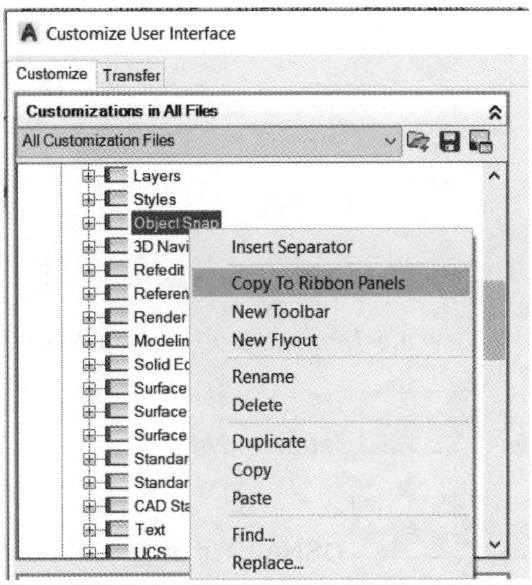

d) Select ***Yes*** in the *CUI Editor – Confirm Copy to Ribbon Panels Node* Window, if one appears.

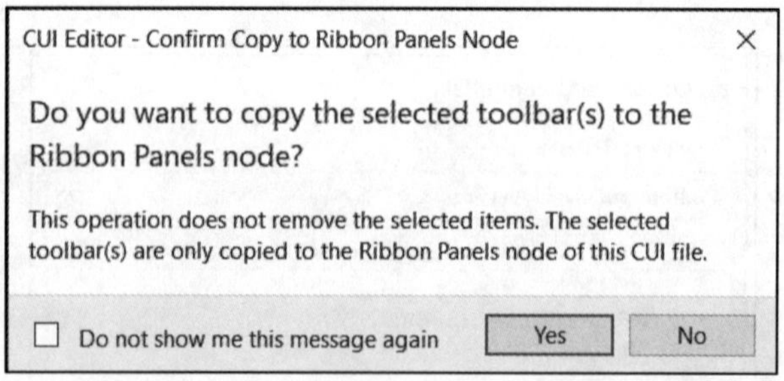

e) Expand the *Ribbon* and *Panels* in the tree view on the left side of the window.

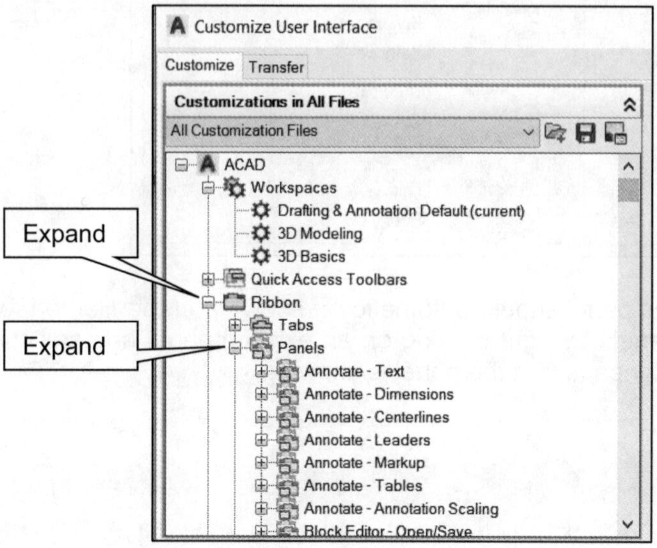

f) Find the *Object Snap* panel within *Panels*. Right click and select ***Copy***.

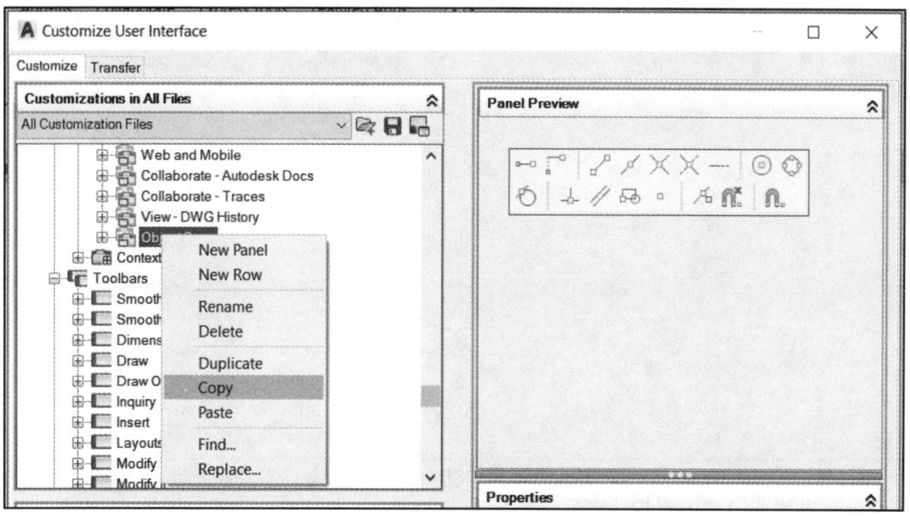

g) Within the *Tabs* root, right click on the *Home 2D* tab and select ***Paste***.
h) Select ***OK***.

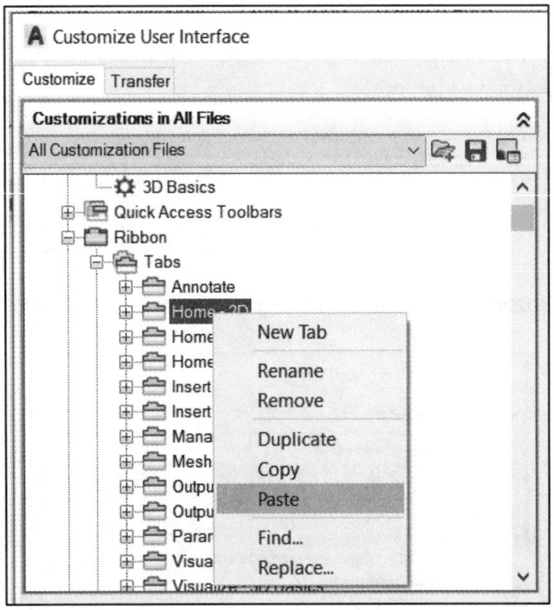

i) The *Object Snap* panel should automatically show up in the *Home* tab. You can hide or show panels by right clicking on an existing panel and selecting *Panels*. The check mark means that the panel is showing.

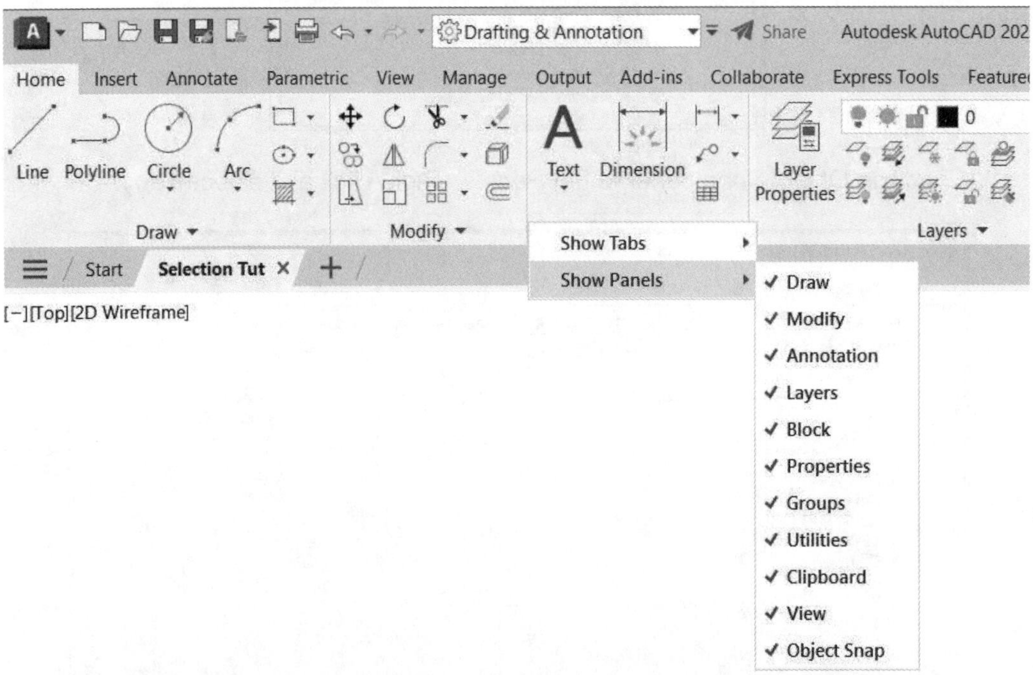

Note: You may rearrange the panels by clicking on the *Panel name* and dragging it to a new location.

5) Enter your ***World coordinate system***.

6) Draw a **Circle** of <u>diameter</u> **2** whose center is located at **5,4**.

7) **COpy** the circle to create the three outer circles. Look at the initial drawing to get the distances. Try to do this without looking at the How? box.

How?

a) <u>Command:</u> **co** or **copy** 
b) Select objects: Select the circle.
c) Select objects: **Enter**
d) Specify base point or [Displacement/mOde/Multiple] <Displacement>: m
e) Specify base point or [Displacement/mOde/Multiple] <Displacement>: Select any point in the drawing area.
f) Specify second point or [Array] <use first point as displacement>: **@2.5,2**
g) Specify second point or [Array/Exit/Undo] <Exit>: **@2.5,-2**
h) Specify second point or [Array/Exit/Undo] <Exit>: **@-3.5,0**
i) Specify second point or [Array/Exit/Undo] <Exit>: **Enter**

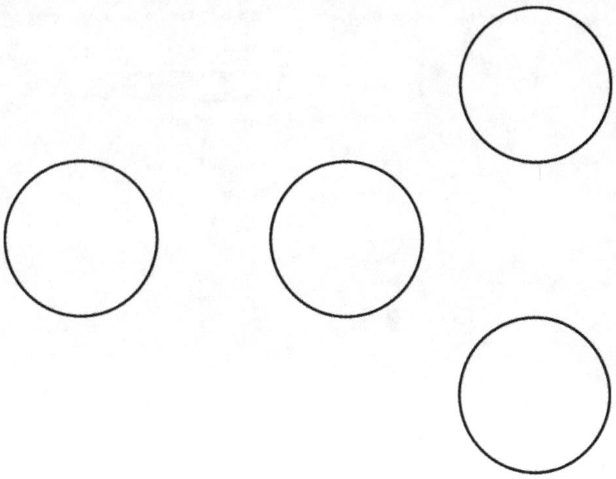

8) **Zoom All**

9) Turn your ***Object Snap*** on 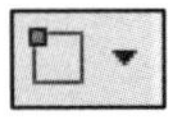 in the *Status Bar* and tell AutoCAD® to automatically detect centers, tangencies and perpendicularities.
   a) Set up your *Object Snap* options by clicking on the arrow next to the *Object Snap* icon in the *Status* bar. Select ***Center***, ***Perpendicular*** and ***Tangent***.

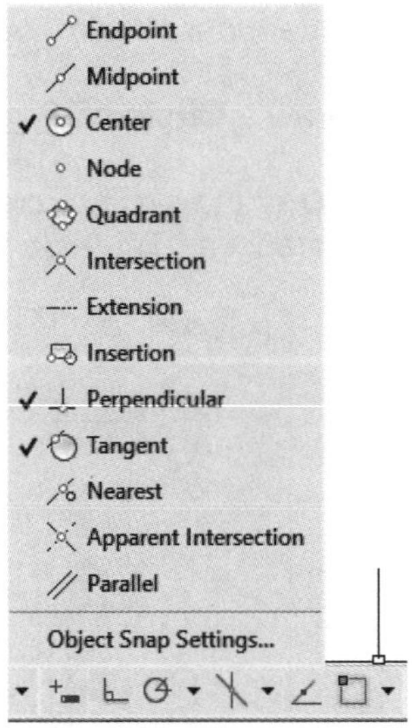

10) Set the size and color of the AutoSnap marker.
   a) Application  - Options window – Drafting tab: Set the *AutoSnap Marker Size* to maximum and then click the ***Colors...*** button.
   b) Drawing Window Colors: Set the autosnap marker color to ***red*** and then click on the ***Apply & Close*** button.
   c) Click ***OK*** in the *Options* and *Drafting Settings* windows.

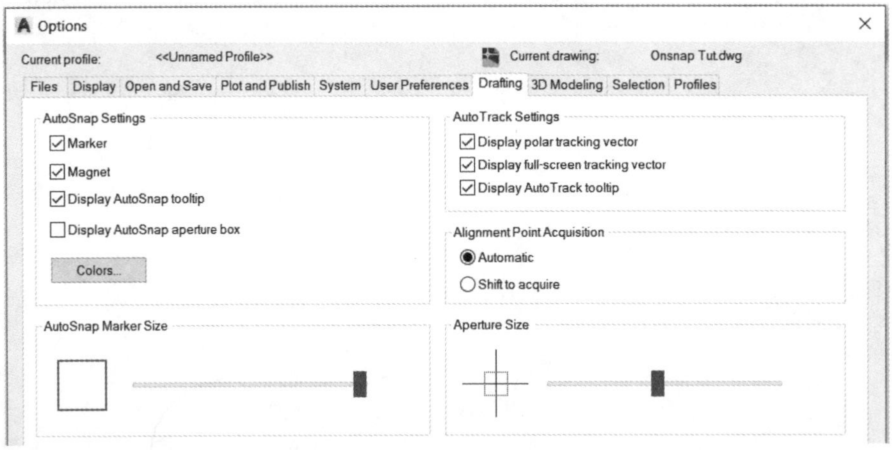

11) Visualize the autosnap markers.
   a) Start a **Line** anywhere in the drawing area.
   b) Move your cursor around the circles and locate each one of the automatic snap markers (Center, Perpendicular, Tangent).
   c) Hit **`Esc`** to exit the LINE command.

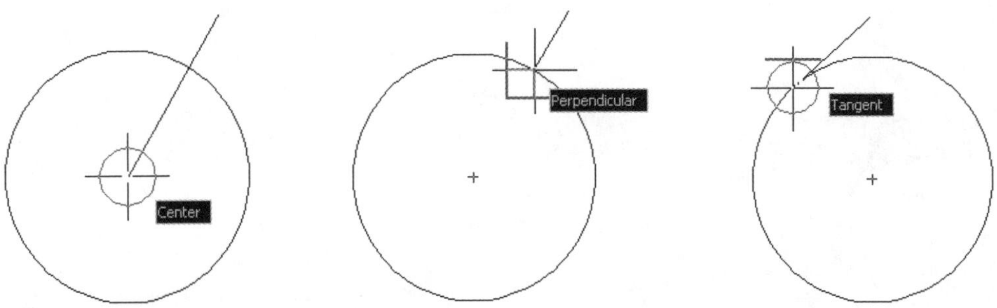

12) Set the autosnap marker size back to 25% of maximum and the color to your preference.

13) Draw 3 **TANgent Line**s around the outer circles.

a) Command: **l** or 
b) `Specify first point:` Move your cursor to one of the circles. Notice that the tangent Osnap marker does not appear. To specifically tell AutoCAD® that you want to detect the tangent, type **tan** or select .
c) `to` Select the circle.
d) `Specify next point or [Undo]:` Move your cursor to the circle at the other end of the line. Again, AutoCAD® will not detect the tangent. Type **tan** or select .
e) `to` Select the circle.
f) `Specify next point or [Undo]:` **Enter**
g) Complete the other two lines.

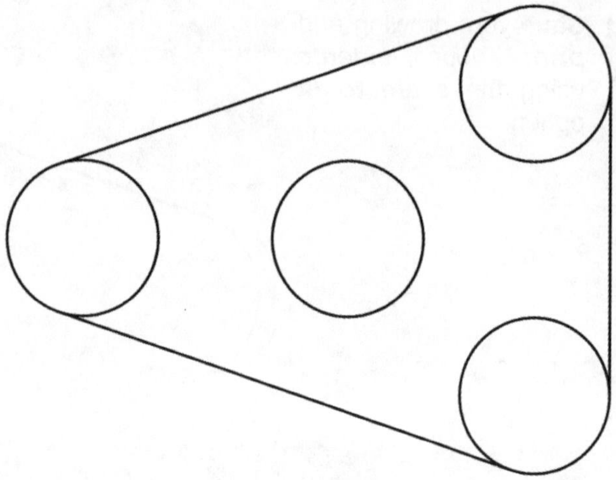

14) Draw the 3 **Line**s from the **CENter** point of the middle circle to **PERpendicular** to the outer tangent lines. Use the Osnap markers to guide you. (Note: To acquire the center of the circle you need to hover over its circumference.)

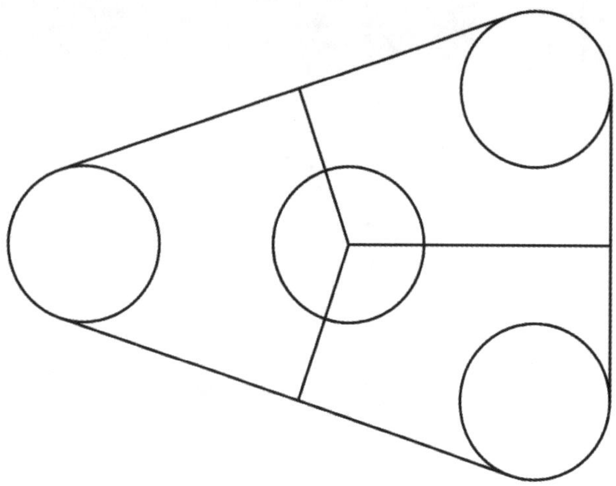

2.20.2) Trimming

1) **TRim** the unwanted lines. First, set your **TRIMEXTENDMODE** to **1**.
   a) Command: **TRIMEXTENDMODE**
   b) `Enter new value for TRIMEXTENDMODE <0>:` **1**
   c) Command: **TRim** or *Modify* panel: 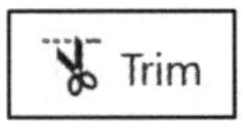

   d) `[cutting edges/Crossing/mOde/Project/eRase]:` Select all the lines that you want to trim.

> **Problems?**
> - If AutoCAD® will not let you trim the outer circles, you did not draw the tangent lines correctly.

   e) `[cutting edges/Crossing/mOde/Project/eRase]:` **Enter**

2) ***Save*** your drawing and ***print*** your ***extents*** using the ***scale to fit*** option.

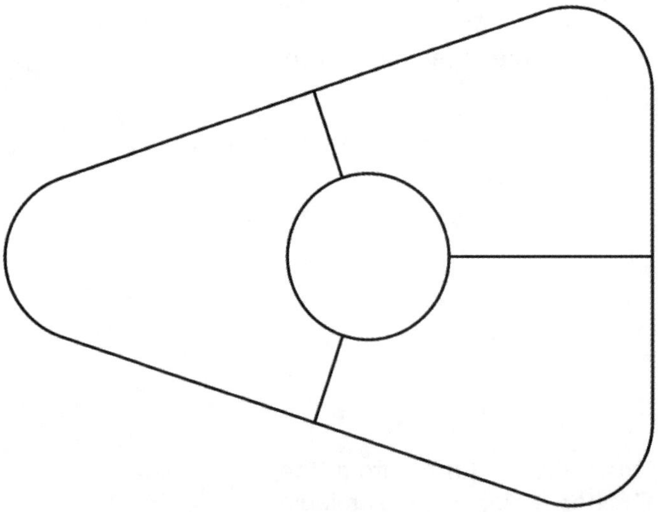

2.21) POLAR TRACKING

Polar tracking restricts cursor movement to specified angles. When you are creating or modifying objects, you can use polar tracking to display temporary alignment paths defined by the polar angles you specify. Figure 2.21-1 shows a polar tracking path restricting a line to be along a 15-degree angle. Once a polar tracking path has been snapped to, a distance from the previous point may be entered in the *Command* window. This will place the next point along the polar path at the specified distance.

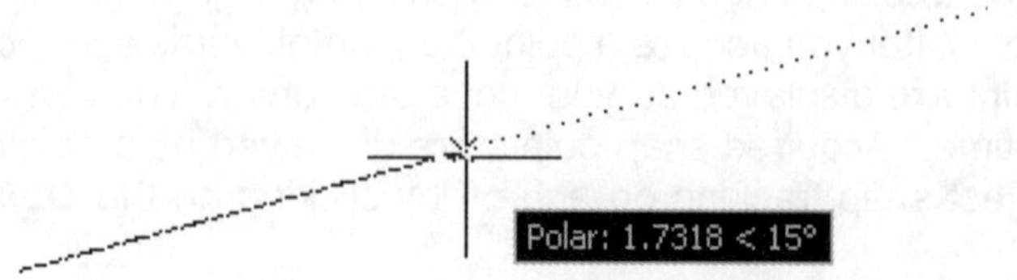

Figure 2.21-1: Polar tracking path

Polar angles are relative to the orientation of the WCS or the current user coordinate system (UCS). You can turn your polar tracking on and off by clicking on the ***Polar Tracking*** 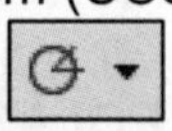 icon in the *Status Bar*. To change the increment of the tracking angle you can use the **POLARANG** command or click on the arrow next to the *Polar Tracking* icon and select ***Tracking Settings...***. Figure 2.21-2 shows the *Polar Tracking* settings window.

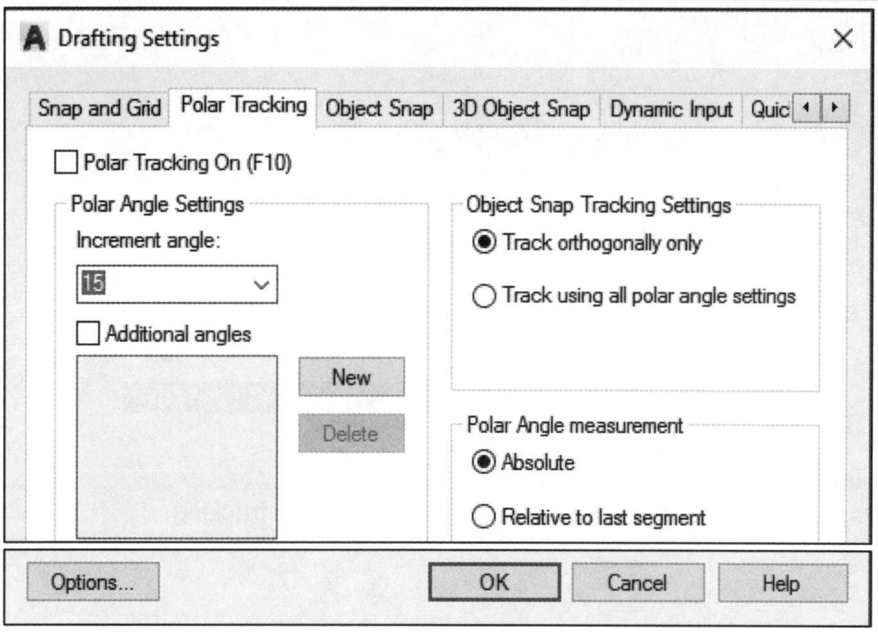

Figure 2.21-2: Polar tracking settings

Polar snap restricts cursor movement to specified increments along a polar tracking path. You can turn on the polar snap by setting your **SNAPTYPE** variable to 1 (a value of 0 is for standard snap). You can set the polar snap distance with the **POLARDIST** command.

2.22) OBJECT SNAP TRACKING

Object snap tracking enables you to track along alignment paths that are based on object snap points. After you acquire a point, horizontal, vertical, or polar alignment paths relative to the point are displayed as you move the cursor. You can acquire up to seven snap points at a time. Acquired snap points are displayed as a small plus sign (+). You can turn your object snap tracking on and off by clicking on the ***Object Snap Tracking***  icon in the *Status Bar* or by hitting `F11`. Figure 2.22-1 shows a line being drawn with the help of object snap tracking. The end of the line will be drawn where the center of the circle aligns with the endpoint of the existing line.

A temporary track point is a point that is not associated with the geometry directly, but with the alignment paths that come off the geometry. You can select a temporary track point by typing **TT** or selecting the ***Temporary Track Point***  icon in the *Object Snap* panel and then selecting the point.

Object snap tracking is set to create paths at 0, 90, 180, and 270 degrees. However, you can use polar tracking angles instead by setting the **POLARMODE** variable to 2.

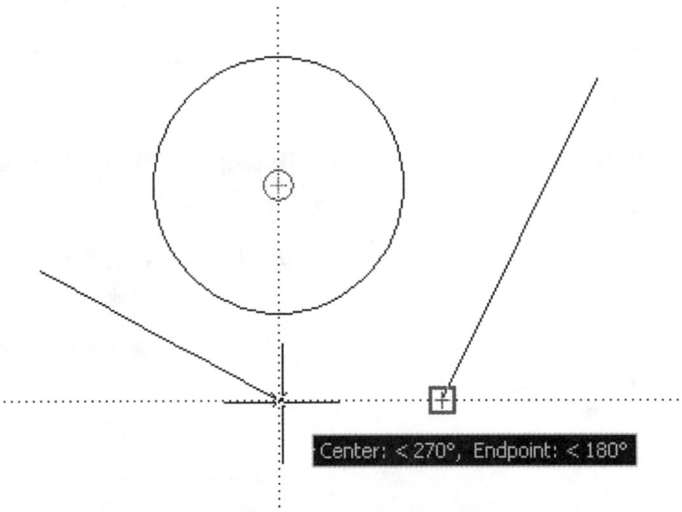

Figure 2.22-1: Using object snap tracking

2.23) TRACKING TUTORIAL

The objective of this tutorial is to familiarize the user with AutoCAD's tracking ability. AutoCAD® allows you to track along polar paths. Polar paths are created at angle increments that you specify. Distances along a polar path may be entered to identify the location of the next point. Object snap tracking is also available. This allows you to place a point at the intersection of multiple paths. These paths extend from acquired object snap points.

2.23.1) Polar tracking

1) View the *Tracking* video and read sections 2.21) and 2.22).

2) Open ***set-mm.dwt*** and Save As **Tracking Tut.dwg**

3) <u>Status Bar:</u>
   a) Turn your ***Object Snap*** and ***Polar Tracking*** <u>on</u>.
   b) Turn your ***Dynamic Input*** <u>off</u>.

4) Set your polar tracking angle increment to 15 degrees.
   a) <u>Command:</u> **polarang**
   b) `Enter new value for POLARANG <90>:` **15**

5) <u>Object Snap Panel:</u> Access the ***Osnap settings*** and activate the snaps shown.

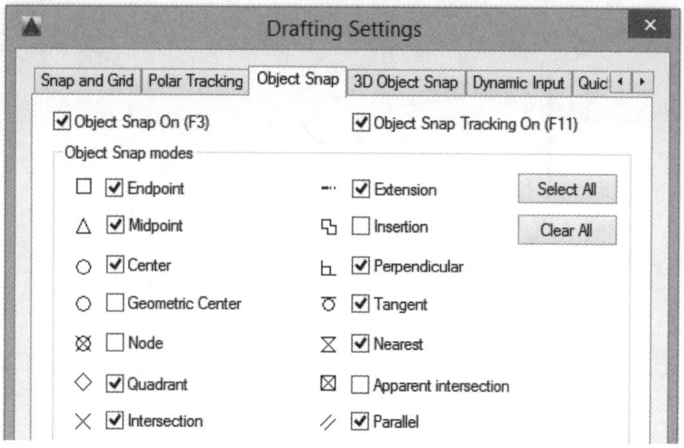

6) Enter your ***World Coordinate System*** and **Zoom All**

7) Draw the following object using polar tracking. The object is symmetric.
   a) Start a **Line** at **30,30**.
   b) Move your cursor around the drawing area until you snap to the 60-degree polar path.
   c) Type **40** and then hit **`Enter`**.
   d) Use polar tracking to complete the object.

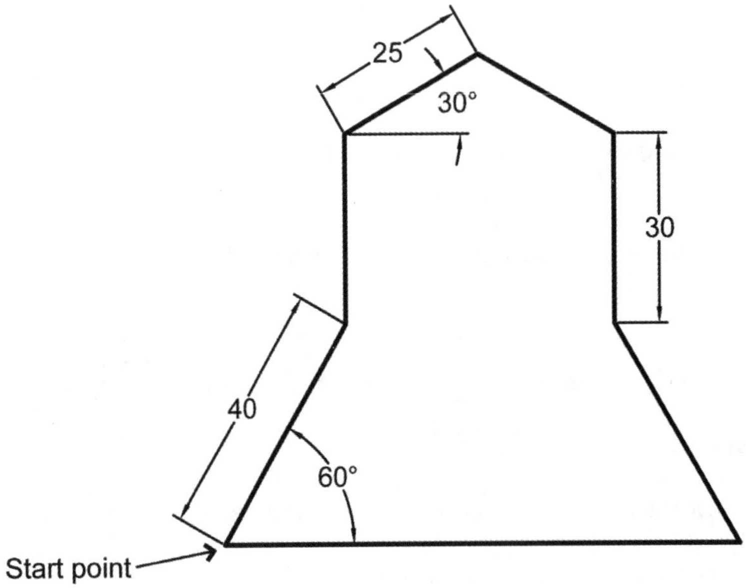

8) **MIrror** your entire drawing. The first point of the mirror line should be **140,20**. Use the **90°** polar path to snap the second point of the mirror line. Do not erase the original drawing.

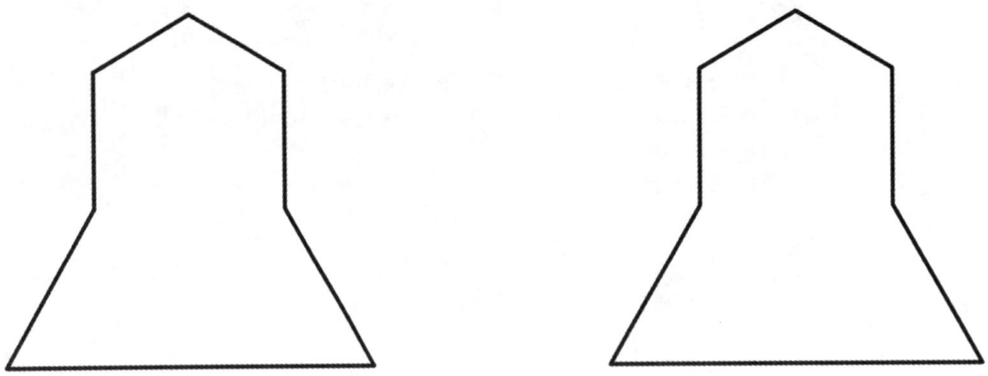

9) *Status Bar:* Turn your ***Object Snap Tracking*** on.

10) Set your **POLARMODE** variable to **2**. (This allows you to track using polar paths.)

11) Draw an octagon that is aligned on a 15 degree path from *Point 1* and a 90 degree path from *Point 2*.

a) Command: **POLygon** or *Draw* panel: 
b) `Enter number of sides <4>:` **8**
c) `Specify center of polygon or [Edge]:` Acquire Point 1 by moving your cursor over it. A small cross will appear when the point is acquired. Move the cursor out along the 15 degree polar path. Acquire point 2. Move the cursor along the 90 degree polar path until the 15 degree path appears. Select the point where the paths intersect.
d) `Enter an option [Inscribed in circle/Circumscribed about circle] <I>:` **i**
e) `Specify radius of circle:` **15**

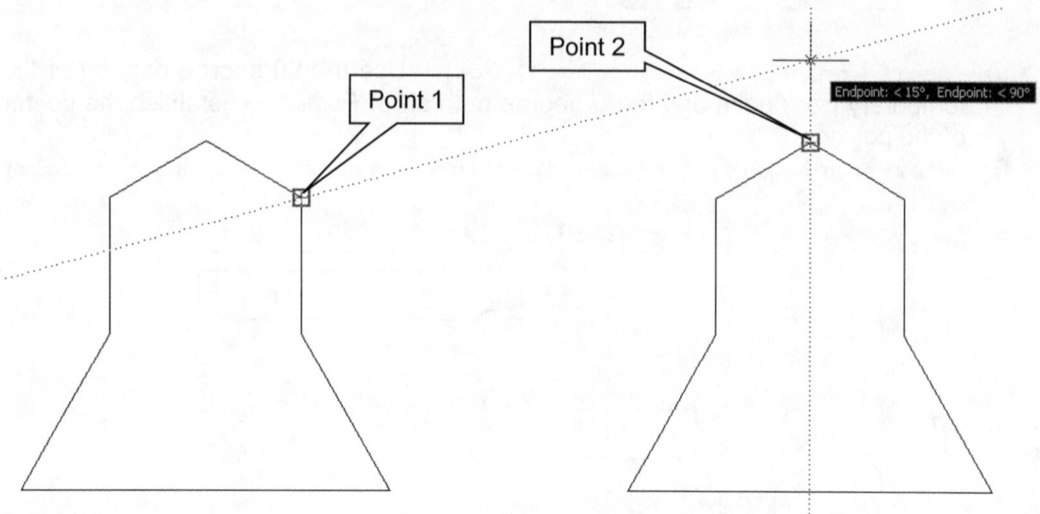

12) Draw a hexagon in the middle of the two main objects using a temporary tracking point.

a) Command: **POLygon** or *Draw* panel: 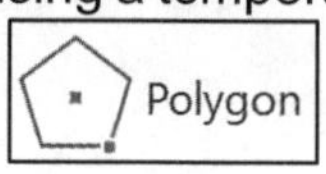

b) `Enter number of sides <8>:` **6**
c) `Specify center of polygon or [Edge]:` Select the ***Temporary Track Point***  icon in the *Object Snap* panel
d) `Specify temporary OTRACK point:` Acquire the intersection of the two extensions shown in the following figure and then select the point where the extensions cross.

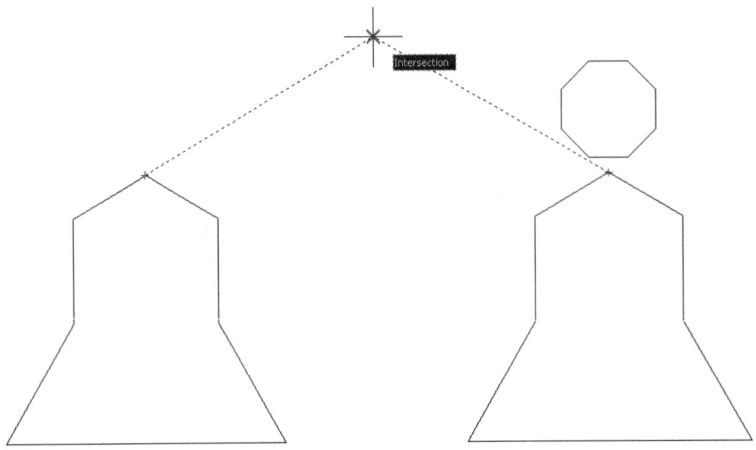

e) `Specify center of polygon or [Edge]:` Use the 90 degree path off of the temporary track point and the 0 degree path off of *Point 1* to establish the center of the polygon.

f) `Enter an option [Inscribed in circle/Circumscribed about circle] <I>:` **i**

g) `Specify radius of circle:` **30**

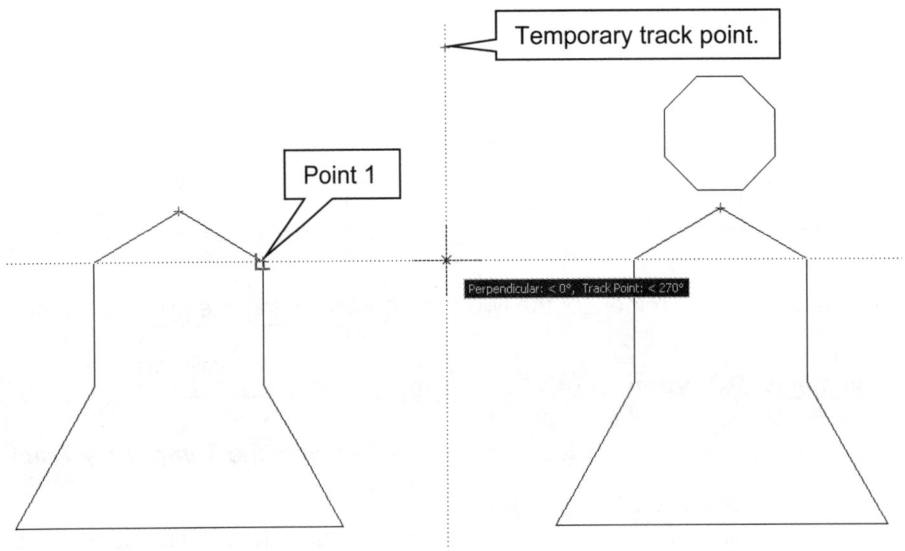

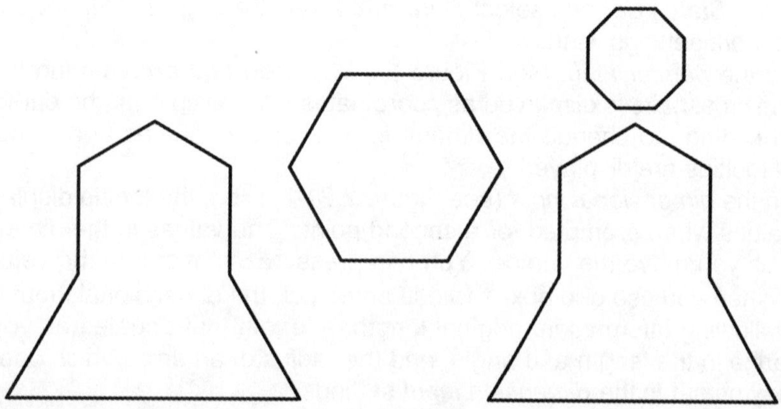

13) 

and ***print*** your drawing.

2.24) DYNAMIC INPUT

Dynamic input provides a command interface near the cursor to help you keep your focus in the drawing area. When the dynamic input is on, a tooltip displays information near the cursor that is dynamically updated as the cursor moves. You can enter a response in the tooltip area instead of in the *Command* window. If you press the `Down Arrow` key, you can view and select options. Pressing the `Up Arrow` key displays recent input. Figure 2.24-1 shows the use of dynamic inputs in the creation of a line.

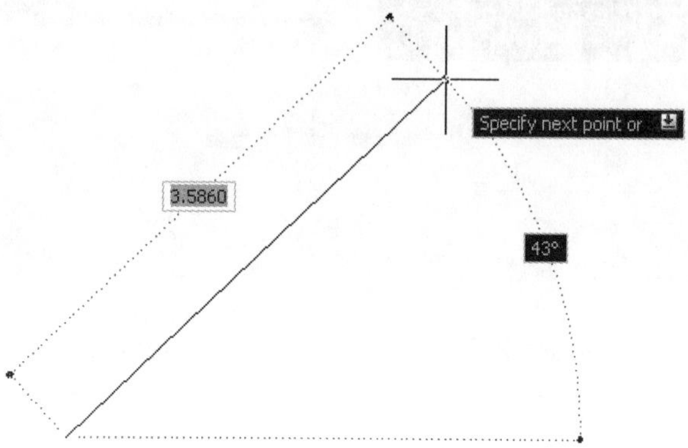

Figure 2.24-1: An example of dynamic inputs

The dynamic input may be turned on and off by clicking on the ***Dynamic Input***  icon in the *Status Bar* or by using the `F12` key. If the *Dynamics Input* icon is not showing up in the *Status Bar*, you will need to add it by clicking on 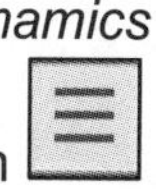 in the *Status Bar* and selecting Dynamic Input. To set the dynamic input controls, right click on the *Dynamic*

Input icon in the *Status Bar* and select ***Dynamic Input Settings...***. Figure 2.24-2 shows the *Dynamic Input* settings window.

When the *pointer input* (see Figure 2.24-2) is on and a command is active, the location of the crosshairs is displayed as coordinates in a tooltip near the cursor. Use the *pointer input* settings to change the default format for coordinates and to control when *pointer input* tooltips are displayed.

When the *dimensional input* (see Figure 2.24-2) is on, the tooltip displays distance and angle values when prompted for a second point. The values in the dimensional tool tips change as you move the cursor. You can press **`Tab`** to move to the value you want to change. When you use grip boxes to edit an object, the dimensional input tooltips can display the following information: original length, a length that updates as you move the grip, the change in the length and angle, and the radius of an arc. Which one of these is displayed may be set in the *dimension input* settings.

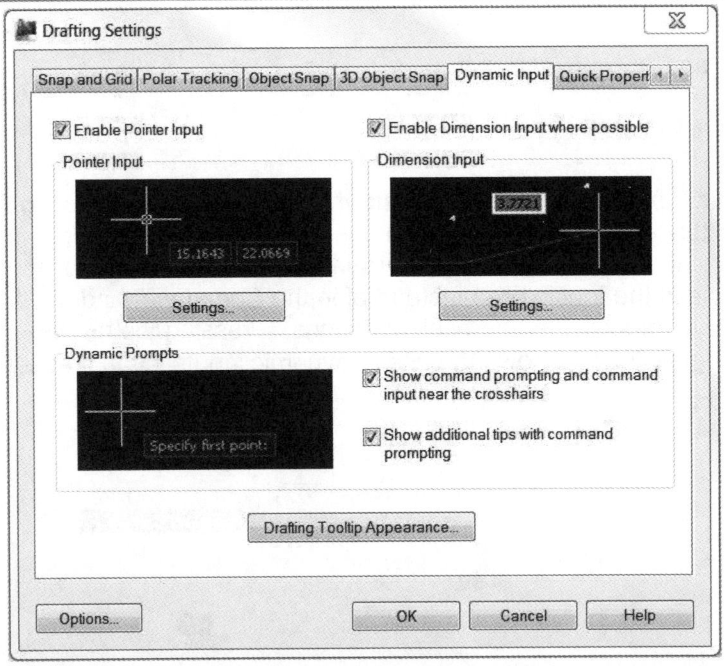

Figure 2.24-2: Dynamic input settings

2.25) DYNAMIC INPUT TUTORIAL

The objective of this tutorial is to familiarize the user with using dynamic inputs and the different settings that are available. The dynamic input allows you to enter commands and select options in an area near the cursor and the object being drawn.

2.25.1) Dynamic input settings

1) Read section 2.24)

2) 

set-inch.dwt and 

Dynamic input Tut.dwg

3) <u>Status Bar:</u>

   a) Turn your ***Dynamic Input***  <u>on</u>.

   b) Turn your ***Polar Tracking*** 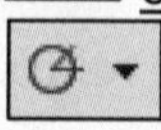 and ***Object Snap Tracking***  <u>off</u>.

4) Activate a **1** x 1 **GRID** and **Zoom All**

5) Change the dynamics input settings.
   a) <u>Status Bar:</u> Right click on the ***Dynamic Input*** icon and select ***Dynamic Input Settings…***
   b) <u>Drafting Settings window – Dynamic Input tab:</u> Select the ***Settings…*** button under *Pointer Input.*
   c) <u>Pointer Input Settings window:</u> Activate the ***Polar format***, ***Absolute coordinates*** and ***When a command asks for a point*** radio buttons.
   d) Select ***OK*** in both windows.

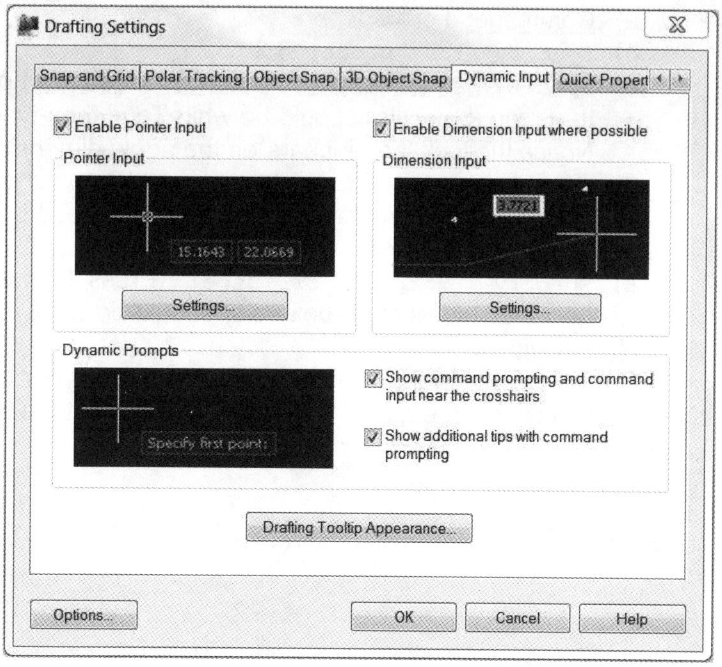

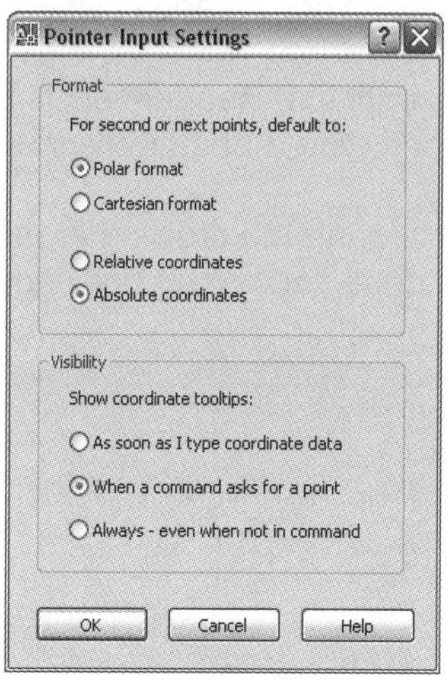

6) Draw a **Line** from (2,2) to (3,3) with the *dynamic input* on.
   a) Command: **l** or **line**
   b) `Specify first point:` Move your cursor around the drawing area. Notice the coordinates near the cursor. When finished, enter the first point without taking your cursor down to the *Command* window **2,2**.
   c) `Specify next point or [Undo]:` Move your cursor around the screen and see the length of the line and angle change. When finished enter the second point **3,3** without taking your cursor down to the *Command* window and then **`Enter`** to exit the command.
   d) `Specify next point or [Undo]:` **`Enter`**
   e) Note the coordinate of the second point is relative to the WCS.

7) Pointer Input Settings window: Change *Absolute coordinates* to ***Relative coordinates***.

8) Draw a **Line** from **4,4** to **5,5** as in step 6).

9) **Zoom All**. (Notice that the second point is relative to the first point and not to the WCS.)

10) Pointer Input Settings window: Change *Relative coordinates* to ***Absolute coordinates***.

2.25.2) Locking a coordinate

1) We will be drawing a **Line** from 3,2 that is 3 inches long at a 45 degree angle. From the end of the previous line, draw a Line that is 2 inches long at a 30 degree angle.
   a) Command: **l** or 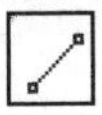
   b) `Specify first point:` **3,2**
   c) `Specify next point or [Undo]:` Press the **`Tab`** key until the angle dimension turns red (box color should be white) and then type **45** and hit the **`Tab`** key again. Notice the lock that appears on the angle dimension.
   d) `Specify next point or [Undo]:` Move your cursor around the drawing area. Notice that the length of the line changes, but the angle does not. When finished, type **3** and hit **`Enter`**.
   e) `Specify next point or [Undo]:` Press the **`Tab`** key until the linear dimension becomes highlighted (box color should be white) and then type **2** and hit the **`Tab`** key again.
   f) `Specify next point or [Undo]:` Move your cursor around the drawing area. Notice that the angle of the line changes, but the length does not. When finished, type **30** and hit **`Enter`** twice.

2) 

2.26) GRIP BOXES

Object grips or grip boxes are usually blue boxes that appear on a selected object if no command is active. Once the grip boxes appear, you can use them to MOVE, COPY, SCALE, ROTATE, MIRROR and STRETCH the object. To understand how grip boxes work, let's look at a simple line (Figure 2.26-1). If you click on the line, grip boxes will appear at the ends and the middle. If you click on the middle grip box, you can move the entire line. If you click on one of the end grips, you can stretch the line. For more advanced options, click on a grip and then right click to access a shortcut menu.

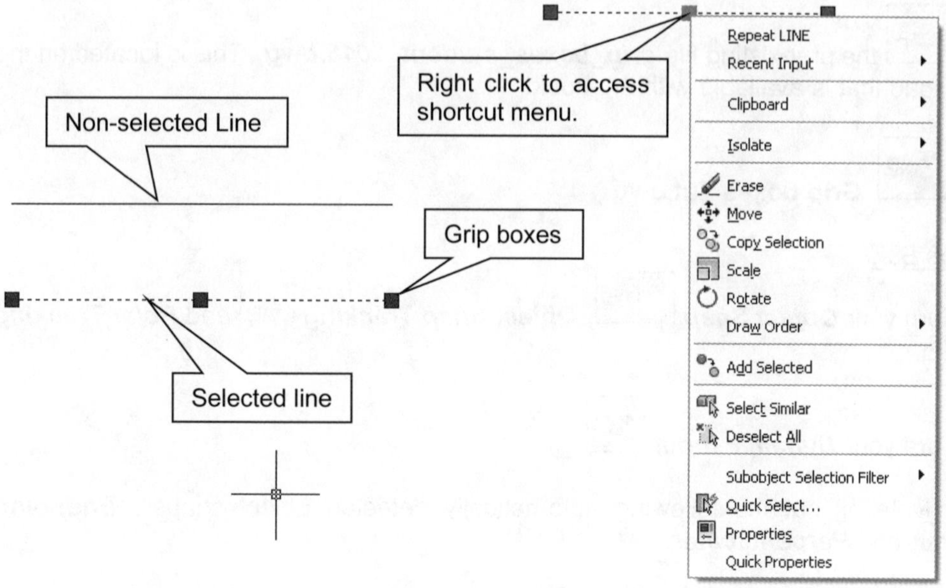

Figure 2.26-1: Grip boxes

The grip box mode may be turned off by setting the **GRIPS** variable to 0 and turned on by setting it to 1. Additional midpoint grips on polyline segments may be shown by setting GRIPS to 2. The size of the grip boxes are controlled by the **GRIPSIZE** variable. Grip box settings are also available in the *Selections* tab of the *Options* window.

2.27) GRIP BOX TUTORIAL

The objective of this tutorial is to use object grips or grip boxes and the *Properties* window to edit a drawing. Grip boxes allow you to quickly modify an object without having to enter a command.

2.27.1) Preparing to draw

1) Read section 2.26).

2) 

the preexisting file ***grip_boxes_student_2018.dwg***. This is located on the download that is available with the book.

3) 

Grip boxes Tut.dwg

4) <u>*Status Bar*:</u>
   a) Turn your ***Object Snap*** , ***Object Snap Tracking***  and ***Polar Tracking*** 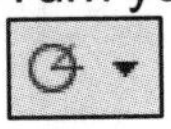 <u>on</u>.
   b) Turn your ***Dynamic Input***  <u>off</u>.

5) <u>Deactivate</u> all but the following automatically detected object snaps: ***Endpoint***, ***Center***, and ***Perpendicular***.

2.27.2) Fixing the drawing

We need to fix the areas indicated in the figure.

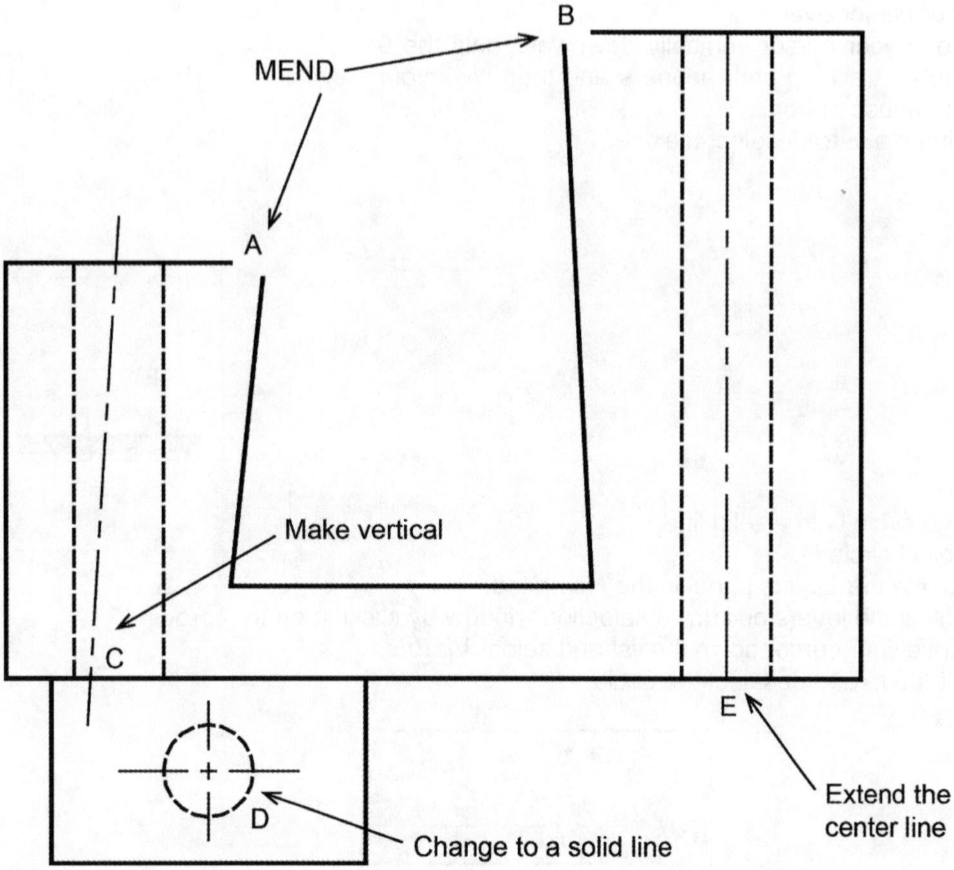

1) Repair corner A.
   a) Select the almost vertical line at corner A.
   b) Click on the top grip box.
   c) Move your cursor and see the end of the line moves.
   d) Move your cursor over to right end of the horizontal line at corner A. Once the END snap marker appears, click your left mouse button.
   e) Hit the `Esc` to deselect the line.

2) Use the same procedure to repair corner B.

3) Make line C vertical.
   a) Select line C (the centerline).
   b) Click on the bottom grip box.
   c) Acquire the top end of the centerline by moving your cursor over it.
   d) Move your cursor vertically downward until the 0 degree tracking path appears and then click your left mouse button.
   e) Hit the **Esc** to deselect the line.

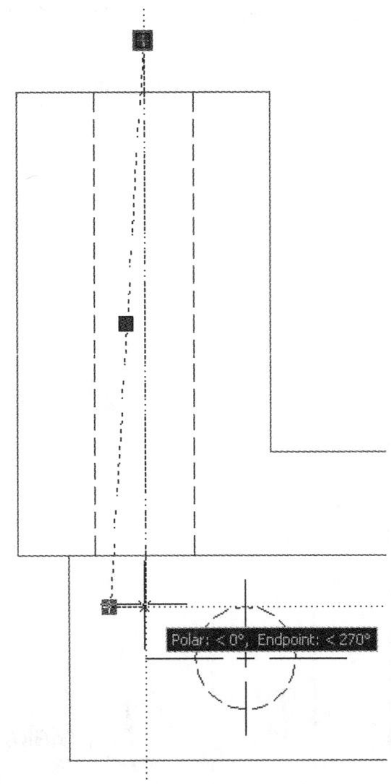

4) Change circle D to a solid line.
   a) Select circle D.
   b) Locate the *Layers* panel in the *Home* tab.
   c) Select the layers pull down selection window by clicking on the arrow.
   d) Move your cursor down the list and select ***Visible***.
   e) Hit the **Esc** to deselect the circle.

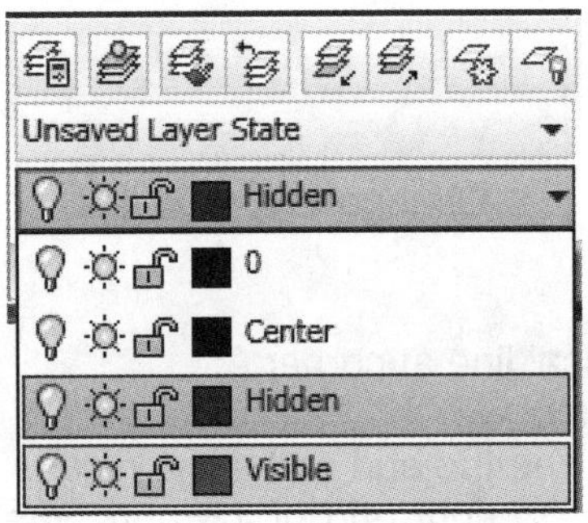

5) Extend Line E past the top and bottom horizontal visible/solid lines.

a) Command: **len** (lengthen) or *Modify* Panel: 
b) `Select on object or [DElta/Percent/Total/DYnamic]:` **de**
c) `Enter delta length or [Angle] <0.0000>:` **10**
d) `Select an object to change or [Undo]:` Select Line E near the top.
e) `Select an object to change or [Undo]:` Select Line E near the bottom.
f) `Select an object to change or [Undo]:` **Enter**

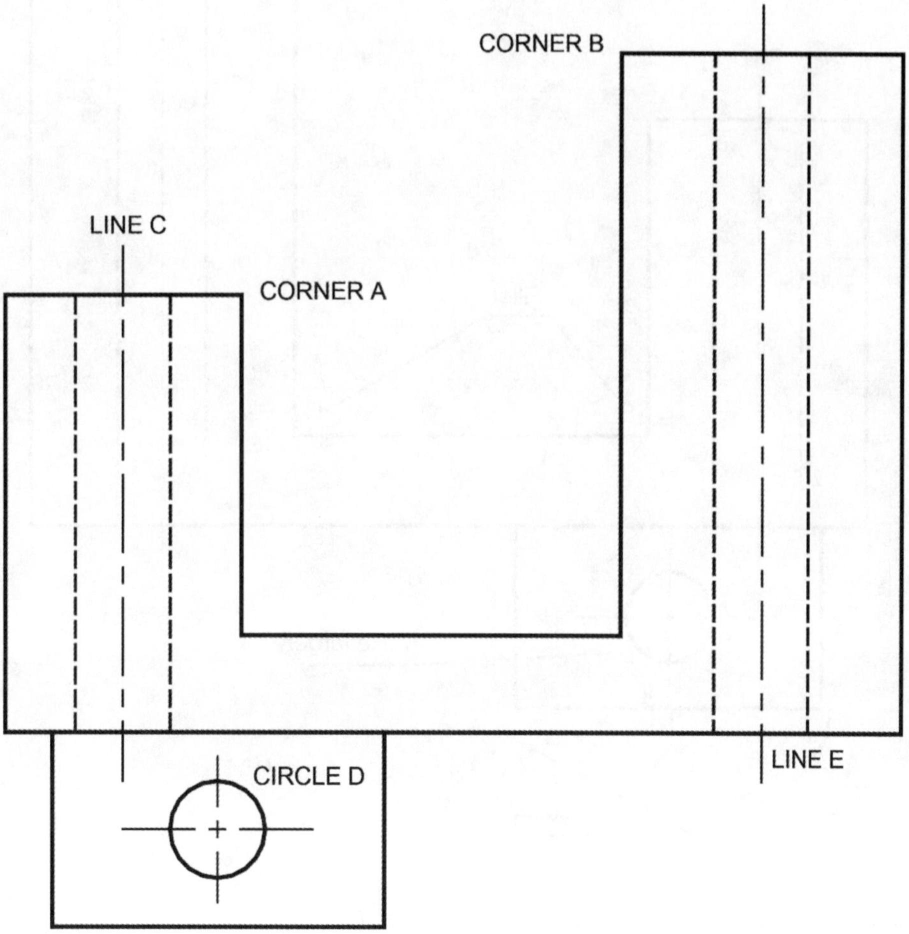

2.27.3) Modifying the drawing shape

The following figure lists the modifications that we will perform.

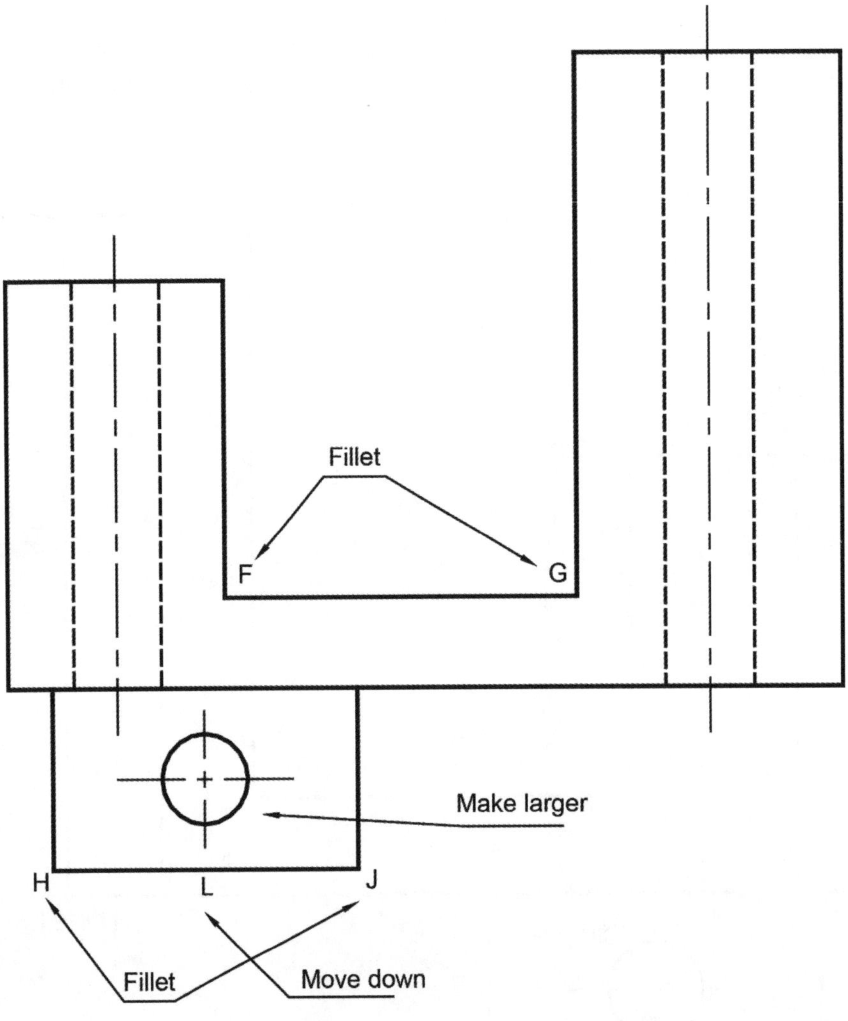

1) Apply an R5 (radius = 5) **Fillet** to corners F and G.
   a) Command: **Fillet** or *Modify* panel: 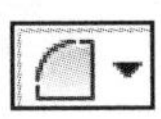
   b) `Select first object or [Undo/Polyline/Radius/Trim/Multiple]:` **r**
   c) `Specify fillet radius <10.0000>:` **5**
   d) `Select first object or [Undo/Polyline/Radius/Trim/ Multiple]:` Select one of the two lines that make up corner F.
   e) `Select second object or shift-select to apply corner:` Select the other line that makes up corner F.
   f) Command: Hit the **Space** bar to repeat the last command and apply the same fillet to corner G.

2) Apply a **R10 Fillet** to corners H and J. This time use the **Multiple** option.

3) Change the size of Circle D.
   a) Select Circle D.
   b) *View* tab – *Palettes* panel: 

   c) *Properties* window: Change the circle's *Diameter* to **30** and click on the graphics screen to watch the changes occur. Close the window when you are done.
   d) Hit the **`Esc`** to deselect the circle.

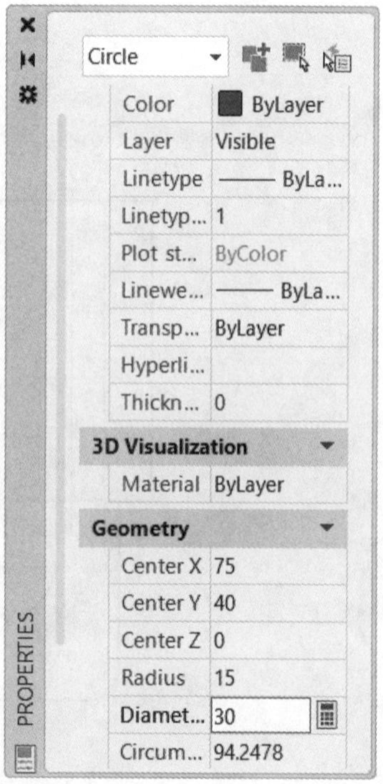

4) On your own, **LENgthen** the vertical centerline of circle D in both directions by **2.5** units.

5) Move line L and the fillets down by 20 mm.
   a) Use a window to select line L and both fillets.
   b) Left click on the middle grip box.
   c) Right click on the middle grip box and select ***Move*** from the shortcut menu.
   d) `Specify move point or [Base point/Copy/Undo/eXit]:` Use polar tracking to move line L and the fillets down **20** mm.

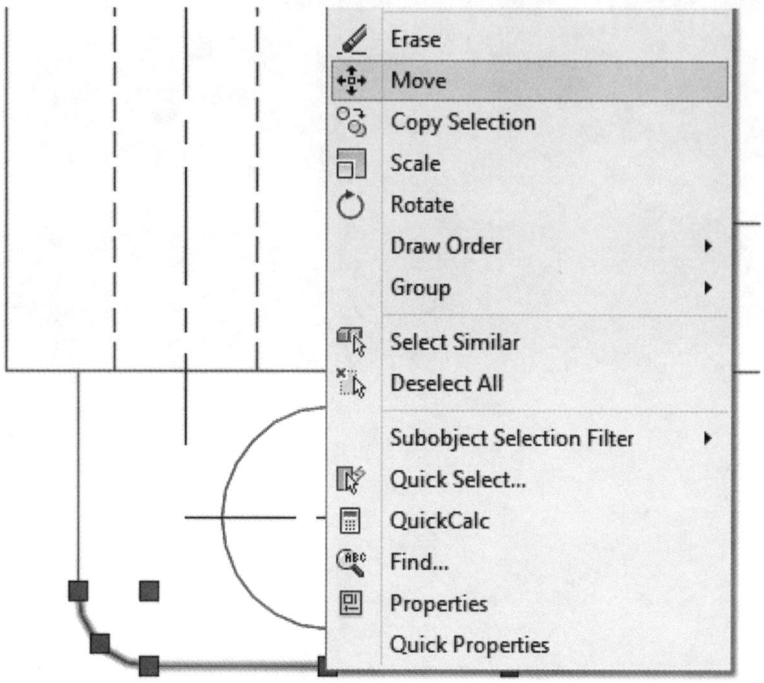

6) Use grip boxes to connect the ends of the vertical lines to the fillets.

7) 

and **print** your drawing.

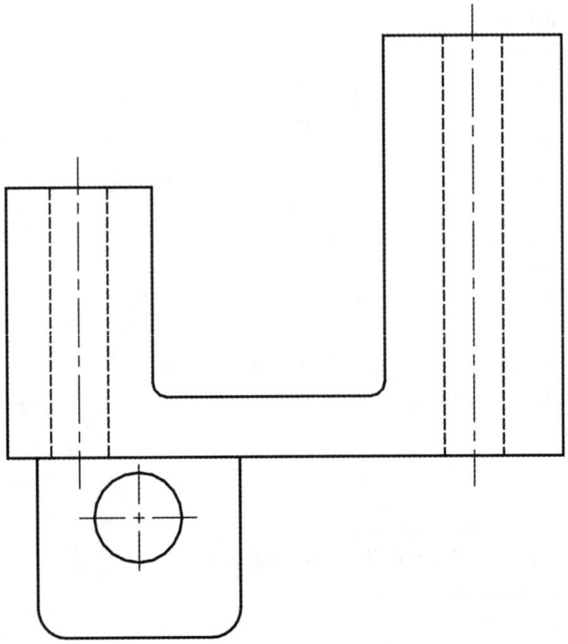

2.28) PARAMETRIC DRAWING

The commands located in the *Parametric* panel allow you to apply geometric and dimensional constraints to 2D drawings (shown in Figure 2.28-1). The power of parametric drawing becomes apparent during the design phase of a part. Parametric drawing allows you to apply key functional constraints and play with or adjust the rest of the part design without worrying about losing the constraints that you have already applied.

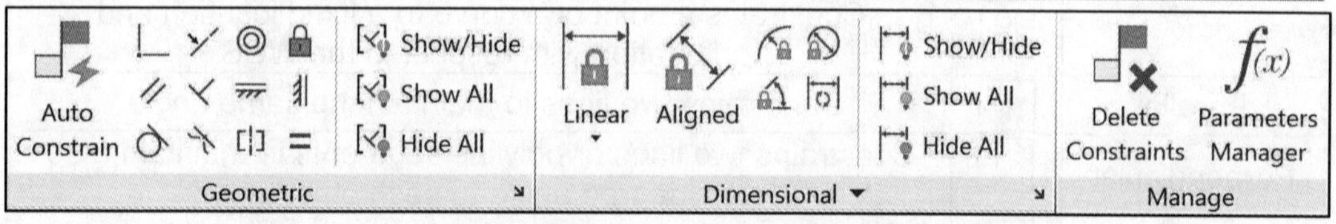

Figure 2.28-1: Parametric panel

2.28.1) Geometric constraints

Geometric constraints control the orientation relationship between two elements or of a single element. For example, you are able to force an element to be horizontal, or you can make two lines be perpendicular to each other. Table 2.28-1 describes the available geometric constraints. This command may be accessed through the *Parametric* ribbon tab or by using the **GEOMCONSTRAINT** command.

Constraint Type	Icon	Purpose
Coincident		Constrains two points to coincide, or a point to lie on an object or an extension of an object.
Colinear		Constrains two lines to lie on the same infinite line.
Concentric		Constrains two circles, arcs or ellipses to have the same center point.
Fix		Constrains a point or a curve to a fixed location and orientation with respect to the WCS.
Parallel		Constrains two lines to maintain the same angle.
Perpendicular		Constrains two lines or polyline segments to maintain a 90 degree angle to each other.
Horizontal		Constrains a line or a pair of points to lie parallel to the *x*-axis of the current UCS.
Vertical		Constrains a line or a pair of points to lie parallel to the *y*-axis of the current UCS.
Tangent		Constrains two curves to maintain a point of tangency to each other or their extensions.
Smooth		Constrains a spline to be contiguous and maintain G2 continuity with another spline, line, arc or polyline.
Symmetric		Constraints two curves or points on objects to maintain symmetry about a selected line.
Equal	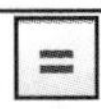	Constrains two line or polyline segments to maintain equal lengths, or circles and arcs to maintain equal radii.

Table 2.28-1: Geometric Constraints

2.28.2) Dimensional constraints

Dimensional constraints control size and angle. You can apply a dimensional constraint between two elements, two points on one element or to control the overall size or angle of an element. The size of the element will automatically change if the value of the dimension is changed. The dimension contains both a name and a value. This allows you the ability to relate one dimension to another through an equation (see Figure 2.28-2). Dimensional constraints may be accessed in the *Parametric* ribbon tab or by using the **DIMCONSTRAINT** command.

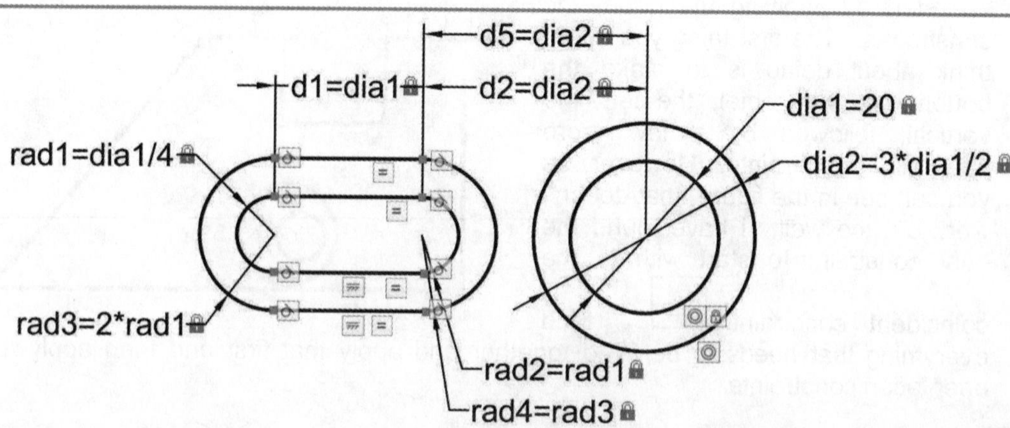

Figure 2.28-2: Example of parametric constraints.

2.29) APPLYING PARAMETRIC CONSTRAINTS TUTORIAL

The objective of this tutorial is to familiarize you with applying geometric and dimensional constraints to a pre-drawn part.

2.29.1) Applying geometric constraints

1) Read section 2.28).

2) 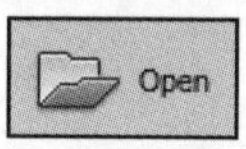

the preexisting drawing ***parametric_student_2018.dwg***.

3) 

Apply Parametric Tut.dwg

4) Our goal is to make the drawing on the left look like the drawing on the right without having to redraw it.

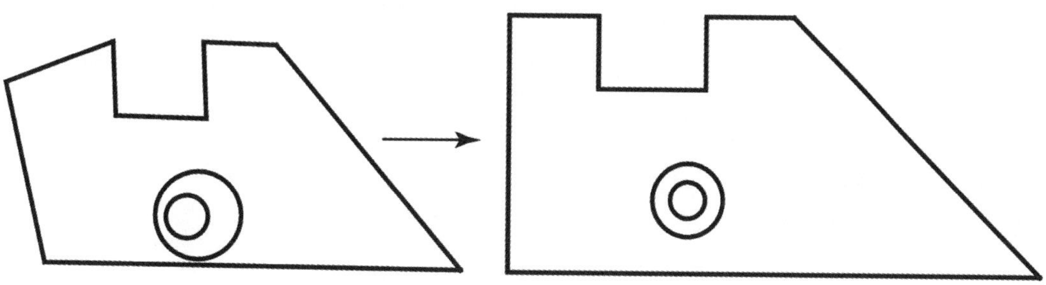

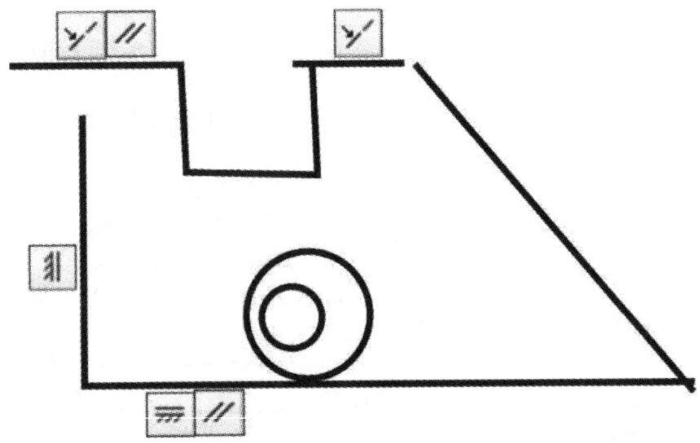

5) We start by applying the geometric constraints. The first thing you might think about doing is to make the bottom line horizontal, the left line vertical, followed by a few more orientation constraints. However, as you can see in the figure, that doesn't work out too well. I have found the best constraint to start with is the coincident constraint . Find everything that needs to be fixed together and apply that first and then apply the orientation constraints.

6) Apply a **COINCIDENT** constraint to every corner.

   a) <u>*Parametric* ribbon tab – *Geometric* panel:</u> 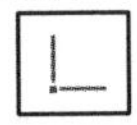

   b) `Select the first point or [Object/Autoconstrain] <Object>:` Hover over the bottom line near the bottom left corner of the part. Once you get this symbol  at the corner, select the line.

   c) `Select the second point or [Object] <Object>:` Hover over the left vertical line near the bottom left corner of the part. Once you get this symbol  at the corner, select the line. A blue square should appear at the corner. (If the blue square does not appear, select the connecting line.)

   d) Apply a coincident constraint to the remaining corners using a similar procedure.

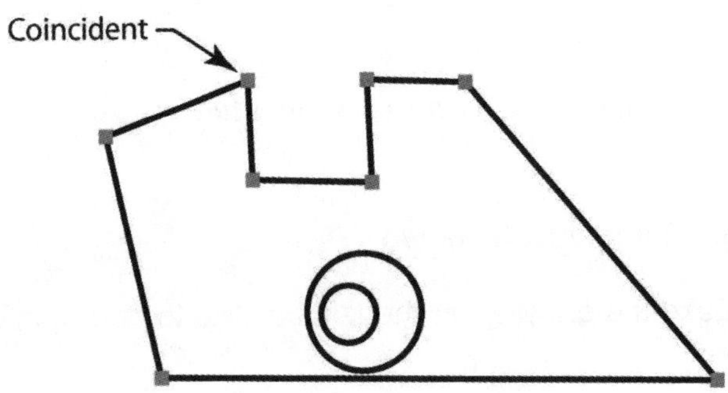

7) Make the bottom line ***HORIZONTAL*** and the left line ***VERTICAL*** as shown in the following figure.

   a) *Parametric* ribbon tab – *Geometric* panel:
   b) Select an Object or [2Points] <2Points>: Select the bottom line.
   c) Apply a vertical constraint to the left line using a similar procedure.

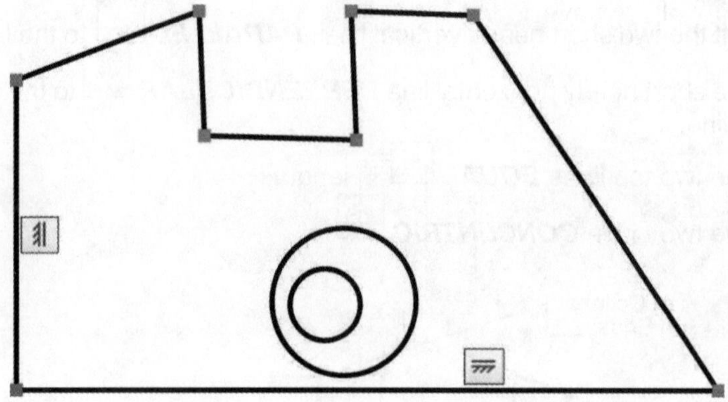

8) On your own, apply the following constraints. See the figures below and on the following page to guide you.

   a) ***FIX*** the bottom horizontal line.

   b) Apply a ***COLINEAR*** constraint to the top two lines.

   c) Make the right side top line ***PARALLEL*** to the bottom line.

   d) Make left the two short nearly vertical lines ***PARALLEL*** to the left vertical line.

   e) Make the short nearly horizontal line ***PERPENDICULAR*** to the right side short vertical line.

   f) Make the two top lines ***EQUAL*** in length.

   g) Make the two circle ***CONCENTRIC***.

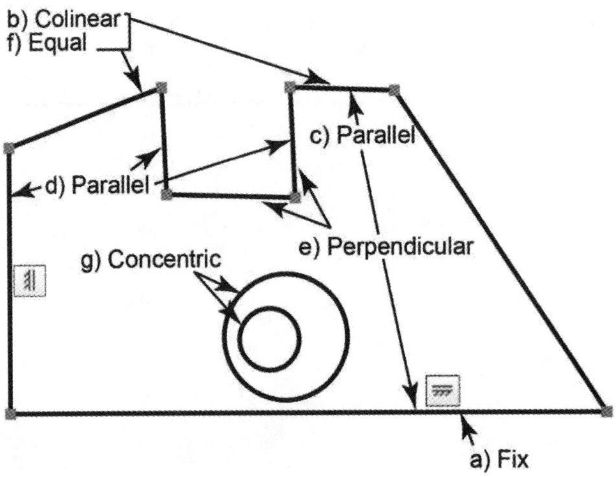

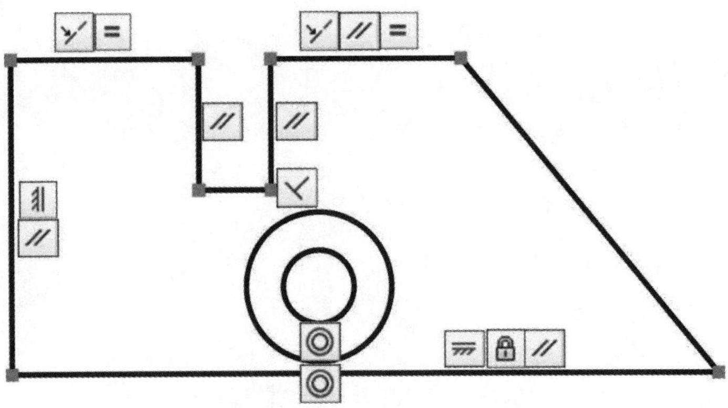

9) 

2.29.2) Applying dimensional constraints

Now that our part is completely constrained geometrically, let's add some size constraints.

1) Add ***LINEAR*** dimensions to the part.

a) <u>Command:</u> **dclinear** *or* <u>*Parametric* ribbon tab – *Dimensional* panel:</u>
b) `Specify first constraint point or [Object] <Object>:` Hover over the top horizontal line near the left corner of the part. Once you get this symbol  at the corner, select the line.
c) `Specify second constraint point:` Hover over the bottom horizontal line near the left corner of the part. Once you get this symbol  at the corner, select the line.
d) `Specify dimension line location:` Pull the dimension away from the part and click the left mouse button.
e) `Dimension text = 67` Don't worry about the dimension value right now, just hit **`Enter`**.
f) Place the rest of the linear (**DCLINEAR**) dimensions shown in the figure using a similar procedure. To place the linear dimensions between the lines and the center of the circle, select the line first and then the border of the circle.

Don't worry if your dimensions are named differently than the following figure.

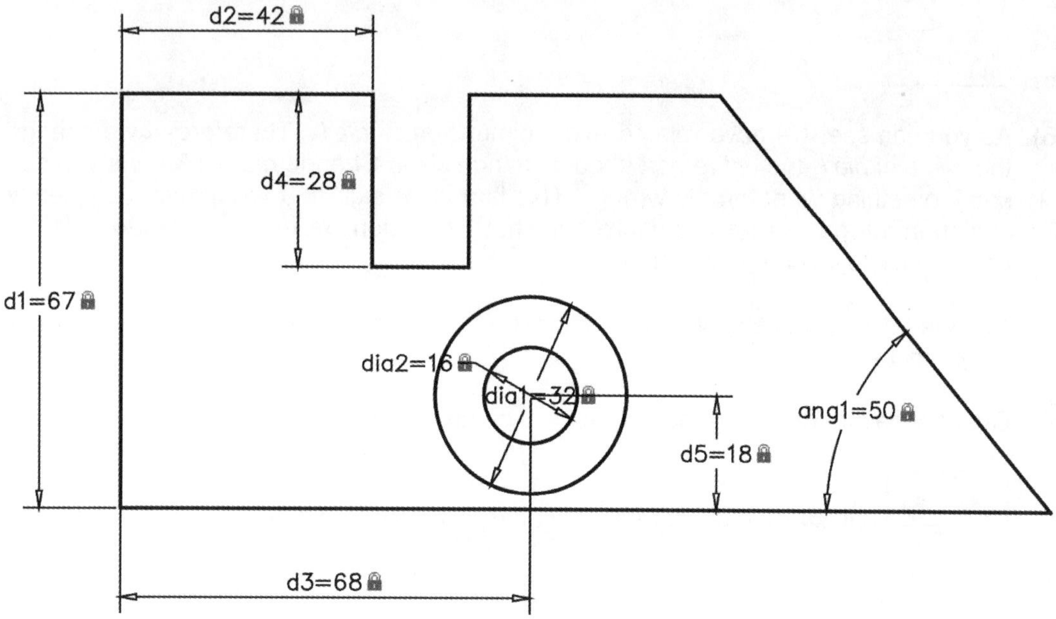

2) On your own, add the angular (**DCANGULAR**)  and diameter (**DCDIAMETER**)  dimensions. Read the command prompt for guidance.

3) Double click on the angular dimension and type **ang1=45** and then hit `Enter`.

4) Use the same procedure to set both the dimension NAME and VALUE of all the constraints to be the same as those shown in the figure below. NOTE: You may need to create some temporary dummy names if you have a duplicate dimension name. You should start with the diameter dimension since every other dimension is based off of those dimensions.

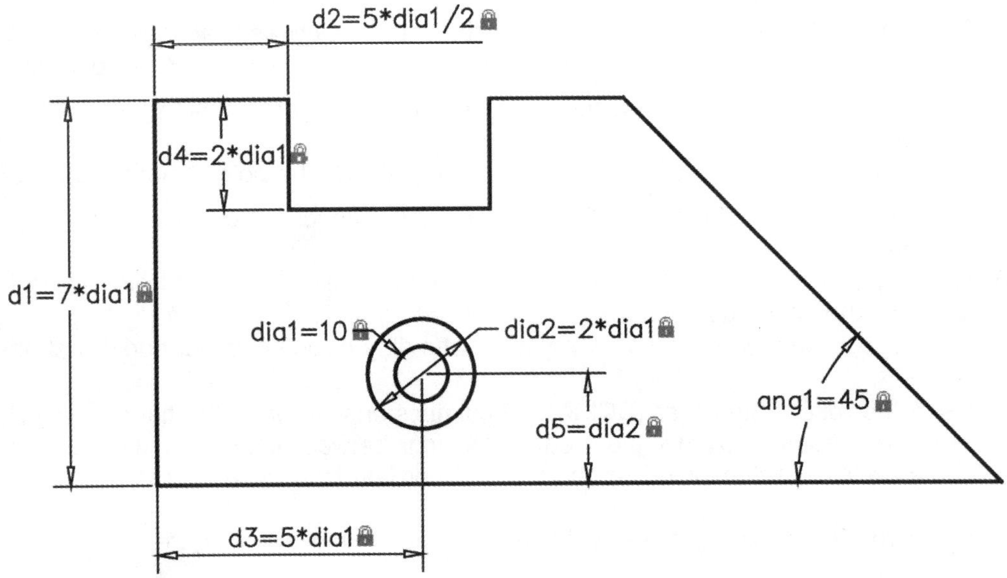

5) 

6) As you can see, we have related every dimension to *dia1*. Therefore, if we change the value of *dia1*, the entire part should change size. Change *dia1* to **30**. As you can see, something went terribly wrong. This is a clear sign that we did not completely constrain our part. Can you figure out what dimension we missed? **Undo** until the part is back to its correct shape and size.

7) Add the LINEAR dimension that controls the total length of the bottom line and set its length to **15*dia1**.

8) Change *dia1* to **30**. This time the result is completely different.

9) 

and ***print*** your drawing using the ***scale to fit*** option.

2.30) AUTOMATIC PARAMETRIC CONSTRAINTS TUTORIAL

The objective of this tutorial is to familiarize the reader with apply parametric constraints to an already correctly drawn part.

1) 

set-mm.dwt and 

Auto Parametric Tut.dwg

2) Draw the following object using the proper OSNAPS. Do not include the dimensions, but draw it to the correct size. ®

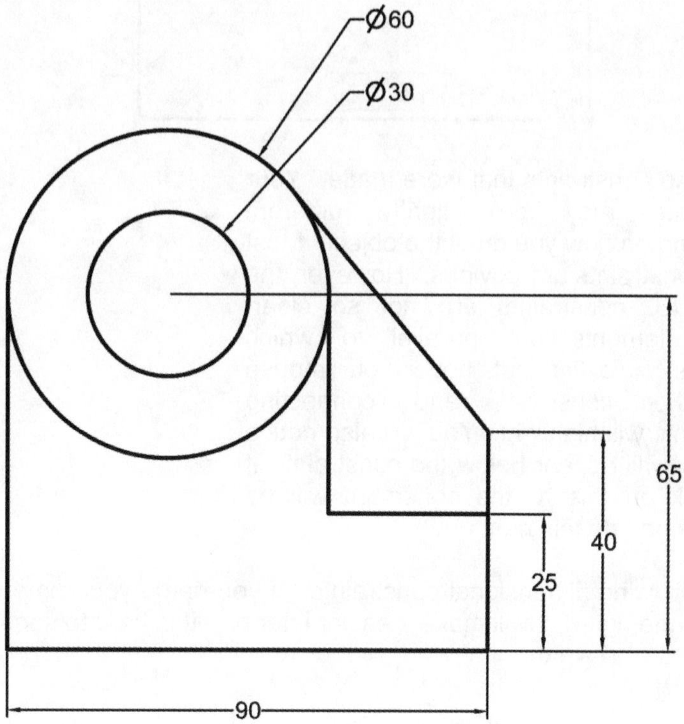

3) Automatically apply the geometric constraints based on your drawing.

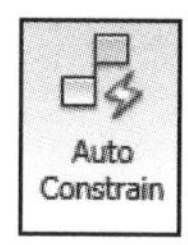

a) Command: **autoconstrain** or *Parametric* tab – *Geometric* panel:
b) `Select objects or [Settings]:` **all**
c) `Select objects or [Settings]:` **Enter**

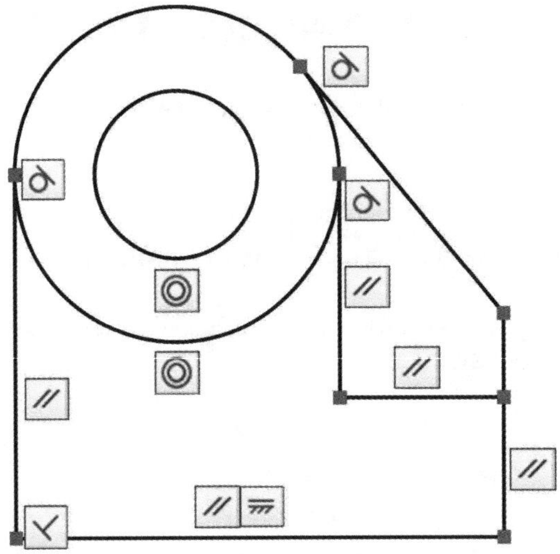

d) Notice the constraints that were made. Your constraints may be slightly different depending on how you drew the object. Most of the constraints are obvious. However, the PARALLEL constraints are not so clear. Which elements are parallel to which elements? To find out, hover your mouse over the constraint and connecting constraints will highlight. You will also notice that an X will appear below the constraint. If you click on this X, the constraint will be hidden (don't do this right now).

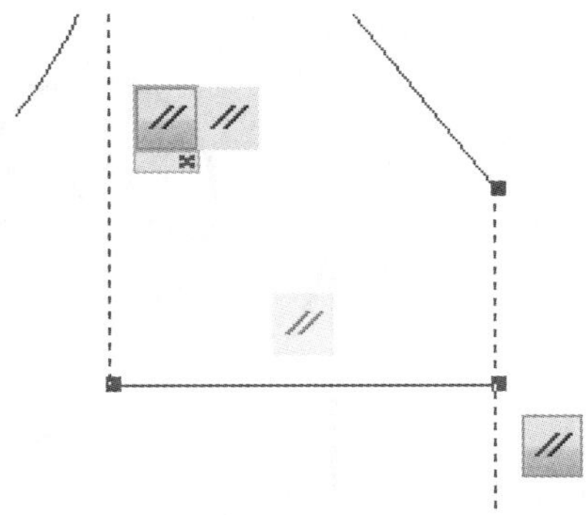

4) Apply the following dimensional constraints. If you name your dimensions the same as shown in the figure, it will make it easier later on. It is hard to see in the figure, but **dia1 = 30** and **dia2 = 60**.

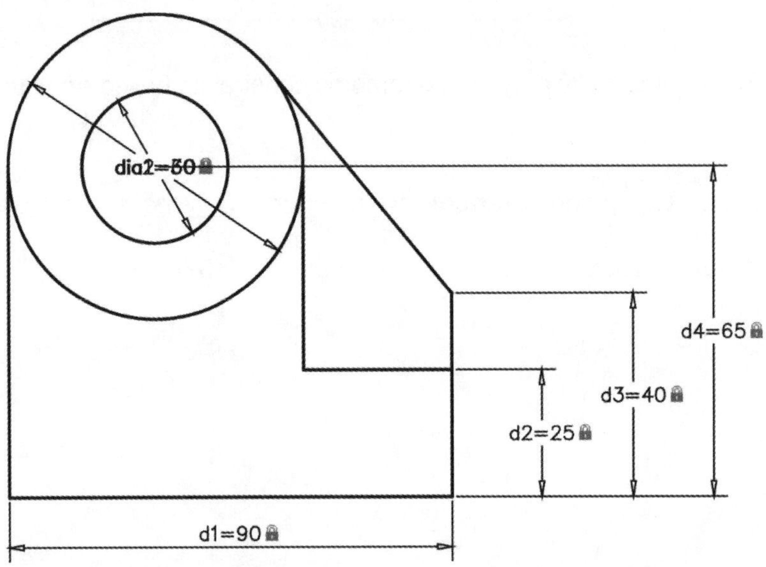

5) Apply functional relationships between the dimensional constraints.

a) Command: **parameters** or *Parametric* tab – *Geometric* panel: 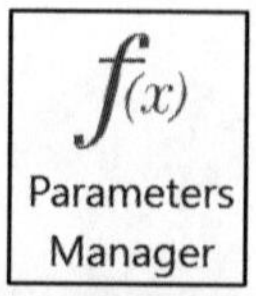

b) *Parameters Manager* window: Input the following functional relationships between the dimensional constraints. The *Parameters Manager* allows you to change the name and value of every dimension (double click to change the value). Refer to the above figure to relate the name to the original value.

c) ***Close*** the *Parameters Manager* window.

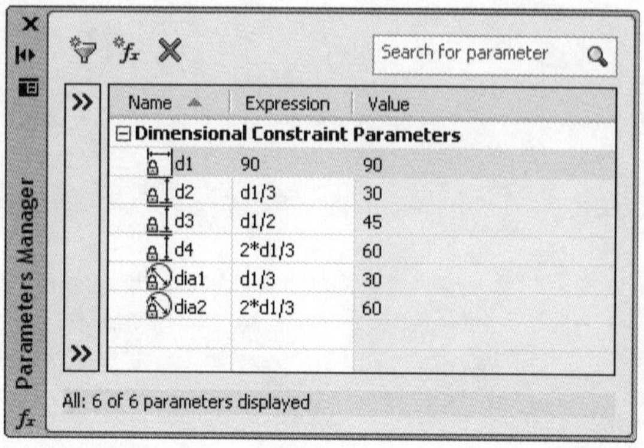

6) Change **d1** to **60** and make sure all the constraints are properly applied.

7) ***Save*** and ***print*** your drawing using the ***scale to fit*** option.

NOTES:

DRAWING IN AUTOCAD QUESTIONS

Name: ________________________________ Date: ______________

User interface

Q2-1) The shortcut menu is accessed by

a) Hitting the space bar
b) Left clicking
c) Right clicking
d) Hitting the enter key

Q2-2) The window and tab that you need to access in order to change the drawing area's color?

a) Options-Selection
b) Options-Drafting
c) Options-Files
d) Options-Display

Q2-3) This key allows you to quickly repeat your last command.

a) space bar
b) esc
c) tab
d) enter

Q2-4) Circle all the ways that you can use to access AutoCAD's commands.

a) Ribbon panels
b) Command window
c) Tool palettes
d) Application button search box

Q2-5) A place that gives you quick access to commands that are frequently turned on and off.

a) Ribbon panels
b) Command window
c) Tool palettes
d) Status bar

Starting and setting up a drawing

Q2-6) The system variable that determines whether the *Select Template* window or the *Create New Drawing* window appears when starting a new drawing.

a) drawing
b) startup
c) template
d) create

Q2-7) The command that is used to select your unit of measure and precision.

a) limits
b) precision
c) measure
d) units

Q2-8) The command that is used to set your paper size.

a) limits
b) precision
c) measure
d) units

Name: ______________________________ Date: ______________

Coordinates

Q2-9) Which coordinate system is stationary and cannot be translated or rotated?

a) WCS
b) UCS
c) CCS
d) LCS

Q2-10) Which coordinate system may be translated and rotated by the user to make drawing easier?

a) WCS
b) UCS
c) CCS
d) LCS

Q2-11) An absolute coordinate is measured relative to the ....

a) origin
b) last point entered
c) bottom left corner of your paper
d) cursor

Q2-12) A relative coordinate is measured relative to the ....

a) origin
b) last point entered
c) bottom left corner of your paper
d) cursor

Q2-13) A relative coordinate is indicated by placing the following symbol before your coordinate.

a) #
b) &
c) @
d) <

Printing

Q2-14) Which printing option prints everything that you can currently see?

a) limits
b) extents
c) display
d) window
e) scale to fit

Q2-15) Which printing option will expand/reduce your drawing to fit the paper?

a) limits
b) extents
c) display
d) window
e) scale to fit

Q2-16) Which printing option prints everything within your defined paper size?

a) limits
b) extents
c) display
d) window
e) scale to fit

Q2-17) Which printing option prints everything that has been drawn?

a) limits
b) extents
c) display
d) window
e) scale to fit

Name: ________________________________ Date: ______________

Draw commands

Q2-18) An arc may be defined by its START, END and .... (circle all that apply)

a) radius
b) direction
c) diameter
d) angle

Q2-19) What is the typed command used to access text settings?

a) textsettings
b) edit
c) style
d) font

Q2-20) A polygon that is drawn on the outside of a circle is said to be ...

a) inscribed
b) circumscribed
c) outward
d) inward

Q2-21) A circle may be defined by its CENTER and .... (circle all that apply)

a) radius.
b) diameter.
c) circumference.
d) three points.

Modify commands

Q2-22) What is the rotation basepoint used in the example shown?

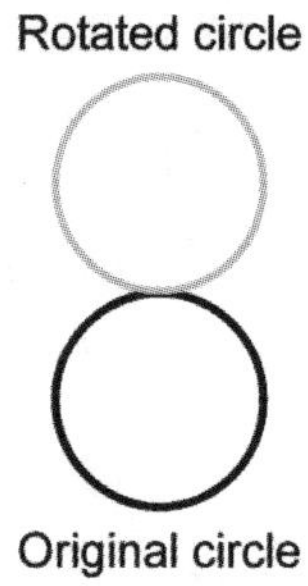

a) circle center
b) top quadrant
c) right quadrant
d) bottom quadrant

Q2-23) What is the scale basepoint used in the example shown?

a) lower left corner
b) upper left corner
c) rectangle center
d) upper right corner

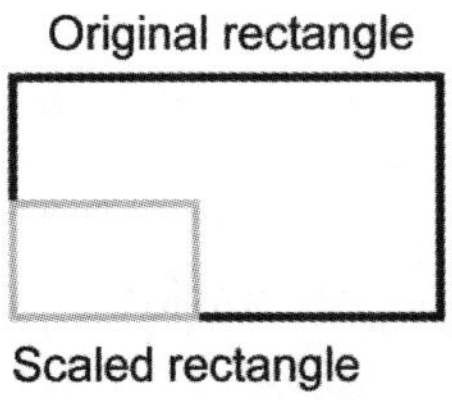

Q2-24) When moving an object using relative coordinates, the first base point may be .... (circle all that apply)

a) the origin.
b) a point on the object.
c) the point that you are moving the object to.
d) any point.

Name: ______________________________ Date: _____________

Selecting objects

Q2-25) What type of selection window selects everything touching and inside the defined window?

a) standard window
b) crossing window
c) lasso window
d) polygon window

Q2-26) Clicking and dragging the mouse from right to left produces a ....

a) standard window.
b) crossing window.
c) polygon window.
d) fence.

Q2-27) Clicking and dragging the mouse from left to right produces a ....

a) standard window.
b) crossing window.
c) polygon window.
d) fence.

Q2-28) Clicking, holding and dragging the mouse produces a ....

a) standard window.
b) crossing window.
c) lasso window.
d) fence.

Q2-29) When AutoCAD is waiting for you to select an object, the crosshairs turn into a ....

a) hand.
b) pickbox.
c) arrow.
d) lasso.

Q2-30) You know when an object is selected because it becomes ....

a) highlighted
b) invisible
c) blinks
d) bigger

Q2-31) After selecting several objects to erase, what command would you type if you wanted to remove an object(s) from the selection set?

a) add
b) delete
c) remove
d) eliminate

Q2-32) What key do you need to hold down if you want to remove an object(s) from the current selection set?

a) ctrl
b) esc
c) tab
d) shift

Name: ______________________________ Date: ______________

Object snaps

Some of the following questions refer to the object snap panel shown.

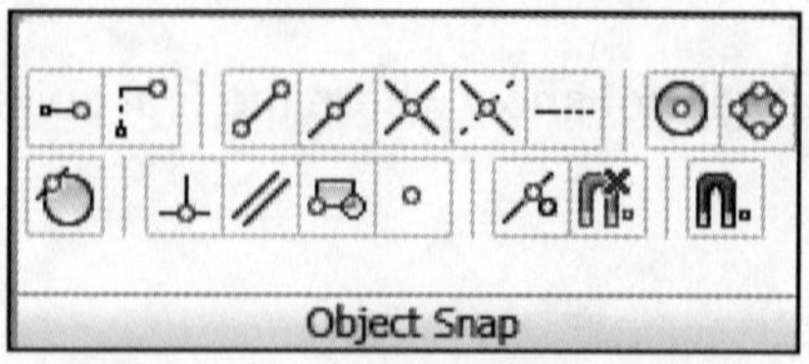

Q2-33) Object snaps not only speed up the drawing process, you cannot draw .... without them unless you enter coordinates.

a) accurately
b) neatly
c) efficiently
d) with the mouse

Q2-34) You may access the object snap settings by right clicking on the *Object Snap* icon in the status bar, clicking on the arrow next to the icon, or by typing what command?

a) snapset
b) snap
c) osnap
d) object

Q2-35) *Object Snap* panel: Top row, ninth icon from the left?

a) endpoint
b) quadrant
c) nearest
d) tangent

Q2-36) *Object Snap* panel: Top row, third icon from the left?

a) endpoint
b) quadrant
c) nearest
d) tangent

Q2-37) *Object Snap* panel: Second row, sixth icon from the left?

a) endpoint
b) quadrant
c) nearest
d) tangent

Q2-38) Which is the window and tab where you can access the *Autosnap Marker* size?

a) options-files
b) options-display
c) options-drafting
d) options-selection

Q2-39) The object snap that will not show where the first point of a line is located until the second point is selected.

a) endpoint
b) quadrant
c) nearest
d) tangent

Name: ______________________________ Date: ____________

Tracking and dynamic input

Q2-40) This enables you to snap along angled track lines.

a) temporary tracking
b) object snap tracking
c) polar tracking
d) dynamic input

Q2-41) What typed command allows you to change the polar tracking angle.

a) pangle
b) anglepo
c) setang
d) polarang

Q2-42) This icon, located in the status bar, allows you to create tracking lines off of object snap points.

a) temporary tracking
b) object snap tracking
c) polar tracking
d) dynamic input

Q2-43) What letters do you type to indicate that you want to create a temporary track point?

a) tm
b) tt
c) tp
d) pt

Q2-44) What key do you press to cycle through the dynamic input dimensions?

a) esc
b) shift
c) ctrl
d) tab

Grip boxes

Q2-45) Clicking once on an object, while not currently in a command, accesses the ....

a) grip boxes
b) properties window
c) the command used to create the object
d) modify commands

Q2-46) The grip box options may be accessed by .... on one of the boxes.

a) left clicking
b) right clicking
c) double clicking
d) dragging

Q2-47) The command used to make a line longer by a prescribed length.

a) extend
b) lengthen
c) stretch
d) grow

DRAWING IN AUTOCAD PROBLEMS

Name: ________________________________ Date: _______________

P2-1) (May be attempted after completing the *Drawing using Coordinates Tutorial* in section 2.10) Write down the **relative Cartesian coordinates** needed to create the following object in the direction indicated in the figure. Assume that the start point is created by clicking the mouse; therefore, we do not know its exact coordinate position. Dimensions are given in millimeters.

Start point: Click mouse anywhere

Next point:

Next point:

Next point:

Next point:

Next point:

Next point:

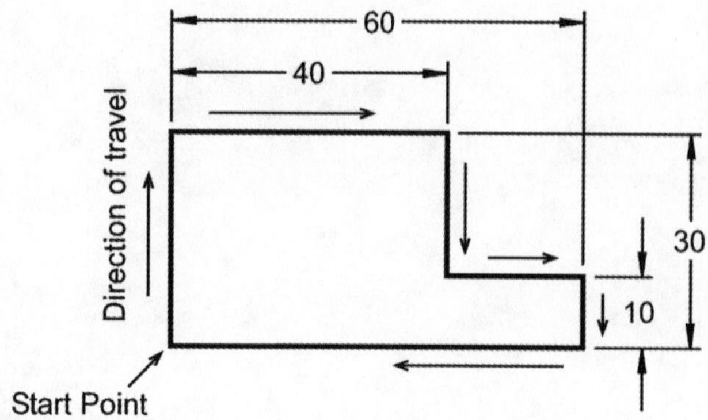

Write down the **relative polar coordinates** needed to create the following object.

Start point: Click mouse anywhere

Next point:

Next point:

Next point:

Next point:

Next point:

Next point:

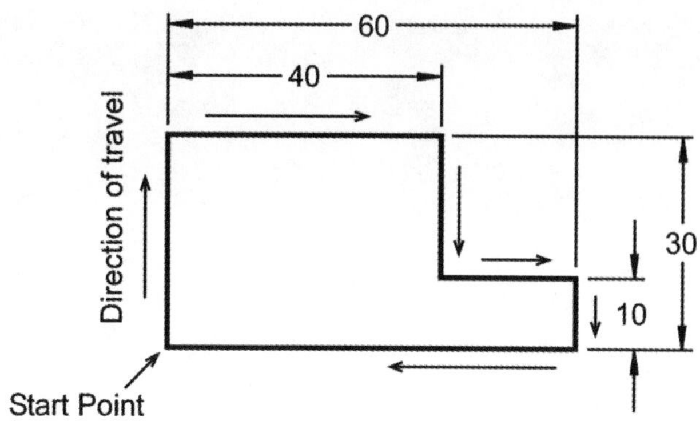

NOTES:

Name: ______________________________ Date: ______________

P2-2) May be attempted after completing the *Drawing using Coordinates Tutorial* and the *Printing Tutorial* in sections 2.10 and 2.12. Fill in the table below with the appropriate relative coordinates needed to draw this object in AutoCAD and then draw the object in AutoCAD. Print using a window and the scale to fit option. Dimensions are in inches.

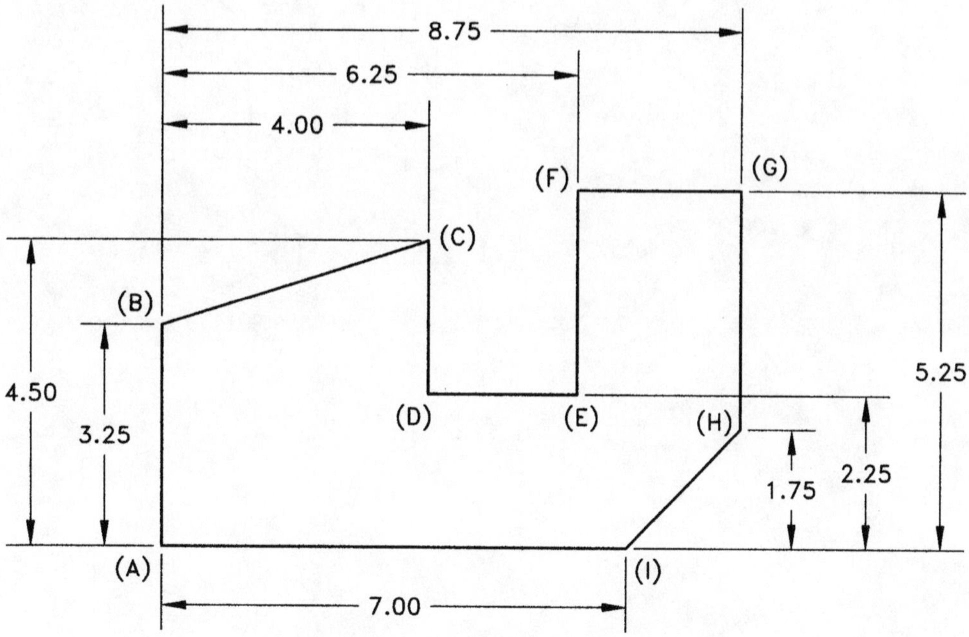

To Point	Relative Coordinate
A to B	@
B to C	@
C to D	@
D to E	@
E to F	@
F to G	@
G to H	@
H to I	@
I to A	@

NOTES:

Name: ______________________________ Date: ______________

P2-3) May be attempted after completing the *Drawing using Coordinates Tutorial* and the *Printing Tutorial* in sections 2.10 and 2.12. Fill in the table below with the appropriate relative coordinates needed to draw this object in AutoCAD and then draw the object in AutoCAD. Print using a window and the scale to fit option. Dimensions are in millimeters.

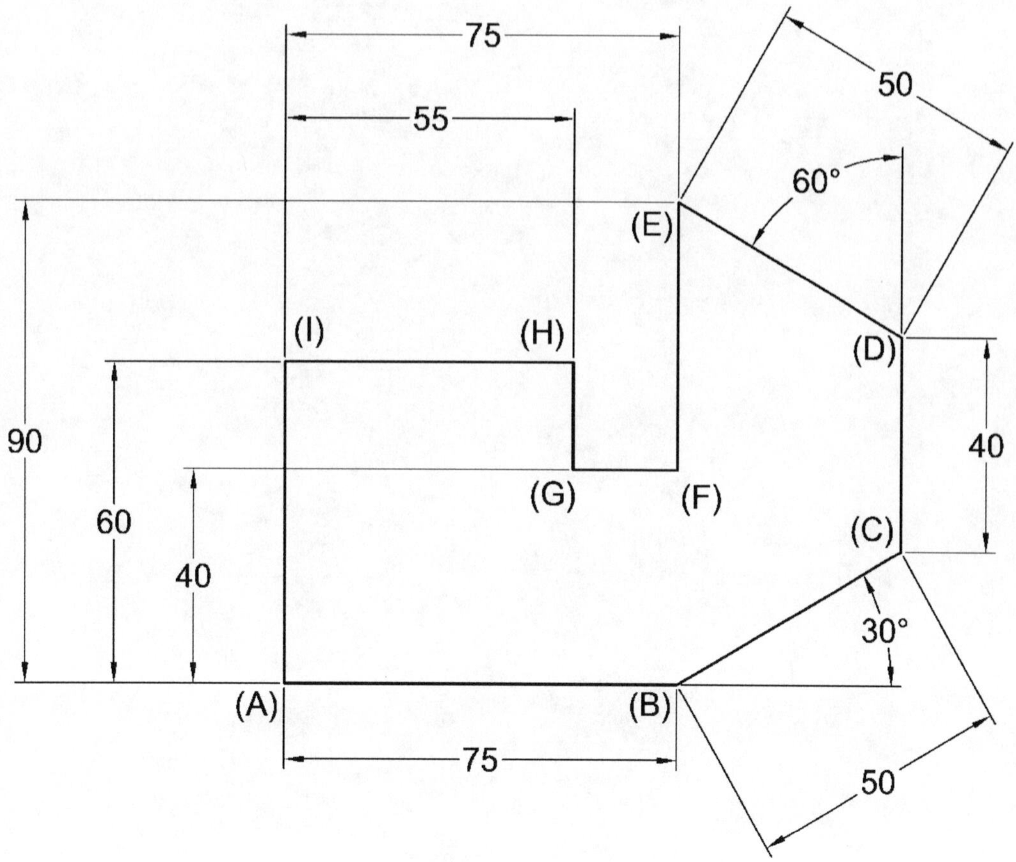

To Point	Relative Coordinate
A to B	@
B to C	@
C to D	@
D to E	@
E to F	@
F to G	@
G to H	@
H to I	@
I to A	@

NOTES:

Name: ______________________________________ Date: ________________

P2-4) May be attempted after completing the *Drawing using Coordinates Tutorial* and the *Printing Tutorial* in sections 2.10 and 2.12. Draw the following object using relative Cartesian and/or relative polar coordinates. Draw the object starting at the point indicated and in the direction indicated. To connect the start point and end point, type CLOSE while still in the LINE command. Write down the relative coordinates used to create the object in the table. Print using a window and the scale to fit option. Dimensions are in millimeters.

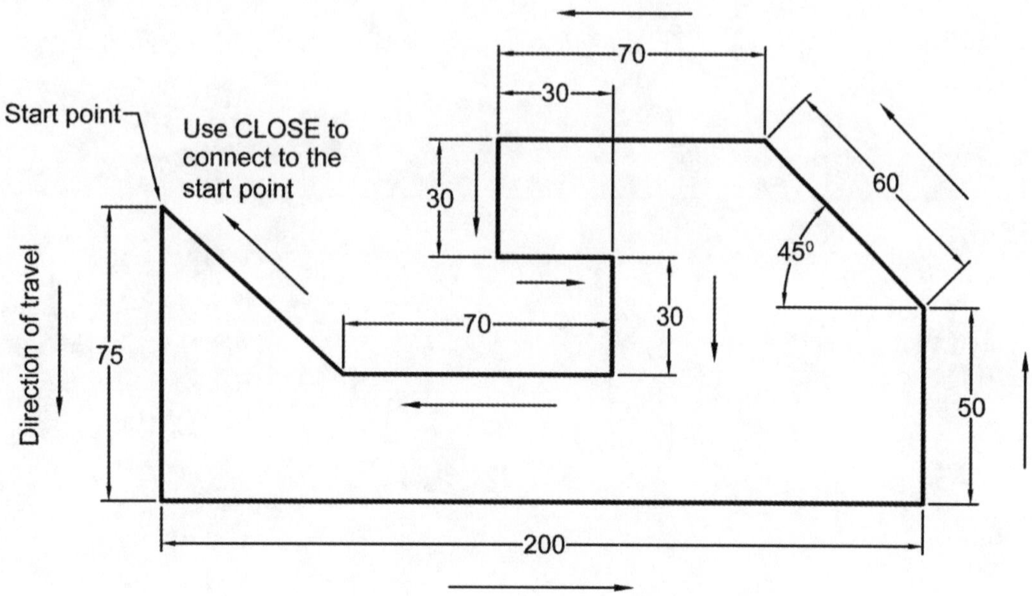

To Point	Relative Coordinate
Start point to next point	@
to Next point	@
to Next point	@
to Next point	@
to Next point	@
to Next point	@
to Next point	@
to Next point	@
to Next point	@
to Next point	CLOSE

NOTES:

P2-5) May be attempted after completing the *WCS/UCS Coordinate Systems*, *Drawing using Coordinates* and the *Printing Tutorials* in sections 2.9, 2.10 and 2.12. Draw the following object in AutoCAD. HINT: To draw the circle and square, try changing your UCS to one of the corners of the main body. Print using a window and the scale to fit option. Dimensions are in inches.

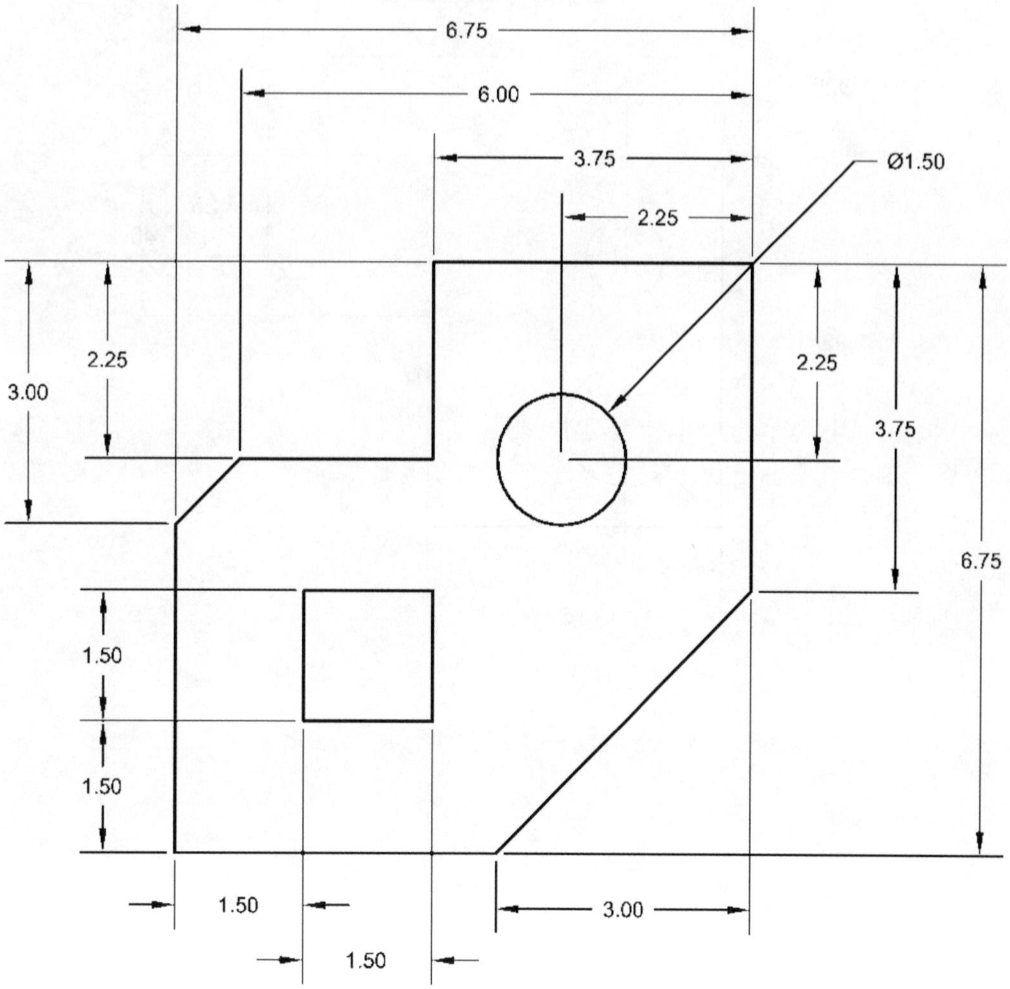

P2-6) May be attempted after completing the *WCS/UCS Coordinate Systems*, *Drawing using Coordinates* and the *Printing Tutorials* in sections 2.9, 2.10 and 2.12. Draw the following object in AutoCAD. HINT: To draw the circles, try changing your UCS to the corners of the main body. Print using a window and the scale to fit option. Dimensions are in millimeters.

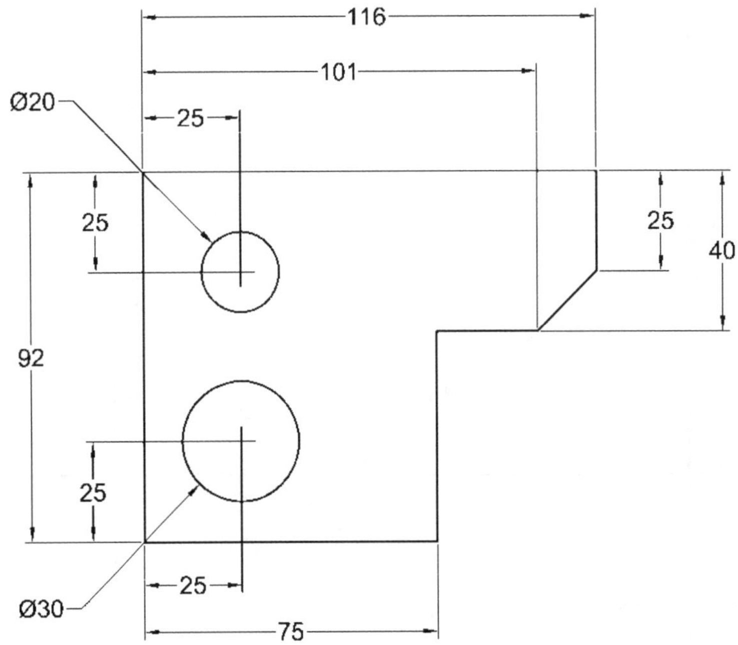

P2-7) May be attempted after completing the *Object Snap Tutorial* in section 2.20. Draw the following object using object snap commands where necessary. Put your name on the drawing and then print it using a *Window* and the *Scale to Fit* option. Dimensions are in millimeters.

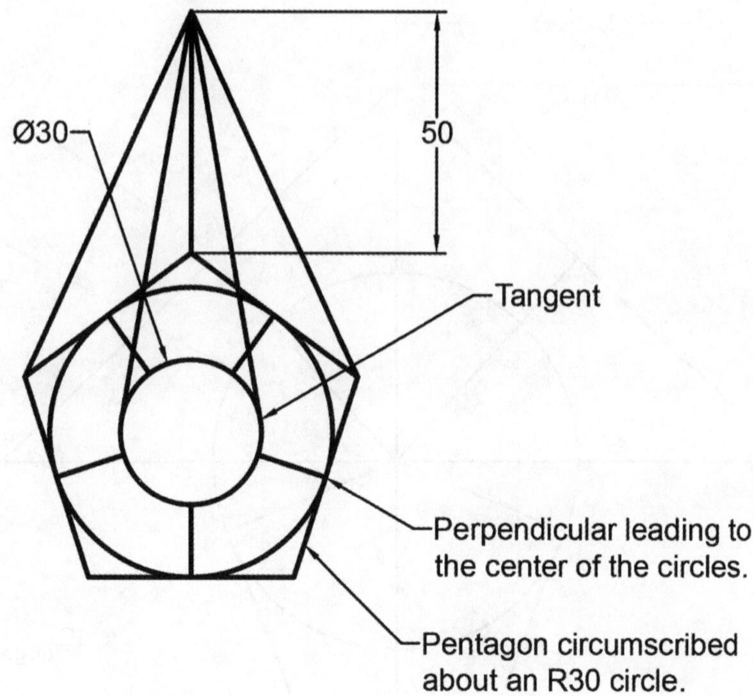

P2-8) May be attempted after completing the *Object Snap Tutorial* in section 2.20. Draw the following object in AutoCAD using object snap commands where necessary. Put your name on the drawing and then print it using a *Window* and the *Scale to Fit* option. Dimensions are in inches.

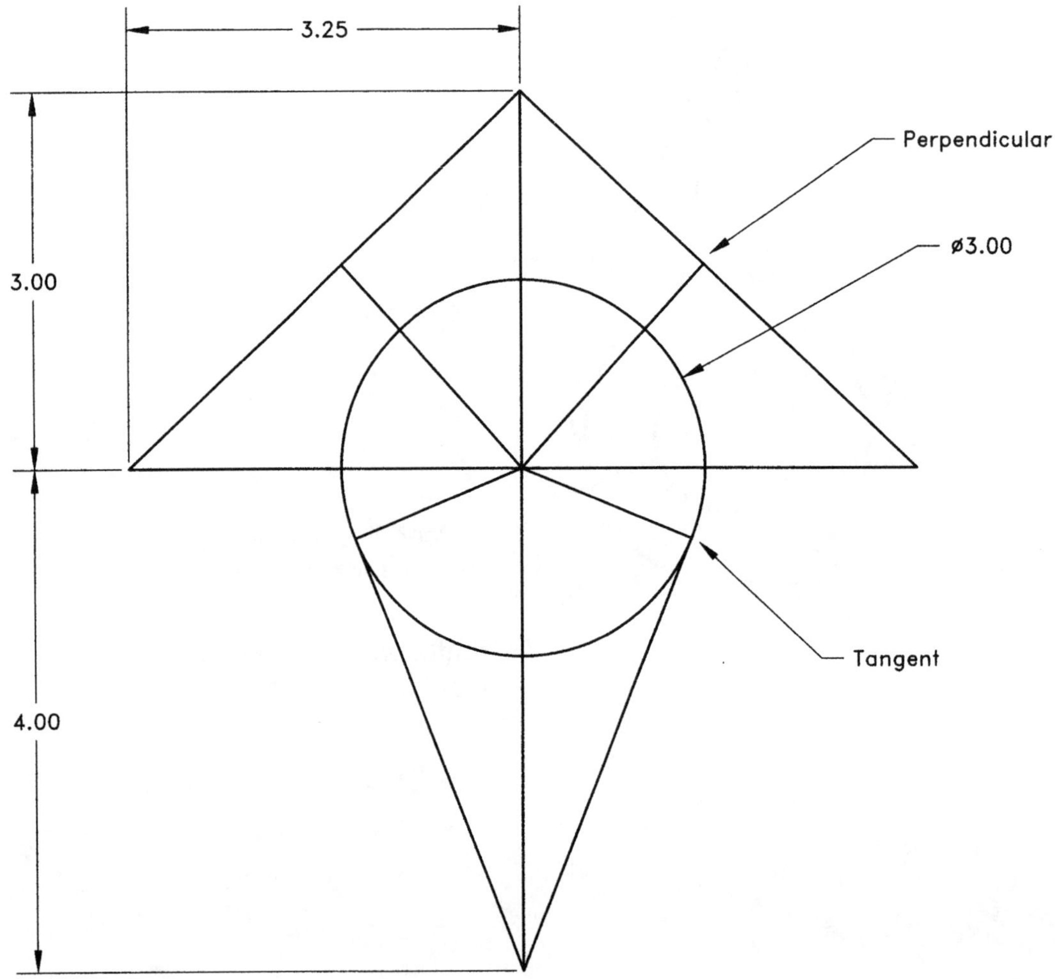

P2-9) May be attempted after completing the *Object Snap Tutorial* in section 2.20. Draw the following object in AutoCAD using object snap commands where necessary. Put your name on the drawing and then print it using a *Window* and the *Scale to Fit* option. Dimensions are in inches. Hint: To create the arc, choose the start point, then the end point, and then the radius. Remember that arcs are drawn according to the right hand rule. Dimensions are in inches.

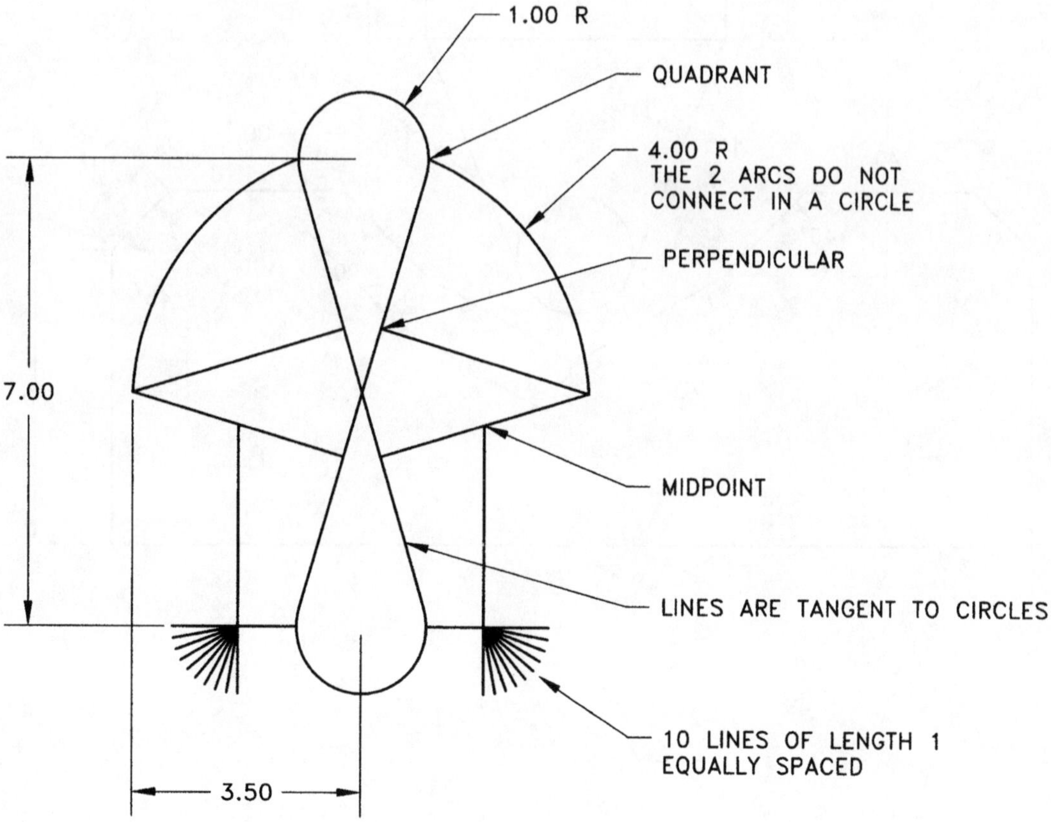

P2-10) May be attempted after completing the *Tracking Tutorial* in section 2.23. Draw the following object with the help of track points. Put your name on the drawing and then print using a 1 to 1 scale. Dimensions are in millimeters.

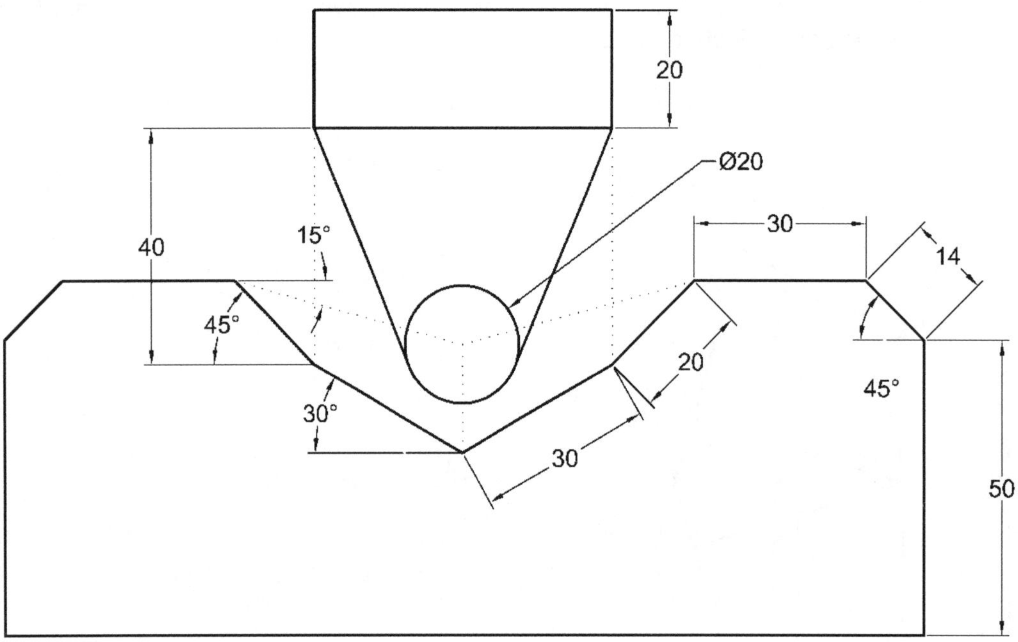

P2-11) May be attempted after completing the *Object Snap Tutorial* in section 2.20. Draw the following object in AutoCAD. Put your name on the drawing and then print it using a *Window* and the *Scale to Fit* option. Dimensions are in millimeters.

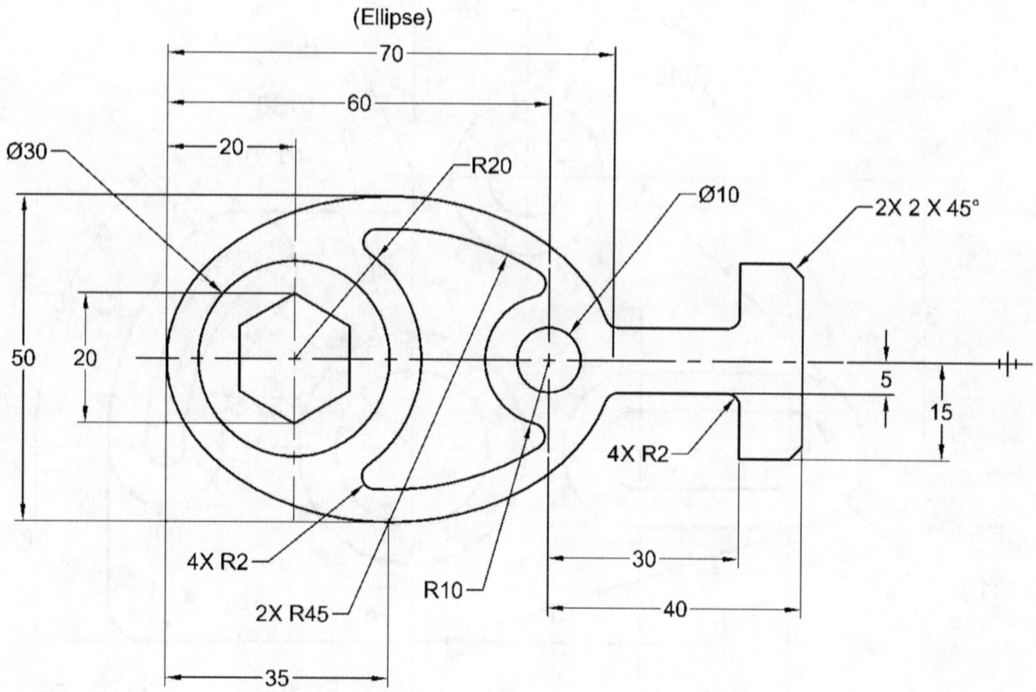

P2-12) May be attempted after completing the *Object Snap Tutorial* in section 2.20. Draw the following object in AutoCAD. Put your name on the drawing and then print it using a *Window* and the *Scale to Fit* option. Dimensions are in millimeters.

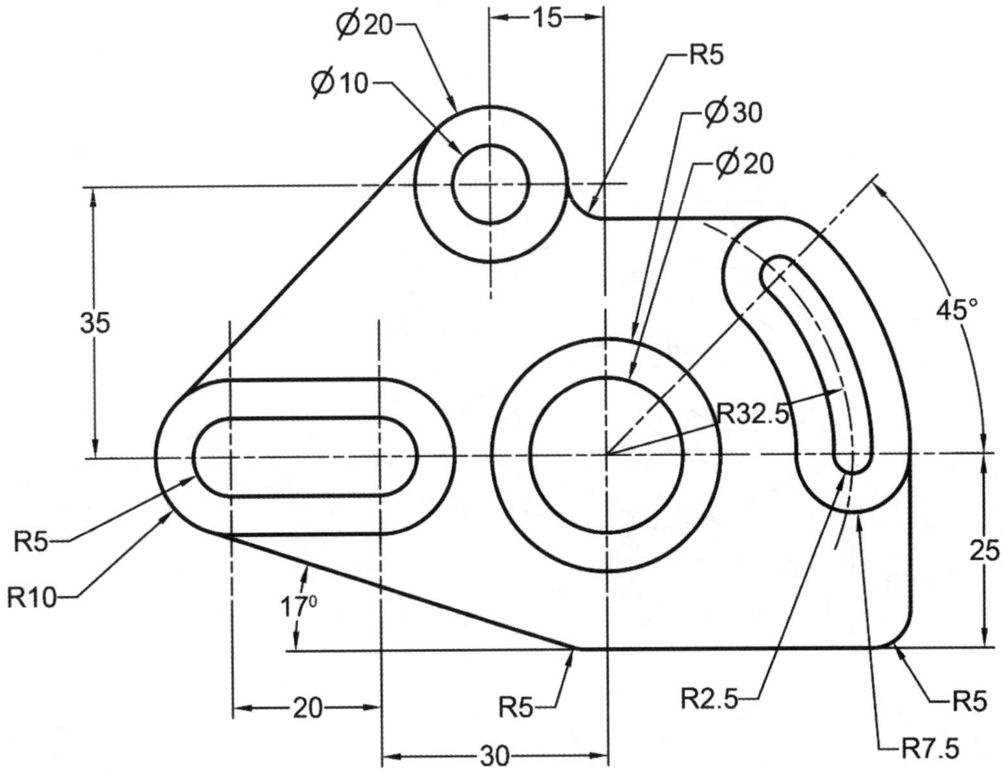

CHAPTER 3

READING ORTHOGRAPHIC PROJECTIONS

CHAPTER OUTLINE

CHAPTER SUMMARY

In this chapter, you will learn how to read orthographic projections. An orthographic projection describes the shape of an object. It is a two-dimensional representation of a three-dimensional object. Different line types are used to indicate visible features, hidden features, and symmetry. By the end of this chapter, you will be able to read a technically correct orthographic projection and visualize its three-dimensional form.

3.1) ORTHOGRAPHIC PROJECTION INTRODUCTION

An *orthographic projection* enables us to represent a three-dimensional object in two dimensions (see Figure 3.1-1). An orthographic projection is a drawing that shows different sides of an object on a sheet of paper (i.e., in two dimensions). The drawing is formed by projecting the edges of the object onto a projection plane from different viewing perspectives.

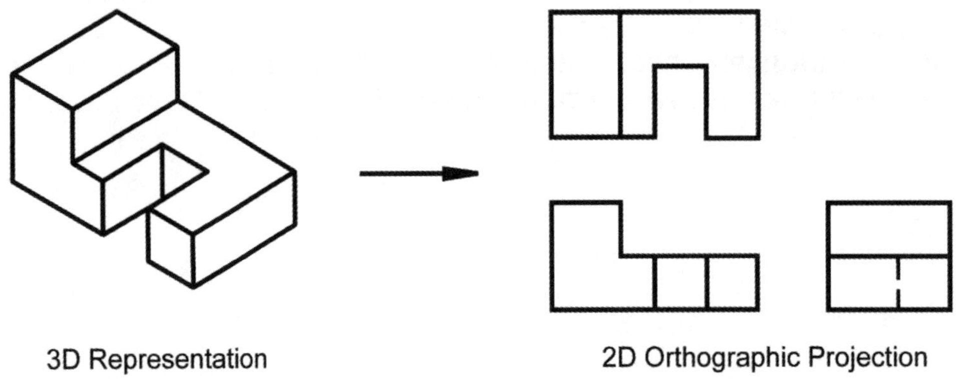

Figure 3.1-1: Orthographic projection.

3.1.1) The Six Principal Views

The six principal viewing directions of an orthographic projection and their associated view names are shown in Figure 3.1-2. These viewing directions are used to create the six principal views. Each principal view is created by looking at the object in the directions indicated in Figure 3.1-2 and drawing what is seen as well as what is hidden from view.

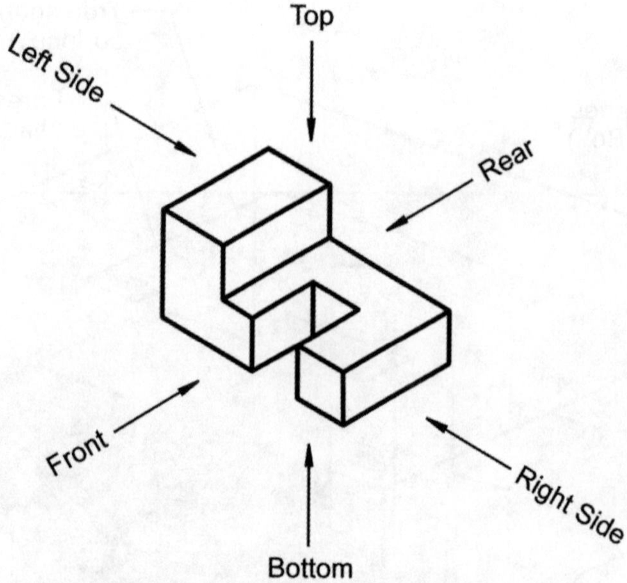

Figure 3.1-2: The six principal viewing directions

3.2) THE GLASS BOX METHOD

The glass box method is a very convenient way of visualizing how an orthographic projection is created. To obtain an orthographic projection, an object is placed in an imaginary glass box as shown in Figure 3.2-1. The sides of the glass box represent the six principal planes. Images of the object are projected onto the sides of the box to create the six principal views. The box is then unfolded to lie flat, showing all views in a two-dimensional plane. Figure 3.2-2 shows the glass box being unfolded to create the orthographic projection of the object.

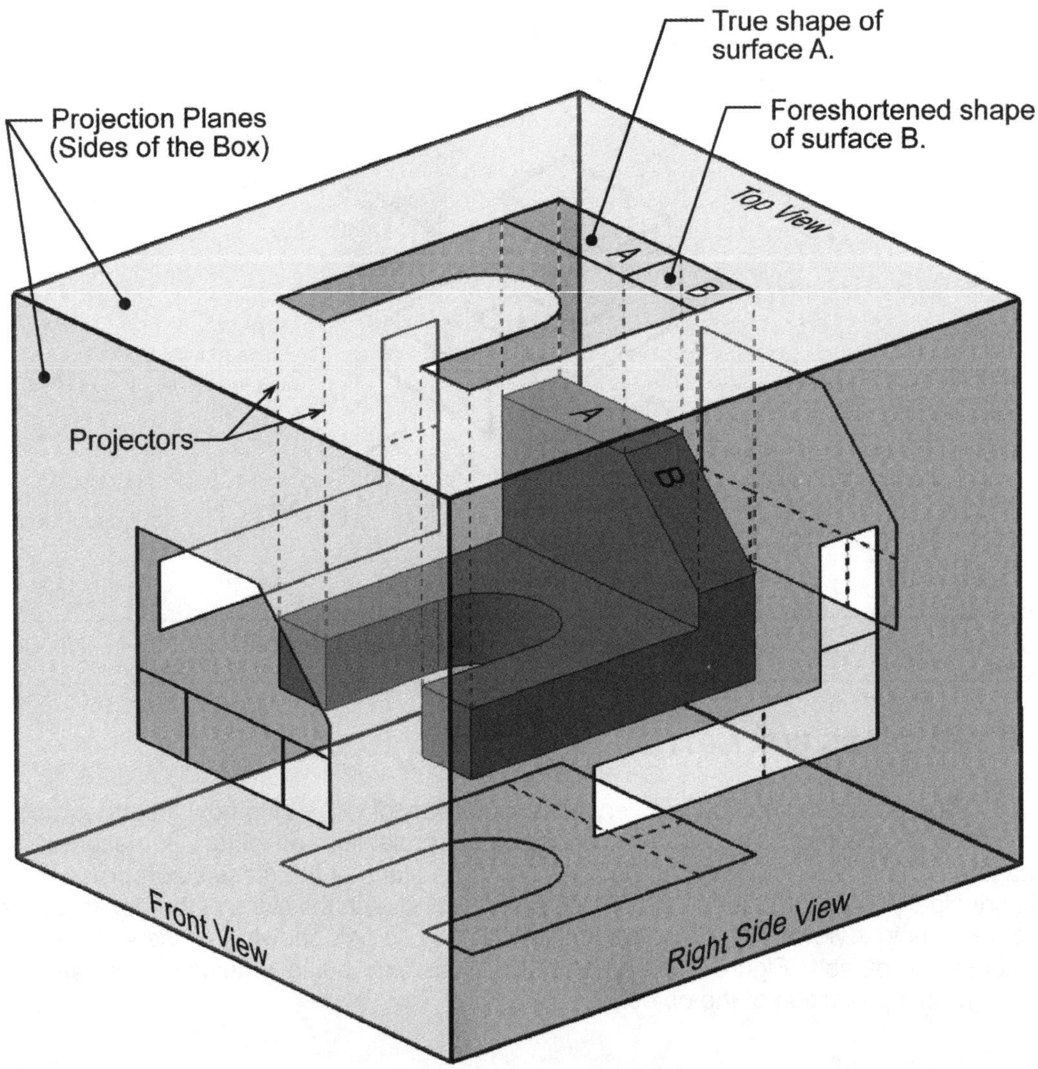

Figure 3.2-1: Object in a glass box

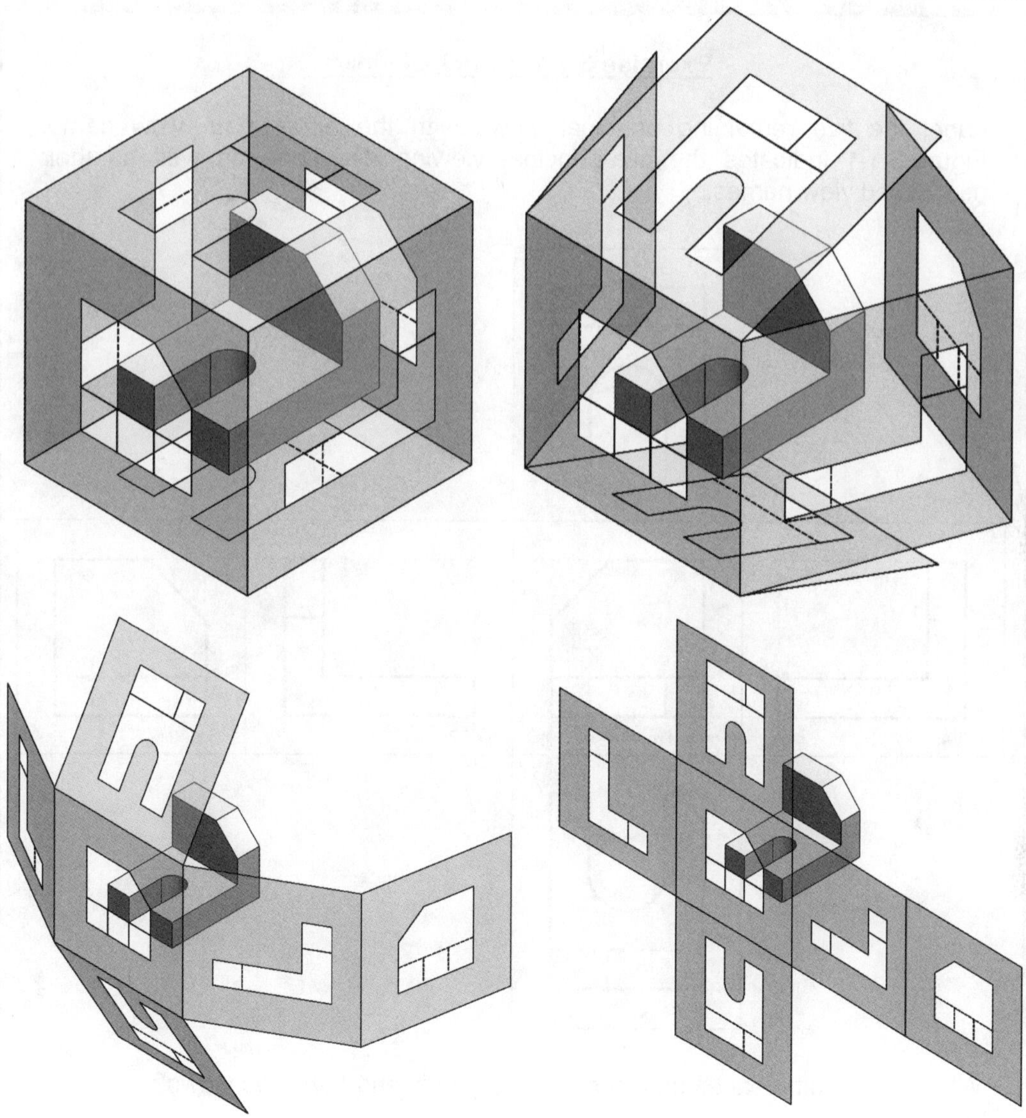

Figure 3.2-2: Glass box being unfolded

Exercise 3.2-1: Principal views

Label the five remaining principal views with the appropriate view name. Figure 3.1-1 indicates the six principal viewing directions as well as their associated view names.

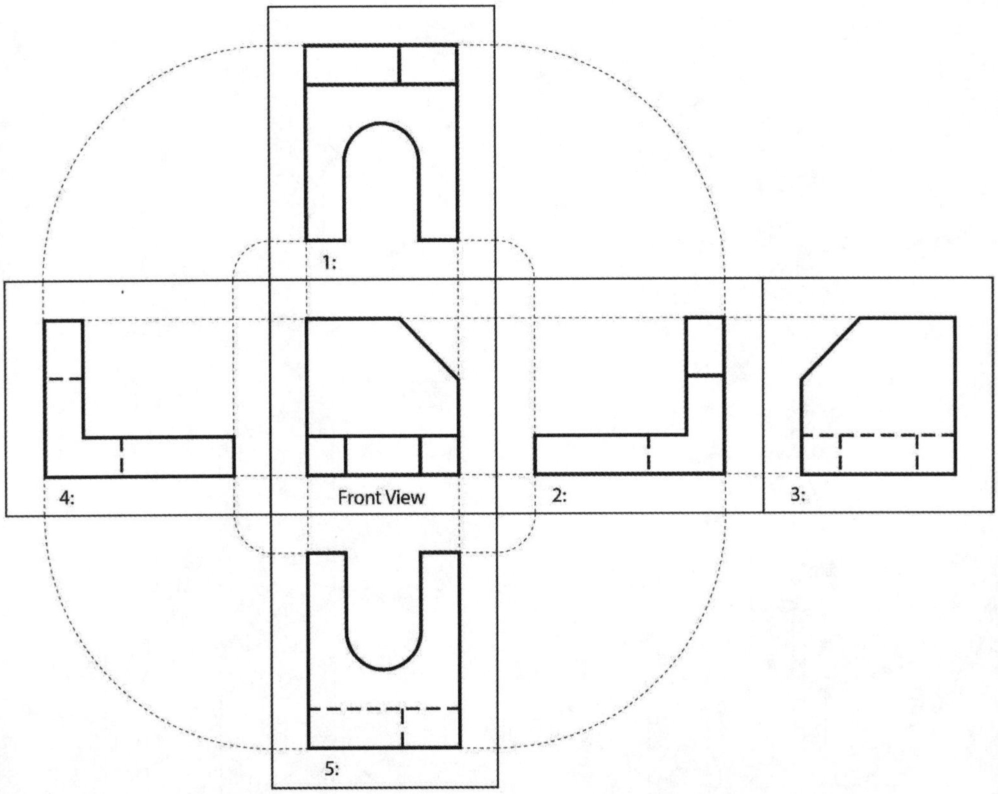

What are the differences between the *Right Side* and *Left Side* views?

What are the differences between the *Top* and *Bottom*, and *Front* and *Rear* views?

Which view(s) have the least number of hidden or dashed lines?

3.3) LINE TYPES USED IN AN ORTHOGRAPHIC PROJECTION

***Line type* and *line weight* provide valuable information to the print reader.** For example, the type and weight of a line can answer the following questions: Is the feature visible or hidden from view? Is the line part of the object or part of a dimension? Is the line indicating symmetry? There are four commonly used line types: continuous, hidden, center, and phantom. Important lines are thicker than less important thin lines. The following is a list of common line types and widths used in a basic orthographic projection that has no section views or dimensions.

1. Visible lines: **Represent visible edges and boundaries.** The visible line type is **continuous,** and the line weight is **thick**. For example, Figure 3.3-1 shows a solid cylinder. Notice that the visible lines are thicker than the center lines.
2. Hidden lines: **Represent edges and boundaries that cannot be seen.** The hidden line type is **dashed,** and the line weight is **medium thick**. For example, Figure 3.3-4 shows a part with a hole in it. In the view shown, the hole cannot be seen. So, hidden lines are used to indicate where the hole is located even though it cannot be seen.
3. Center lines: **Represent axes, center points, planes of symmetry, circle of centers, and paths of motion.** A *circle of centers* is a circle that indicates where the centers of all the holes in a hole pattern lie. A *path of motion* indicates the path a feature takes when moving from one position to the next. The center line type is **long dash – short dash,** and the line weight is **thin**. Figure 3.3-1 shows center lines being used to indicate axes of symmetry. Figure 3.3-2 shows a center line indicating the line of symmetry on a symmetric part. At the ends of the center line, a symmetry symbol is placed to further emphasize that the part is symmetric. Figure 3.3-3 shows center lines being used for a circle of centers, and Figure 3.3-4 shows a center line indicating the path of motion.

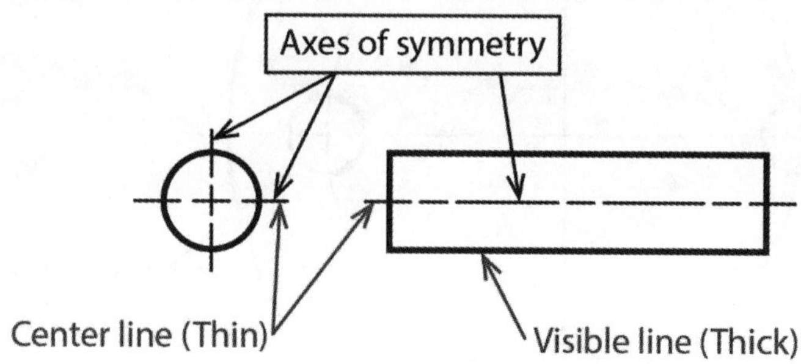

Figure 3.3-1: Axes of symmetry

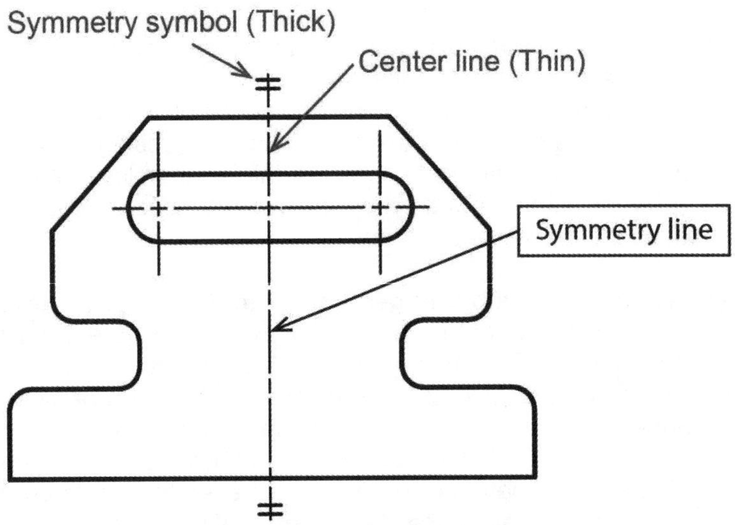

Figure 3.3-2: Part symmetry

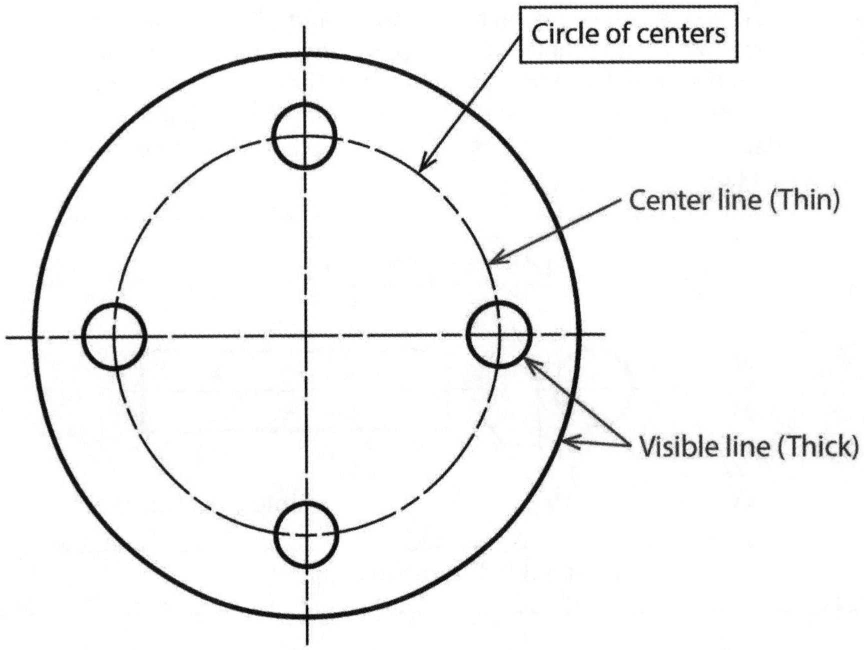

Figure 3.3-3: Circle of centers

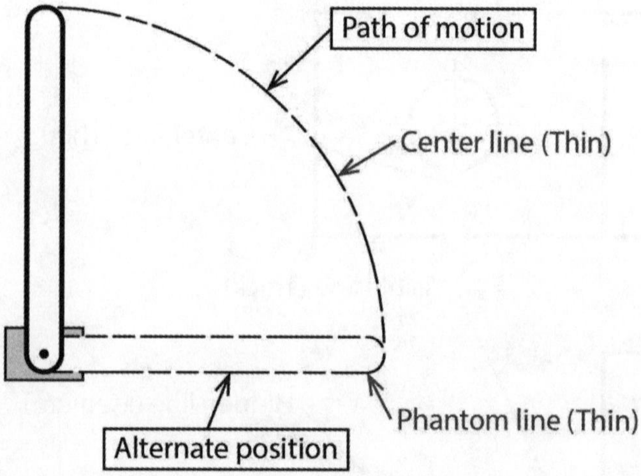

Figure 3.3-4: Paths of motion and alternate position

4. <u>Phantom lines:</u> **Used to indicate imaginary features such as alternate positions of moving parts, adjacent positions of related parts, repeated detail, reference planes between adjacent views, and filleted and rounded corners.** The line type is **long dash – short dash – short dash,** and the line weight is usually **thin**. Figure 3.3-2 shows a rotating bar. Phantom lines are used to show an alternate position of the bar. Figure 3.3-5 shows a part outlined in visible lines. This is the part that is being described. The part that it is sitting on is a related part shown in phantom lines. This part is not being described. The purpose is only to show how they mate. Figure 3.3-6 shows a spring whose center coils are omitted, and a phantom line is used to indicate repeated details. Figure 3.3-7 shows phantom lines being used to indicate changes in surface direction.

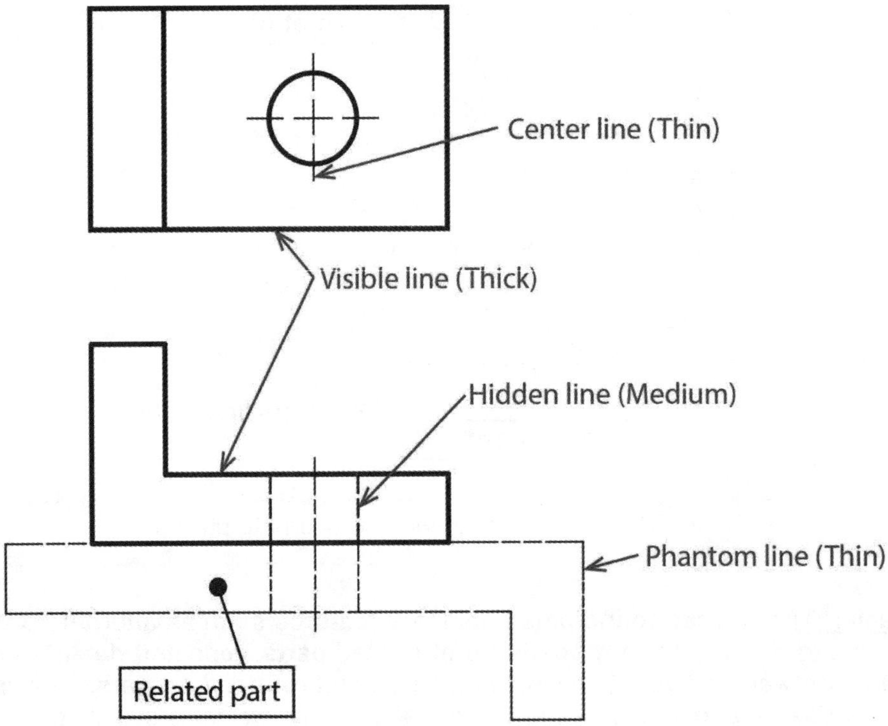

Figure 3.3-5: Related part.

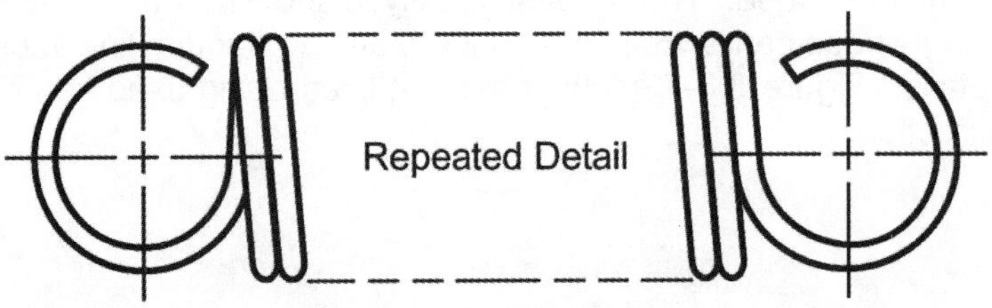

Figure 3.3-6: Repeated detail.

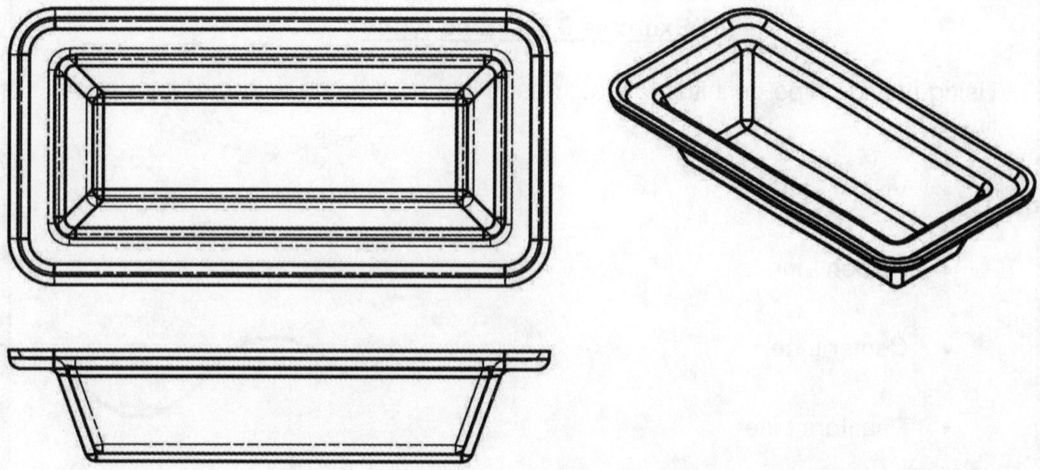

Figure 3.3-7: Phantom lines used to indicate a change in surface direction.

5. <u>Break lines:</u> **Used to show imaginary breaks in objects.** A break line is usually made up of a series of connecting arcs. The line type is **continuous,** and the line weight is usually **thick**. Figure 3.3-8 shows an eye bolt with a long shaft. Drawing the entire shaft will not give the reader any extra information. Therefore, a break line is used to break and shorten the shaft.

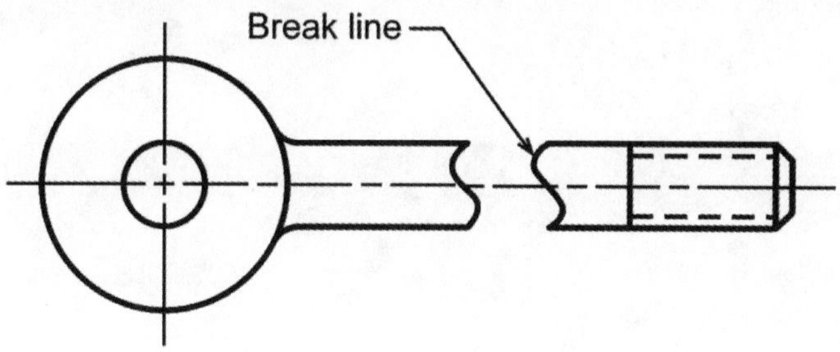

Figure 3.3-8: Using break lines.

Try Exercise 3.3-1, 3.3-2, 3.3-3, and 3.3-4

Exercise 3.3-1: Line types

Using the line type definitions, match each line type name with the appropriate line type.

- Visible Line
- Hidden Line
- Center Line
- Phantom Line
- Break Line

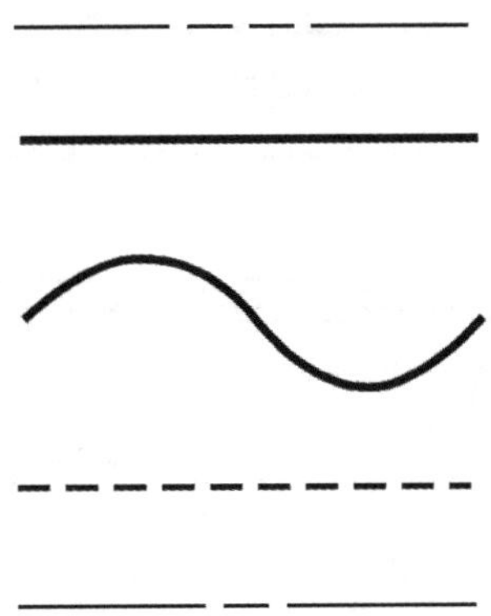

Exercise 3.3-2: Line identification

In the following orthographic projection, identify the line type of each line that is pointed to. Then, identify the associated feature (using a letter) of the selected lines.

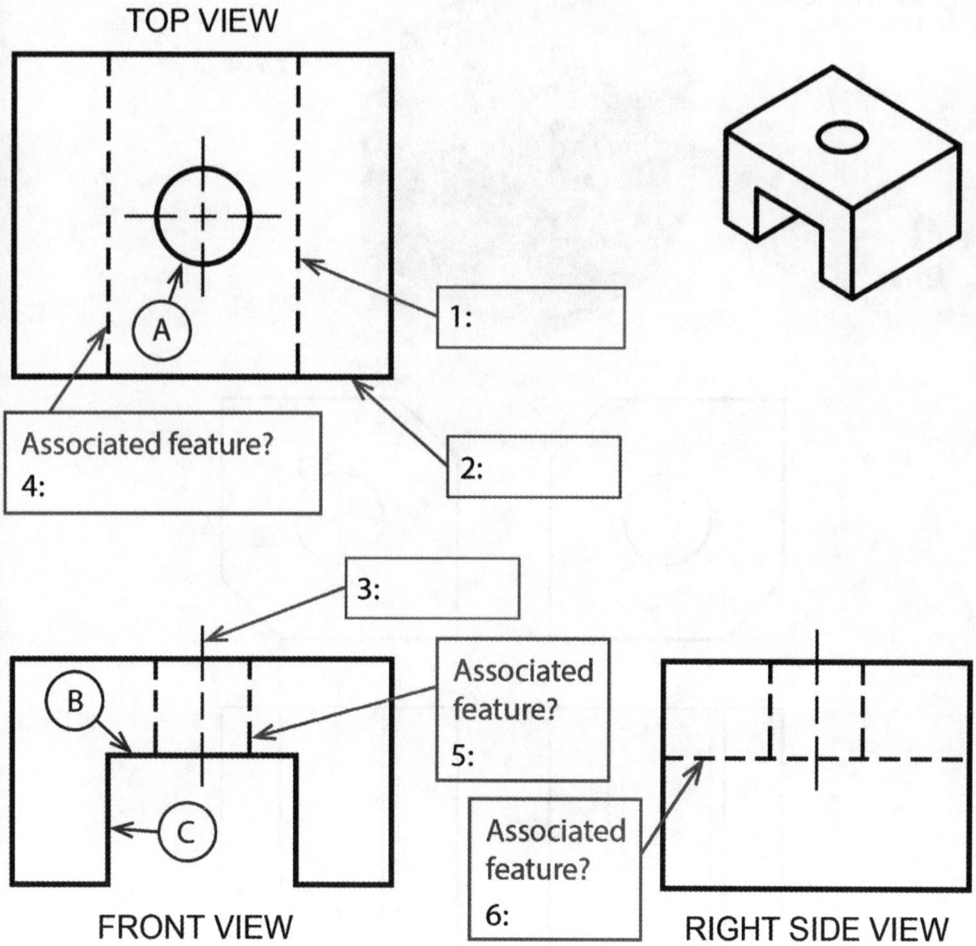

Exercise 3.3-3: View Identification

Match the object with its correct front, top and right-side views. Note that views should not be aligned on an orthographic projection as shown in this problem.

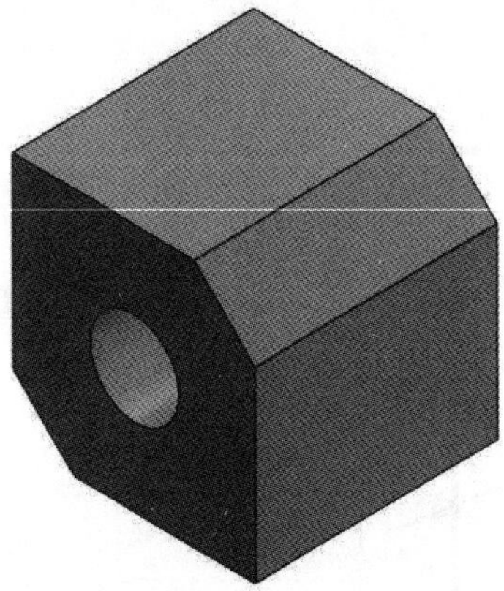

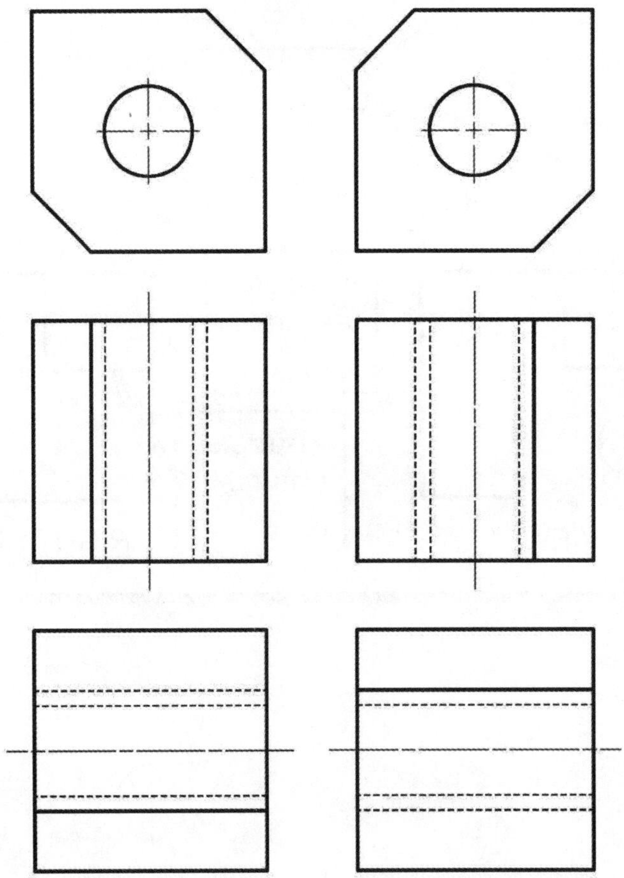

Exercise 3.3-4: Surface Identification

In the following orthographic projection, identify the surfaces identified in the pictorial on the shown views.

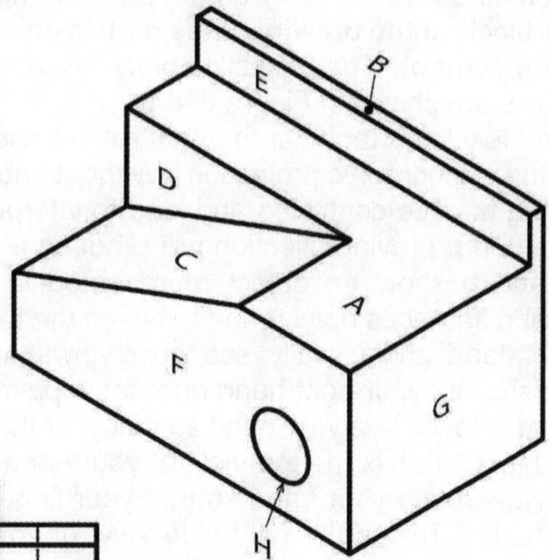

Top View

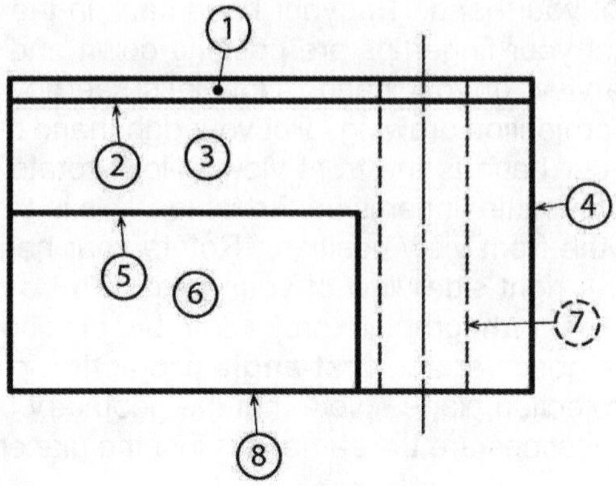

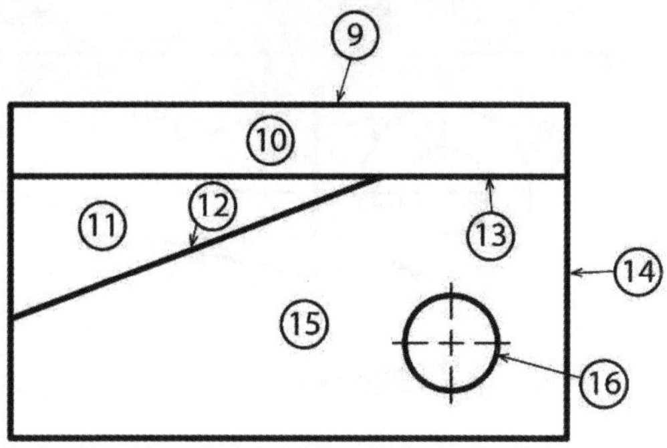

Front View

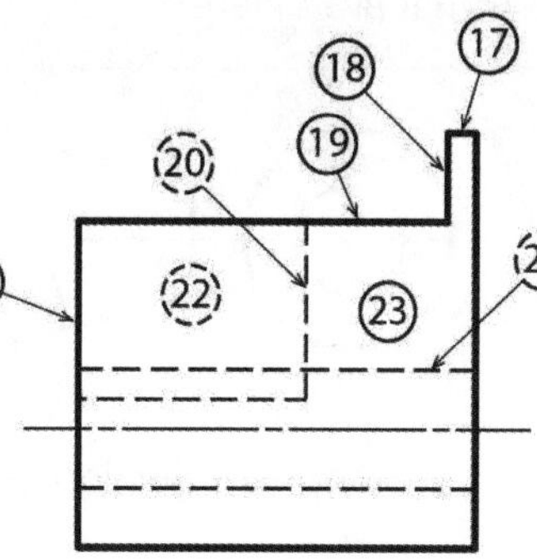

Right Side View

	A	B	C	D	E	F	G	H
Top								
Front								
Right Side								

3.4) PROJECTION SYMBOL

The two internationally recognized systems of projection used to create orthographic projections are third-angle projection and first-angle projection. In the United States, we use third-angle projection to create an orthographic projection. In some parts of Europe, and elsewhere, first-angle projection is used. To inform the print reader what projection method was used to create the drawing, the projection symbol is placed in the projection block. **If the drawing uses metric units, the text "SI" is placed in front of the projection symbol.** The projection block is placed to the left of the title block. The projection symbols are shown in Figure 3.4-1.

It is extremely important that the print reader knows which projection method was used to create the orthographic projection. Without knowledge of the projection method, reading a drawing may be confusing and lead to interpretation mistakes. The glass box method described in a previous section will produce a drawing in third-angle projection. Figure 3.4-2a and b show an object represented in both third-angle and first-angle projection. What differences do you see between the two methods?

To understand and visually see how views are created using the third-angle projection standard, put your right hand on a table palm up. You are looking at the front view of your hand. Now rotate your hand so that your thumb points up and your little finger is touching the table. This is the top view of your hand. Put your hand back in the front view position. Now rotate your hand so that your fingertips are pointing down and your wrist is off the table. This is the right side view of your hand. Now let's see how that changes when we are creating a first-angle projection drawing. Put your right hand on the table with your palm down. The back of your hand is the front view. Now, rotate your hand so that your thumb is pointing up and your little finger is on the table. This is the top view of your hand. Put your hand back in the front view position. Rotate your hand so that your fingers are pointing up. This is the right side view of your hand. To be more technical, **third-angle projection** forms the orthographic projection by placing the projection plane between the object and the observer and **first-angle projection** places the object between the observer and the projection plane. Note that the geometry of the views for both first-angle and third-angle projections are the same, it is just the placement of the views that are different.

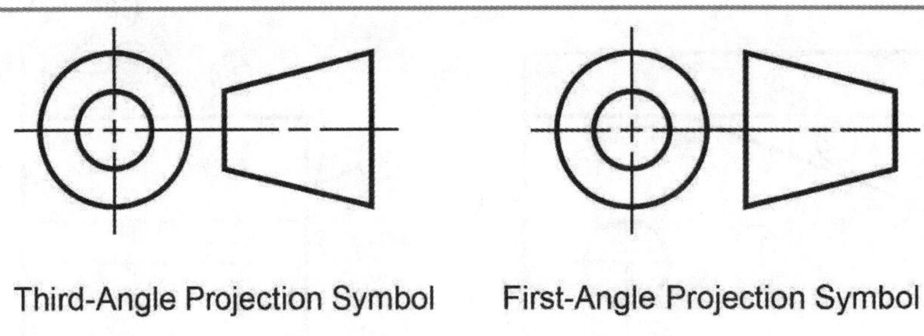

Figure 3.4-1: First and third-angle projection symbols

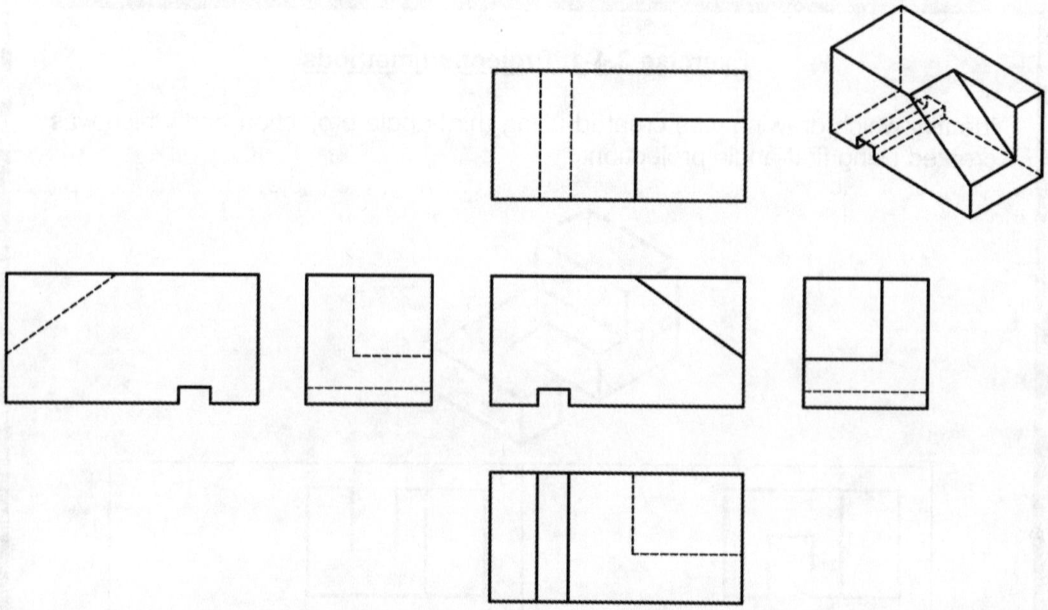

Figure 3.4-2a: Third-angle projection method

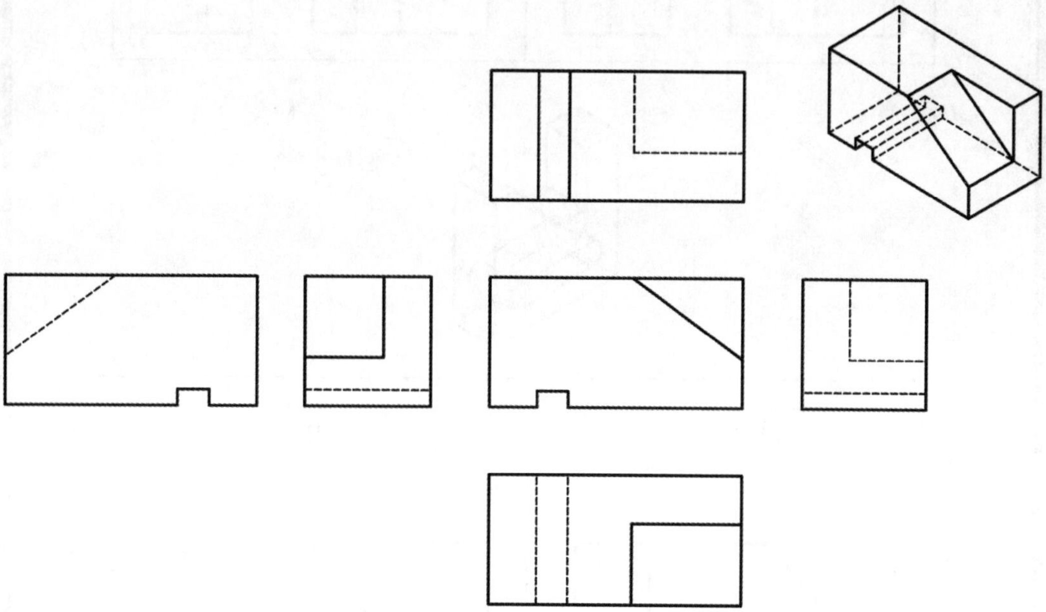

Figure 3.4-2b: First-angle projection method

Try Exercise 3.4-1.

Exercise 3.4-1: Projection methods

Identify which drawing was created using third-angle projection and which was created using first-angle projection.

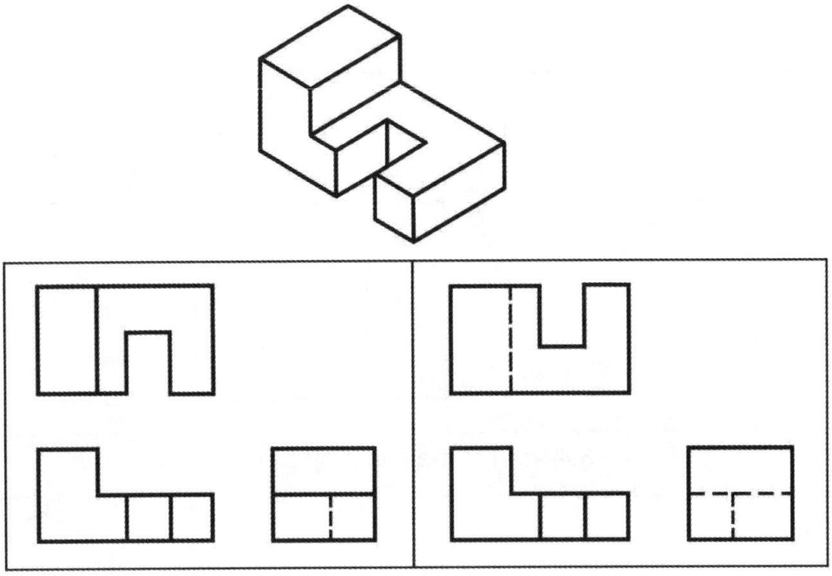

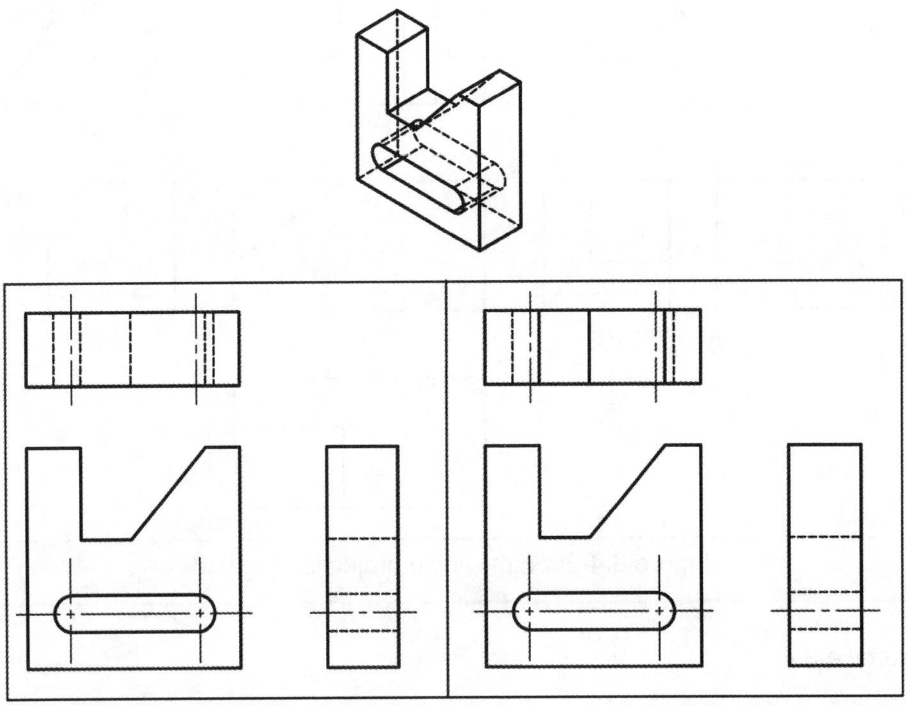

READING ORTHOGRAPHIC PROJECTIONS QUESTIONS – SET1

Name: ______________________________________ Date: _________________

Orthographic projection and principal views

Q3-1) An orthographic projection is a _______ representation of a three-dimensional object. Fill in the blank.

Q3-2) What are the standard views?

- ___________________
- ___________________
- ___________________

Line types

Q3-3) Line type provides valuable information to the print reader. (True, False)

Q3-4) Visible lines are used to indicate …

a) edges and boundaries that you can see.
b) edges and boundaries that you cannot see.
c) imaginary features.
d) symmetric features.

Q3-5) Hidden lines are used to indicate …

a) edges and boundaries that you can see.
b) edges and boundaries that you cannot see.
c) imaginary features.
d) symmetric features.

Projection methods

Q3-6) In the United States, is 1st or 3rd angle projection used as the standard?

NOTES:

READING ORTHOGRAPHIC PROJECTIONS QUESTIONS – SET2

Q3-7) List the 6 principal views.

- ________________
- ________________
- ________________
- ________________
- ________________
- ________________

Q3-8) The FRONT and TOP views are aligned (vertically, horizontally). Circle the correct answer.

Q3-9) The FRONT and RIGHT SIDE views are aligned (vertically, horizontally). Circle the correct answer.

Q3-10) Line weight does not provide any information to the print reader. (True, False)

Q3-11) Center lines are used to indicate .... (Circle all that apply.)

a) axes of symmetry.
b) paths of motion.
c) circle of centers.
d) change in surface direction.

Q3-12) Phantom lines are used to indicate .... (Circle all that apply.)

a) alternate positions.
b) repeated detail.
c) related parts.
d) change in surface direction.

Q3-13) Break lines are used to show an imaginary ___________ in an object.

Q3-14) The symbol "SI" that is placed in front of the projection symbol lets us know that the drawing is using (inches, mm). Circle the correct answer.

Q3-15) The projection symbol, indicating the projection method used to create the drawing, is placed in the _______________ block. Fill in the blank.

READING ORTHOGRAPHIC PROJECTIONS PROBLEMS

Name: ______________________________ Date: _____________

P3-1) Match the solid part with its correct orthographic projection.

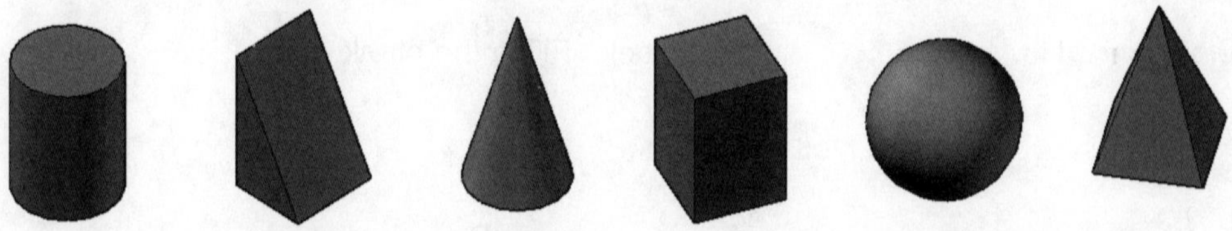

A B C D E F

1. ________

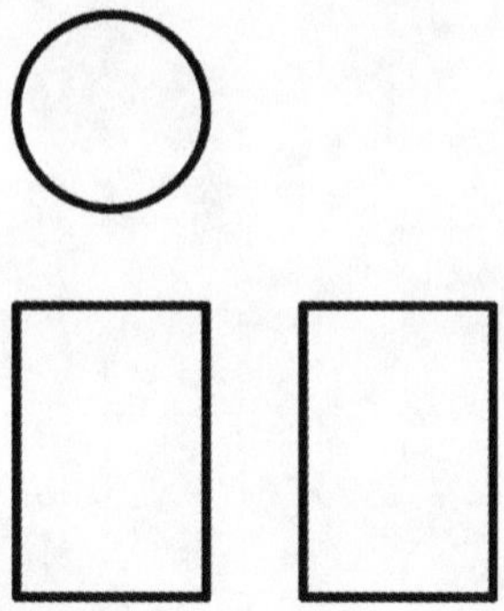

2. ________

3. ________

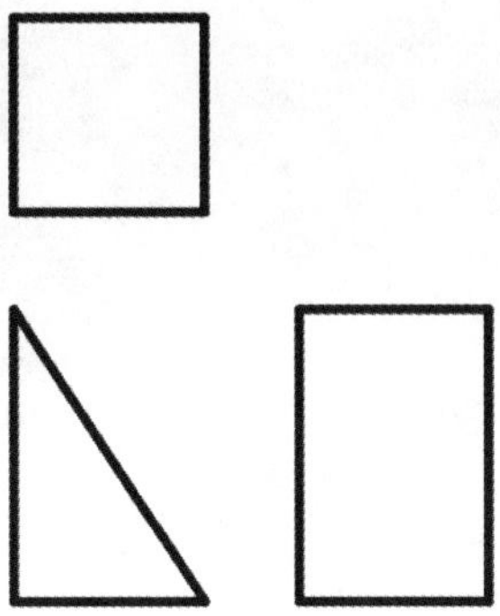

4. ________

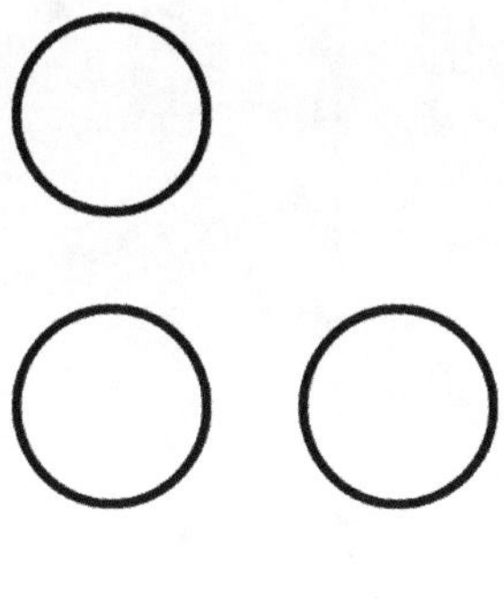

5. ________

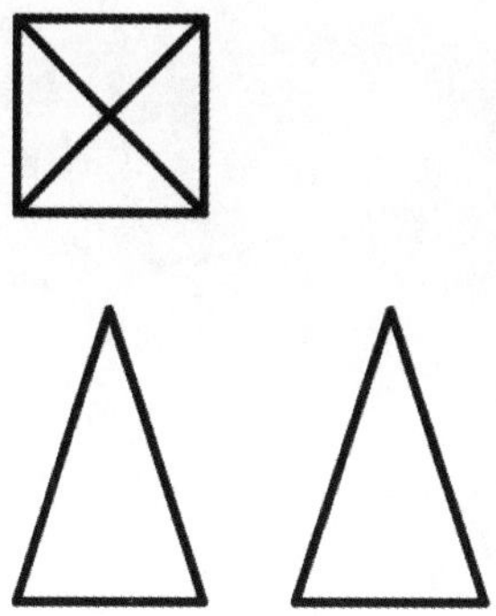

6. ________

NOTES:

Name: ______________________________ Date: ______________

P3-2) Match the solid part with its correct orthographic projection.

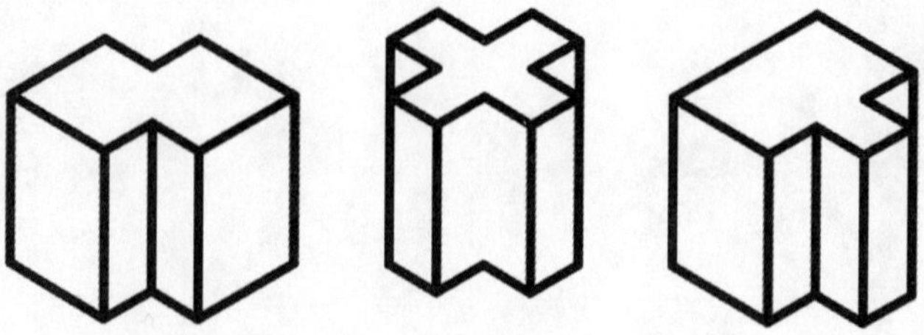

A B C

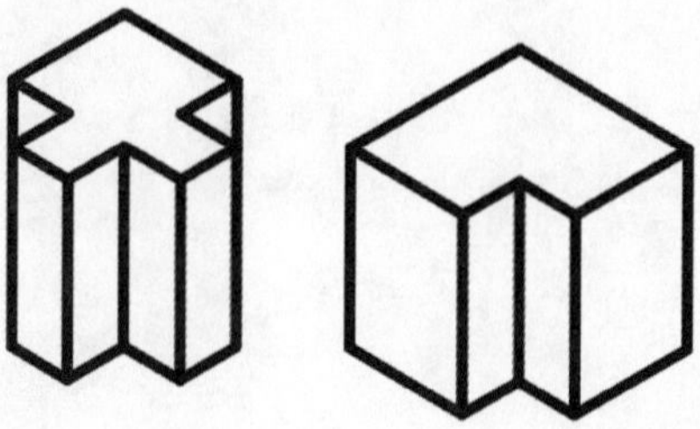

D E

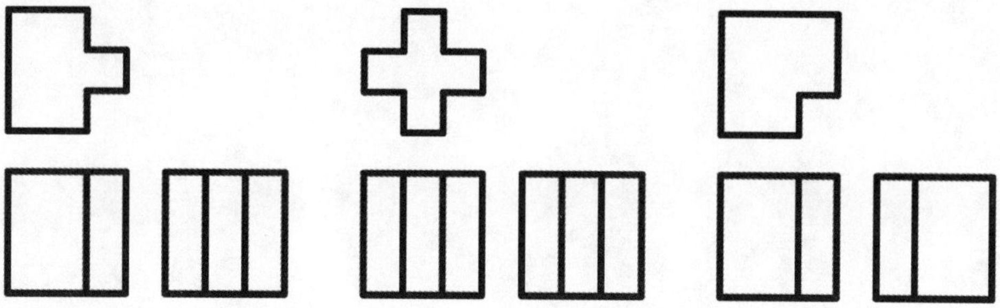

1. ________ 2. ________ 3. ________

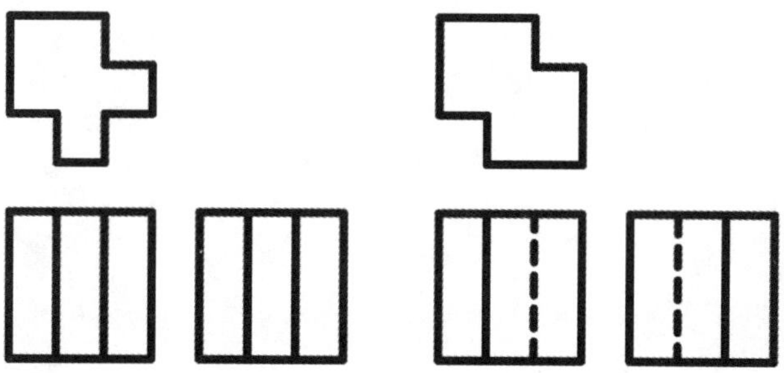

4. ________ 5. ________

NOTES:

Name: ______________________________ Date: ______________

P3-3) Match the solid part with its correct orthographic projection.

A

B

C

D

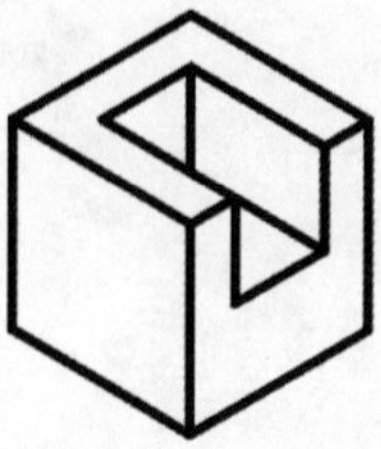

E

F

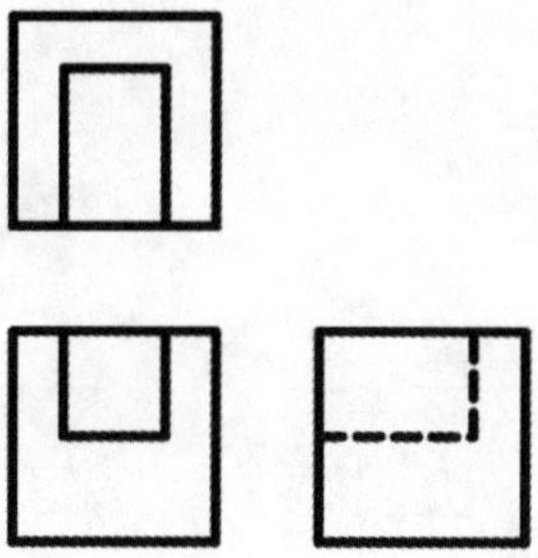

1. ________

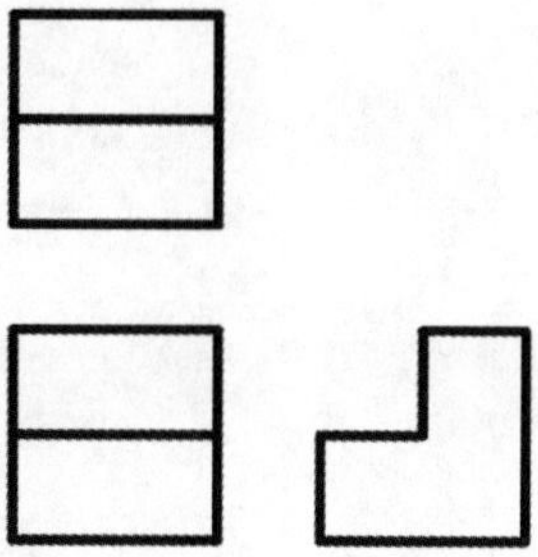

2. ________

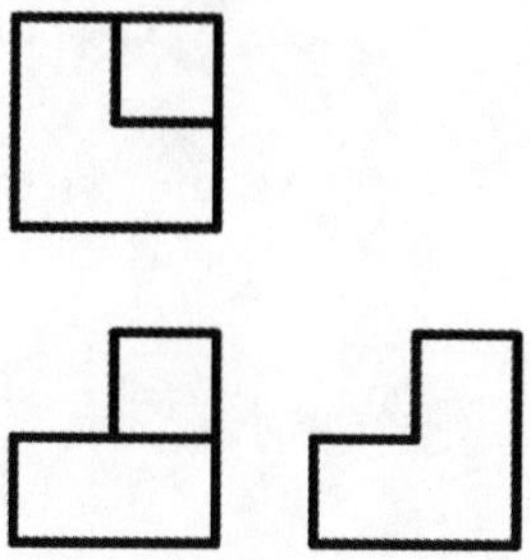

3. ________

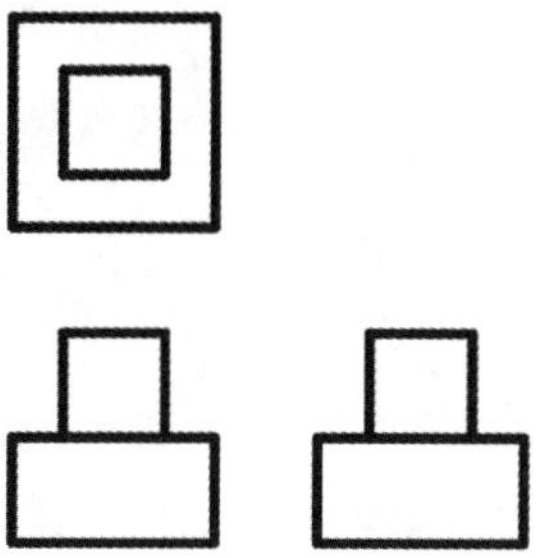

4. ________

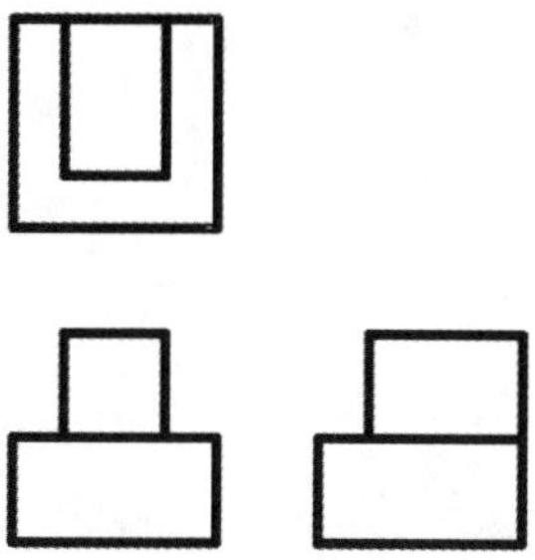

5. ________

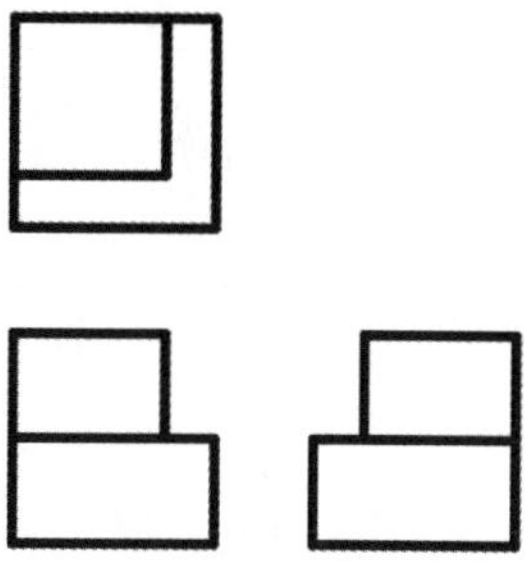

6. ________

NOTES:

Name: ______________________________ Date: ______________

P3-4) Answer the following question related to the orthographic projection shown. Note that the front view is vertically aligned with the top and bottom view and horizontally aligned with the right-side view, left-side view, and the rear view.

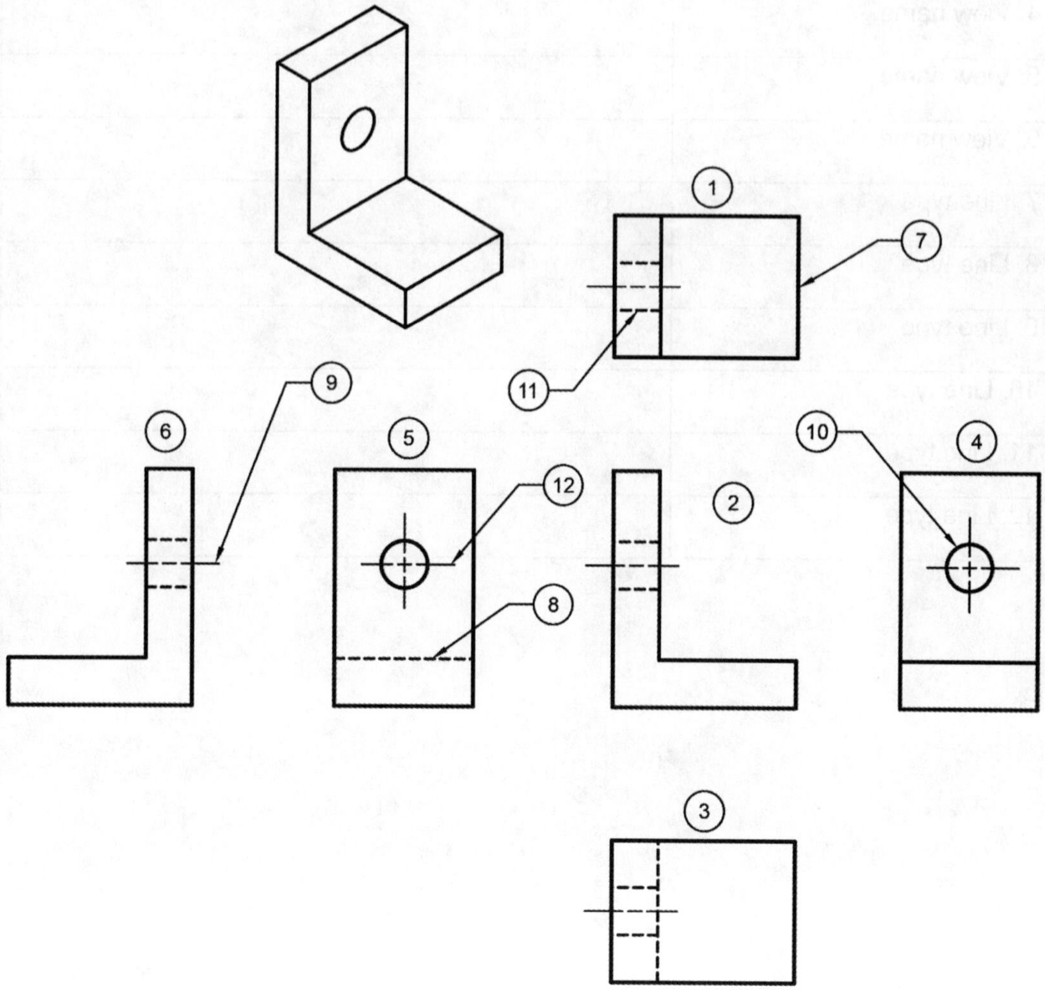

1. View name	
2. View name	
3 View name	
4. View name	
5. View name	
6. View name	
7. Line type	
8. Line type	
9. Line type	
10. Line type	
11. Line type	
12. Line type	

Name: ______________________________ Date: ______________

P3-5) Answer the following question related to the orthographic projection shown. Note that the front view is vertically aligned with the top and bottom view and horizontally aligned with the right-side view, left-side view, and the rear view.

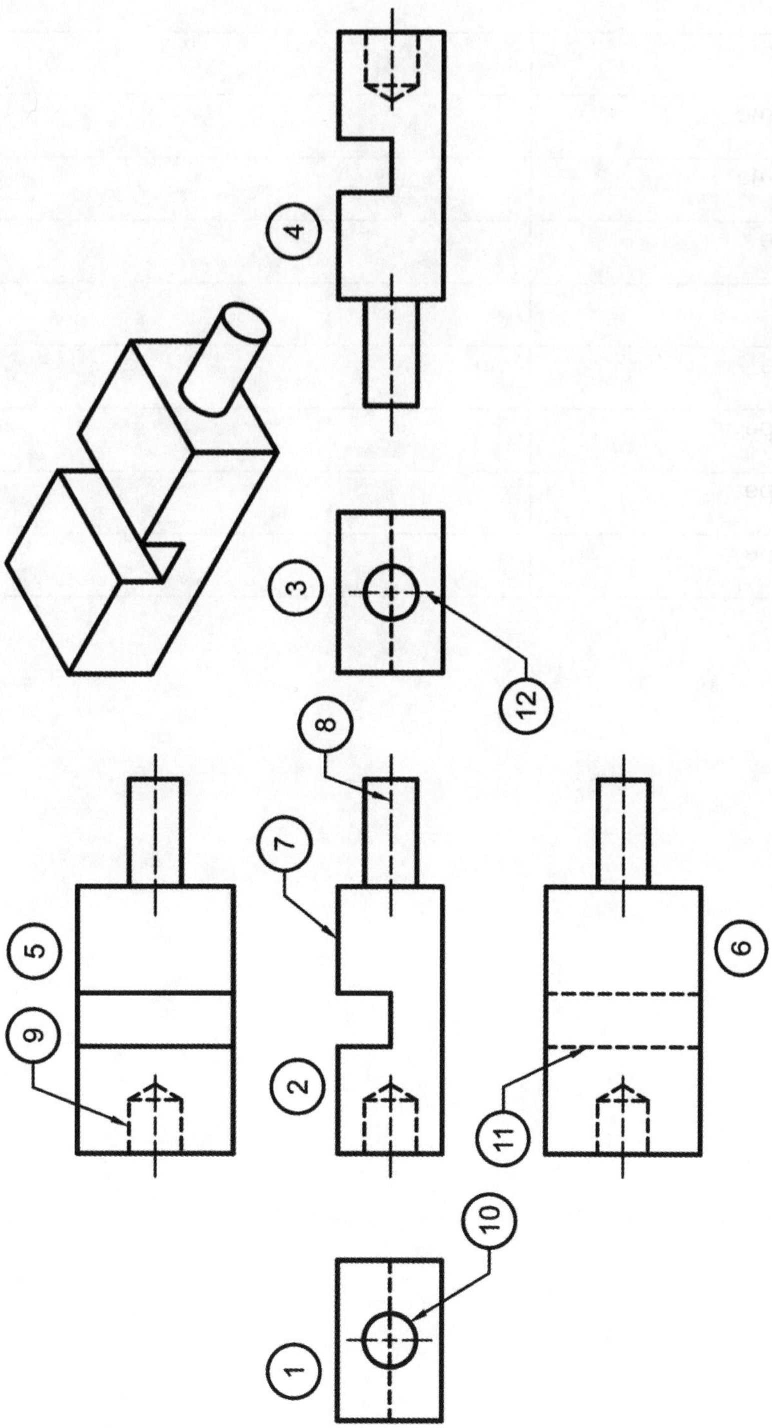

1. View name	
2. View name	
3 View name	
4. View name	
5. View name	
6. View name	
7. Line type	
8. Line type	
9. Line type	
10. Line type	
11. Line type	
12. Line type	

Name: ______________________________ Date: ______________

P3-6) Answer the following question related to the orthographic projection shown. Note that the front view is vertically aligned with the top and bottom view and horizontally aligned with the right-side view, left-side view, and the rear view.

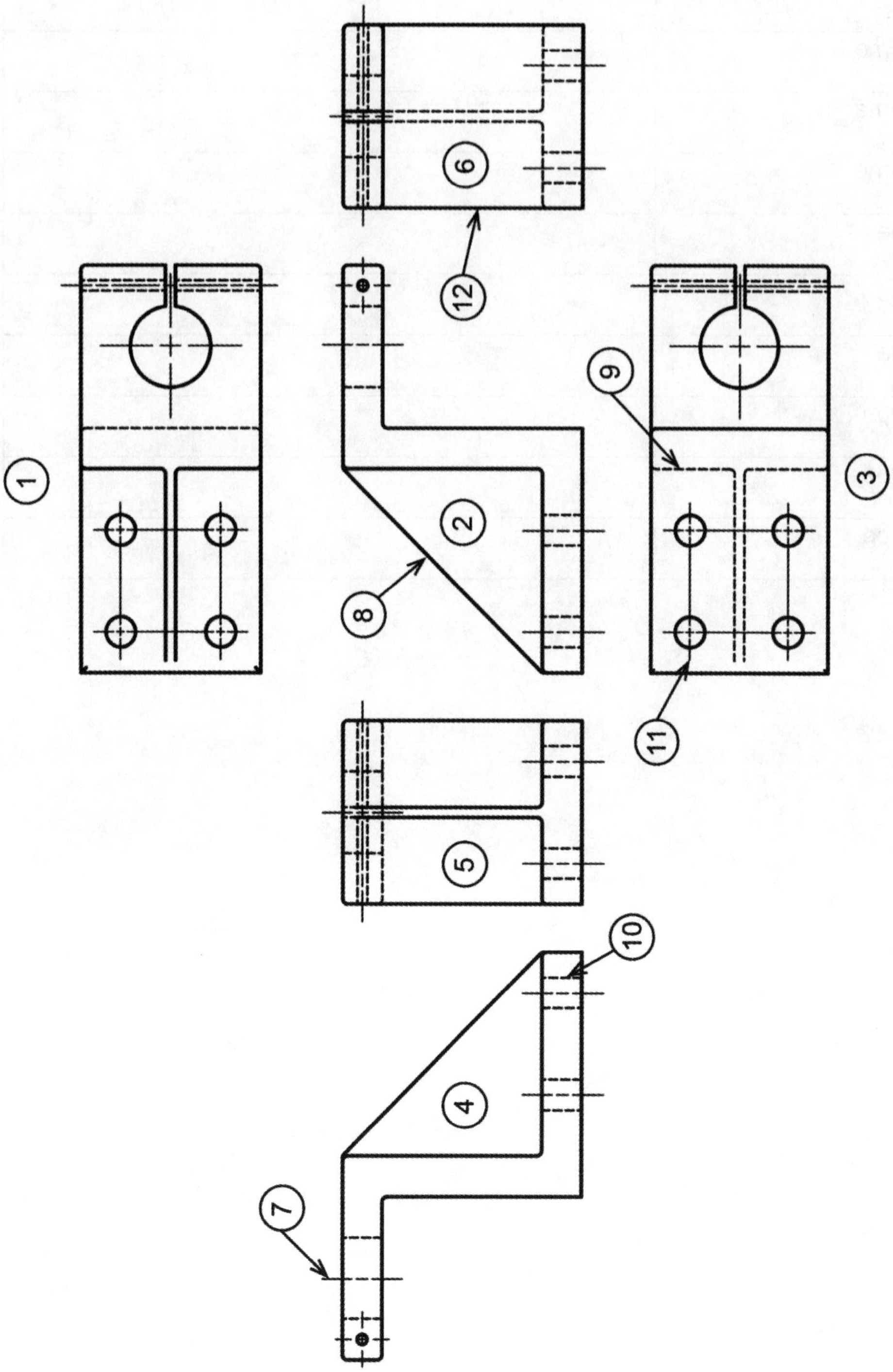

1. View name	
2. View name	
3 View name	
4. View name	
5. View name	
6. View name	
7. Line type	
8. Line type	
9. Line type	
10. Line type	
11. Line type	
12. Line type	

Name: ______________________ Date: ______________

P3-7) Match the numbers in the orthographic projection with the letters in the pictorial.

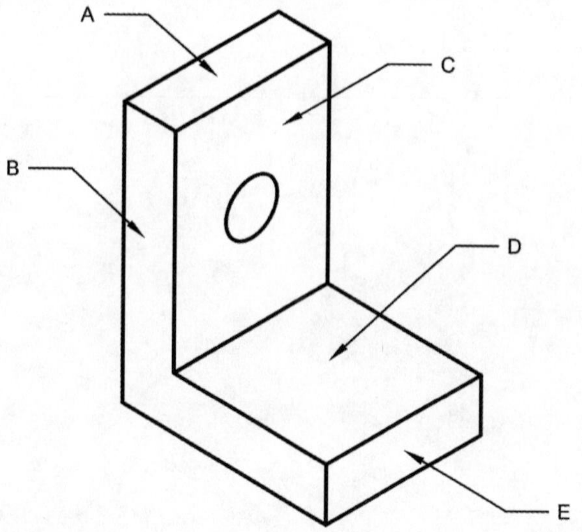

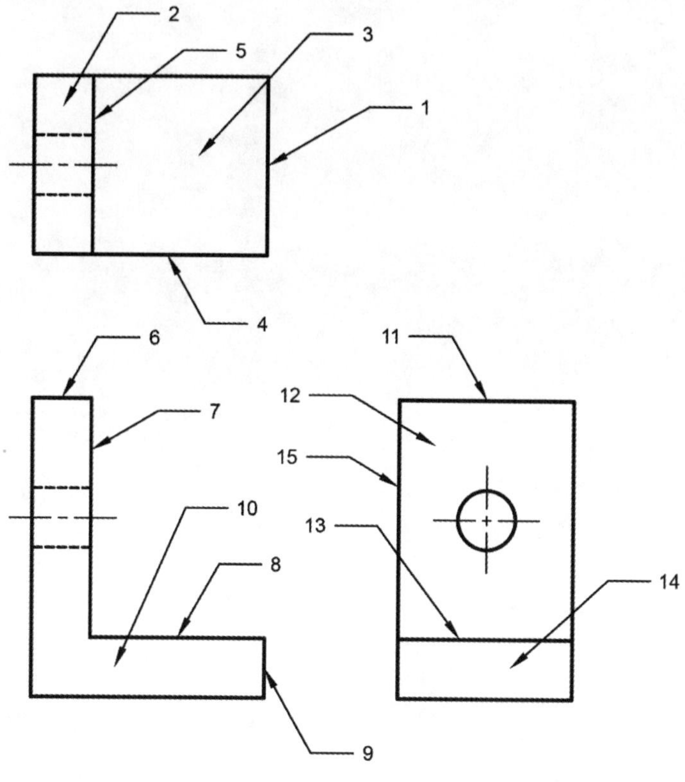

	A	B	C	D	E
FRONT			7		
TOP			5		
RIGHT SIDE			12		

NOTES:

Name: ______________________________ Date: ______________

P3-8) Match the numbers in the orthographic projection with the letters in the pictorial.

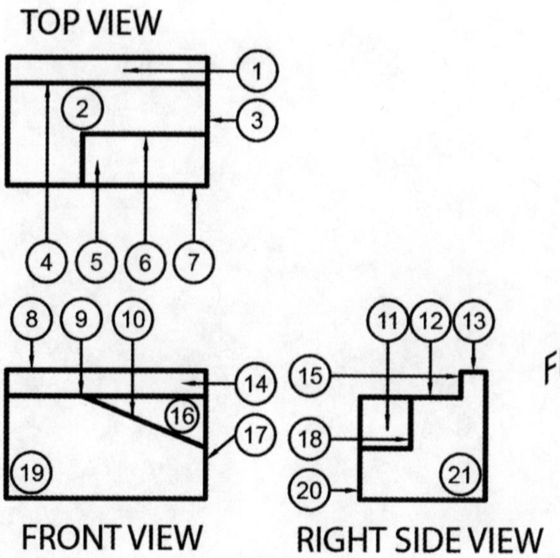

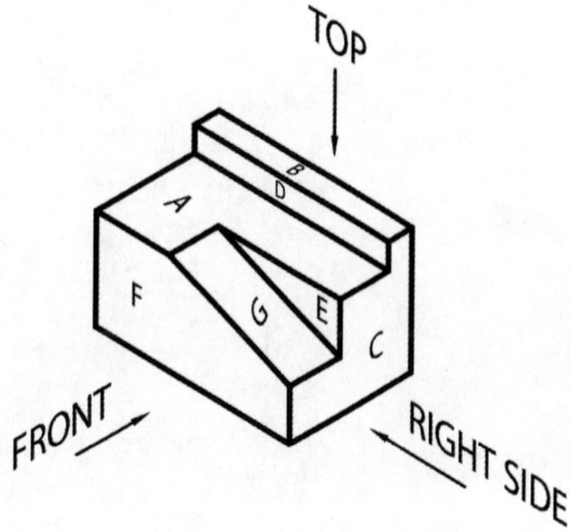

	A	B	C	D	E	F	G
FRONT							
TOP							
RIGHT SIDE							

NOTES:

Name: ______________________________ Date: _____________

P3-9) Match the numbers in the orthographic projection with the letters in the pictorial.

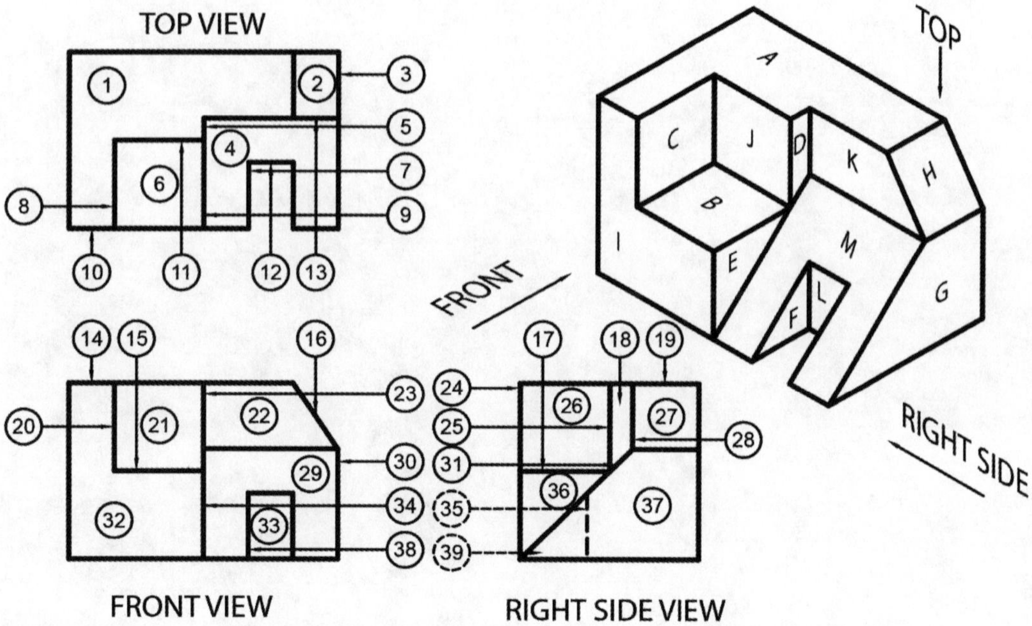

	FRONT	TOP	RIGHT SIDE
A			
B			
C			
D			
E			
F			
G			
H			
I			
J			
K			
L			
M			

NOTES:

Name: ______________________________ Date: ____________

P3-10) Match the object with its correct front, top and right-side views. Note that views should not be aligned on an orthographic projection as shown in this problem.

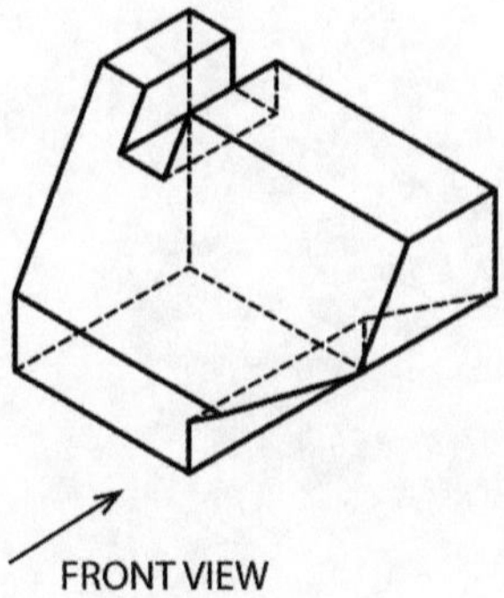

FRONT VIEW

TOP VIEW

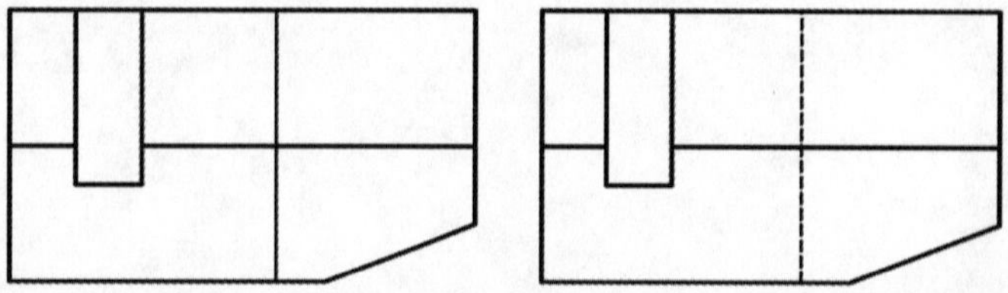

FRONT VIEW

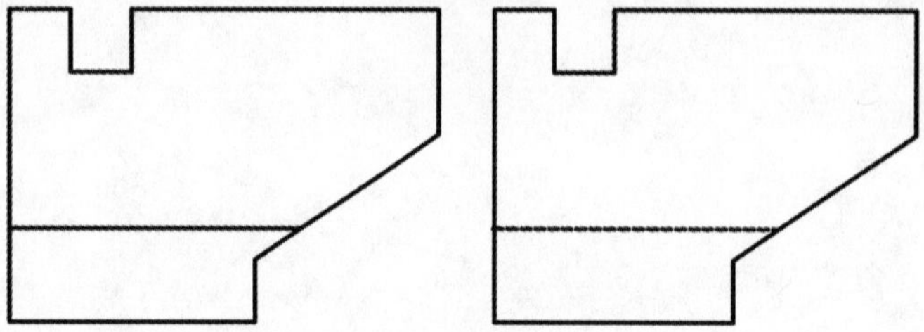

RIGHT SIDE VIEW

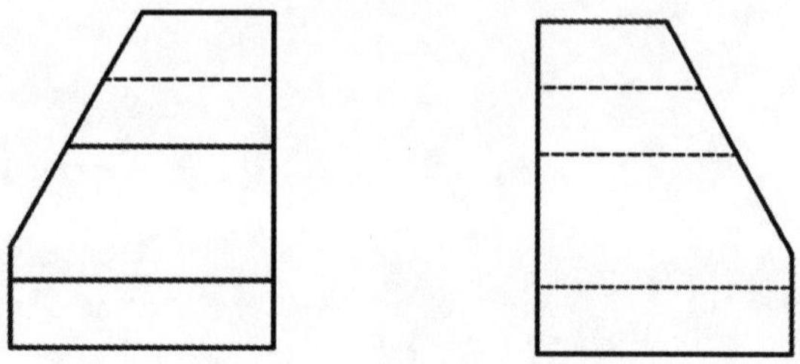

BOTTOM VIEW

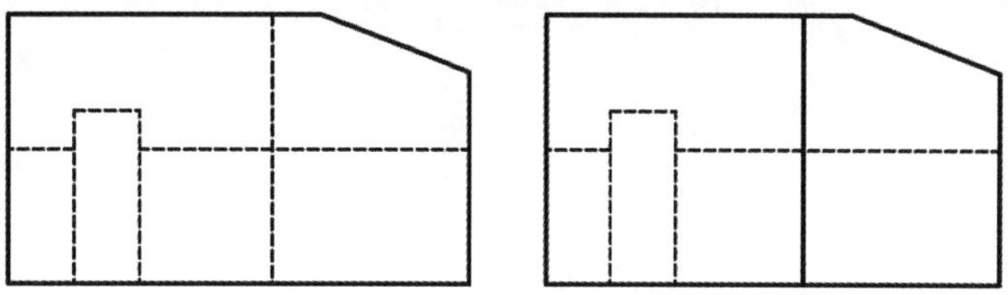

NOTES:

Name: ______________________________ Date: _____________

P3-11) Match the object with its correct front, top and right-side views. Note that views should not be aligned on an orthographic projection as shown in this problem.

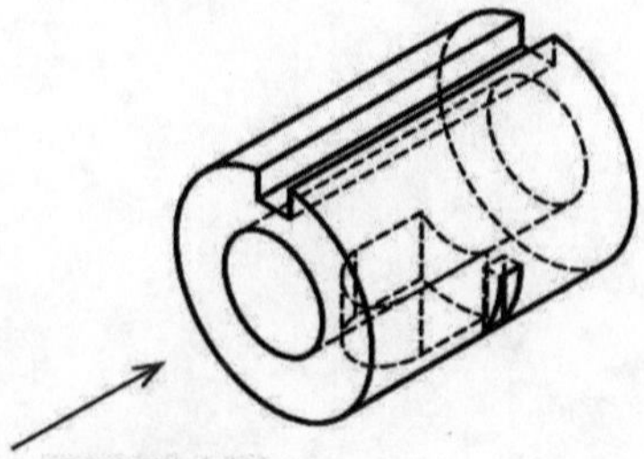

FRONT VIEW

FRONT VIEW

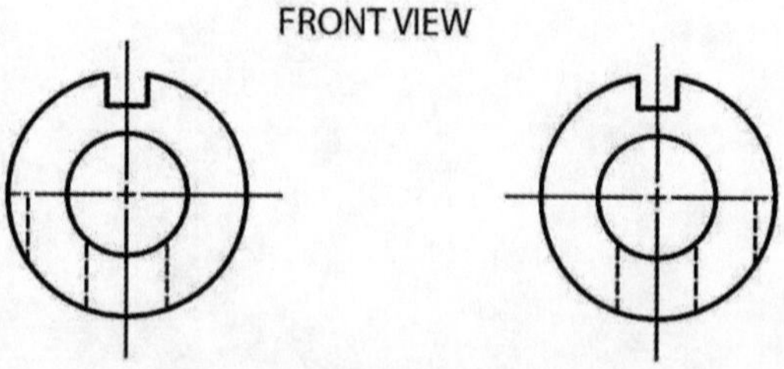

TOP VIEW

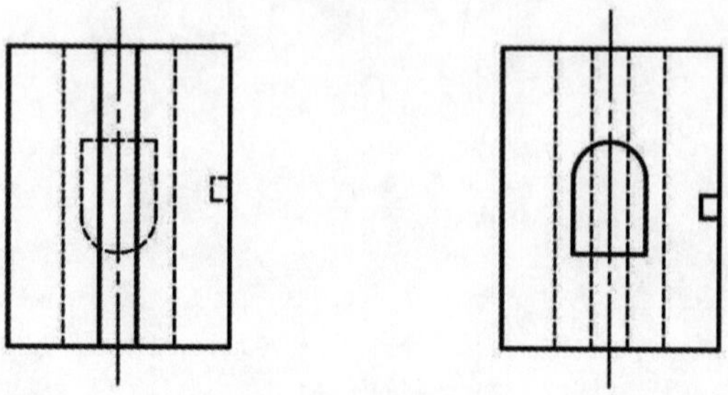

RIGHT SIDE VIEW

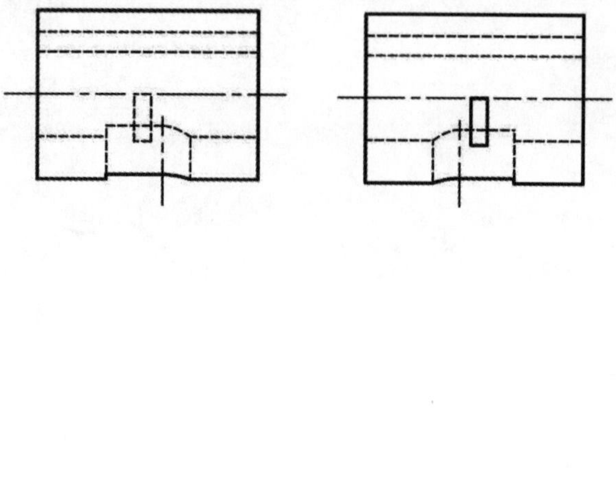

NOTES:

Name: ______________________________ Date: _____________

P3-12) Circle the correct front, top and right side views. Note that this problem does not show correct view alignment.

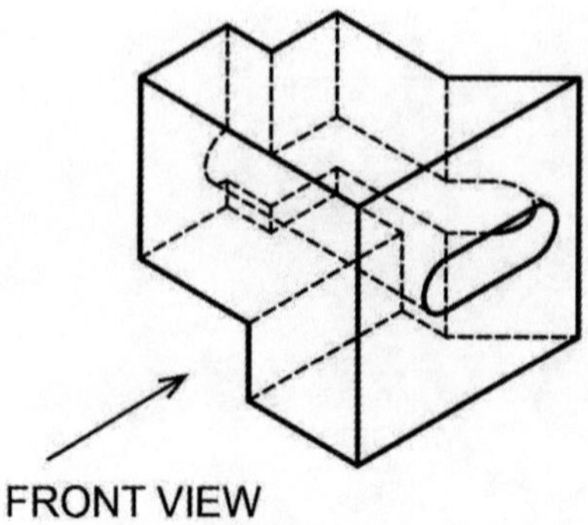

FRONT VIEW

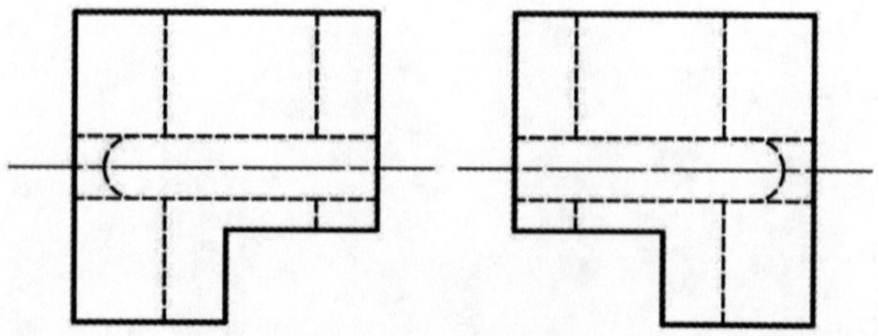

TOP VIEW

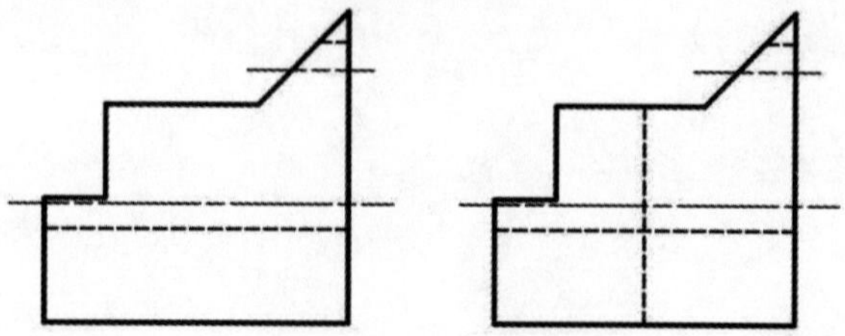

RIGHT SIDE VIEW

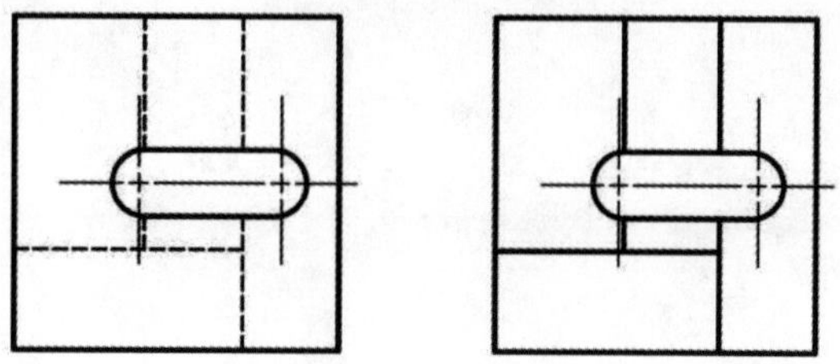

NOTES:

CHAPTER 4

CREATING ORTHOGRAPHIC PROJECTIONS

CHAPTER OUTLINE

CHAPTER SUMMARY

In this chapter, you will learn how to create orthographic projections. An orthographic projection describes the shape of an object. It is a two-dimensional representation of a three-dimensional object. Different line types are used to indicate visible features, hidden features, and symmetry. By the end of this chapter, you will be able to create a technically correct orthographic projection and visualize its three-dimensional form.

4.1) CREATING ORTHOGRAPHIC PROJECTIONS REVIEW

An orthographic projection is formed by projecting the edges of the object onto a projection plane from different viewing perspectives as shown in Figure 4.1-1. Orthographic projections allow us to represent the shape of an object usually using three views; however, a part may be represented completely with only one or two views. These views together with dimensions and notes are sufficient to manufacture the part.

4.1.1) The Glass Box Method Review

To obtain an orthographic projection, an object is placed in an imaginary glass box as shown in Figure 4.1-1. The sides of the glass box represent the six principal planes. Images of the object are projected onto the sides of the box to create the six principal views. The box is then unfolded to lie flat, showing all views in a two-dimensional plane. Figure 4.1-1 shows the glass box being unfolded to create the orthographic projection of the object.

4.2) THE STANDARD VIEWS

When constructing an orthographic projection, we need to include enough views to completely describe the true shape of the part. The more complex a part, the more views are needed to completely describe its shape. Most objects require three views to be completely described. **The standard views used in an orthographic projection are the *front, top,* and *right side* views.** The other views (bottom, rear, left side) are omitted since they usually do not add any new information.

It is not always necessary to use three views. Some objects can be completely described in one or two views. For example, a sphere only requires one view, and a block only requires two views. No matter how many views are used, the viewing directions should be chosen to minimize the use of hidden lines and convey maximum clarity.

4.2.1) The Front View

The *front view* shows the most features or characteristics of the object. It usually contains the least number of hidden lines. The exception to this rule is when the object has a predefined or generally accepted front view. All other views are based on the orientation chosen for the front view. The top, front, and bottom views are all aligned vertically and share the same width dimension. The left side, front, right side, and rear views are all aligned horizontally and share the same height dimension.

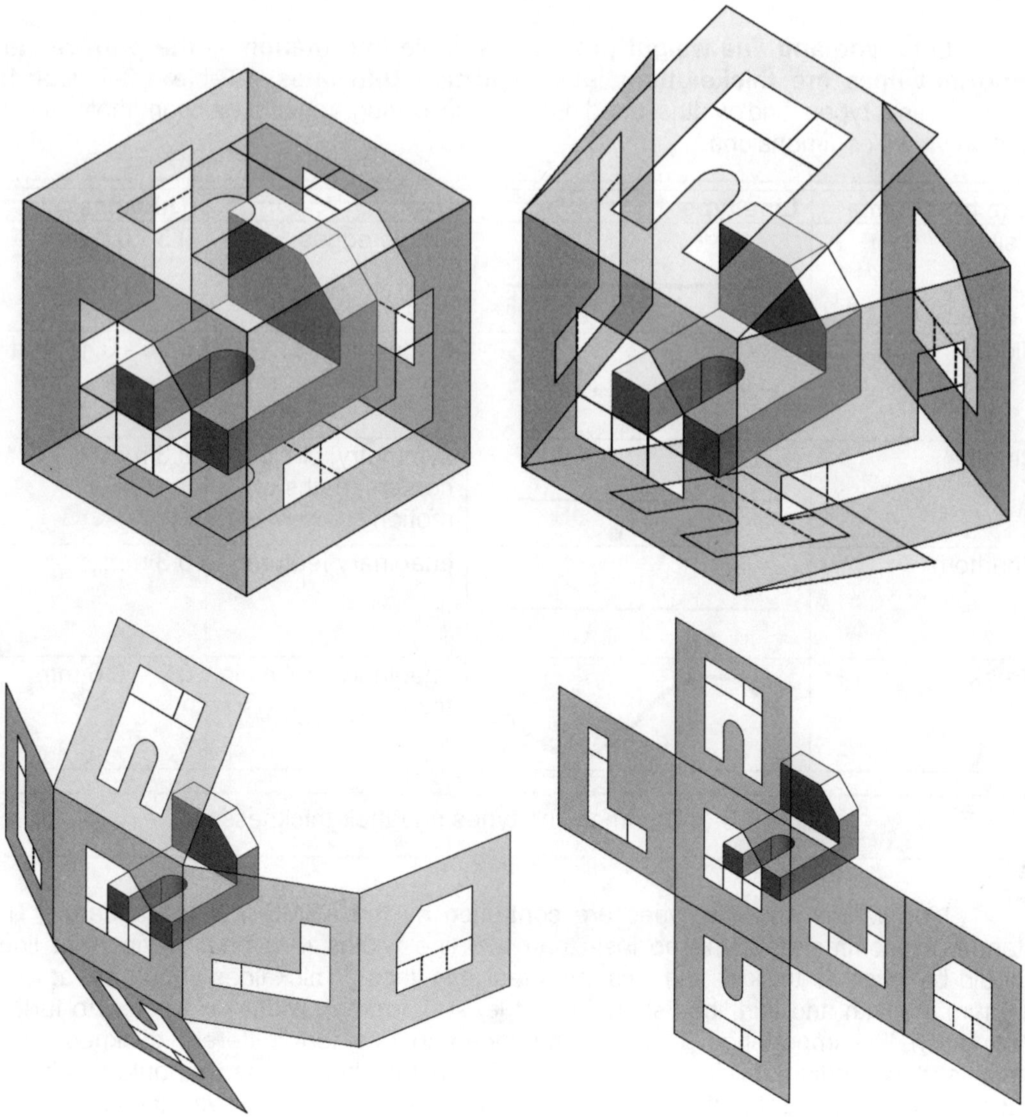

Figure 4.1-1: Glass box being unfolded.

4.3) LINE TYPES USED IN AN ORTHOGRAPHIC PROJECTION

***Line type* and *line weight* provide valuable information to the print reader. Important lines are thicker than less important thin lines.** Table 4.3-1 lists the common line types and widths used in a basic orthographic projection that has no section views or dimensions.

Line type name	**Line type**	**Use**	**Thickness**
Visible		visible edges	0.5 - 0.6 mm
Hidden		hidden edges	0.35 - 0.45 mm
Center		symmetry, circle of centers, paths of motion	0.3 mm
Phantom		imaginary features	0.3 mm
Break		imaginary brakes in the part	0.5 – 0.6 mm

Table 4.3-1: Common line types and their thicknesses

Line widths and line types are controlled by the ASME Y14.2 standard. The standard recommends using no less than two line widths in a print. Important lines should be twice as thick as the less important thin lines. Thick lines should be at least 0.6 mm in width and thin lines should be at least 0.3 mm in width. However, to further distinguish line importance, it is recommended to use four different thicknesses or weights: thin, medium, thick, and very thick. The actual line thickness should be chosen such that there is a visible difference between the line weights; however, they should not be too thick or thin making it difficult to read the print. The thickness of the lines should be adjusted according to the size and complexity of the part.

4.4) RULES FOR LINE CREATION

The following rules and guidelines for line creation should be followed in order to create lines that are effective in communicating the drawing information. However, due to computer automation, some of the rules may be hard to follow. The rules of line creation and use are in accordance with the ASME Y14.2 and ASME Y14.3 standards.

4.4.1) Hidden Lines

Hidden lines represent edges and boundaries that cannot be seen.

Rule 1. The length of the hidden line dashes may vary slightly as the size of the drawing changes as shown in Figure 4.4-1. For example, a very small part may require smaller dashes in order for the hidden line to be recognized.

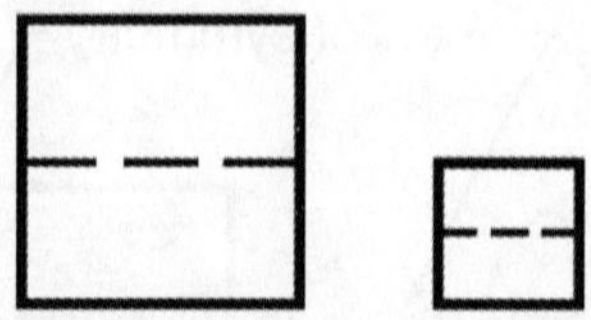

Figure 4.4-1: Dash size

Rule 2. Hidden lines should always begin and end with a dash, except when the hidden line begins or ends at a parallel visible line. Figure 4.4-2 shows a few examples of hidden line configurations.

Rule 3. Hidden line dashes should join at corners (see Figure 4.4-2).

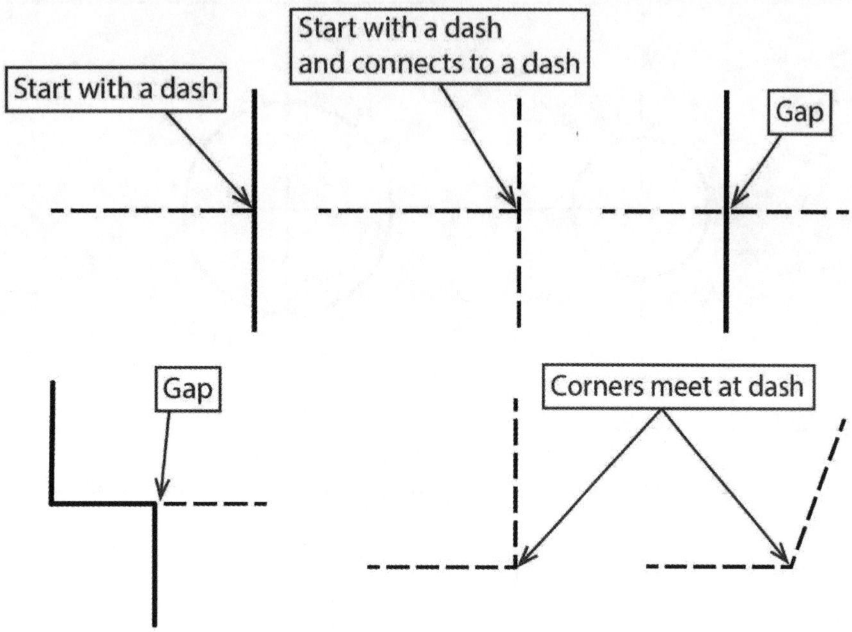

Figure 4.4-2: Drawing hidden lines.

4.4.2) Center Lines

Center lines are used to identify planes and axes of symmetry. Short center lines may be left unbroken if it is certain that they won't be confused with another line type. However, every measure should be taken to produce a break.

Rule 1. Center lines should start and end with long dashes (see Figure 4.4-3).

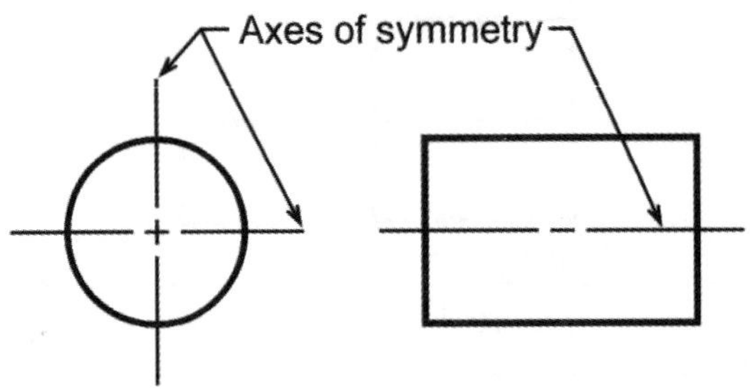

Figure 4.4-3: Axes of symmetry

Rule 2. Center lines should intersect by crossing either the long dashes or the short dashes (see Figure 4.4-4).

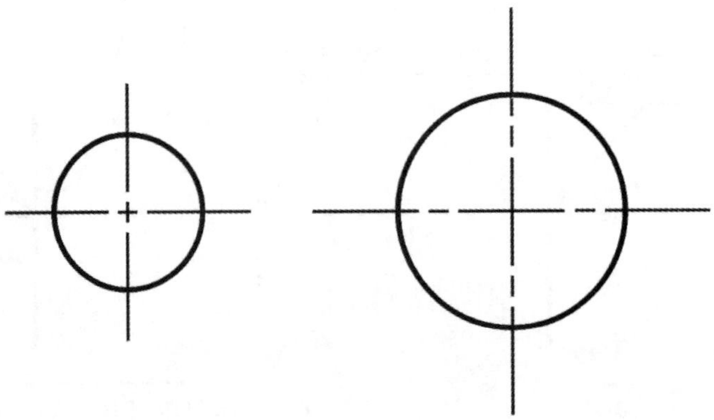

Figure 4.4-4: Crossing center lines.

Rule 3. Center lines should extend a short distance beyond the object or feature. They should not terminate at other lines of the drawing (see Figure 4.4-5).

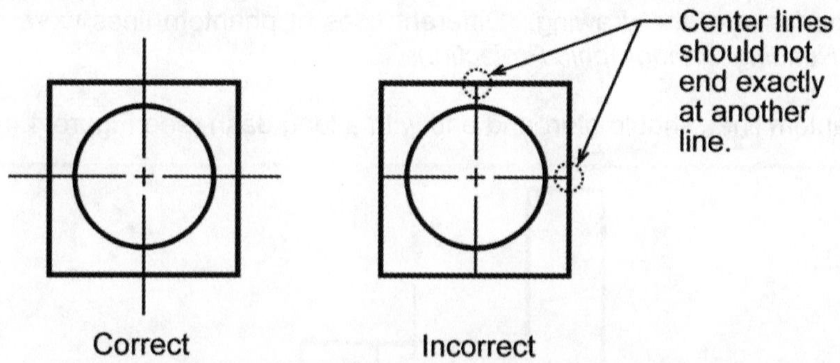

Figure 4.4-5: Terminating center lines.

Rule 4. Center lines may be connected within a single view to show that two or more features lie in the same plane as shown in Figure 4.4-6. However, they should not extend through the space between views.

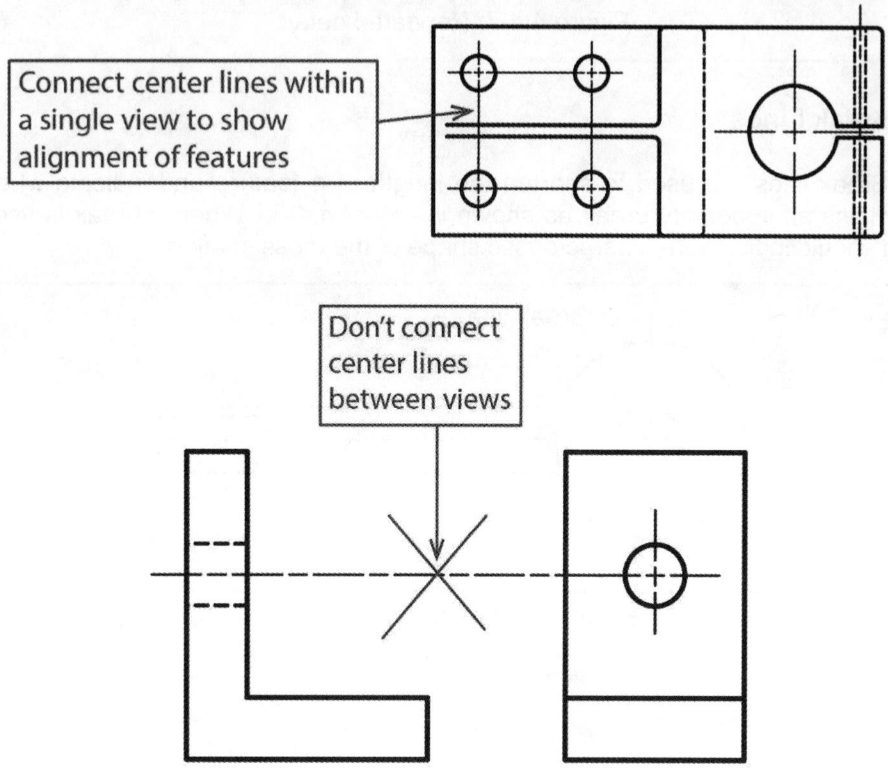

Figure 4.4-6: Connecting center lines.

4.4.3) Phantom Lines

In general, phantom lines are used to indicate things that are missing, imaginary, or are not the focus of the drawing. Different uses of phantom lines were described in the chapter *Reading Orthographic Projections*.

Rule 1. Phantom lines should start and end with a long dash (see Figure 4.4-7).

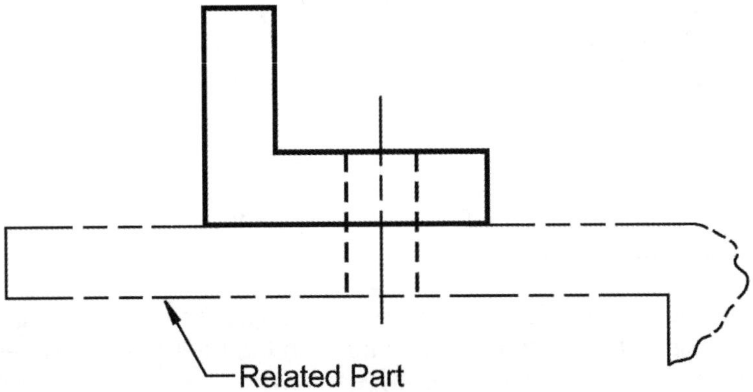

Figure 4.4-7: Repeated detail.

4.4.4) Break Lines

Break lines are used to shorten the length of a feature and indicate where the part contains an imaginary break as shown in Figure 4.4-8. When a break is used, the drawing should indicate the characteristic shape of the cross section.

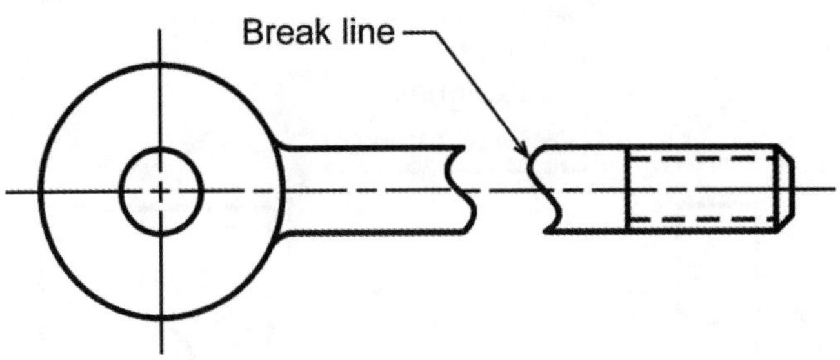

Figure 4.4-8: Using break lines.

There are two types of break lines. A break line may be a series of connecting arcs, as shown in Figure 4.4-8 and 4.4-9, or a straight line with a jog in the middle as shown in Figure 4.4-9. If the distance to traverse is short, a series of connecting arcs is used. This series of arcs is the same width as the visible lines on the drawing. If the distance is long, a thin straight line with a jog is used.

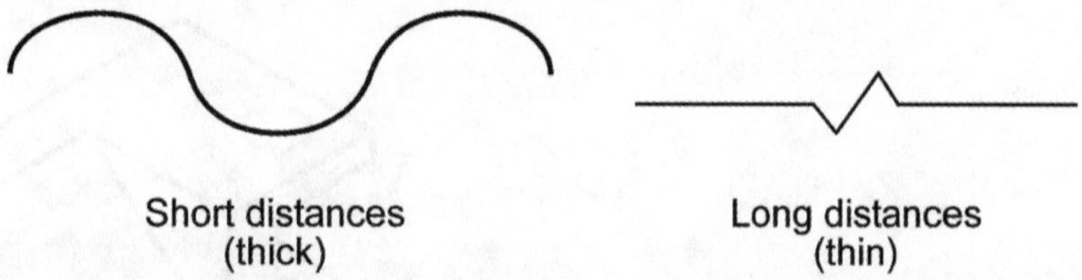

Figure 4.4-9: Types of break lines.

4.4.5) Line Type Precedence

Some lines are considered more important than other lines. **Two lines may occur in the same place; however, only the line that is considered to be the most important is shown.** Lines in order of precedence/importance are as follows:

1. Cutting plane line
2. Visible line
3. Hidden line
4. Center line

Try Exercise 4.4-1

Exercise 4.4-1: Line use in an orthographic projection

Fill the following dotted orthographic projection with the appropriate line types.

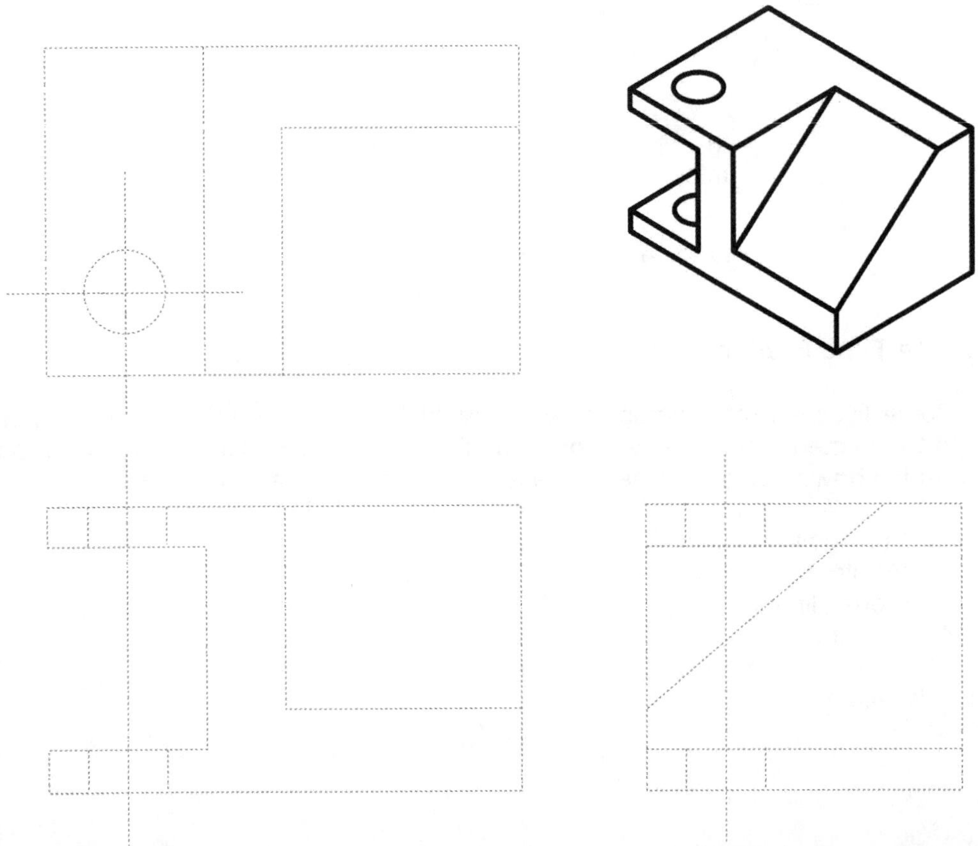

4.5) CREATING AN ORTHOGRAPHIC PROJECTION

The steps presented in this section are meant to help you create a technically correct orthographic projection using the third-angle projection standard. Once you become experienced and proficient at creating orthographic projections, you will develop short cuts and may not need to follow the steps exactly as written. These steps are visually illustrated in Figure 4.5-1.

1. **Choose a front view**. This is the view that shows the most about the object.
2. **Decide how many views are needed** to completely describe the object. If you are unable to determine which views will be needed, draw the standard views (front, top and right side).
3. **Draw the visible features of the front view.**
4. **Draw projectors off of the front view** horizontally and vertically in order to create boundaries for the top and right side views.
5. **Draw the top view**. Use the vertical projectors to fill in the visible and hidden features.
6. **Project from the top view back to the front view.** Use the vertical projectors to fill in any missing visible or hidden features in the front view.
7. **Draw a 45° projector** off of the upper right corner of the box that encloses the front view.
8. **From the top view, draw projectors over to the 45° line and down** in order to create the boundaries of the right side view.
9. **Draw the right side view.**
10. **Project back to the top and front view** from the right side view as needed.
11. **Draw center lines where necessary.**

Following the aforementioned steps will ensure that the orthographic projection is technically correct. That is, it will ensure that:

- √ The front and top views are vertically aligned.
- √ The front and right side views are horizontally aligned.
- √ Every point or feature in one view is aligned on a projector in any adjacent view (i.e., front and top, or front and right side).
- √ The distance between any two points of the same feature in the related views (i.e., top and right side) are equal.

Figure 4.5-1 identifies the *adjacent* and *related* views. Adjacent views are two adjoining views aligned by projectors. Related views are views that are adjacent to the same view.

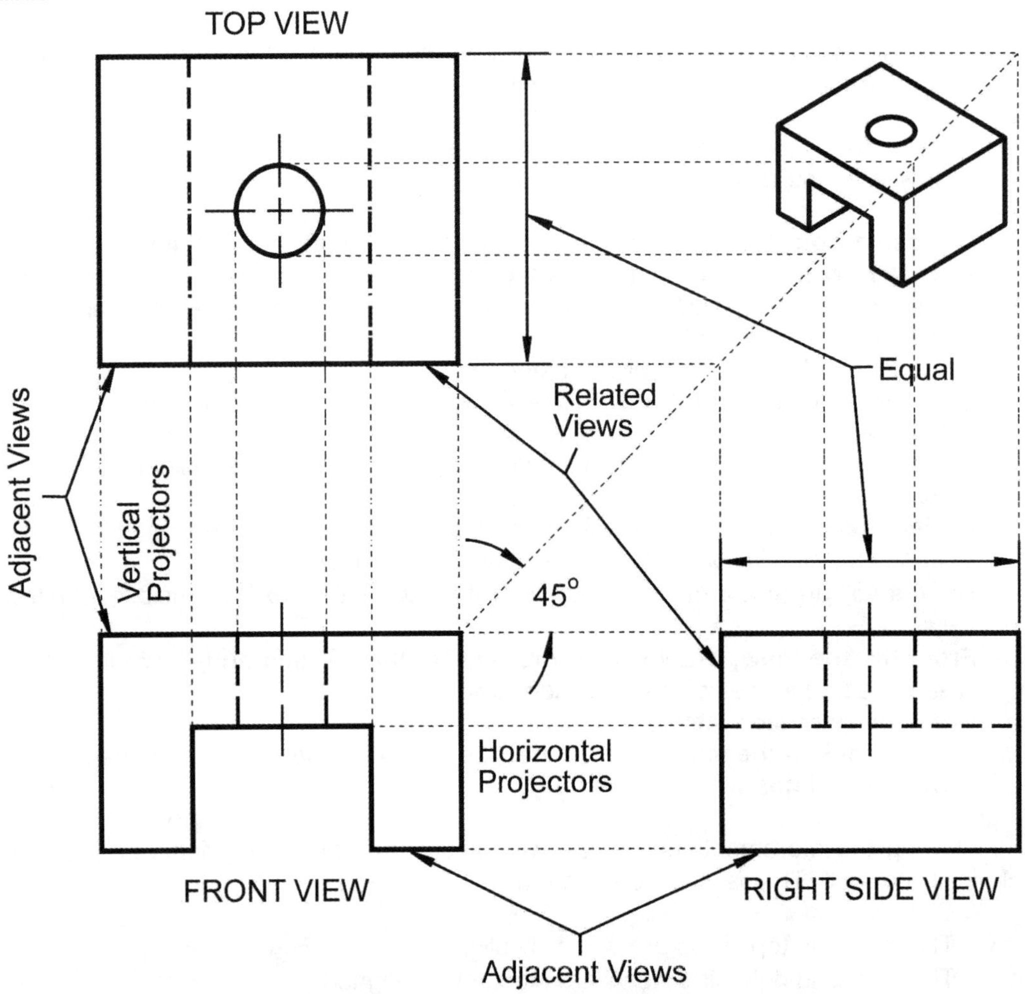

Figure 4.5-1: Features of a technically correct orthographic projection

4.5.1) Projection Symbol

Two internationally recognized systems of projection used to create orthographic projections are third-angle projection and first-angle projection. In the United States, we use third-angle projection to create an orthographic projection. This is the method of creating orthographic projections that is described in this chapter. It is extremely important to let the print reader know which projection method was used to create the orthographic projection. The third angle projection symbol and its proportions are given in Figure 4.5-2. If the drawing uses metric units, the text "SI" is placed in front of the projection symbol.

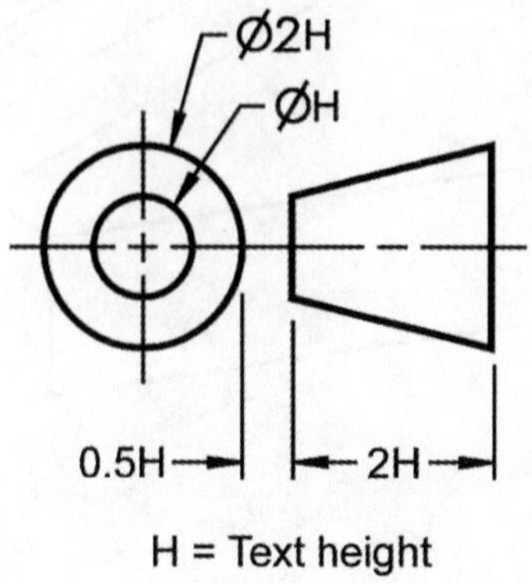

Figure 4.5-2: Projection symbol proportions.

Video Exercise 4.5-1: Beginning Orthographic Projection

This video exercise will take you through creating an orthographic projection for the object shown.

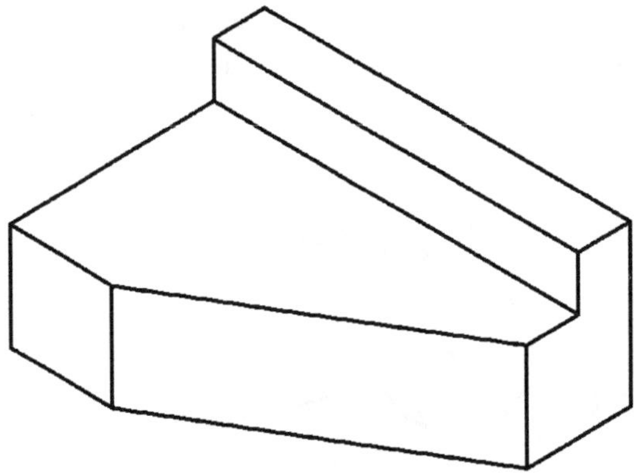

Video Exercise 4.5-2: Intermediate Orthographic Projection

This video exercise will take you through creating an orthographic projection for the object shown.

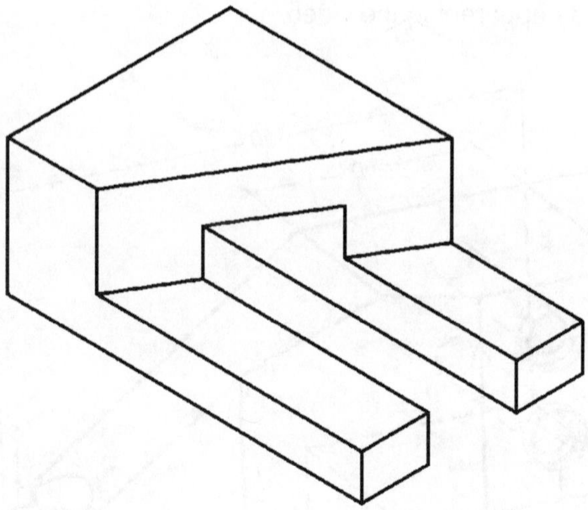

Video Exercise 4.5-3: Advanced Orthographic Projection

This video exercise will take you through creating an orthographic projection for the object shown. Note: The object is not completely dimensioned; however, the missing dimensions will be made apparent in the video.

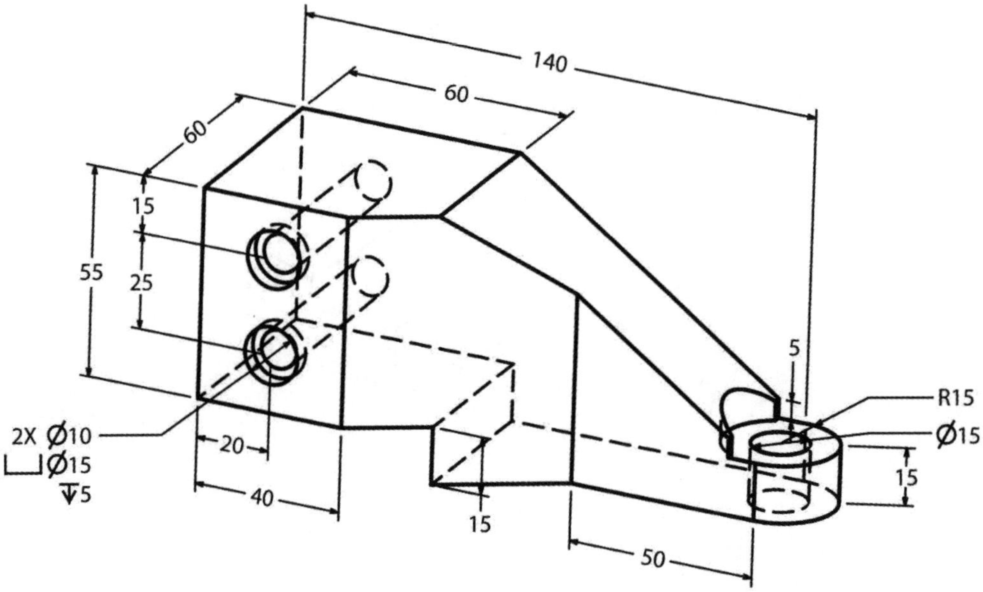

Exercise 4.5-4: Missing lines 1

Name: ______________________________ Date: ______________

Fill in the missing lines in the front, right side, and top views. **Hint:** The front view has one missing visible line. The right side view has one missing visible line and two missing hidden lines. The top view has five missing visible lines and two missing hidden lines.

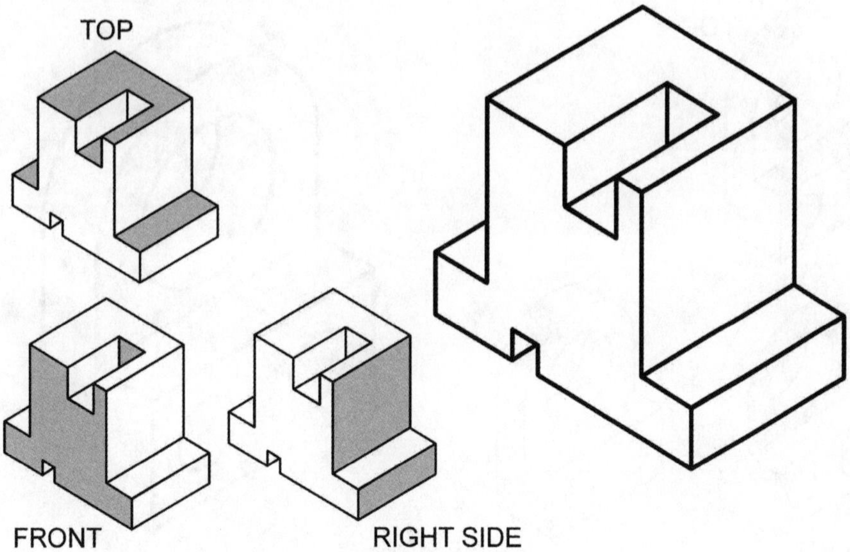

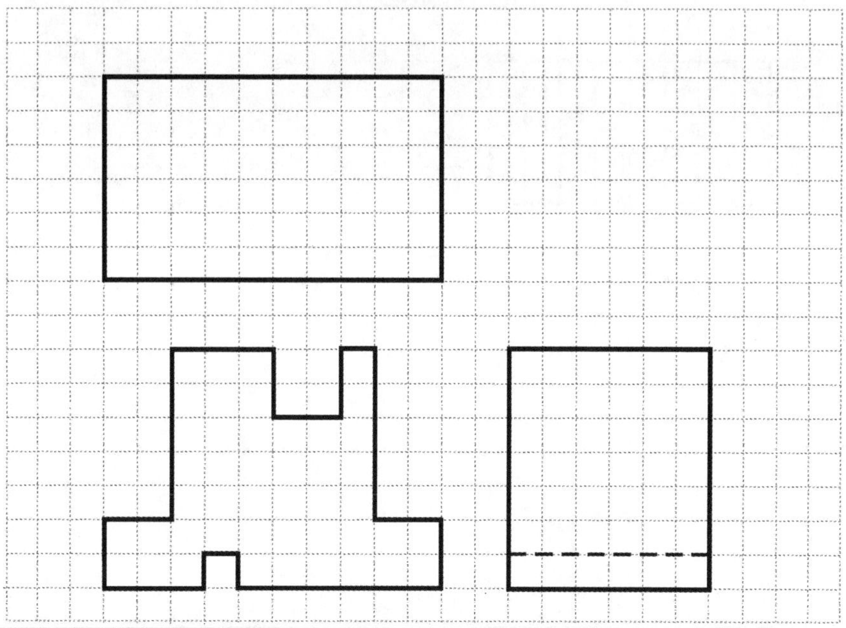

Exercise 4.5-5: Missing lines 2

Name: ______________________________ Date: _______________

Fill in the missing lines in the top, front, and right side views. **Hint:** The top view has one missing visible line. The front view has four missing visible lines and four missing center lines. The right side view has two missing hidden lines and one missing center line.

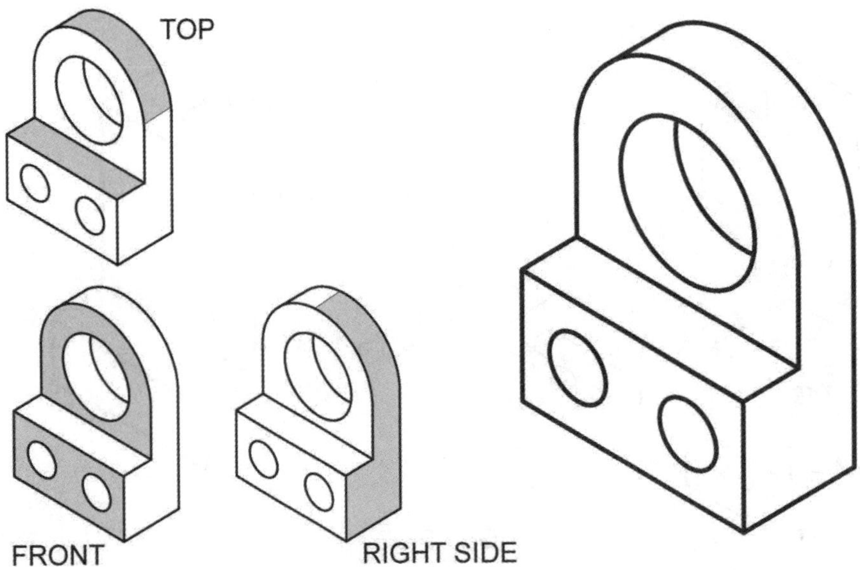

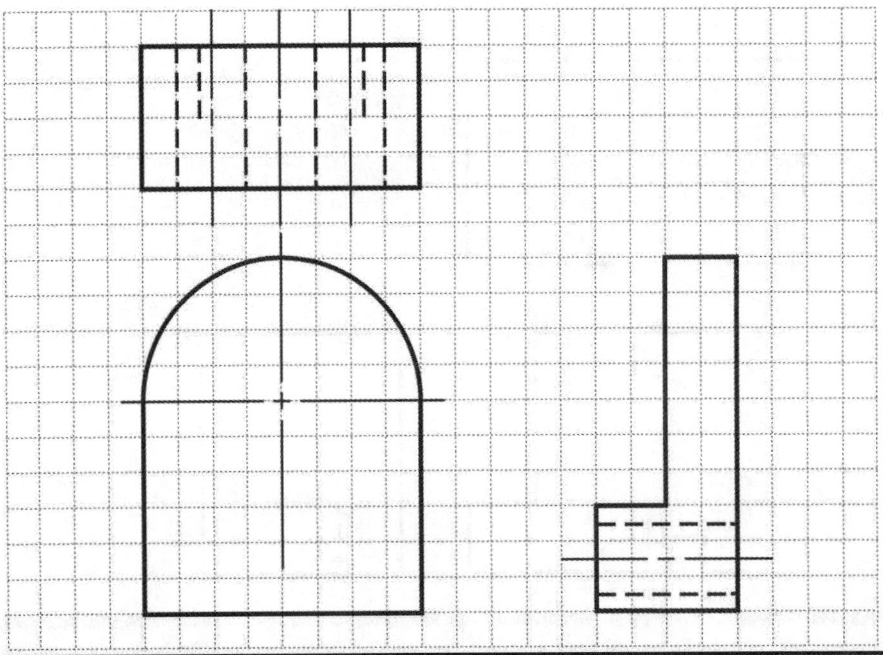

4.6) APPLYING WHAT WE HAVE LEARNED

Exercise 4.6-1: Drawing an orthographic projection 1

Name: ______________________________ Date: ______________

Shade in the surfaces that will appear in the front, top, and right side views. Estimating the distances, draw the front, top, and right side views. Identify the surfaces with the appropriate letter in the orthographic projection.

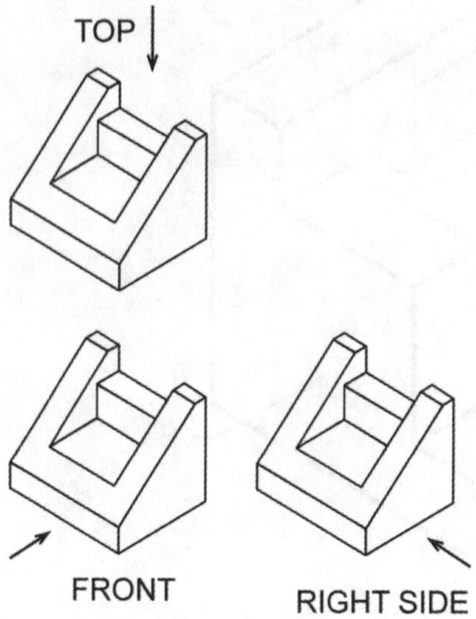

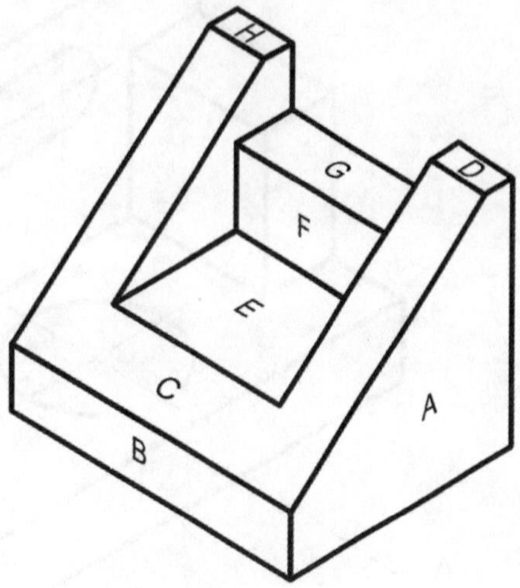

Exercise 4.6-2: Drawing an orthographic projection 2

Name: ______________________________________ Date: _________________

Identify the best choice for the front view. Estimating the distances, draw the front, top, and right side views.

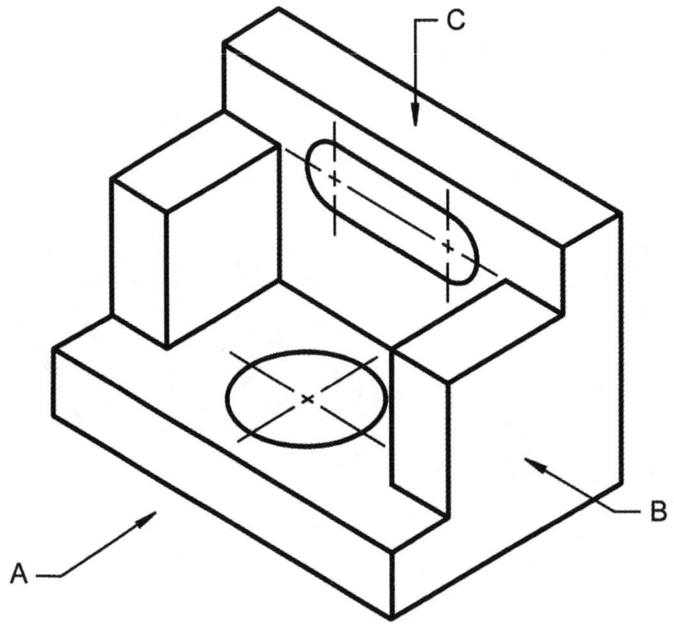

CREATING ORTHOGRAPHIC PROJECTIONS QUESTIONS – SET1

Name: ________________________________ Date: ______________

Orthographic projection

Q4-1) The standard views used in an orthographic projection are … Choose all that apply.

a) front
b) top
c) back
d) right side
e) left side
f) bottom

Q4-2) You need to draw at least 3 views to completely describe the shape of an object. (True, False)

Line types, uses, and creation

Q4-3) To indicate line importance, lines are drawn using different line ....

a) texture
b) thicknesses
c) colors
d) symbols

Q4-4) Center lines should always start and end with a long dash? (True, False)

Creating orthographic projections

Q4-5) Are the front and right side views aligned vertically or horizontally?

Q4-6) Are the front and top views aligned vertically or horizontally?

NOTES:

CREATING ORTHOGRAPHIC PROJECTIONS QUESTIONS – SET2

Name: ______________________________ Date: _____________

Q4-7) The view that generally shows the most characteristics of the part and contains the least number of hidden lines.

a) front
b) top
c) right side

Q4-8) Which is the thickest line type on a non-sectioned orthographic projection.

a) visible
b) hidden
c) center line
d) dimension

Q4-9) Which line type has a medium thickness of 0.35 – 0.45 mm?

Q4-10) Center lines should not connect between views but may connect within a single view. (True, False)

Q4-11) Should a center line end at the boundary of an object? (Yes, No)

Q4-12) Dashes in lines such as hidden lines and center lines may be shorted in length if the part is small. (True, False)

Q4-13) Break lines are drawn in exactly the same way if they traverse a short distance or a long distance. (True, False)

Q4-14) If a **hidden** line and **center** line appear in exactly the same location on a drawing, which one do you delete?

Q4-15) When creating an orthographic projection, what view is chosen first?

Q4-16) A ___________ degree projector is used to relate the features of the top and right side views.

Q4-17) Projection or construction lines are not shown on the final drawing. (True, False)

CREATING ORTHOGRAPHIC PROJECTIONS PROBLEMS

Name: ________________________________ Date: ______________

P4-1) Sketch the front, top and right side views of the following object. Use the grid provided.

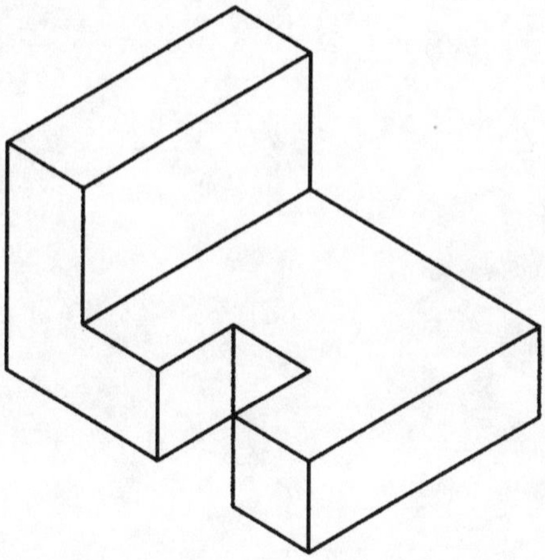

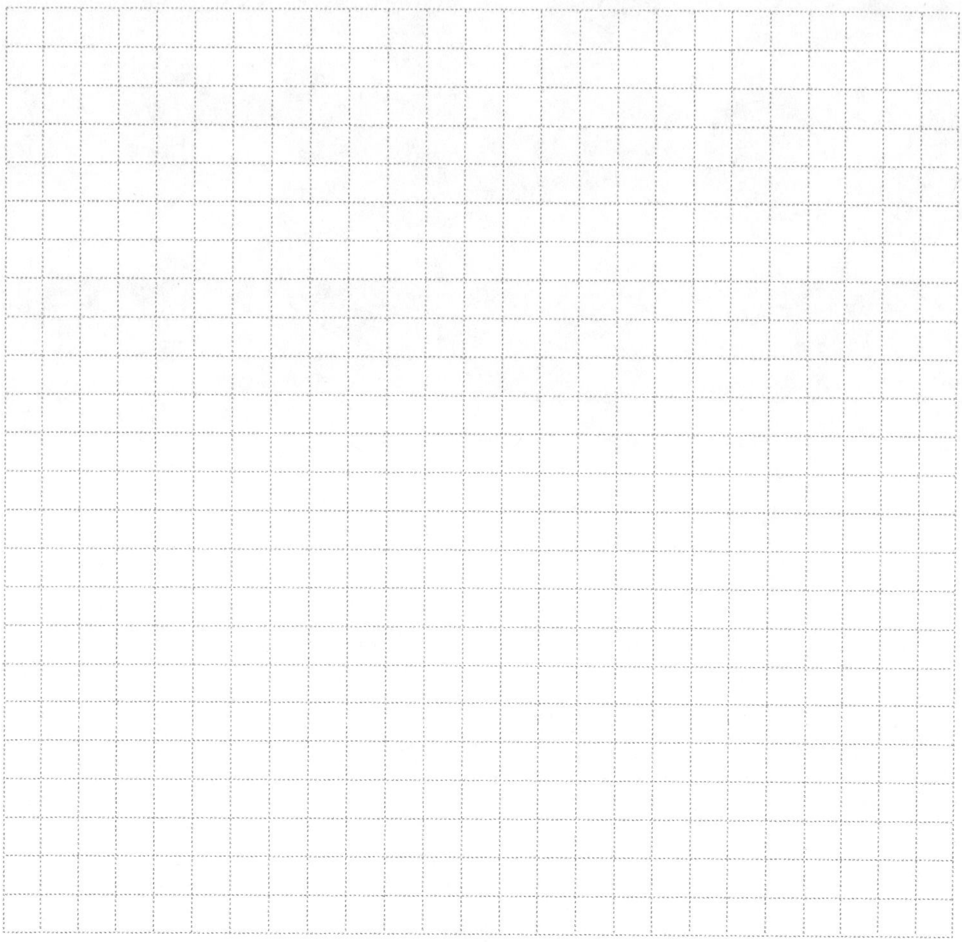

NOTES:

Name: ______________________________ Date: ______________

P4-2) Sketch the front, top and right side views of the following object. Use the grid provided.

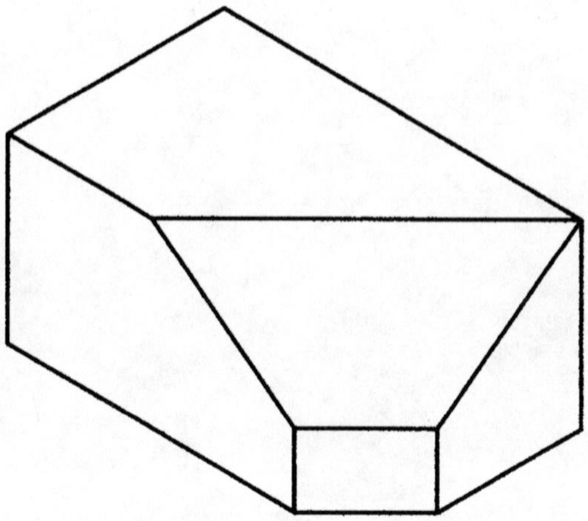

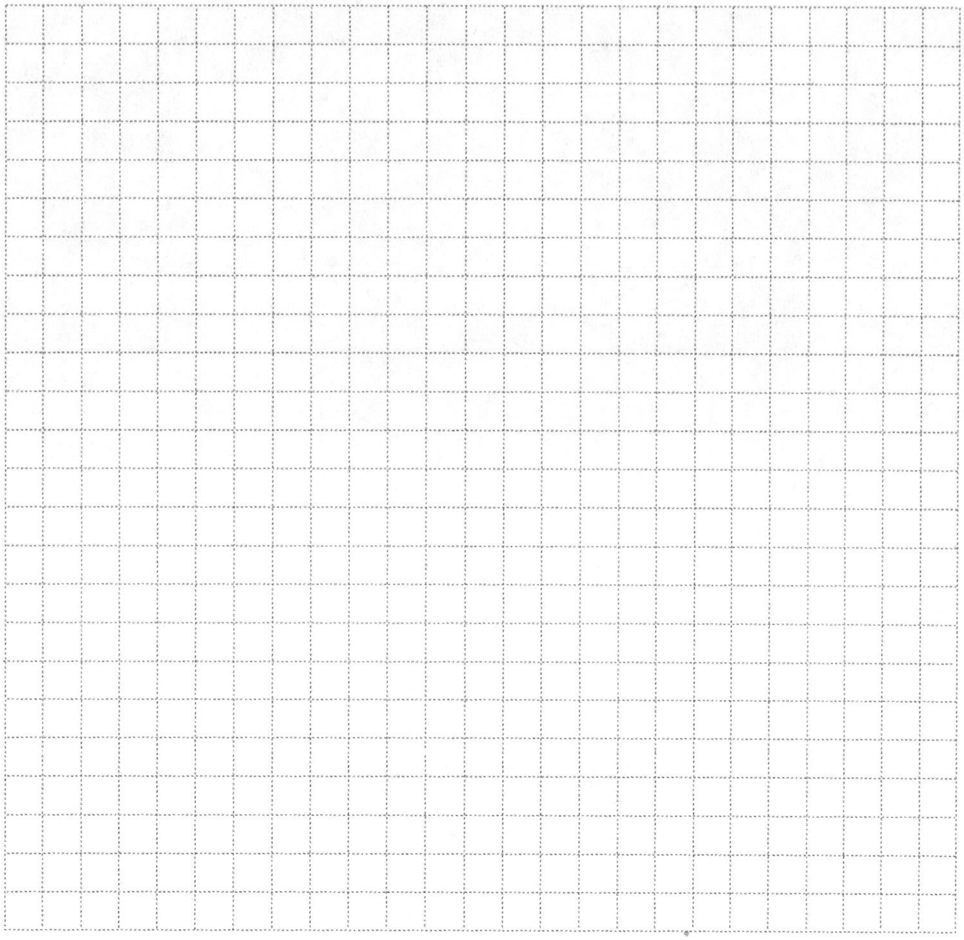

NOTES:

Name: ______________________________ Date: _____________

P4-3) Sketch the front, top and right side views of the following object. Use the grid provided.

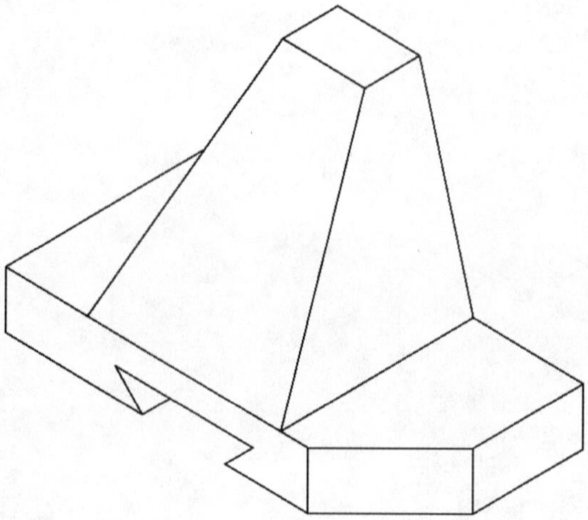

NOTES:

Name: ______________________________ Date: ______________

P4-4) Sketch the front, top and right side views of the following object. Use the 5x5 mm grid provided.

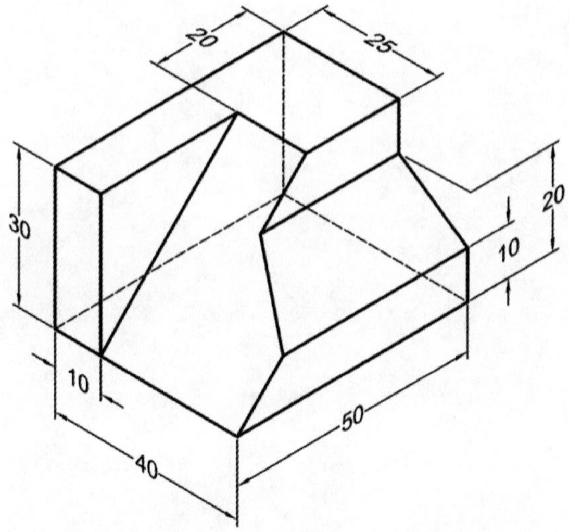

NOTES:

Name: ______________________________ Date: ______________

P4-5) Sketch the front, top and right side views of the following object. Use the grid provided.

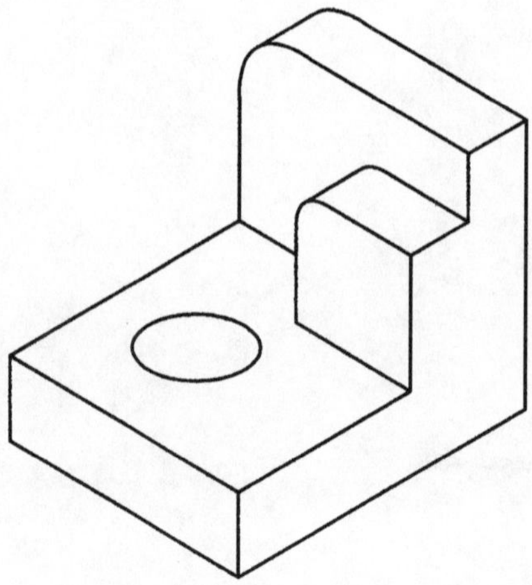

NOTES:

Name: ______________________________ Date: ______________

P4-6) Sketch the front, top and right side views of the following object. Use the grid provided.

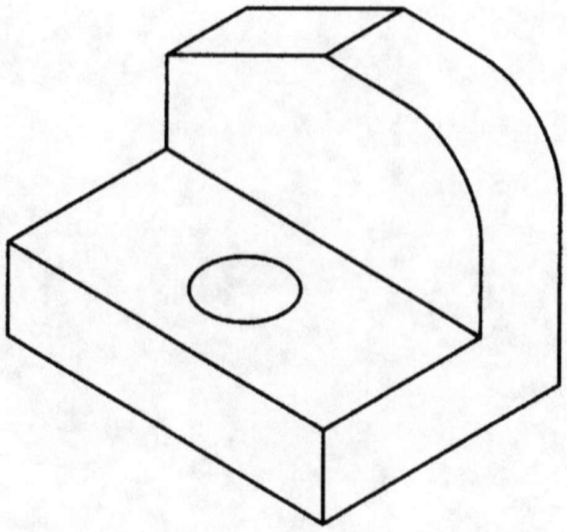

NOTES:

Name: ______________________________ Date: _____________

P4-7) Sketch the front, top and right side views of the following object. Use the grid provided.

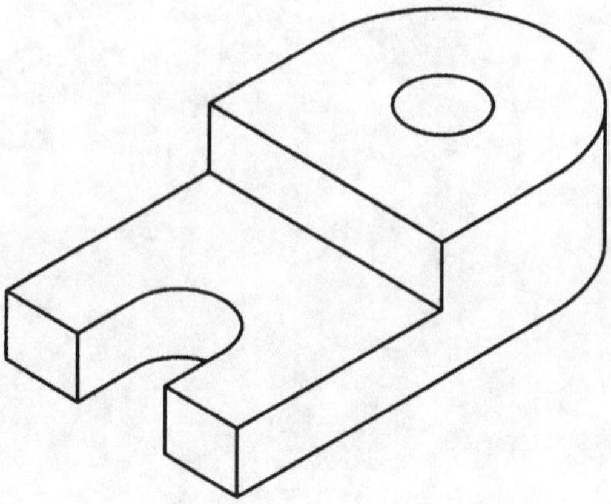

NOTES:

Name: ________________________________ Date: ______________

P4-8) Sketch the front, top and right side views of the following object. Use the grid provided.

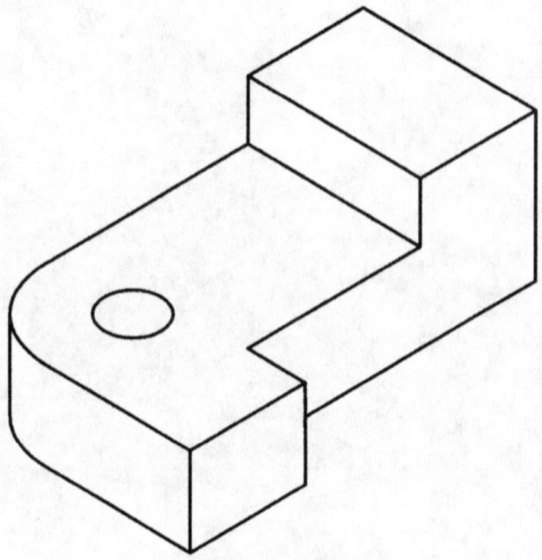

NOTES:

Name: ___________________________________ Date: _______________

P4-9) Sketch the front, top and right side views of the following object. Use the grid provided.

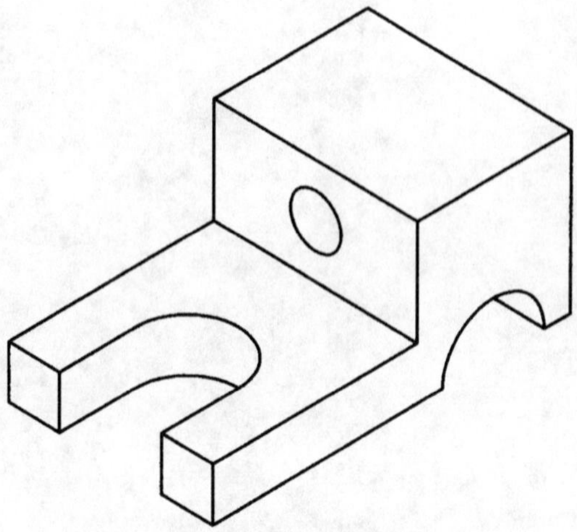

NOTES:

Name: ______________________________ Date: ______________

P4-10) Sketch the front, top and right side views of the following object. Use the grid provided.

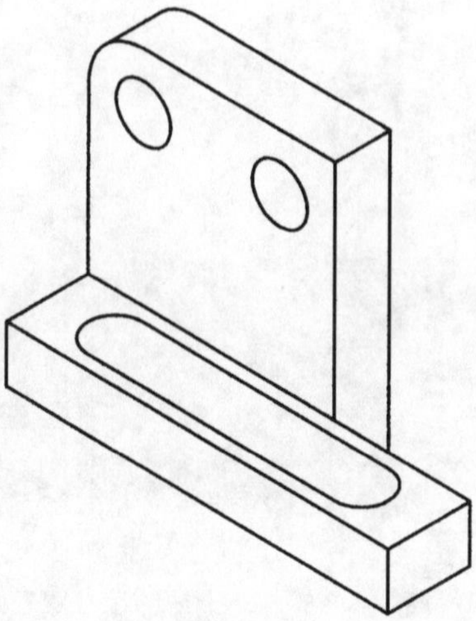

NOTES:

Name: ___________________________________ Date: _______________

P4-11) Sketch the front, top and right side views of the following object. Use the grid provided.

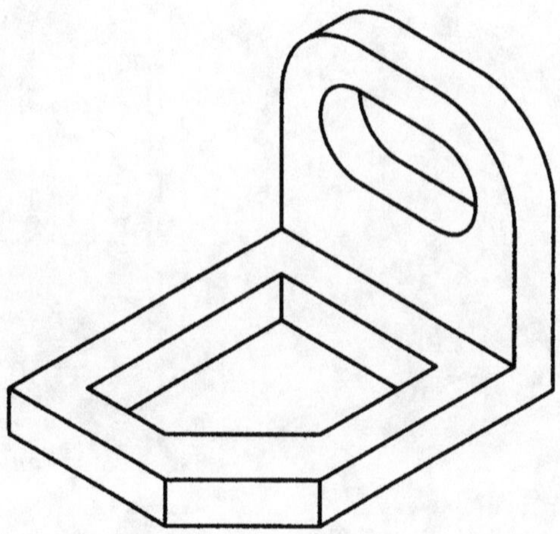

NOTES:

Name: ______________________________ Date: ______________

P4-12) Sketch the front, top and right side views of the following object. Use the grid provided.

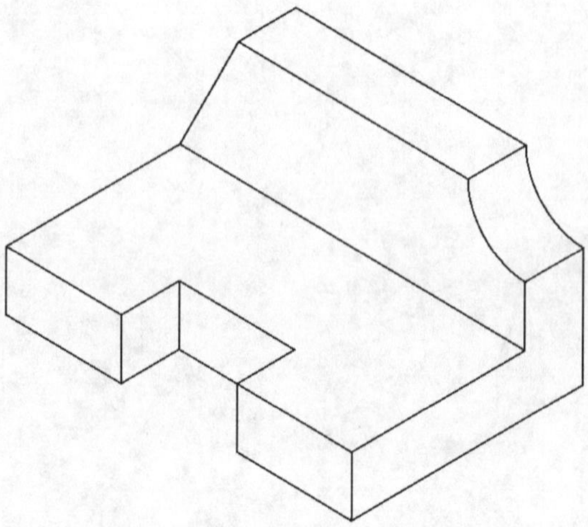

NOTES:

Name: ________________________________ Date: ______________

P4-13) Sketch the front, top and right side views of the following object. Use the grid provided.

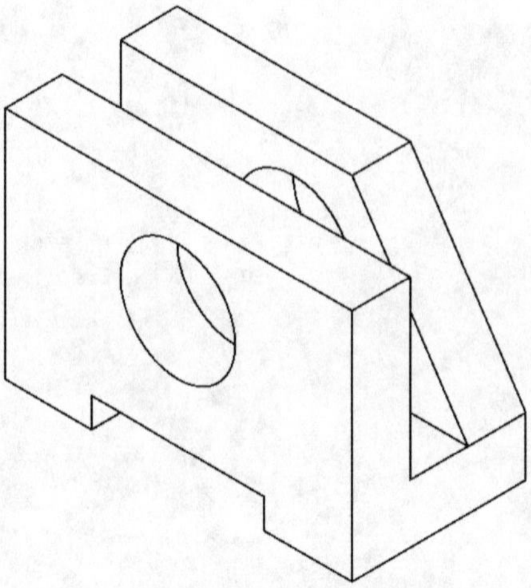

NOTES:

Name: ________________________________ Date: ______________

P4-14) Sketch the front, top and right side views of the following object. Use the grid provided.

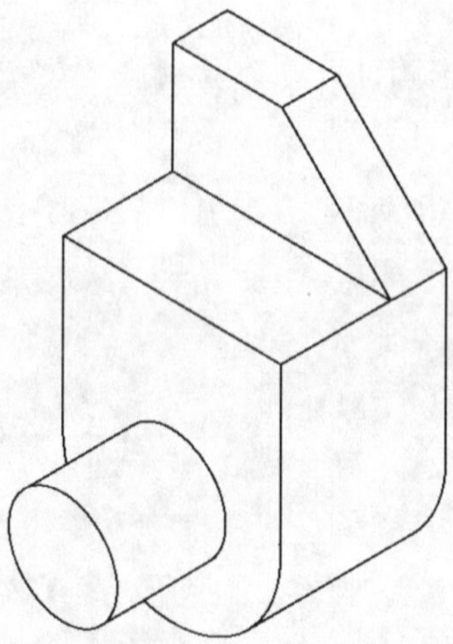

NOTES:

Name: ______________________________ Date: ______________

P4-15) Sketch the front, top and right side views of the following object. Use the grid provided.

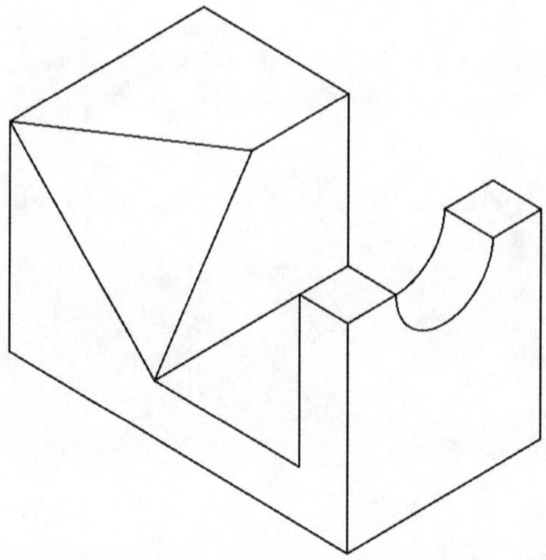

NOTES:

Name: ___________________________ Date: ____________

P4-16) Sketch the front, top and right side views of the following object. Use the grid provided.

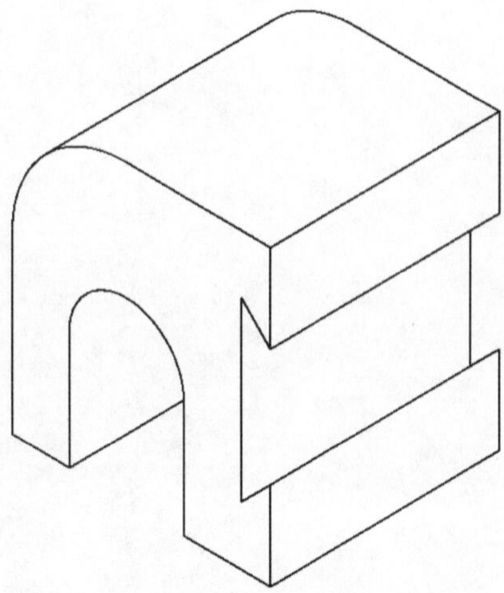

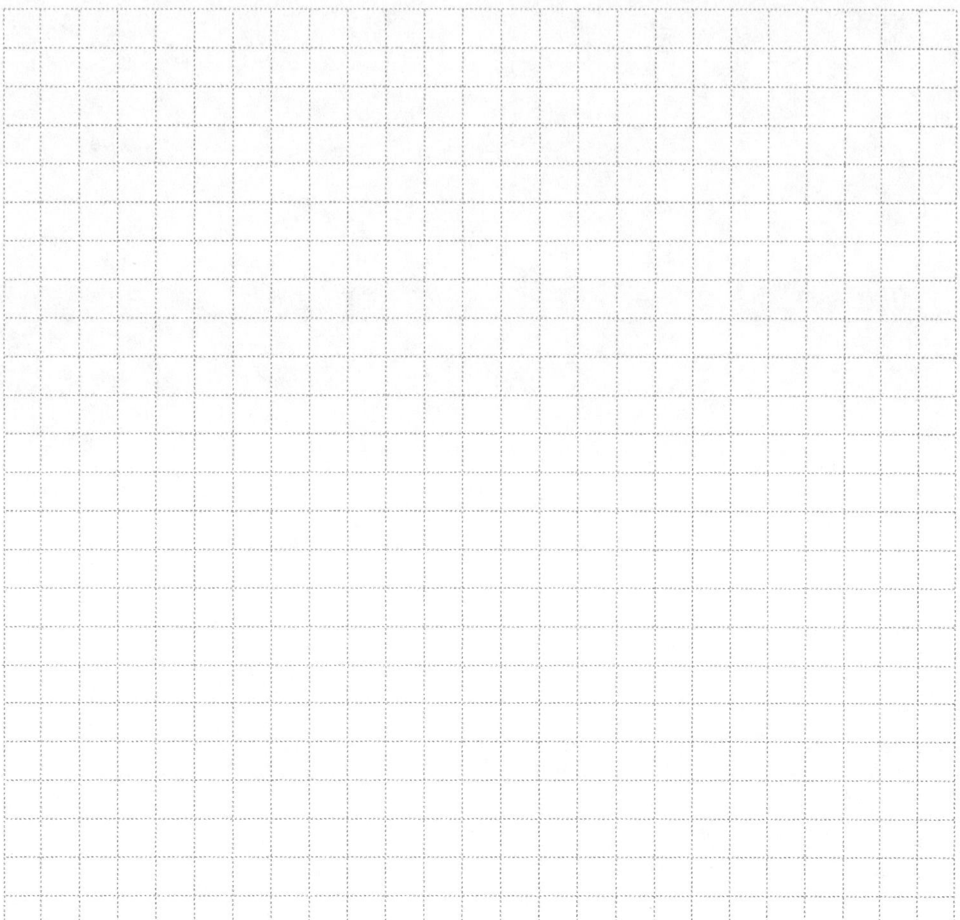

NOTES:

Name: ________________________________ Date: ______________

P4-17) Sketch the front, top and right side views of the following object. Use the grid provided.

NOTES:

Name: ______________________________ Date: ______________

P4-18) Sketch the front, top and right side views of the following object. Use the grid provided.

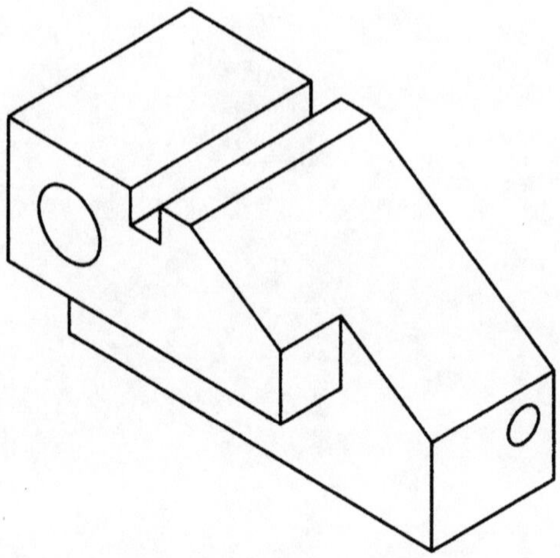

NOTES:

Name: ______________________________ Date: _______________

P4-19) Given two complete views, sketch in the missing view.

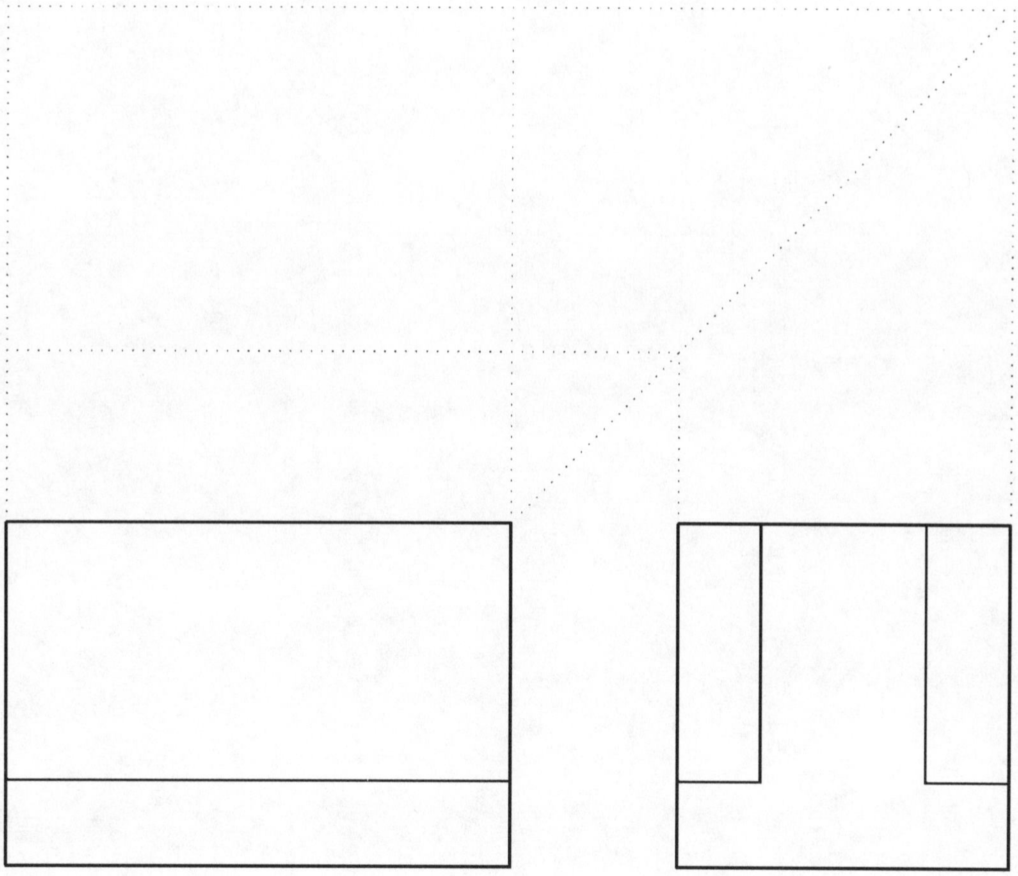

NOTES:

Name: ______________________________ Date: ______________

P4-20) Given two complete views, sketch in the missing view.

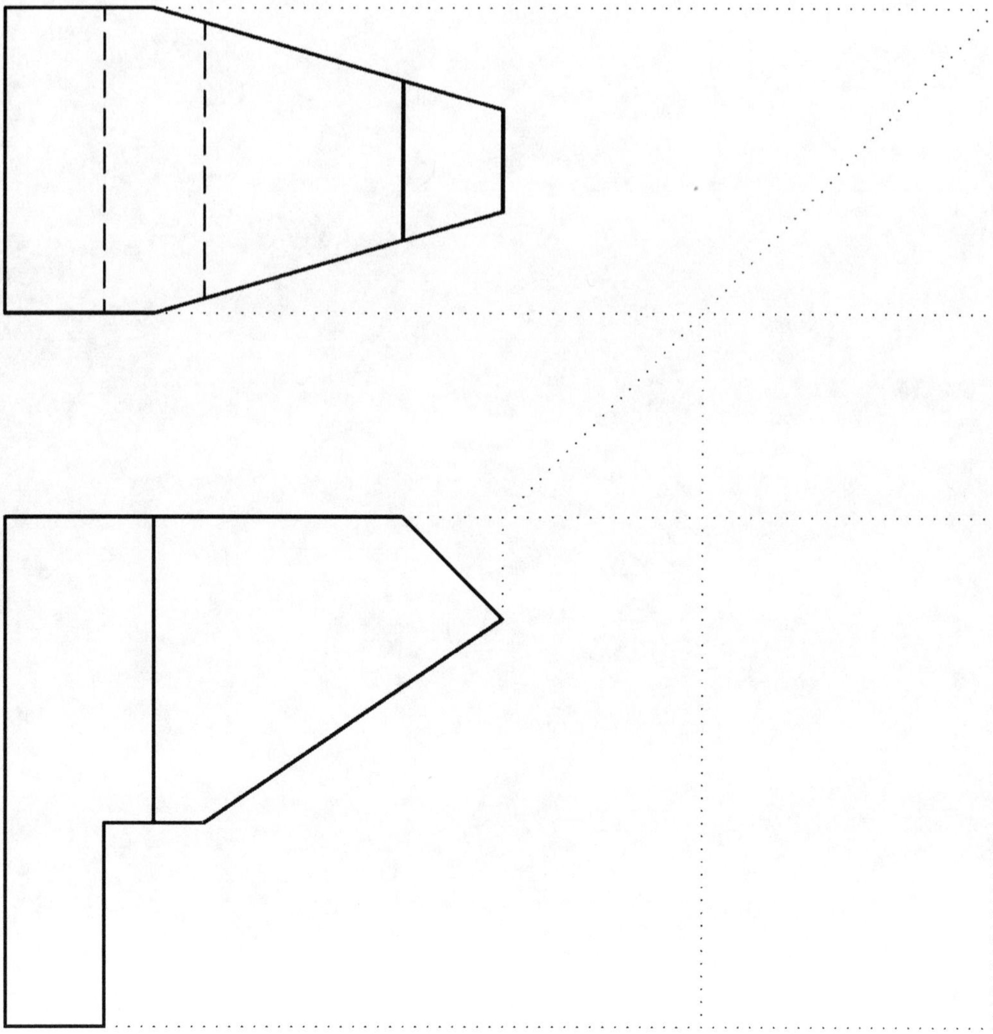

NOTES:

Name: ______________________________ Date: ______________

P4-21) Given two complete views, sketch in the missing view.

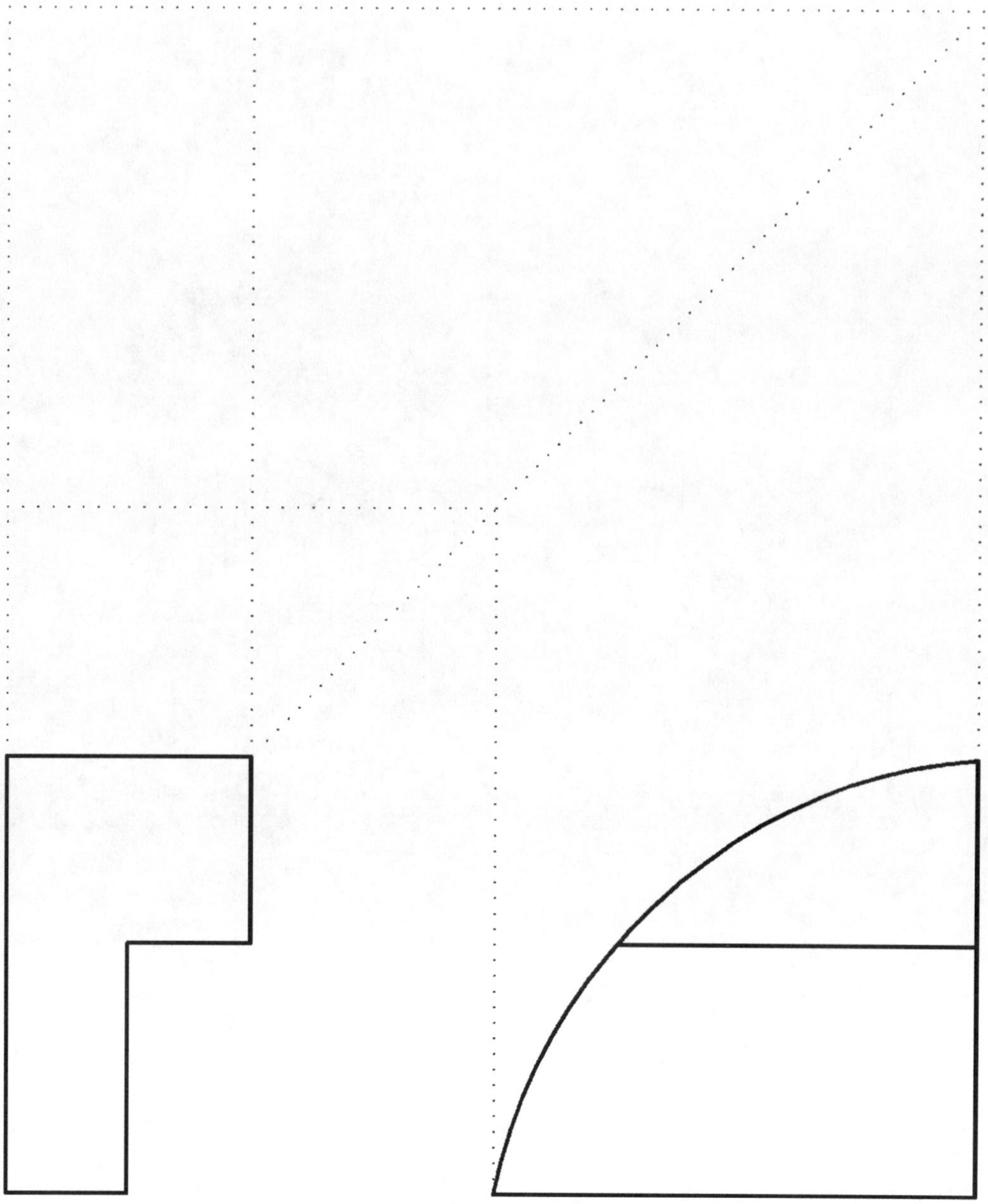

NOTES:

Name: ______________________________ Date: ______________

P4-22) Given two complete views, sketch in the missing view.

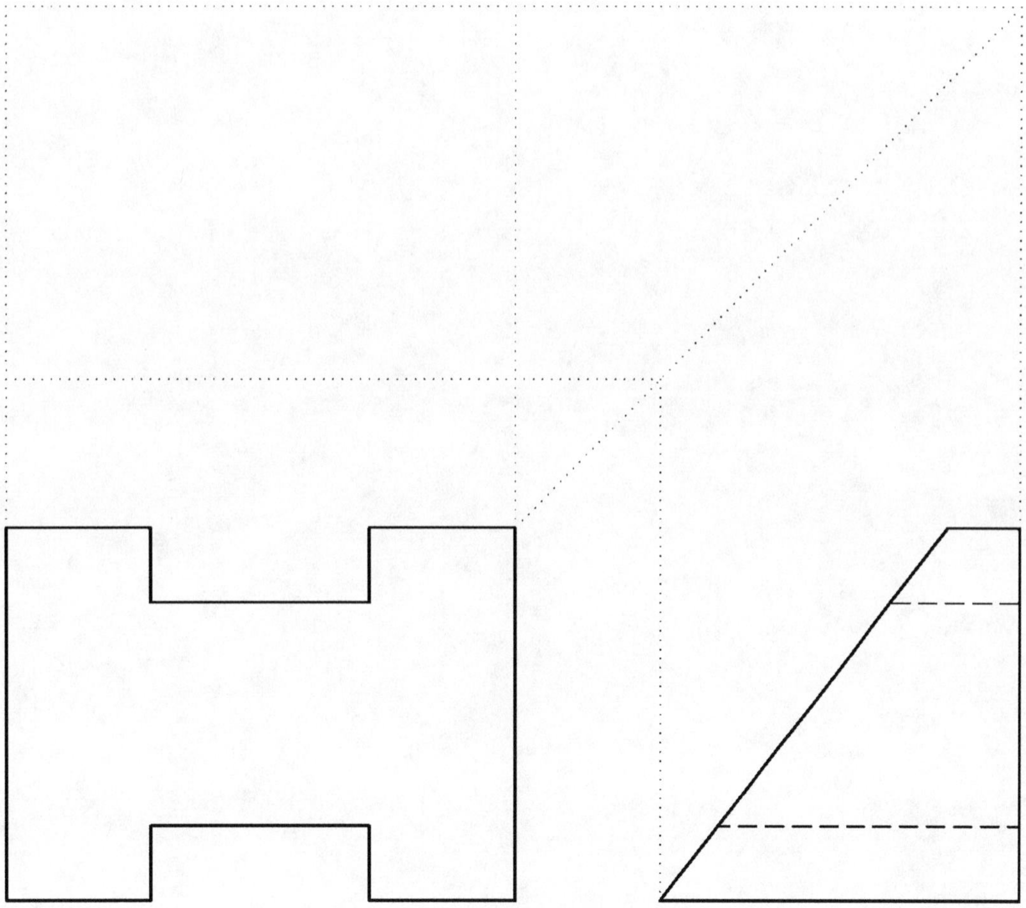

NOTES:

Name: ______________________ Date: ______________

P4-23) Given two complete views, sketch in the missing view.

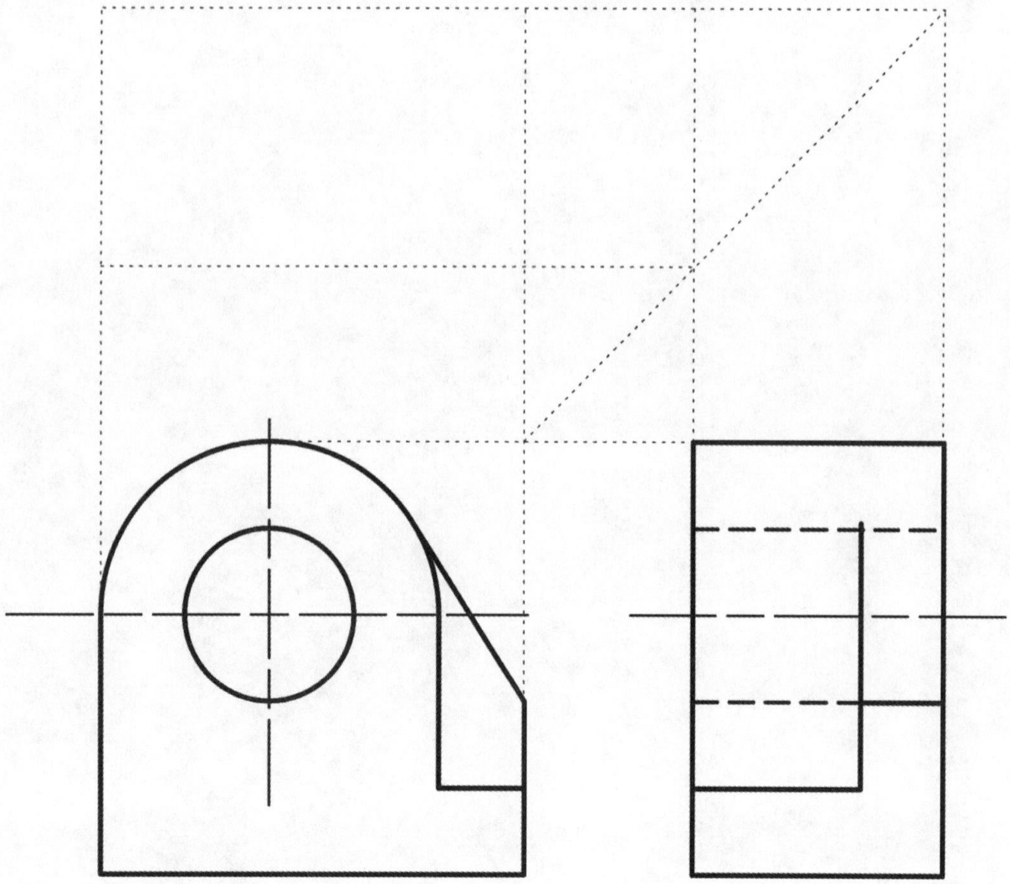

NOTES:

Name: ________________________________ Date: ______________

P4-24) Given two complete views, sketch in the missing view.

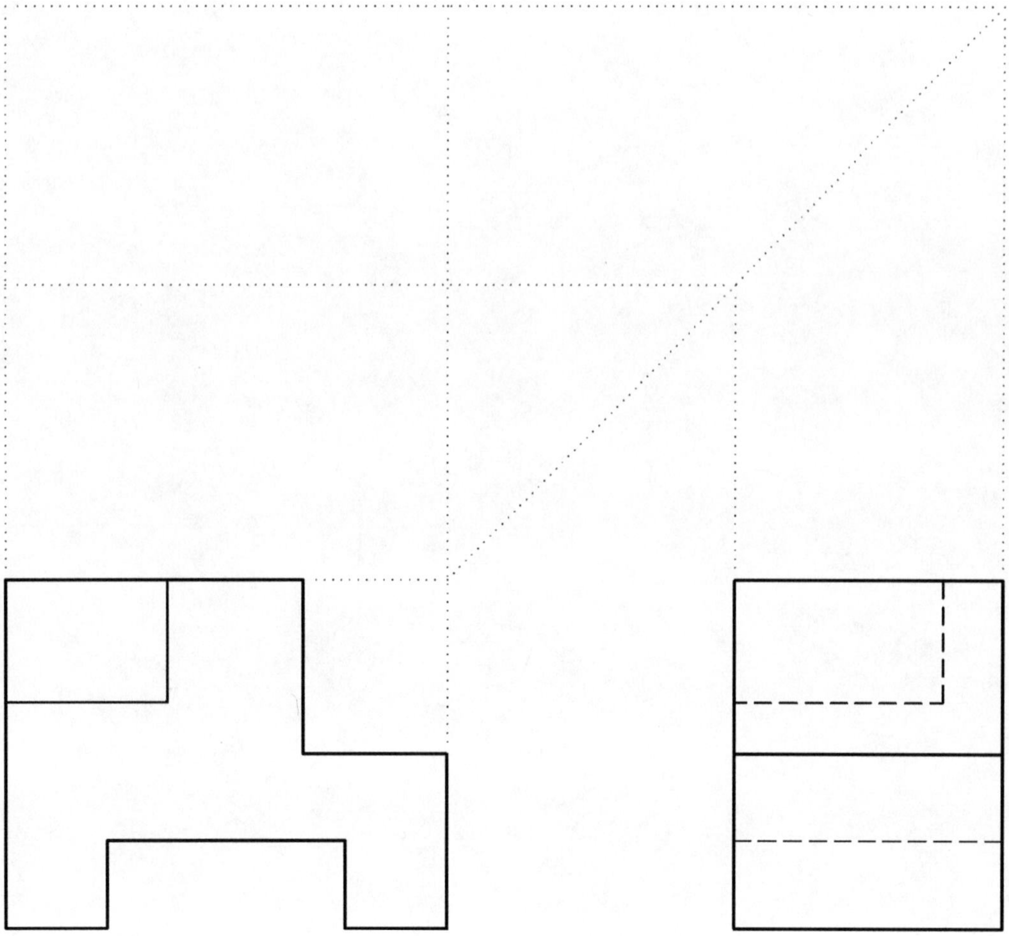

NOTES:

Name: ______________________________ Date: ______________

P4-25) Given two complete views, sketch in the missing view.

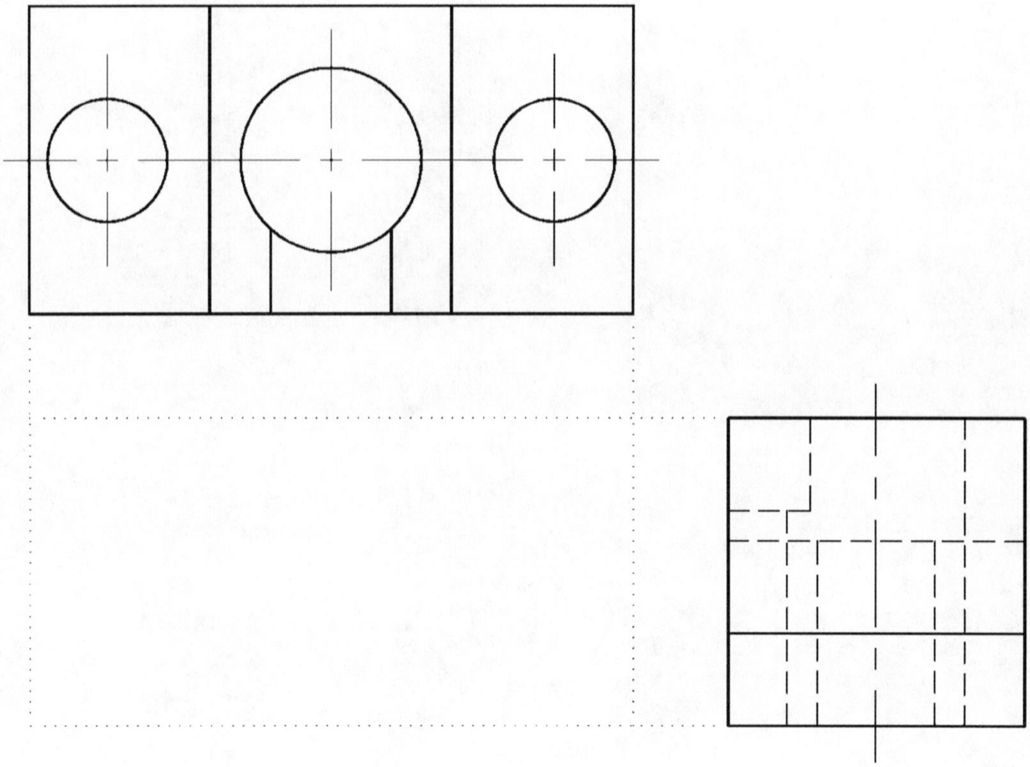

NOTES:

Name: ______________________________ Date: ______________

P4-26) Given two complete views, sketch in the missing view.

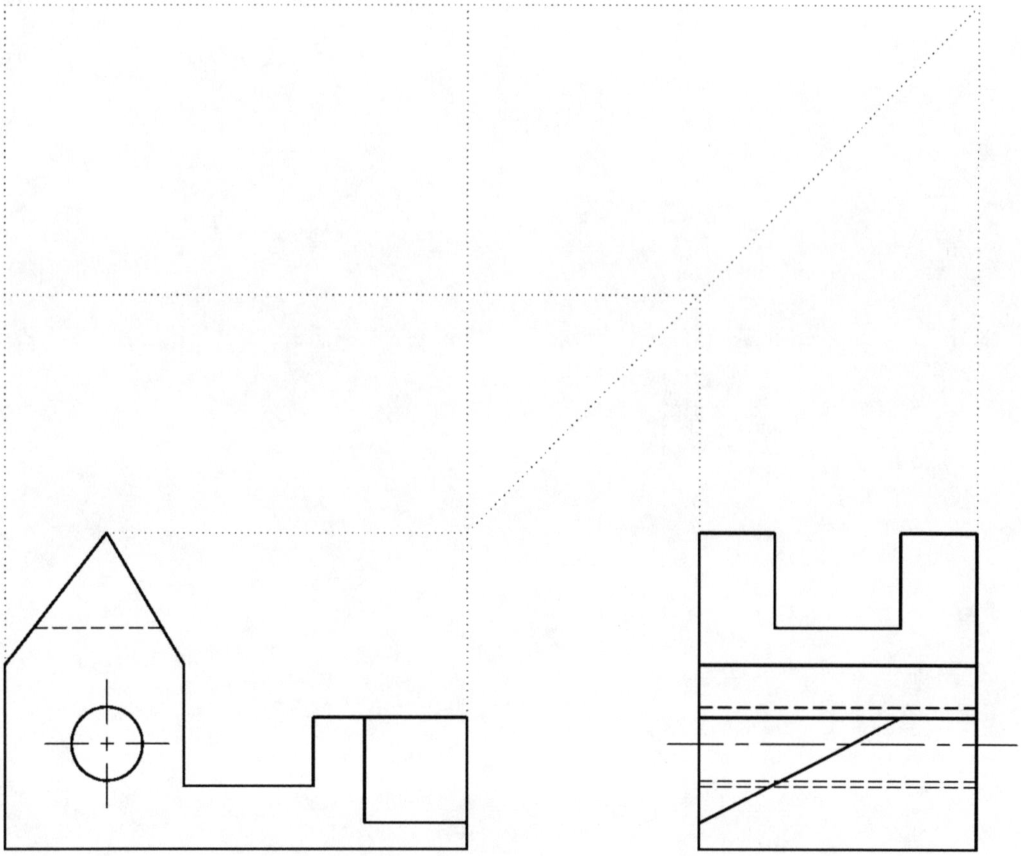

NOTES:

P4-27) Create an orthographic projection of the following object. Draw the three standard views.

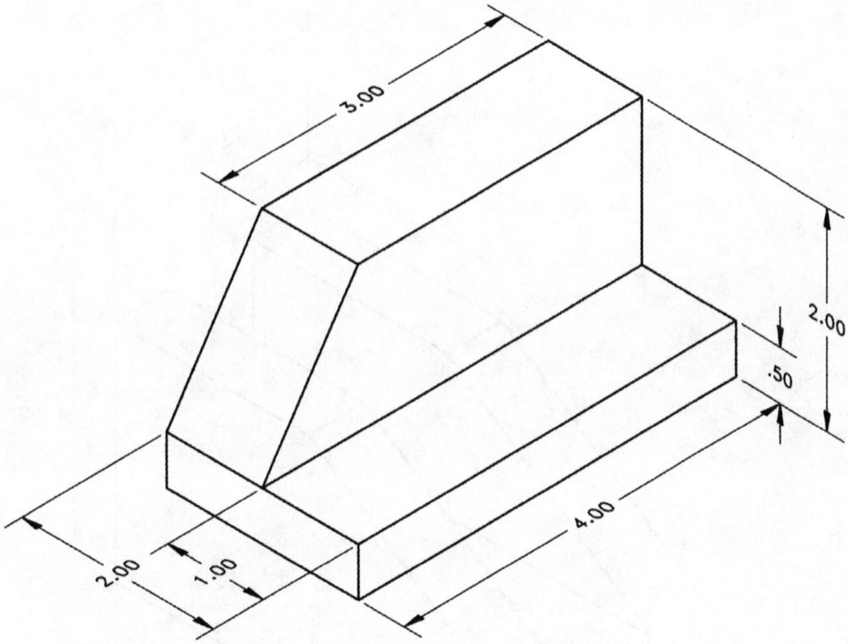

P4-28) Create an orthographic projection of the following object. Draw the three standard views.

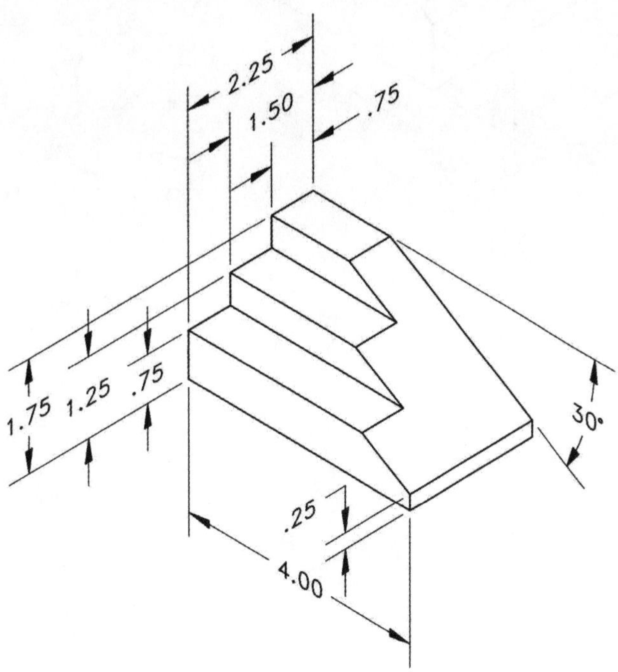

P4-29) Create an orthographic projection of the following object. Draw the three standard views.

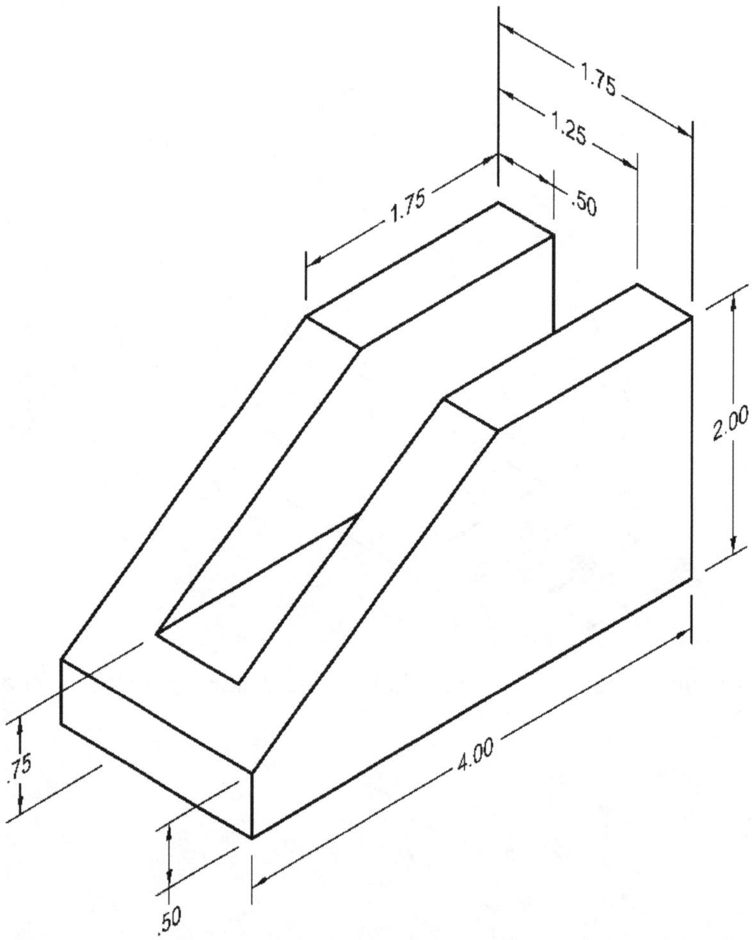

P4-30) Create an orthographic projection of the following object. Draw the three standard views.

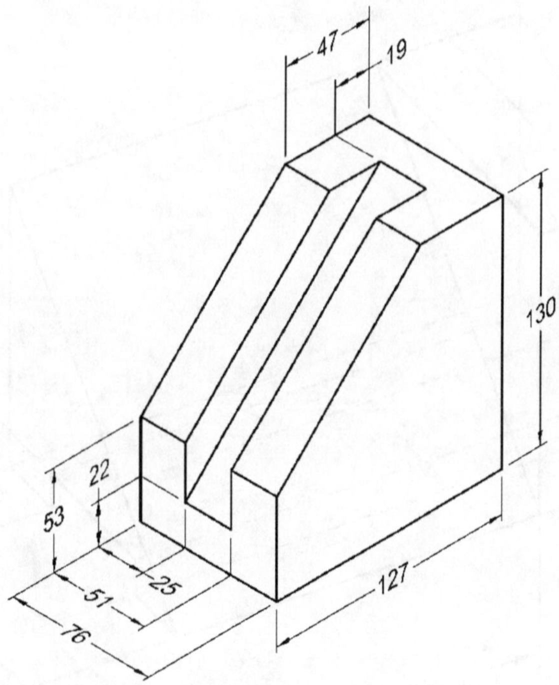

P4-31) Create an orthographic projection of the following object. Draw the three standard views.

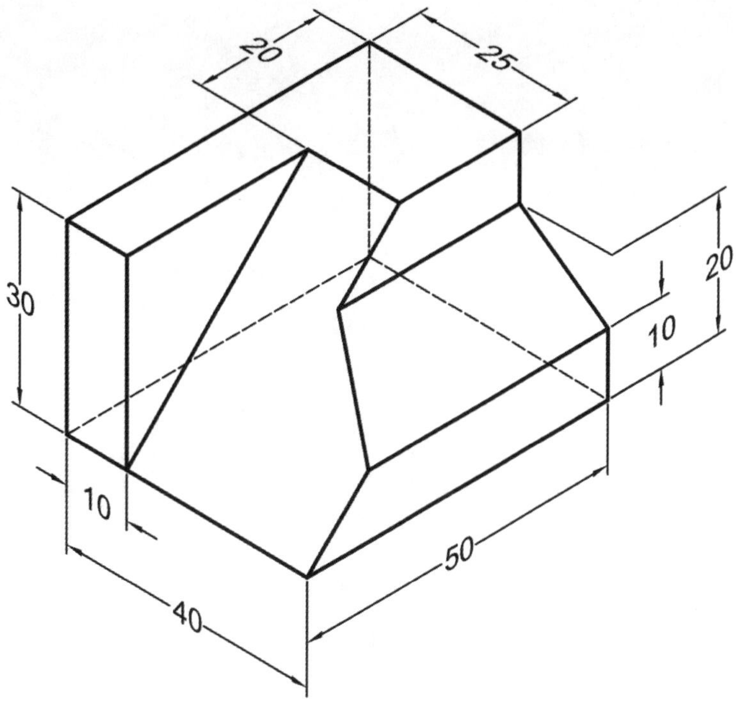

P4-32) Create an orthographic projection of the following object. Draw the three standard views.

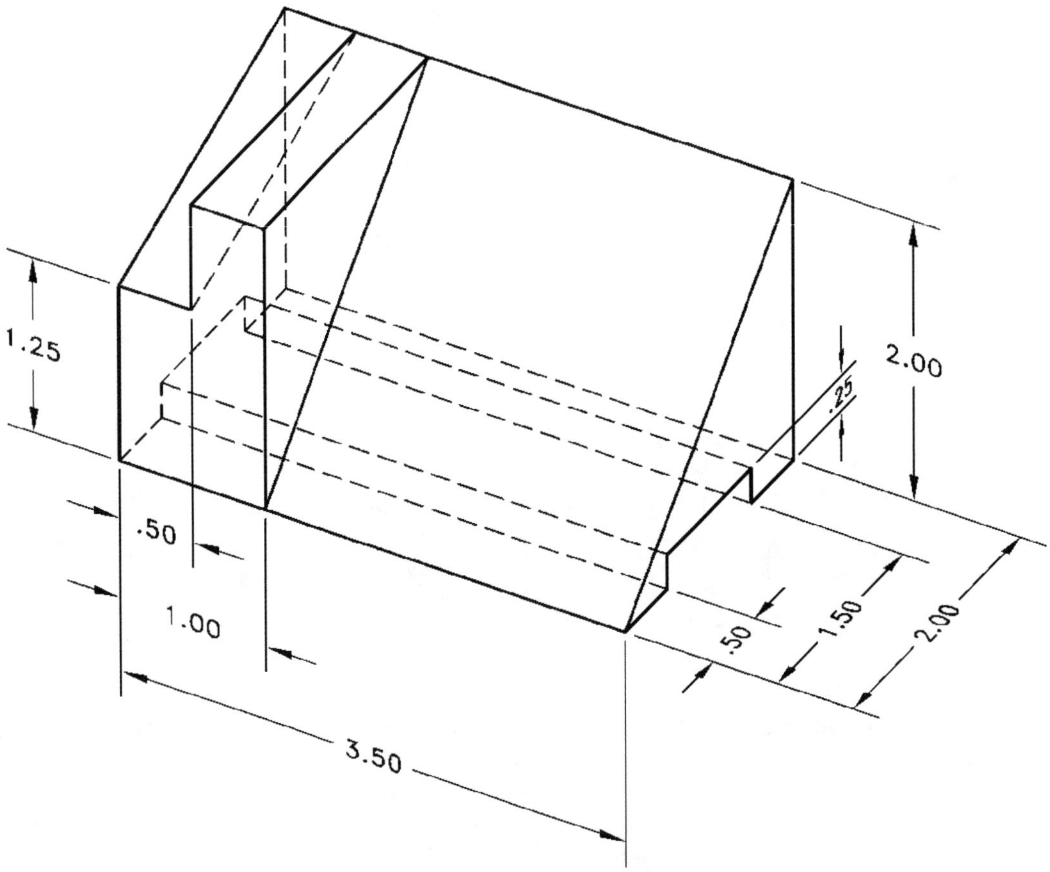

P4-33) Create an orthographic projection of the following object. Draw the three standard views.

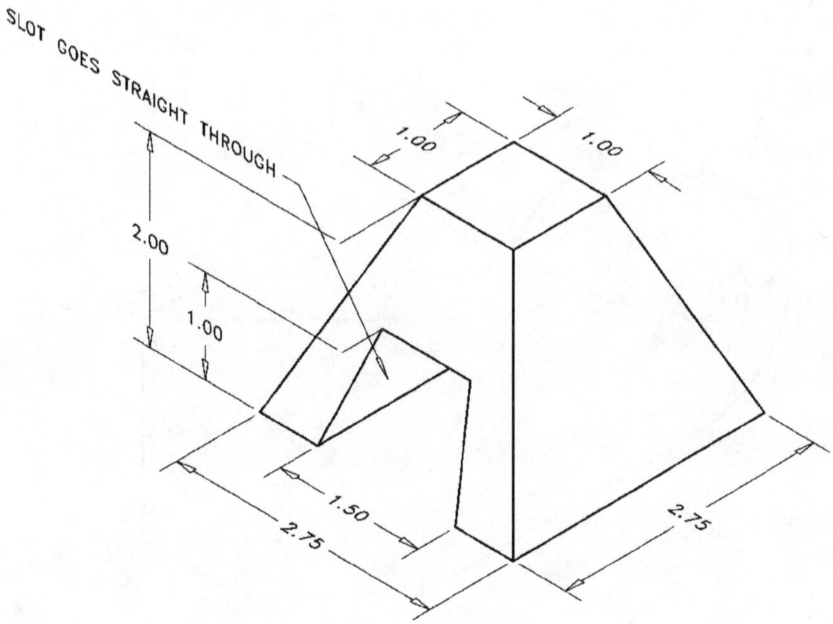

P4-34) Create an orthographic projection of the following object. Draw the three standard views.

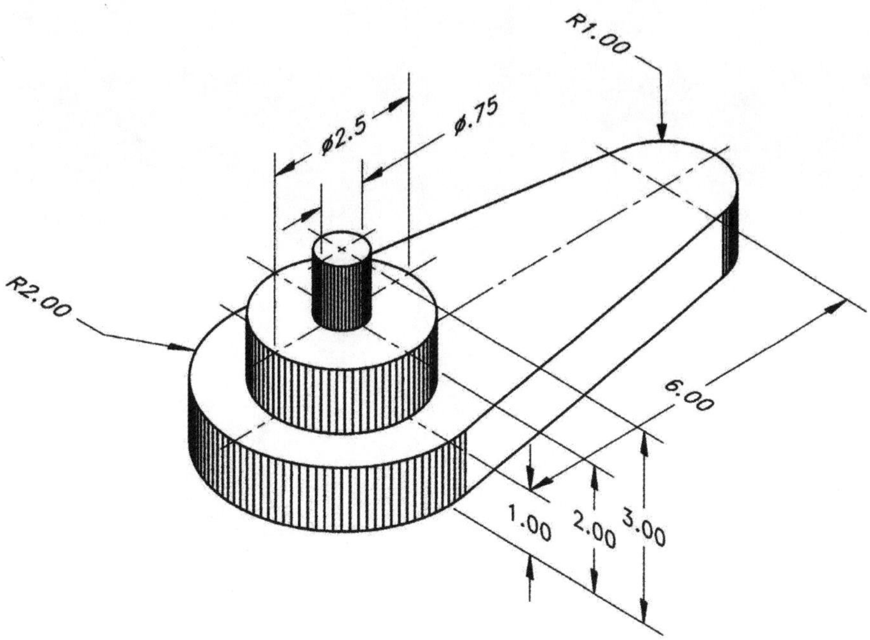

P4-35) Create an orthographic projection of the following object. Draw the three standard views.

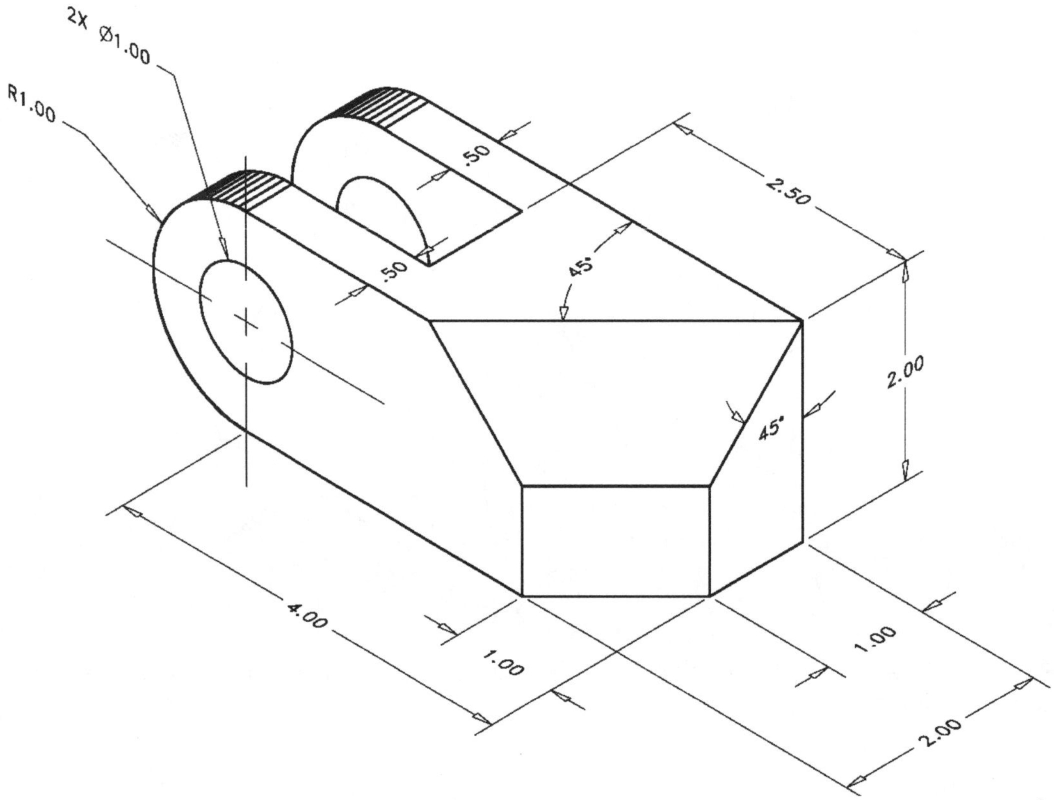

P4-36) Create an orthographic projection of the following object. Draw the three standard views.

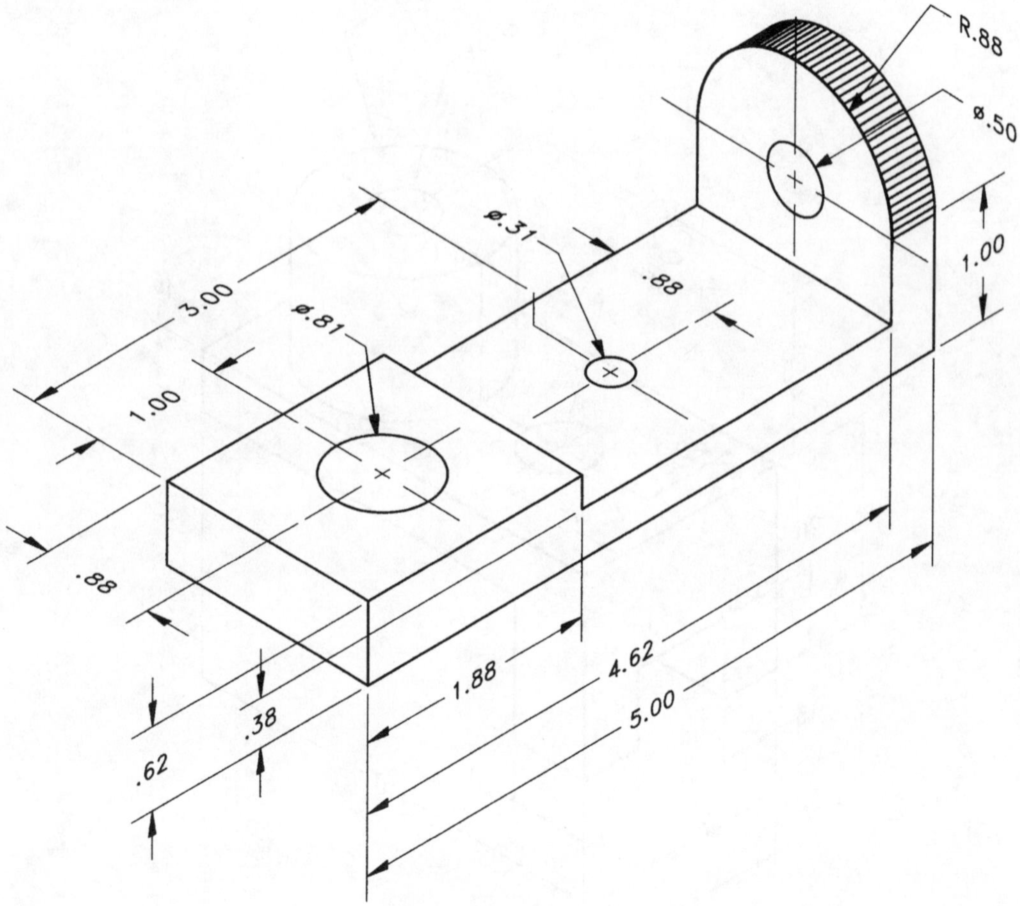

P4-37) Create an orthographic projection of the following object. Draw the three standard views.

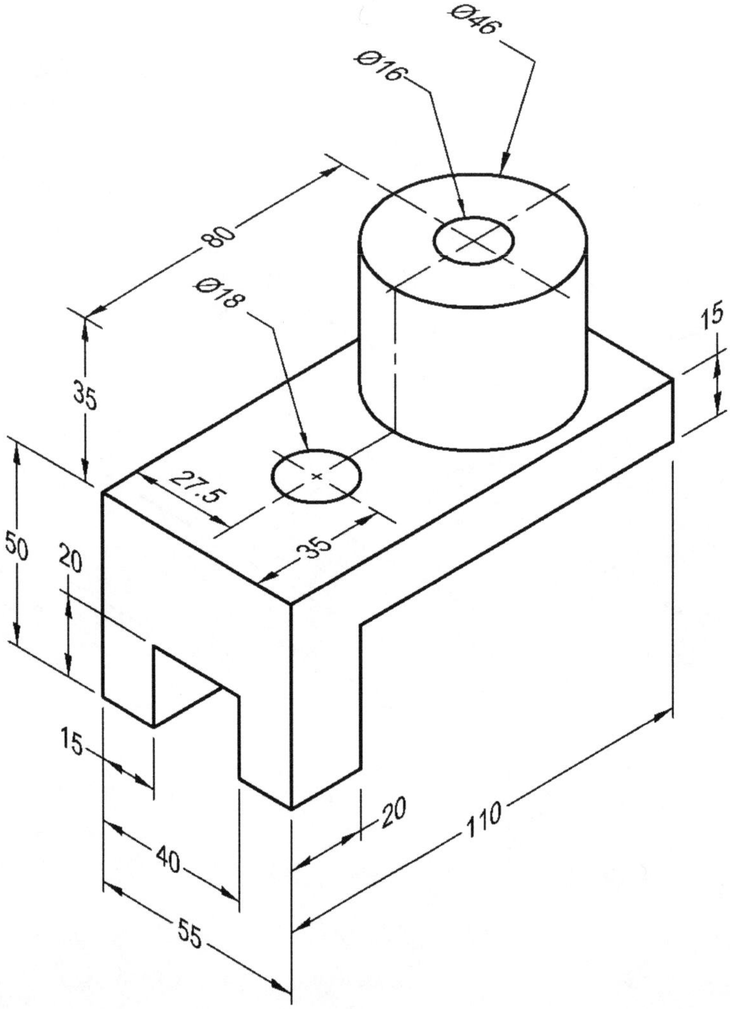

P4-38) Create an orthographic projection of the following object. Draw the three standard views.

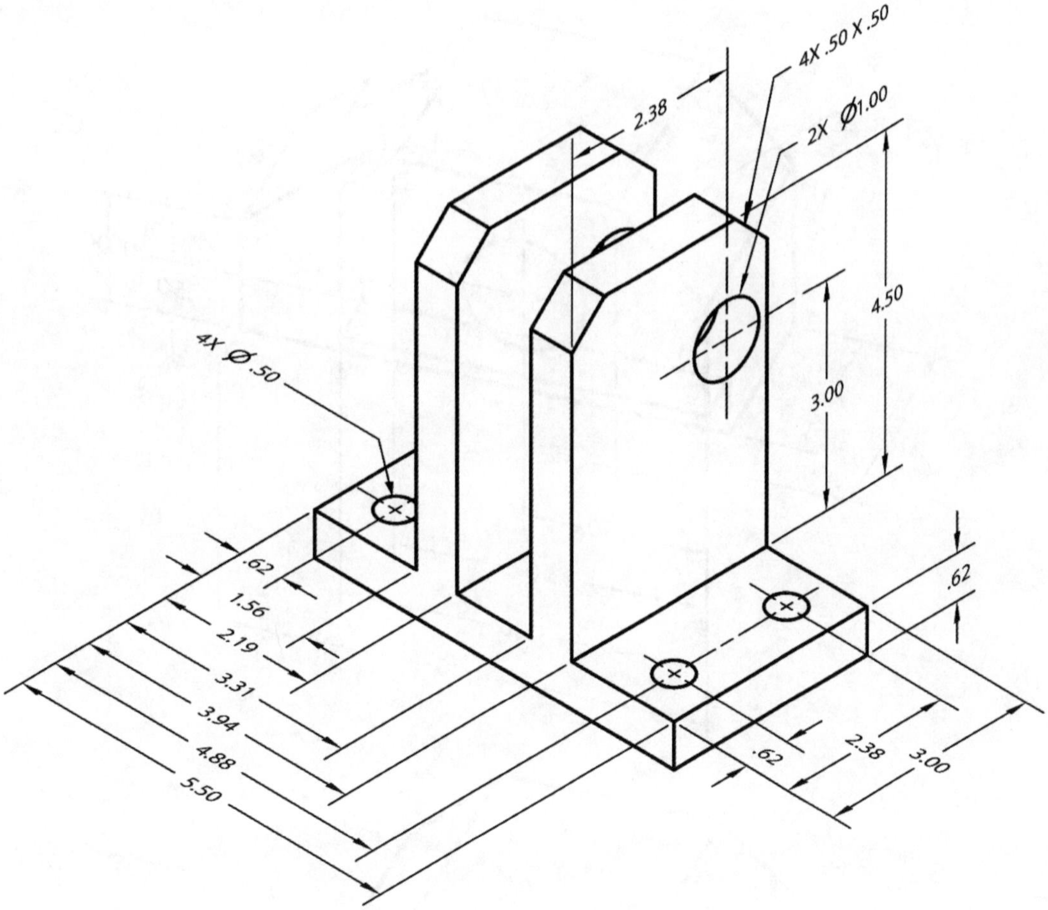

P4-39) Create an orthographic projection of the following object. Draw the three standard views.

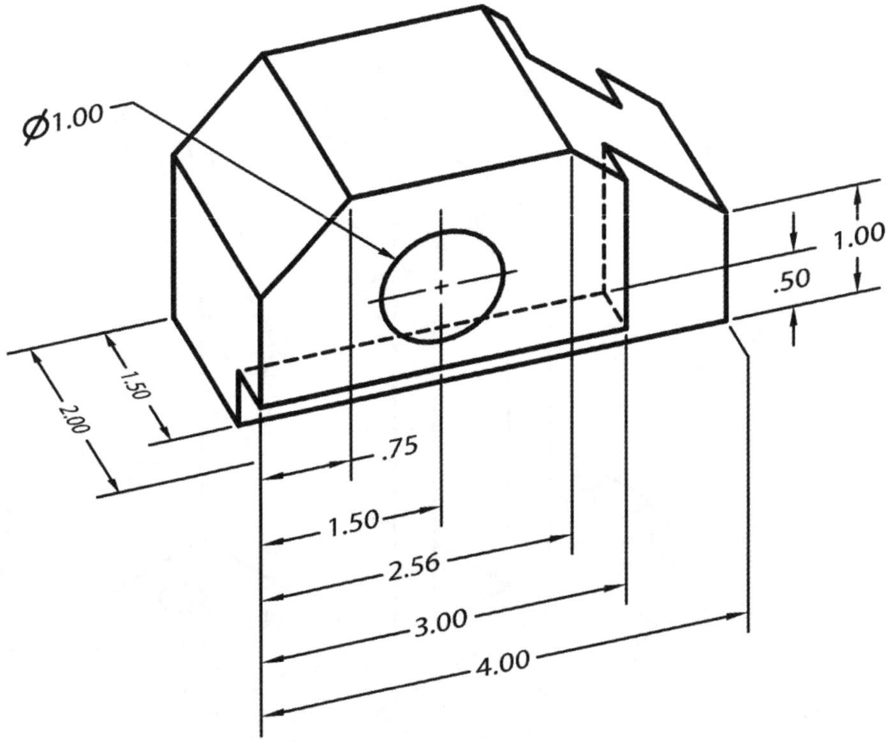

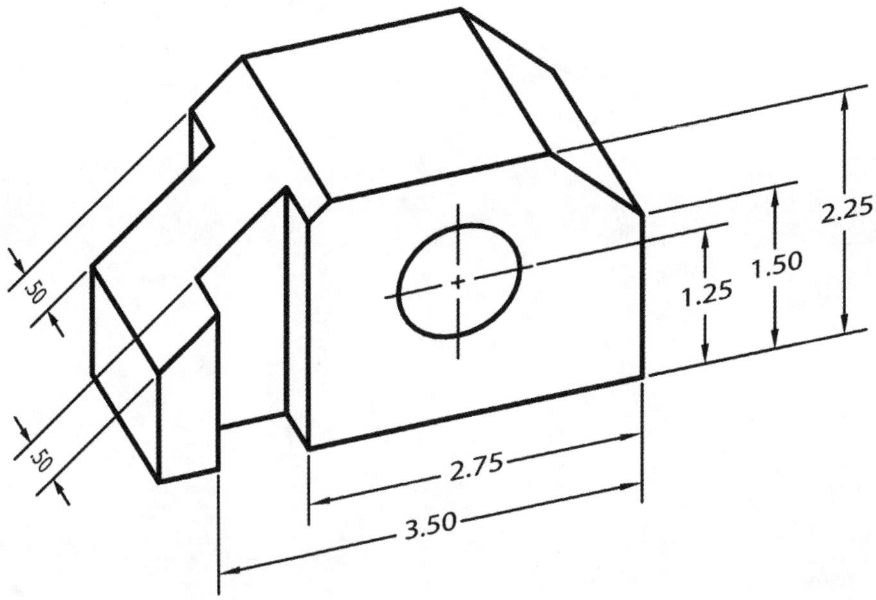

P4-40) Create an orthographic projection of the following object. Draw the three standard views.

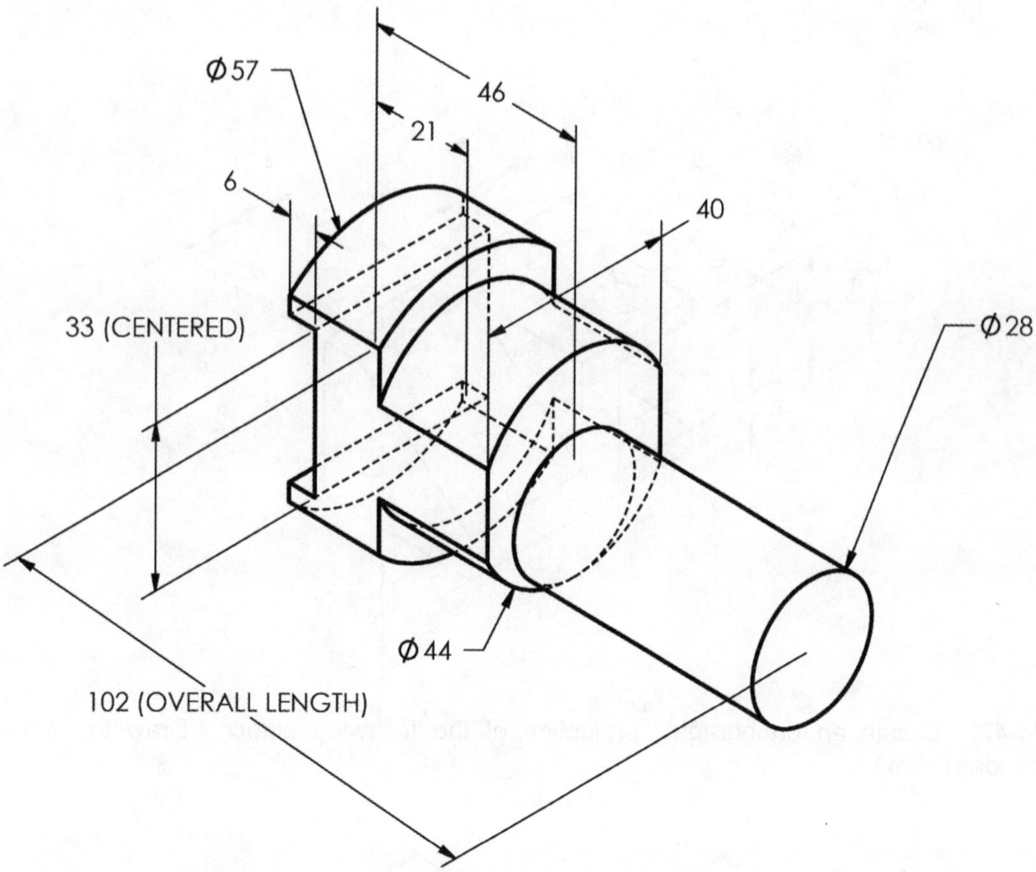

P4-41) Create an orthographic projection of the following object. Draw the three standard views.

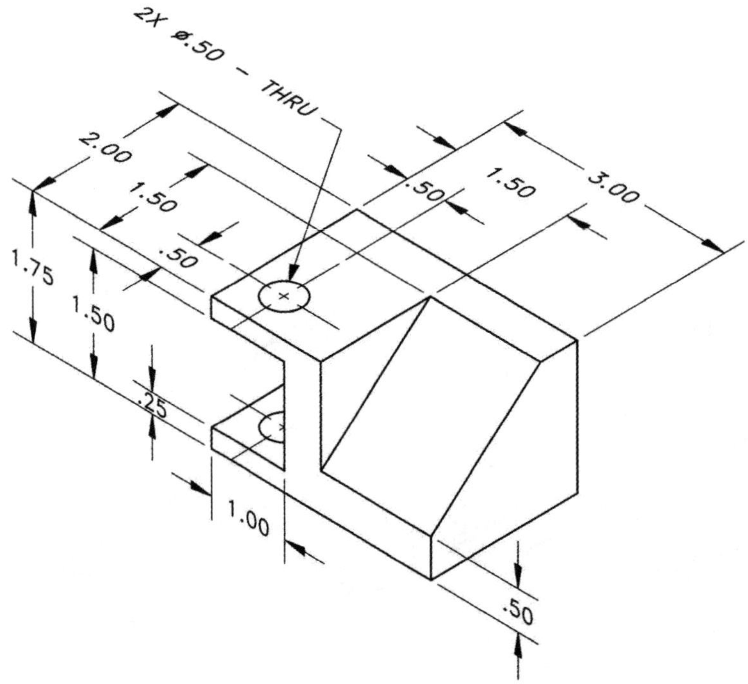

P4-42) Create an orthographic projection of the following object. Draw the three standard views.

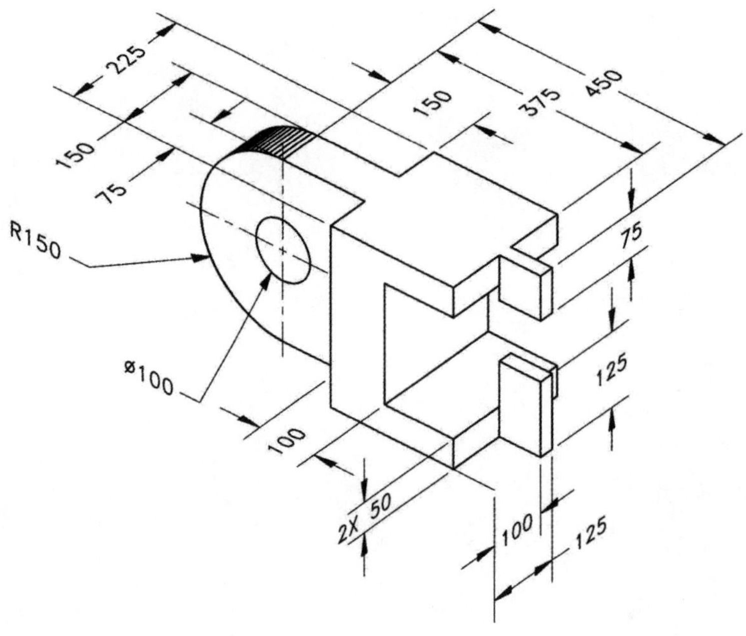

P4-43) Create an orthographic projection of the following object. Draw the three standard views.

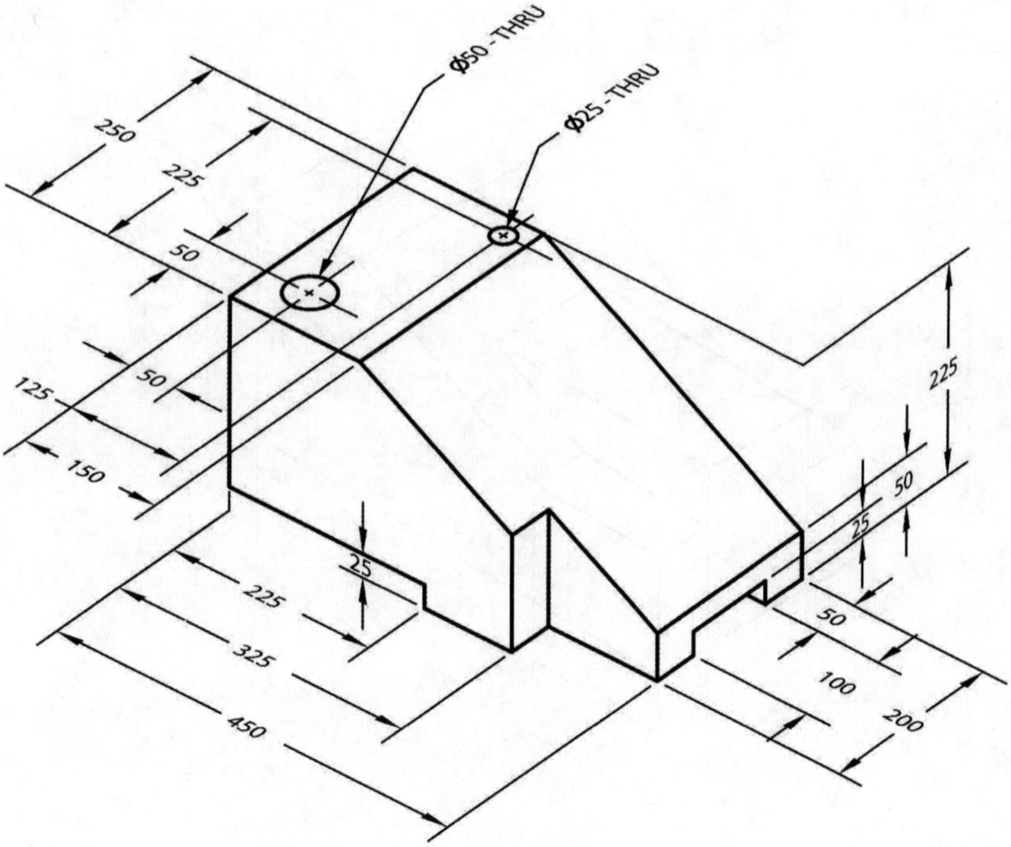

P4-44) Create an orthographic projection of the following object. Draw the three standard views.

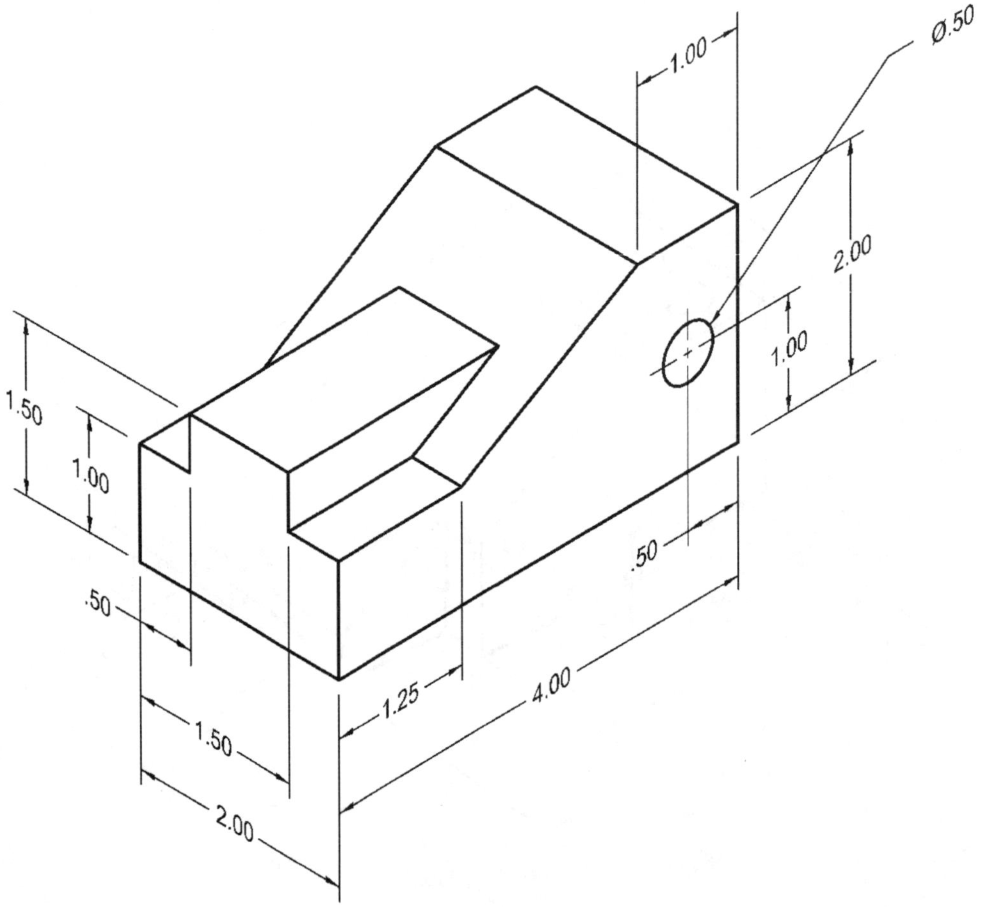

SP4-1) Sketch the front, top and right side views of the following object. Use the grid provided. The answer to this problem is given in the *Independent Learning Content*.

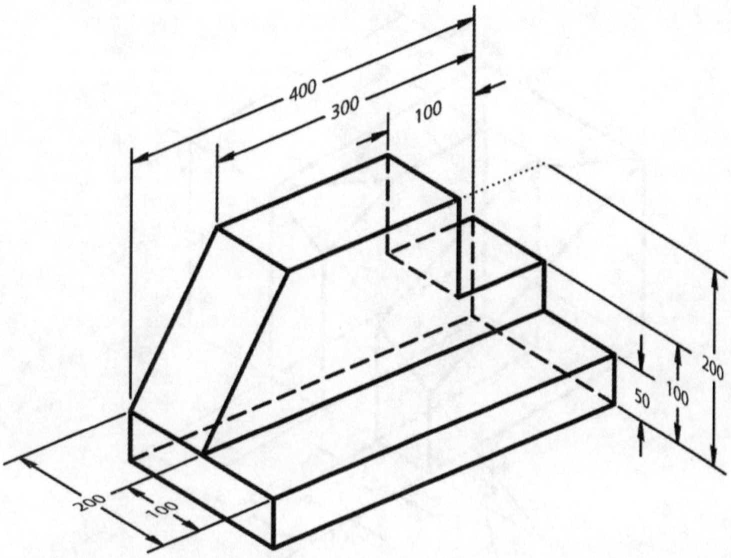

SP4-2) Sketch the front, top and right side views of the following object. Use the grid provided. The answer to this problem is given in the *Independent Learning Content*.

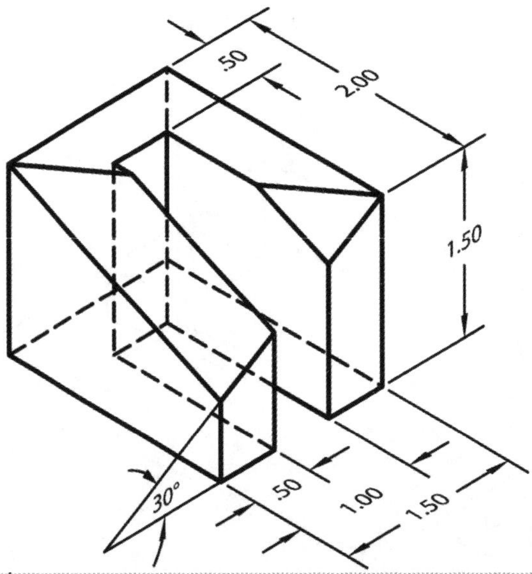

SP4-3) Sketch the front, top and right side views of the following object. Use the grid provided. The answer to this problem is given in the *Independent Learning Content*.

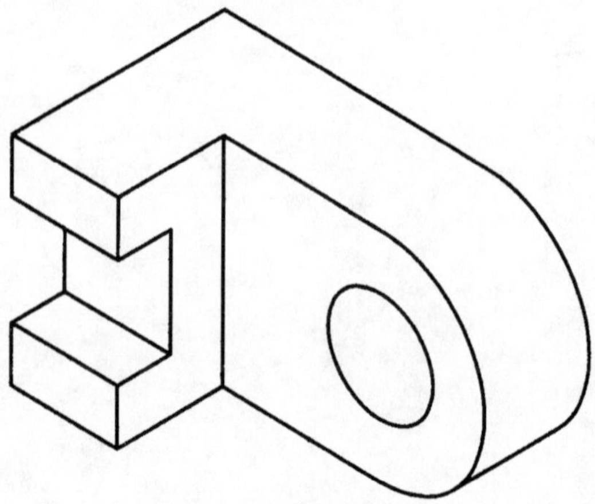

NOTES:

CHAPTER 5

CREATING ORTHOGRAPHIC PROJECTIONS IN AUTOCAD®

CHAPTER OUTLINE

CHAPTER SUMMARY

In this chapter you will learn how to draw an orthographic projection in AutoCAD®. Layers will be used which allow a drawing to contain different line types and to print using different line widths. You will draw a title block and border that can be repeatedly used. By the end of this chapter, you will be able to create a technically correct orthographic projection using proper line types and weights.

5.1) INTRODUCTION

An orthographic projection is a 2-D representation of a 3-D part. The line types and line weights used to create the orthographic projection give valuable information to the drawing or print reader. AutoCAD® enables you to draw orthographic projections using different line types and to print drawings using different line weights. This is accomplished by using layers.

5.2) LAYERS

Layers are like transparencies, one placed over the top of another. Each transparency/layer contains a different line type or a different part of the drawing. One layer may be used to create visible lines, while another layer may be used to create hidden lines. One layer may draw objects in red while another layer may draw objects in blue and so on. Assigning a different line type and color to each layer helps you control and organize the drawing. Before beginning to draw, many layers will be created, and their properties assigned. While drawing, the current or active layer (the layer you are drawing on) will be switched from one to another depending on what feature of the drawing you are working on.

Figure 5.2-1 shows an orthographic projection that uses different line types and line weights. The line type for each layer is set directly as a layer property. The line thickness is controlled by the color in which it is drawn. Figure 5.2-2 shows a possible layer organization scheme that could be used to create the orthographic projection shown in Figure 5.2-2.

Layers not only facilitate the use of line types and weights, but they can also help you visualize, create, and edit your work. For example, layers can be turned on or off. This is very useful when using a projection/construction line. Construction lines are helpful in the creation of an orthographic projection. However, they are not part of the final drawing. It would be tedious if you had to erase all the construction lines individually. A better way is to create a separate *Construction* layer and just turn it off (make it invisible) when they are no longer needed. Layers can also be locked. This means that you can see the layer, but you cannot select any of the objects on the layer. This is very useful when your drawing is very complex, and you need to isolate objects that are on a particular layer.

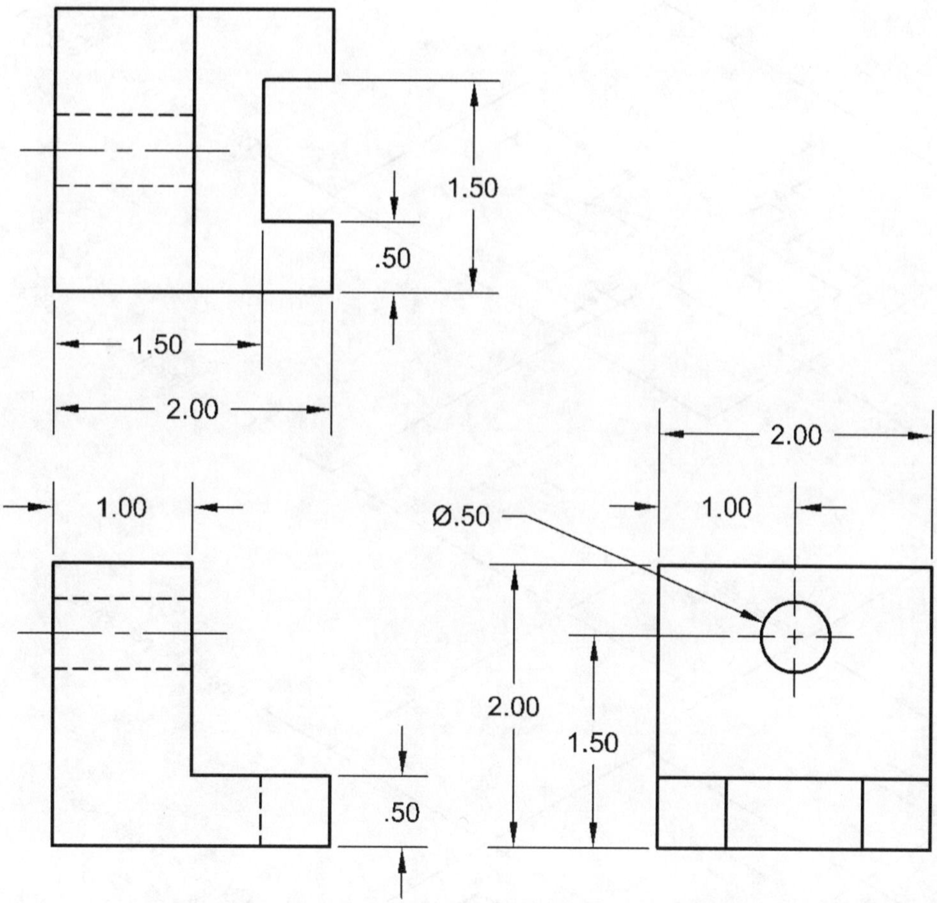

Figure 5.2-1: A typical orthographic projection

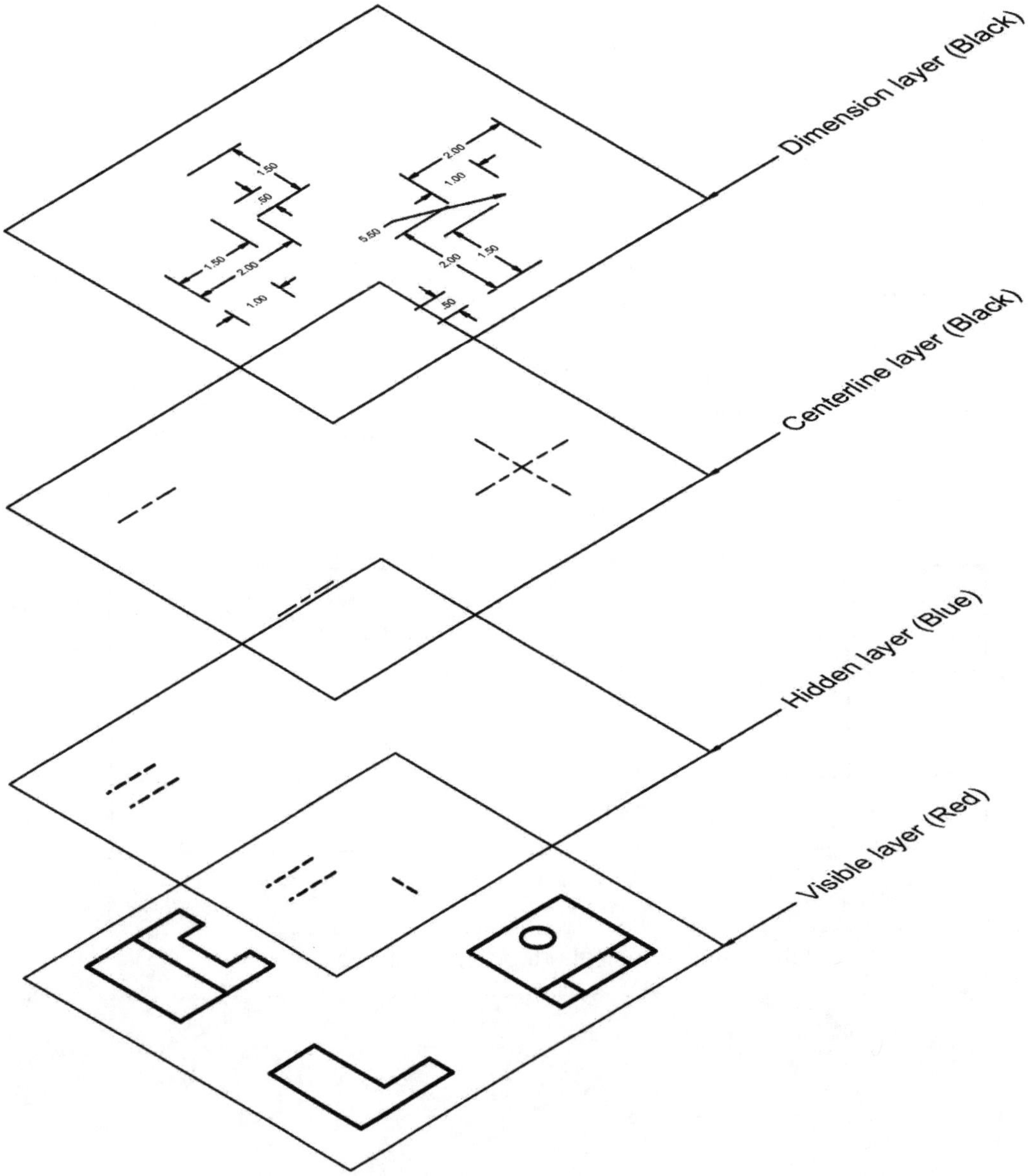

Figure 5.2-2: Layer organization of an orthographic projection

5.2.1) The *Layers* panel

The *Layers* panel is shown in Figures 5.2-3. The most frequently used commands/areas in the *Layers* panel are the *Layers Properties Manager* icon and the *Layers pull-down selection* menu. The *Layers Properties Manager* is used to create, name, assign line types and manage layers. The *Layers* menu allows you to quickly switch from one layer to the next and turn layers on and off.

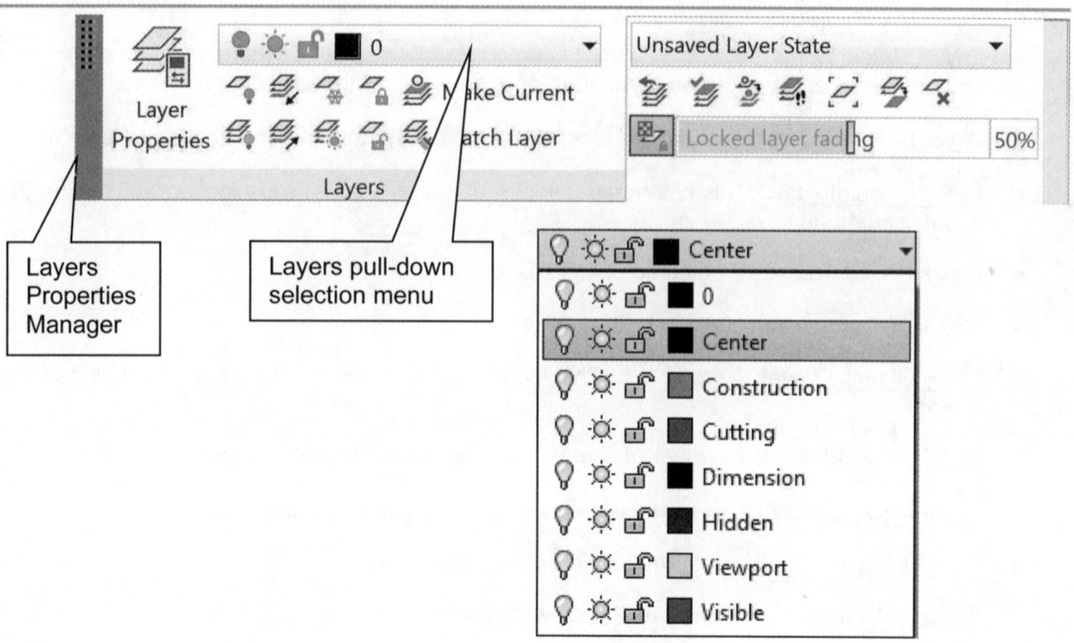

Figure 5.2-3: The *Layers* panel

The icons/features of the *Layers* panel are:

- Layers Properties Manager window:  This icon brings up a *Layers Properties Manager* window. This window is the place where layers are created, and the layer properties are assigned.
- Layer pull-down selection window: This pull-down window shows all of the available layers, allows you to switch between layers and enables you to change an object from one layer to another. To the left of each layer name is a set of quick access layer status settings that may be turned on or off. To turn these settings on and off, just click on them. Reading from left to right these settings are:
    - On/Off:  The ON\OFF status of a layer is indicated by the light bulb. If it is yellow, the layer is ON and the objects on this layer can be seen. If it is gray, the layer is OFF and the objects on this layer cannot be seen.
    - Freeze/Thaw: 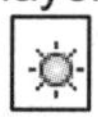 The FREEZE/THAW status of a layer is indicated by two suns. The big yellow sun freezes/thaws all viewports and the small sun freezes/thaws only the current

viewport. If a layer is FROZEN, the sun will turn into a snowflake. Objects on a frozen layer are not displayed, regenerated, or plotted. Freezing layers shortens regenerating time.

- Lock/Unlock: The LOCK/UNLOCK status of a layer is indicated by the pad lock. If the lock is open, the layer is UNLOCKED. The objects on this layer can be seen and selected. If the lock is closed, the layer is LOCKED. The objects on this layer can be seen but not selected.

- Layer States menu: Unsaved Layer State This is where you can save the current settings for layers in a named layer state and then restore those settings later.
- Layer Isolate: This command locks all layers except the one you choose to isolate.
- Layer Unisolate: This command unlocks all the layers that were locked while using the *Layer Isolate* command.
- Freeze: Freezes a selected object's layer.
- Off: Turns a selected object's layer off.
- Make Object's Layer Current: This icon sets the layer of a selected object to be the current one.
- Match: Matches the layer of a selected object to a destination layer.
- Layer Previous: This icon switches you back to your previous layer.
- Turn All Layers On: Turns all the drawing layers on.
- Thaw All Layers: Thaws all the drawing layers.
- Lock: Locks a selected object's layer.
- Unlock: Unlocks a selected object's layer.
- Change to Current Layer: Changes the layer of a selected object to the current one.
- Copy Objects to New Layer: Creates duplicates of the selected objects on a specified layer.
- Layer Walks: Allows you to see all the objects on an individual layer while hiding the objects on the other layers.
- Isolate to Current Viewport: Freezes select layers in all viewports except the current viewport.
- Merge: Merges selected layers into a target layer.
- Delete: Deletes all objects on a selected layer and then purges the layer.
- Locked Layer Fading: Locked layer fading 50% The locked layer fading may be set using this slider bar.

5.2.2) Layer properties

The *Layer Properties Manager* window is the place where you can create layers and set their properties. This window may be accessed using the command **LAYER** or by clicking on the *Layer Properties Manager* 

icon in the *Layers* panel. Figure 5.2-4 shows the *Layer Properties Manager* window with the important features identified. Most of the features are self-explanatory except for the layer filter. The *New Property Filter* window is a place where you may create filters based on one or more layer properties. Right clicking on any layer name(s) accesses a shortcut menu with several useful commands as shown in Figure 5.2-5.

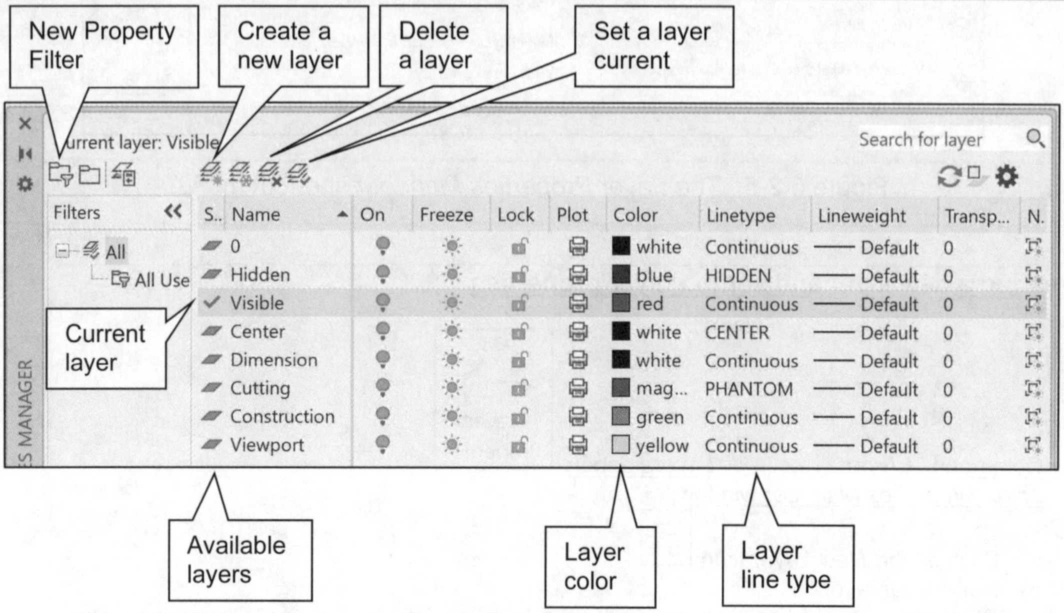

Figure 5.2-4: The *Layer Properties Manager* window

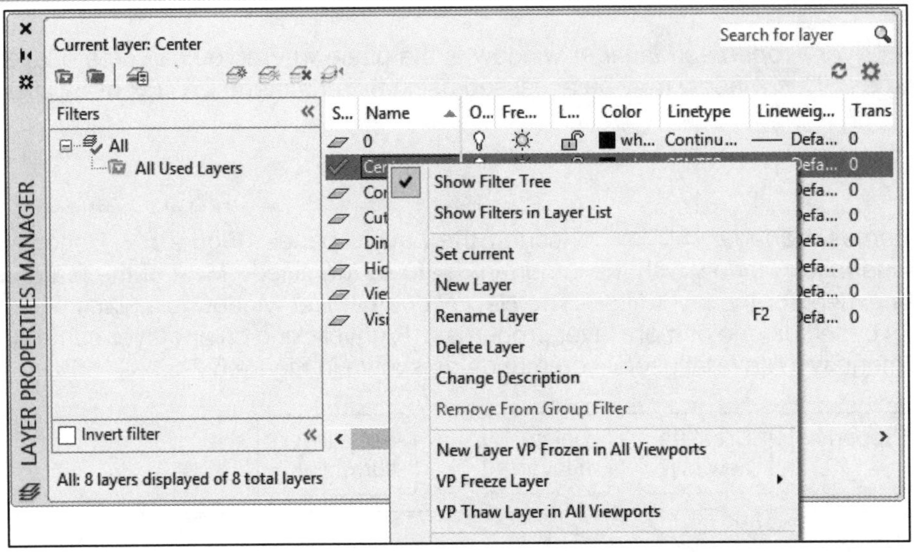

Figure 5.2-5: The *Layer Properties Manager* shortcut menu

Creating a new layer and setting layer properties

1) Command: **LAyer** or *Layers* panel:
2) *Layer Properties Manager* window:

   a) Click on the *New Layer* icon 
   b) Name your layer.
   c) Click on the square colored box under the heading *Color*. A *Select Color* window will appear.

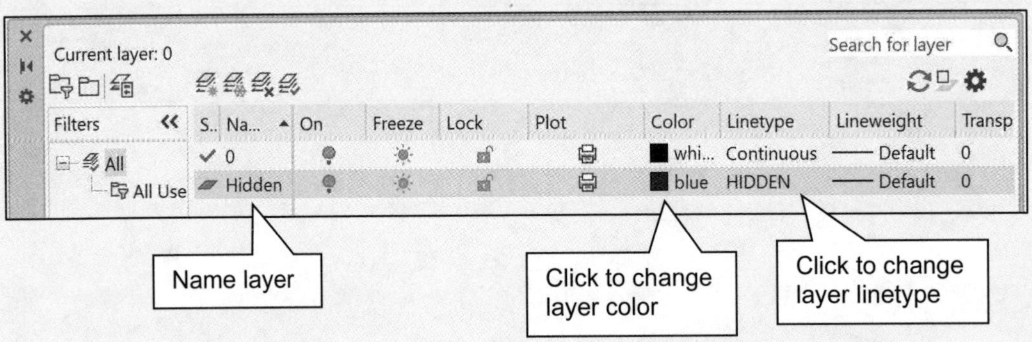

3) *Select Color* window – *Index Color* tab:
   a) Select a color for your layer. It is best to select a standard color. Note: The color *White* and *Black* are the same.
   b) ***OK***

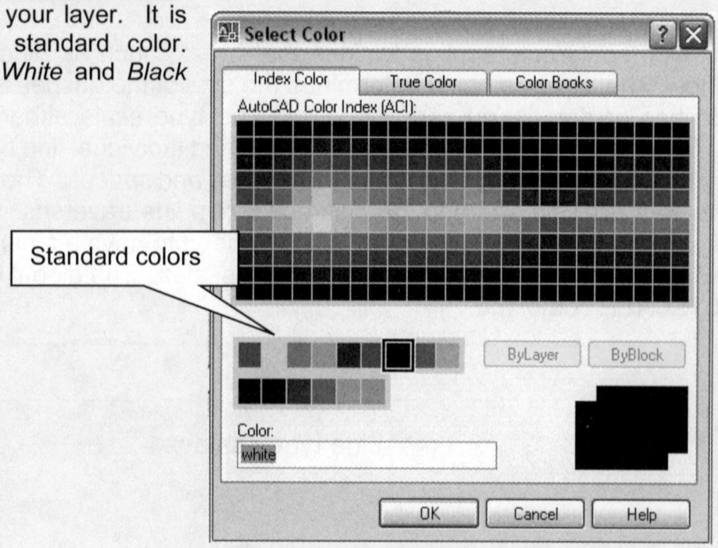

4) *Layer Properties Manager* window: Click on the name of the line type under the heading *Linetype*. A *Select Linetype* window will appear.

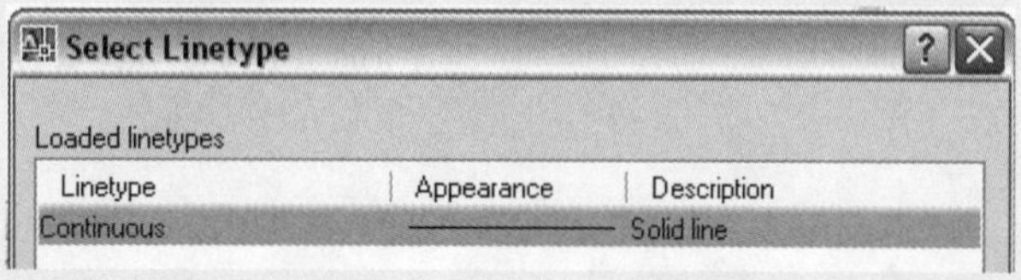

5) *Select Linetype* window: If the line type that you wish to use is not *Continuous*, click on ***Load...*** to select a different line type. A *Load or Reload Linetypes* window will appear.

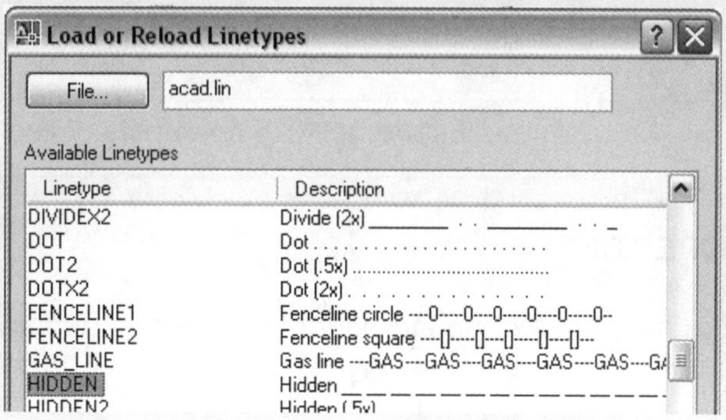

6) *Load or Reload Linetypes* window:
   a) Scroll down until you find the desired line type and select it.
   b) ***OK***

7) *Select Linetype* window:
   a) Select the line type that you wish to assign to the layer.
   b) ***OK***.

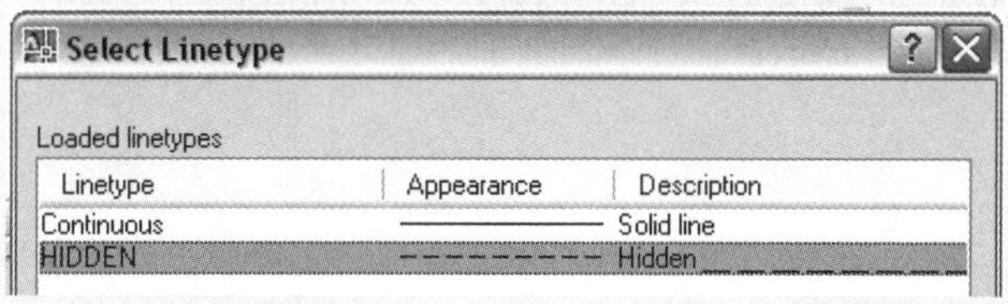

8) *Layer Properties Manager* window: Close the window.

5.3) LINE TYPE SCALE

Line type scale only applies to lines that break, such as hidden lines, centerlines and phantom lines. The line type scale determines the size of the dashes and the size of the spaces between dashes or dots. You can control the line type scale either globally (for all lines) or individually for each object. By default, both global and individual line type scales are set to 1.00. The smaller the line type scale, the smaller the dashes and spaces. The line type scale is adjusted according to your drawing size and the distance that a line traverses. A short line segment that does not break and is displayed as continuous will need to have a smaller line type scale. Figure 5.3-1 shows a centerline at three different line type scales. The global line type scale may be set using the **LTSCALE** command.

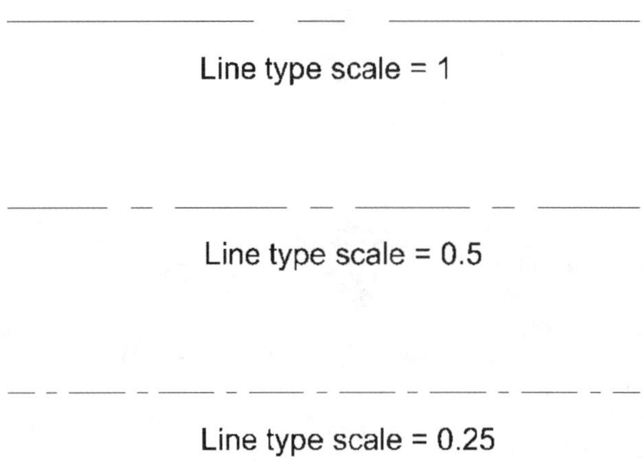

Figure 5.3-1: The effects of line type scale

5.4) PROPERTIES

The properties of an individual object may be changed by selecting the object and then selecting the *Properties* icon 

in the *View* tab - *Palettes* panel. Figure 5.4-1 shows the *Properties* window of a circle. Several properties such as object layer, line type scale, and radius or diameter may be changed. Different objects will have different options available in the *Properties* window. Properties may also be changed using the **CHPROP** command.

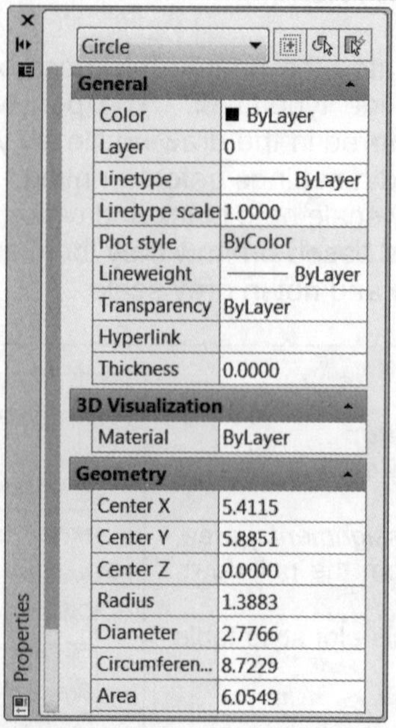

Figure 5.4-1: Properties window for a circle

5.4.1) The *Properties* panel

The *Properties* panel (Figure 5.4-2) is located in the *Home* tab. It allows you to change the color, line type and line weight of a selected object. It is my suggestion that these properties always remain on ByLayer (the default properties of the object's layer). If you need to change one of these properties, your first action should be to move the object to a layer that has those properties. This creates a much more organized drawing. Changing the ByLayer settings in the properties toolbar should be reserved for occasional use only. Two useful commands found in the *Properties* panel are *Match Properties* and *List*. The ***LIST*** command lists the property data for a selected object.

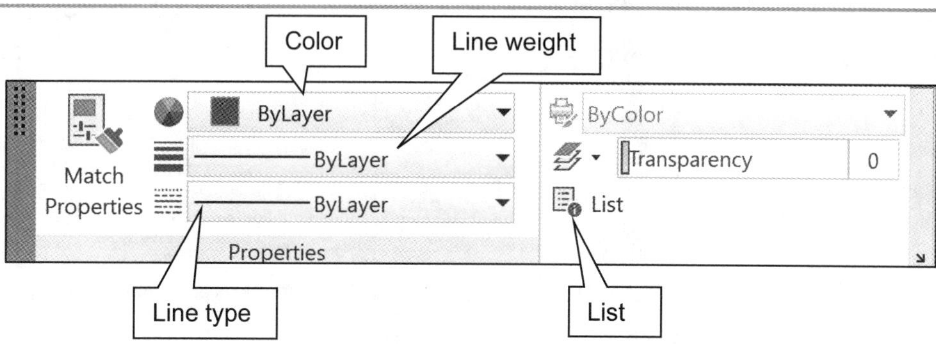

Figure 5.4-2: The *Properties* panel

5.5) PRINTING USING PEN WIDTHS

The color of an object dictates the printed thickness of that object. This is why we will specify a different color to each line type/layer. The pen widths are stored in files that are computer specific. They are not stored in the drawing file. If you are using a public computer, it is a good idea to check the pen width settings before printing.

You may print in color, grey scale or in black and white. If you are printing to an inkjet and in color, you need to choose colors based on how they look. If you are printing to a laser printer it is best to print in black and white and not in grey scale.

Setting pen widths

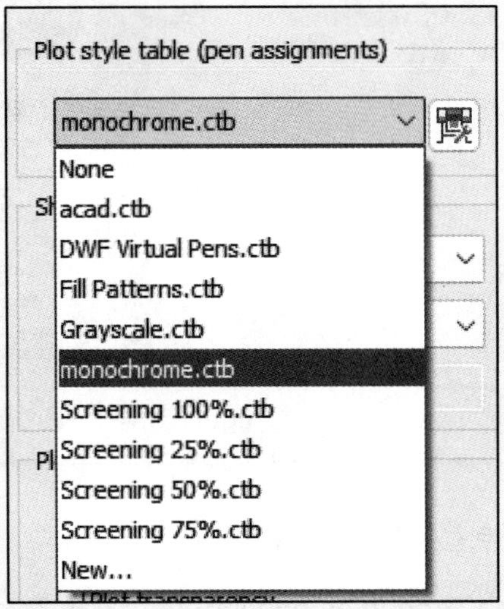

1) _Menu browser:_ ***Print – Page Setup...***
2) _Page Setup Manager window:_ ***Modify...***
3) _Page Setup – Model window:_
   a) In the *Plot style table (pen assignments)* area, select ***monochrome.ctb*** from the pull-down menu.
   b) _Question window_ (Assign this plot style table to all layouts?): ***Yes***
   c) Select the ***Edit...*** icon next to the pull-down menu.
4) _Plot Style Table Editor – monochrome.ctb window:_
   a) _Plot styles field:_ Select a color
   b) _Lineweight field:_ Select the appropriate line weight using the pull-down menu.
   c) Repeat for all colors that you are using. Note that the print color in the *Properties* area is always *Black* no matter what the *Plot styles* color is.
   d) ***Save & Close***
5) _Page Setup – Model window:_ ***OK***
6) _Page Setup Manager window:_ ***Close***

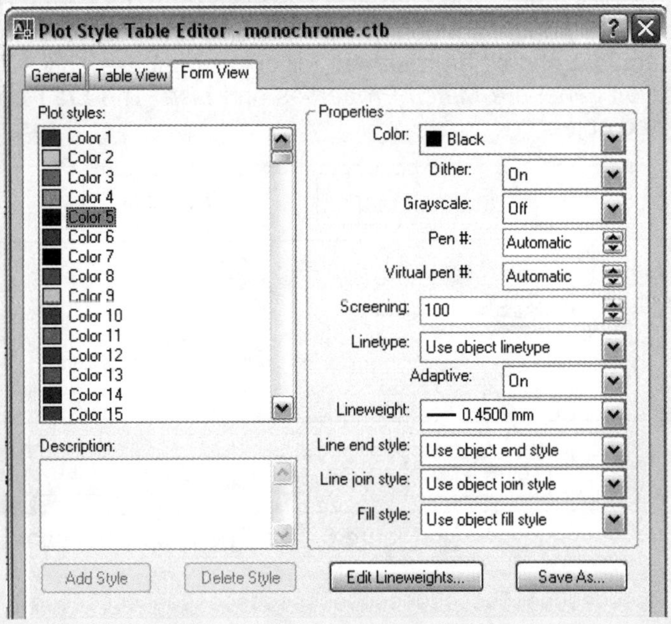

5.6) CREATING LAYERS TUTORIAL

The objective of this tutorial is to create a set of standard layers that will be used to create orthographic projections. These layers will be saved to a template file so that they can be used repeatedly.

5.6.1) Setting drawing parameters

1) View the *Layers & Penwidths* video and read sections 5.1) through 5.5).

2) Open your ***set-inch.dwt***. Your *set-inch* template file should have the following settings. If it does not, change them at this point.
   - **UNITS**
     a. Units = inches
     b. Precision = 0.00
   - **LIMITS** = 11,8.5
   - **STyle**
     a. Text font = Arial
     b. Text height = 0.12
     c. Make sure the ***Annotative*** toggle is checked.

3) Set the global line type scale to 0.5.
   a) Command: **ltscale**
   b) `Enter new linetype scale factor <1.0000>:` **0.5**

5.6.2) Creating layers

1) Command: **la** or *Layers panel:*

2) *Layer Properties Manager* window:
   a) Click on the *New Layer* icon 
   b) Name your layer **Hidden**.
   c) Click on the square colored box under the heading *Color* that is associated with the *Hidden* layer. A *Select Color* window will appear.

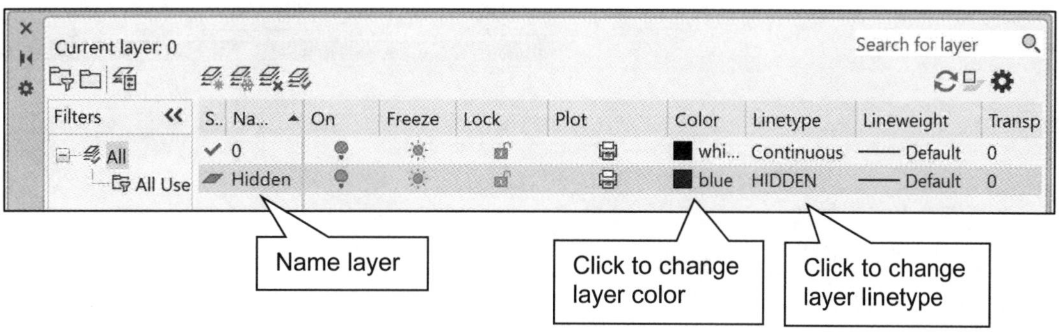

3) <u>*Select Color* window – *Index Color* tab:</u>
   a) Select the color ***Blue*** from the standard colors bar.
   b) ***OK***

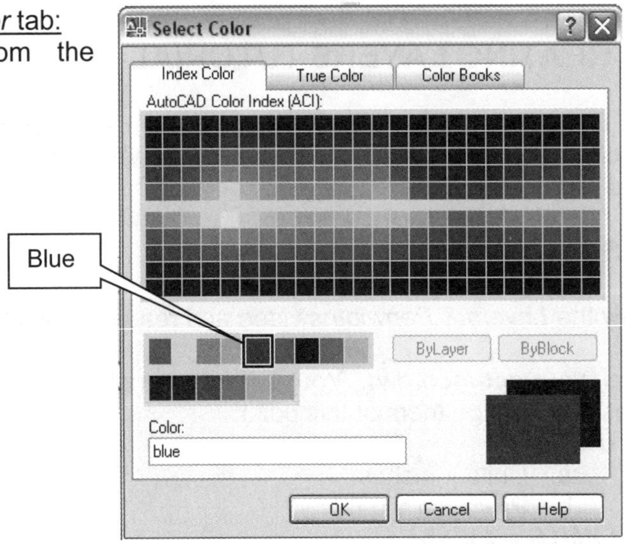

4) <u>*Layer Properties Manager* window:</u> Click on the name of the line type under the heading *Linetype* that is associated with the *Hidden* layer. A *Select Linetype* window will appear.

5) <u>*Select Linetype* window:</u> Click on ***Load…***. A *Load or Reload Linetypes* window will appear.

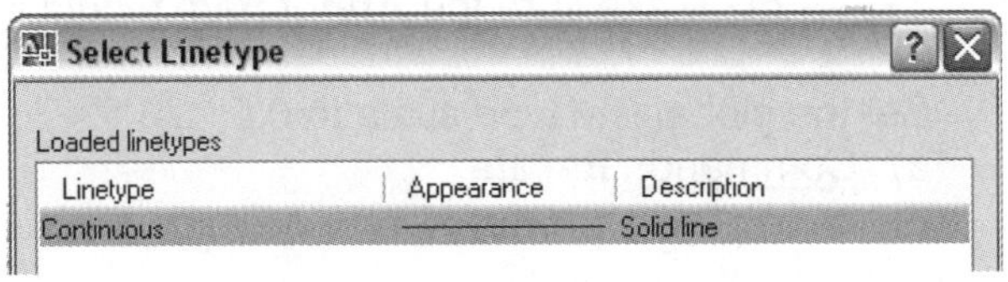

6) <u>*Load or Reload Linetypes* window:</u>
   a) Scroll down until you find the ***HIDDEN*** line type and select it.
   b) ***OK***

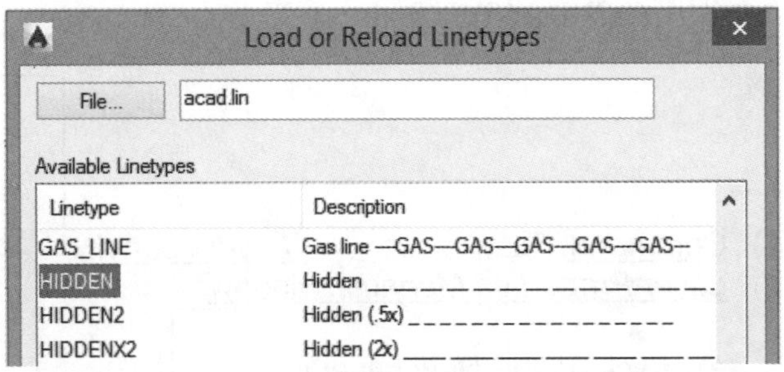

7) <u>*Select Linetype* window:</u>
   a) Select the ***HIDDEN*** line type.
   b) ***OK***.

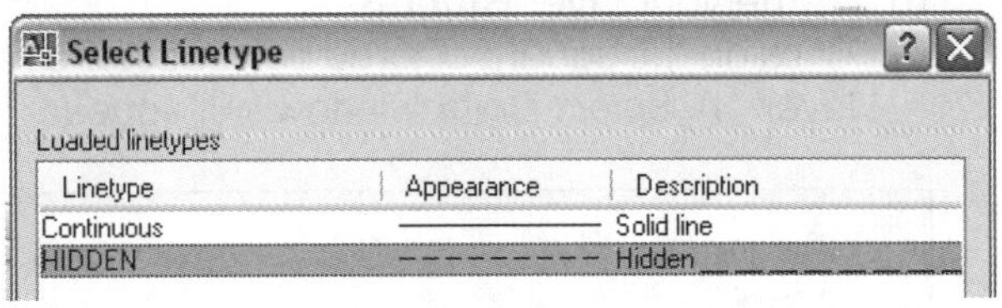

8) In a similar fashion, create the following layers.
- **Visible**, color = ***red***, linetype = ***Continuous***
- **Center**, color = ***white***/black, linetype = ***CENTER***
- **Dimension**, color = ***white***/black, linetype = ***Continuous***
- **Cutting**, color = ***magenta***, linetype = ***PHANTOM***
- **Construction**, color = ***green***, linetype = ***Continuous***
- **Viewport**, color = ***yellow***, linetype = ***Continuous***

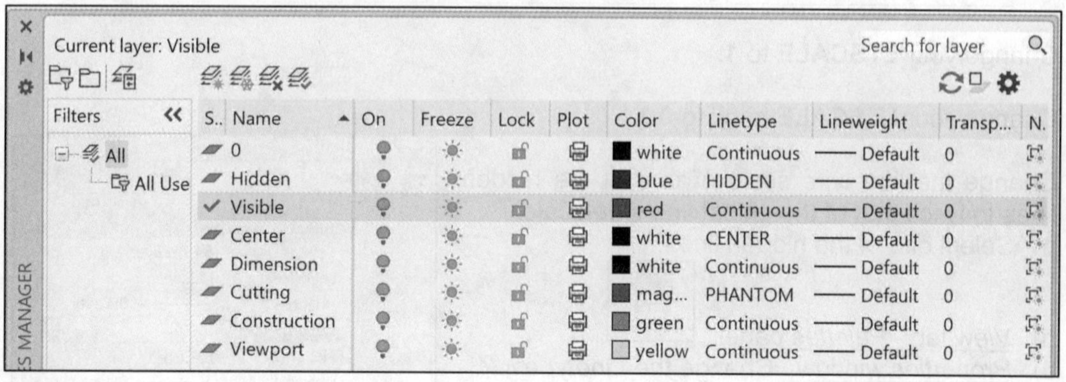

9) 

set-inch.dwt.

5.6.3) Drawing on different layers

1) 

Layers Tut.dwg.

2) Draw a line on each layer to see if the layer properties were set correctly.
   a) Set the ***Visible*** layer to be current.
      i. Layers panel: Expand the *Layer pull-down* menu and select ***Visible***.
   b) Draw a **Line**. It should be red.
   c) Set the ***Hidden*** layer to be current and draw 2 **Lines**. They should be blue and dashed.
   d) Repeat for all the other layers.

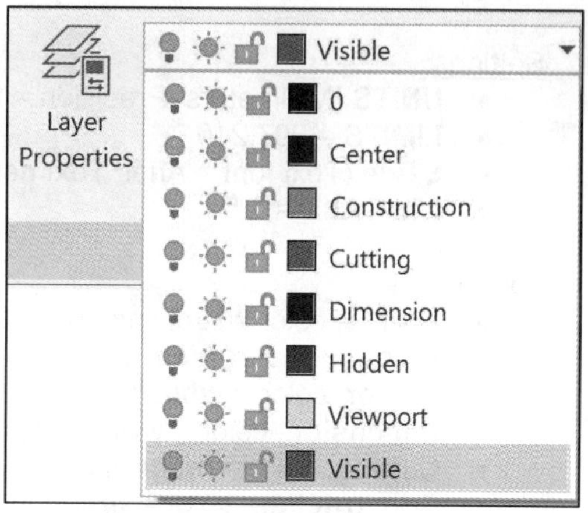

5.6.4) Line type scale

1) Change the global line type scale (**LTSCALE**) to **0.25**. Notice that the dashes and spaces between the dashes become smaller.

> **How?**
> a) Command: **ltscale**
> b) `Enter new linetype scale factor <0.5000>:` **0.25**

2) Change your **LTSCALE** to **1**.

3) Change your **LTSCALE** back to **0.5**.

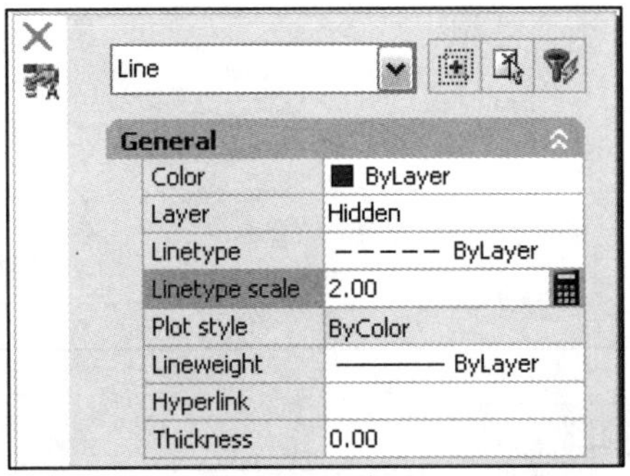

4) Change the line type scale of one of the hidden lines to twice that of the global line type scale.
   a) Select one of the hidden lines.
   b) *View* tab - *Palettes* panel: 

   c) *Properties* window: Change the *Linetype scale* to **2**.

5) ***Save*** and ***print*** your drawing.

Exercise 5.6-1: Creating layers

Open your ***set-mm.dwt***, make sure that it has the following settings and create the layers indicated. Then, resave your template file.

Settings:
- **UNITS** (Millimeters, Precision = 0)
- **LIMITS** = 297,210
- **STyle** (Text font = Arial, Text height = 3, Annotative)
- **LTSCALE** = 0.5

Layers:
- **Visible**, color = ***red***, linetype = ***Continuous***
- **Hidden,** color = ***blue***, linetype = ***HIDDEN***
- **Center**, color = ***white***/black, linetype = ***CENTER***
- **Dimension**, color = ***white***/black, linetype = ***Continuous***
- **Cutting**, color = ***magenta***, linetype = ***PHANTOM***
- **Construction**, color = ***green***, linetype = ***Continuous***
- **Viewport**, color = ***yellow***, linetype = ***Continuous***

5.7) BLOCKING

Blocks are a grouping of objects that can be used repeatedly. The command **BLOCK** allows you to define a particular drawing as an entity. It groups all the lines, circles, and other geometric shapes into one entity. This means that you can insert this group into a drawing without having to redraw it. The commands that are relevant for creating and using blocks are grouped in the *Block* panel shown in Figure 5.7-1.

Figure 5.7-1: *Block* panel

The commands contained in the *Block* panel and the other commands related to blocking are:

- **INSERT:** 

The INSERT command allows you to retrieve an existing block or wblock.
- **BLOCK:** 

The BLOCK command allows you to create a grouping of objects that can be used repeatedly in the current drawing. Blocks are inserted as entities, which means that they can't be edited by erasing parts of them or breaking lines within them unless you use the BEDIT command or EXPLODE the block first.
- **BEDIT:** 

The block edit command allows you to select and edit an existing block. The block edit command temporarily adds a *Block Editor* tab to the ribbon as shown in Figure 5.7-2.

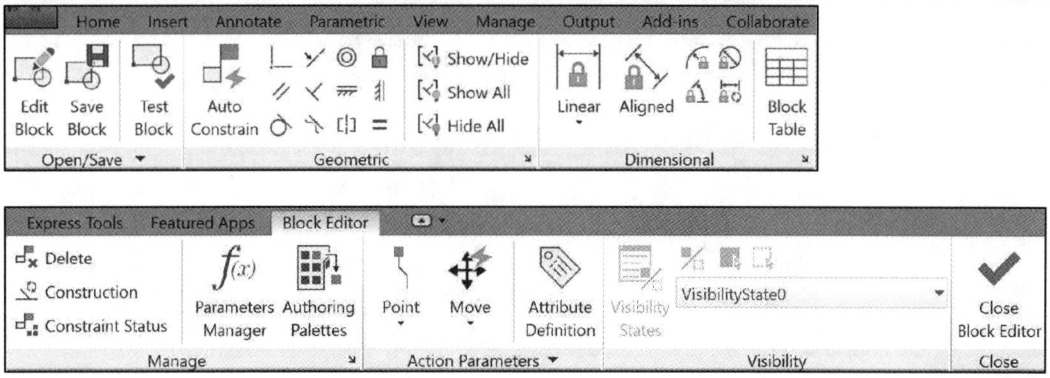

Figure 5.7-2: *Block Editor* tab

- **<u>WBLOCK:</u>** This command writes a block to a file. This allows you to use the block in all drawings not just the current one.

- **<u>EXPLODE:</u>**  Allows you to separate a block into its individual parts. The EXPLODE command may be accessed in the *Modify* panel.

- **<u>BASE</u>** <u>(Set Base point):</u>  Set the insertion base point for the current drawing. The base point is the reference point used when creating and inserting your block. This point should not be arbitrary. It should have some relationship with the block and with the object or space in which it will be inserted.

<u>Creating blocks</u>

1) <u>Command:</u> **block** or <u>*Block* panel:</u> 

2) <u>*Block Definition* window:</u>
   a) Name the block.
   b) <u>*Base point* area:</u> Pick a base point/insertion point. This can be accomplished by directly entering a coordinate or by selecting the ***Pick point*** icon.
   c) <u>*Objects* area:</u>
      i. Select all objects that you wish to include in the block definition using the ***Select objects*** icon. (The objects may also be selected before entering the BLOCK command.)
      ii. Activate either the *Retain* (keeps the original object as is), *Convert to block* (converts the original object to a block) or *Delete* (deletes the original object) radio button.
   d) <u>*Behavior* area:</u> Activate ***Allow exploding*** and ***Annotative*** checkboxes.
   e) If necessary, set the *Block units.*
   f) ***OK***

Note: A block is defined within the current drawing and cannot be used in other drawings unless a WBLOCK is created.

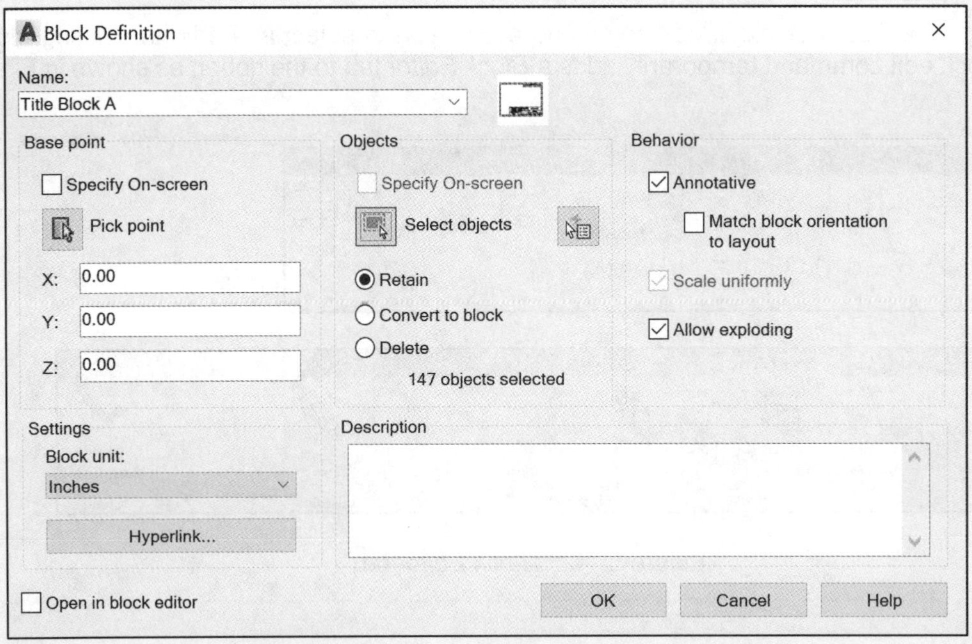

Creating a wblock

1) Command: **wblock**
2) *Write Block* window:
   a) Select the ***Block*** radio button.
   b) Select the block you wish to write to a file in the pull-down menu.
   c) Select a location for the file by clicking on the file path icon.
   d) Select the *Insert units*.
   e) ***OK***

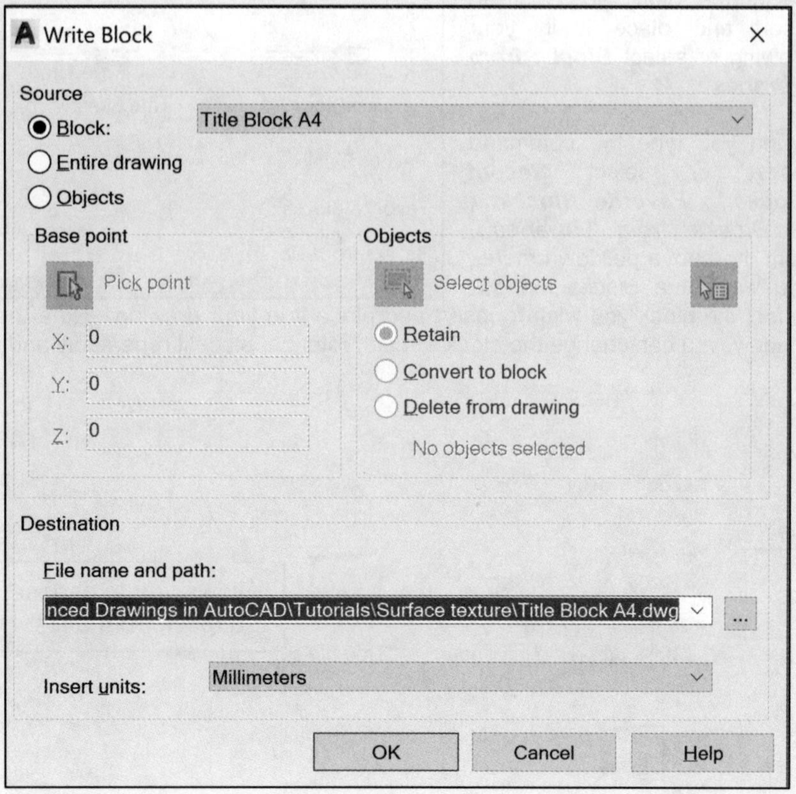

<u>Inserting a block or wblock</u>

1) <u>Command:</u> **insert** or <u>*Block* panel:</u> 

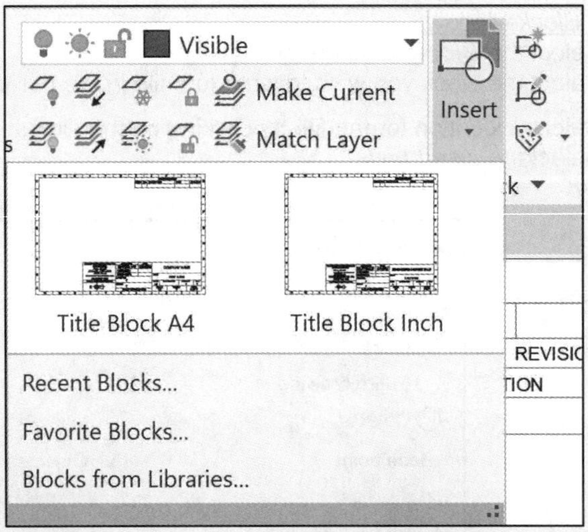

a) When you select the Insert icon, you will get a dropdown menu that has your drawing block. Select the block you wish to insert and place it in your drawing or select ***Blocks from Libraries***.

b) When you type the command **insert** or select ***Recent Blocks..., Favorite Blocks...,*** *or* ***Blocks from Libraries...*** from the above pulldown menu, you will get a *Blocks* window. Select the block you wish to insert and place it in your drawing. Note that, from this window, you can change the block's scale, rotation, place it repeatedly and explode it.

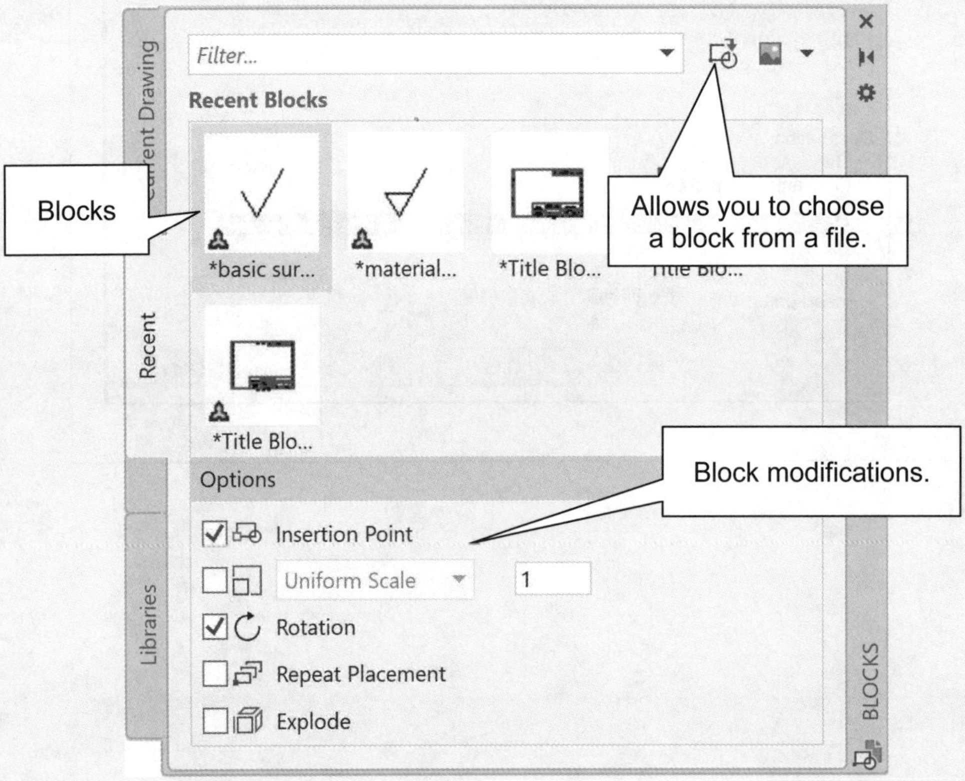

5.8) MODEL AND LAYOUT SPACE

5.8.1) Model space

In model space, you draw your design at a 1:1 scale. You specify whether one unit represents one millimeter, one centimeter, one inch, one foot, or whatever unit is most convenient. If you are going to create a 2-D orthographic projection, you can create both the model (drawing) and annotations (dimensions), and print entirely from within model space. This method is simple but has several limitations including:

- It is suitable for drawings that are viewed from only one direction. 2-D drawings are only viewed from one direction, but 3-D drawings may have many viewing directions.
- It does not support multiple views and view dependent layer settings.
- Scaling the annotations and title block requires computation. This is because if you change the scale of the model the annotations change with it.

With this method, you always draw geometric objects at full scale (1:1) and text, dimension and other annotations at a scale that will appear at the correct size when the drawing is plotted.

5.8.2) Layout space

In paper/layout space, you can place objects and annotations that are not part of your design such as a title block and dimensions. In paper space, you see what will be printed (usually on an 8.5 x 11 sheet of paper). Therefore, objects from the model space that are larger than the paper are scaled to fit the available printing area.

You can plot objects that are in the model space from paper space using viewports. A viewport is a rectangular window that views the object from a specified line of sight. Viewports are most useful when working with a 3-D model. In this situation, you can create several viewports that view the 3-D model from several different vantage points. When looking at a 2-D drawing, you really only want to view the *xy* plane. A situation where you might use multiple viewports with a 2-D drawing is if you are showing part of the model at a different scale. The command VIEWPORTS may be used to create additional viewports.

In paper space, each layout viewport is like a picture frame containing a photograph of the model. Each layout viewport contains a view that displays the model at an independent scale and orientation that you specify. You can also specify different layers properties in each layout viewport. The advantages of plotting from paper space are:

- You can plot multiple viewports.
- The size and location of the objects within each viewport is completely within your control.
- With annotative scaling, it is not necessary to calculate the appropriate dimension and text scale. Annotative scaling will be discussed in detail in the "*Dimensioning in AutoCAD®*" chapter. Figure 5.8-1 shows an example of what you would see in paper space before plotting.

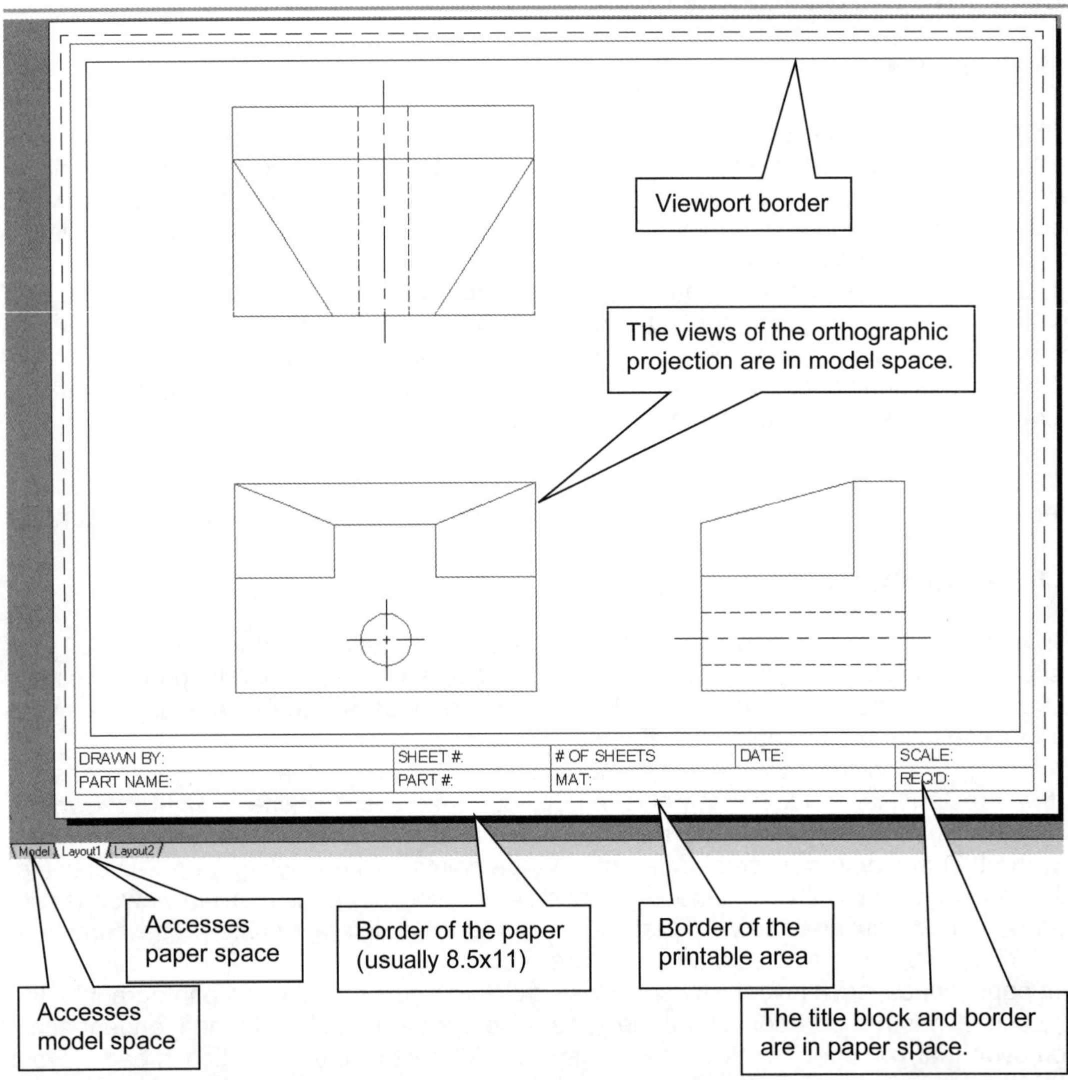

Figure 5.8-1: Paper space

5.9) CENTERLINES

Center lines are used to indicate axis of symmetry among other things. AutoCAD® has specialized commands for creating center marks for circles and arcs as well as center lines for axes of symmetry. Both the **CENTERLINE** and **CENTERMARK** commands create lines that are associative. Which means that they are attached to and change with the particular geometry that was used to define them. Figure 5.9-1 shows the *Centerlines* panel which is located in the *Annotate* tab.

Center lines and center marks may be edited through the use of grip boxes or in the *Properties* window 

(*View* tab – *Palettes* panel). If you click on either a center mark or center line, grip boxes will appear allowing you to extend or shorten the line. Figure 5.9-2 shows a grip boxes modification example. Several of the center mark or center line features may be adjusted within the *Properties* window. For example, for a center mark, the cross size and cross gap may be changed. Figure 5.9-3 shows the *Properties* window for both a center mark and a center line.

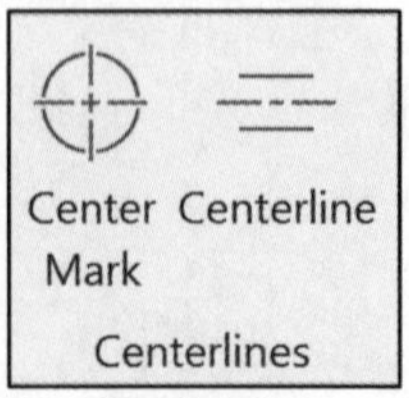

Figure 5.9-1: Centerlines panel

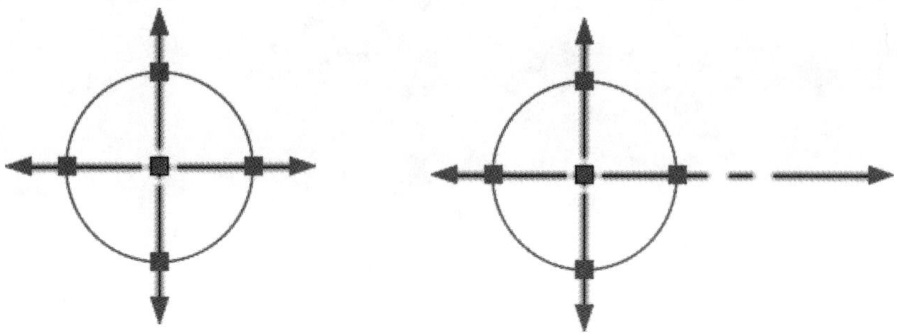

Figure 5.9-2: Grip box modification of a center mark

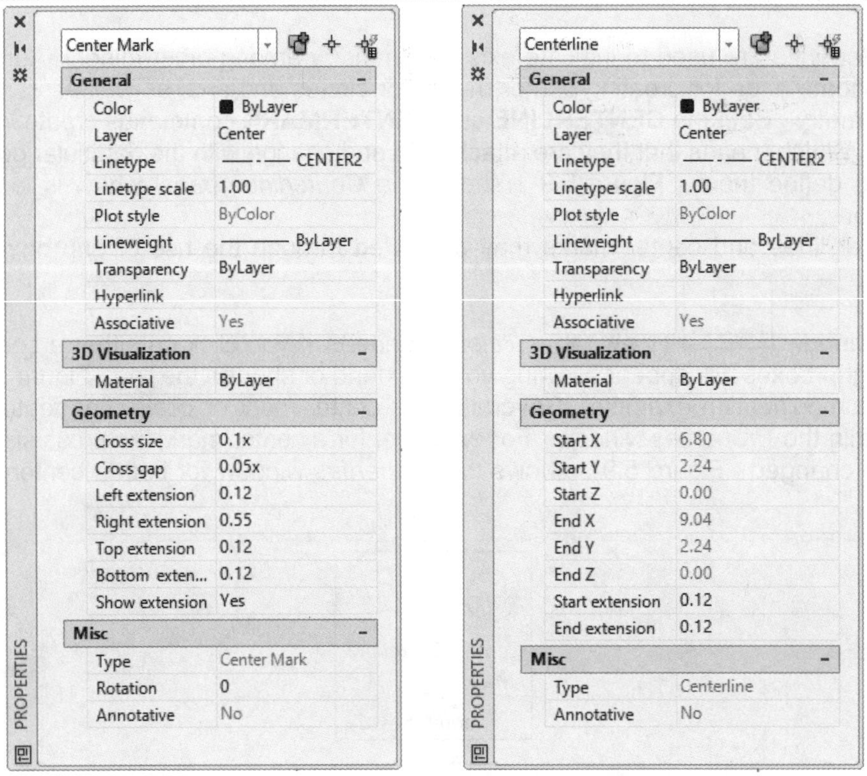

Figure 5.9-3: Center mark and center line *Properties* window

5.10) TITLE BLOCK TUTORIAL

Every engineering drawing should have both a border and a title block. The border defines the drawing area, and the title block gives pertinent information about the part or assembly being drawn. There are several different types of title blocks, but they all contain similar information. The information that is included depends on the drawing type, field of engineering, and viewing audience. The title block specified in the ASME Y14.100 standard is described in the chapter on "*Introduction to Engineering Drawings*".

5.10.1) Blocking a title block

1) View the *Blocking* video and read section 5.7).

2) 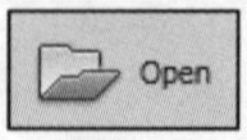

titleblock_student_A_2018.dwg. You will see a basic title block meant to fit an A sized sheet (i.e. 8.5 x 11.)

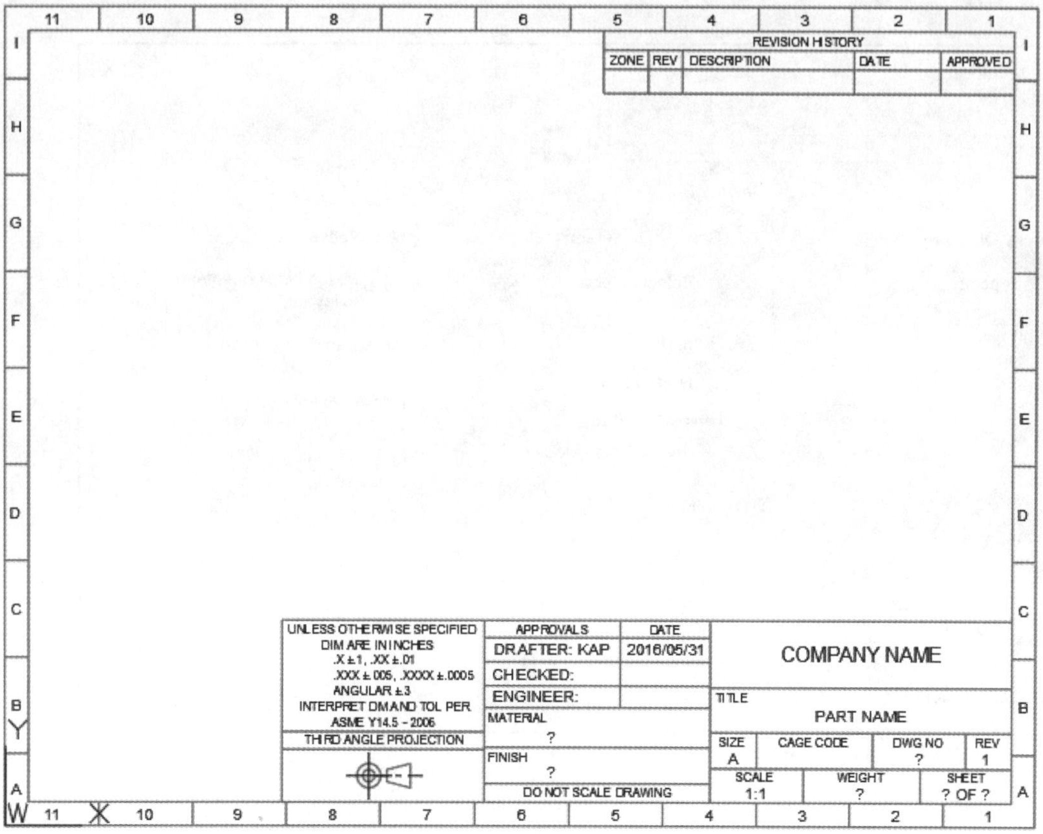

3) Fill in all the standard information into your title block. To edit the text, just double click on it, or you can use the command **DDEDIT**.
   a) COMPANY NAME = Enter your company or university name.
   b) DRAFTER = Enter your initials.

4) **Zoom All**

5) 

6) **BLOCK** your title block and border.

   a. <u>Command:</u> **block** or <u>*Home* Ribbon - *Block* panel:</u> 

   b. <u>*Block Definition* window:</u>
      i. Name the block **Title Block A**.
      ii. Enter a *Base point* of **0.00, 0.00, 0.00**
      iii. Select all objects that make up your title block and border by selecting the 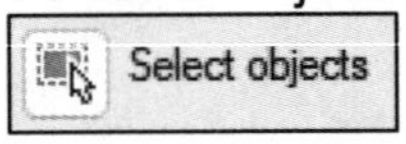

      icon. Hit the `Enter` key after you have selected your objects to return to the *Block Definition* window.
      iv. Activate the ***Retain*** radio button.
      v. Activate the ***Annotative*** and ***Allow exploding*** checkboxes.
      vi. Set the *Block units* to ***Inches***.
      vii. ***OK***

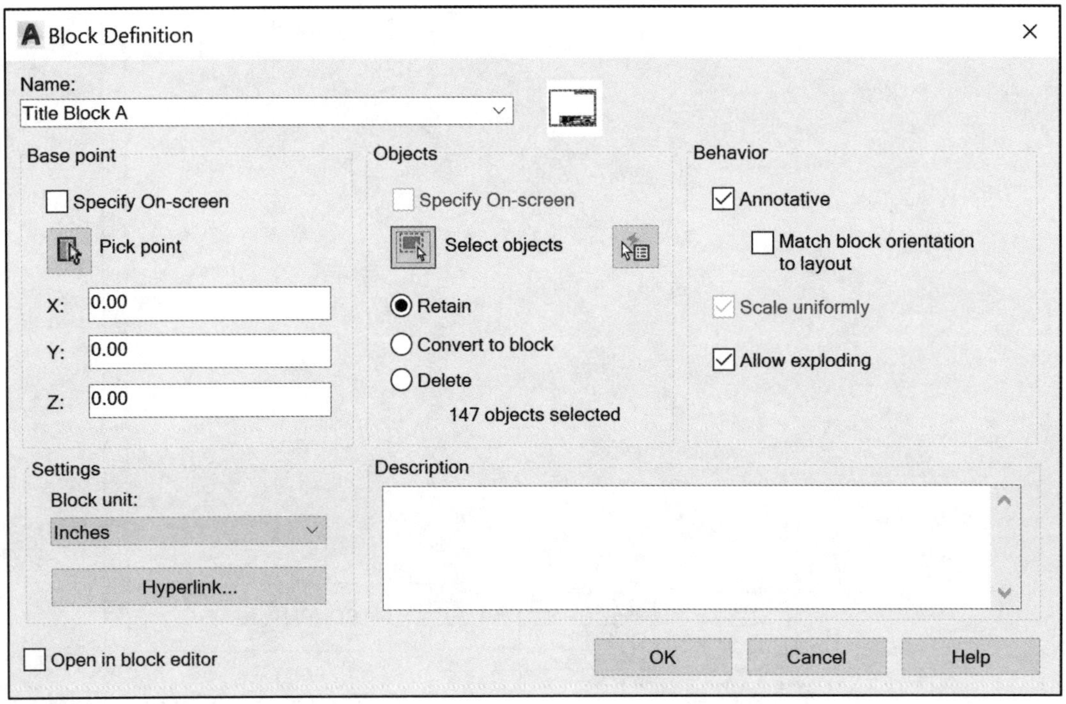

7) Write the *Title Block A* block to a file.
   a) <u>Command:</u> **wblock**
   b) <u>*Write Block* window:</u>
      i. Select the ***<u>B</u>lock*** radio button.
      ii. Select the ***Title Block A*** block from the pull-down menu.
      iii. Select a location for the file by clicking on the file path icon and name the file **Title Block A**.
      iv. Select ***Inches*** as the insert units.
      v. ***OK***

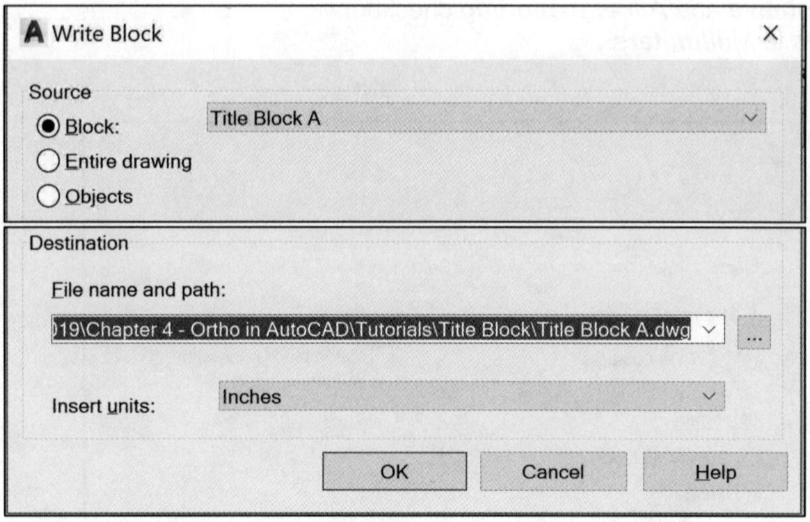

5.10.2) Blocking a metric title block

The Metric sheet size that is closest to an A size sheet (i.e. 11 x 8.5 inches) is the A4 sheet which is 297 x 210 mm (i.e. 11.7 x 8.3 inches).

1) View the *Blocking* video and read section 5.7).

2) 

titleblock_student_A4_2018.dwg and 

Title Block A4.dwg. You will see a basic title block meant to fit an A4 sized sheet (i.e. 297 x 210 mm)

3) Fill in all the standard information into your title block. To edit the text, just double click on it, or you can use the command **DDEDIT**.
   a) COMPANY NAME = Enter your company or university name.
   b) DRAFTER = Enter your initials.

4) **Zoom All**

5) 

6) **BLOCK** your title block and border.

   a. Command: **block** or *Block* panel: 

   b. *Block Definition* window:
      i. Name the block **Title Block A4**.
      ii. Enter a *Base point* of **0.00, 0.00, 0.00**
      iii. Select all objects that make up your title block and border using the ***Select objects*** icon. Hit the `Enter` key after you have selected your objects to return to the *Block Definition* window.
      iv. Activate the ***Retain*** radio button.
      v. Activate the ***Annotative*** and ***Allow exploding*** checkboxes.
      vi. Set the *Block units* to ***Millimeters***.
      vii. ***OK***

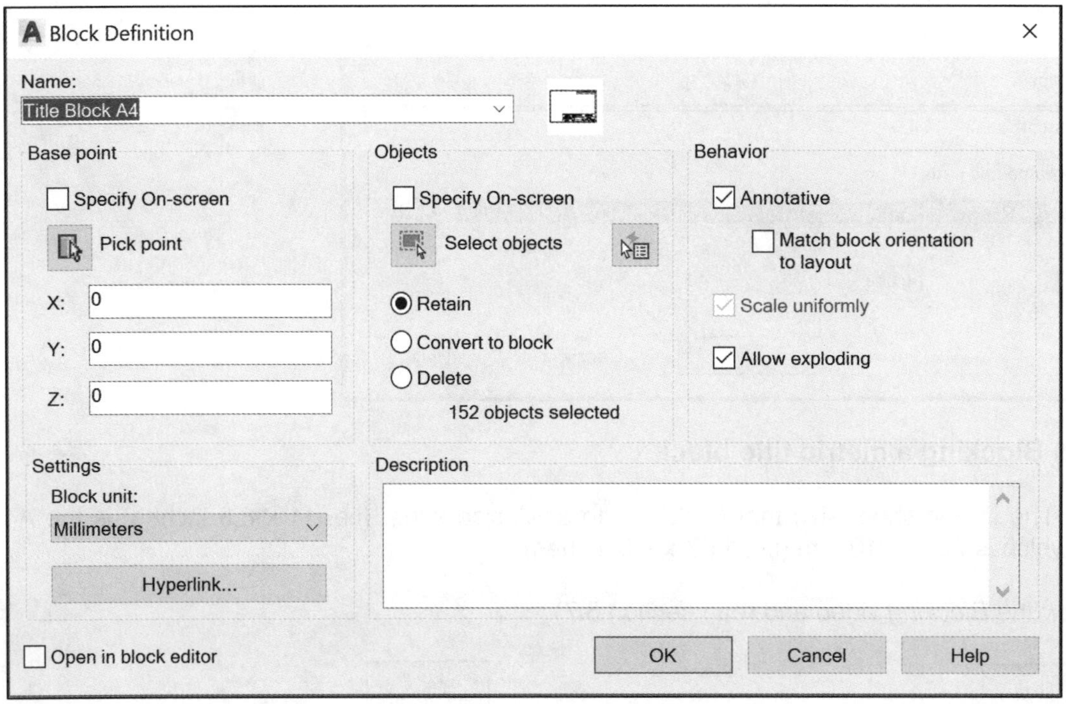

7) Write the *Title Block mm* block to a file.
   c) <u>Command:</u> **wblock**
   d) <u>*Write Block* window:</u>
      i. Select the ***Block*** radio button.
      ii. Select the ***Title Block A4*** block from the pull-down menu.
      iii. Select a location for the file by clicking on the file path icon and name the file **Title Block A4**.
      iv. Select ***mm*** as the insert units.
      v. ***OK***

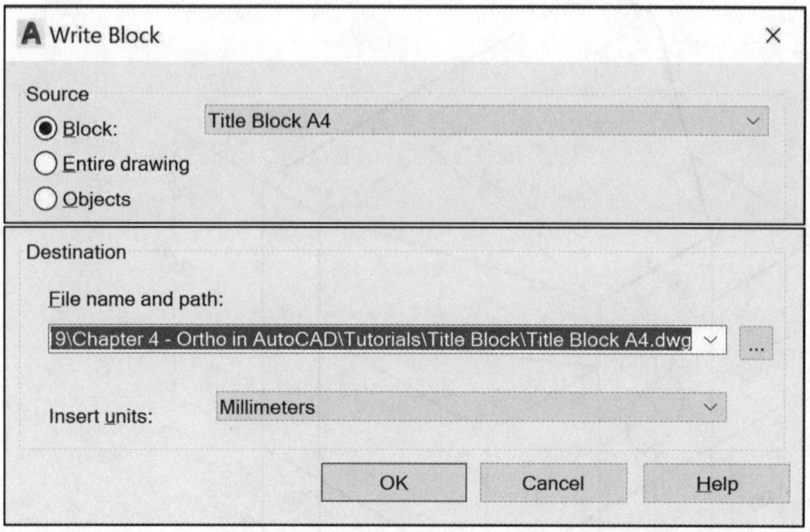

<u>**Exercise 5.10-1: Creating Blocks**</u>

Open ***titleblock_student_B_2018***. This is a title block that will fit a B sized sheet of paper (17 x 11 inches). Open ***titleblock_student_A3_2018***. This is a title block that will fit an A3 sized sheet of paper (420 x 297 mm). **Block** and **Wblock** each title block for use later.

5.11) ORTHOGRAPHIC PROJECTION TUTORIAL

By the end of this tutorial, you will have created and printed an orthographic projection of the part shown using proper pen widths. We will draw the orthographic projection using the procedure explained in the chapter on "*Orthographic Projections*". We will start by drawing the front view and use projectors to construct the top and right side views. Visible, hidden, and centerlines will be drawn on their own layer. Once the drawing is complete, we will use both the model space and the layout space to plot the drawing.

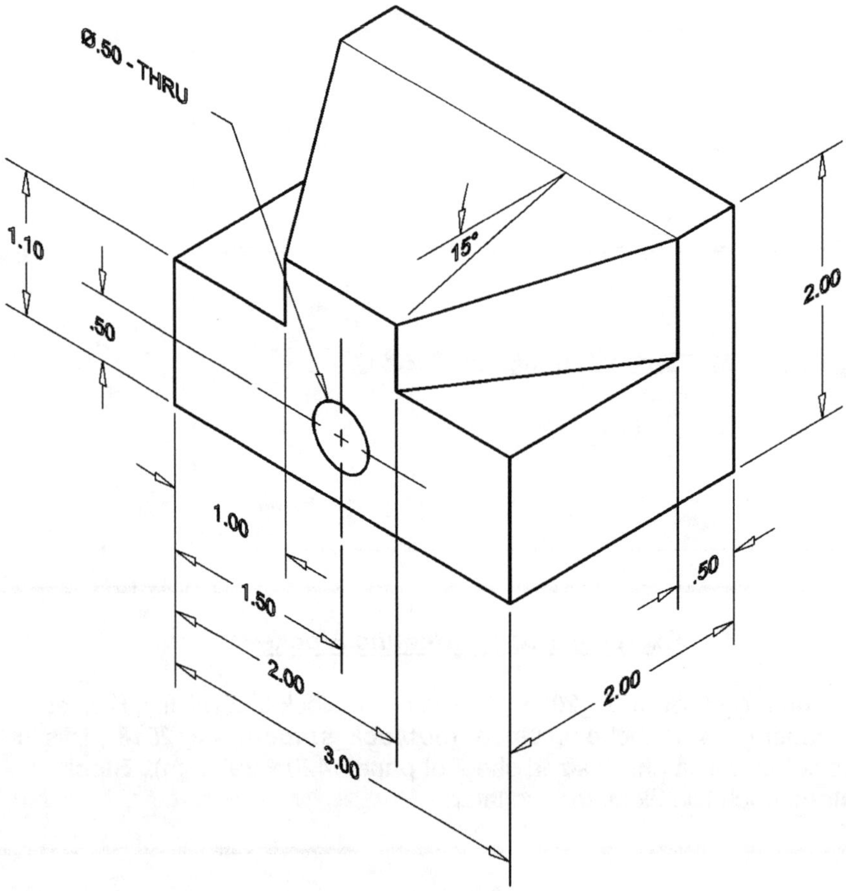

5.11.1) Draw the front view

1) View the *Model - Layout, Printing from model space,* and *Printing from layout space* videos and read sections 5.8) and 5.9).

2) Take some time to sketch what you think the FRONT, TOP and RIGHT SIDE views of the above object will look like.

3) 

set-inch.dwt and 

Ortho Tut.dwg. Save periodically throughout this tutorial.

4) Enter your WCS (Located in the ***Visualize*** tab. You can also access the World Coordinate system using the command **UCS**.)

> **Note:** If the ***Visualize*** tab is not active perform the following steps.
> a) **Right click** on the ribbon.
> b) Select **Show Tab**
> c) Select **Visualize**

5) If you are using *Dynamic Input*, set the *Pointer Input Format* to **Absolute coordinates**.

6) In the ***Viewport*** layer, draw a **RECtangle** that indicates the edges of your limits/paper (11x8.5).

7) **Zoom All**

8) In your ***Visible*** layer, draw the visible lines of the front view.
   a) Draw a **RECtangle** that is **3** inches long and **2** inches wide near the bottom left corner of your drawing area.
   b) Set your **UCS** origin to the bottom left corner of the front view.
   c) Draw the 2 **Lines** within the rectangle.
   d) Draw the **Circle**. (Note: ∅ = diameter)

> **Note:** Some visible features are missing, but this is all we can do for now.

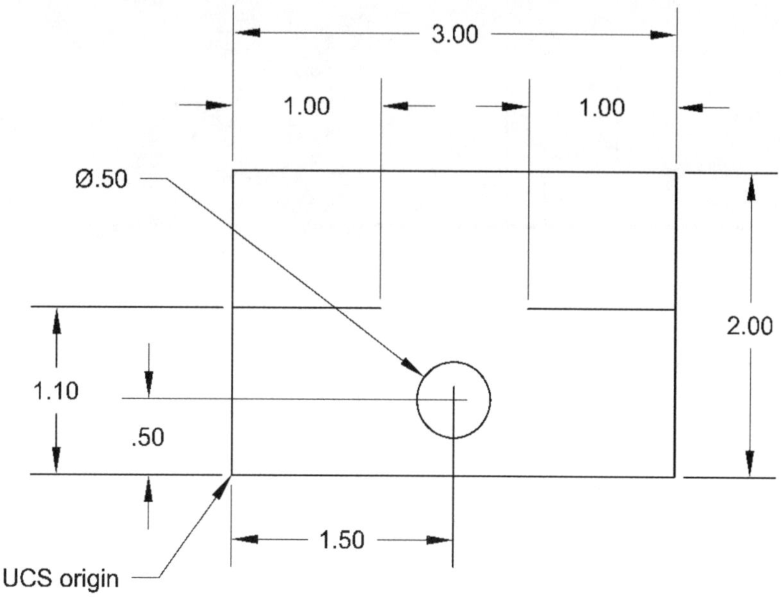

5.11.2) Drawing the right side view

1) Turn your ***Object Snap*** on and set the following object snaps to be automatically detected (Endpoint, Midpoint, Center, Quadrant, Intersection, Nearest, Perpendicular, Extension).

2) In the ***Construction*** layer, draw horizontal and vertical construction lines (**XLine**) off of every edge and boundary of the front view.
   a) Create the horizontal projectors.
      i. Command: **xl** or *Draw* panel: 
      ii. `Specify a point or [Hor/Ver/Ang/Bisect/Offset]:` **h**
      iii. `Specify through point:` Select every corner, edge and quadrant that should have a horizontal projector coming off of it.
      iv. `Specify through point:` **`Enter`**
   b) Create the vertical projectors.
   c) Move the visible lines of the front view above the construction lines.
      i. *Home* tab - *Modify* panel: 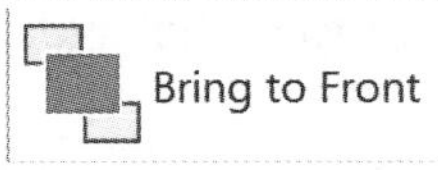

      ii. `Select objects:` Using a window, select all the visible lines of the front view.
      iii. `Select objects:` **`Enter`**

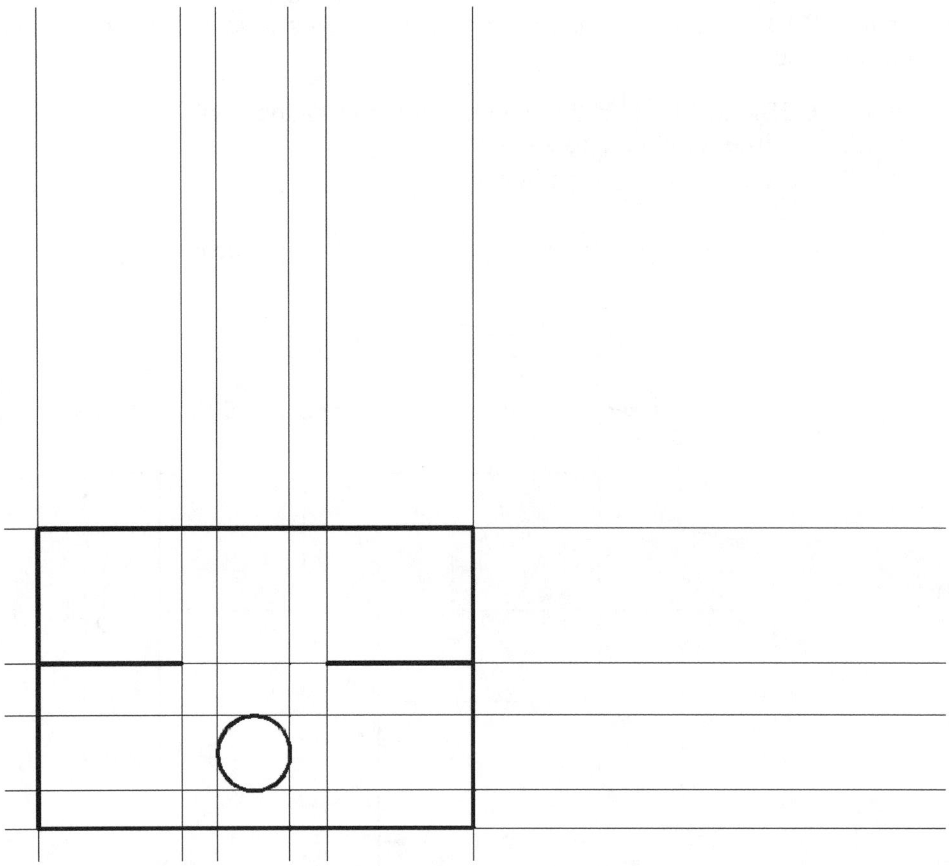

3) In the ***Visible*** layer, draw the visible features of the L-shaped part of the right side view.

How?

1) <u>Command:</u> **line** or 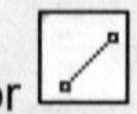
2) `Specify first point:` Select a point that is **NEArest** *Projector 1*. (See the figure below.)
3) `Specify next point or [Undo]:` **@2<0**
4) `Specify next point or [Undo]:` Select a point that is **PERpendicular** to *Projector 2*.
5) `Specify next point or [Close/Undo]:` **@.5<180**
6) `Specify next point or [Close/Undo]:` Select a point that is **PERpendicular** to *Projector 3*.
7) `Specify next point or [Close/Undo]:` **@1.5<180**
8) `Specify next point or [Close/Undo]:` Close the shape by snapping to the **ENDpoint**.
9) `Specify next point or [Close/Undo]:` **Enter**

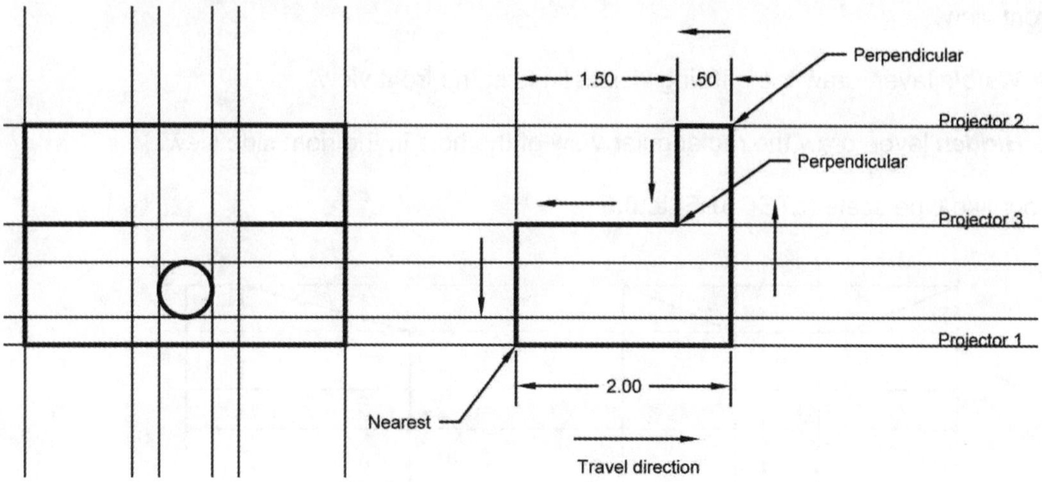

4) Draw the angled feature of the right side view using the following commands.
   a) Turn the ***Polar Tracking*** on and set **POLARANG** to ***15*** degrees.
   b) Use a polar tracking path and the **EXTension** snap to construct the angled line.
   c) Connect the angled line with the L-shaped body.

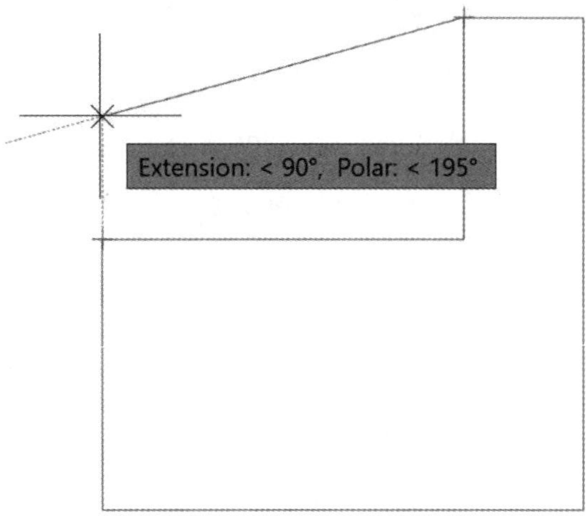

5) In the ***Construction*** layer, project the angled feature of the right side view back to the front view.

6) In the ***Visible*** layer, draw the missing visible lines in the front view.

7) In the ***Hidden*** layer, draw the rectangular view of the hole in the right side view.

8) Set your line type scale (**LTSCALE**) to **0.5**.

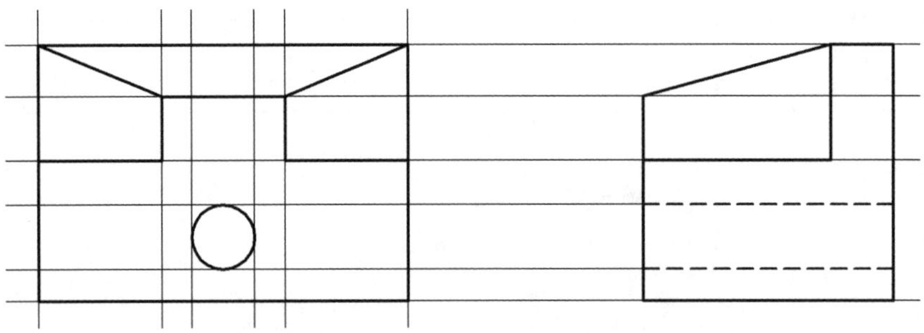

5.11.3) Drawing the top view

1) In the ***Construction*** layer, draw the projectors needed to complete the top view.
   a) Draw a 45° projector off the upper right corner of the front view.
      i. <u>Command:</u> **xl** or <u>*Draw* panel:</u> 
      ii. `Specify a point or [Hor/Ver/Ang/Bisect/Offset]:` **a**
      iii. `Enter angle of xline (0) or [Reference]:` **45**
      iv. `Specify through point:` Select the upper right corner of the front view.
      v. `Specify through point:` **`Enter`**
   b) Draw vertical projectors up from the right side view and horizontal projectors over to where the top view will be located.
   c) Use the 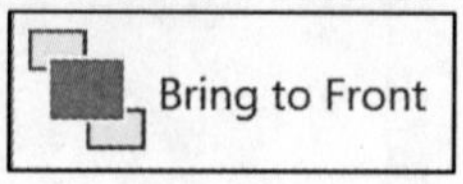

icon to bring the lines of the right side view to the front.

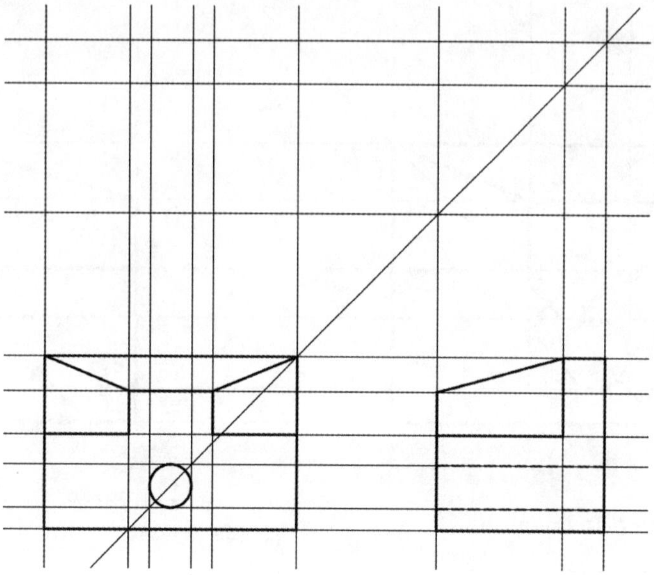

2) Draw the visible and hidden features of the top view.

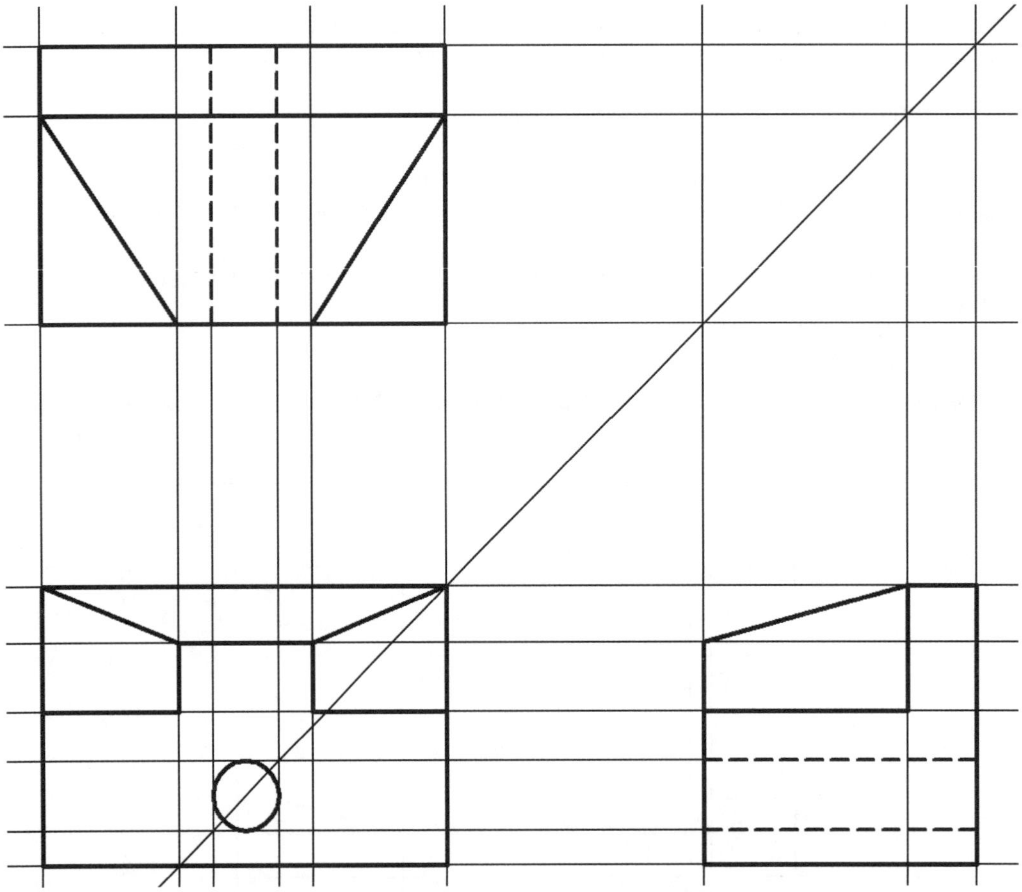

3) Turn the ***Construction*** layer off.

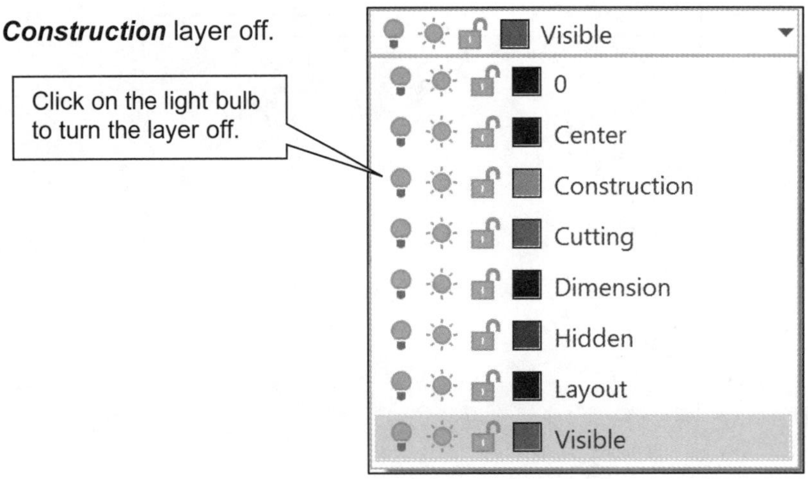

5.11.4) Drawing centerlines

1) In the ***Center*** layer, add the center mark for the hole in the front view.
    a) *Annotate* Tab – *Centerlines* panel: 

 or **CENTERMARK**
    b) `Select circle or arc to add centermark:` Click on the circle.

2) Add the centerlines in the right side and top views.
    a) *Annotate* Tab – *Centerlines* panel: 

 or **CENTERLINE**
    b) `Select first line:` Click on one of the lines that will define the centerline location.
    c) `Select second line:` Click on the other line.

Note: Don't worry if your centerlines don't look correct. We will fix them later.

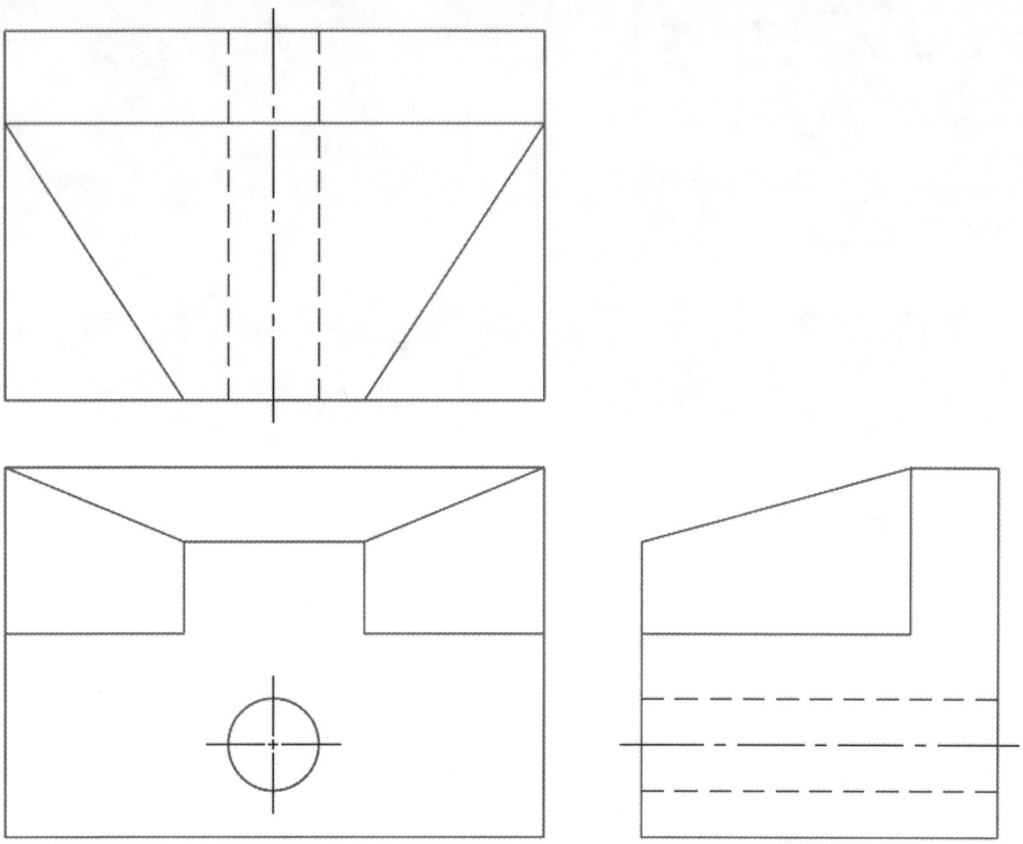

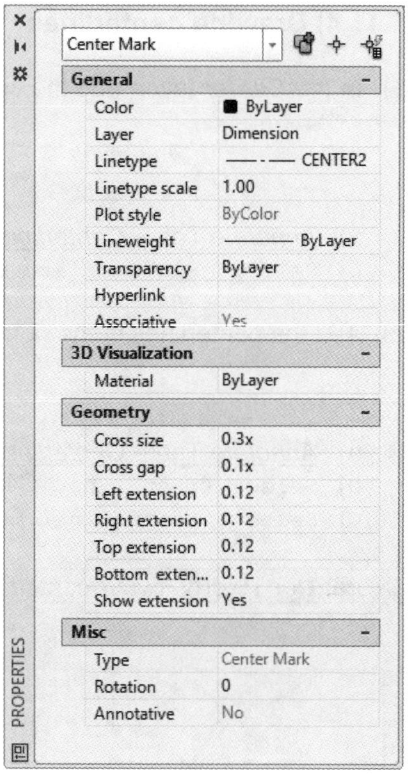

3) Notice that the center mark and centerlines have very small dashes. Let's fix that.
   a) Click on the center mark.
   b) <u>*View* tab – *Palettes* panel:</u> 

   c) Change the *Cross size* to **0.3x** and the *Cross gap* to **0.1x**.
   d) Change all of the *extensions* to **0.12**.

4) Fix the centerlines.
   a) Click on both of the centerlines.
   b) <u>*View* tab – *Palettes* panel:</u> 

   c) Change the *Linetype* to **CENTER** instead of CENTER2.
   d) Change the *Start* and *End extension* to **0.12**.

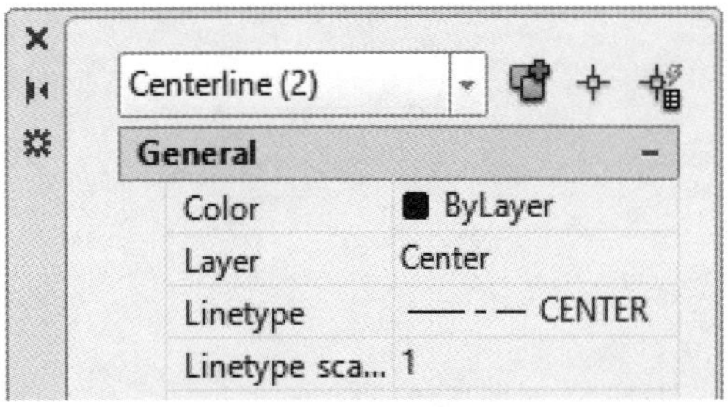

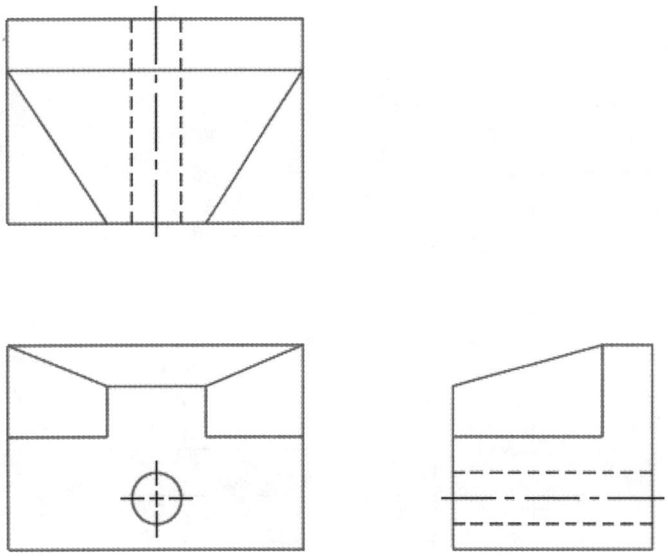

5) Make sure that all three views are within the limits rectangle that you drew.

6) 

5.11.5) Printing the layout

1) Select the ***Layout1*** tab at the bottom of your drawing screen.

2) Insert your inch title block.

   a) <u>Command:</u> **insert** or <u>*Block* panel:</u> 

and then ***Blocks from Libraries…*** If this is your first time inserting a block it will automatically go to the file navigation window; otherwise, it will go directly to the *Blocks* window.

   b) If you are in the *Blocks* window, select  to navigate the file. **Open** the ***Title Block A*** block file.

   c) Check the ***Insertion Point*** check box. This will allow you to choose an insertion point on the screen.

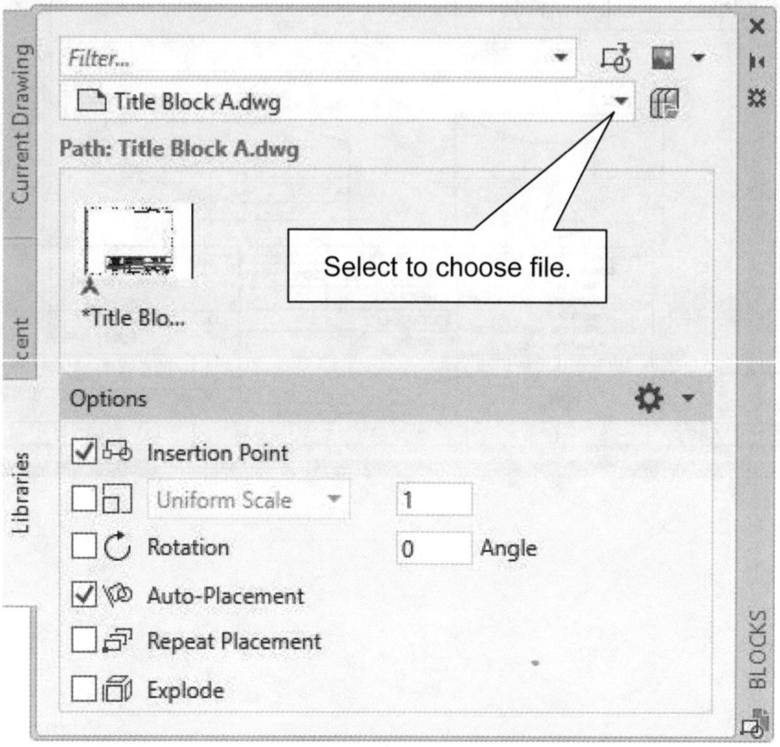

   d) Select the ***Title Block A*** picture and manually specify an insertion point to be just inside the lower left corner of the printable area. The printable area is indicated by a light line. This should be the biggest rectangle shown on the page. The size of this area depends on the type of printer being used. (See the figure below.)

3) Notice the features of the layout (see the figure below). At this point, you should see:
   - The border of the 8.5x11 sheet of paper.
   - The border of the printable area. The size of the printable area is printer dependent.
   - The viewport border.
   - The orthographic projection is in model space.
   - The rectangle that you drew to indicate the 11x8.5 limits (yellow). Therefore, the objects in the model are not being shown at a 1:1 scale relative to paper space.
   - Note that your title block may be too big. We will take care of that later.

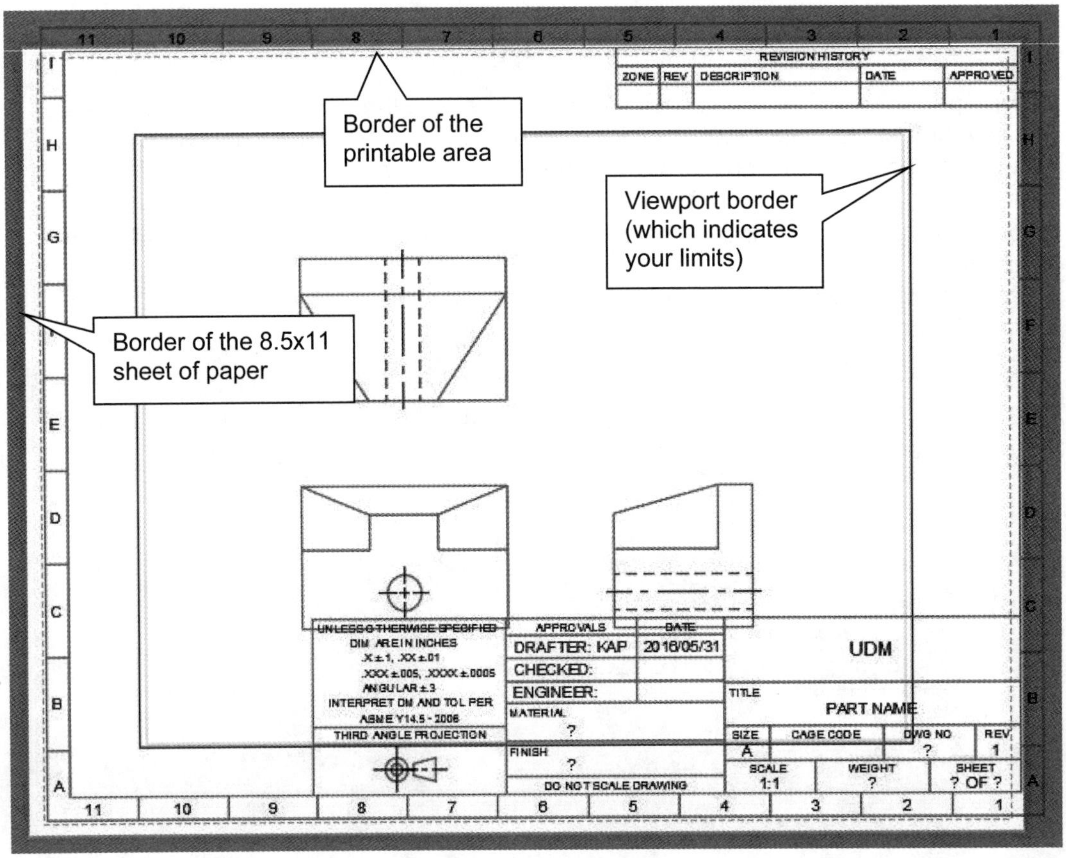

4) Set your pen widths and page size.

   a) <u>*Application button:*</u>  ***Print – Page Setup...*** or <u>Layout Tab:</u> 

   b) <u>*Page Setup Manager* window:</u> ***Modify...***
   c) <u>*Page Setup – Layout1* window:</u>
      i. Select a printer.
      ii. Plot the ***Layout***.
      iii. Select a ***1:1*** scale.
      iv. <u>*Plot style table (pen assignments)* area</u>: Select ***monochrome.ctb*** from the pull-down menu.
      v. Select the **Edit...**  icon next to the pull-down menu. A *Plot Style Table Editor* window will appear.
   d) <u>*Plot Style Table Editor – monochrome.ctb* window:</u>
      iii. <u>*Plot styles* field:</u> Select ***Color 1*** (red – visible line color).
      iv. <u>*Lineweight* field:</u> Select ***0.6000 mm*** from the pull-down menu.
      v. Follow the same procedure to set the widths of the other line types.
         - ***Color 5*** (blue – hidden) = ***0.45 mm***
         - ***Color 7*** (black – center and dimension lines) = ***0.3 mm***
      vi. ***Save & Close***
   e) <u>*Page Setup – Layout1* window:</u> ***OK***
   f) <u>*Page Setup Manager* window:</u> ***Close***

Note: Every setting except the pen widths are saved within the drawing file and will not change unless you change them. The pen widths are computer specific and will have to be re-entered if you change computers.

Note: You may also set pen width within the Layers Properties Manager if you find this easier (see figure below). However, this method gives you a limited number of pen widths. Therefore, you notice that the hidden line is given a pen width of 0.50 mm when a better width is 0.45 mm.

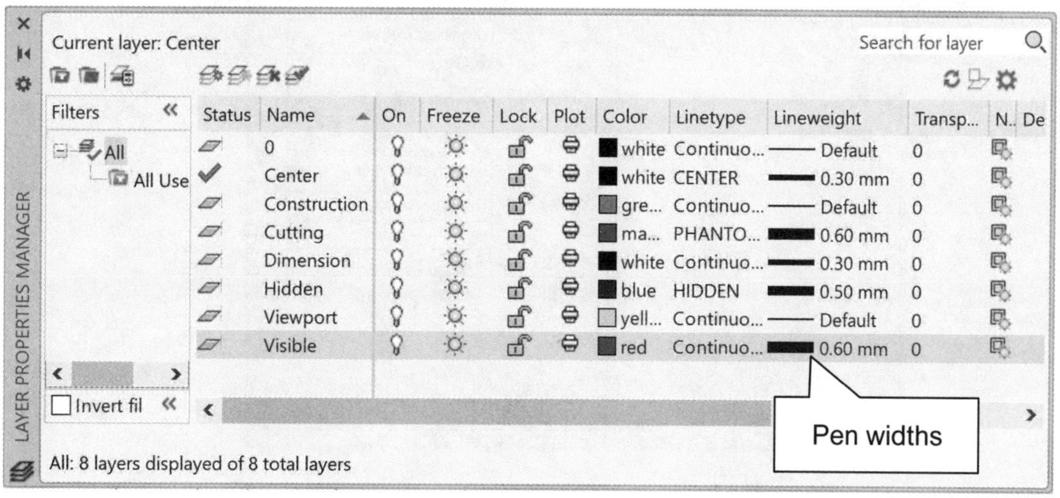

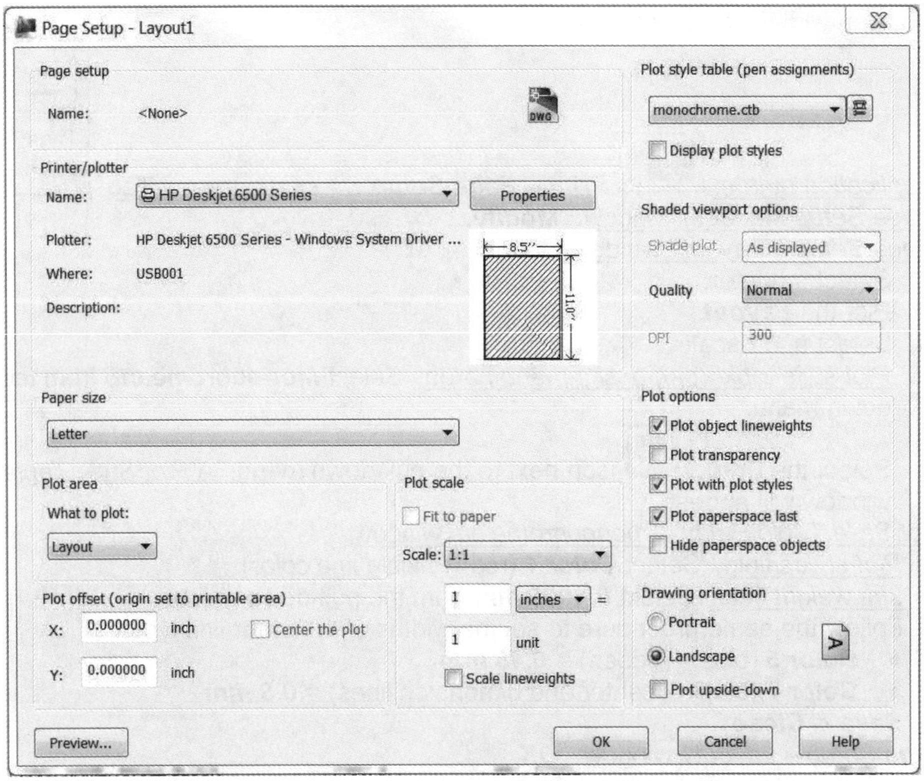
Page Setup - Layout1
Page setup
Name: <None>
Printer/plotter
Name: HP Deskjet 6500 Series
Properties
Plotter: HP Deskjet 6500 Series - Windows System Driver ...
Where: USB001
Description:
8.5″
11.0″
Paper size
Letter
Plot area
What to plot:
Layout
Plot offset (origin set to printable area)
X: 0.000000 inch
Y: 0.000000 inch
Center the plot
Plot scale
Fit to paper
Scale: 1:1
1 inches =
1 unit
Scale lineweights
Plot style table (pen assignments)
monochrome.ctb
Display plot styles
Shaded viewport options
Shade plot As displayed
Quality Normal
DPI 300
Plot options
Plot object lineweights
Plot transparency
Plot with plot styles
Plot paperspace last
Hide paperspace objects
Drawing orientation
Portrait
Landscape
Plot upside-down
Preview...
OK
Cancel
Help

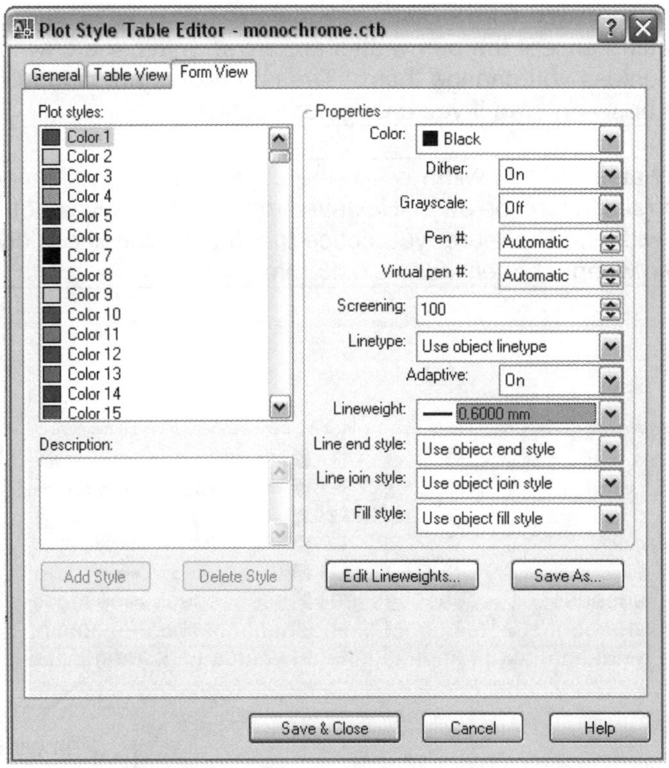
Plot Style Table Editor - monochrome.ctb
General
Table View
Form View
Plot styles:
Color 1
Color 2
Color 3
Color 4
Color 5
Color 6
Color 7
Color 8
Color 9
Color 10
Color 11
Color 12
Color 13
Color 14
Color 15
Description:
Properties
Color: Black
Dither: On
Grayscale: Off
Pen #: Automatic
Virtual pen #: Automatic
Screening: 100
Linetype: Use object linetype
Adaptive: On
Lineweight: 0.6000 mm
Line end style: Use object end style
Line join style: Use object join style
Fill style: Use object fill style
Add Style
Delete Style
Edit Lineweights...
Save As...
Save & Close
Cancel
Help

5) Move your viewport border to the ***Viewport*** layer.

6) If your title block extends beyond the printable area, **Scale** your title block using the lower left-hand corner as the base point. The scale percentage depends on your printer selection. For me it was 93%.

7) Use the **Move** command to center your title block within the printable area.

8) Click on the viewport border to activate its grip boxes. Using the grip boxes, resize the viewport border so that it is just inside your title block border. **Caution!** Don't make it the same size as your title block border. We will need to access the viewport border often.

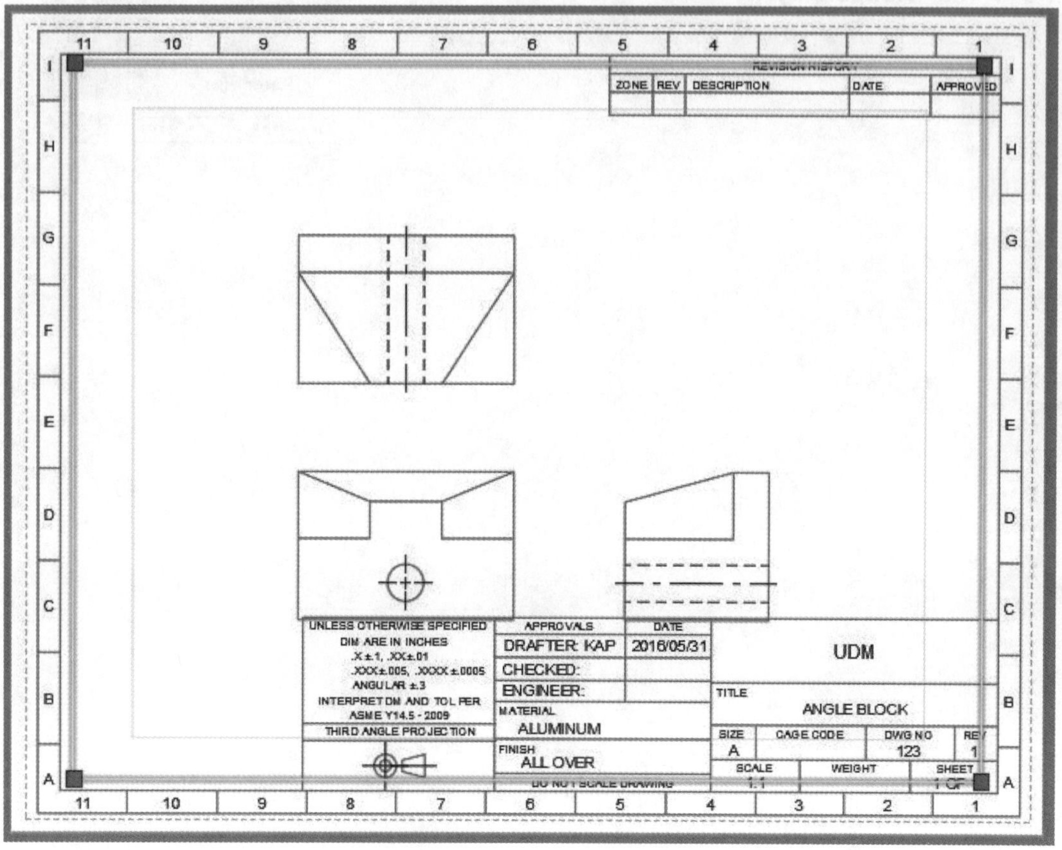

9) With the view port still selected, notice that a *Viewport Scale* is added to the *Status* bar. The *Viewport Scale* indicates the scale at which objects within the view port are shown relative to

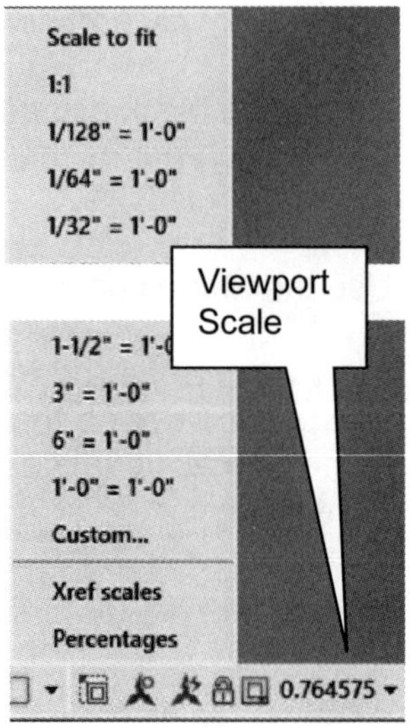

the paper space. If you have more than one view port, each view port may have a different scale.

10) Click on the *Viewport Scale* and change it to ***1:1***.

11) Double click inside the viewport border. This activates the model space and the viewport border will thicken. Use the **Pan** and **Move** commands so that the orthographic projection is centered within the title block border. Double click outside the viewport border to re-enter paper space.

12) Turn ***OFF*** your *Viewport* layer.

13) Fill in your title block. In order to enter text, we need to break the title block into its individual entities.

a) Command: **explode** or *Modify* panel: 
b) `Select objects:` Select any part of the title block.
c) `Select objects:` **`Enter`**

14) Edit your text by using the DDEDIT command or by double clicking on the word to edit. Enter the following information.
a) PART NAME = ANGLE BLOCK
b) SIZE = A
c) SCALE = 1:1
d) DWG NO = 123
e) WEIGHT = delete the ?.
f) SHEET = 1 OF 1
g) DATE = Enter the appropriate date
h) MATERIAL = ALUMINUM
i) FINISH = ALL OVER

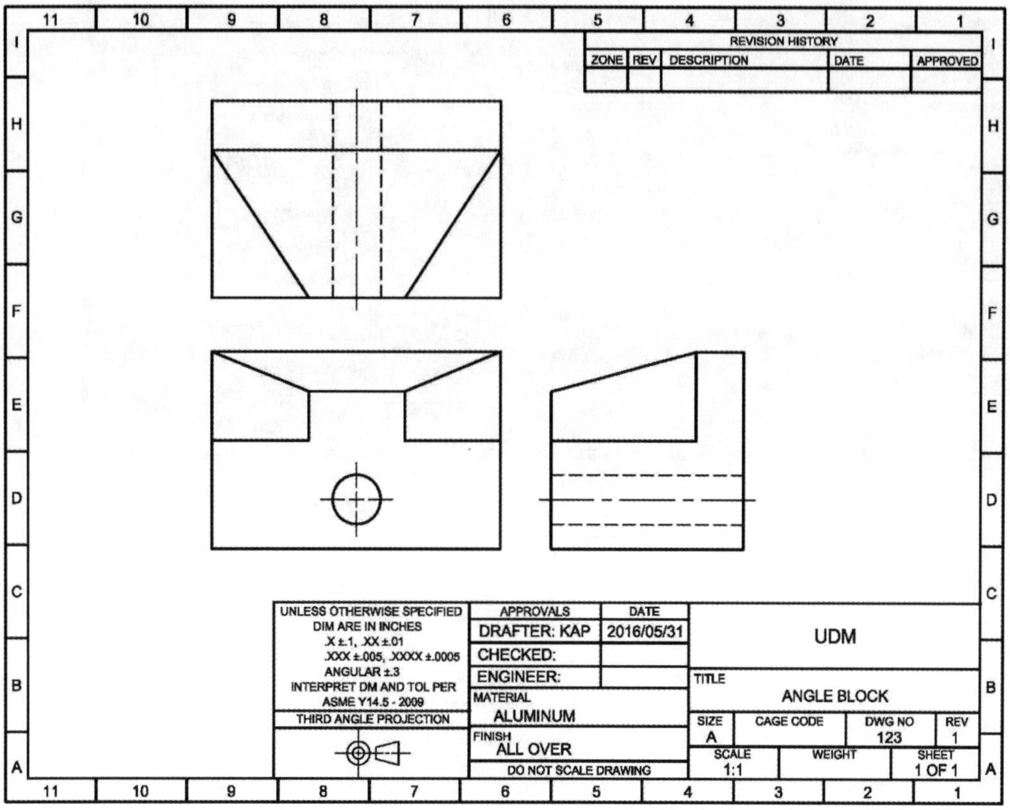

15) Plot your drawing.
   a) Application button: ***Print – Plot...***.
   b) Plot - Layout1 window: ***Preview...***
   c) Hit `Esc` to exit print preview.
   d) If the preview did not appear as you expected, adjust your settings and ***Preview...*** the drawing again. Check to make sure your pen widths are set correctly and your line breaks look right.
   e) Plot - Layout1 window: Select ***OK*** when everything is set correctly.

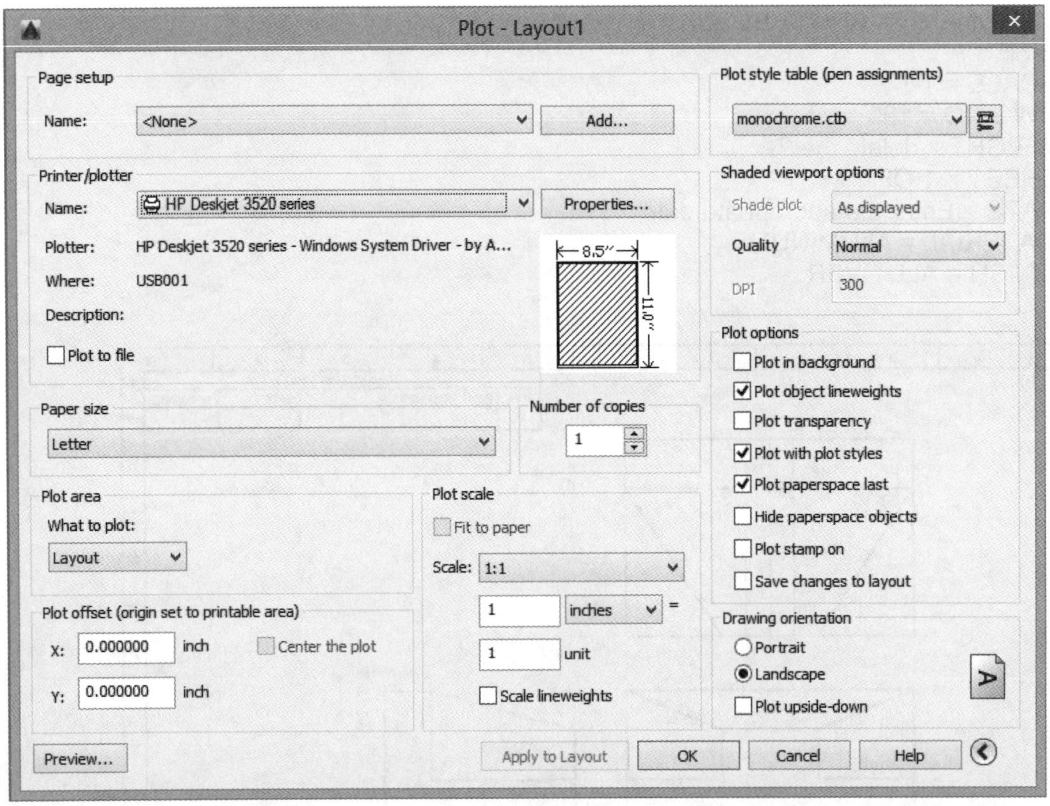

16) Switch back to your model space by clicking the ***Model*** tab at the bottom of the drawing screen. Notice that your title block disappears. This is because layout objects do not appear in the model space.

17) 

5.11.6) Printing a metric drawing

1) 

ortho_metric_student_2018.dwg. This file contains a metric version of the orthographic projection completed in the previous sections.

2) 

Ortho Metric Tut.dwg

3) Verify that the drawing is indeed metric. On the ***Viewport*** layer, draw a limits **RECtangle** that is **297 x 210** mm whose lower left corner starts at **0,0**.

4) **Zoom All**

5) Enter ***Layout*** space.

6) Move your viewport border to the ***Viewport*** layer.

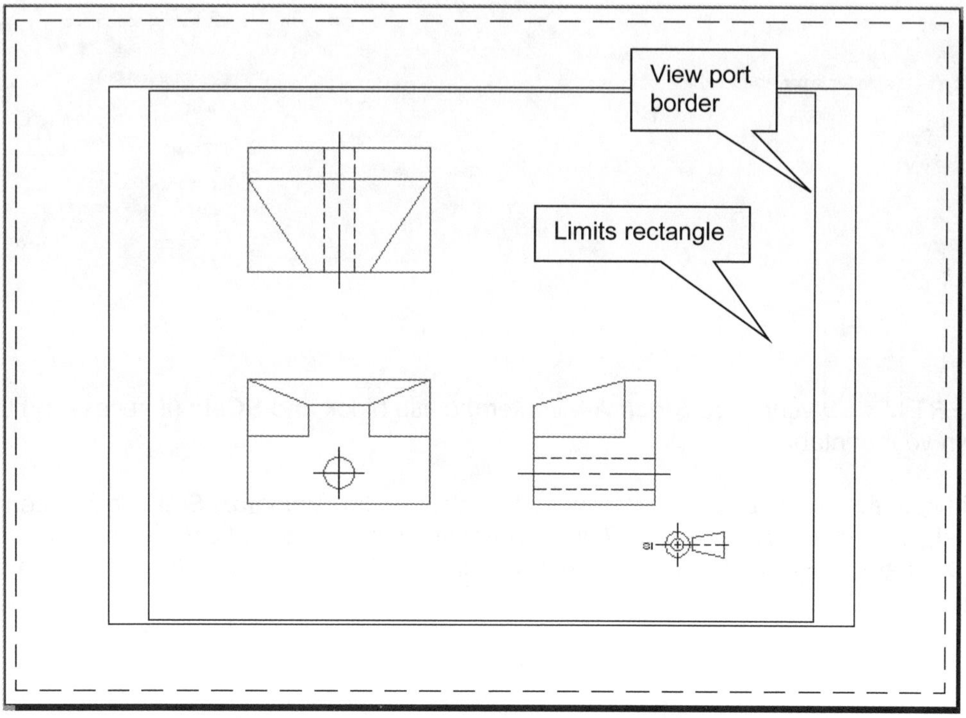

7) Enter the *Page Setup – Layout1* window (***Print – Page Setup...- Modify***) and set the following parameter.
   a) Paper size = ***ISO A4 (297.00 x 210.00 MM).***
   b) Plot scale area:
      i. Scale = ***1:1***
   c) Plot style = ***monochrome.ctb***
   d) ***OK***
   e) ***Close***

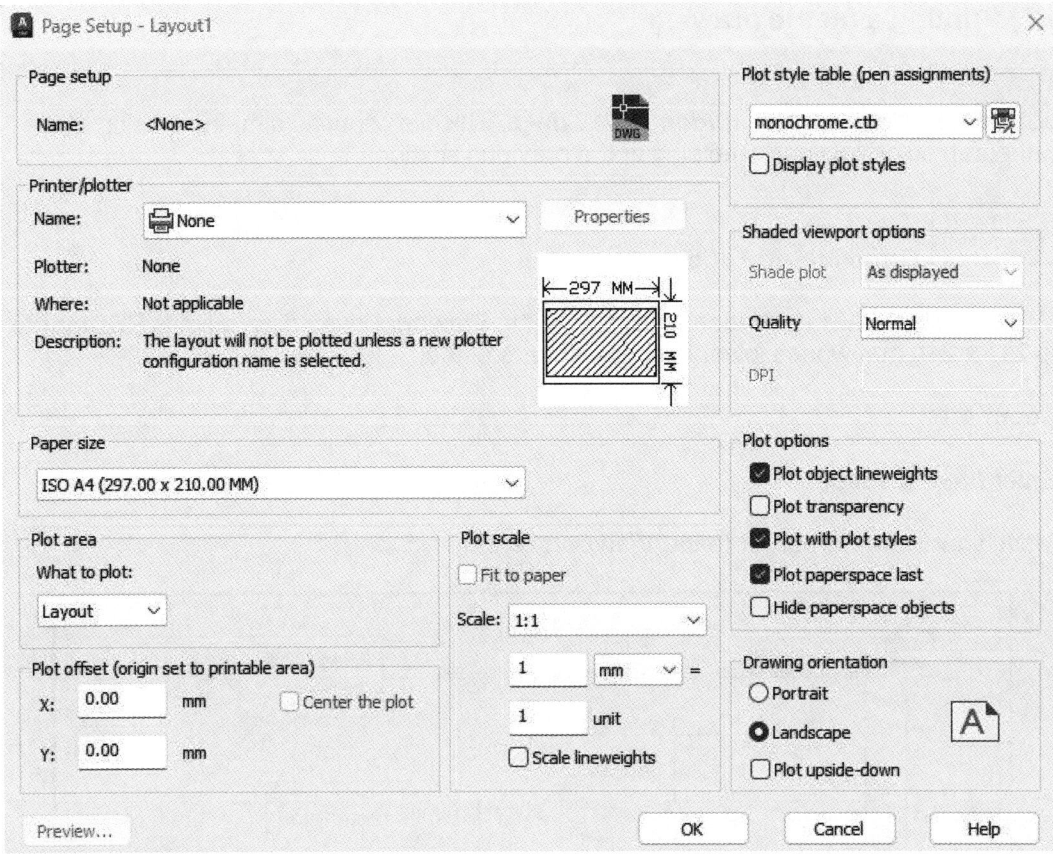

8) **INSERT** 

your ***Title Block A4,*** center the title block and **SCale** (if necessary) to fit within your printable area.

9) Fill in your title block, adjust your view port border, set the ***Viewport Scale*** to 1:1, center your model, turn the ***Viewport*** layer ***off***, fill in your title block, ***save*** and ***print*** your drawing. Note, you will have to **EXPLODE** your title block in order to fill in the fields. (See figure on the next page.)

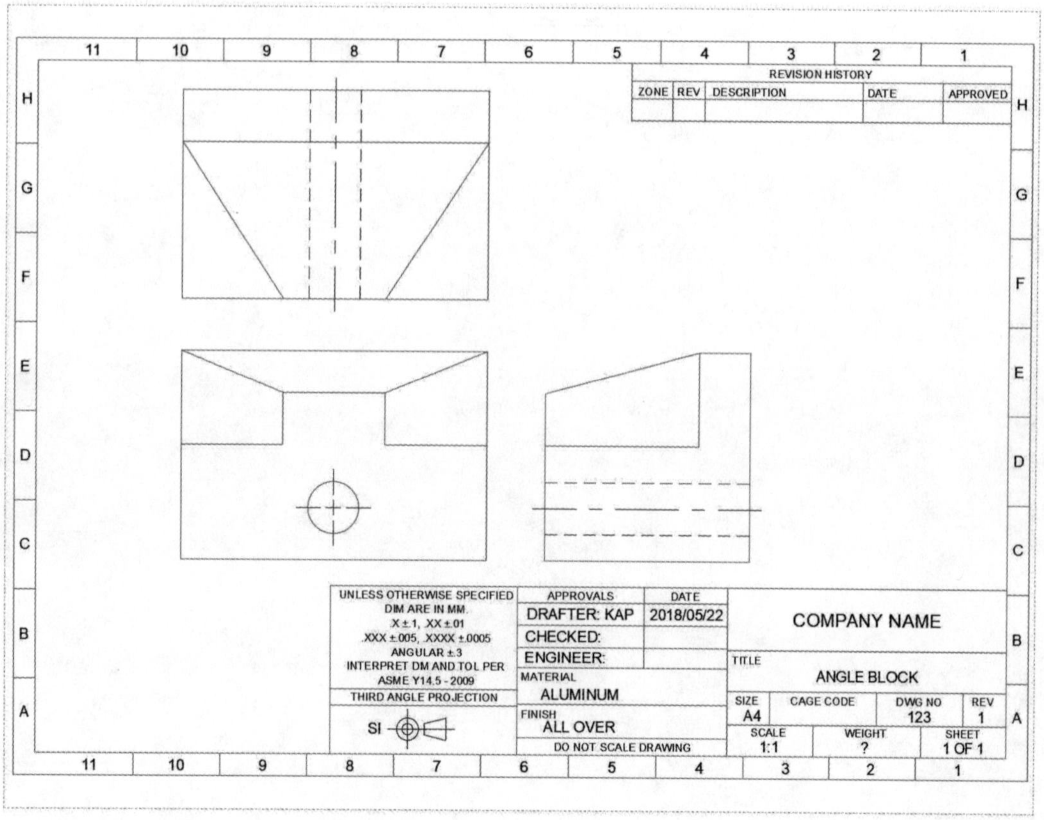

REVISION HISTORY
ZONE
REV
DESCRIPTION
DATE
APPROVED
UNLESS OTHERWISE SPECIFIED
DIM ARE IN MM.
X ±.1, XX ±.01
.XXX ±.005, .XXXX ±.0005
ANGULAR ±.3
INTERPRET DIM AND TOL PER
ASME Y14.5 - 2009
THIRD ANGLE PROJECTION
SI
APPROVALS
DATE
DRAFTER: KAP
2018/05/22
CHECKED:
ENGINEER:
MATERIAL
ALUMINUM
FINISH
ALL OVER
DO NOT SCALE DRAWING
COMPANY NAME
TITLE
ANGLE BLOCK
SIZE
A4
CAGE CODE
DWG NO
123
REV
1
SCALE
1:1
WEIGHT
?
SHEET
1 OF 1

NOTES:

ORTHOGRAPHIC PROJECTIONS IN AUTOCAD® QUESTIONS

Name: ________________________________ Date: ______________

Layers

Q5-1) The layer you are drawing on is said to be ....

1. on.
2. first.
3. on top.
4. current.

Q5-2) What layer property controls an entity's printed width?

a) line type
b) layer name
c) color
d) pen style

Q5-3) The construction layer is used to create projection lines. When the orthographic projection is complete, we do not need these lines anymore. The easiest way to not show the projections lines is to turn the construction layer to the ________ state.

a) freeze
b) thaw
c) off
d) on

Q5-4) Lines occurring on a LOCKED or OFF layer may not be selected. Which layer status still allows you to see the lines?

Q5-5) The place/window where you can change a layer's color, linetype and status.

a) Layer properties manager
b) Layers manager
c) Layer status manager

Q5-6) The typed command that is used to control the length of the dashes and spaces of the different line types.

a) ltscale
b) scale
c) dashscale
d) setscale

Q5-7) To change the line type scale of an individual object, you must enter the .... window.

a) scale
b) properties
c) line type
d) page setup

Blocking

Q5-8) A grouping of objects that may be reused.

a) group
b) nest
c) pair
d) block

Q5-9) What typed command is used to write a block to a file?

a) block
b) create
c) wblock
d) insert

Q5-10) The command used to break a block up into its individual components.

a) ungroup
b) explode
c) break apart
d) Insert

Name: ________________________________ Date: ______________

Model/layout space and printing

Q5-11) The space where you see exactly what is going to be printed. (circle all that apply)

a) model
b) layout
c) paper
d) real

Q5-12) An area within layout space that allows you to view objects within model space and to scale these objects with respect to the printed page.

a) viewport
b) model view
c) paper space

Q5-13) How do you access model space while still remaining in paper space?

a) Click on the model tab.
b) Double click within the viewport border.
c) Type "model"
d) Click on the viewport border.

Q5-14) The typed command that allows you to create a new viewport.

a) viewports
b) port
c) newport
d) newview

Q5-15) What pen styles table is used if you want to print in black and white?

a) color
b) gray
c) black and white
d) monochrome

Q5-16) The typed command used to edit existing text.

a) ddedit
b) edit
c) text edit
d) tedit

NOTES:

ORTHOGRAPHIC PROJECTIONS IN AUTOCAD® PROBLEMS

P5-1) Create an orthographic projection of the following object. Draw the three standard views. Dimensions given in inches.

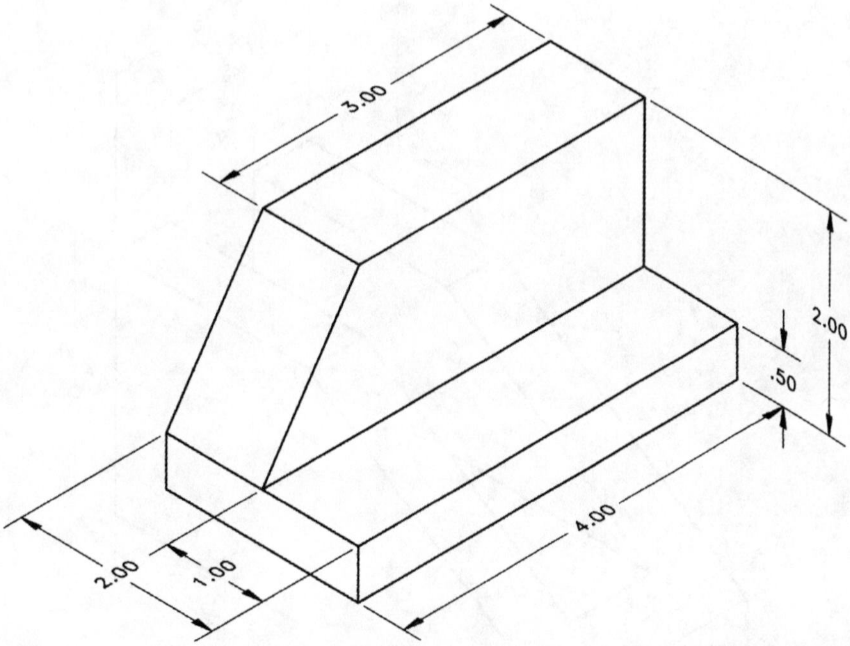

P5-2) Create an orthographic projection of the following object. Draw the three standard views. Dimensions given in inches.

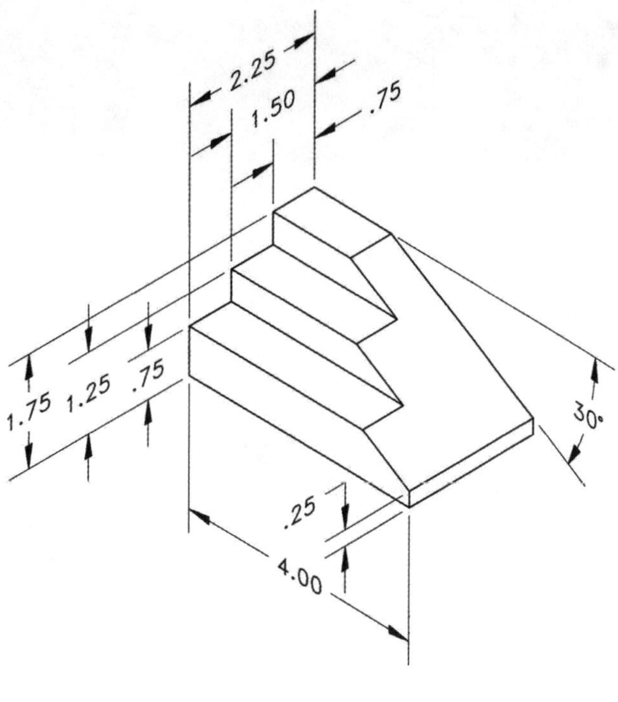

P5-3) Create an orthographic projection of the following object. Draw the three standard views. Dimensions given in inches.

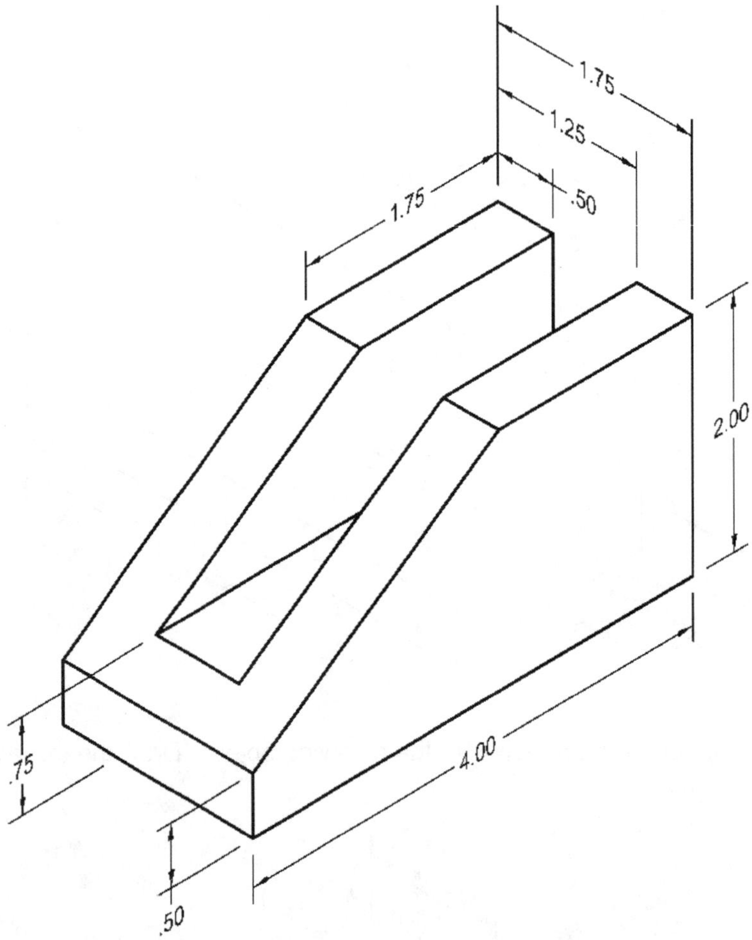

P5-4) Create an orthographic projection of the following object. Draw the three standard views. Dimensions given in millimeters.

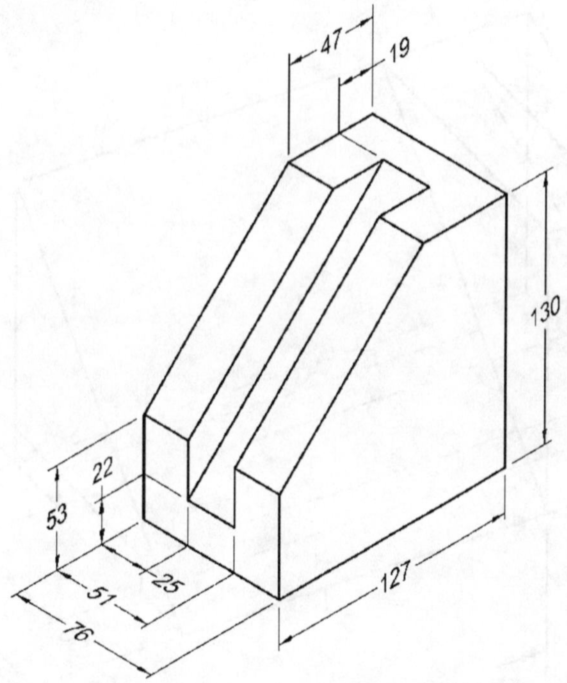

P5-5) Create an orthographic projection of the following object. Draw the three standard views. Dimensions given in millimeters.

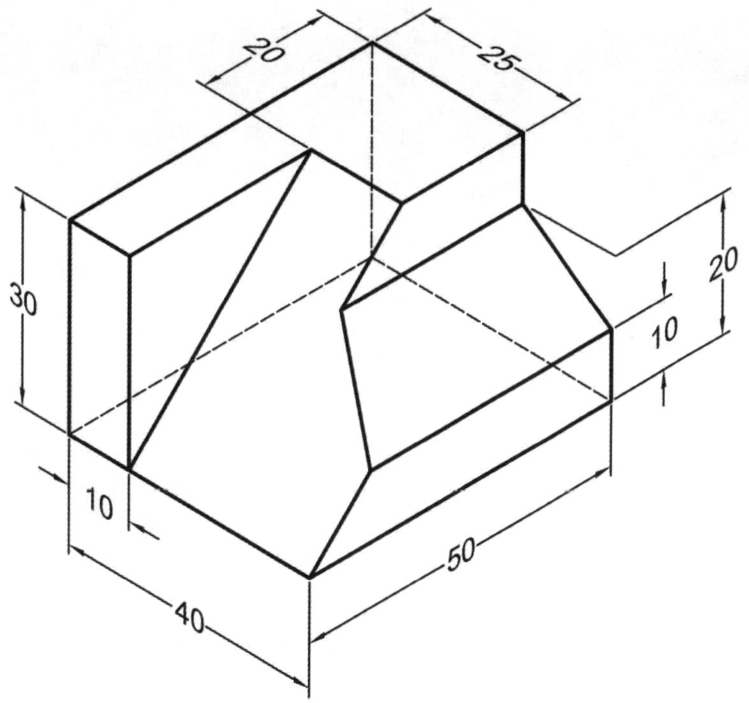

P5-6) Create an orthographic projection of the following object. Draw the three standard views. Dimensions given in inches.

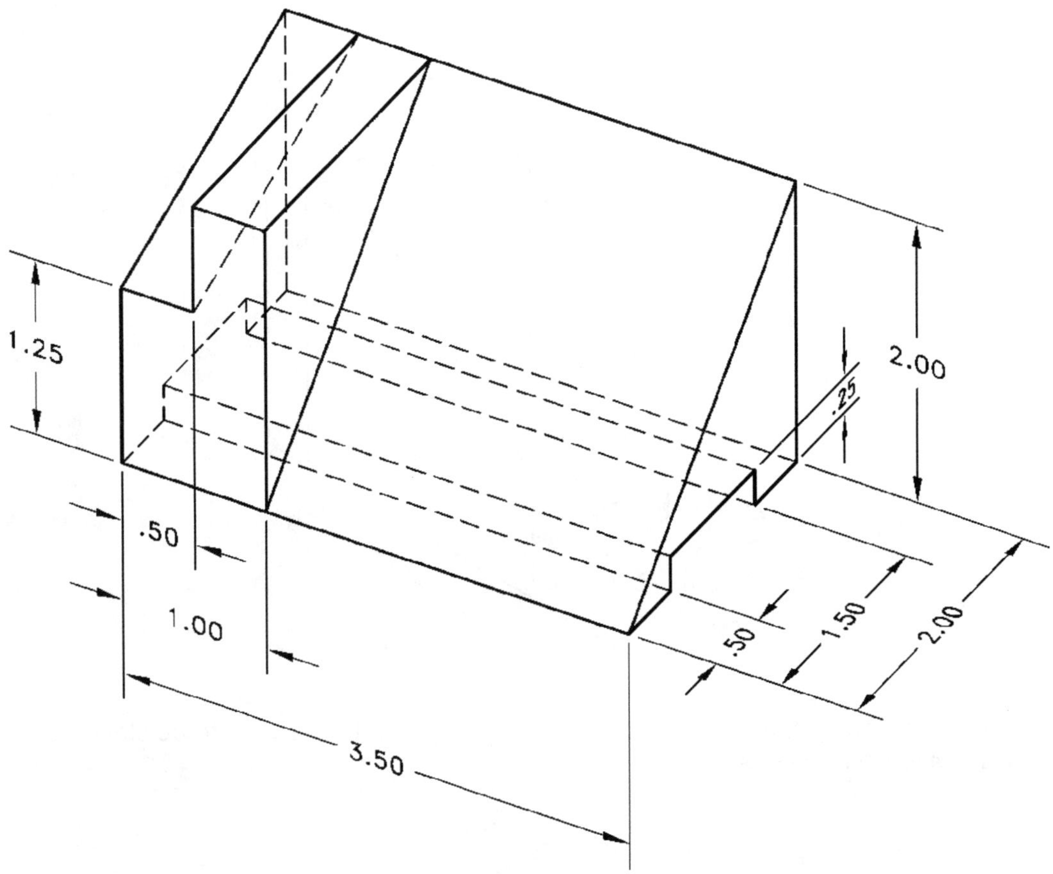

P5-7) Create an orthographic projection of the following object. Draw the three standard views. Dimensions given in inches.

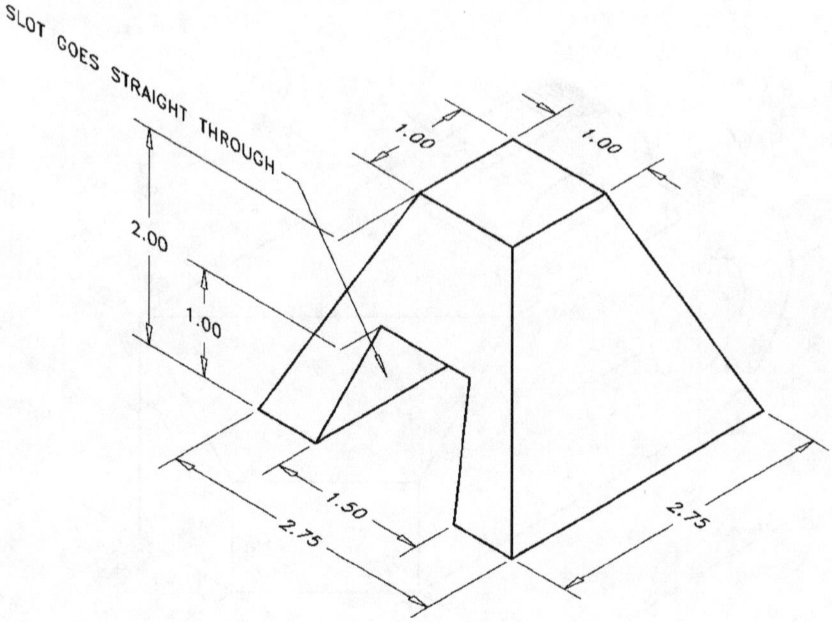

P5-8) Create an orthographic projection of the following object. Draw the three standard views. Dimensions given in inches.

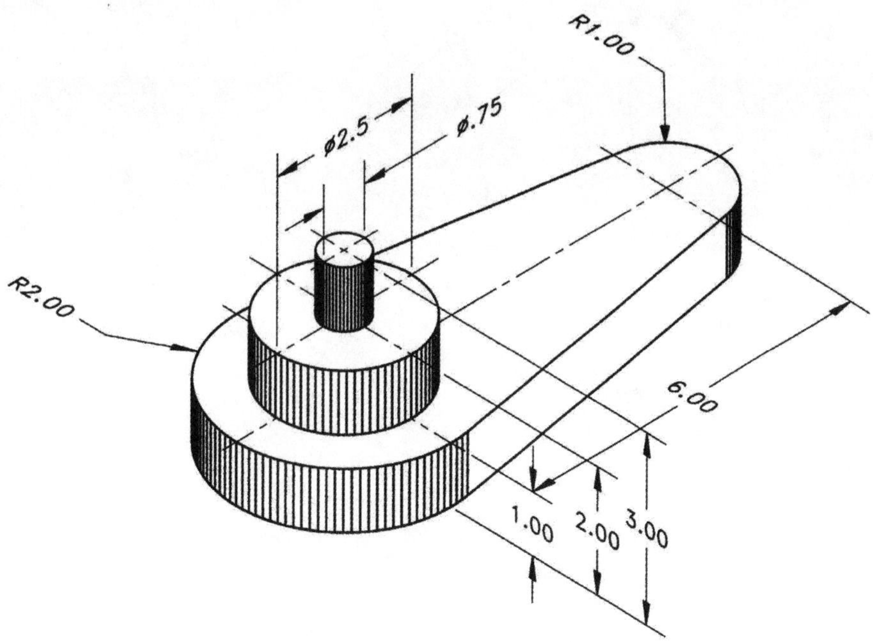

P5-9) Create an orthographic projection of the following object. Draw the three standard views. Dimensions given in inches.

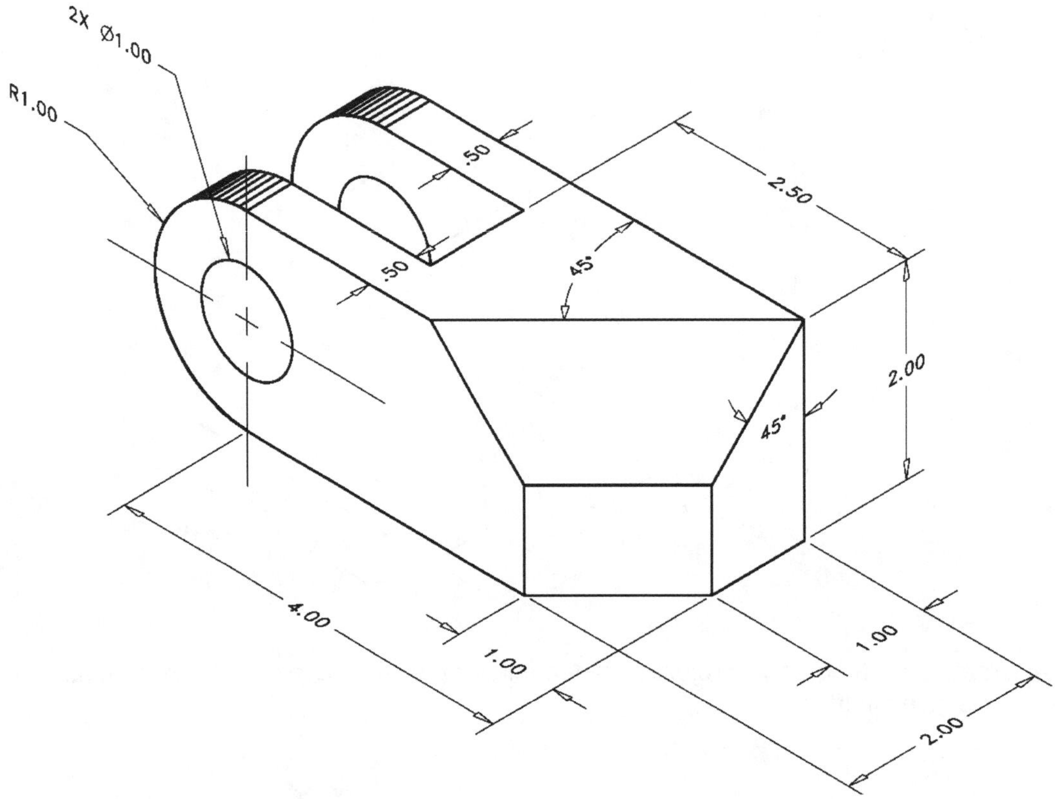

P5-10) Create an orthographic projection of the following object. Draw the three standard views. Dimensions given in inches.

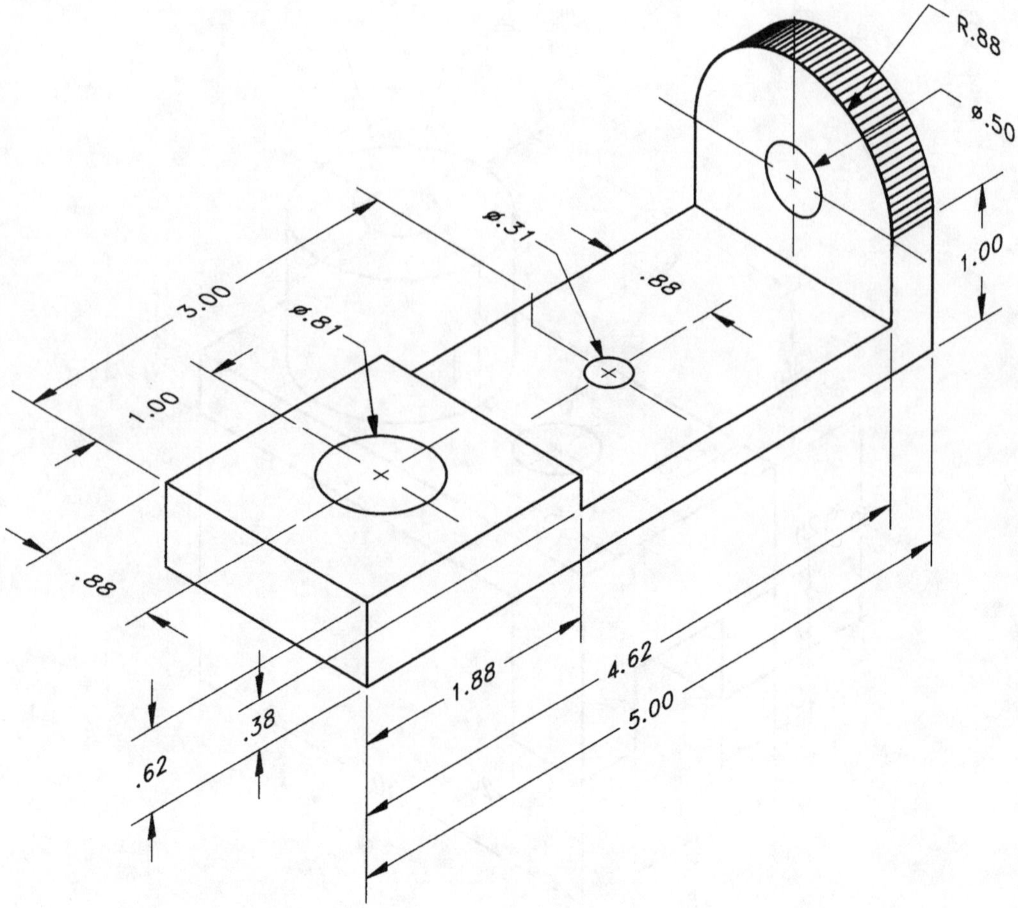

P5-11) Create an orthographic projection of the following object. Draw the three standard views. Dimensions given in millimeters.

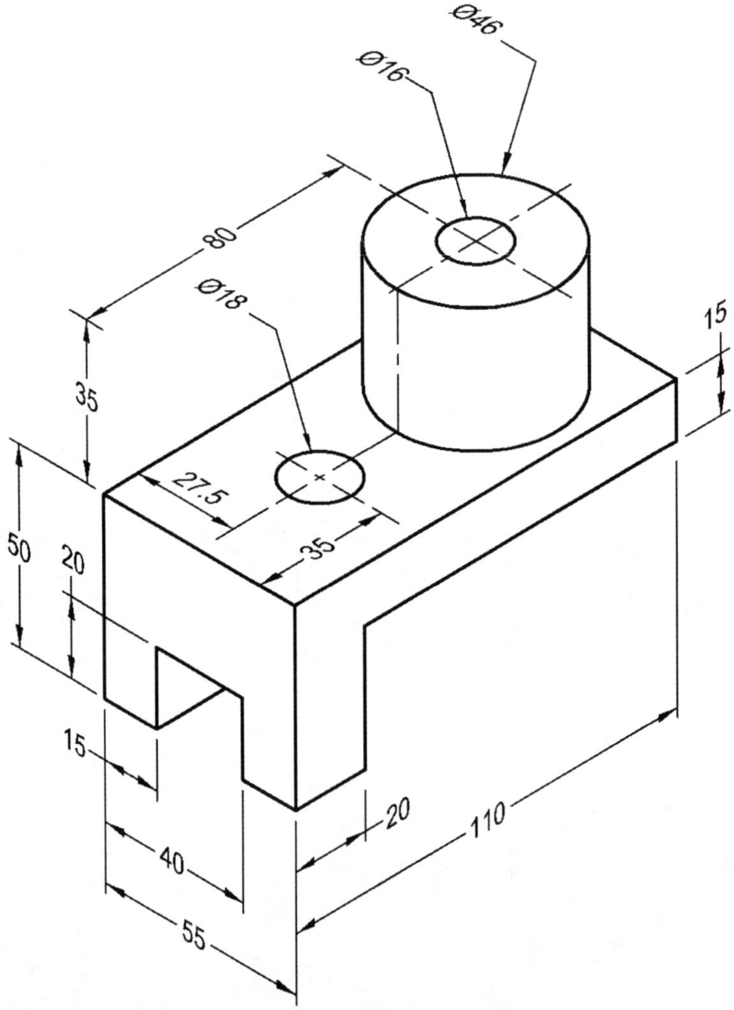

P5-12) Create an orthographic projection of the following object. Draw the three standard views. Dimensions given in inches.

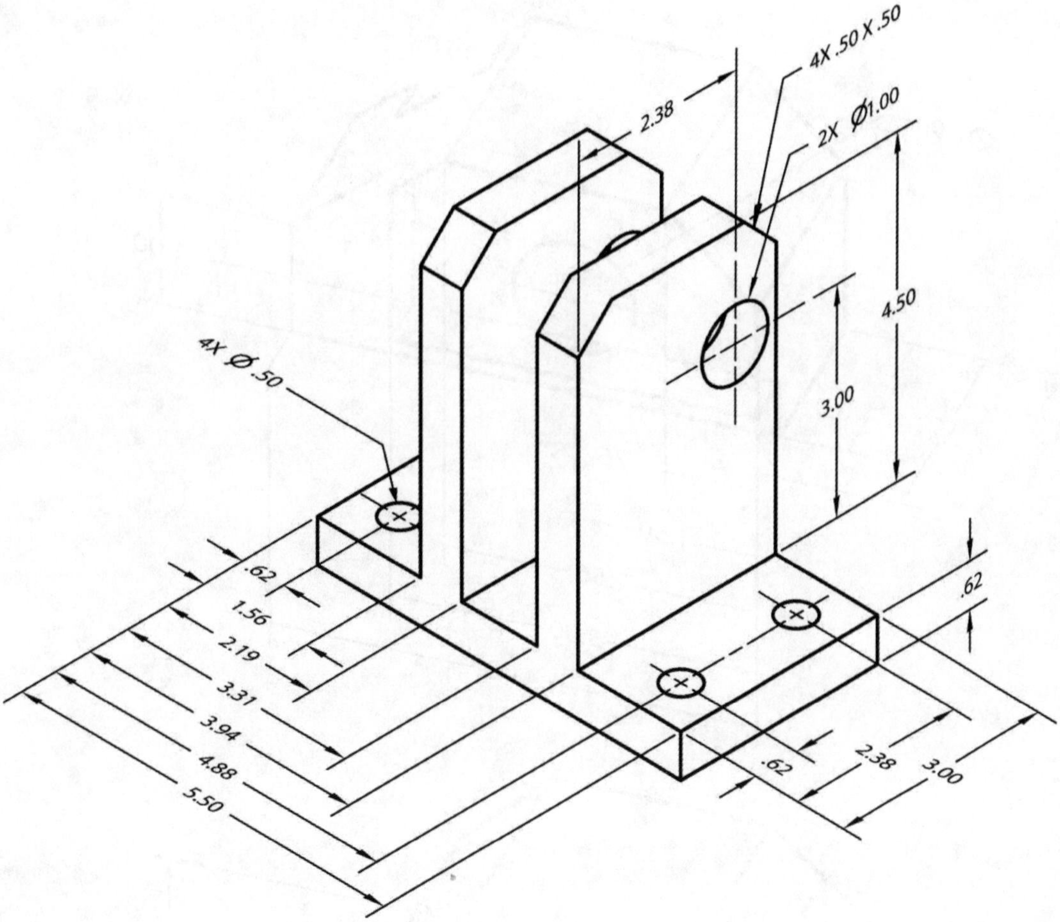

P5-13) Create an orthographic projection of the following object. Draw the three standard views. Dimensions given in inches.

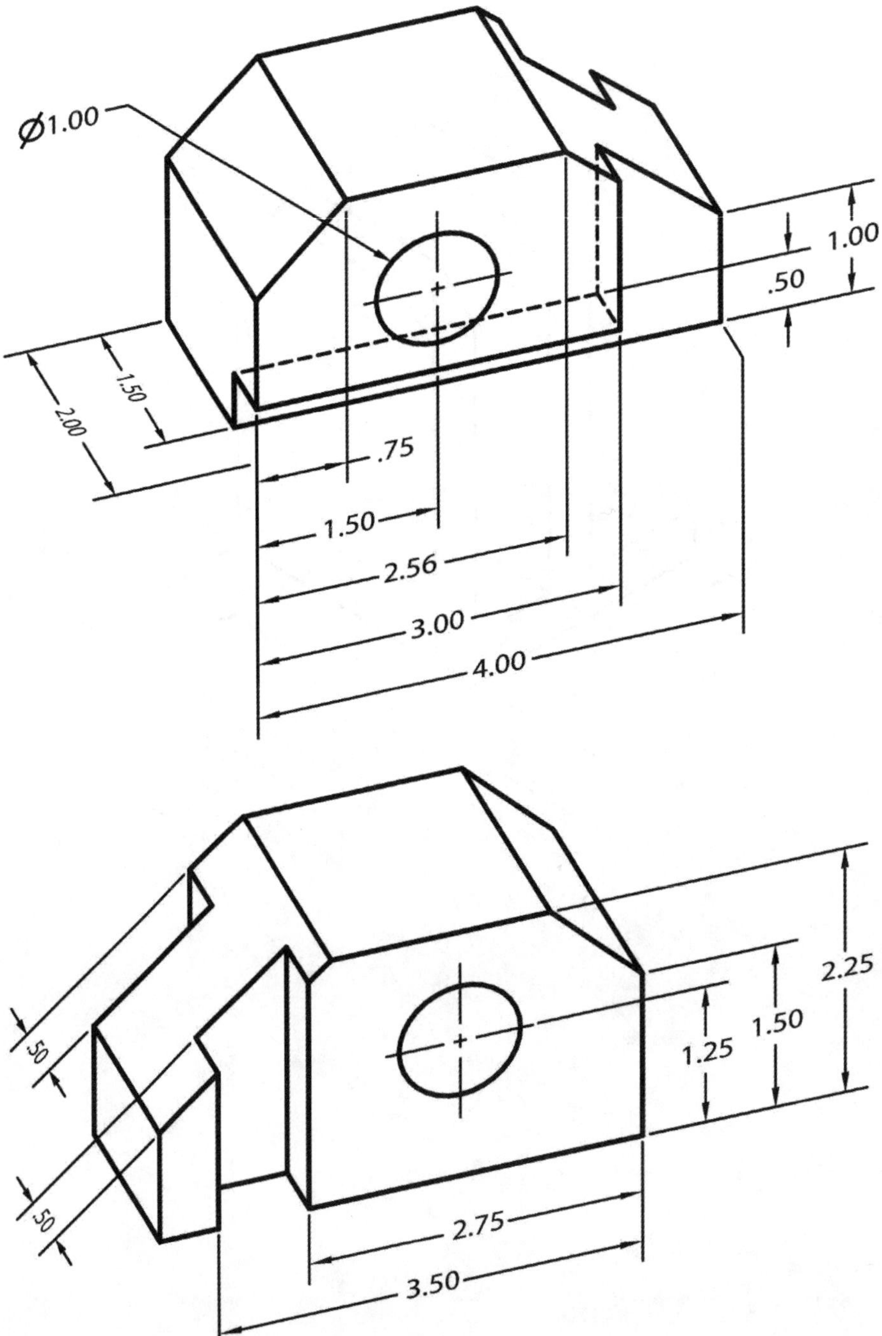

P5-14) Create an orthographic projection of the following object. Draw the three standard views. Dimensions given in millimeters.

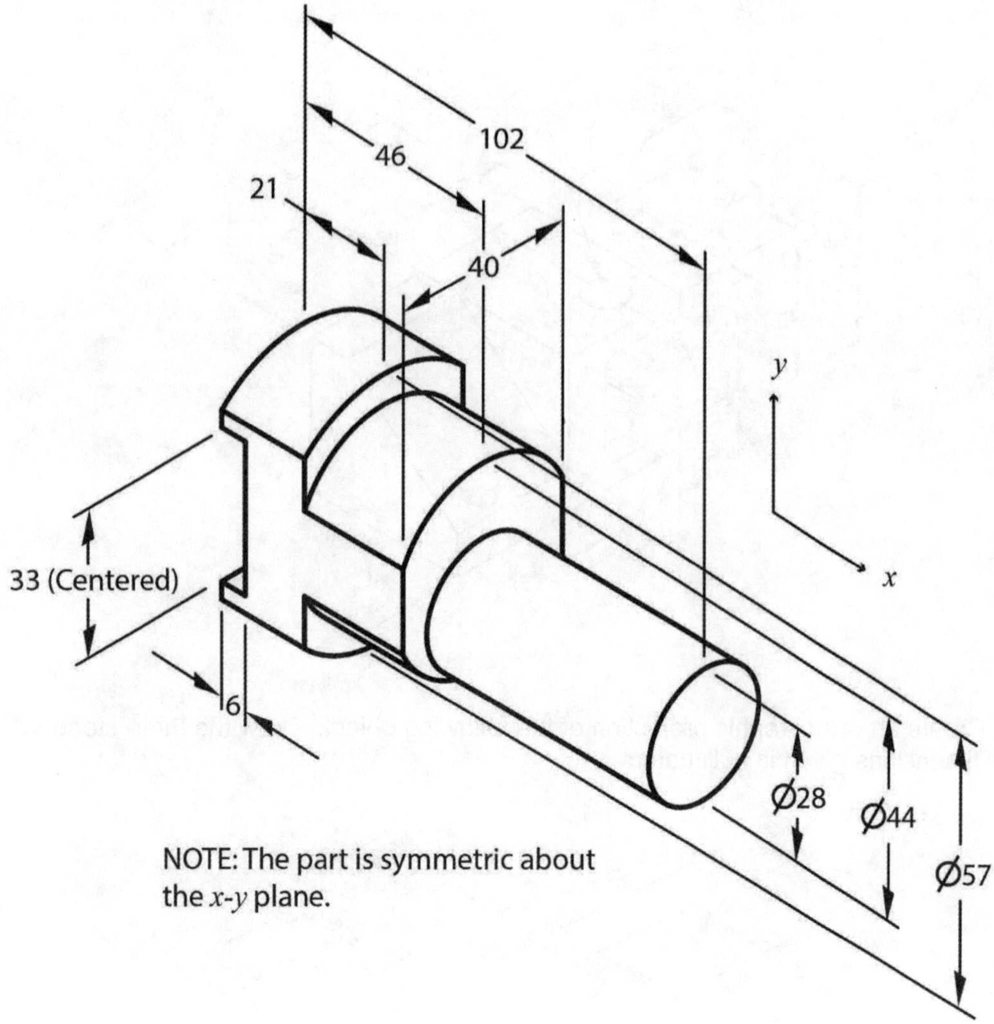

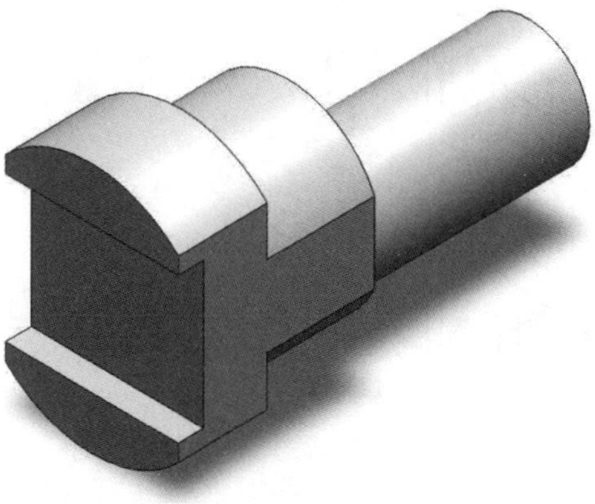

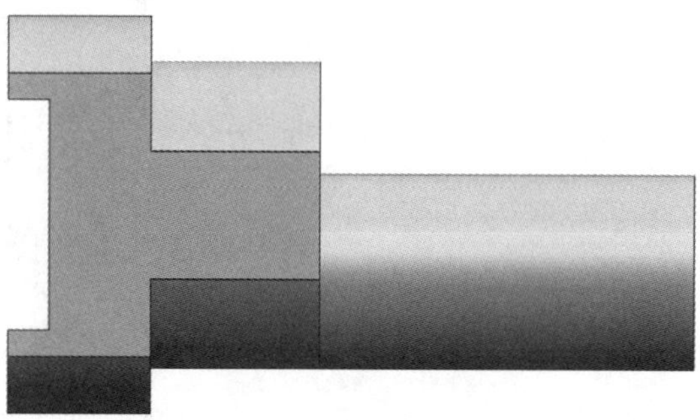

P5-15) Create an orthographic projection of the following object. Draw the three standard views. Dimensions given in inches.

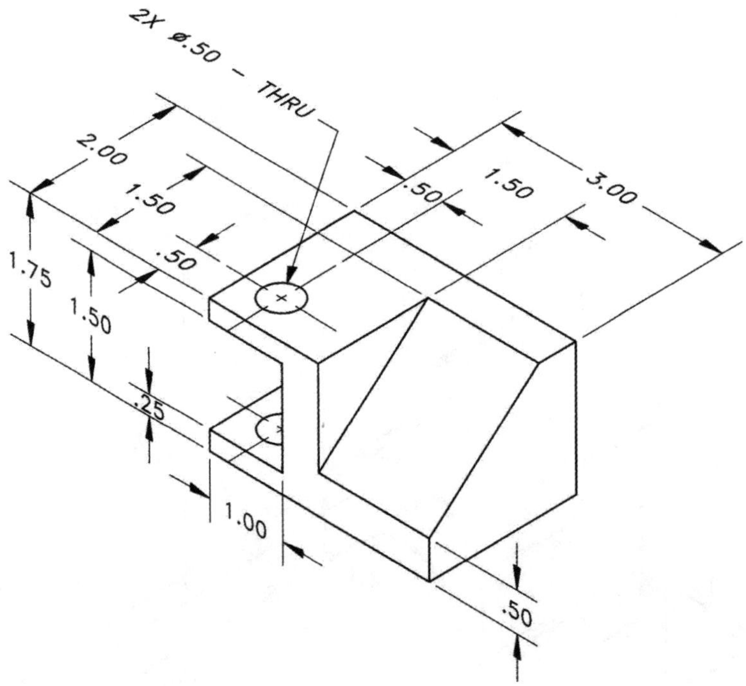

P5-16) Create an orthographic projection of the following object. Draw the three standard views. Dimensions given in millimeters.

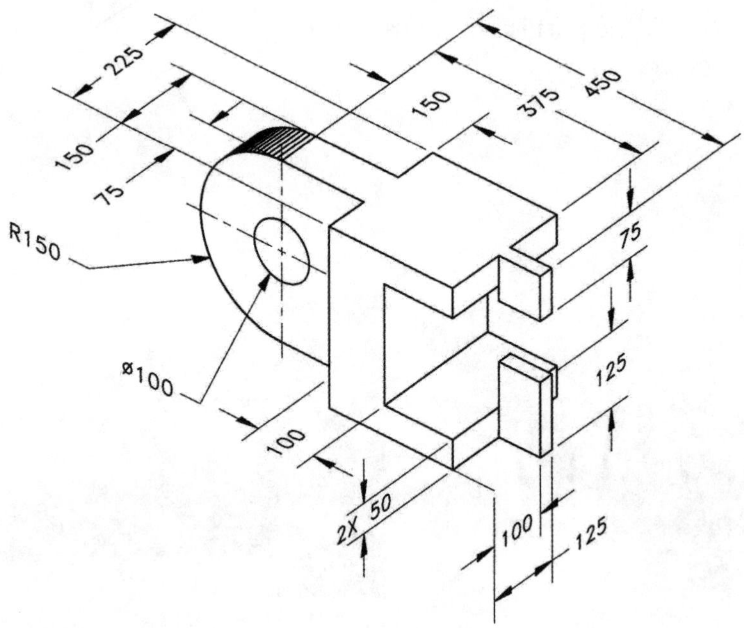

P5-17) Create an orthographic projection of the following object. Draw the three standard views. Dimensions given in millimeters.

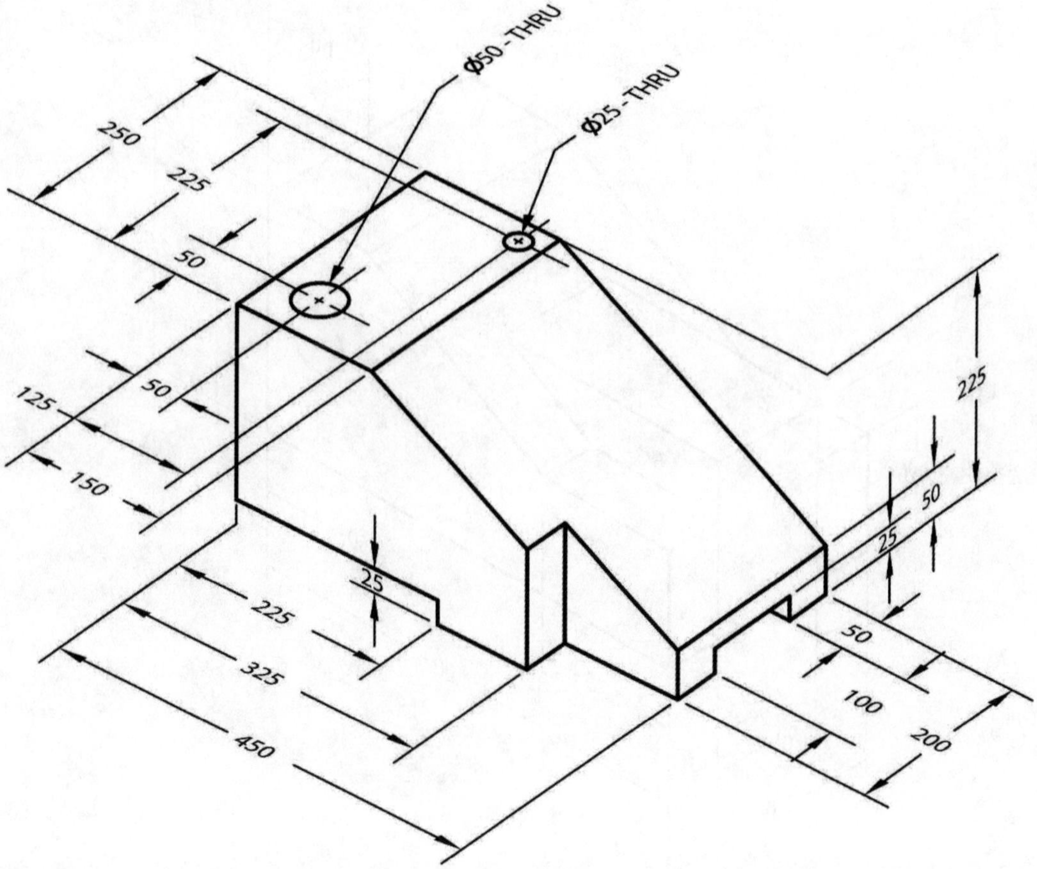

P5-18) Create an orthographic projection of the following object. Draw the three standard views. Dimensions given in inches.

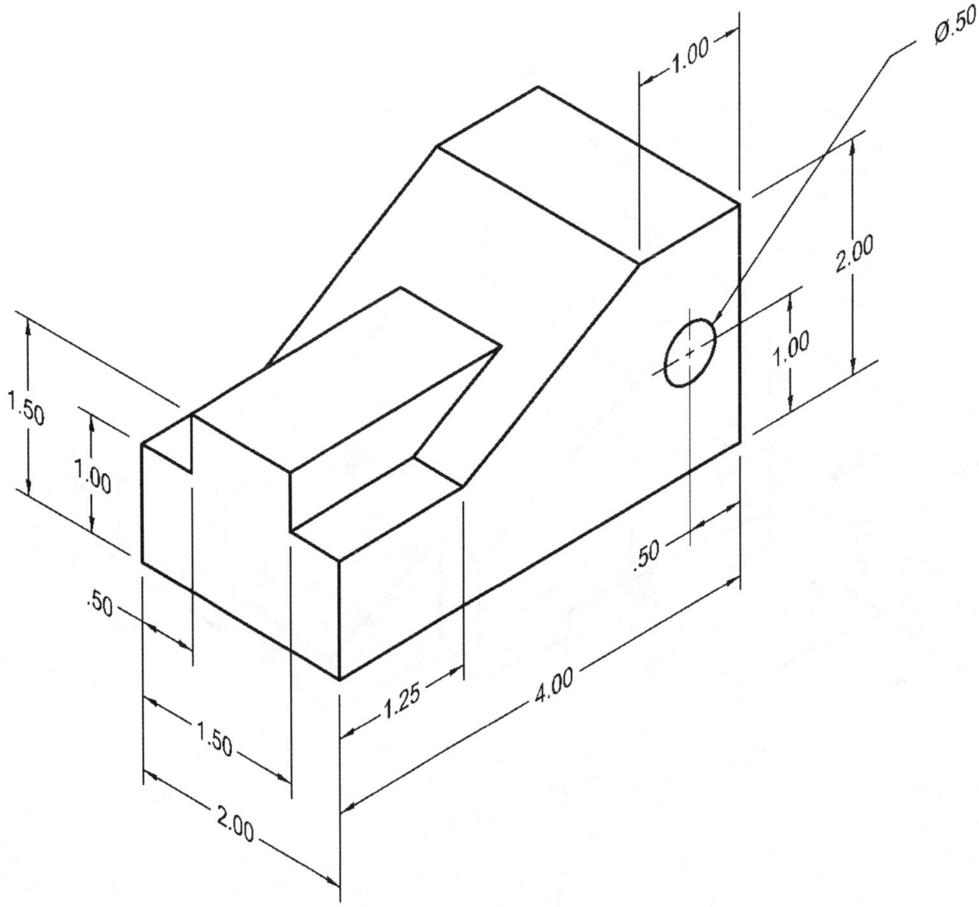

CHAPTER 6

READING PICTORIAL DRAWINGS

CHAPTER OUTLINE

CHAPTER SUMMARY

In this chapter you will learn about pictorial drawings. A pictorial drawing is a representation of an object created in two dimensions, which appears three dimensional. Pictorials are very helpful when trying to interpret a complex part print. By the end of this chapter, you will be able to recognize different types of pictorials.

6.1) PICTORIALS INTRODUCTION

Pictorials are pseudo three-dimensional drawings. That is, they are drawings of an object created in two dimensions, but our brain interprets them as three-dimensional. A pictorial of a part is often included on a detailed drawing to help with the visualization of the part (see Figure 6.1-1). Pictorials are also used to illustrate how parts fit together in an exploded assembly drawing (see Figure 6.1-2).

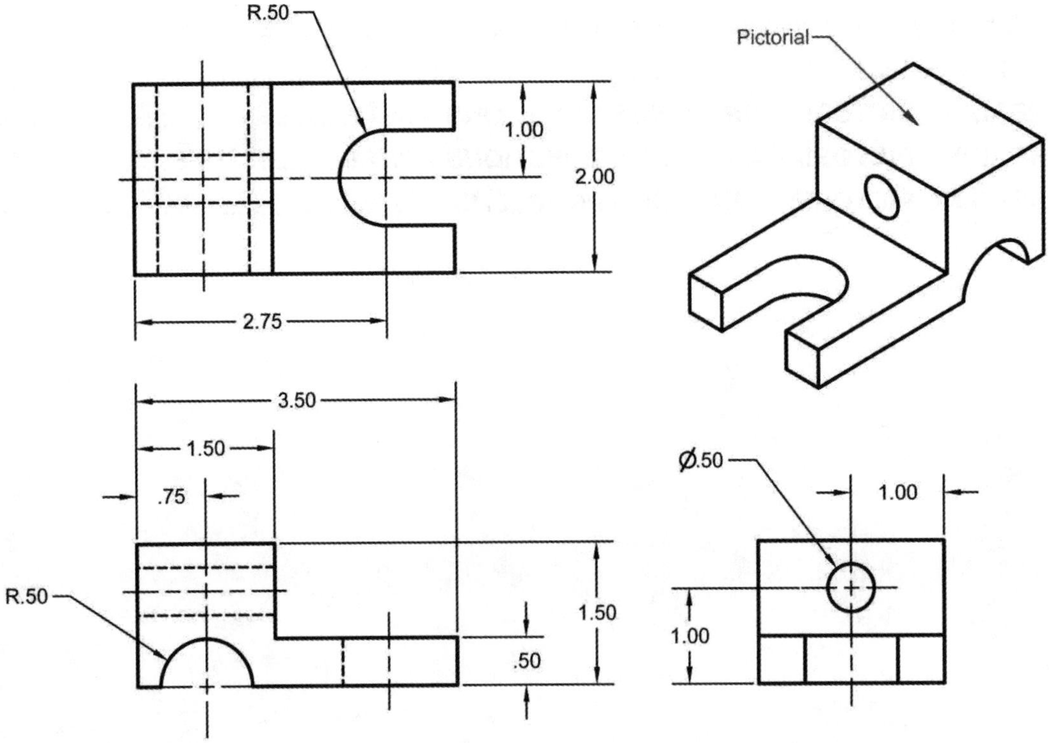

Figure 6.1-1: Pictorial representation added to a detailed drawing

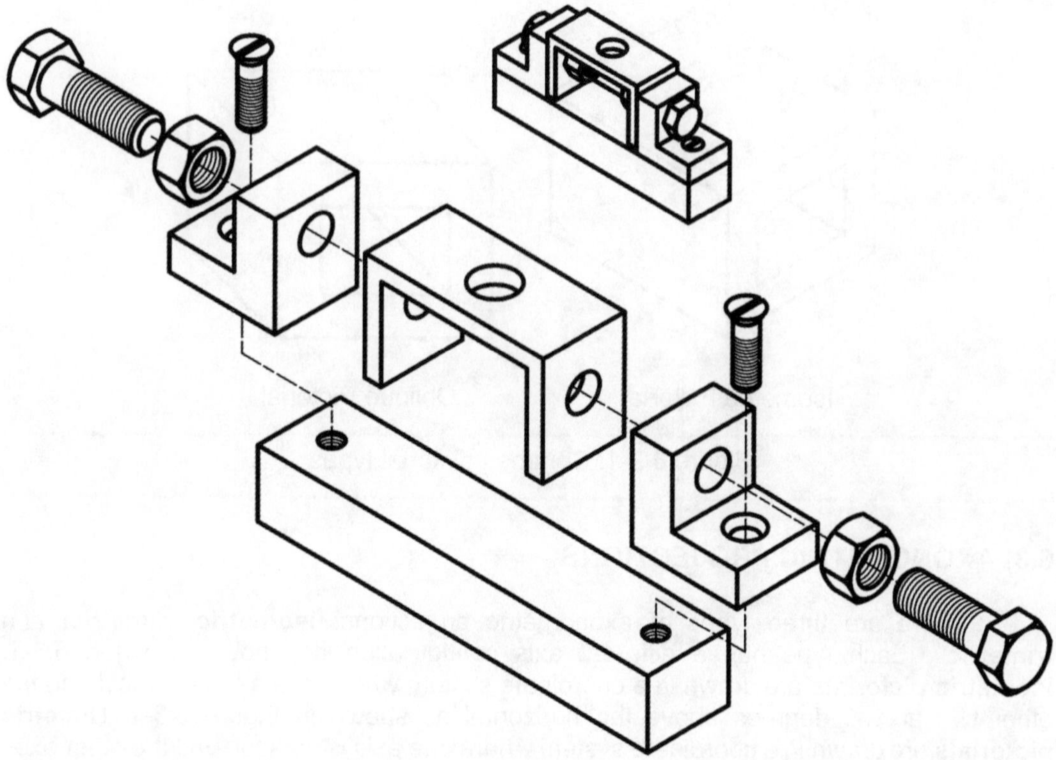

Figure 6.1-2: Exploded assembly drawing

6.2) PICTORIAL TYPES

There are three basic types of pictorial drawings: **axonometric**, **oblique**, and **perspective**. Before computer assisted drawing, the two most used pictorials in engineering drawings were *isometric* and *oblique* (see Figure 6.2-1). Notice that their orientations are different but they both look three dimensional. Different types of pictorials may use different scales on one or more axis directions to make the drawing look more realistic. For example, in Figure 6.2-1, the isometric pictorial uses the same scale on all axes, but the cabinet oblique pictorial uses a half scale in the depth direction to portray a more realistic rendering of the object. The scale that each axis uses is not important to remember when you are just interpreting the drawing. It will become more important when you start drawing pictorials yourself.

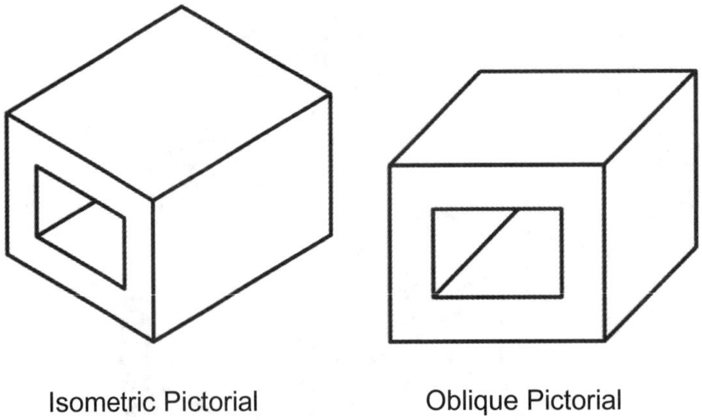

Figure 6.2-1: Common pictorial types

6.3) AXONOMETRIC PROJECTIONS

There are three types of axonometric projections: **isometric**, **dimetric**, and **trimetric**. Each type has a different axis configuration as shown in Figure 6.3-1. **Isometric pictorials** are drawn in a coordinate system where one axis is vertical and the other two are 30 degrees above the horizontal as shown in Figure 6.3-1. **Dimetric pictorials** are drawn in a coordinate system where one axis is vertical, and the other axes are drawn at an angle that is equal and may vary between 0 and 45 degrees above the horizontal as shown in Figure 6.3-1. **Trimetric pictorials** are drawn in a coordinate system where one axis is vertical, and the other axes may vary in angle above the horizontal as shown in Figure 6.3-1.

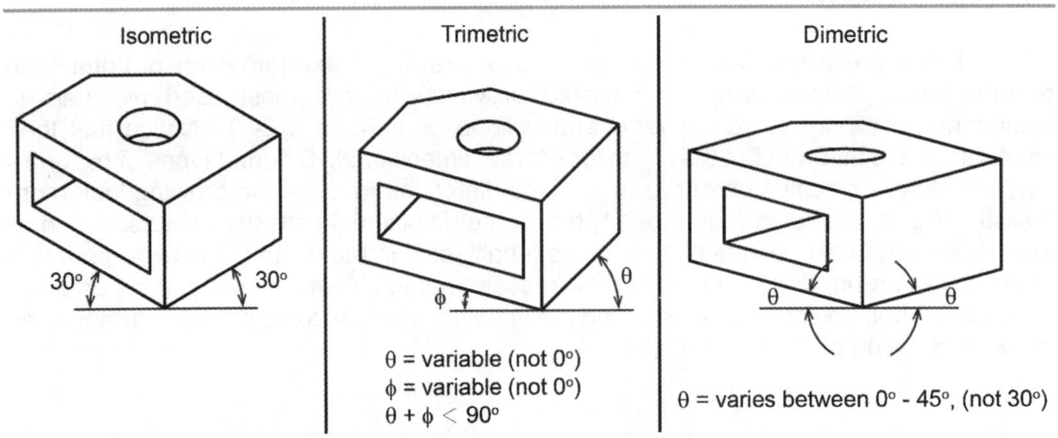

Figure 6.3-1: Axonometric projection types

Try Exercise 6.3-1

Exercise 6.3-1: Axonometric pictorial identification

Identify what type of axonometric pictorial is used to represent the following object.

______________ ______________ ______________

6.4) OBLIQUE PROJECTIONS

There are three types of oblique pictorials: **cavalier**, **cabinet**, and **general** as shown in Figure 6.4-1. All three types draw one side of the part flat and full-scale on the plane of paper as if you are looking at that side straight on. The other features that seem to go into the paper are drawn at different scales depending on the pictorial type. A **cavalier projection** is an oblique projection where all features are drawn at full scale. A **cabinet projection** is an oblique projection where all features drawn on the angled axis are drawn at half scale. A **general oblique projection** is where all features drawn on the angled axis are drawn at a scale but not at full or half scale. Figure 6.4-1 shows an example of each type of oblique pictorial.

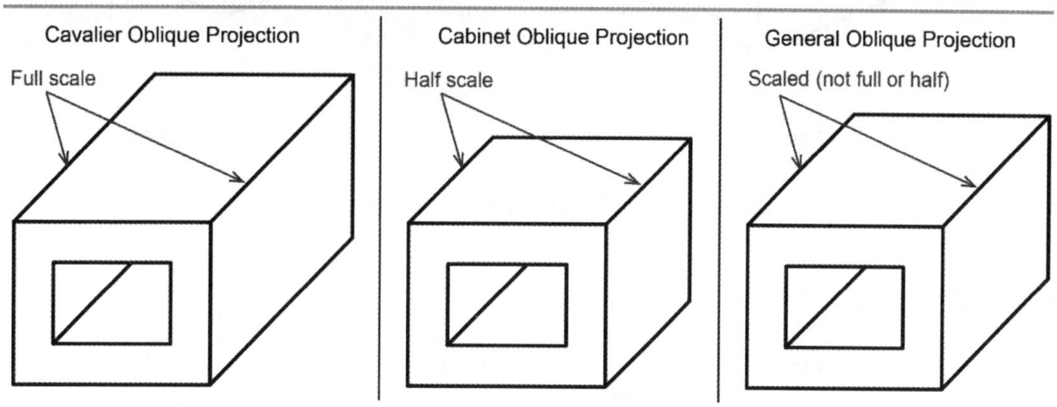

Figure 6.4-1: Oblique pictorial types

6.5) PERSPECTIVE PROJECTIONS

A perspective projection is one in which the projectors are not parallel, instead they converge to a point of sight as shown in Figure 6.5-1. This means that edges that are parallel on the real object will not necessarily be parallel in a perspective projection. There are three types of perspective projections: **one-point**, **two-point**, and **three-point**.

6.5.1) Types of perspective projections

In a **one-point perspective**, the height and width of the object are shown vertically and horizontally, and the depth axis will converge to a single vanishing point (see Figure 6.5-1). In **two-point perspective projection** the height is shown vertically and the width and depth axes each converge to their own vanishing point. In **three-point perspective projection** the height, width, and depth axes will each converge to their own vanishing point. Figure 6.5-1shows examples of each type of perspective projection.

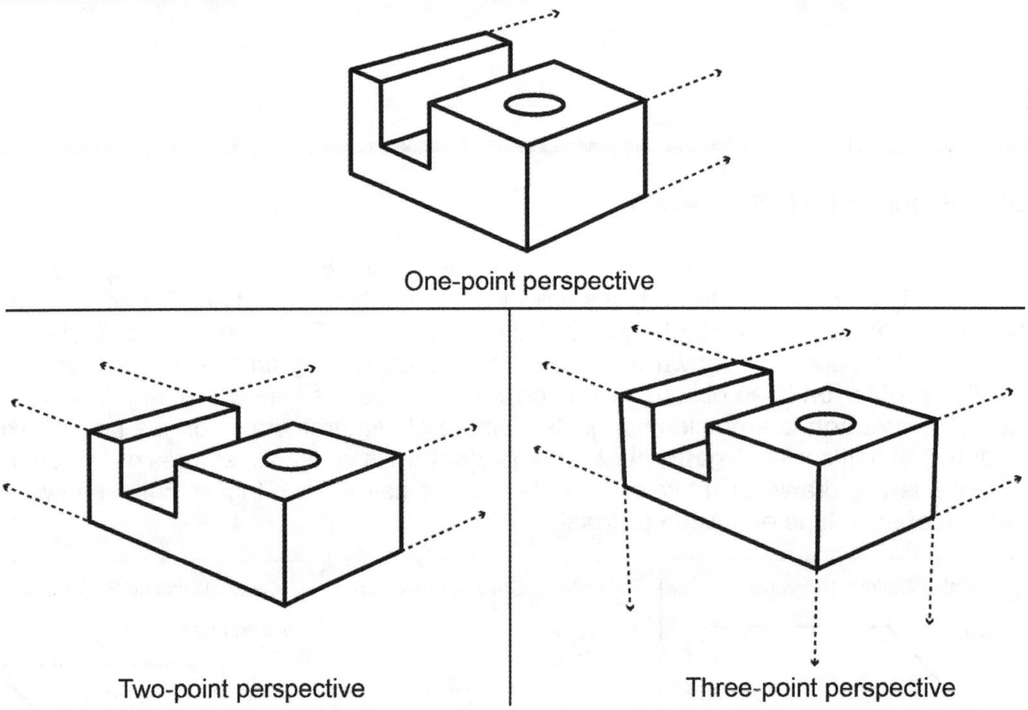

Figure 6.5-1: Perspective projection types

6.6) VISUALIZATION

Visualization is the ability to picture in your mind how a 3D part would look like as a 2D orthographic projection and vice versa. Being able to visualize a part is important for two reasons. First, if you are given a part print you should have the skills to turn that drawing into a 3D object in your mind. Second, if you create an orthographic projection automatically, you should be able to verify its correctness.

Exercise 6.6-1: Pictorial matching

Based on the orthographic projection shown, circle the pictorial that represents the true shape of the object.

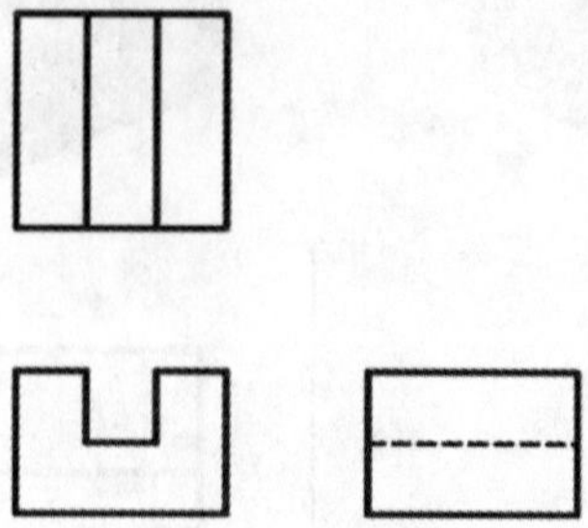

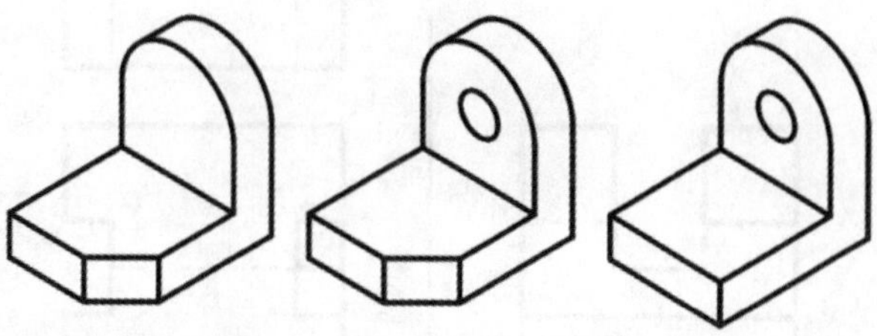

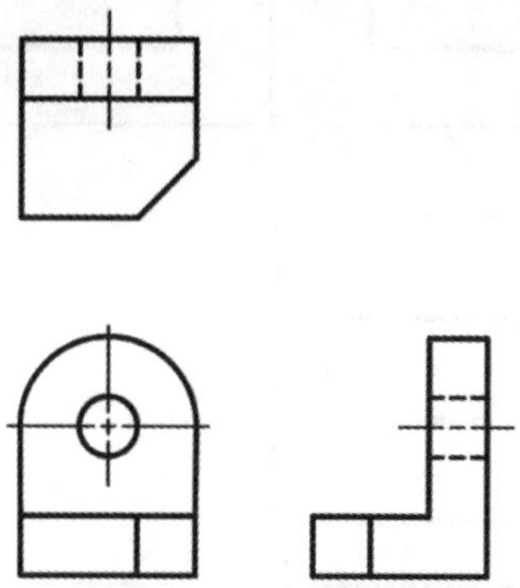

Exercise 6.6-2: Orthographic projection matching

Based on the pictorials shown, circle the orthographic projection that represents the true shape of the object.

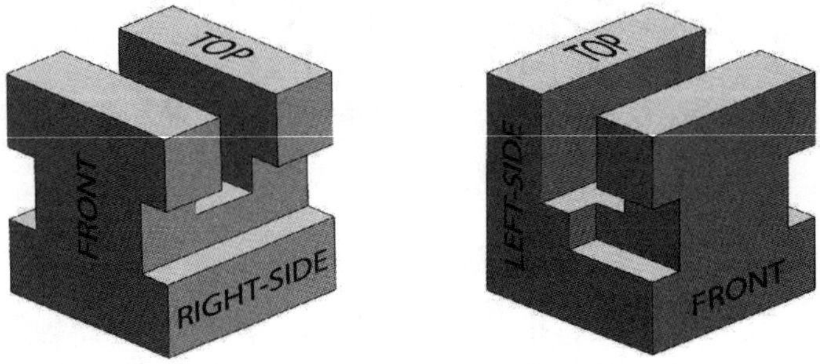

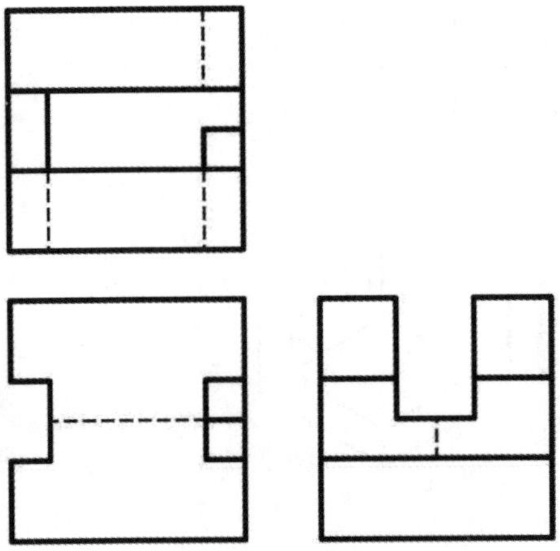

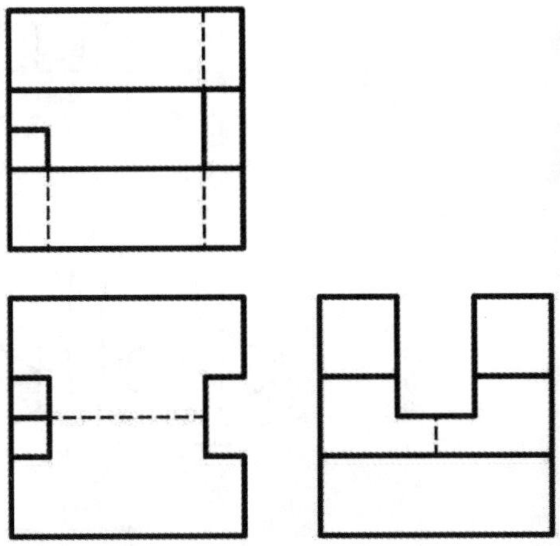

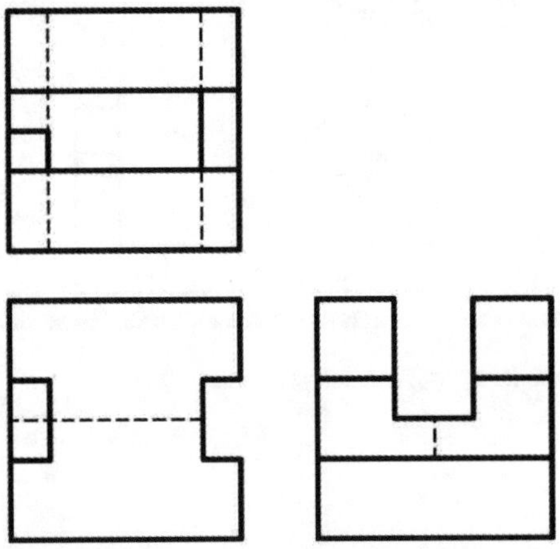

READING PICTORIAL DRAWINGS QUESTIONS – SET1

Name: ______________________________ Date: _____________

Q6-1) A pictorial drawing is a two-dimensional rendering of a part, but the drawing still looks ____________. Fill in the blank.

Q6-2) List the three different types of pictorials.

Q6-3) Pictorials help a print reader ______________ a part.

NOTES:

READING PICTORIAL DRAWINGS QUESTIONS – SET2

Name: ________________________________ Date: ______________

Q6-4) List the three different types of axonometric projections.

Q6-5) List the three different types of oblique projections.

Q6-6) List the three different types of perspective projections.

Q6-7) Visualization is the ability to imagine, in your mind, how a 2-D orthographic projection will look in ____________ and vice versa.

NOTES:

READING PICTORIAL DRAWINGS PROBLEMS

Name: ______________________________ Date: ______________

P6-1) Match the correct pictorial to the orthographic projection.

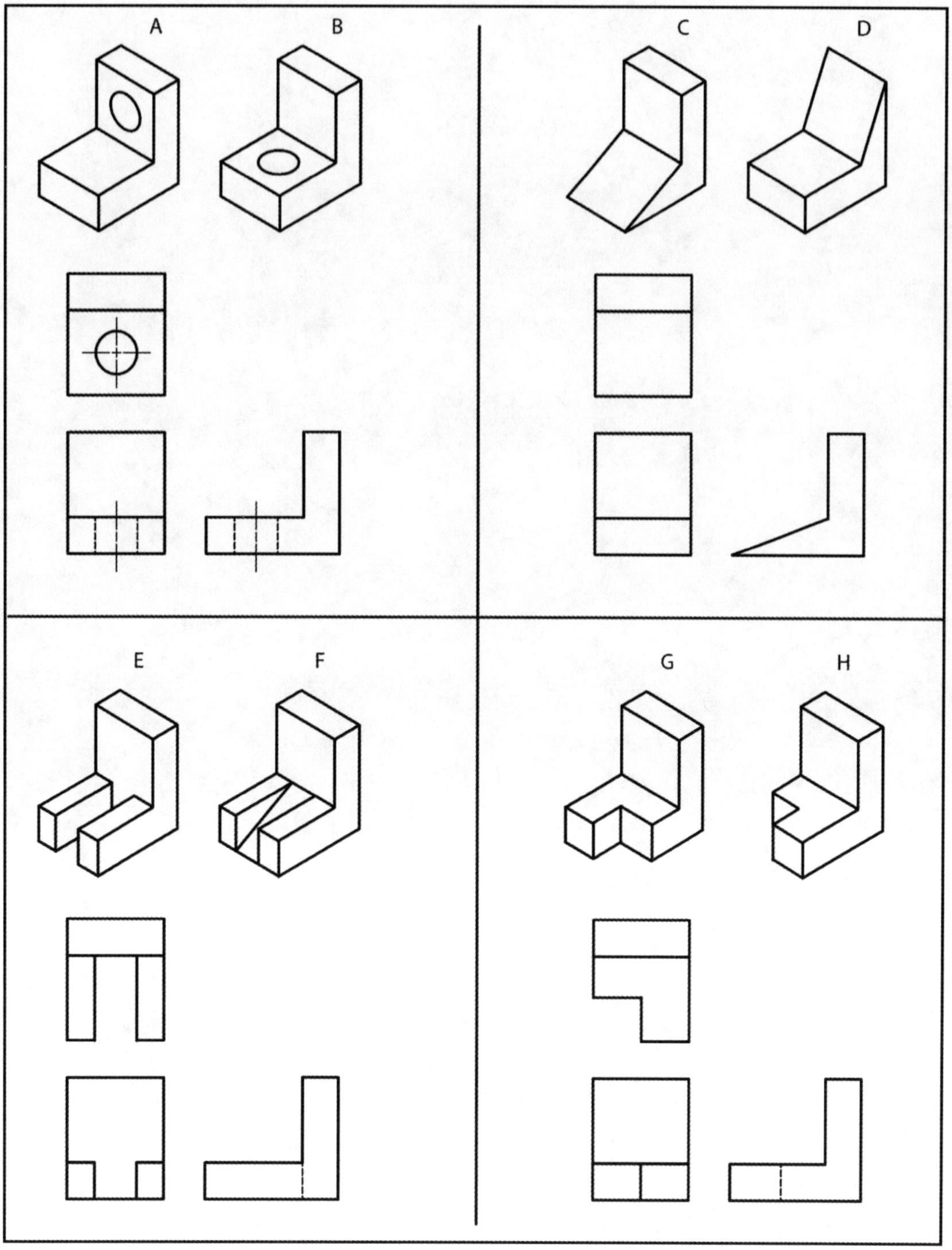

NOTES:

Name: ______________________________ Date: ______________

P6-2) Match the correct pictorial to the orthographic projection.

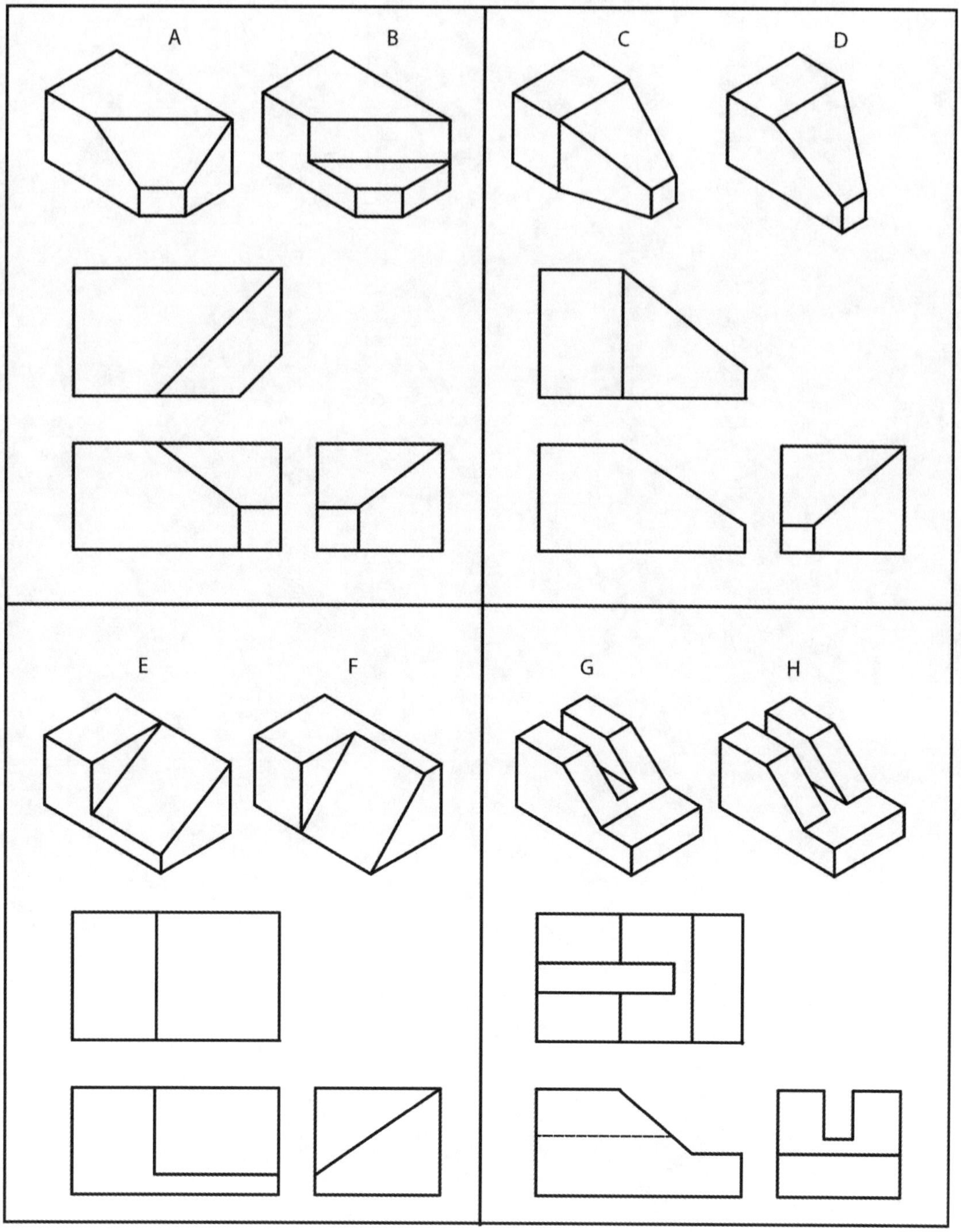

NOTES:

Name: ______________________________ Date: ______________

P6-3) Match the correct pictorial to the orthographic projection.

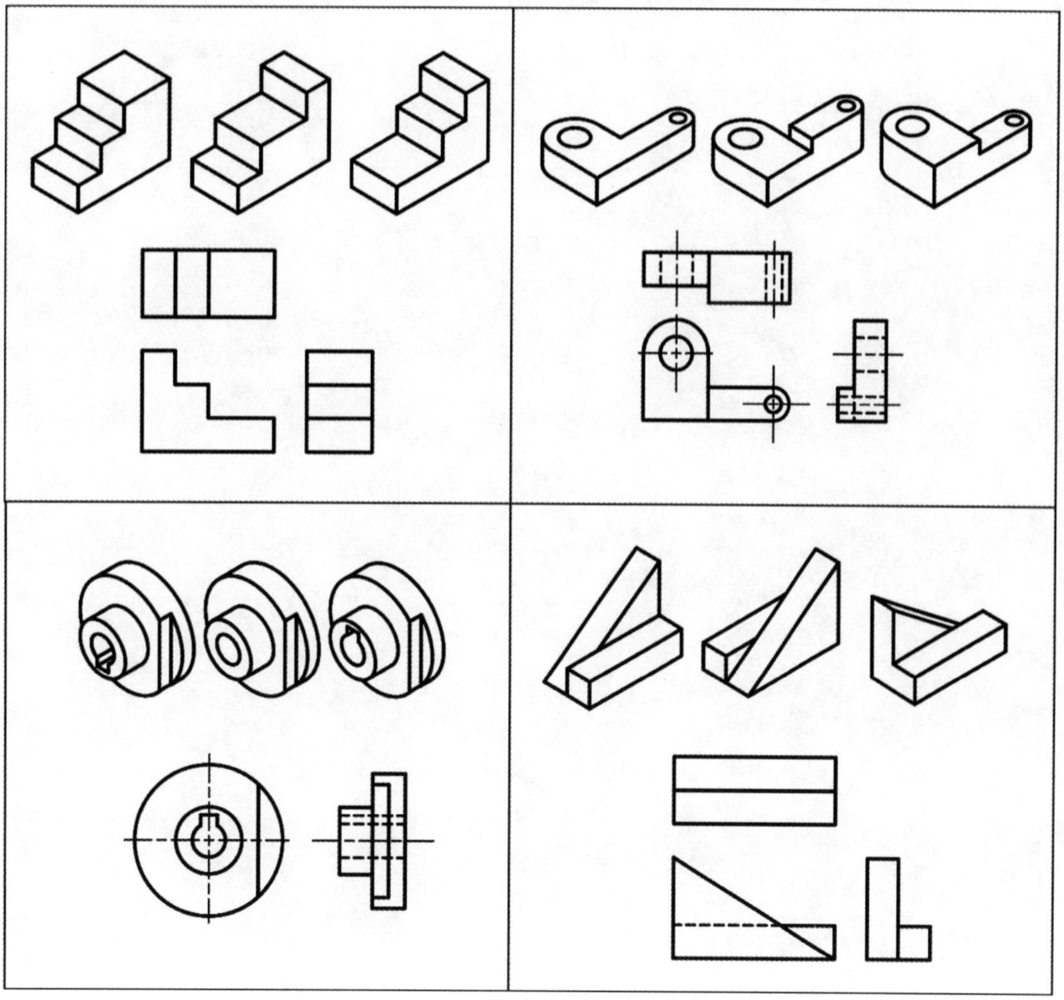

NOTES:

Name: ______________________________ Date: _____________

P6-4) Match the correct orthographic projection to the given pictorial.

A

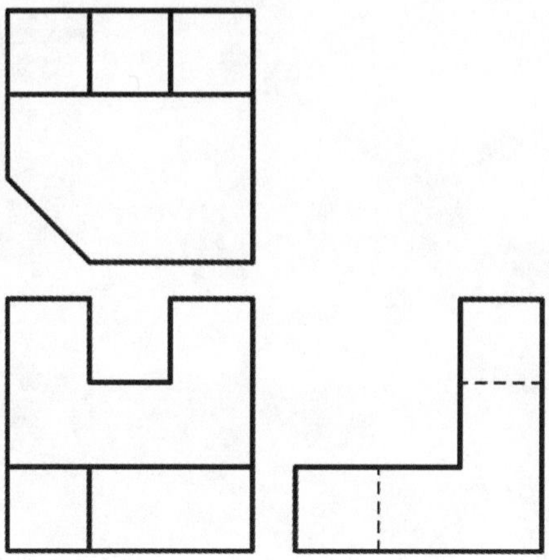

B

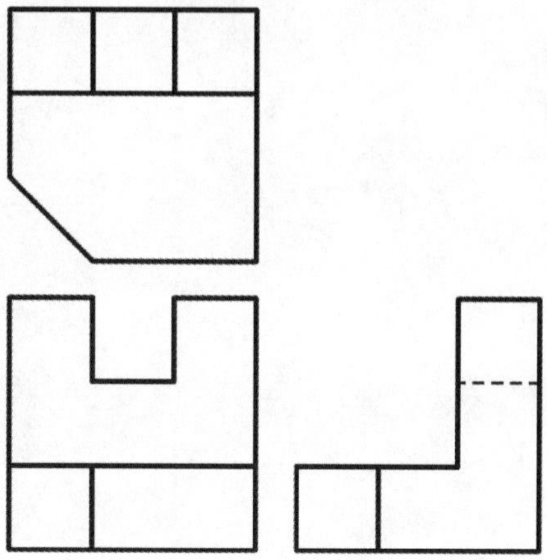

C

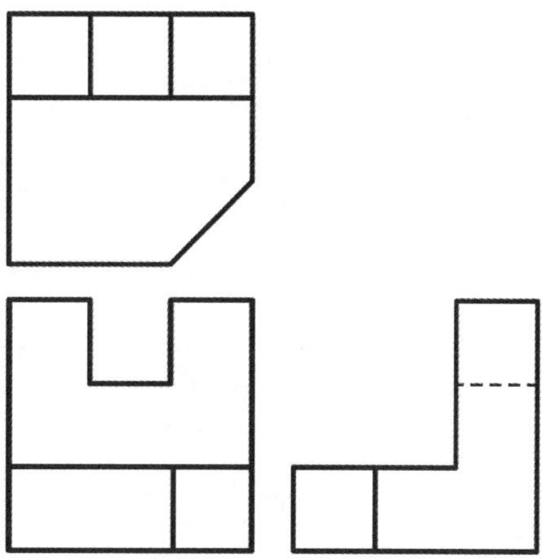

NOTES:

CHAPTER 7

CREATING PICTORIAL DRAWINGS

CHAPTER OUTLINE

CHAPTER SUMMARY

In this chapter you will learn how to create pictorial drawings. Pictorials are very helpful when you are trying to communicate design ideas to an audience that is unfamiliar with orthographic projections. By the end of this chapter, you will be able to sketch isometric and oblique pictorials based on an orthographic projection of the part.

7.1) PICTORIAL TYPES

Pictorials are very useful when trying to communicate design ideas to an audience that may not know how to read an orthographic projection. Being able to efficiently and effectively create a pictorial sketch will enable you to get your idea across to your design team quickly and with less possibility of misinterpretation (see Figure 7.1-1).

In the chapter on reading pictorials, we learned that there are three basic types of pictorial drawings: **axonometric**, **oblique**, and **perspective**. Each of these three pictorial types differ in their relationship between the object and the point of sight. Choosing a pictorial type depends on your part geometry, the pictorials available in your software package, and your ability to draw one type more easily than another. The procedure for creating isometric and cabinet oblique pictorials will be discussed in subsequent sections in detail. Most computer drawing and modeling packages are set up to create pictorial drawings. Some programs let you choose the type of pictorial; however, many others create the pictorial based on your current model view which rarely coincides with one of the three types of pictorials mentioned. The pictorial types discussed in this book and how they are constructed are in accordance with the ASME – Y14.3 standard.

Figure 7.1-1: Pictorial sketches of design ideas

7.2) AXONOMETRIC PROJECTIONS

There are three types of axonometric projections: **isometric**, **dimetric**, and **trimetric**. Each type has a different axonometric axes configuration as shown in Figure 7.2-1. The type of axonometric projection used should be chosen based on which type will give the clearest description of the object.

An axonometric projection creates a pictorial by using projectors that are perpendicular to the plane of projection and parallel to each other. All the principal edges in an axonometric pictorial are drawn on or parallel to the axonometric axes as shown in Figure 7.2-1. On the real object, the principal edges are 90° apart and lie on or parallel to the *x-y-z* coordinate system. In order to produce the illusion of a three-dimensional object, the axonometric axes are not 90° apart. They will vary in degrees depending on the type of pictorial being used. When looking at Figure 7.2-1, notice how each type of axonometric pictorial uses axes that are angled differently. Also, notice that the holes in the object are interpreted by the brain as circular. However, if you look closely, circular features such as holes, cylinders, and radii are drawn as ellipses.

7.2.1) Types of axonometric pictorials

Isometric pictorials are drawn in a coordinate system where one axis is vertical and the other two are 30 degrees above the horizontal as shown in Figure 7.2-1. The height of the object is drawn along the vertical axis and the width and depth are drawn along the axes that are at a 30-degree angle from the horizontal. Isometric pictorials are drawn at a uniform scale which means that the scale of all features drawn on the three isometric axes are the same. The most realistic looking scale is 80%. However, Features drawn at an angle to the axes are not at the same scale as lines and features along or parallel to the axes.

Dimetric pictorials are drawn in a coordinate system where one axis is vertical, and the others are angled above the horizontal. The angle is the same for both angled axes which can vary between 0 and 45 degrees as shown in Figure 7.2-1. If the angle becomes 30 degrees, it is identified as an isometric pictorial. The height of the object is drawn along the vertical axis and the width and depth are drawn along angled axes. The scaling of a dimetric pictorial is equal along the angled axes but may be different on the vertical axis. Features at an angle to the dimetric axes will naturally be at a different scale.

Trimetric pictorials are drawn in a coordinate system where one axis is vertical, and the other axes may vary in angle above the horizontal as shown in Figure 7.2-1. The varying axis angles are not equal to each other and may not be zero degrees. If the angle becomes equal, it is identified as a dimetric pictorial. The sum of the two angles of the non-vertical axes may not exceed 90 degrees. The height of the object is drawn along the vertical axis, and the width and depth are drawn along the angled axes. Each axis may use a different scale.

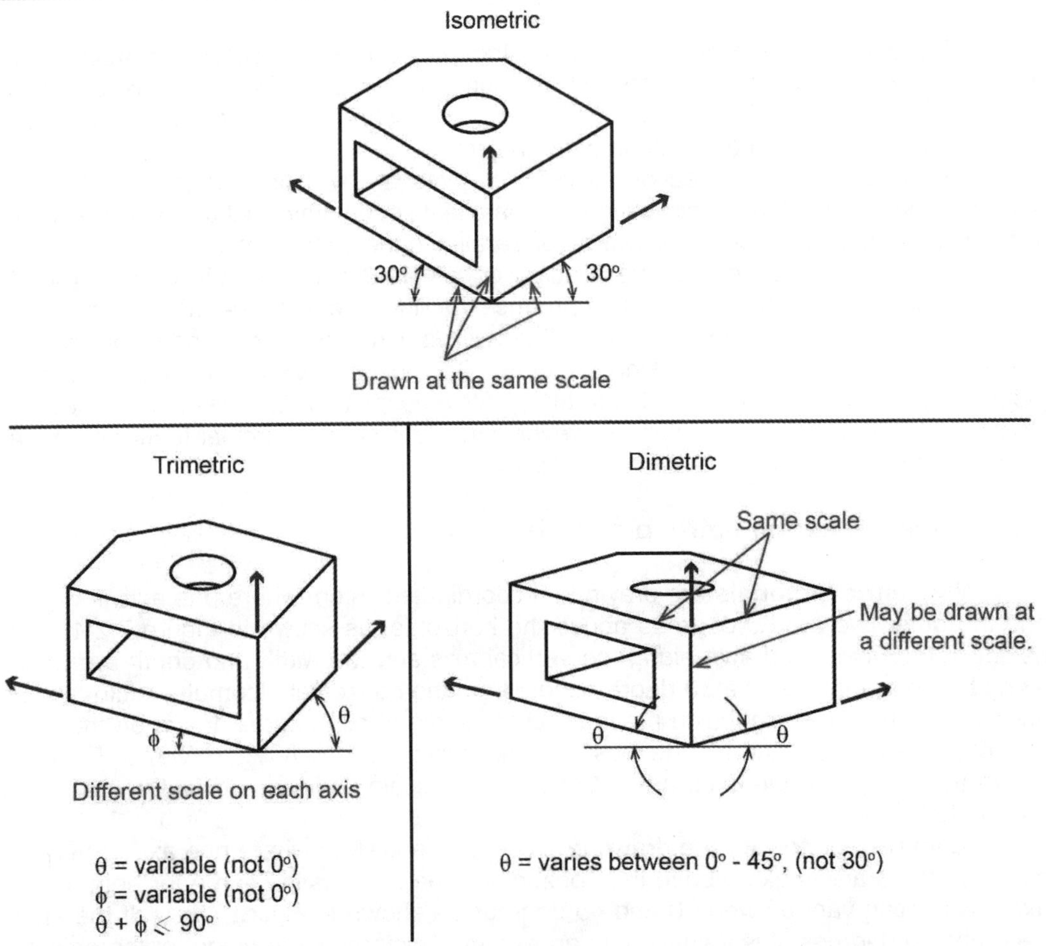

Figure 7.2-1: Axonometric projection types

7.3) OBLIQUE PROJECTIONS

There are three types of oblique pictorials: **cavalier**, **cabinet**, and **general** as shown in Figure 7.3-1. Each type is created by drawing the height in a vertical axis, the width along the horizontal axis and the depth along the axes that is at an angle from the horizontal. The features drawn on the axes that are parallel to the projection plane (i.e., vertical and horizontal axes) are drawn at full scale and true shape. The linear features drawn on the angled axis may be full scale (cavalier projection) or may be drawn foreshortened. The most common is a half scale cabinet projection. The cabinet projection approach looks the most realistic (see Figure 7.3-1).

An oblique projection creates a pictorial by using projectors that are not perpendicular to the plane of projection but are parallel to each other. All the principal edges are drawn on or parallel to the oblique axes as shown in Figure 7.3-1. On the real object, the principal edges are 90° apart and lie on or parallel to the *x-y-z* coordinate system. Oblique pictorials are drawn in a coordinate system where two of the axes make a 90-degree angle with each other. Only one of the axes is at an angle from the horizontal. The angle of this axis may range between 0 and 90 degrees; however, the most commonly used angle is 45 degrees.

7.3.1) Types of oblique pictorials

A **cabinet pictorial** is an oblique projection where all features drawn on the vertical and horizontal axes are at full scale; this is true for all oblique pictorials. In a cabinet pictorial, all features drawn on the angled axis are half scale. A **cavalier pictorial** is an oblique projection where all features drawn parallel to the oblique pictorial axes are drawn at full scale. A **general oblique pictorial** is where all features drawn on the angled axis are drawn at a scale but not at full or half scale. Figure 7.3-1 shows an example of each type of oblique pictorial.

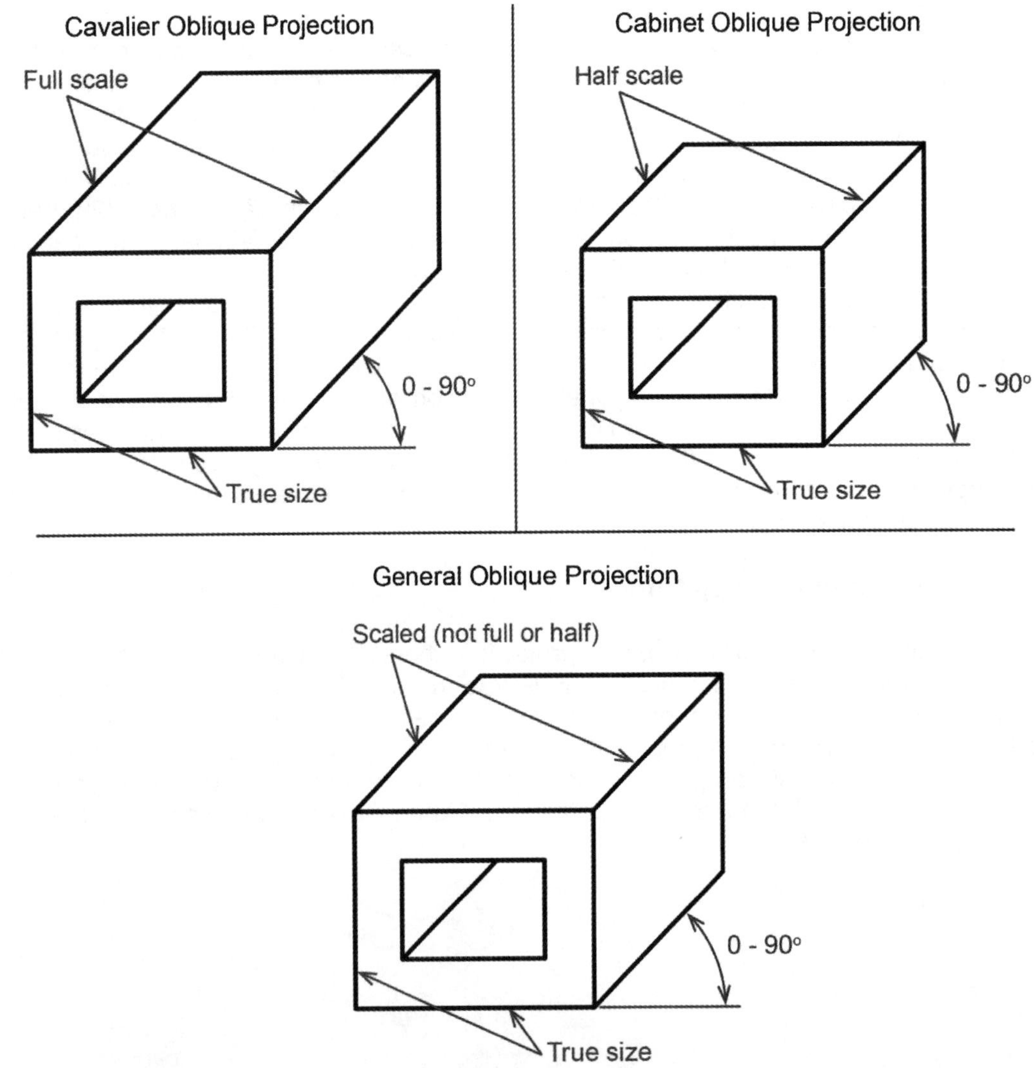

Figure 7.3-1: Oblique pictorial types

7.4) VISUALIZATION

With solid modeling becoming the main method of constructing part prints, teaching visualization skills has been de-emphasized. However, being able to visualize a part is important for two reasons. First, if you create a part print from a solid model, it is important that you can inspect the computer-generated drawing and be able to determine whether or not the CAD program created a technically correct orthographic projection. Second, if you are given a part print you should have the skills to turn that drawing into a solid model. By practicing pictorial sketching, visualization skills will improve.

7.5) DRAWING ISOMETRIC PICTORIALS

Isometric pictorials are drawn in a coordinate system where the axes are 60° apart as shown in Figure 7.5-1. The height of the object is drawn along the vertical axis, and the width and depth are drawn along the axes that are at a 30-degree angle above the horizontal. The linear features on or parallel to these three axes are drawn at 80% of full scale to more accurately represent true size. However, isometric pictorials may be drawn at any scale as long as the scale is uniform on all axes. Note that even though round features such as holes appear to the eye as being perfectly circular, they are really ellipses (see Figure 7.5-2).

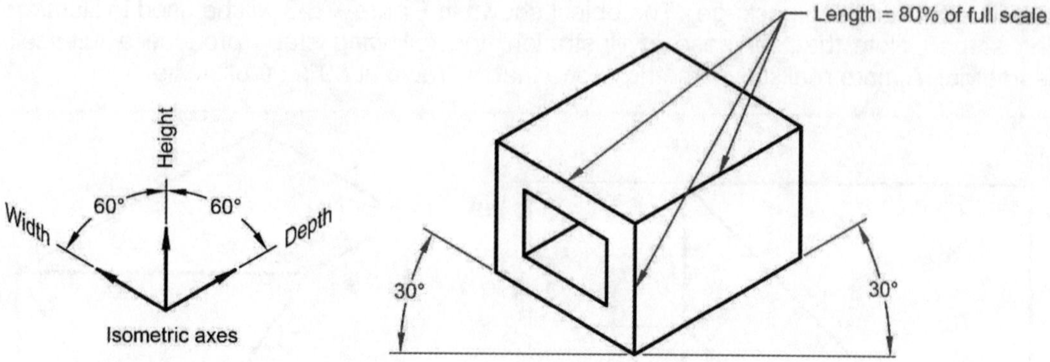

Figure 7.5-1: Isometric pictorial axes

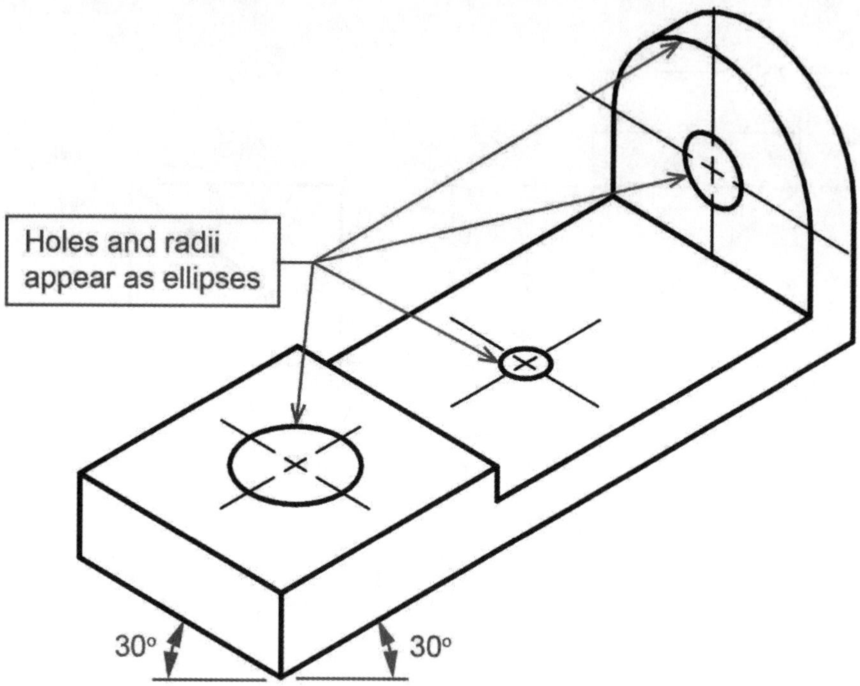

Figure 7.5-2: Isometric pictorial

7.5.1) Drawing linear features in an isometric pictorial

The steps used to draw an isometric pictorial depend on the method of its creation. For example, you may use pencil and paper to sketch an isometric pictorial, or a computer drawing and/or solid modeling package such as AutoCAD® or SolidWorks®. If you are sketching an isometric pictorial, it is best to start with a box that contains or frames in your part. When using a 2-D drawing package, it is best to start with an isometric grid that will guide you along the appropriate axes. If you are using a 3-D modeling package, you don't have to draw a pictorial at all because it will automatically generate one for you. The following steps describe a method that may be used to draw an isometric drawing by hand or with a 2-D drawing package. The object shown in Figure 7.5-3 will be used to illustrate the steps. Note that, for ease of illustration, the following steps produce a full-scale isometric. A more realistic isometric is one that is drawn at 80% of full scale.

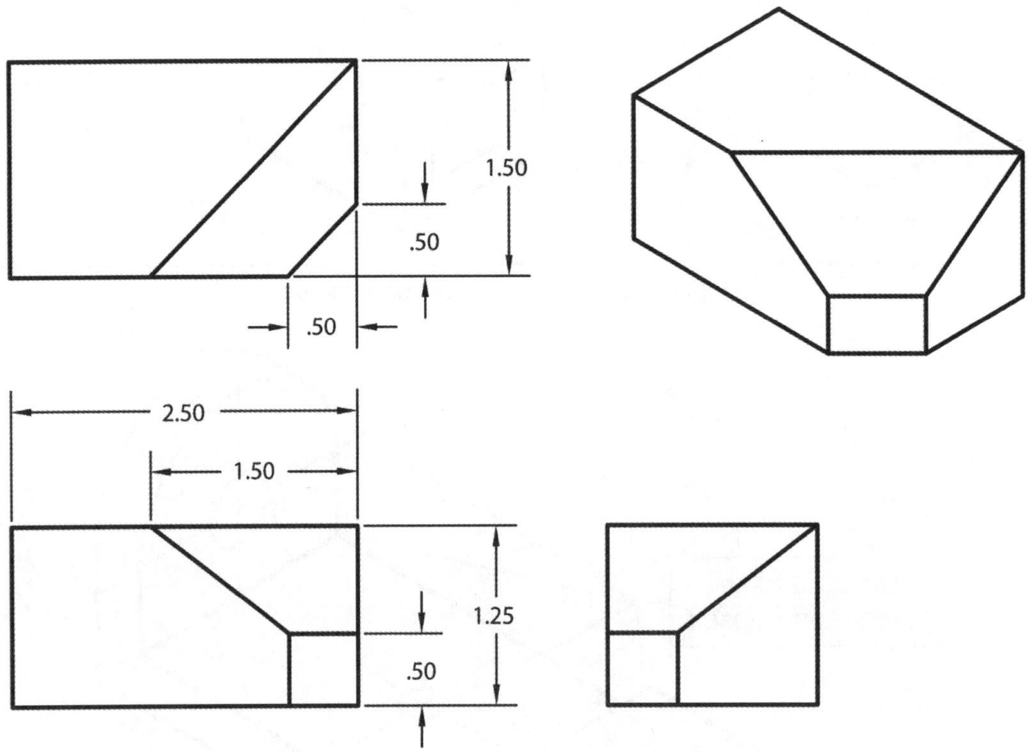

Figure 7.5-3: Isometric pictorial

Step 1) Draw three construction lines that represent the isometric axes (see Figure 7.5-4).

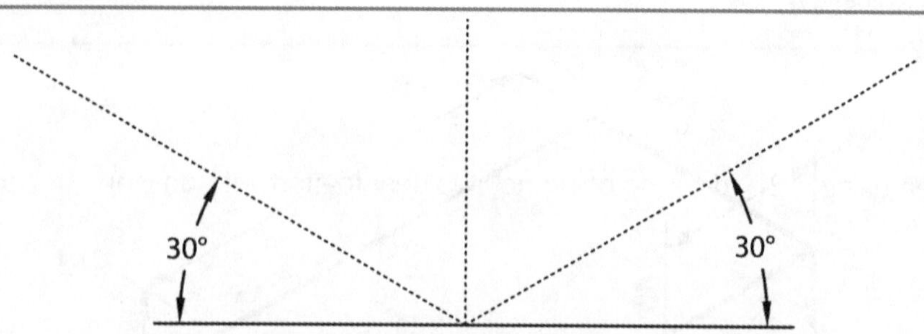

Figure 7.5-4: Creating an isometric pictorial step 1

Step 2) Draw a box whose sides are parallel to the three axes and whose dimensions are equal to the maximum height, width, and depth dimensions of the object (see Figure 7.5-5).

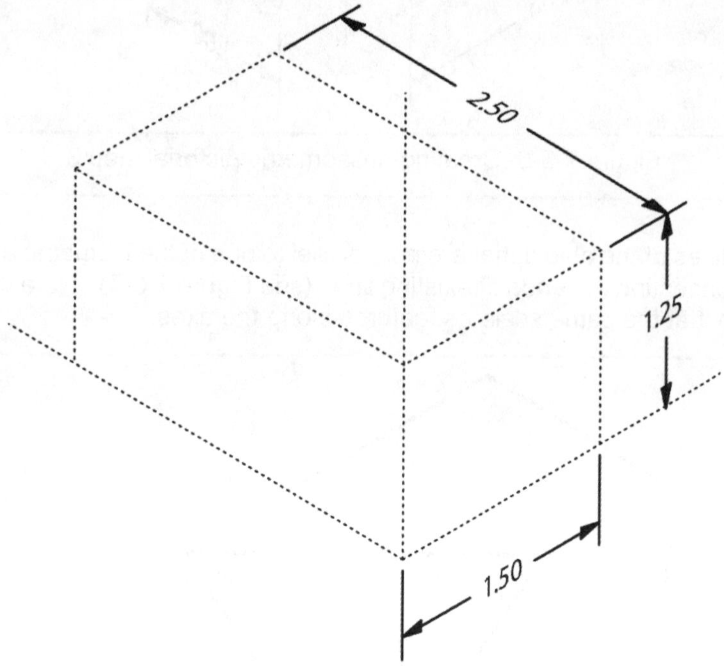

Figure 7.5-5: Creating an isometric pictorial step 2

Step 3) Draw the lines of the object that are parallel to the axes. All of these lines will be drawn at the same scale (see Figure 7.5-6). In this case, we are drawing them at full scale.

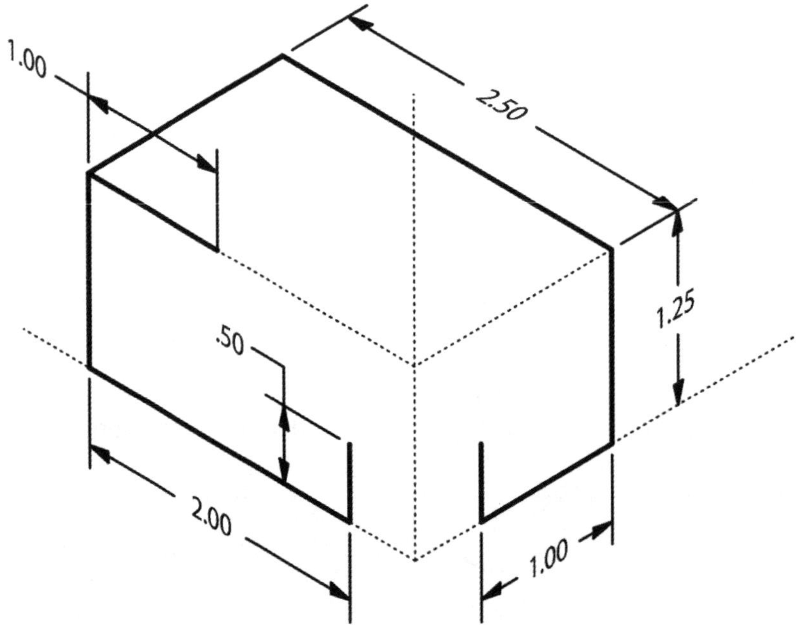

Figure 7.5-6: Creating an isometric pictorial step 3

Step 4) The lines of the object that are not parallel to one of the isometric axes are added by connecting the ends of existing lines (see Figure 7.5-7). Note that these lines are not at the same scale as features along the axes.

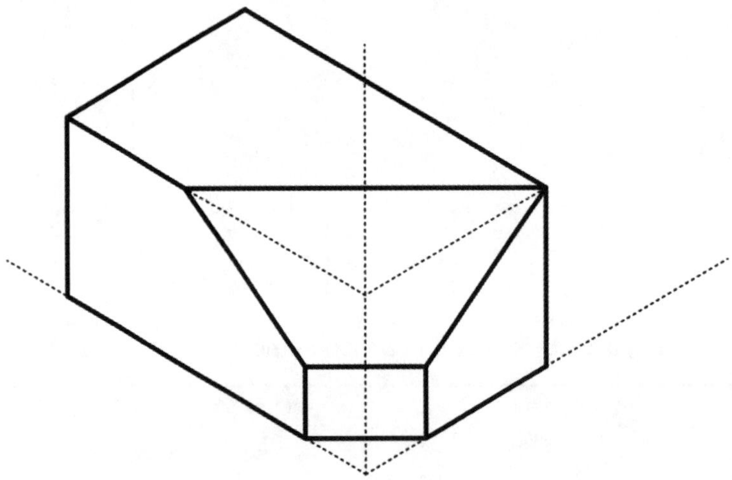

Figure 7.5-7: Creating an isometric pictorial step 4

Step 5) Erase or remove the construction lines.

Step 6) If the drawing is produced in a computer drawing package, it should be scaled by 80%.

If you plan to sketch an isometric pictorial by hand, a 30/60 triangle, an isometric (80%) ruler, and an isometric ellipse template will help.

Try Exercise 7.5-1 and view Video Exercise 7.5-2

7.5.2) Drawing circles and radii in an isometric pictorial

Circular features of an object are drawn as ellipses in an isometric pictorial. The object shown in Figure 7.5-8 will be used to illustrate the steps used to create isometric circular features. Note that, for illustrative purposes, the following steps produce a full scale isometric.

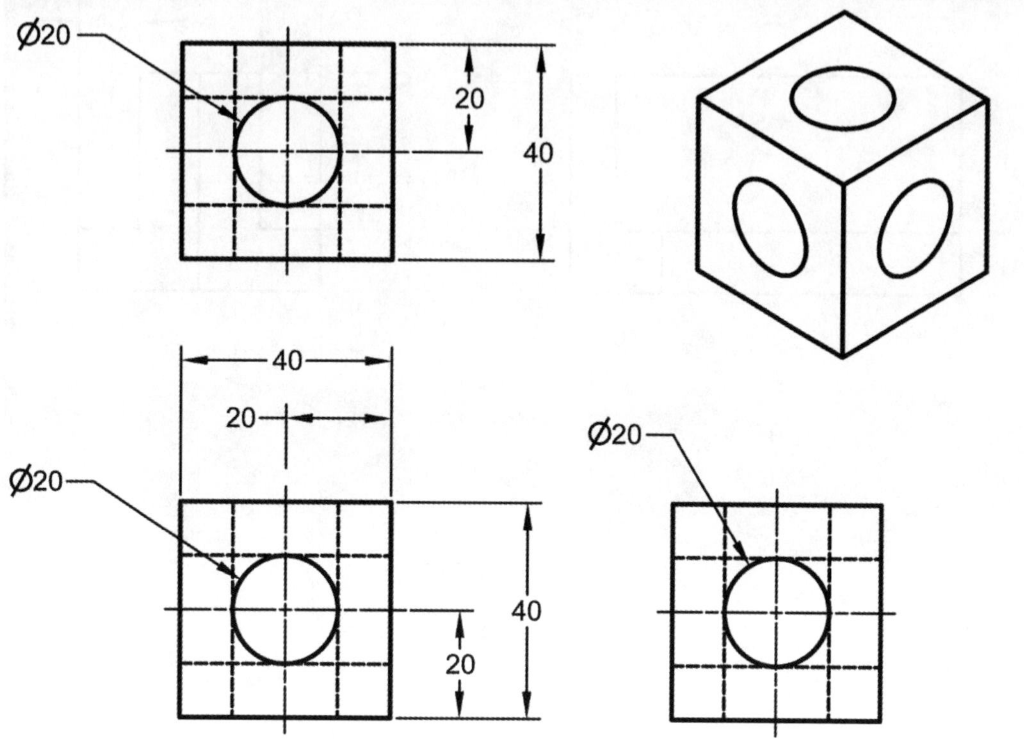

Figure 7.5-8: Creating circular features

Video Exercise 7.5-1: Beginning Isometric Pictorial

This video exercise will take you through creating an isometric pictorial based on the orthographic projection shown.

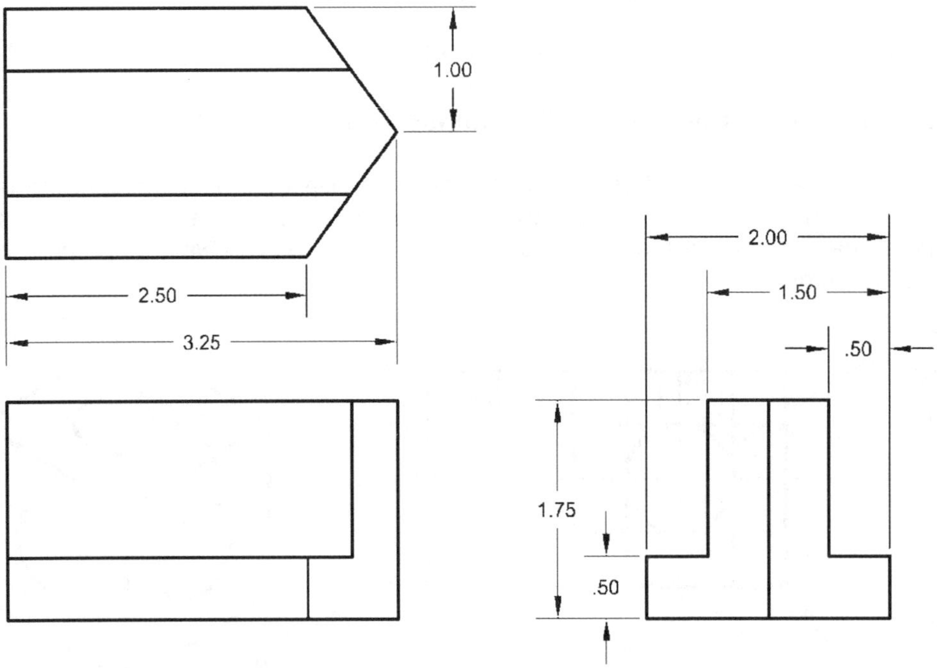

Exercise 7.5-2: Isometric pictorial linear features

Create an isometric pictorial of the following object. The grid spacing is 10 mm.

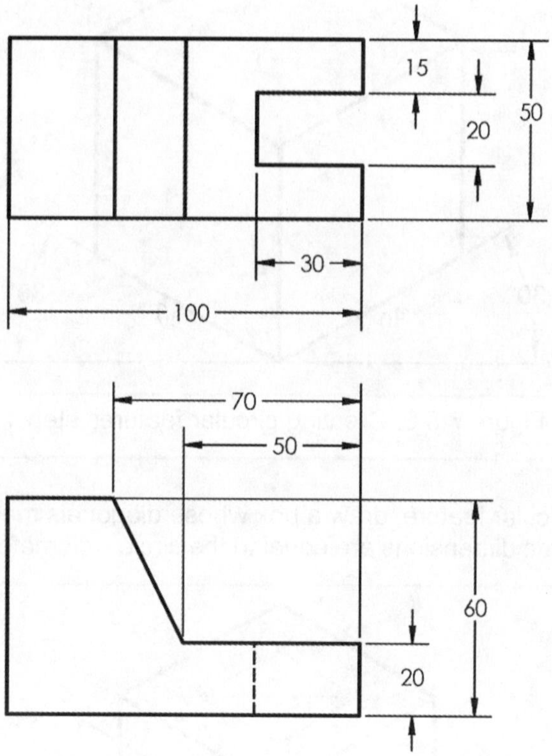

Step 1) Draw the linear features of the object using the procedure previously described (see Figure 7.5-9).

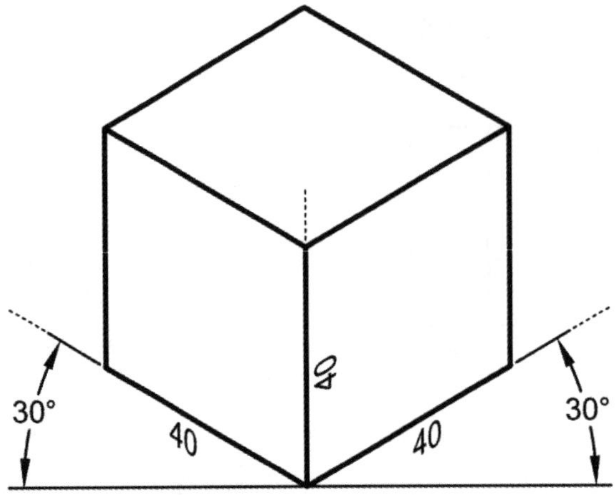

Figure 7.5-9: Creating circular features step 1

Step 2) For each circular feature, draw a box whose diagonals meet at the center of the circle and side dimensions are equal to the circle's diameter (see Figure 7.5-10).

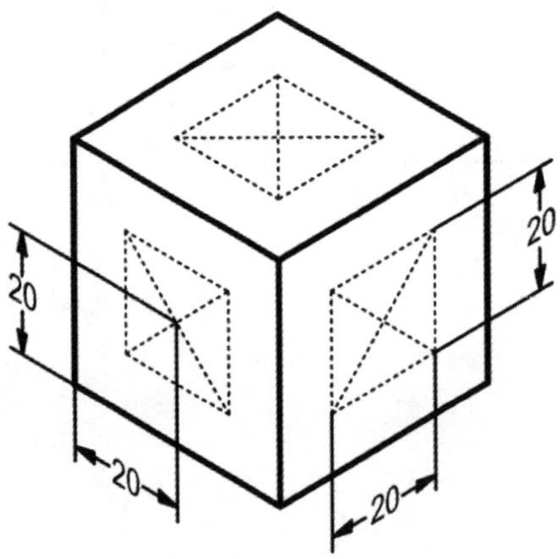

Figure 7.5-10: Creating circular features step 2

Step 3) Draw an ellipse in the box whose major axis is aligned with the long diagonal of the box. The ellipse touches the box at the midpoint of its sides (see Figure 7.5-11).

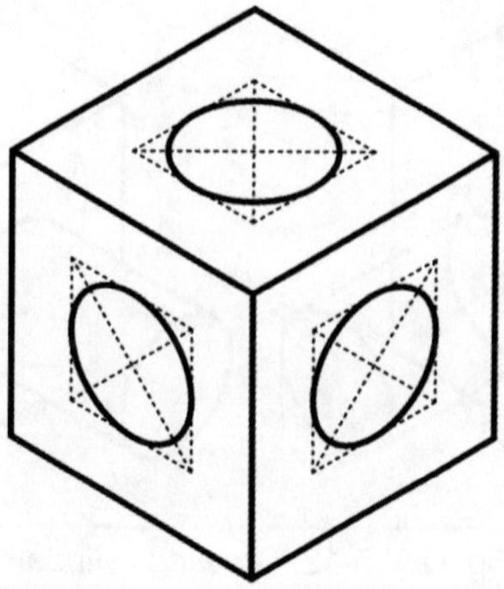

Figure 7.5-11: Creating circular features step 3

Step 4) Erase or remove the construction lines.

Step 5) If the drawing is produced in a 2-D drawing package, it should be scaled by 80%.

The same procedure is used to create radii except that the unwanted part of the ellipse is erased or trimmed. To sketch a more accurate isometric pictorial, an isometric ellipse template should be used.

7.5.3) Drawing cylinders in an isometric pictorial

Drawing cylinders in an isometric pictorial is just a matter of drawing two isometric circles and adding some connecting lines (see Figure 7.5-12).

Step 1) Draw a defining box whose height is equal to the height of the cylinder and whose width and depth dimensions are equal to the diameter of the cylinder.

Step 2) Draw the diagonals and ellipses in the boxes that define the beginning and end of the cylinder.

Step 3) Draw two lines that connect the two ellipses. The lines will start and end at the intersection between the ellipse and the major axis diagonal.

Step 4) Erase all construction lines and any lines that fall behind the cylinder.

Step 5) If the drawing is produced in a computer drawing package, it should be scaled by 80%.

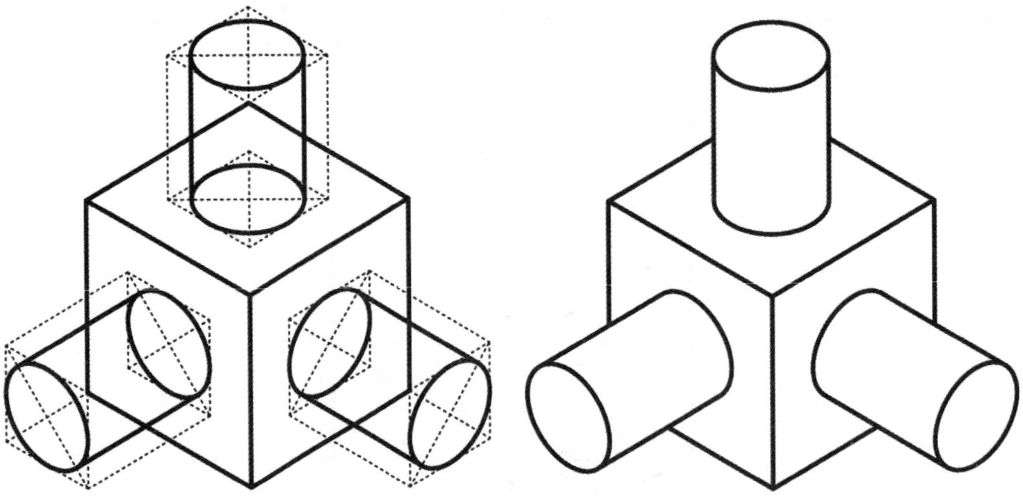

Figure 7.5-12: Drawing cylinders

Try Exercise 7.5-3 and view Video Exercises 7.5-4 and 7.5-5

Video Exercise 7.5-3: Beginning Isometric Pictorial – Circular Features

This video exercise will take you through creating an isometric pictorial based on the orthographic projection shown.

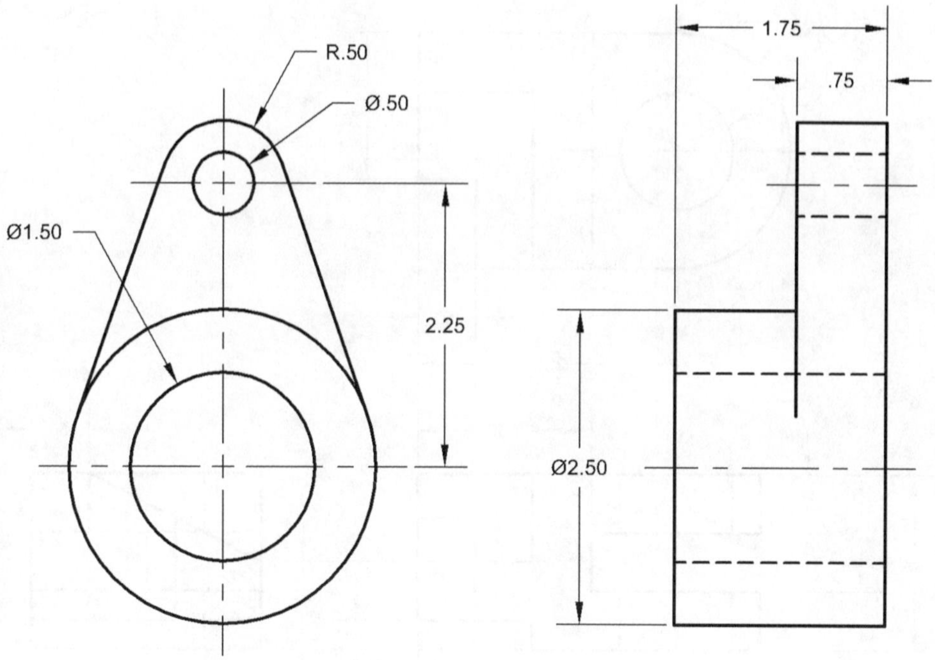

Video Exercise 7.5-4: Intermediate Isometric Pictorial – Circular Features

This video exercise will take you through creating an isometric pictorial based on the orthographic projection shown.

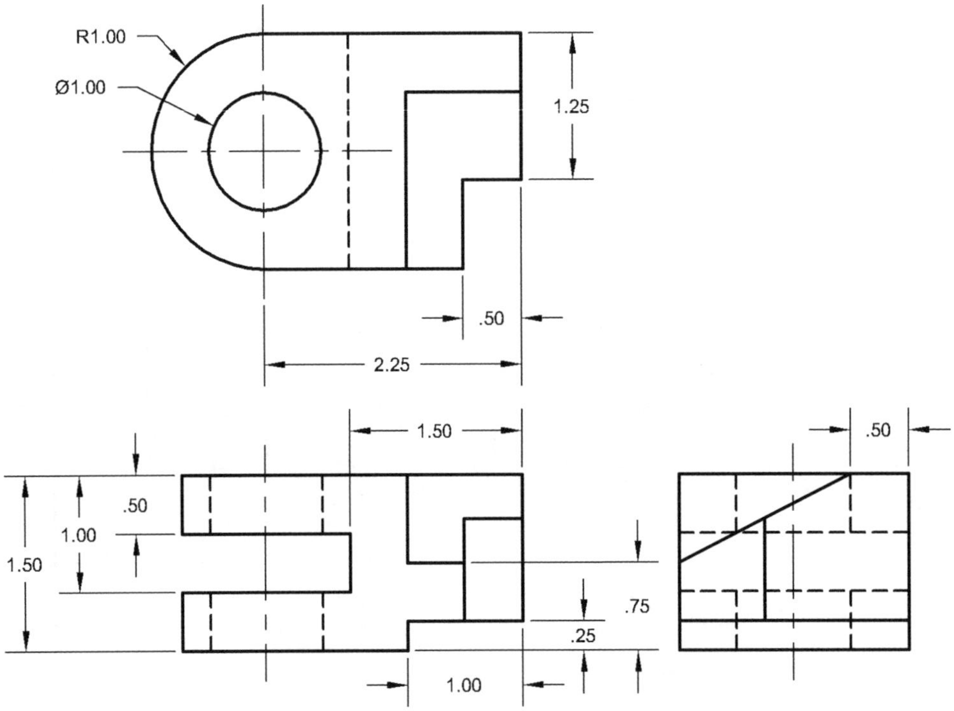

Exercise 7.5-5: Isometric pictorial circular features

Create an isometric pictorial of the following object. The grid spacing is 10 mm.

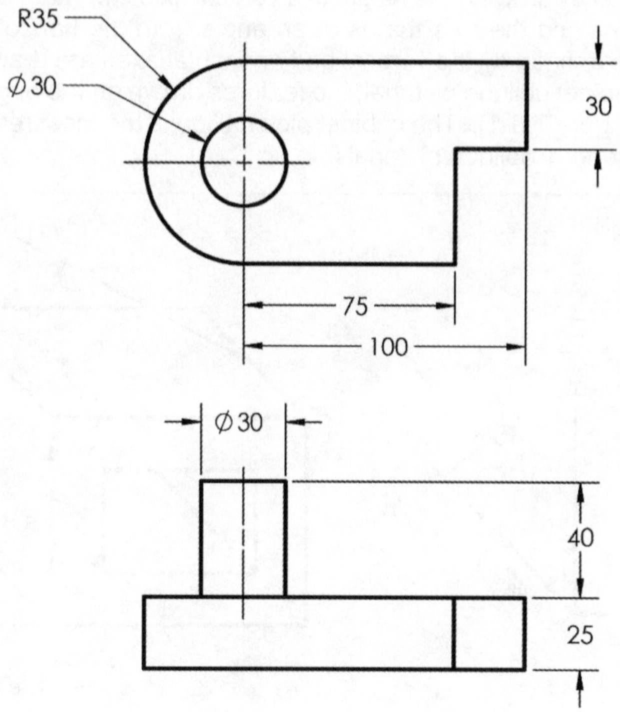

7.6) DRAWING CABINET OBLIQUE PICTORIALS

Oblique pictorials are drawn in a coordinate system where only one axis is at an angle above the horizontal. The angle of this axis may range between 0 and 90 degrees; however, the most commonly used angle is 45 degrees, as shown in Figure 7.6-1. Oblique pictorials are created by drawing the height in a vertical axis, the width along the horizontal axis and the depth along the axis that is at an angle from the horizontal. The features drawn on the plane defined by the vertical and horizontal axes are drawn at full scale and true shape. In a cabinet oblique pictorial, the features drawn on the angled axis are drawn at half scale (see Figure 7.6-1). The cabinet pictorial looks the most realistic as compared to the cavalier or general oblique pictorials.

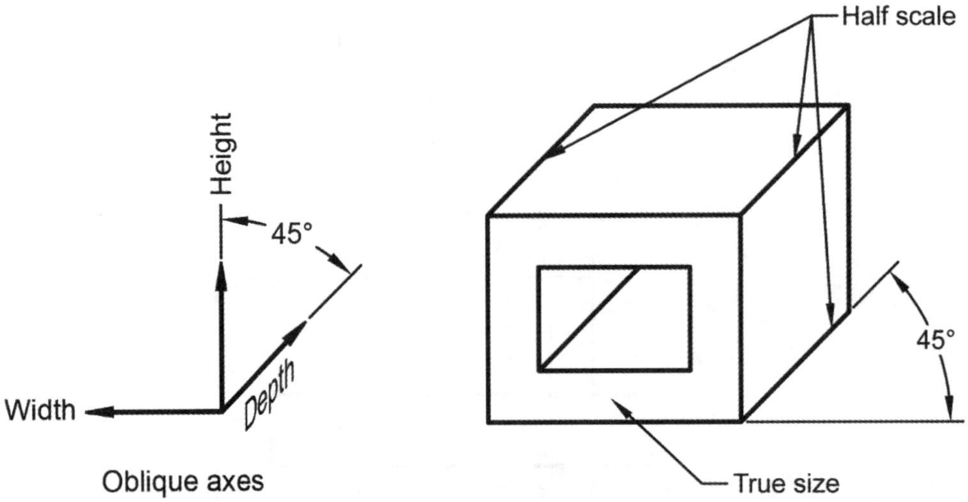

Figure 7.6-1: Oblique pictorial axes

7.6.1) Drawing features of a cabinet oblique pictorial

Just as with an isometric pictorial, the steps used to draw an oblique pictorial depend on the method of its creation. The following steps describe a method that may be used to draw a cabinet oblique pictorial by hand. Most CAD packages are not set up to draw oblique pictorials, so this is more challenging. The object shown in Figure 7.6-2 will be used to illustrate the steps.

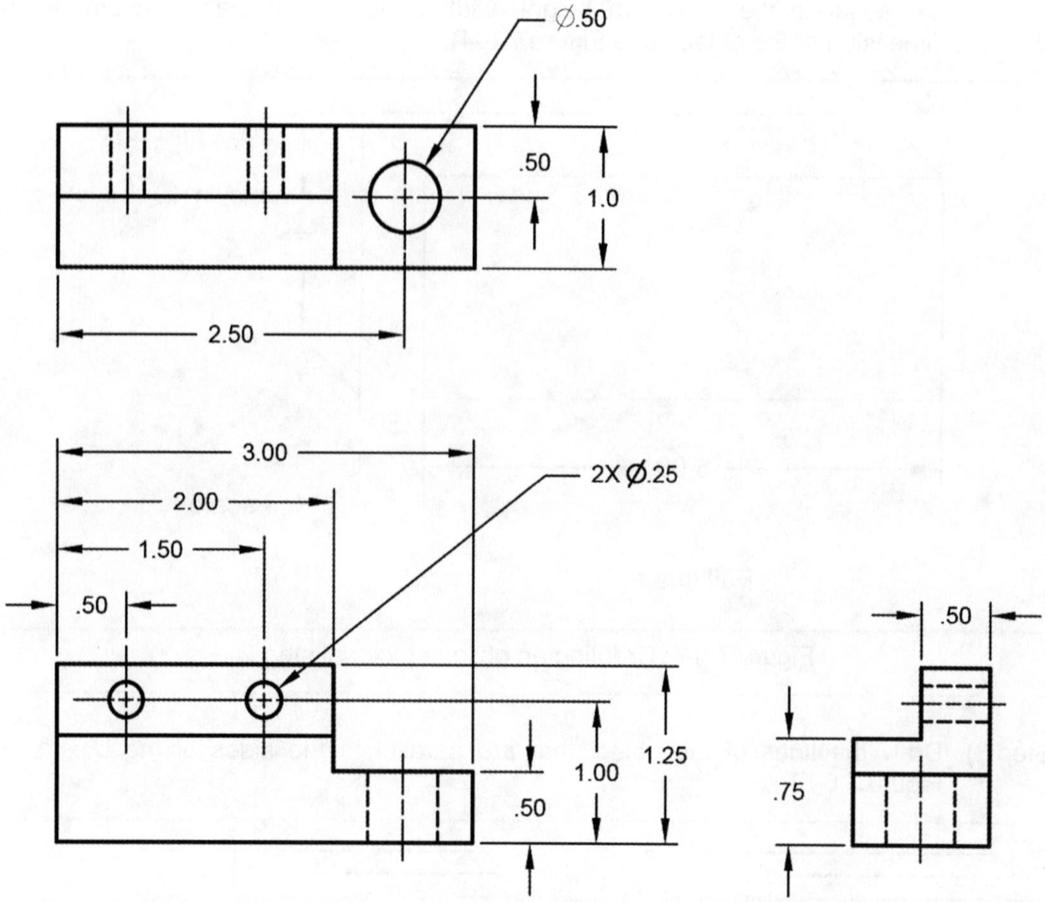

Figure 7.6-2: Cabinet oblique pictorial

Step 1) Draw three construction lines that represent the oblique axes (see Figure 7.6-3). We will use an angle of 45° for the third axis.

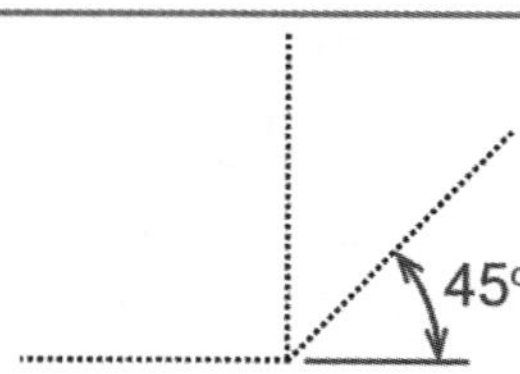

Figure 7.6-3: Creating a cabinet oblique pictorial step 1

Step 2) Draw a box whose sides are parallel to the three axes and whose dimensions are equal to the maximum height, width, and half of the maximum depth dimension of the object (see Figure 7.6-4).

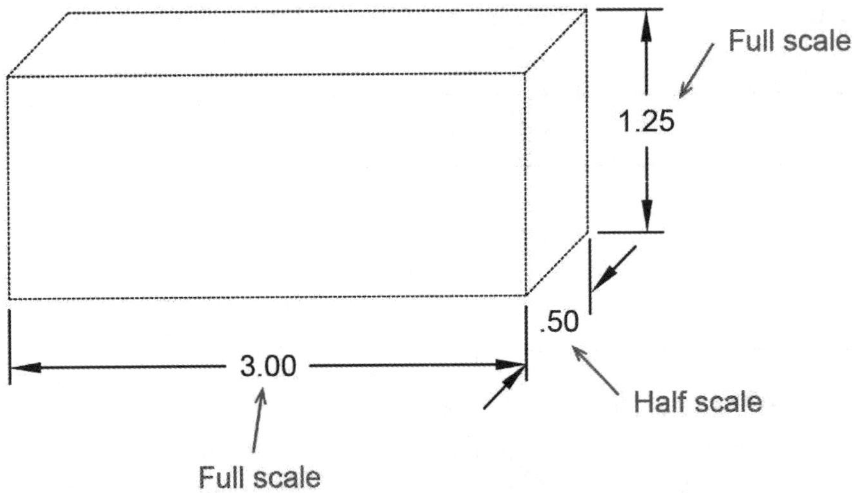

Figure 7.6-4: Creating an oblique pictorial step 2

Step 3) Draw the lines of the object that are parallel to the sides of the box (see Figure 7.6-5).

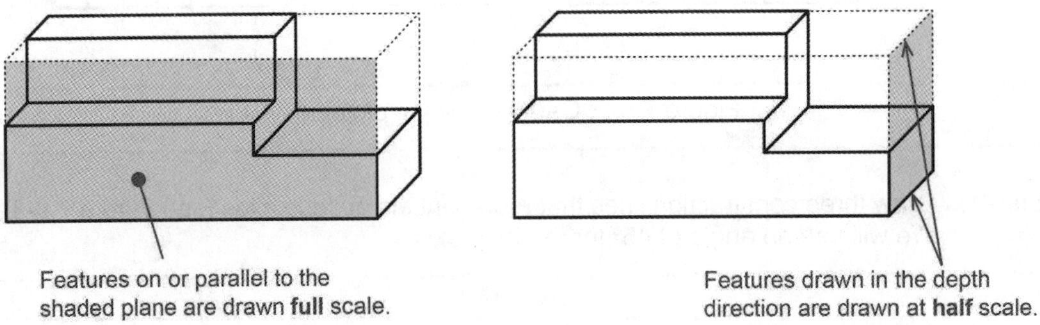

Figure 7.6-5: Creating an oblique pictorial step 3

Step 4) Add any lines of the object that are not parallel to one of the axes by connecting the ends of existing lines. Note that these lines are not at the same scale as the features on the axes.

Step 5) Add any circular features. Note that the circular features that are drawn on a plane created by the horizontal and vertical axes, are circular and true size and shape. Any circular features that are not parallel to these axes are not true shape (see Figure 7.6-6). The procedure for drawing these circular features is similar to that of an isometric circular feature except for the scaling of the depth direction which is half the diameter of the circle.

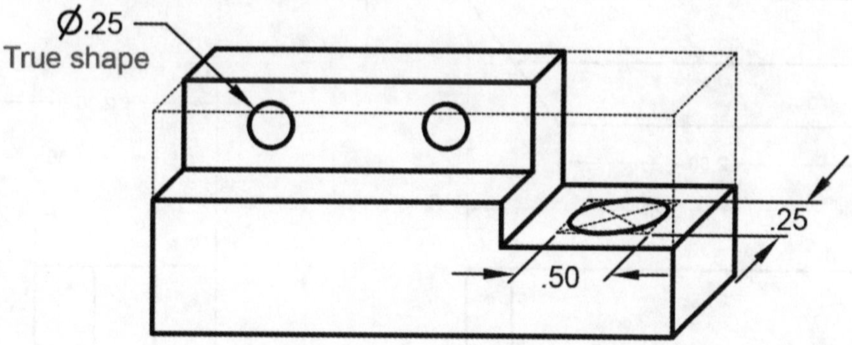

Figure 7.6-6: Creating an oblique pictorial step 5

Step 6) Erase or remove the construction lines.

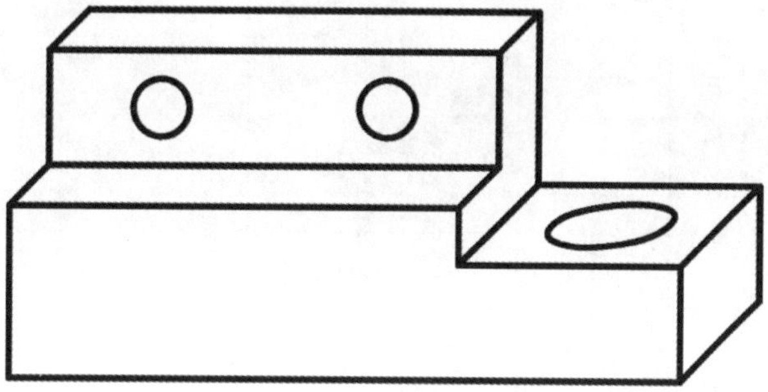

Figure 7.6-7: Creating an oblique pictorial step 6

If you plan to sketch a cabinet oblique pictorial by hand, a 45°/90° triangle, a half scale ruler, and a 45° ellipse template should be used.

Try Exercise 7.6-1 and 7.6-2, and watch Video Exercise 7.6-3 and 7.6-4

Video Exercise 7.6-1: Beginning Oblique Pictorial

This video exercise will take you through creating cabinet oblique pictorial based on the orthographic projection shown.

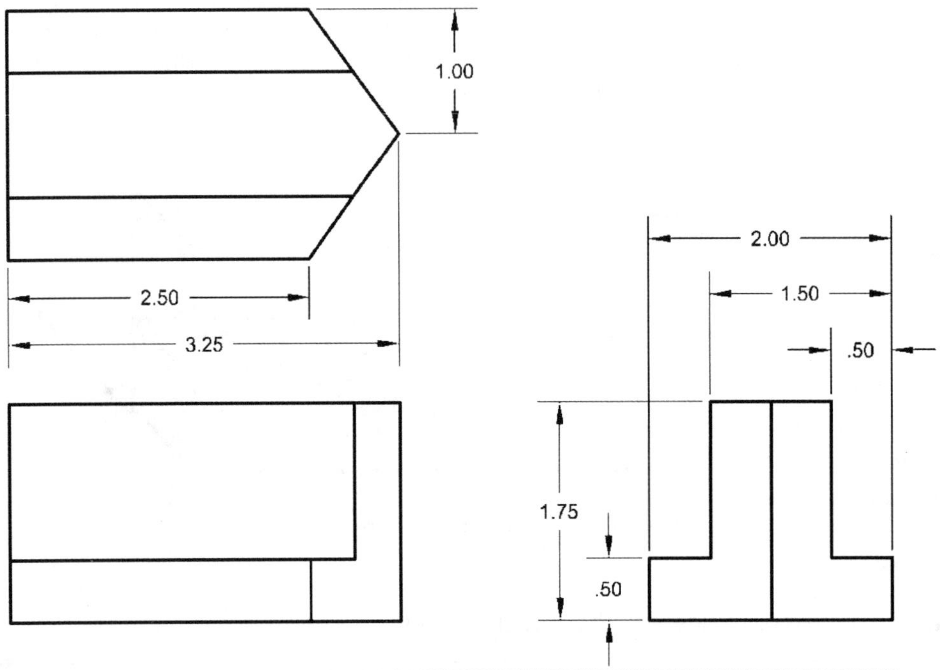

Video Exercise 7.6-2: Cabinet Oblique Pictorial – Circular Features

This video exercise will take you through creating cabinet oblique pictorial based on the orthographic projection shown.

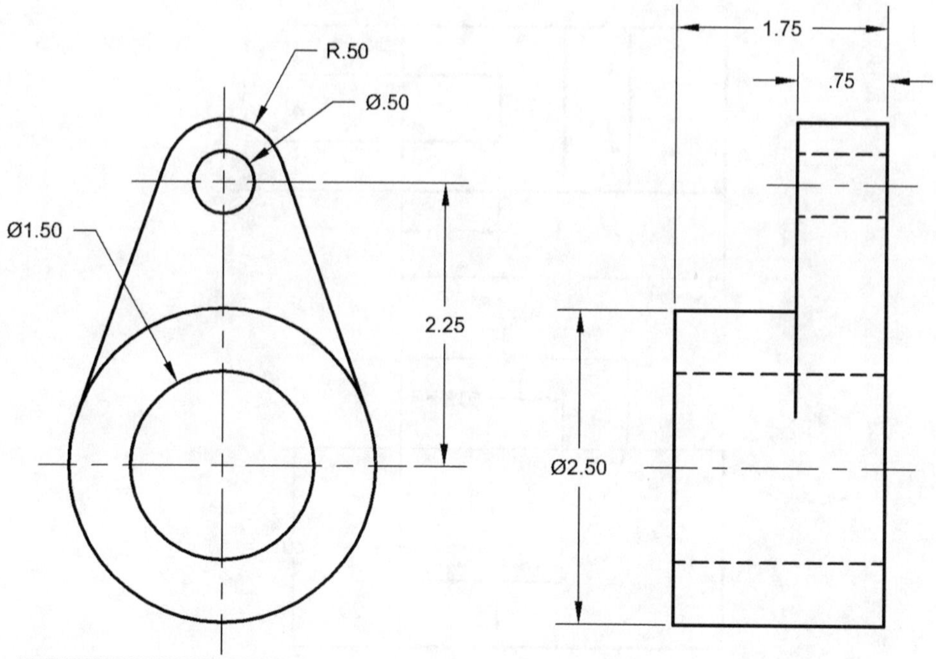

Exercise 7.6-3: Cabinet oblique pictorial linear features

Create a cabinet oblique pictorial of the following object. The grid spacing is 10 mm.

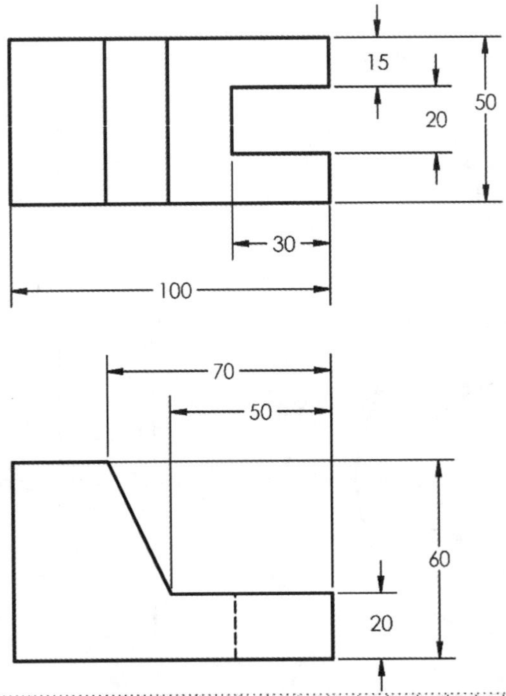

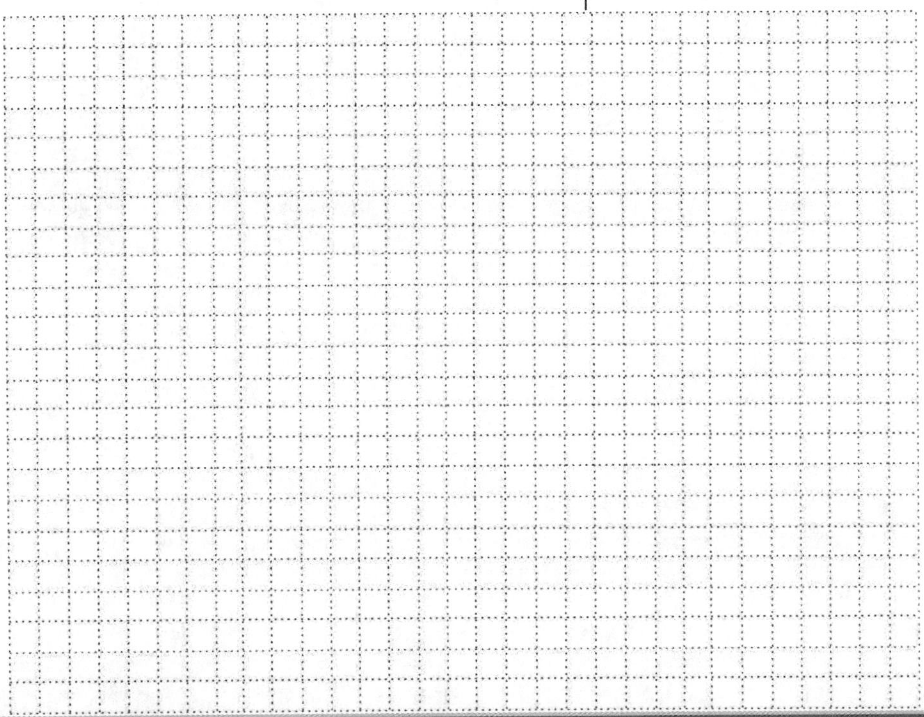

Exercise 7.6-4: Cabinet oblique pictorial circular features

Create a cabinet oblique pictorial of the following object. The grid spacing is 10 mm.

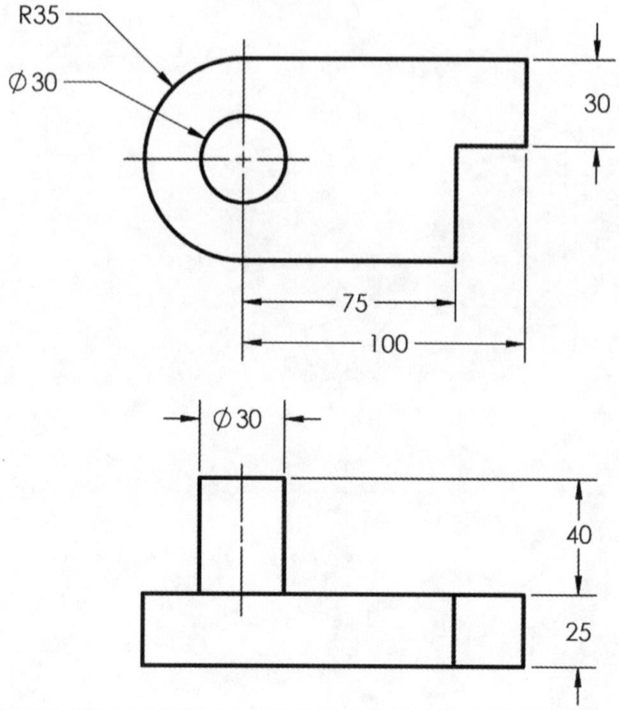

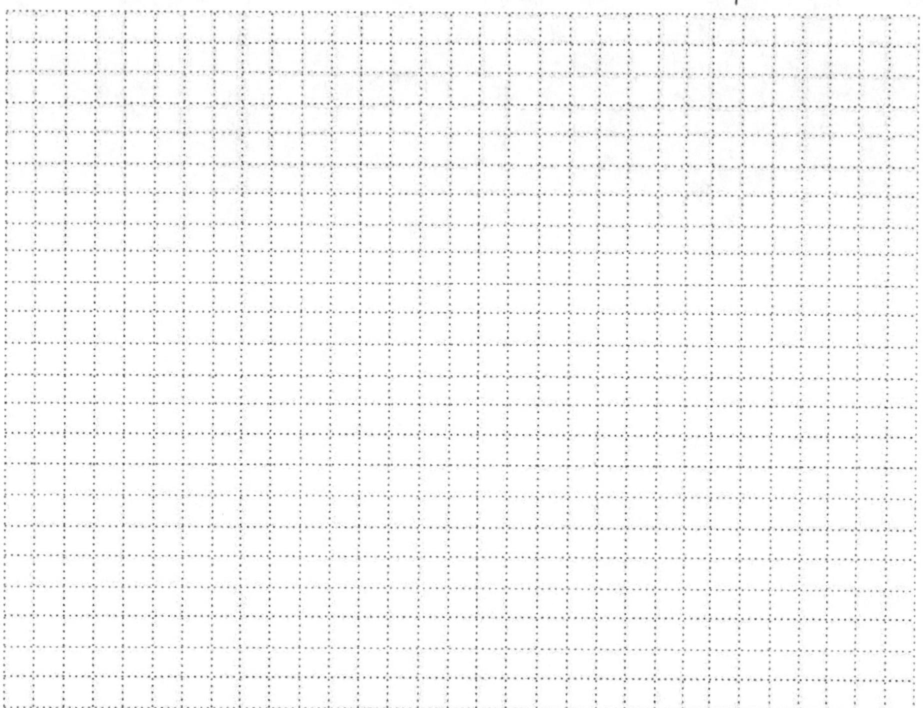

NOTES:

7.7) APPLYING WHAT WE HAVE LEARNED

Exercise 7.7-1: Creating pictorials 1

Name: ______________________________ Date: ________________

Create an isometric pictorial of the following object. The grid spacing is 0.25 inches.

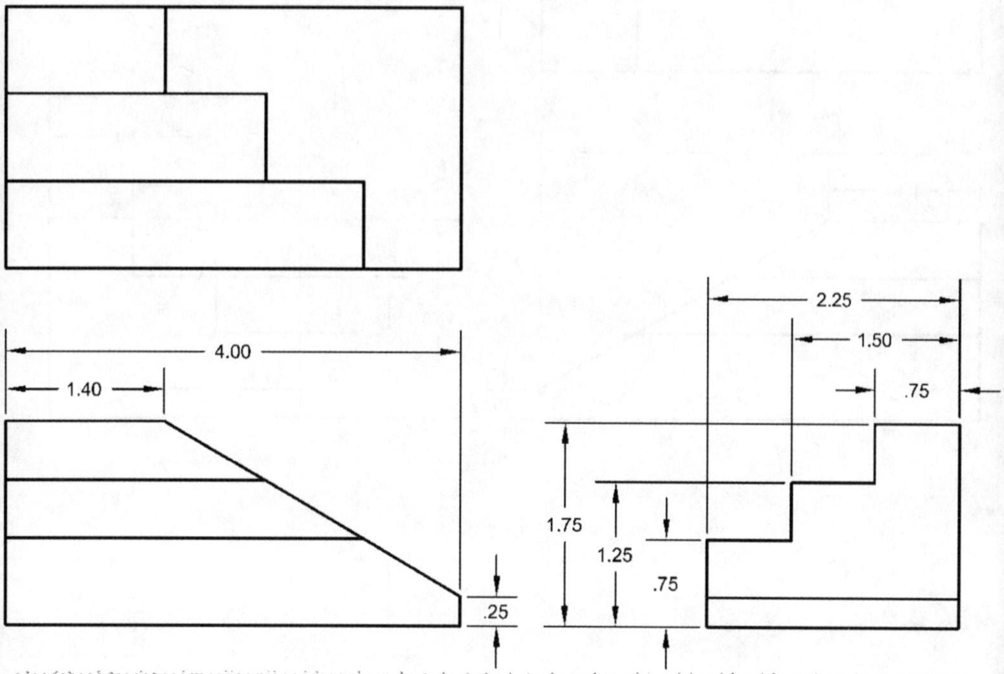

Create a cabinet oblique pictorial of the following object. The grid spacing is 0.25 inches.

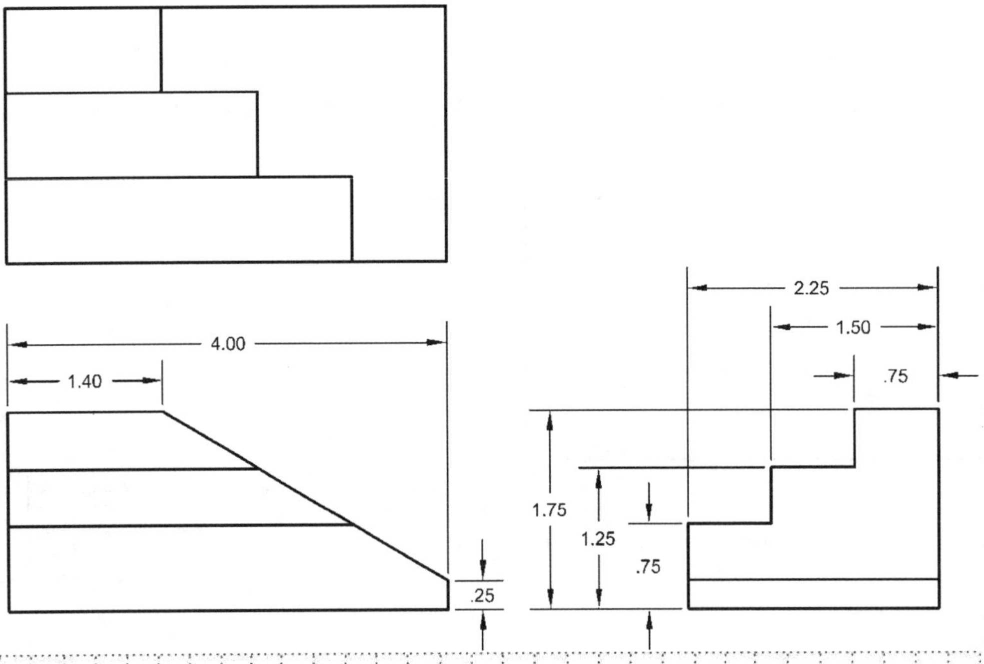

Exercise 7.7-2: Creating pictorials 2

Name: ______________________________ Date: ________________

Create an isometric pictorial of the following object. The grid spacing is 10 mm.

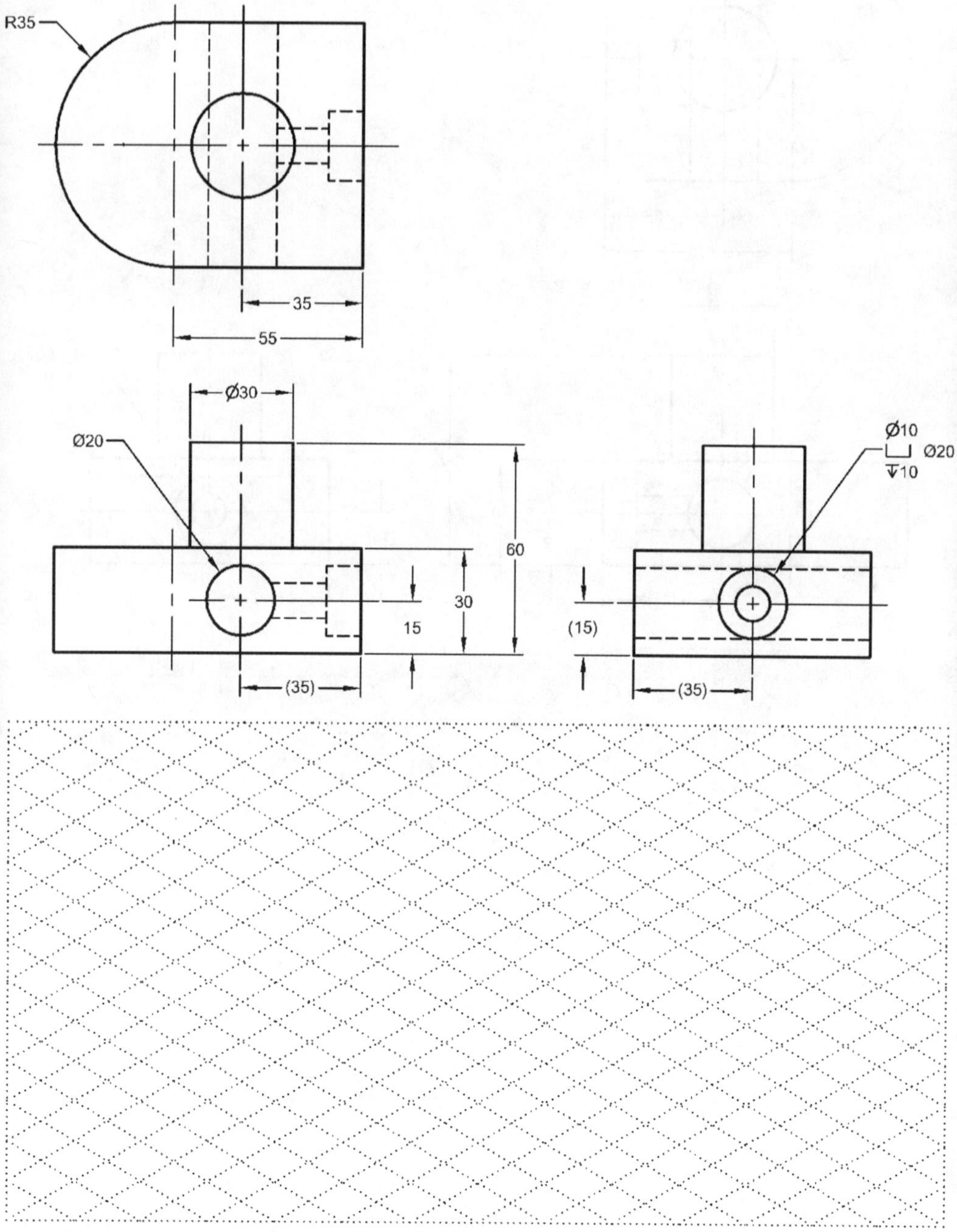

Create a cabinet oblique pictorial of the following object. The grid spacing is 10 mm.

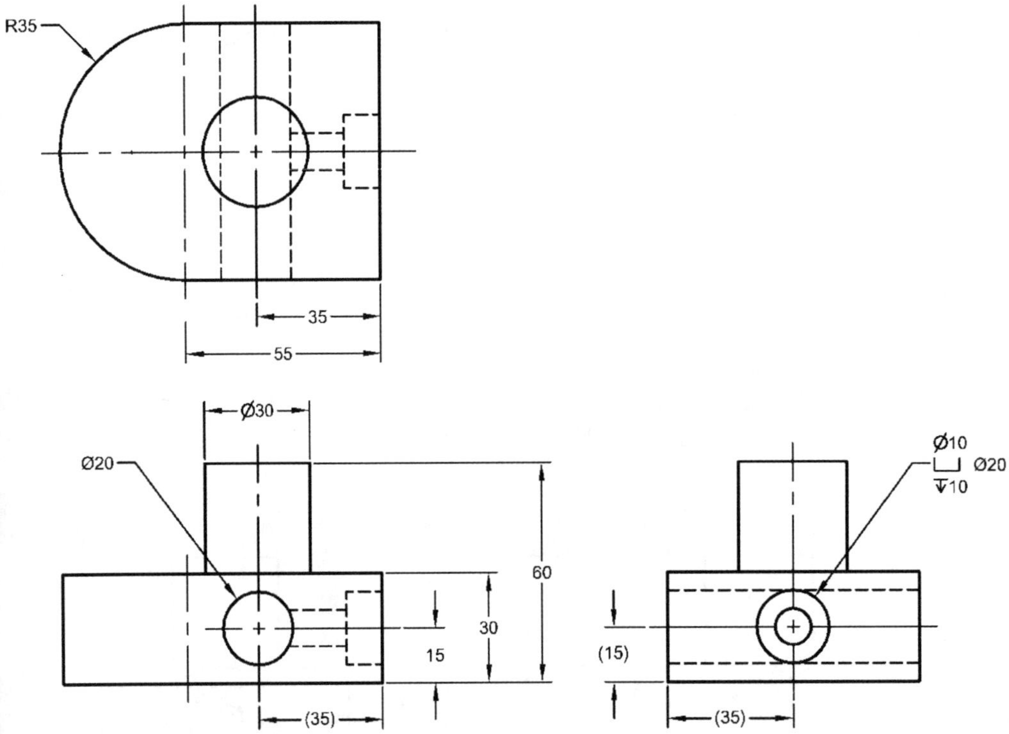

CREATING PICTORIAL DRAWINGS QUESTIONS – SET1

Name: ________________________________ Date: ______________

Q7-1) A pictorial may be included on a detailed drawing. (True, False)

Q7-2) Two of the isometric axes are drawn .... degrees above the horizontal.

a) 10
b) 15
c) 30
d) 45

Q7-3) Two of the oblique pictorial axes are drawn horizontally and vertically. The other axis is most commonly drawn .... degrees above the horizontal.

a) 10
b) 15
c) 30
d) 45

Q7-4) Circular features in an isometric pictorial are drawn as _______________. Fill in the blank.

NOTES:

CREATING PICTORIAL DRAWINGS QUESTIONS – SET2

Name: ________________________________ Date: ______________

Q7-5) Pictorials help us ... (Circle all that apply.)

a) be expressive.
b) visualize a part or assembly.
c) communicate ideas.

Q7-6) Why is developing the ability to sketch pictorials by hand important?

Q7-7) An isometric pictorial looks more realistic if it is drawn at a .... percent scale.

a) 30
b) 50
c) 80
d) 90

Q7-8) The diagonals of the box used to guide you in drawing the circular feature align with the ______________ and ______________ axes of the ellipse.

Q7-9) The width dimension along the angled axes in a cabinet oblique is drawn ___________ scale.

NOTES:

CREATING PICTORIAL DRAWINGS PROBLEMS

Name: ______________________________________ Date: ________________

P7-1a) Draw a full-scale isometric pictorial by hand or in a drawing package per instructions. The grid spacing is 0.25 inch.

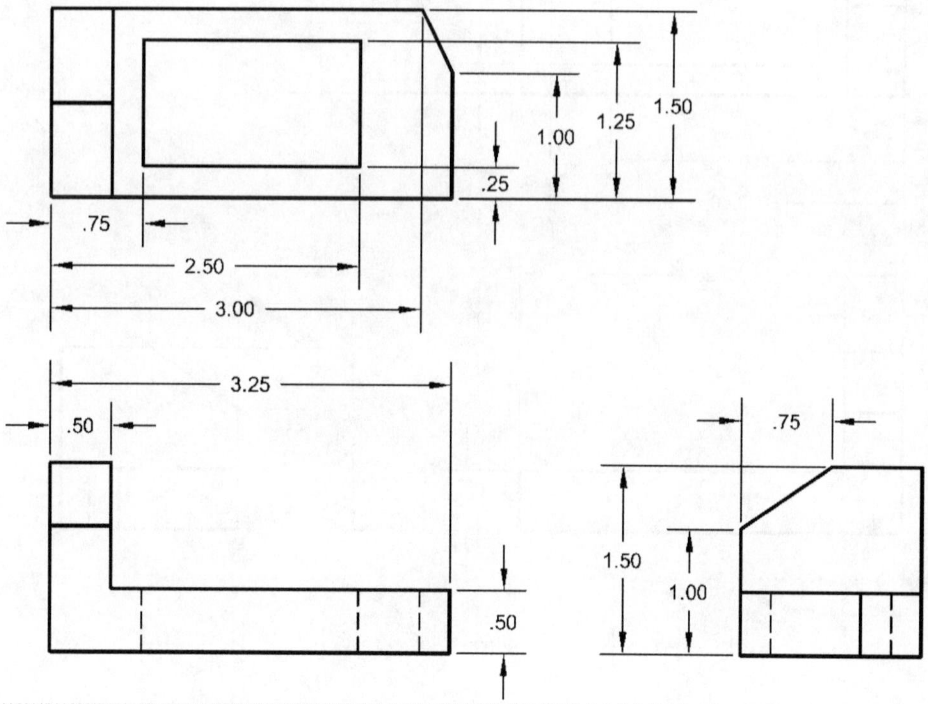

P7-1b) Draw a full-scale cabinet oblique pictorial by hand or in a drawing package per instructions. The grid spacing is 0.25 inch.

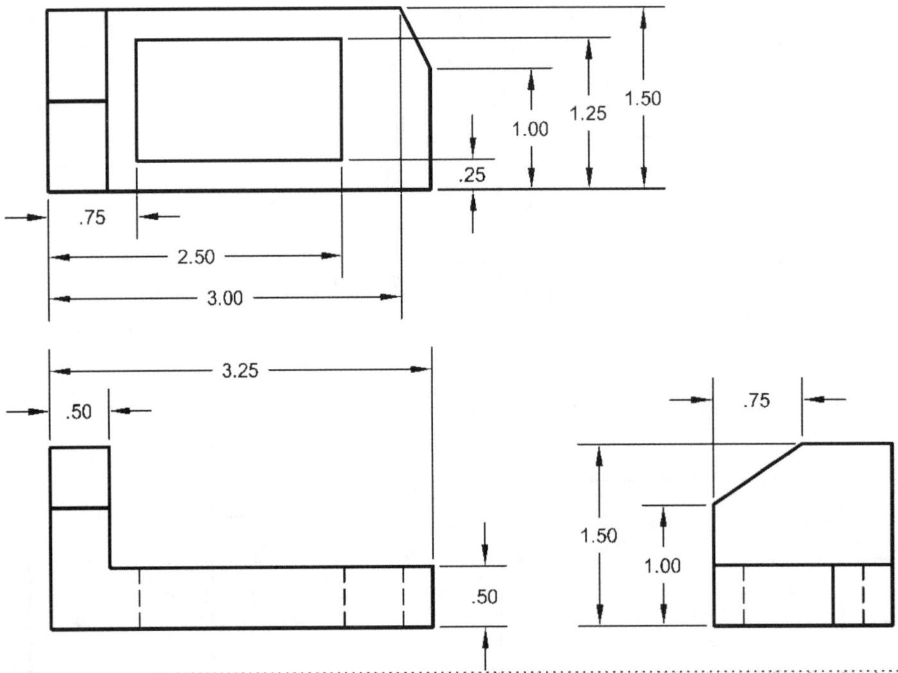

Name: ______________________________ Date: ______________

P7-2a) Draw a full-scale isometric pictorial by hand or in a drawing package per instructions. The grid spacing is 10 mm.

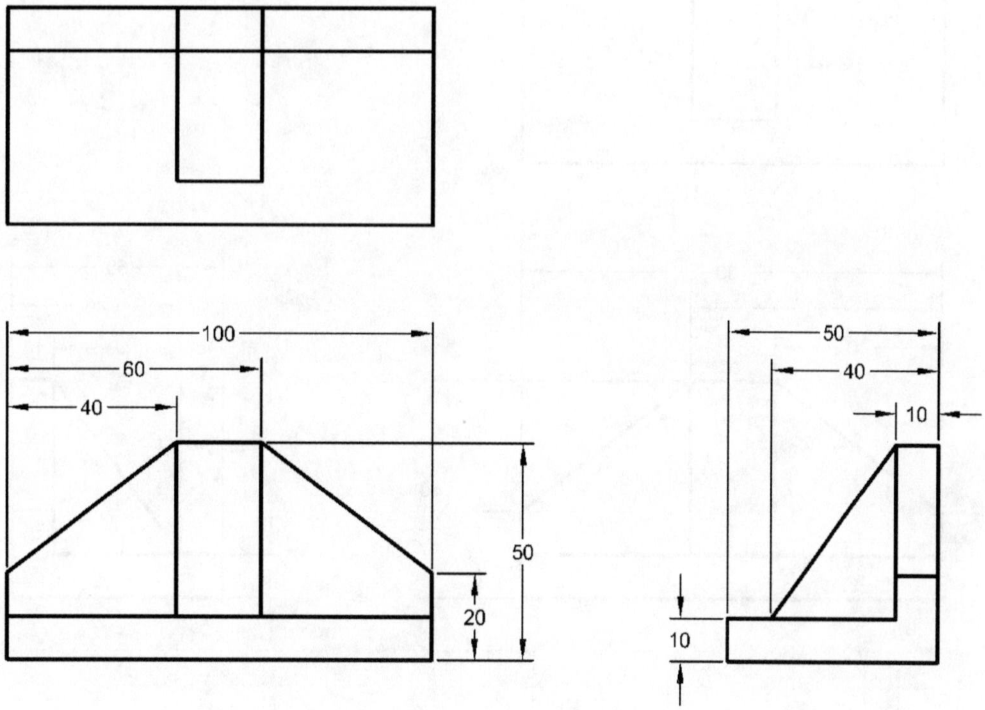

P7-2b) Draw a full-scale cabinet oblique pictorial by hand or in a drawing package per instructions. The grid spacing is 10 mm.

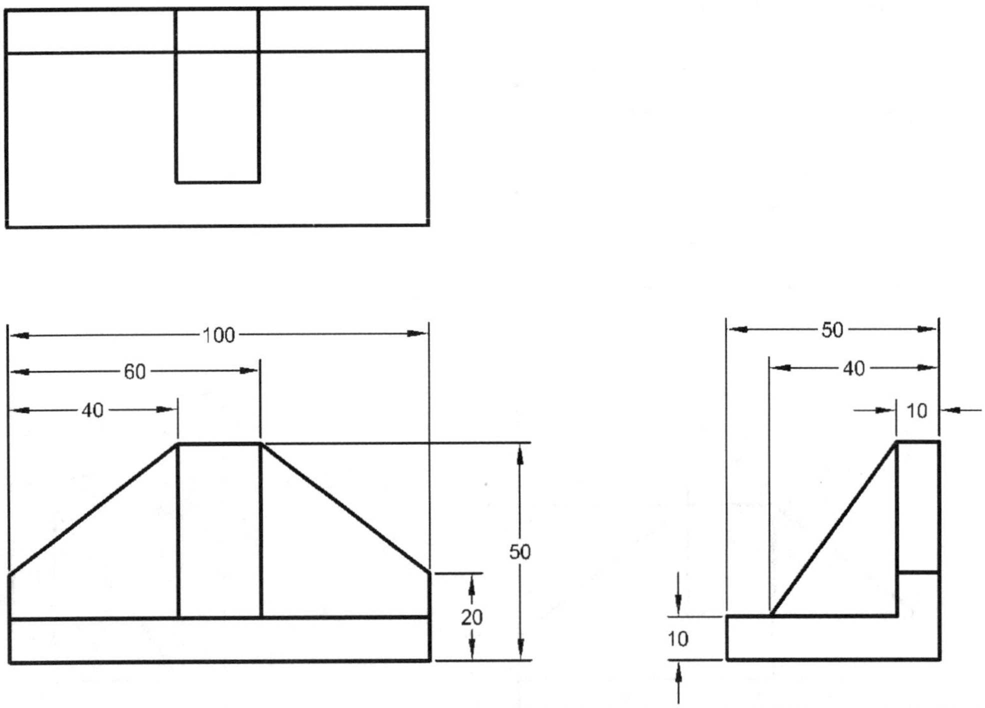

Name: ______________________________ Date: ______________

P7-3a) Draw a full-scale isometric pictorial by hand or in a drawing package per instructions. The grid spacing is 0.25 inch.

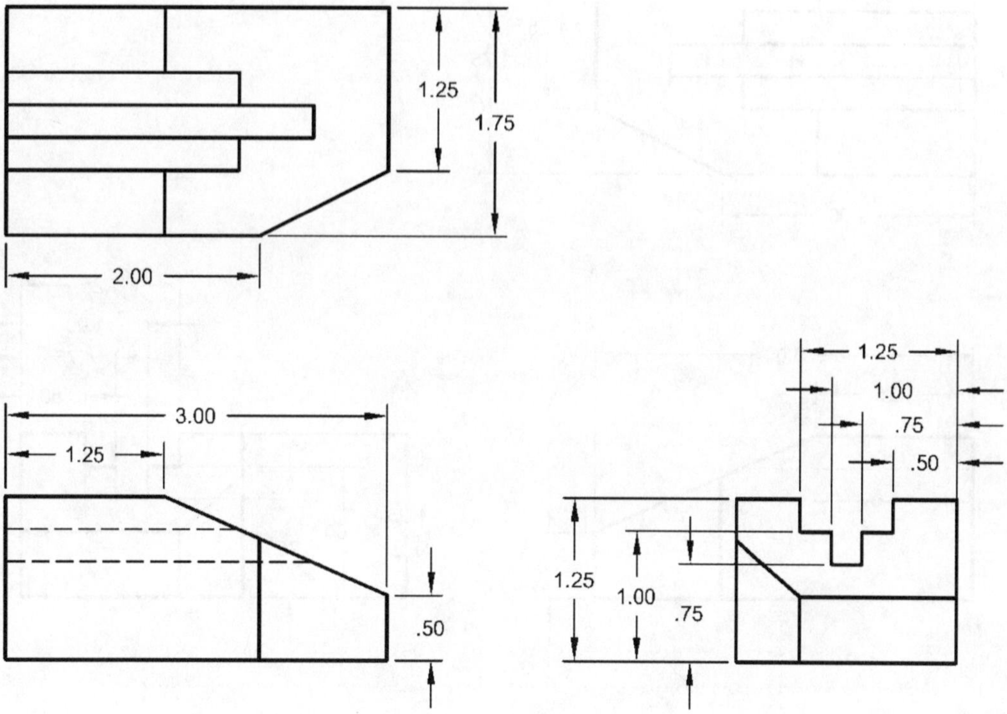

P7-3b) Draw a full-scale cabinet oblique pictorial by hand or in a drawing package per instructions. The grid spacing is 0.25 inch.

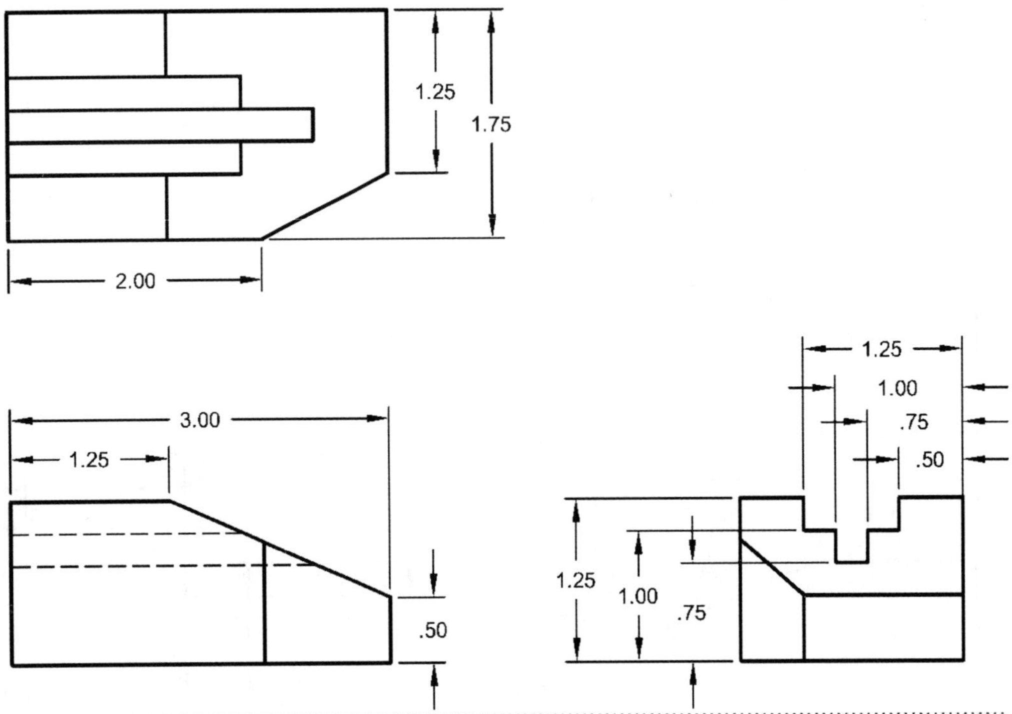

Name: ______________________________ Date: ______________

P7-4a) Draw a full-scale isometric pictorial by hand or in a drawing package per instructions. The grid spacing is 10 mm.

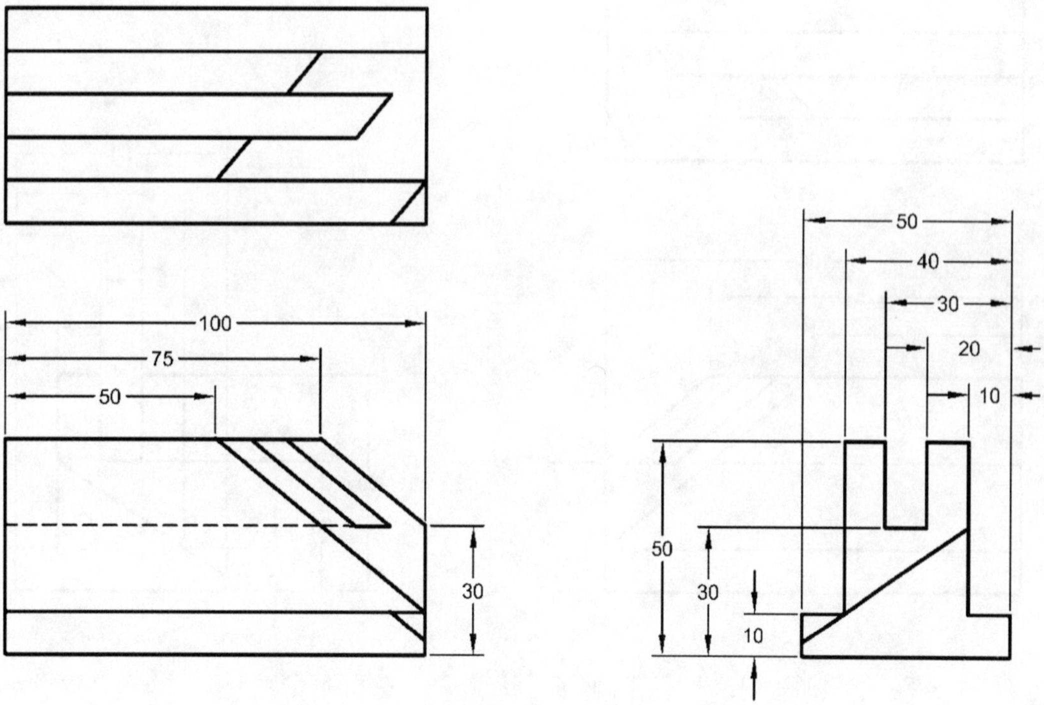

P7-4b) Draw a full-scale cabinet oblique pictorial by hand or in a drawing package per instructions. The grid spacing is 10 mm.

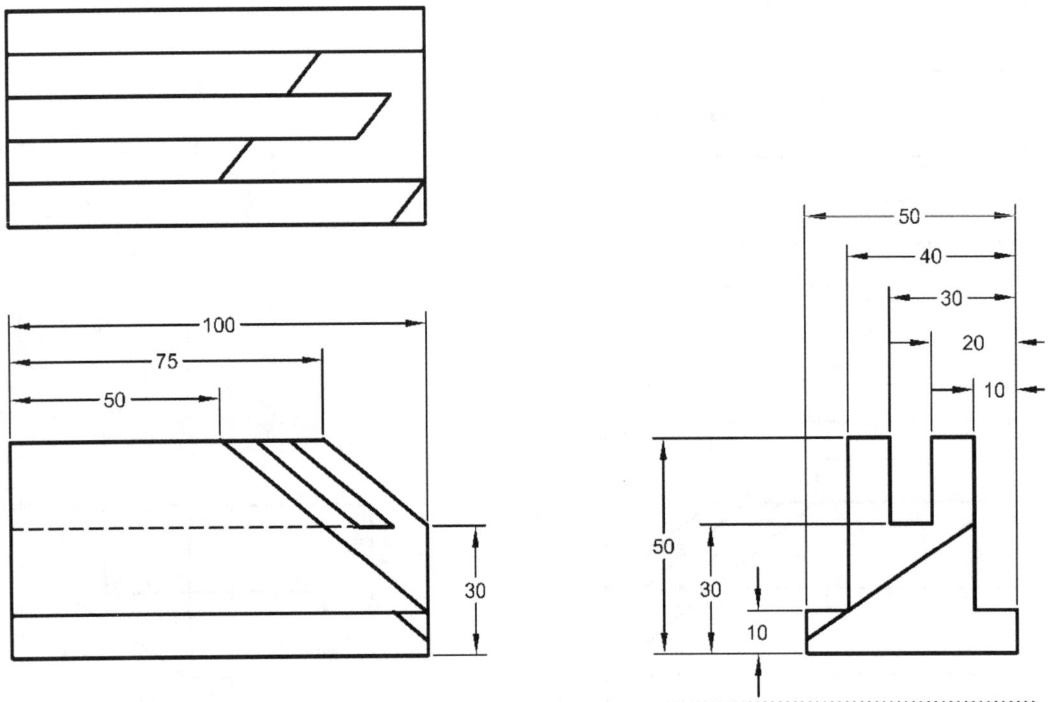

Name: ______________________________ Date: ______________

P7-5a) Draw a full-scale isometric pictorial by hand or in a drawing package per instructions. The grid spacing is 0.25 inch.

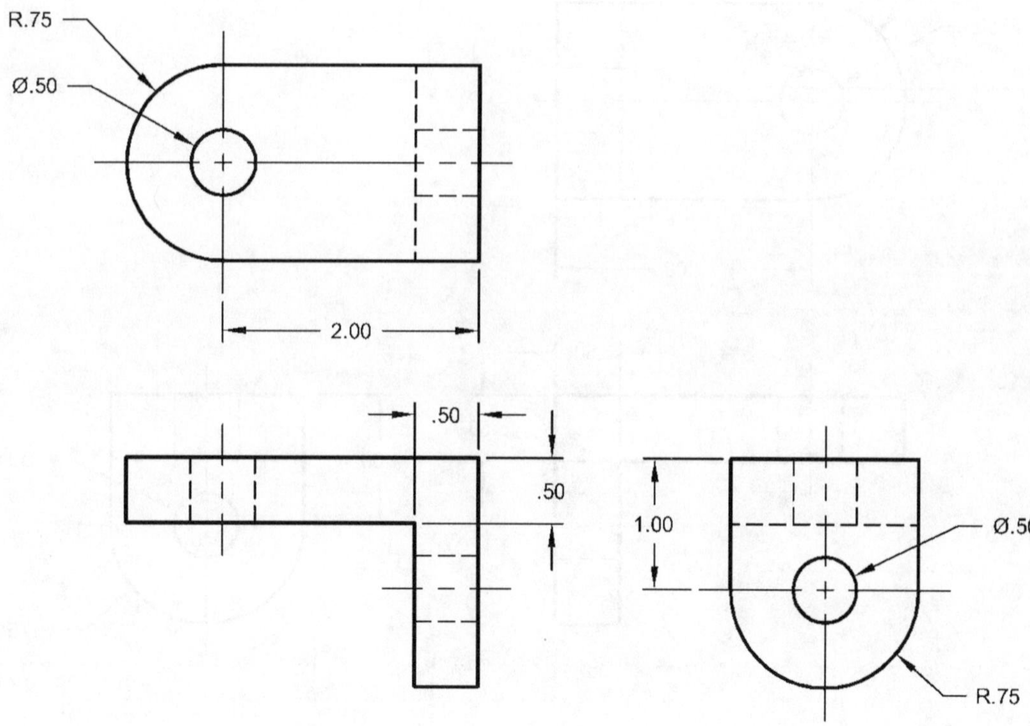

P7-5b) Draw a full-scale cabinet oblique pictorial by hand or in a drawing package per instructions. The grid spacing is 0.25 inch.

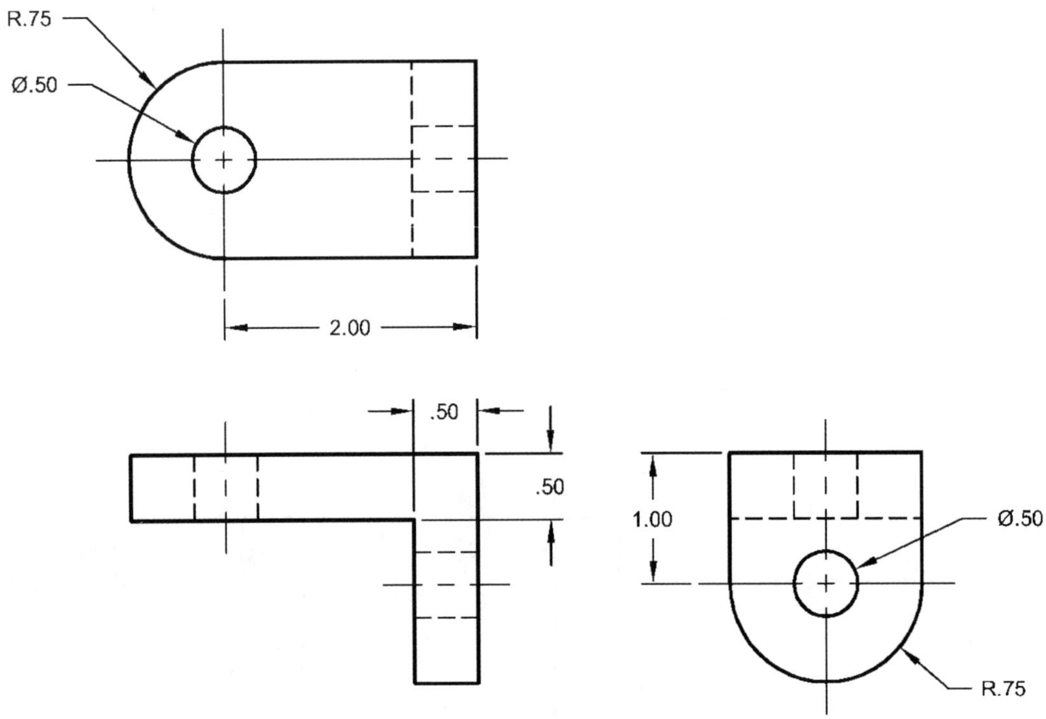

Name: ______________________________ Date: ______________

P7-6a) Draw a full-scale isometric pictorial by hand or in a drawing package per instructions. The grid spacing is 10 mm.

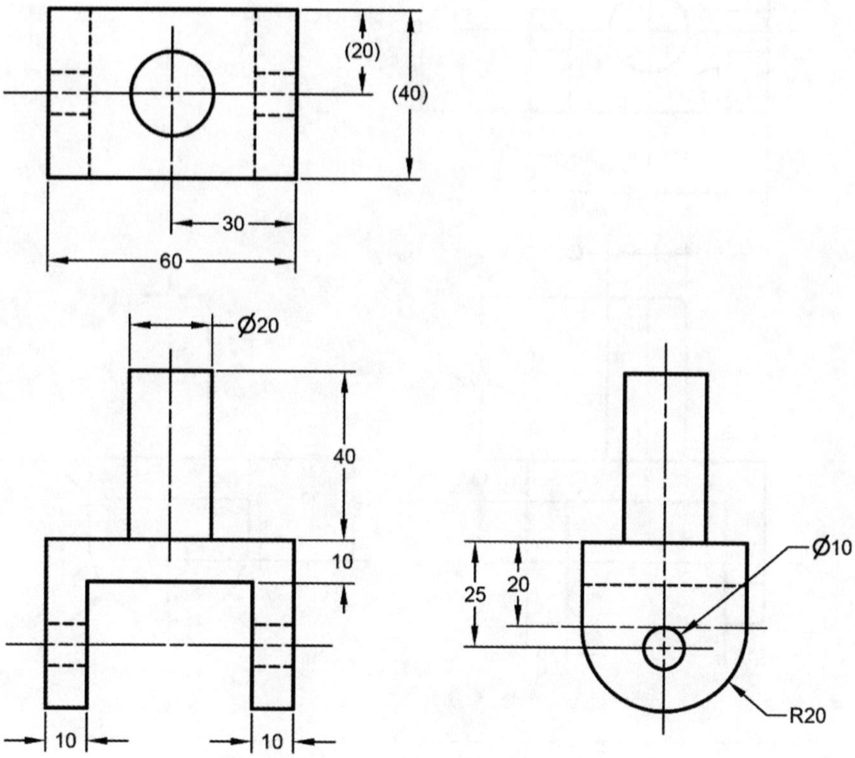

P7-6b) Draw a full-scale cabinet oblique pictorial by hand or in a drawing package per instructions. The grid spacing is 10 mm.

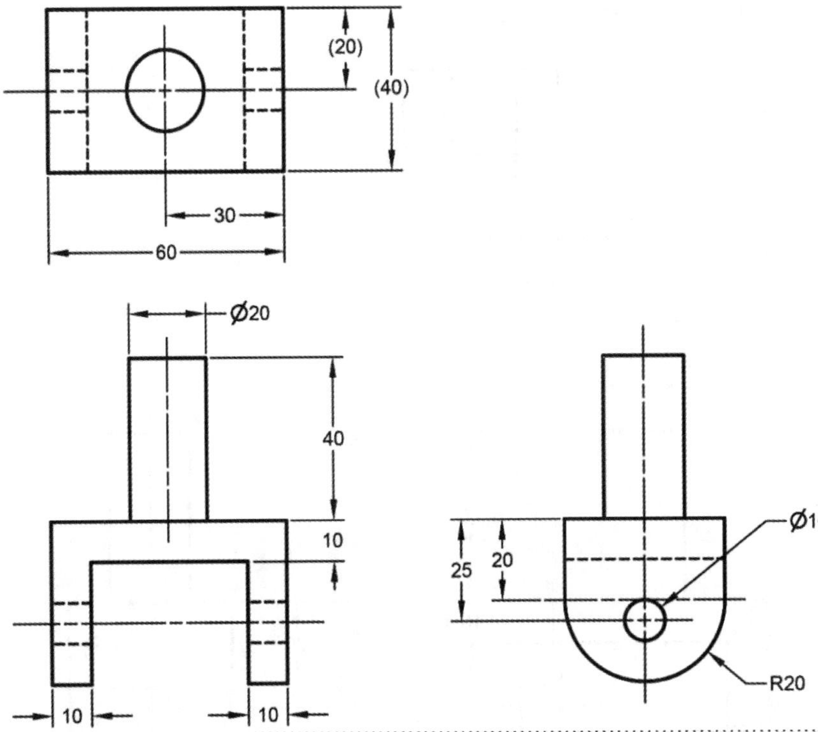

P7-7a) Draw a full-scale isometric pictorial by hand or in a drawing package per instructions.

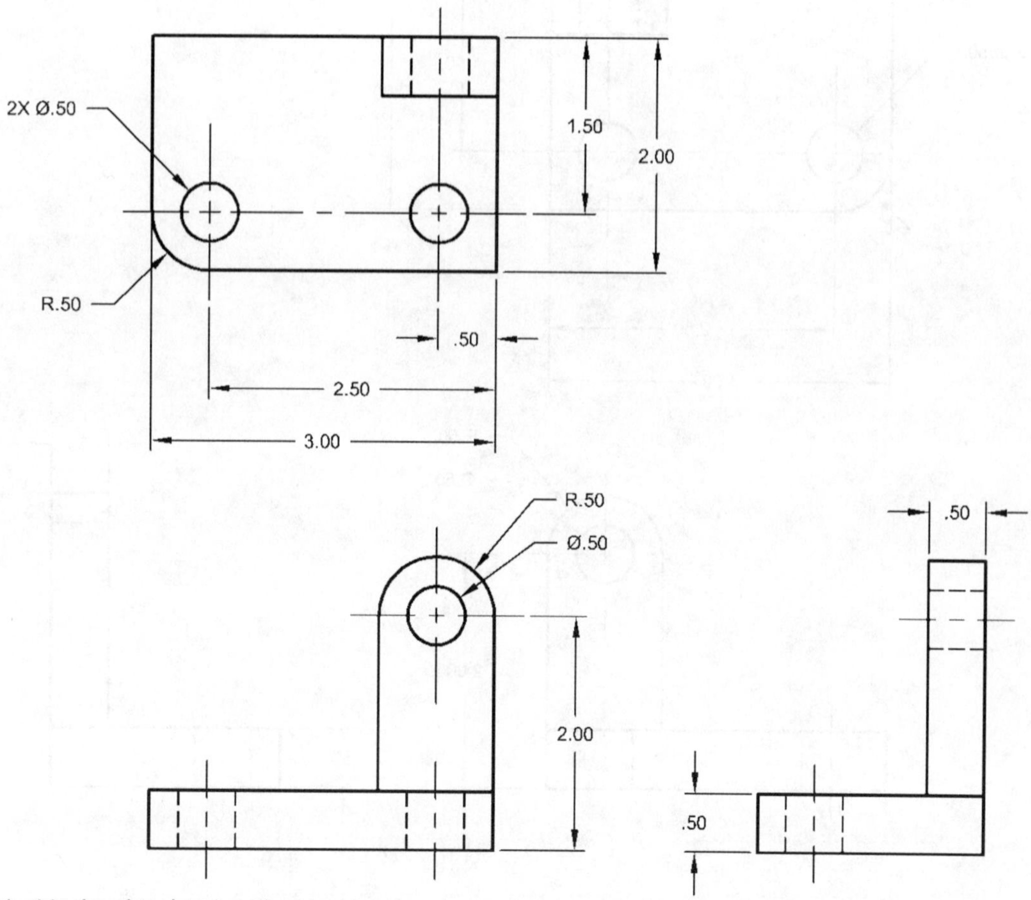

P7-7b) Draw a full-scale cabinet oblique pictorial by hand or in a drawing package per instructions.

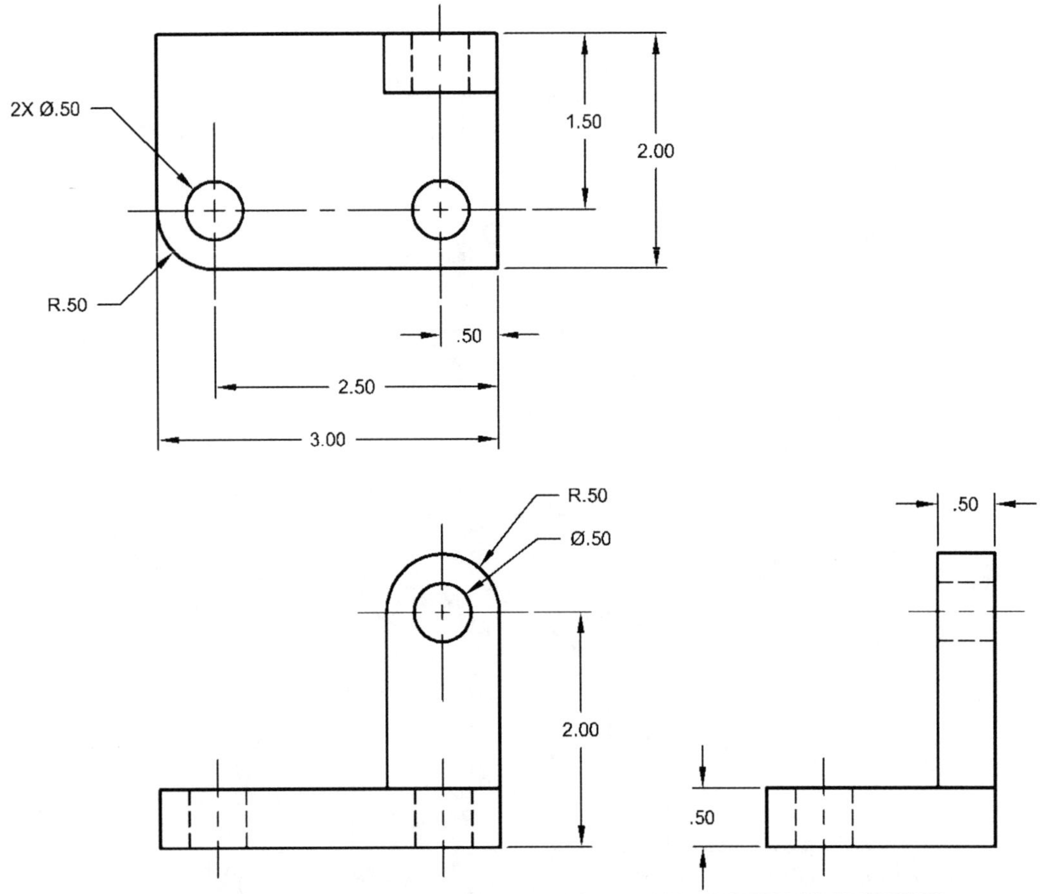

P7-8a) Draw a full-scale isometric pictorial by hand or in a drawing package per instructions.

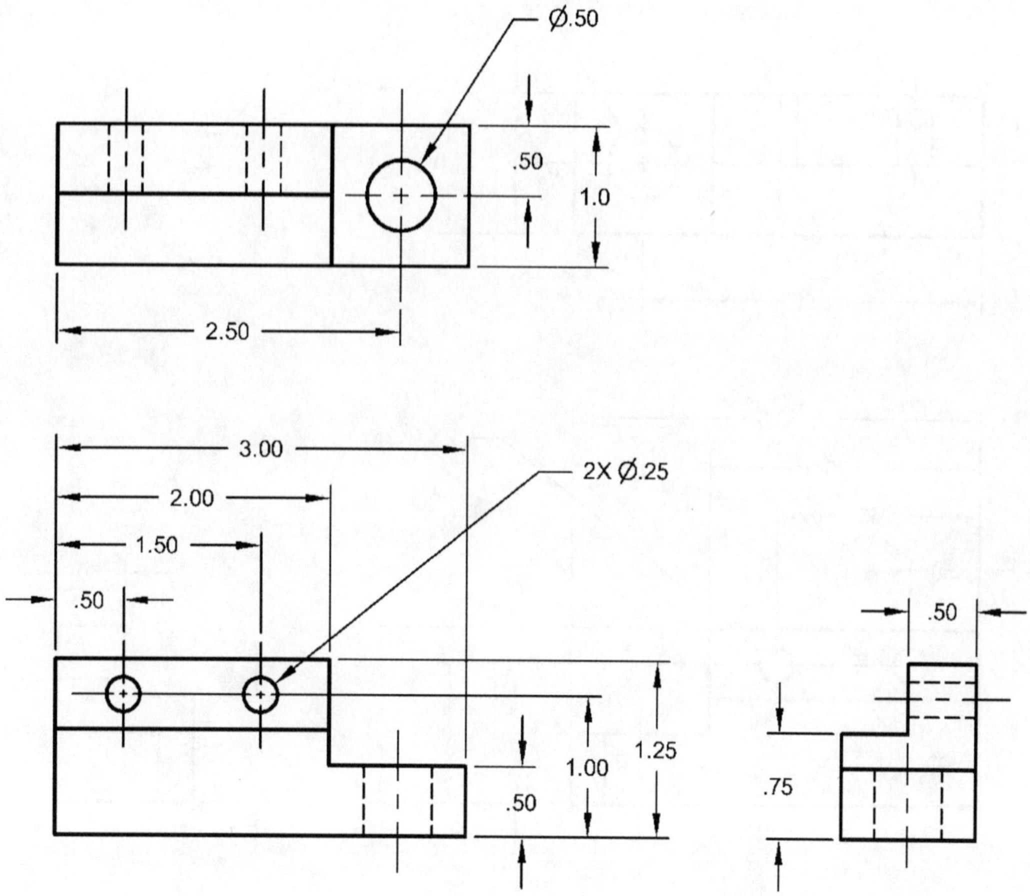

P7-8b) Draw a full-scale cabinet oblique pictorial by hand or in a drawing package per instructions.

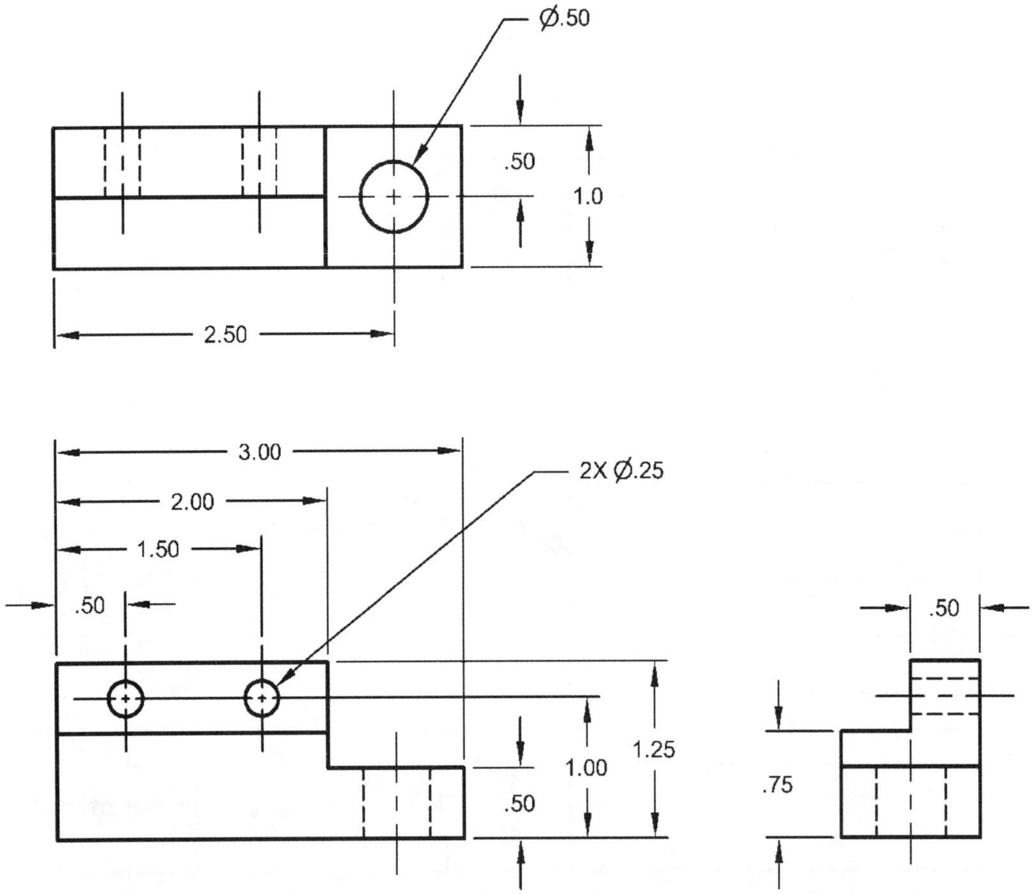

P7-9a) Draw a full-scale isometric pictorial by hand or in a drawing package per instructions.

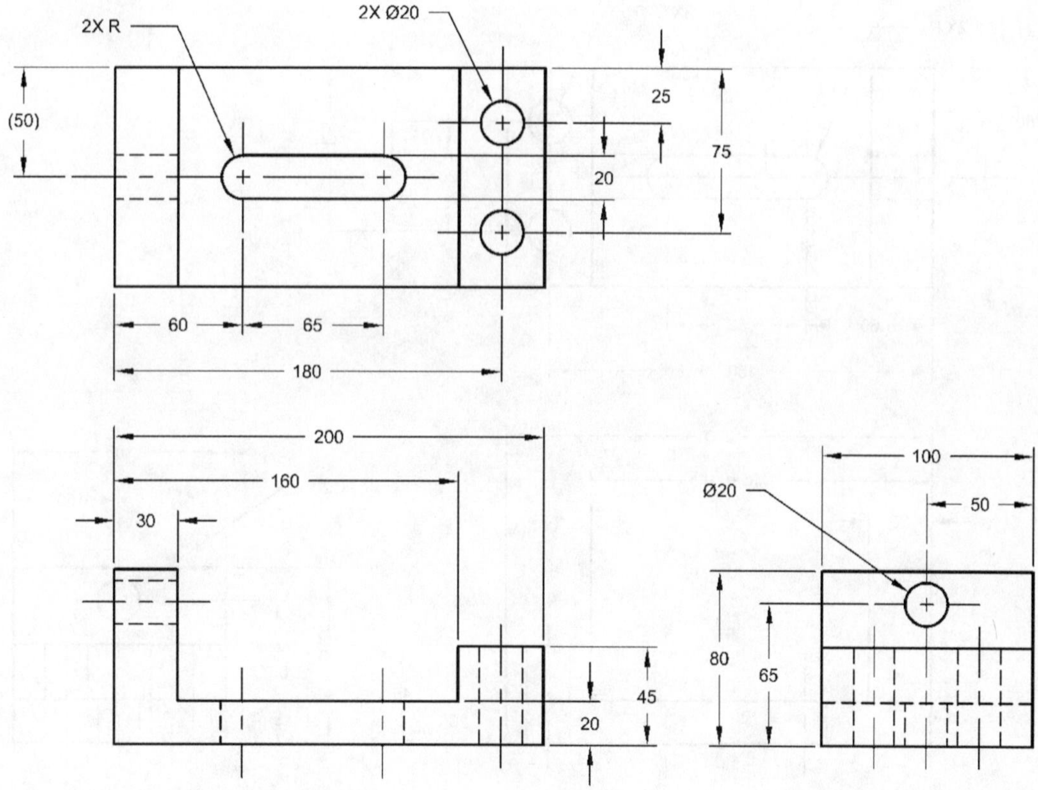

P7-9b) Draw a full-scale cabinet oblique pictorial by hand or in a drawing package per instructions.

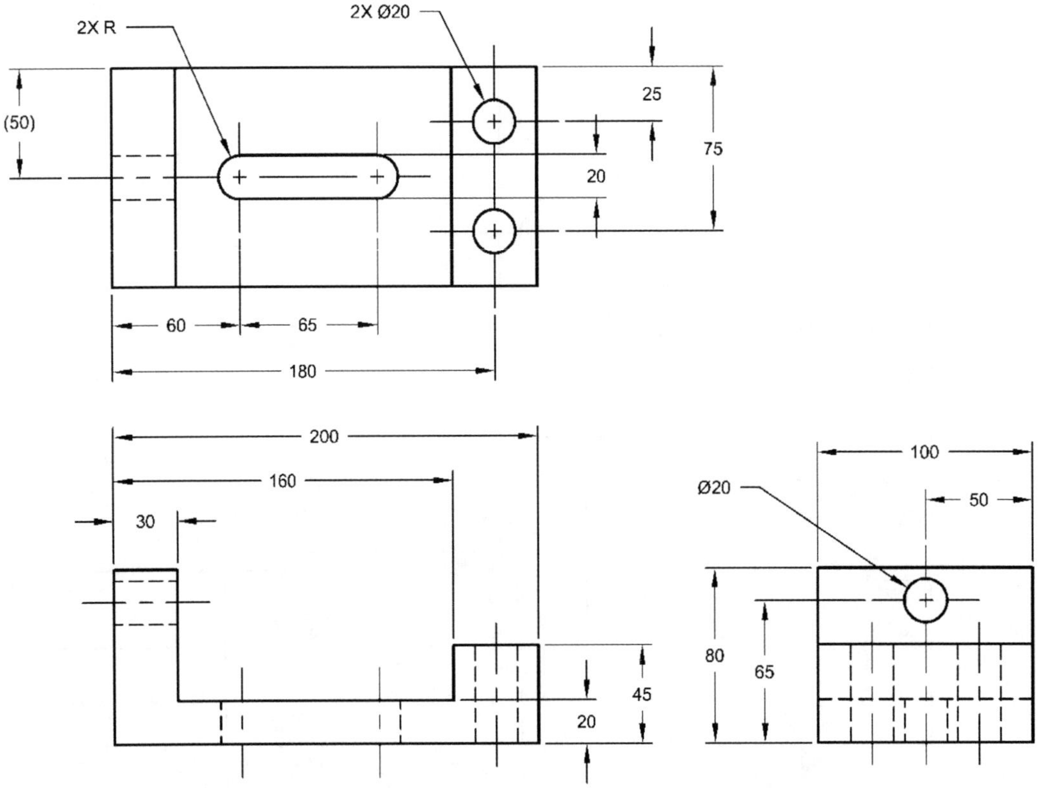

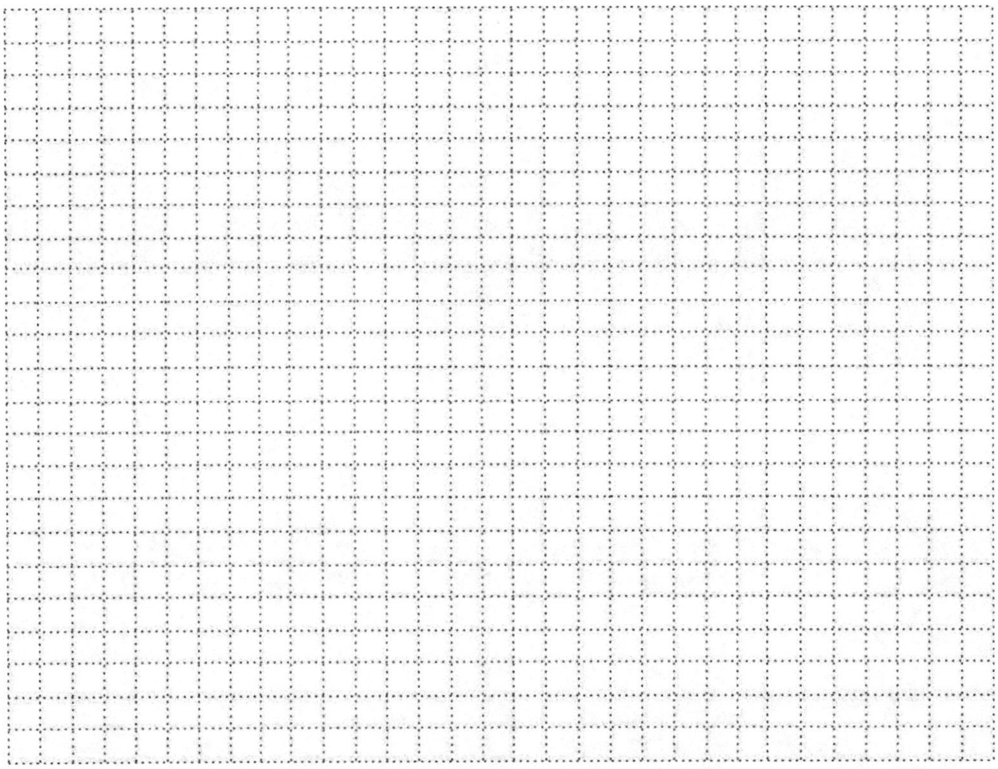

P7-10a) Draw a full-scale isometric pictorial by hand or in a drawing package per instructions.

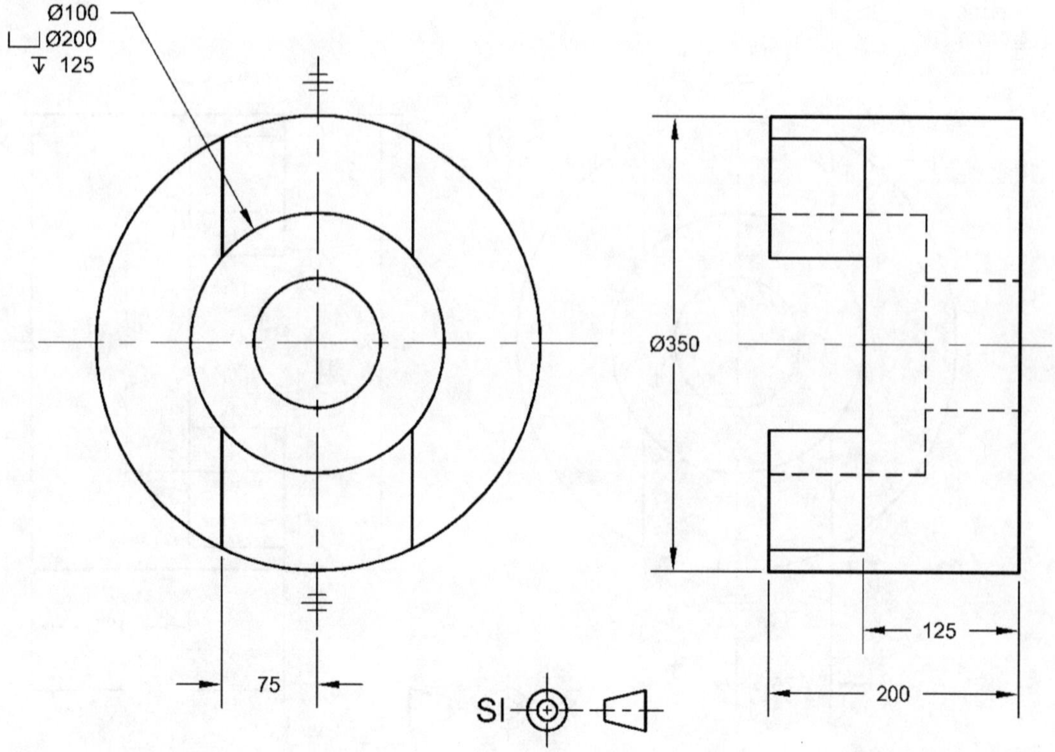

P7-10b) Draw a full-scale cabinet oblique pictorial by hand or in a drawing package per instructions.

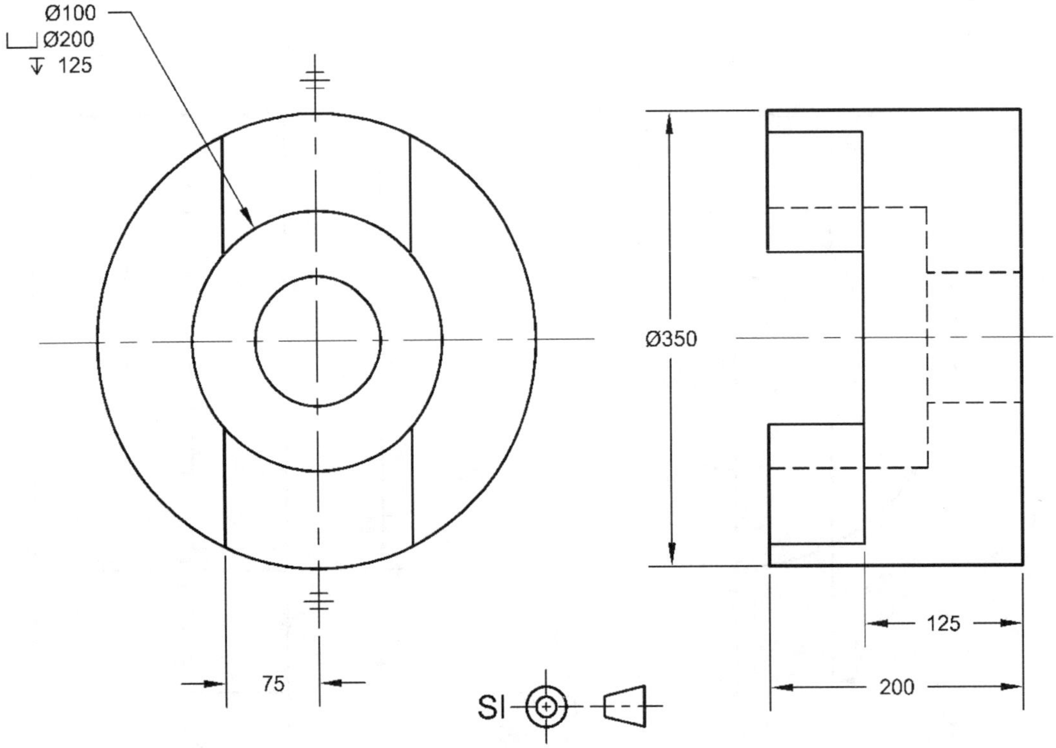

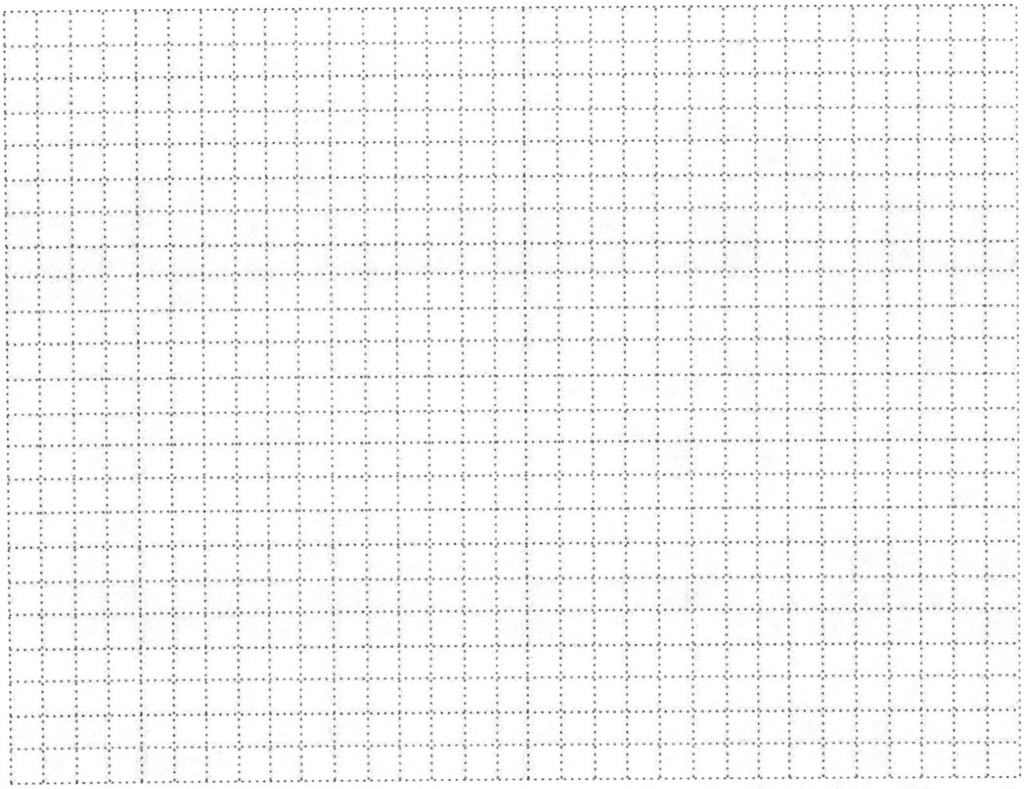

P7-11a) Draw a full-scale isometric pictorial by hand or in a drawing package per instructions.

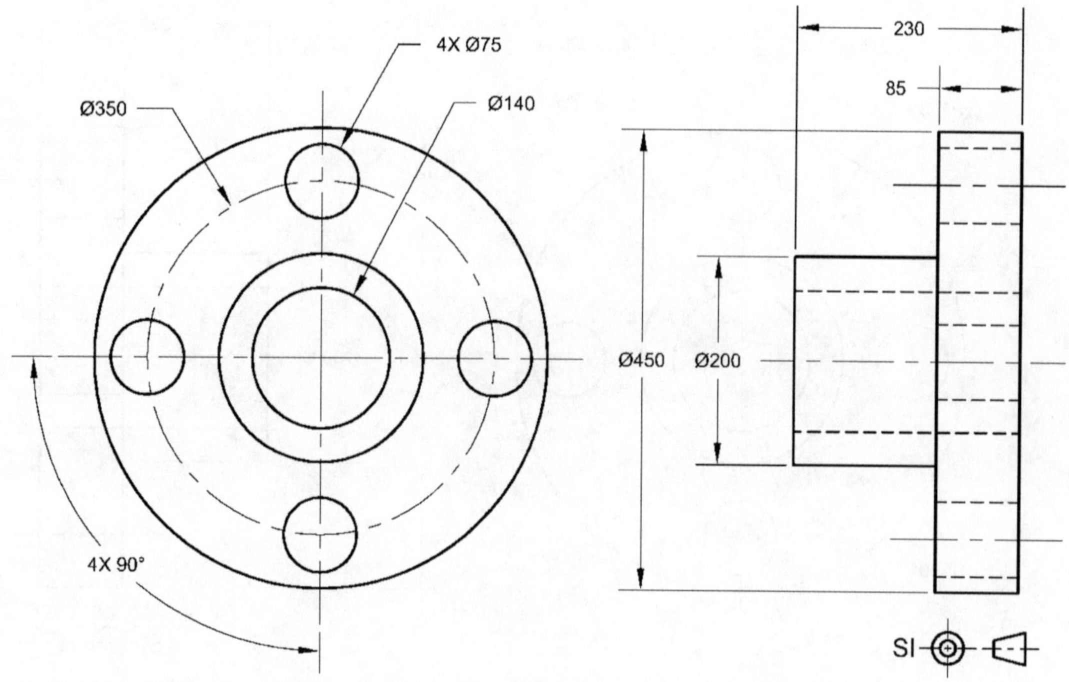

P7-11b) Draw a full-scale cabinet oblique pictorial by hand or in a drawing package per instructions.

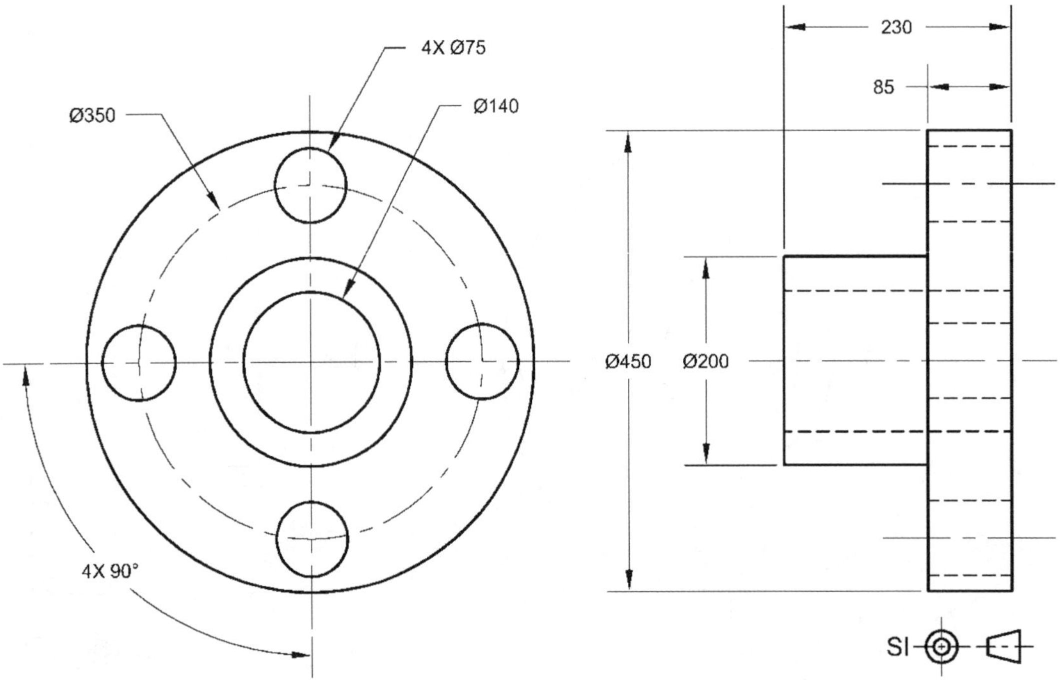

P7-12a) Draw a full-scale isometric pictorial by hand or in a drawing package per instructions. Include all hidden lines.

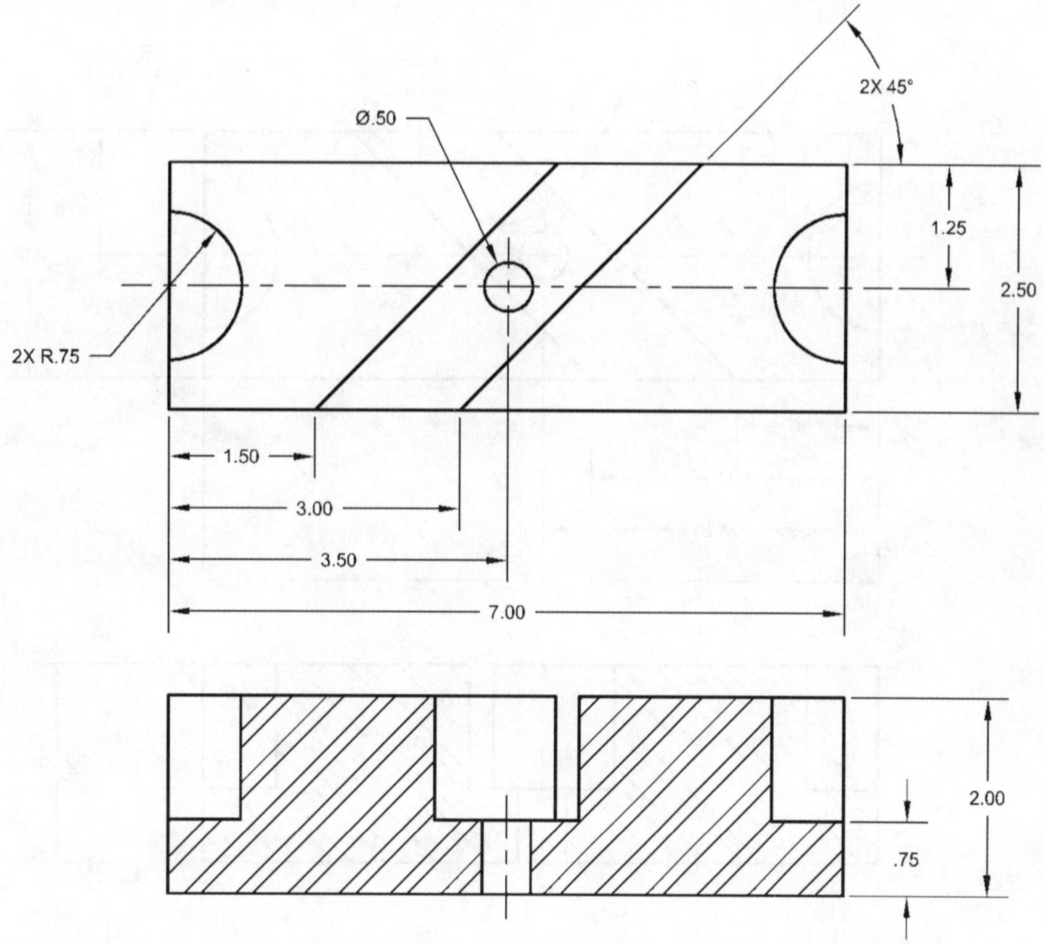

P7-12b) Draw a full-scale cabinet oblique pictorial by hand or in a drawing package per instructions. Include all hidden lines.

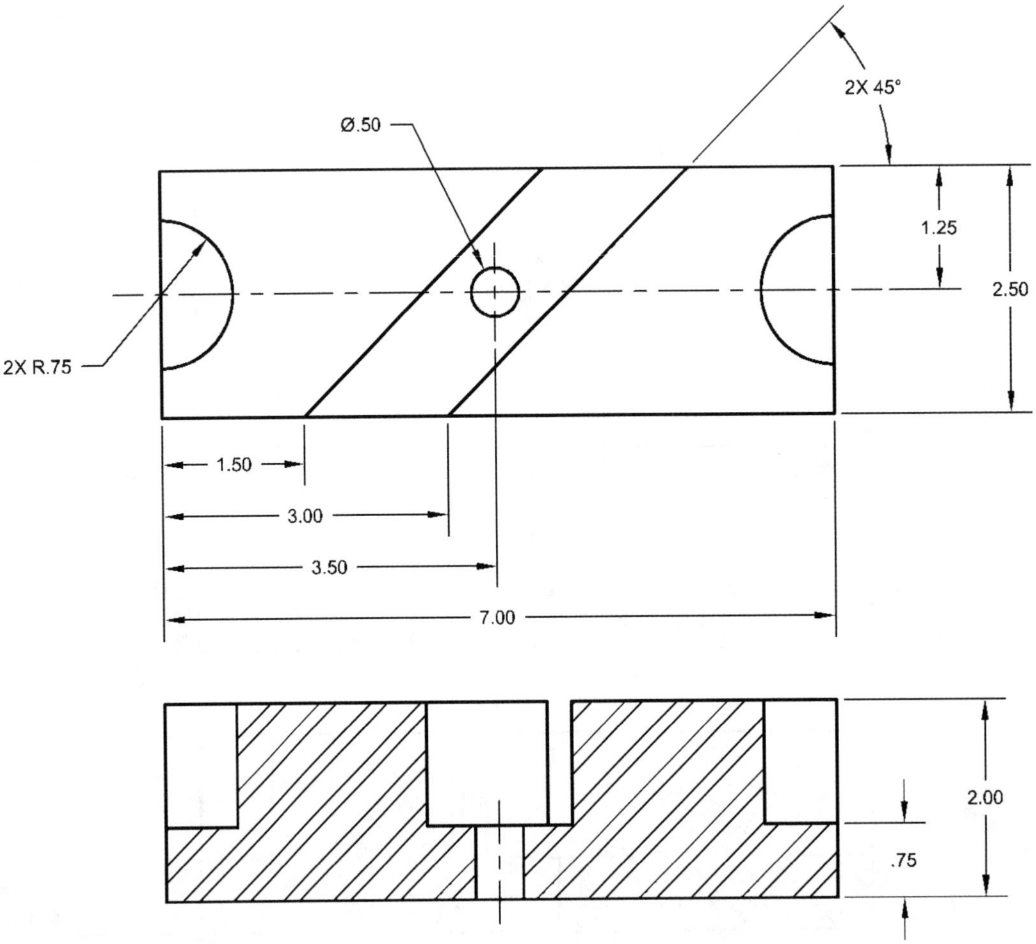

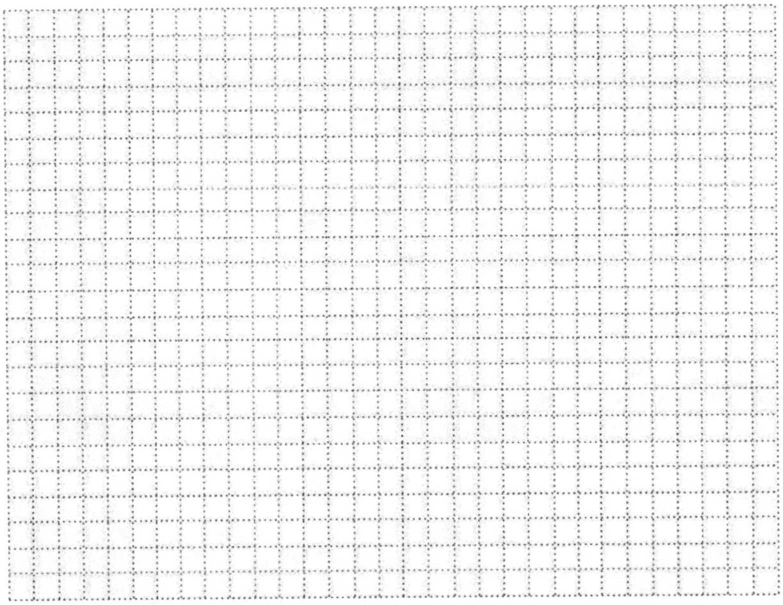

SP7-1a) Draw a full-scale isometric pictorial by hand or in a drawing package. The answer to this problem is on the *Independent Learning content*.

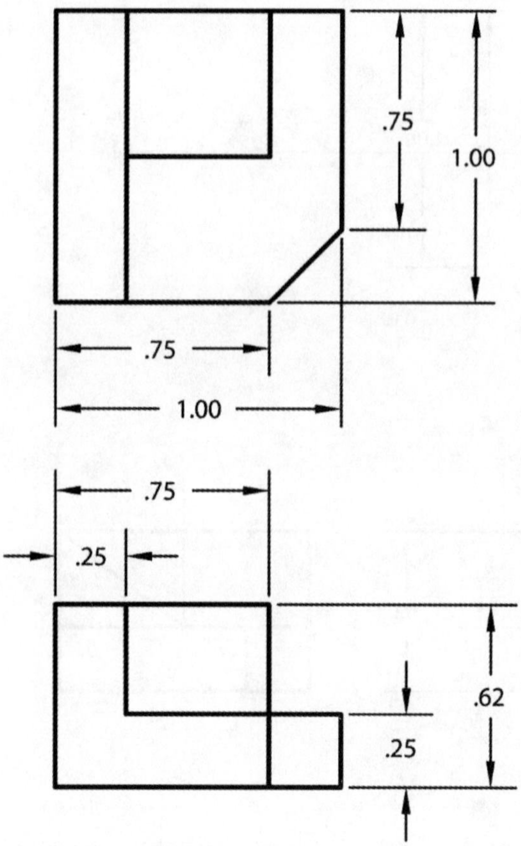

SP7-1b) Draw a full-scale cabinet oblique pictorial by hand or in a drawing package. The answer to this problem is on the *Independent Learning content*.

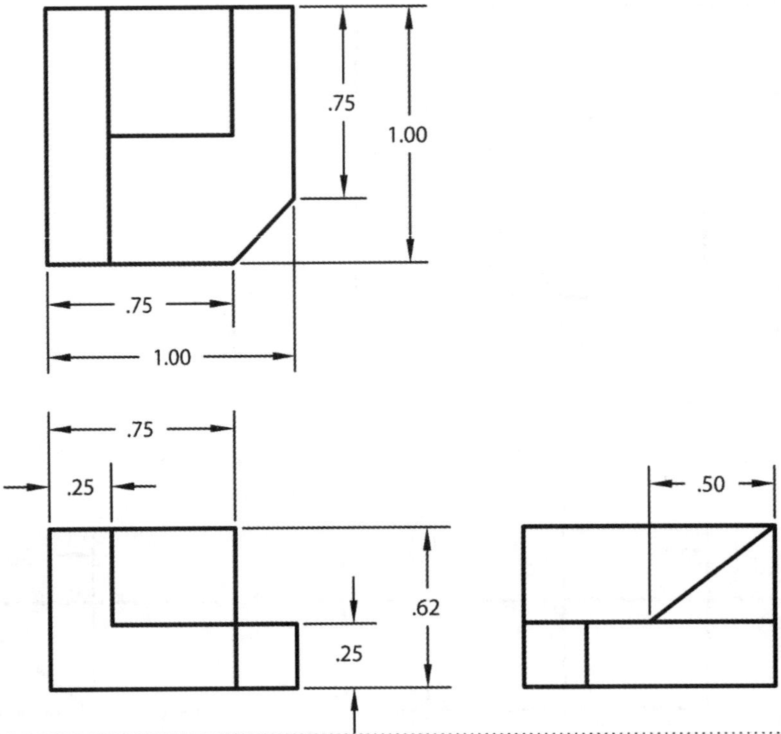

SP7-2a) Draw a full-scale isometric pictorial by hand or in a drawing package. The answer to this problem is on the *Independent Learning content*.

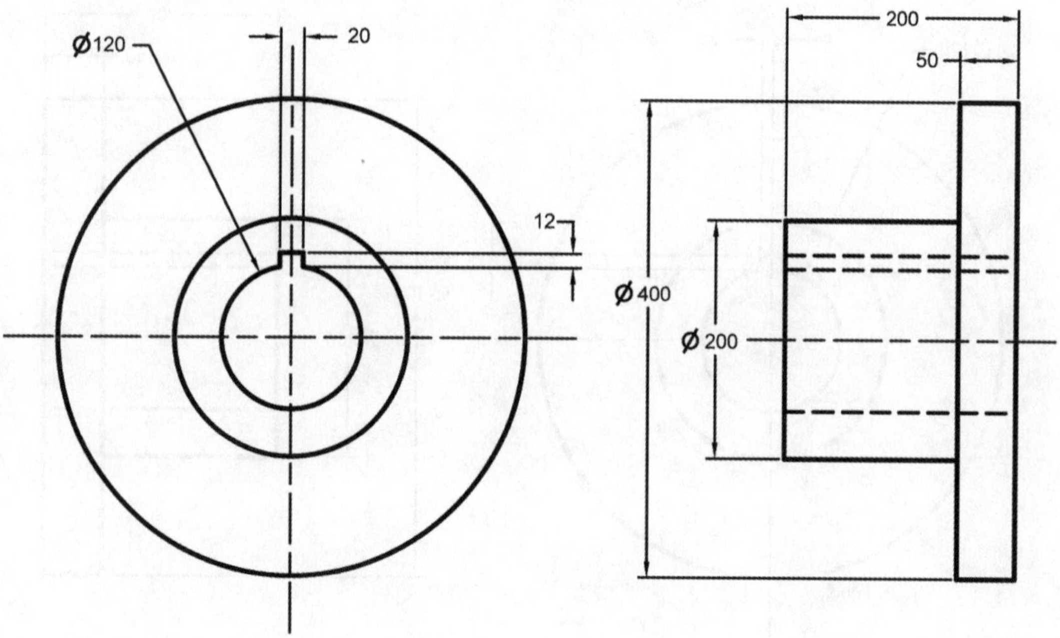

SP7-2b) Draw a full-scale cabinet oblique pictorial by hand or in a drawing package. The answer to this problem is on the *Independent Learning content*.

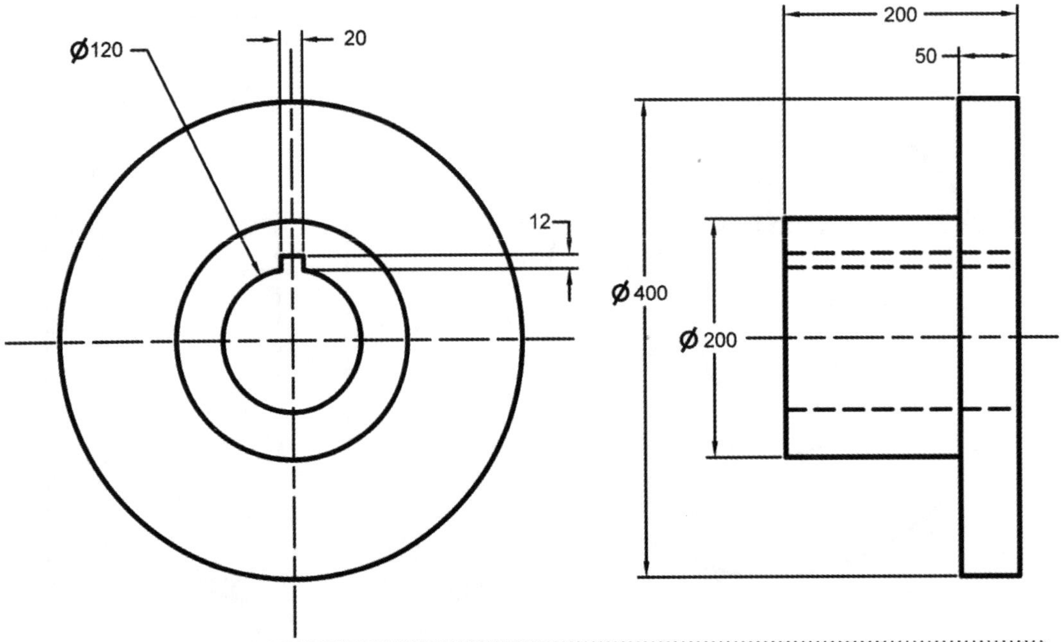

CHAPTER 8

CREATING PICTORIAL DRAWINGS IN AUTOCAD®

CHAPTER OUTLINE

CHAPTER SUMMARY

In this chapter you will learn how to use the isometric grid/snap and isocircles to create an isometric pictorial. The isometric snap option allows you to create a grid that aligns itself with the isometric pictorial axes. By the end of this chapter, you will be able to create an isometric pictorial that consists of lines, circles and radii.

8.1) ISOMETRIC SNAP

To facilitate the creation of an isometric pictorial, you may activate AutoCAD's isometric snap. Once the isometric snap is activated, the grid and snap will act along the isometric axes. Remember, these axes are oriented at 30 degrees above the horizontal. Figure 8.1-1 shows AutoCAD's isometric grid with an illustration of the isometric axes. An isometric pictorial may be created by following the isometric grid and snap directions. *Polar Tracking* set at increments of 30 degrees may also be helpful in the construction of an isometric pictorial.

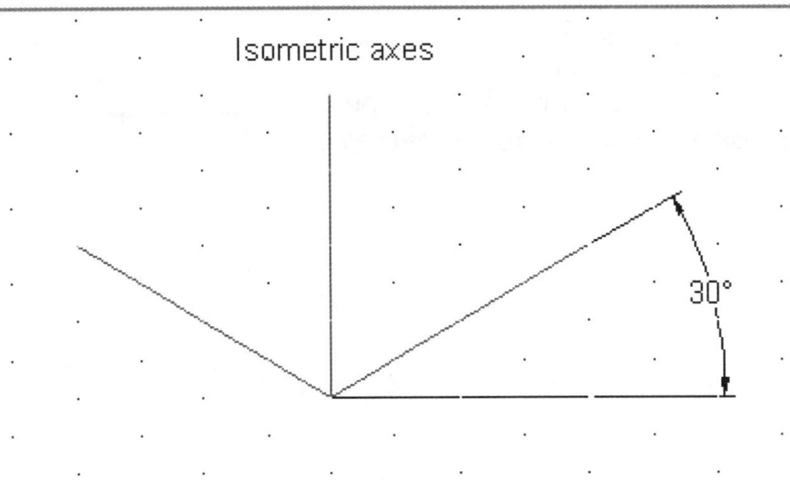

Figure 8.1-1: Isometric grid

Activating the isometric snap

1) Command: **SNap**
2) `Specify snap spacing or [ON/OFF/Aspect/Legacy/Style/Type] <10>:` **s**
3) `Enter snap grid style [Standard/Isometric] <S>:` **i**
4) `Specify vertical spacing <10>:` Specify the isometric snap spacing.

8.2) ISOCIRCLES

In an isometric pictorial, circular features are represented by an ellipse. The axes of the ellipse are not always horizontal and vertical. The angle of the ellipse axes depends on the isoplane in which the ellipse resides. Figure 8.2-1 shows a cube with a hole in each side. The representative ellipses and their defining boxes are shown. Notice the orientation of the ellipses and their associated isoplanes.

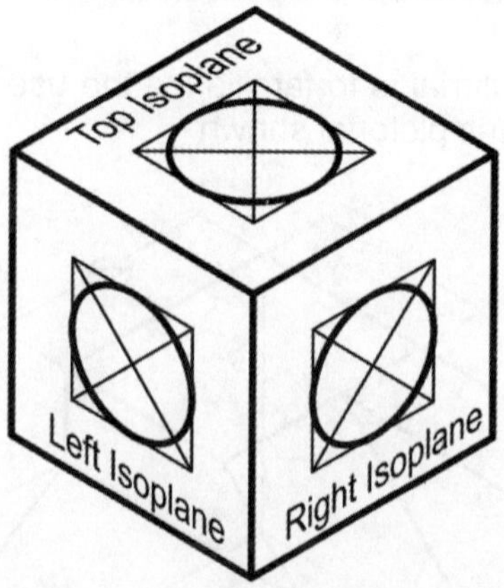

Figure 8.2-1: Isoplanes and ellipse orientation

AutoCAD® makes creating the ellipses or isocircles used to represent circular features very easy. **ISOCIRCLE** is an option within the **ELLIPSE** command. When creating isocircles, you need to specify the desired isoplane. You may toggle between isoplanes by pressing `Ctrl+E` or by clicking on the appropriate *Isoplane* icon  in the *Status Bar* (See Figure 8.2-2). You will know what isoplane you are currently in by looking at the crosshairs of your cursor.

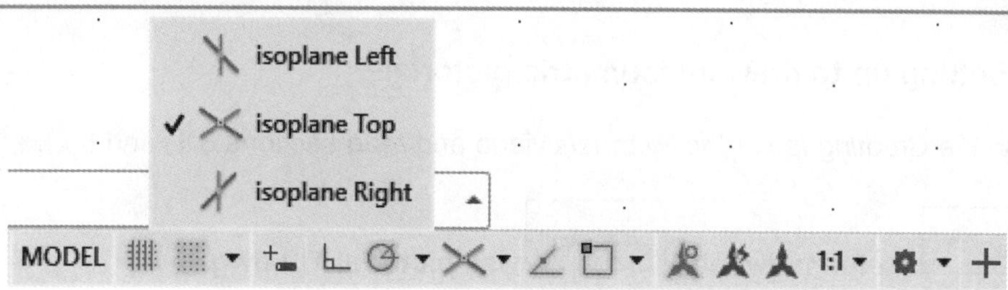

Figure 8.2-2: Status bar isoplanes commands

Creating isocircles

1) Command: **ELlipse** or *Draw* panel: 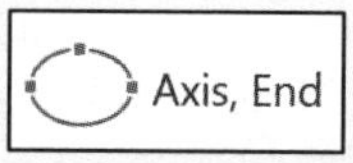

2) `Specify axis endpoint of ellipse or [Arc/Center/Isocircle]:` **i**
3) `Specify center of isocircle:` Specify the center of the isocircle.
4) `Specify radius of isocircle or [Diameter]:` Press `Ctrl+E` to toggle to the correct isoplane. Enter the radius of the circle that the isocircle is representing.

8.3) ISOMETRIC PICTORIAL TUTORIAL

The objective of this tutorial is to familiarize the user with the isometric snap and grid. You will draw the isometric pictorial shown.

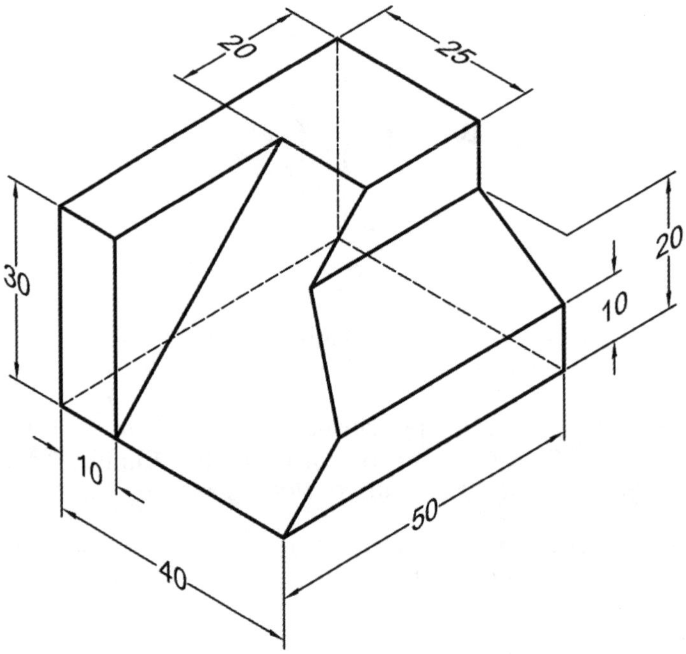

8.3.1) Setting up to draw an isometric pictorial

1) View the *Creating Isometric Pictorials* video and read sections 8.1) and 8.2).

2) 

set-mm.dwt and 

Iso pictorial Tut.dwg.

3) Turn your **GRID** on and set the spacing to be **10** mm.

4) Set your isometric snap.
   a) <u>Command:</u> **SNap**
   b) `Specify snap spacing or [ON/OFF/Aspect/Legacy/Style/Type] <10>:` **s**
   c) `Enter snap grid style [Standard/Isometric] <S>:` **i**
   d) `Specify vertical spacing <10>:` **5**

5) Notice that the crosshairs and grid are now at a 30 degree angle, in line with the isometric axes.

6) Turn your **Polar Tracking** on and set your polar tracking angle (**POLARANG**) to 30 degree increments.

8.3.2) Drawing the isometric pictorial

1) In your ***Construction*** layer, draw the object's defining box. Use the isometric grid/snap and polar tracking to guide you.

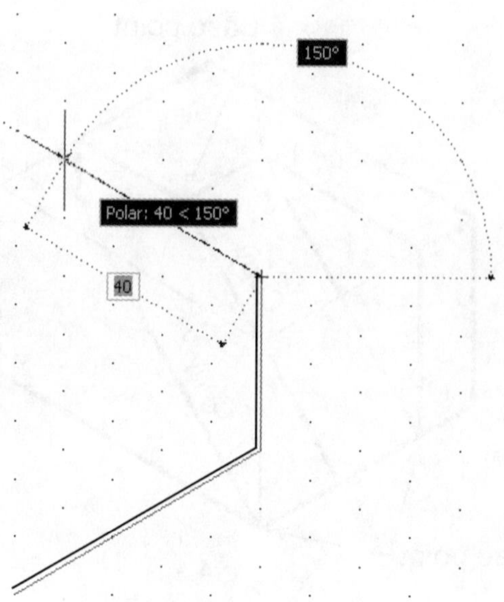

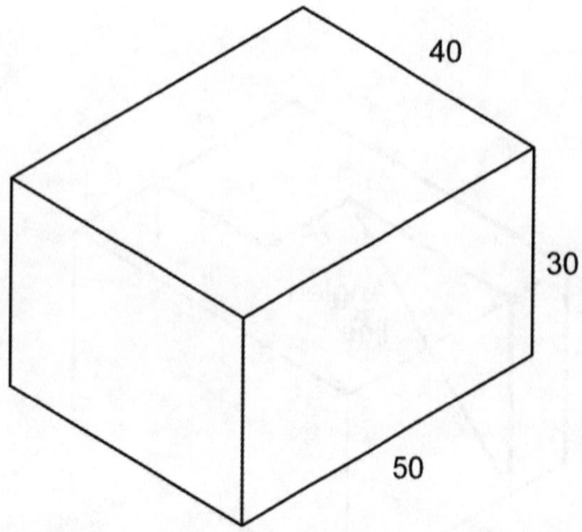

2) In your ***Visible*** layer, draw the features that are parallel to the sides of the defining box. You may want to deactivate your object snap while working with your snap to make it easier.

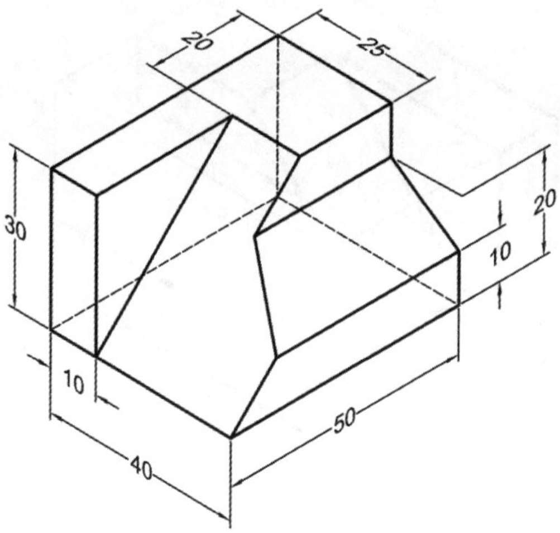

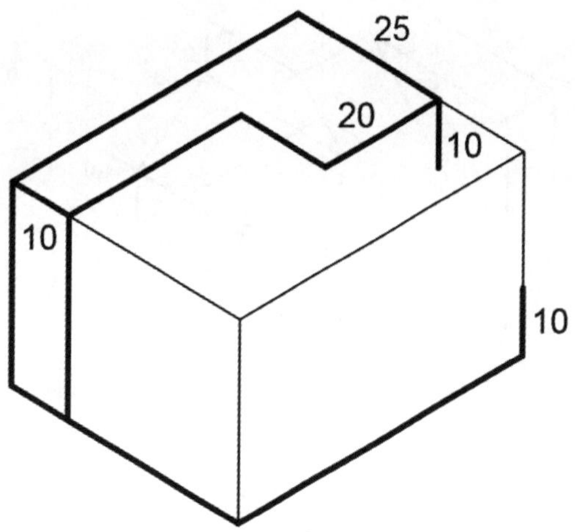

3) Draw the angled line shown in the left side figure shown below.

4) **Copy** the angled line as shown in the right side figure. It may be helpful to temporarily turn off the **Snap** and turn your **object snap** on.

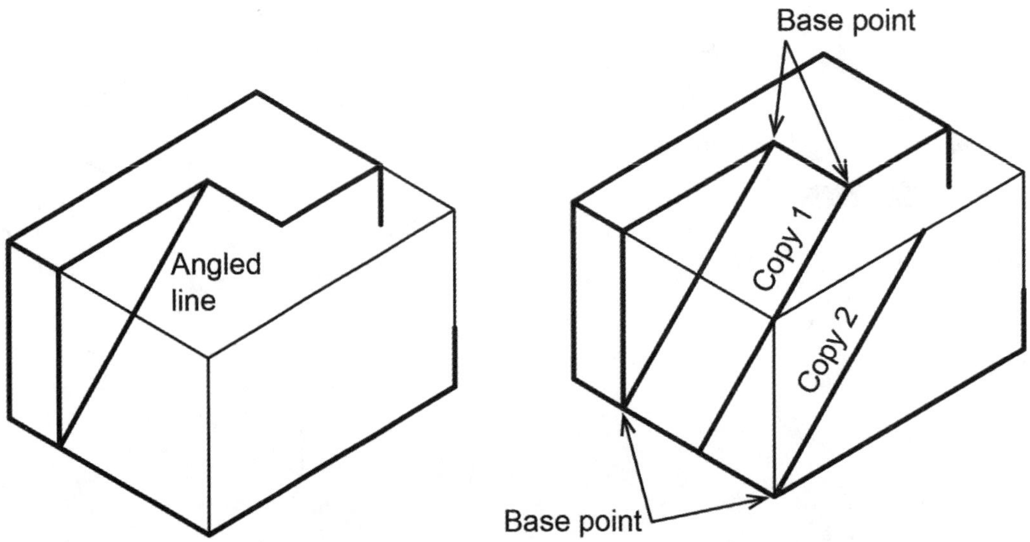

5) Add the additional lines shown. You may want to draw the lines long and then **trim** off the excess.

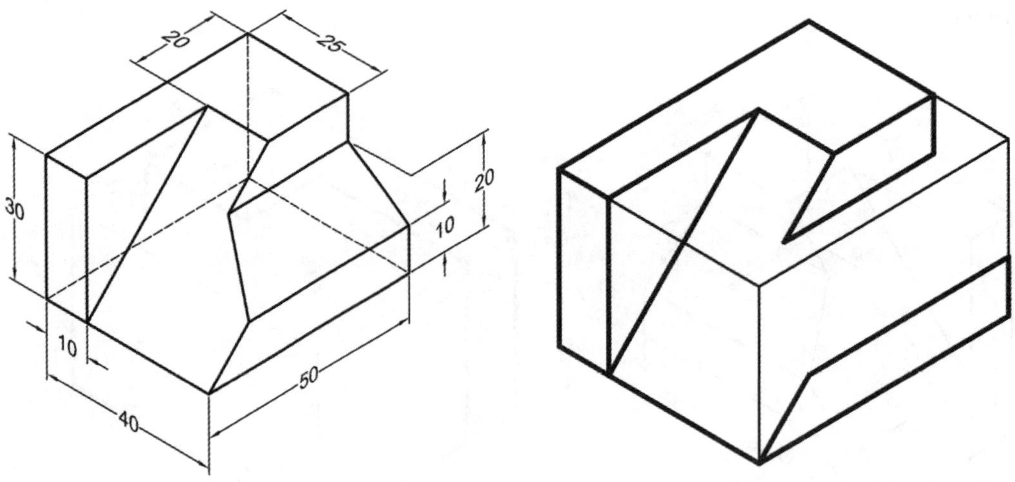

6) If you turned your object snap off, turn it back on. Add the remaining lines, **trim** unwanted lines, and turn off your ***Construction*** layer as shown in the figure.

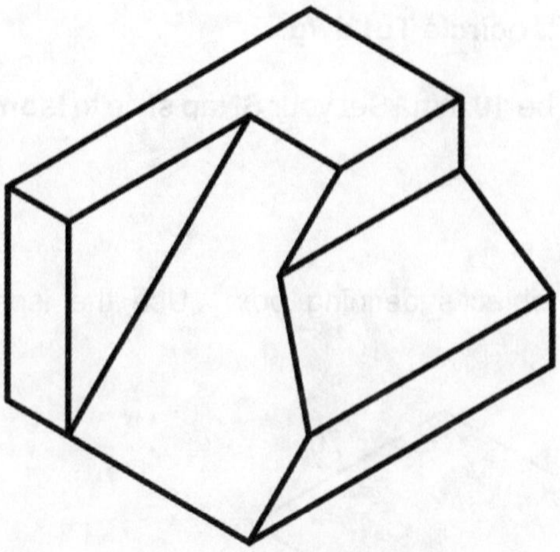

8.4) ISOCIRCLE TUTORIAL

The objective of this tutorial is to familiarize the user with creating isocircles. You will draw an isometric pictorial of the object shown.

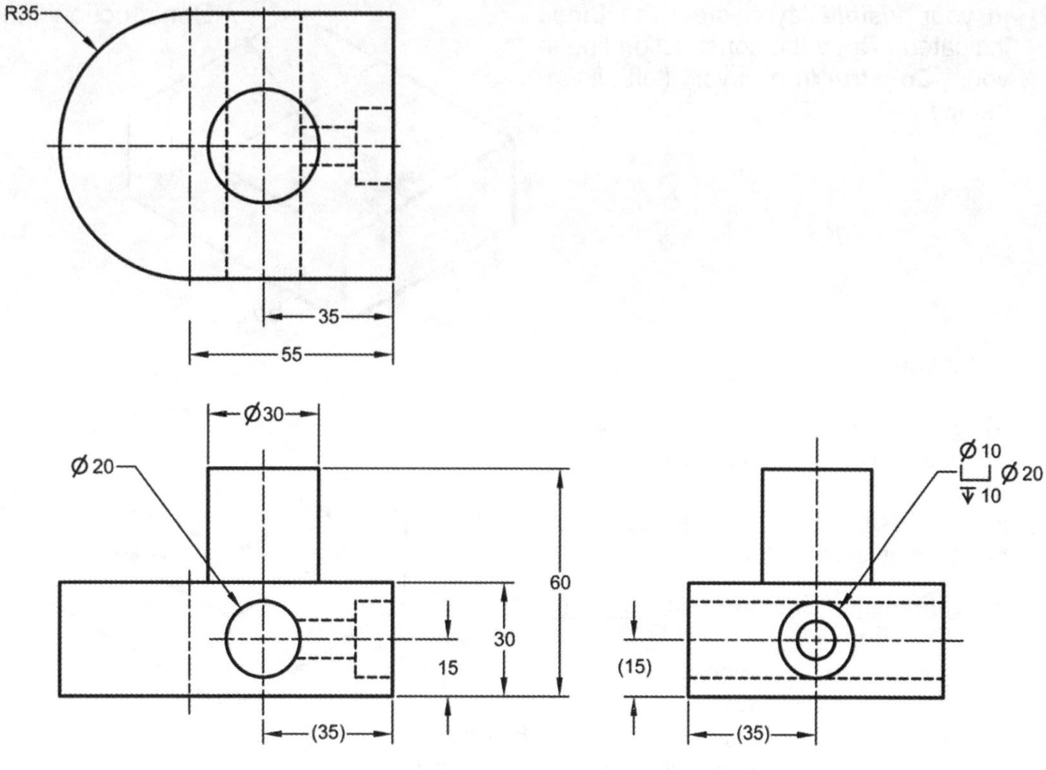

8.4.1) Setting up to draw an isometric pictorial

1) 

set-mm.dwt and 

Isocircle Tut.dwg.

2) Turn your **GRID** on and set the spacing to be **10** mm. Set your **SNap** style to **Isometric** and set the snap spacing to **5** mm.

8.4.2) Drawing the isometric pictorial

1) In your ***Construction*** layer, draw the object's defining box. Use the isometric grid/snap to guide you.

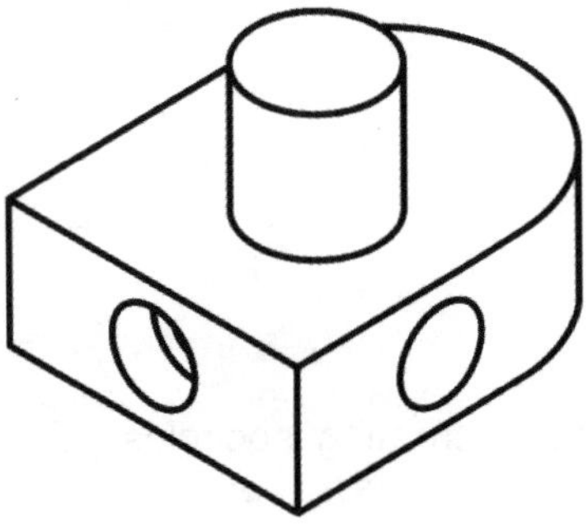

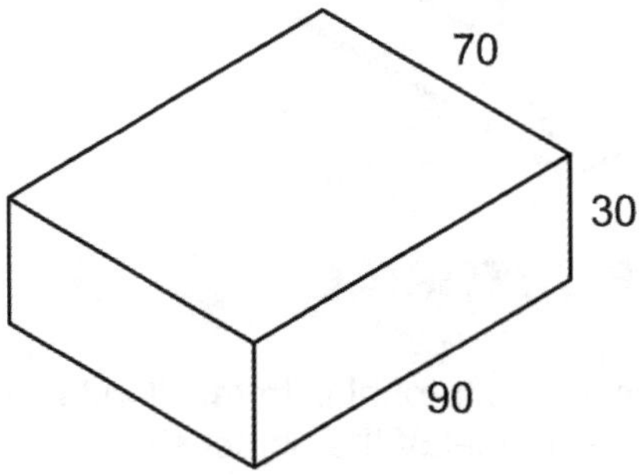

2) In your ***Visible*** layer, draw the **Lines** indicated. Draw the construction line in your ***Construction*** layer (left figure below).

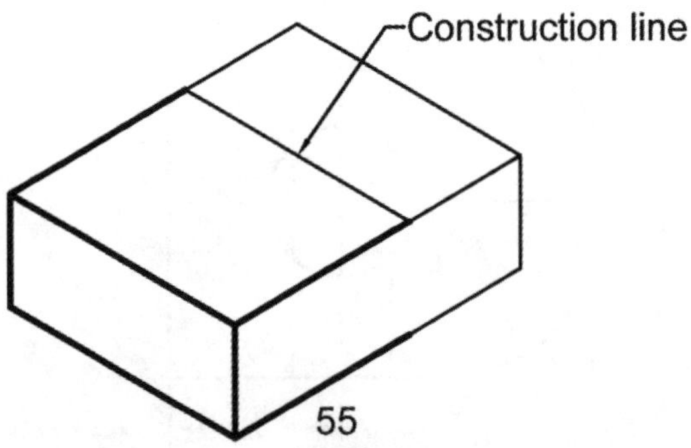

3) Enter your top isoplane.

   a) <u>*Status bar*:</u> 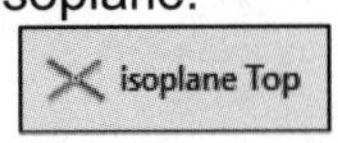

or `Ctrl+E` until the cursor is on the top

4) In your ***Visible*** layer, draw the large radius of the base (right figure below).

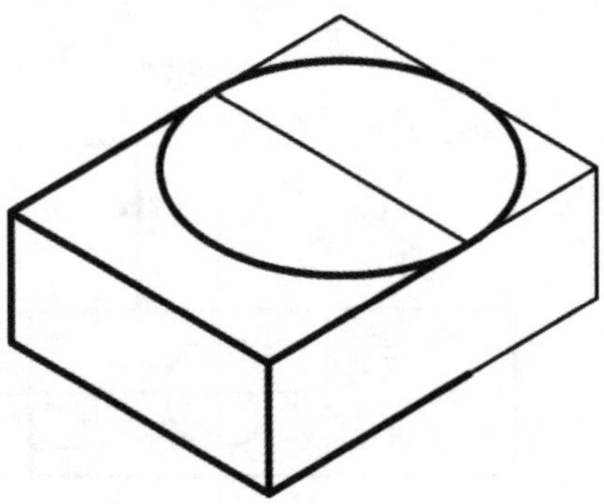

   a) <u>Command:</u> **ELlipse** or <u>*Draw* panel:</u>  (Axis, End)

   b) `Specify axis endpoint of ellipse or [Arc/Center/Isocircle]:` **i**

   c) `Specify center of isocircle:` **MIDpoint**
   `of` Select the midpoint of the construction line.

   d) `Specify radius of isocircle or [Diameter]:` **35**

5) **COpy** the isocircle as shown.

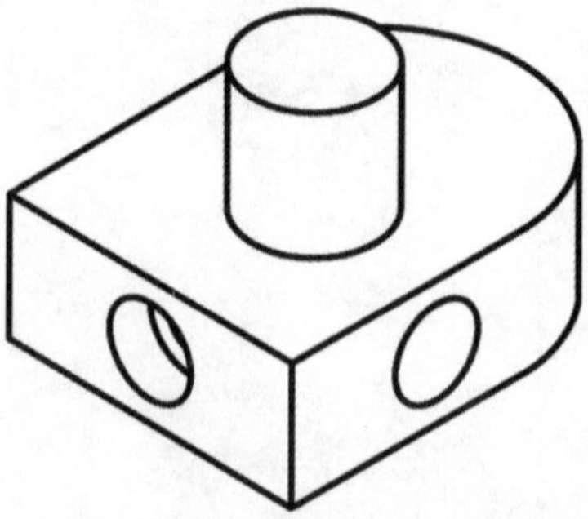

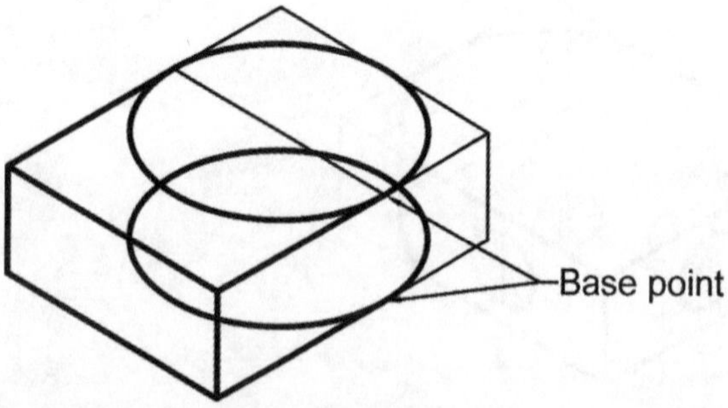

6) Draw a vertical **Line** from the **QUADrant**s of the isocircles and then **TRim** off any unwanted lines as shown in the figure on the left side.

7) With the help of a construction line, draw an **Isocircle** of radius **10** mm as shown in the figure on the right side. The isocircle center is at the midpoint of the construction line. Enter the appropriate isoplane.

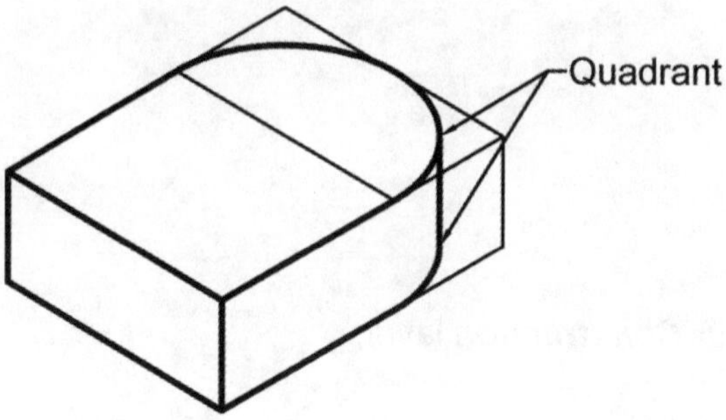

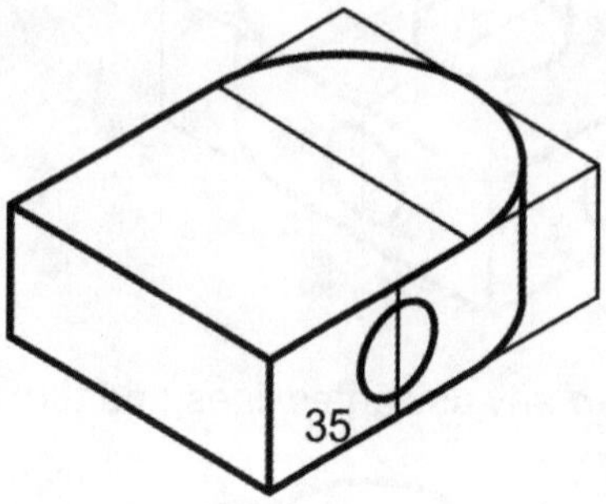

8) Add an **Isocircle** of radius **10** mm to represent the counterbored hole. (See left side figure.)

9) **COpy** the counterbore isocircle using a first base point of anywhere and a second base point of **@10<30**. (See right side figure.)

10) Use the **CENter** of the copied isocircle to create the **Isocircle** of the drill (radius = **5** mm). (See right side figure.)

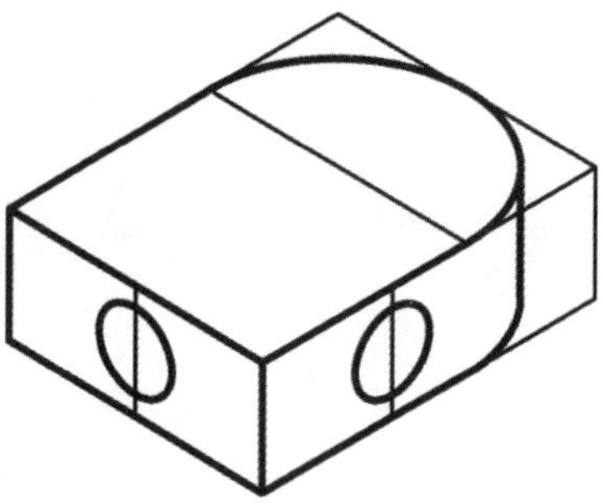

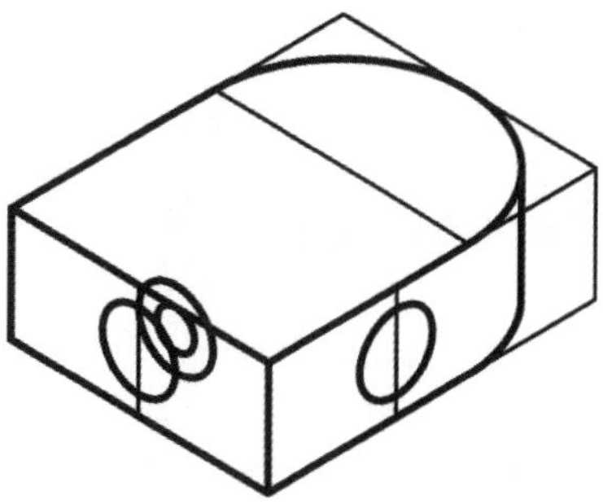

11) **TRim** off any unwanted lines.

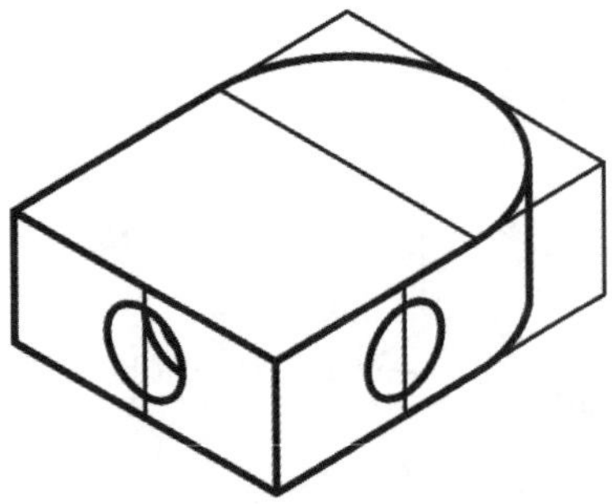

12) Draw an **Isocircle** that represents the base of the cylinder (radius = **15 mm**). **COpy** this isocircle using a second base point of **@30<90**. Draw vertical **Lines** between the **QUADrants** of the isocircles.

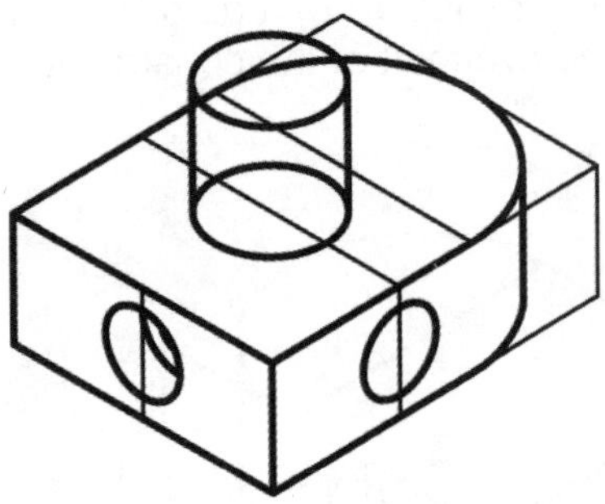

13) **TRim** any unwanted lines and turn off your ***Construction*** layer.

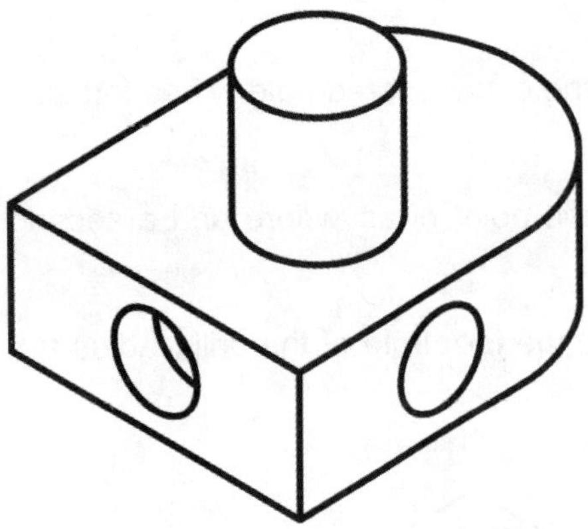

CREATING PICTORIALS IN AUTOCAD® QUESTIONS

Name: ________________________________ Date: ______________

Q8-1) A circular feature in an isometric pictorial is represented by an ...

a) circle.
b) ellipse.
c) cylinder.
d) radius.

Q8-2) What typed command and options are used to access the isometric snap? The answer is the (command) followed by the first (option) and then the second (option).

a) grid-style-isometric
b) snap-style-standard
c) isometric-isocircle-ellipse
d) snap-style-isometric

Q8-3) What typed command is used to change the polar tracking angle increment?

a) polarincrement
b) polartracking
c) polarang
d) angle

Q8-4) How do you toggle between isoplanes?

a) ctrl+E
b) ctrl+T
c) tab+E
d) shift+T

Q8-5) Within the ELLIPSE command, what option allows you to create a circular feature in an isometric pictorial?

a) axis-end
b) isocircle
c) isoplane
d) isometric

NOTES:

CREATING PICTORIALS IN AUTOCAD® PROBLEMS

P8-1) Draw an 80% scale isometric drawing of the following object. Dimensions are in inches.

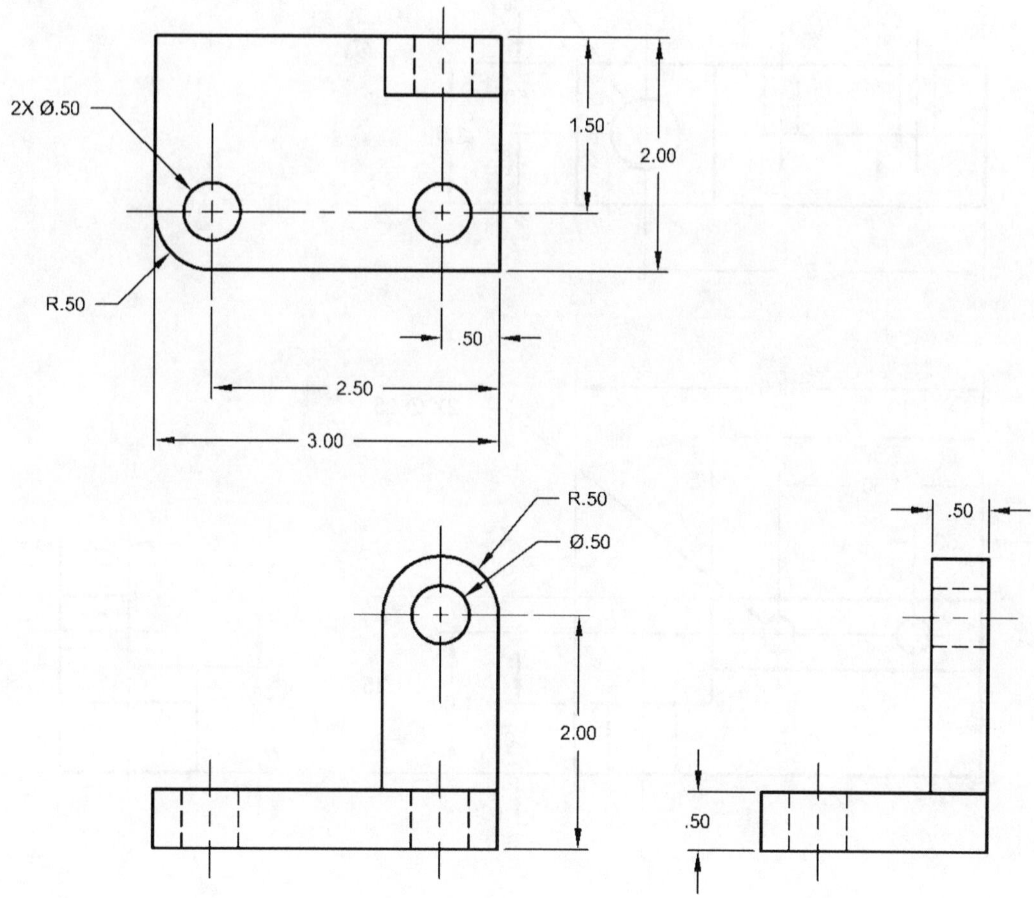

P8-2) Draw an 80% scale isometric drawing of the following object. Dimensions are in inches.

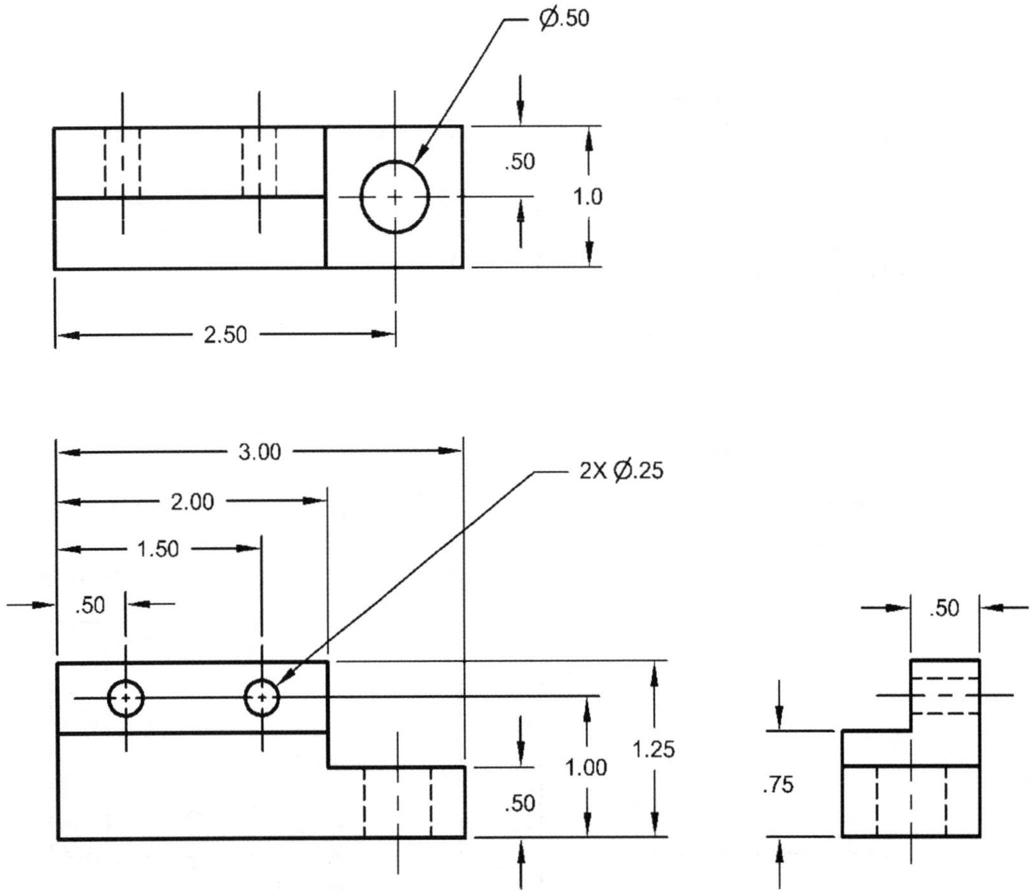

P8-3) Draw an 80% scale isometric drawing of the following object. Dimensions are in millimeters.

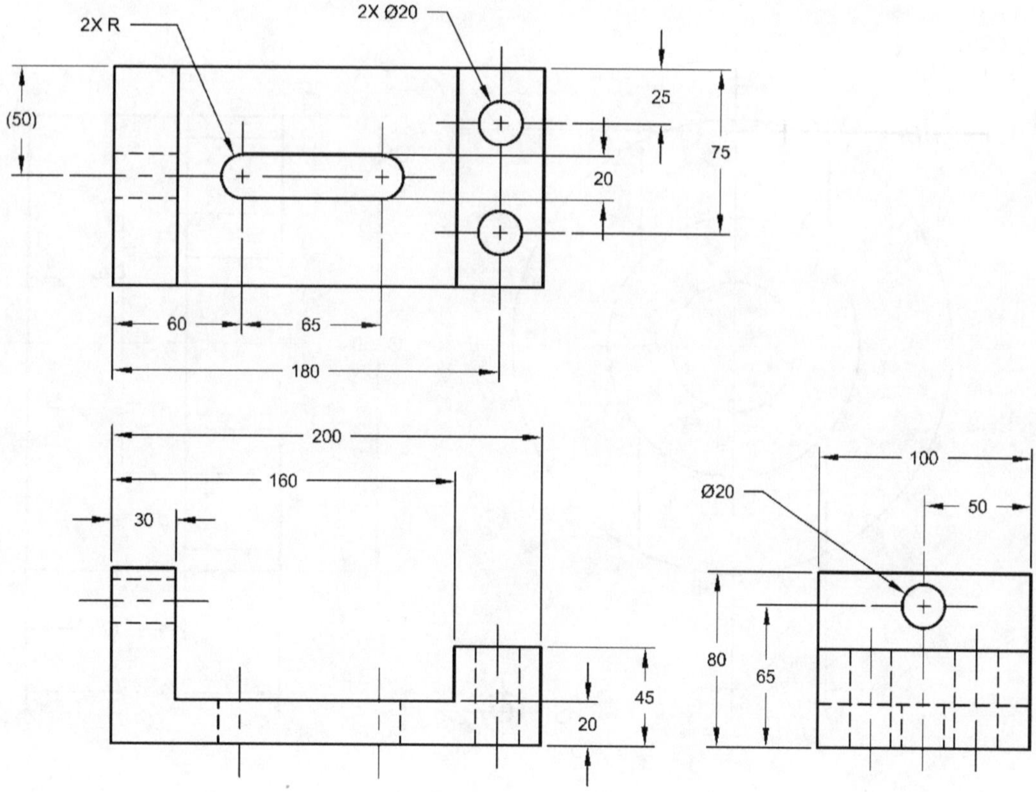

P8-4) Draw an 80% scale isometric drawing of the following object. Dimensions are in millimeters.

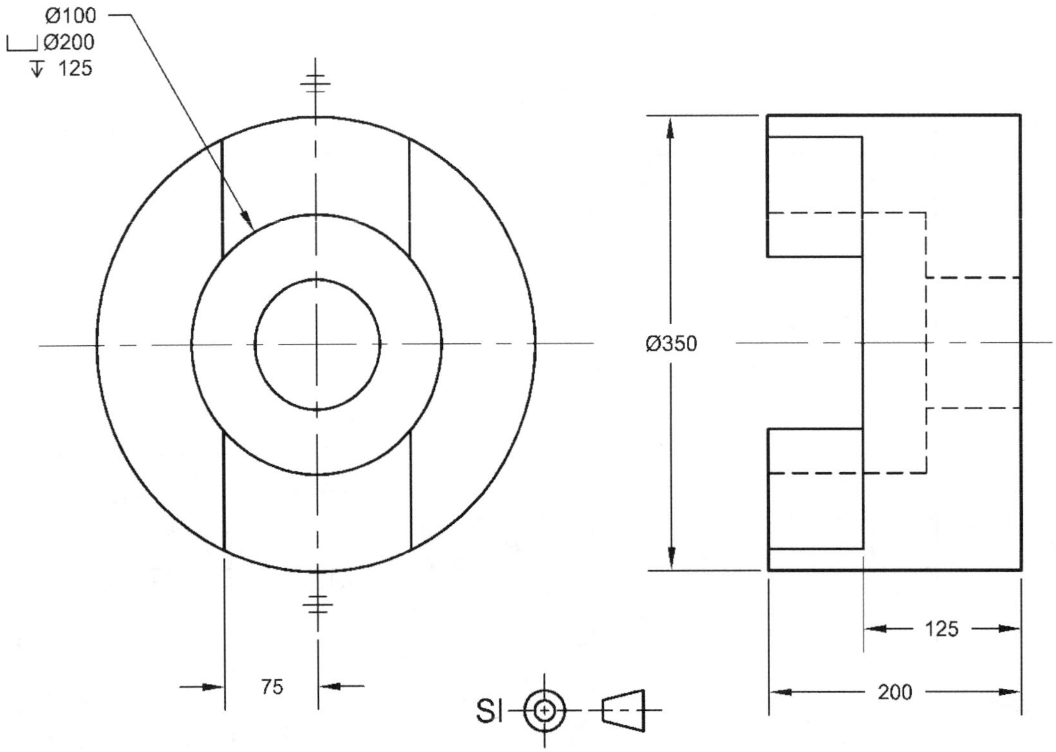

P8-5) Draw an 80% scale isometric drawing of the following object. Dimensions are in millimeters.

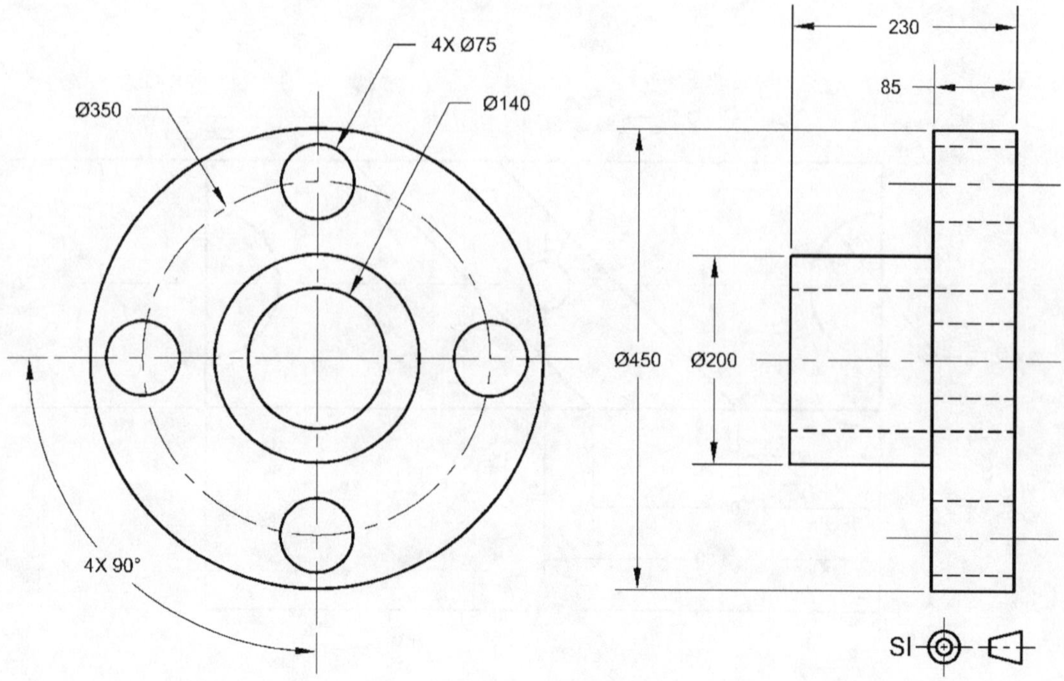

P8-6) Draw an 80% scale isometric drawing of the following object. Include all hidden lines. Dimensions are in inches.

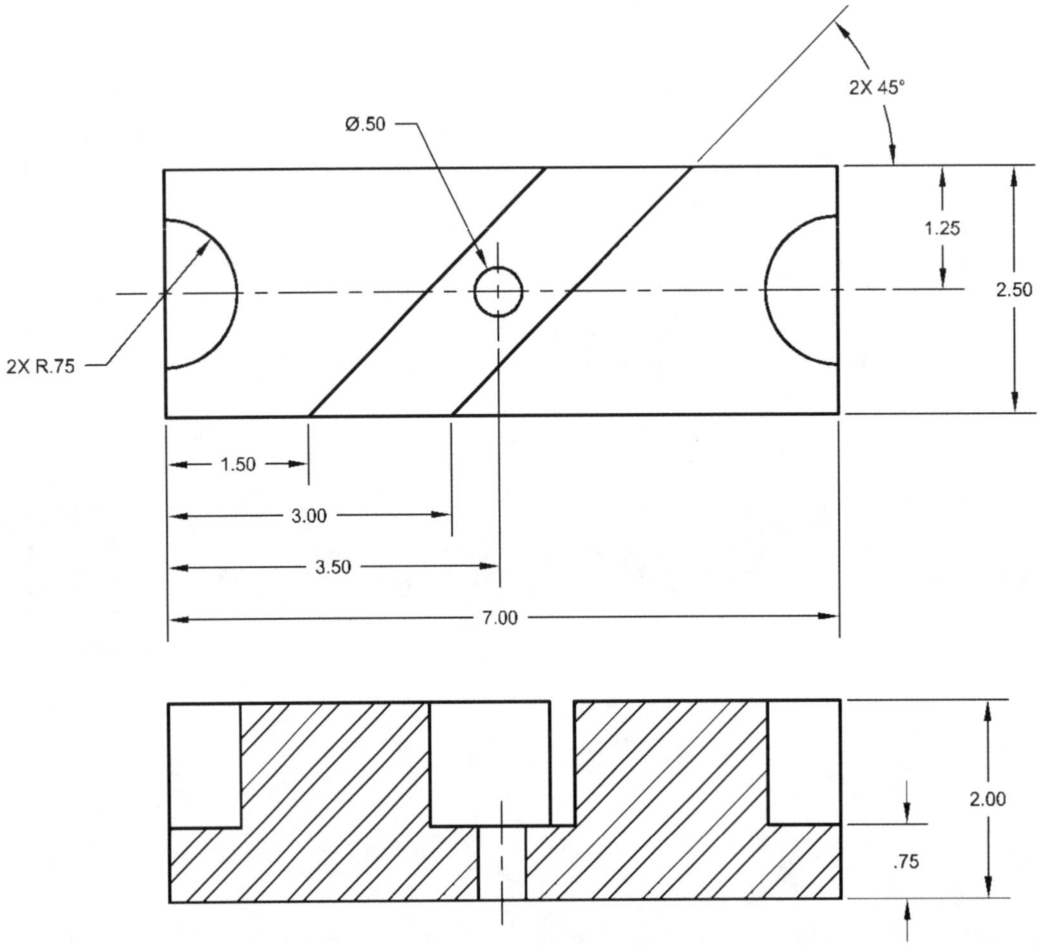

CHAPTER 9

READING DIMENSIONS

CHAPTER OUTLINE

CHAPTER SUMMARY

In this chapter you will learn how to read the dimensions on an orthographic projection. This may seem like a simple task; however, dimensions give more information than just the size of a feature. Dimensions affect how a part is manufactured. The type and placement of the dimensions and the dimension text is highly controlled by ASME standards (American Society of Mechanical Engineers). By the end of this chapter, you will be able to read standard dimensions and interpret their meaning.

9.1) DETAILED DRAWINGS

In addition to the shape description of an object given by an orthographic projection, engineering drawings must also give a complete size description using dimensions. This enables the object to be manufactured. **An orthographic projection, complete with all the dimensions and specifications needed to manufacture the object is called a *detailed drawing*.** Figure 9.1-1 shows a simple example of a detailed drawing.

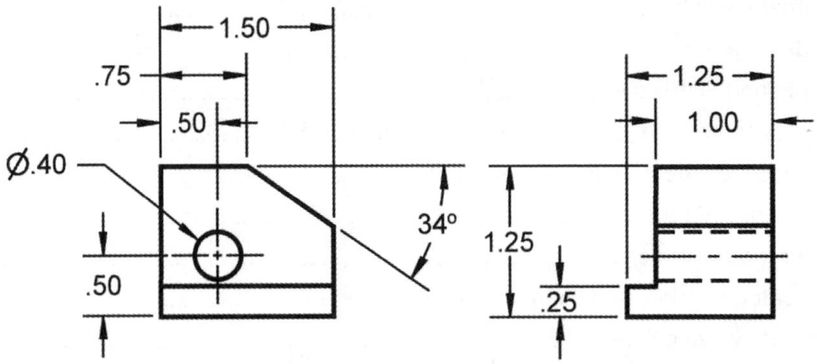

Figure 9.1-1: Detailed drawing

9.2) DIMENSIONING STANDARD

Dimensions are placed on an orthographic projection in accordance to a set of rules. Dimensions and notes give all the information needed to manufacture and inspect the part. The rules controlling how and where to place dimensions are given by the ASME Y14.5 standard. This standard was created to establish a uniform way of dimensioning an engineering drawing. Following the standard also minimizes errors that could occur while reading or interpreting an engineering drawing. When a drawing conforms to the standard, it is noted in the tolerance block as shown in Figure 9.2-1. Note that standards are updated periodically; therefore, it is necessary to place the date of the standard being used.

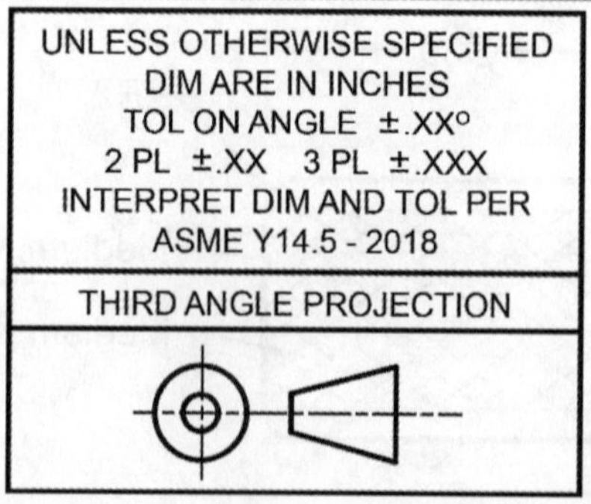

Figure 9.2-1: ASME Y14.5 designation

9.3) DIMENSION APPEARANCE

Dimensions require the use of *dimension*, *extension,* and *leader lines*. Figure 9.3-1 shows the use of dimension and extension lines. Figure 9.3-2 shows the use of leader lines.

- Dimension line: A dimension line is a thin solid line terminated by arrowheads, which indicates the direction and extent of a dimension. A number is placed near the midpoint to specify the feature's size.
- Extension line: An extension line is a thin solid line that extends from a point on the drawing to which the dimension refers.
- Leader line: A leader line is a straight inclined thin solid line that is usually terminated by an arrowhead. It is used to direct a dimension, note, symbol, item number, or part number to the intended feature on a drawing.

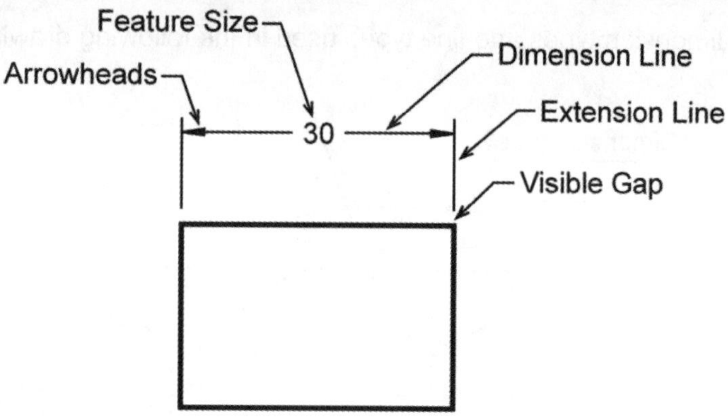

Figure 9.3-1: Features of a dimension

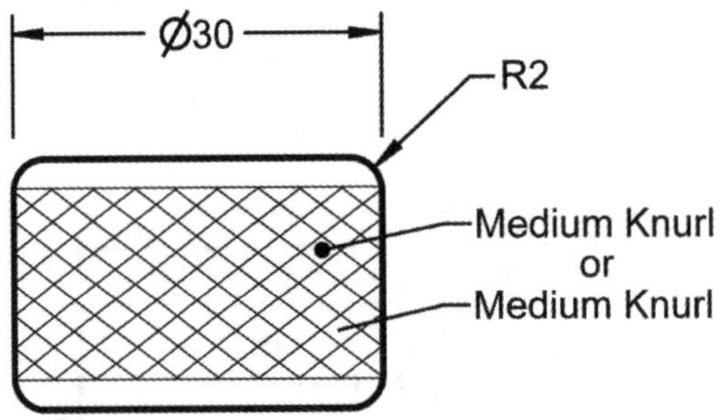

Figure 9.3-2: Leader line configurations

9.3.1) Types of Dimensions

Dimensions are given in the form of *linear distances*, *angles*, and *notes*.

- Linear distances: A linear dimension is used to give the distance between two points.
- Angles: An angular dimension is used to give the angle between two surfaces or features of a part.
- Notes: Notes are used to dimension diameters, radii, chamfers, threads, and other features that cannot be dimensioned by the other two methods. Notes can be local (i.e., applies to one feature), or general (i.e., applies to the whole drawing).

Try Exercise 9.3-1

Exercise 9.3-1: Dimension appearance

Identify the dimension types and line types used in the following drawing.

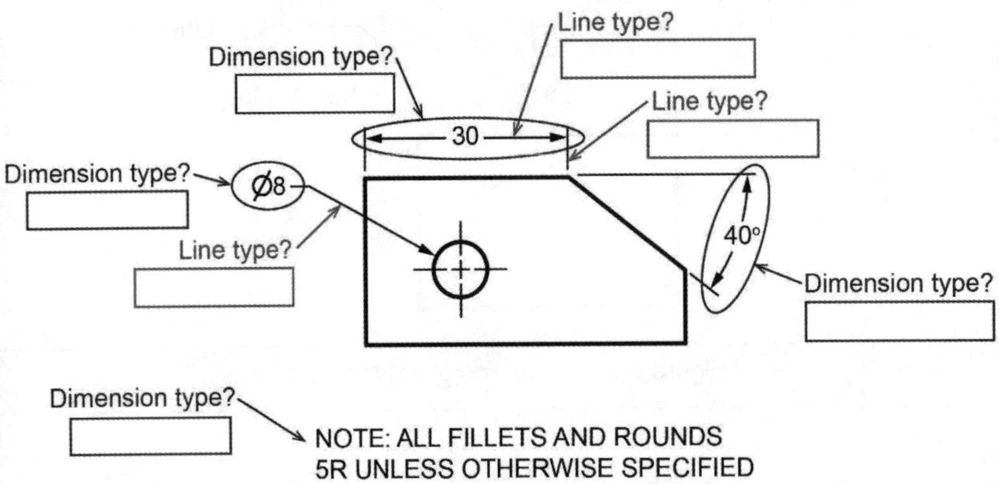

9.3.2) Units

The units of measure used on engineering drawings are either **inches** or **millimeters**. In general, **inch dimensions are given to two decimal places and millimeters are given to zero decimal places**. The decimal places mentioned are for noncritical dimension values. If the dimension values need to be more accurate, they will use more decimal places. In most cases you can determine if the drawing is using inches or millimeters by looking at the projection block. If there is an SI next to the projection symbol, the units are millimeters (see Figure 9.3-3). In some situations, the drafter will put a general note stating the units of the drawing. If none of these methods are present, look at the number of decimal places. If most of the dimension have two decimal places, then it is most likely in inches. If most of the dimensions have zero or one decimal place, then it is most likely in millimeters.

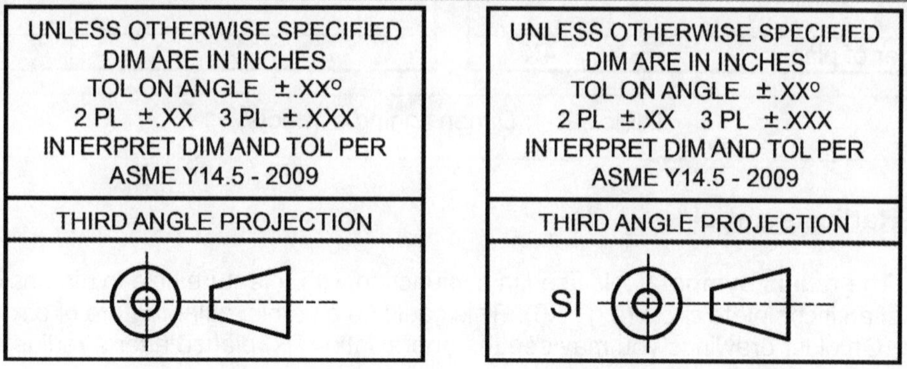

Inch drawing   Millimeter drawing

Figure 9.3-3: Unit designation in the projection block

9.4) DIMENSIONING SYMBOLS

Dimensioning symbols replace text and are used to minimize language barriers. Many companies produce parts all over the world. A print made in the U.S.A. may have to be read in several different countries. The goal of using dimensioning symbols is to eliminate the need for language translation. Table 9.4-1 shows some commonly used dimensioning symbols. The following sections illustrate the standard ways the dimensioning symbols are used and explain their meaning.

9.4.1) Diameter symbol

The **diameter symbol** (∅) is used in conjunction with a feature size (e.g., ∅4). This combination is used to dimension the diameter of a complete circle. This could be the diameter of a hole or cylinder. On older drawings you may see the abbreviation "DIA" placed after a diameter size.

Term	Symbol
Diameter	∅
Spherical diameter	S∅
Radius	R
Spherical radius	SR
Reference dimension	(8)
Counterbore / Spotface	⌴
Countersink	⌵
Number of places	4X

Term	Symbol
Depth / Deep	↧
Dimension not to scale	<u>10</u>
Square (Shape)	□
Arc length	$\frown{5}$
Conical Taper	⌲
Slope	⌳
Symmetry	⌯ or =

Table 9.4-1: Dimensioning symbols

9.4.2) Radius symbol

The **radius symbol** (R) is used in conjunction with a feature size to dimension the radius of an incomplete circle (e.g., R6). This could be a semicircular feature or a rounded corner. On older drawings you may see the abbreviation "R" placed after a radius size.

9.4.3) Depth and THRU symbols

The symbol **THRU** is most commonly used to indicate a hole that goes all the way through the part.

The **depth symbol** (↧) is commonly used to indicate the depth of a blind hole (i.e., a hole that doesn't go all the way through the part). Note that holes are usually made with a twist drill and therefore will have a point at the bottom of the hole. The depth symbol is used to indicate the depth of the full diameter not the total depth.

Try Exercise 9.4-1

Exercise 9.4-1: Diameter and Radius dimensions

Answer the following questions about the dimensions on the detailed drawing shown.

1. What units are being used?
2. How many linear dimensions?
3. How many leader line note dimensions?
4. How many diameter dimensions?
5. How many radius dimensions?
6. How many angular dimensions?
7. What is the depth of the ∅25 blind hole?
8. What is the diameter of the cylinder?
9. Does the ∅30 diameter hole go all the way through the part?

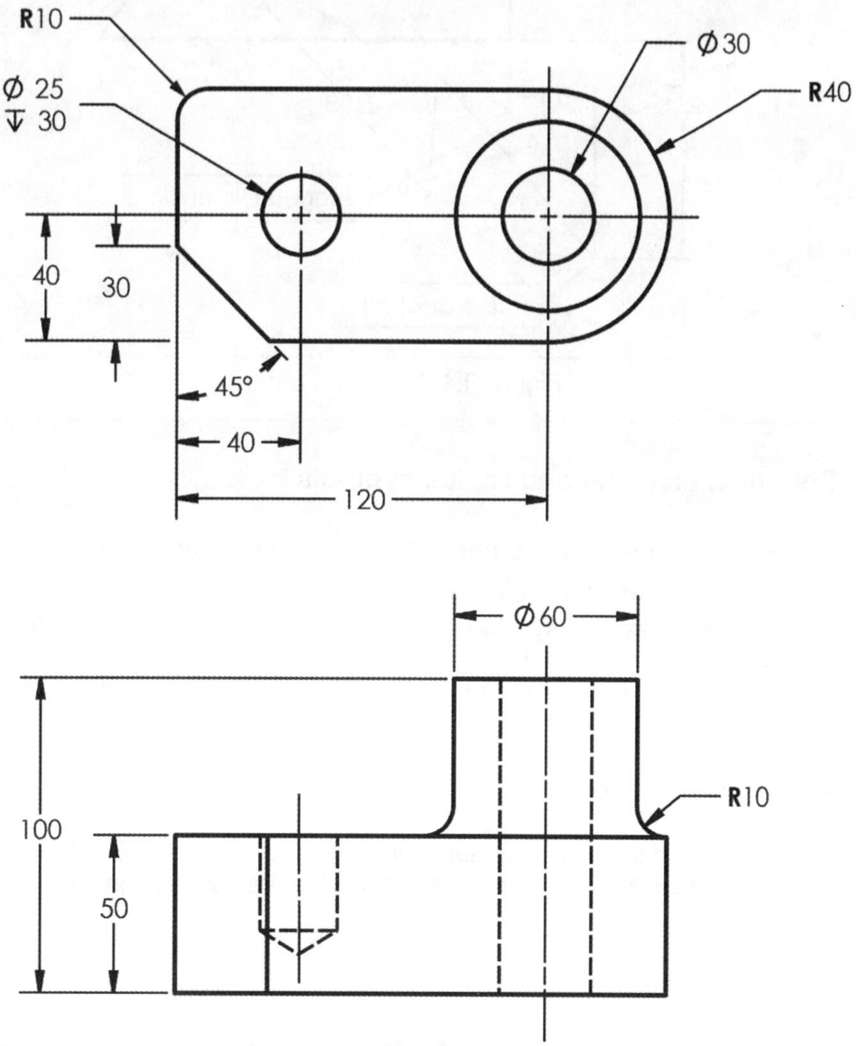

9.4.4) Radius center and jogged dimension symbols

The **center of a radius** is indicated by using a small cross (+). If the center of the radius is not apparent based on the drawing, the cross (+) is used and dimensioned. If the center of the radius is outside the drawing or interferes with another view, the dimension lines may be foreshortened. In this case, a false center and jogged dimensions are used to give the size and location from the false center as shown in Figure 9.4-2.

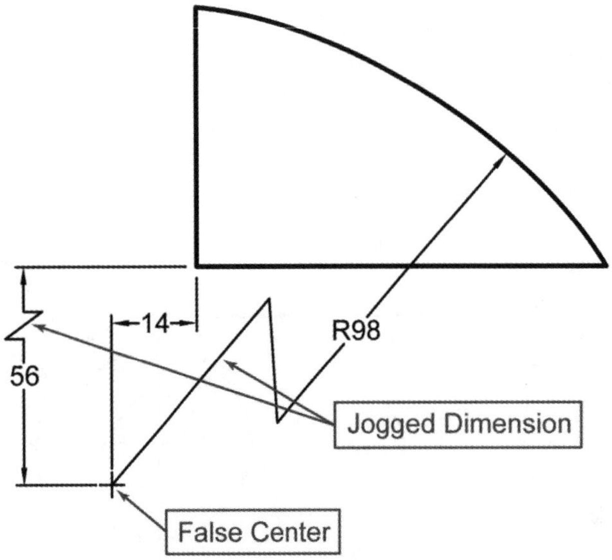

Figure 9.4-2: Jogged radius

9.4.5) Spherical diameter and radius symbols

The **spherical diameter symbol** (S∅) is used in conjunction with a feature size to dimension the diameter of a complete sphere (e.g., S∅10).

The **spherical radius symbol** (R) is used in conjunction with a feature size to dimension the radius of an incomplete sphere (e.g., SR8). This could be a spherical end on a solid part that is a hemisphere, but could be smaller or bigger than a perfect hemisphere.

9.4.6) Arc length symbol

The **arc length symbol** in conjunction with a feature size is used to dimension the length of an arc. The symbol is placed above the feature size as shown in Figure 9.4-3.

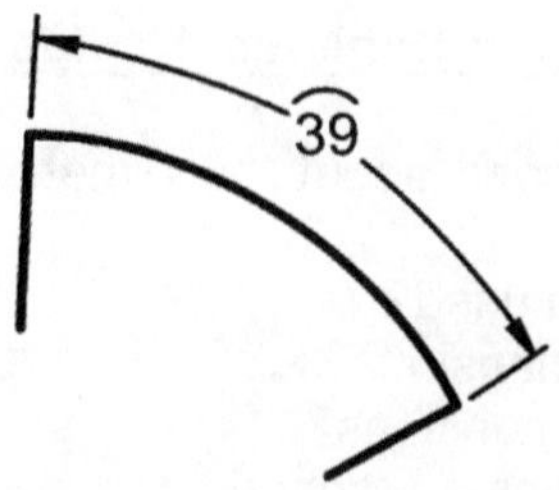

Figure 9.4-3: Arc length

9.4.7) Reference Dimension

A reference dimension gives a feature size that is already specified on the drawing in another way. If a reference dimension is used, the size value is placed within parentheses, e.g., (10). This is done because duplicate dimensions may cause confusion. If a change is made to one dimension, the reference dimension may be overlooked causing informational conflict. If the reference dimension and the dimension it references do not match, the reference dimension should be ignored.

Try Exercise 9.4-2

9.4.8) Repeated features and chamfer symbol

The **repeated feature symbol** (X) and **chamfer symbol** (X) use the same symbol but these two things are very different. A **repeated feature** is a feature that occurs 2 or more times on a part. A repeated feature is specified by using the symbol "X" along with the number of times the feature is repeated. There is no space between the number of times the feature is repeated and the "X" symbol; however, there is a space between the symbol "X" and the dimension of the feature (e.g., 8X ∅10).

A **chamfer** is a beveled or angled edge. Chamfers are dimensioned by a linear dimension and an angle, or by two linear dimensions. The symbol "X" is placed between the two dimensions (e.g., 2 X 45°). Notice that there is a space between the "X" symbol and the linear dimension. The space is inserted so that it is not confused with a repeated feature.

Try Exercise 9.4-3 and 9.4-4

Exercise 9.4-2: Spherical Radius dimensions

Answer the following questions about the dimensions on the detailed drawing shown.

1. What units are being used?
2. How many linear dimensions?
3. How many radius dimensions?
4. Which radii dimensions are spherical radii?
5. What is the diameter of the cylinder?
6. Which radii need to have a dimensioned radius center?
7. Why is the ∅90 diameter in parentheses?

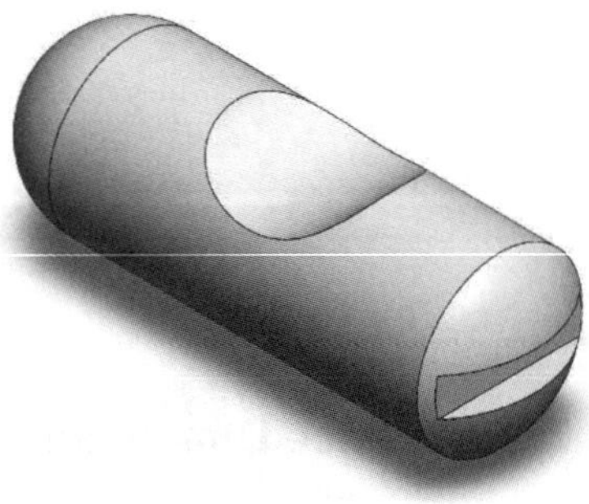

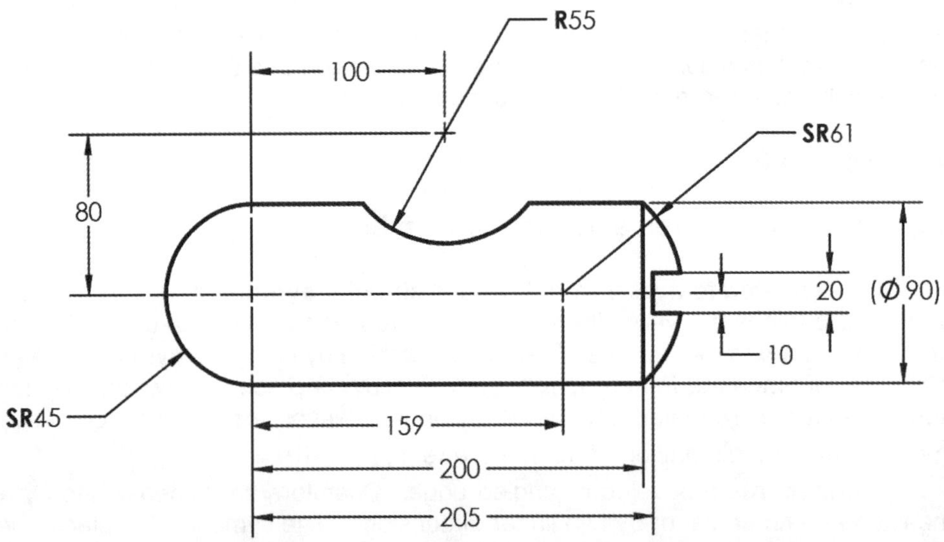

Exercise 9.4-3: Repeated feature and chamfer dimensions 1

Identify which of the dimensions is a repeated feature dimension and which is a chamfer dimension.

4 X 4 = ______________________

4X 4 = ______________________

Exercise 9.4-4: Repeated features and chamfer dimensions 2

Answer the following questions about the dimensions on the detailed drawing shown.

1. How many diameter dimensions?
2. How many times is the radius dimension repeated?
3. How many times is the ∅15 hole repeated?
4. What is the angle between the ∅15 holes? Is it the same between all the ∅15 holes?
5. What is the diameter of the circle of centers for the ∅15 holes?
6. How many times is the ∅10 hole repeated?
7. What is the angle between the ∅10 holes? Is it the same between all the ∅10 holes?
8. For the dimension 3X 20° (=60°) dimension, what do you think the (=60°) means?
9. What is the diameter of the circle of centers for the ∅10 holes?
10. Is the chamfer dimension 4 by 2, or 2 by 2?
11. How many chamfers are on the part?

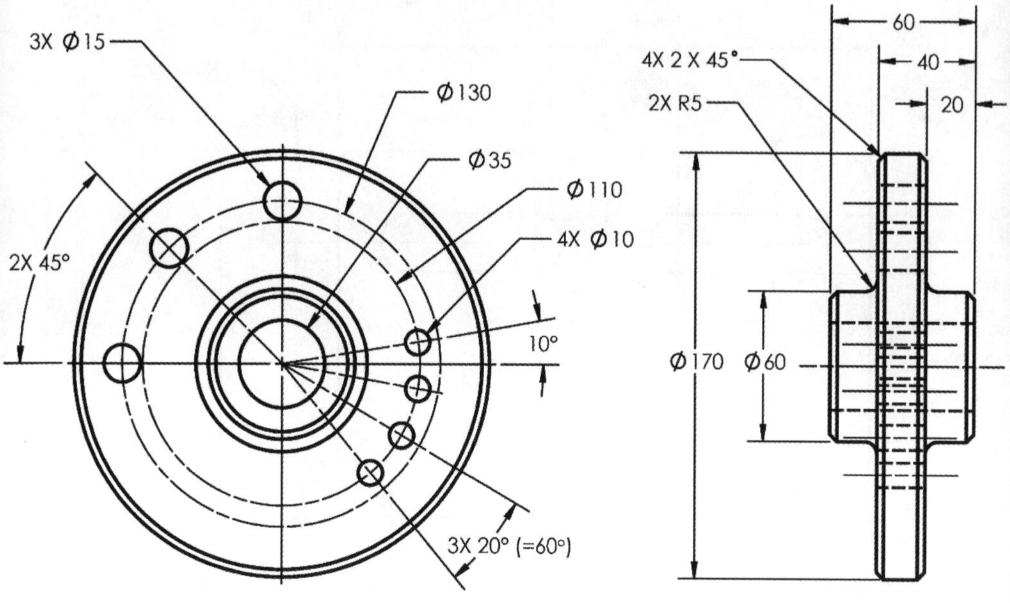

9.4.9) Symmetry symbol

The **symmetry symbol** (⌯ or =) is used to indicate that a part is symmetric about an axis. The center line of symmetry is indicated by using a center line with the symmetry symbol "⌯" or "=" placed at both ends of the center line. On older drawings you might see the symbol "℄" used instead. If a part is symmetric, dimensions only need to be given on one side of the center line of symmetry.

Try Exercise 9.4-5

Exercise 9.4-5: Symmetry

Answer the following questions about the dimensions on the detailed drawing shown.

1. Circle the symmetry symbols.
2. What is the distance from the center line of symmetry and the left edge of the part?
3. What is the size of the bottom right radius?
4. What do you think the dimension 2X R means? Why is there no radius size given?

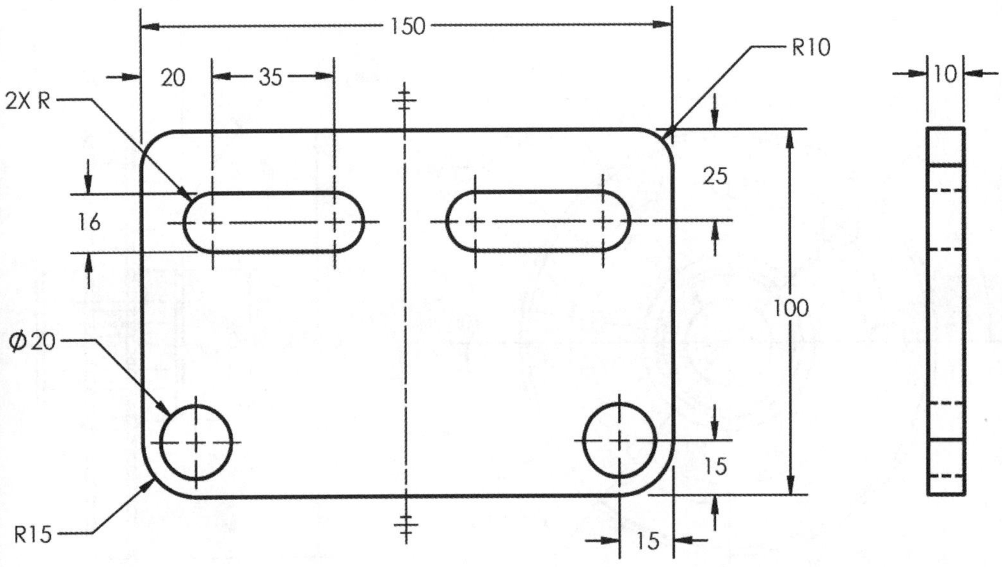

9.4.10) Counterbores and countersinks symbols

A counterbore is created by drilling a hole and then drilling a bigger flat bottom hole in the same place whose depth is less than the original drilled hole as shown in Figure 9.4-4. Counterbored holes are often used to recess the heads of a screw or bolt as shown in Figure 9.4-5. Counterbored holes are specified by giving the diameter (∅) of the drill, the diameter (∅) of the counterbore which is preceded by the **counterbore symbol** (⌴), and the depth (↧) of the counterbore in a note as shown in Figure 9.4-4.

Spot faced holes are similar to counterbored holes. The only difference is that the machining operation occurs on a curved surface. Therefore, the depth of the counterbore drill is not given in the note. It must be specified in the rectangular view as shown in Figure 9.4-6.

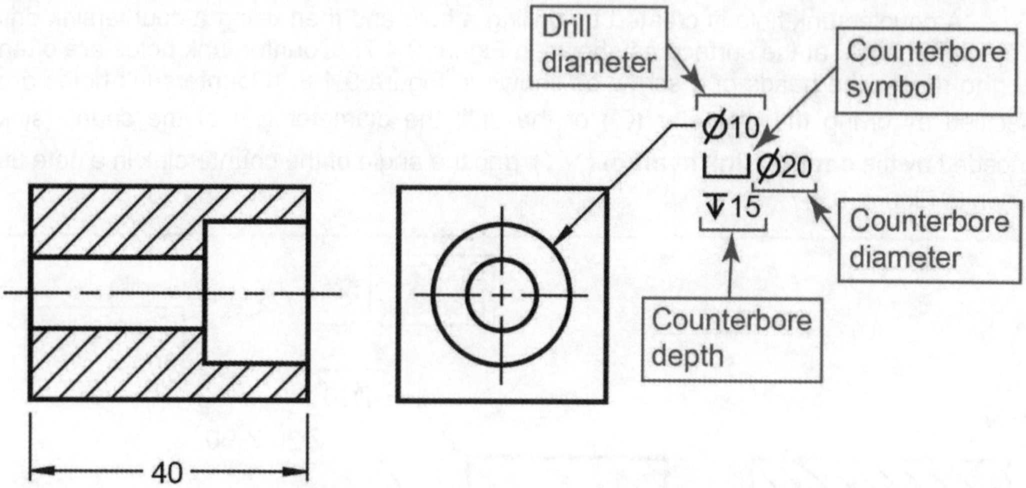

Figure 9.4-4: Counterbored holes.

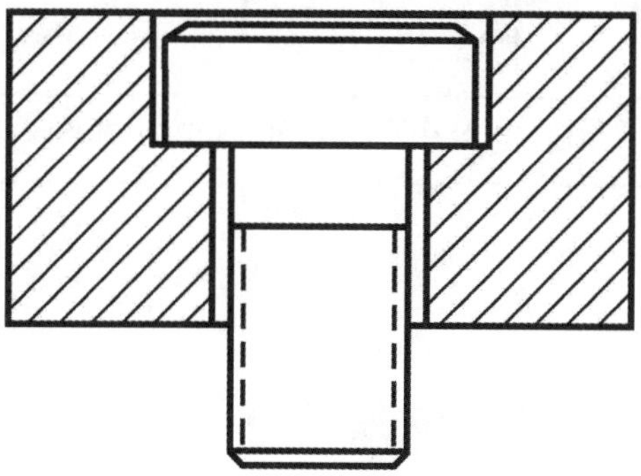

Figure 9.4-5: Counterbore used to recess head of screw

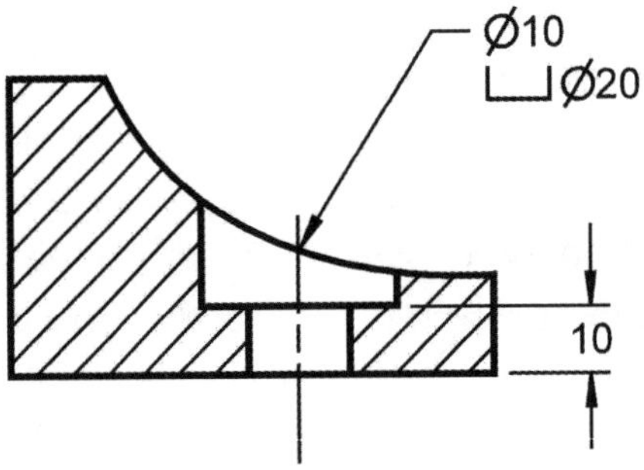

Figure 9.4-6: Spot faced holes.

A countersunk hole is created by drilling a hole and then using a countersink drill to create an angle at the surface as shown in Figure 9.4-7. Countersunk holes are often used to recess the heads of a screw as shown in Figure 9.4-8. Countersunk holes are specified by giving the diameter (⌀) of the drill, the diameter (⌀) of the countersink preceded by the **countersink symbol** (⌵), and the angle of the countersink in a note as shown in Figure 9.4-7.

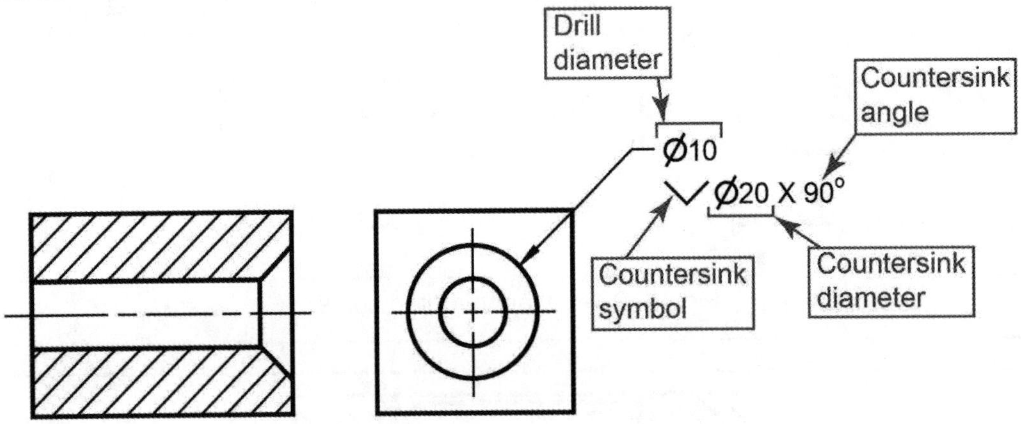

Figure 9.4-7: Countersunk holes.

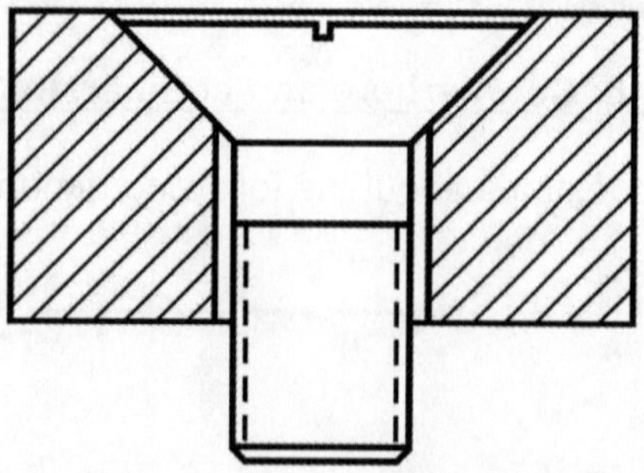

Figure 9.4-8: Countersink used to recess head of screw

Try Exercise 9.4-6

9.4.11) General drawing notes

General drawing notes give additional information that is used to complement conventional dimensions. **General notes apply to the entire drawing.** Unlike a general note, a local note is positioned near and points to the specified area to which it applies such as a leader line and dimension. Listed below are a few examples of general drawing notes. General notes are usually placed in the bottom left corner of the drawing area.

NOTE: ALL FILLETS AND ROUNDS R3 MM UNLESS OTHERWISE SPECIFIED.

NOTE: REMOVE BURRS AND BREAK SHARP EDGES.

NOTE: APPLICABLE STANDARDS: ASME Y14.5-2009, ASME Y14.41-2003

Exercise 9.4-6: Counterbore and countersink dimensions

Answer the following questions about the following dimensions.

⌀10
⌴⌀15
↧8

Drill diameter = ____________________

Counterbore diameter = ____________________

Counterbore depth = ____________________

⌀15
⌵⌀25 X 88°

Drill diameter = ____________________

Maximum Countersink diameter = ____________________

Countersink angle = ____________________

9.5) DATUM DIMENSIONING

When reading a print, the dimensions give you clues to the part's function and mating relationships. Figure 9.5-1 shows examples of this. Most of the time, features on a part are located with respect to functionally important features or surfaces which are called datum features. **A datum feature is a functionally important feature or surface.** Datum features on a drawing are identified by a datum feature symbol as shown in Figure 9.5-2. A letter is used to identify and differentiate between the datum features. If no datum feature symbols are given, datums may be identified by the use of dimensions. Usually, datum features are the origin of all the dimensions.

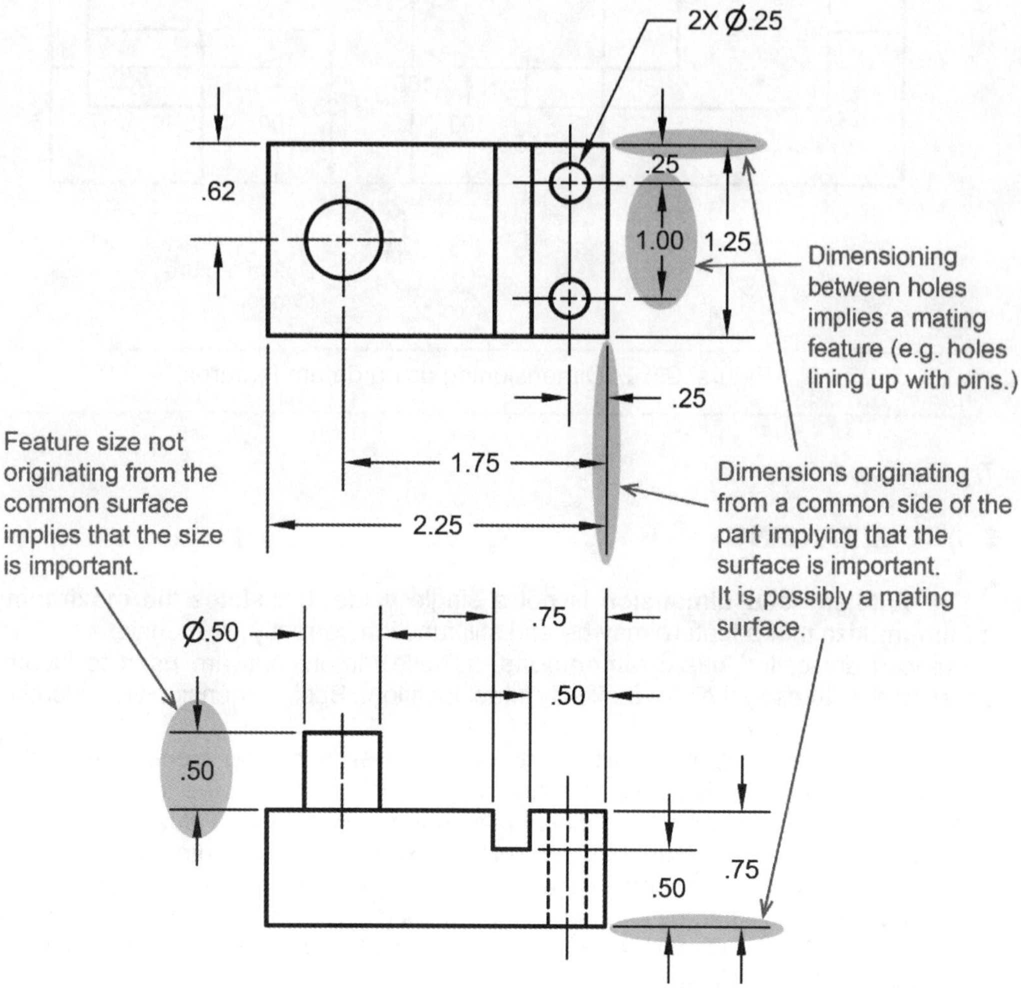

Figure 9.5-1: Dimensions imply function

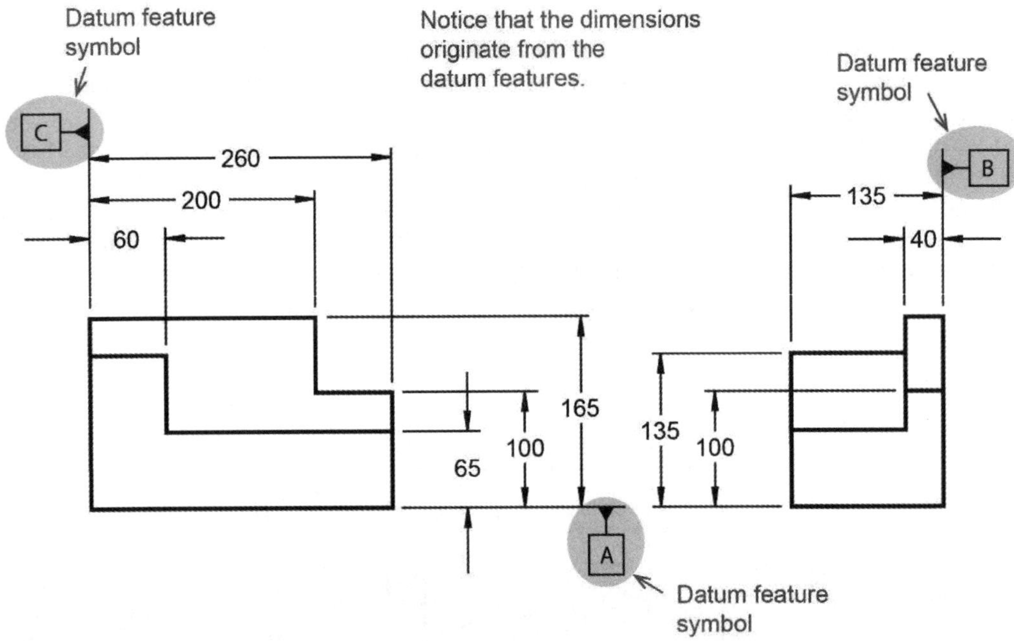

Figure 9.5-2: Dimensioning using datum features.

Try Exercise 9.5-1

9.6) TOLERANCING

A **toleranced dimension** is not a single value, but states the **maximum and minimum size** that a feature may be and still function correctly. Dimensions that are not toleranced are called **basic dimensions**. These dimensions are used to locate and dimension features to their theoretically exact location. Basic dimensions are identified by placing them in a box.

Tolerances may be explicitly stated or covered by the block tolerance. If a dimension is not explicitly stated and there is no block tolerance, the tolerance is implied and depends on the number of decimal places in the dimension value. The exceptions are basic dimensions, reference dimensions, maximum/minimum dimensions, and stock sizes. A basic dimension provides a nominal location or size from which permissible variations are established by geometric tolerances (GD&T). GD&T will not be covered in this chapter. Figure 9.6-1 illustrates a few different examples of explicit and implied tolerances, and basic dimensions.

Try Exercise 9.6-1 and 9.6-2

Exercise 9.5-1: Datum Features

This part has three datum features.

1. Based on the dimensions, identify the datum features.
2. Identify the corresponding datum feature in the adjacent and related views.

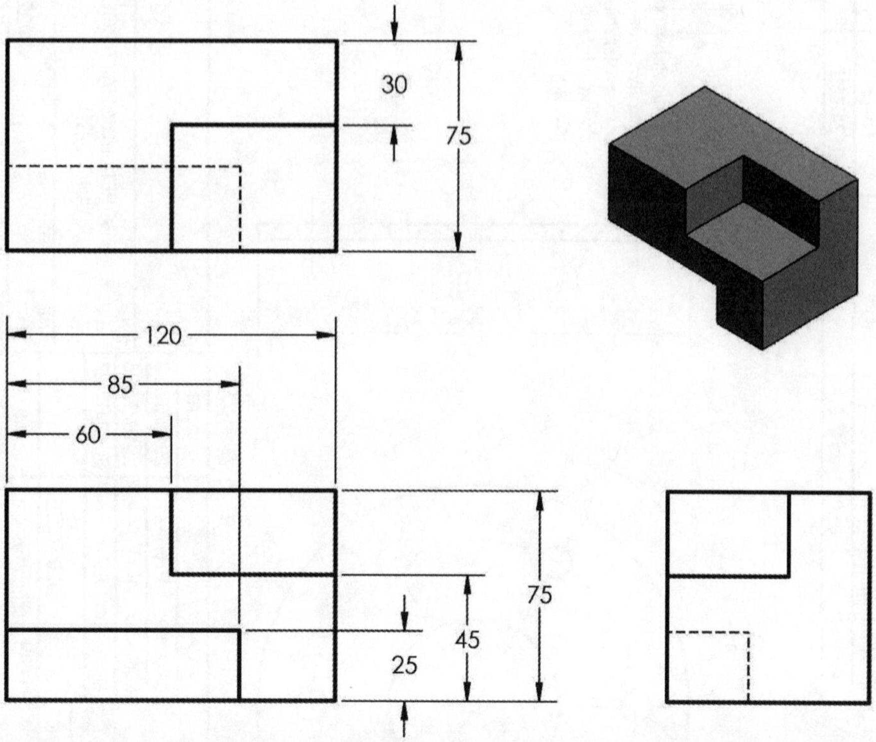

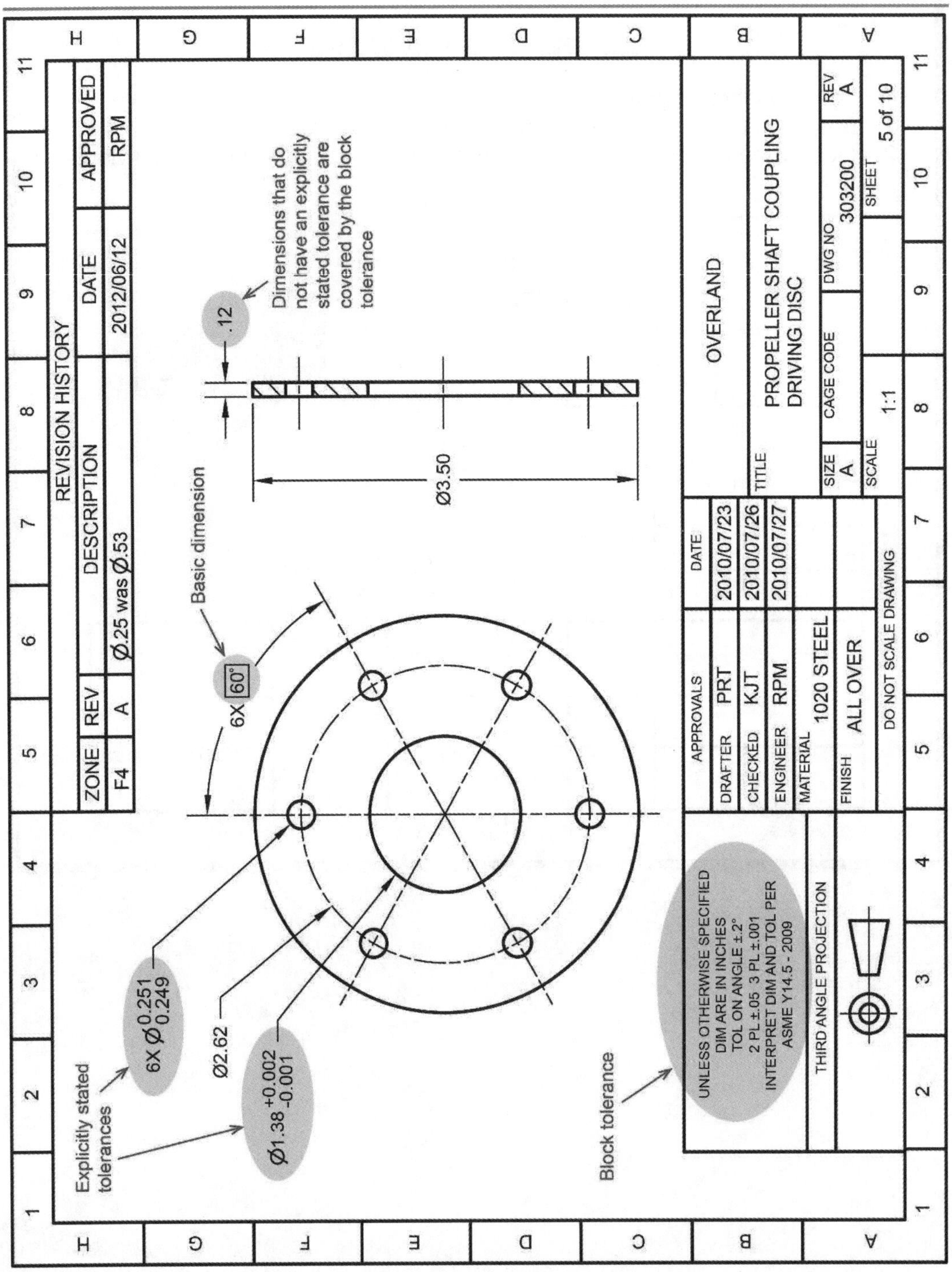

Figure 9.5-3: Tolerances

Exercise 9.6-1: Tolerances

Identify which dimensions have explicitly stated tolerances, which are covered by the block tolerance, which dimensions are implied, and which are basic dimensions.

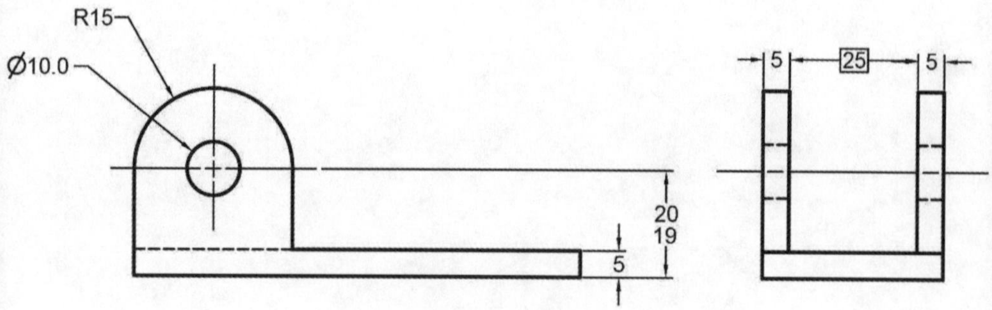

UNLESS OTHERWISE SPECIFIED
DIM ARE IN MM
TOL ON ANGLE ±.2°
1 PL ± 0.1
INTERPRET DIM AND TOL PER
ASME Y14.5 - 2009

Exercise 9.6-2: Dimension accuracy

Consider the figure shown below.

- Does the arrow indicate an increasing or decreasing accuracy?
- Write down the range in which the dimension values are allowed to vary.

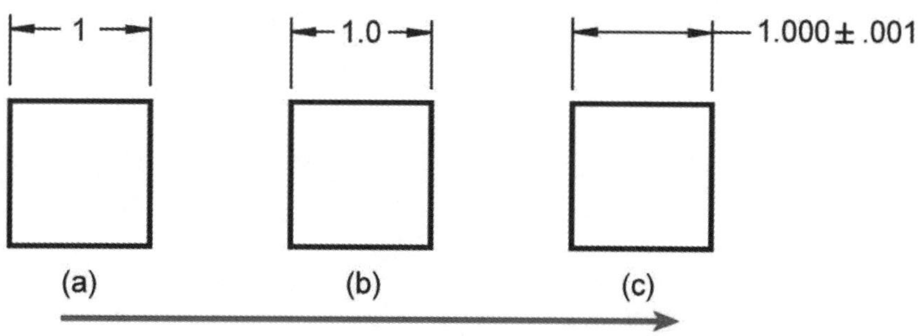

NOTES:

READING DIMENSIONS QUESTIONS – SET1

Name: ________________________________ Date: ______________

Dimension appearance

Q9-1) Dimensions generally take the form of ... (Circle all that apply.)

a) linear dimensions
b) extension lines
c) angular dimensions
d) notes

Q9-2) Which line type does not ever have arrowheads? (dimension, extension, leader)

Units

Q9-3) What unit of measure is most commonly used on English drawing?

Q9-4) What unit of measure is most commonly used on metric drawing?

Dimensioning symbols

Q9-5) What is this symbol? ∅

a) radius
b) depth
c) counterbore
d) diameter
e) symmetry

Q9-6) What is this symbol? R

a) radius
b) depth
c) counterbore
d) diameter
e) symmetry

Q9-7) Is the following dimension a repeated feature dimension or a chamfer dimension?

2X 45°

NOTES:

READING DIMENSIONS QUESTIONS – SET2

Name: ______________________________ Date: _____________

Q9-8) A detailed drawing is an orthographic projection with .... (Circle all that apply.)

a) dimensions.
b) notes.
c) manufacturing specifications.
d) everything necessary to manufacture and inspect the part as intended by the designer.

Q9-9) What is this symbol? ↧

a) repeated feature
b) depth
c) counterbore
d) countersink
e) symmetry

Q9-10) What is this symbol? ⌵

a) repeated feature
b) depth
c) counterbore
d) countersink
e) symmetry

Q9-11) What is this symbol? ⌯ or =

a) repeated feature
b) depth
c) counterbore
d) countersink
e) symmetry

Q9-12) X is the symbol used for repeated features. What else is this symbol used for?

a) chamfer
b) concentricity
c) counterbore
d) symmetry

Q9-13) A reference dimension is given within ....

a) brackets.
b) double quotes.
c) parentheses.
d) single quotes.

NOTES:

READING DIMENSIONS PROBLEMS

Name: ______________________________ Date: ______________

P9-1) Answer questions about the following drawing.

a) How many linear dimensions?

b) How many diameter dimensions? This is not the same thing as the number of features.

c) How many notes-leader line dimensions?

d) Based on the dimensions, identify the three datums on the drawing.

e) If you were inspecting the thickness of this part and find that it measures 0.124 in, would it pass inspection?

f) If you were inspecting the height of this part and find that it measures 2.009 in, would it pass inspection?

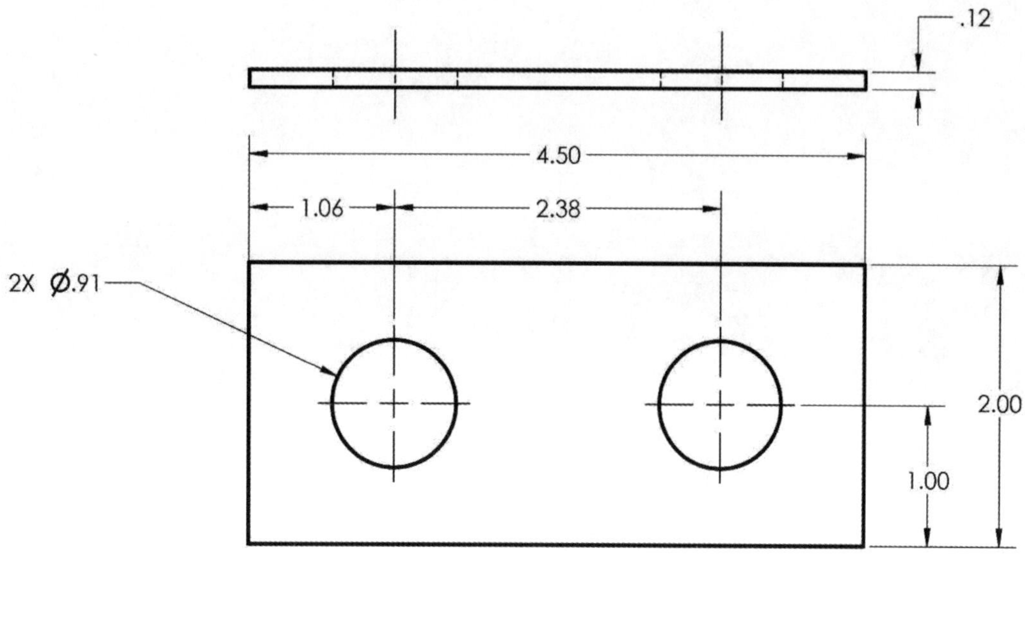

NOTES:

Name: ______________________________ Date: ______________

P9-2) Answer questions about the following drawing.

a) How many linear dimensions?

b) How many diameter dimensions? Do not count the thread dimension.

c) How many notes-leader line dimensions?

d) How many explicitly stated toleranced dimensions are there?

e) Based on the dimensions, identify the three datums on the drawing.

f) If you were inspecting the overall thickness of this part and find that it measures 1.002 in, would it pass inspection?

g) If you were inspecting the diameter of the two big holes and find that the right hole measures 0.6255 in, would it pass inspection?

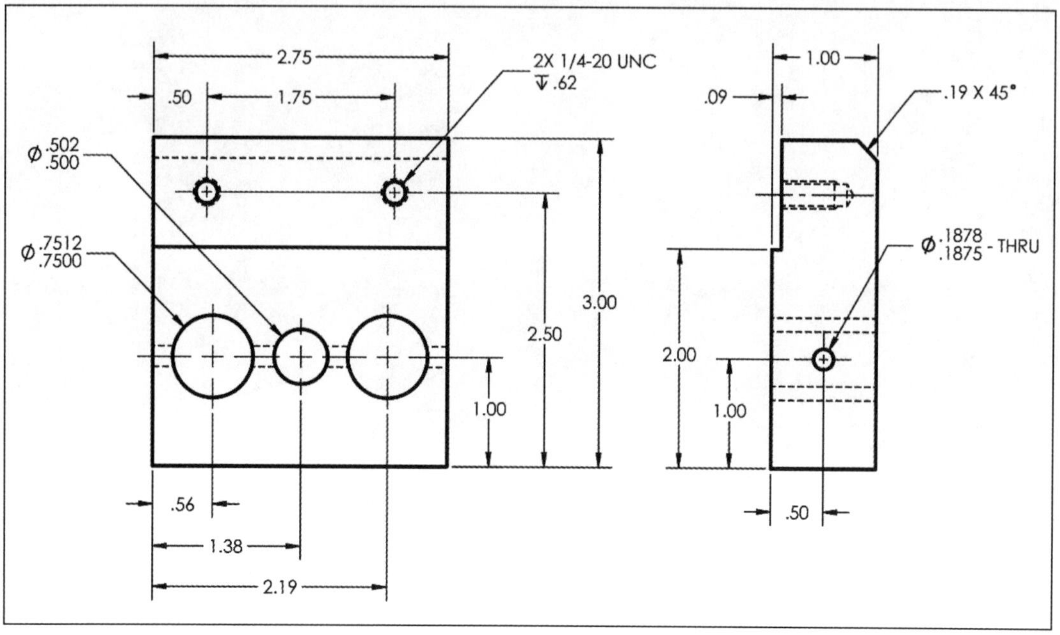

NOTES:

Name: ______________________________ Date: ______________

P9-3)

Answer the following questions related to the counterbore figure.

a) Drill diameter = ________________

b) Counterbore diameter = ________________

c) Counterbore depth = ________________

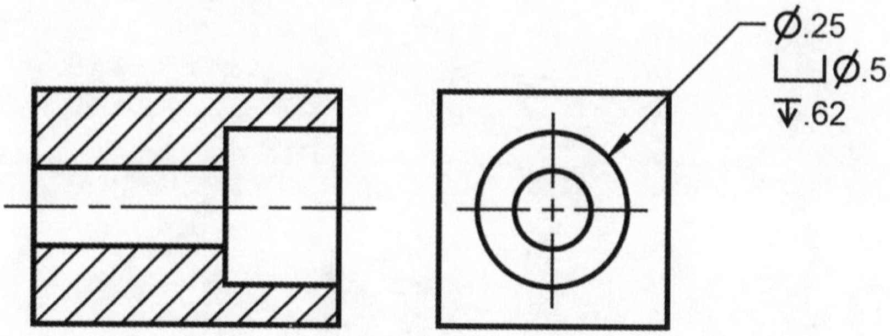

Answer the following questions related to the countersink figure.

d) Drill diameter = ________________

e) Drill depth = ________________

f) Countersink maximum diameter = ________________

g) Countersink angle = ________________

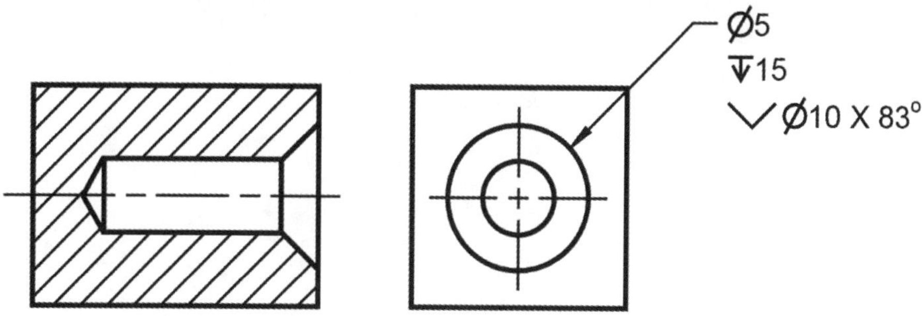

NOTES:

CHAPTER 10

CREATING DIMENSIONS

CHAPTER OUTLINE

CHAPTER SUMMARY

In this chapter you will learn how to dimension an orthographic projection using proper dimensioning techniques. This may seem like a simple task; however, dimensioning a part is not as easy as inserting the sizes used to draw the part. Dimensions affect how a part is manufactured. A small change in how an object is dimensioned may produce a part that will not pass inspection. The type and placement of the dimensions and the dimension text is highly controlled by ASME standards (American Society of Mechanical Engineers). By the end of this chapter, you will be able to dimension a moderately complex part using proper dimensioning techniques. Dimensioning complex/production parts requires the knowledge of x-y coordinate tolerancing and GD&T (Geometric Dimensioning & Tolerancing). Tolerancing is covered in another chapter.

10.1) LEARNING TO DIMENSION

Dimensioning a part correctly requires conformance to many rules. It is very tempting to dimension an object using the measurements needed to draw or model the part. But, these are not necessarily the dimensions required to manufacture it. Generally accepted dimensioning standards should be used when dimensioning any object. In basic terms, dimensions should be given in a clear and concise manner and should include all the information needed to produce and inspect the part exactly as intended by the designer. There should be no need to measure the size of a feature directly from the drawing.

The dimensioning standards presented in this chapter are in accordance with the **ASME Y14.5** standard. When a drawing conforms to the standard, it should be noted in the tolerance block. Other common sense practices will also be presented.

10.2) DIMENSION APPEARANCE

10.2.1) Lines Used in Dimensioning

Dimensions require the use of *dimension*, *extension* and *leader lines* as described in the previous chapter. In this section we will focus on rules and practices that help in placing dimensions that are readable and conform to the standard. **All lines used in dimensioning are drawn thin so that the print reader does not confuse them with visible lines.** Thin lines should be drawn at approximately **0.016 inch (0.3 mm)**.

Extension lines indicate from which points you are measuring and are used to indicate the extent of the dimension line. To make sure these lines don't get confused for a feature on the part, **a small gap between the extension line and part is used**. This means that the extension line does not touch the part at the point of measurement. They may cross the part if the feature being measured is inside the part. However, **long extension lines should be avoided.**

A leader line is used to direct a dimension, note, symbol, item number, or part number to the intended feature on a drawing. Leader lines should not be drawn vertical or horizontal, except for a short horizontal portion extending to the first or last letter of the note. The horizontal part should not underline the note and may be omitted entirely. Leader lines may be terminated by an arrow if it ends on the outline of an object or without an arrowhead or with a dot (∅1.5 mm, minimum) if it ends within the outline of an object. You should avoid creating long leaders, crossing leaders, or leaders that are parallel to features on the drawing.

Try Exercise 10.2-1

Exercise 10.2-1: Line use in dimensioning

Shown is a dimensioned view/part. Answer the questions posed.

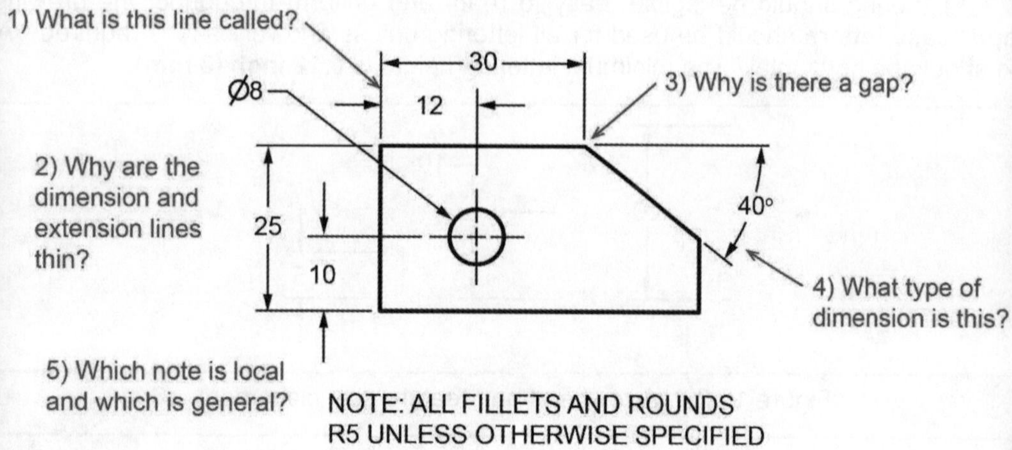

Answers:

1)

2)

3)

4)

5)

10.2.2) Arrowheads, lettering, and symbols

The length and width **ratio of an arrowhead should be 3 to 1** and the width should be proportional to the line thickness. A single style of arrowhead should be used throughout the drawing. Arrowheads are drawn between the extension lines if possible. If space is limited, they may be drawn on the outside. Figure 10.2-1 shows the most common arrowhead configurations.

Lettering should be legible, easy to read, and uniform throughout the drawing. **Upper case letters** should be used for all lettering unless a lower case is required. All text should be horizontal. The minimum lettering height is **0.12 inch (3 mm)**.

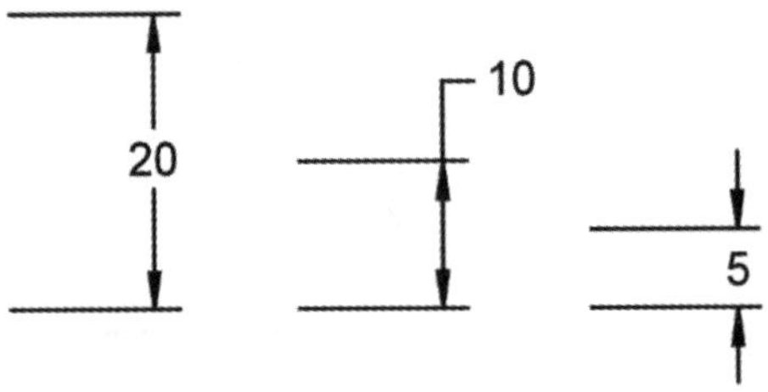

Figure 10.2-1: Arrowhead and feature size placement.

Dimensioning symbols replace text and are used to minimize language barriers. A table in the previous chapter shows all the symbols that may be used on a print.

Try Exercise 10.2-2

<u>**Exercise 10.2-2: Dimension Symbols**</u>

Without referring to the table in the previous chapter, try to identify these common dimensioning symbols..

- ∅ =
- R =
- (10) =
- ⌵ =
- ⊔ =
- 6X =
- ↧ =

10.3) FEATURE DIMENSIONS

The following section illustrates the standard ways common features are dimensioned.

10.3.1) Dimensioning holes, cylinders, arcs, and rounded features

A circle is dimensioned by its diameter and an arc by its radius using a leader line and a note or linear dimension. Diameter dimensions of solid parts, such as a cylinder, is given as a linear dimension. A diameter dimension is preceded by the symbol "∅", and a radial dimension is preceded by the symbol "R". Figure 10.3-1 illustrates diameter and radius dimensions.

Holes are dimensioned by giving their diameter and the center is located in the circular view. Cylinders are dimensioned by giving their diameter and length in the rectangular view, and the center is located in the circular view. By giving the diameter of a cylinder in the rectangular view, it is less likely to be confused with a hole. See Figure 10.3-2 for an illustration of how holes and cylinders are dimensioned differently.

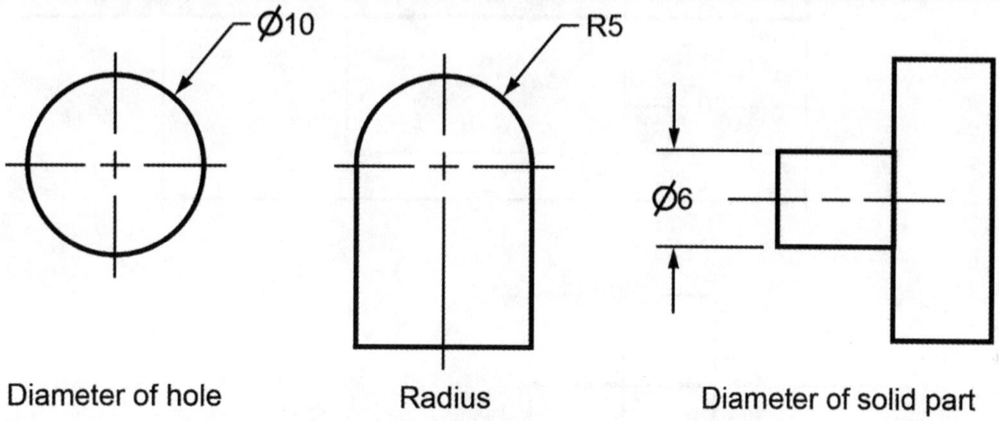

Figure 10.3-1: Diameter and radius dimensions

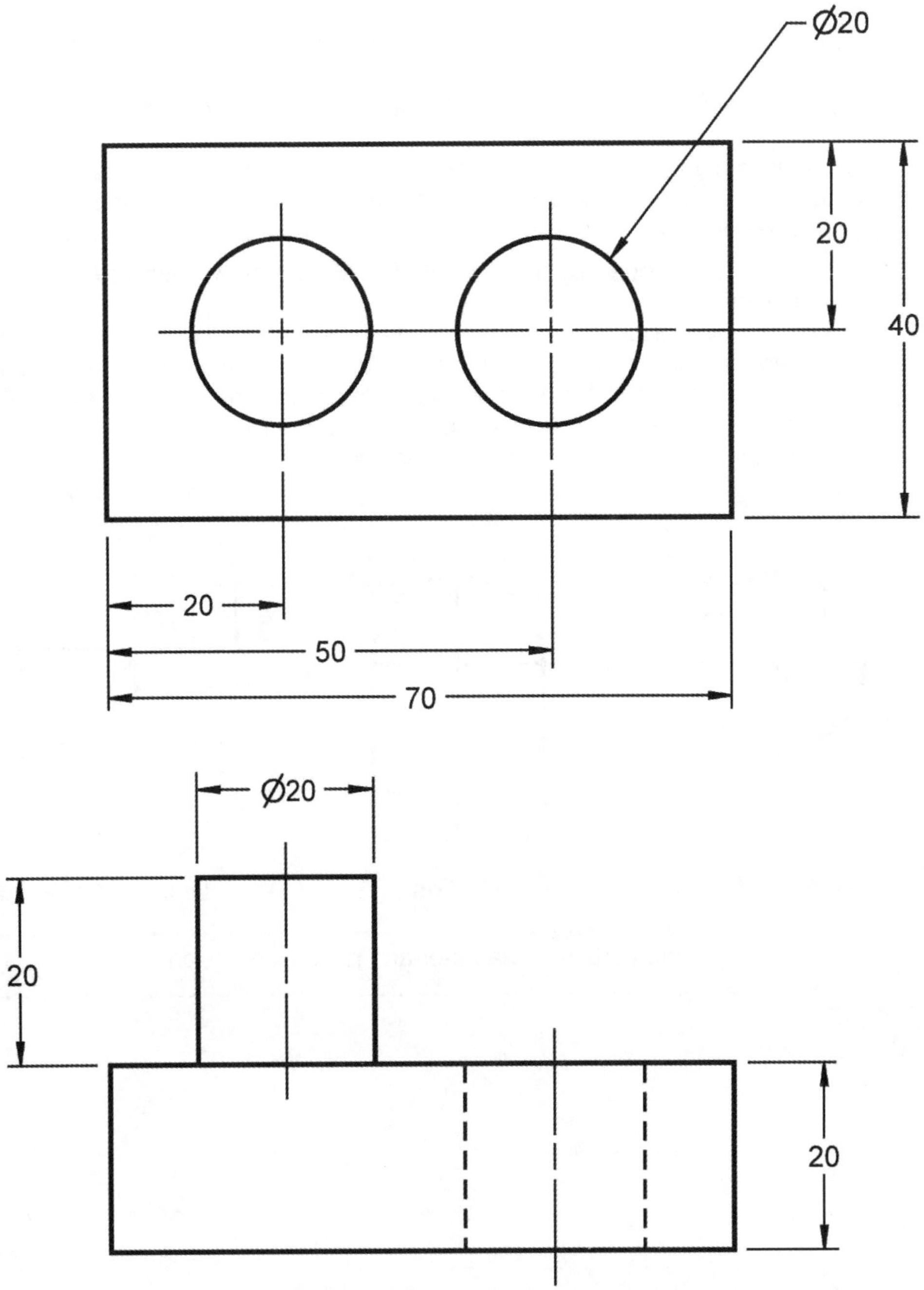

Figure 10.3-2: Dimensioning holes and cylinders

The depth (↧) of a blind hole is specified under the hole's diameter dimension and is the depth of the full diameter from the surface of the object. Figure 10.3-3 illustrates how to dimension a blind hole. If a hole goes completely through the feature and it is not clearly shown on the drawing, the abbreviation "THRU" follows the dimension.

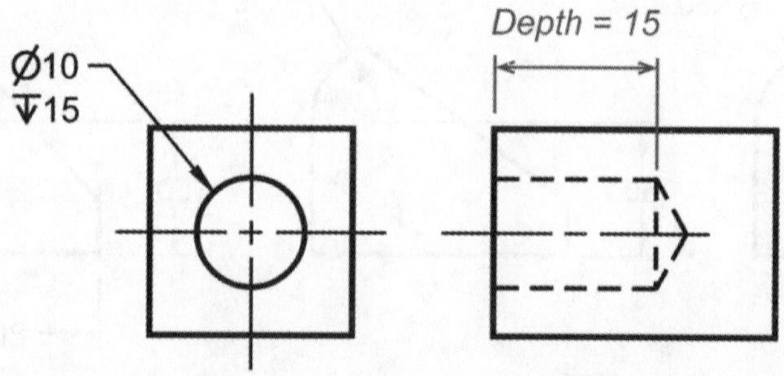

Figure 10.3-3: Dimensioning a blind hole.

A complete sphere is dimensioned by its diameter and an incomplete sphere by its radius. A spherical diameter is indicated by using the symbol "SØ" and a spherical radius by the symbol "SR". Figure 10.3-4 illustrates the spherical diameter and spherical radius dimensions.

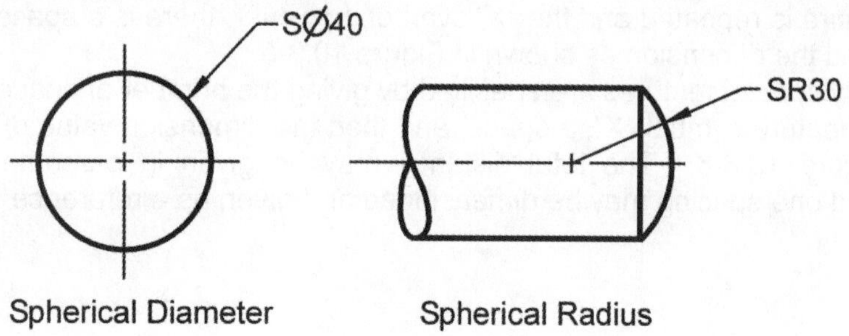

Figure 10.3-4: Dimensioning spherical features.

If a dimension is given to the center of a radius, a small cross is shown at the center. Where the center location of the radius is unimportant, the drawing must clearly show that the arc location is controlled by other dimensioned features such as tangent surfaces. Figure 10.3-5 shows several different radius configurations.

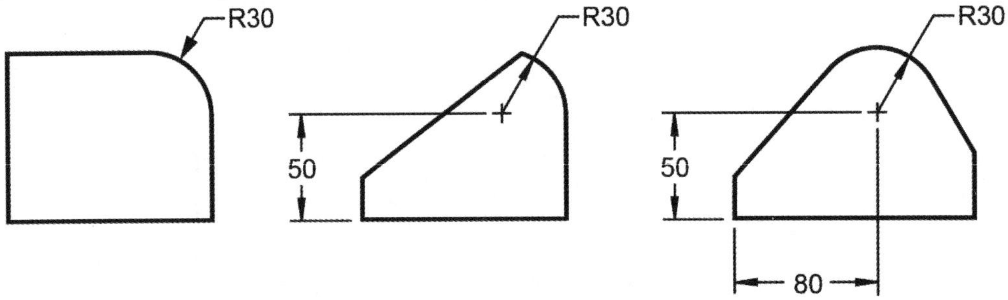

Figure 10.3-5: Dimensioning radial features.

Try Exercise 10.3-1

10.3.2) Repeated features, chamfers, and symmetry

Repetitive features or dimensions are specified by using the symbol "X" along with the number of times the feature is repeated. There is no space between the number of times the feature is repeated and the "X" symbol; however, there is a space between the symbol "X" and the dimension as shown in Figure 10.3-6.

Equally spaced features are specified by giving the number of spaces followed by the repeated feature symbol "X", a space, and then the dimension value of the space as shown in Figure 10.3-6. The total distance may be given in parentheses after the dimension and one spacing may be dimensioned and given as a reference value.

Exercise 10.3-1: Dimensioning circular features

The part shown has missing dimensions. Fill in the dimension for the following features.

1. The blind hole.
2. The cylinder.
3. The two radii and location of their center if necessary.

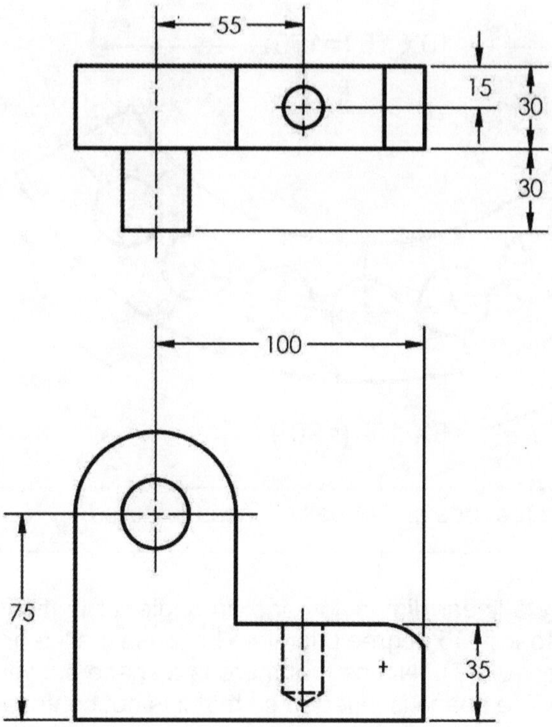

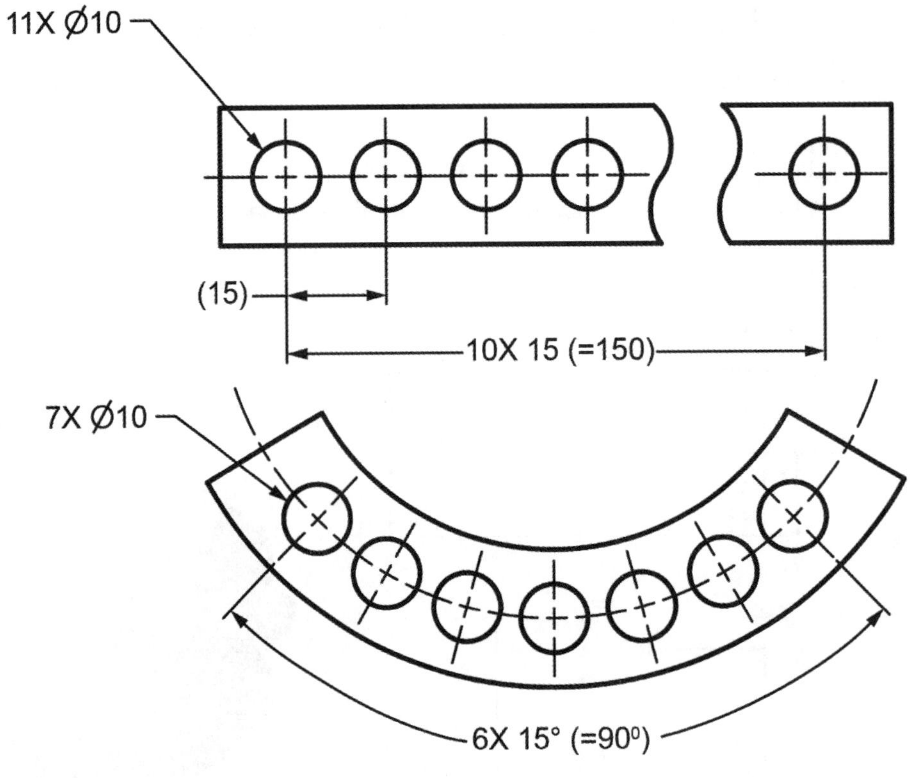

Figure 10.3-6: Repeated features and equally spaced features

Chamfers are dimensioned by a linear dimension and an angle, or by two linear dimensions. A note may be used to specify 45 degree chamfers because the linear value applies in either direction (see Figure 10.3-7). Notice that there is a space between the 'X' symbol and the linear dimension. The space is inserted so that it is not confused with a repeated feature.

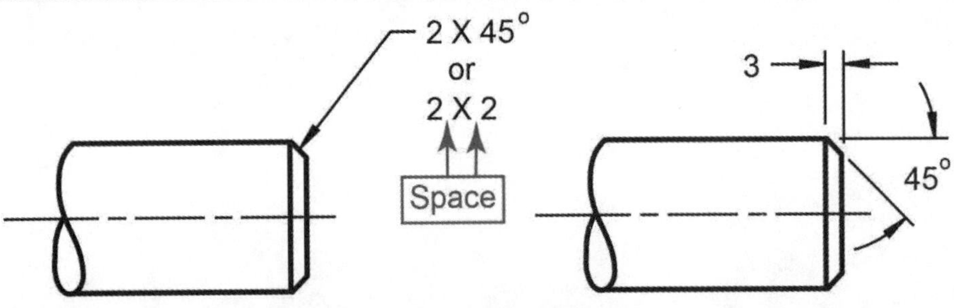

Figure 10.3-7: Chamfers.

a) If a part is symmetric, dimensions on one side of the center line of symmetry need only be given. The center line of symmetry is indicated by using the symbol "$\overline{\underline{+}}$" or "=". Figure 10.3-8 illustrates the use of the symmetry symbol.

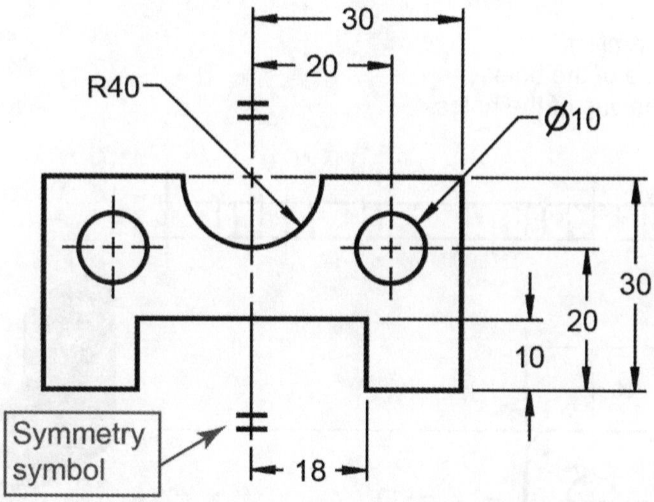

Figure 10.3-8: Center line of symmetry.

Try Exercise 10.3-2

10.3.3) Slots and solid parts with rounded ends

Solid parts that have rounded ends are dimensioned by giving their overall dimensions (see Figure 10.3-9). If the ends are partially rounded, a radius size is also given. For fully rounded ends, a radius is indicated but the value is not given. This is because the width of the part is two times the radius.

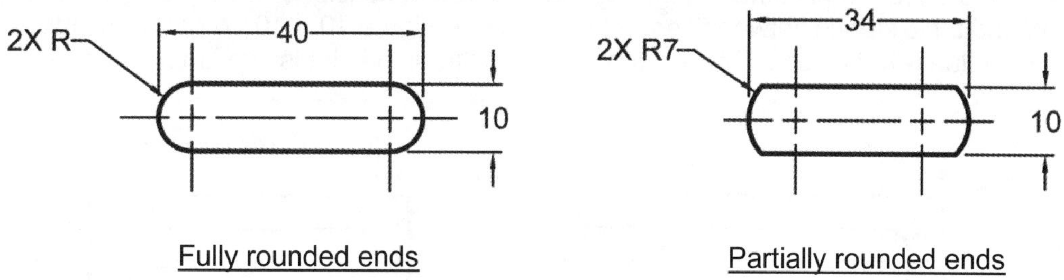

Figure 10.3-9: Rounded ends

Exercise 10.3-2: Dimensioning repeated features and chamfers

The part shown has missing dimensions. Fill in the dimension for the following features.

1. The chamfers
2. The size of the holes
3. The spacing of the holes

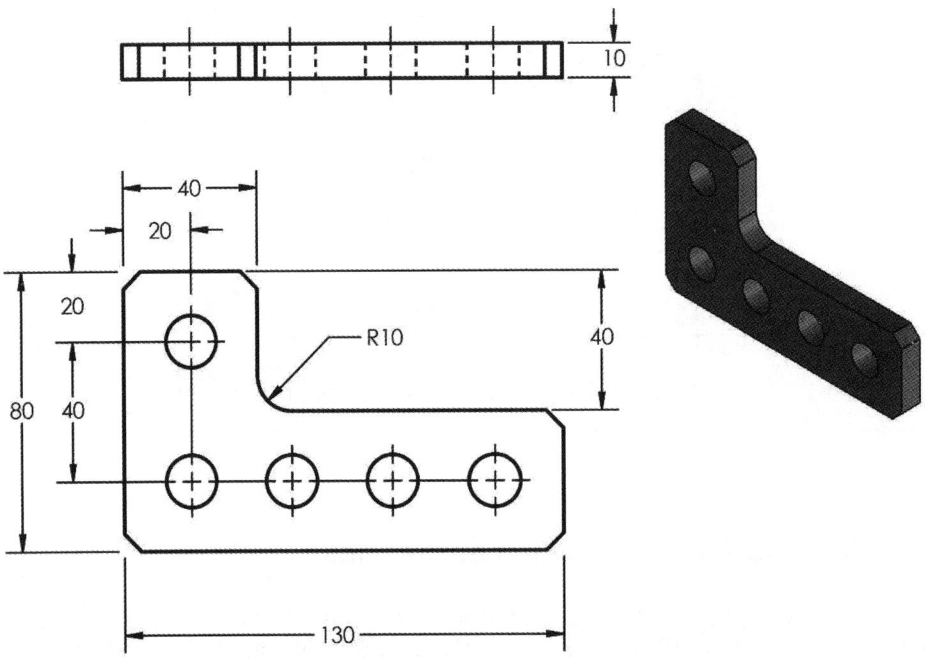

Slots are dimensioned by giving their overall dimensions or by giving the overall width and the distance between centers as shown in Figure 10.3-10. A radius is indicated but the value is not given. This is because the width of the slot is two times the radius.

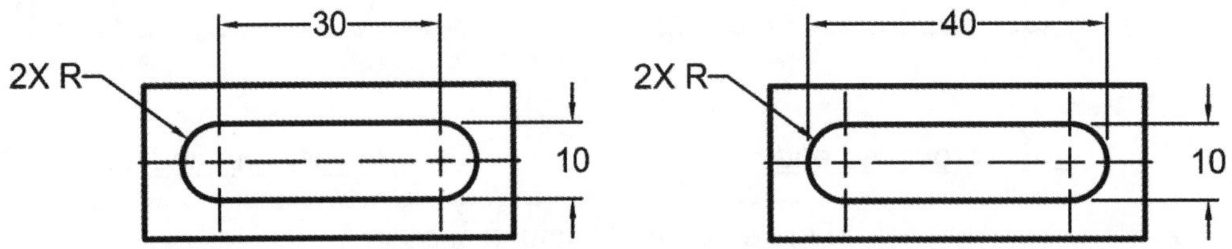

Figure 10.3-10: Slots

10.3.4) Counterbores and countersinks

Counterbored holes are specified by giving the diameter (∅) of the drill, the diameter (∅) of the counterbore (⌴), and the depth (↧) of the counterbore in a note as shown in Figure 10.3-11. If the thickness of the material below the counterbore is significant, this thickness rather than the counterbore depth is given.

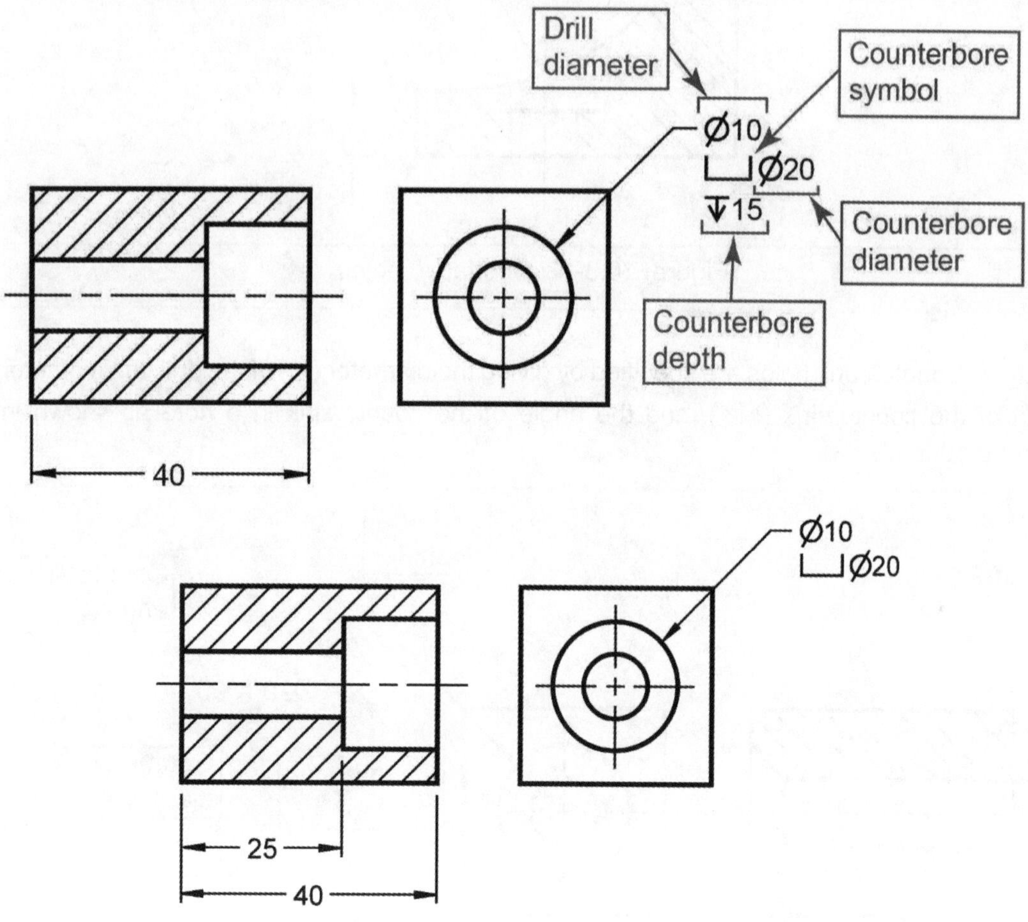

Figure 10.3-11: Counterbored holes.

Spotfaced holes are similar to counterbored holes. The difference is that the machining operation occurs on a curved surface. Therefore, the depth of the counterbore drill is not given in the note. It must be specified in the rectangular view as shown in Figure 10.3-12.

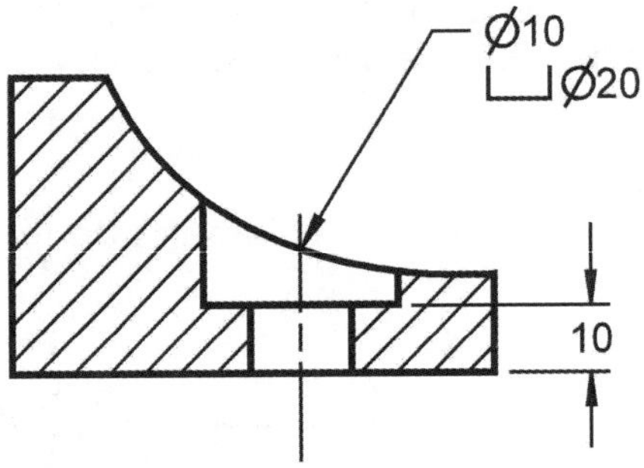

Figure 10.3-12: Spotfaced holes.

Countersunk holes are specified by giving the diameter (∅) of the drill, the diameter (∅) of the countersink (⌵), and the angle of the countersink in a note as shown in Figure 10.3-13.

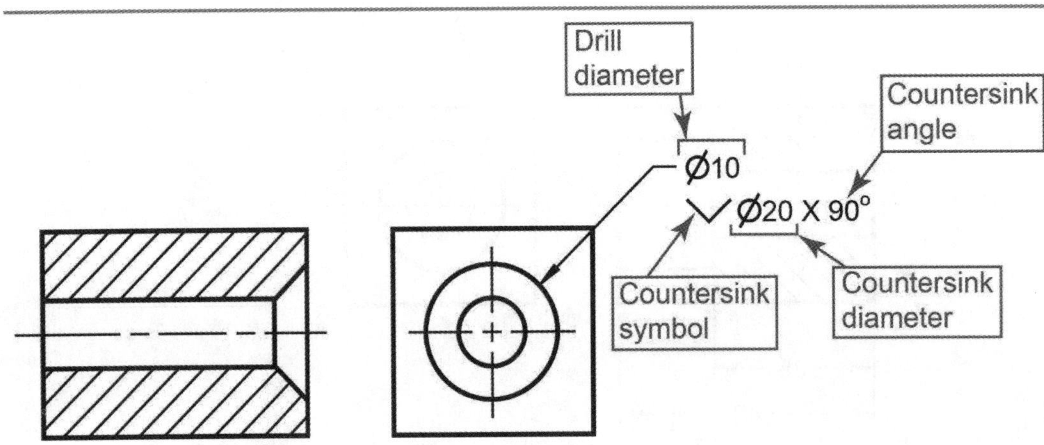

Figure 10.3-13: Countersunk holes.

Try Exercise 10.3-3

Exercise 10.3-3: Dimensioning slots, counterbores, and countersinks

The part shown has missing dimensions. Fill in the dimension for the following features.

1. The counterbores
   a. Drill diameter = 26 mm
   b. Counterbore diameter = 45 mm
   c. Counterbore depth = 15 mm
2. The countersinks
   a. Drill diameter = 5.5 mm
   b. Countersink max. diameter = 10 mm
   c. Countersink angle = 90 degrees
3. The slot size and location
   a. Radius = 15 mm
   b. Distance between centers = 80 mm

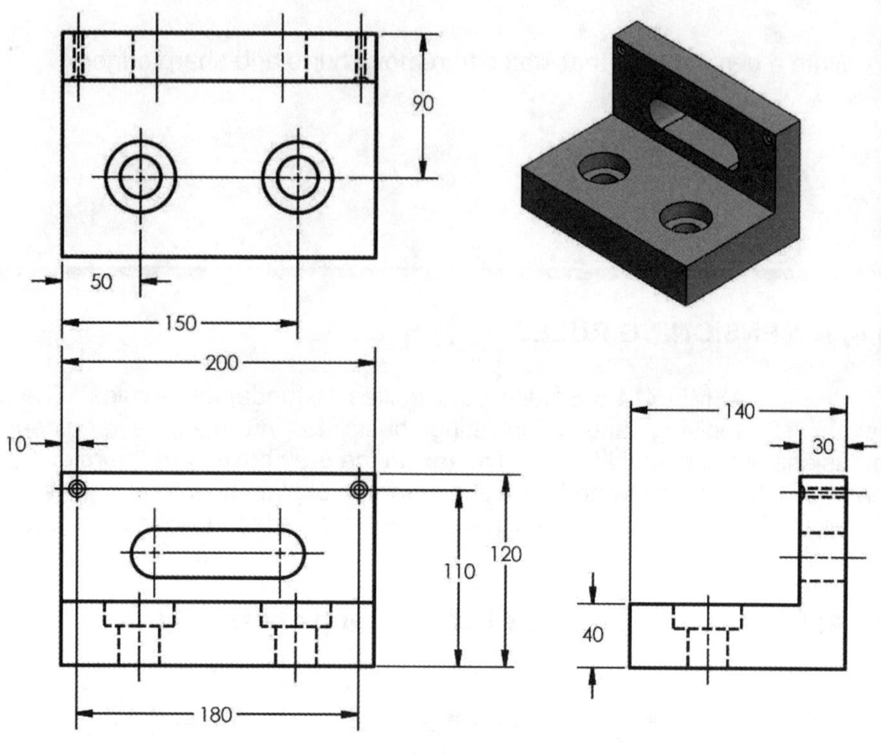

10.3.5) Drawing Notes

Drawing notes give additional information that is used to complement conventional dimensions. Drawing notes provide information clarifying the manufacturing requirements for the part. They cover information such as treatments and finishes among other manufacturing processes. A note may also be used to give blanket dimensions, such as the size of all rounds and fillets on a casting, or a blanket tolerance. Notes may apply to the entire drawing or to a specific area. A **general note** applies to the entire drawing. A general note area is identified with the heading "NOTE:". A **local note** is positioned near and points to the specified area to which it applies.

Exercise 10.3-9: Drawing notes

Write a general drawing note that states that all fillets and rounds have a 3 mm radius unless otherwise specified.

Write a general note that states to remove burrs and sharp edges.

10.4) DIMENSIONING RULES

The ASME Y14.5M standard specifies 16 fundamental rules. The rules that are relevant to applying and interpreting basic to intermediate engineering drawing dimensions are explained below. The text in the grey boxes are the rules from the ASME standard. The text following the rule is meant to explain how to apply the rule. Note that the order of the rules presented here is not the order that they are presented in the standard.

10.4.1) Dimension placement, spacing, and readability

Rule 1) Dimensions should be arranged for maximum readability.

Dimensions should be easy to read and minimize the possibility for conflicting interpretations and should be placed in such a way as to enhance the communication of your design. Dimensions should be given clearly and in an organized fashion. They should not be crowded or hard to read.

The following are guidelines that govern the logical and practical arrangement of dimensions to ensure maximum legibility:

a) The **spacing** between dimension lines **should be uniform** throughout the drawing. The space between the first dimension line and the part should be at least 10 mm; the space between subsequent dimension should be at least 6 mm. However, the above spacing is only intended as a guide.

b) **Do not dimension inside an object** or have the dimension line touch the object unless clearness is gained.

c) **Dimension text should be horizontal** which means that it is read from the bottom of the drawing.

d) Dimension text should not cross dimension, extension, or visible lines.

e) Dimension lines should not cross extension lines or other dimension lines. To avoid this, **shorter dimensions should be placed before longer ones**. Extension lines can cross other extension lines or visible lines. However, this should be minimized. Where extension lines cross other lines, the extension lines are not broken. If an extension line crosses an arrowhead or is near an arrowhead, a break in the extension line is permitted.

Try Exercise 10.4-1.

f) Extension lines and centerlines should not connect between views.

g) Leader lines should be straight, not curved, and **point to the center of the arc or circle at an angle between 30°-60°**. The leaders should *float up* or, in other words, lead from the arrow up to the text.

Try Exercise 10.4-2.

h) Dimensions should be grouped whenever possible.

i) Dimensions should be placed between views, unless clearness is promoted by placing some outside.

j) Dimensions should be attached to the view where the shape is shown best.

k) Do not dimension hidden lines.

Try Exercise 10.4-3

Exercise 10.4-1: Spacing and readability 1

Consider the incorrectly dimensioned object shown. There are 5 types of dimensioning mistakes. List them and then dimension the object correctly.

1)

2)

3)

4)

5)

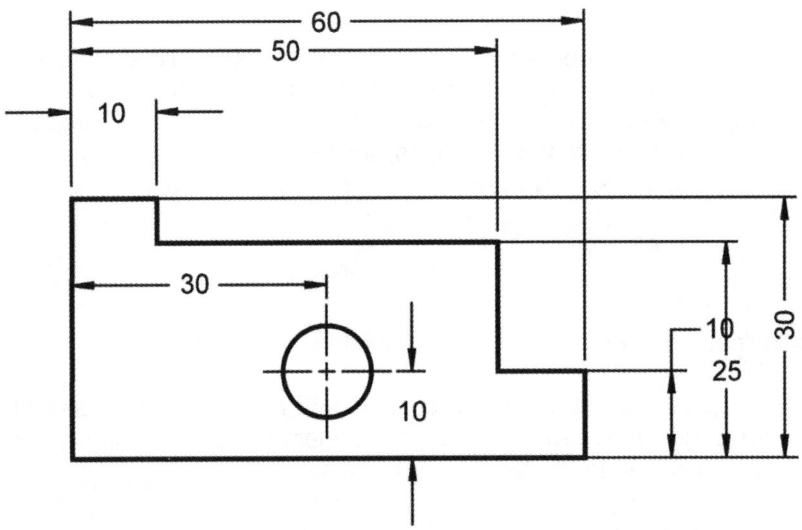

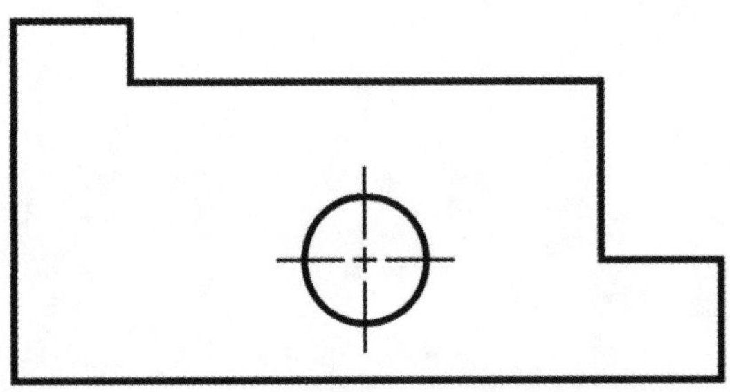

Exercise 10.4-2: Spacing and readability 2

Consider the incorrectly dimensioned object shown. There are 4 types of dimensioning mistakes. List them and then dimension the object correctly.

1)

2)

3)

4)

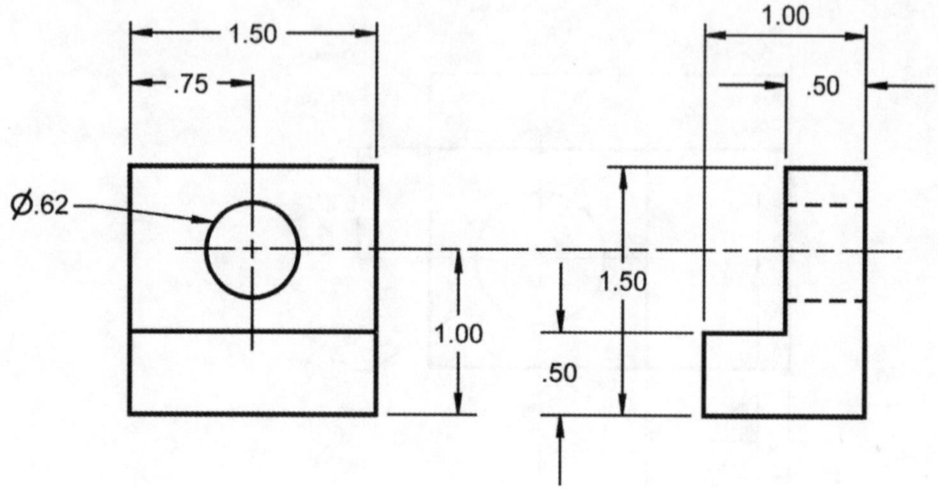

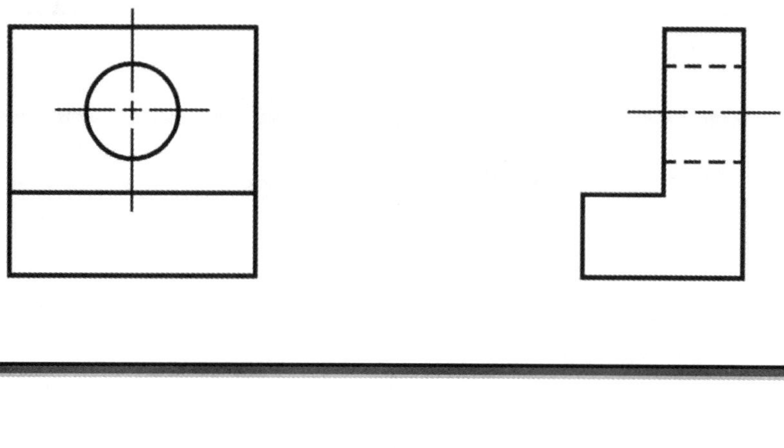

Exercise 10.4-3: Dimension placement

Consider the incorrectly dimensioned object shown. There are 6 types of dimensioning mistakes. List them and then dimension the object correctly.

1)

2)

3)

4)

5)

6)

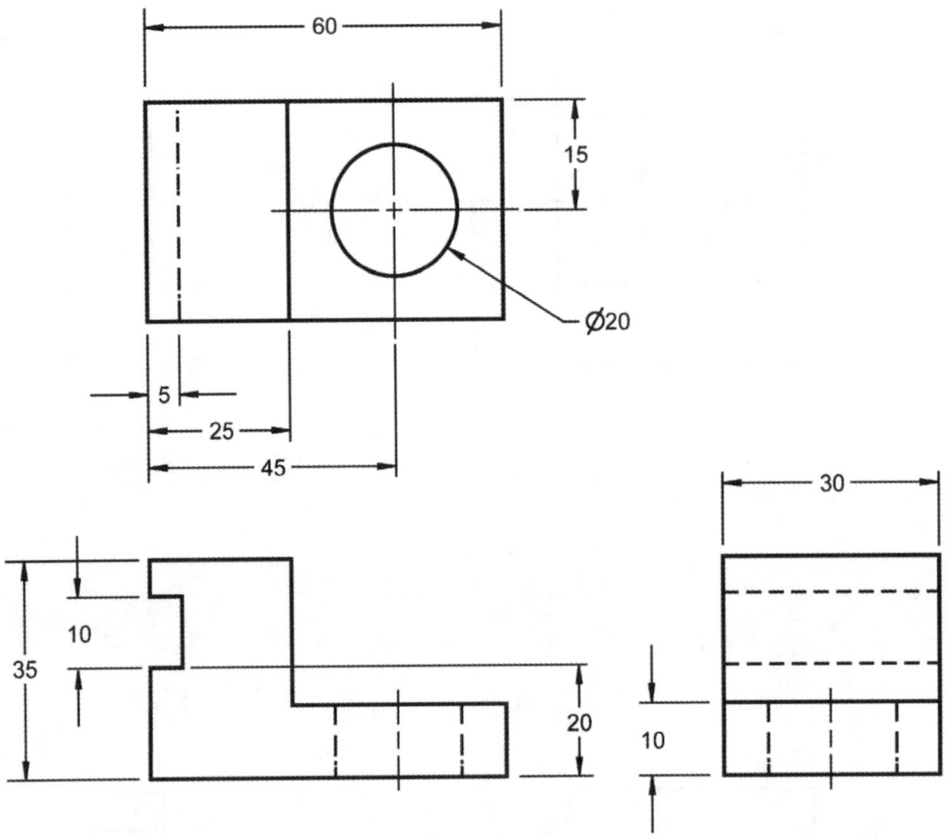

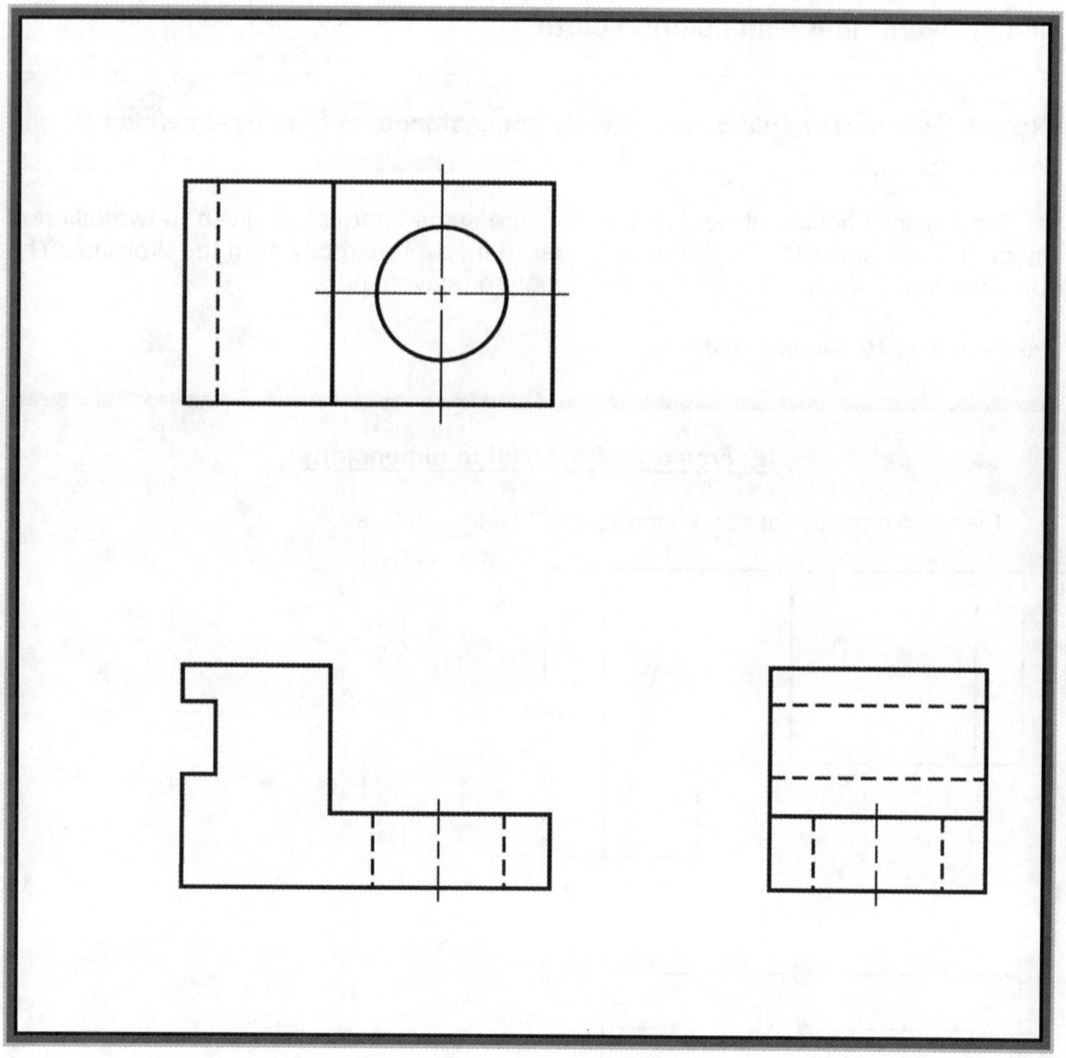

10.4.2) Over/Under dimensioned parts

Rule 2) Your part should be completely dimensioned, but not over defined.

Dimensions should not be duplicated or the same information given in two different ways. It is not allowable for the print reader to measure directly from the drawing. The standard does list a few exceptions, but none are relevant here.

Try Exercises 10.4-4 and 10.4-5

Exercise 10.4-4: Missing dimensions

Find and draw the missing dimensions. There are three.

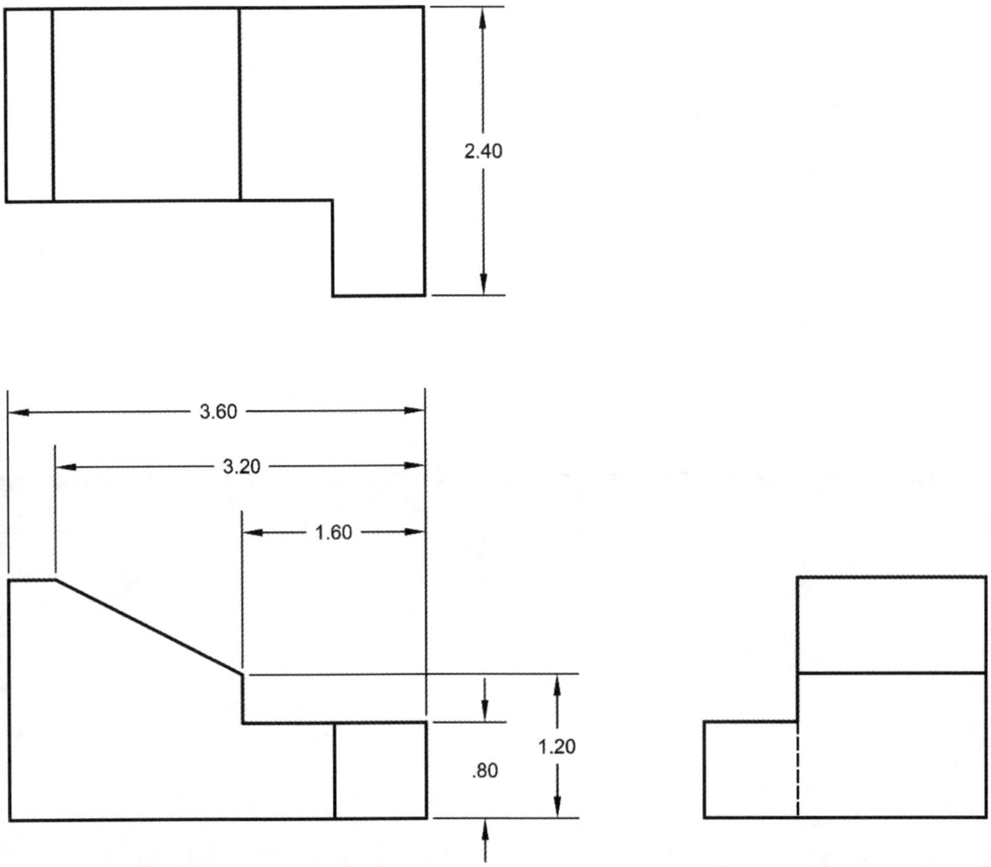

Exercise 10.4-5: Duplicate dimensions

Find the duplicate dimensions and cross out the ones that you feel should be omitted.

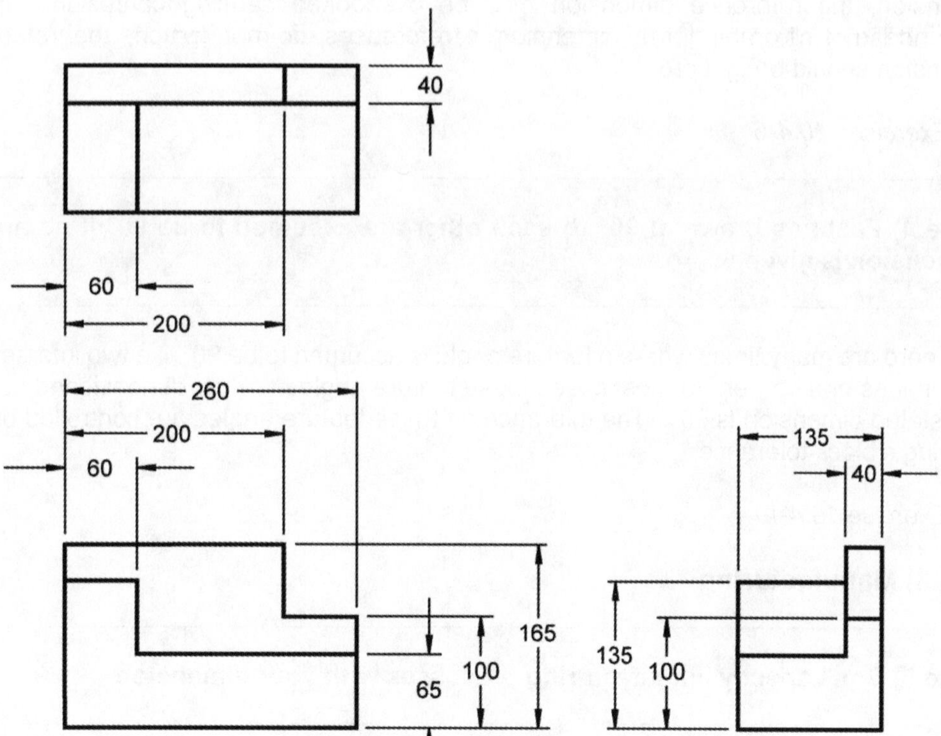

Rule 3) The use of reference (duplicated) dimension should be minimized.

If a reference dimension is used, the size value is placed within parentheses, e.g., (10). Duplicate dimensions may cause needless trouble. If a change is made to one dimension, the reference dimension may be overlooked causing confusion. If the reference dimension and the dimension it references do not match, the reference dimension should be ignored.

Try Exercises 10.4-6

Rule 4) Features drawn at 90° to each other are assumed to be 90° if no angle dimension is given.

There are many times where a feature angle is assumed to be 90° like two intersecting center lines or a corner. In most cases these feature angles are not dimensioned but the non-stated dimension is 90°. The tolerance on these feature angles are controlled by the drawing's block tolerance.

Try Exercise 10.4-7

10.4.3) Manufacturing

Rule 5) Don't specify manufacturing processes with your dimension.

Examples of words that specify manufacturing processes are "DRILL", "REAM", and "PUNCH". These should not be placed with the feature size. On old prints, you may see a hole dimension specified as ".12 DRILL". This dimension specifies a manufacturing process. The dimension should read "∅.12". The exception is when the process is essential to the definition of the engineering requirements.

Exercise 10.4-6: Reference dimensions

Match the reference dimension with the dimension it references. Are there any inconsistencies?

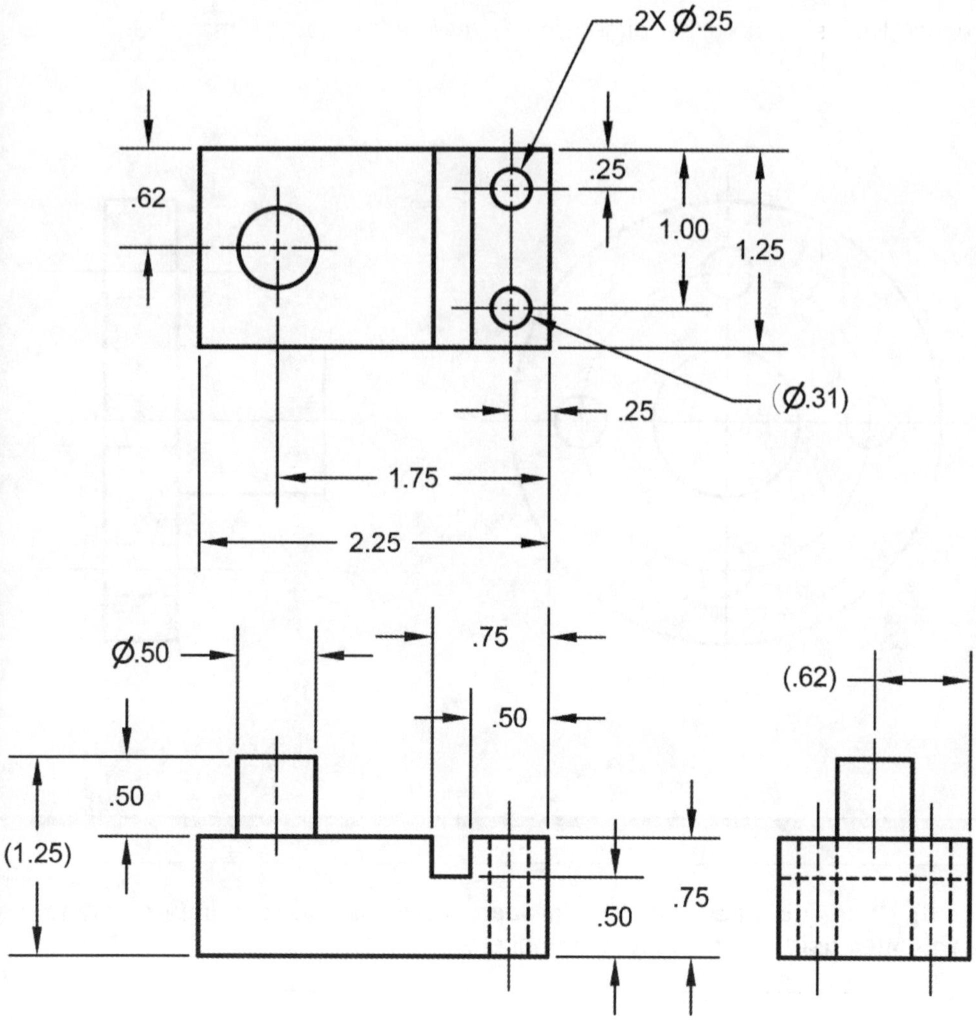

Exercise 10.4-7: Dimensioning

Dimension the following object.

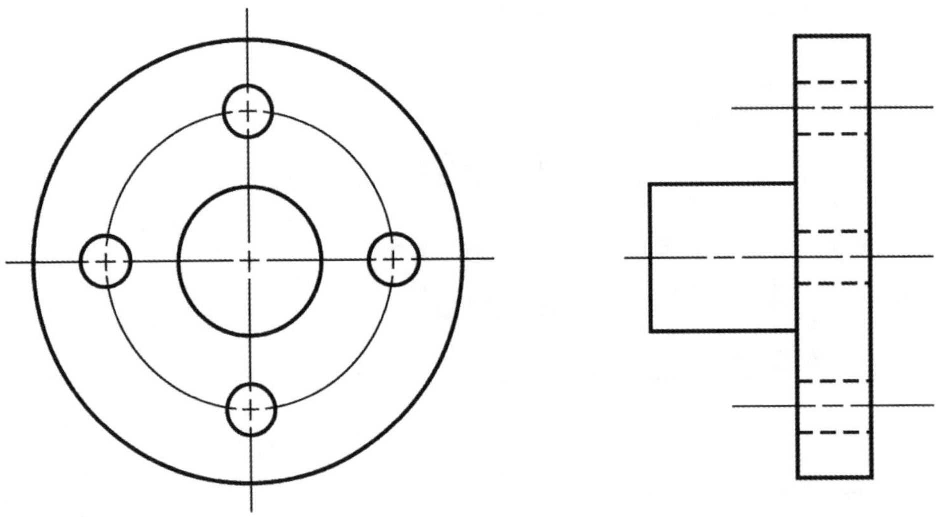

Rule 6) Parts identified by drill, broach, gage, or code numbers/letters are dimensioned using their actual decimal size.

Sometimes you may encounter a drawing that specifies standard drills, broaches, gages, or codes by a number or letter. The number or letter may be shown in parentheses next to the dimension, but the decimal size must be shown as the primary dimension.

Your choice of dimensions will directly influence the method used to manufacture a part. However, your **choice of dimensions should depend on the function and the mating relationship of the part**, and then on manufacturing. Learning the topics in this section and the upcoming sections will guide you when choosing your dimension units, decimal places and the dimension's starting point. Even though dimensions influence how the part is made, the manufacturing process is not specifically stated on the drawing. Listed are a few examples of how dimension placement and dimension text influence how the part gets manufactured.

- ✓ **Increasing the number of decimal places** (e.g., 1.00 goes to 1.000) **will increase the cost of manufacturing.** Some manufacturing processes are not as accurate as other processes (e.g., *casting* is not very accurate, *grinding* is more accurate). More accurate processes are generally more expensive.
- ✓ **Identifying a datum feature** (i.e., a surface from which most dimensions originate) **will influence the surfaces used in the manufacturing process.**
- ✓ **Dimension placement influences error build up.** Using datum dimensioning minimizes error build up.

a) On drawings where all the dimensions are given either in millimeters or inches, individual identification of the units is not necessary. However, the drawing should contain a note stating UNLESS OTHERWISE SPECIFIED, ALL DIMENSIONS ARE IN MILLIMETERS (or INCHES). If some inch dimensions are used on a millimeter drawing or vice versa, the abbreviations **IN** or **mm** shall follow the dimension value.

b) Metric dimensions are given in '**mm**' and typically given to **0 or 1 decimal** place (e.g., 10, 10.2). When the dimension is less than a millimeter, a zero should precede the decimal point (e.g., 0.5).

c) English dimensions are given in '**inches**' and typically given to **2 decimal places** (e.g. 1.25). A zero is not shown before the decimal point for values less than one inch (e.g. .75).

There is no such thing as an "exact" measurement. **The more accurate a dimension is, the more expensive it is to manufacture.** To cut costs it is necessary to round off fractional dimensions. If, for example, we are rounding off to the second decimal place and the third decimal place number is less than 5, we truncate after the second decimal place. If the number in the third decimal place is greater than 5, we round up and increase the second decimal place number by 1. If the number is exactly 5, whether or not we round up depends on if the second decimal place number is odd or even. If it is odd, we round up and if it is even, it is kept the same.

Try Exercise 10.4-8 and 10.4-9

Exercise 10.4-8: Rounding off

Round off the following fractions to two decimal places according to the rules stated above.

(5/16) .3125 →	(1/8) .125 →
(5/32) .1562 →	(3/8) .375 →

Exercise 10.4-9: Advanced dimensioning

Consider the incorrectly dimensioned object shown. There are 7 types of dimensioning mistakes. List them and then dimension the object correctly.

1)

2)

3)

4)

5)

6)

7)

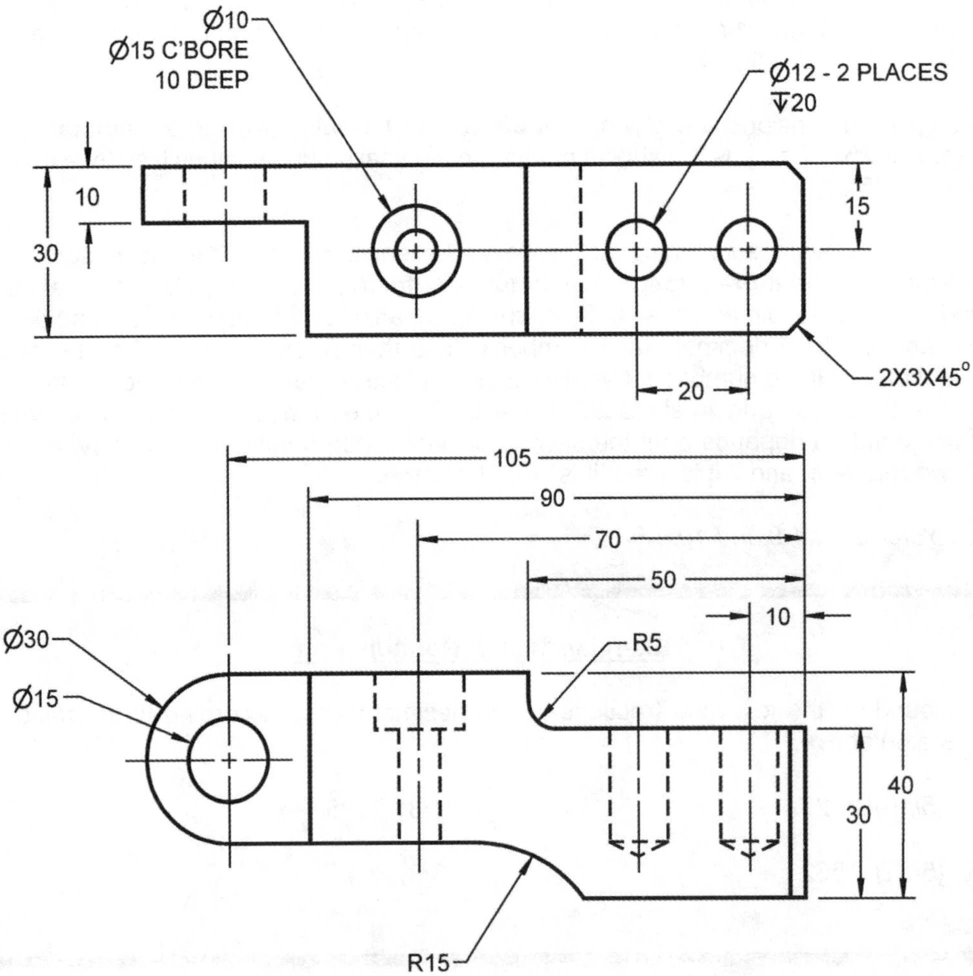

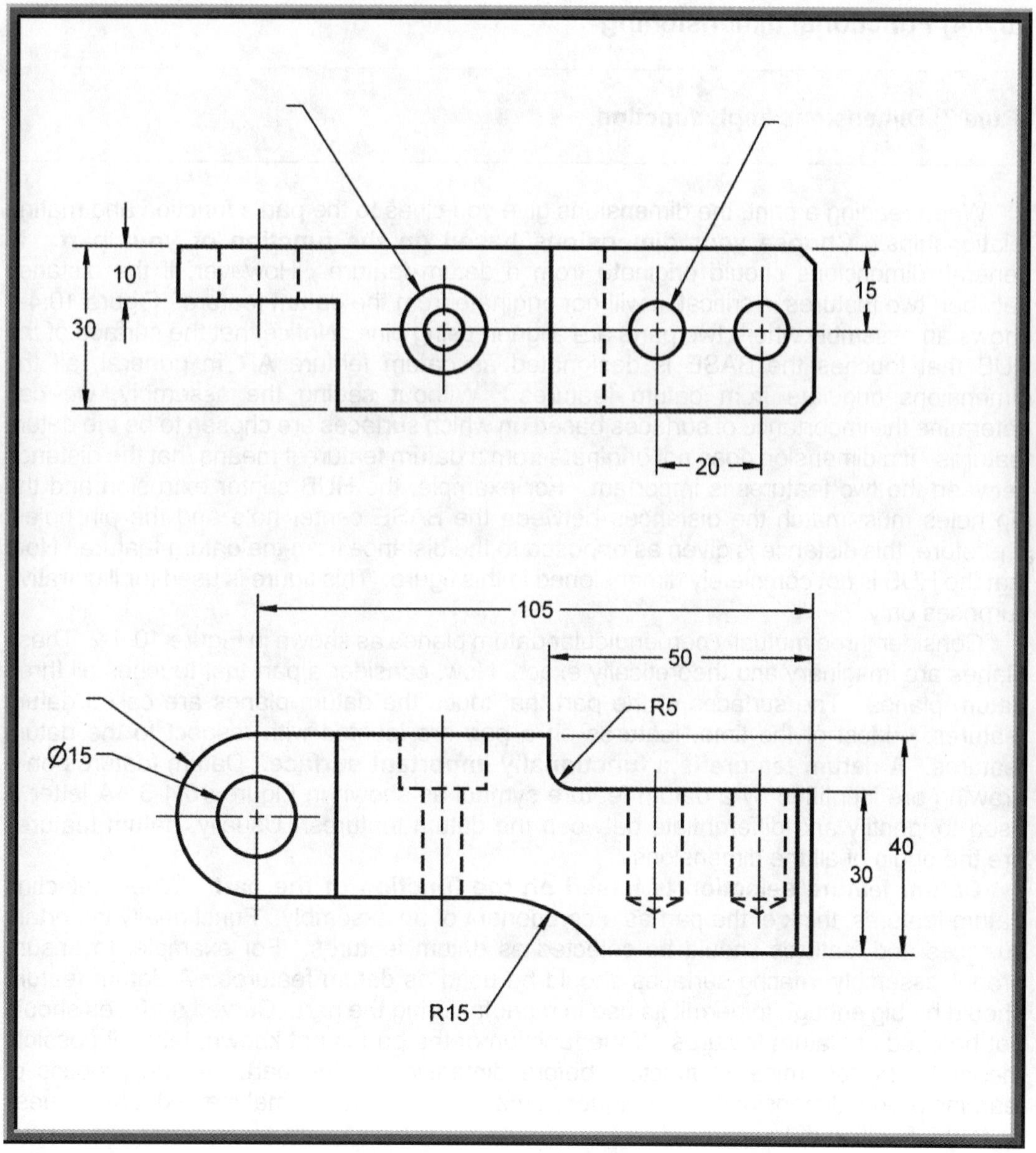
10
30
15
20
105
50
R5
Ø15
40
30
R15

10.4.4) Functional dimensioning

Rule 7) Dimensions imply function.

When reading a print, the dimensions give you clues to the part's function and mating relationships. **Choose your dimensions based on the function of your part.** In general, dimensions should originate from a datum feature. However, if the distance between two features is critical, it will not originate from the datum feature. Figure 10.4-1 shows an assembly where two parts are aligned using pins. Notice that the surface of the HUB that touches the BASE is designated as datum feature A. In general, all the dimensions originate from datum features. Without seeing the assembly, we can determine the importance of surfaces based on which surfaces are chosen to be the datum features. If a dimension does not originate from a datum feature it means that the distance between the two features is important. For example, the HUB center extrusion and the pin holes must match the distances between the BASE center hole and the pin holes. Therefore, this distance is given as opposed to the distance from the datum feature. Note that the HUB is not completely dimensioned in this figure. This figure is used for illustrative purposes only.

Consider three mutually perpendicular datum planes as shown in Figure 10.4-2. These planes are imaginary and theoretically exact. Now, consider a part that touches all three datum planes. The surfaces of the part that touch the datum planes are called datum features. Most of the time, features on a part are located with respect to the datum features. **A datum feature is a functionally important surface.** Datum features on a drawing are identified by a datum feature symbol as shown in Figure 10.4-3. A letter is used to identify and differentiate between the datum features. Usually, datum features are the origin of all the dimensions.

Datum feature selection is based on the function of the part. When selecting datum features, think of the part as a component of an assembly. Functionally important surfaces and features should be selected as datum features. For example, to ensure proper assembly, mating surfaces should be used as datum features. A datum feature should be big enough to permit its use in manufacturing the part. Curved surfaces should not be used as datum features. If the function of the part is not known, take all possible measures to determine its function before dimensioning the part. In the process of learning proper dimensioning techniques, it may be necessary to make an educated guess as to the function of the part.

Try Exercise 10.4-10 and Video Exercises 10.4-11, 10.4-12, 10.4-13, and 10.4-14

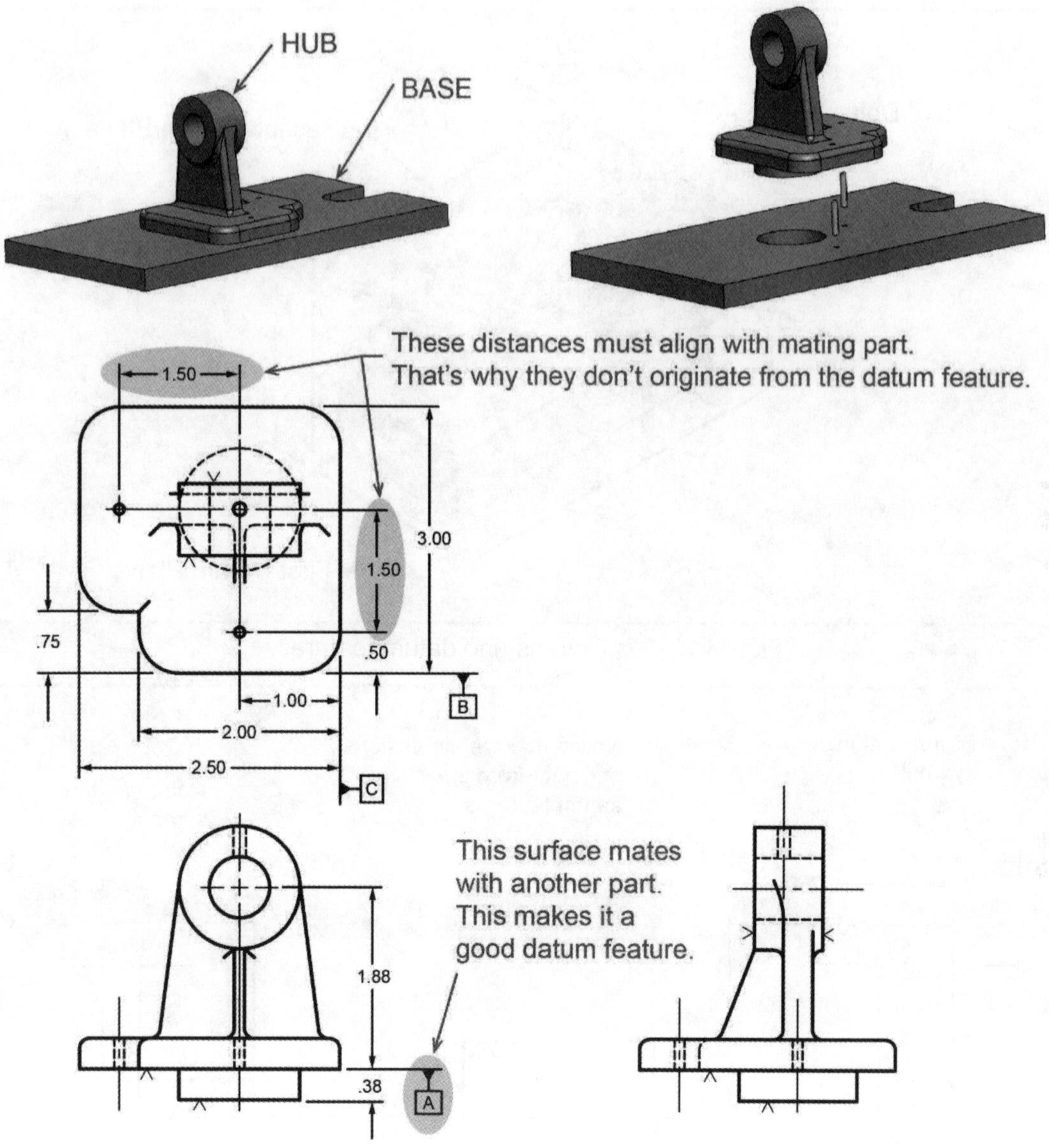

Figure 10.4-1: Dimensions indicate function.

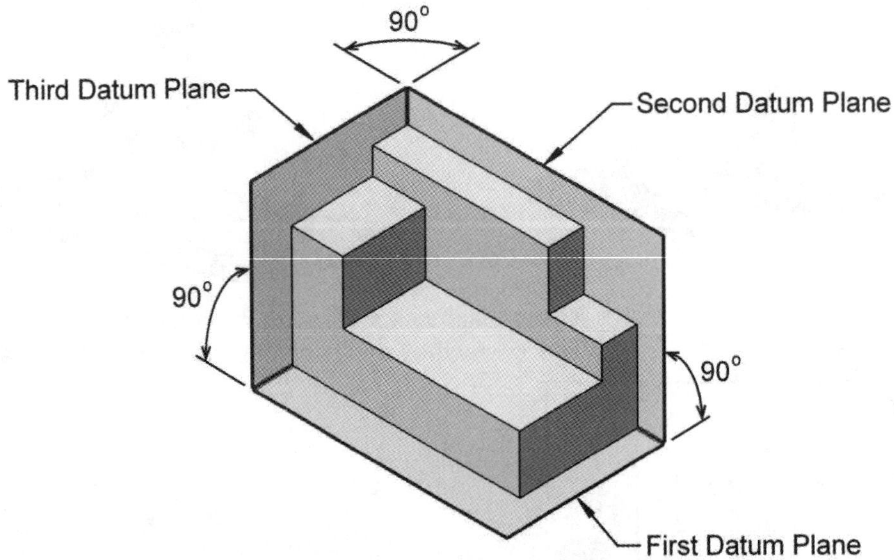

Figure 10.4-2: Datums and datum features.

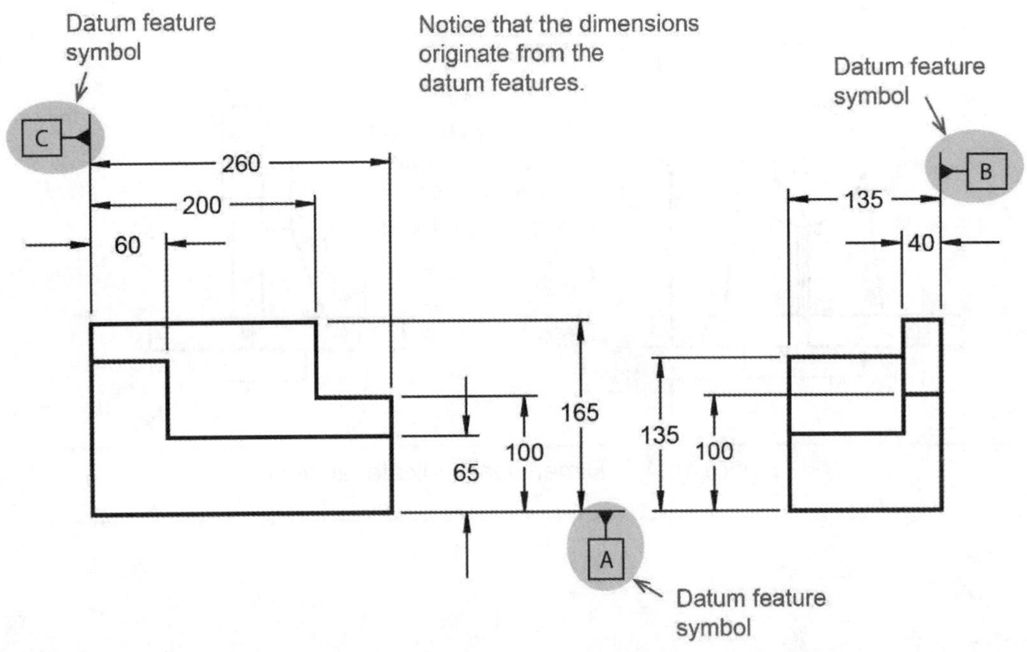

Figure 10.4-3: Dimensioning using datum features.

Exercise 10.4-10: Dimension choice

Consider the incorrectly dimensioned object shown. There are 4 types of dimensioning mistakes. List them and then dimension the object correctly.

1)

2)

3)

4)

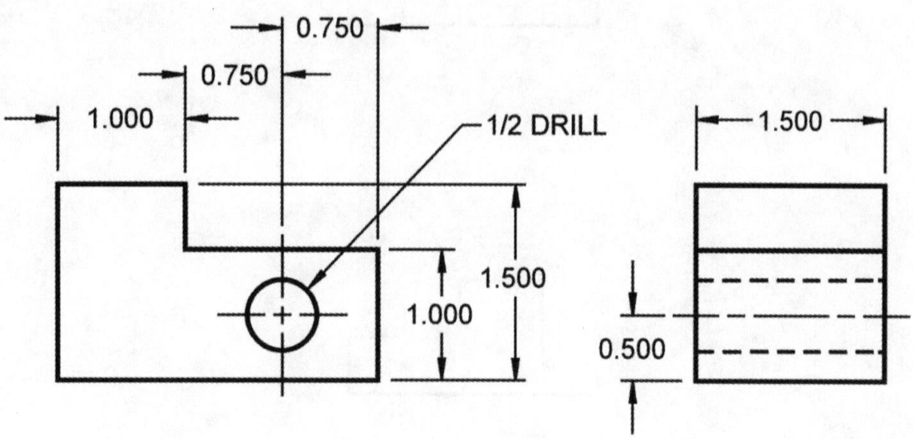

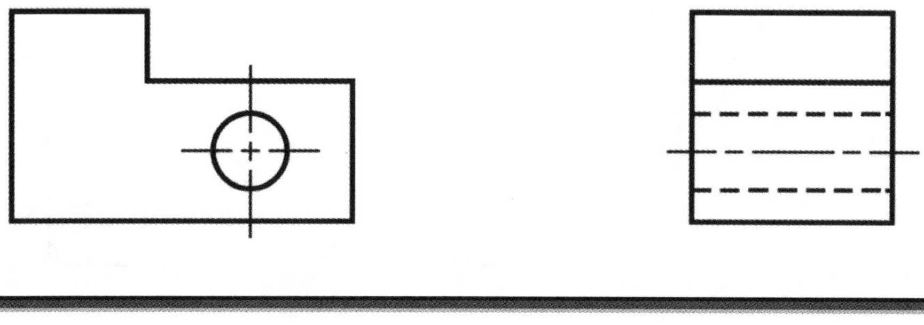

Video Exercise 10.4-11: Beginning Dimensioning

This video exercise will take you through dimensioning the following objects using proper dimensioning techniques.

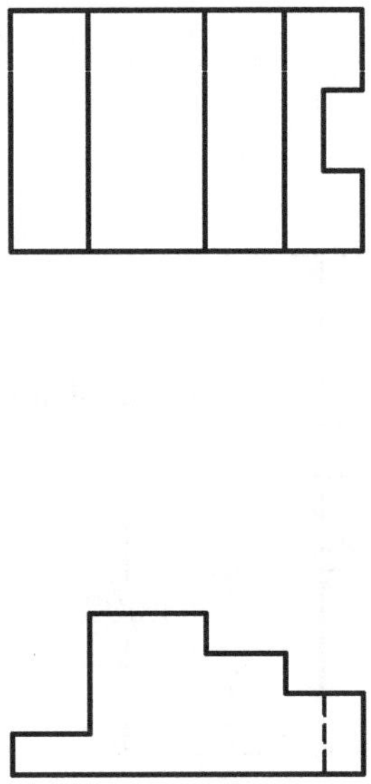

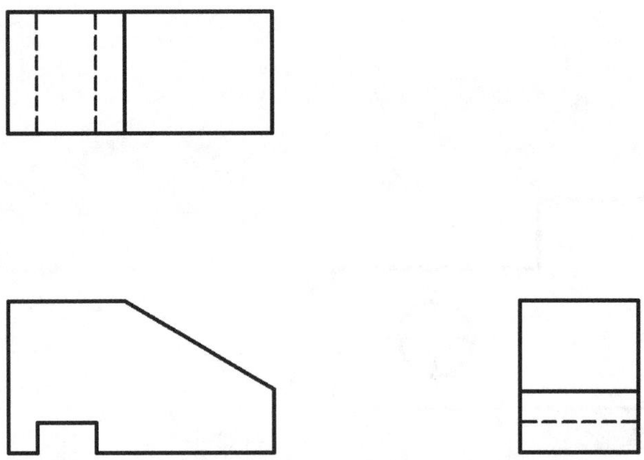

Video Exercise 10.4-12: Intermediate Dimensioning

This video exercise will take you through dimensioning the following objects using proper dimensioning techniques.

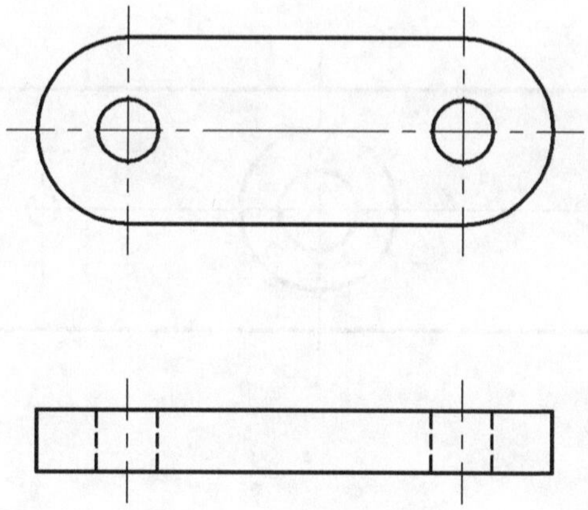

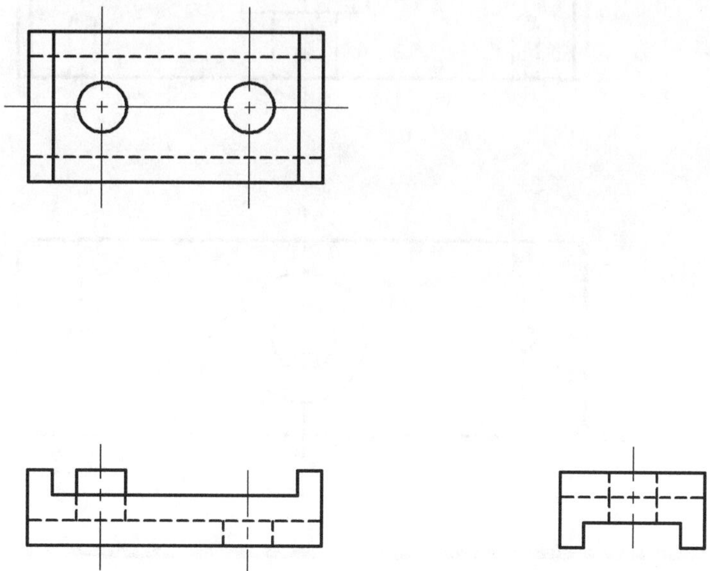

Video Exercise 10.4-13: Advanced Dimensioning 1

This video exercise will take you through dimensioning the following objects using proper dimensioning techniques.

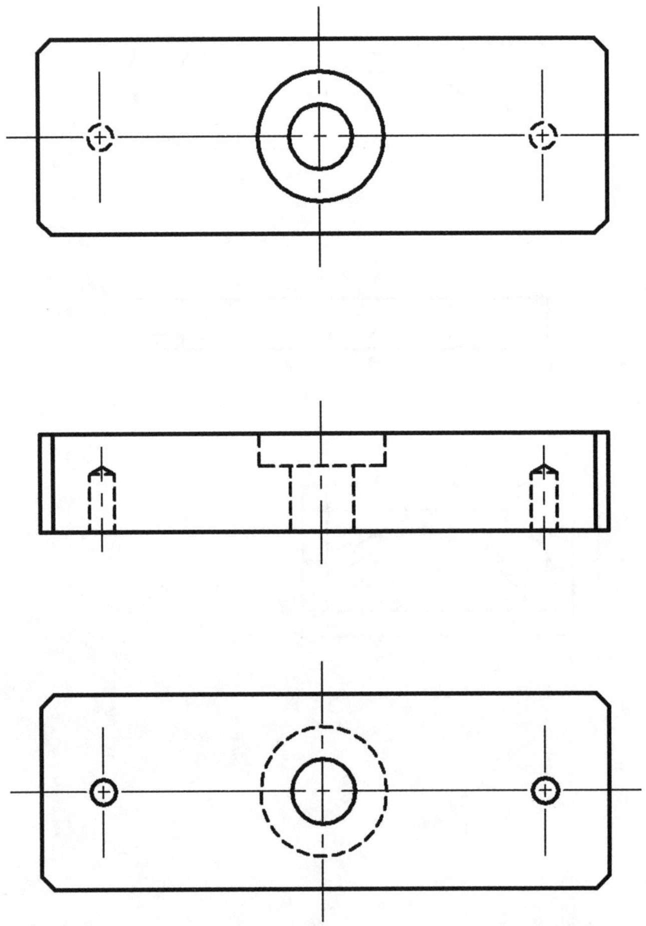

Video Exercise 10.4-14: Advanced Dimensioning 2

This video exercise will take you through dimensioning the following objects using proper dimensioning techniques.

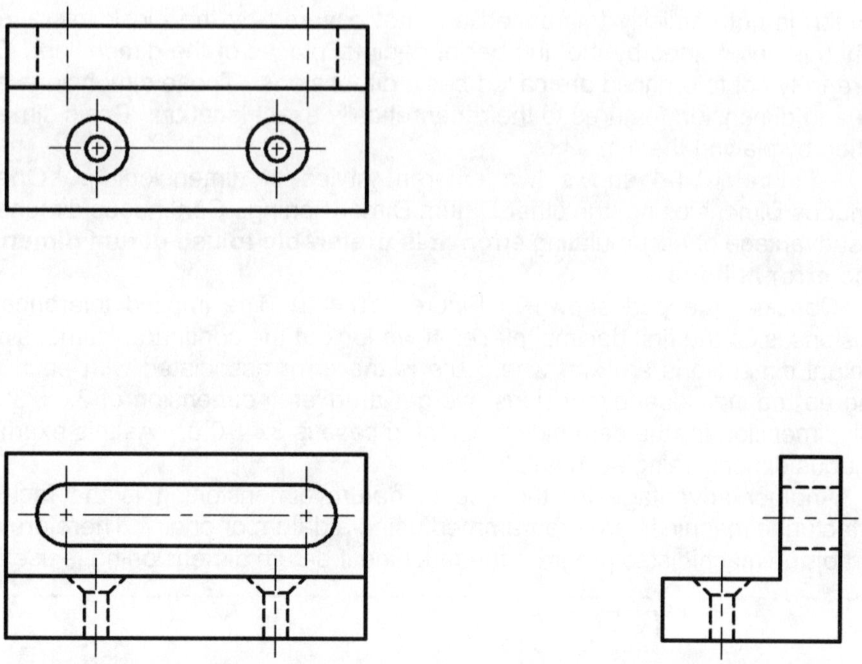

10.4.5) Tolerancing

Rule 8) Every dimension is toleranced.

A toleranced dimension is not a single value, but states the maximum and minimum size that a feature may be and still function correctly. If a dimension does not have an explicitly stated tolerance, it is most likely covered by the block tolerance. If a dimension is not explicitly toleranced and not covered by the block tolerance, then its tolerance is determined by the number of decimal places of the dimension. Dimensions that are truly not toleranced are called basic dimensions. These dimensions are used to locate and dimension features to their theoretically exact location. Basic dimensions are identified by placing them in a box.

Figure 10.4-4 shows two different styles of dimensioning. One is called Continuous Dimensioning, the other Datum Dimensioning. Continuous dimensioning has the disadvantage of accumulating error. **It is preferable to use datum dimensioning to reduce error buildup.**

Consider the part shown in Figure 10.4-4. The implied tolerance of all the dimensions is on the first decimal place. If we look at the continuous dimensioning case, the actual dimensions are x.*e*, where 0.*e* is the error associated with each dimension. Adding up the individual dimensions, we get an overall dimension of 3x + 3*(0.*e*). The overall dimension for the datum dimensioning case is 3x + 0.*e*. As this example shows, continuous dimensioning accumulates error.

Another advantage for the use of datum dimensioning is the fact that many manufacturing machines are programmed using a datum or origin. Therefore, it makes it easier for the machinist to program the machine if datum dimensioning is used.

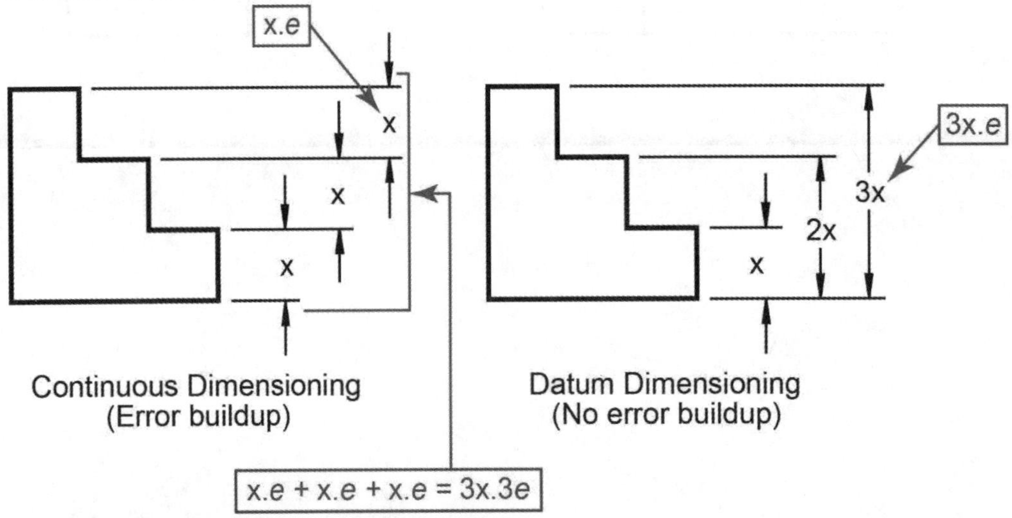

Figure 10.4-4: Error buildup.

10.5) APPLYING WHAT WE HAVE LEARNED

Exercise 10.5-1: Dimensioning 1

Name: ______________________________ Date: ______________

Dimension the following object using proper dimensioning techniques. Did we need to draw the right side view?

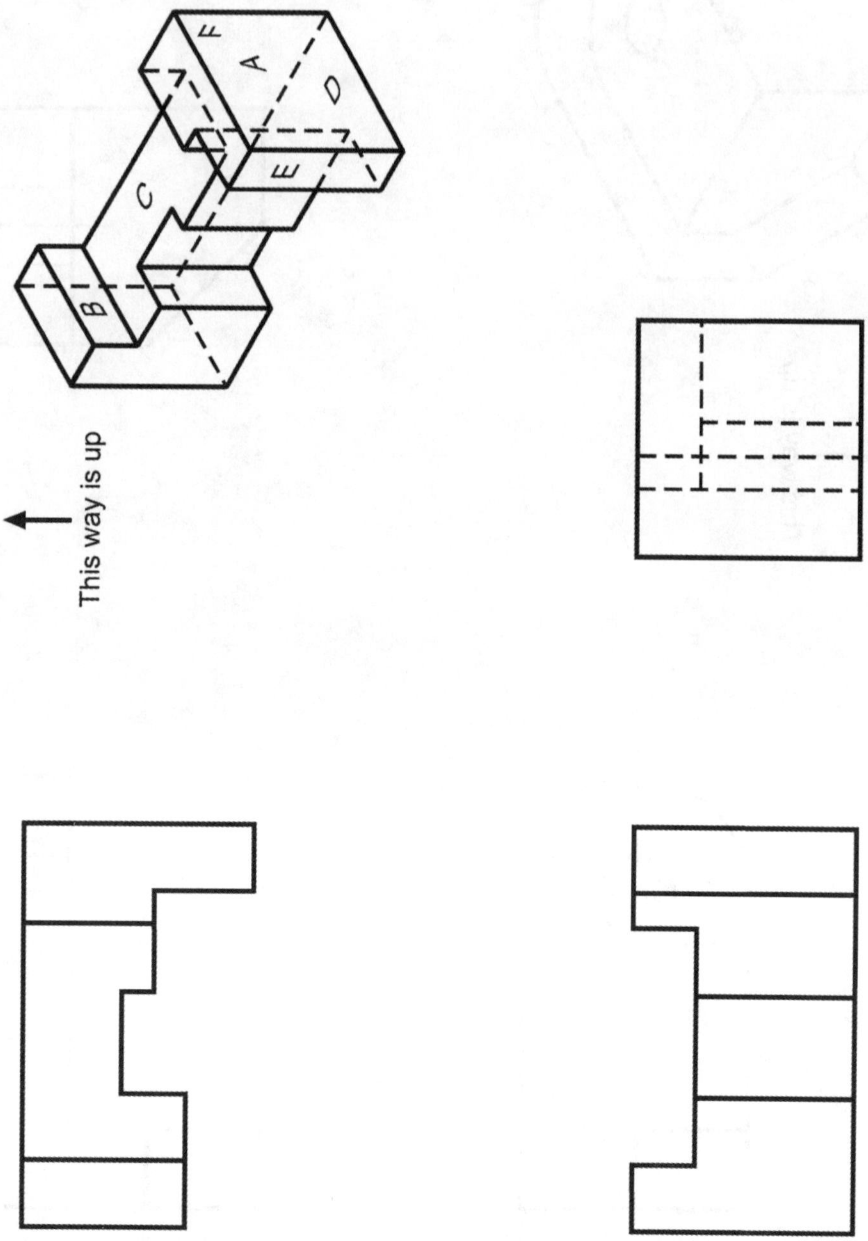

Exercise 10.5-2: Dimensioning 2

Name: ______________________________ Date: _____________

Dimension the following object using proper dimensioning techniques.

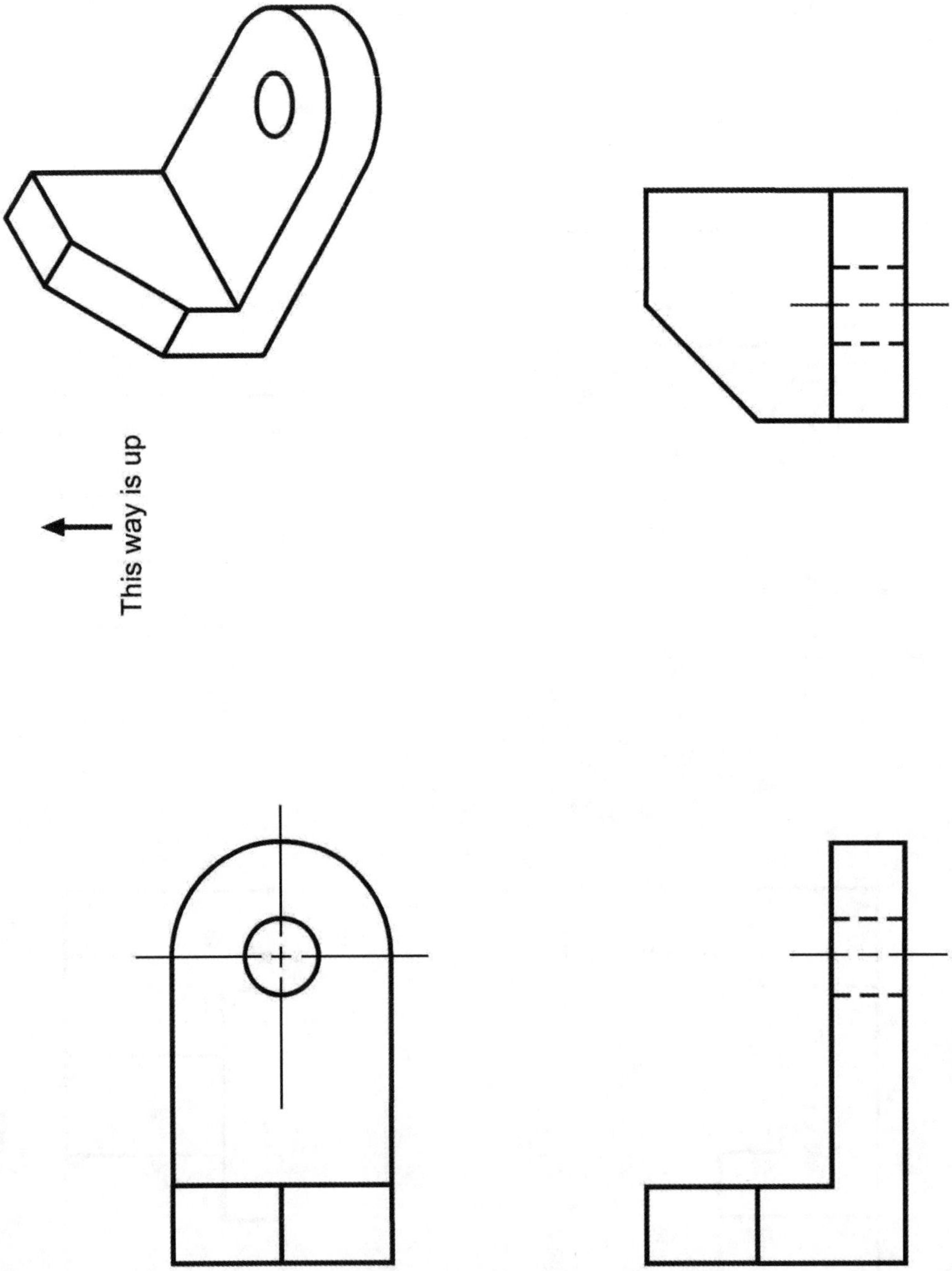

Exercise 10.5-3: Dimensioning 3

Name: ______________________________ Date: ______________

Dimension the following object using proper dimensioning techniques.

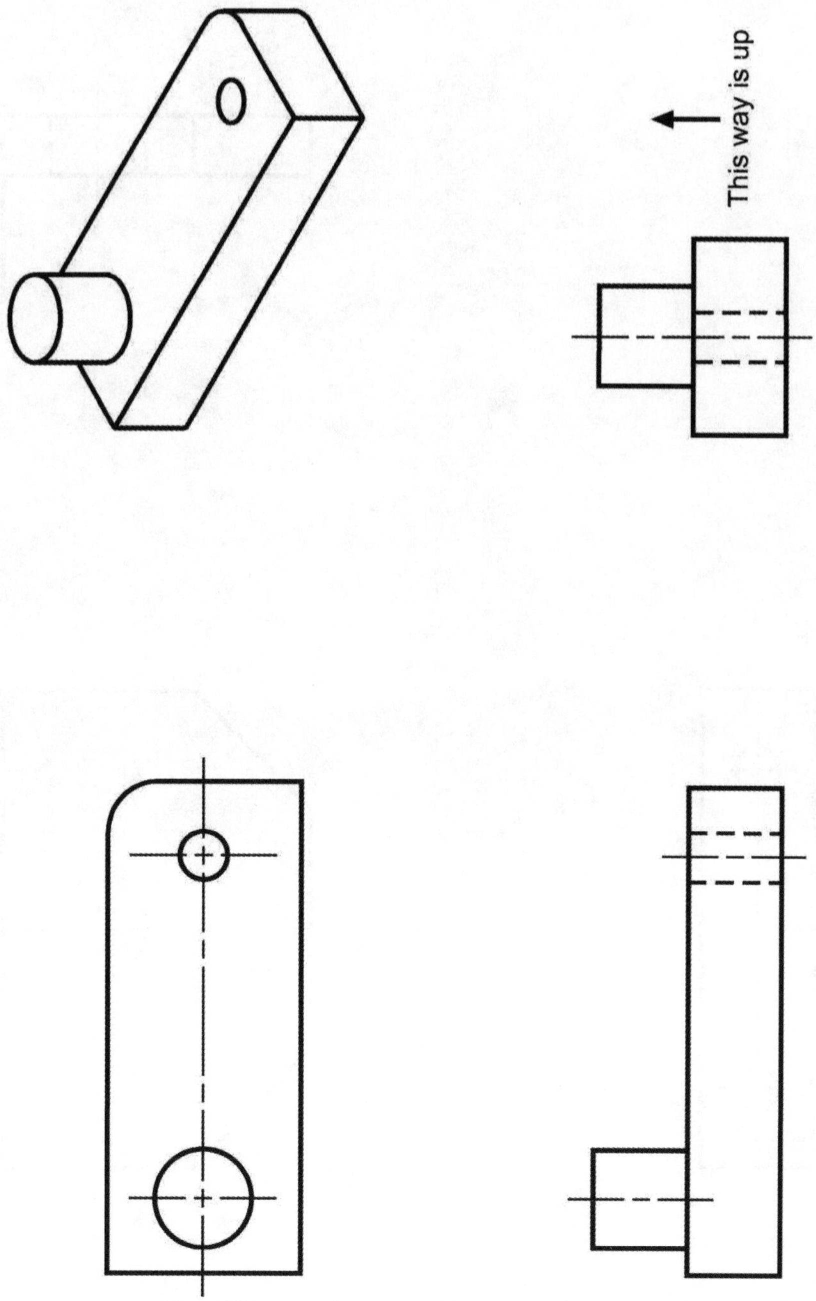

Exercise 10.5-4: Dimensioning 4

Name: ______________________________ Date: ______________

Dimension the following object using proper dimensioning techniques.

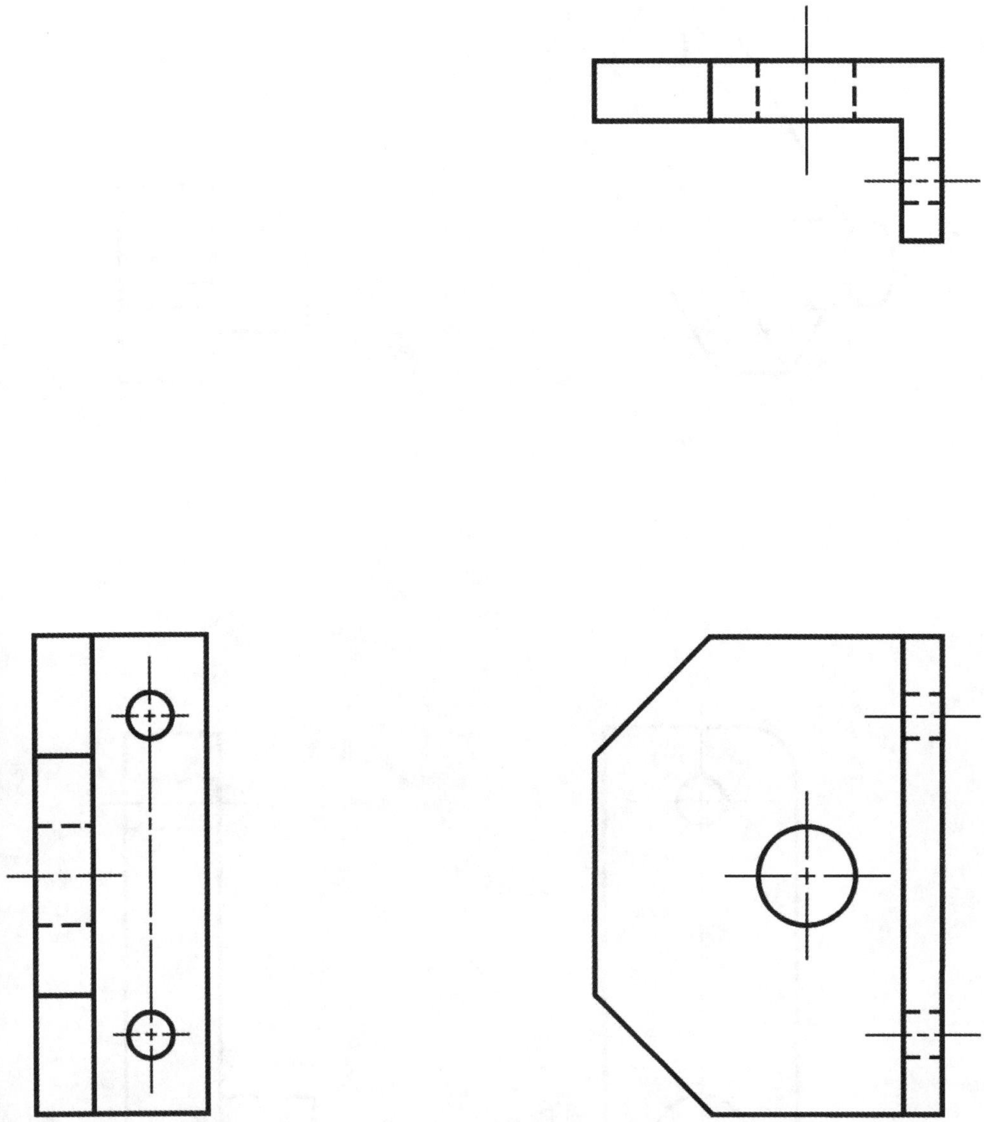

CREATING DIMENSIONS QUESTIONS – SET 1

Name: ______________________________ Date: _____________

Dimension appearance

Q10-1) Dimension and extension lines are thin so that they will not be mistaken for .... lines.

a) visible
b) hidden
c) center
d) cutting plane

Q10-2) All dimension text should be ....

a) vertical
b) horizontal
c) lower case
d) bold

Dimensioning and locating features

Q10-3) Is a complete circle such as a hole dimensioned by its diameter or radius?

Q10-4) The size of a slot radius is given in the radius dimension. (True, False)

Q10-5) A _______ is located in the circular view. (Circle all that apply.)

a) hole
b) cylinder

Q10-6) The diameter of a _______ is given in the circular view. (Circle all that apply.)

a) hole
b) cylinder

Dimensioning Rules

Q10-7) All dimensions should be placed on the view where the shape is best described. (True, False)

Q10-8) It is acceptable to duplicate the same dimension on multiple views to ensure clarity. (True, False)

Q10-9) Dimensioning hidden lines under some circumstances is allowed. (True, False)

Dimensioning/manufacturing

Q10-10) Datum dimensioning is preferred over continuous dimensions because it ...

a) reduces dimensioning time.
b) reduces error build up.
c) increases calculation time.
d) increases set up time.

Q10-11) A surface of the part that touches the datum plane is called a ...

a) datum.
b) simulated datum.
c) baseline.
d) datum feature.

Q10-12) Non-critical inch dimensions usually have .... decimal places.

a) 0
b) 1
c) 2
d) 3

Q10-13) Non-critical mm dimensions usually have .... decimal places. (Circle all that apply.)

a) 0
b) 1
c) 2
d) 3

CREATING DIMENSIONS QUESTIONS – SET 2

Name: ______________________________ Date: ____________

Dimension appearance

Q10-14) Leader lines should not be … (Choose all that apply.)

a) horizontal.
b) straight.
c) curved.
d) vertical.

Q10-15) Lettering should measure ….. on the printed drawing.

a) 2 mm
b) 3 mm
c) 4 mm
d) 5 mm

Dimensioning and locating features

Q10-16) Write the dimension text for 3 repeated holes with a diameter of 10 mm.

Q10-17) Write the dimension text for a 2 mm chamfer dimension with equal sides.

Q10-18) Write the dimension text for a 1/2 inch blind hole that is 1 inch deep.

Q10-19) Write the dimension text for a counterbore that has a 1/4 inch drill and a 1/2 in counterbore that is 1/2 inch deep.

Q10-20) Write the dimension text for a countersink that has a 10 mm drill and a countersink that has a maximum diameter of 20 mm with a 90 degree angle.

Dimensioning Rules

Q10-21) Dimension lines should never cross extension lines. (True, False)

Q10-22) Dimensions should be placed inside the object if space allows. (True, False)

Q10-23) Which of the following is NOT a general rule for dimensioning?

a. Avoid dimensioning to hidden lines
b. Place dimensions between views if possible
c. Use the fewest number of dimensions to describe the object
d. Include redundant dimensions to ensure accuracy

Q10-24) Where should overall dimensions typically be placed?

a. Closest to the object
b. Inside the object's boundaries
c. Farthest from the object
d. Next to hidden lines

Dimensioning/manufacturing

Q10-25) How many zeros to the right of the decimal does two thousandths of an inch have?

Q10-26) (Continuous, Datum) dimensioning is preferred to minimize error build up. (Circle the appropriate answer.)

CREATING DIMENSIONS PROBLEMS

Name: ______________________________ Date: ______________

P10-1) The following object is dimensioned incorrectly. Identify the incorrect dimensions and list all mistakes associated with them. Then, dimension the object correctly using proper dimensioning techniques. There are five mistakes.

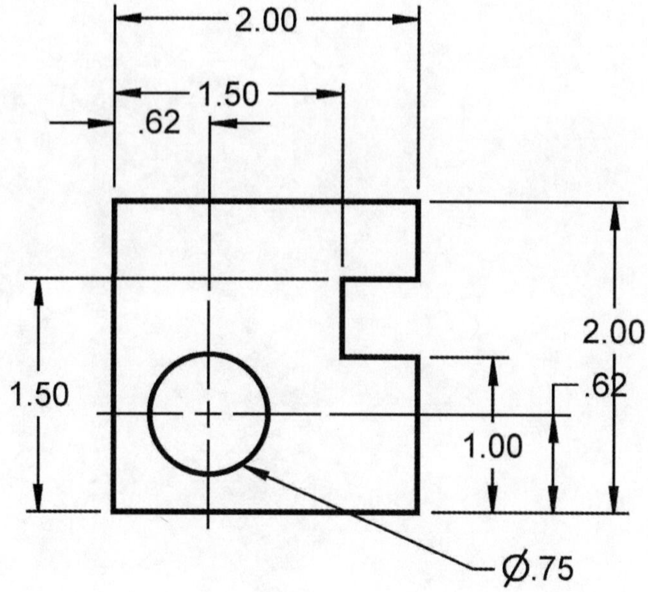

1)

2)

3)

4)

5)

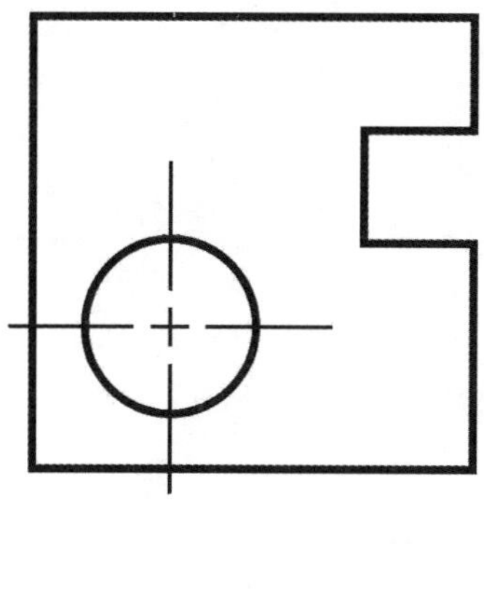

NOTES:

Name: ______________________________ Date: _____________

P10-2) The following object is dimensioned incorrectly. Identify the incorrect dimensions and list all mistakes associated with them. Then, dimension the object correctly using proper dimensioning techniques. There are four mistakes.

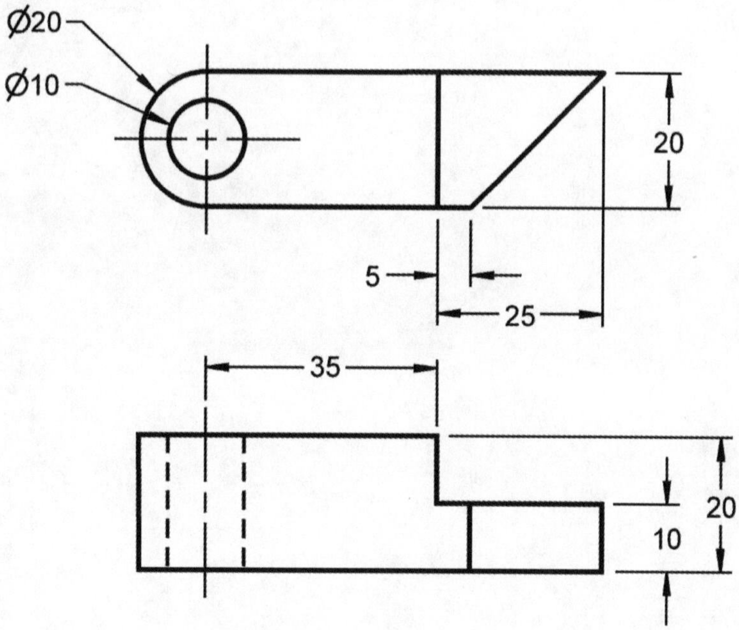

1)

2)

3)

4)

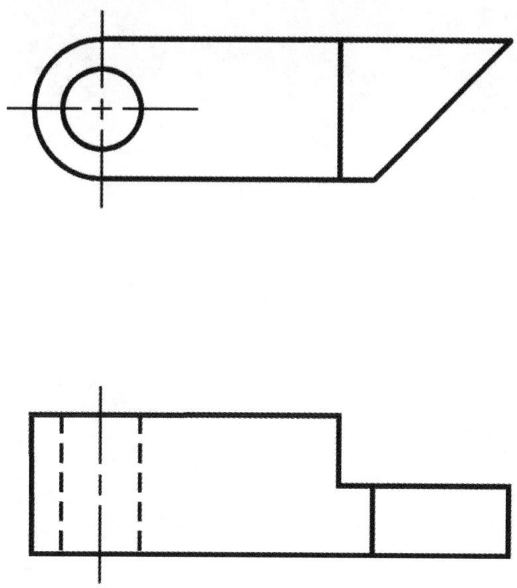

NOTES:

Name: ______________________________ Date: ______________

P10-3) The following object is dimensioned incorrectly. Identify the incorrect dimensions and list all mistakes associated with them. Then, dimension the object correctly using proper dimensioning techniques. There are six mistakes.

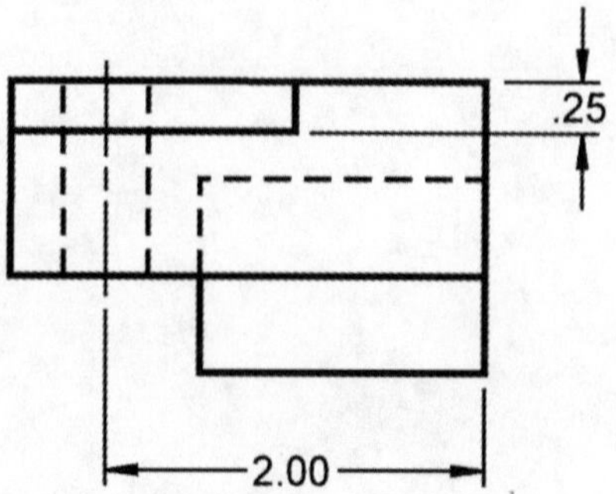

1)

2)

3)

4)

5)

6)

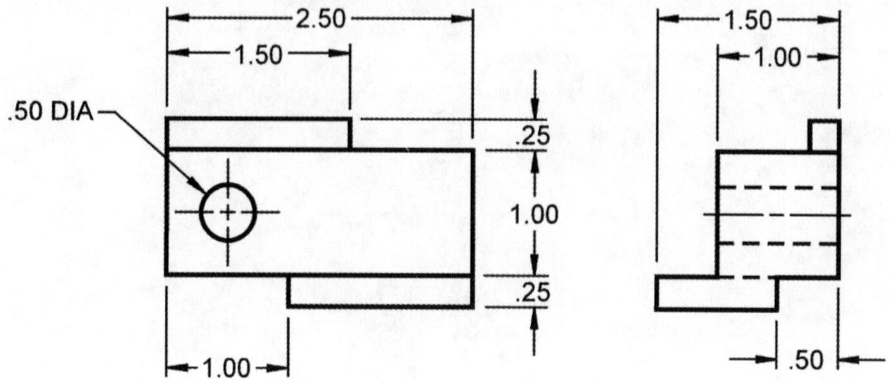

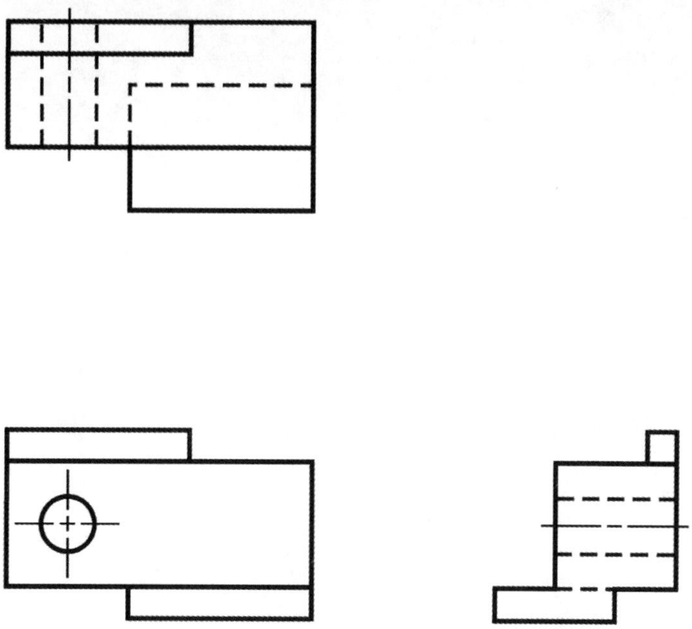

NOTES:

Name: ______________________________ Date: _____________

P10-4) The following object is dimensioned incorrectly. Identify the incorrect dimensions and list all mistakes associated with them. Then, dimension the object correctly using proper dimensioning techniques. There are four mistakes.

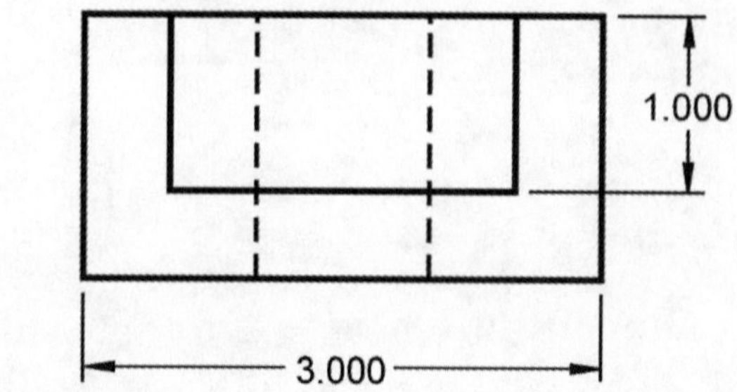

1)

2)

3)

4)

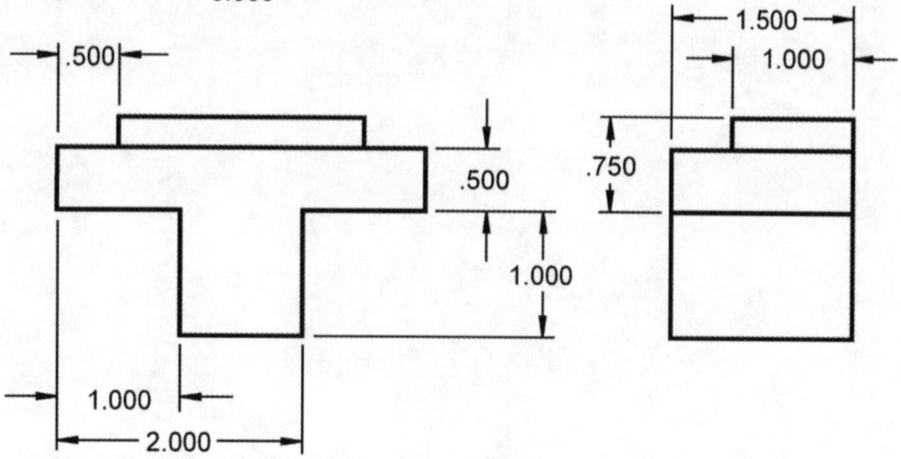

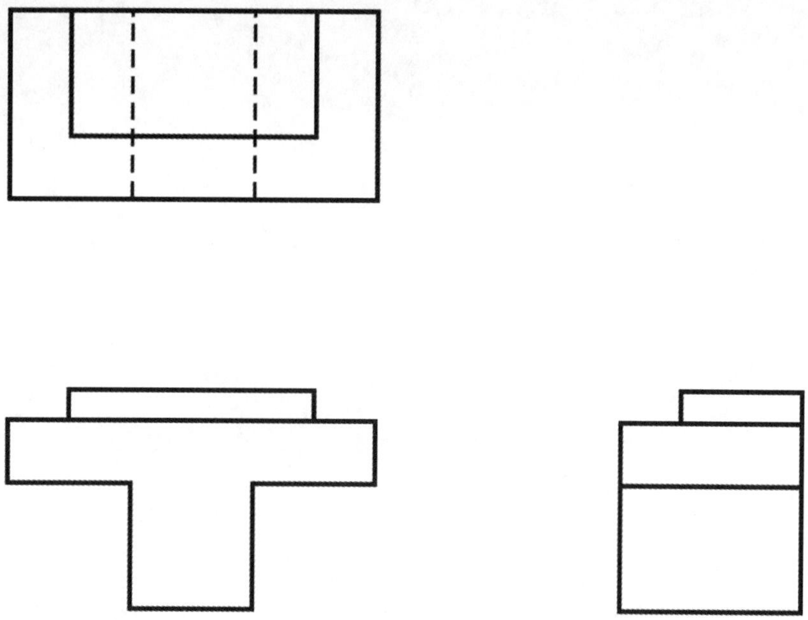

NOTES:

Name: ______________________________ Date: ______________

P10-5) The following object is dimensioned incorrectly. Identify the incorrect dimensions and list all mistakes associated with them. Then, dimension the object correctly using proper dimensioning techniques. There are five mistakes.

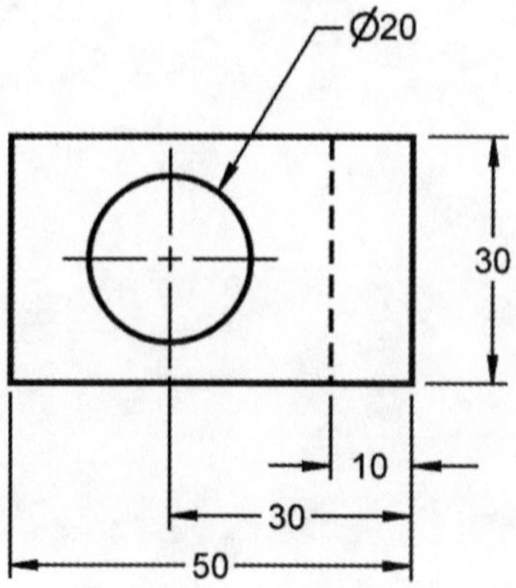

1)

2)

3)

4)

5)

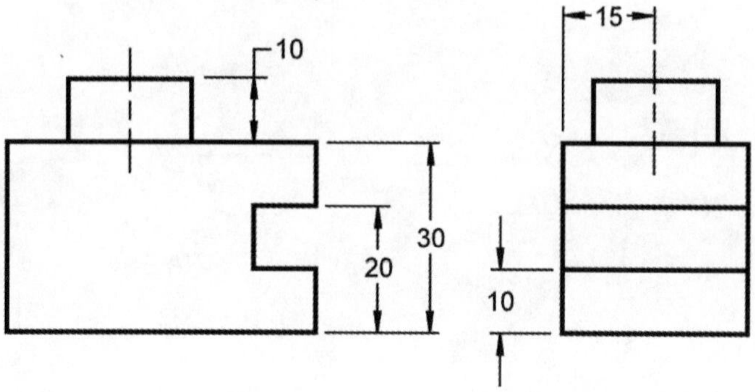

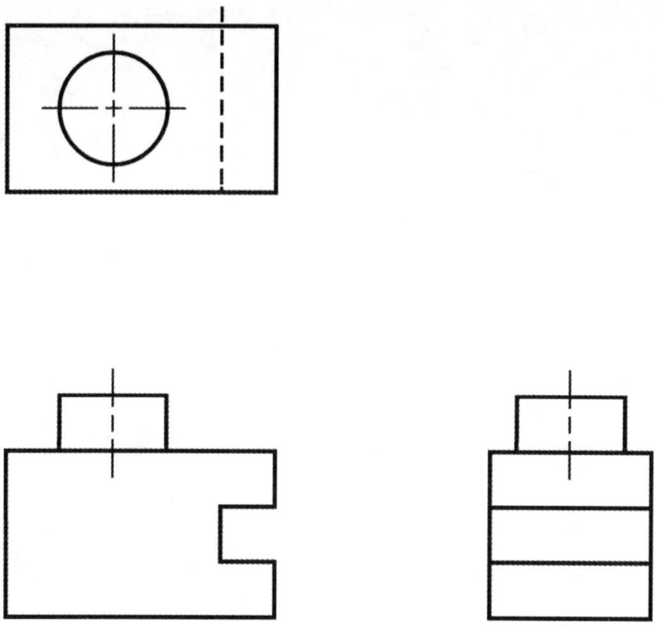

NOTES:

Name: ______________________________ Date: ______________

P10-6) Completely dimension the objects shown (by hand) using proper dimensioning techniques. Wherever a numerical dimension value is required, place an 'x' or make up a number. Use dimensioning symbols where necessary.

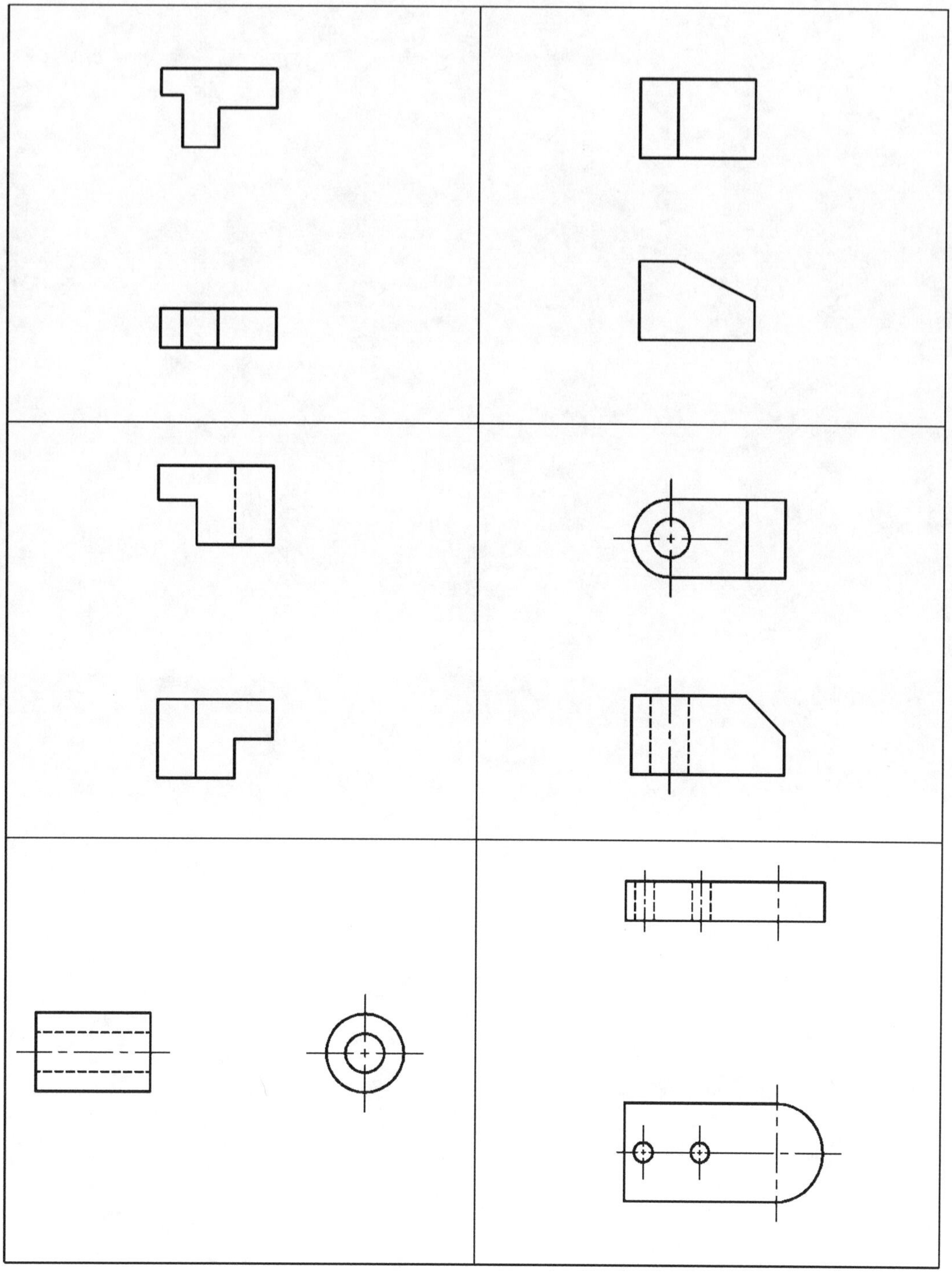

NOTES:

Name: ______________________________ Date: ______________

P10-7) Completely dimension the objects shown (by hand) using proper dimensioning techniques. Wherever a numerical dimension value is required, place an 'x' or make up a number. Use dimensioning symbols where necessary.

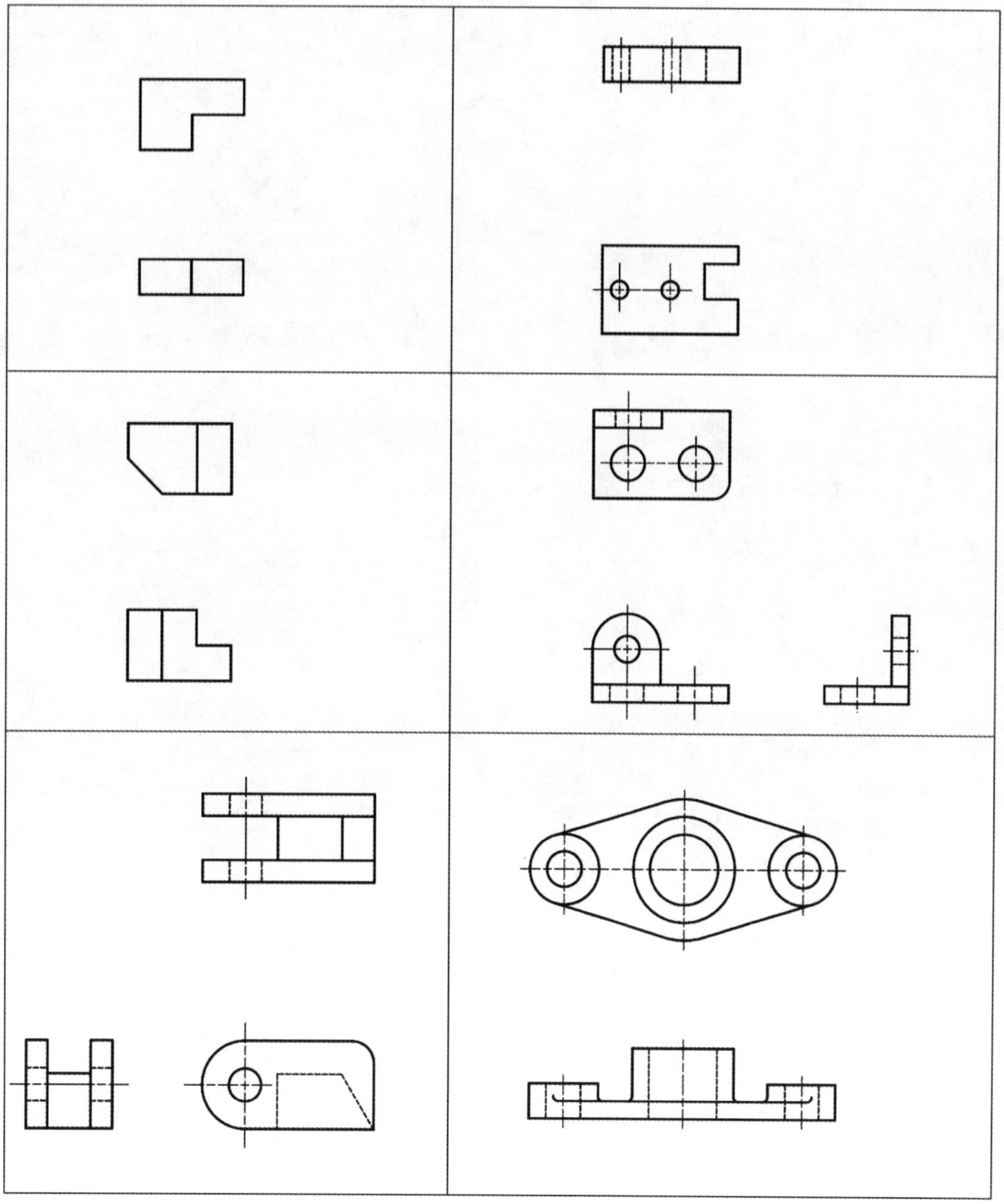

NOTES:

Name: ______________________________ Date: _____________

P10-8) Completely dimension the objects shown (by hand) using proper dimensioning techniques. Wherever a numerical dimension value is required, place an ‘x’ or make up a number. Use dimensioning symbols where necessary.

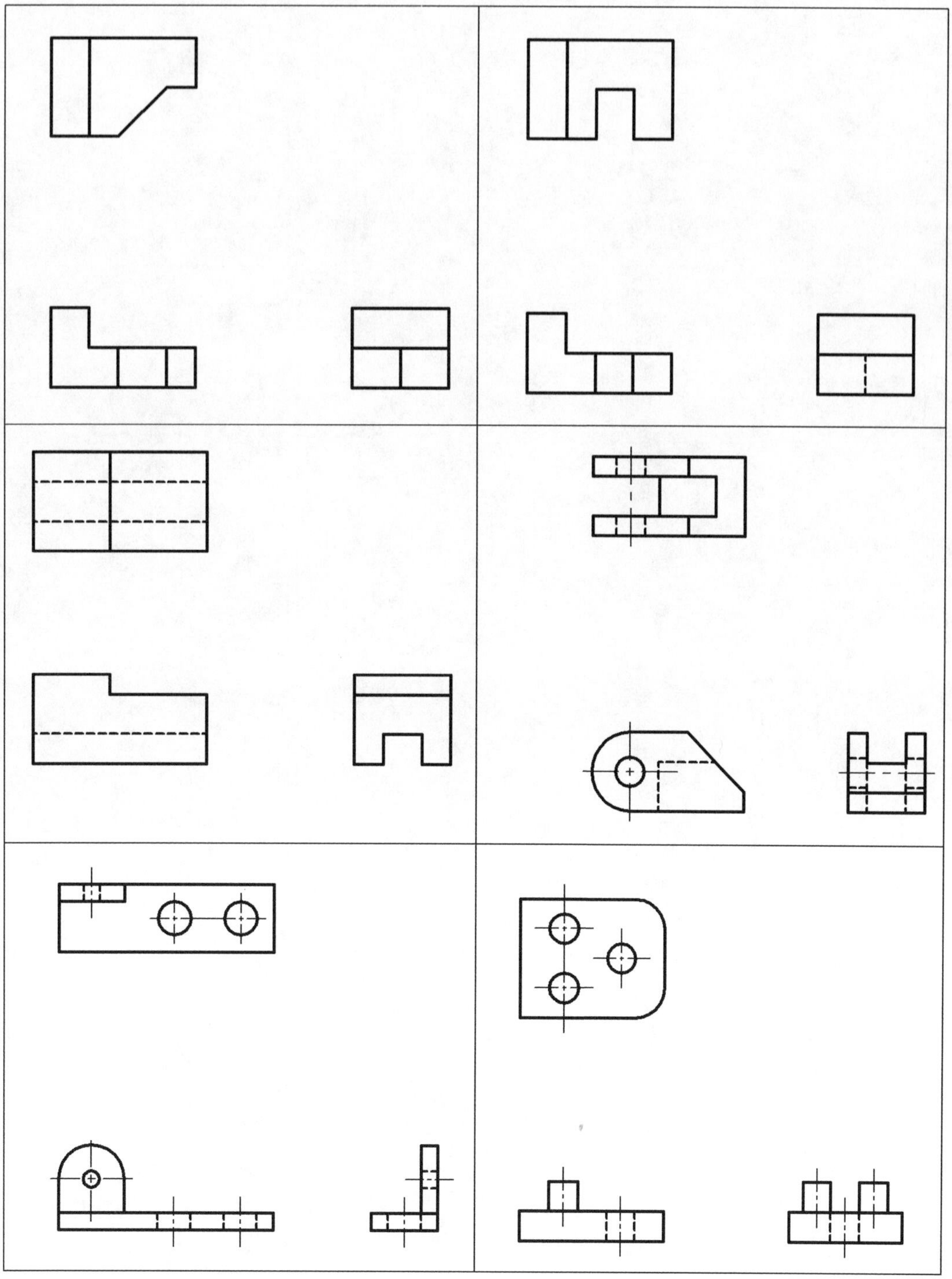

NOTES:

Name: ______________________________ Date: _____________

P10-9) Completely dimension the objects shown (by hand) using proper dimensioning techniques. Wherever a numerical dimension value is required, place an 'x' or make up a number. Use dimensioning symbols where necessary.

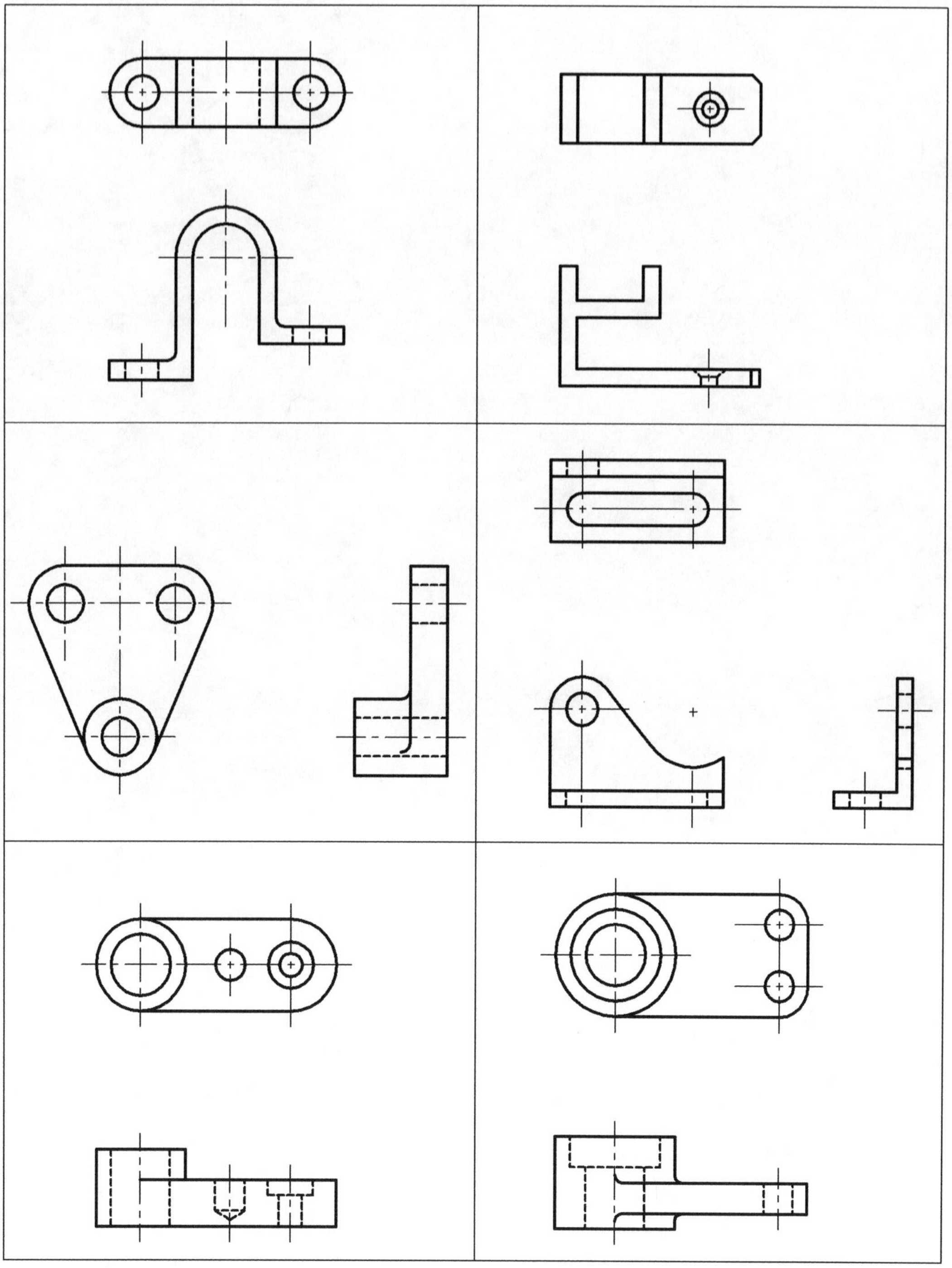

NOTES:

P10-10) Draw the necessary views and completely dimension the part shown. Do not base your 2-D dimension placement on the 3-D dimensions shown. Use proper dimensioning techniques to dimension your object.

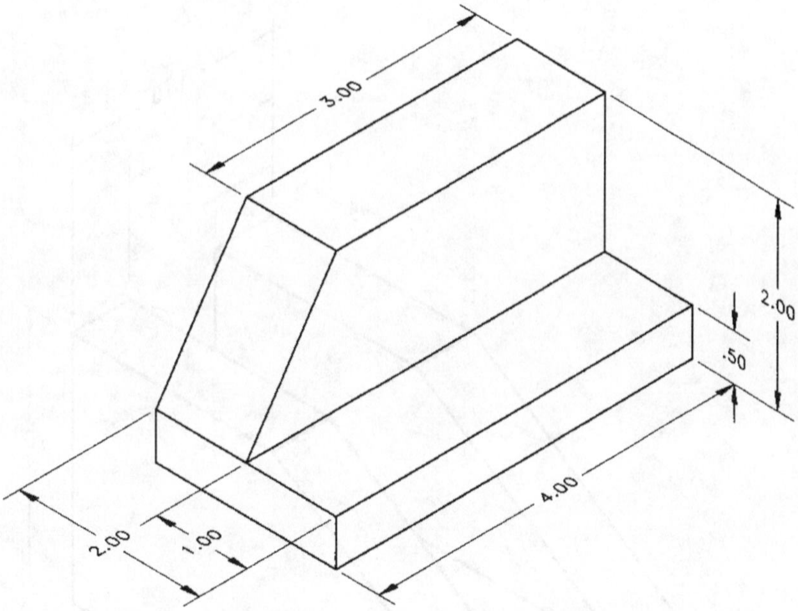

P10-11) Draw the necessary views and completely dimension the part shown. Do not base your 2-D dimension placement on the 3-D dimensions shown. Use proper dimensioning techniques to dimension your object.

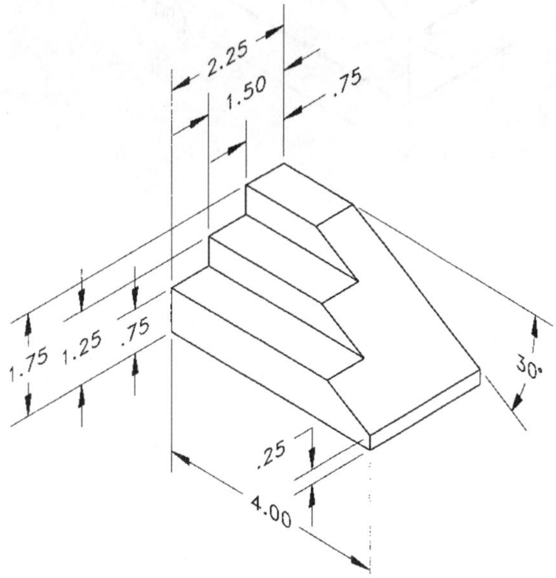

P10-12) Draw the necessary views and completely dimension the part shown. Do not base your 2-D dimension placement on the 3-D dimensions shown. Use proper dimensioning techniques to dimension your object.

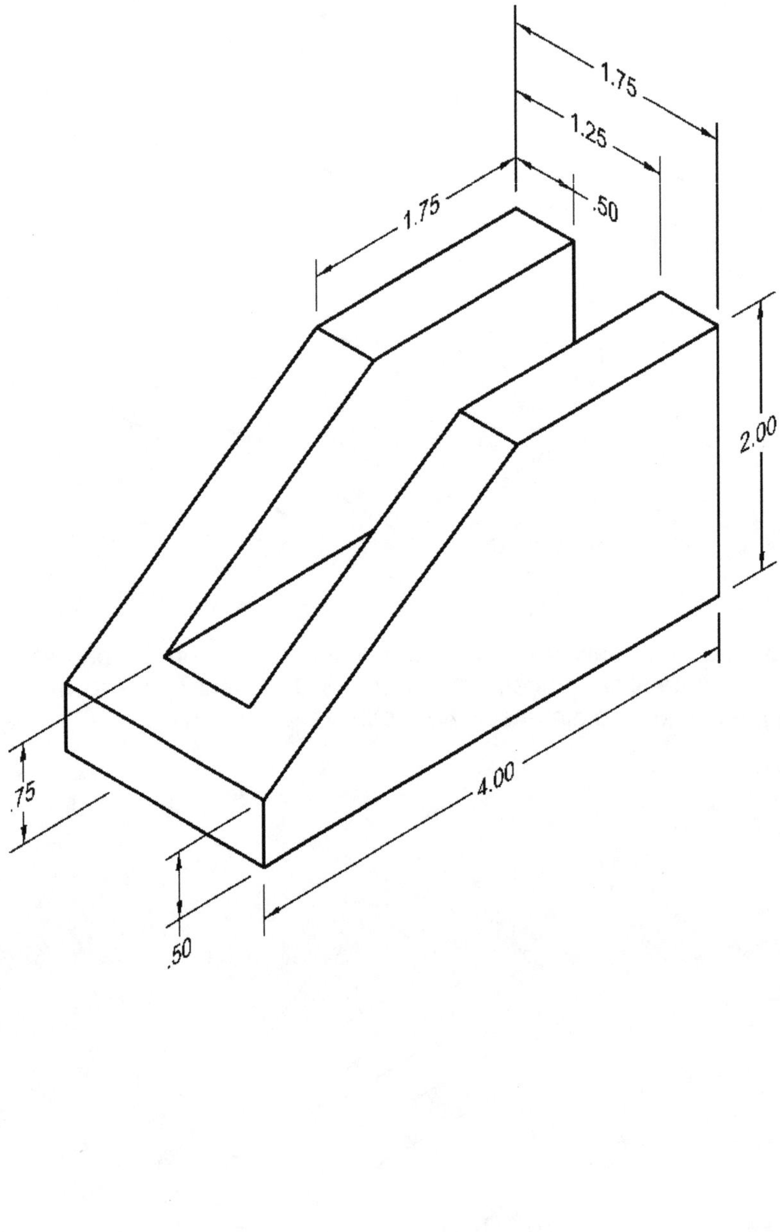

P10-13) Draw the necessary views and completely dimension the part shown. Do not base your 2-D dimension placement on the 3-D dimensions shown. Use proper dimensioning techniques to dimension your object.

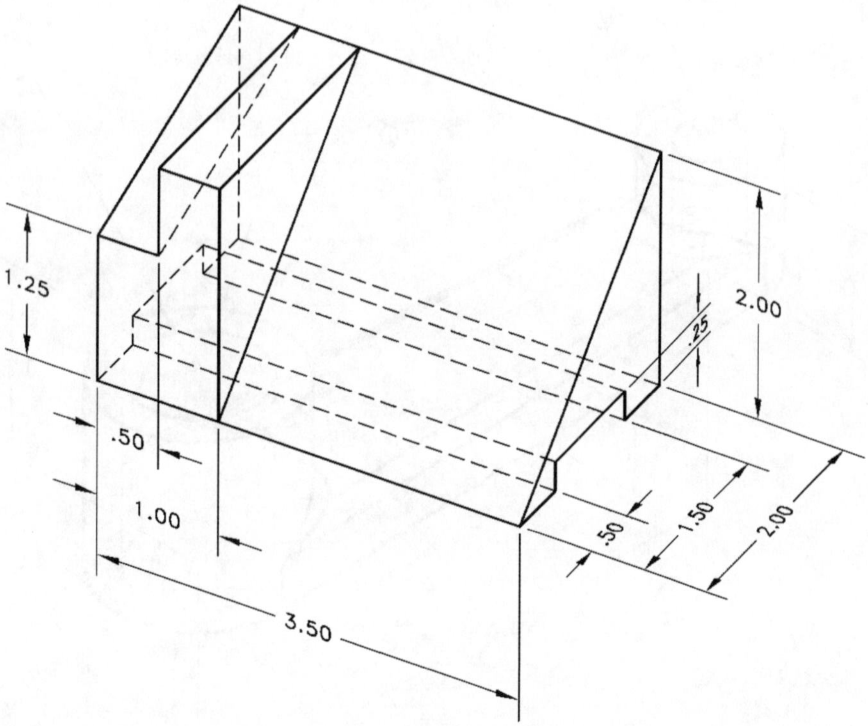

P10-14) Draw the necessary views and completely dimension the part shown. Do not base your 2-D dimension placement on the 3-D dimensions shown. Use proper dimensioning techniques to dimension your object.

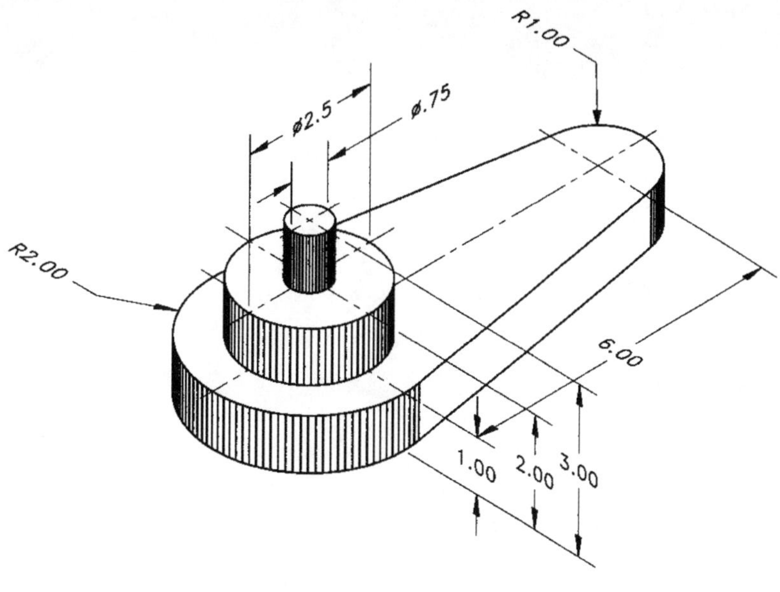

P10-15) Draw the necessary views and completely dimension the part shown. Do not base your 2-D dimension placement on the 3-D dimensions shown. Use proper dimensioning techniques to dimension your object.

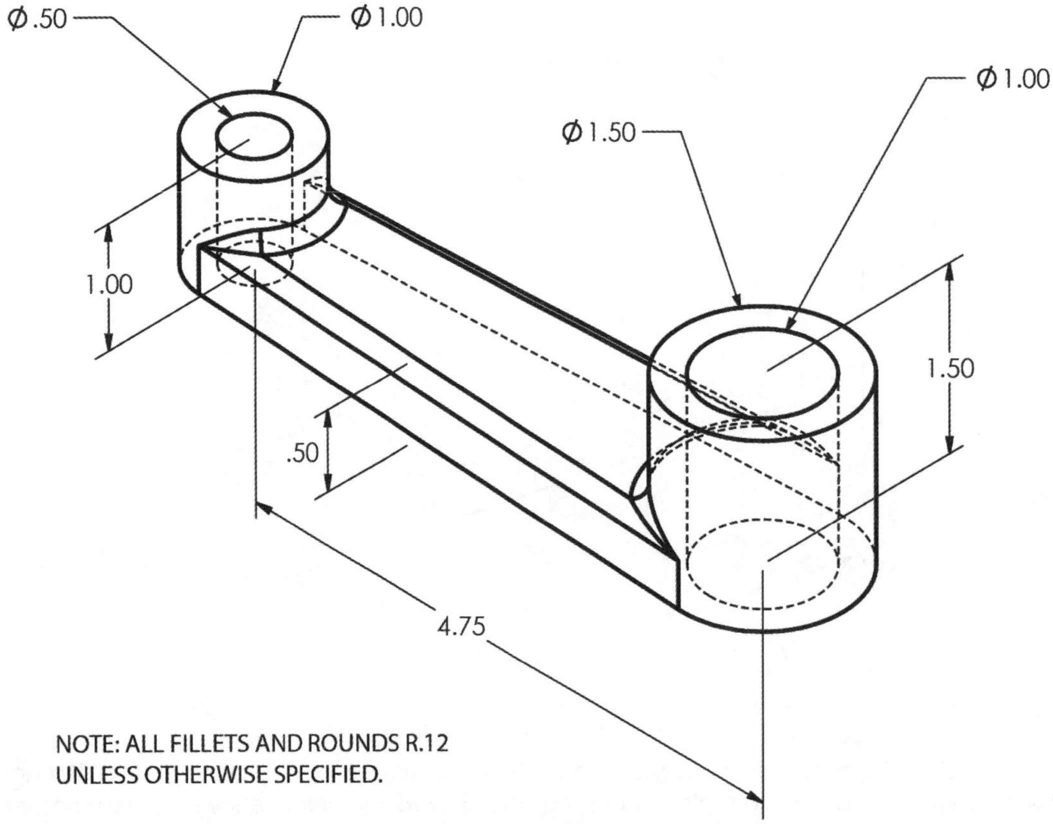

P10-16) Draw the necessary views and completely dimension the part shown. Do not base your 2-D dimension placement on the 3-D dimensions shown. Use proper dimensioning techniques to dimension your object.

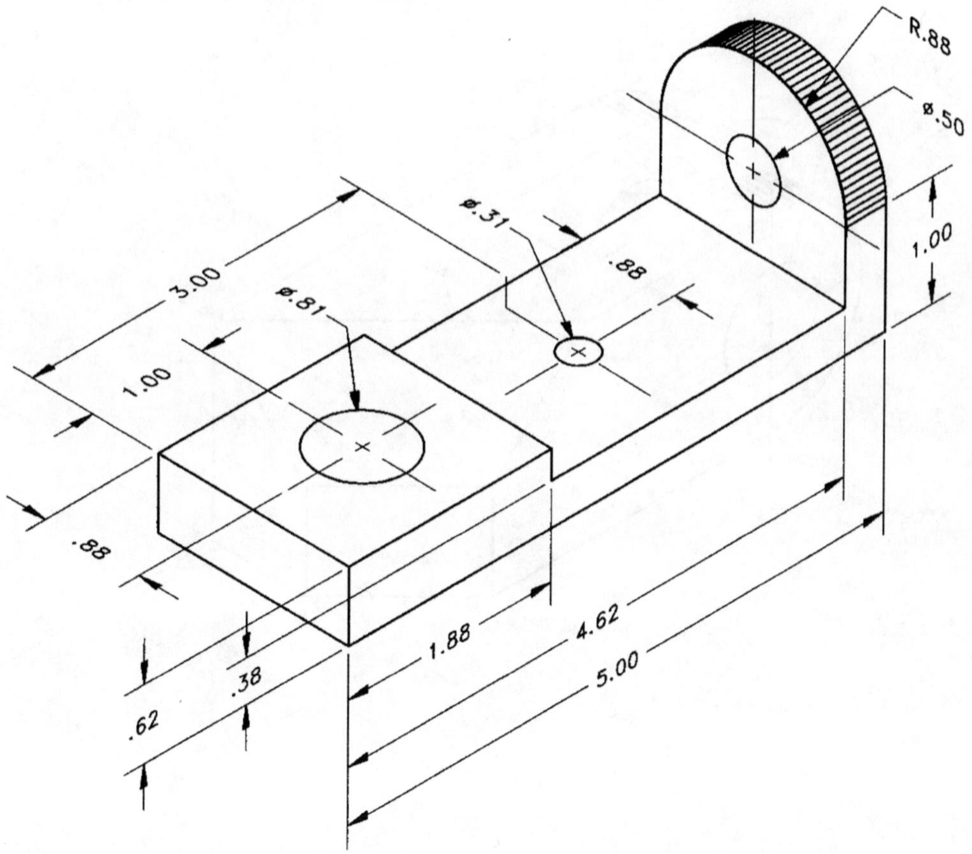

P10-17) Draw the necessary views and completely dimension the part shown. Do not base your 2-D dimension placement on the 3-D dimensions shown. Use proper dimensioning techniques to dimension your object.

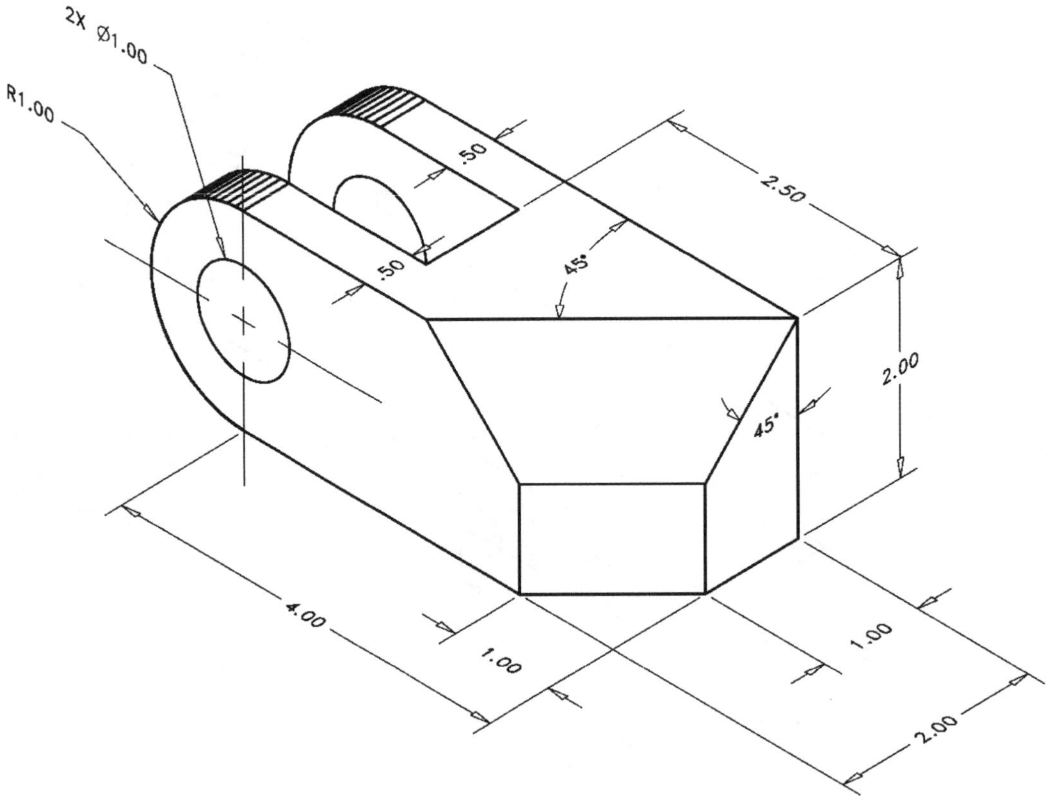

P10-18) Draw the necessary views and completely dimension the part shown. Do not base your 2-D dimension placement on the 3-D dimensions shown. Use proper dimensioning techniques to dimension your object.

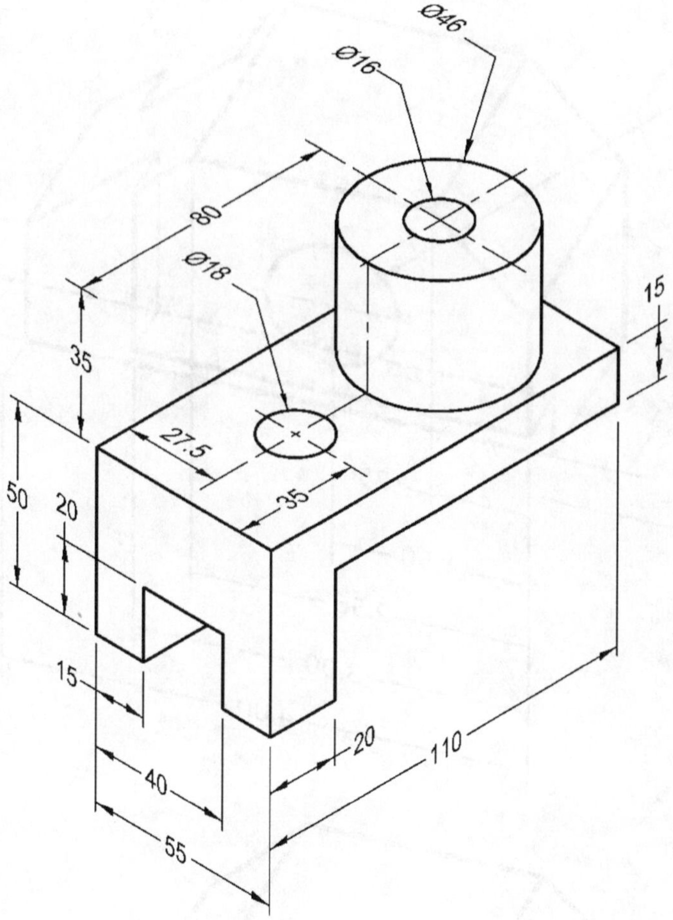

P10-19) Draw the necessary views and completely dimension the part shown. Do not base your 2-D dimension placement on the 3-D dimensions shown. Use proper dimensioning techniques to dimension your object.

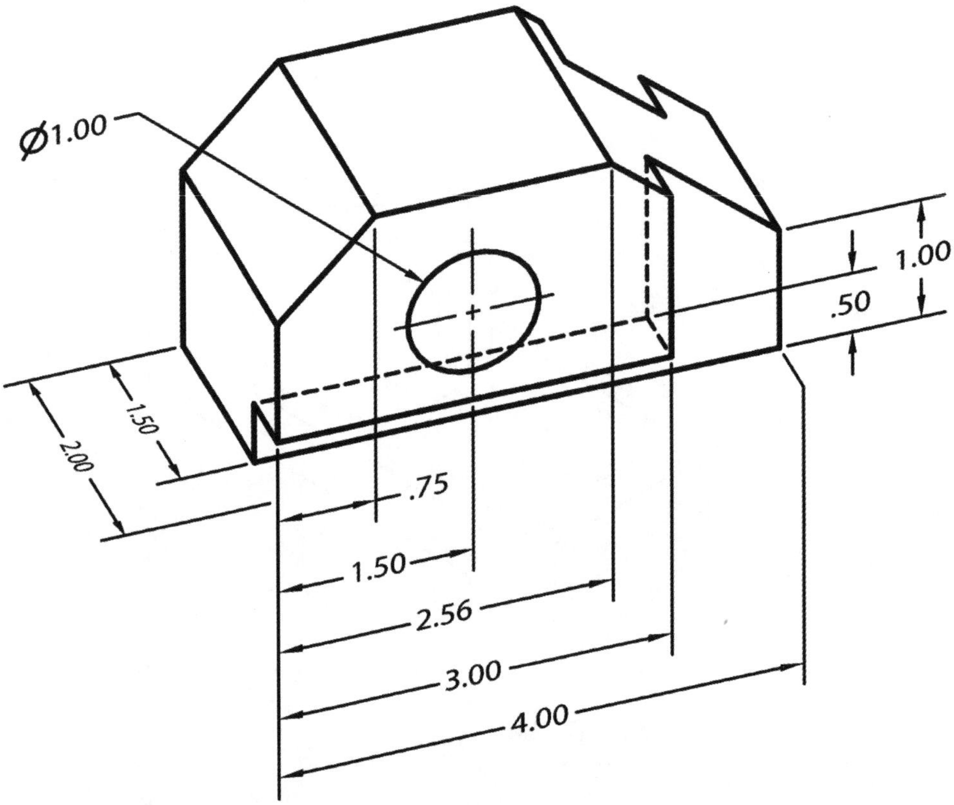

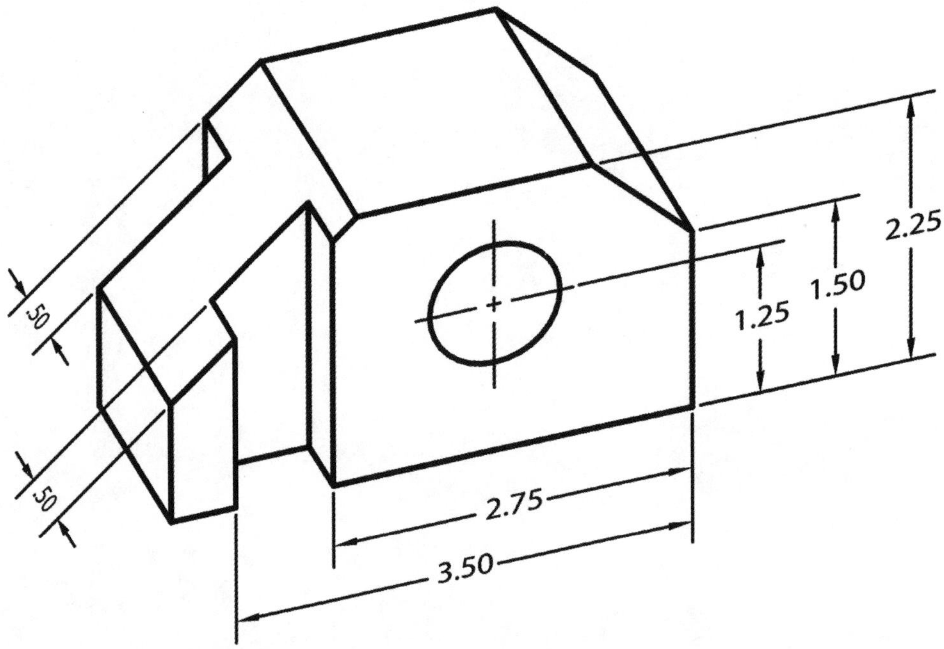

P10-20) Draw the necessary views and completely dimension the part shown. Do not base your 2-D dimension placement on the 3-D dimensions shown. Use proper dimensioning techniques to dimension your object.

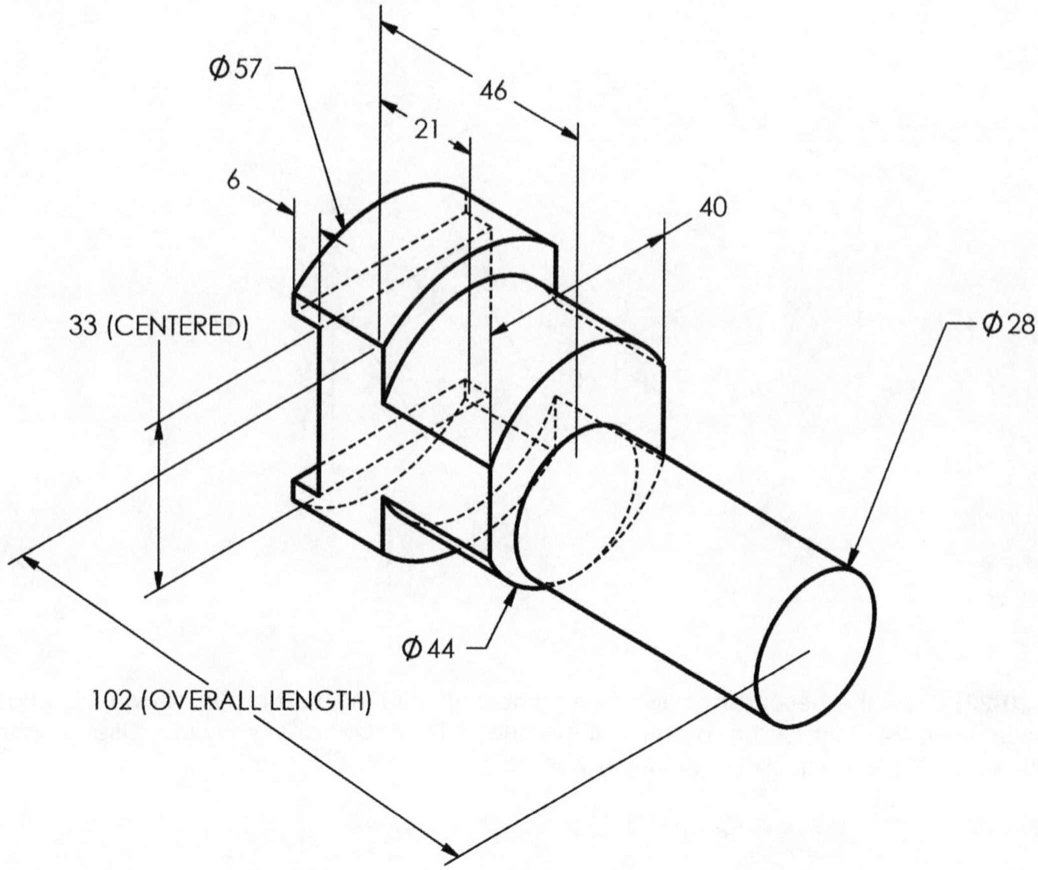

P10-21) Draw the necessary views and completely dimension the part shown. Do not base your 2-D dimension placement on the 3-D dimensions shown. Use proper dimensioning techniques to dimension your object.

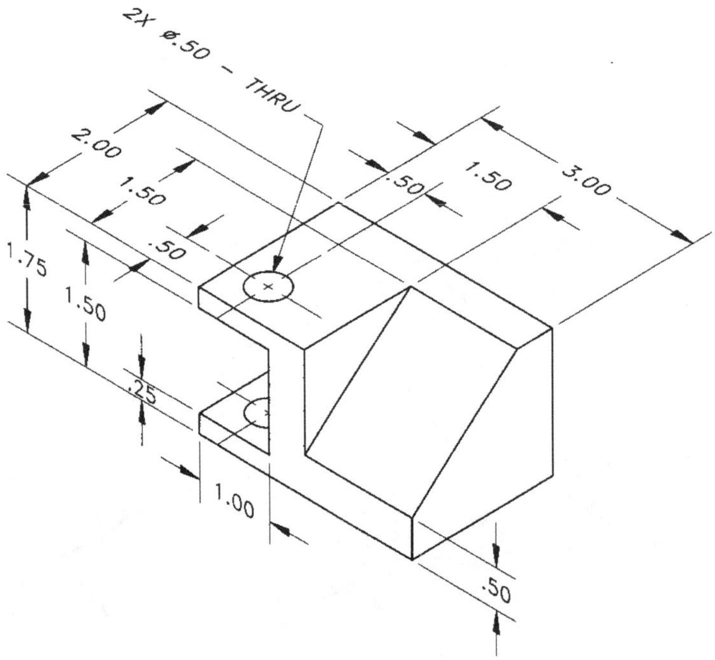

P10-22) Draw the necessary views and completely dimension the part shown. Do not base your 2-D dimension placement on the 3-D dimensions shown. Use proper dimensioning techniques to dimension your object.

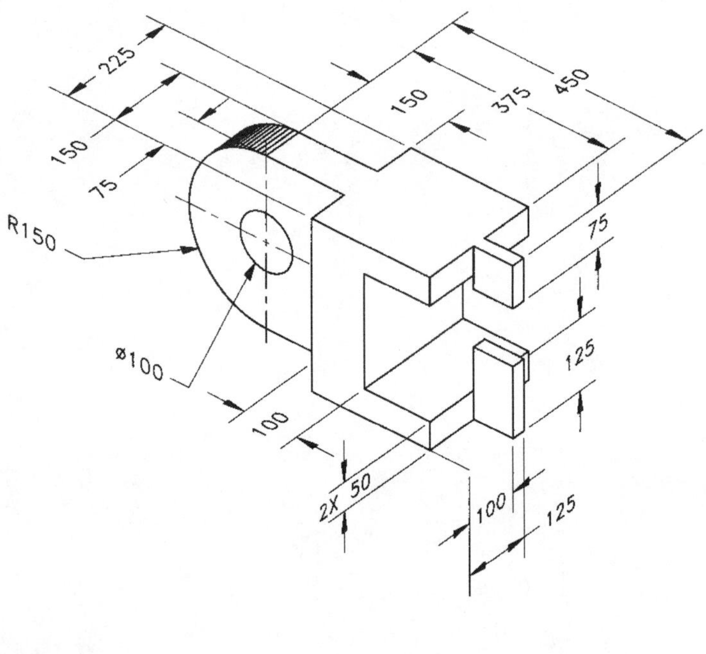

P10-23) Draw the necessary views and completely dimension the part shown. Do not base your 2-D dimension placement on the 3-D dimensions shown. Use proper dimensioning techniques to dimension your object.

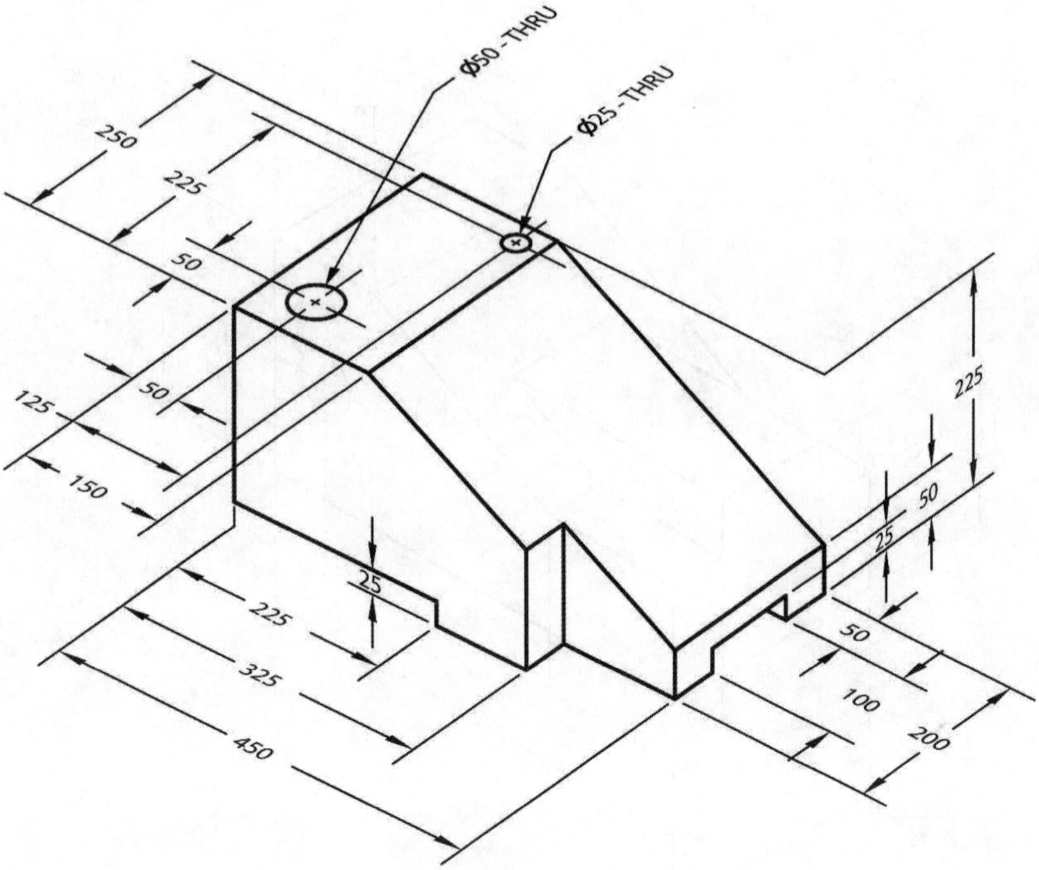

P10-24) Draw the necessary views and completely dimension the part shown. Do not base your 2-D dimension placement on the 3-D dimensions shown. Use proper dimensioning techniques to dimension your object.

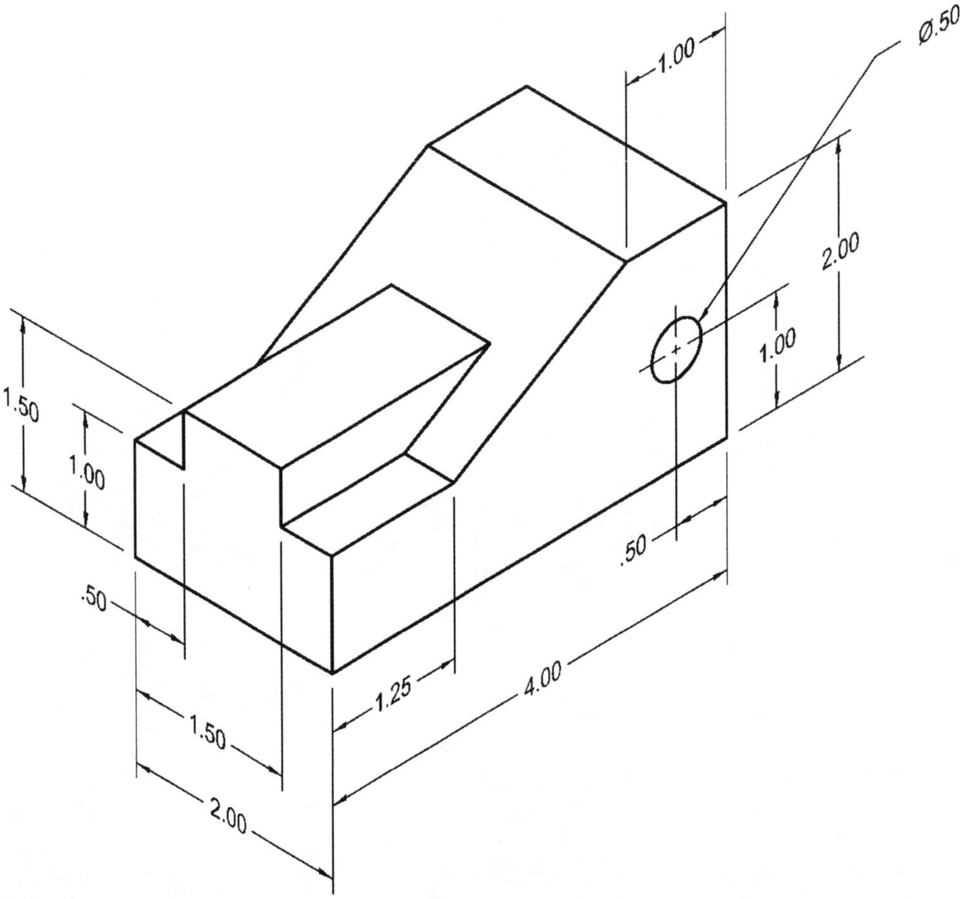

P10-25) Draw the necessary views and completely dimension the part shown. Do not base your 2-D dimension placement on the 3-D dimensions shown. Use proper dimensioning techniques to dimension your object.

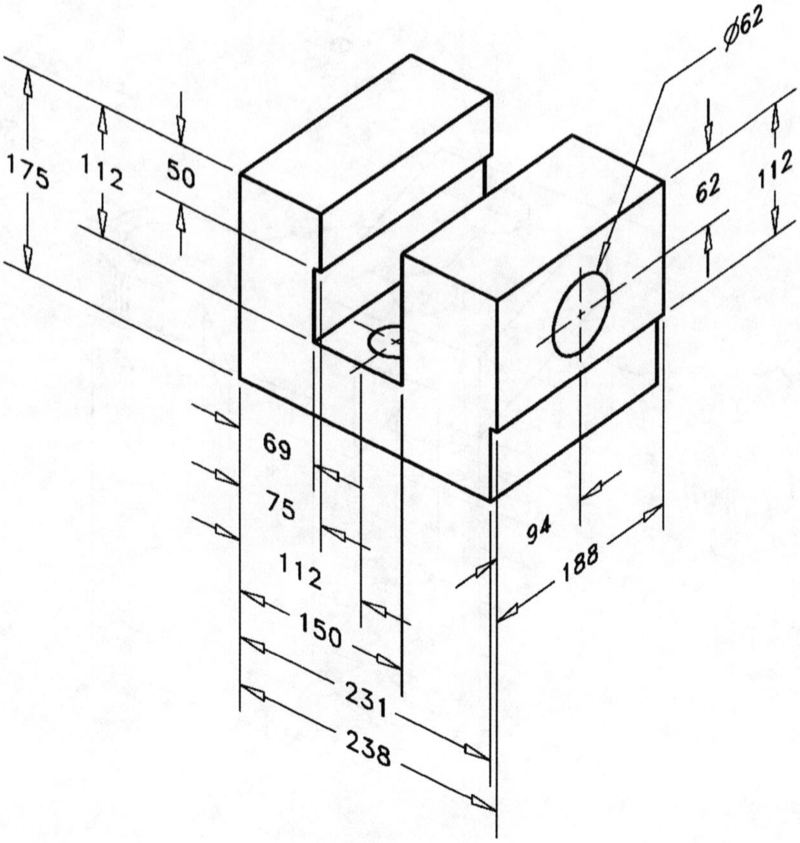

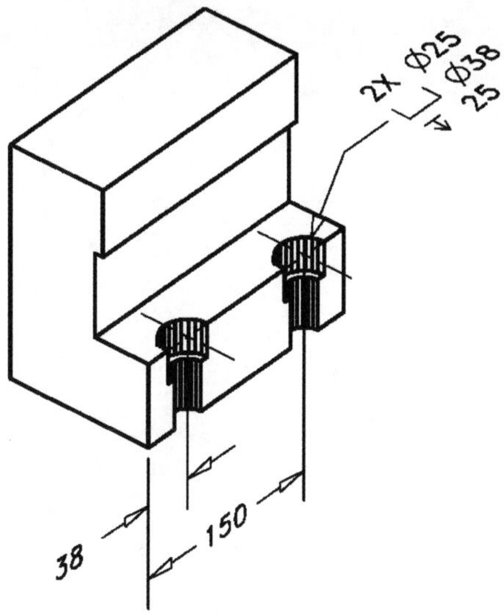

P10-26) Draw the necessary views and completely dimension the part shown. Do not base your 2-D dimension placement on the 3-D dimensions shown. Use proper dimensioning techniques to dimension your object.

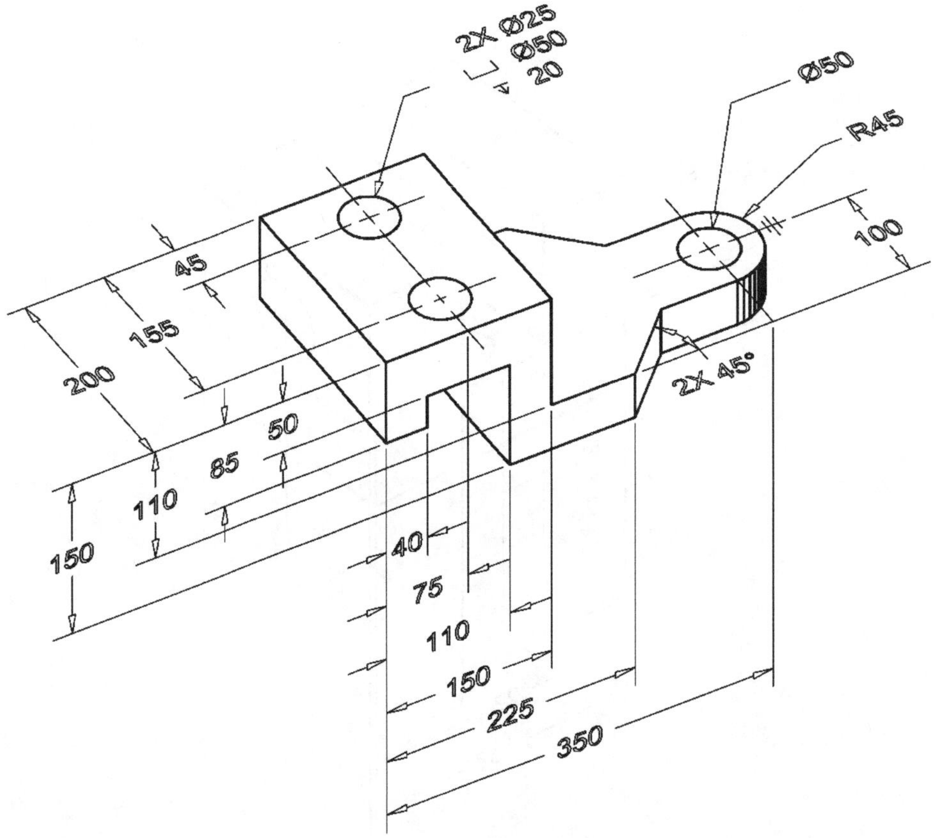

P10-27) Draw the necessary views and completely dimension the part shown. Do not base your 2-D dimension placement on the 3-D dimensions shown. Use proper dimensioning techniques to dimension your object.

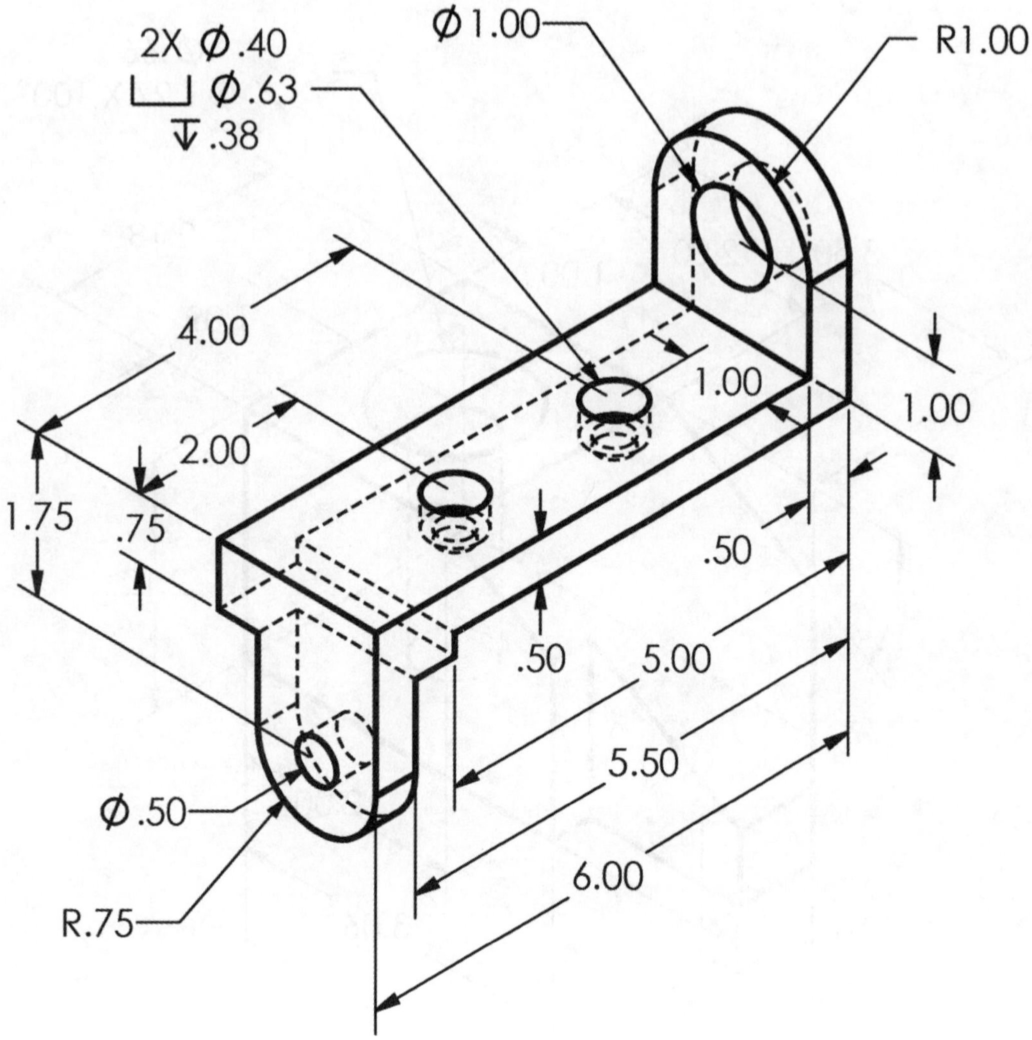

P10-28) Draw the necessary views and completely dimension the part shown. Do not base your 2-D dimension placement on the 3-D dimensions shown. Use proper dimensioning techniques to dimension your object.

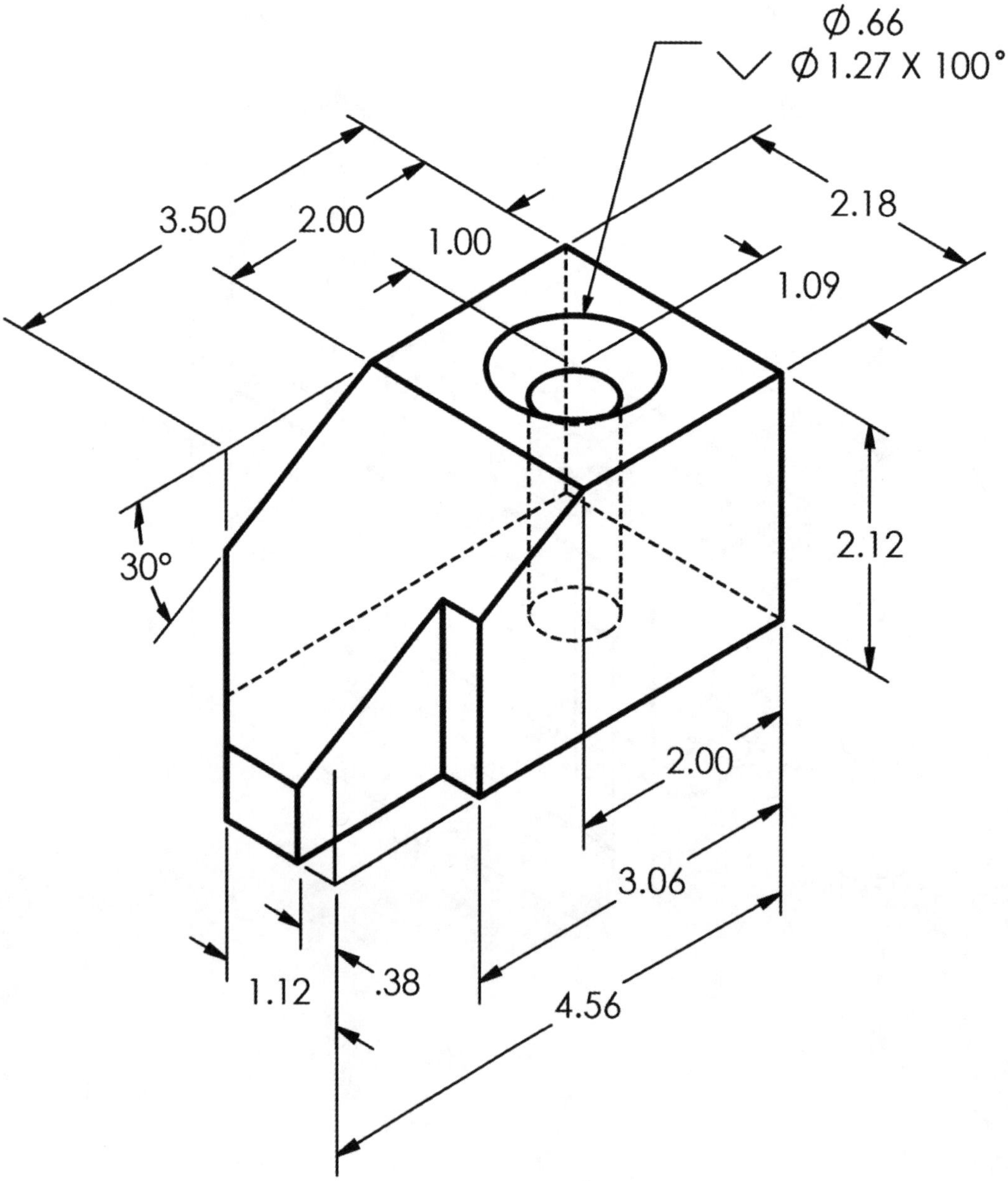

SP10-1) Completely dimension the objects shown (by hand) using proper dimensioning techniques. Wherever a numerical dimension value is required, place an 'x' or make up a number. Use dimensioning symbols where necessary. The answer to this problem is given on the *Independent Learning Content*.

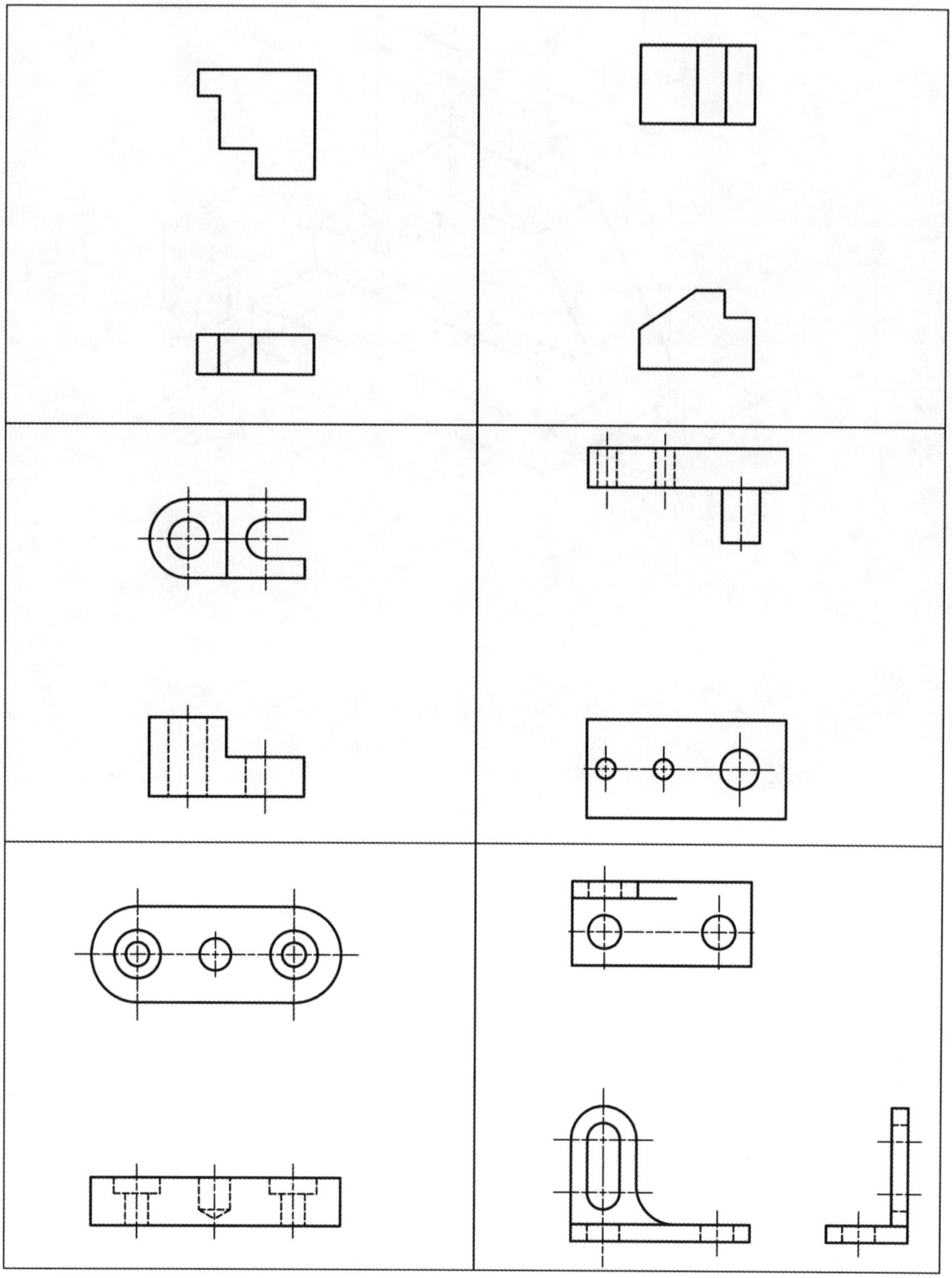

SP10-2) Draw the necessary views and completely dimension the part shown. Do not base your 2-D dimension placement on the 3-D dimensions shown. Use proper dimensioning techniques to dimension your object. The answer to this problem is given on the *Independent Learning Content*.

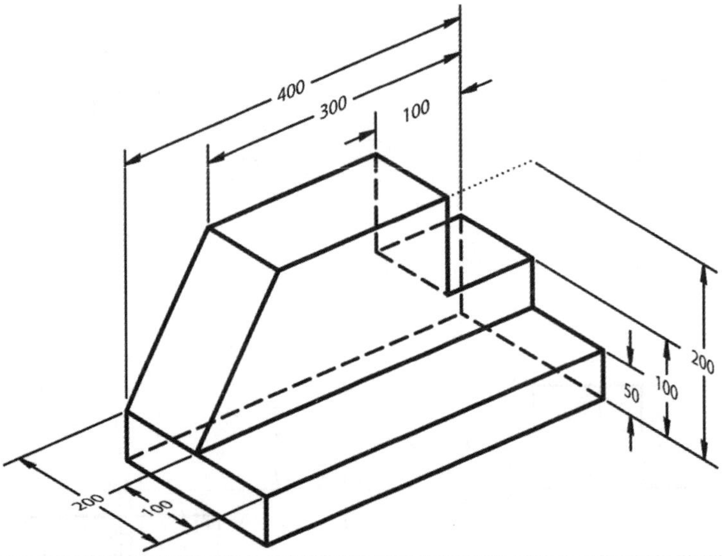

SP10-3) Draw the necessary views and completely dimension the part shown. Do not base your 2-D dimension placement on the 3-D dimensions shown. Use proper dimensioning techniques to dimension your object. The answer to this problem is given on the *Independent Learning Content*.

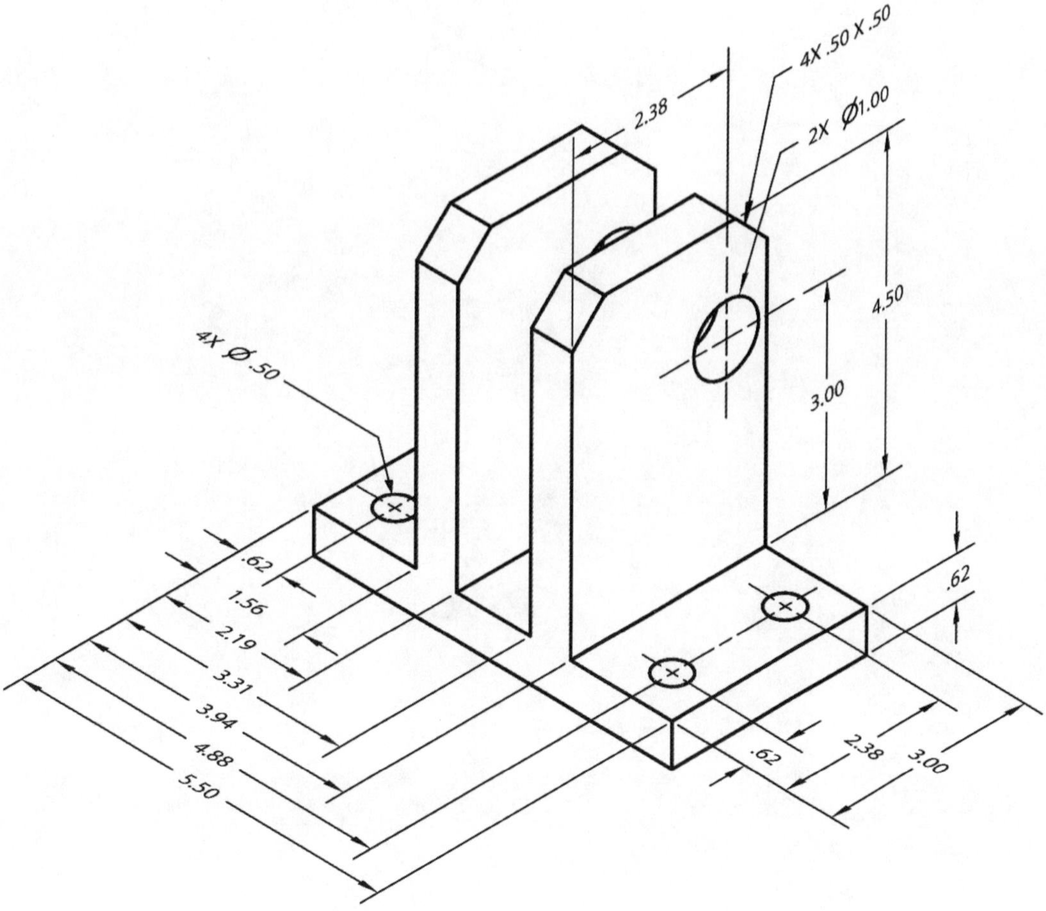

NOTES:

CHAPTER 11

DIMENSIONING IN AUTOCAD®

CHAPTER OUTLINE

CHAPTER SUMMARY

In this chapter you will learn how to dimension a part in AutoCAD®. AutoCAD® makes creating linear, angular, diameter and radius dimensions quite easy. By default, these dimensions are associative. This means that the dimension values change if the geometry they are attached to changes. In order to maintain the associativity between dimension and geometry, it is often necessary to edit the dimension text of more complex features after the dimension has been created. By the end of this chapter, you will be able to create, place and edit dimensions using a predefined dimensioning style.

11.1) INTRODUCTION

Dimensioning a part in AutoCAD® is quite automated. It is as easy as selecting the geometry you wish to dimension and then selecting the dimension's location. AutoCAD® will create the dimension lines, extension lines, arrow heads and dimension text. This is both good and bad. It makes dimensioning an object very fast. However, new users may find it frustrating when trying to fine tune the dimension settings to achieve dimensions that look just the way they want them to look. Dimension appearance and properties may be adjusted in the *Dimension Styles Manager* window. Some experimentation with these dimension settings may be required.

There are several ways to access AutoCAD's dimensioning commands. The *Dimension* pull-down menu, dashboard and toolbar contain commands that allow you to create a variety of dimension types. Dimensioning commands may also be typed in at the *Command* prompt or the *Dim* prompt. The *Dim* prompt is similar to the *Command* prompt except that it is used solely for creating and modifying dimensions using keyed in commands. One disadvantage with this method is that you are unable to draw or modify objects from the *Dim* prompt.

Dimensions are created as single entities and, with the exception of multileaders, are associated with the geometries used to create them. They are similar to blocks. If, for some reason, you need to edit the individual line and arrows of a dimension, it must be EXPLODED first. However, the associativity or connection to the geometry is broken if the dimension is exploded.

In this chapter annotative objects will be introduced. If an object is annotative, its scale or size will change with the view port scale. For example, using annotative text allows your printed text to always remain 1/8 of an inch high (or whatever value you set it to) no matter what scale you are using to print. AutoCAD® will automatically adjust the height of the text. Objects that may be defined as annotative include text, dimensions, multileaders, hatches and blocks.

11.2) DIMENSION COMMANDS

11.2.1) Dimensions panel

Figure 11.2-1 shows the *Dimensions* panel which is located in the *Annotate* tab.

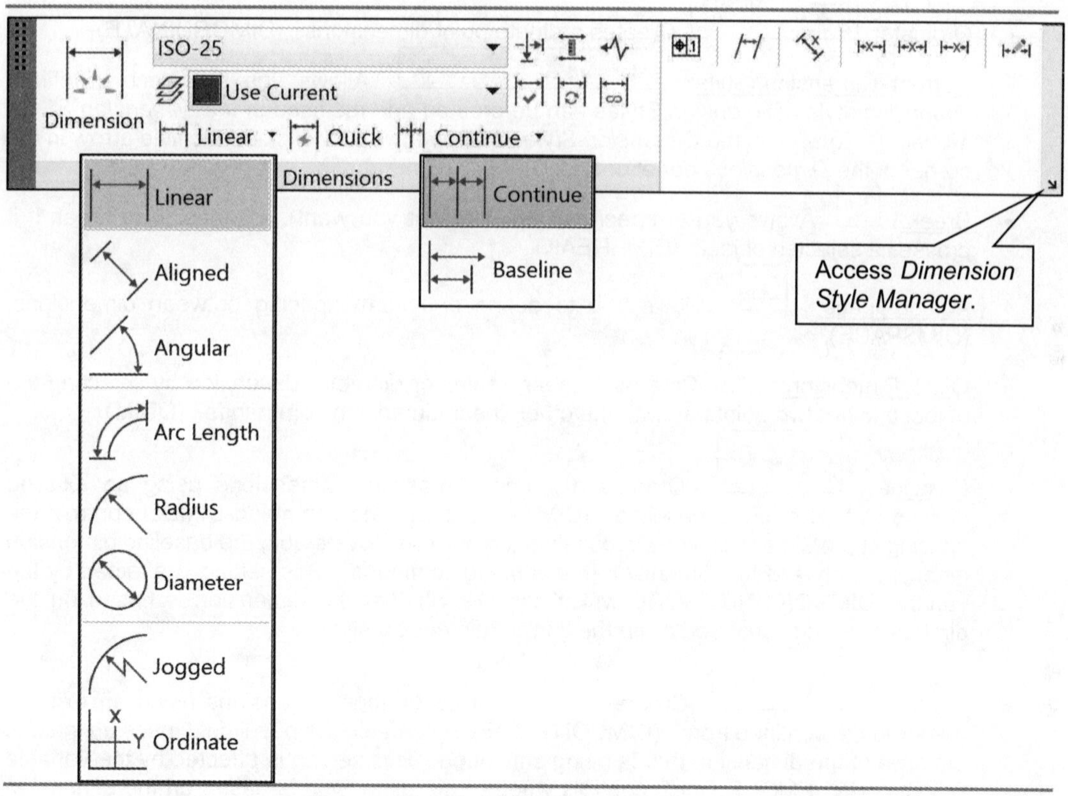

Figure 11.2-1: The *Dimensions* panel

The commands located in the *Dimensions* panel are:

- Dimension: 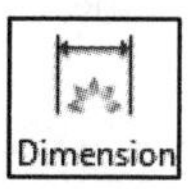

Allows you to apply various types of dimensions. (DIM)
- Linear: 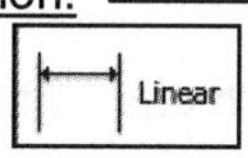

Creates horizontal or vertical linear dimensions. (DIMLINEAR)
- Aligned: 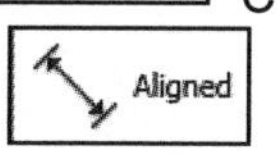

Creates linear aligned dimensions. (DIMALIGNED)
- Angular: 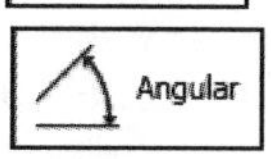

Creates an angular dimension. (DIMANGULAR)
- Arc Length: 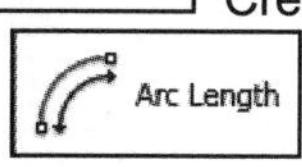

Creates an arc length dimension. (DIMARC)
- Radius: 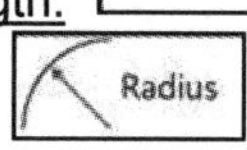

Creates a radius dimension. (DIMRADIUS)

- Diameter: Creates a diameter dimension. (DIMDIAMETER)
- Jogged: Creates jogged dimensions for circles and arcs. (DIMJOGGED)
- Ordinate: Creates ordinate point dimensions. (DIMORDINATE)
- Current Dimension Style: Standard Allows you to select a defined dimension style. Dimension Styles can be created and modified in the *Dimension Styles Manager*. To access the *Dimension Styles Manager* window click on the little arrow in the corner of the *Dimensions* panel or type DIMSTYLE.
- Break: Allows you to specify whether or not you want a dimension to break if it crosses a selected object. (DIMBREAK)
- Adjust Space: Allows you to define a uniform spacing between dimensions. (DIMSPACE)
- Quick Dimension: Creates a linear, radius or diameter dimension by selecting the object and not two points as with the other linear dimension commands. (QDIM)
- Baseline: Creates a series of baseline dimensions using an existing dimension to define the baseline. (DIMBASELINE) The command DIMDLI controls the spacing of the dimension lines in baseline dimensions. By default, the baseline dimension inherits the style of the dimension that is being continued. This setting is affected by the variable DIMCONTINUEMODE which controls whether the dimension is based on the dimension being continued or on the current dimension style.
- Continue: Creates a series of continuous dimensions using an existing dimension to continue from. (DIMCONTINUE) By default, the baseline dimension inherits the style of the dimension that is being continued. This setting is affected by the variable DIMCONTINUEMODE which controls whether the dimension is based on the dimension being continued or on the current dimension style.
- Inspection: Allows you to add or remove an inspection dimension from a selected dimension. (DIMINSPECT)
- Update: Redraws the dimensions with the current dimension style settings. (-DIMSTYLE)
- Jogged Line: Adds a jog to a linear dimension. (DIMJOGLINE)
- Reassociate: Associates or reassociates a selected dimension to an object or a point on an object. (DIMREASSOCIATE)
- Tolerance: Allows you to create a GD&T feature control frame. (TOLERANCE)
- Oblique: Makes the extension lines of a linear dimension oblique. This is useful when dimensioning pictorials. (DIMEDIT)
- Text Angle: Allows you to rotate the dimension text to a specified angle. (DIMTEDIT)
- Left Justify: Places the dimension text on the left side. (DIMTEDIT)

- Center Justify: Places the dimension text in the center. (DIMTEDIT)
- Right Justify: Places the dimension text on the right side. (DIMTEDIT)
- Override: Allows you to override dimension style variables. (DIMOVERRIDE)

11.2.2) The Leaders panel

Figure 11.2-2 shows the *Leaders* panel which is located in the *Annotate* tab.

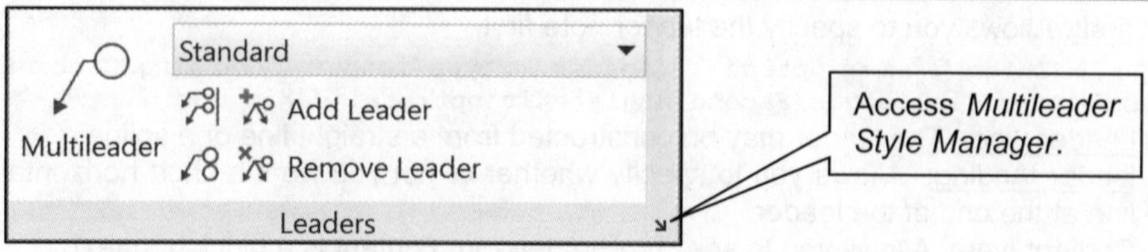

Figure 11.2-2: The *Leaders* panel

The commands located in the *Leaders* panel are:

- Multileader: Creates various types of leaders and notes. (MLEADER)
- Current Multileader Style: Allows you to select a defined multileader style. Multileader Styles can be created and modified in the *Multileader Styles Manager*. To access the *Multileader Styles Manager* window click on the little arrow in the corner of the *Leaders* panel or type **MLEADERSTYLE**.
- Add Leader: Adds a leader(s) to an existing multileader. (MLEADEREDIT)
- Remove Leader: Removes a leader from an existing multileader. (MLEADEREDIT)
- Align: Aligns several existing multileaders with a line created within the command. (MLEADERALIGN)
- Collect: Collects the content of several multileaders and creates a single multileader. (MLEADERCOLLECT)

The *multileader* command may be accessed in the following way.

- *Leaders* panel: 

- *Command* window: **mleader**

Multileader options (`Specify leader arrowhead location or [leader Landing first/Content first/Options] <Options>:`).

- leader Landing first: Allows you to specify the location of the short horizontal line at the end of a leader first.
- Content first: Allows you to specify the leader note first.
- Options: `Enter an option [Leader type/leader lAnding/Content type/Maxpoints/First angle/Second angle/eXit options] <eXit options>:`
  - Leader type: The leader may be constructed from a straight line or a spline.
  - leader lAnding: Allows you to specify whether or not you want a short horizontal line at the end of the leader.
  - Content type: Allows you to specify whether your content is a block or mtext.
  - Maxpoints: Allows you to create leader lines that consist of several straight line segments, or specify how many defining points you want for your spline.
  - First angle / Second angle: Allows you to specify at least 2 angles that you wish to use to draw your leader lines.

11.3) DIMENSION STYLES

11.3.1) Dimension Style Manager

The *Dimension Style Manager* (Figure 11.3-1) is used to create new dimension styles, set the current style, modify styles, set overrides on the current style, and compare styles. The *Dimension Style Manager* window may be accessed using the **DDIM** or **DIMSTYLE** commands. It may also be accessed from the *Dimensions* panel. The features of the *Dimension Style Manager* window are (see figure 11.3-1):

- Current dimension style: The current dimension style is the style that is applied to dimensions you create.
- Styles: This is a list of styles that are available.
- List: Allows you to display all styles or only the styles that are in use.
- Preview of: Shows a preview of what the dimensions will look like.
- Set Current: Sets a selected style to be current.
- New...: Allows you to create a new style.
- Modify...: Allows you to modify the current style.
- Override...: Allows you to set temporary override settings to the current style.
- Compare...: Allows you to compare styles.

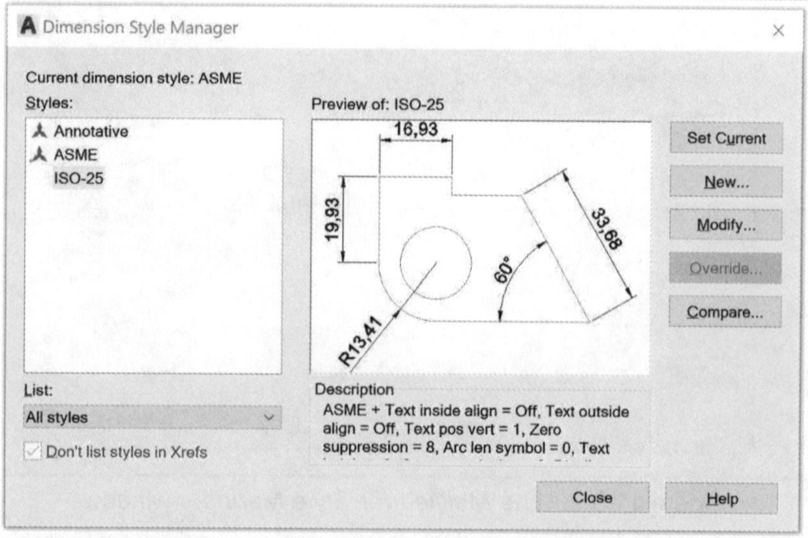

Figure 11.3-1: The *Dimension Style Manager* window

The default metric drawing dimension style is ISO-25. ISO stands for 'International Standards Organization'. The United States follows ASME's standards. ASME stands for 'American Society of Mechanical Engineers'. The ASME standard related to dimensioning is close to the ISO standard; therefore, we can use the ISO standard as a starting point when we create a new ASME dimension style.

11.3.2) Multileader Style Manager

The *Multileader Style Manager* (Figure 11.3-2) is used to create new multileader styles, set the current style and modify styles. The *Multileader Style Manager* window may be accessed using the **MLEADERSTYLE** command. It may also be accessed from the *Leaders* panel. The features of the *Multileader Style Manager* window are (see Figure 11.3-2):

- Current multileader style: The current multileader style is the style that is applied to multileaders that you create.
- Styles: This is a list of styles that are available.
- List: Allows you to display all styles or only the styles that are in use.
- Preview of: Shows a preview of what the multileader will look like.
- Set Current: Sets a selected style to be current.
- New...: Allows you to create a new style.
- Modify...: Allows you to modify the current style.

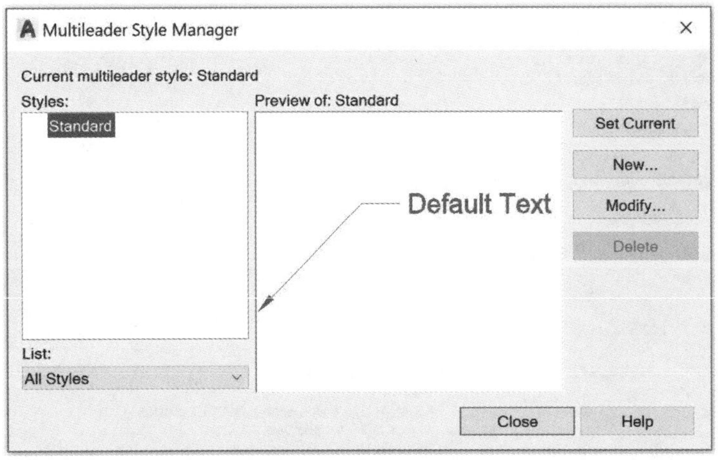

Figure 11.3-2: The *Multileader Style Manager* window

11.4) DIMENSION VARIABLES

Dimension appearance may be modified by changing the value of the following dimension variables. Only the most commonly used variables are listed. These variables may also be set in the *Dimension Styles Manager*. However, it is not uncommon to change some of these variables on the fly.

11.4.1) Dimension scale

- **DIMSCALE:** This command sets the overall size or scale factor of the dimensions. The following variables are controlled directly by the DIMSCALE variable. There is usually no need to change them individually.
  - **DIMASZ:** Controls the size of the arrows.
  - **DIMEXE:** Controls the length of the extension lines beyond dimension lines.
  - **DIMEXO:** Controls the gap between the extension line and the object.
  - **DIMGAP:** Controls the space between the dimension text and the dimension line.
  - **DIMTXT:** Controls the height of the dimension text unless the current style has a fixed height.

11.4.2) Dimension and extension lines

- **DIMSOXD:** Suppresses the placement of dimension lines outside of the extension lines.
  - 0 = Off
  - 1 = On
- **DIMTOFL:** Draws dimension lines between extension lines even if the text is placed outside the extension lines.
  - 0 = Off
  - 1 = On

- **DIMATFIT:** Determines how dimension text and arrows are arranged when space is not sufficient to place both within the extension lines.
  - 0 = Places both text and arrows outside the extension lines.
  - 1 = Moves arrows first and then text.
  - 2 = Moves text first, then arrows.
  - 3 = Moves either text or arrows, whichever fits best.
- **DIMCLRD:** Assigns a color to dimension lines, arrowheads and dimension leader lines.

11.4.3) Dimension text

- **DIMTIH:** Forces the dimension text inside the extension lines to be positioned horizontally, rather than aligned.
  - 0 = Off
  - 1 = On
- **DIMTIX**: Forces dimension text inside extension lines.
  - 0 = Off
  - 1 = On
- **DIMDEC**: Sets the number of decimal places displayed for the primary units.
- **DIMJUST**: Controls the horizontal positioning of the dimension text.
  - 0 = Above the dimension line and center justifies it between the extension lines.
  - 1 = Next to the first extension line.
  - 2 = Next to the second extension line.
  - 3 = Above the dimension line and next to the first extension line.
  - 4 = Above the dimension line and next to the second extension line.
- **DIMTAD**: Controls the vertical position of the text relative to the dimension lines.
  - 0 = Centered between the extension lines.
  - 1 = Above the dimension line except when the dimension line is not horizontal and DIMTIH = 1. The distance from the dimension line to the bottom of the text is controlled by DIMGAP.
  - 2 = On the side of the dimension line farthest away from the dimension origin(s).
  - 3 = According to the JIS (Japanese Industrial Standards).
- **DIMTMOVE**: Sets dimension text movement rules.
  - 0 = Moves the dimension line with the dimension text.
  - 1 = Adds a leader when the dimension text is moved.
  - Allows text to be moved freely without a leader.
- **DIMTOH**: Controls the position of the dimension text outside the extension lines.
  - 0 or Off= Aligns the text with the dimension line.
  - 1 or On= Draws the text horizontally.
- **DDEDIT**: Edits single line text, dimension text and feature control frames.
- **DIMTEDIT**: Moves and rotates dimension text.
- **DIMCLRT**: Assigns colors to dimension text.

11.4.4) Diameter and radial dimensions

- **DIMCEN:** Controls size of the center marks drawn by diameter and radial dimensions.
- **DIMJOGANG:** Determines the angle of the transverse segment of the dimension line in a jogged radius dimension.

11.4.5) Angular dimensions

- **DIMADEC:** Controls the number of decimal places displayed in angular dimensions.
- **DIMAUNIT:** Sets the units format for angular dimensions.

11.4.6) Alternative units

- **DIMALT:** Adds an additional dimension text in an alternative unit.
  - 0 = Off
  - 1 = On
- **DIMALTD:** Controls the number of decimal places in the alternative unit.
- **DIMALTF:** Controls the conversion factor of the alternative unit. For example, the conversion factor from inches to millimeters is 25.4.

11.4.7) Toleranced dimensions

- **DIMLIM:** Presents dimensions in limit form.
- **DIMTOL:** Presents dimensions in tolerance form.
- **DIMTM:** Sets the negative tolerance value.
- **DIMTP:** Sets the positive tolerance value.

11.4.8) Miscellaneous

- **DIMARCSYM:** Controls whether or not an arc symbol will be placed above an arc length dimension.
  - 0 = Before the dimension text.
  - 1 = Above the dimension text.
  - 2 = Will not display the arc length symbol.

11.5) ASSOCIATIVE DIMENSIONS

Associative dimensions are dimensions that are associated with a geometric object or a particular feature of your part. This means that if the feature is changed, the associated dimension value will change. For example, if the diameter of a circle is 10 mm then the diameter dimension value will read ∅10. If you subsequently change the diameter of the circle to 20 mm within the *Properties* window, the dimension value will automatically change to ∅20. Associativity is broken if you manually type in the dimension text, replace the dimension text or EXPLODE the dimension. Leader dimensions are not associative. The dimension commands that are related to associativity are:

- **DIMDISASSOCIATE:** Removes associativity from a selected dimension.
- **DIMREASSOCIATE:** Associates a selected dimension to geometric objects.
- **DIMREGEN:** Updates the locations of all associative dimensions.
- **DIMASSOC:** Controls the associativity of dimensions and whether dimensions are exploded.

11.6) ANNOTATIVE OBJECTS

Annotative objects are objects that can support multiple viewport scales. Consider the following situation. I start a metric drawing and set my text height to 3 mm. If I print at a 1:1 scale, my text height will measure 3 mm on the printed page. However, if I print at a 1:2 scale my text height will only measure 1.5 mm. Annotative text adjusts its height so that no matter what viewport scale you select the text will always measure 3 mm on the printed page. Figure 11.6-1 shows an example of regular text and annotative text at three different viewport scales. Notice that the regular text height increases or decreases depending on the viewport scale, and the annotative text height never changes.

How does this work? If you select the annotative text, you will see not just one instance of the text, but three or however many viewport scales it supports. Figure 11.6-2 shows the selected annotative text and the instances that it supports. Objects that may be defined as annotative include text, dimensions, multileaders, hatches and blocks. The principle is the same for all annotative objects.

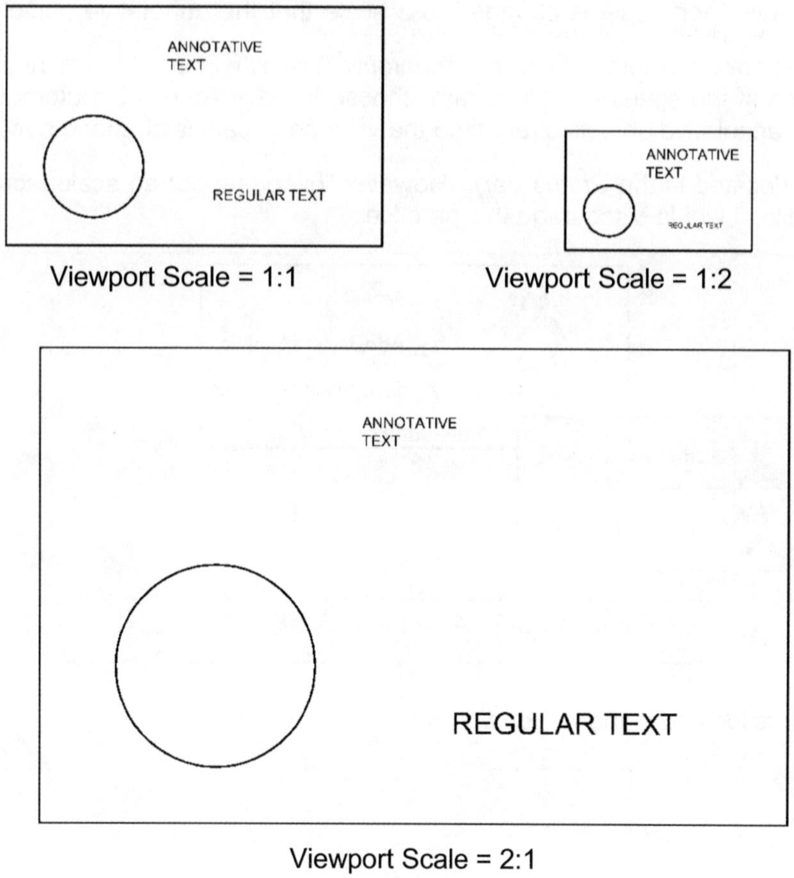

Figure 11.6-1: Annotative text

Figure 11.6-2: Annotative text instances

11.6.1) Annotative object scale

An annotative object, by default, only supports a 1:1 scale. Supported scales may be added or removed from an annotative object by using the commands located in the *Annotation Scaling* panel as shown in Figure 11.6-3.

If the view port scale is changed to a scale that the annotative object does not support, it will not be visible unless the *Annotative Visibility* icon is turned on. This icon is located in the status bar. You may choose to have AutoCAD automatically add scales to the annotative objects every time the view port scale is changed by turning this icon on (located in the *Status bar*). However, every supported scale increases the size of your file. I would discourage this practice.

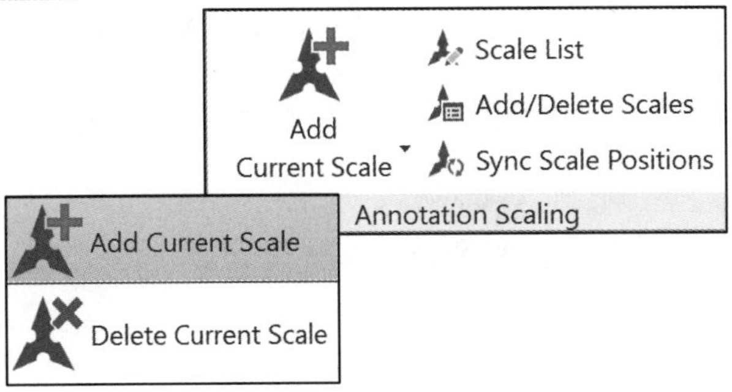

Figure 11.6-3: *Annotation Scaling* panel

The commands located in the *Annotation Scaling* panel are:

- Add Current Scale: 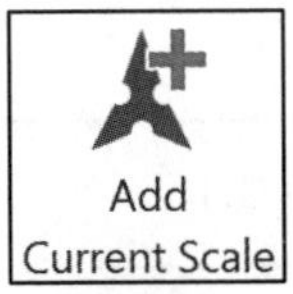

Allows you to add a scale that the object will support.
- Delete Current Scale: 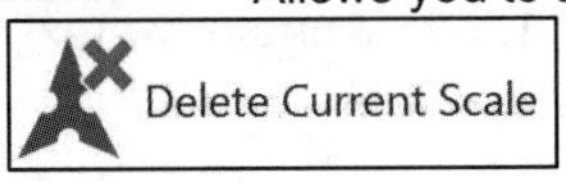

Allows you to delete a supported scale from an object.
- Scale List: 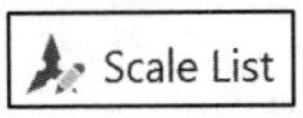

Brings up the *Edit Scale List* window which lists all scales available. It also allows you to add or delete scales. (SCALELISTEDIT)
- Add/Delete Scales: 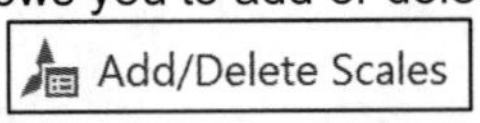

Brings up the *Annotation Object Scale* window which lists all scales supported by the selected object(s). It also allows you to add or delete supported scales. (OBJECTSCALE)
- Synchronize Scale Positions: 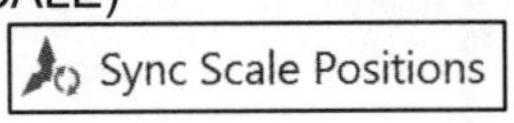

Resets the positions of all scale representations.

11.7) DIMENSIONING TUTORIAL

The objective of this tutorial is to familiarize the user with creating a variety of dimension types. This tutorial will also take the user through the steps required to create a new dimension style. We will first dimension the object using the ISO-25 standard. The differences between the ISO standard and the ASME standard will be pointed out and then we will create an ASME dimension style and use that style to dimension the object. The last section of this tutorial will illustrate the dimensions associativity and annotative properties.

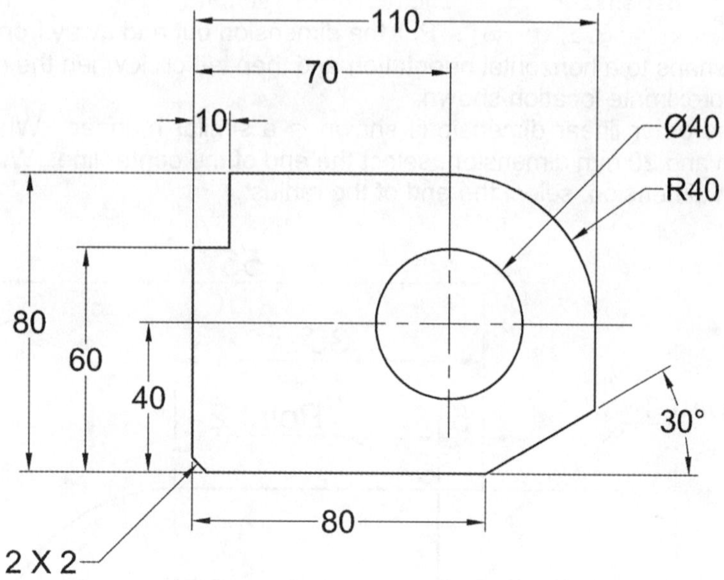

11.7.1) Drawing the object

1) View the *Creating Dimension*, *Multileaders*, *Associativity* and *Annotative Objects* videos and read section 11.1) through 11.6).

2)  ***set-mm.dwt*** drawing template. Verify the following settings…
   - **STyle**: Text style = ***Arial***, Text height = **3** mm, ***Annotative***.
   - **LIMITS** = **297, 210**

3)  **Dim Tut.dwg**

4) Draw the object given in the previous figure (without the dimensions) using the appropriate layers. Make sure to include the center mark.

5) Turn your ***Object Snap*** on and have it automatically detect, at minimum, *Endpoint* and *Intersection*.

6) **Zoom** in to better view your drawing.

11.7.2) Drawing linear dimensions

1) Set the ***Dimension*** layer as current and activate the ***Annotate*** tab.

2) Add the linear dimensions.

   a) Command: **dimlinear** or *Dimensions* panel: 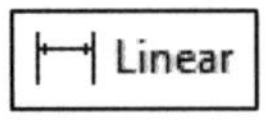

   b) `Select objects or specify first extension line origin or <Select object>:` Select *Point1*.
   c) `Specify second extension line origin or [Undo]:` Select *Point2*.
   d) `Specify dimension line location or second line for angle [Mtext, Text, text aNgle, Undo]:` Pull the dimension out and away from the object so that it snaps to a horizontal orientation and then left click when the dimension is in the approximate location shown.
   e) Add the other linear dimensions shown in a similar manner. When adding the 35 mm and 20 mm dimension, select the end of the center line. When adding the 55 mm dimension, select the end of the radius.

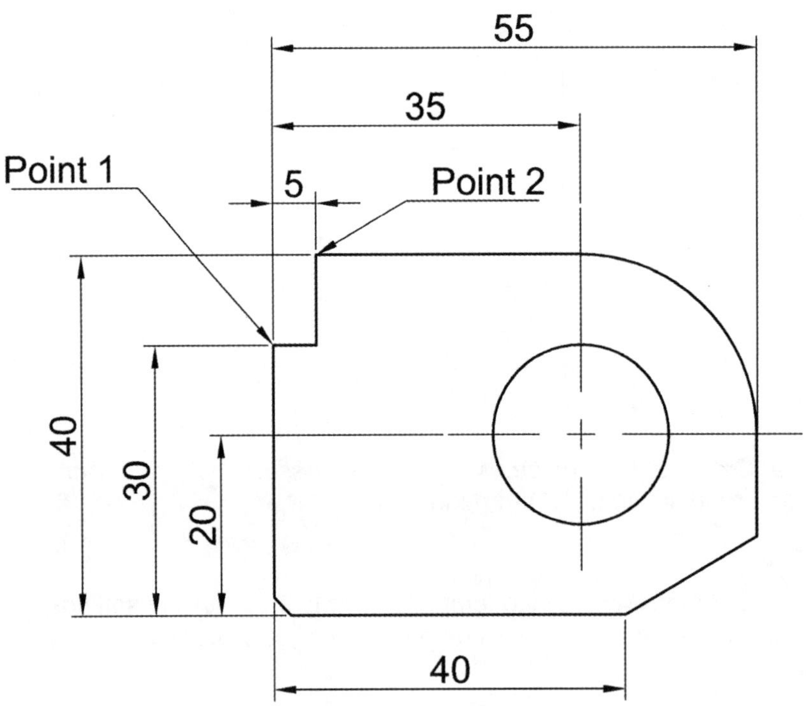

3) Space the linear dimensions evenly.

   a) Command: **dimspace** or *Dimensions* panel: 
   b) `Select base dimension:` Select the 5 mm dimension.
   c) `Select dimensions to space:` Select the 35 mm and then the 55 mm dimension.
   d) `Select dimensions to space:` **Enter**
   e) `Enter value or [Auto] <Auto>:` **a**
   f) Notice that the AUTO option spaces the dimensions too close.
   g) Repeat the above process using **8** mm as the spacing.
   h) Evenly space the vertical linear dimensions.

11.7.3) Drawing diameter, radius, and angular dimensions

1) Dimension the radius and diameter.

   a) Command: **dimradius** or *Dimensions* panel: 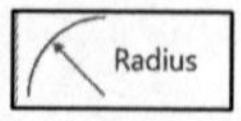

   b) `Select arc or circle:` Select the circle.
   c) `Specify radius dimension location or [Mtext, Text, Angle]:` Pull the dimension out and away from the object and left click when the dimension is in the approximate position shown. Notice that the radius symbol "R" is automatically placed in front of the dimension value.
   d) Repeat the process to add the ∅20 diameter dimension (**DIMDIAMETER**, 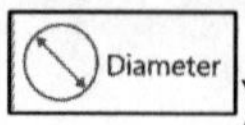

).

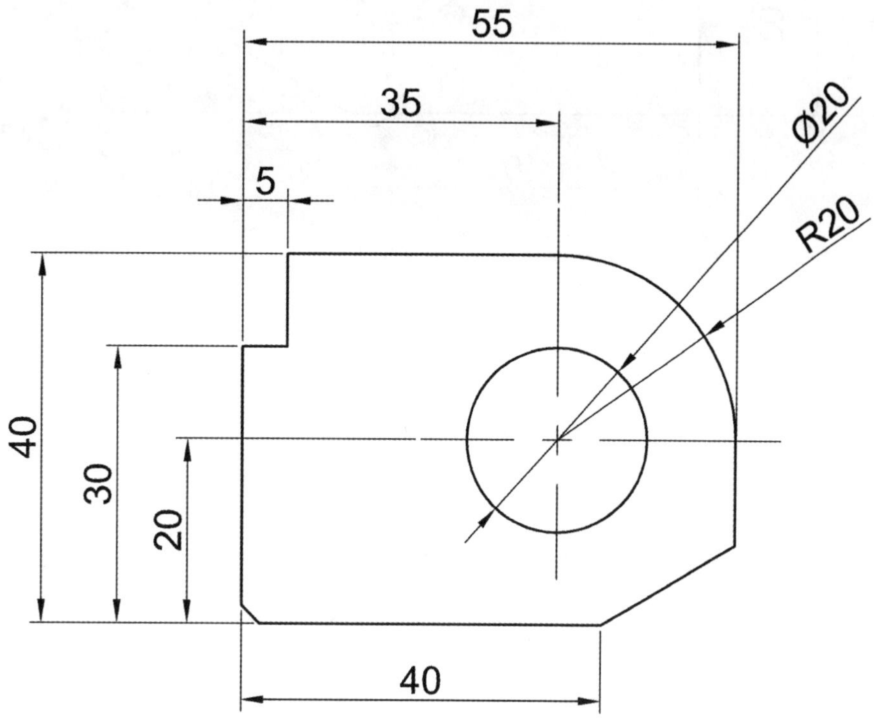

2) Dimension the angled feature.

a) Command: **dimangular** or *Dimensions* panel: 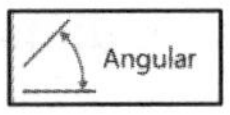

b) `Select arc, circle, line, or <specify vertex>:` Select *Line1*.

c) `Select second line:` Select *Line 2*.

d) `Specify dimension arc line location or [Mtext, Text, Angle, Quadrant]:` Pull the dimension out and away from the object and left click when the dimension is in the approximate position shown. Notice that the degree symbol "o" is automatically placed behind the dimension value.

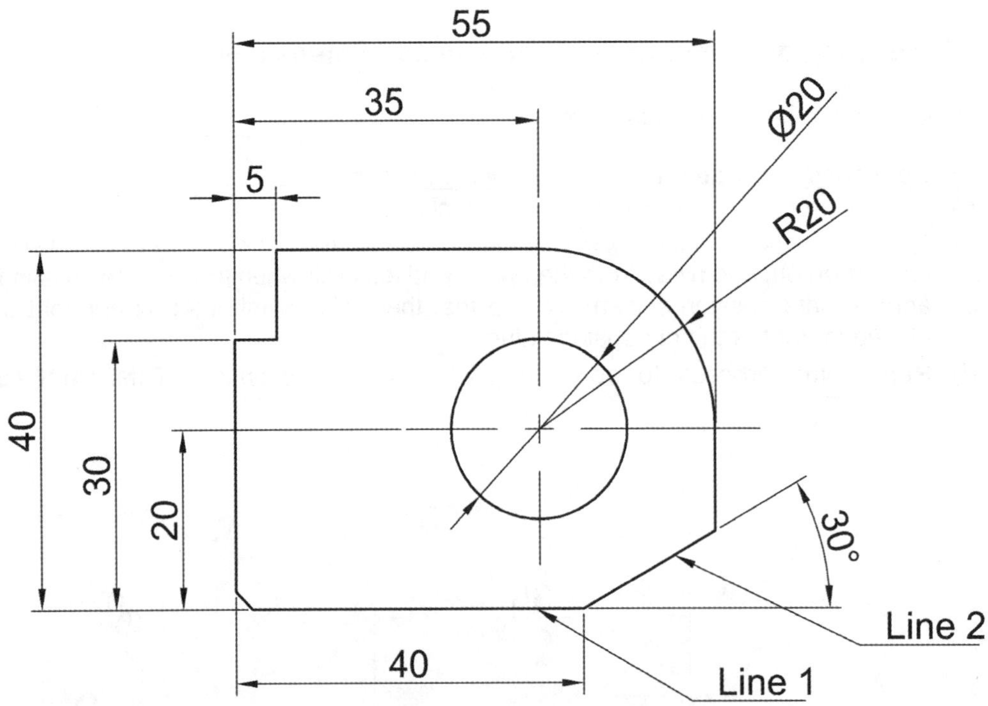

11.7.4) Drawing leaders

1) Dimension the chamfer.

- Command: **mleader** or *Leaders* panel: 

- `Specify leader arrowhead location or [leader Landing first/Content first/Options] <Options>:` **mid**
  `of` Select the angled line of the chamfer near the middle (see the figure below).
- `Specify leader landing location:` Pull the leader out away from the object and click (see figure).
- *Text Editor* tab: In the ribbon, select the ***Annotative*** icon above where you enter the text height, set the text height to **3** mm, select ***Arial*** as the font, and then enter the text **2 X 2.** When you are done select 

.

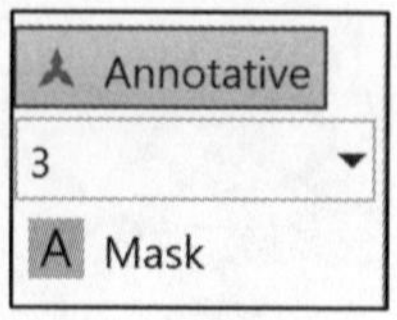

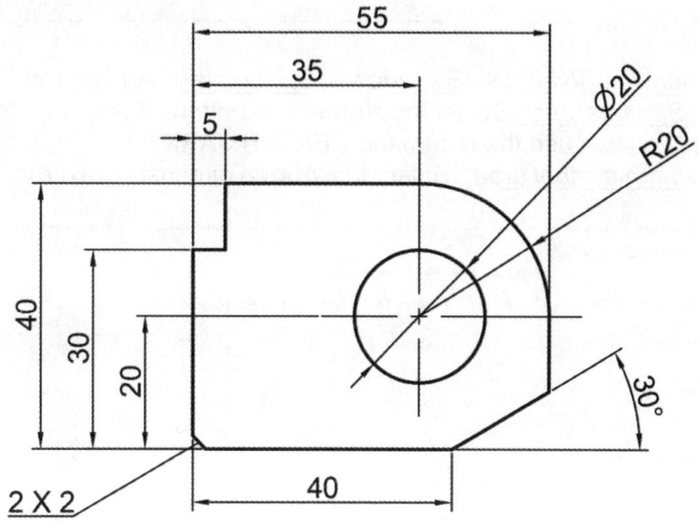

11.7.5) Creating a new dimension style

The ISO-25 standard used to create the above drawing is different from the ASME standard that we need to use. Notice the following:

- The dimension text is not always horizontal.
- The dimension text is next to or above the dimension line (there is no break allowing space for the text).
- The diameter and radius dimension text is aligned with the leader line.
- The diameter dimension leader line goes through the circle.
- The multileader does not appear to have an arrow head.
- The multileader landing underlines the text.

We will fix all of the above problems by creating our own dimension and multileader styles.

1) Create a new ASME dimension style.

   a) Command: **ddim** or *Dimensions* panel:
   b) *Dimension Style Manager* window: **New…**
   c) *Create New Dimension Style* window:
      i. *New Style Name* field: **ASME**
      ii. *Start With* field: ***ISO-25***
      iii. *Use for* field: ***All dimensions***
      iv. Activate the ***Annotative*** checkbox.
      v. ***Continue***

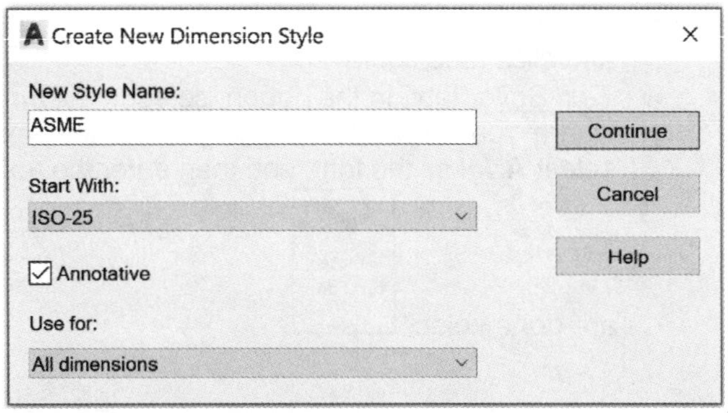

   d) *New Dimension Style: ASME* window – *Symbols and Arrows* tab:
      i. *Center marks* area: Select the ***None*** radio button. If you need to place a center mark, you can use the command CENTERMARK.
      ii. *Arc length symbol* area: Select the ***Above*** dimension text radio button.

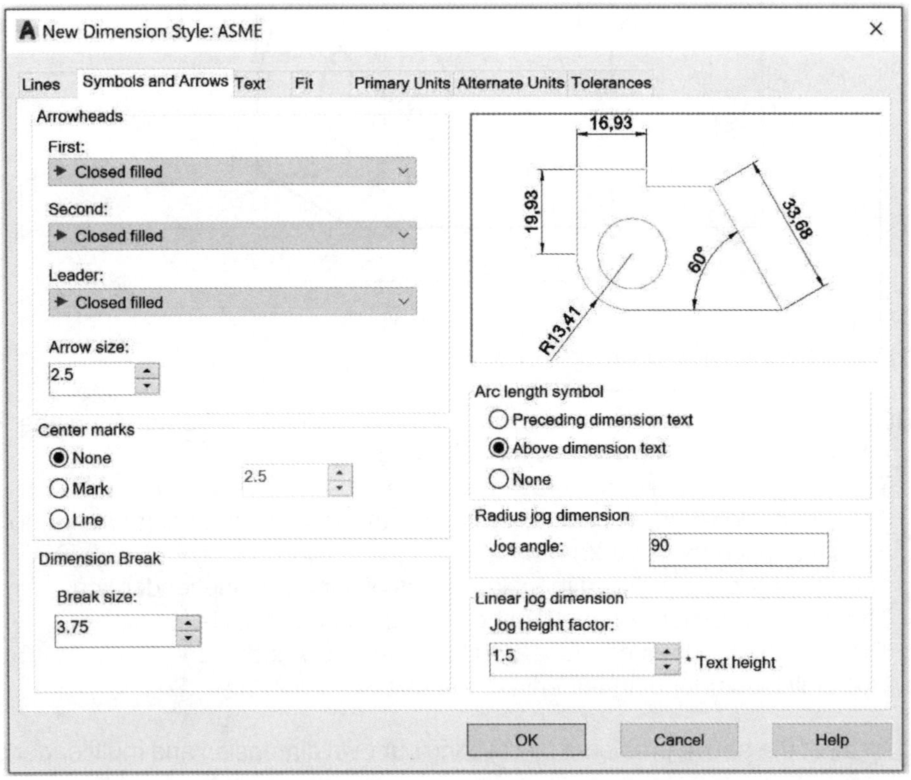

e) _New Dimension Style: ASME_ window – _Text_ tab:
   i. _Text placement_ area – _Vertical_ field: ***Centered***
   ii. _Text alignment_ area: Select the ***Horizontal*** radio button. Notice the preview area changes as you change the settings.

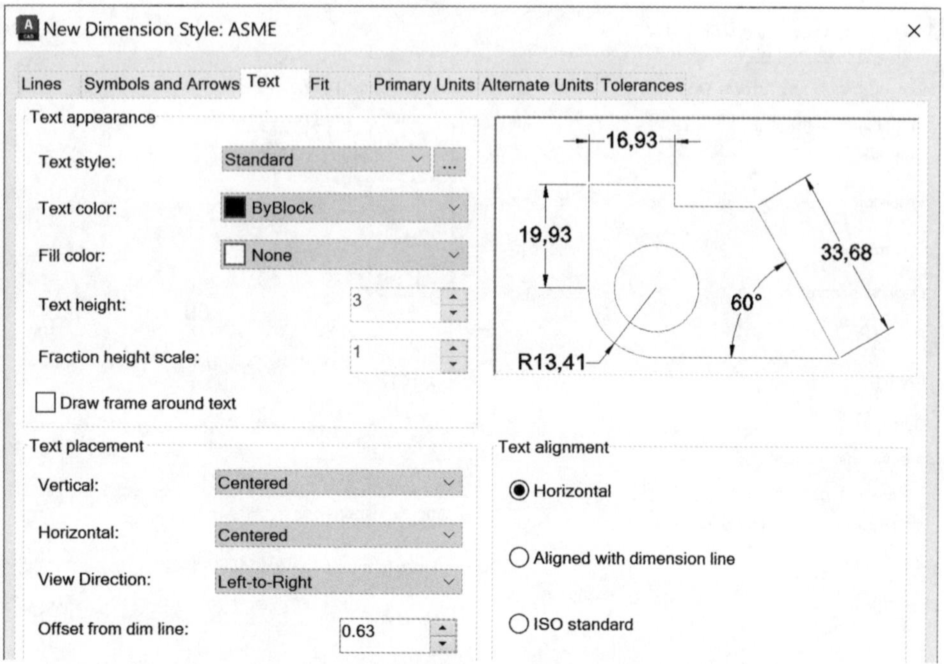

f) _New Dimension Style: ASME_ window – _Fit_ tab:
   i. _Fine tuning_ area: Deselect the ***Draw dim line between ext lines*** checkbox.

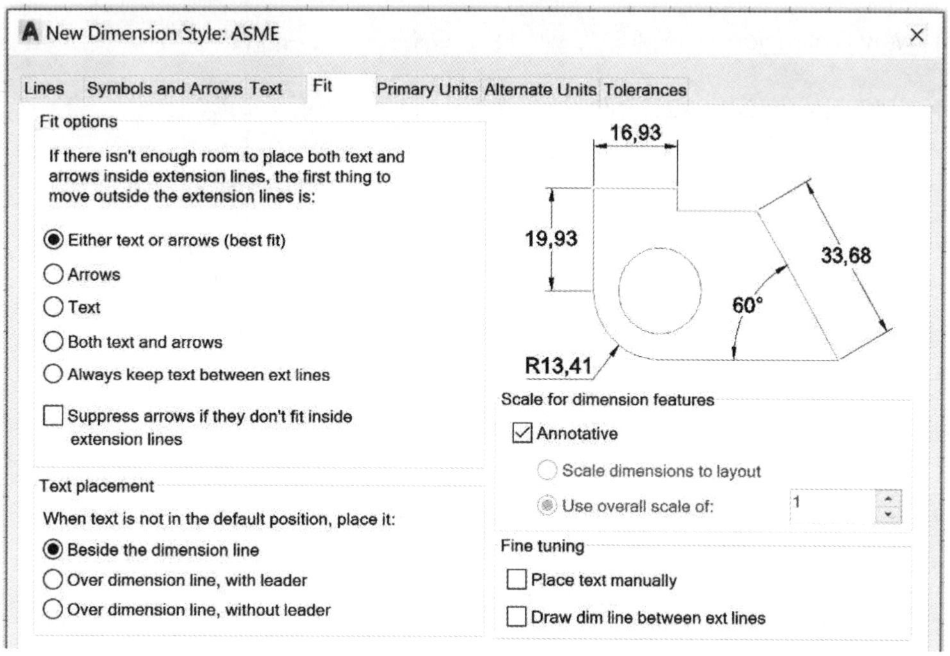

g) *New Dimension Style: ASME* window – *Primary Units* tab:
   i. *Linear dimensions* area - *Precision* field: Set the precision to ***0***.
   ii. *Linear dimensions* area - *Decimal separator* field: Select ***'.'(Period)***.
   iii. *Zero suppression* area: Deselect the ***Trailing*** checkbox (in both the *Linear dimensions* field and the *Angular dimensions* field).

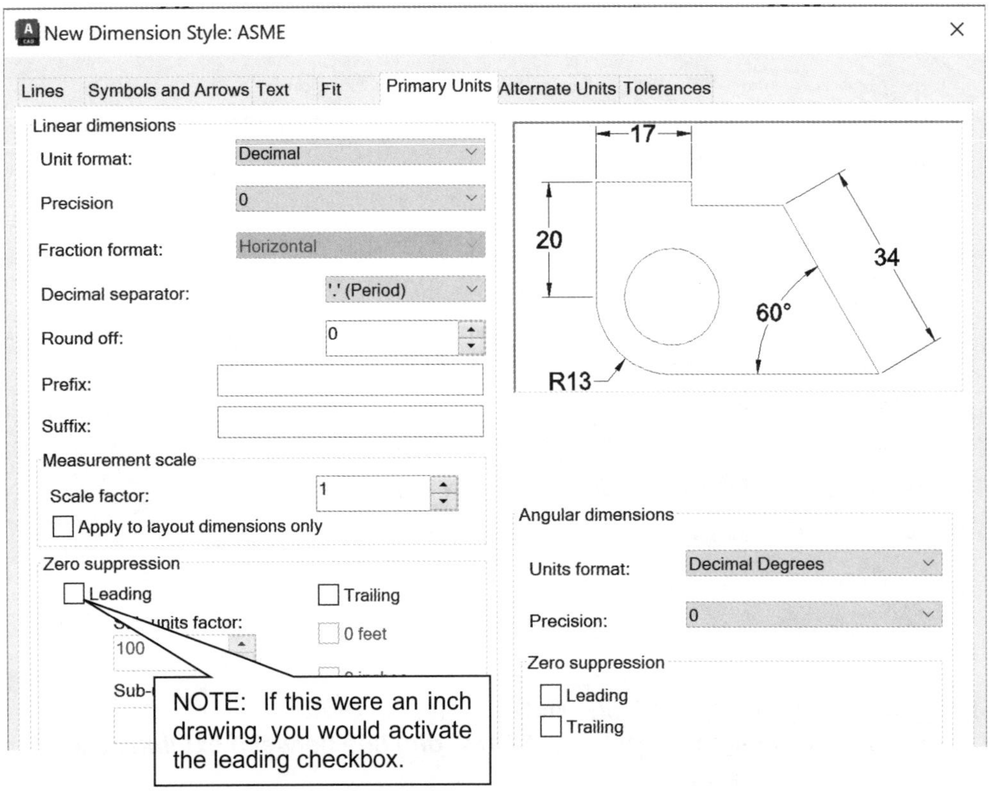

h) *New Dimension Style: ASME* window: ***OK***

i) *AutoCAD Alert* window: ***OK***

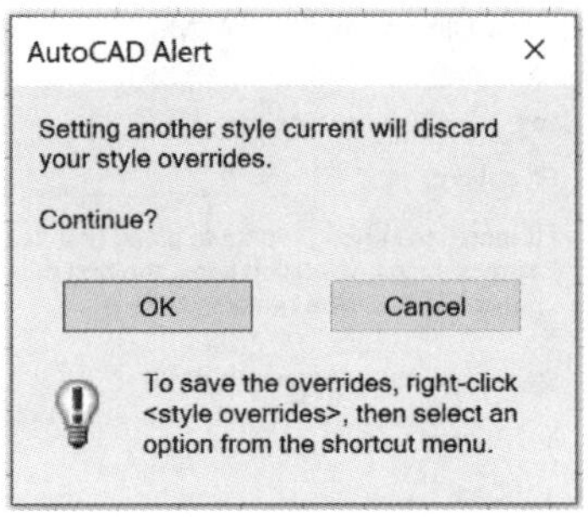

j) *Dimension Style Manager* window: Notice that the ASME style has been added to the *Styles* field.
   i. Select the ***ASME*** style and then select the ***Set Current*** button.
   ii. ***Close***

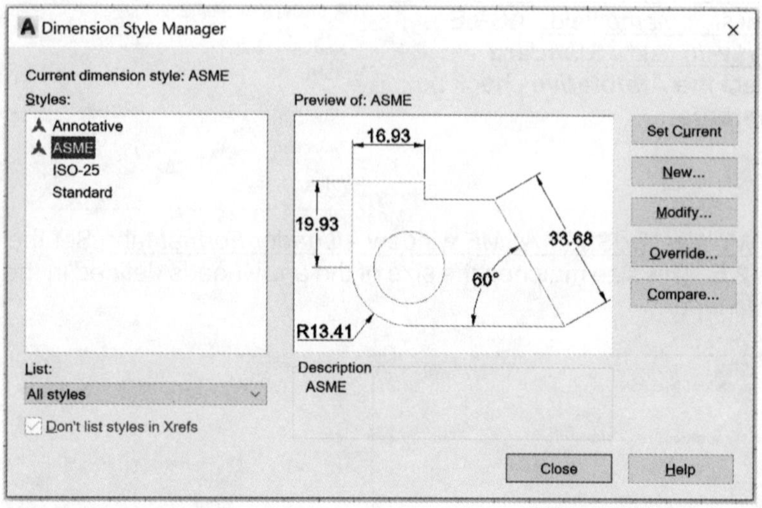

2) Update your dimensions to the ASME style.
   a) *Dimensions* panel: 
   b) `Select objects:` **all**
   c) `Select objects:` **`Enter`**
   d) Notice that all the dimensions change except for the leader.

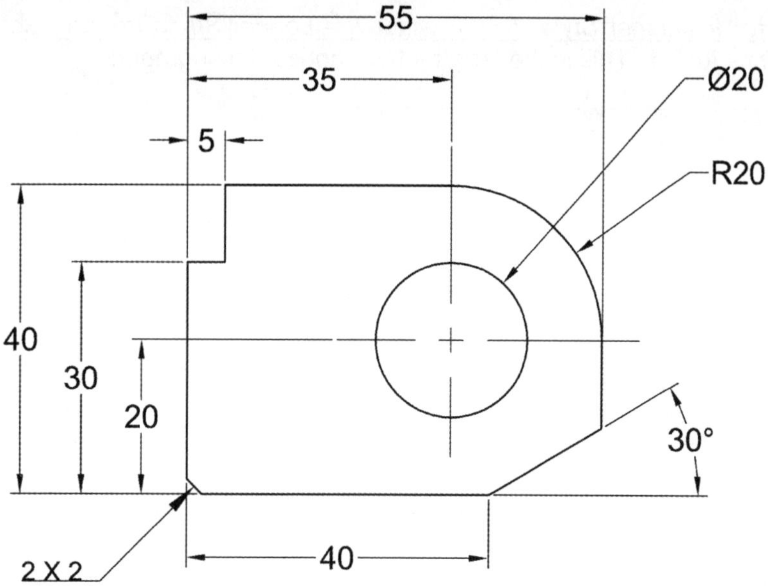

Problem? If the UPDATE command does not work on the radius and diameter dimensions, you will have to erase and redraw the dimensions.

3) Create a new multileader style.

   a) <u>Command:</u> **mleaderstyle** or <u>*Leaders* panel:</u> 
   b) <u>*Multileader Style Manager* window:</u> **New …**
   c) <u>*Create New Multileader Style* window:</u>
      i. <u>*New style name* field:</u> **ASME**
      ii. <u>*Start with* field:</u> ***Standard***
      iii. Select the ***Annotative*** check box.
      iv. ***Continue***

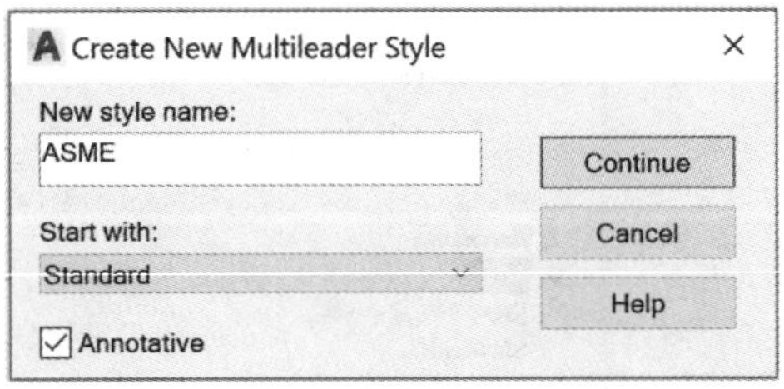

   d) <u>*Modify Multileader Style: ASME* window – *Leader Format* tab:</u> Set the *Arrowhead Size* to ***2.5***. This size matches the size of the arrowheads defined in the *Dimension Style Manager*.

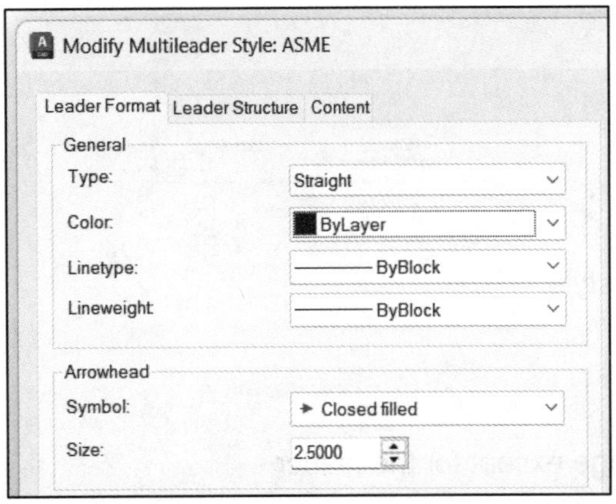

   e) <u>*Modify Multileader Style: ASME* window – *Leader Structure* tab:</u> Set the *landing distance* to ***2.5***. This is the length of the horizontal segment.

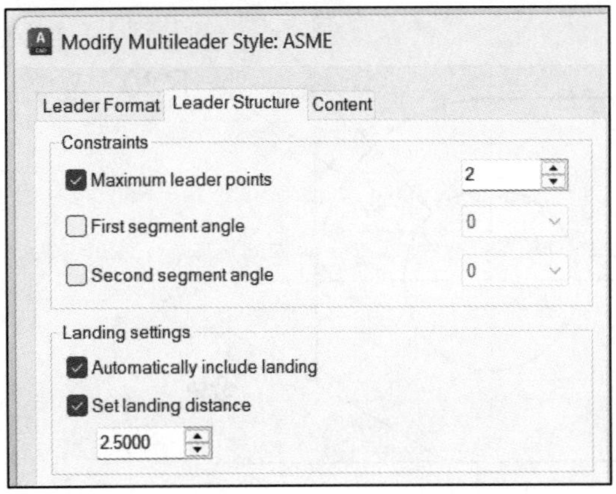

f) *<u>Modify Multileader Style: ASME</u>* <u>window</u> – *<u>Content</u>* <u>tab:</u>
   i. Set the *Right Horizontal attachment* to ***Middle of top line.*** This defines how the text is placed relative to the landing.
   ii. Set the Landing gap to **2** mm.
   iii. Select ***OK***.

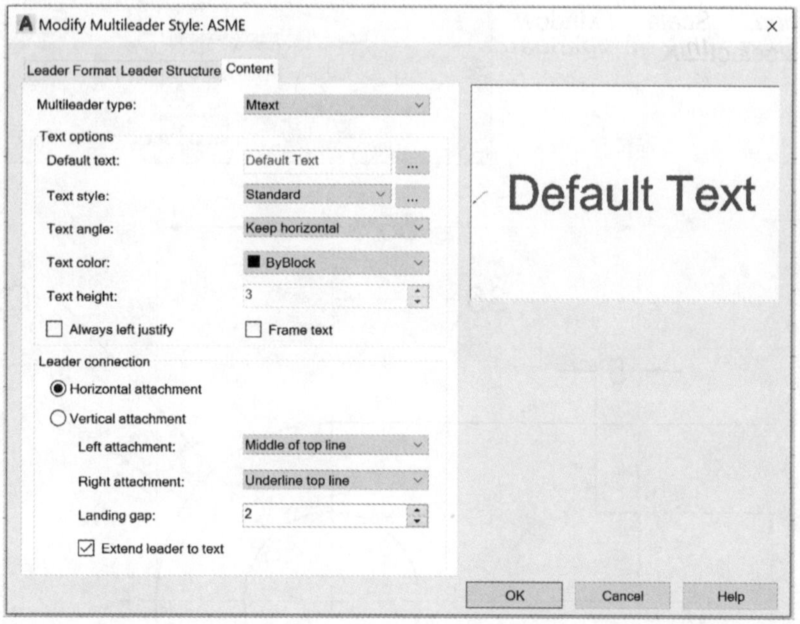

g) *<u>Multileader Style Manager</u>* <u>window:</u> Notice that the ASME style has been added to the *Styles* field.
   i. Select the ***ASME*** style and then select the ***Set Current*** button.
   ii. ***Close***

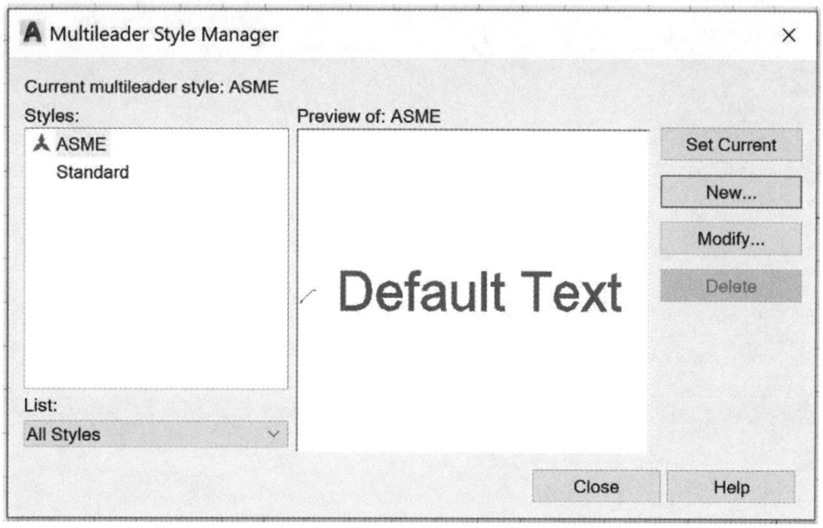

4) Try to update  the chamfer dimension. Notice that multileaders do not update. **ERASE** the dimension and create a new one. If a *Select Annotation Scale* window appears select ***OK***.

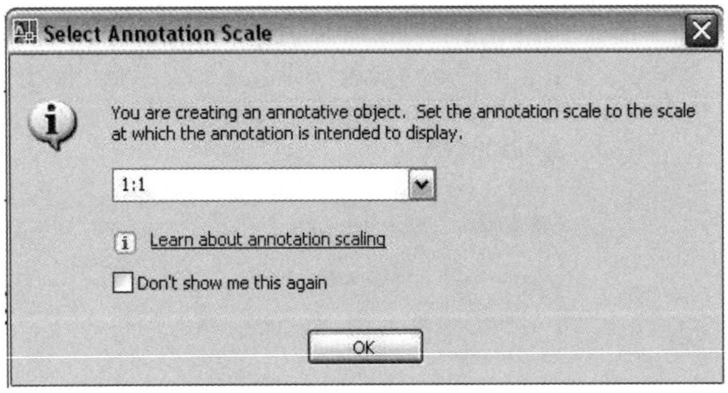

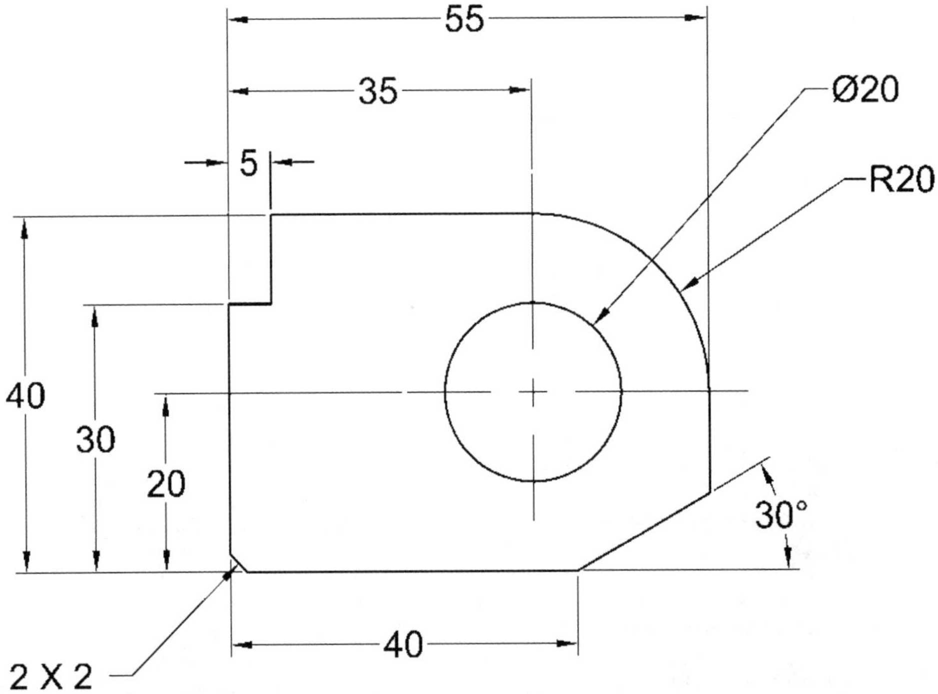

11.7.6) Annotative objects

1) Hover your mouse over the dimensions in the drawing. A  symbol will appear if the dimension is defined as annotative.

2) Enter paper space (*Layout1*) and prepare your drawing to print 1:1 scale.

> **How?**
> 1) Enter ***Layout1***.
> 2) Enter the *Page Setup – Layout1* window (***Print – Page Setup...- Modify***) and set the following parameter.
>   a) Paper size = ***A4***
>   b) What to plot: ***Layout***
>   c) *Plot scale* area:
>   a. Scale = ***1:1***
>   b. ***1 mm*** = ***1*** units
>   d) Plot style = ***monochrome.ctb***
>   e) Set your pen width

3) **INSERT** your metric title block and border. **EXPLODE** the title block and fill in the following information:
    - Part name = **DIMENSIONING TUTORIAL**
    - SIZE -= **A4**
    - DWG NO = **34**
    - Scale = **1:1**
    - WEIGHT = delete the ?
    - SHEET = **1 OF 1**
    - DATE = Fill in the appropriate date
    - MATERIAL = delete the ?
    - FINISH = delete the ?

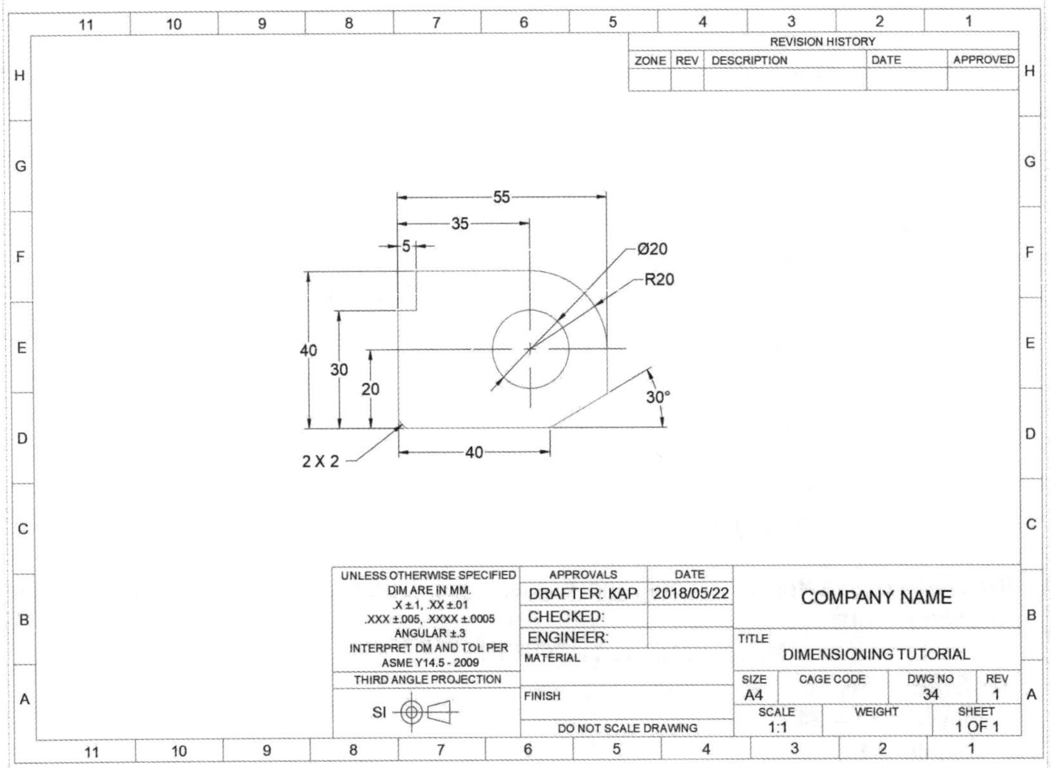

4) Adjust your view port border so that it just fits in your title block, but it is still accessible. We will need to click on it later.

5) Place the view port border on the ***Viewport*** layer.

6) Click on the view port border and set the *Viewport Scale* to ***1:1***, center your model, turn the *Viewport* layer ***OFF***, and ***print*** your drawing at a **1:1** scale.

7) Measure the size of the text on your printout and confirm that it is 3 mm high.

8) Turn the *Viewport* layer ON.

9) Click on your view port border and change the *Viewport Scale:* to **2:1**. Your dimensions may disappear. This is because the dimensions are annotative objects and they do not, as of yet, support a 2:1 scale. To see your dimensions, click on the ***Show annotation objects***  icon in the *Status* bar. Notice that your model and dimension size has doubled. If you were to print your drawing now, the text height would measure 6 mm on the paper. However, we would like the text to always be 3 mm high no matter what view port scale is used.

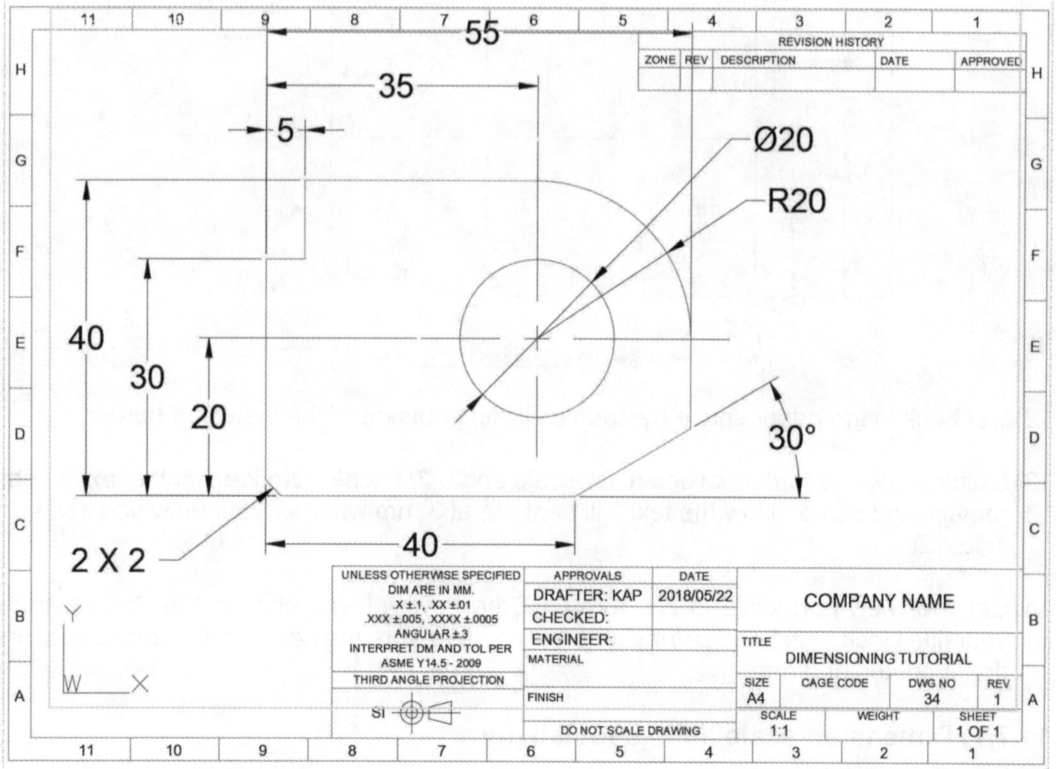

10) Add a 2:1 scale support to the annotative dimensions.
   a) Double click inside your view port border to enter model space.
   b) Select all of your dimensions.
   c) <u>*Annotate* tab - *Annotation Scaling* panel:</u> 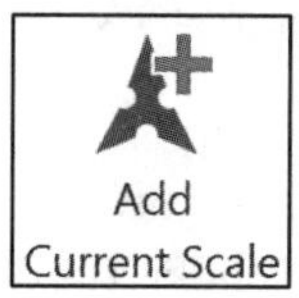

   d) Click on one of the dimensions. Notice that it now shows two instances of the dimension. One instance for the 1:1 scale and one for the 2:1 scale.

11) Using the grip boxes, manually space your dimensions to a more appropriate spacing. Notice that the 1:1 scale dimensions and 2:1 scale dimensions will be spaced differently.

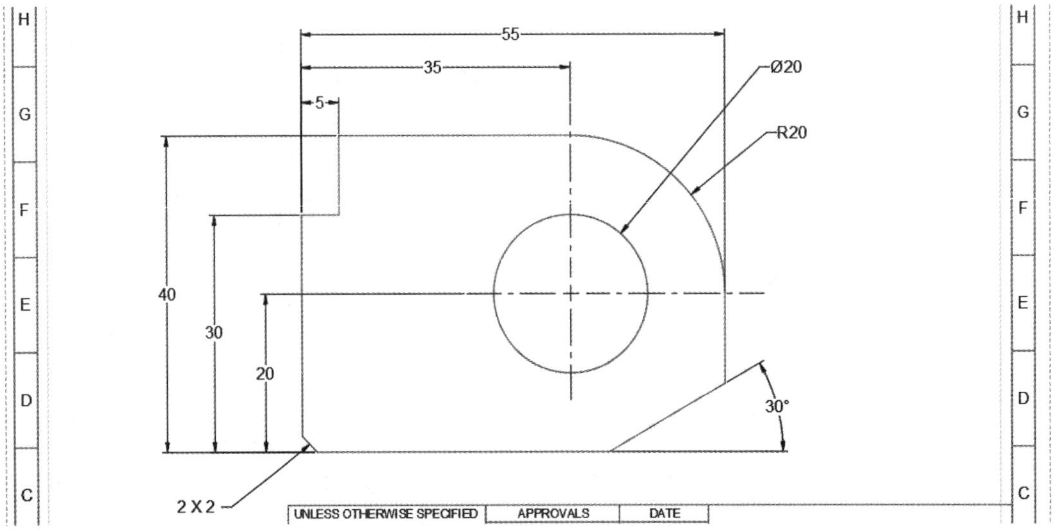

12) Get back to the paper space by double clicking outside of the view port border.

13) Switch back and forth between a ***1:1*** scale and a ***2:1*** scale. Notice that the text height remains the same. Now the text will print out at 3 mm whether your view port scale is 1:1 or 2:1.

14) Set your view port scale to ***2:1***, turn ***OFF*** the *Layout* layer, change the *Scale* field in your title block to **2:1** and ***print*** your drawing. Measure the height of the text to confirm that it printed at 3 mm.

11.7.7) Dimension scale and associativity

1) Set your view port scale to ***1:1***.

2) Enter model space from within paper space, select all the objects in your drawing, including the dimensions, and **SCale** them by a factor of **2**.

3) You should notice three things.
   - The dimension values have increased by a factor of two. This is called associativity. The dimensions are associated with the object and the dimension values will change when the object changes.
   - The dimension physical size did not get scaled.
   - The chamfer or leader dimension gets scaled with the model and the text does not change to 4 X 4. Multileaders are not associative.

4) **Undo** the scaling and this time **SCale** everything, except for the chamfer dimension, by a scale of **2**.

5) Select the chamfer dimension and use the grip boxes to move it back into position and edit the text (**DDEDIT**) so that it reads **4 X 4**.

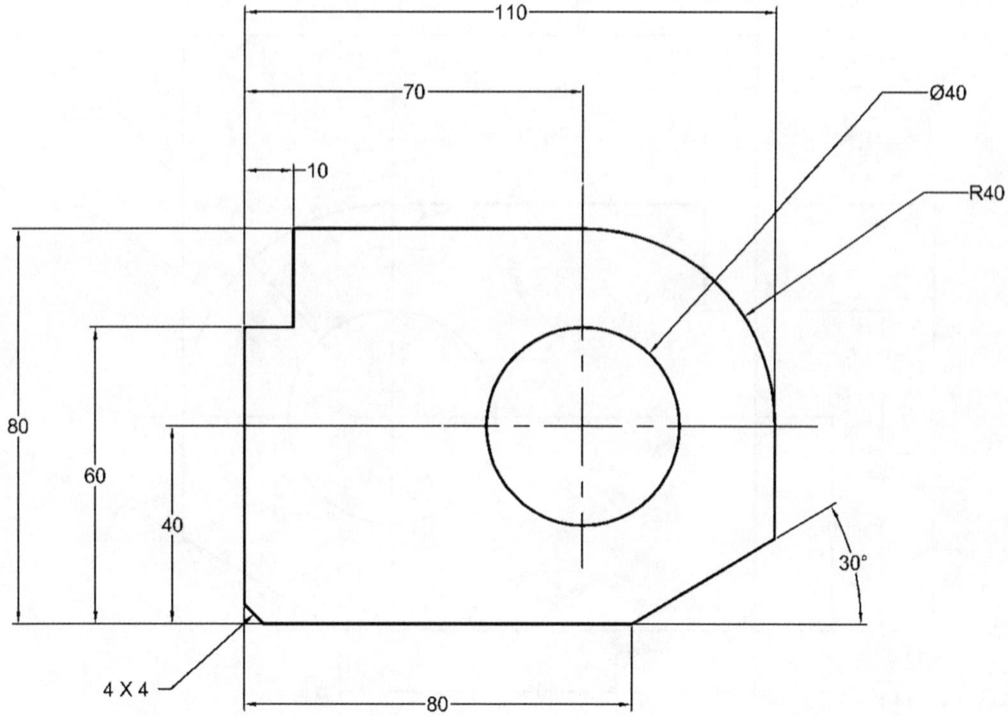

6) Notice that the 10 mm dimension value is outside the extension lines. Sometimes it is desirable to force the text between the extension lines.
   a) Command: **dimtix**
   b) `Enter new value for DIMTIX <OFF>:` **on**
   c) Update  only the 10 mm dimension.
   d) Turn your **DIMTIX** off.

Problem? If the UPDATE command does not work, you will have to erase and redraw the dimension being modified.

7) Set the spacing between the linear dimensions to 10 mm. If necessary, use grip boxes to move the other dimensions to a more appropriate location.

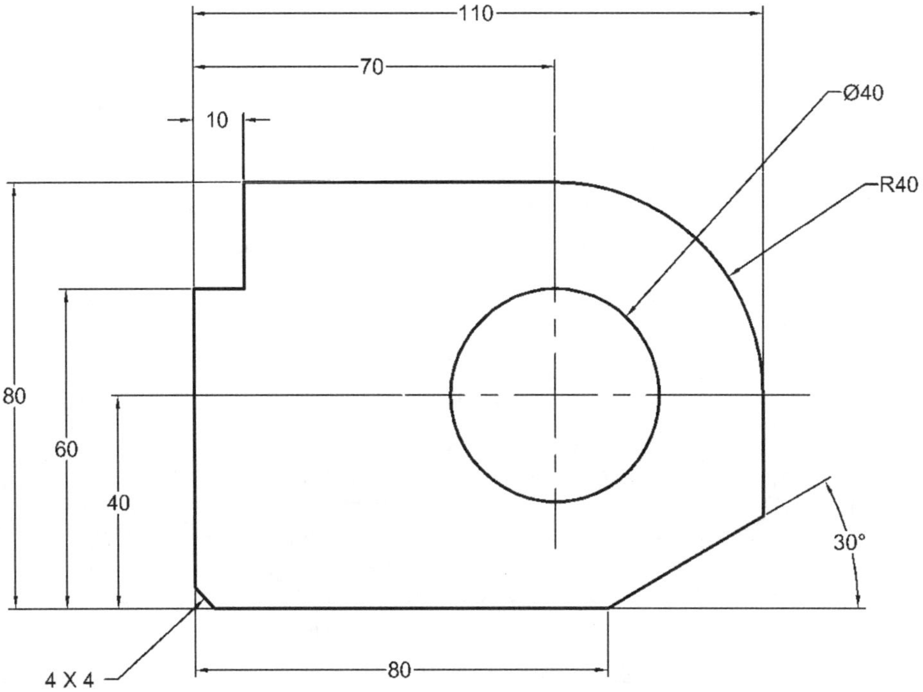

8) Enter the appropriate scale in your title block, ***save*** and ***print*** your drawing.

Exercise 11.8-1: Dimension styles

Create an annotative ASME **dimension** and **multileader styles** (as in the above tutorial) in your ***set-mm.dwt*** and your ***set-inch.dwt***. Once the style is created and set to be the current dimension style, resave your template file. For the *set-inch.dwt*, use a 0.00 precision and suppress the leading zero. For the inch multileader, use the same setting as the *Standard* style.

11.8) EDITING DIMENSION TEXT TUTORIAL

The objective of this tutorial is to familiarize the user with editing dimension text. We will be adding text to a dimension without influencing its associativity. We will also be adding dimension symbols.

1) 

dim_edit_student_2018.dwg and 

Dim Edit Tut.dwg. By the end of the tutorial, we will add all the dimensions shown. The initial drawing will contain no dimensions.

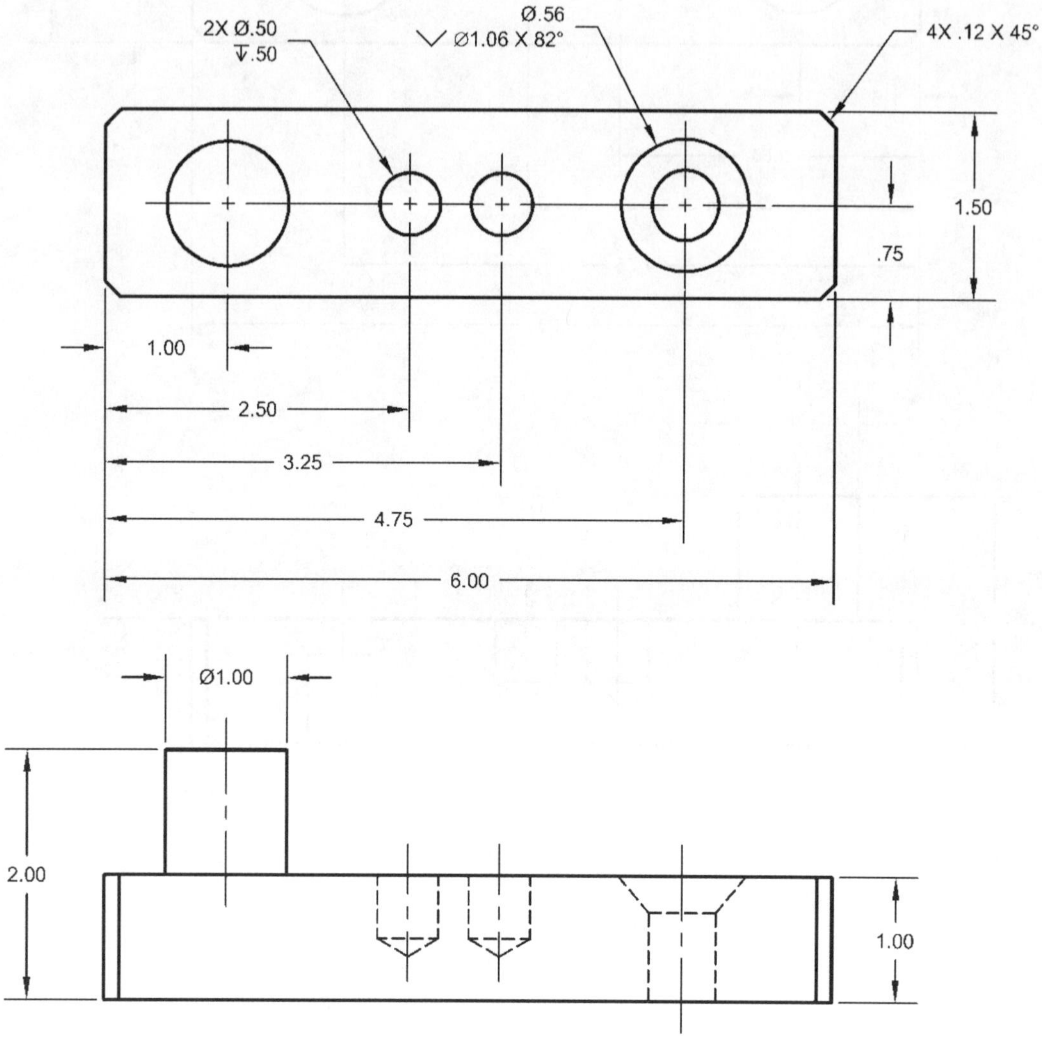

2) Dimension the part as shown. To force the dimension text between the extension lines use the dimension variable **DIMTIX**. Remember that the `Space` bar repeats the last command used.

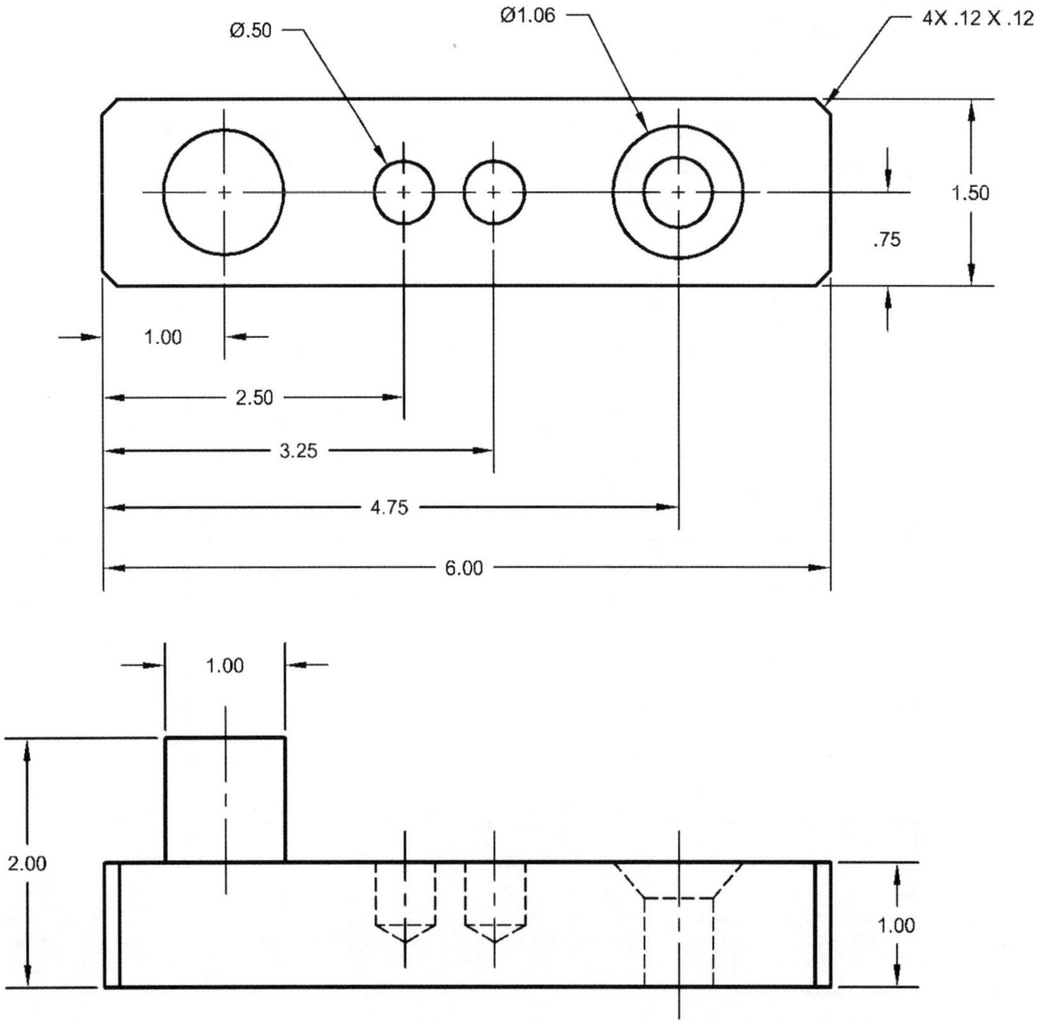

3) Add a diameter symbol to the 1.00 diameter cylinder dimension.
   a) <u>Command:</u> **ddedit**
   b) `Select an annotation object or [Undo]:` Select the 1.00 dimension text of the cylinder. Move the cursor to the front of the text.
   c) *<u>Text Editor</u>* <u>tab:</u>
      i. The symbols menu is available by selecting the **@** icon. Select ***Diameter*** from the menu.

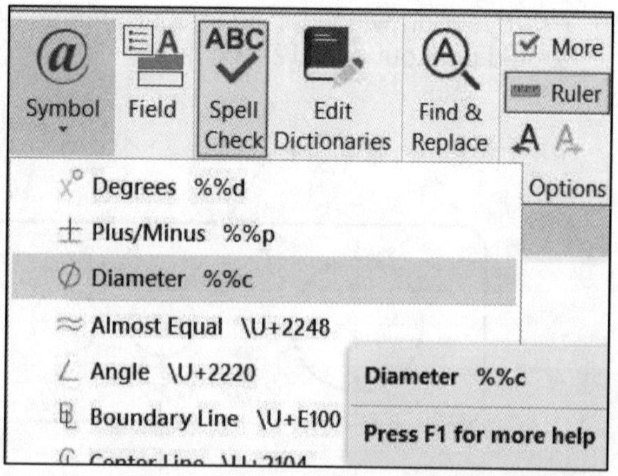

      ii. 

   d) The dimension text should now read **∅1.00**.

4) On your own, change the chamfer dimension from 4X .12 X .12 to **4X .12 X 45°**. Insert a degree symbol in the same way that you inserted a diameter symbol.

5) Add the repeated feature and depth text to the ∅.50 dimension text.
   a) <u>Command:</u> **ddedit**
   b) `Select an annotation object or [Undo]:` Select the ∅.50 dimension text. Type **2X** and a space. Then use the **`Right arrow`** to position your cursor at the end of the dimension text. Press **`Enter`** to start a new line of text and type **x.50**. Make sure that the **x** is in lower case.
   c) *<u>Text Editor</u>* <u>tab:</u>
      i. Highlight the lower case **x** and change its font to ***gdt***.
      ii. Align the text to the right.
      iii. 

6) On your own, change the countersink dimension text. The following is a list of useful *gdt* font symbols.

i = ⌯ n = ∅ v = ⌴ w = ⌵ x = ↧

7) Space the dimension evenly.

8) 

9) ***Print*** your drawing indicating your print scale in the title block. Your dimensions text should print out as 0.12 inch high.

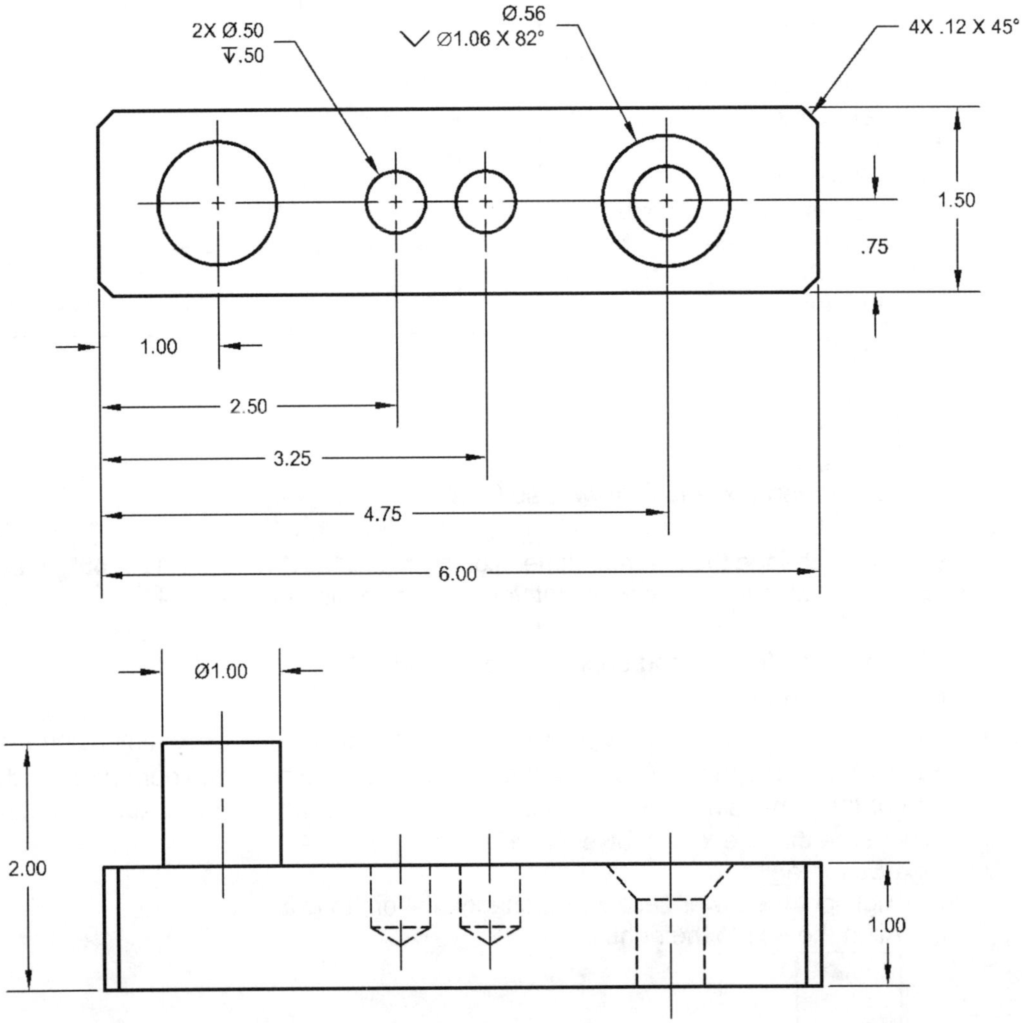

DIMENSIONING IN AUTOCAD® QUESTIONS

Name: ________________________________ Date: ______________

Q11-1) Dimension text should be aligned ...

a) vertically.
b) horizontally.
c) with the part.
d) it doesn't matter.

Q11-2) A radius or diameter dimension leader should always point to the ... of the arc or circle.

a) center
b) edge
c) tangent
d) quadrant

Q11-3) The name of the window used to create and modify dimension styles.

a) Dimension manager
b) Dimension creation manager
c) Dimension style manager

Q11-4) The name of the command that allows you to apply any changes made to the current dimension style.

a) update
b) newstyle
c) set current
d) edit

Q11-5) The ribbon panel that contains commands that allow you to add and remove an annotative object's supported scales.

a) annotation objects
b) annotation support
c) scaling
d) annotation scaling

Q11-6) The organization that controls the United States' dimensioning standard.

a) ISO
b) ASME
c) ANSI
d) SI

Q11-7) The typed command used to edit dimension text.

a) edit
b) tedit
c) ddedit
d) ddim

Q11-8) An object that will adjust its scale as the viewport scale changes.

a) annotative
b) associative
c) scalable
d) parametric

Q11-9) A dimension that is linked to and will change with the geometry is ...

a) annotative
b) associative
c) scalable
d) parametric

Q11-10) A dimension type that does not have associativity.

a) linear
b) radius
c) angular
d) multileader

Q11-11) The typed command used to force dimension text between the extension lines.

a) ddim
b) dimext
c) dimtix
d) dimexo

DIMENSIONING IN AUTOCAD® PROBLEMS

Print each drawing using the appropriate pen widths and insert your titleblock.

P11-1) Using a CAD package, draw the necessary views and completely dimension the part shown. Do not base your 2-D dimension placement on the 3-D dimensions shown. Use proper dimensioning techniques to dimension your object. Dimensions given in inches.

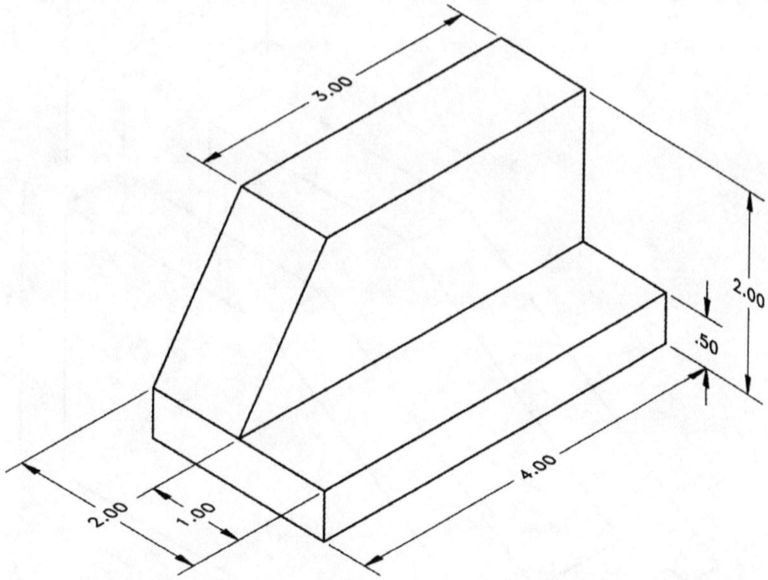

P11-2) Using a CAD package, draw the necessary views and completely dimension the part shown. Do not base your 2-D dimension placement on the 3-D dimensions shown. Use proper dimensioning techniques to dimension your object. Dimensions given in inches.

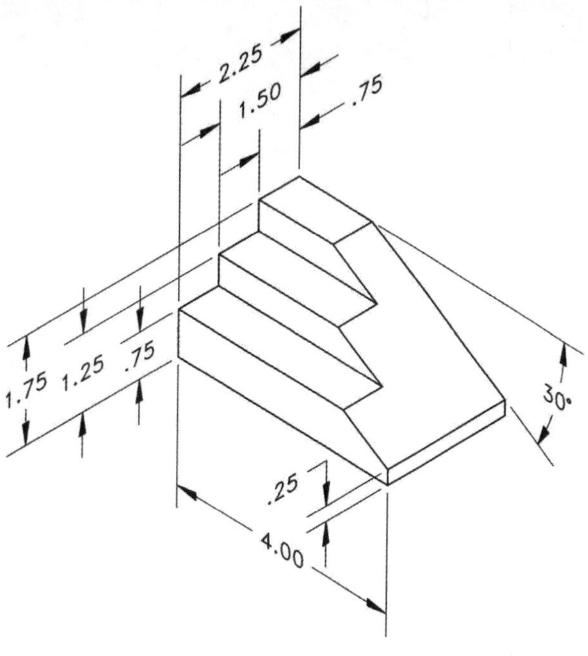

P11-3) Using a CAD package, draw the necessary views and completely dimension the part shown. Do not base your 2-D dimension placement on the 3-D dimensions shown. Use proper dimensioning techniques to dimension your object. Dimensions given in inches.

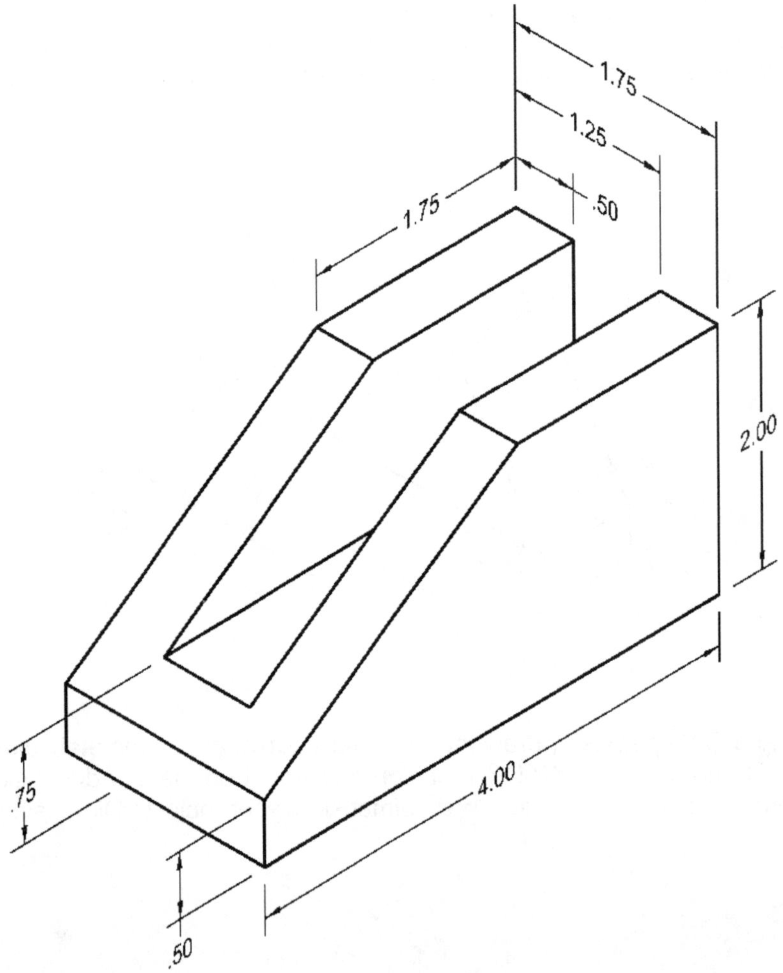

P11-4) Using a CAD package, draw the necessary views and completely dimension the part shown. Do not base your 2-D dimension placement on the 3-D dimensions shown. Use proper dimensioning techniques to dimension your object. Dimensions given in inches.

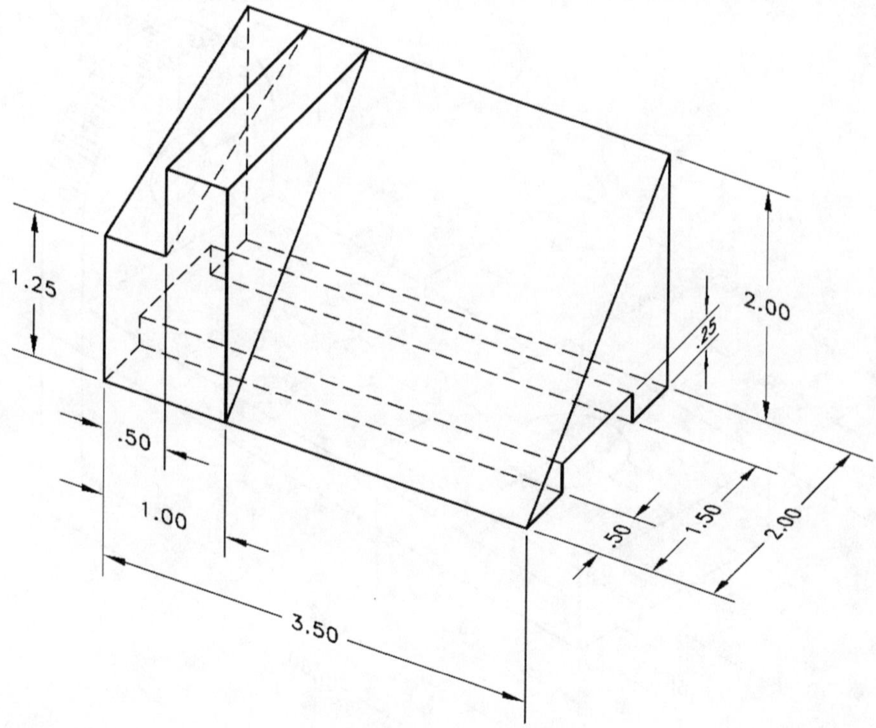

P11-5) Using a CAD package, draw the necessary views and completely dimension the part shown. Do not base your 2-D dimension placement on the 3-D dimensions shown. Use proper dimensioning techniques to dimension your object. Dimensions given in inches.

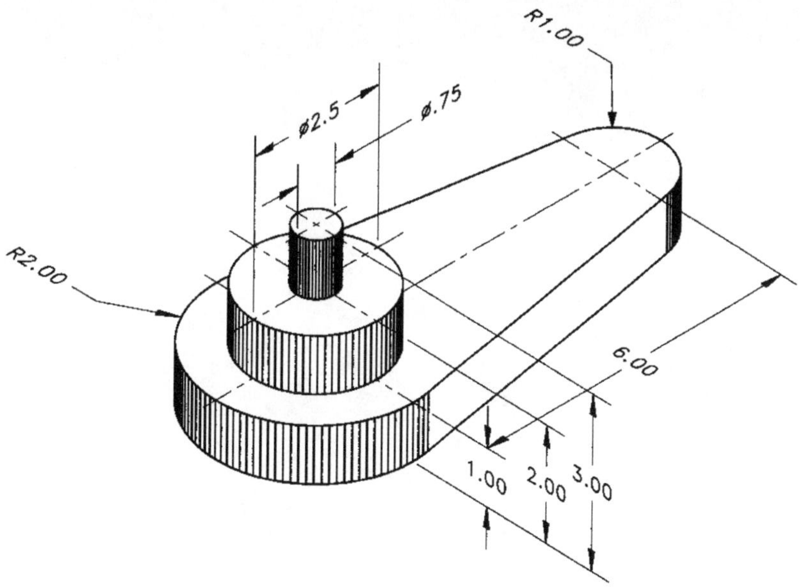

P11-6) Using a CAD package, draw the necessary views and completely dimension the part shown. Do not base your 2-D dimension placement on the 3-D dimensions shown. Use proper dimensioning techniques to dimension your object. Dimensions given in inches.

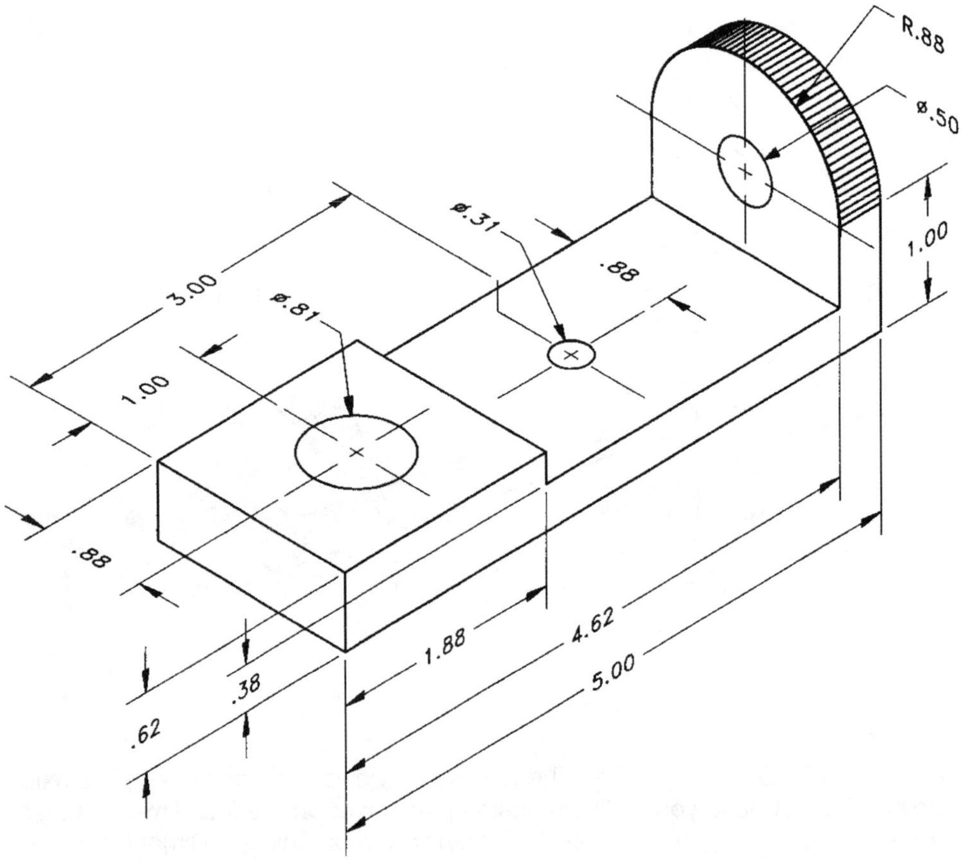

P11-7) Using a CAD package, draw the necessary views and completely dimension the part shown. Do not base your 2-D dimension placement on the 3-D dimensions shown. Use proper dimensioning techniques to dimension your object. Dimensions given in inches.

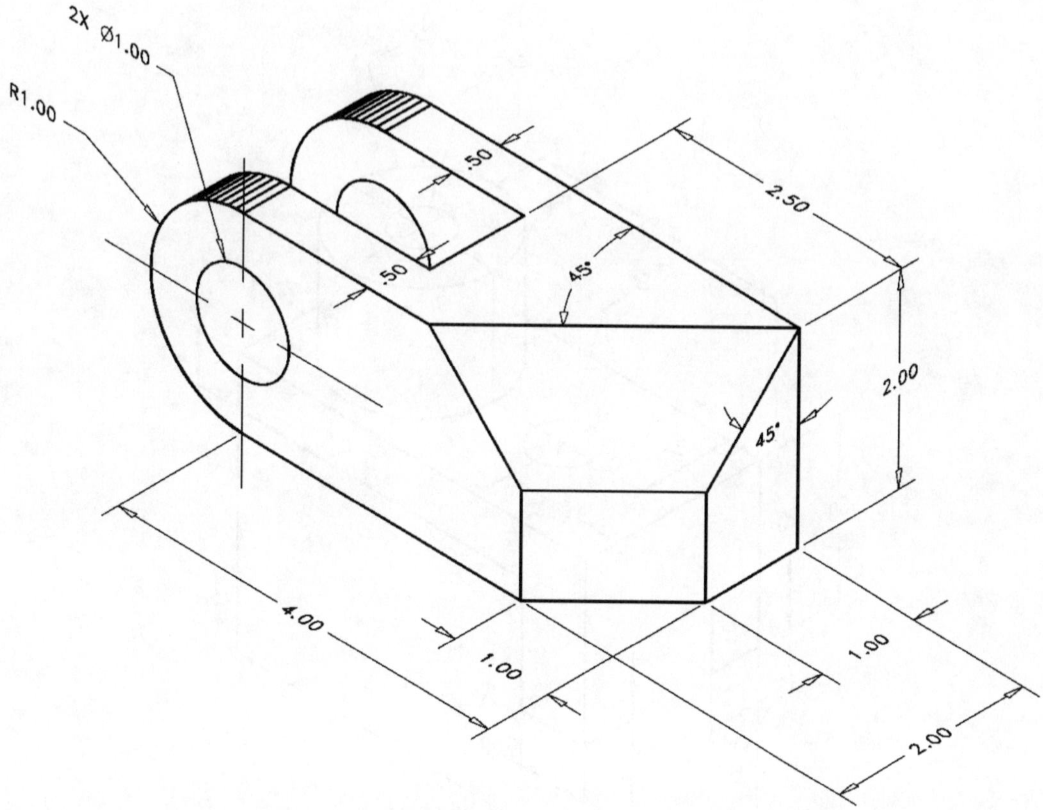

P11-8) Using a CAD package, draw the necessary views and completely dimension the part shown. Do not base your 2-D dimension placement on the 3-D dimensions shown. Use proper dimensioning techniques to dimension your object. Dimensions given in millimeters.

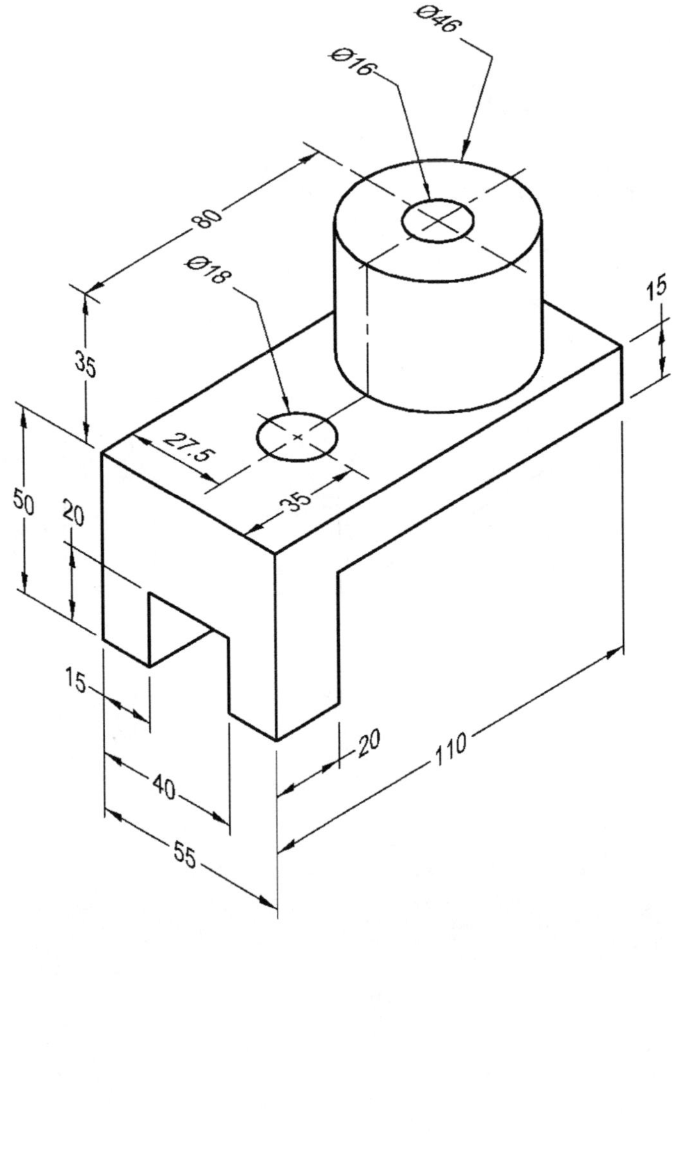

P11-9) Using a CAD package, draw the necessary views and completely dimension the part shown. Do not base your 2-D dimension placement on the 3-D dimensions shown. Use proper dimensioning techniques to dimension your object. Dimensions given in inches.

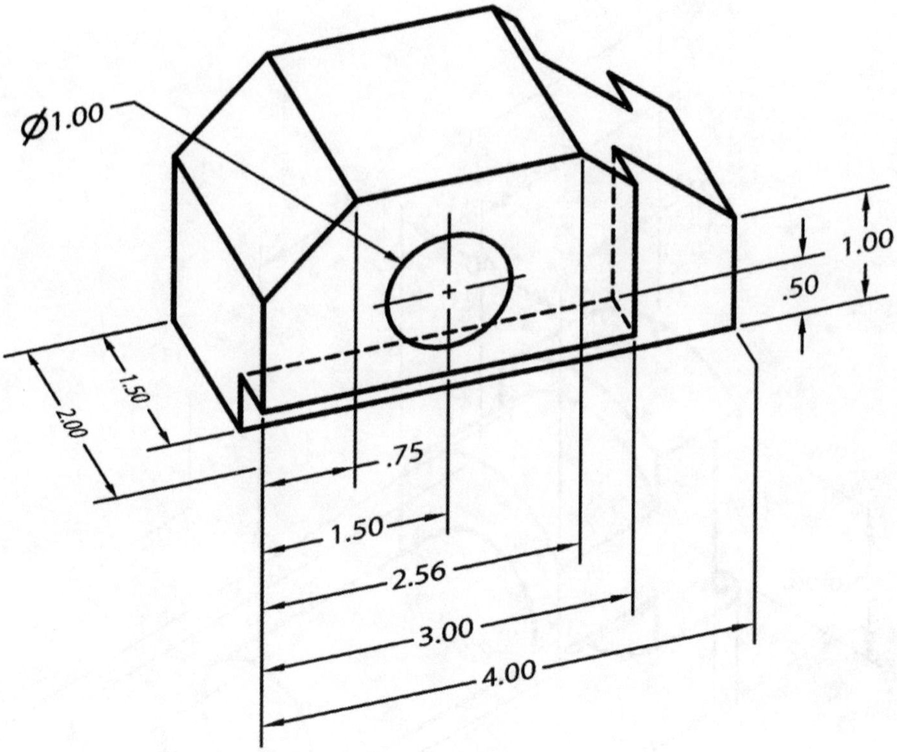

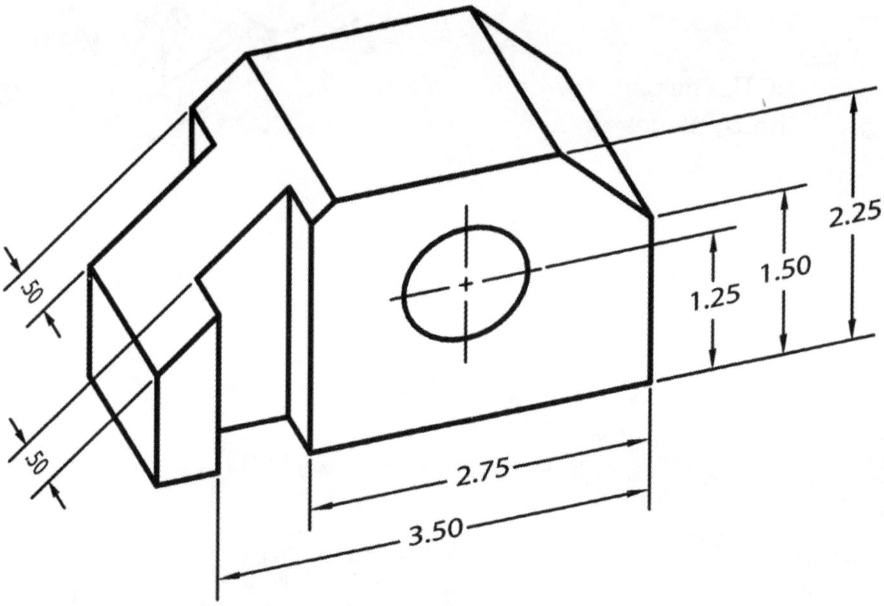

P11-10) Using a CAD package, draw the necessary views and completely dimension the part shown. Do not base your 2-D dimension placement on the 3-D dimensions shown. Use proper dimensioning techniques to dimension your object. Dimensions given in millimeters.

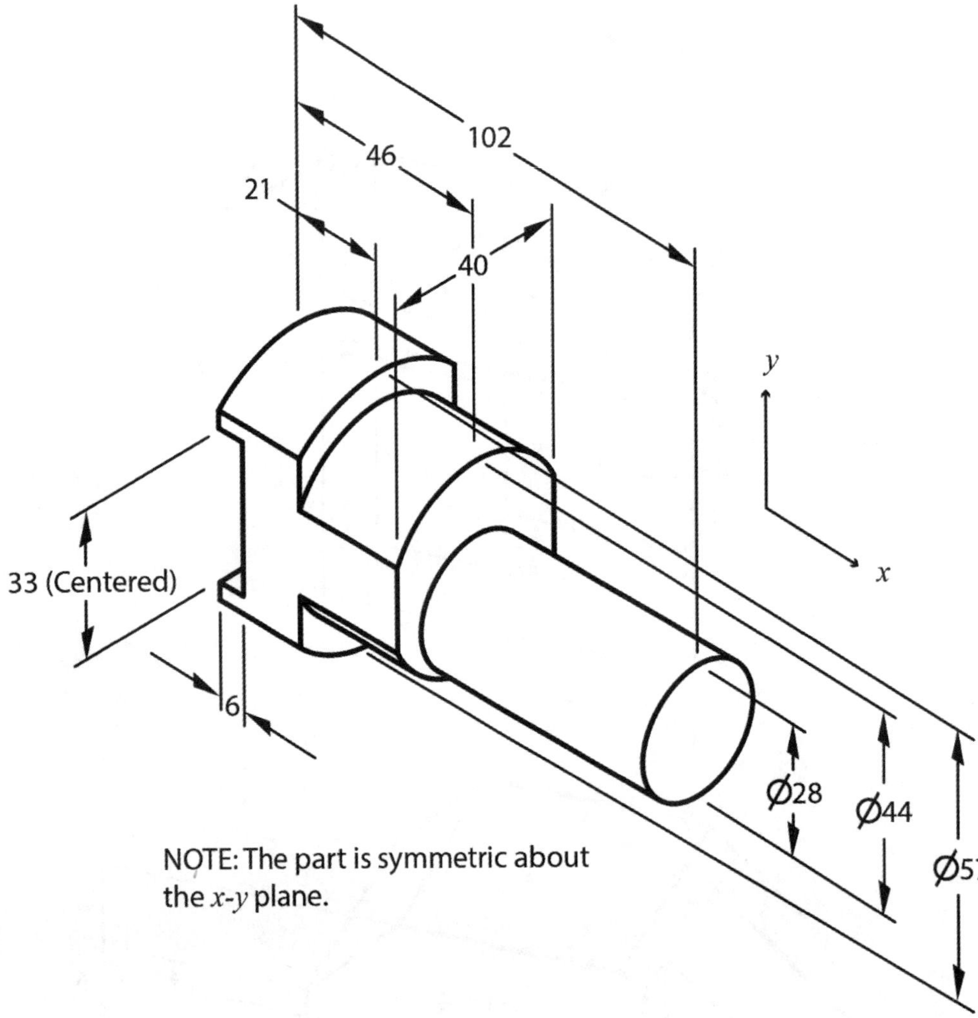

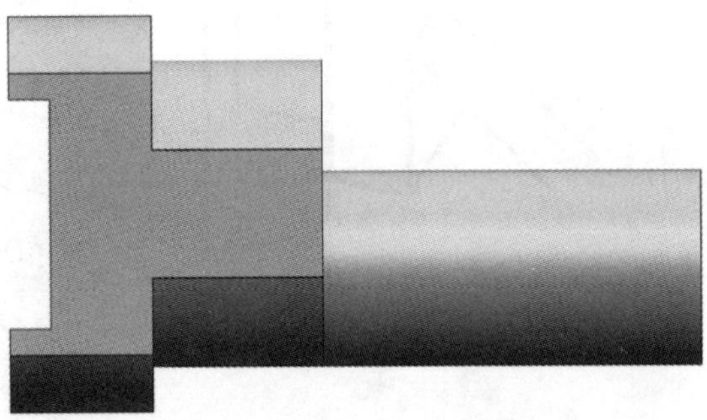

P11-11) Using a CAD package, draw the necessary views and completely dimension the part shown. Do not base your 2-D dimension placement on the 3-D dimensions shown. Use proper dimensioning techniques to dimension your object. Dimensions given in inches.

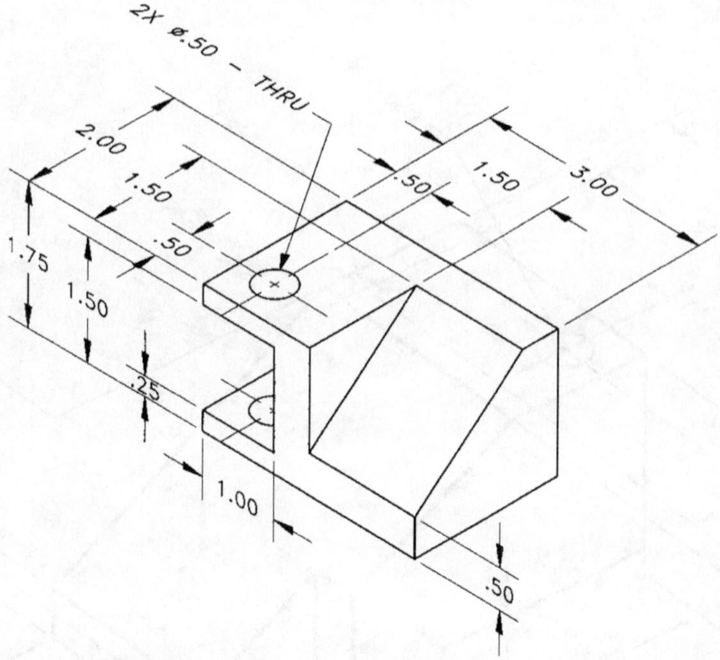

P11-12) Using a CAD package, draw the necessary views and completely dimension the part shown. Do not base your 2-D dimension placement on the 3-D dimensions shown. Use proper dimensioning techniques to dimension your object. Dimensions given in millimeters.

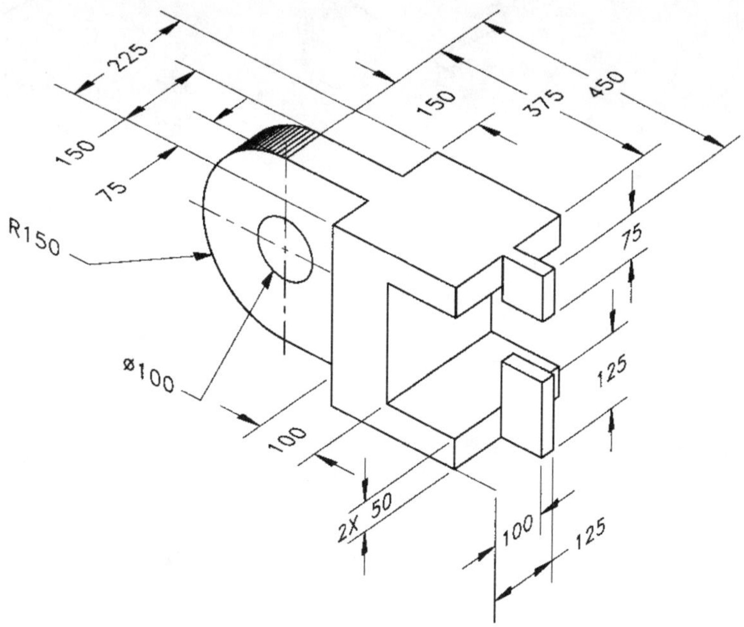

P11-13) Using a CAD package, draw the necessary views and completely dimension the part shown. Do not base your 2-D dimension placement on the 3-D dimensions shown. Use proper dimensioning techniques to dimension your object. Dimensions given in millimeters.

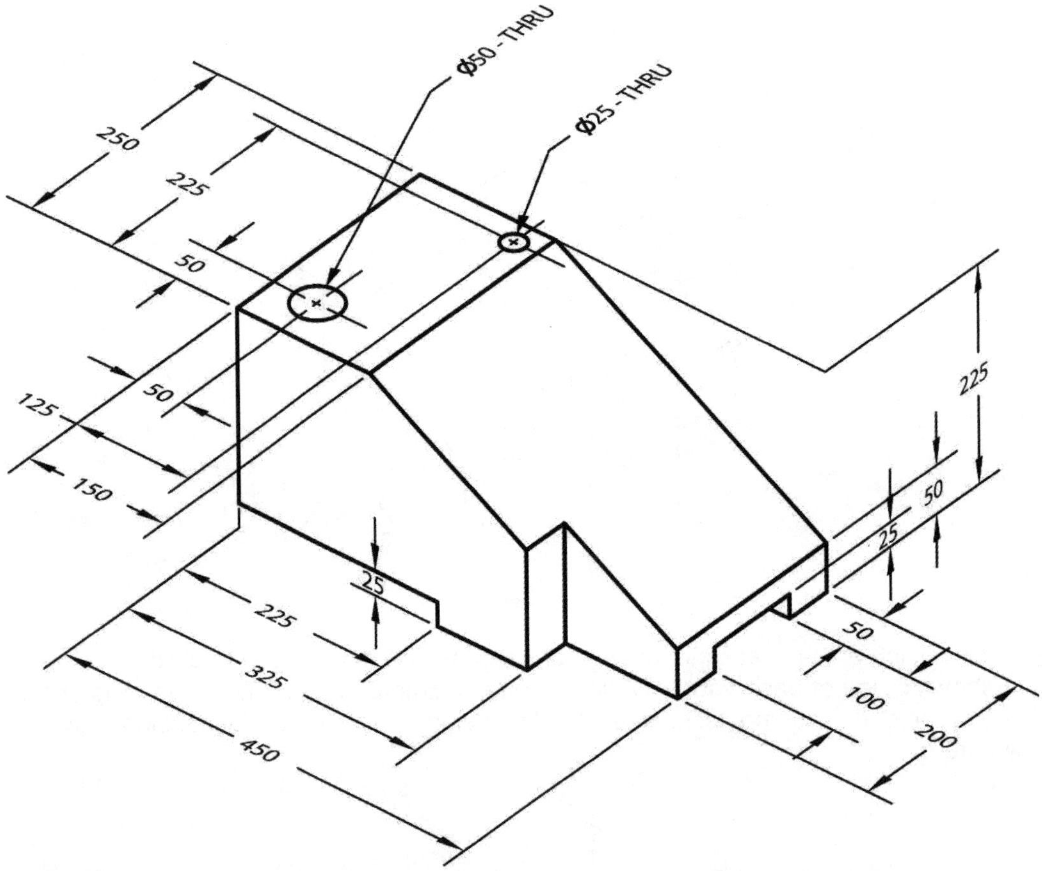

P11-14) Using a CAD package, draw the necessary views and completely dimension the part shown. Do not base your 2-D dimension placement on the 3-D dimensions shown. Use proper dimensioning techniques to dimension your object. Dimensions given in inches.

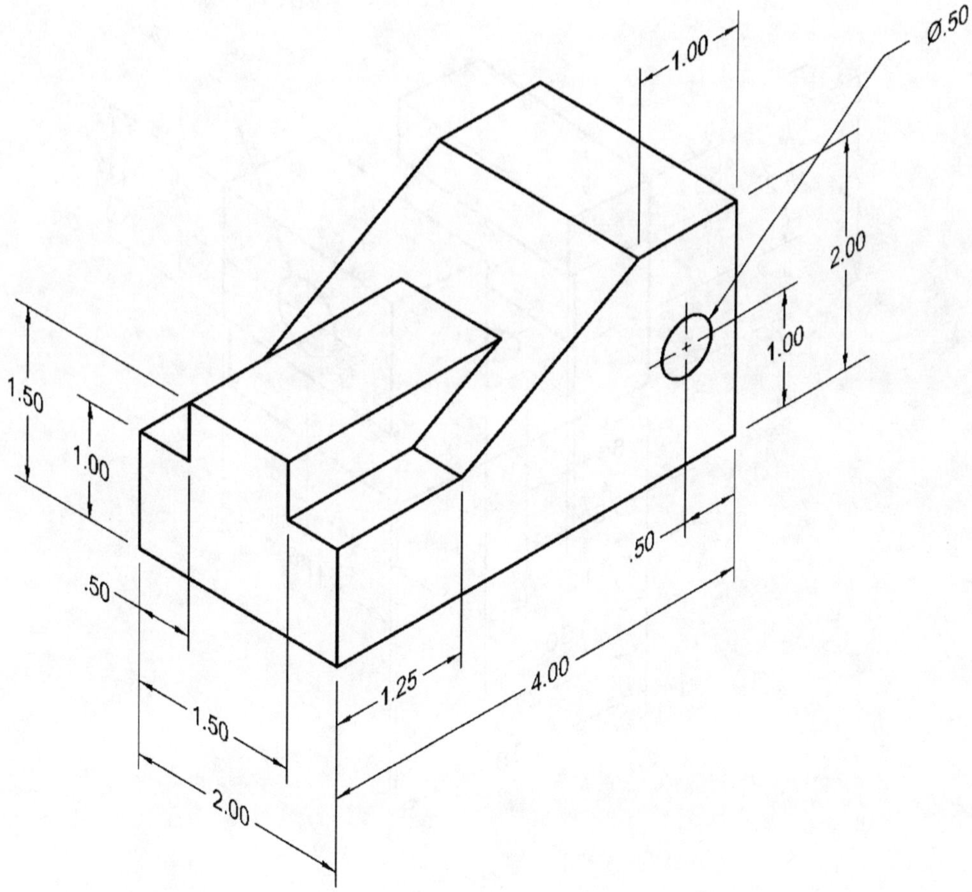

P11-15) Using a CAD package, draw the necessary views and completely dimension the part shown. Do not base your 2-D dimension placement on the 3-D dimensions shown. Use proper dimensioning techniques to dimension your object. Dimensions given in millimeters.

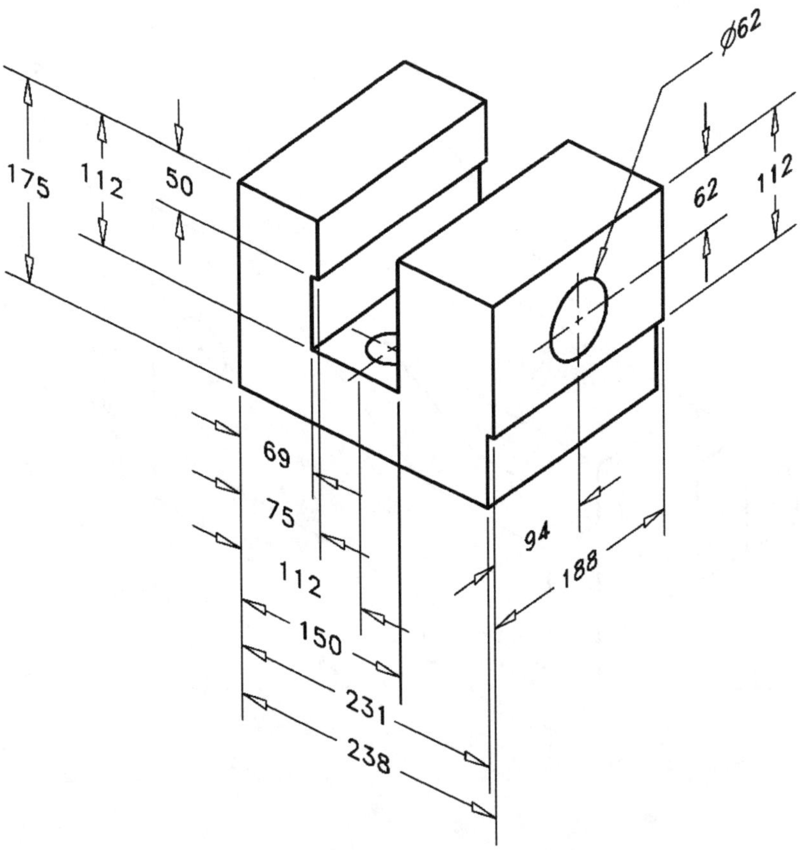

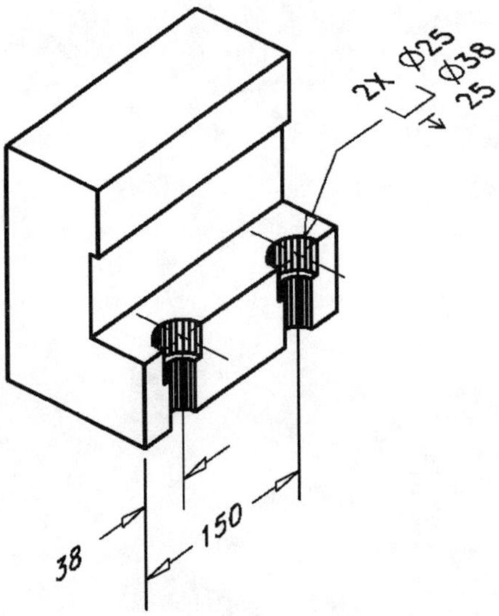

P11-16) Using a CAD package, draw the necessary views and completely dimension the part shown. Do not base your 2-D dimension placement on the 3-D dimensions shown. Use proper dimensioning techniques to dimension your object. Dimensions given in millimeters.

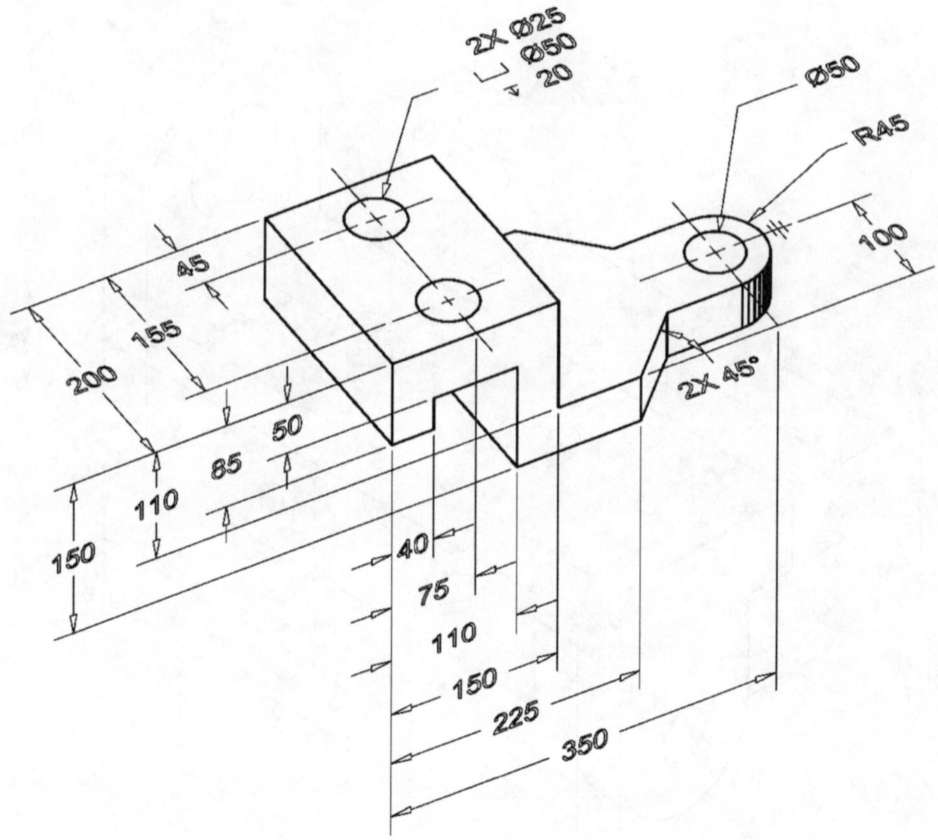

P11-17) Using a CAD package, draw the necessary views and completely dimension the part shown. Do not base your 2-D dimension placement on the 3-D dimensions shown. Use proper dimensioning techniques to dimension your object. Dimensions given in inches.

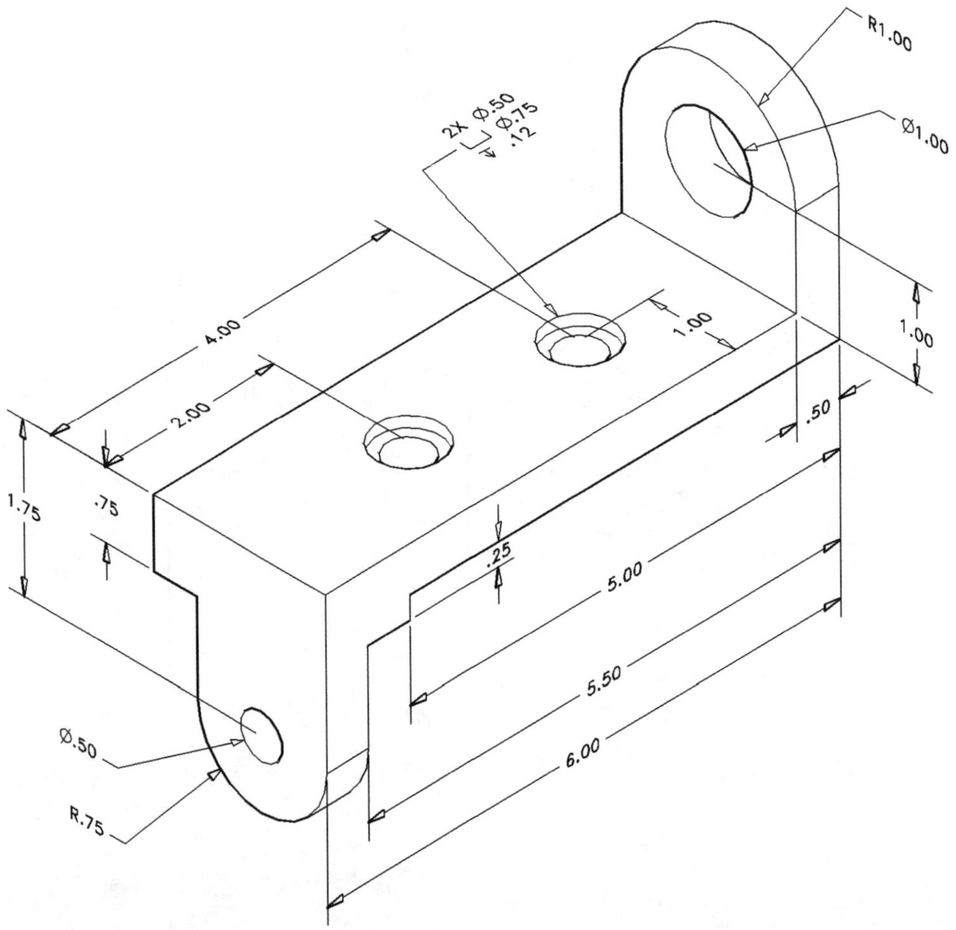

P11-18) Using a CAD package, draw the necessary views and completely dimension the part shown. Do not base your 2-D dimension placement on the 3-D dimensions shown. Use proper dimensioning techniques to dimension your object. Dimensions given in inches.

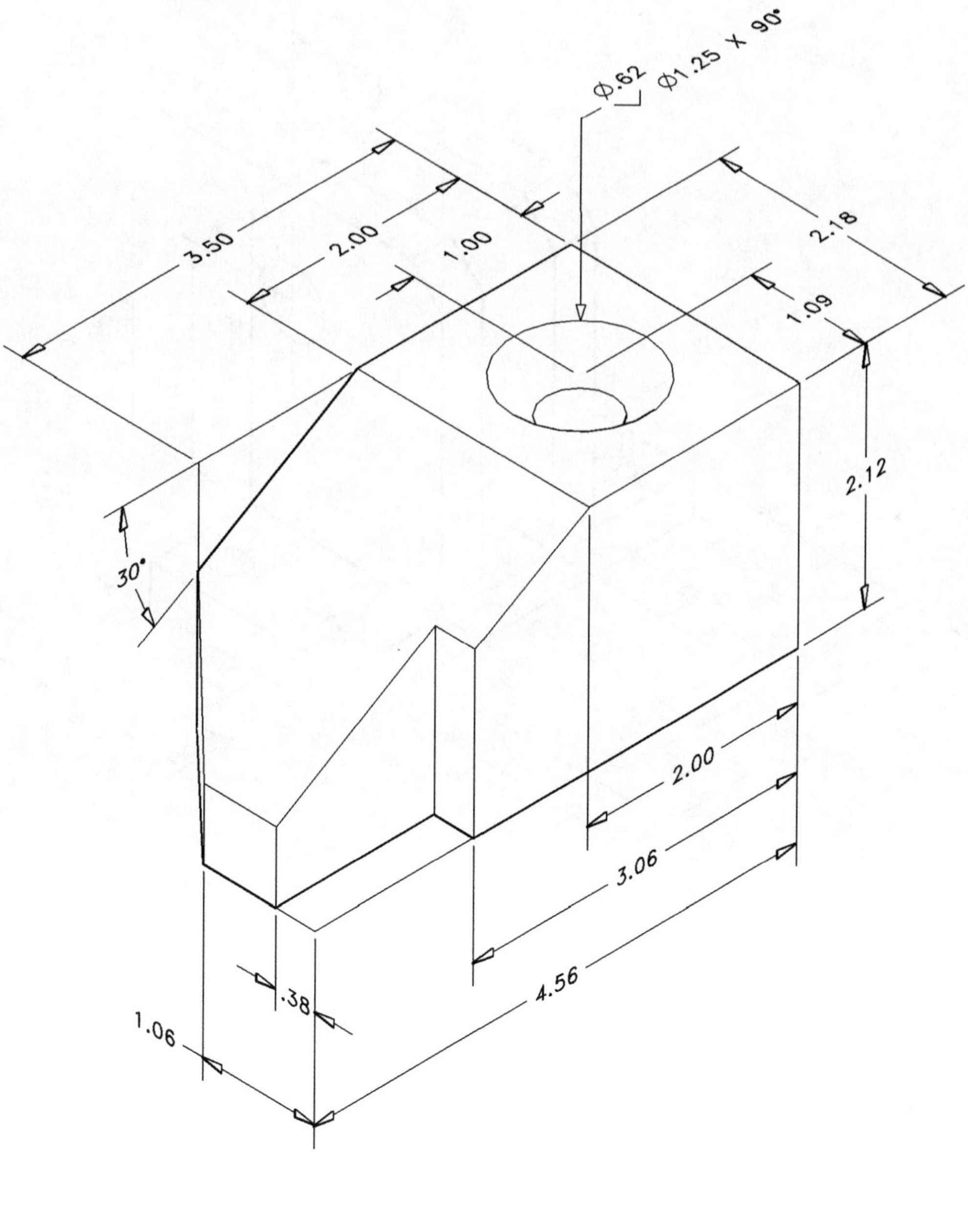

SP11-19) Draw the necessary views and completely dimension the part shown. Do not base your 2-D dimension placement on the 3-D dimensions shown. Use proper dimensioning techniques to dimension your object. The answer to this problem is given on the *Independent Learning Content*. Dimensions given in inches.

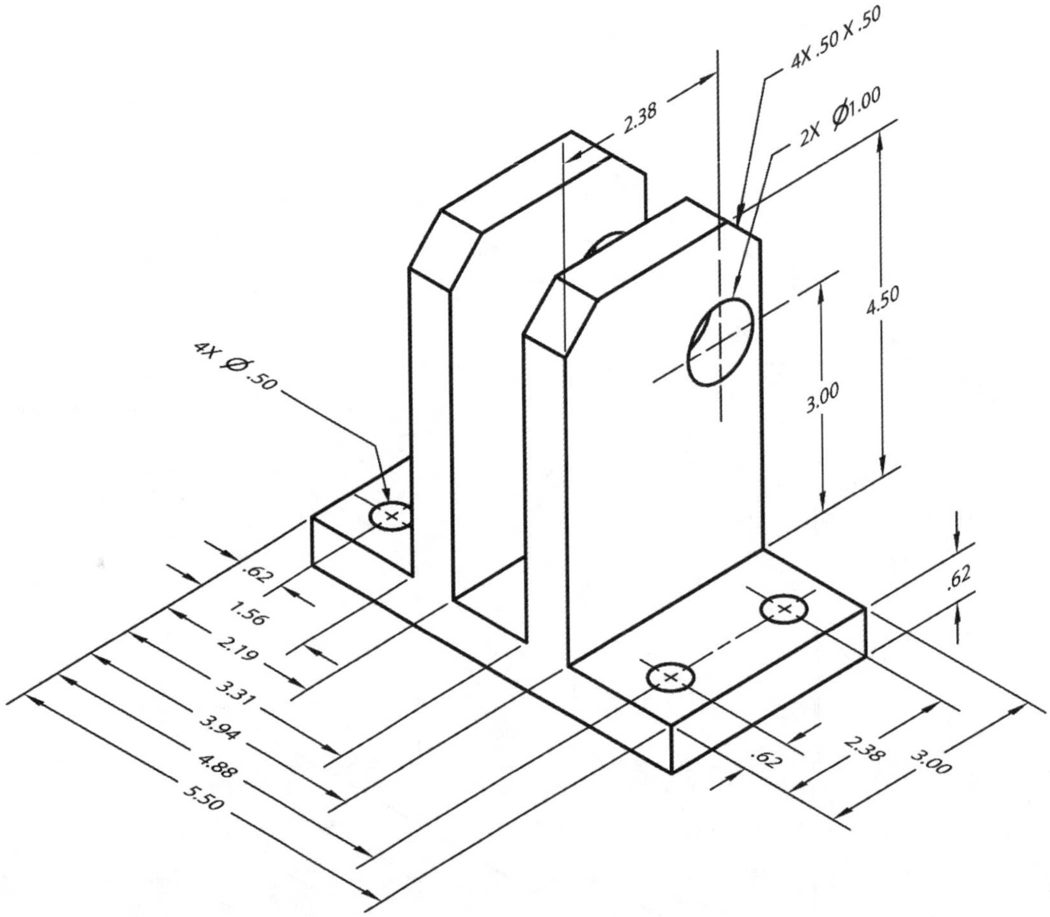

CHAPTER 12

READING SECTION VIEWS

CHAPTER OUTLINE

CHAPTER SUMMARY

Section views allow you to see inside an object. In this chapter you will learn how to recognize and read various types of sectional views. This includes understanding what the different section line symbols indicate.

12.1) SECTION VIEWS

A section view or section looks inside an object. Sections are used to clarify the interior construction of a part that cannot be clearly described by hidden lines in exterior views. It is a cut away view of an object. Often, objects are more complex and interesting on the inside than on the outside. **By taking an imaginary cut through the object and removing a portion, the inside features may be seen more clearly.** For example, a geode is a rock that is very plain and featureless on the outside but cut into it and you get an array of beautiful crystals.

A section view is created by cutting a part with an imaginary cutting plane. The portion of the part that is between the observer and the cutting plane is mentally discarded exposing the interior construction as shown in Figure 12.1-1.

A sectional view is projected perpendicular to the cutting plane and conforms to the standard arrangement of views. A cutting plane line is used to show where the part is being cut. The cutting plane line ends in arrows pointing in the direction of sight (see Figure 12.1-2). Section line symbols are used to indicate where the material has been cut and the type of material that the part is made from. If there is more than one section, they are labeled with capital letters such as A, B or C. These letters are placed near the arrows of the cutting plane line. The sectional view is then labeled with the corresponding letter (e.g., SECTION A-A) as shown in Figure 12.1-2.

Figure 12.1-1: Creating a section view.

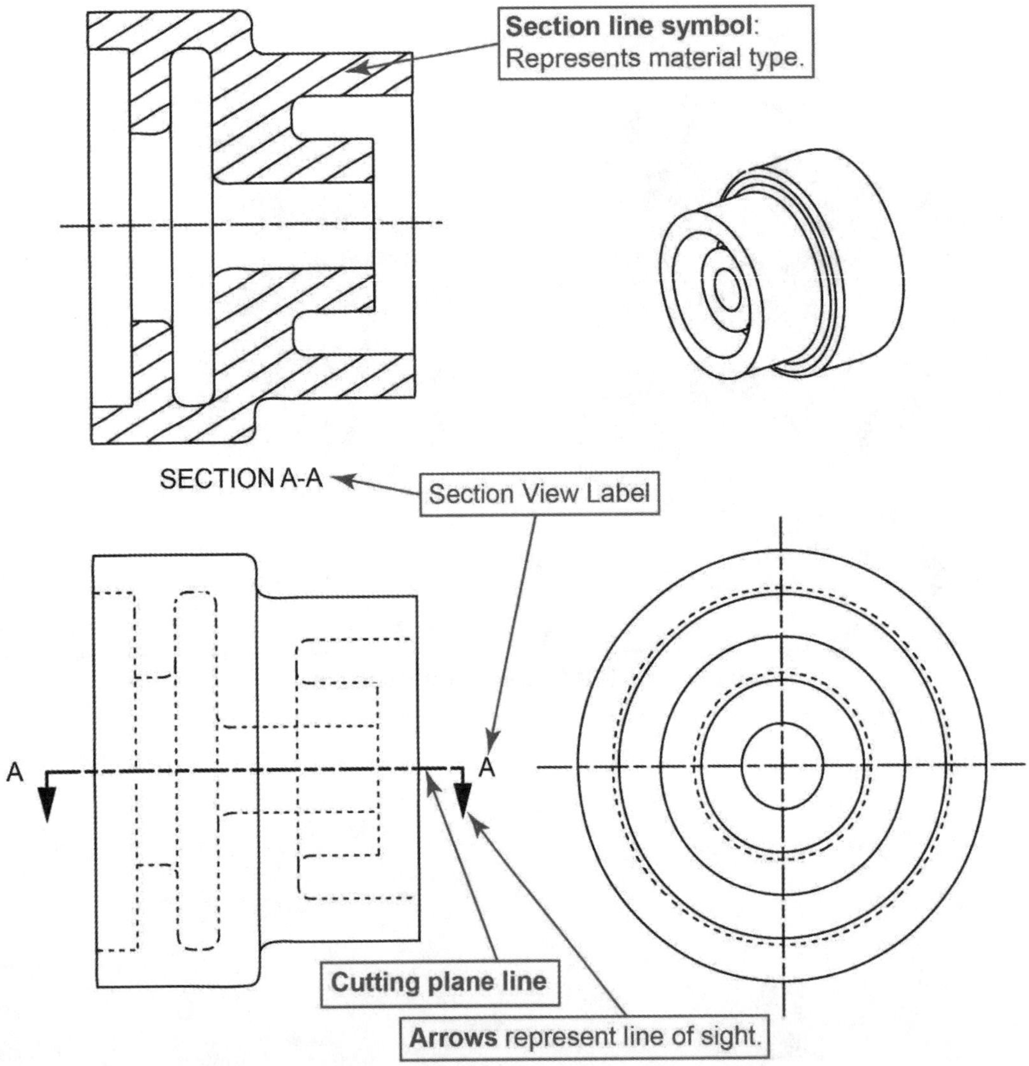

Figure 12.1-2: Sectional view.

12.2) LINES USED IN A SECTION VIEW

- <u>Cutting Plane Line</u>

A cutting plane line is used to show where the object is being cut and represents the edge view of the cutting plane. **Arrows are placed at the ends of the cutting plane line to indicate the direction of sight.** The arrows point to the portion of the object that is kept (see Figure 12.1-2).

- <u>Section Line Symbols</u>

Section line symbols are used to indicate where the cutting plane cuts the material (see Figure 12.1-2). Cut material is that which makes contact with the cutting plane. Section line symbols also indicate the type of material used to make the part. The most common section line symbols are shown in Figure 12.2-1.

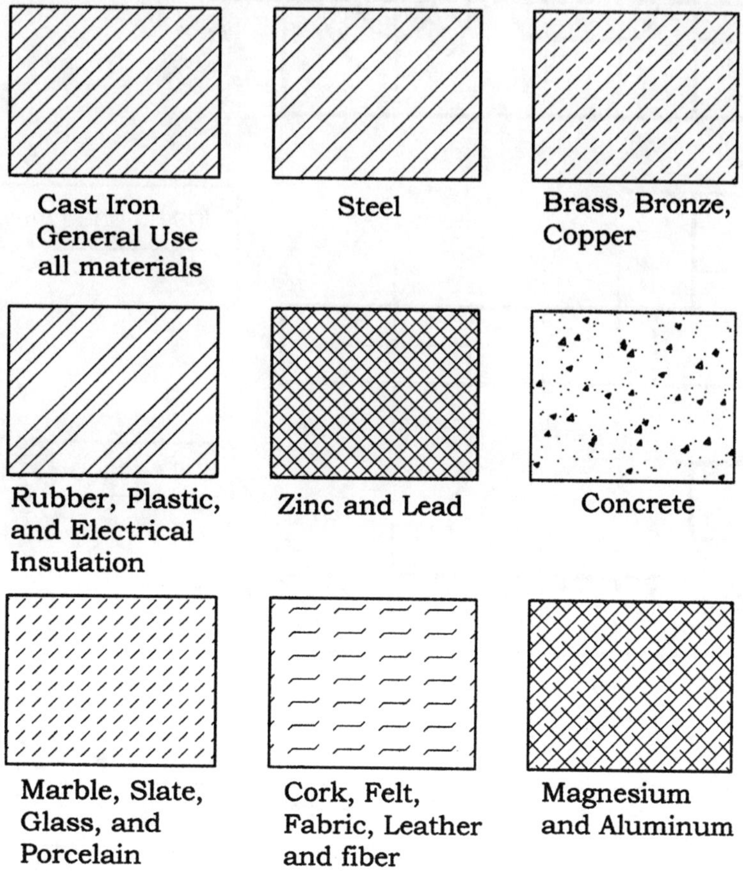

Figure 12.2-1: Section line symbols.

12.3) BASIC SECTIONS

Many types of sectioning techniques are used. The type of section view that was used typically depends on the type of part and the information that needs to be conveyed.

12.3.1) Full section

In a full section, the cutting plane passes fully through the object. The half of the object that is between the observer and the cutting plane is mentally removed. This exposes the cut surface and the interior features of the remaining portion. Figure 12.3-1 shows an example of a full section.

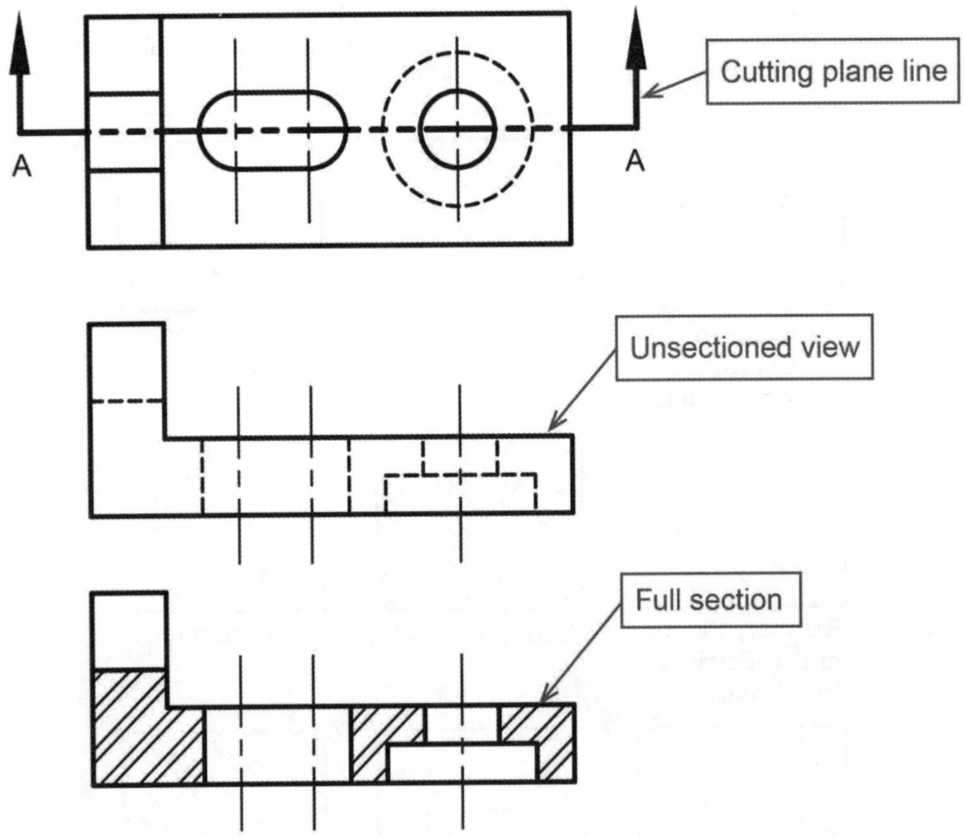

SECTION A-A

Figure 12.3-1: Full section.

12.3.2) Half section

A half section exposes the interior of one half of an object while retaining the exterior of the other half. In a half section, two cutting planes pass through the object at right angles to each other. Therefore, only a quarter of the object is mentally removed. Figure 12.3-2 shows an example of a half section.

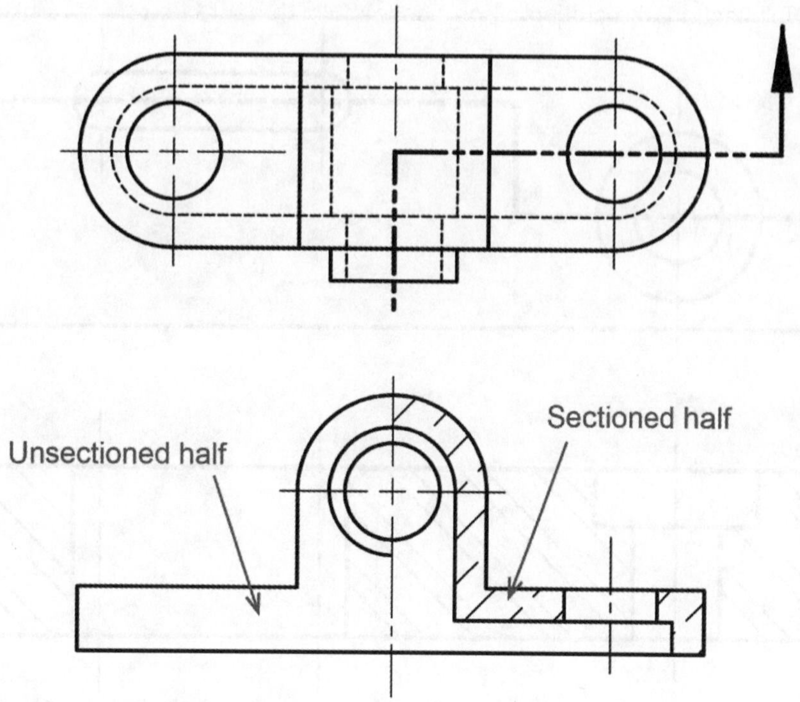

Figure 12.3-2: Half section.

12.3.3) Offset section

An offset section is produced by bending the cutting plane to show features that don't lie in the same plane. The section is drawn as if the offsets in the cutting plane were in one plane. Notice that the bends are not indicated in the section view. Figure 12.3-3 shows an offset section.

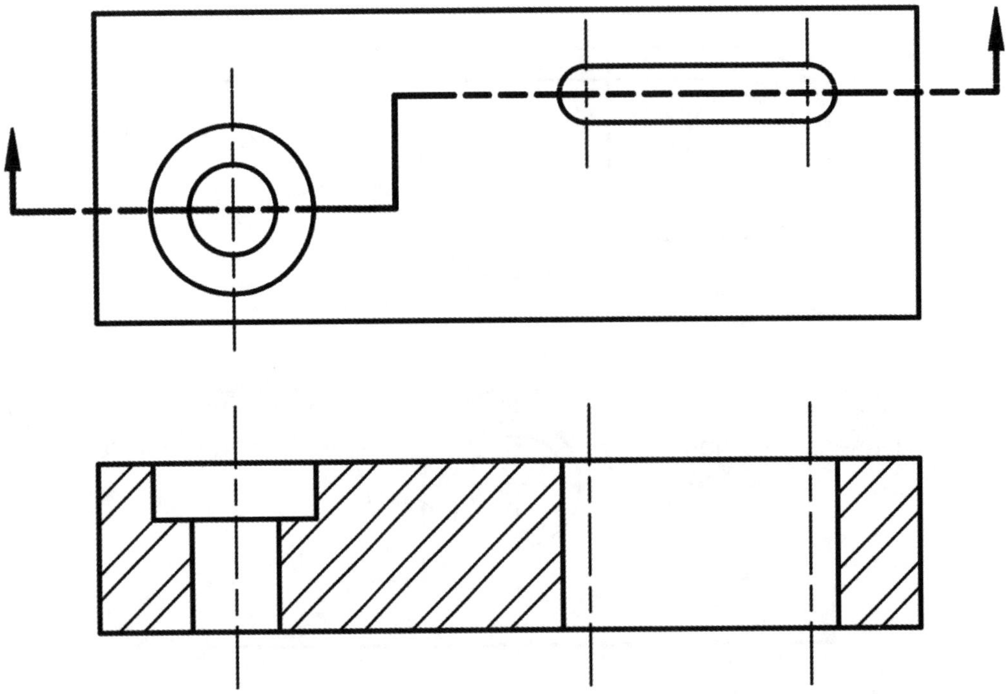

Figure 12.3-3: Offset section.

Try Exercises 12.3-1 and 12.3-2

Exercise 12.3-1: Identifying parts of a section view

Identify the different lines used in this full section view.

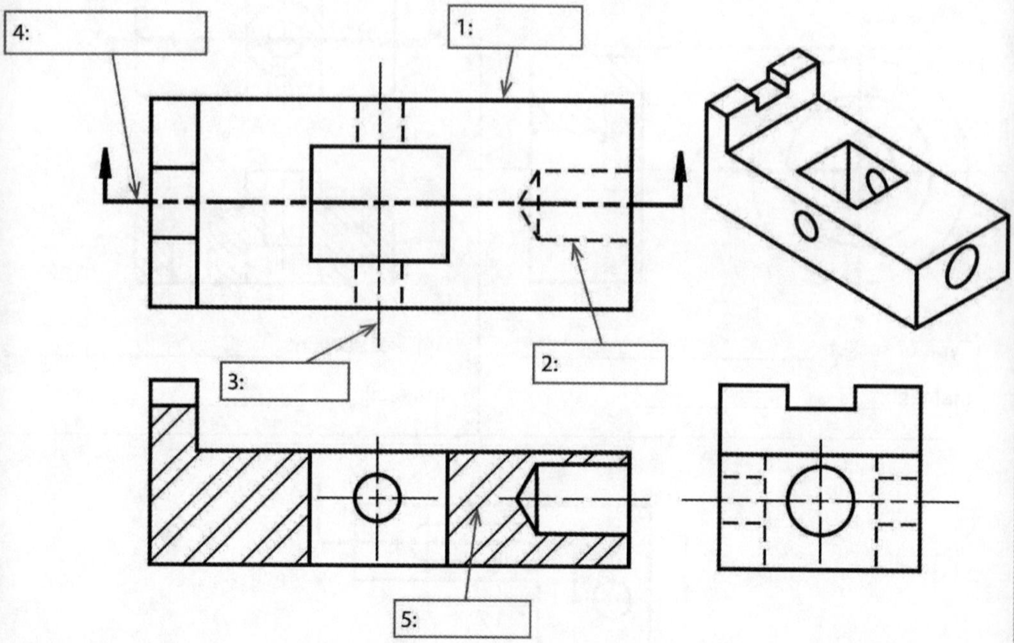

Exercise 12.3-2: Types of section views

Identify the type of section view used and the material that the part is made of.

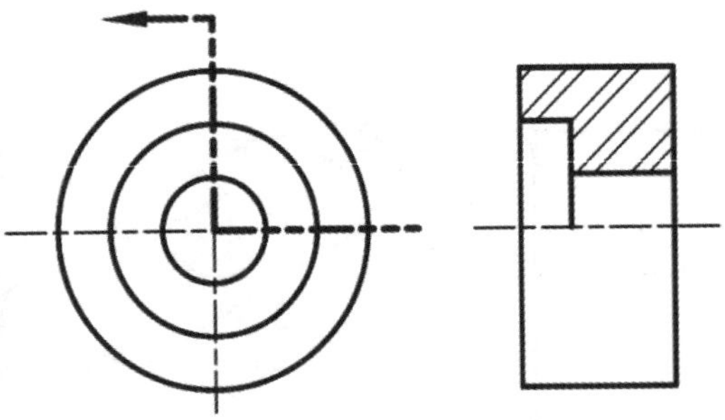

Type of section: ____________________

Material: ________________

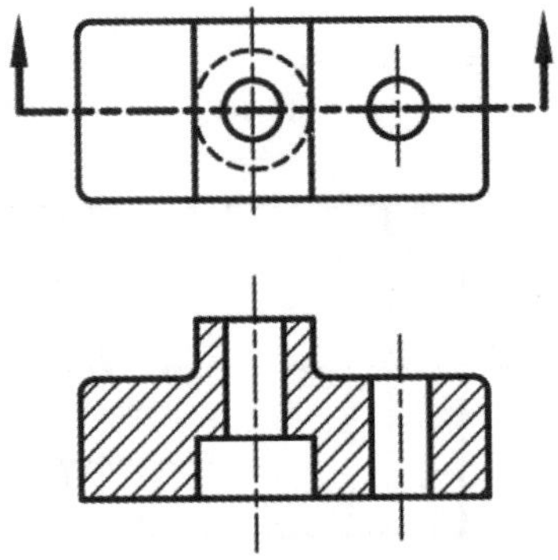

Type of section: ____________________

Material: ________________

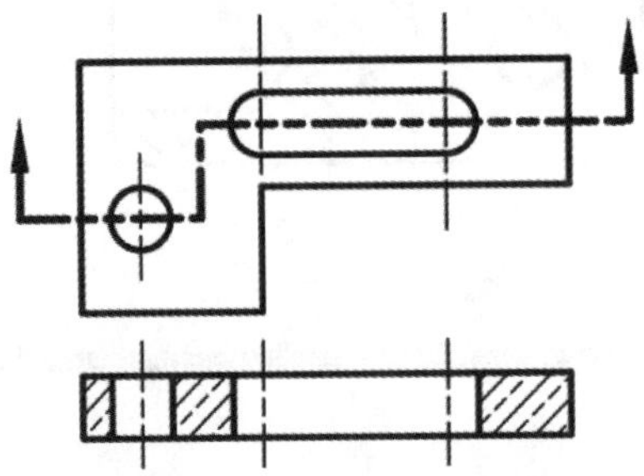

Type of section: ____________________

Material: ________________

12.4) ADVANCED SECTIONS

Advanced section view techniques are used to create a section view in special situations. These techniques are used if the basic sections don't show one or more features clearly.

12.4.1) Aligned section

In order to include angled elements in a section, the cutting plane may be bent so that it passes through those features. The plane and features are then revolved, according to the convention of revolution, into the original plane.

- Convention of Revolution: Features are revolved into the projection plane, usually a vertical or horizontal plane, and then projected. The purpose of this is to show true distances from a center or to show features that would otherwise not be seen. Figure 12.4-1 shows an aligned section employing the convention of revolution.

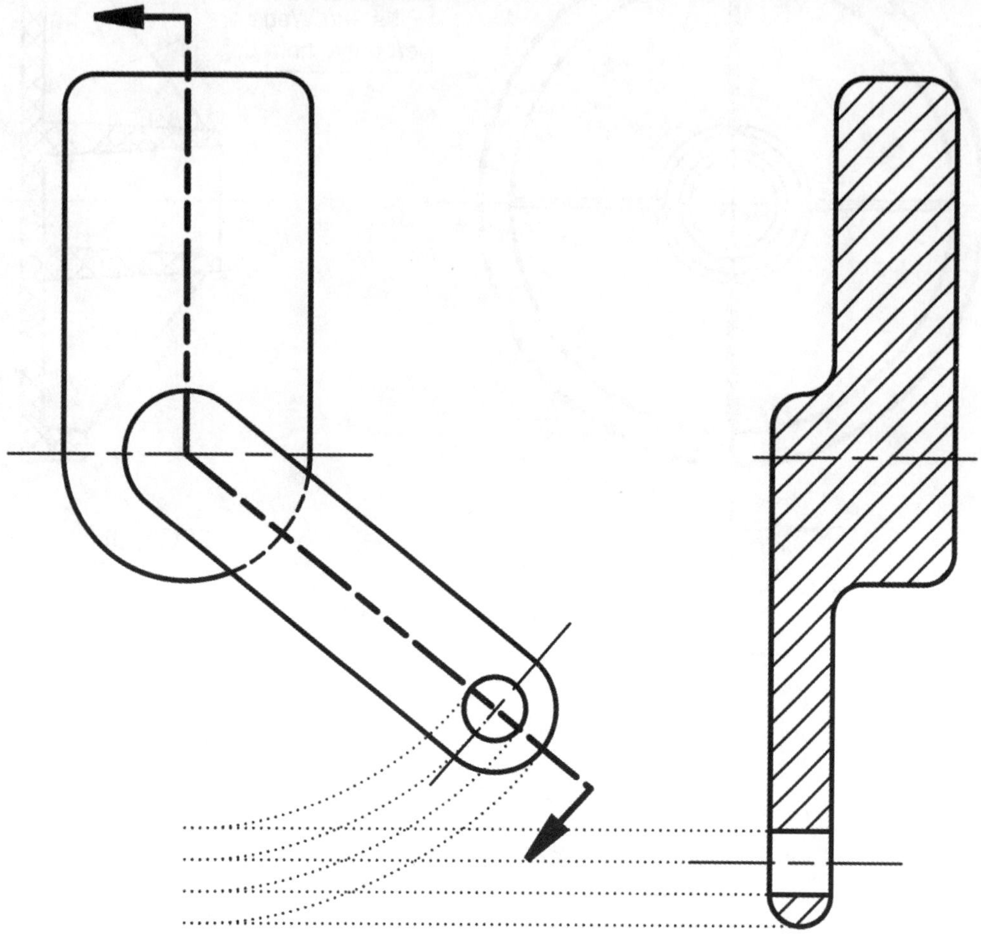

Figure 12.4-1: Aligned section.

12.4.2) Rib and web sections

To avoid a false impression of thickness and solidity, ribs and webs and other similar features are not sectioned even though the cutting plane passes along the center plane of the rib or web as indicated in Figure 12.4-2.

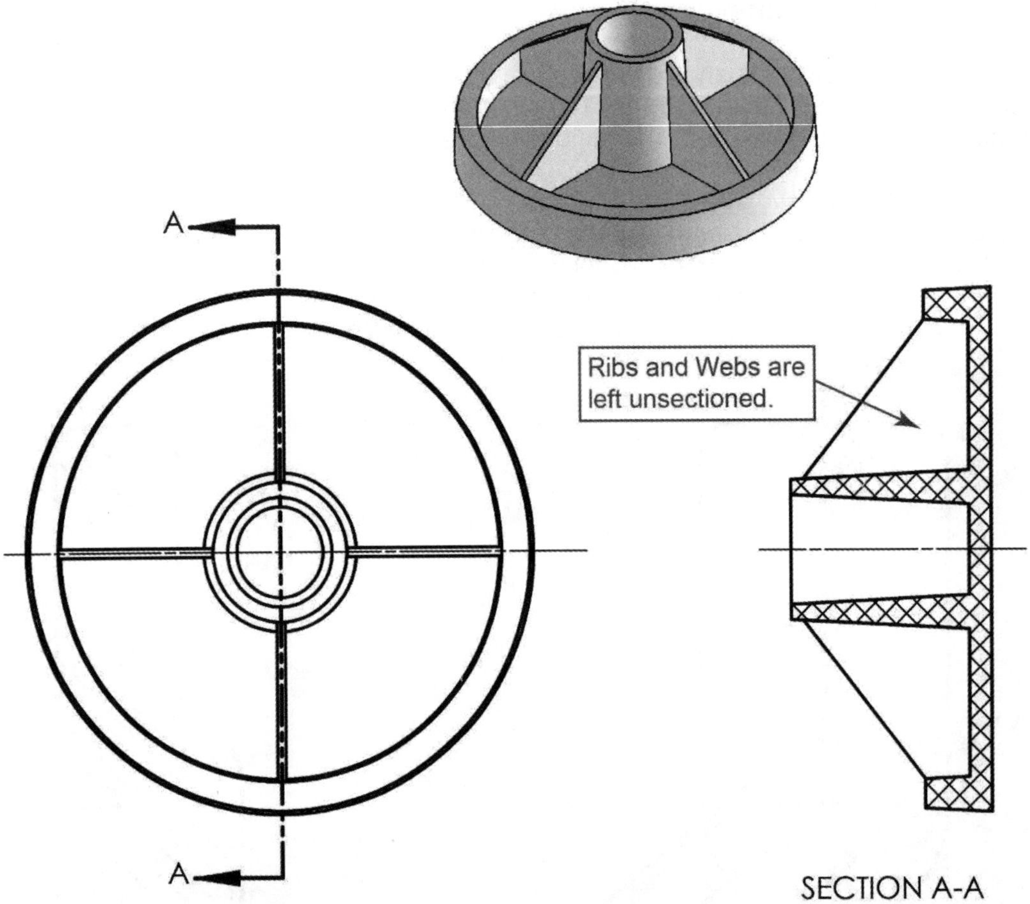

Figure 12.4-2: Rib and web sections.

12.4.3) Broken-out section

Sometimes only a portion of the object needs to be sectioned to show a single feature of the part. This technique is called a broken-out section. It's used to clarify a single feature. Figure 12.4-3 and Figure 12.4-4 show examples of a broken-out section.

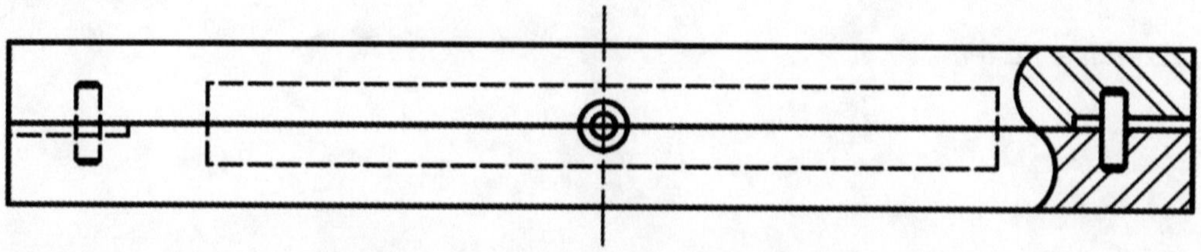

Figure 12.4-3: Broken-out section.

12.4.4) Removed section

A removed section is one that is not in direct projection of the view containing the cutting plane. Removed sections are labeled (e.g., SECTION A-A) so that you know which cutting plane line the view refers to. Frequently, removed sections are drawn to an enlarged scale, which is indicated beneath the section title. Section B-B in Figure 12.4-4 is a removed section view.

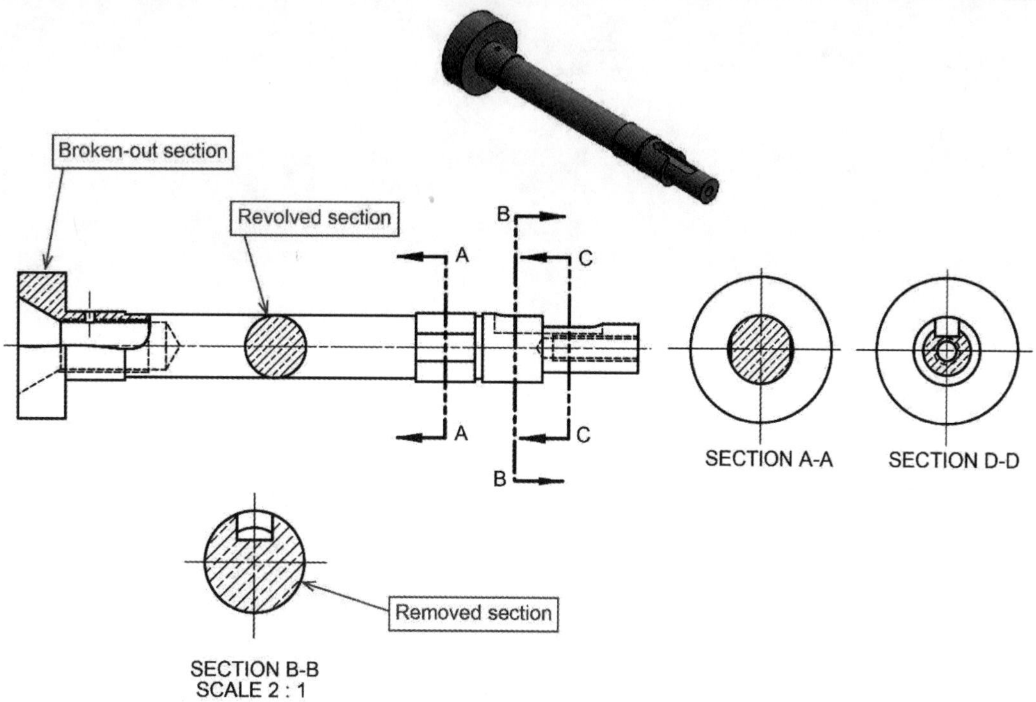

Figure 12.4-4: Removed and revolved sections.

12.4.5) Revolved section

The cross-sectional shape of a bar, arm, spoke or other elongated objects may be shown in the longitudinal view by means of a revolved section. A revolved section view is cut and revolved in place. This creates a section view that is superimposed on the view that would normally contain the cutting plane line as shown in Figure 12.4-4.

Try Exercise 12.4-1

Exercise 12.4-1: Advanced Sections

Identify the type of section used and the material that the part is made of.

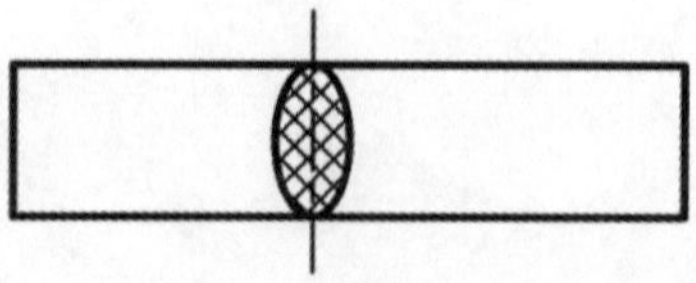

Type of section: ____________________

Material: ____________________

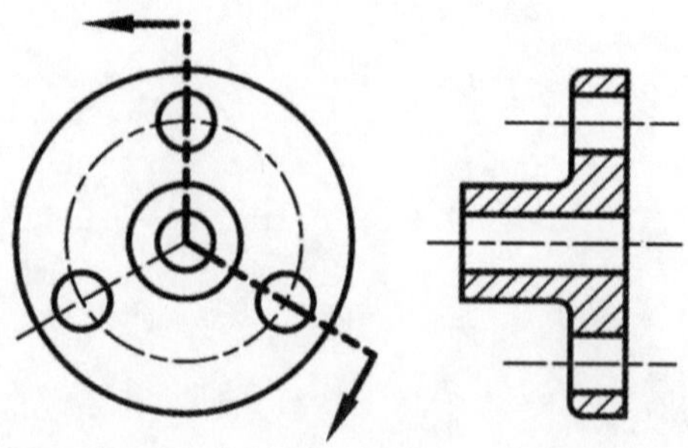

Type of section: ____________________

Material: ____________________

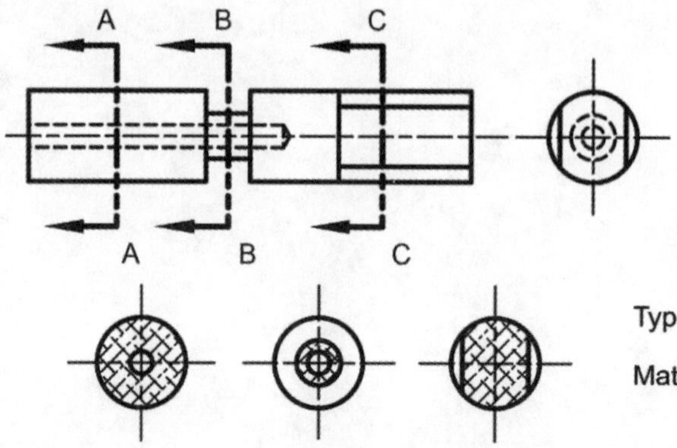

SECTION A-A SECTION B-B SECTION C-C

Type of section: ____________________

Material: ____________________

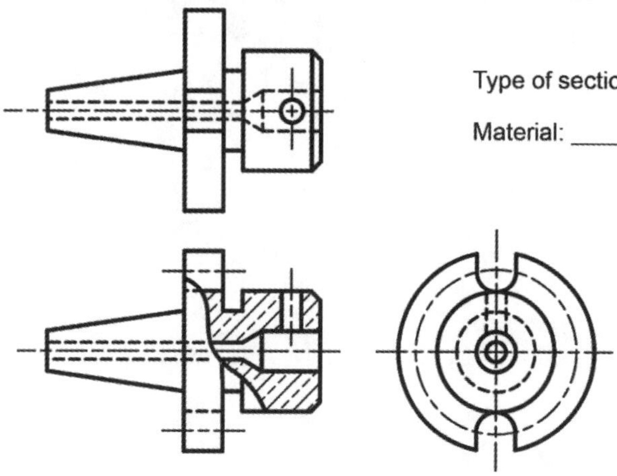

Type of section: ____________________

Material: ____________________

NOTES:

READING SECTION VIEWS QUESTIONS – SET 1

Name: ______________________________ Date: _____________

Q12-1) The purpose of a section view is to see what is on the _______ of a part.

a) outside
b) inside
c) backside
d) other side

Q12-2) A cutting plane line indicates where the part is being ....

a) viewed.
b) cut.
c) rotated.
d) drawn.

Q12-3) Section lines are used to indicate .... (Choose all that apply.)

a) cut material.
b) line of sight.
c) type of material.
d) size of the part.

Q12-4) A full section usually removes one _______ of the object.

a) half
b) quarter
c) third

Q12-5) If a cutting plane cuts the length of a rib, section lines are shown. (True, False)

Q12-6) A broken-out section only sections a portion of the part. (True, False)

NOTES:

READING SECTION VIEWS QUESTIONS – SET 2

Name: ___________________________________ Date: ________________

Q12-7) Are the arrows at the end of a cutting plane line pointing to the part of the object that is being removed or viewed?

Q12-8) The following section line symbol is used to indicate that the part is made from ....

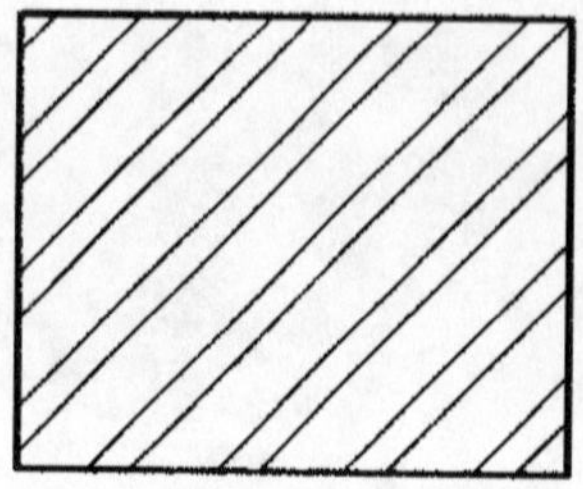

a) Brass
b) Steel
c) Aluminum
d) Concrete

Q12-9) A half section removes one _______ of the object.

a) half
b) quarter
c) third

Q12-10) The *convention of revolution* is used when creating an aligned section so that the angled features may be shown ....

a) at an angle.
b) aligned with the feature.
c) true size.
d) at a scaled size.

Q12-11) A removed section may be shown at an increased scale. (True, False)

NOTES:

READING SECTION VIEW PROBLEMS

Name: ______________________________ Date: ______________

P12-1) Answer the following question regarding the section view shown.

Type of section? ____________________

What material is the part made of? ____________________

In the view that shows the cutting plane line, circle the section of the part that is being viewed.

This part contains which type of feature, counterbores or countersinks?

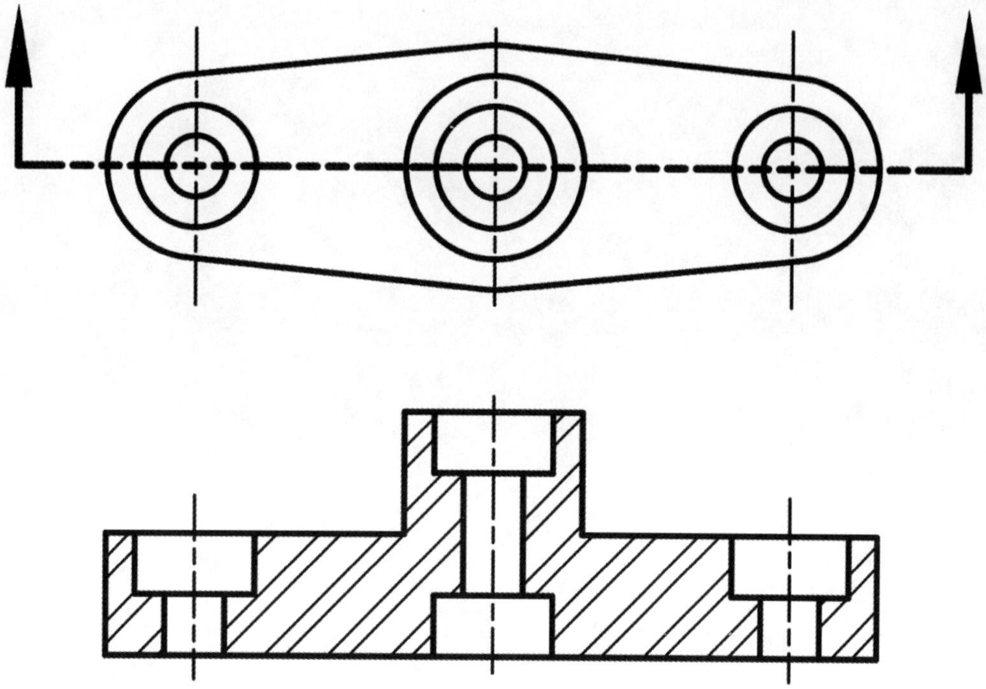

NOTES:

Name: ______________________________ Date: ______________

P12-2) Answer the following question regarding the section view shown.

What two sectioning techniques are used? ________________ ________________

What material is the part made of? ____________________

In the view that shows the cutting plane line, circle the section of the part that is being viewed.

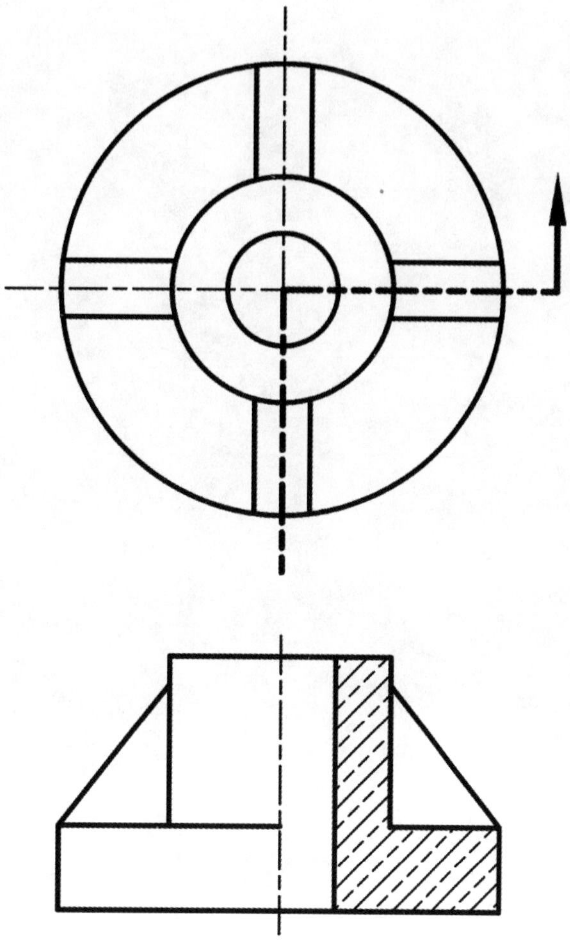

NOTES:

Name: ______________________________ Date: ______________

P12-3) Circle the correct section views out of the three possibilities. One for each cutting plane.

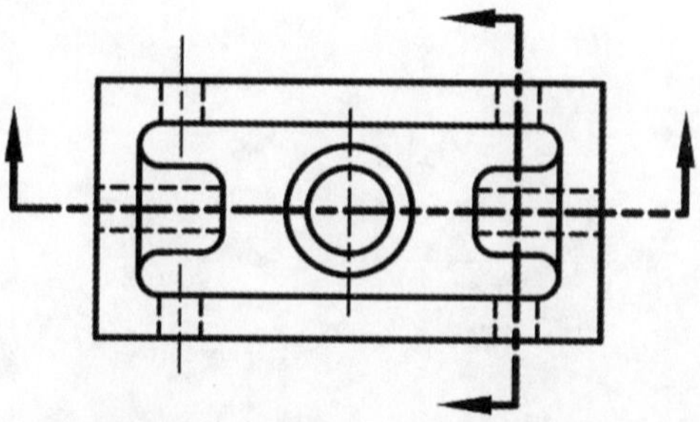

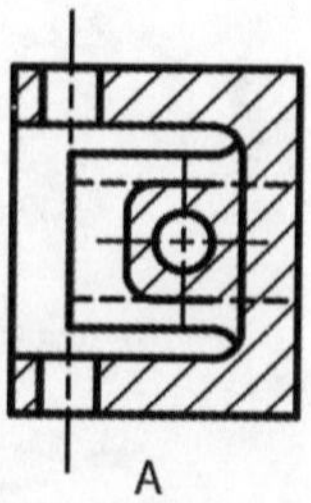

A

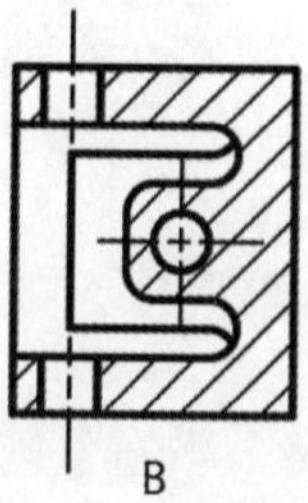

B

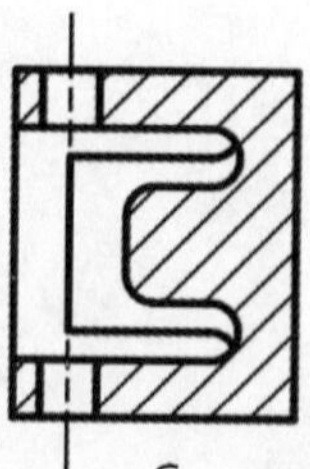

C

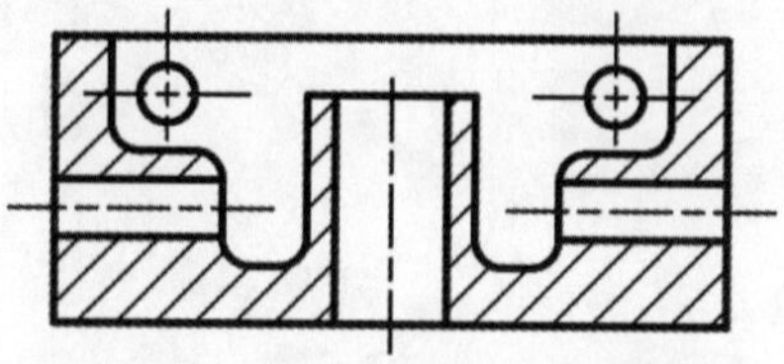

D

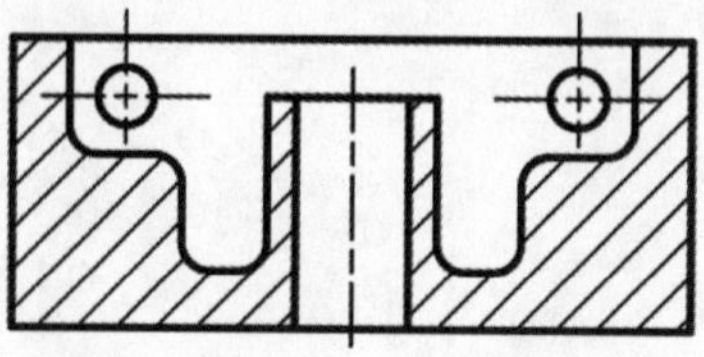

E

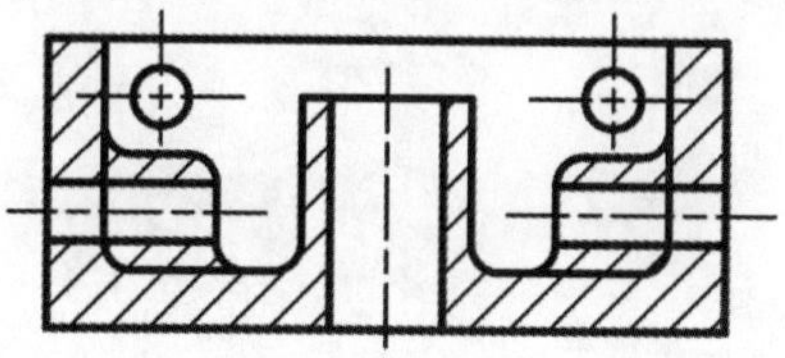

F

NOTES:

Name: ______________________________ Date: ______________

P12-4) Circle the correct section view out of the three possibilities.

Would a half section have been effective in this case? (Yes, No)

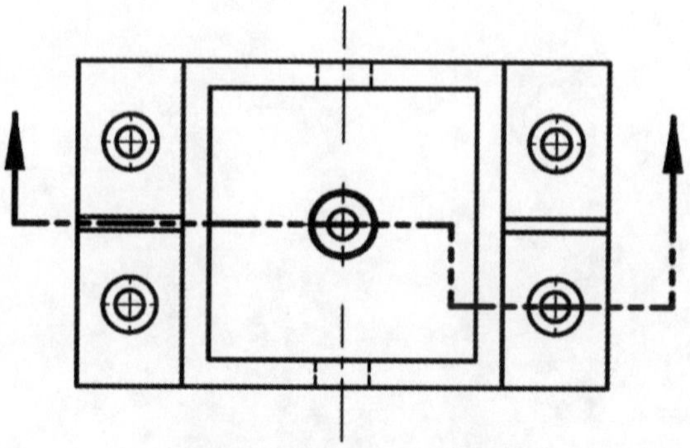

A

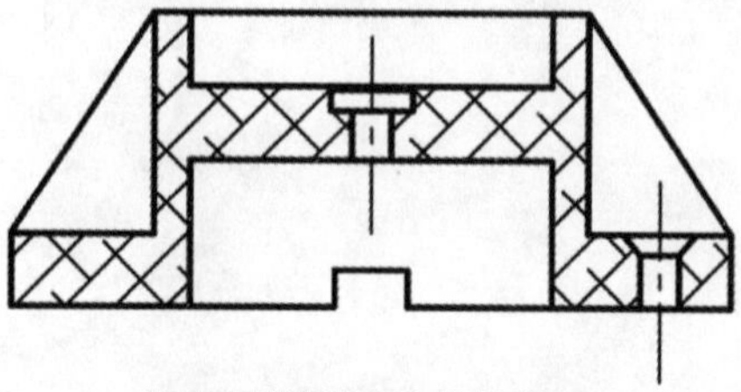

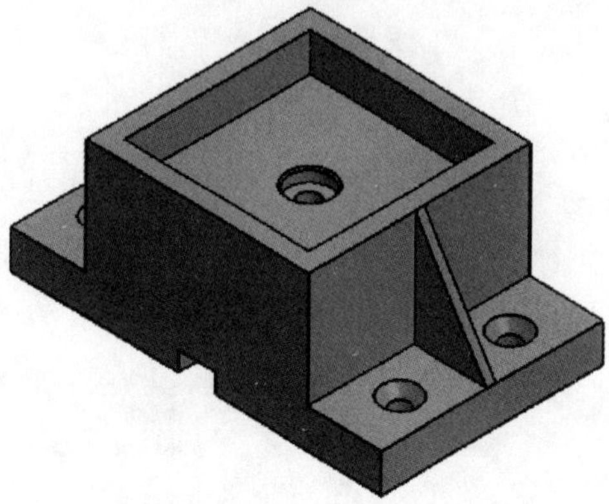

B

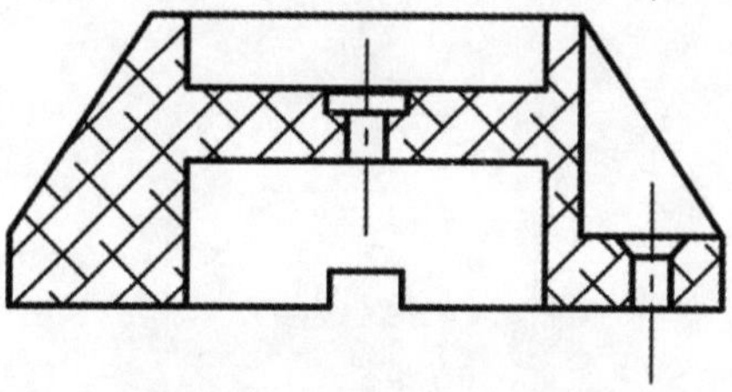

C

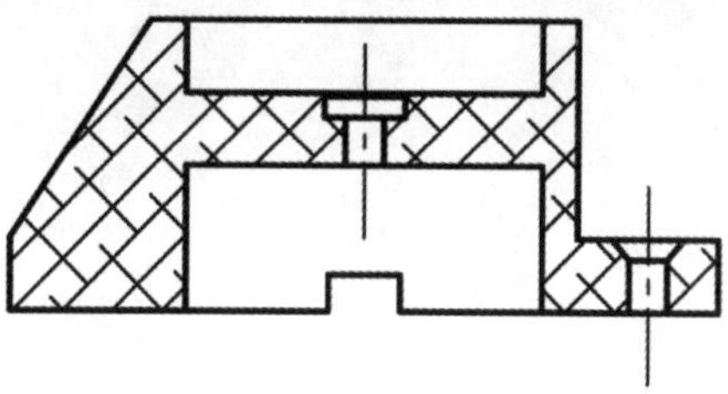

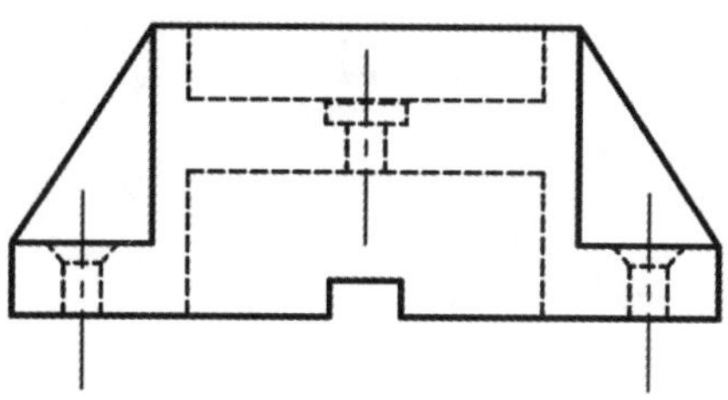

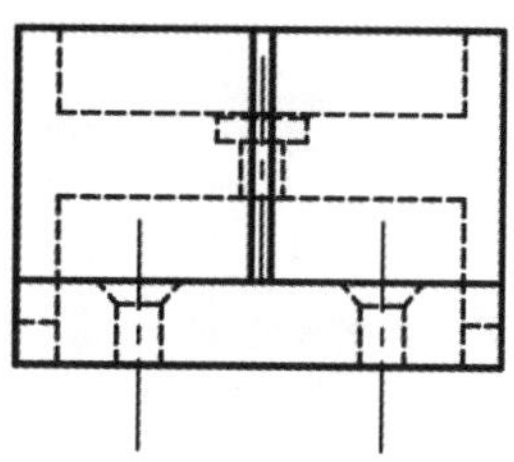

NOTES:

Name: ______________________________ Date: ______________

P12-5) Circle the correct section view out of the three possibilities.

What type of sectioning technique is being used?

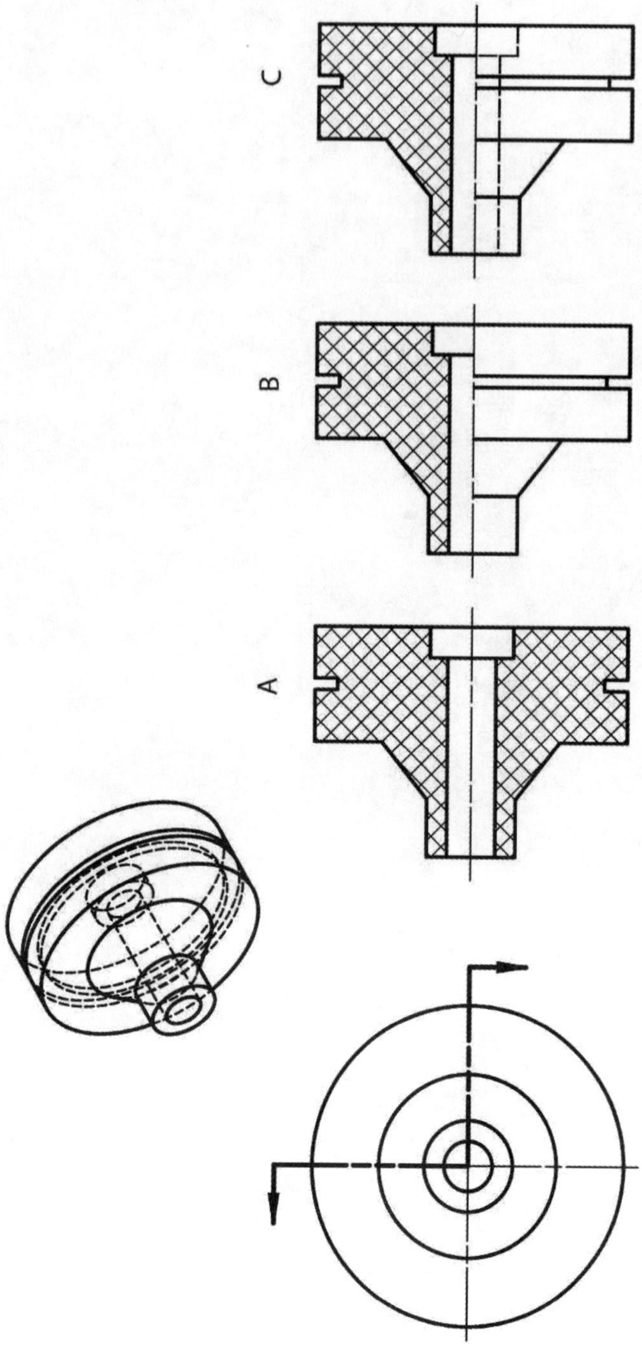

NOTES:

Name: ______________________________ Date: ______________

P12-6) Circle the correct section view out of the two possibilities for both section A-A and section B-B.

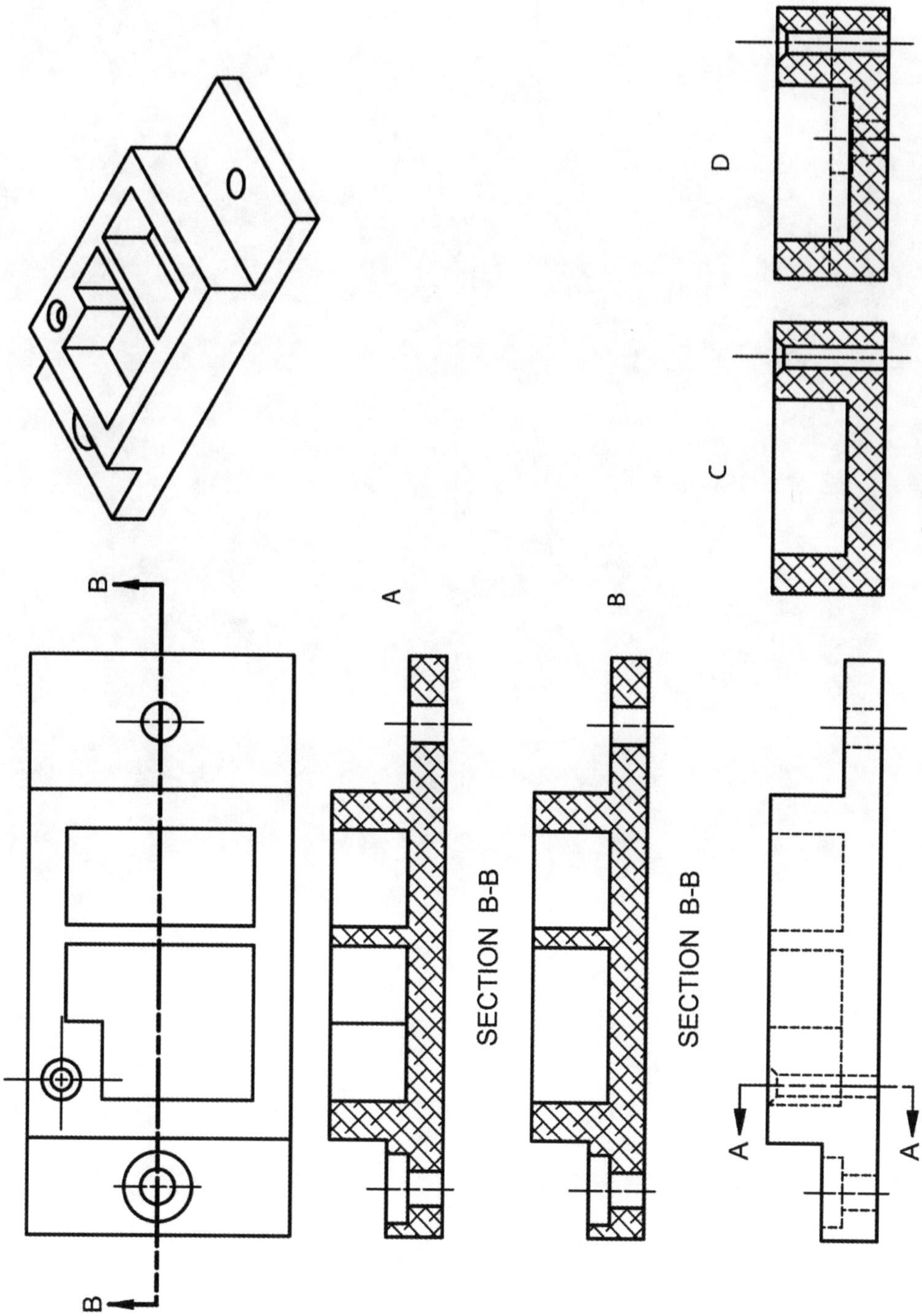

NOTES:

CHAPTER 13

CREATING SECTION VIEWS

CHAPTER OUTLINE

CHAPTER SUMMARY

In this chapter you will learn how to create various types of sectional views. Using a section view within an orthographic projection can be very useful for parts that have complex interior geometry. By the end of this chapter, you will be able to create several different types of section views. You will also be able to choose which type of section is the most appropriate for a given part.

13.1) CREATING SECTION VIEWS

Sections are used to clarify the interior construction of a part that cannot be clearly described by hidden lines in exterior views. It is often necessary to use section views to avoid dimensioning hidden features or if there are so many hidden lines that it is hard to interpret the drawing.

To produce a section view, decide where and how you want to cut the part using an imaginary cutting plane. Mentally, remove the portion of the part that is between the observer and the cutting plane and draw what you see. Figure 13.1-1 shows how a cutting plane cuts a part producing a full section view.

A standard section view should be projected perpendicular to the cutting plane and conform to the standard arrangement of views. However, there are some types of section views that are removed from the line of projection (e.g., removed section, revolved section).

A cutting plane line is used to show where the part is being cut. The cutting plane line ends in arrows pointing in the direction of sight. Section line symbols are used to indicate where the material has been cut and type of material (see Figure 13.1-1). If there is more than one section, they need to be labeled with capital letters such as A, B or C. These letters are placed near the arrows of the cutting plane line. The sectional view is then labeled with the corresponding letter (e.g., SECTION A-A) as shown in Figure 13.1-1. Letters that should not be used to label sections are I, O, Q, S, X and Z. These letters are often used for other purposes and may lead to misinterpretation.

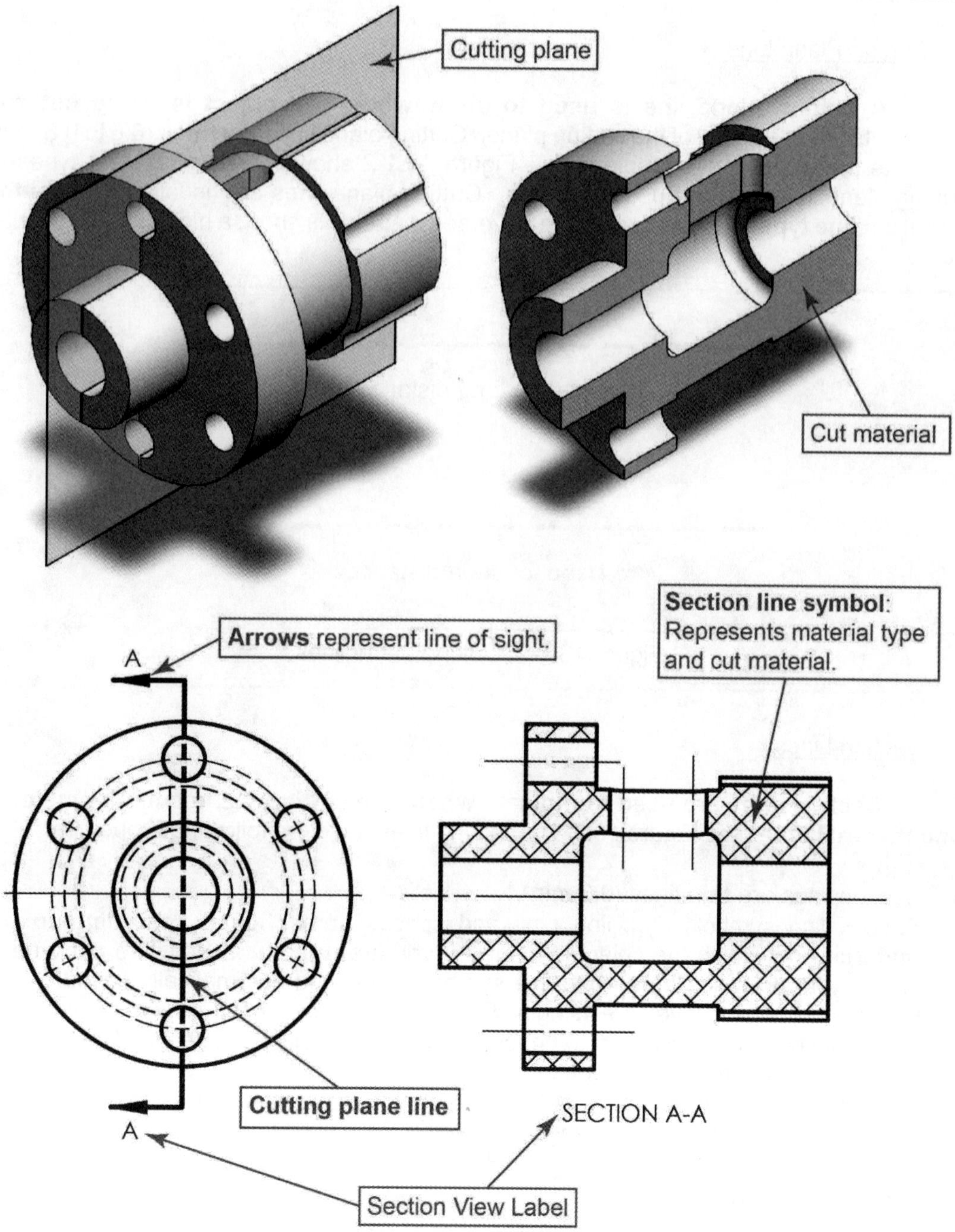

Figure 13.1-1: Creating a section view.

13.1.1) Lines used in section views

- <u>Cutting Plane Line</u>

A cutting plane line is used to show where the object is being cut and represents the edge view of the cutting plane. Cutting plane lines are **thick** (0.6 to 0.8 mm) and take precedence over centerlines. Figure 13.1-2 shows the two different types of cutting plane lines that are used on prints. Cutting plane lines are usually drawn as the **phantom line type**; however, when the traversed distance is short, a hidden line type may be used.

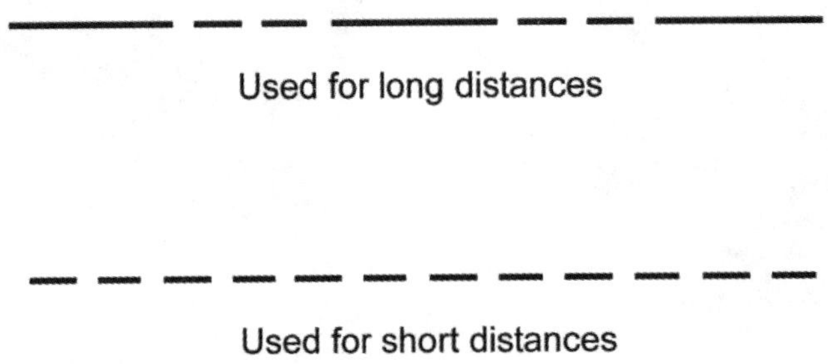

Figure 13.1-2: Cutting plane lines.

- <u>Section Lines</u>

Section lines are used to indicate where the cutting plane cuts the material and material type (see Figure 13.1-1). Section lines have the following properties:

√ Section lines are **thin** lines (0.3 mm).
√ Section line symbols (i.e., line type and spacing) are **chosen according to the material** from which the object is made. If you are using a 3D software package to create your drawing, the section line symbol is selected automatically based on the material of the part. If you are using a 2D drawing package, they will have an extensive library of section line symbols to choose from. Commonly used section line symbols are shown in the previous chapter.
√ Section lines are drawn at a **45° angle** to the horizontal unless there is some advantage in using a different angle.

13.1.2) Rules of sectioning

Rule 1. A section lined area is always completely bounded by a visible outline.

Rule 2. The section lines in all sectioned areas should be parallel. Section lines shown in opposite directions indicate a different part.

Rule 3. All the visible edges behind the cutting plane should be shown.

Rule 4. Hidden features should be omitted in all areas of a section view. Exceptions include threads and broken out sections.

13.2) BASIC SECTIONS

In this section we will learn how to create the basic types of section views (i.e., full, half, and offset sections). The type chosen depends on the situation and what information needs to be conveyed.

13.2.1) Full section

To create a full section, the cutting plane passes fully through the object. Full sections are used in many cases to avoid having to dimension hidden lines as shown in Figure 13.2-1.

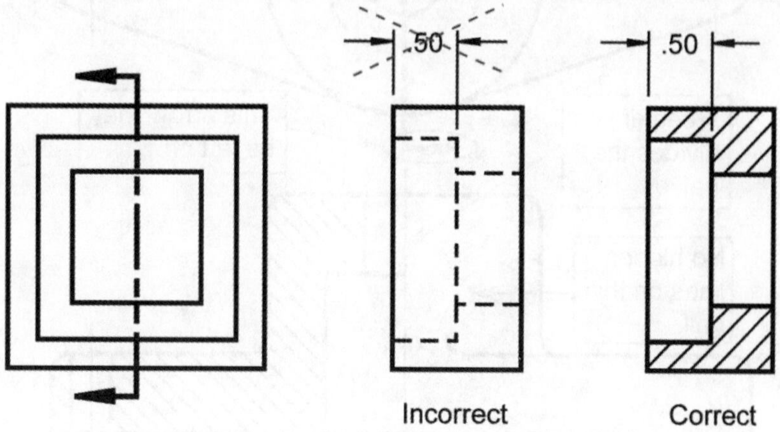

Figure 13.2-1: Full section.

13.2.2) Half section

Half sections are used mainly for symmetric objects. A half section is obtained by passing two cutting planes through the object at right angles to each other, such that the intersection of the two planes coincides with the axis of symmetry. Therefore, only a quarter of the object is mentally removed. On the sectional view, **a centerline is used to separate the sectioned and unsectioned halves**. Hidden lines should not be shown on either half. Figure 13.2-2 shows an example of a half section.

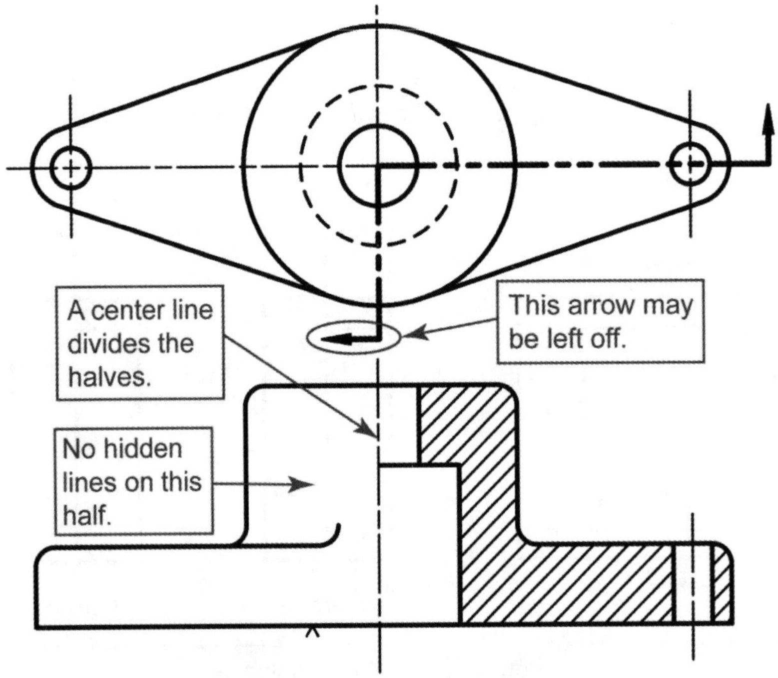

Figure 13.2-2: Half section.

13.2.3) Offset section

An offset section is produced by bending the cutting plane to show features that don't lie in the same plane. The section is drawn as if the offsets in the cutting plane were in one plane. The bends in the cutting plane line are not shown in the section view. Figure 13.2-3 shows an offset section.

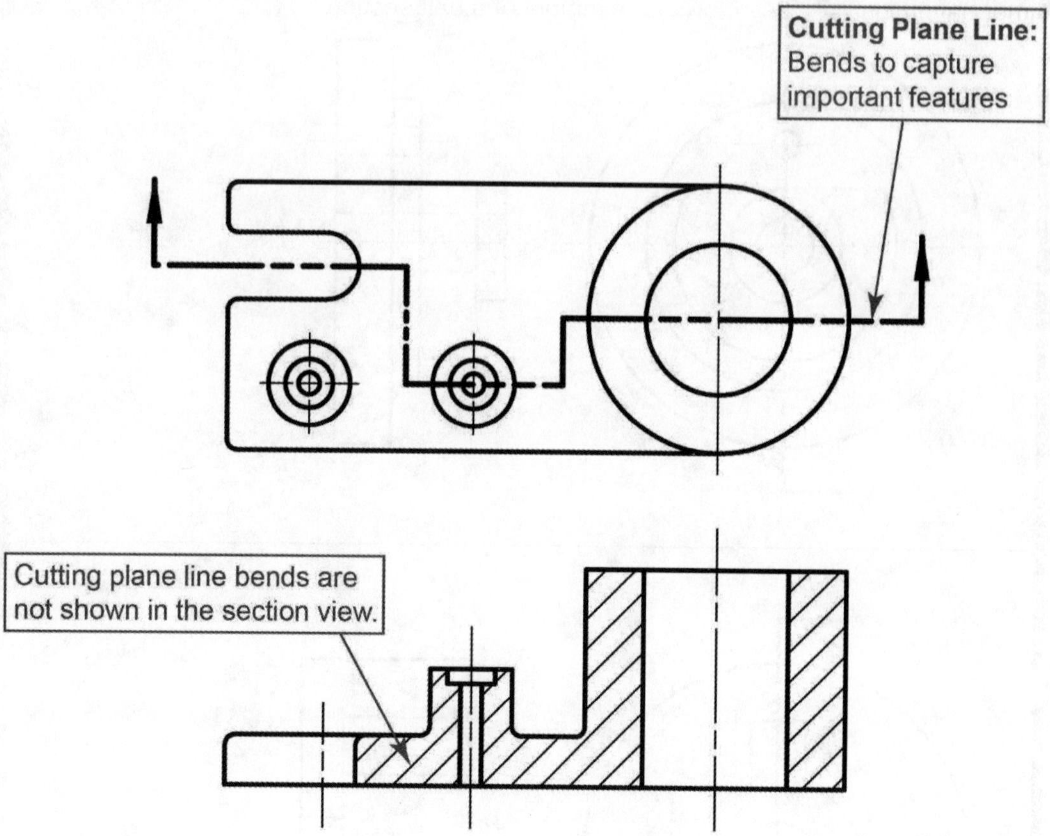

Figure 13.2-3: Offset section.

Watch Video Exercises 13.2-1, and 13.2-2 and try Exercises 13.2-3 and 13.2-4

Video Exercise 13.2-1: Full Section

The following video exercise will take you through creating a full section of the objects shown.

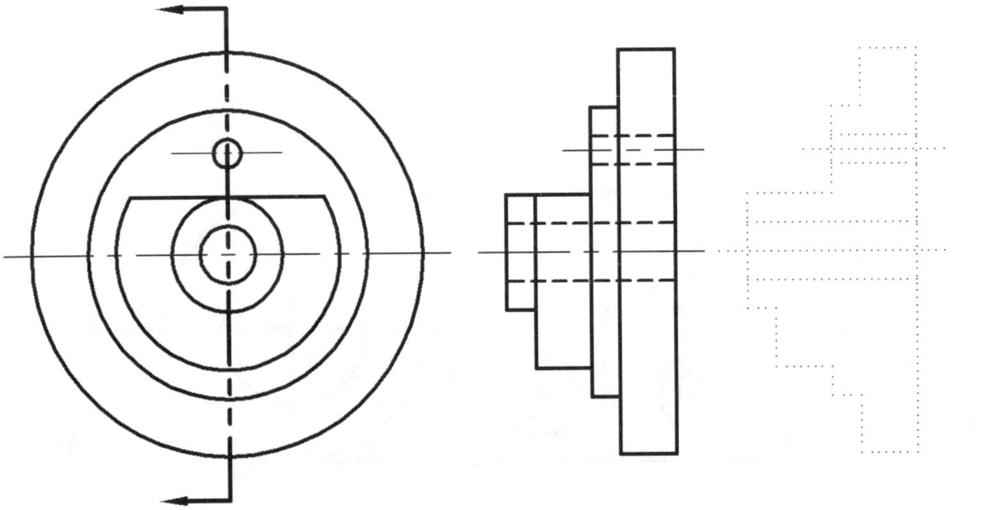

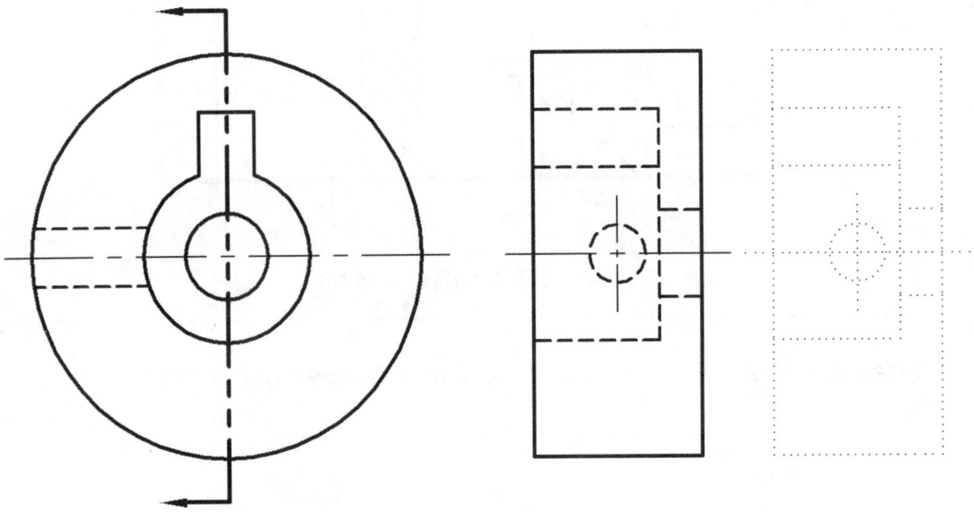

Video Exercise 13.2-2: Half Section

The following video exercise will take you through creating a half section of the objects shown.

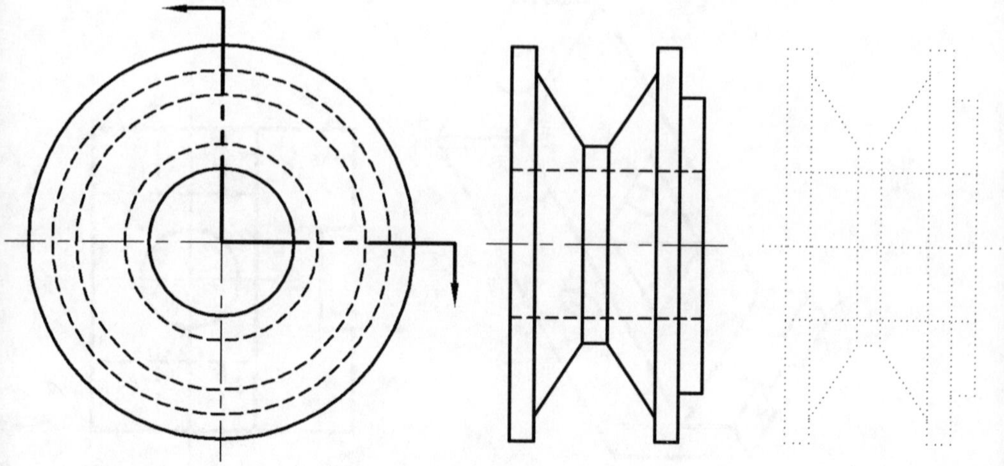

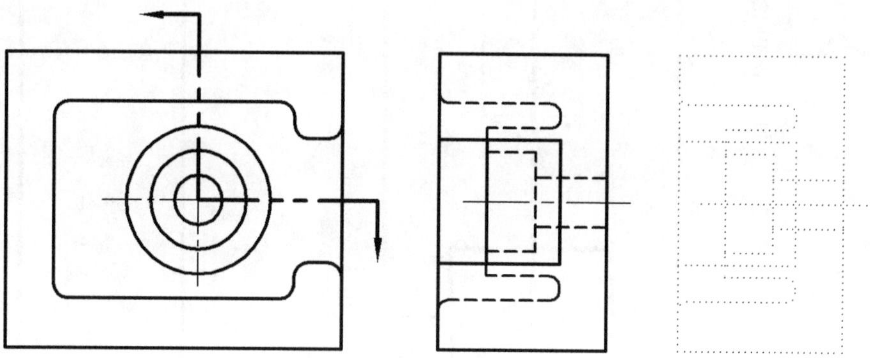

Exercise 13.2-3: Full section

Given the top and right-side views, sketch the front view as a full section. The material used is steel.

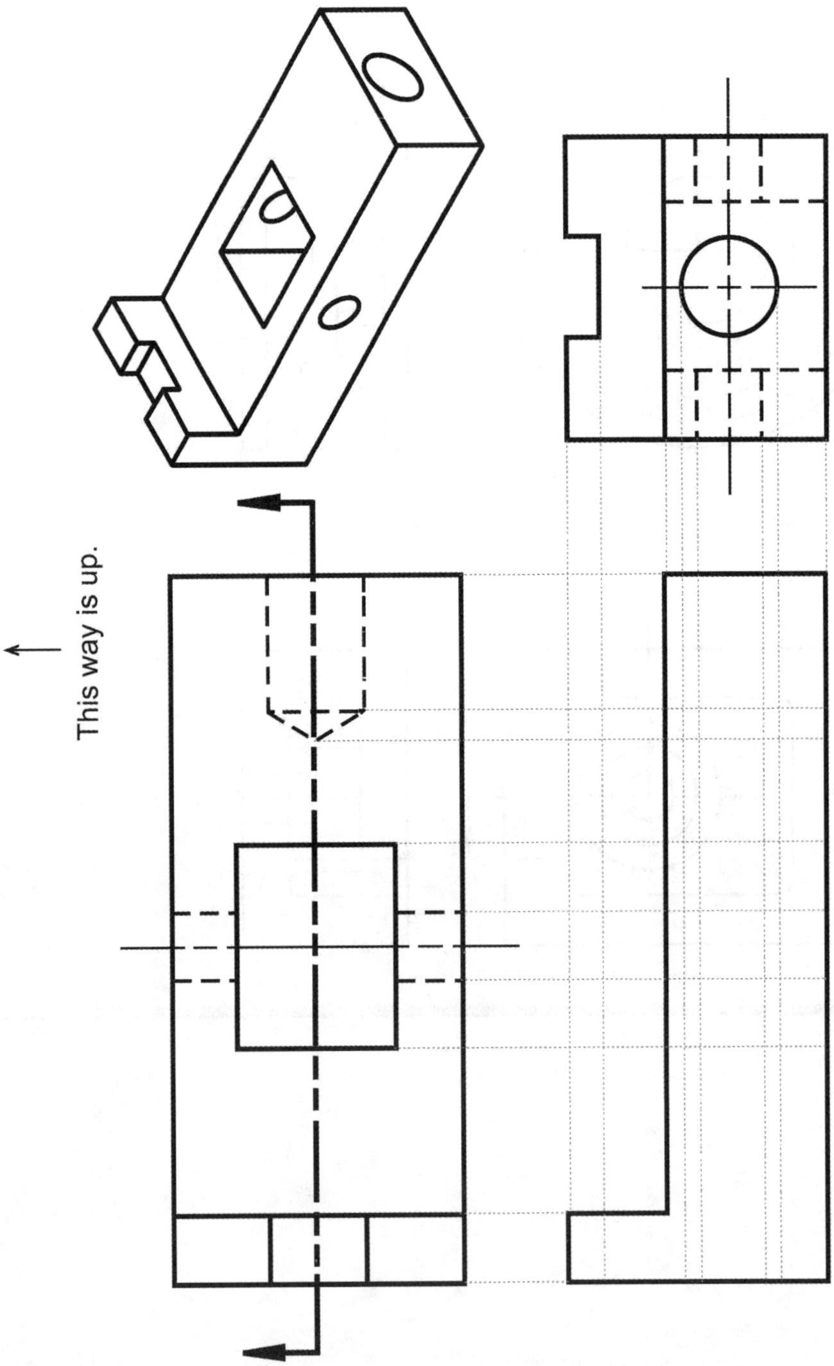

Exercise 13.2-4: Half Section

Given the two views, sketch the half section. The material used is cast iron.

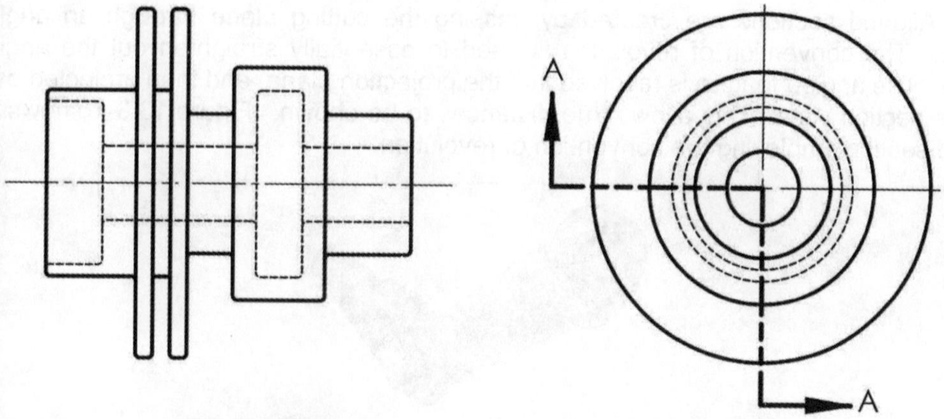

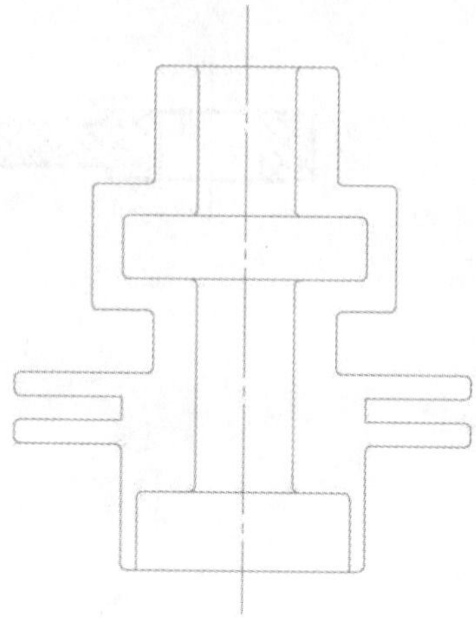

SECTION A-A

13.3) ADVANCED SECTIONS

If the basic sectioning techniques don't show a part or feature clearly, there are several advanced sectioning techniques that can be implemented.

13.3.1) Aligned section

Aligned sections are created by passing the cutting plane through an angled feature. The convention of revolution is used to essentially straighten out the angled feature. The angled feature is revolved into the projection plane, and then projected over into the section view. This allows true distances to be shown. Figure 13.3-1 shows an aligned section employing the convention of revolution.

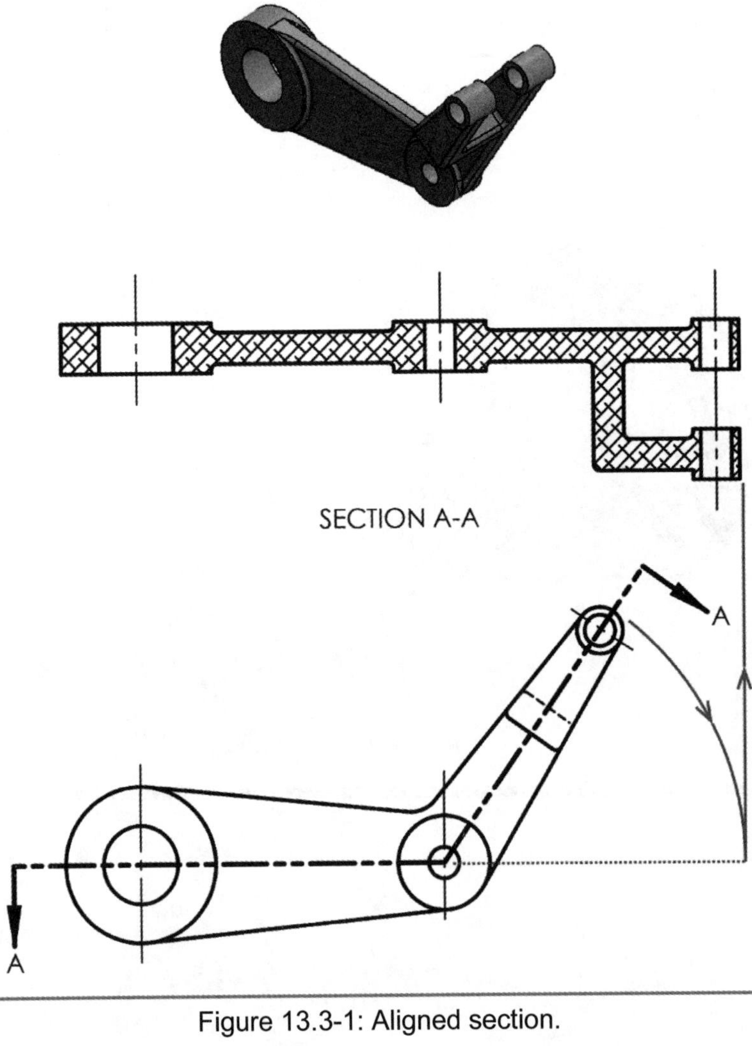

Figure 13.3-1: Aligned section.

13.3.2) Rib and web sections

Ribs, webs, and other similar features are not sectioned even though the cutting plane passes along the center plane of the rib or web. However, if the cutting plane passes crosswise through the rib or web, the member is shown in section as indicated in Figure 13.3-2.

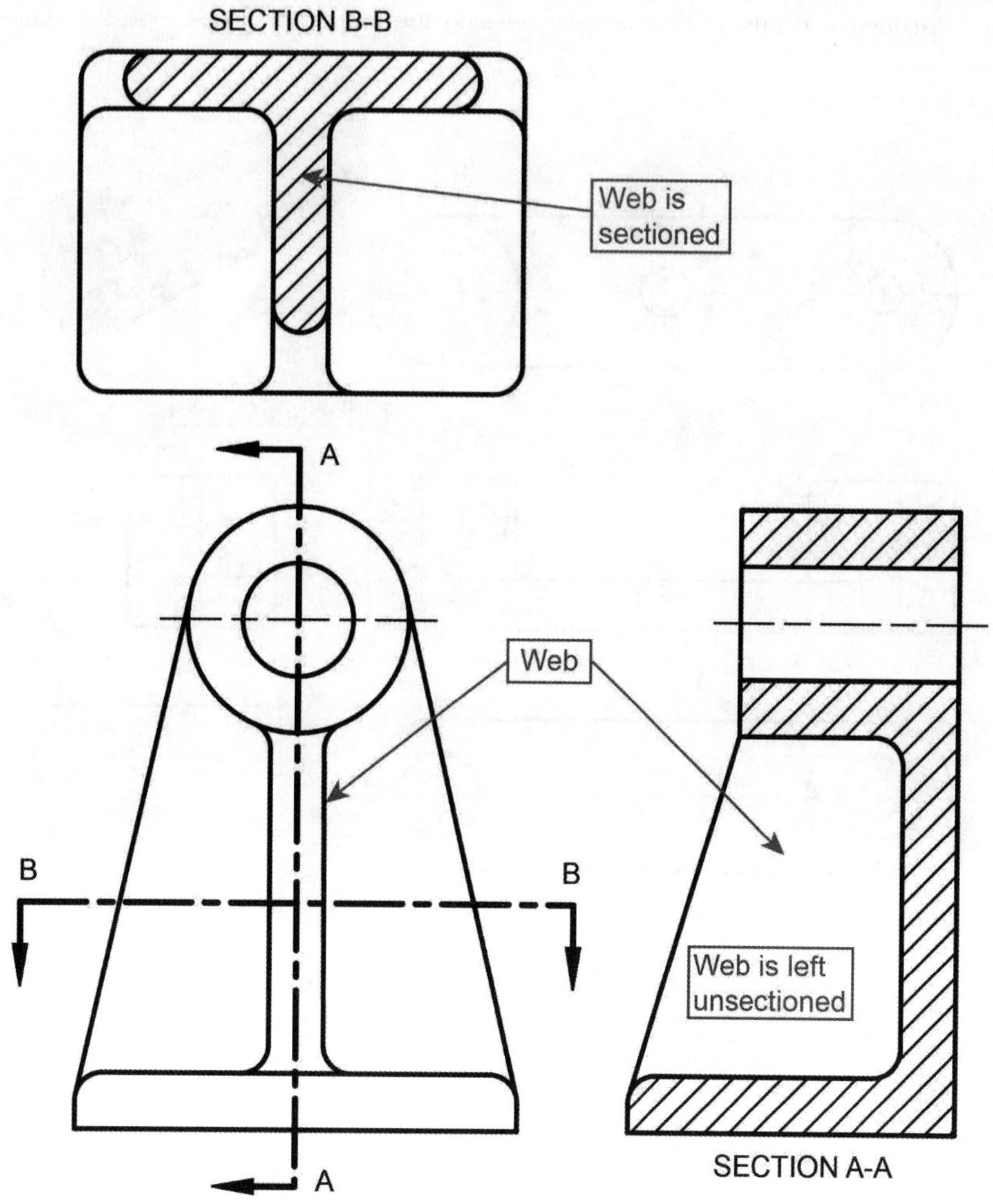

Figure 13.3-2: Rib and web sections.

13.3.3) Broken-out section

Sometimes only a portion of the object needs to be sectioned to show a single feature of the part. In this case, the sectional area is bound on one side by a break line. Usually, hidden lines are not shown anywhere on a section view. This rule does not apply to a broken-out section view. Hidden lines are shown in the unsectioned area of a broken-out section. Figure 13.3-3 shows an example of a broken-out section.

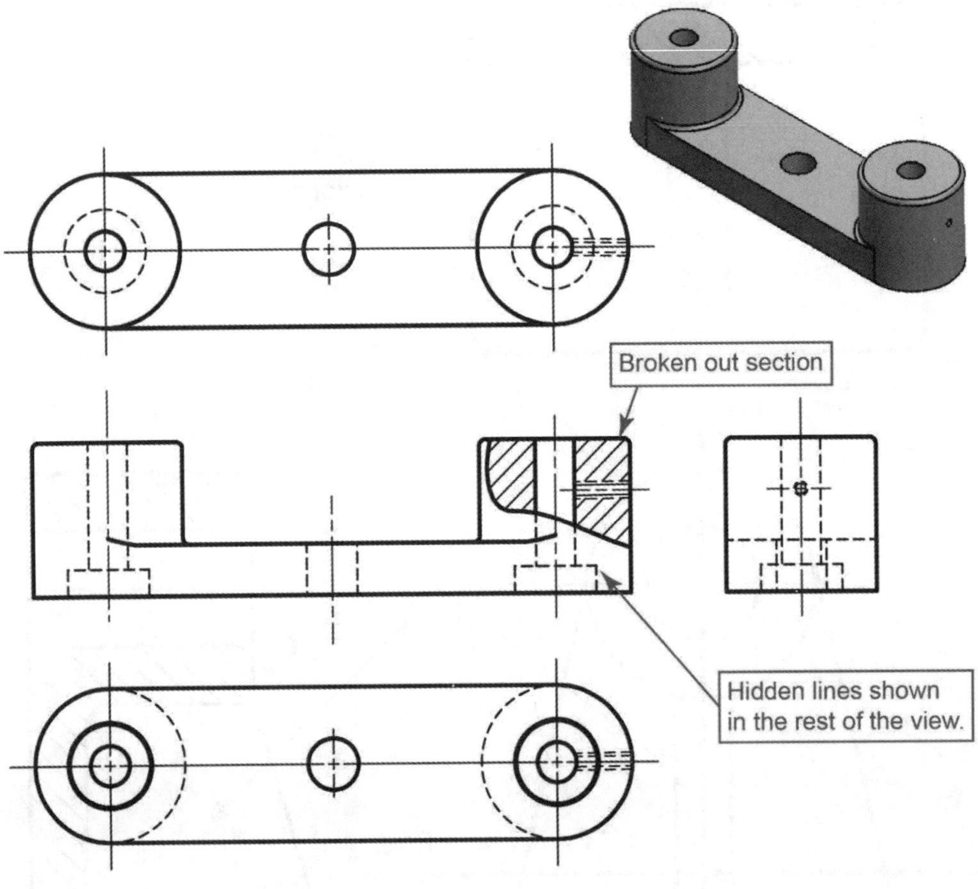

Figure 13.3-3: Broken-out section.

13.3.4) Removed section

A removed section is one that is not in direct projection of the view containing the cutting plane (see Figure 13.3-4). Removed sections should be labeled (e.g., SECTION A-A) according to the letters placed at the ends of the cutting plane line. They should be arranged in alphabetical order from left to right. Frequently, removed sections are drawn to an enlarged scale, which is indicated beneath the section title.

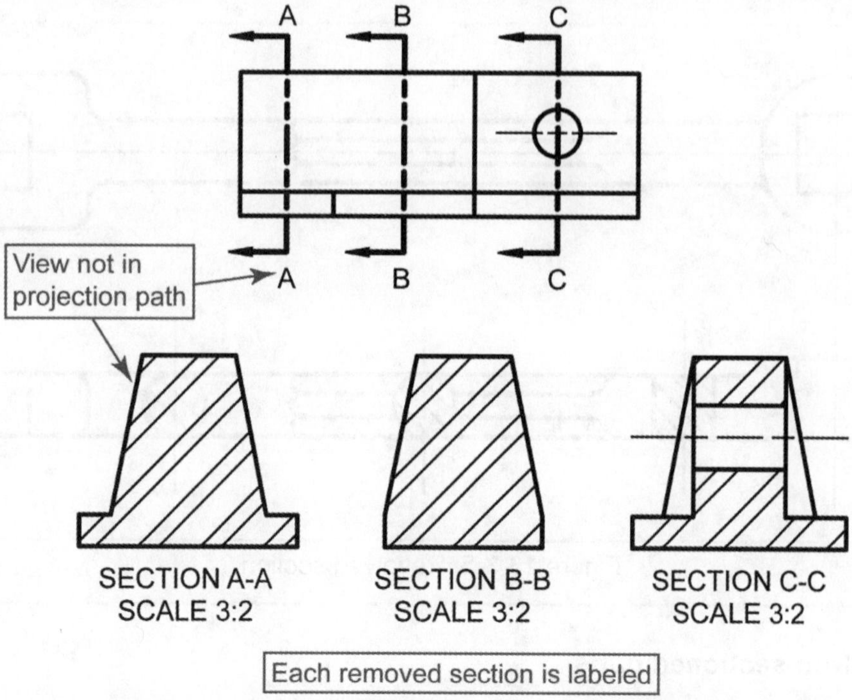

Figure 13.3-4: Removed section.

13.3.5) Revolved section

The cross-sectional shape of a bar, arm, spoke, or other elongated objects may be shown in the longitudinal view by means of a revolved section. The visible lines adjacent to a revolved section may be broken out if desired. The super imposition of the revolved section requires the removal of all original lines covered by the section as shown in Figure 13.3-5. The true shape of a revolved section should be retained after the revolution regardless of the direction of the lines in the view.

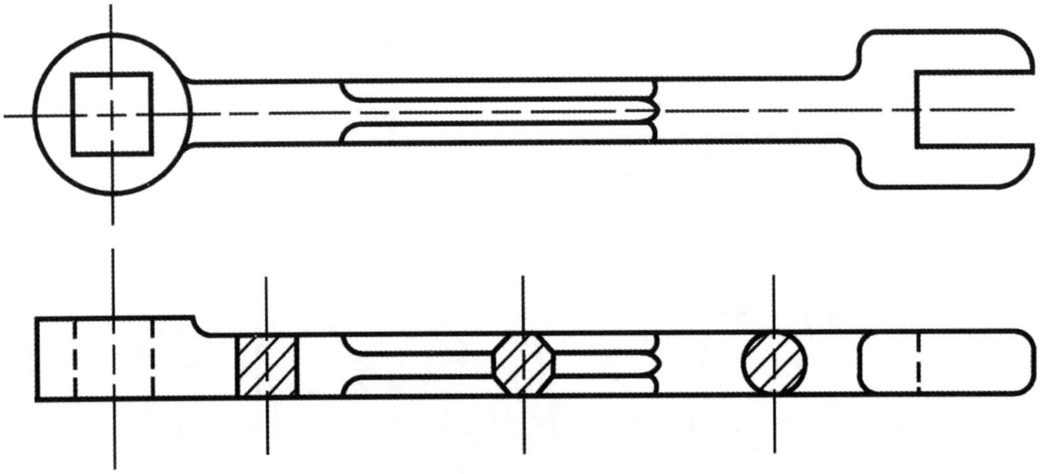

Figure 13.3-5: Revolved section.

13.3.6) Non-sectioned parts

It is common practice to show standard parts like nuts, bolts, rivets, shafts, and screws 'in the round' or un-sectioned. This is done because they have no internal features, and the section view would actually show less information. Other non-sectioned parts include bearings, gear teeth, dowels, and pins.

13.3.7) Thin sections

For extremely thin parts of less than 4 mm thickness, such as sheet metal, washers, and gaskets, section lines are ineffective; therefore, the parts should be shown in solid black or without section lines.

Watch Video Exercise 13.3-1 and try Exercises 13.3-2 through 13.3-3.

Video Exercise 13.3-1: Aligned Section

The following video exercise will take you through creating an aligned section of the object shown.

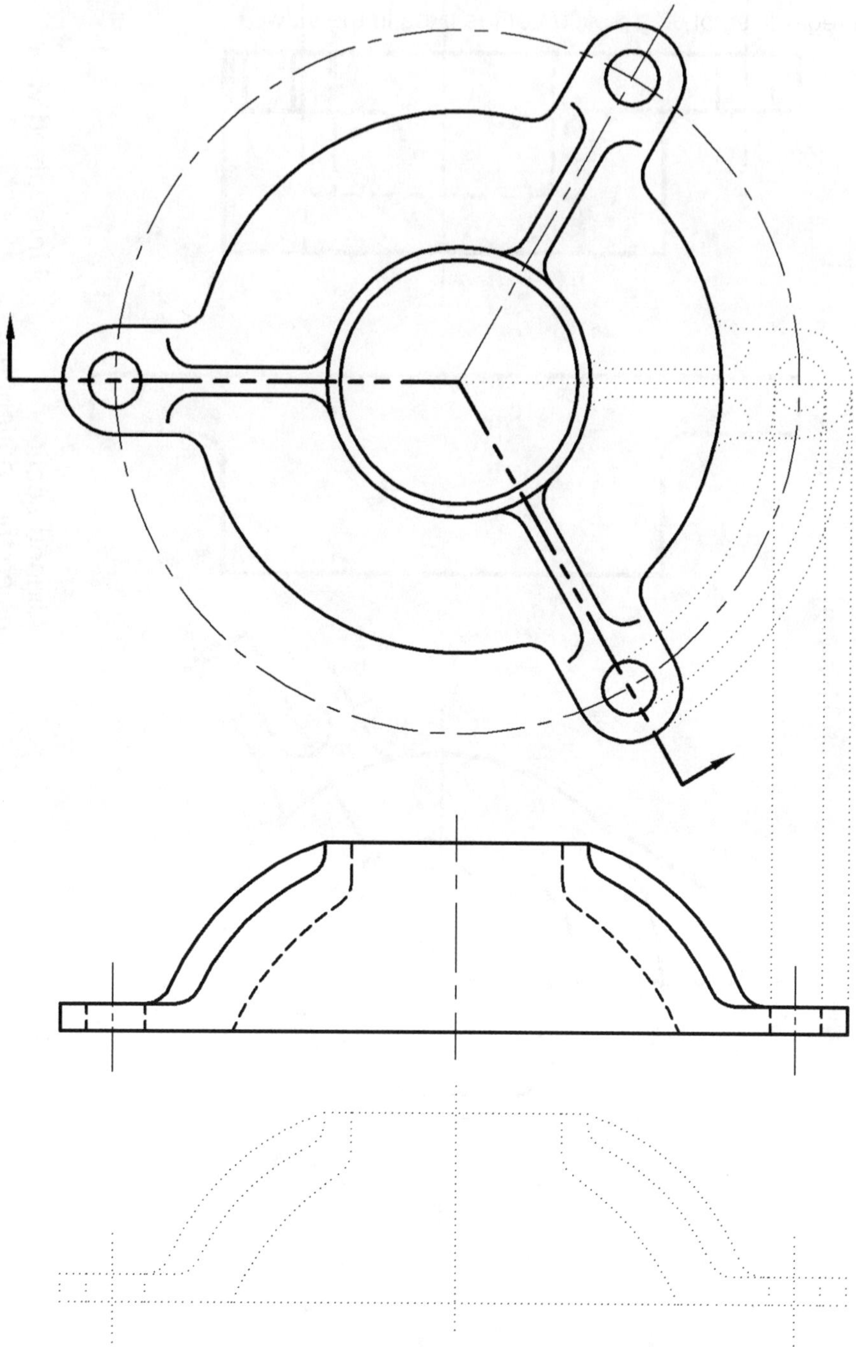

Exercise 13.3-2: Aligned section

Given the front and un-revolved right-side views, sketch the right-side view as an aligned section using the conventions of revolution. The material is cast iron.

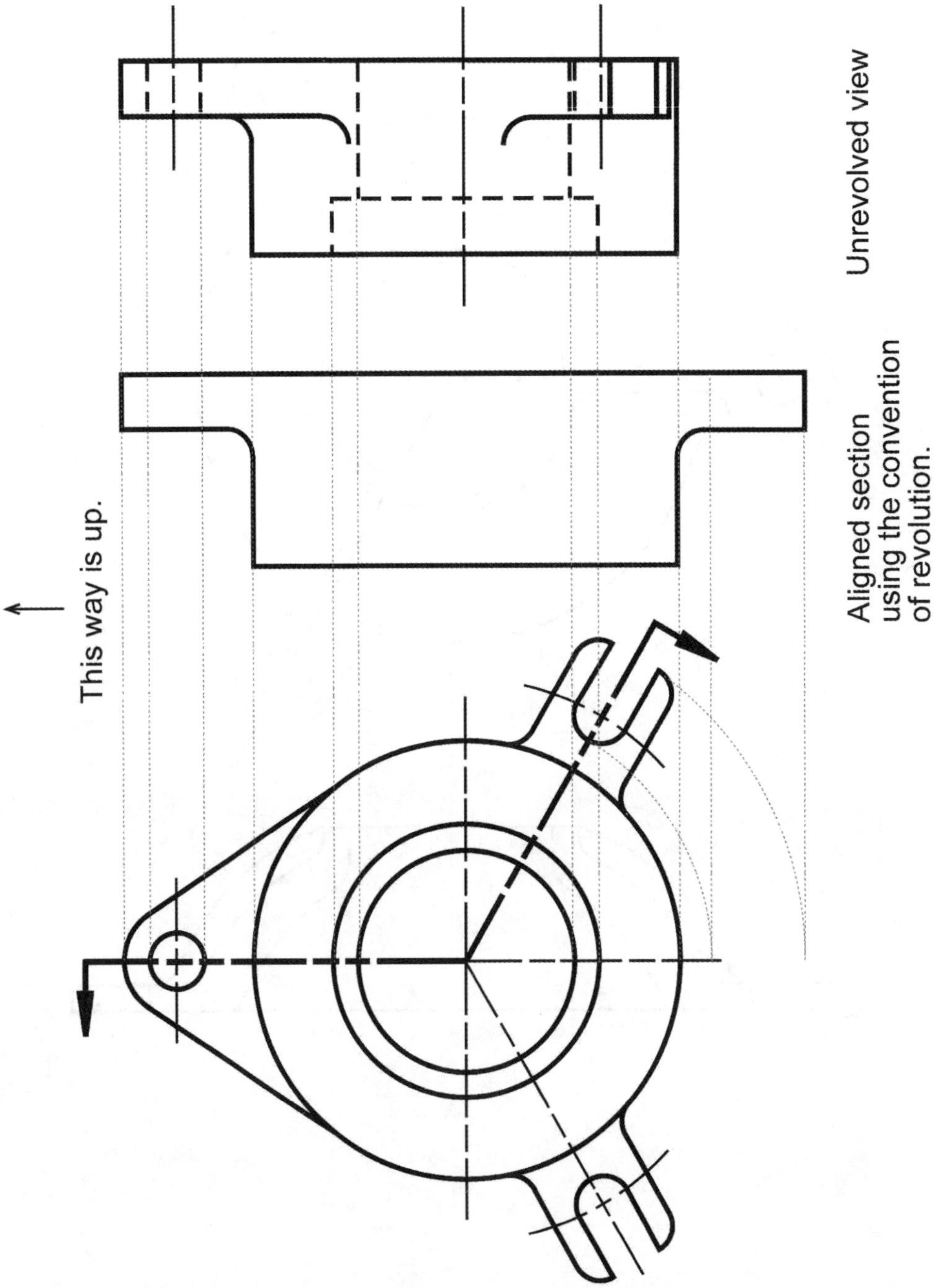

Exercise 13.3-3: Section techniques

- What features are not clearly shown in the drawing?
- What type of section would be most effective for this part?
- Draw the section view(s). The part is made of steel.

Section type(s): ______________________________

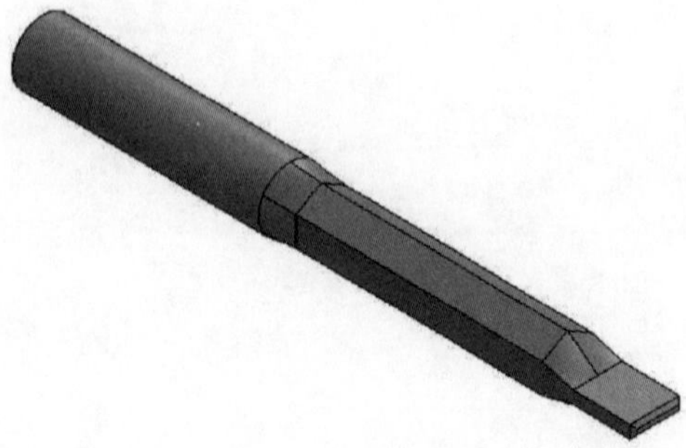

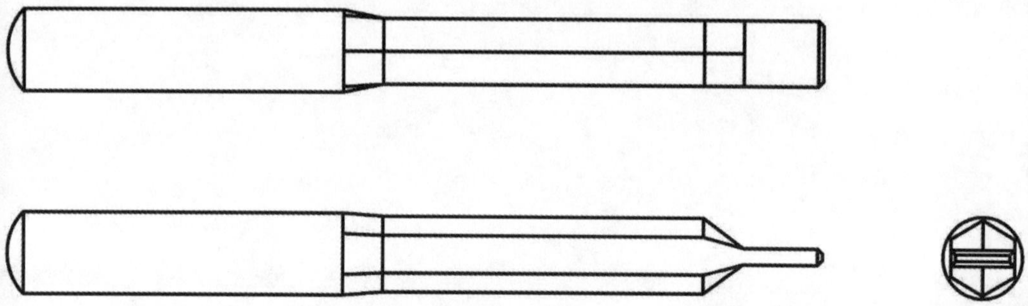

NOTES:

13.4) APPLYING WHAT WE HAVE LEARNED

Exercise 13.4-1: Full and Half section

Name: ________________________ Date: ________________

Given the front and right-side views, sketch the top view as a full section and create a half sectioned front view. The material is brass.

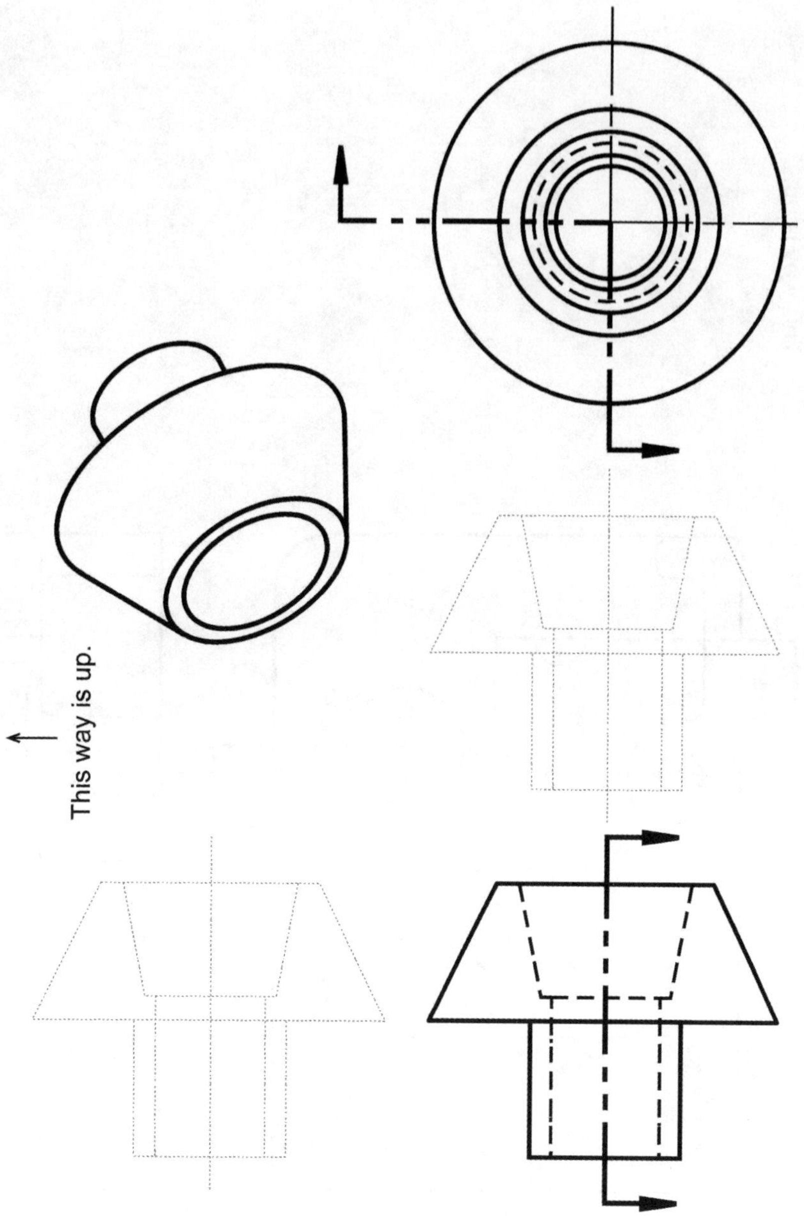

Exercise 13.4-2: Offset section

Name: ______________________________ Date: _______________

Given the front and top views, sketch the three missing section views in their appropriate places. The material is cast iron.

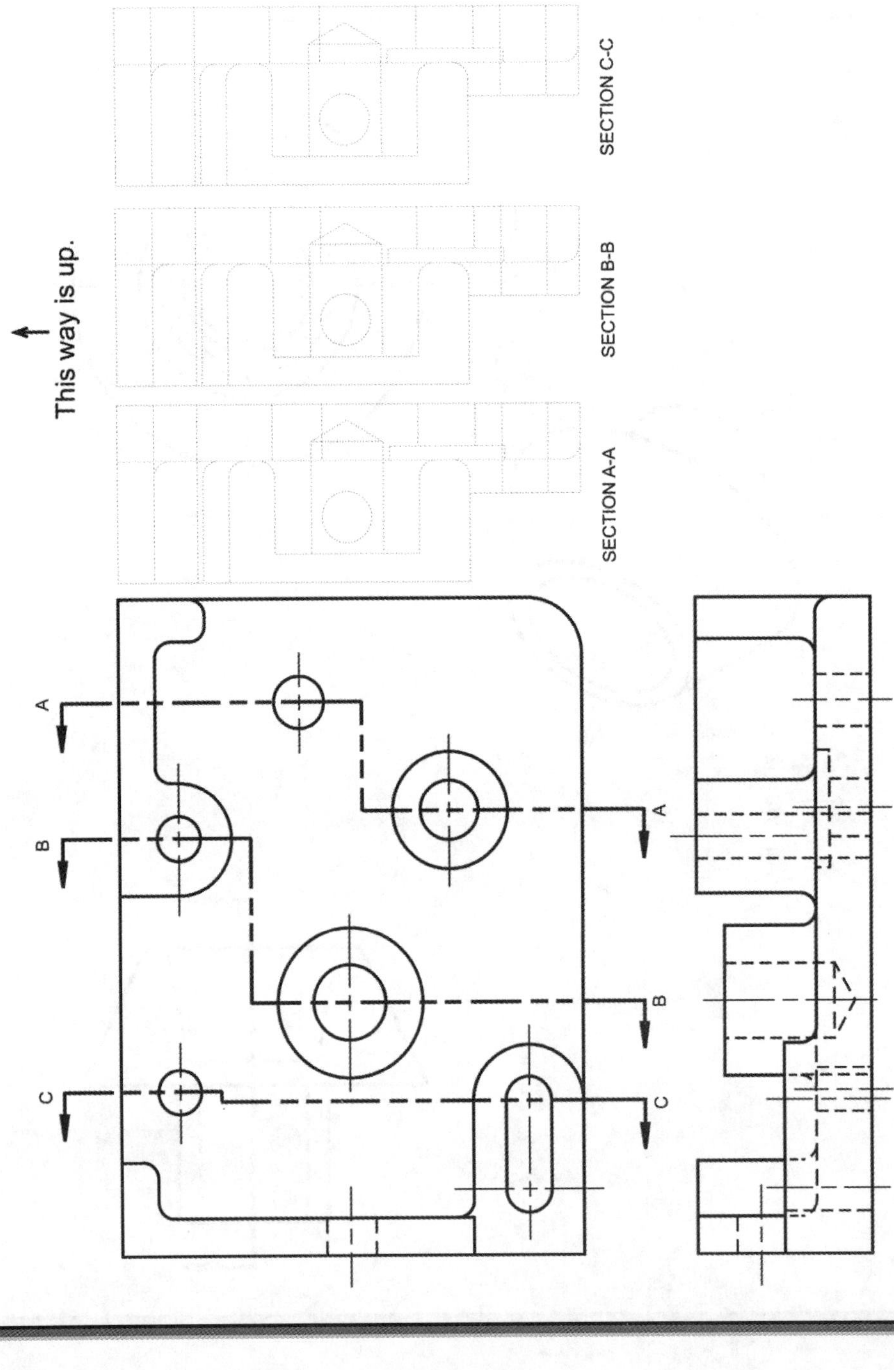

Exercise 13.4-3: Advanced section

Name: ______________________________ Date: ________________

- Draw the section view. The part is made of cast iron.

Section type(s): ____

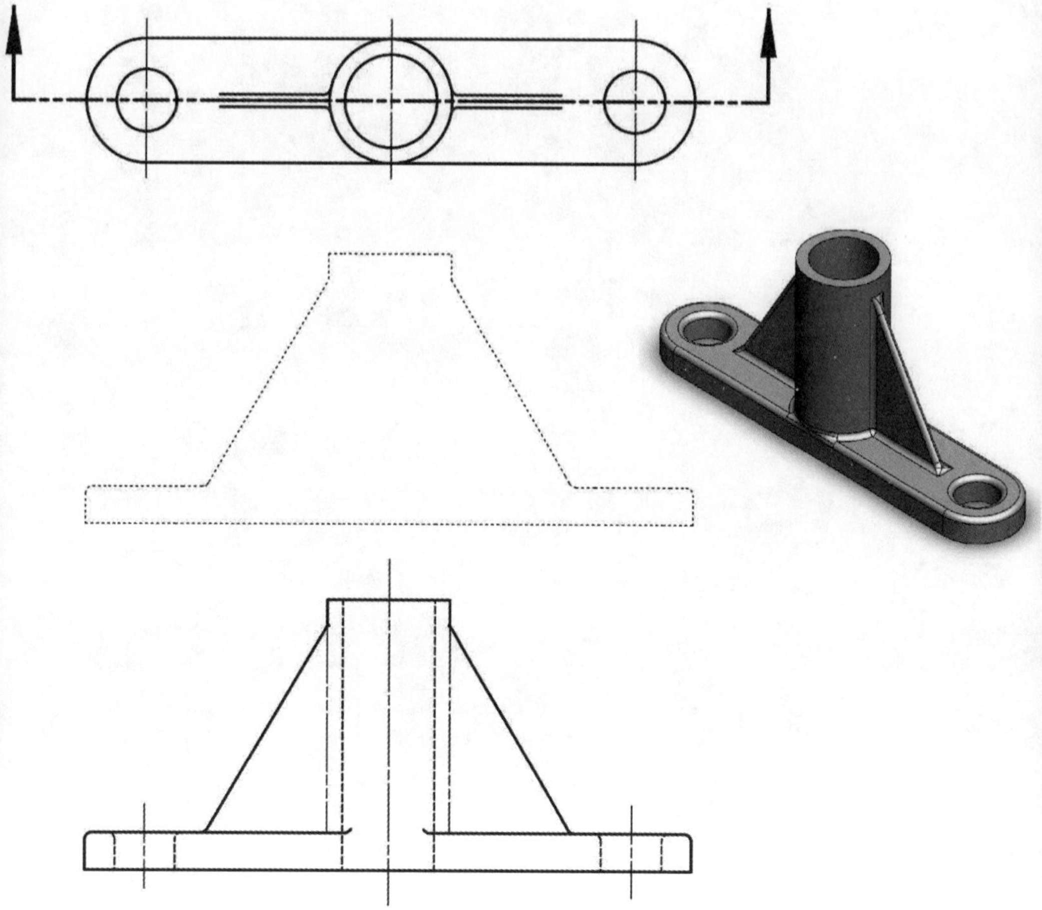

NOTES:

CREATING SECTION VIEWS QUESTIONS – SET 1

Name: ______________________________ Date: _____________

Q13-1) Which side of the part is mentally removed? (right, left)

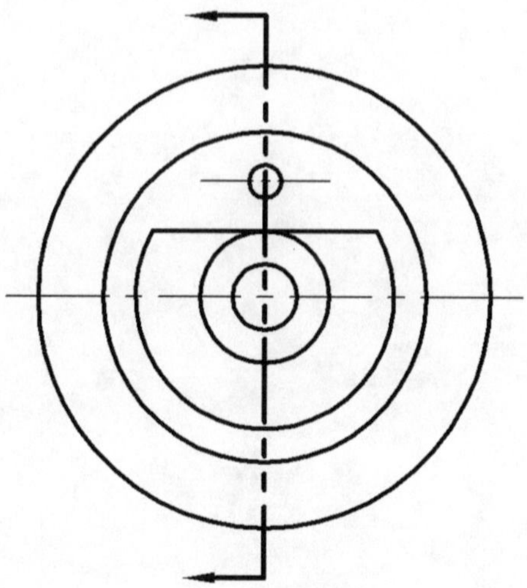

Q13-2) Section lines are drawn thin and angled at 45°. (True, False)

Q13-3) In general, hidden lines should be shown in a section view. (True, False)

Q13-4) The sectioned and non-sectioned halves of a half section are separated by a ________ line.

a) visible
b) hidden
c) cutting plane
d) center

Q13-5) Which type of section view is usually shown at an enlarged scale?

a) Full
b) Offset
c) Aligned
d) Removed

NOTES:

CREATING SECTION VIEWS QUESTIONS – SET 2

Name: ______________________________ Date: _____________

Q13-6) Which letter from the following list should not be used when labeling a section view?

A, B, F, I, H, W

Q13-7) Which line type is used when a cutting plane line traverses a short distance? (phantom, hidden)

Q13-8) Visible edges behind the cutting plane are not shown. (True, False)

Q13-9) Is it permissible to show hidden lines on some portion of a half section? (yes, no)

Q13-10) Is it permissible to show hidden lines on some portion of a broken section? (yes, no)

Q13-11) The **convention of revolution** is used when creating a (an) ...

a) full section
b) half section
c) offset section
d) aligned section
e) revolved section

Q13-12) A _____________ section is always labeled (for instance SECTION A-A.)

Q13-13) Bolts are usually not sectioned. (True, False)

NOTES:

CREATING SECTION VIEW PROBLEMS

Name: ______________________________ Date: ______________

P13-1) Sketch the sectional view as indicated. The material of the part is Steel.

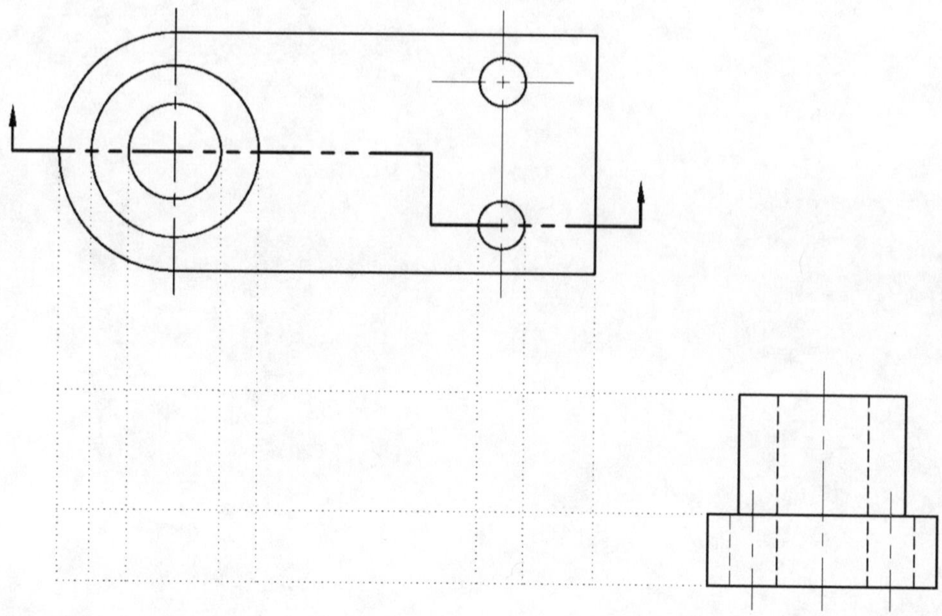

P13-2) Sketch the sectional view as indicated. The material of the part is Aluminum.

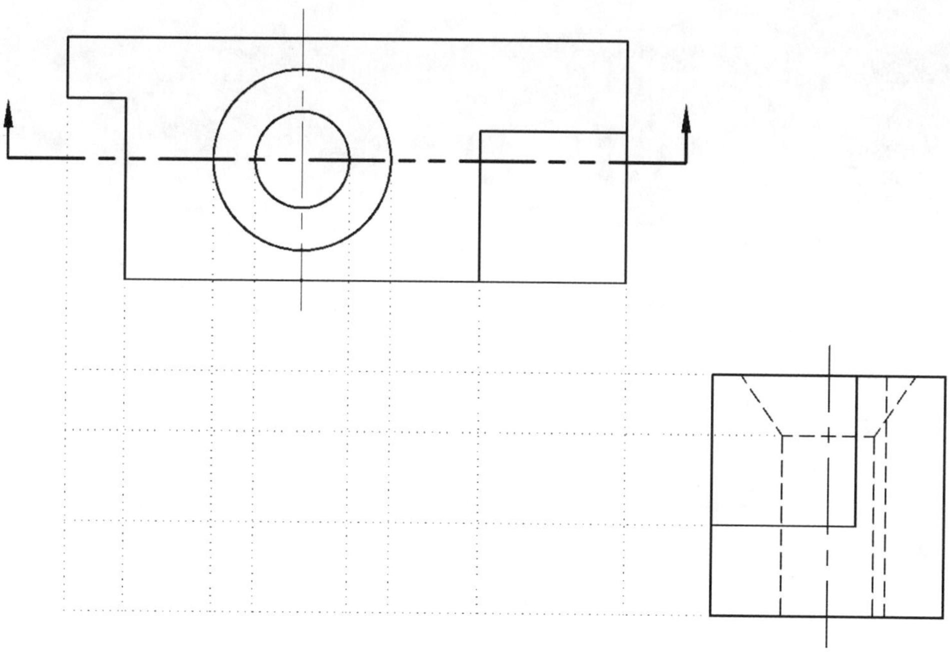

NOTES:

Name: ______________________ Date: ______________

P13-3) Sketch the sectional view as indicated. The material of the part is Rubber.

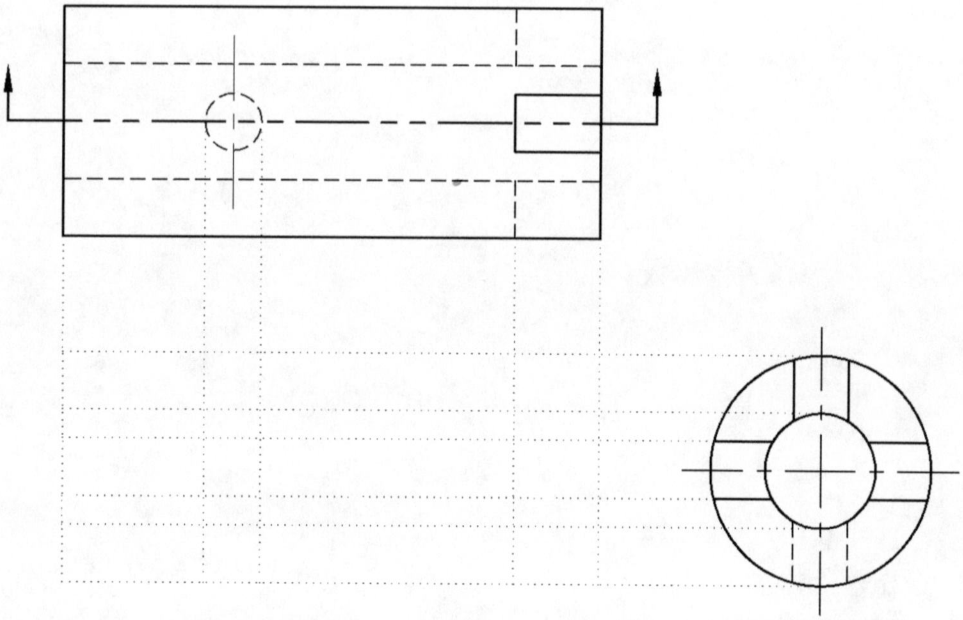

P13-4) Sketch the sectional view as indicated. The material of the part is Brass.

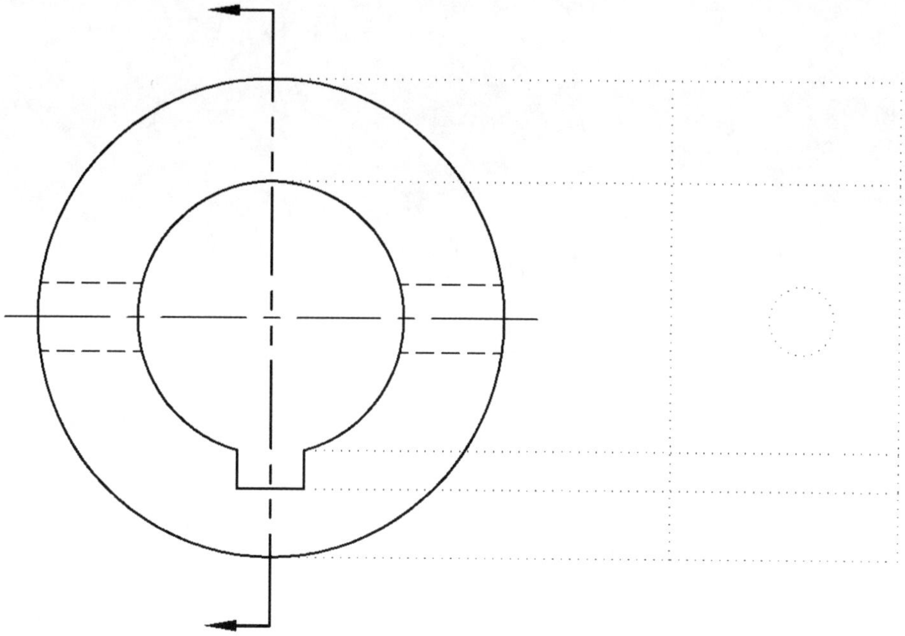

NOTES:

Name: ______________________________ Date: _____________

P13-5) Sketch the sectional view as indicated. The material of the part is Aluminum.

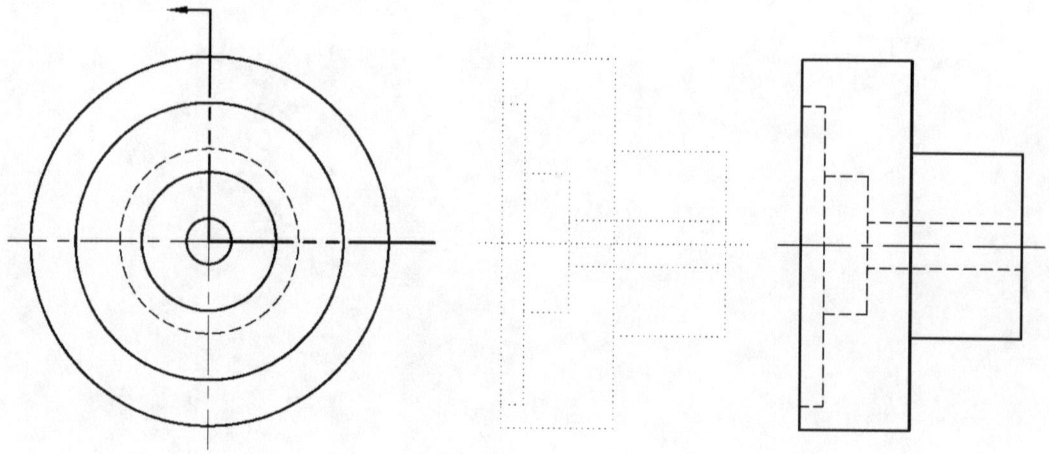

P13-6) Sketch the sectional view as indicated. The material of the part is Cast Iron.

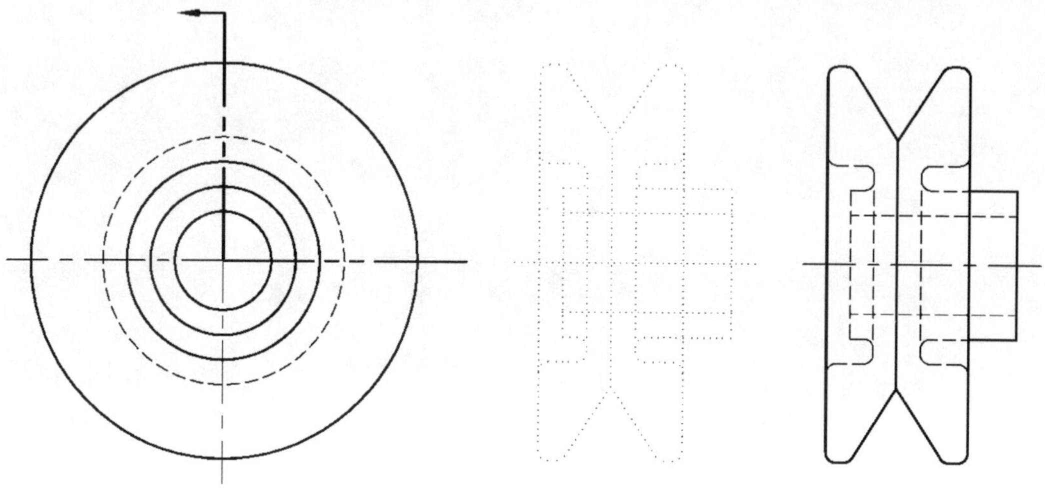

NOTES:

Name: ______________________________ Date: ______________

P13-7) Sketch the sectional view as indicated. The material of the part is Cast Iron.

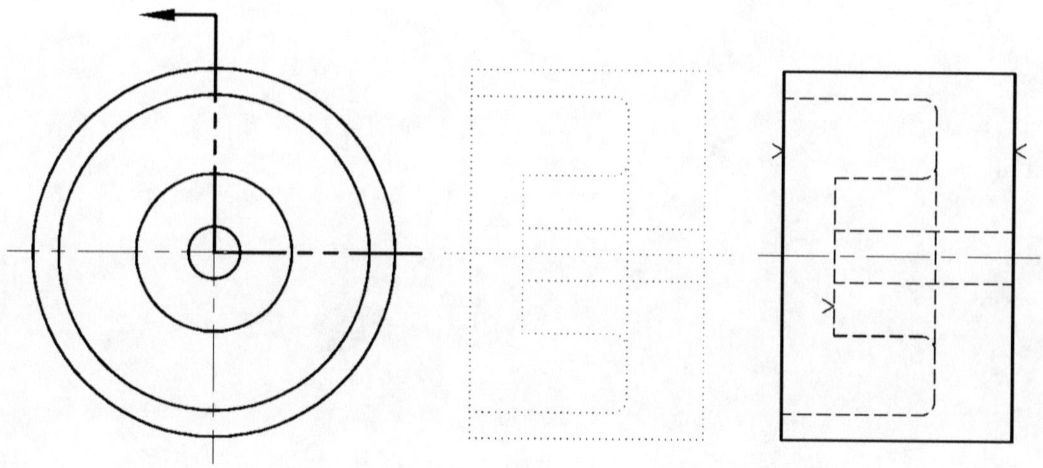

P13-8) Sketch the sectional view as indicated. The material of the part is Brass.

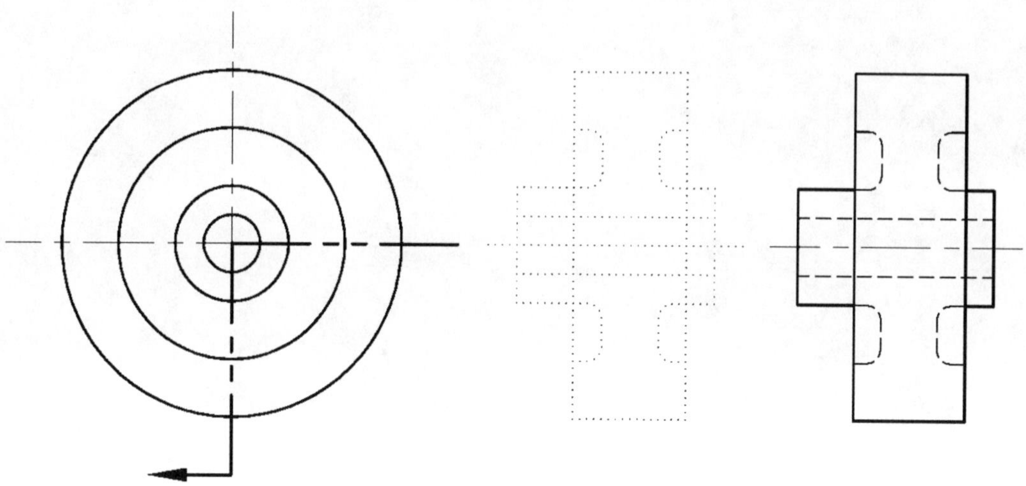

NOTES:

Name: ______________________________ Date: ______________

P13-9) Sketch the sectional view as indicated. The material of the part is Rubber.

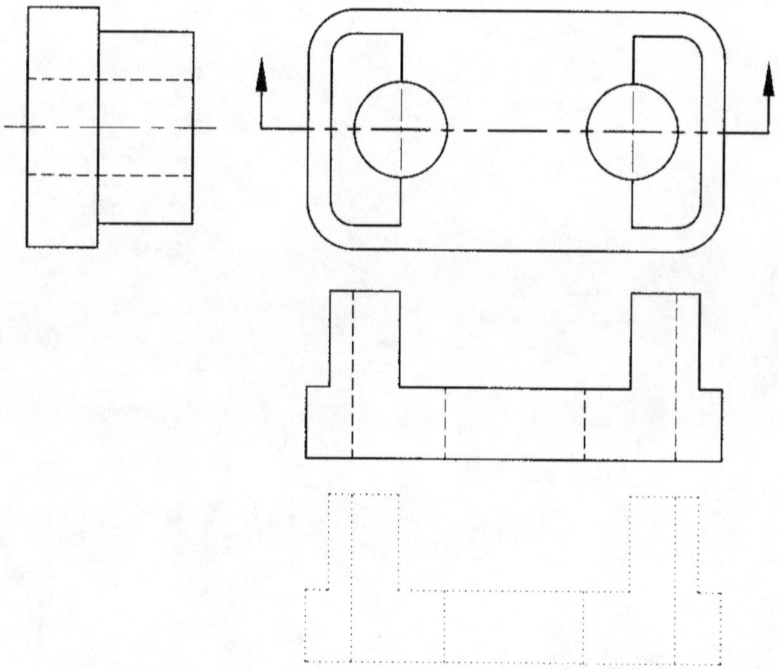

P13-10) Sketch the sectional view as indicated. The material of the part is Steel.

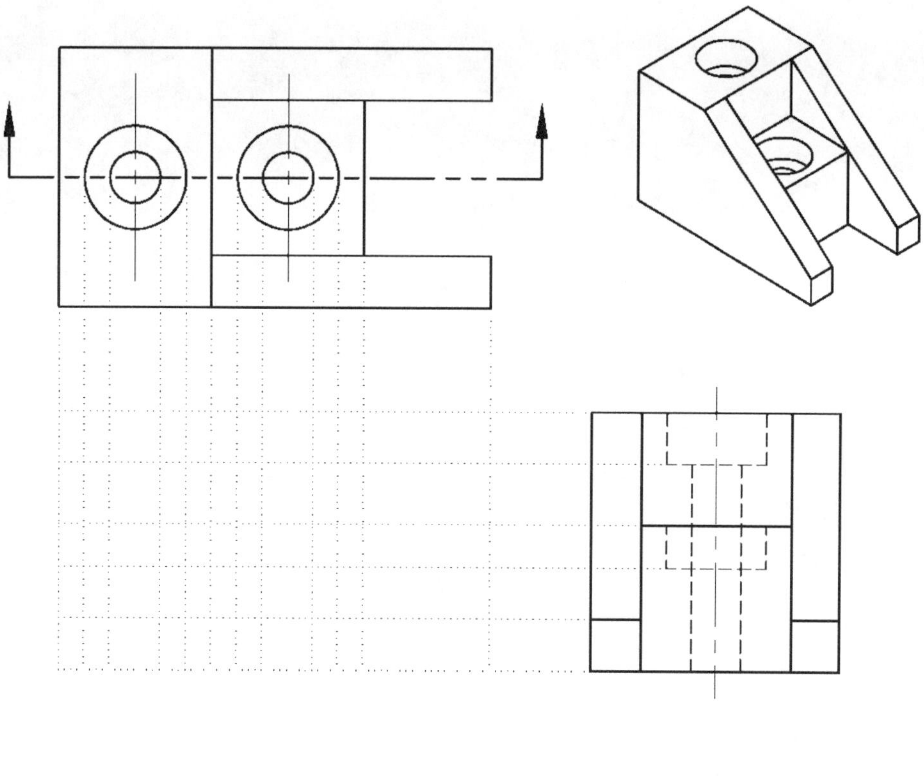

NOTES:

Name: ______________________________ Date: ______________

P13-11) Sketch the sectional view as indicated. The material of the part is Steel.

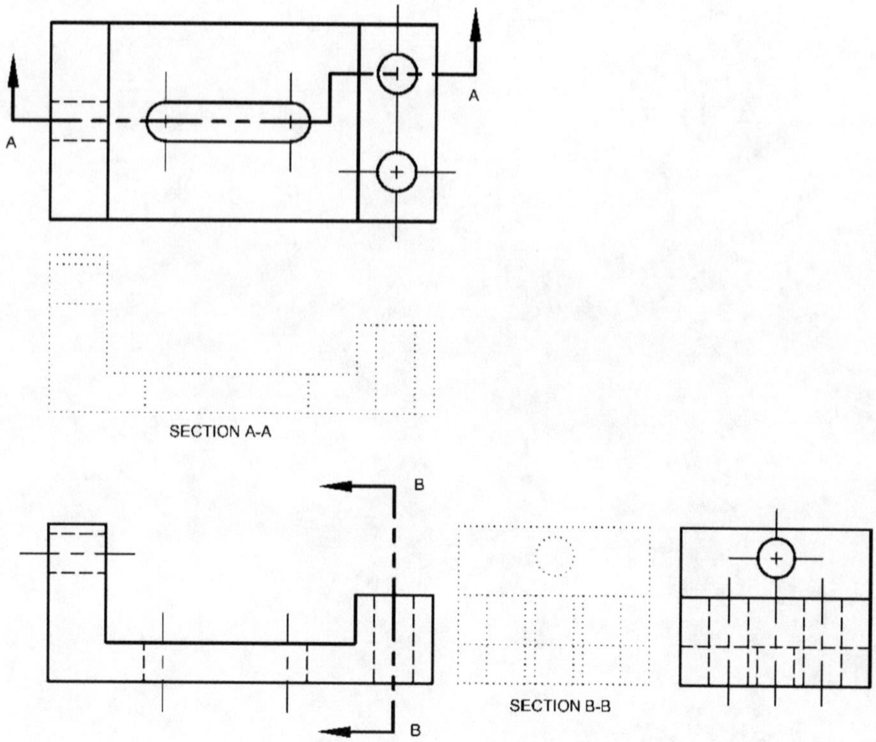

P13-12) Sketch the sectional view as indicated. The material of the part is Aluminum.

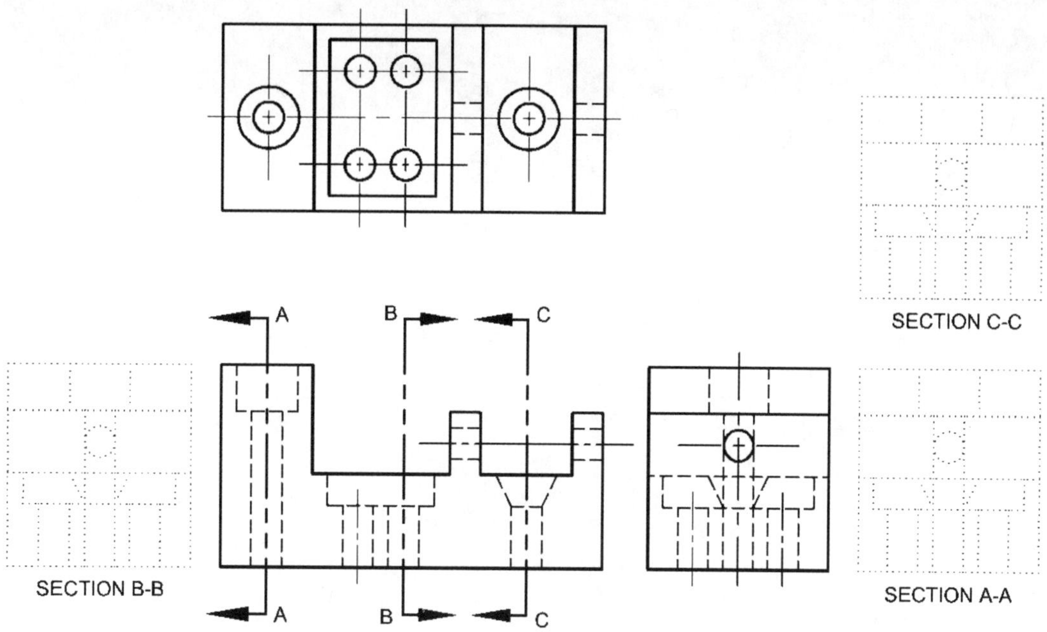

NOTES:

Name: ______________________________ Date: ______________

P13-13) Sketch the sectional view as indicated. The material of the part is Cast Iron.

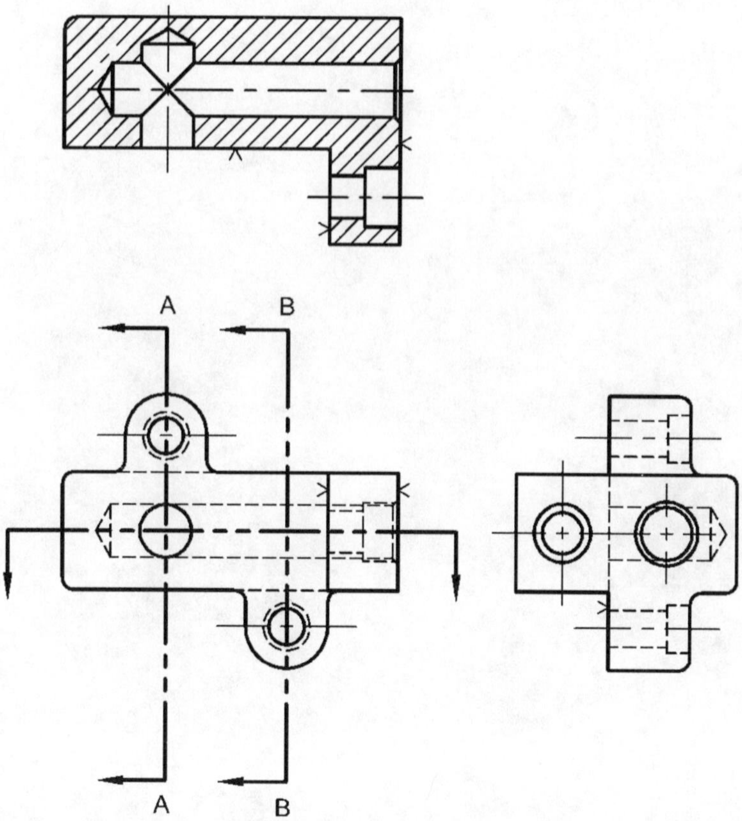

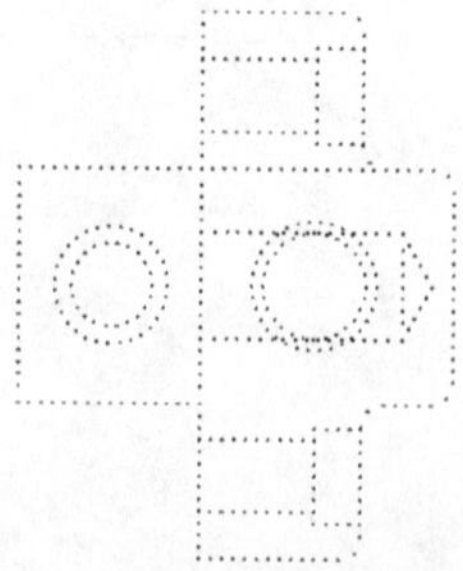

SECTION B-B

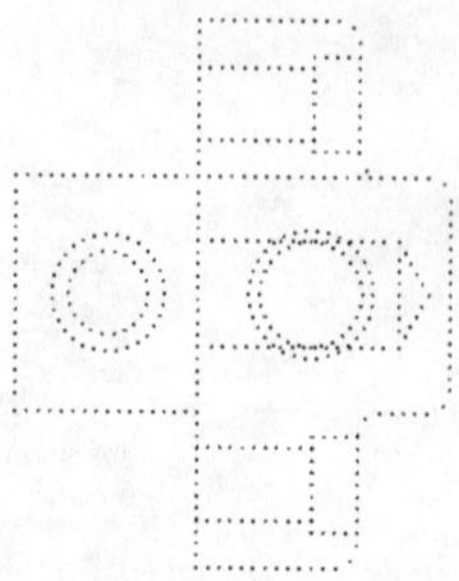

SECTION A-A

NOTES:

Name: ______________________________ Date: ______________

P13-14) Sketch the sectional view as indicated. The material of the part is Steel.

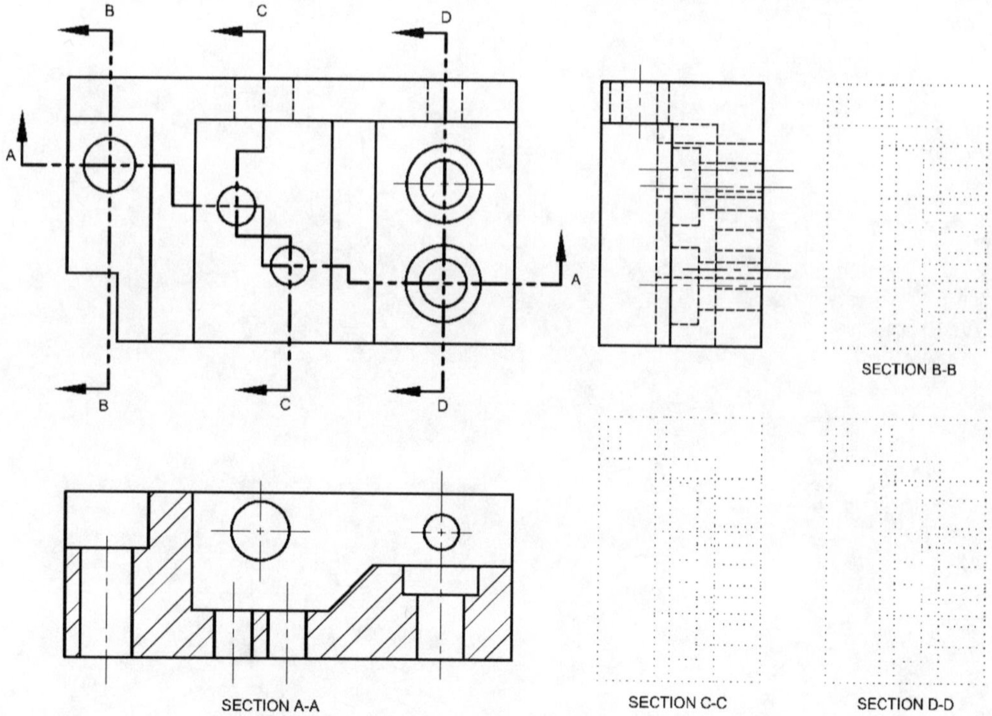

P13-15) Sketch the sectional view as indicated. The material of the part is Cast Iron.

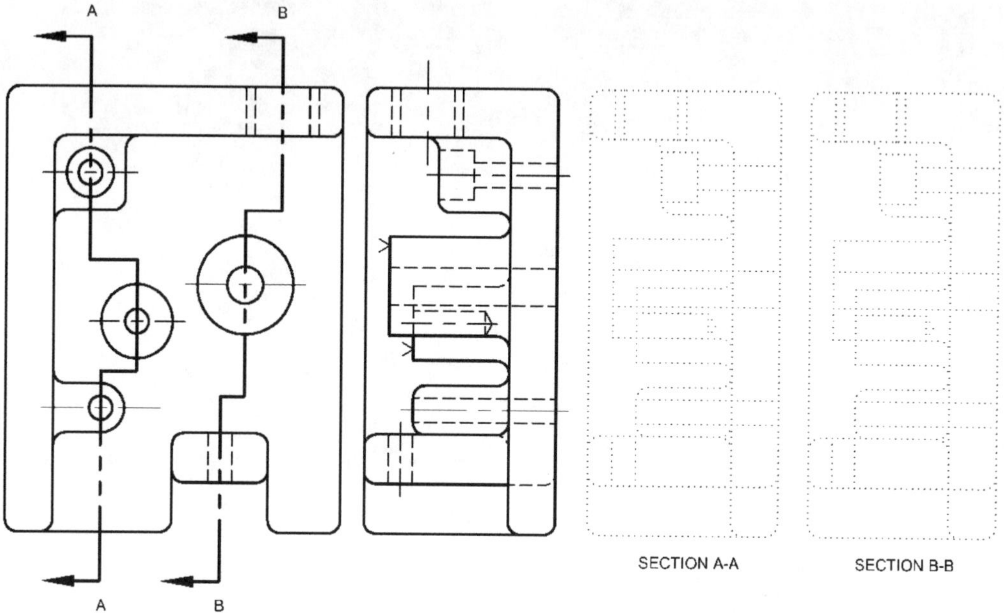

NOTES:

Name: ________________________________ Date: ______________

P13-16) Sketch the sectional view as indicated. The material of the part is Steel. Remember to include centerlines.

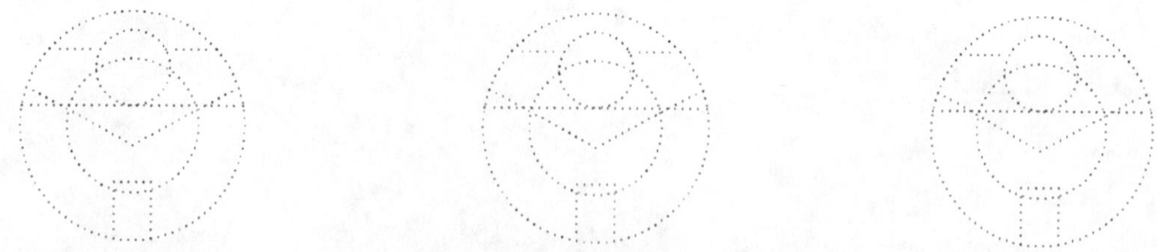

SECTION A-A SECTION B-B SECTION C-C

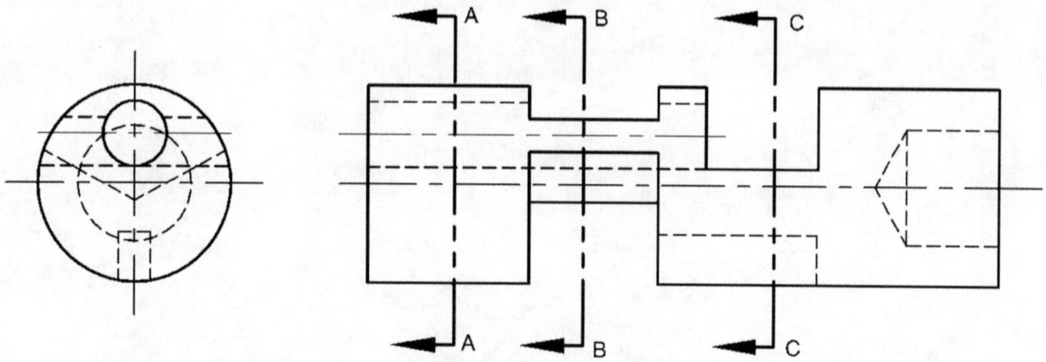

P13-17) Sketch the sectional view as indicated. The material of the part is Aluminum.

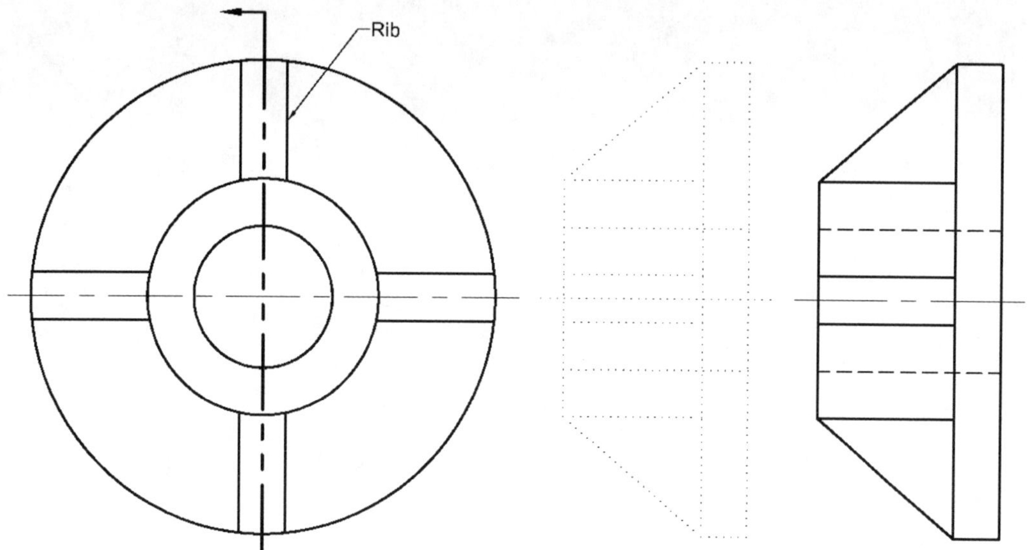

NOTES:

Name: ______________________________ Date: ______________

P13-18) Sketch an aligned section view using the conventions of revolution. The unsectioned right side view is shown true shape. The material of the part is Cast Iron.

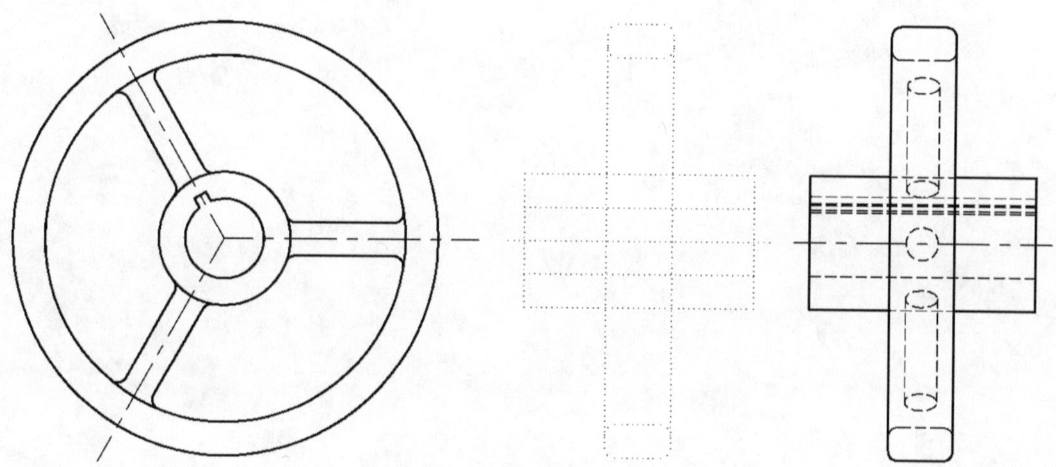

P13-19) Sketch an aligned section view using the conventions of revolution. The unsectioned right side view is shown true shape. The material of the part is Cast Iron.

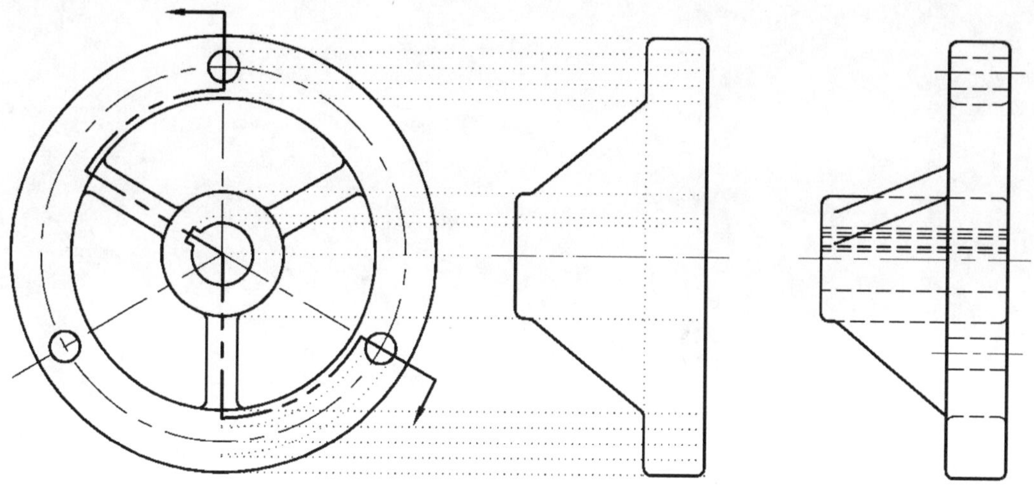

Aligned section using the conventions of revolution.

Unrevolved view

NOTES:

P13-20) Draw the following object converting the front view into an offset section. It is not necessary to include the dimensions. The material of the part is Steel.

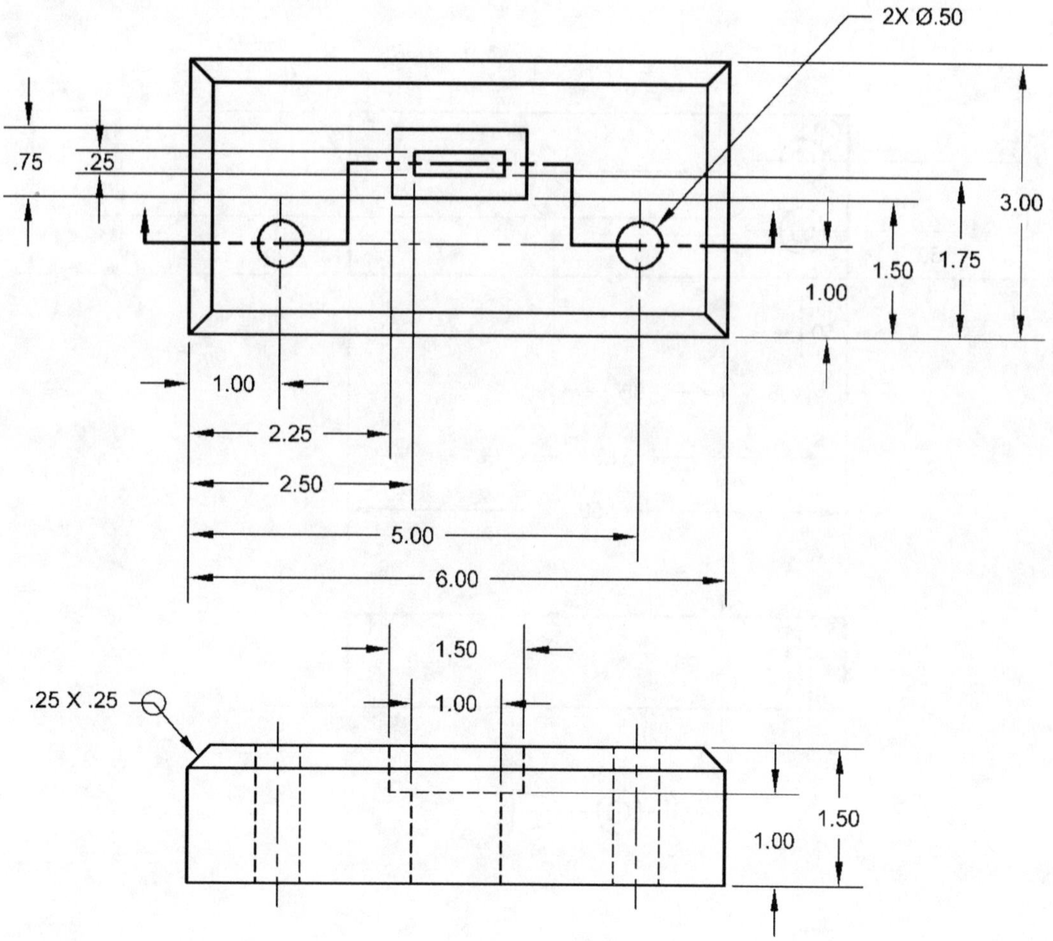

P13-21) Draw the following object converting the front view into an offset section. It is not necessary to include the dimensions. The material of the part is Aluminum.

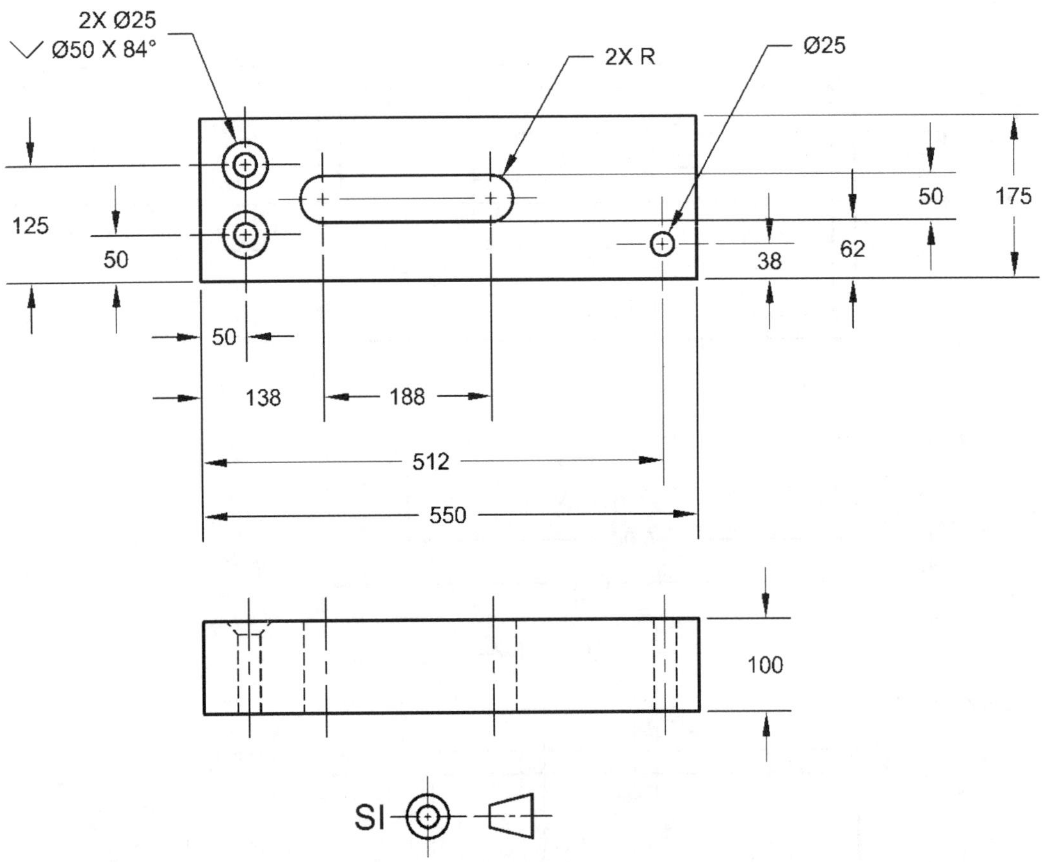

P13-22) Draw the following object converting the front view into an offset section. Capture as many features as possible. Draw the appropriate cutting plane line. It is not necessary to include the dimensions. The material of the part is Plastic.

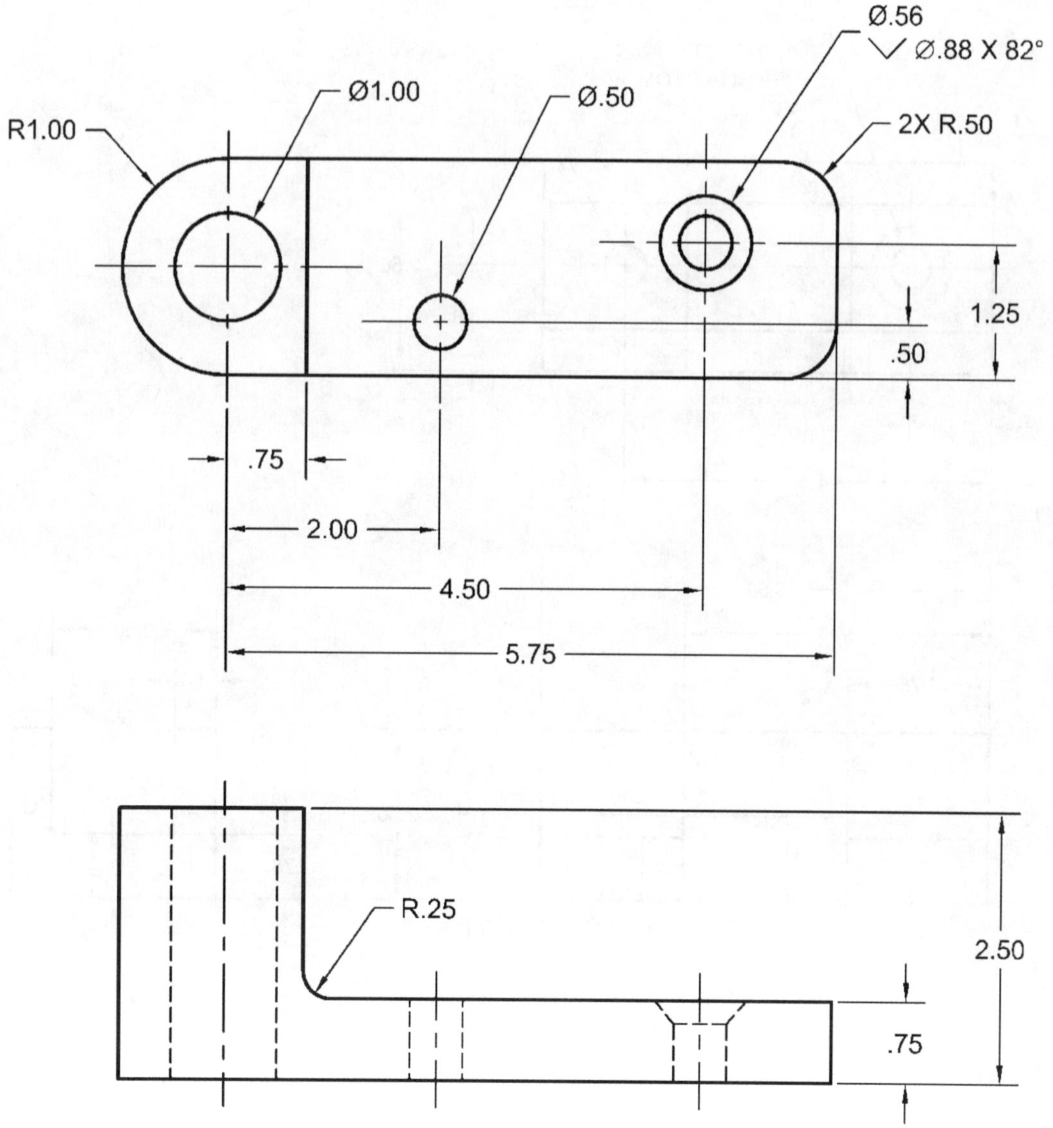

P13-23) Draw all three views of the following object converting the front view into a full section. Draw the appropriate cutting plane line. It is not necessary to include the dimensions. The material of the part is Steel.

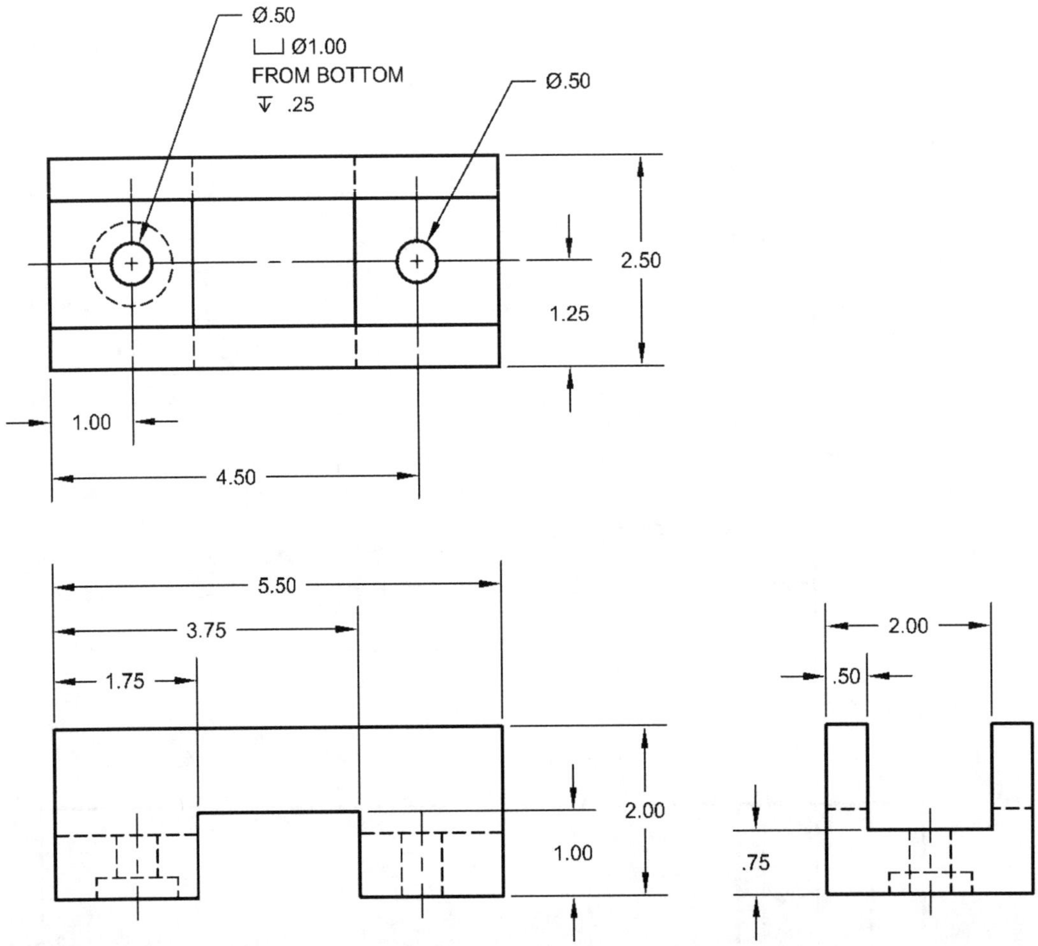

P13-24) Draw the following object converting the front view into a full section. Draw the appropriate cutting plane line. It is not necessary to include the dimensions. The material of the part is Cast Iron.

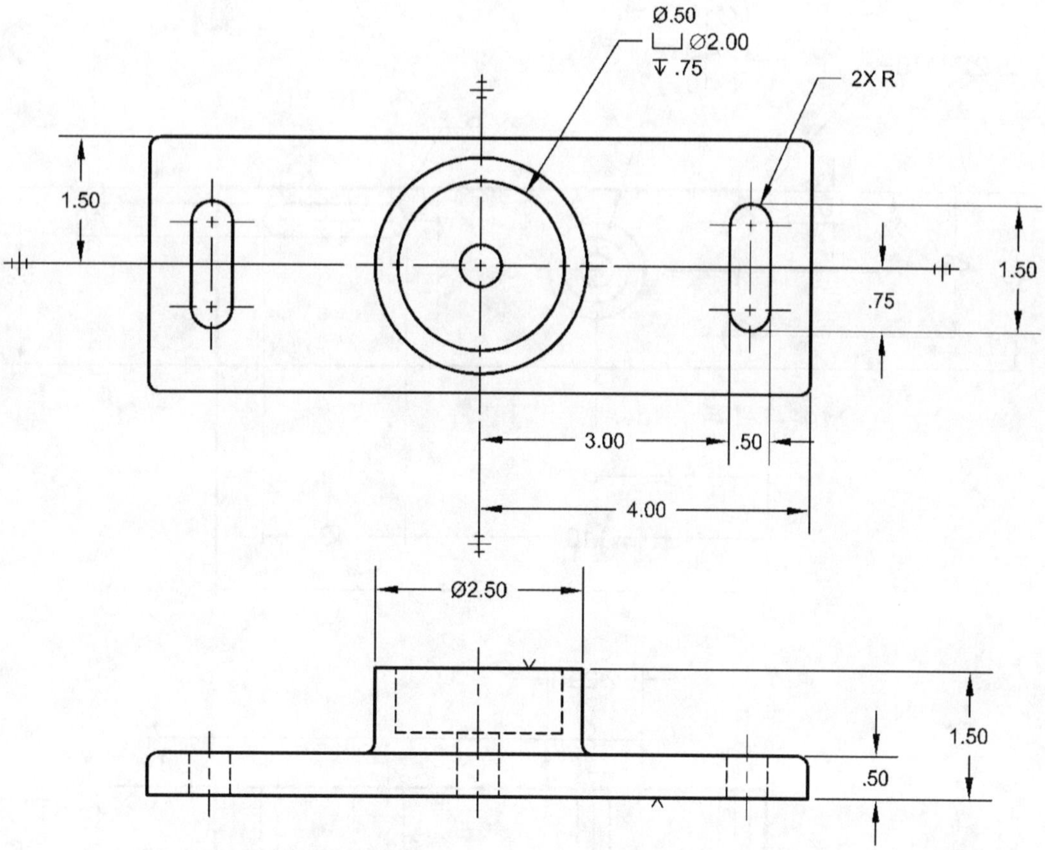

NOTE: ALL ROUNDS AND FILLETS .12 R

P13-25) Draw the following object converting the front view into an offset section. Capture as many features as possible. Draw the appropriate cutting plane line. It is not necessary to include the dimensions. The material of the part is Steel.

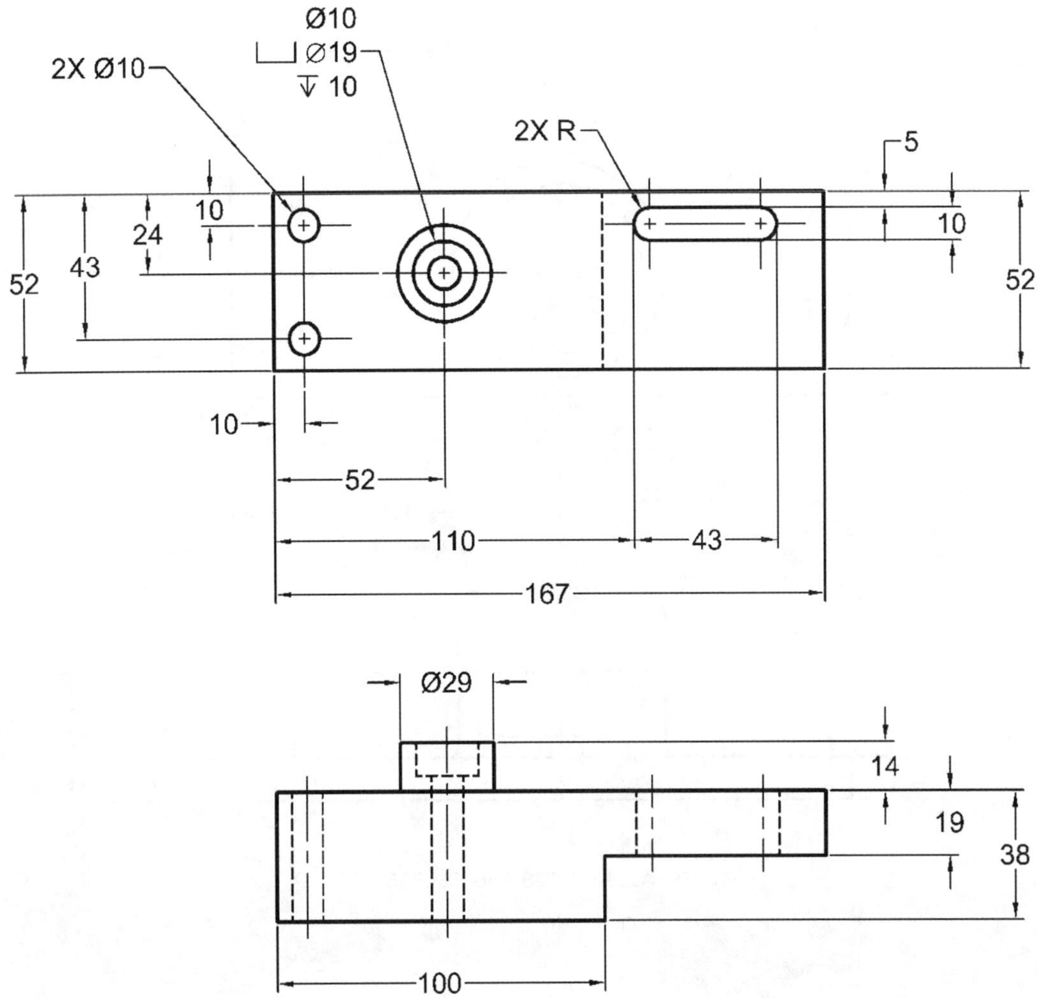

P13-26) Draw the following object converting the front view into an offset section. Capture as many features as possible. Draw the appropriate cutting plane line. It is not necessary to include the dimensions. The material of the part is Cast Iron.

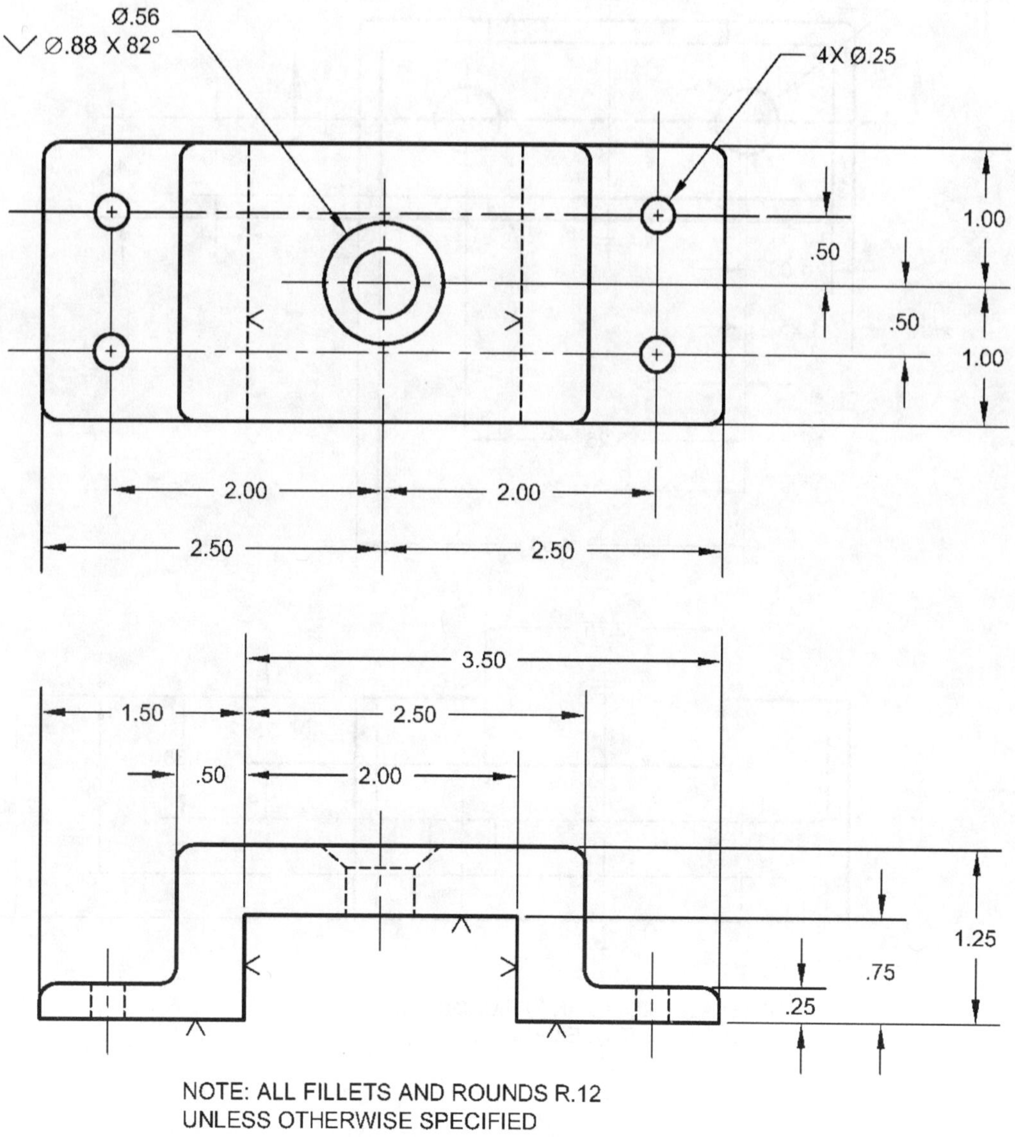

P13-27) Draw the following object converting the front view into a full section. It is not necessary to include the dimensions. The material of the part is Cast Iron.

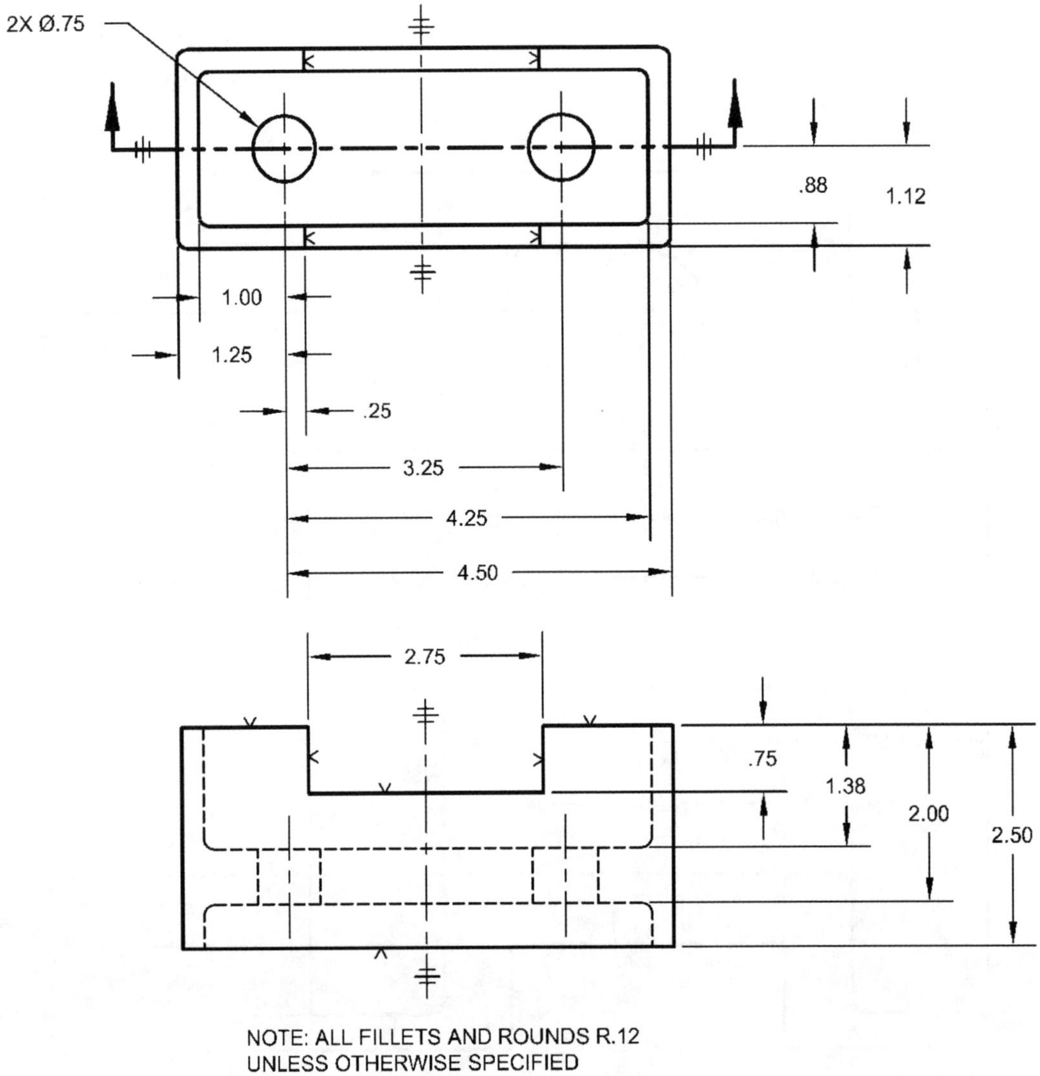

P13-28) Draw the following object converting the front view into a full section. It is not necessary to include the dimensions. The material of the part is Cast Iron.

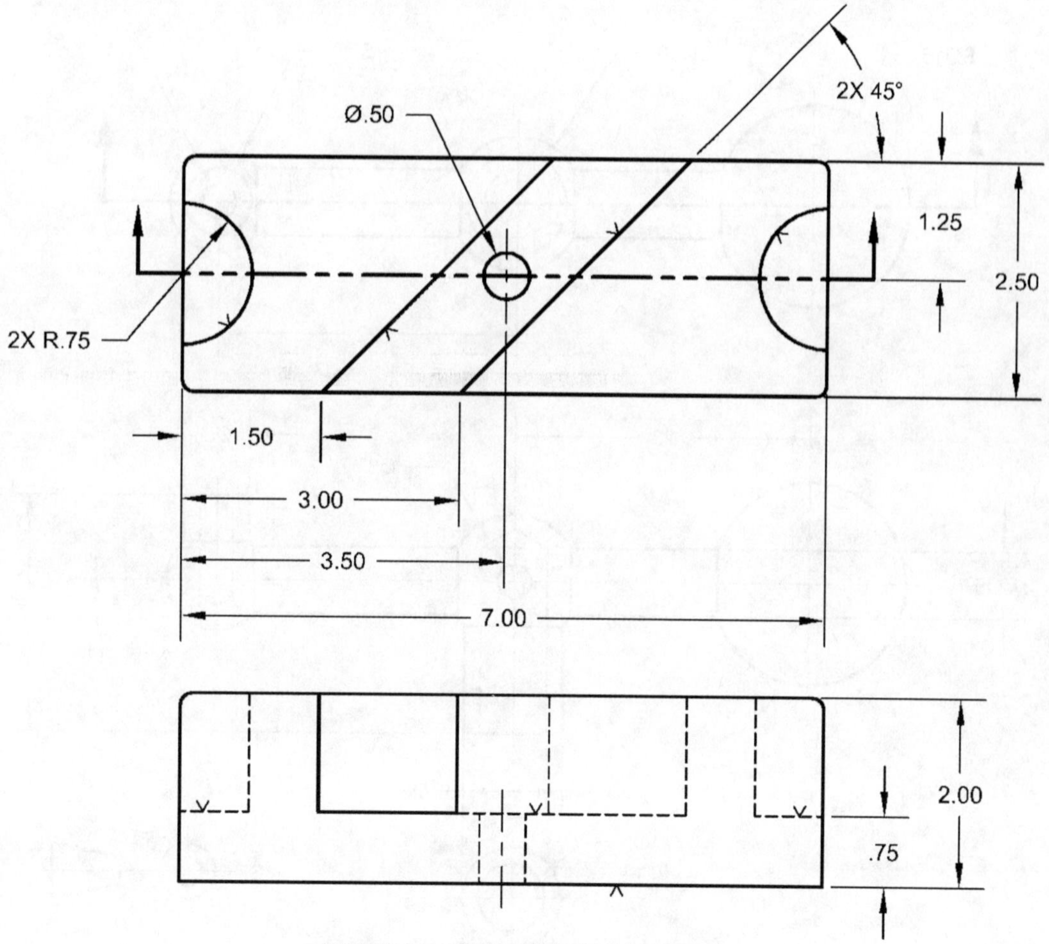

NOTE: ALL FILLETS AND ROUNDS R.12
UNLESS OTHERWISE SPECIFIED.

P13-29) Draw the following object converting the front view into a full section. It is not necessary to include the dimensions. The material of the part is Plastic.

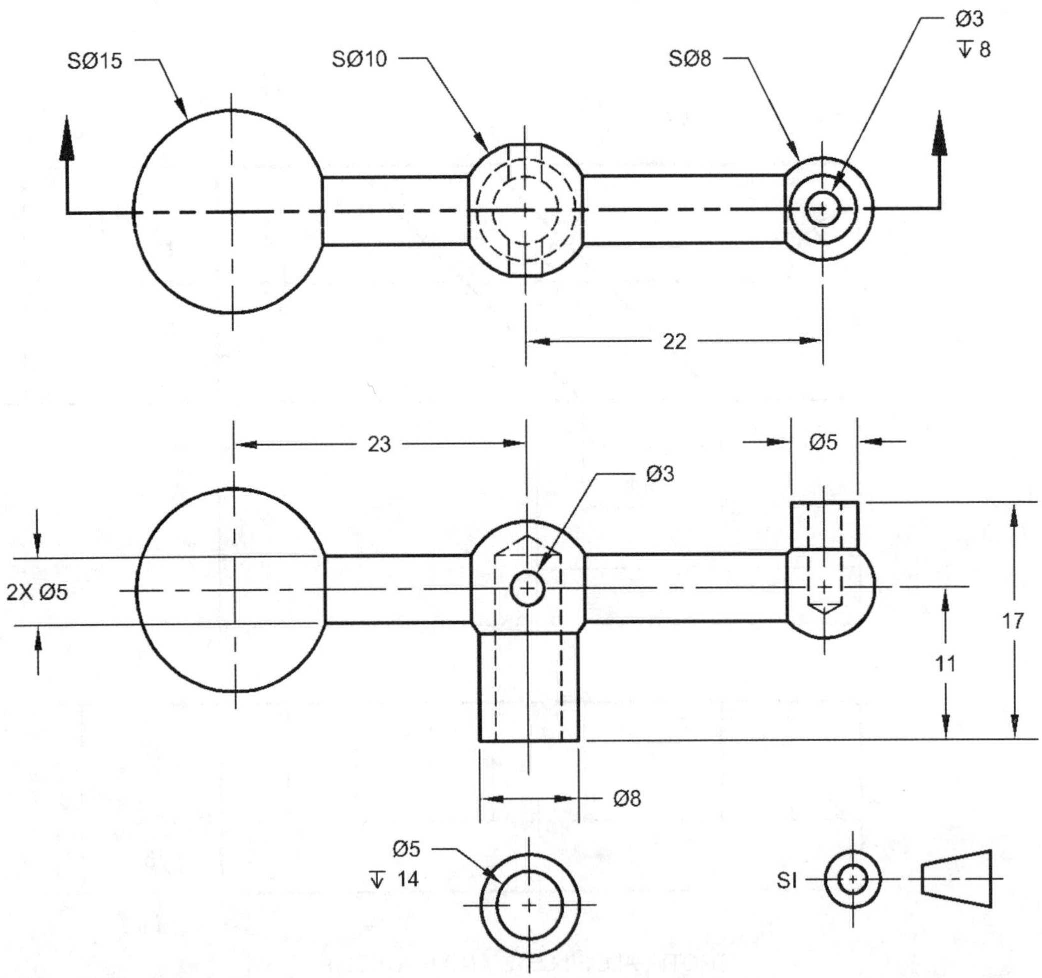

P13-30) Draw the following object converting the right side view into a half section. Draw the appropriate cutting plane line. It is not necessary to include the dimensions. The material of the part is Brass.

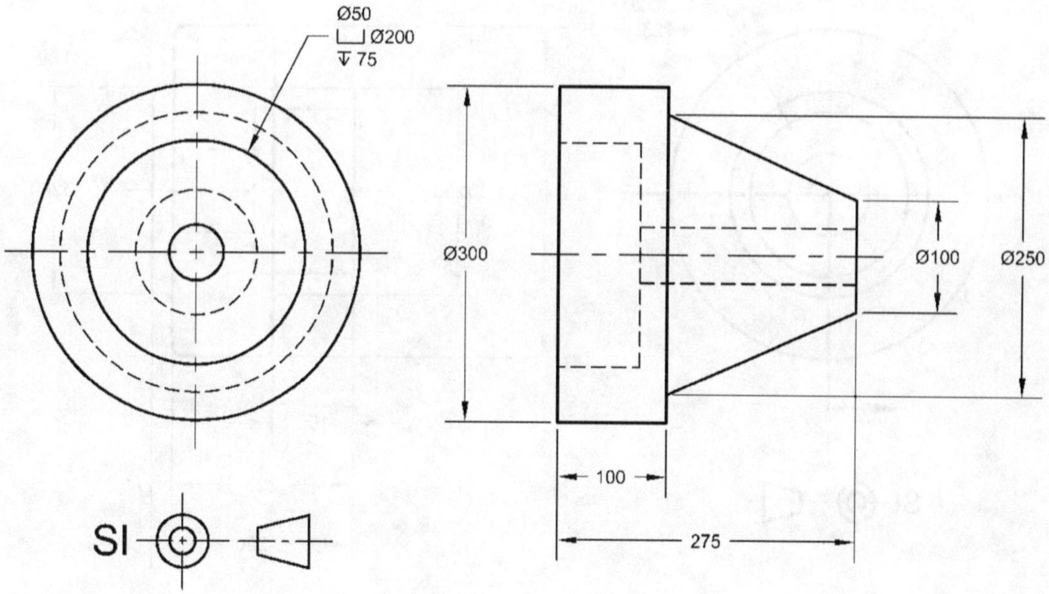

P13-31) Draw the following object converting the right side view into a half section. It is not necessary to include the dimensions. The material of the part is Steel.

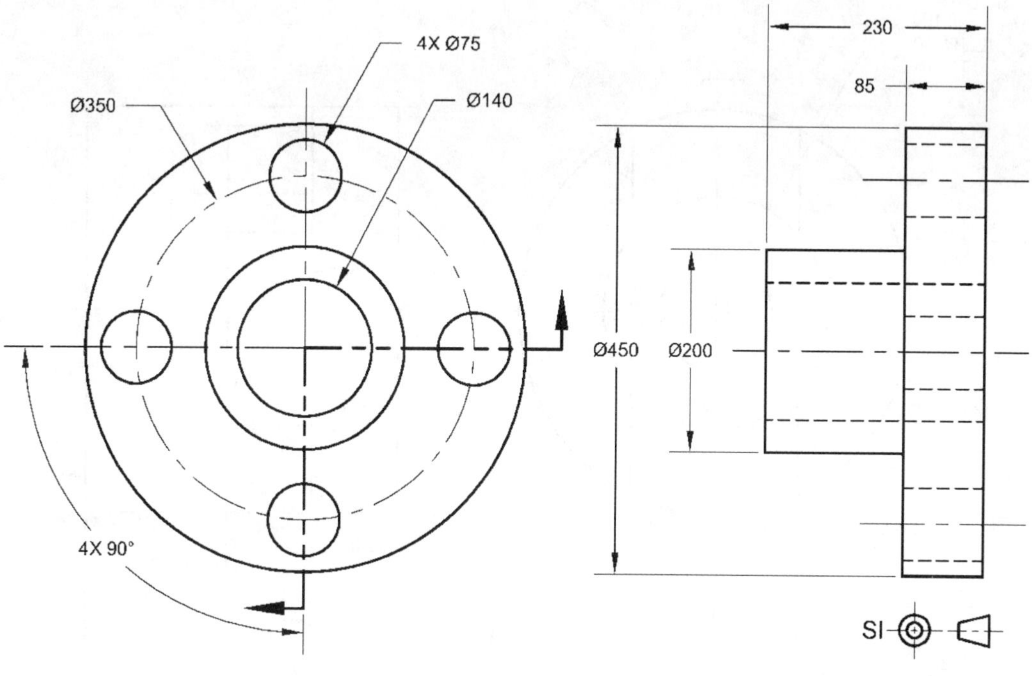

P13-32) Draw the following object converting the right side view into a half section. It is not necessary to include the dimensions. The material of the part is Aluminum.

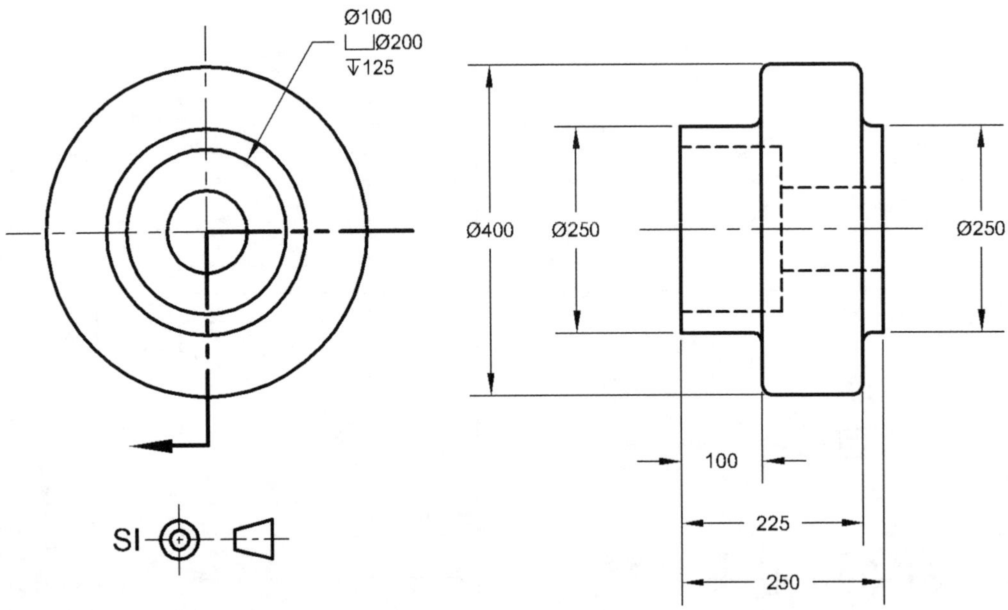

P13-33) Draw the following object converting the right side view into a half section. Draw the appropriate cutting plane line. It is not necessary to include the dimensions. The material of the part is Steel.

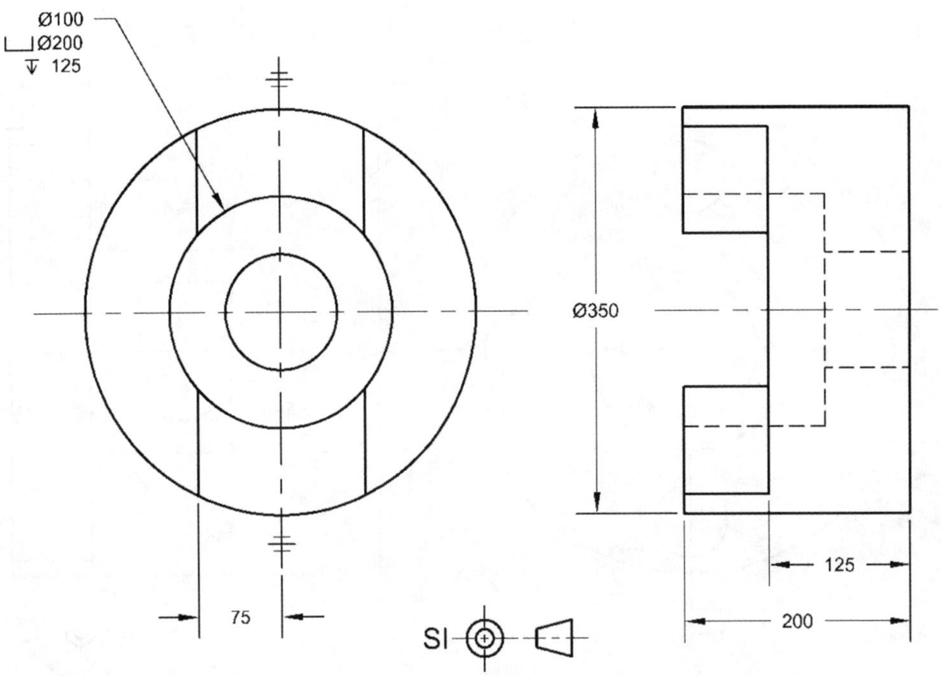

P13-34) Draw the following object converting the left side view into a half section. Draw the appropriate cutting plane line. It is not necessary to include the dimensions. The material of the part is Steel.

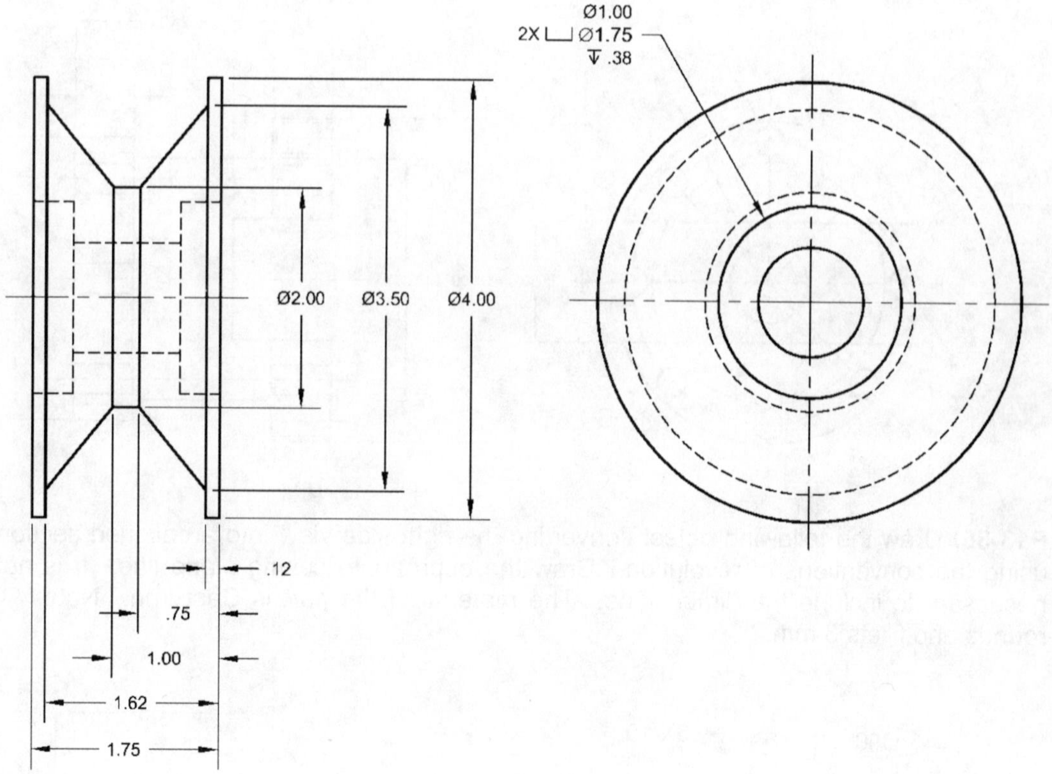

P13-35) Draw the following object converting the right side view into a half section. It is not necessary to include the dimensions. The material of the part is Aluminum.

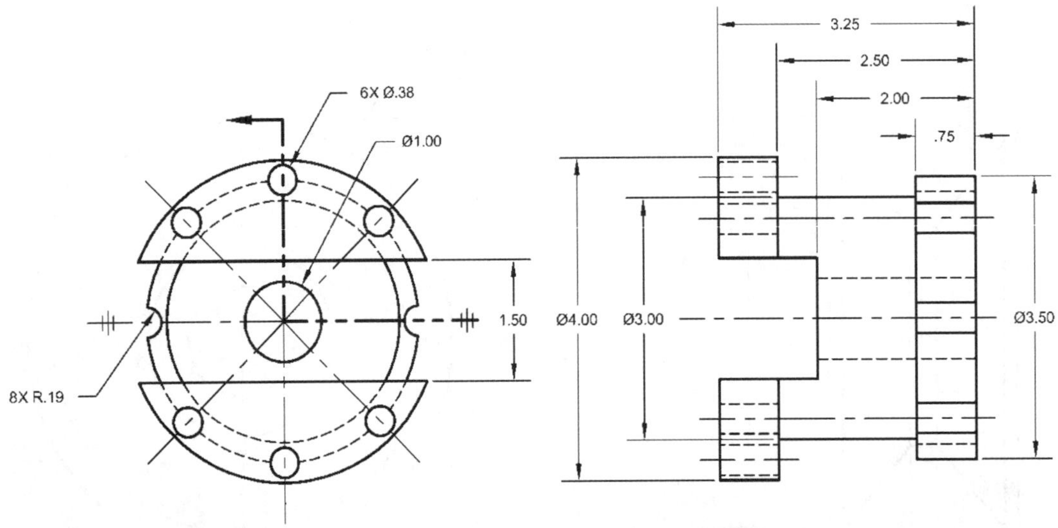

P13-36) Draw the following object converting the right side view into an aligned section using the conventions of revolution. Draw the appropriate cutting plane line. It is not necessary to include the dimensions. The material of the part is Cast iron. Note: All rounds and fillets 3 mm.

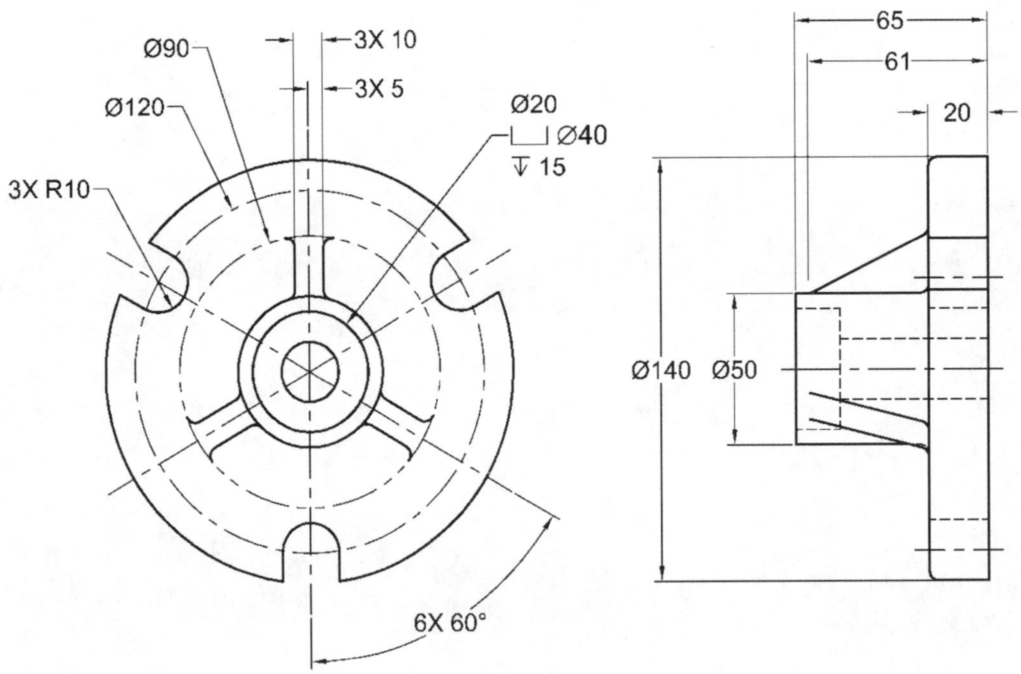

SP13-1) Sketch the sectional view as indicated. The material of the part is Steel. The answer to this problem is given on the *Independent Learning Content*.

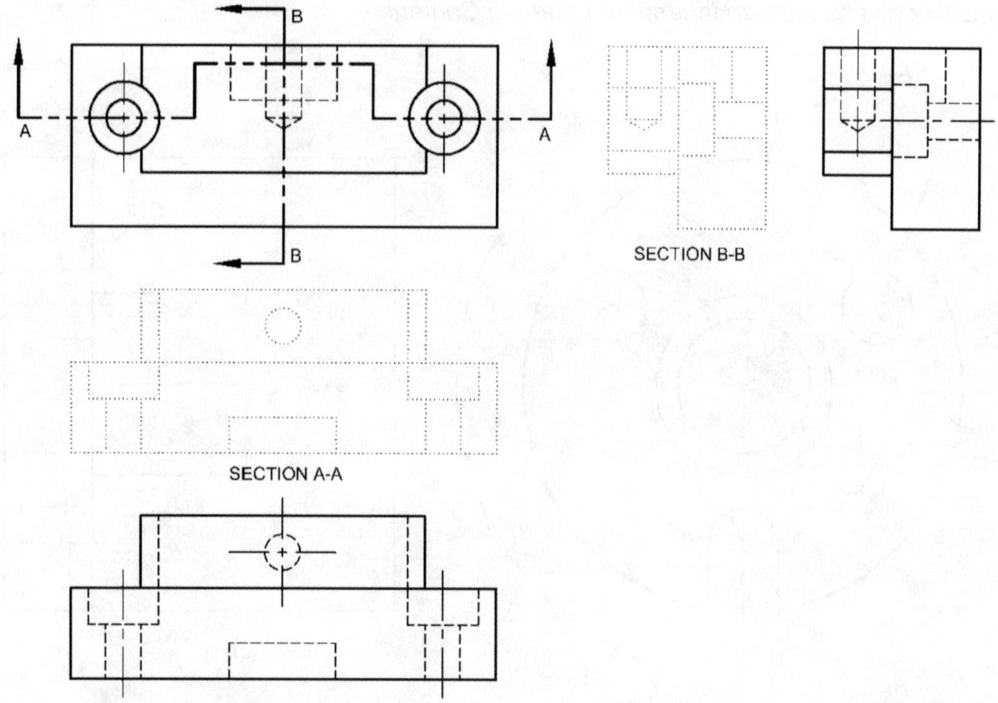

SP13-2) Sketch the sectional view as indicated. The material of the part is Rubber. The answer to this problem is given on the *Independent Learning Content*.

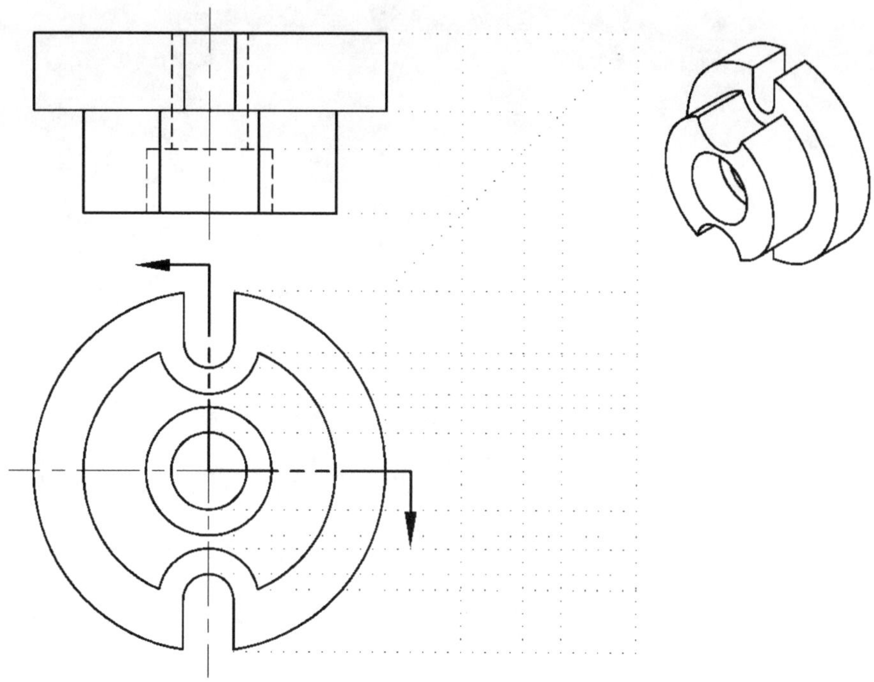

SP13-3) Draw the following object converting the right side view into an aligned section using the conventions of revolution. Draw the appropriate cutting plane line. It is not necessary to include the dimensions. The material of the part is Steel. The answer to this problem is given on the *Independent Learning Content*.

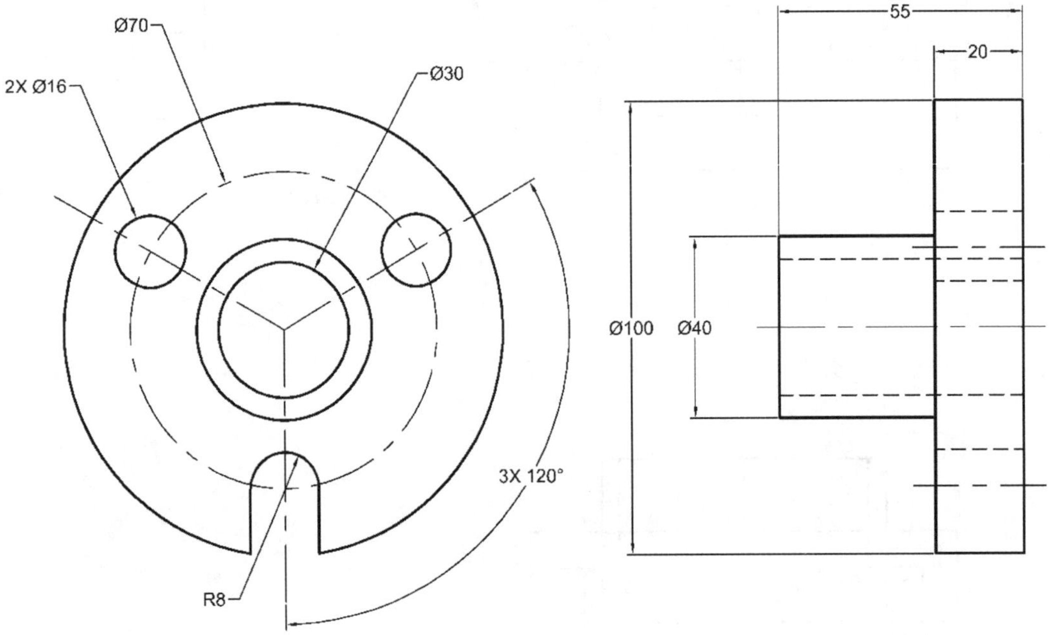

CHAPTER 14

CREATING SECTION VIEWS IN AUTOCAD®

CHAPTER OUTLINE

CHAPTER SUMMARY

In this chapter you will learn how to create section views in AutoCAD®. Creating a section view in AutoCAD's 2-D environment consists of creating section lines, or hatches as they are called in AutoCAD®, and drawing a cutting plane line. There are many different predefined hatch patterns available. By the end of this chapter, you will be able to draw cutting plane lines and place section lines within a bounded area.

14.1) INTRODUCTION

When drawing a section view, it is necessary to draw cutting plane lines and section lines. The *Phantom* line type is used to create the cutting plane line and it is printed thick. Cutting plane lines are thicker than visible lines. Therefore, they are placed on their own layer. Section lines on the other hand are thin and may be placed on the dimension layer. AutoCAD® makes drawing section lines very easy. The command used to create section lines is **HATCH**. Section lines or hatch symbols are predefined and may be drawn at different angles and at different scales. The scale controls the distance between the parallel hatch lines.

14.2) CUTTING PLANE LINES

Figure 14.2-1 shows an example of a cutting plane line. The cutting plane line is placed on its own layer and the layer line type is *Phantom*. The thickness of the cutting plane line is between 0.6 and 0.8 mm. The procedure for drawing a cutting plane line is simple. A line is drawn indicating where the part is to be cut and multileaders are used to indicate the view direction. The cutting plane line arrows are usually larger than the arrowheads used in dimensioning, therefore a new multileader style will be created that has a large arrow and no landing.

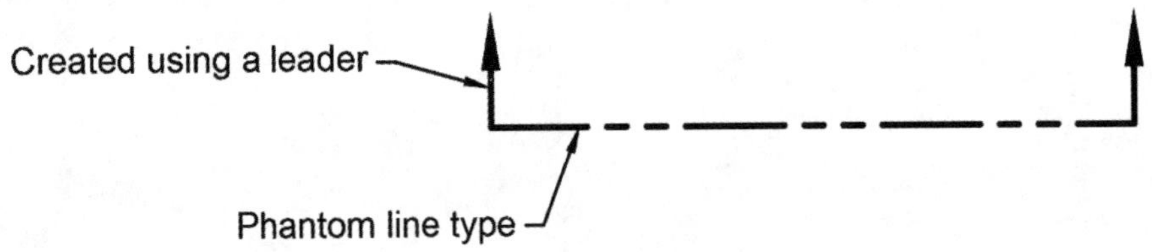

Figure 14.2-1: Cutting plane line

14.3) HATCHES

Section lines are created using hatches. AutoCAD® has many predefined hatches. Some of these are shown in Figure 14.3-1. Several of them are labeled by material. However, the most commonly used hatches are labeled by their standard number.

- ANSI31 = Cast Iron or general use
- ANSI32 = Steel
- ANSI33 = Brass, Bronze, Copper
- ANSI34 = Rubber, Plastic, Electrical Insulation
- ANSI37 = Zinc, Lead
- ANSI38 = Magnesium, Aluminum

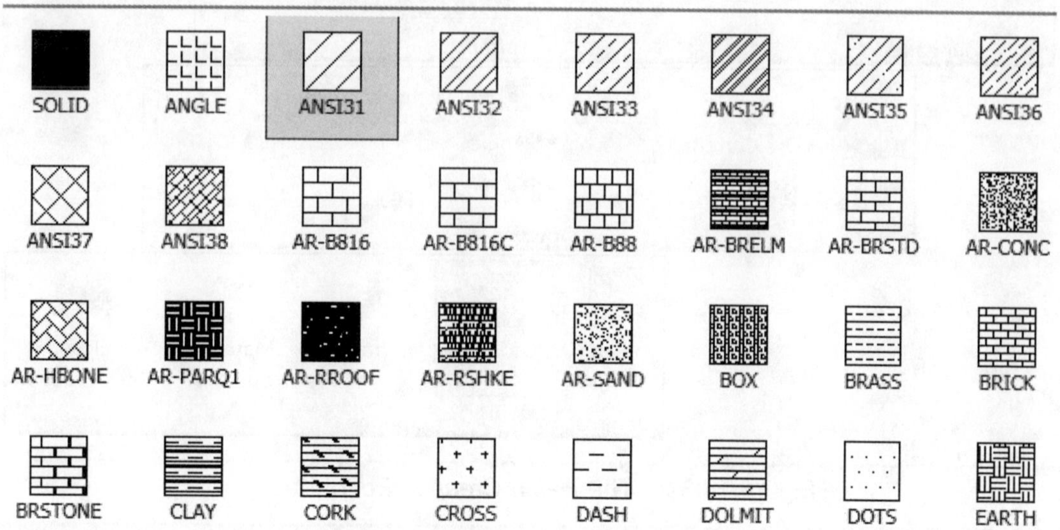

Figure 14.3-1: Hatch patterns

The angle and scale at which the hatches are drawn may be controlled within the *Hatch Creation/Editor* ribbon (Figure 14.3-2). Section lines are usually drawn at 45 degrees. For the ANSI standard hatches, the default angle is 45 degrees. This is indicated by a 0 in the *Angle* field. Any non-zero angle specified in this field is either added to or subtracted from 45 degrees. The scale of the hatch controls the space between the parallel lines. It will be increased or decreased depending on the size of the part.

The hatched area is usually bounded by lines, circles or arcs. The two easiest ways to specify a hatch boundary are the *pick points* method and the *select boundary objects* method.

- Pick points: Specify a point within an area that is enclosed by objects. AutoCAD® will automatically select all objects that bound the area.
- Select boundary objects: Manually select the objects that bound the area. If you want to hatch an area whose boundary is not quite closed, you can set the **HPGAPTOL** system variable to bridge gaps between lines and arcs.

Hatches, by default, are associative. That means that they will be updated when the boundary is changed. Associativity is automatically removed if HPGAPTOL is set to

0 and a change in the boundary results in a gap. Associativity is reapplied if the boundary is mended.

Hatches may also be defined as annotative. That is, they will change their scale depending on the viewport scale used to view the drawing.

The *Hatch Creation* ribbon may be accessed in the following ways:

- *Draw* panel: 
- *Command* window: **HATCH**

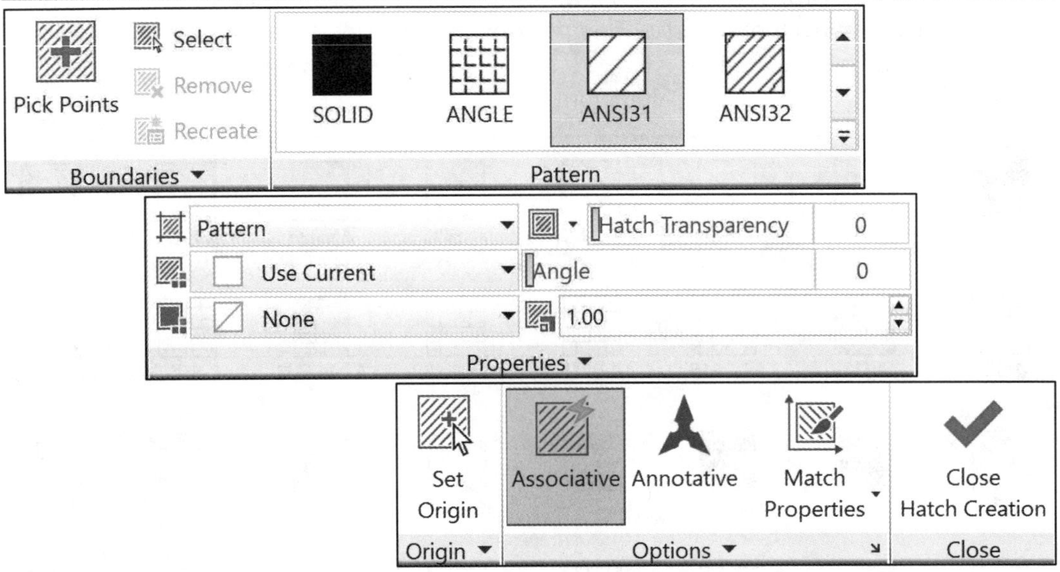

Figure 14.3-2: The *Hatch Creation/Editor* ribbon

Creating hatches

1) Command: **hatch** or *Draw* panel: 
2) `Hatch Pick internal point or [Select objects/Undo/seTtings]:` You may change the hatch area selection method and the hatch settings here. However, most of your modifications will be done in the *Hatch Creation* ribbon that appears and allows you to apply and modify the hatch pattern.
3) *Hatch Editor* ribbon:
   a) *Pattern* panel: Select a hatch pattern. You may view all the predefined patterns by selecting the arrows on the right side of the panel.
   b) *Properties* panel: Enter an angle. This angle is either added to (positive angle) or subtracted from (negative angle) the patterns default angle. The default angle is usually 45 degrees.
   c) *Properties* panel: Enter a scale. The scale is usually the same as your DIMSCALE; however, it also depends on the size of the part and the size of the cut areas.
   d) *Options* panel: Select whether you want your hatch to be annotative and/or associative.
   e) *Boundaries* panel: Select the area in which to place hatches. This may be done in two ways.
      - *Pick points*: 

        This method allows you to pick a point within each bounded area that you wish to place hatches.
      - Select boundary objects: 

        This method allows you to select the objects that will create the boundaries of your sectioned area.
   f) *Boundaries* panel: 

      If you need to modify your hatch boundary you may use the *Remove* icon.
   g) When you are satisfied with the results, select the ***Close Hatch Creation*** icon.

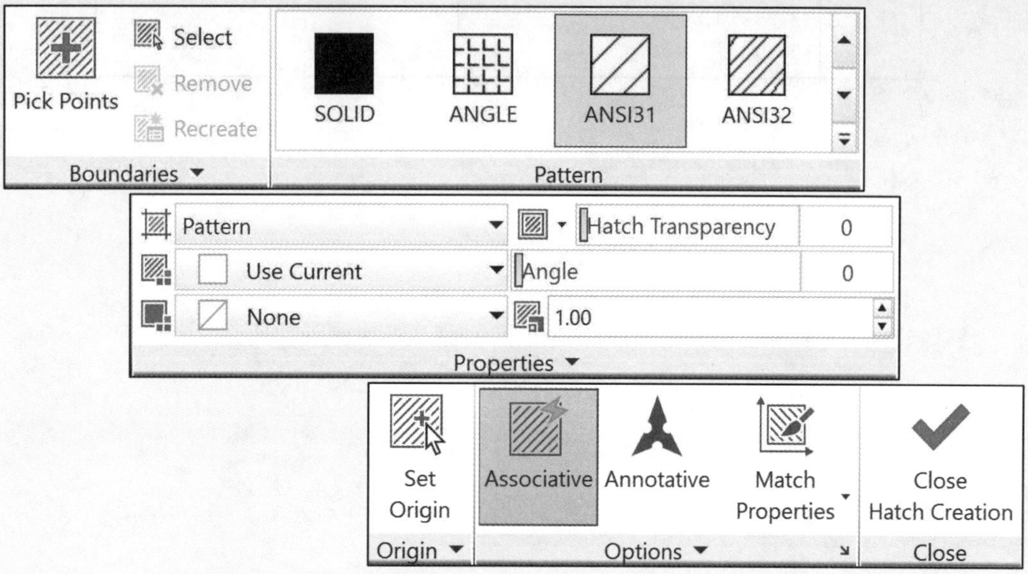

14.4) CREATING HATCHES TUTORIAL

The objective of this tutorial is to familiarize the user with the different methods and options available when creating hatches. It will take you through the different ways of choosing the hatch boundary and show you the affect of changing the hatch angle and scale.

14.4.1) Creating hatches

1) View the *Sectioning* video and read section 14.1) through 14.3).

2) 

set-mm.dwt and 

Creating hatches Tut.dwg.

3) Draw the following object in your ***Visible*** layer. Use annotative text to write your name inside the object. It is not necessary to include the dimensions.

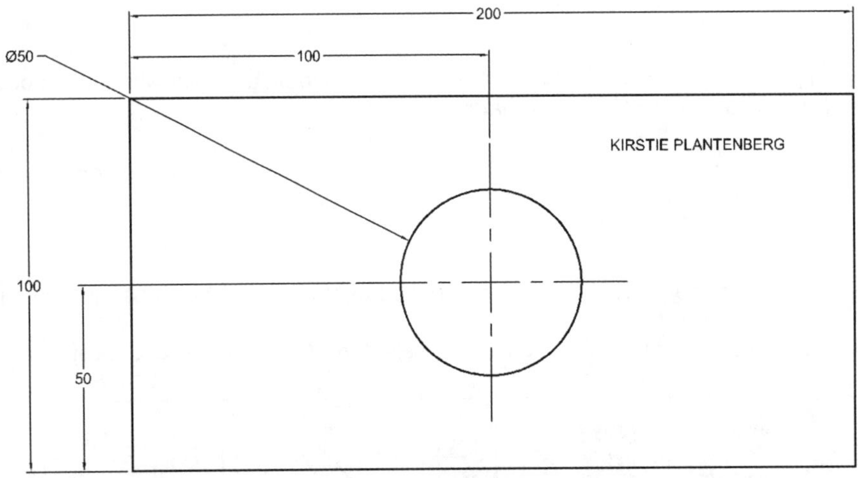

4) Draw section lines using the *Select Boundary* method.
   a) Make your ***Dimension*** layer current.
   b) <u>Command:</u> **hatch** or <u>*Draw* panel:</u> 
   c) <u>*Hatch Creation* ribbon:</u>
      i. <u>*Pattern* panel:</u> Select the hatch pattern ***ANSI31*** (Cast iron).
      ii. <u>*Options* panel:</u> Activate the ***Annotative*** icon.
      iii. <u>*Boundaries* panel:</u> Click on the ***Select boundary objects*** icon 

      and then select every line of your rectangle.
      iv. Select the ***Close Hatch Creation*** icon. (Notice how everything inside the selected boundary is hatched.)

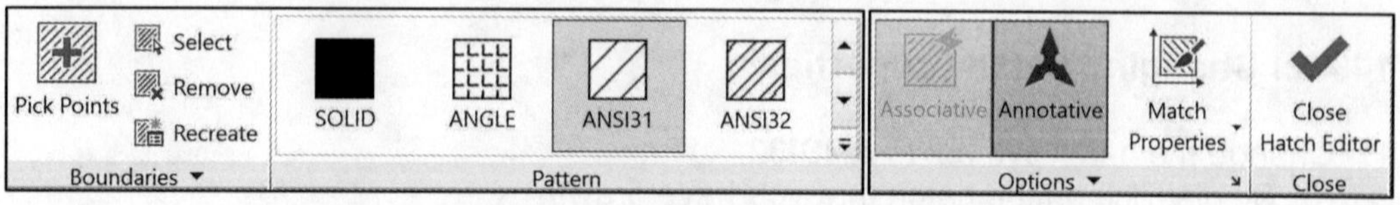

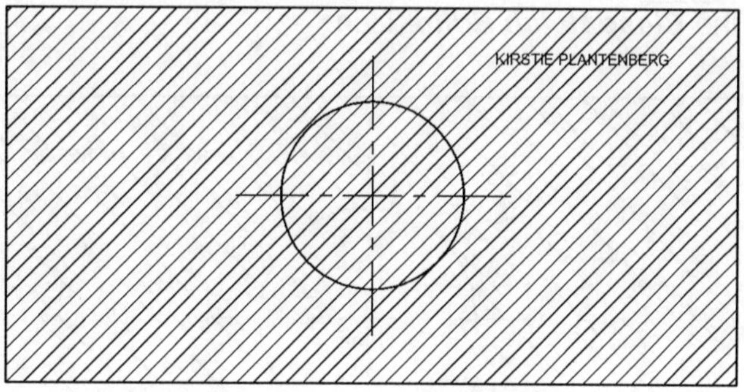

5) Using the ***Select Boundary Objects*** icon 

add the circle and text to the boundary elements. Notice the difference.

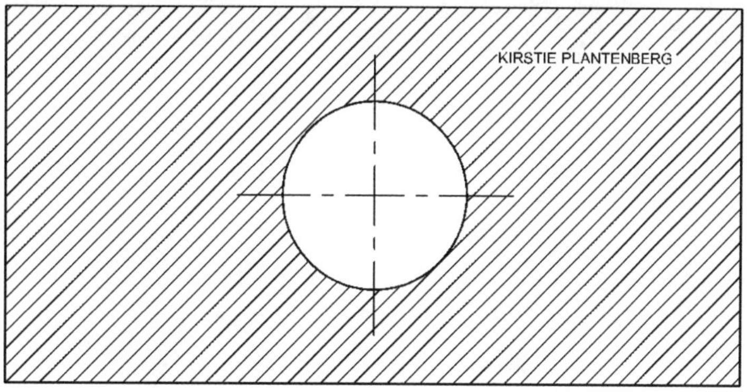

6) Draw section lines using the ***Pick Point*** method.
   a) **Erase** the previous hatch.
   b) <u>Command:</u> **hatch** or <u>*Draw* panel:</u> 
   c) <u>*Hatch Creation* ribbon:</u>
      i. <u>*Pattern* panel:</u> Select the hatch pattern ***ANSI31*** (Cast iron).
      ii. <u>*Options* panel:</u> Select the ***Annotative*** icon.
      iii. <u>*Boundaries* panel:</u> Click on the ***Pick points*** icon  and then select a point that is inside the rectangle but outside the circle.
      iv. Select the ***Close Hatch Creation*** icon. (Notice that the area you indicated is hatched. The hatch stops at any boundary.)

14.4.2) Changing hatch properties

1) Change the hatch symbol to **ANSI32**.
   a) Single click on the hatch that you have drawn.
      i. <u>*Pattern* panel:</u> Select the hatch pattern ***ANSI32*** (Steel).
      ii. Select the ***Close Hatch Editor*** icon.

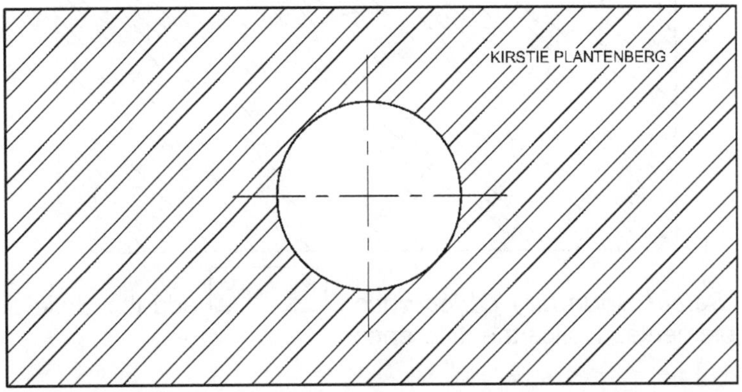

2) On your own edit the hatch and change the pattern to ***ANSI33*** (Brass), the scale to **2** and the angle to be **-15** (this is an actual angle of 45-15 = 30).

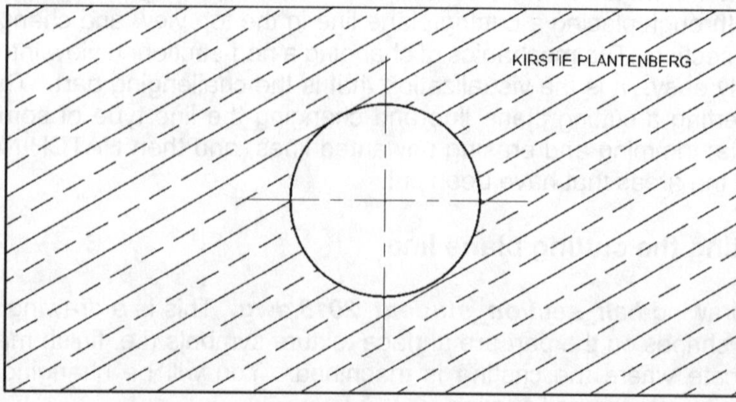

3) Add a 1:2 support scale to the text and hatch.

   a) *Annotate* Tab – *Annotation Scaling* panel: Add/Delete Scales.
   b) Select annotative object: Select the hatch and the text.
   c) *Annotation Object Scale* window: Select **Add...**
   d) *Add Scales to Object* window: Select **1:2** and then **OK**.
   e) *Annotation Object Scale* window: Select **OK**.

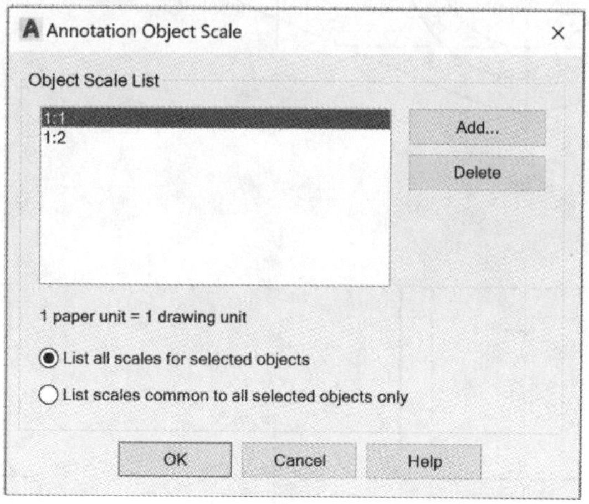

4) Enter paper space and change the viewport scale back and forth between 1:1 and 1:2. Notice that the text and hatch pattern adjust their scale as the view port scale changes.

5) Save your drawing and print a 1:1 drawing using the appropriate pen widths.

6) Re-enter model space and on your own, use the grip boxes to change the shape of the rectangle and notice that the hatch, due to its associativity, changes to match the boundary.

14.5) HALF SECTION TUTORIAL

In this tutorial we will create a section view from an existing orthographic projection. It will take you through placing a cutting plane line in the top view and changing the front view into a half section. The mechanics of changing a non-sectioned view into a sectioned view is relatively easy. It is the visualization that is the challenging part. The procedure consists of inserting a cutting plane line and changing the line type of some lines from hidden to visible, trimming and erasing unwanted lines, and then HATCHING or placing section lines in the areas that have been cut.

14.5.1) Inserting the cutting plane line

1) Open the drawing ***half_section_student_2018.dwg***. This is a drawing of a casting. The little V shapes on the part are surface texture symbols (i.e. finish marks). These marks indicate where the casting is machined. You will be changing the original drawing shown into the half section.

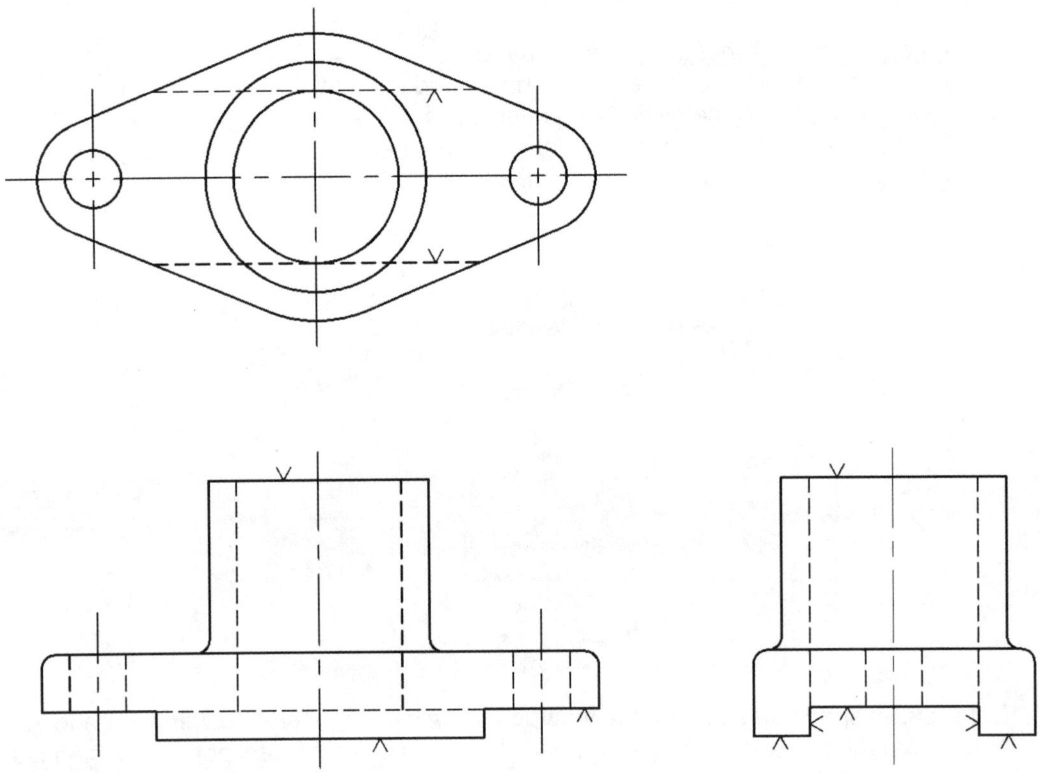

2) 

Half Section Tut.dwg

3) Make the ***Cutting*** layer current.

4) Get rid of the centerlines where the cutting plane line will be placed. Remember, cutting plane lines take precedence over other lines. In the top view, **Erase/TRim** the horizontal centerline to the right of the middle vertical centerline and **TRim** the vertical centerline below the horizontal centerline.

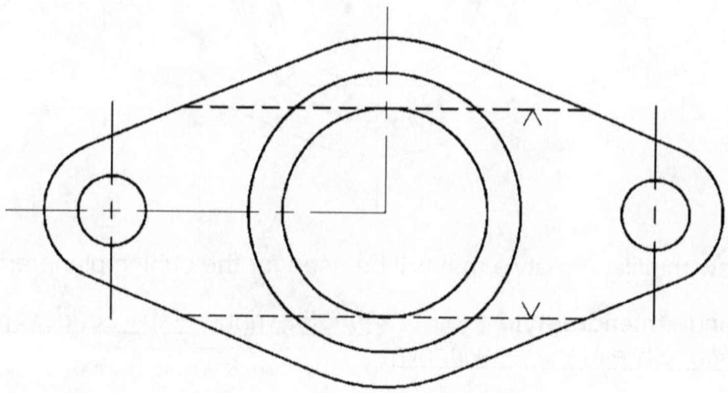

5) In the top view, draw a phantom **Line** (cutting layer) from the **CENter** to the **QUADrant** of the right side radius. Then draw a phantom **Line** from the **CENter** to the **QUADrant** of the bottom radius. (See figure below.)

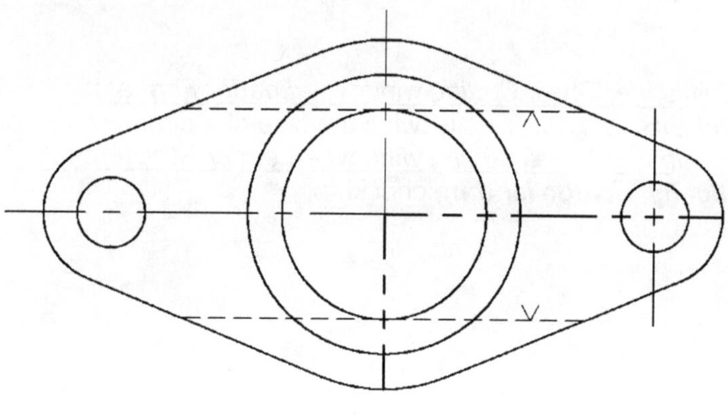

6) **LENgthen** the cutting plane lines **0.40** inches past the edge of the part.

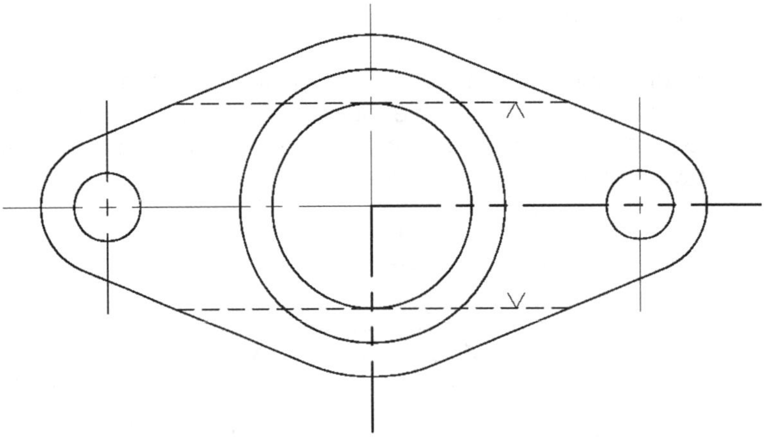

7) Create a new multileader style that will be used for the cutting plane arrows.

   a) Command: **mleaderstyle** or *Annotate* ribbon tab - *Leaders* panel:

   b) *Multileader Style Manager* window: **New ...**
   c) *Create New Multileader Style* window:
      i. *New style name* field: **Cutting**
      ii. *Start with* field: ***Standard***
      iii. Select the ***Annotative*** check box.
      iv. ***Continue***

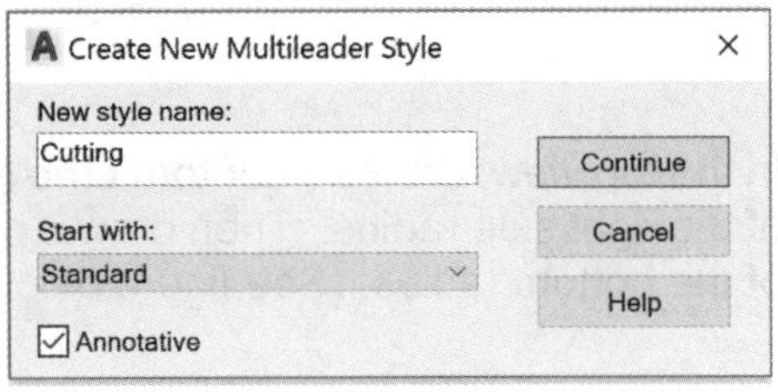

   d) *Modify Multileader Style: Cutting* window – *Leader Format* tab: Set the *Arrowhead Size* to ***0.36***. This is twice the size of a dimension arrowhead.
   e) *Modify Multileader Style: Cutting* window – *Leader Structure* tab: Deactivate the ***Automatically include landing*** checkbox.

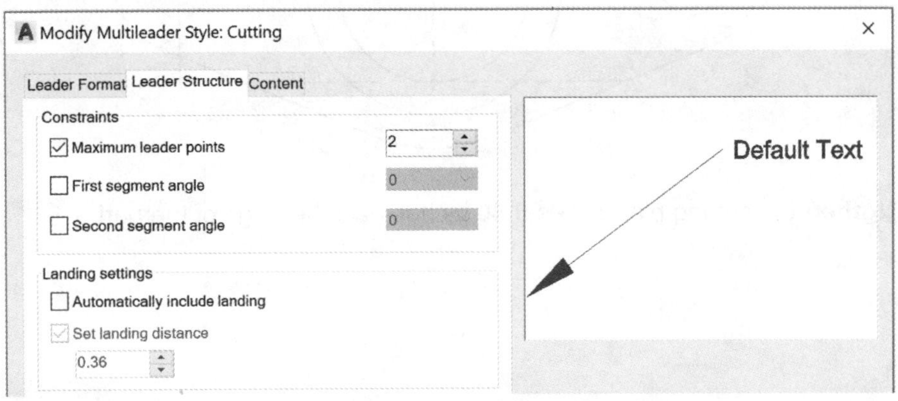

f) *Modify Multileader Style: ASME* window – *Content* tab – *Multileader type* field: Select ***None*** and then select ***OK***.

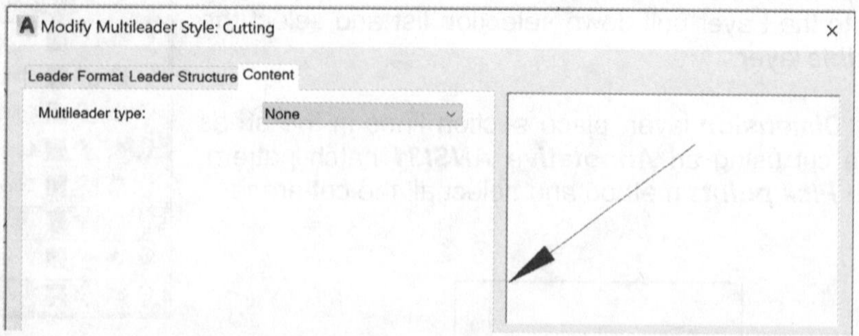

g) *Multileader Style Manager* window:
   i. Select the ***Cutting*** style and then select the ***Set Current*** button.
   ii. ***Close***

8) With the help of ***Object Snap Tracking***, draw two **Multileaders** that are approximately ***0.75*** inch long. One should be horizontal and the other vertical (as shown). These arrows indicate direction of sight.

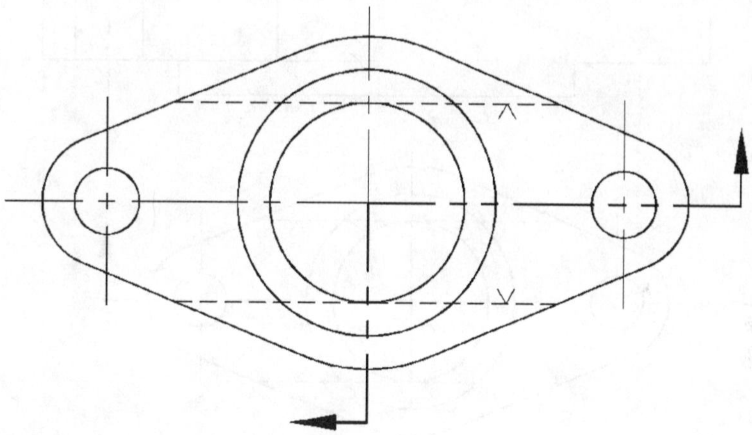

14.5.2) Creating the half section view

1) **Erase/TRim** the hidden lines and any centerline associated with a hidden feature in the left hand side of the front view.

2) **Erase/TRim** any visible lines associated with surface features in the right hand side of the front view (see figure).

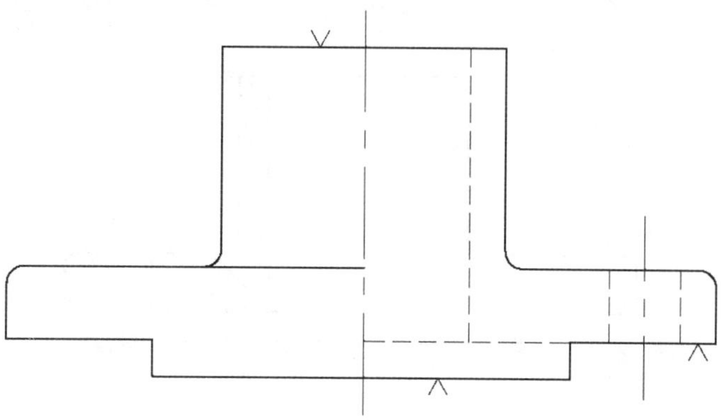

3) Change the hidden lines in the right hand side of the front view into visible lines.
   a) Select all of the hidden lines.
   b) Go to the Layer pull down selection list and select the ***Visible*** layer.

4) In your ***Dimension*** layer, place section lines in the areas that are cut using an ***Annotative ANSI31*** hatch pattern. Use the ***Pick points*** method and select all the cut areas.

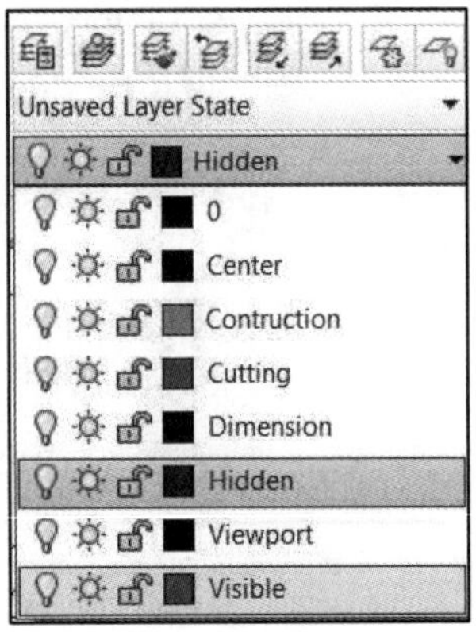

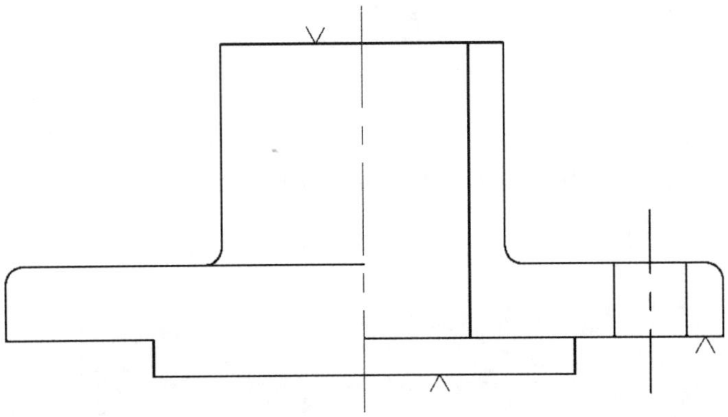

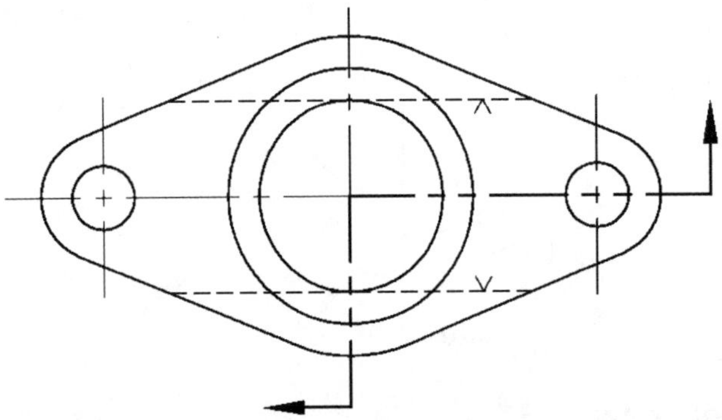

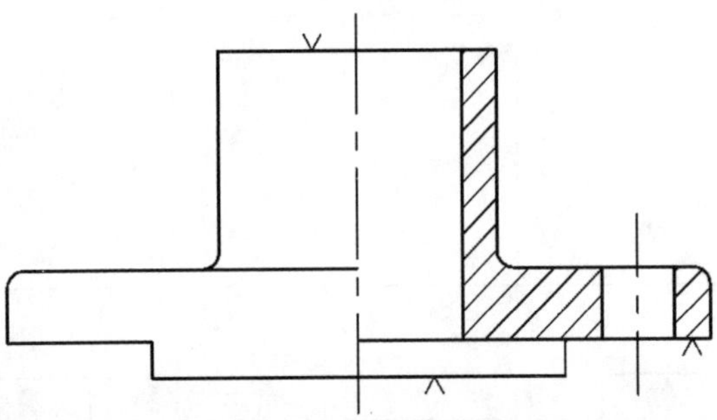

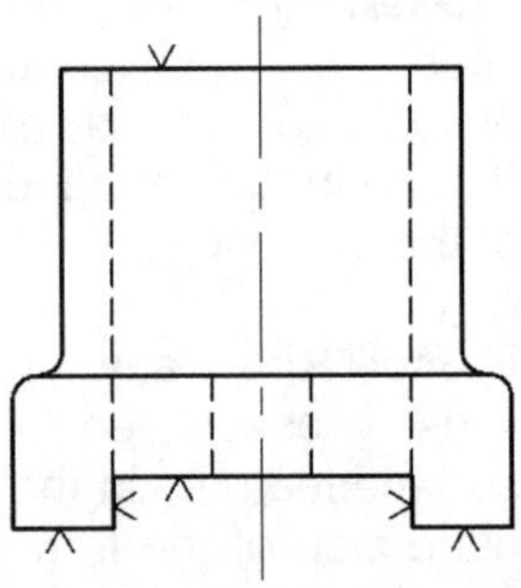

5) ***Save*** your drawing and ***print*** it at a ***1:1*** scale. Include your title block with the appropriate information filled in.

SECTION VIEWS IN AUTOCAD® QUESTIONS

Name: ________________________________ Date: ______________

Q14-1) A _______ line is drawn thicker than the visible lines.

a) section
b) cutting plane
c) hidden
d) center

Q14-2) _______ line patterns are drawn thinner than visible lines.

a) section
b) cutting plane
c) hidden
d) center

Q14-3) Cutting plane line *linetype*.

a) continuous
b) dashed
c) dotted
d) phantom

Q14-4) The typed command used to create section lines.

a) hatch
b) section
c) halogap
d) phantom

Q14-5) ANSI31

a) Cast iron
b) Steel
c) Brass
d) Plastic

Q14-6) ANSI32

a) Cast iron
b) Steel
c) Brass
d) Plastic

Q14-7) ANSI33

a) Cast iron
b) Steel
c) Brass
d) Plastic

Q14-8) The boundary selection method used to create a hatch that stops when it encounters a boundary.

a) pick points
b) select boundary objects
c) recreate boundaries
d) remove boundaries

Q14-9) The boundary selection method that will hatch everything inside the boundary.

a) pick points
b) select boundary objects
c) recreate boundaries
d) remove boundaries

Q14-10) Hatches will change shape if the geometry they are connected to changes. This makes them ...

a) annotative
b) associative
c) reactive
d) shapetive

Q14-11) Hatches will change size based on the viewport scale. This makes them ...

a) annotative
b) associative
c) reactive
d) shapetive

Q14-12) The cutting plane line arrowheads are created using a ...

a) linear dimension
b) diameter dimension
c) multileader dimension
d) angular dimension

Q14-13) The section line angle resulting when a value of -10 degrees is entered into the angle field.

a) -10
b) 25
c) 30
d) 35

SECTION VIEWS IN AUTOCAD® PROBLEMS

P14-1) Draw the following object converting the front view into an offset section. It is not necessary to include the dimensions. The material of the part is Steel. Dimensions given in inches.

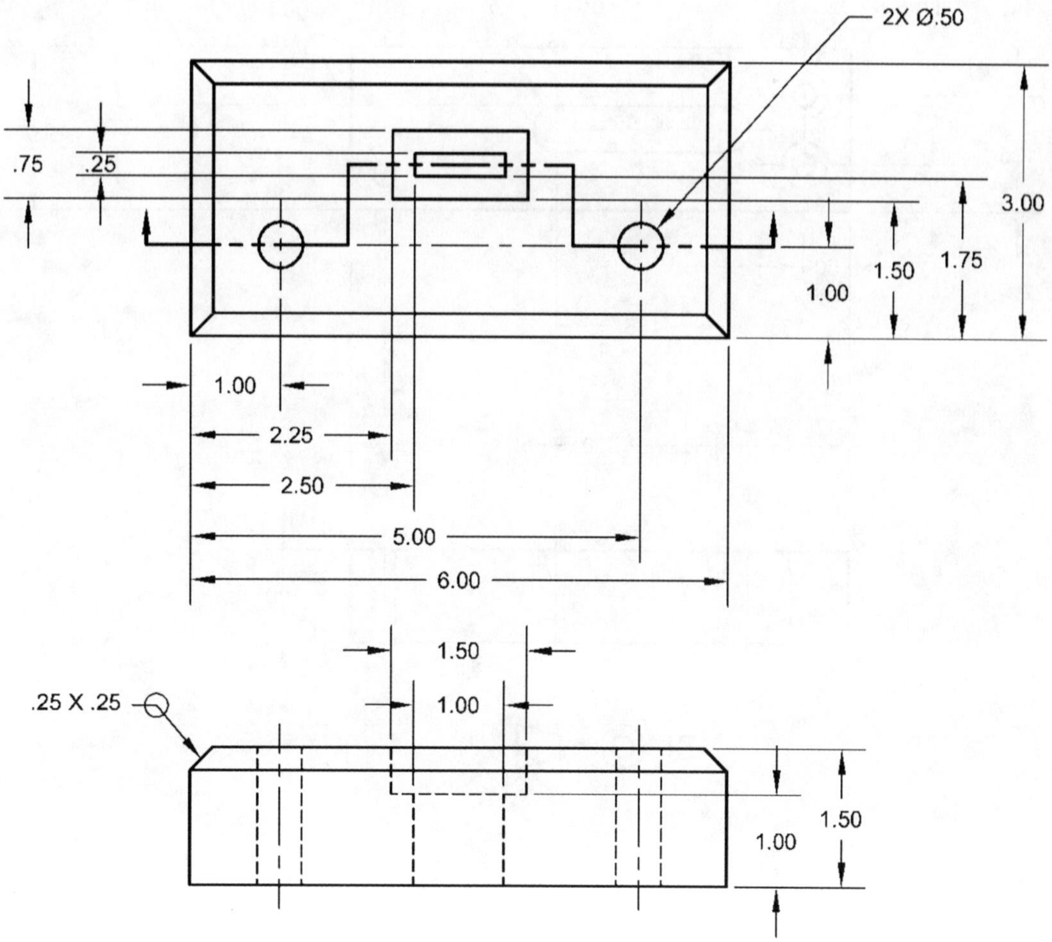

P14-2) Draw the following object converting the front view into an offset section. Capture as many features as possible. Draw the appropriate cutting plane line. It is not necessary to include the dimensions. The material of the part is Aluminum. Dimensions given in millimeters.

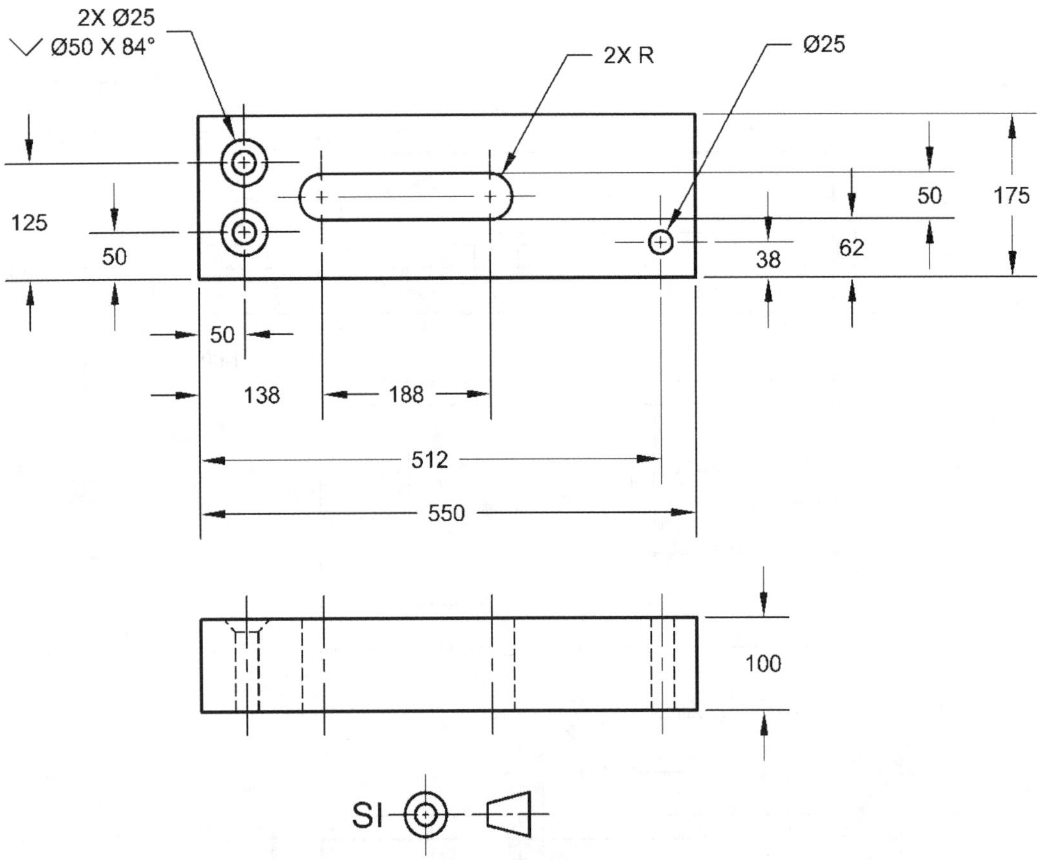

P14-3) Draw the following object converting the front view into an offset section. Capture as many features as possible. Draw the appropriate cutting plane line. It is not necessary to include the dimensions. The material of the part is Plastic. Dimensions given in inches.

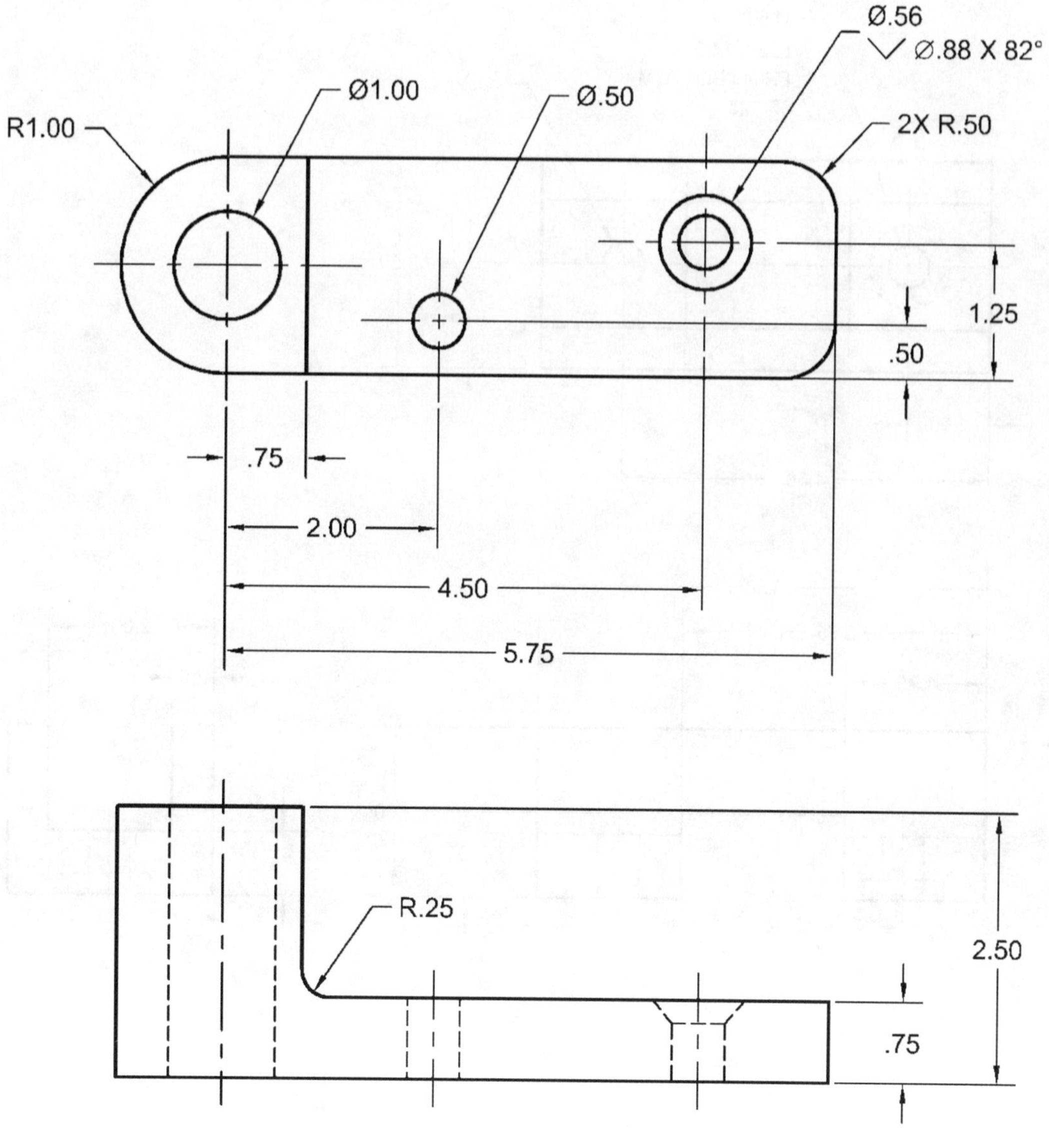

P14-4) Draw all three views of the following object converting the front view into a full section. Draw the appropriate cutting plane line. It is not necessary to include the dimensions. The material of the part is Steel. Dimensions given in inches.

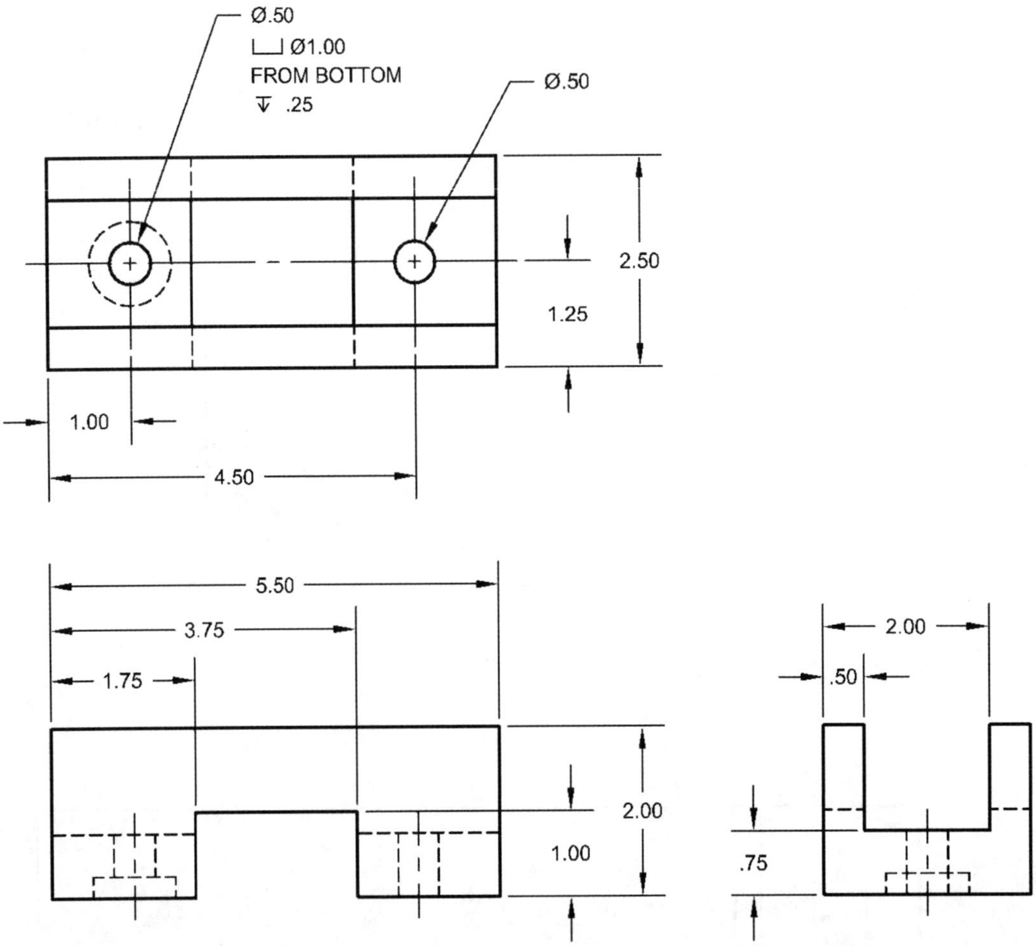

P14-5) Draw the following object converting the front view into a full section. Draw the appropriate cutting plane line. It is not necessary to include the dimensions. The material of the part is Cast Iron. Dimensions given in inches.

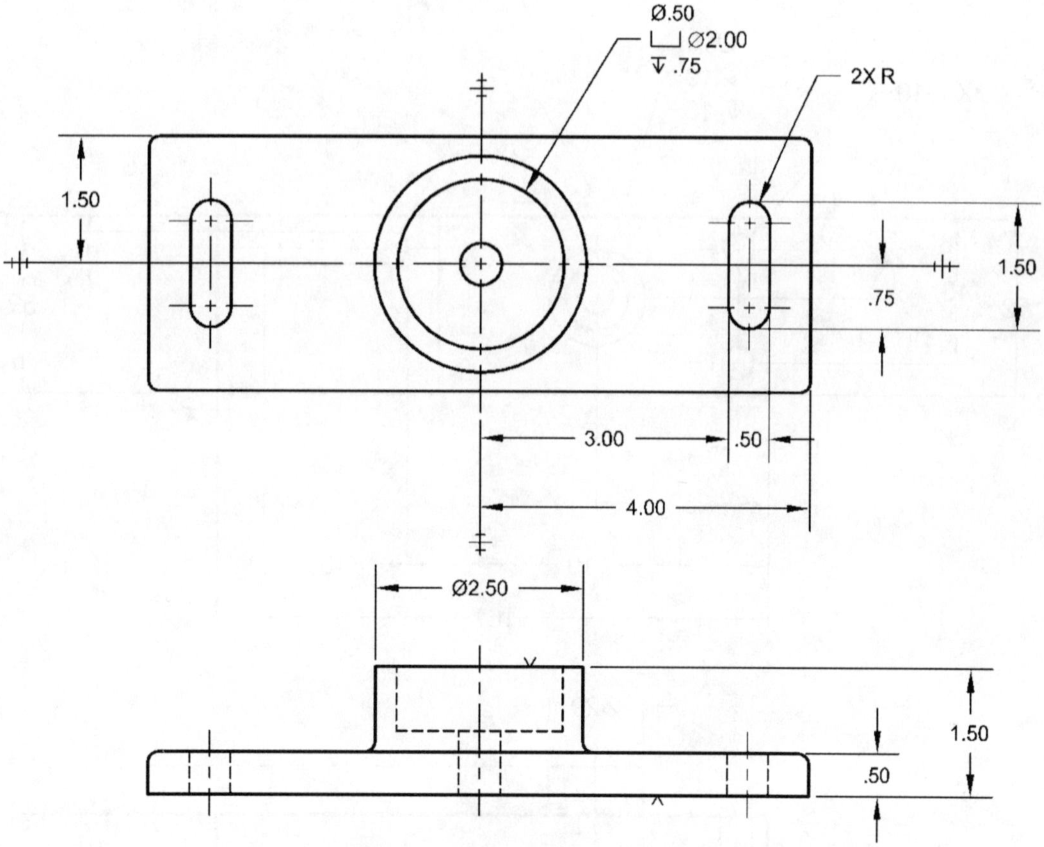

NOTE: ALL ROUNDS AND FILLETS .12 R

P14-6) Draw the following object converting the front view into an offset section. Capture as many features as possible. Draw the appropriate cutting plane line. It is not necessary to include the dimensions. The material of the part is Steel. Dimensions given in millimeters.

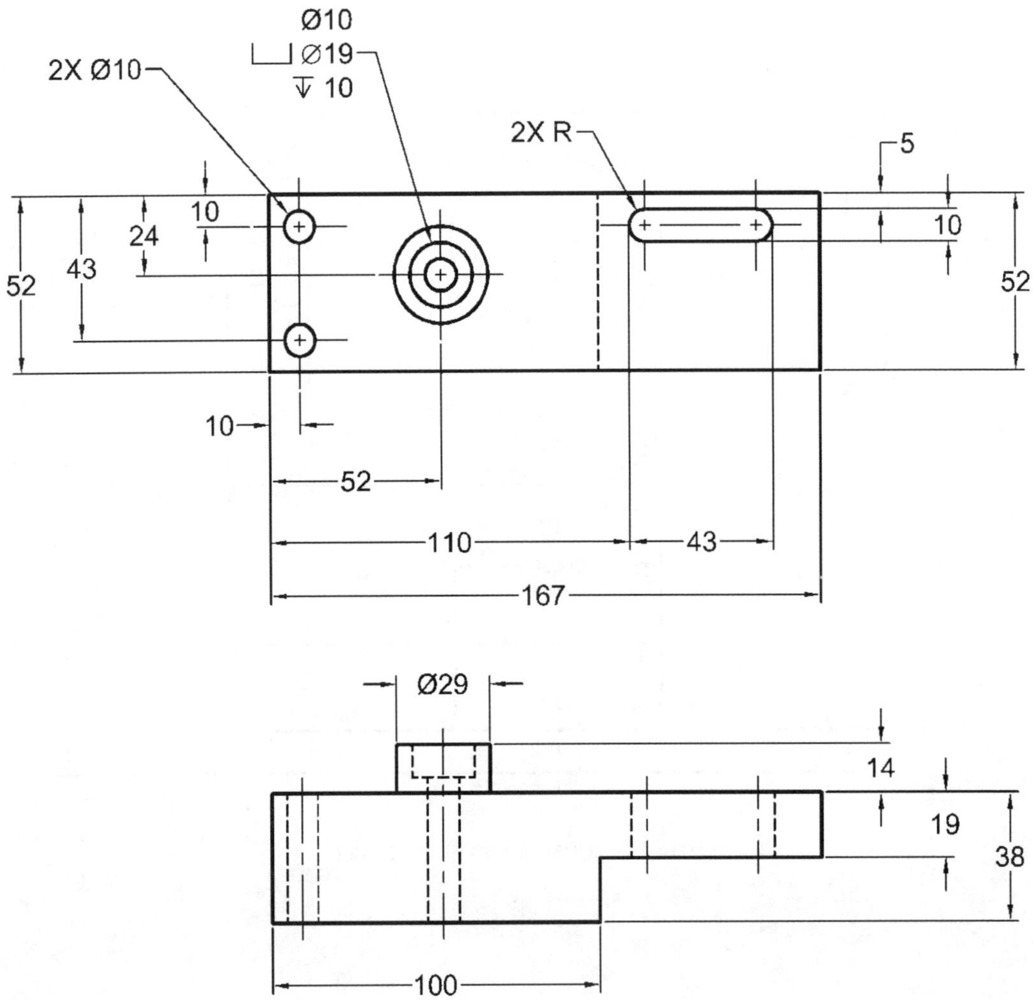

P14-7) Draw the following object converting the front view into an offset section. Capture as many features as possible. Draw the appropriate cutting plane line. It is not necessary to include the dimensions. The material of the part is Cast Iron. Dimensions given in inches.

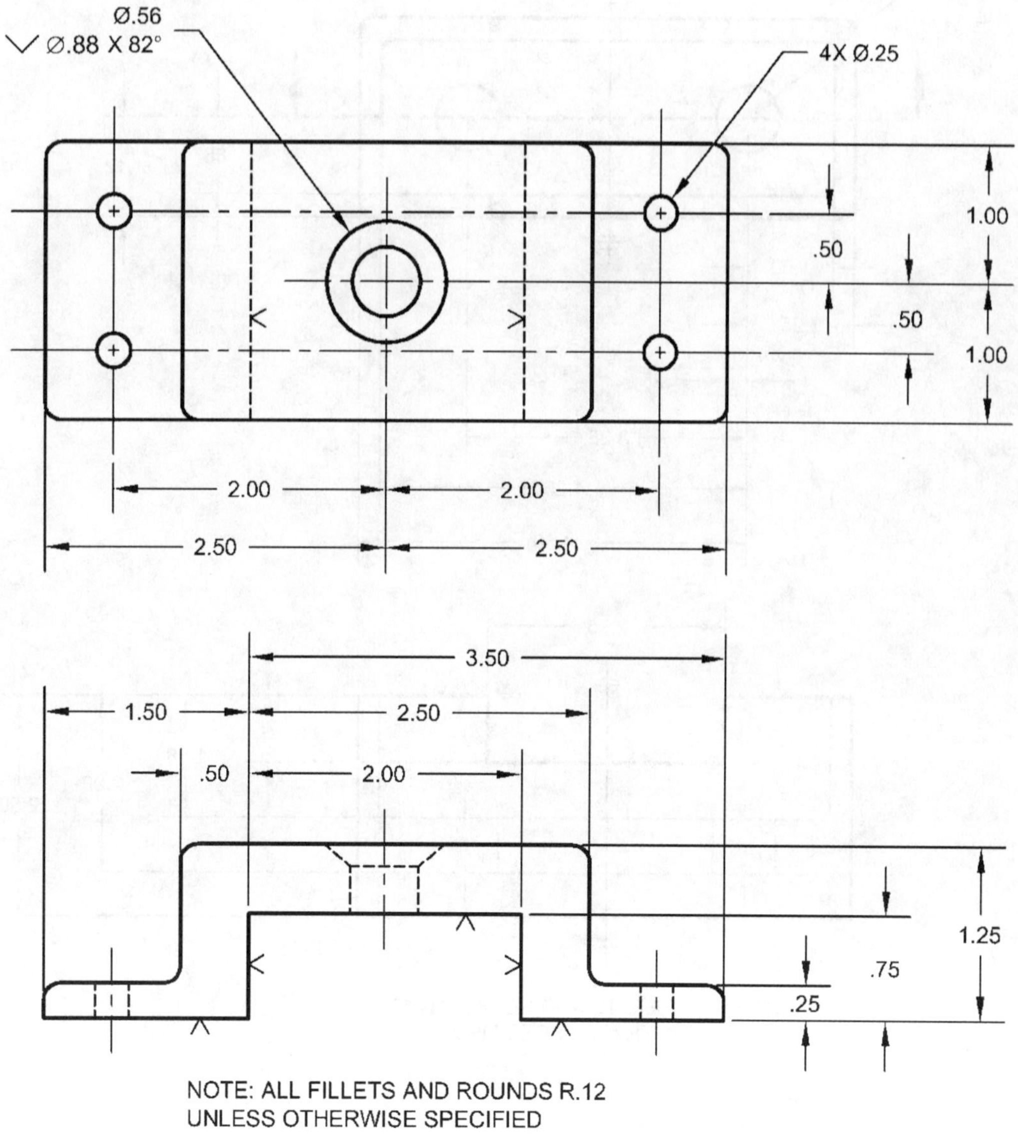

P14-8) Draw the following object converting the front view into a full section. It is not necessary to include the dimensions. The material of the part is Cast Iron. Dimensions given in inches.

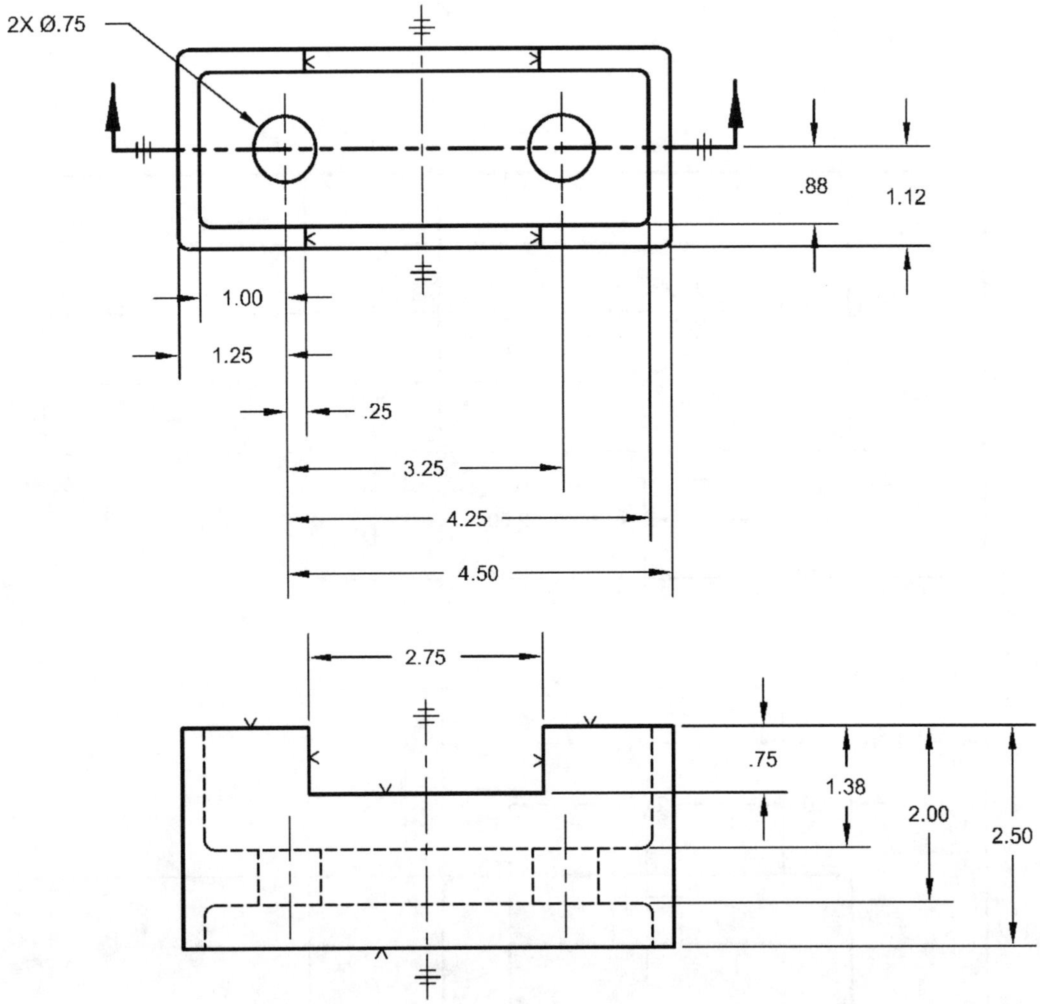

NOTE: ALL FILLETS AND ROUNDS R.12
UNLESS OTHERWISE SPECIFIED

P14-9) Draw the following object converting the front view into a full section. It is not necessary to include the dimensions. The material of the part is Cast Iron. Dimensions given in inches.

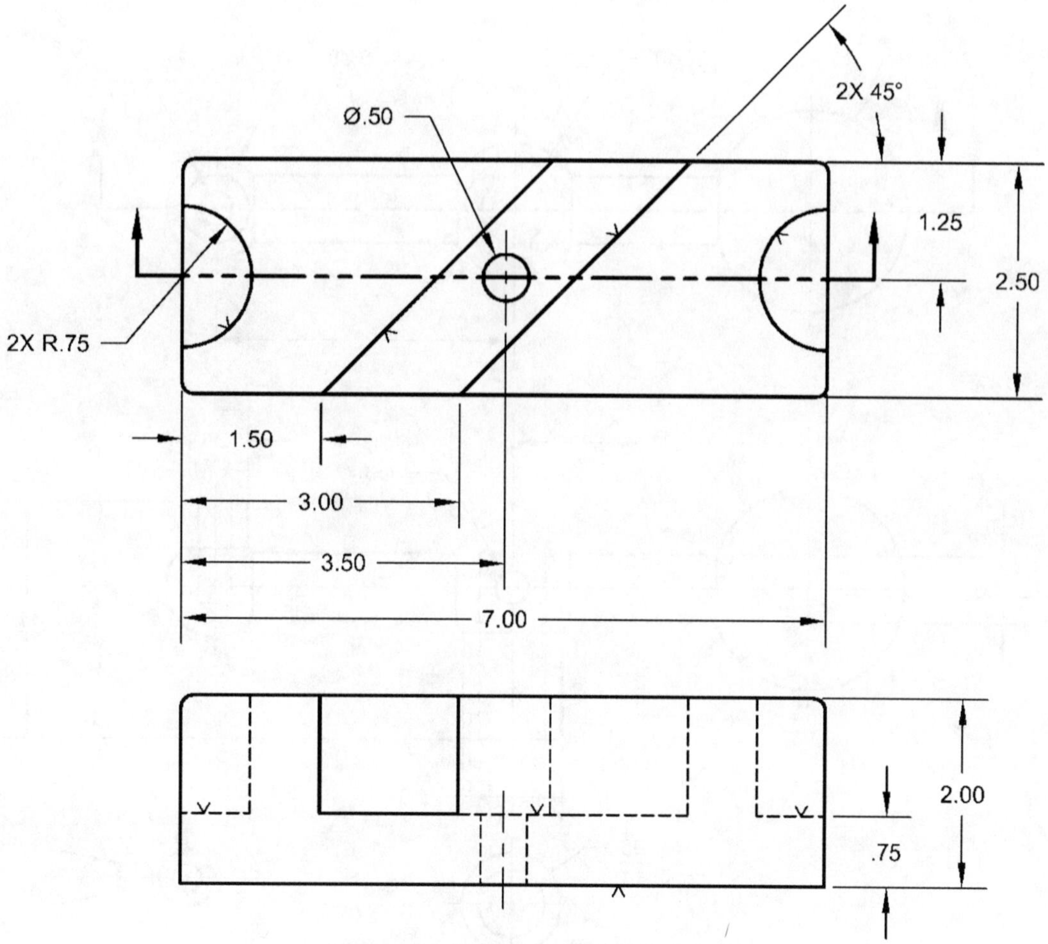

NOTE: ALL FILLETS AND ROUNDS R.12
UNLESS OTHERWISE SPECIFIED.

P14-10) Draw the following object converting the front view into a full section. It is not necessary to include the dimensions. The material of the part is Plastic. Dimensions given in millimeters.

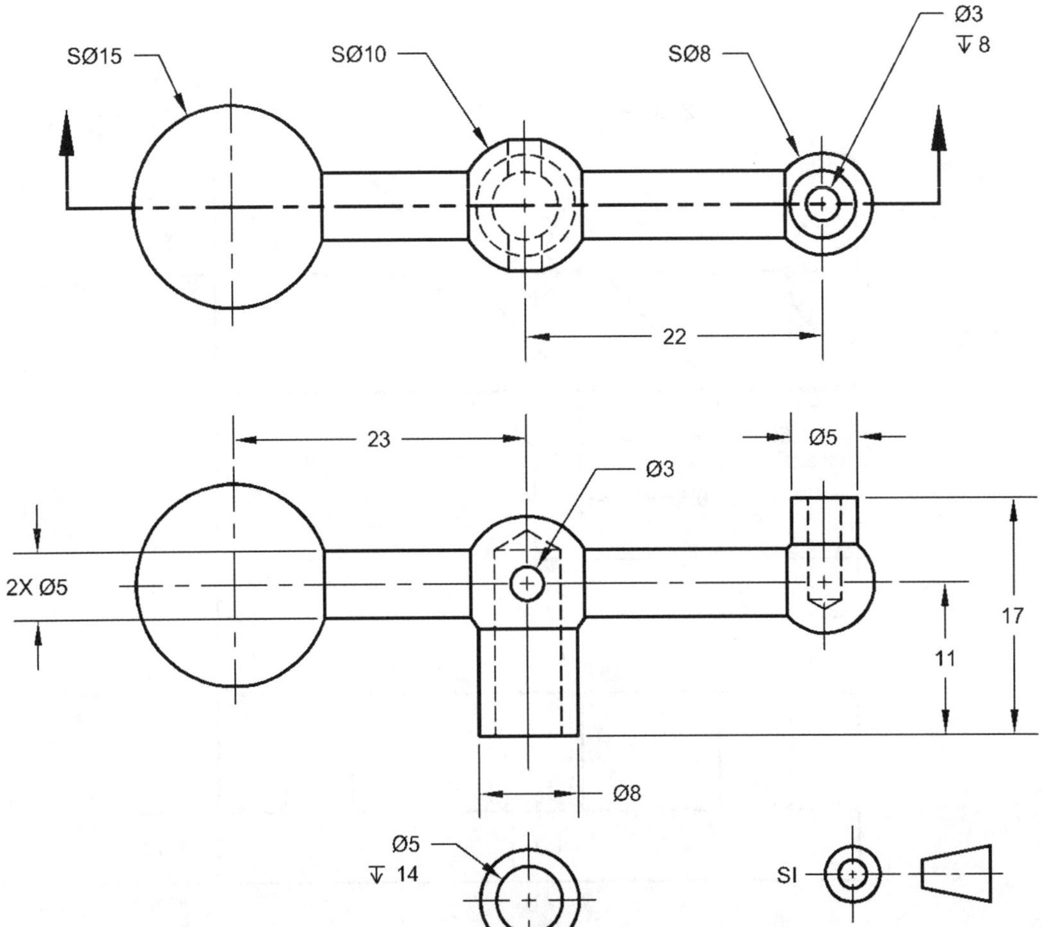

P14-11) Draw the following object converting the right side view into a half section. Draw the appropriate cutting plane line. It is not necessary to include the dimensions. The material of the part is Brass. Dimensions given in millimeters.

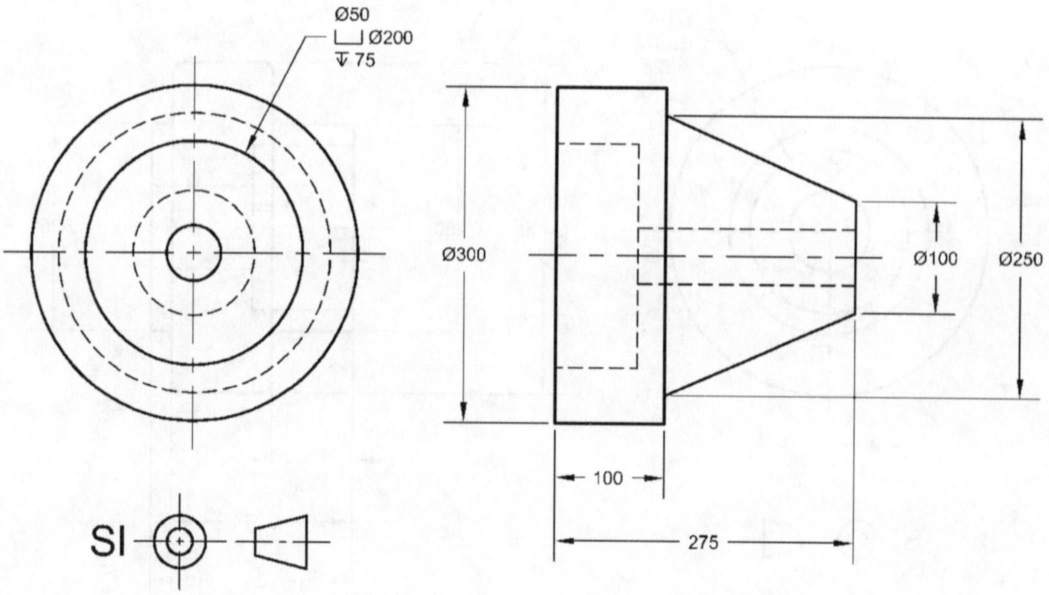

P14-12) Draw the following object converting the right side view into a half section. It is not necessary to include the dimensions. The material of the part is Steel. Dimensions given in millimeters.

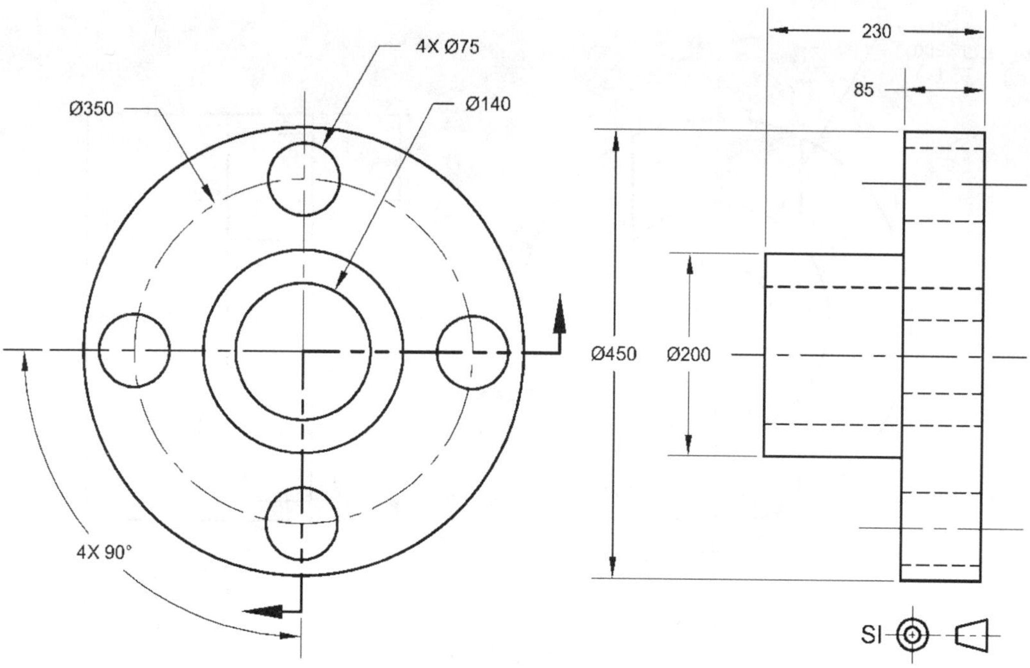

P14-13) Draw the following object converting the right side view into a half section. It is not necessary to include the dimensions. The material of the part is Aluminum. Dimensions given in millimeters.

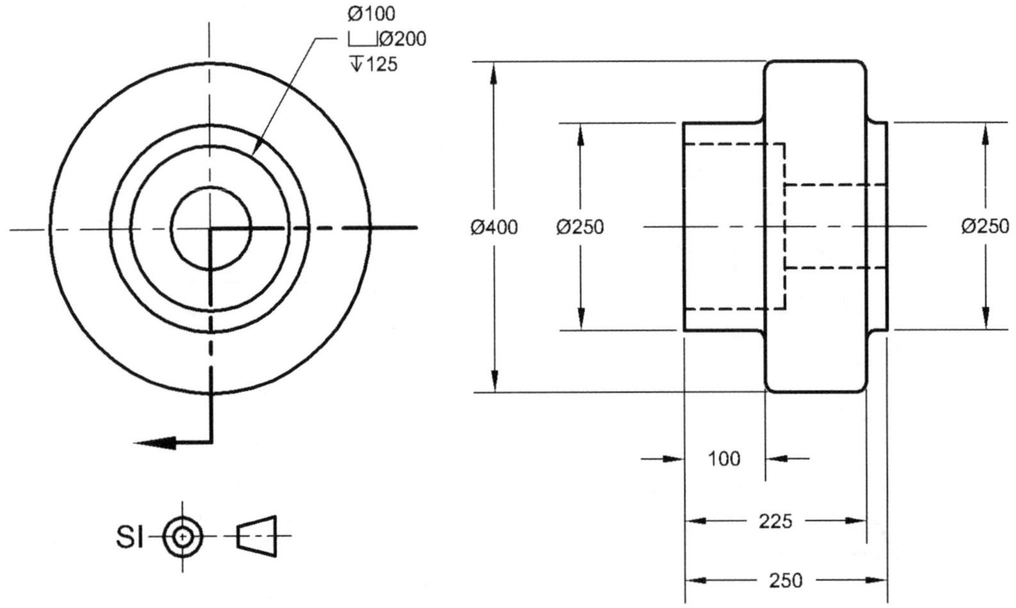

P14-14) Draw the following object converting the right side view into a half section. Draw the appropriate cutting plane line. It is not necessary to include the dimensions. The material of the part is Steel. Dimensions given in millimeters.

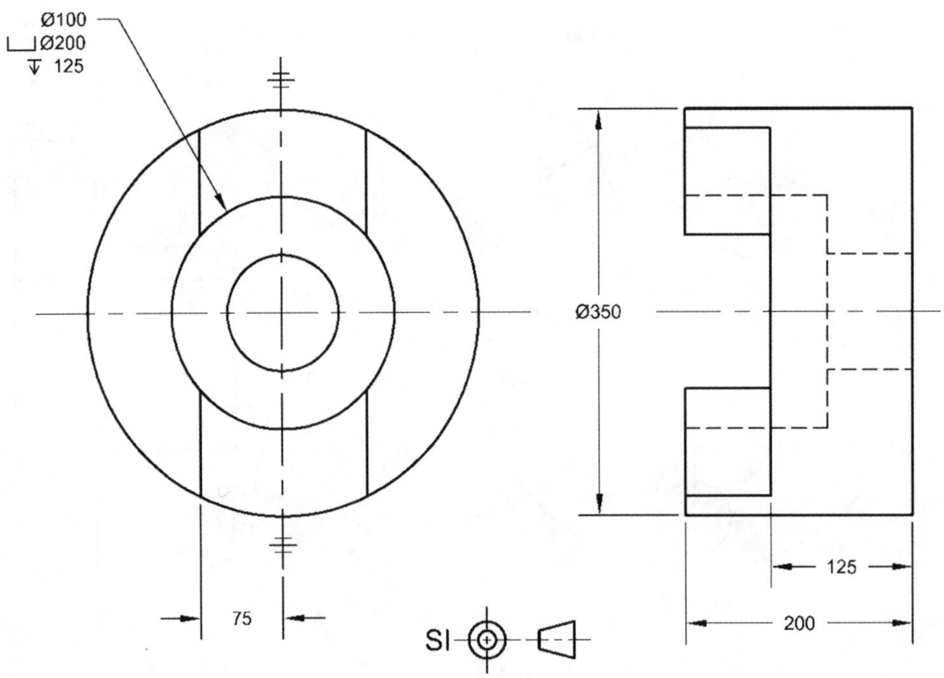

P14-15) Draw the following object converting the left side view into a half section. Draw the appropriate cutting plane line. It is not necessary to include the dimensions. The material of the part is Steel. Dimensions given in inches.

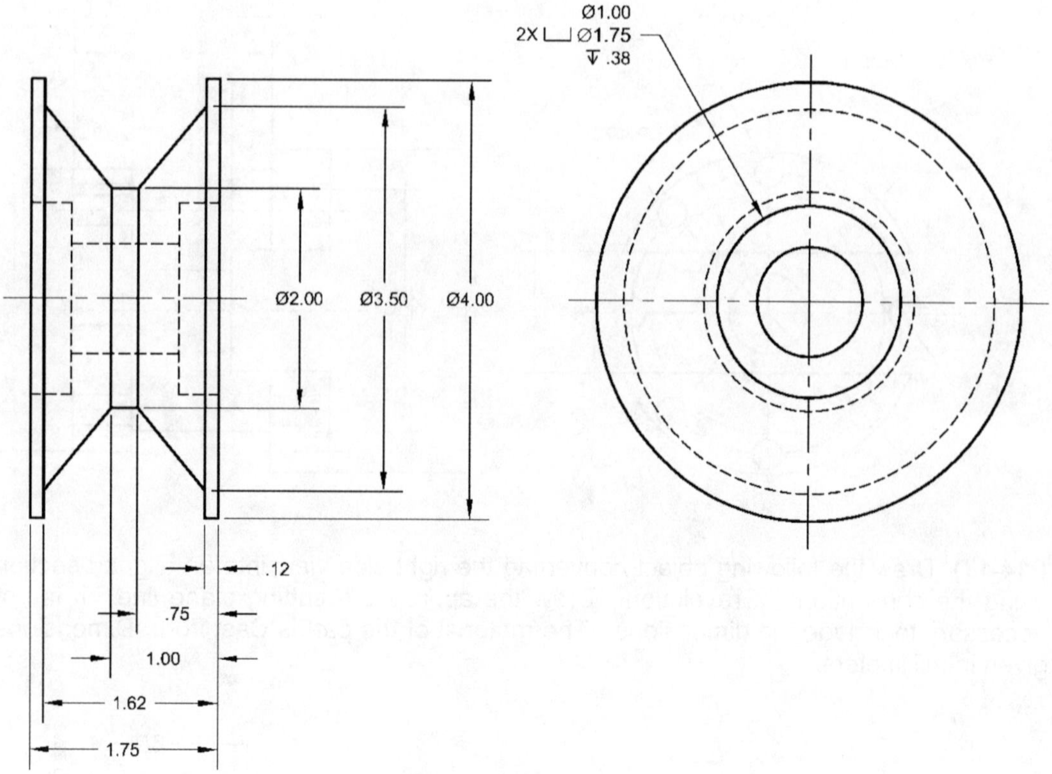

P14-16) Draw the following object converting the right side view into a half section. It is not necessary to include the dimensions. The material of the part is Aluminum. Dimensions given in inches.

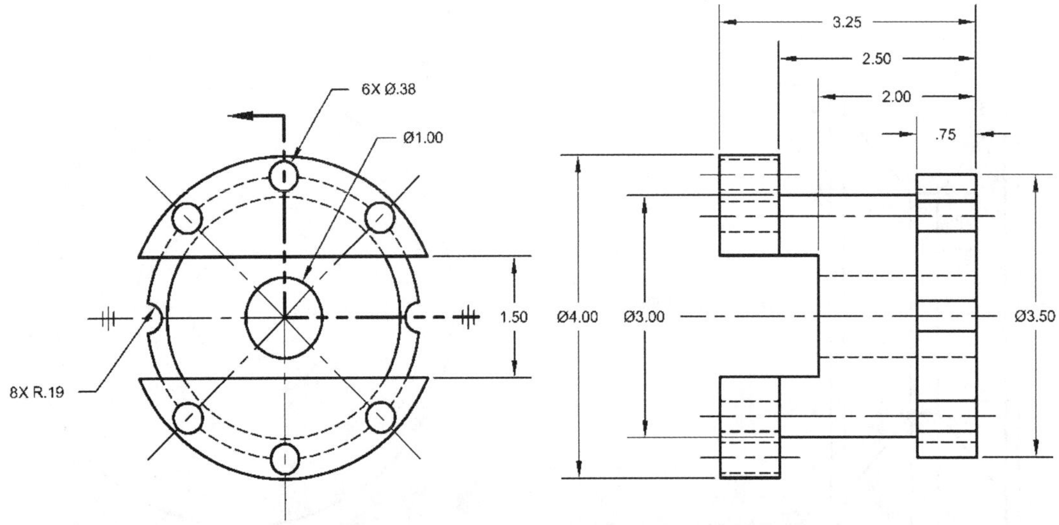

P14-17) Draw the following object converting the right side view into an aligned section using the conventions of revolution. Draw the appropriate cutting plane line. It is not necessary to include the dimensions. The material of the part is Cast iron. Dimensions given in millimeters.

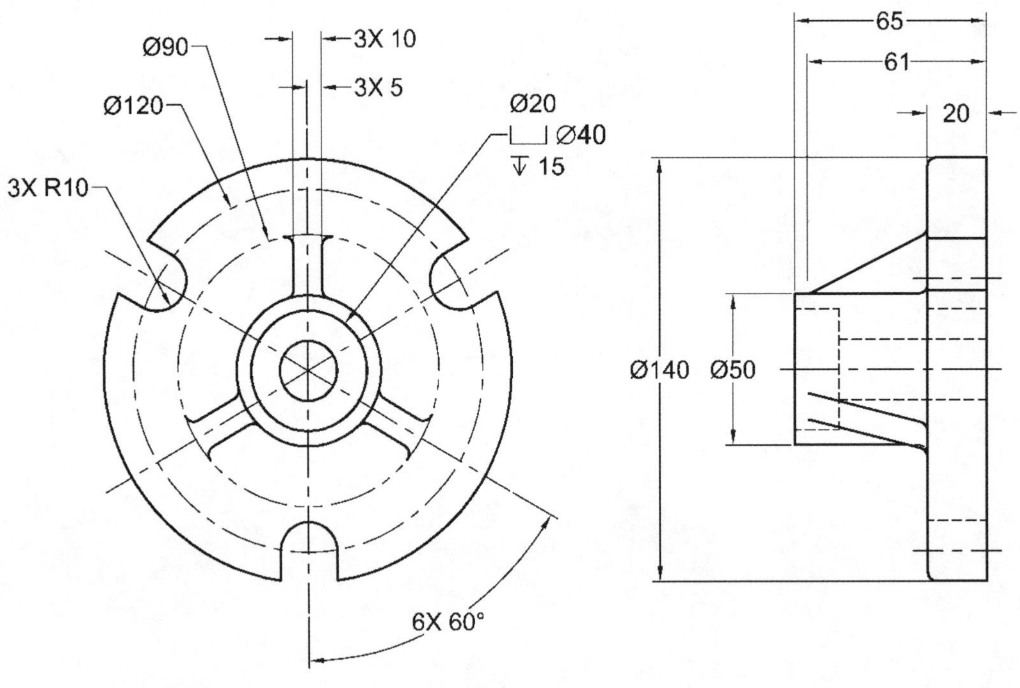

SP14-1) Draw the following object converting the right side view into an aligned section using the conventions of revolution. Draw the appropriate cutting plane line. It is not necessary to include the dimensions. The material of the part is Steel. The answer to this problem is given on the *Independent Learning Content*. Dimensions given in millimeters.

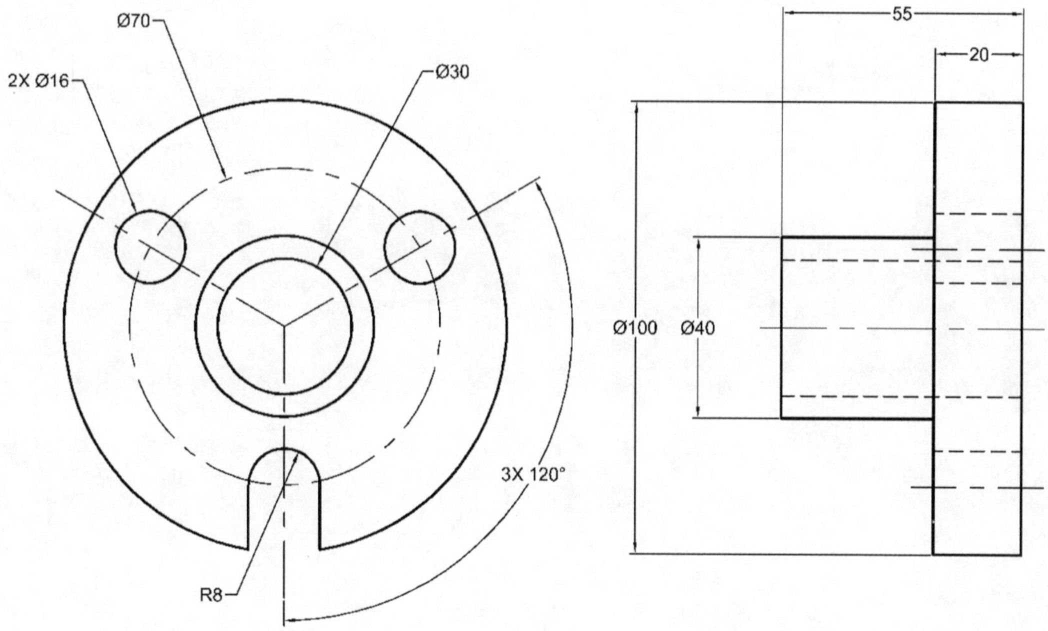

NOTES:

CHAPTER 15

READING ADVANCED DRAWINGS

CHAPTER OUTLINE

CHAPTER SUMMARY

In this chapter you will learn how to read views and parts that are created using advanced drawing techniques. These views include removed and revolved views, detail views, partial views, and auxiliary views. You will also learn how to read orthographic projections of welded and cast parts.

15.1) ADVANCED VIEWS

Advanced views are views created using techniques that were not covered in the orthographic projection chapters. Understanding how to read these views requires some knowledge of how they were created.

15.1.1) Removed and revolved orthographic views

In some instances, the size and location of an orthographic view (e.g., top, right side) may be removed from its normal aligned position. The view may also be rotated and scaled. When a removed or rotated view is used, letter identifications are used to indicate from where the view was taken and its line of sight. Figure 15.1-1 shows an example of a removed view and Figure 15.1-2 shows an example of a removed view that has been rotated. Removed and rotated views are labeled with their view identification and scale. Rotated views are also labeled with their angle of rotation.

15.1.2) Detail views

If a part has intricate features that are small relative to the rest of the part, a detail view is used to clarify these features. A detail view is usually shown at an increased scale. The detail view is identified by using a letter that matches the letter given by the circle indicating where the detail is being taken from. Figure 15.1-3 shows an example of a detail view.

15.1.3) Partial views

Partial views only show a portion of the entire part. They are used to show only pertinent features. They are used instead of drawing the complete view when the complete view does not add any new information. Hidden lines may be left off if they are not important for interpreting the view. Figure 15.1-4 shows an example of a partial orthographic view.

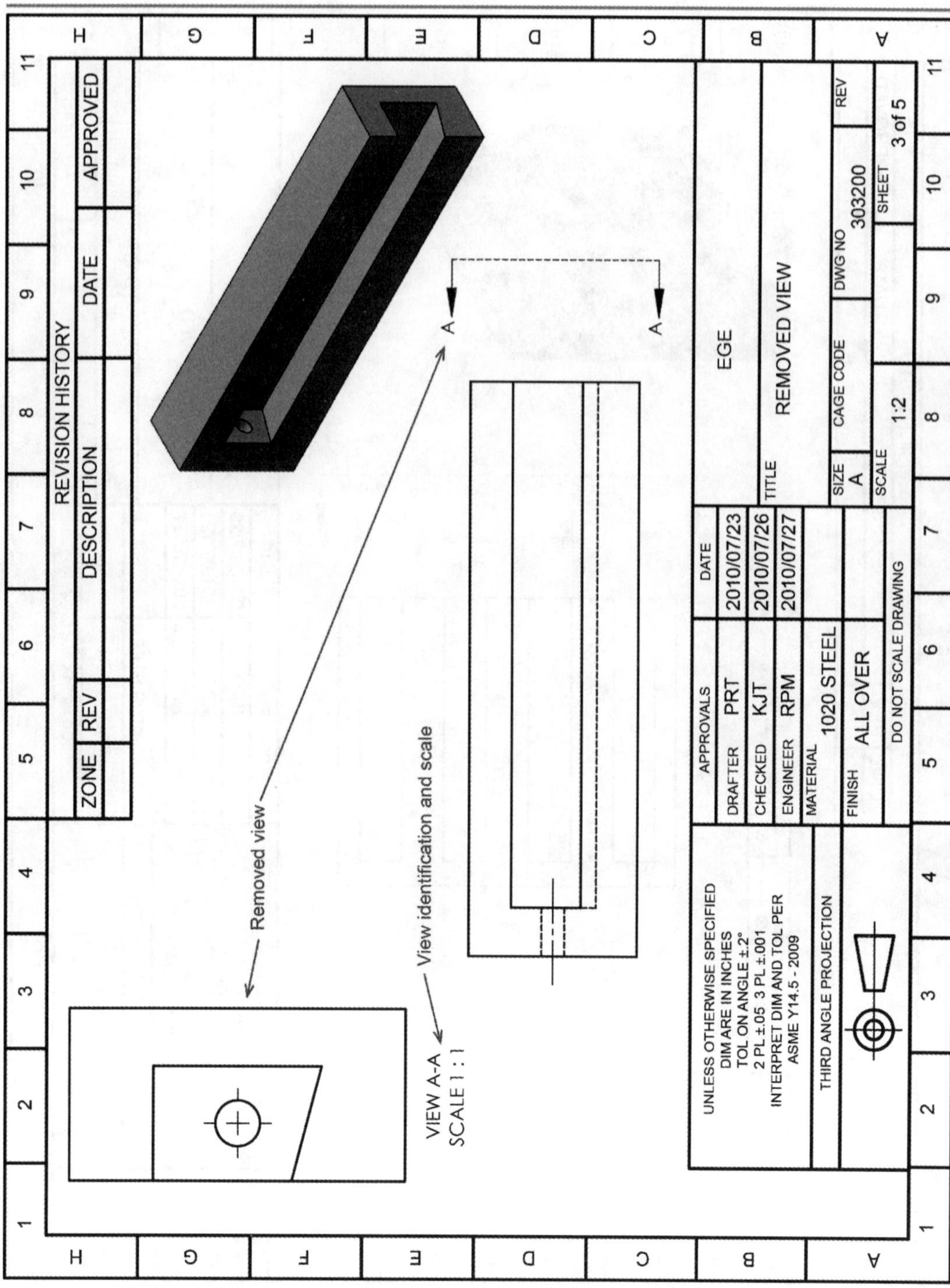

Figure 15.1-1: Removed orthographic view

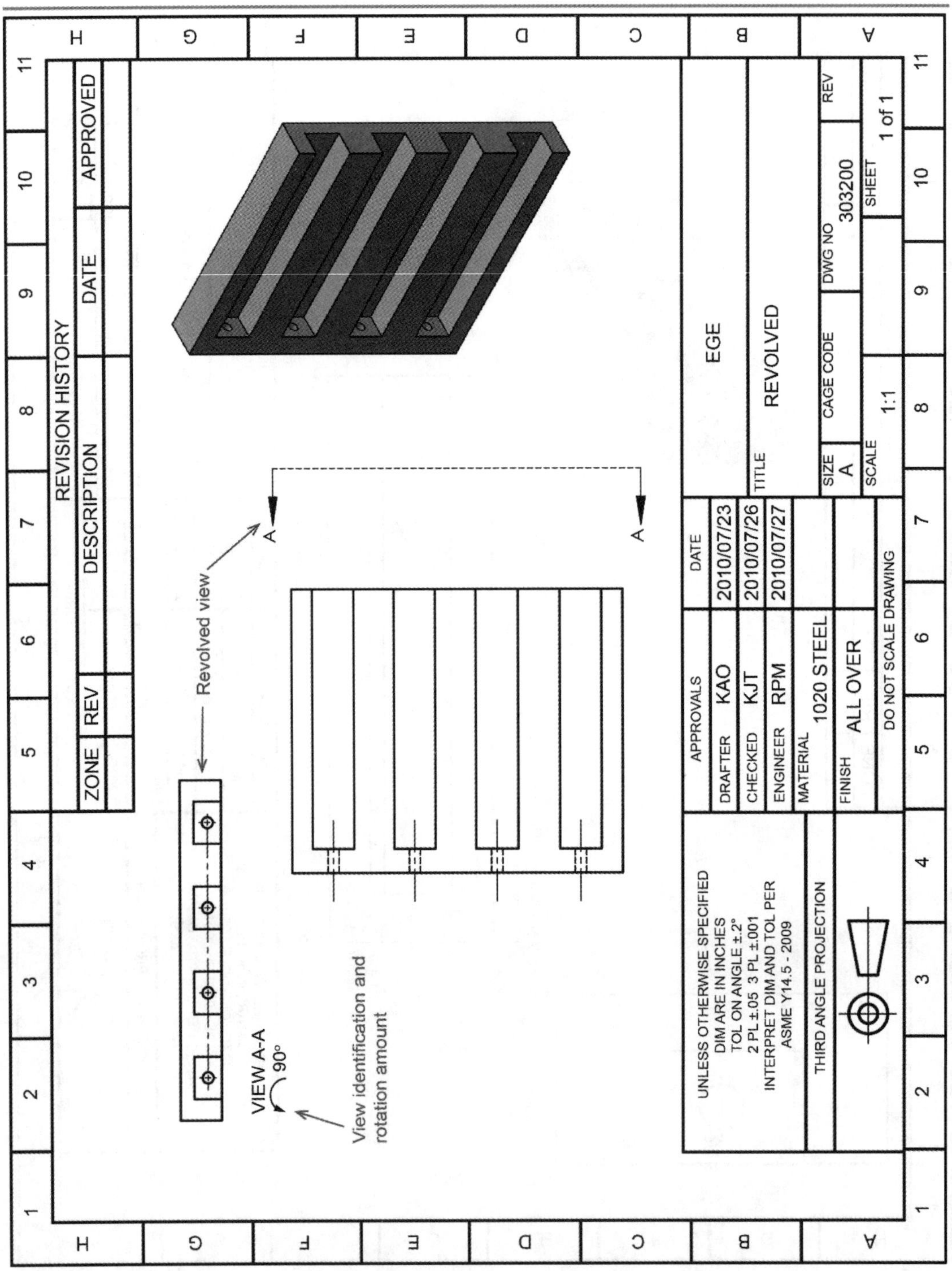

Figure 15.1-2: Revolved orthographic view

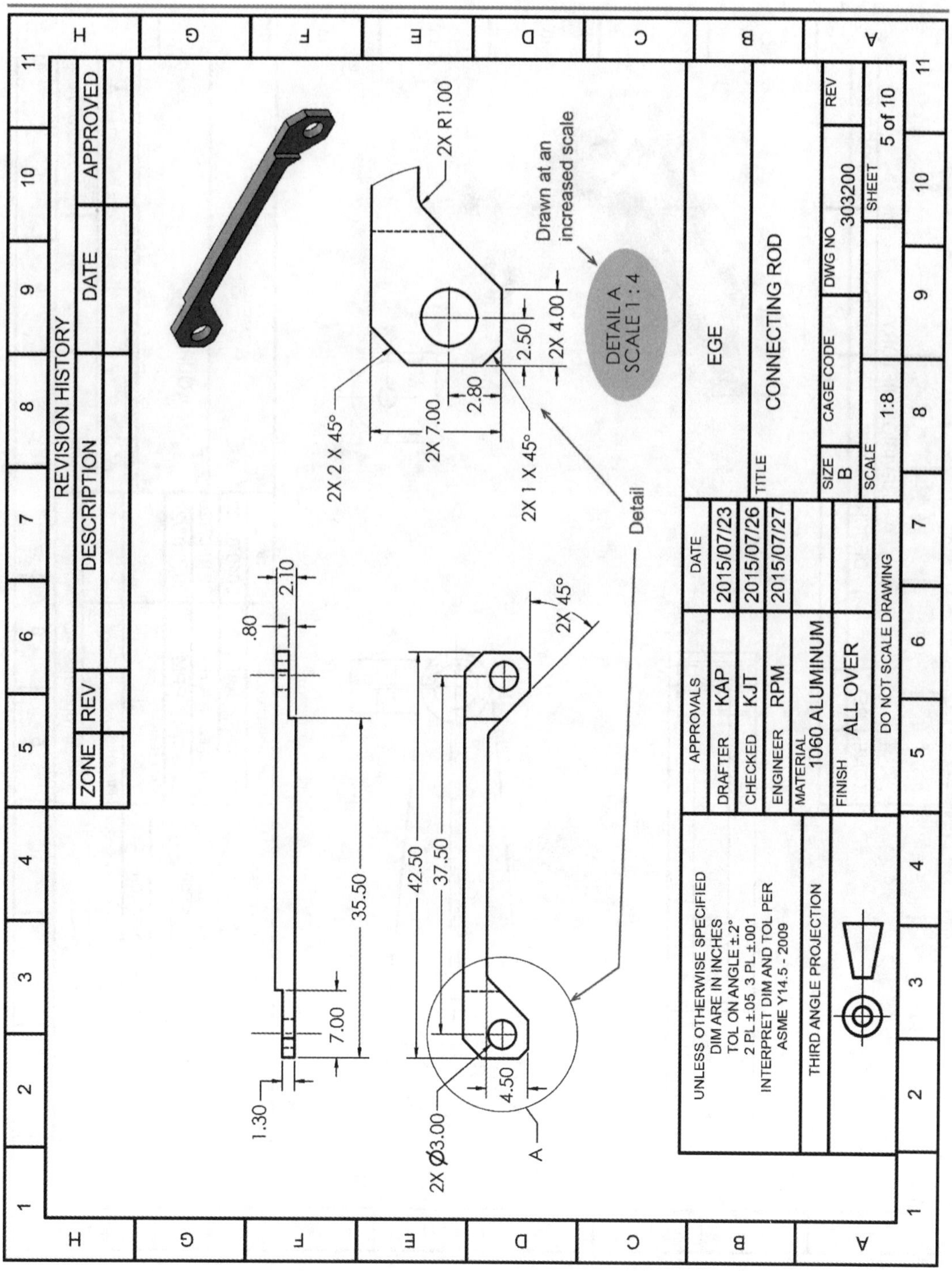

Figure 15.1-3: Detail view

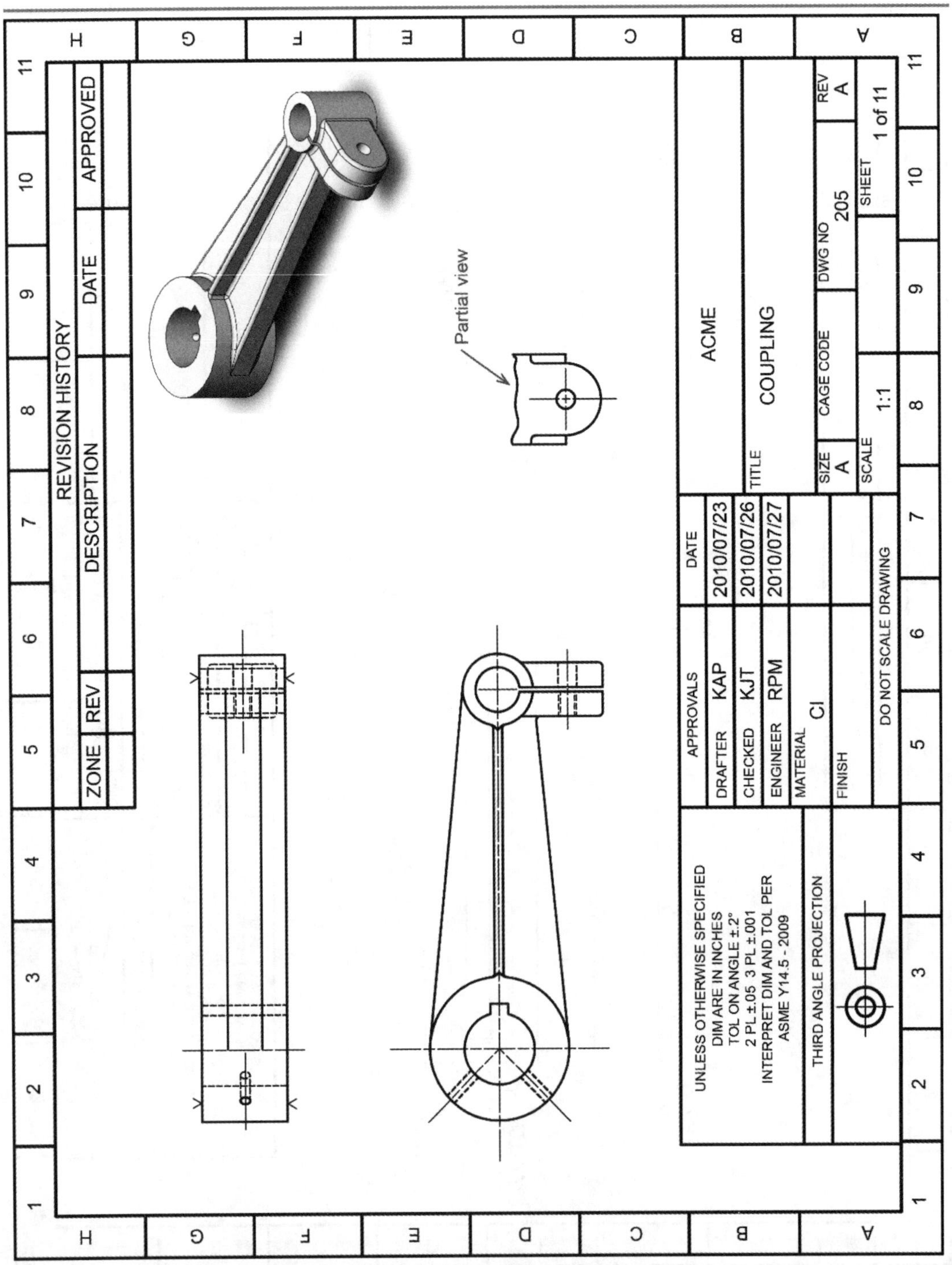

Figure 15.1-4: Partial view

15.1.4) Auxiliary views

Primary views include the six views described in the *Orthographic Projection* chapters (i.e., front, top, right-side, bottom, left-side, rear). **Auxiliary views are views projected at an angle to one of the principal planes**. Figure 15.1-5 shows an object in a glass box. The sides of the box represent the principal planes, and the views projected on the sides are the principal views. The auxiliary plane is at an angle to the principal planes. The view projected on the auxiliary plane is the auxiliary view. Figure 15.1-6 shows the orthographic projection of the object shown in Figure 15.1-5 along with full and partial auxiliary views. Note how the partial auxiliary view differs from the full auxiliary view. Partial auxiliary views are used quite often since these views highlight one or two features, while the rest of the information is given in the principal views.

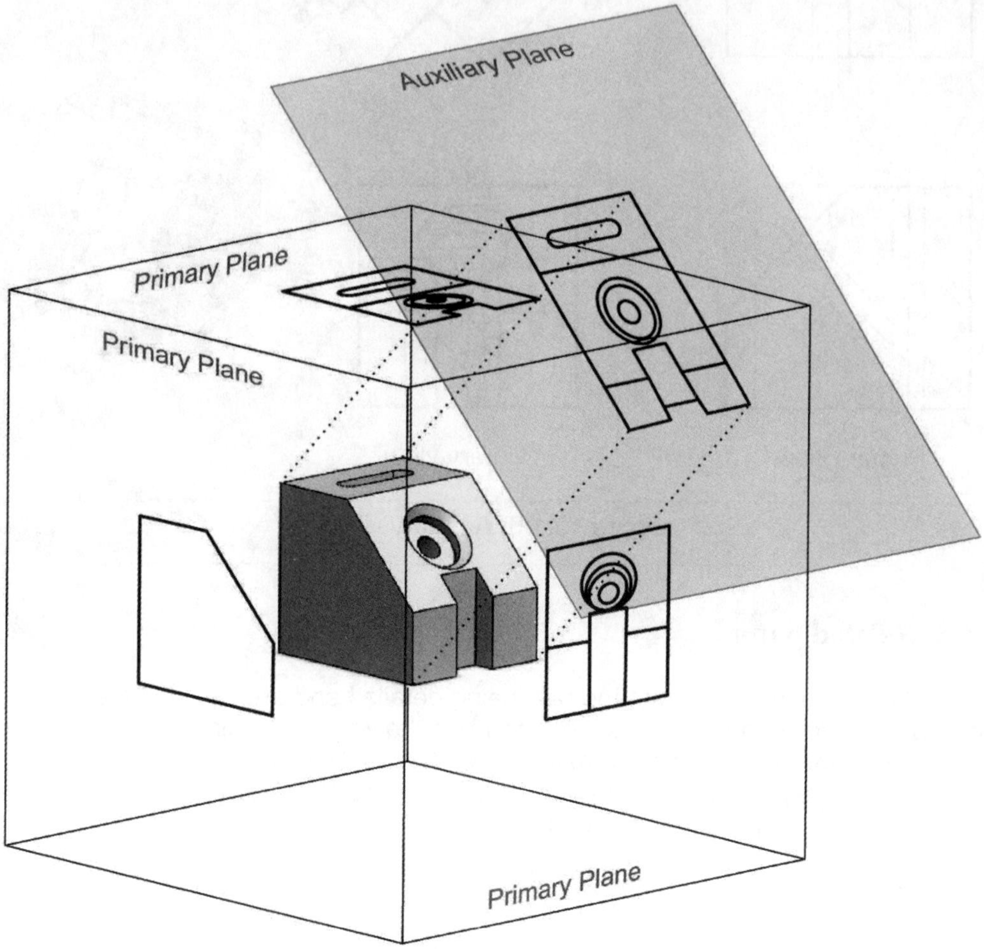

Figure 15.1-5: Auxiliary view projection

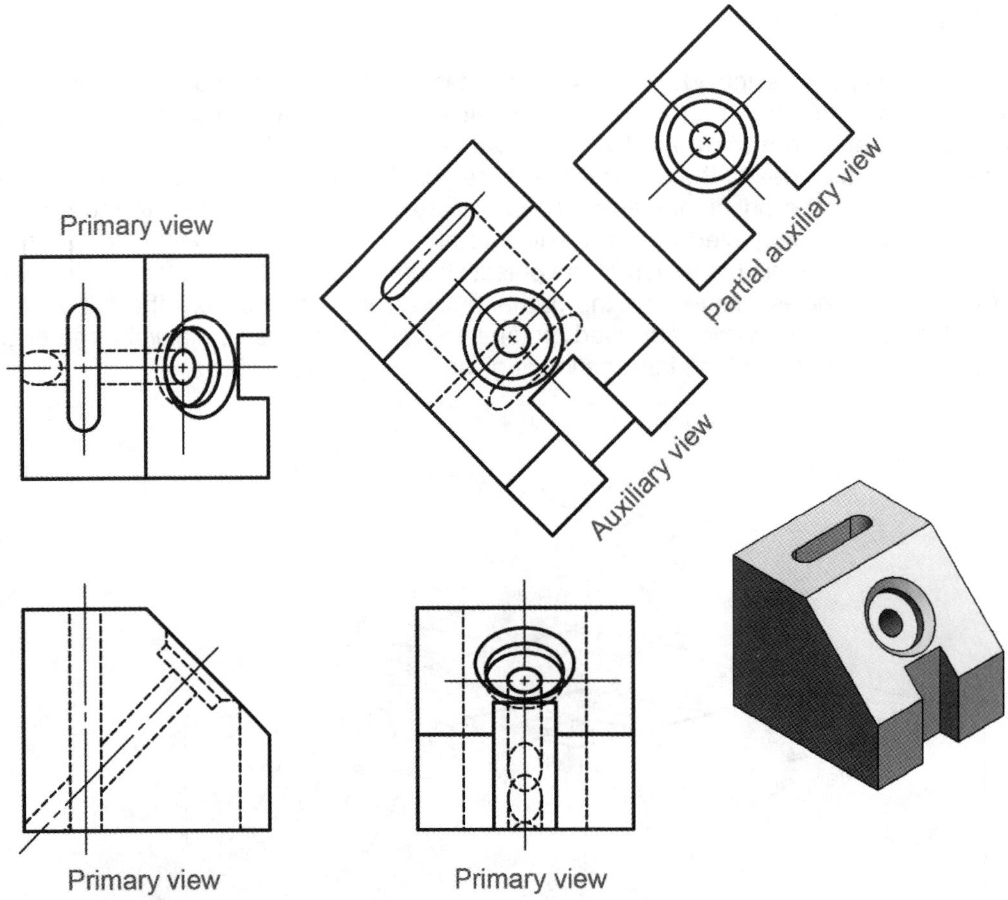

Figure 15.1-6: Auxiliary views

15.1.5) Related parts

The relationship between the part being detailed and another part (i.e., a related part) may be shown in the context of a detailed drawing. If a related part is shown, it usually means that the relationship between the two parts is important. The related part is shown using the phantom line type as shown in Figure 15.1-7. Phantom lines are often used to show imaginary features or parts.

Try Exercises 15.1-1

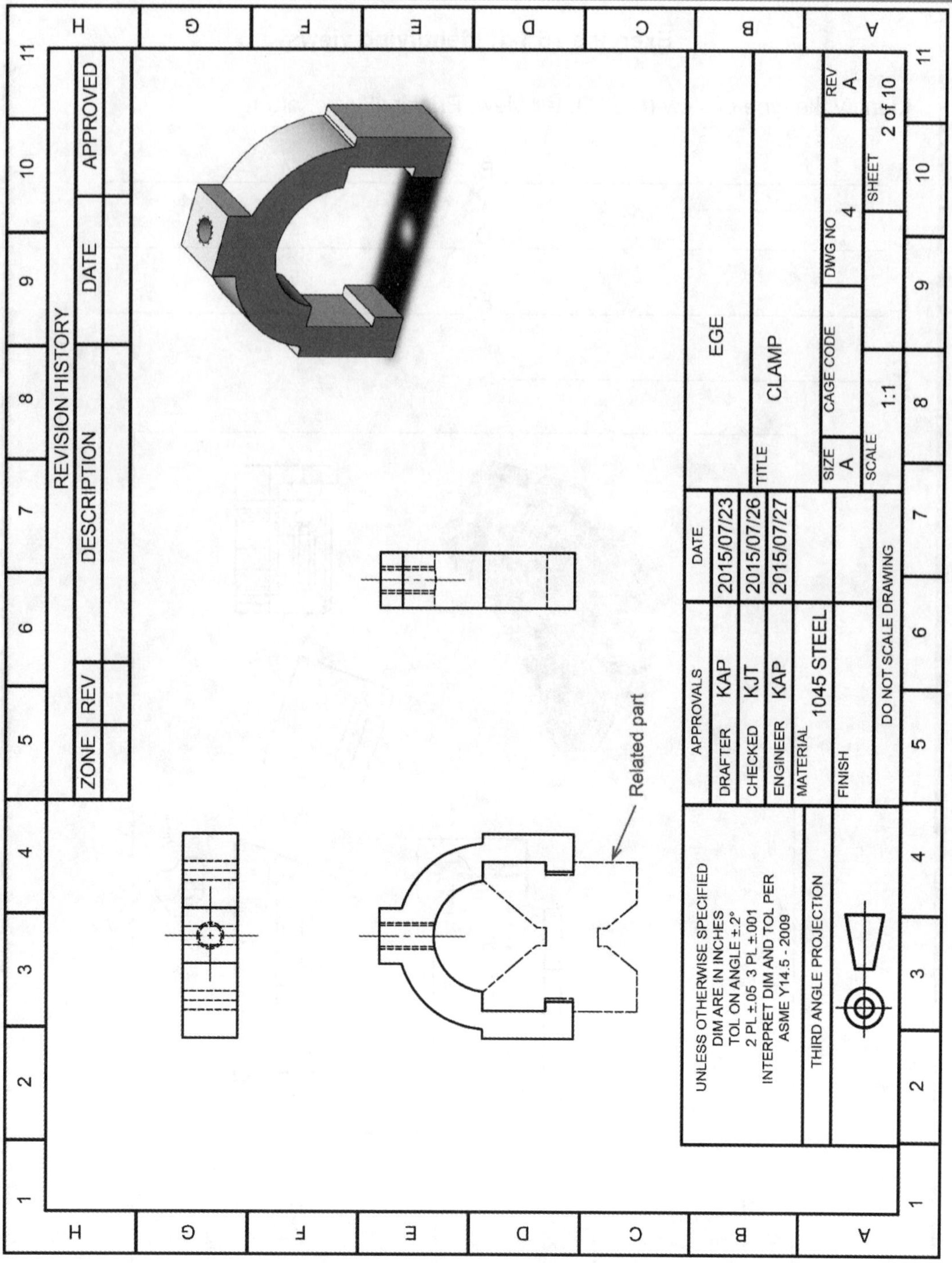

Figure 15.1-7: Related part

Exercise 15.1-1: Identifying views

Identify the type of view (e.g., Detail view, Principal view, etc.)

A:______________________ B: ______________________

C:______________________ D: ______________________

E:______________________ F: ______________________

G:______________________

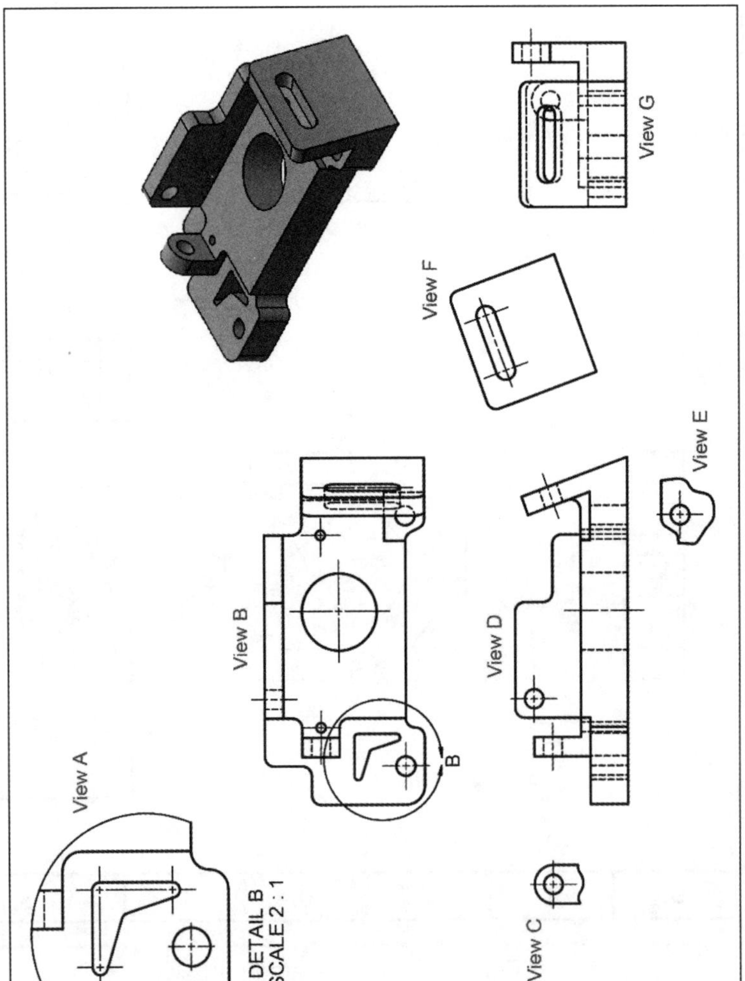

15.2) ADVANCED PART TECHNIQUES

There are several types of parts that require special drawing symbols. For example, cast parts use surface texture symbols and welded parts use weld symbols. We will take a look at cast and molded parts in this section.

15.2.1) Cast and molded parts

In order to fully appreciate the drawing elements of a casting or molded part, it helps to have a basic understanding of the processes used to make these parts. Cast and molded parts are similar in the sense that the parts are made by pouring or injecting a melted substance into a cavity and allowing the substance to solidify. In the case of castings, the material is usually a metal, and it is poured into the mold. In the case of molded parts, the material is usually a polymer, and it is injected into the mold. Cast and molded parts are most often used when the part needed is too complex to economically make the part using another method. Figures 15.2-1 and 15.2-2 show the different components of a casting system. Before we look at a drawing of a cast or molded part, let's go over some definitions.

- **Casting:** A process whereby a part is produced by the solidification of a material in a mold. The solid part produced by this process is also called the *casting.*
- **Mold:** A form made of sand, metal, or other material. The melted material is poured or injected into the mold and allowed to solidify.
- **Parting line:** A line on the drawing that represents the mating surfaces of the mold.
- **Draft:** The taper given to a part so that it can be extracted from the mold.
- **Fillet radius:** A concaved radius on the part connecting two surfaces.
- **Corner radius:** A convex radius on the part connecting two surfaces.

In the tangible world, there are several features that allow you to immediately identify a casting. Figure 15.2-3 shows the casting of a bottle opener. Notice the following features. Cast and molded parts will often have a ridge where the parting line is located. Most sand casted metal parts have slightly rough surfaces from contact with the sand. The smooth surfaces on the casting have been machined after the completed casting process. A cast part will have both fillet and corner radii. These radii are placed in the design to avoid sharp corners which lead to stress concentrations (i.e., an increased possibility for part failure under load.) Also, castings will have surfaces that are angled (i.e. drafted). Drafts allow the part to be extracted from the mold. These drafts proceed from the parting plane (i.e., the plane where the two halves of the mold meet) outward or inward depending on the drawing specifications. The most common material used for metal castings is cast iron. Cast iron is a relatively brittle material; therefore, you will often see supporting ribs and webs to help increase the part's strength.

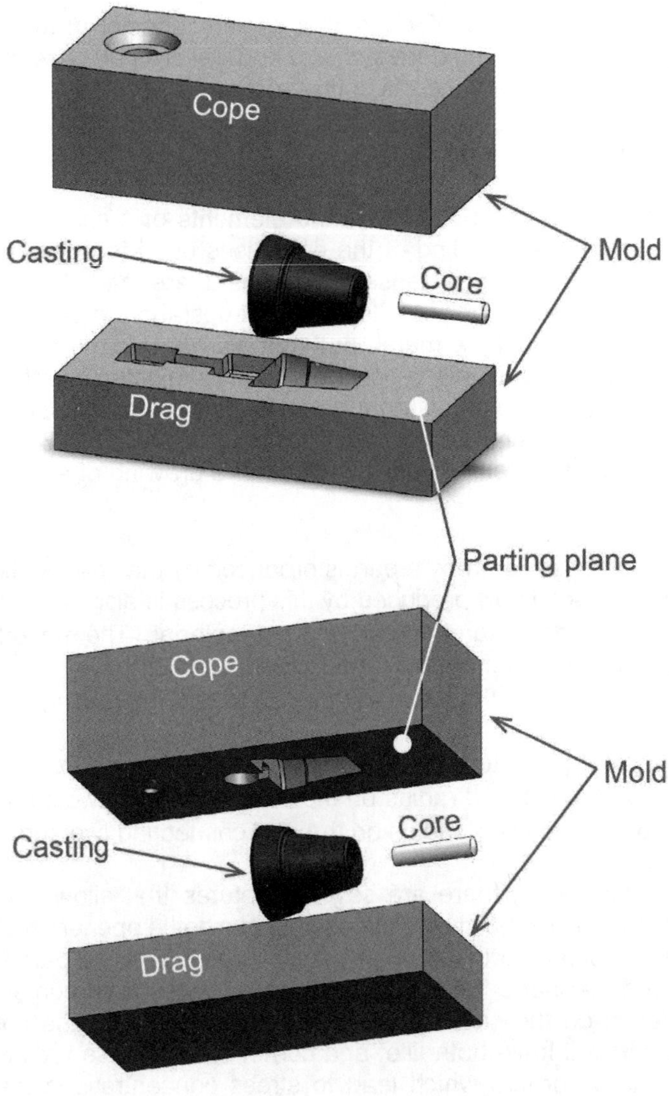

Figure 15.2-1: Casting components – exploded view

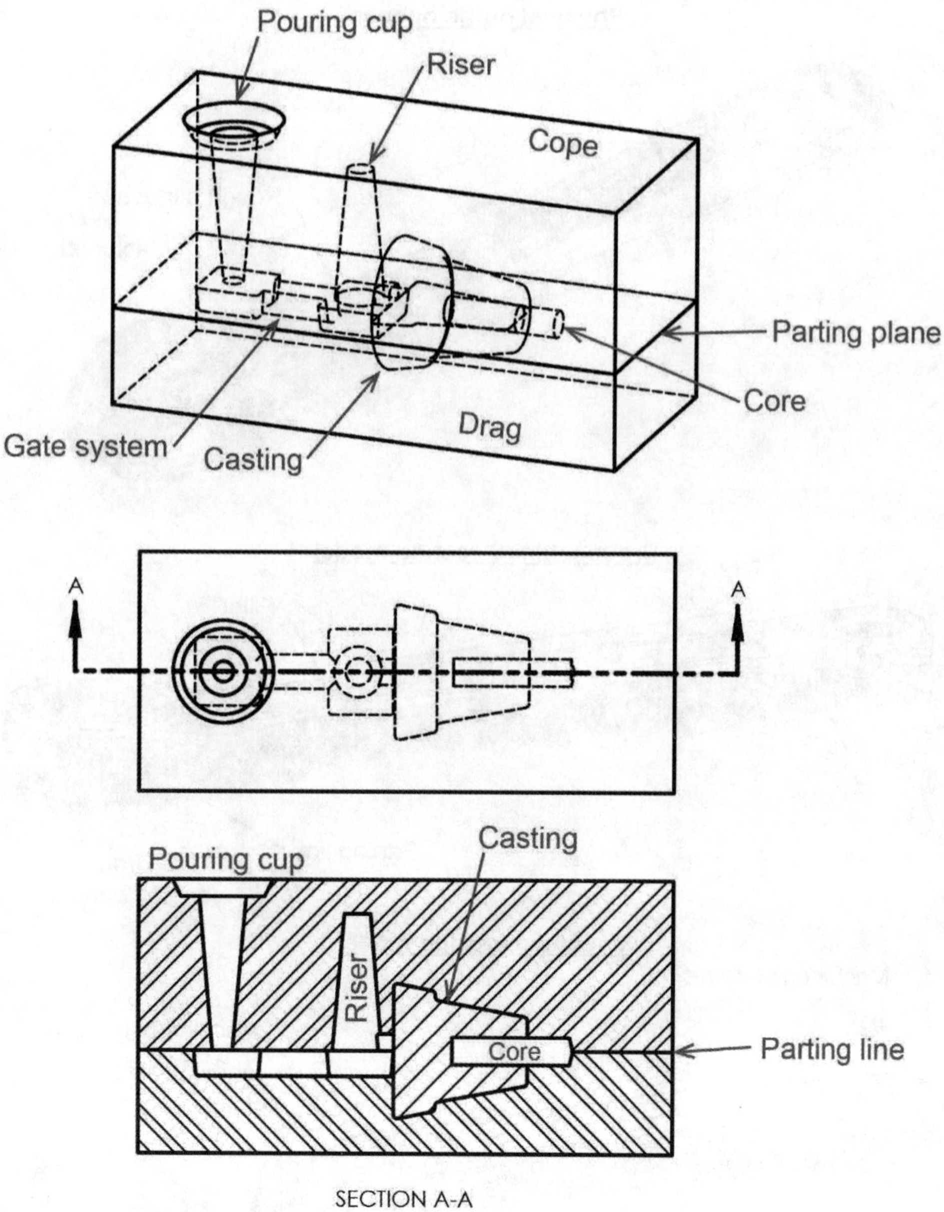

Figure 15.2-2: Casting components

Physical bottle opener

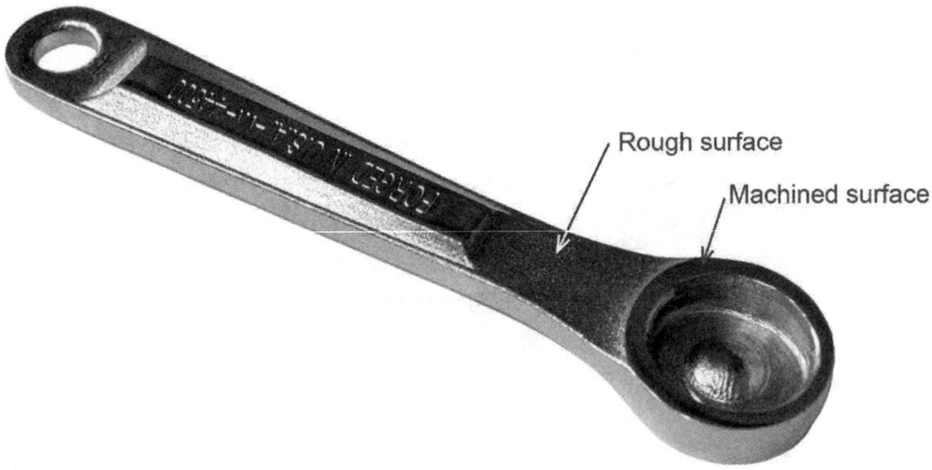

Pre-machined casting model

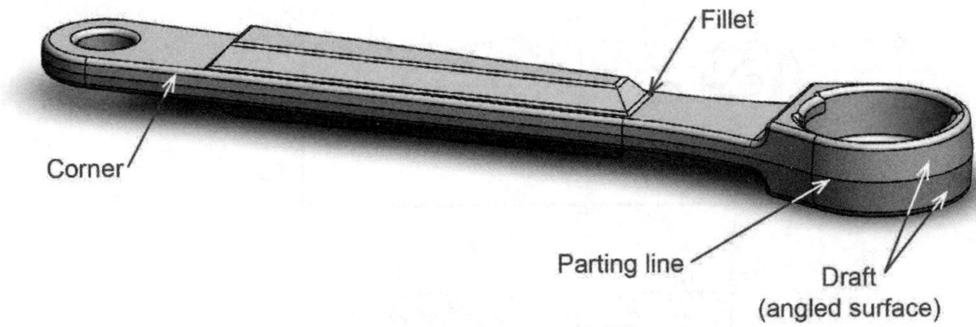

Machined casting model

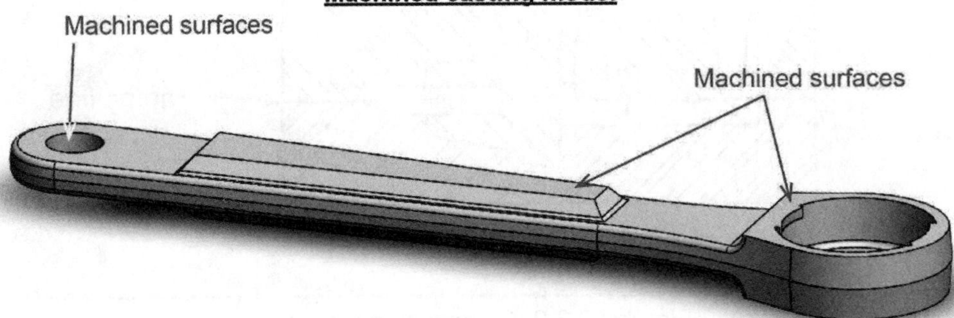

Figure 15.2-3: Bottle opener

In this text we will focus on the *end item drawing.* That means the drawing that shows the part after it has been cast and machined (i.e., in its final state.) Here is a list of features and concepts that you should keep in mind when reading a casting drawing. See Figure 15.2-6 for illustrations of these concepts. Note that the drawing shown in Figure 15.2-6 may not be complete. It is just used for illustration purposes.

- The **radius of fillets and corners** are not dimensioned individually but specified in a note on the drawing as shown in Figure 15.2-6.
- **Dimensions are measured to the mold lines.** This means that if a dimension goes between a fillet or corner radius, the dimension is measuring from the theoretical sharp corner created by the two meeting surfaces.
- A **surface texture value** is specified for all machined surfaces.
- The **die closure tolerance** is either specified in a note or applied directly to the dimension.
- The **parting line** (i.e., where the mold halves meet) is indicated with a phantom line and the parting line symbol.

15.2.1.1) Surface texture symbol

Surface texture symbols are used to indicate surfaces of a casting that will be machined after the casting process. Figure 15.2-4 shows the three basic configurations of the surface texture symbol and Figure 15.2-6 shows their use. Figure 15.2-5 shows a surface texture symbol with roughness specifications. Getting into what each specification means is beyond the scope of this text. Further information may be obtained in the Machinery's handbook.

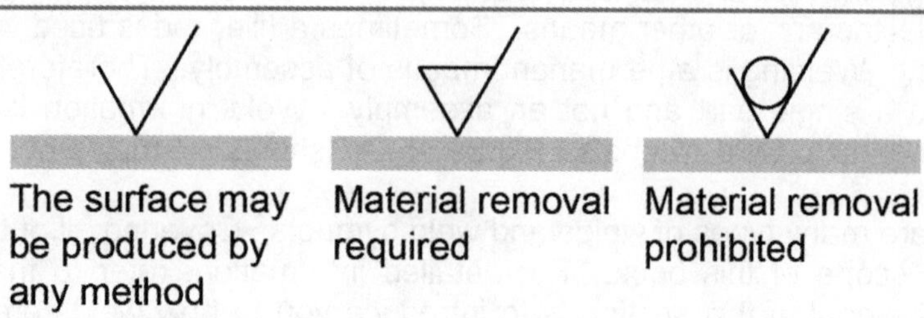

Figure 15.2-4: Surface texture symbols

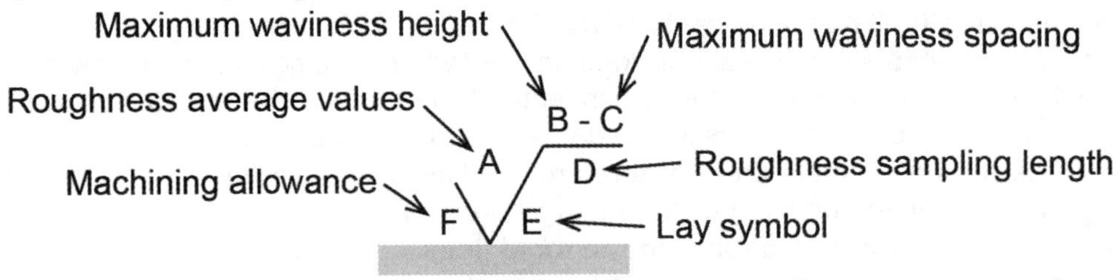

Example

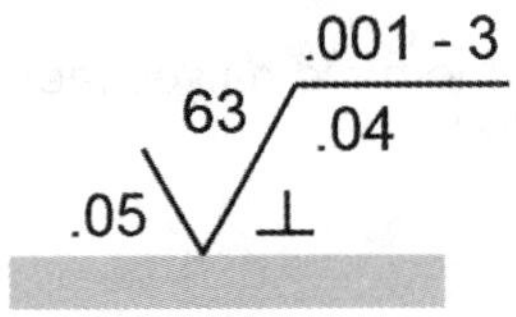

Figure 15.2-5: Surface texture symbols specifications

15.2.2) Welded parts

Welding joins pieces of metal by heating the surfaces to the point of melting using a blowtorch, electric arc, or other means. Sometimes a filler rod is used to add material to the weld joint. Welding is a permanent means of assembly. Therefore, welded parts are considered a single part and not an assembly. Weld information is given on the detailed drawing using weld symbols. Figure 15.2-7 shows examples of some common weld symbols.

There are many types of welds and weld symbols. Covering all of these symbols is beyond the scope of this book. For detailed information, refer to the Machinery's Handbook. The goal of this section is to introduce you to how welds are indicated on drawings. This will allow you to recognize these symbols as welds so that you can look up their exact meaning.

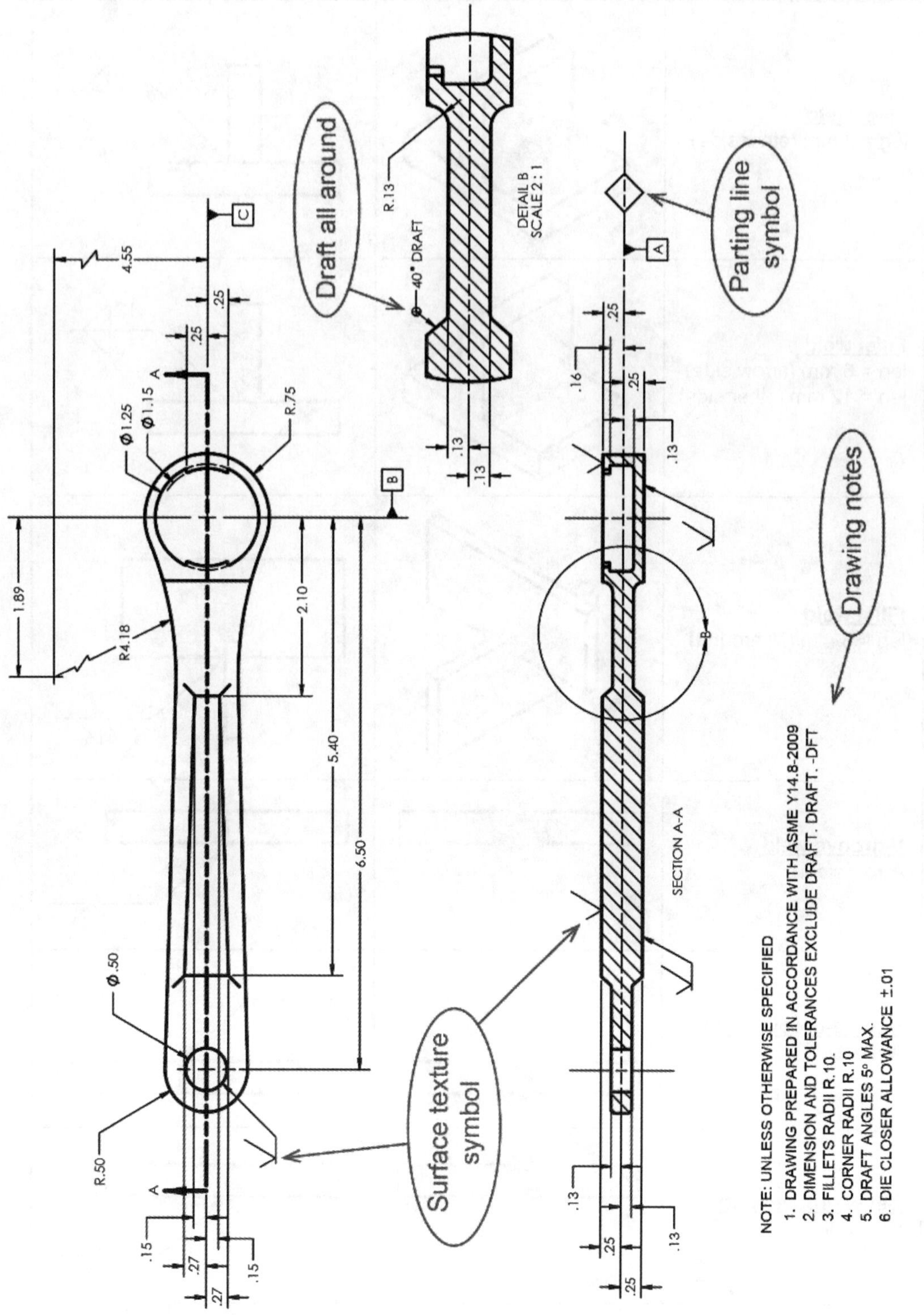

Figure 15.2-6: Bottle opener drawing

Fillet weld leg = 8 mm (other side)	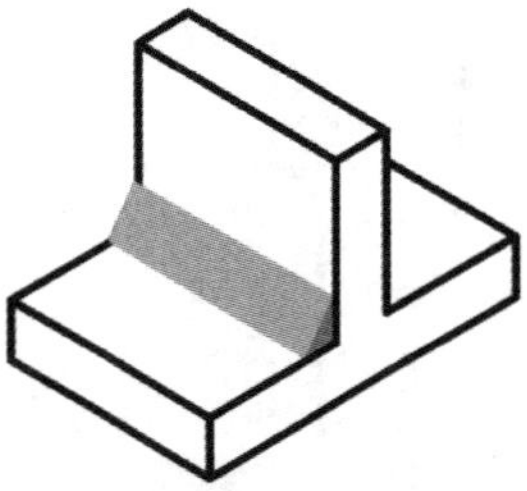	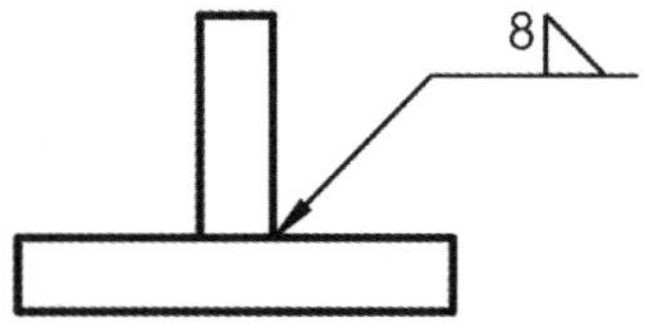
Fillet weld leg = 6 mm (arrow side) leg = 12 mm (other side)	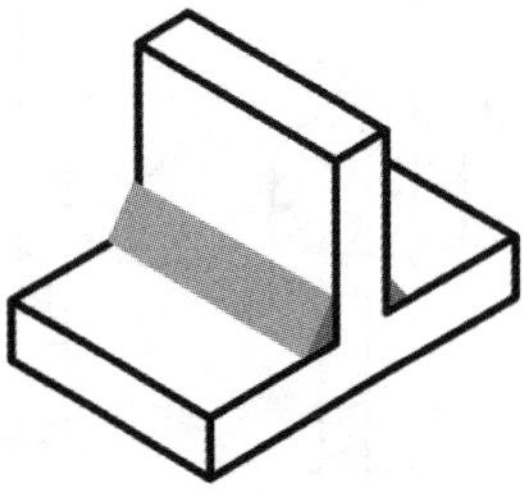	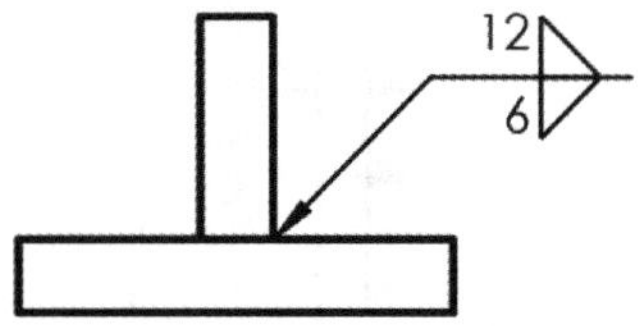
Fillet weld leg = 6 mm (all around)	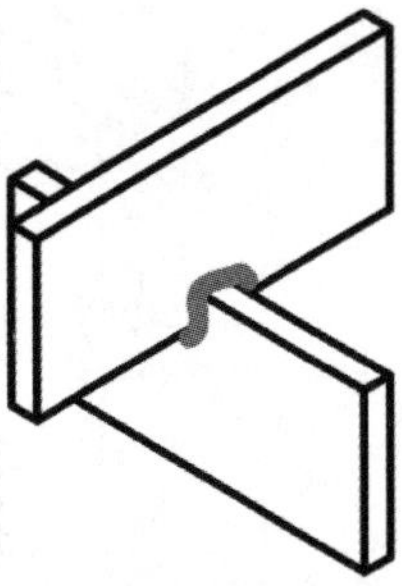	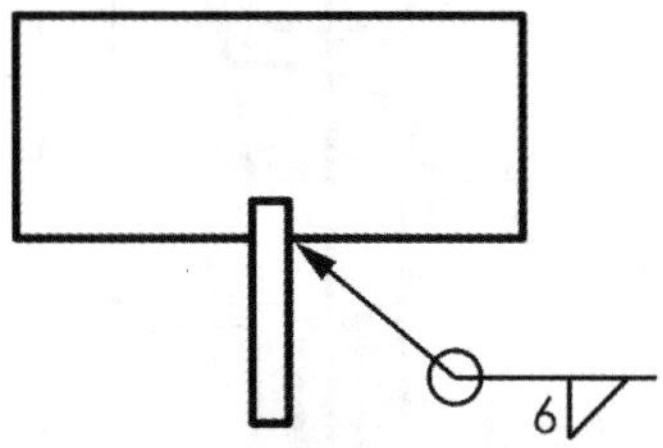
V-groove weld Arrow side	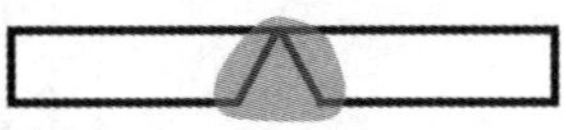	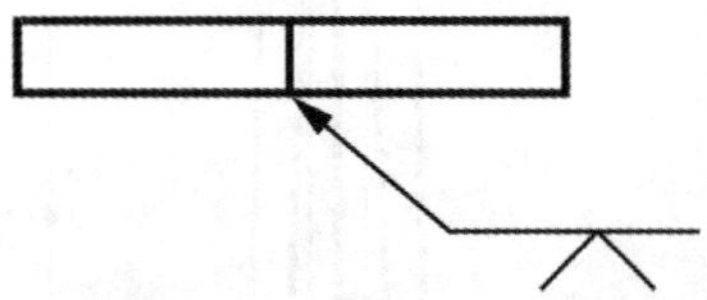
Square-groove weld Arrow side	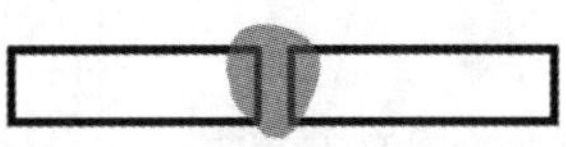	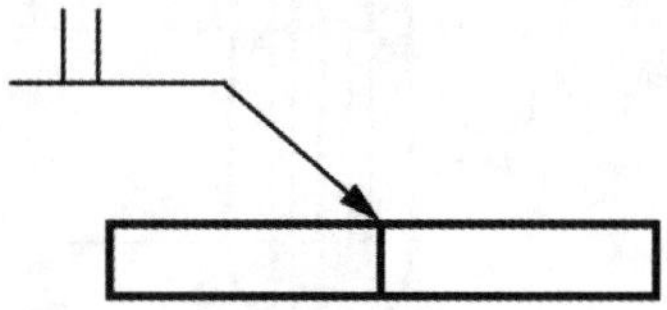
Bevel-groove weld both side		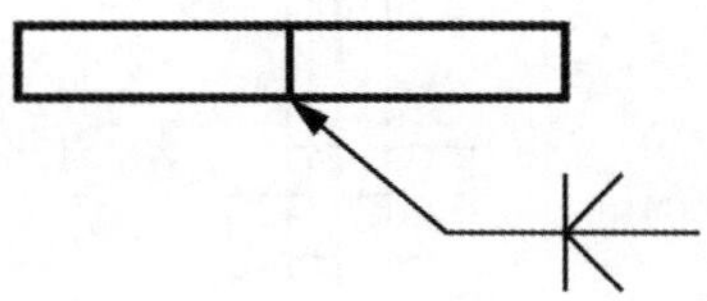

Figure 15.2-7: Weld symbol examples

READING ADVANCED DRAWINGS QUESTIONS – SET 1

Name: ________________________________ Date: ______________

Q15-1) These types of views are not in the projection path. (Circle all that apply.)

a) Removed
b) Revolved
c) Detail
d) Auxiliary

Q15-2) These types of views may be shown at an increased scale. (Circle all that apply.)

a) Removed
b) Revolved
c) Detail
d) Auxiliary

Q15-3) This type of view, for clarity, does not show everything.

a) Removed
b) Revolved
c) Partial
d) Related

Q15-4) This type of part is shown in phantom lines.

a) Adjacent
b) Revolved
c) Partial
d) Related

Q15-5) Why might a detail view use a different scale from the rest of the drawing?

a) To fit on the page
b) To emphasize critical features too small to see clearly
c) To exaggerate defects in manufacturing
d) To follow standard ANSI regulations

Q15-6) This type of view is projected using a plane that is not parallel to one of the principal planes.

a) Removed
b) Revolved
c) Detail
d) Auxiliary

Q15-7) Drawings of castings use these two types of symbols. (Circle two choices.)

a) Parting line
b) Weld
c) Surface texture
d) Draft

READING ADVANCED DRAWINGS QUESTIONS – SET 2

Name: ________________________________ Date: ______________

Q15-8) A partial view is used to focus on a specific feature and reduce clutter in a drawing. (True, False)

Q15-9) Break lines are used to show the boundary of a partial view. (True, False)

Q15-10) What are the purposes of a removed view in an engineering drawing? (Choose all that apply.)

a) To show the exploded assembly
b) To clarify internal features with hidden lines
c) To show a view at a larger scale
d) To eliminate crowding

Q15-11) What is the primary purpose of a detail view in an engineering drawing?

a) To show an assembly of parts
b) To illustrate exploded views of components
c) To enlarge and clarify a specific part of a drawing
d) To provide a bill of materials

Q15-12) How is a detail view typically labeled on an engineering drawing?

a) With roman numerals
b) With a letter (e.g., Detail A)
c) With a number and a title
d) With the full name of the feature

Q15-13) The title of a detail view must include the scale if it differs from the scale of the parent view. (True, False)

Q15-14) What line type is used to represent a related part?

Q15-15) An auxiliary view is projected perpendicular to one of the standard orthographic planes. (True, False)

Q15-16) The draft angle used in castings and molds aids in part release. (True, False)

Q15-17) Weld symbols indicate the side of the weld by placing the weld symbol ….

a) above or below the line.
b) to the right or left of the line.
c) in bold or italics.

Q15-18) The circle at the bend of a weld callout indicates that the weld goes “all around”. (True, False)

READING ADVANCED DRAWING TECHNIQUES PROBLEMS

Name: ______________________________ Date: ______________

P15-1) Answer the following questions about the following drawing.

a) What type of advanced view discussed in this chapter is being used?

b) What is the scale of these views?

c) These advanced views are in the projection path of the front view. (True, False)

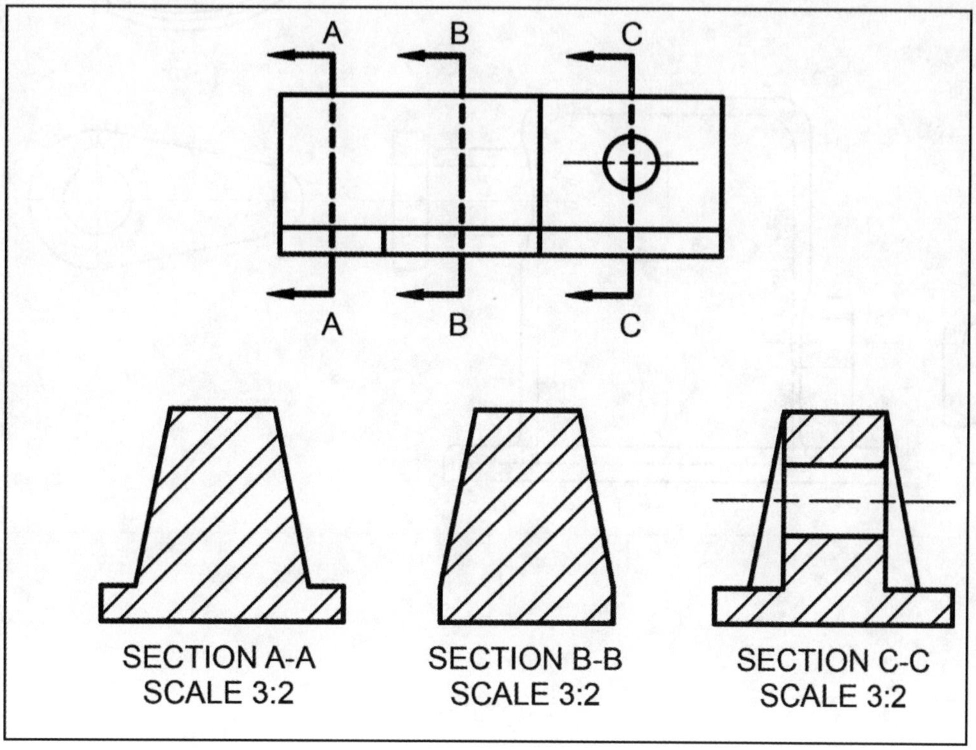

P15-2) Answer the following questions about the following drawing.

a) What type of advanced view technique is being used?

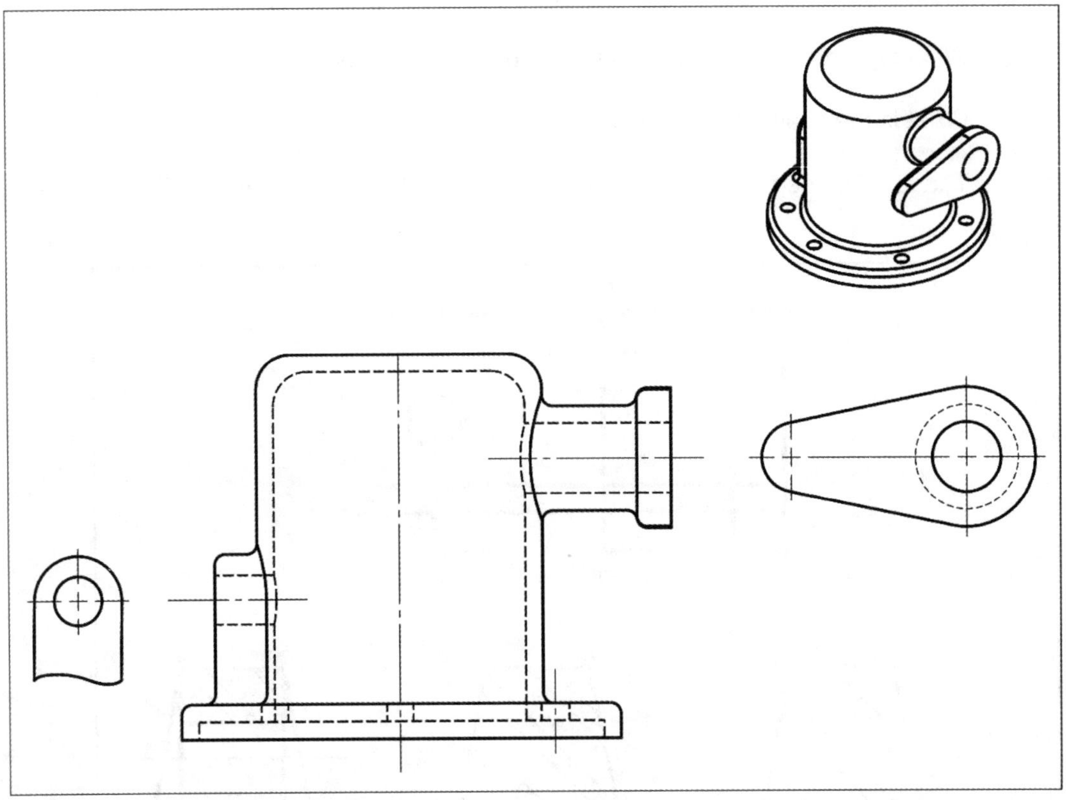

Name: ______________________________ Date: ______________

P15-3) Answer the following questions about the following drawing.

a) What type of advanced view is shown?

b) Is the view a full or partial view?

c) What is the depth of the slot?

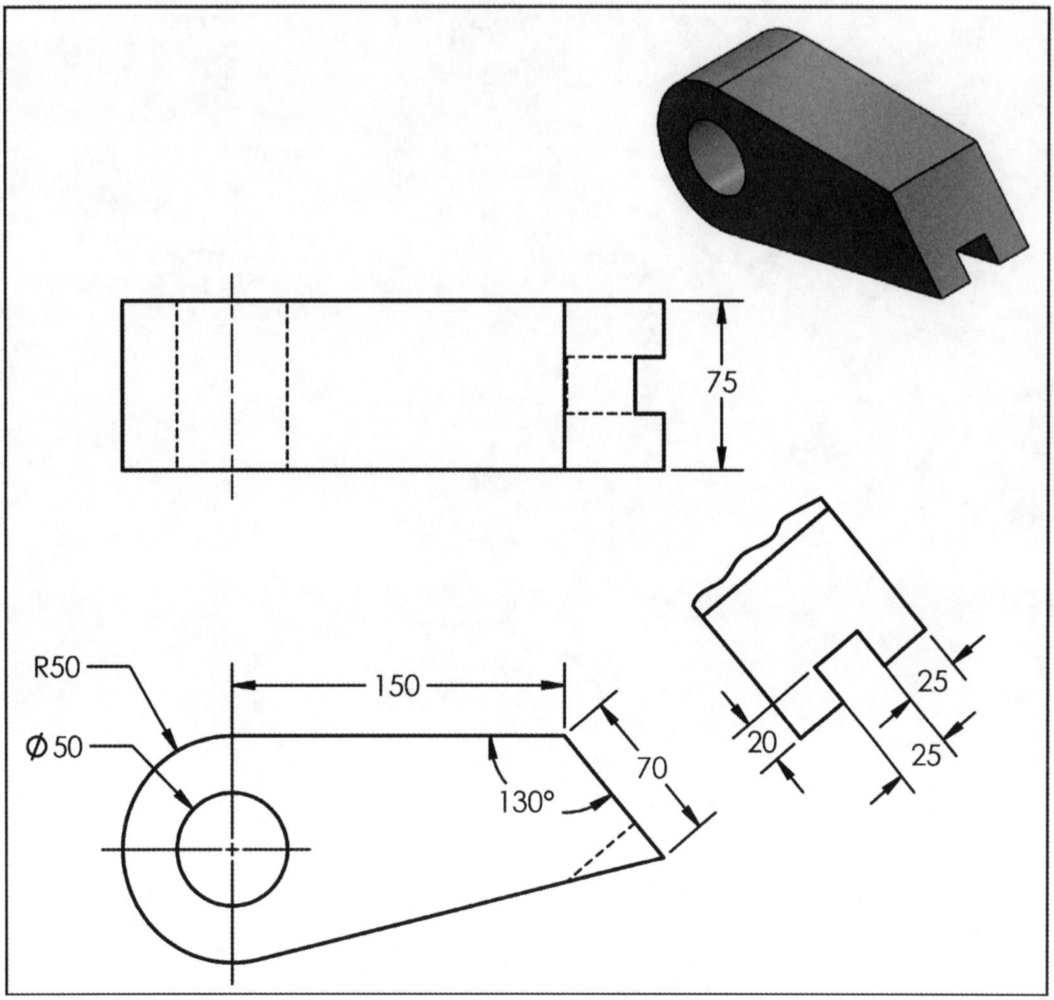

NOTES:

CHAPTER 16

CREATING ADVANCED DRAWINGS

CHAPTER OUTLINE

CHAPTER SUMMARY

In this chapter you will learn how to create auxiliary views. Auxiliary views are created using auxiliary planes which are at an angle to the principal planes. Auxiliary views are used in cases where one or more features are not shown true size in the principal views. Along with learning about auxiliary views you will also learn how to create an orthographic projection of a casting. Castings often have rounded edges and surfaces that are machined post castings. This requires the use of surface roughness symbols.

16.1) AUXILIARY VIEWS

Primary or principal views are created by projecting the part onto the principal planes (e.g., front, top, right side, left side, bottom, and rear views). **Auxiliary views are created by projecting the part onto a plane that is at an angle to one of the principal planes**.

Auxiliary views are used to show the true shape of features that are not parallel to any of the principal planes of projection. Figure 16.1-1 shows a pictorial of an object along with several views. Look at the pictorial to get a sense of the object's shape. Notice the cutouts on the sides of the object and the cylinder on the back side. These features are not shown true size in any of the principal views.

To show the true size of the cutouts, we need to project onto an auxiliary plane that is parallel to the angled face. A full and partial auxiliary views are shown. Note that the partial auxiliary view is all that is needed. The goal is just to show the cutouts and be able to dimension them. We don't need any extra information. If we use a partial view, we don't need to include hidden lines or anything else that will distract the viewer from the information that we are trying to convey. Partial auxiliary views are often used to show only a particular feature that is not described in the principal views.

To show the true size of the cylinder we need to use a secondary auxiliary view. Note that even though the cylinder may appear to be true size in the full auxiliary view used to show the cutouts, it is not. It is at a slight angle. To show the cylinder true size we need to project on to a plane that is parallel to the hidden line shown in the front view (the primary auxiliary view) and then project on to a plane that is parallel to the side of the primary auxiliary view. This secondary auxiliary view shows the cylinder's true size. Notice that the secondary auxiliary view is a partial view. We only need to show and dimension the cylinder.

Watch Video Exercise 16.1-1 and try Exercise 16.1-2.

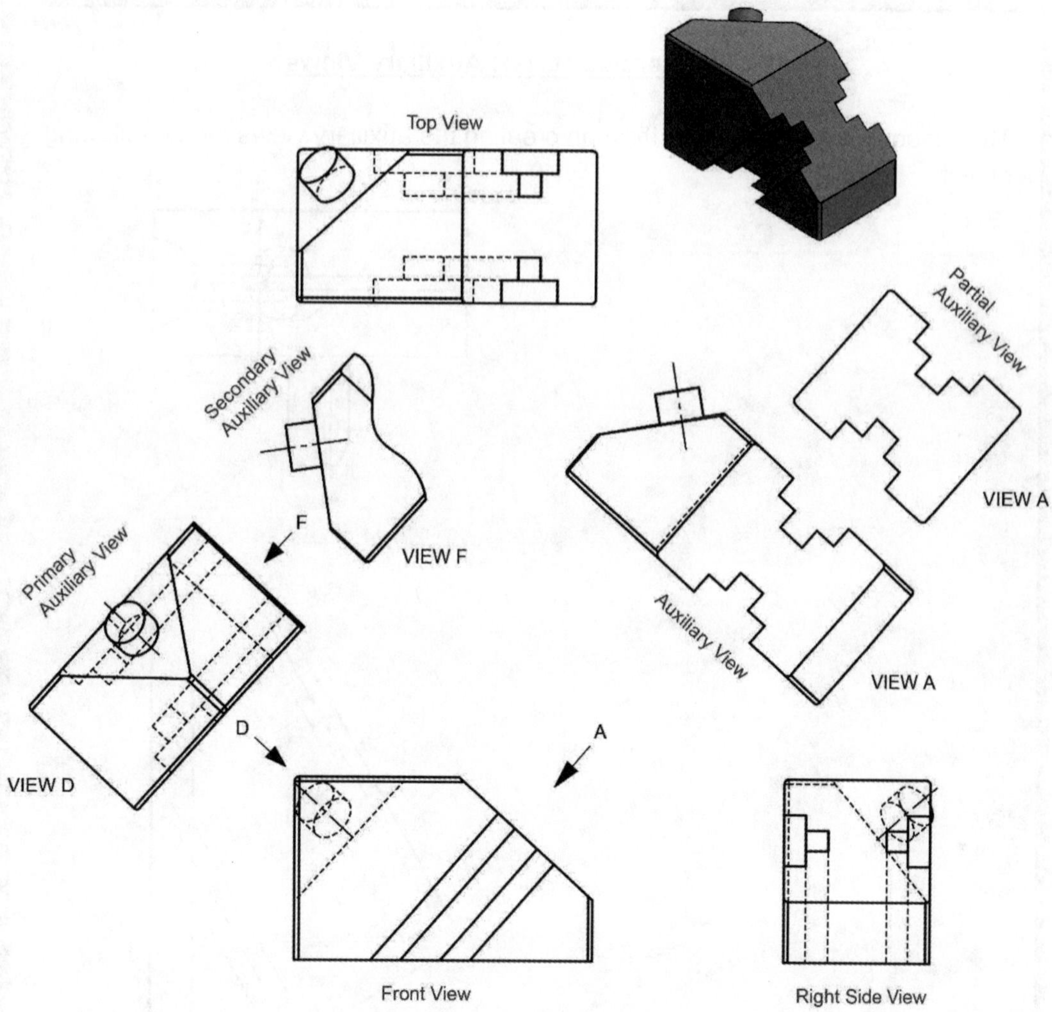

Figure 16.1-1: Auxiliary views

Video Exercise 16.1-1: Auxiliary Views

This video exercise takes you through creating the auxiliary views for the following object.

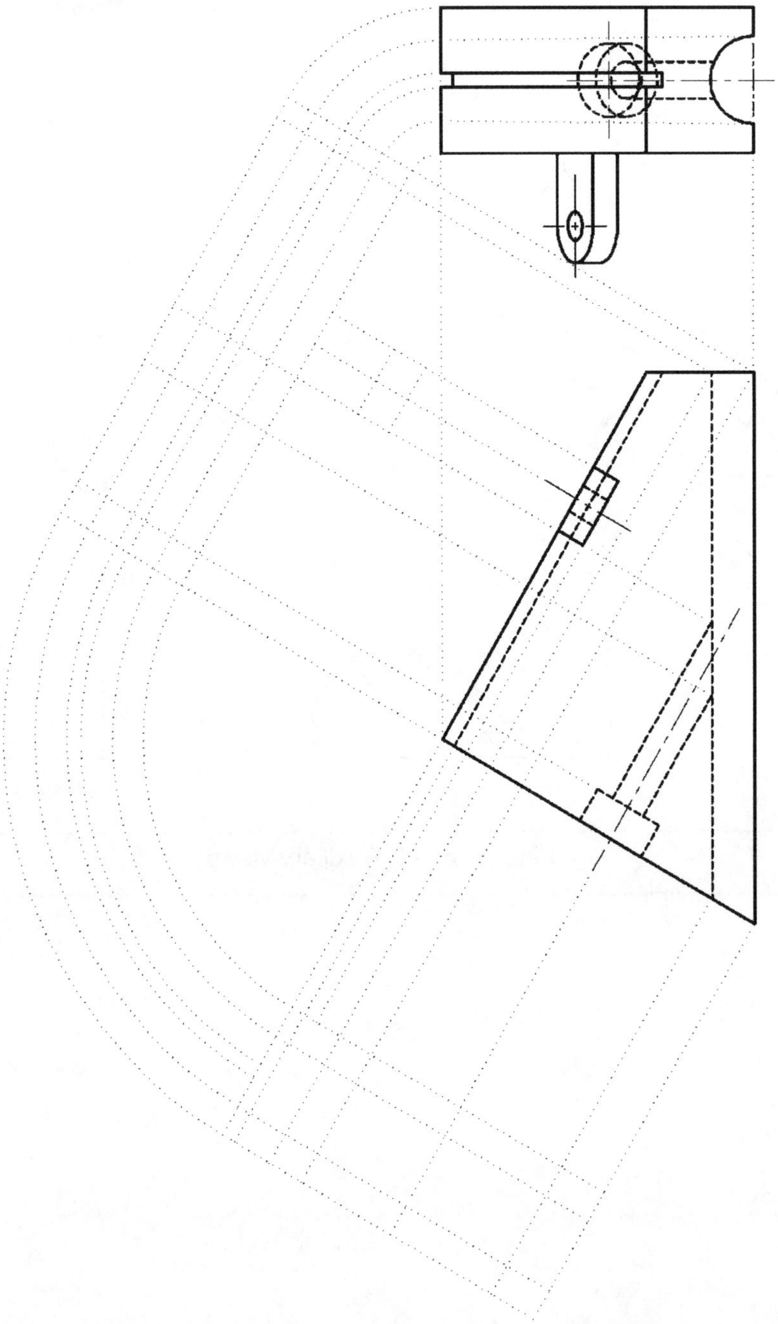

Exercise 16.1-2: Auxiliary view

Draw the auxiliary view for this object.

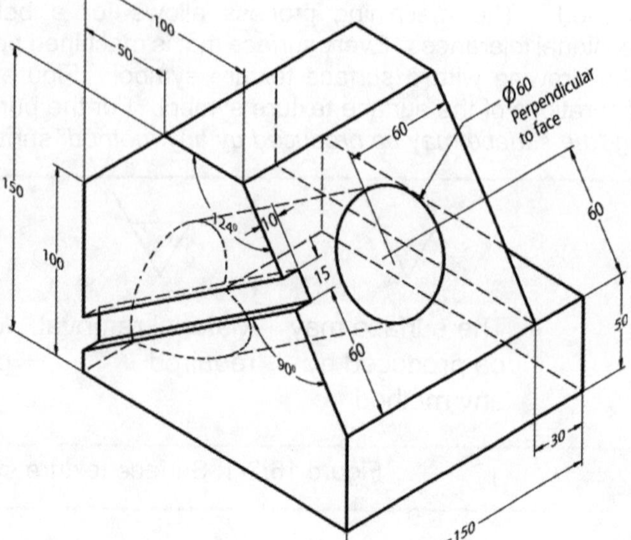

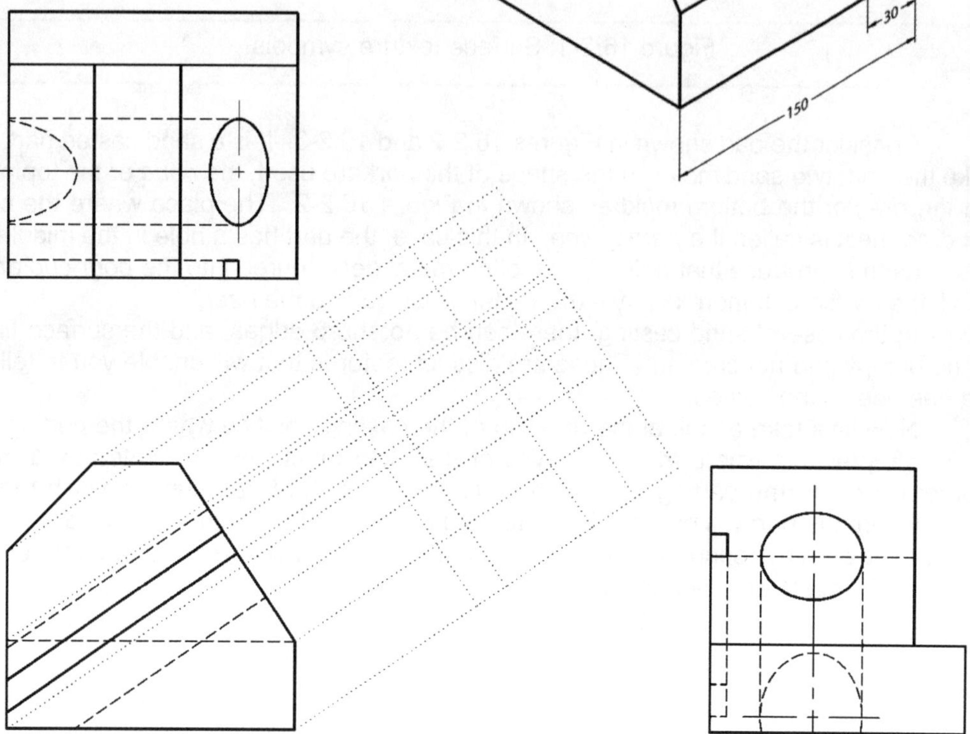

16.2) CASTINGS

Cast and molded parts are similar in the sense that the parts are made by pouring or injecting a melted substance into a cavity and allowing the substance to solidify. The casting process is explained in more detail in the previous chapter.

In the case of metal castings, post casting machining operations are usually performed. The machining process allows for a better finish and more accurate dimensional tolerances. Every surface that is machined post casting needs to be indicated on the drawing with a surface texture symbol. Figure 16.2-1 shows the three basic configurations of the surface texture symbol. For the purpose of this text, we will just be using *"the surface may be produced by any method"* surface texture symbol.

Figure 16.2-1: Surface texture symbols

Consider the part shown in Figures 16.2-2 and 16.2-3. It is a sand casted part. To make the part, two sand molds in the shape of the part are used, the *cope* or the top mold and the *drag* or the bottom mold as shown in Figure 16.2-2. The place where the cope and drag meet is called the *parting line*. In this case, the part has a hole in the middle. A core is used to produce that hole. The molten metal gets poured into the *pour cup* and it fills all the cavities. If there is any extra metal, it will go into the *riser*.

In the case of sand casting, there can be no sharp edges, and the surface finish will be bumpy and not smooth. These are distinct features that will enable you to tell if a part has been sand casted.

Now let's take a look at the drawing of the casting. Notice where the parting line is. This represents where the two halves of the mold meet. It is indicated by using a phantom line and the parting line symbol. Next, notice the three surface finish marks. This is where the part will be machined creating a surface that is smooth. Because sand castings have many rounded corners, there is usually a drawing note that specifies the radii of all the fillets and rounds (or corners).

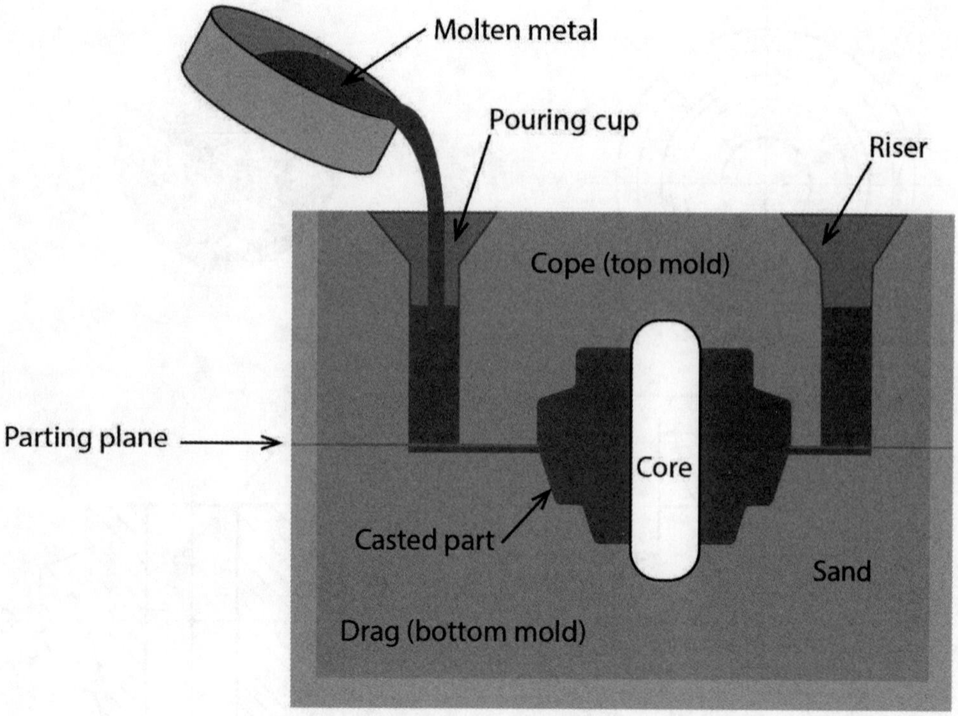

Figure 16.2-2: Casting

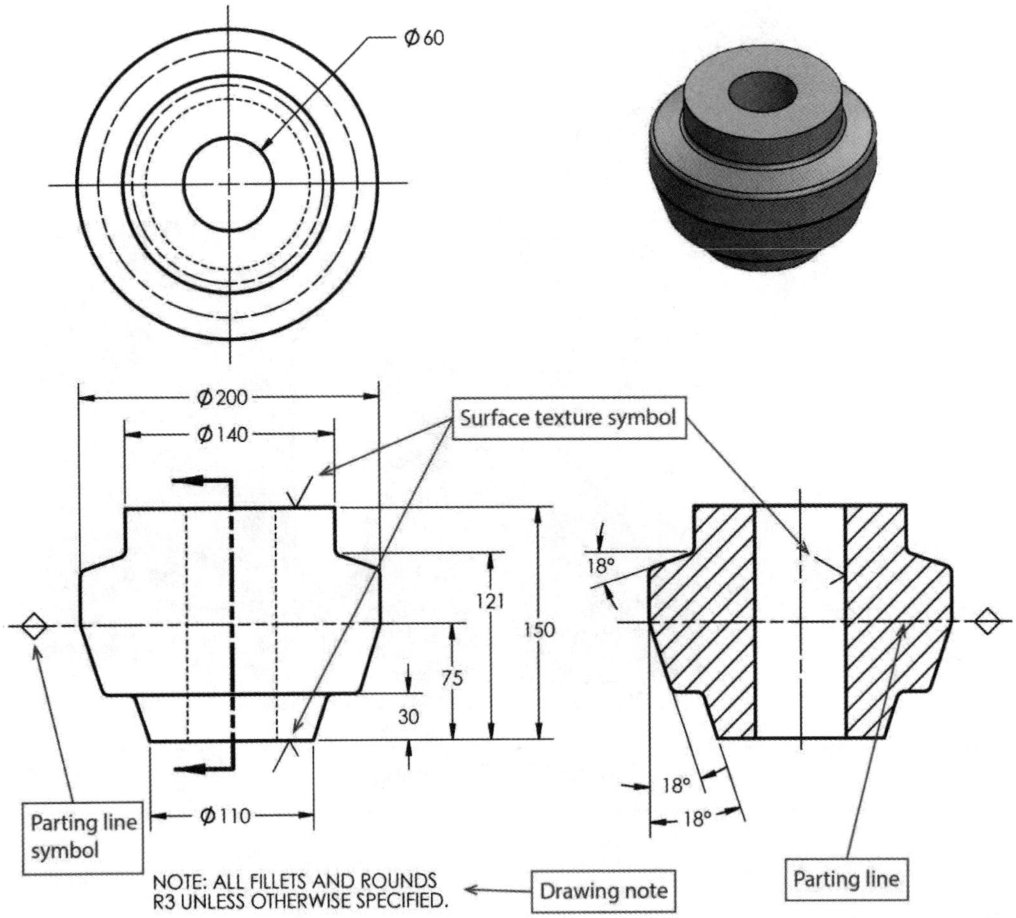

Figure 16.2-3: Casting drawing

Exercise 16.2-1: Surface texture symbol

The following orthographic projection represents a part that has been sand casted. Place a surface texture symbol everywhere that it is needed.

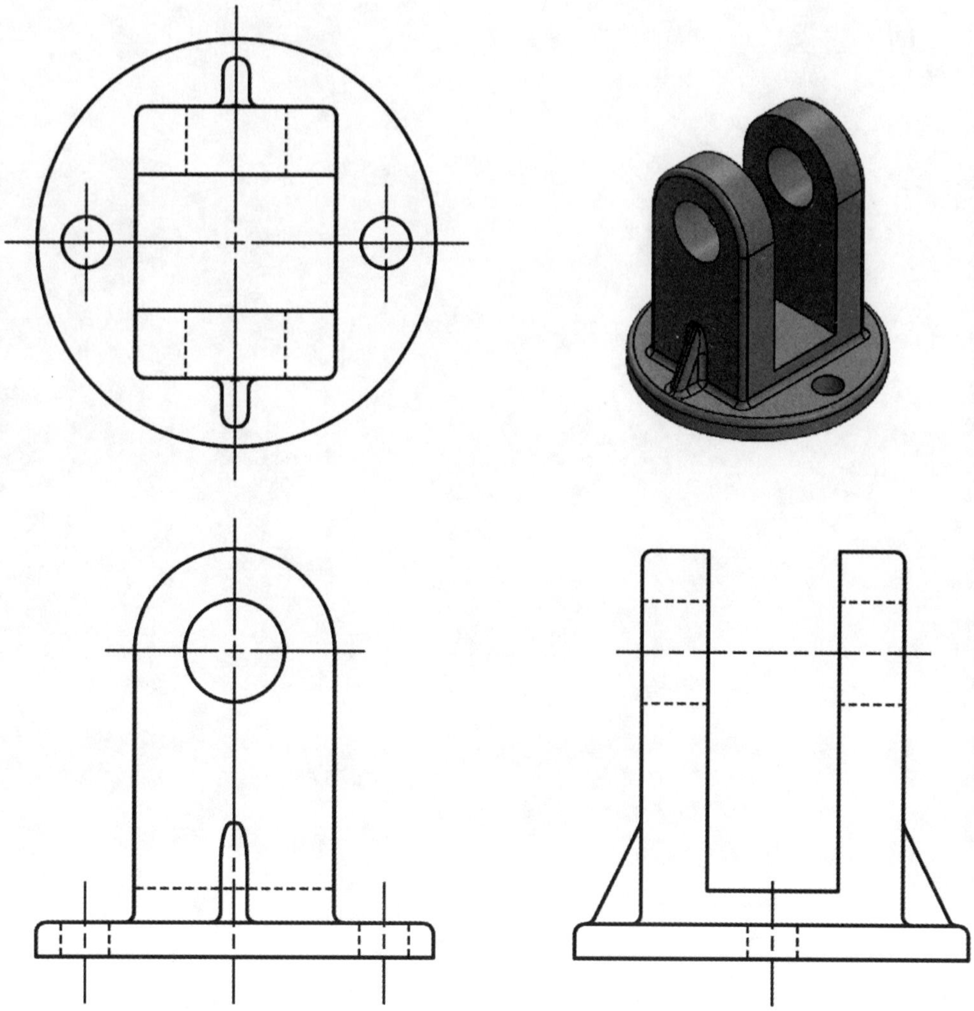

NOTES:

CREATING ADVANCED DRAWINGS QUESTIONS – SET 1

Name: ________________________________ Date: ______________

Q16-1) What is the main purpose of an auxiliary view?

a) To show hidden lines
b) To show the true size of an inclined surface
c) To add perspective to drawings
d) To replace section views

Q16-2) What symbol is used to indicate post casting machining?

Q16-3) The parting line indicates where the cope and drag meet. (True, False)

Q16-4) Which of the following features is typically added to a casting drawing to help in the removal of the part from the mold?

a) Draft angle
b) Chamfer
c) Undercut
d) Fillet radius

Q16-5) What is the purpose of adding fillets in casting design?

a) To reduce the cost of material.
b) To prevent machining errors.
c) To reduce stress concentration and promote smooth metal flow.
d) To increase the part's weight

NOTES:

CREATING ADVANCED DRAWINGS QUESTIONS – SET 2

Name: ______________________________ Date: ______________

Q16-6) Auxiliary views are used to show features that appear foreshortened in the principal views. (True, False)

Q16-7) In which direction is an auxiliary view projected?

a) Parallel to the front view
b) Perpendicular to the top view
c) Perpendicular to the surface being shown in true size
d) At a 45-degree angle from any principal view

Q16-8) What is typically omitted from a partial view to reduce clutter?

a) Visible lines
b) Hidden lines
c) Centerlines
d) Dimension lines

Q16-9) An auxiliary view cannot be used to dimension features of a part. (True, False)

Q16-10) When representing a parting line on a casting drawing, how should it be shown?

a) With a thick solid line.
b) With a centerline.
c) With a chain line or phantom line.
d) It is not shown on the drawing.

Q16-11) All fillets and radii on a casted part must be dimensioned explicitly on the drawing. (True, False)

NOTES:

CREATING ADVANCED DRAWING PROBLEMS

Name: ______________________________ Date: ______________

P16-1) Sketch in a complete auxiliary view in the space indicated.

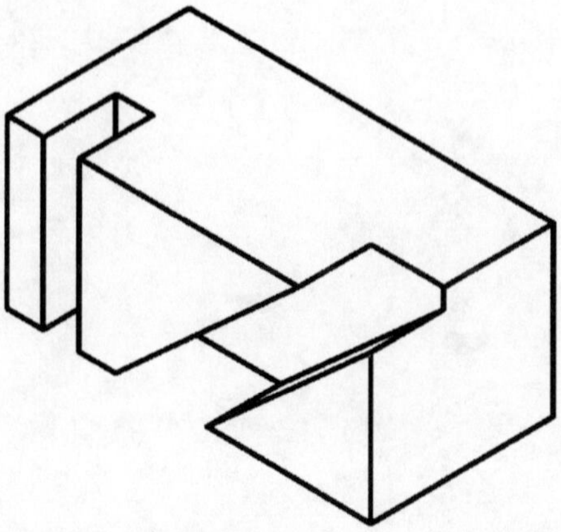

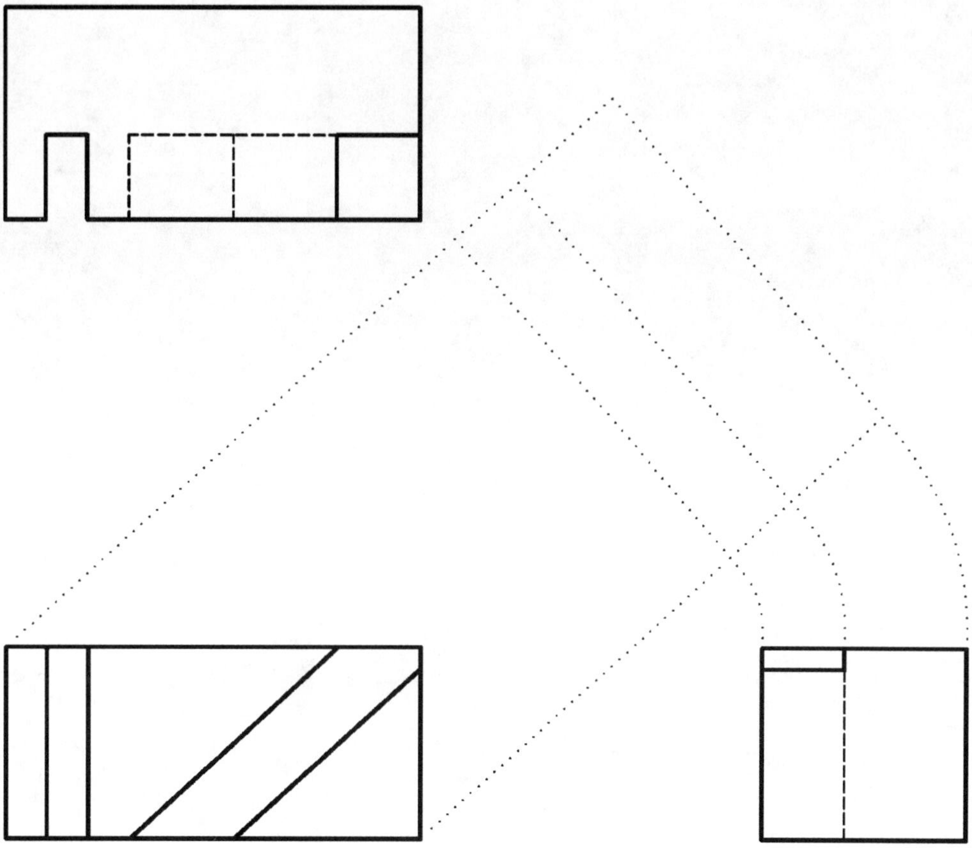

NOTES:

Name: ______________________________ Date: ______________

P16-2) Sketch in a complete auxiliary view in the space indicated.

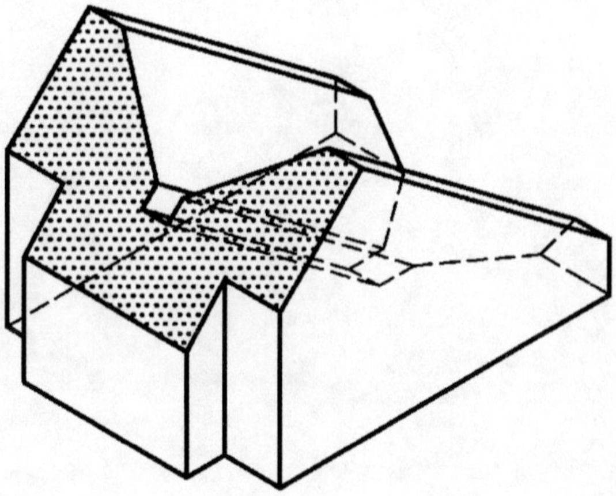

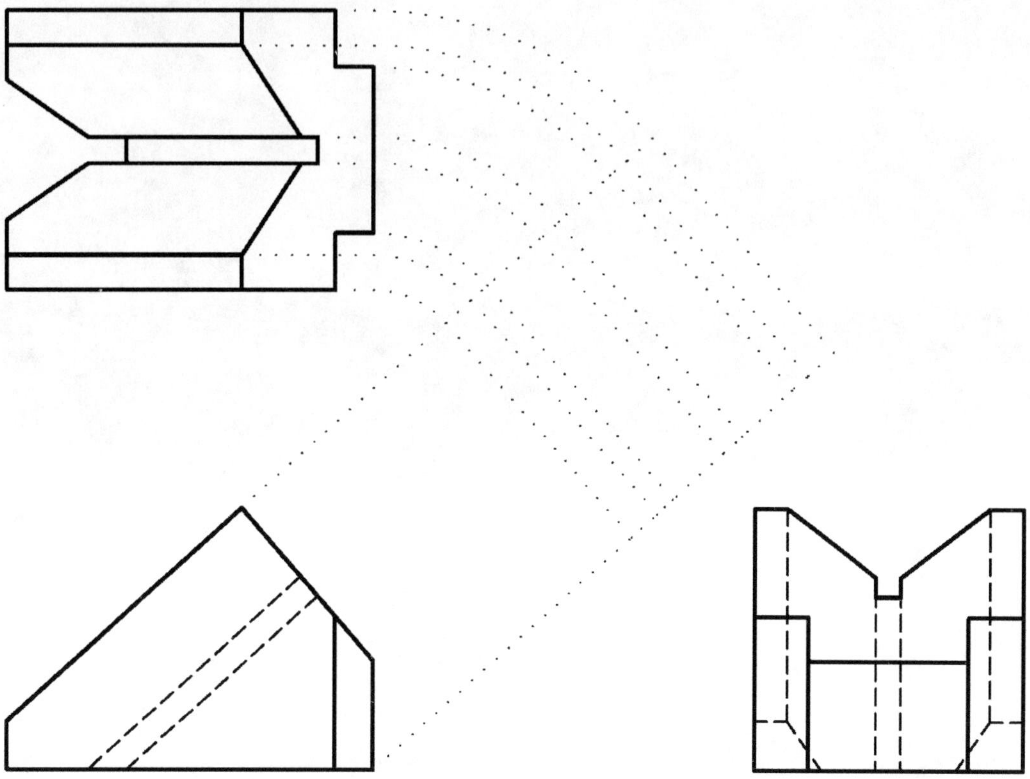

NOTES:

Name: ______________________________ Date: _____________

P16-3) Finish the two incomplete auxiliary views.

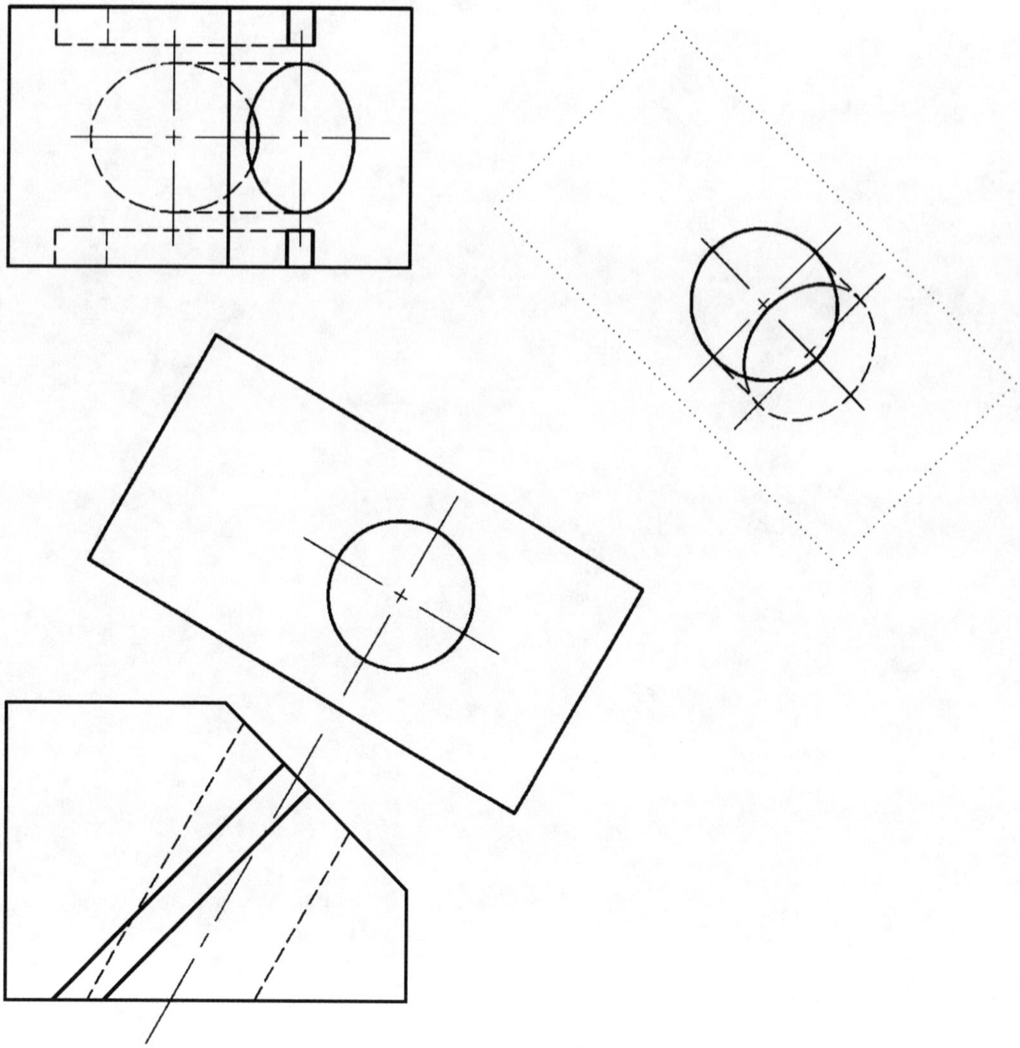

NOTES:

P16-4) Create detailed drawing (orthographic projection + dimensions) of the following object. Draw an auxiliary view that shows the angled surface true shape. Use partial views where appropriate.

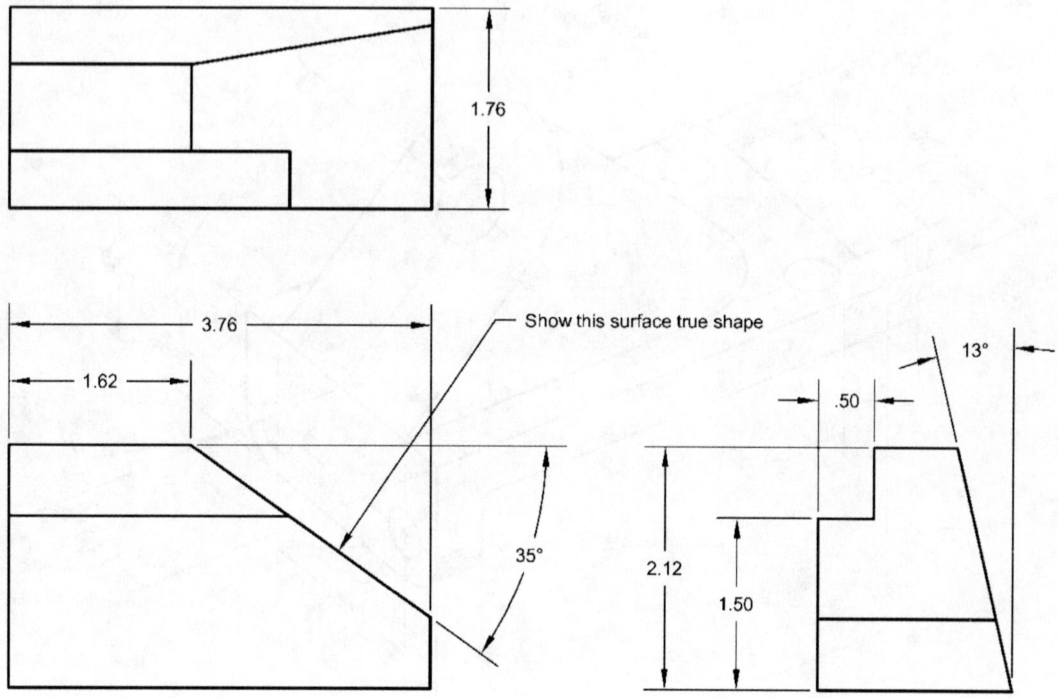

P16-5) Create detailed drawing (orthographic projection + dimensions) of the following object. Draw an auxiliary view that shows the angled surface true shape. Use partial views where appropriate.

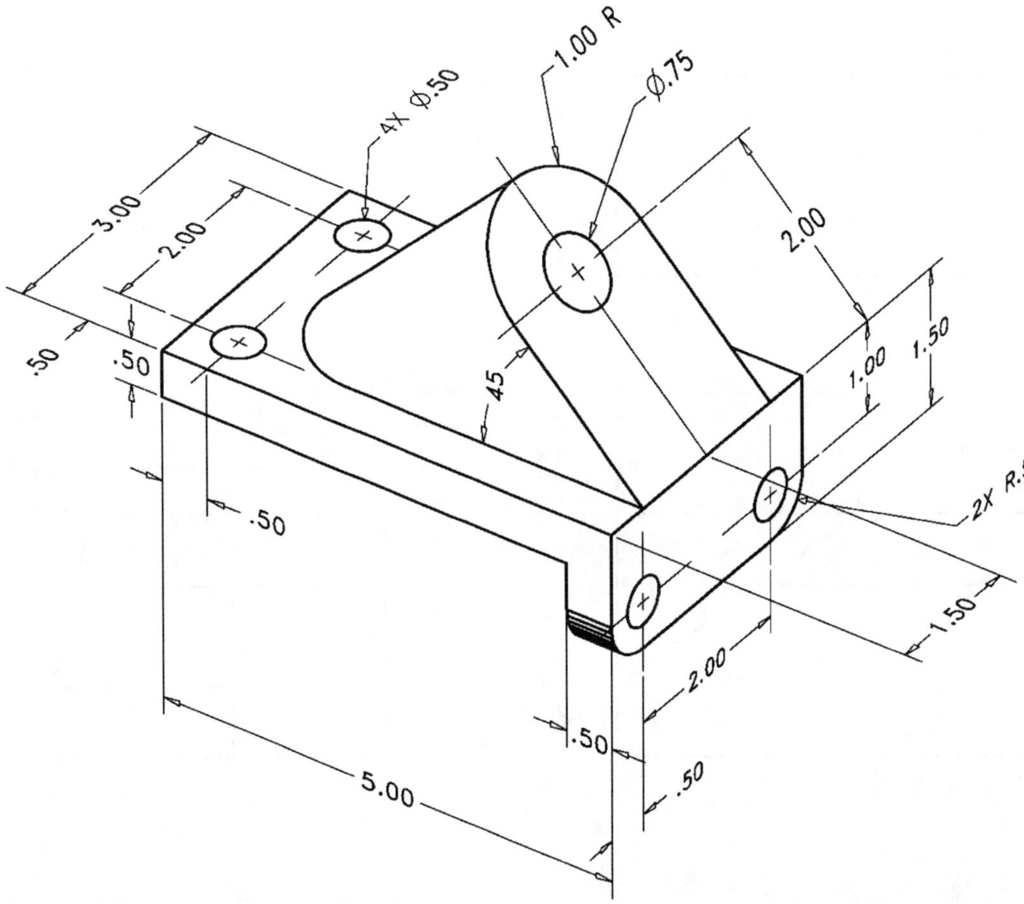

P16-6) Create detailed drawing (orthographic projection + dimensions) of the following object. Draw an auxiliary view that shows the angled surface true shape. Use partial views where appropriate.

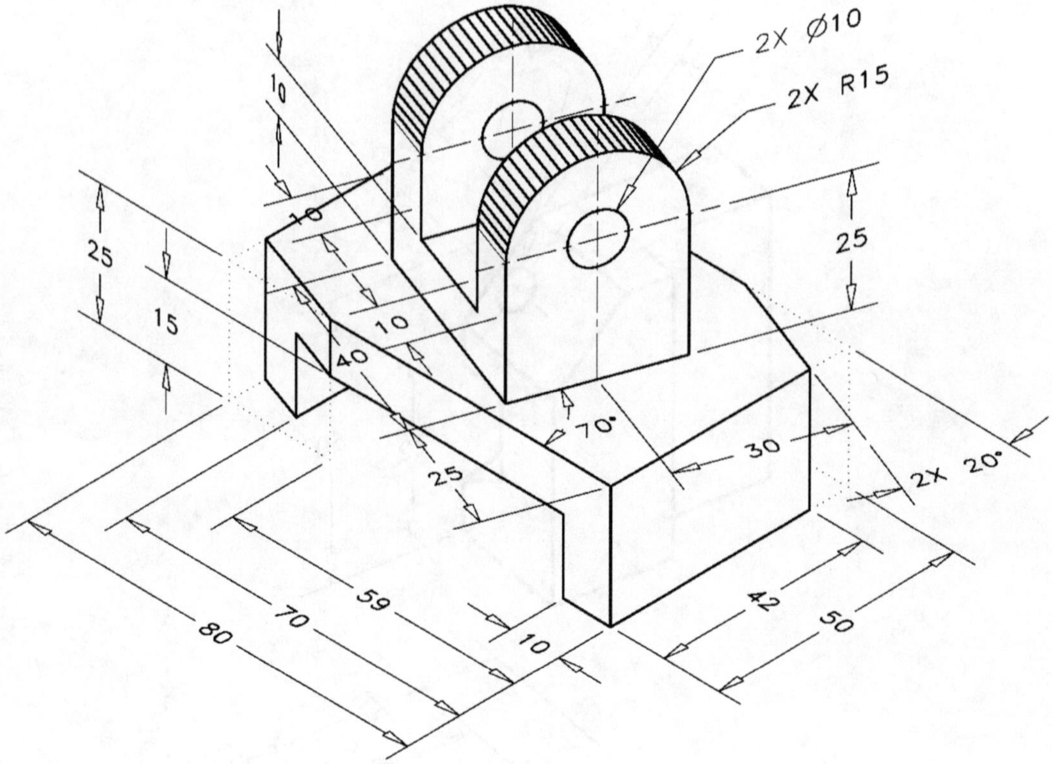

P16-7) Create detailed drawing (orthographic projection + dimensions) of the following object. Draw two auxiliary views that show the angled features true shape. Use partial views where appropriate.

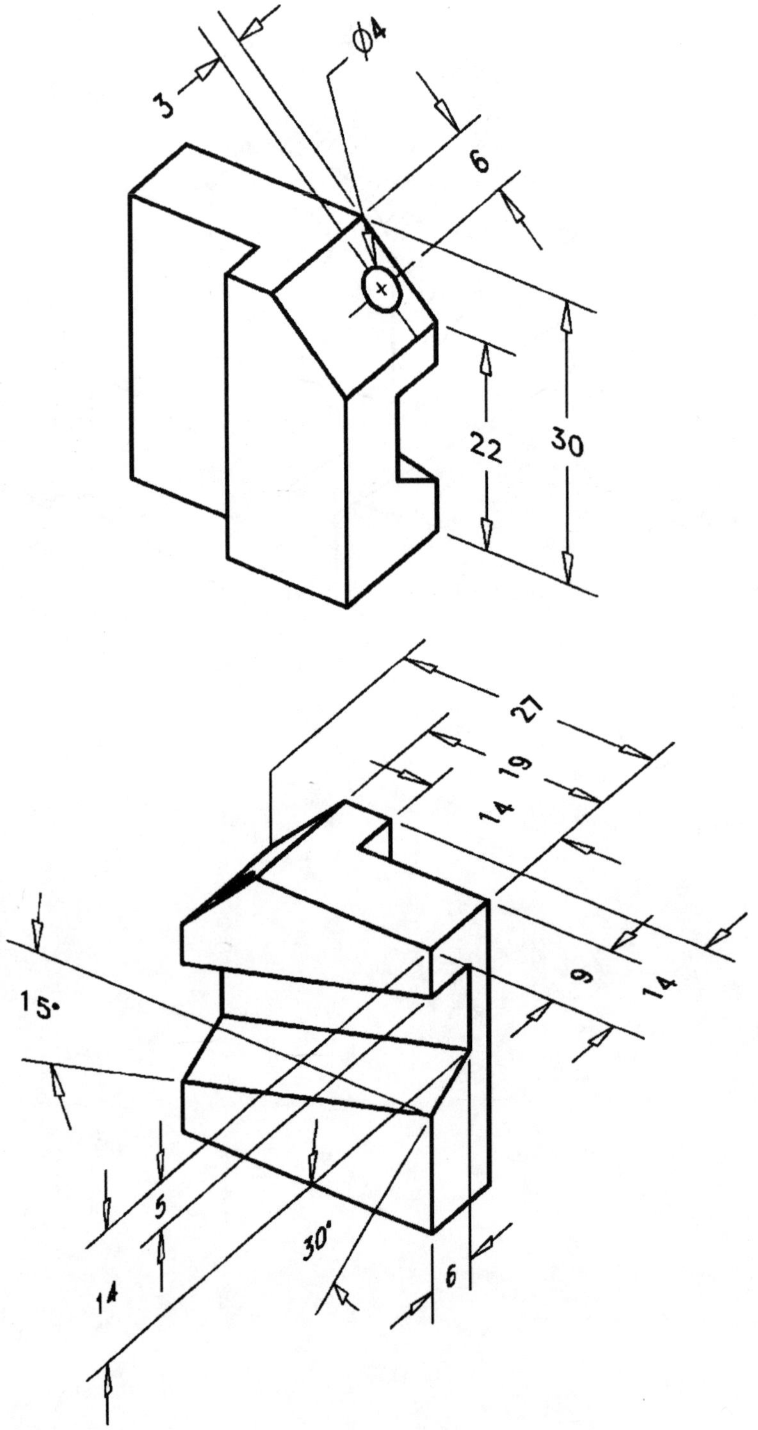

P16-8) Create detailed drawing (orthographic projection + dimensions) of the following object. Draw an auxiliary view that shows the angled feature true shape. Use partial views where appropriate.

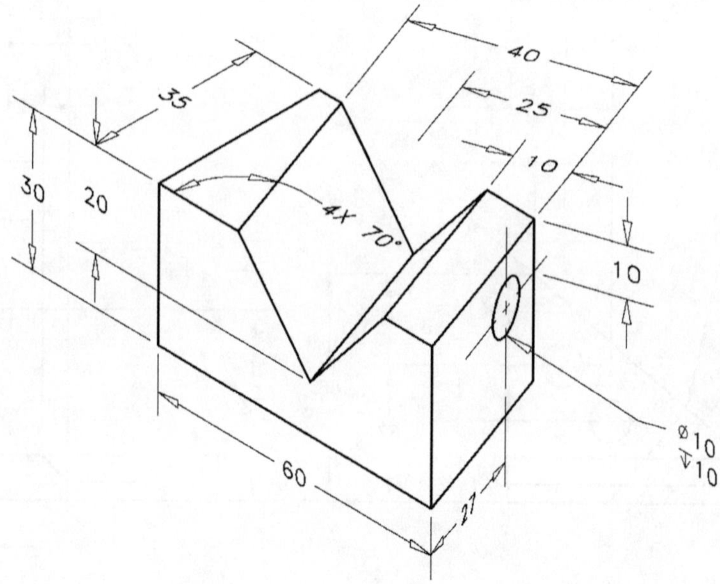

P16-9) Create detailed drawing (orthographic projection + dimensions) of the following object. Draw an auxiliary view that shows the angled surface true shape. Use partial views where appropriate.

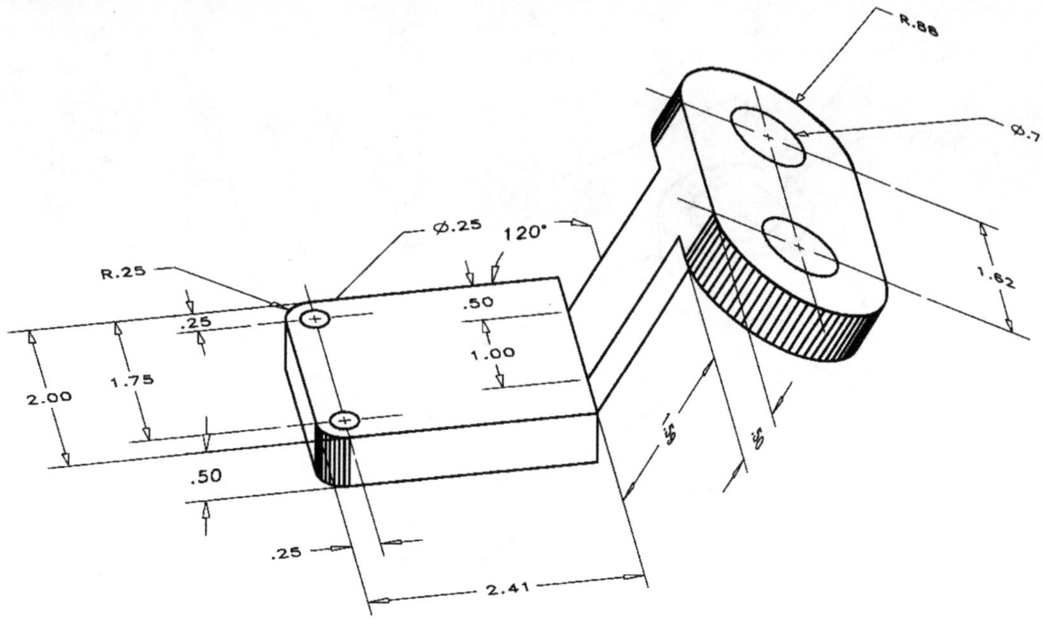

P16-10) Create an orthographic projection of the following object. Draw an auxiliary view that shows the angled surface true shape. Use partial views where appropriate.

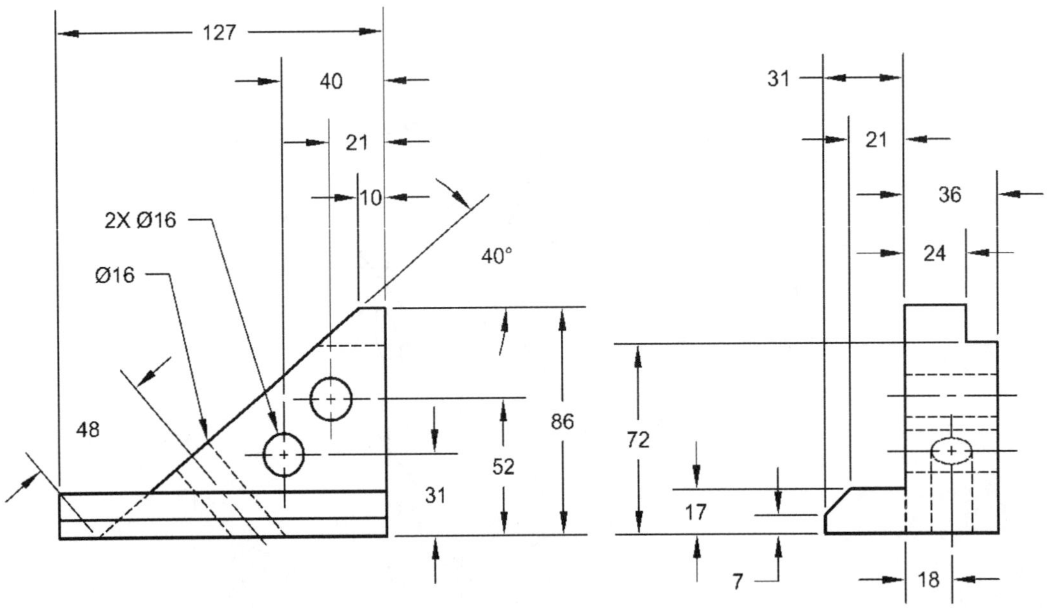

P16-11) Create detailed drawing (orthographic projection + dimensions) of the following object. Draw the three standard views. Place surface roughness symbols on all finished surfaces. Note that all fillets and rounds are R3 unless otherwise specified.

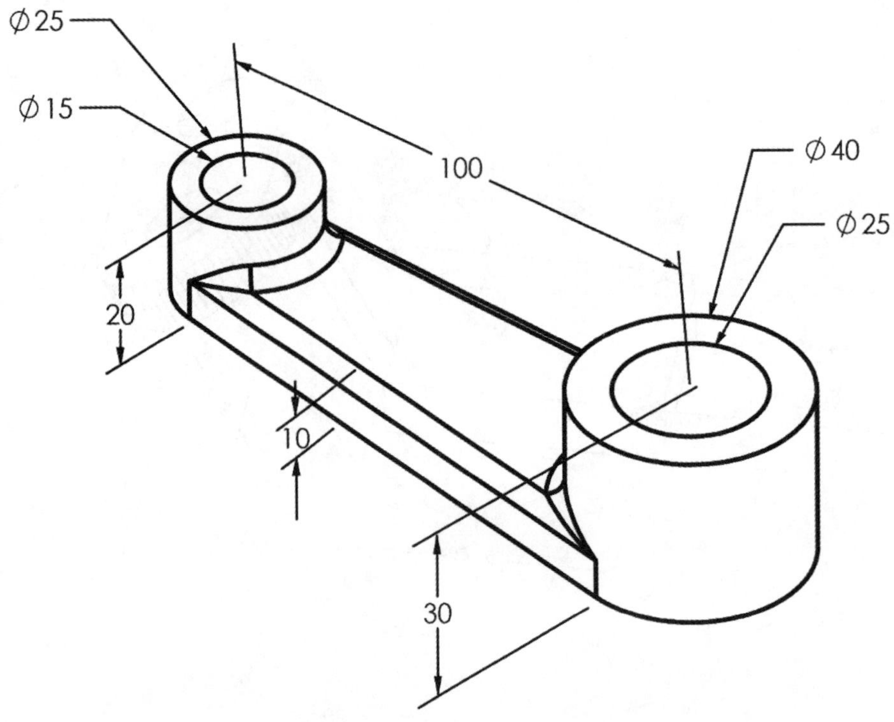

P16-12) Create detailed drawing (orthographic projection + dimensions) of the following object. Draw the three standard views. Place surface roughness symbols on all finished surfaces.

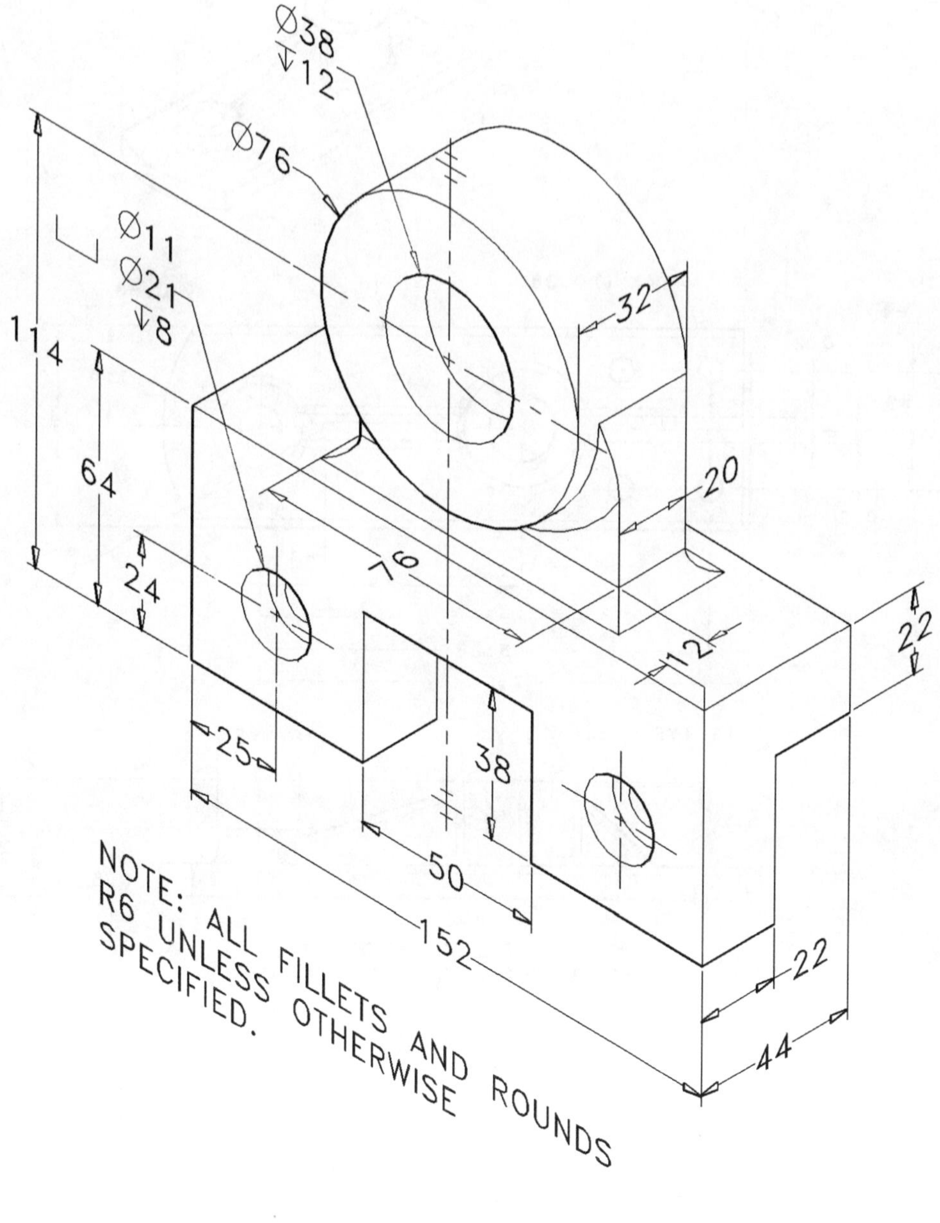

P16-13) Create an orthographic projection of the following object. Draw the three standard views. Place surface roughness symbols on all finished surfaces.

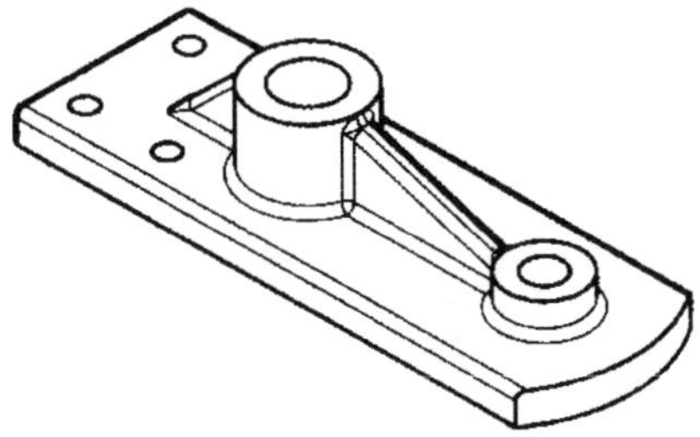

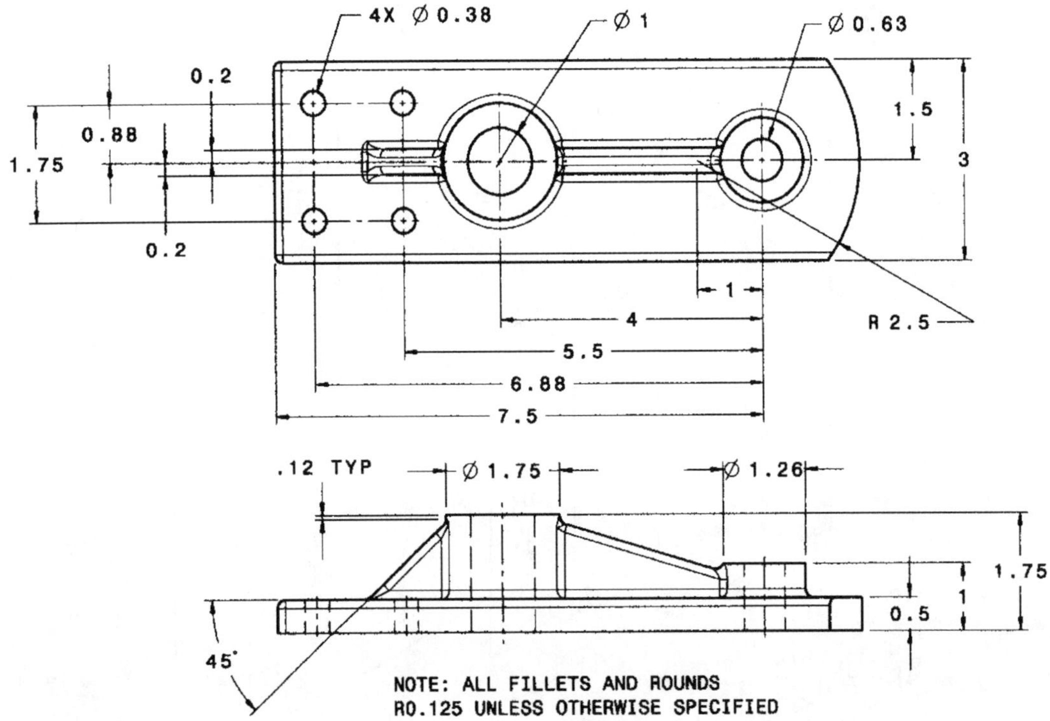

P16-14) Create detailed drawing of the following object. Draw and dimension the required views. Place surface roughness symbols on all finished surfaces.

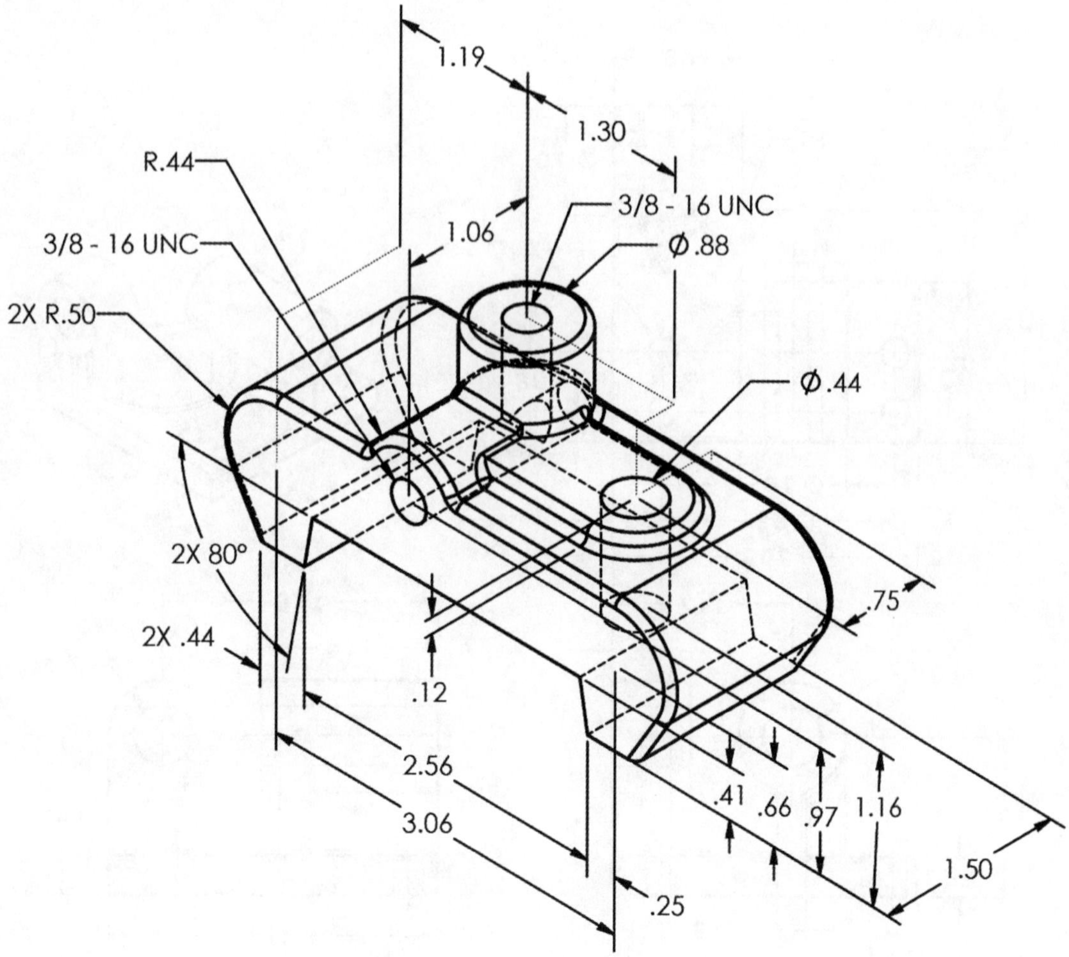

P16-15) Create an orthographic projection of the following object. Draw the three standard views. Place surface roughness symbols on all finished surfaces.

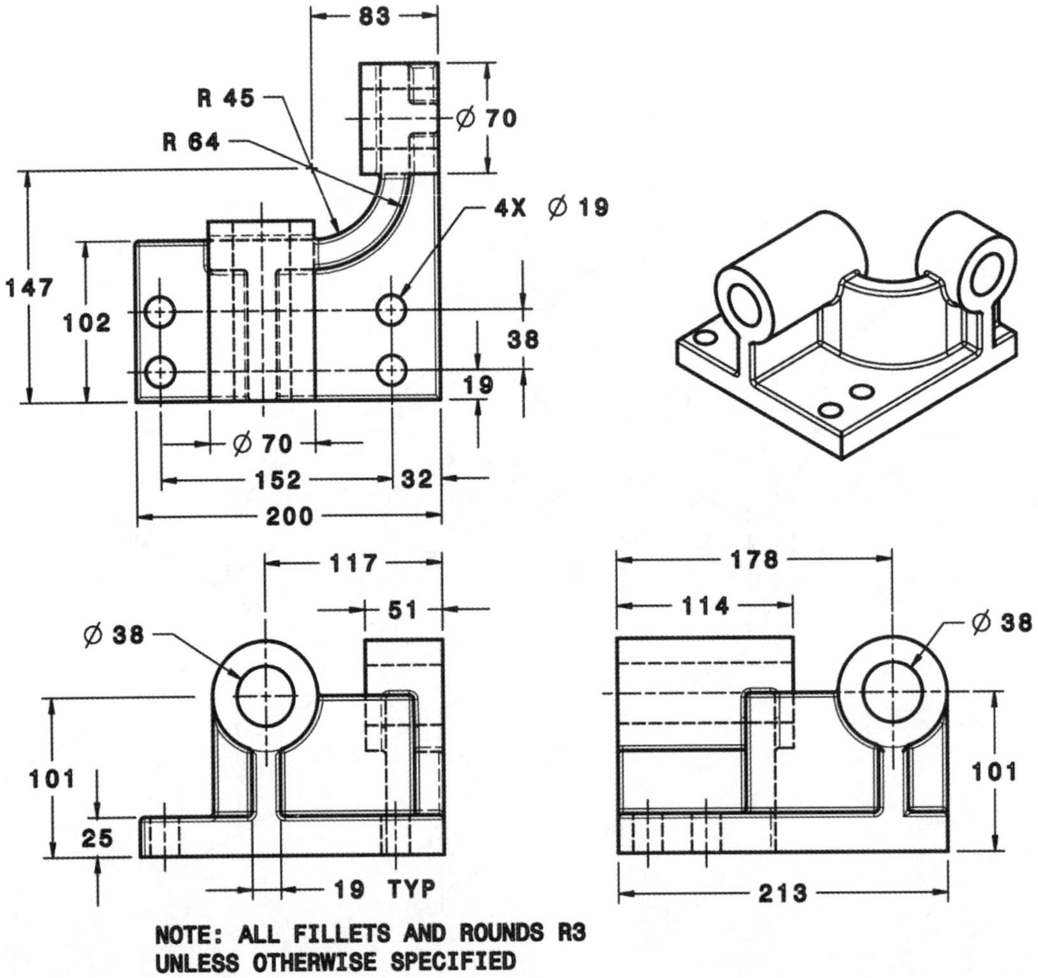

SP16-1) Draw the front, top, and right side view of the given part. Then draw a complete auxiliary view to show the cylinder and cutout true size.

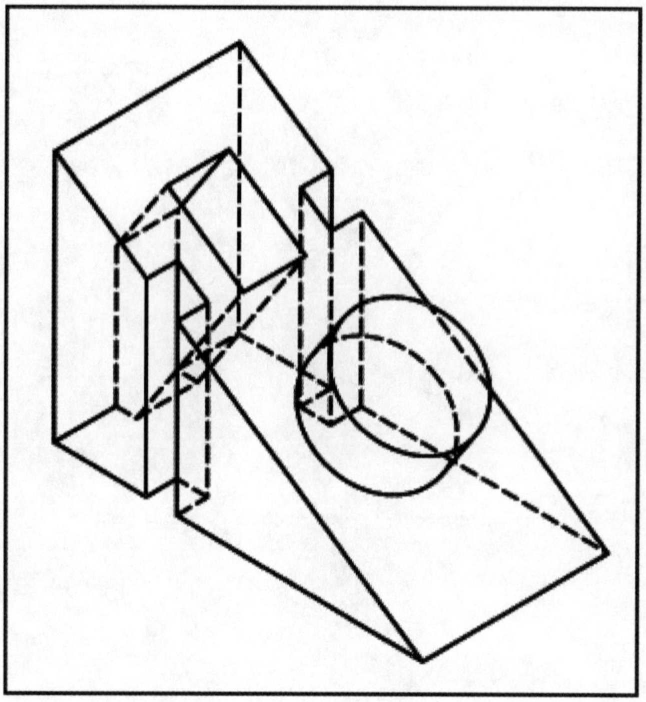

NOTES:

CHAPTER 17

CREATING ADVANCED DRAWINGS IN AUTOCAD®

CHAPTER OUTLINE

CHAPTER SUMMARY

In this chapter you will learn how to create views in AutoCAD® using advanced drawing techniques. These views and techniques include removed and revolved views, detail views, partial views, auxiliary views, castings that include surface texture symbols, and views that include weld symbols.

17.1) INTRODUCTION

Views that are not part of the normal principal views will be covered in this chapter. These views include removed and revolved views, detail views, partial views, and auxiliary views. For the most part, with the exception of auxiliary views, these are not in the projection path of the parent view. Auxiliary views are projected from the parent view, but at an angle. Along with non-standard views, this chapter will cover symbols that are included in castings and weldments.

17.2) REMOVED AND REVOLVED ORTHOGRAPHIC VIEWS

Examples of removed and revolved views are given in the *Advanced Drawing Techniques* chapter. Basically, these are views that are removed from the normal projection path. They may also be scaled and/or rotated. In AutoCAD®, these views should be drawn in the projection path at normal scale to begin with. Then, they can be removed, scaled, and rotated as necessary using the commands **Move**, **SCale**, and **ROtate**.

17.3) DETAIL AND PARTIAL VIEWS

A detail view is a projected view generated from an existing drawing view. A detail view shows a specific portion of the drawing view (it was generated from), at an enlarged scale. Examples of detail views are given in the *Advanced Drawing Techniques* chapter.

AutoCAD® does have the ability to create detail views from model document using the command VIEWDETAIL. A model document is an associative 2-D drawing created from either an AutoCAD® 3-D or Inventor® model. However, AutoCAD® cannot create, automatically, a detail view from a manually created orthographic projection.

To create a detail view of a manually created orthographic projection, simply copy the view, draw a circle around the portion you wish to detail, and then use the **TRim** and **SCale** commands to create the view. You will also want to indicate the portion to be detailed in the original view and label both the circle in the original view and the detail view.

A partial view only shows some of the features of the complete view. Examples of partial views are given in the *Advanced Drawing Techniques* chapter. Depending on the partial view, useful AutoCAD® commands are **TRim** and **Arc**, where the arc is used as the break line.

17.4) AUXILIARY VIEW TUTORIAL

The objective of this tutorial is to draw an orthographic projection with an auxiliary view. Objects often contain inclined surfaces. When the features on these inclined surfaces are not shown true size in any of the principal views (Front, Top, Right Side), an auxiliary view is used. The projection plane used to create the auxiliary view is not vertical or horizontal like those used to create the principal views, but it is parallel to the inclined surface. This allows the features on the inclined surface to be shown true size in the auxiliary view. We will draw the principal views of the orthographic projection in the usual way. The auxiliary view will be created by rotating the user coordinate system.

17.4.1) Drawing the orthographic projection

1)  ***auxiliary_student_2018.dwg*** and  **Auxiliary Tut.dwg**. Use the orthographic projection shown as a guide throughout this tutorial. Important projectors are shown.

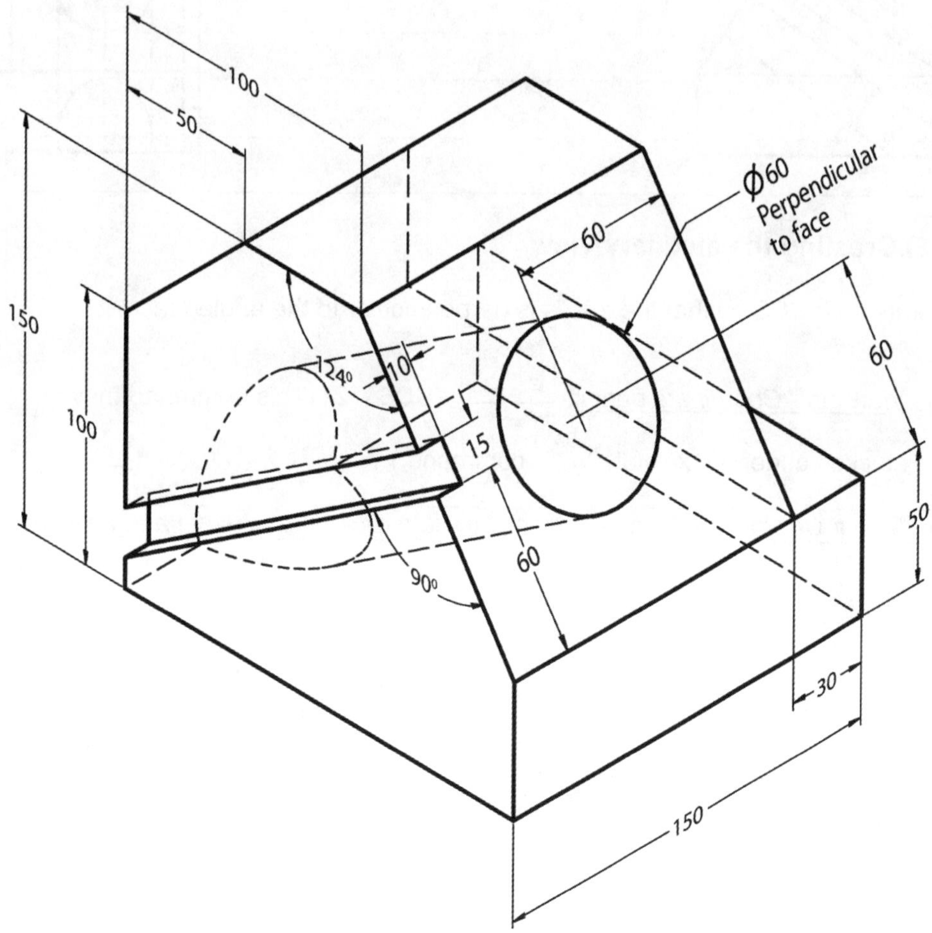

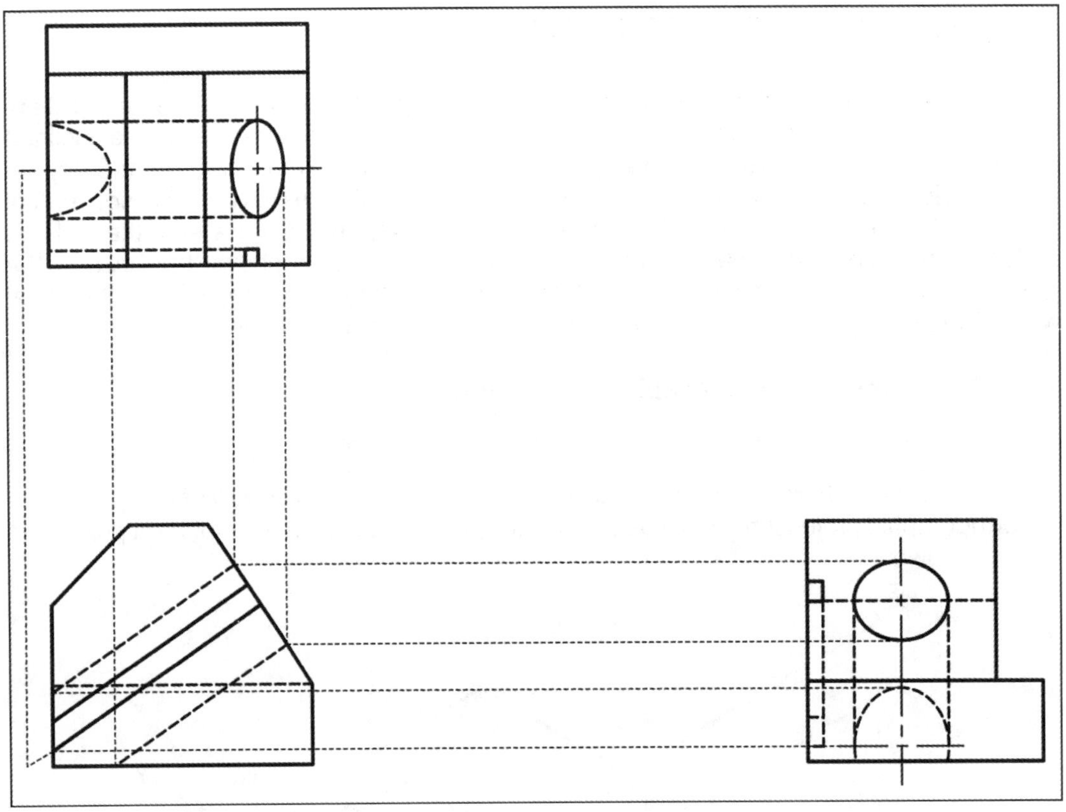

17.4.2) Creating the auxiliary view

1) Rotate your UCS so that the *x* axis is perpendicular to the angled face.

   a) <u>*View* tab - *Coordinate* panel:</u> 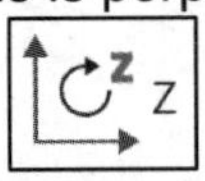 (**UCS – Z**) (This command may be stacked under the x-rotate  command.)

Note: If your *Coordinate* panel is not shown, right click on any panel and activate it.

   b) `Specify rotation angle about Z axis <90>:` **34**

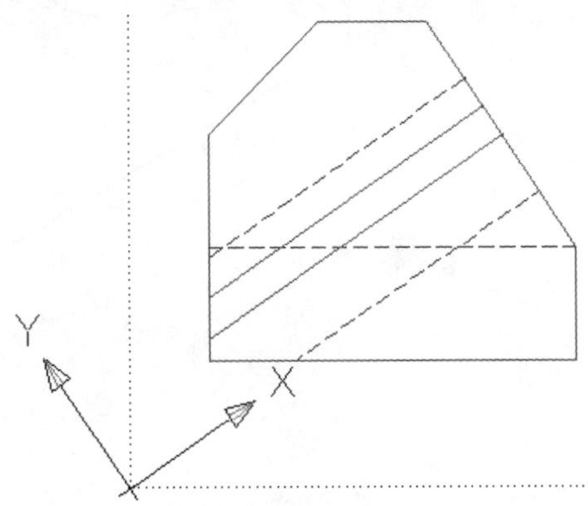

2) In the ***Construction*** layer, draw a set of horizontal construction lines (**XLine**) off of every edge and boundary of the front view.

3) Draw a **Line** that is **NEARest** the bottom projector and **PERpendicular** to the top projector.

4) **OFFSET** the line by **150 mm** in the direction shown.

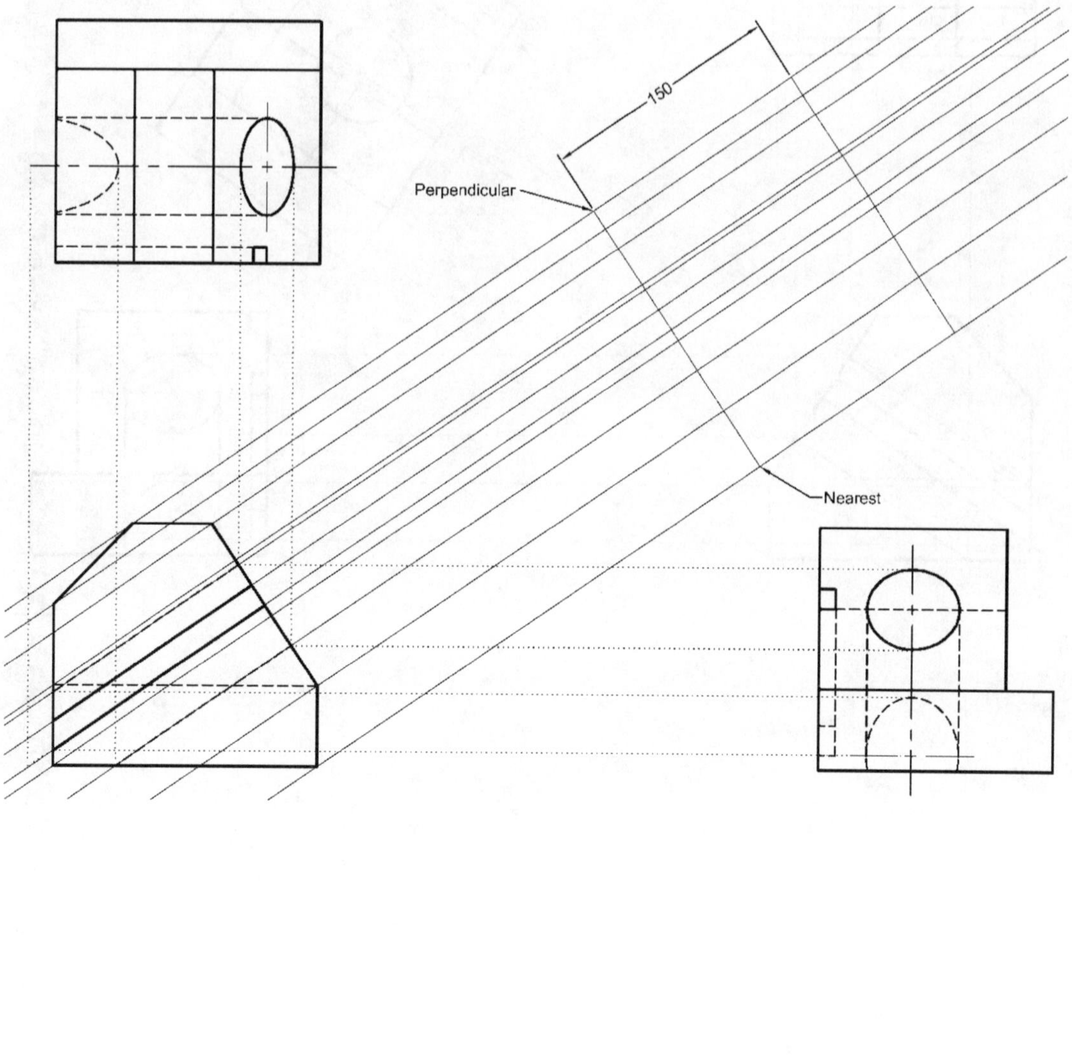

5) Fill in the features of the auxiliary view. Create construction lines where necessary.

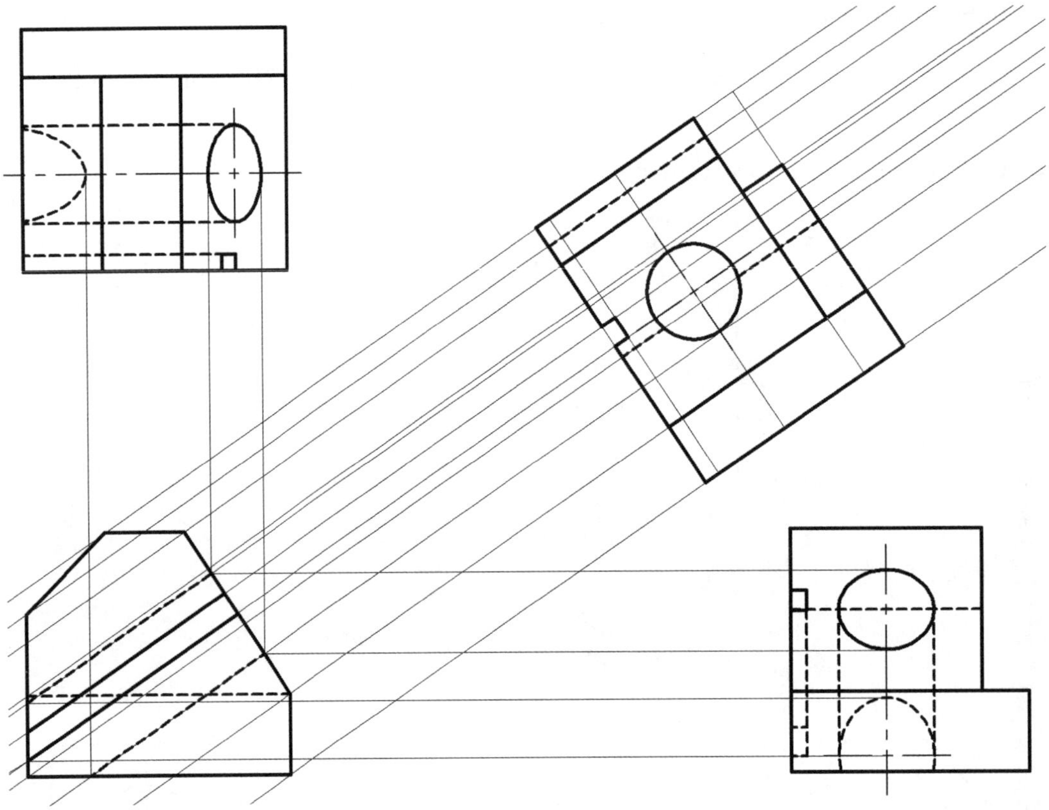

6) In your layout space, insert your metric title block, fill in the appropriate information, set your viewport scale to the appropriate scale and print.

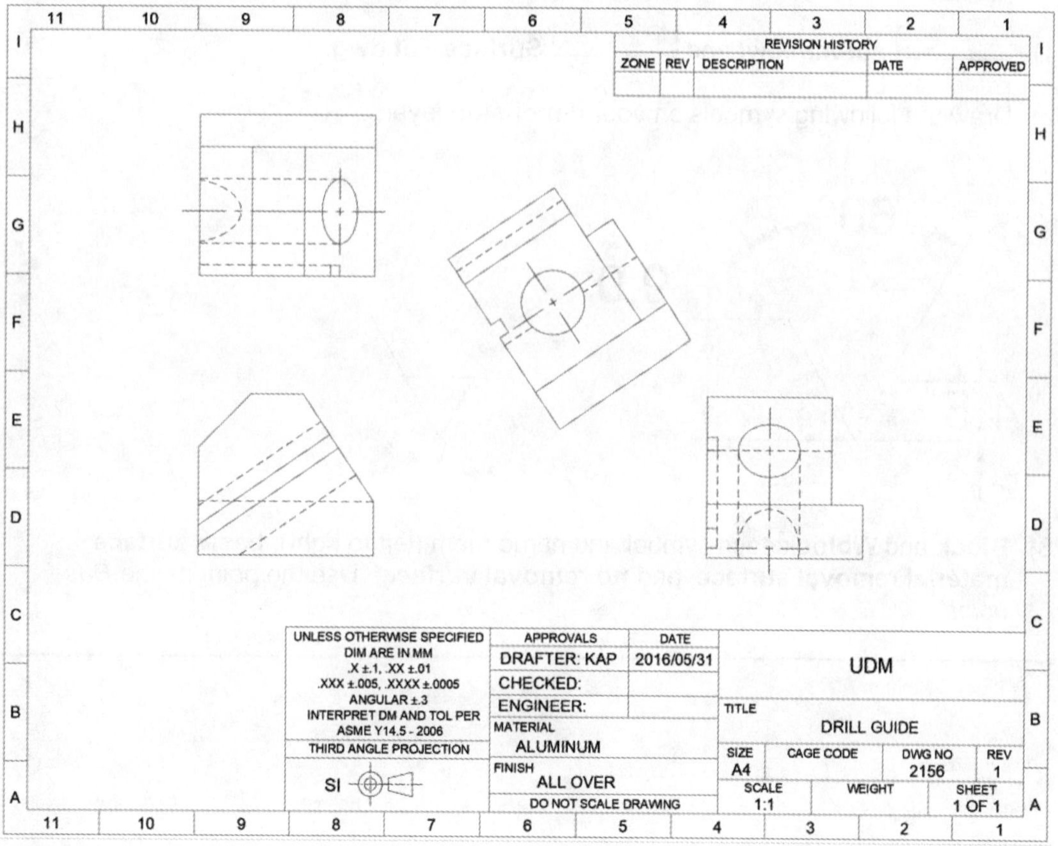

17.5) SURFACE TEXTURE TUTORIAL

1) 

set-mm.dwt and 

Surface Tut.dwg.

2) Draw the following symbols on your **dimension** layer.

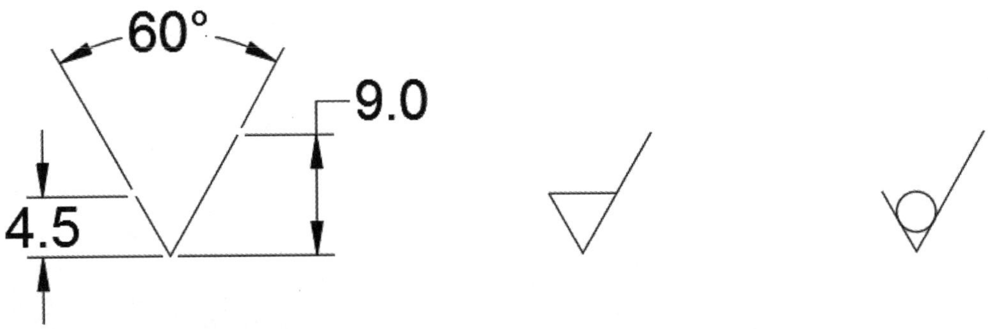

3) **Block** and **Wblock** each symbol and name them (left to right), **basic surface**, **material removal surface**, and **no removal surface**. Use the point as the *Base point*.

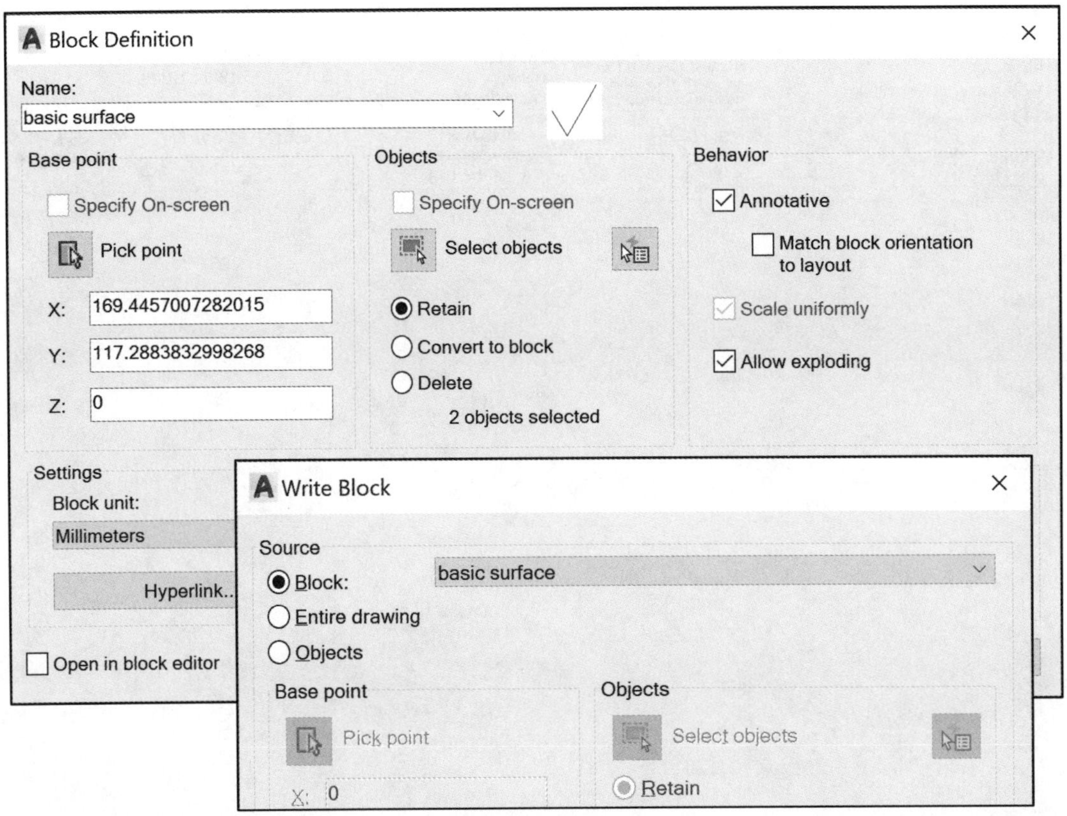

4) 

casting_2018.dwg and 

Casting tut.dwg. Notice that there are two drawings within this file. The drawing on the left represents the part right out of the casting process. No machining has been done. The drawing on the right shows the part after machining.

CASTING BEFORE MACHINING
(Phantom lines indicate surfaces to be machined.)

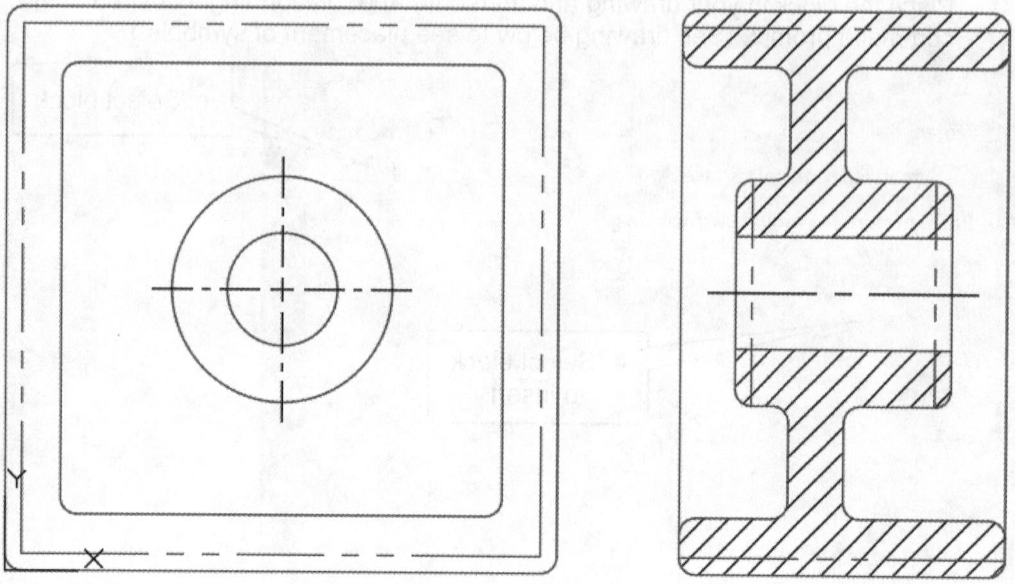

5) On the drawing on the right, **insert** your ***material removal surface*** symbol on the machined surfaces shown in the figure.

   a. <u>*Home* Ribbon – *Block* tab:</u>  or <u>Command prompt:</u> **Insert**

   b. Select **Blocks from Library...**
   c. Select the **material removal** block on your computer.
   d. Select the **Insertion Point** and **Rotation** check boxes.
   e. Click on the **material removal** block.
   f. Place the block in your drawing and then enter the rotation angle desired in the command prompt. (See drawing below to see placement of symbols.)

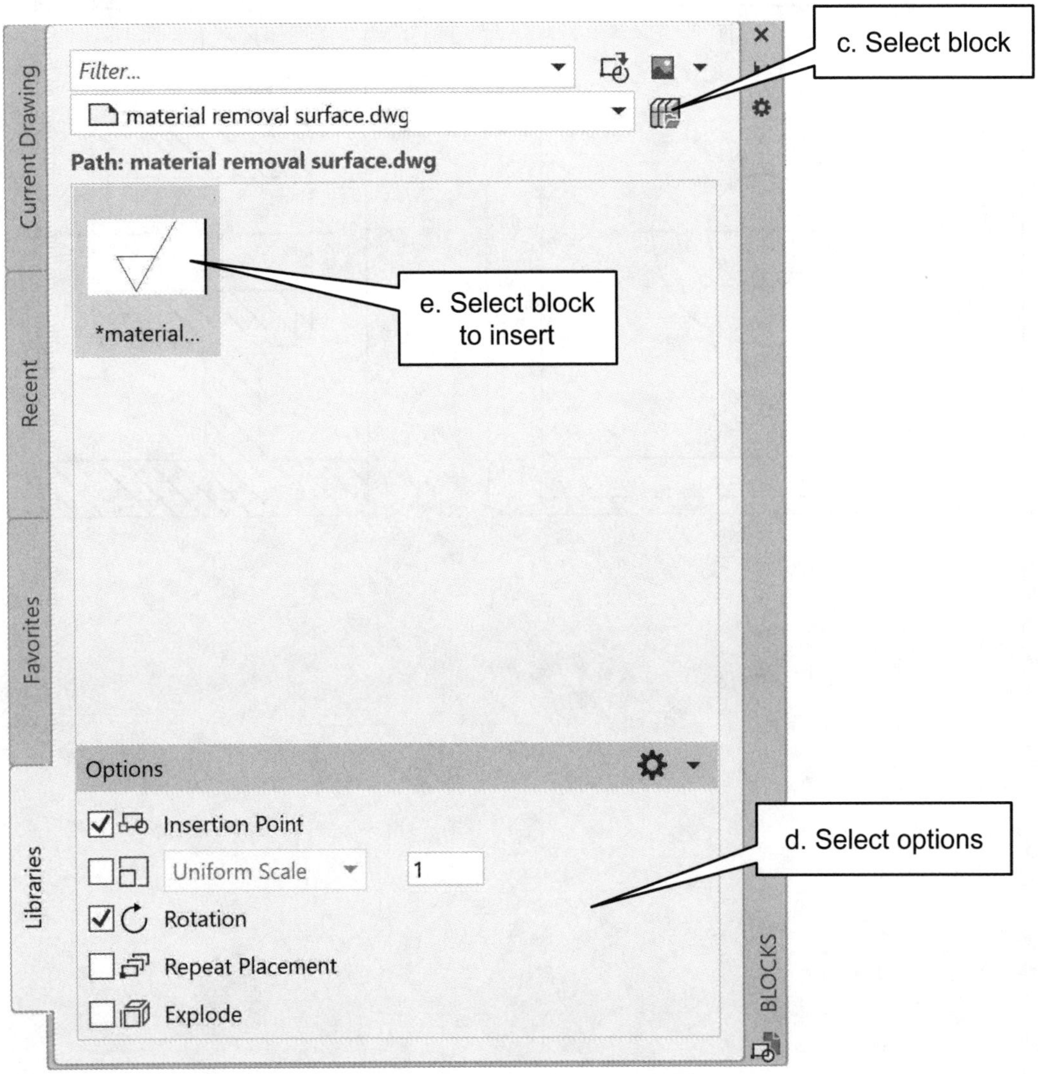

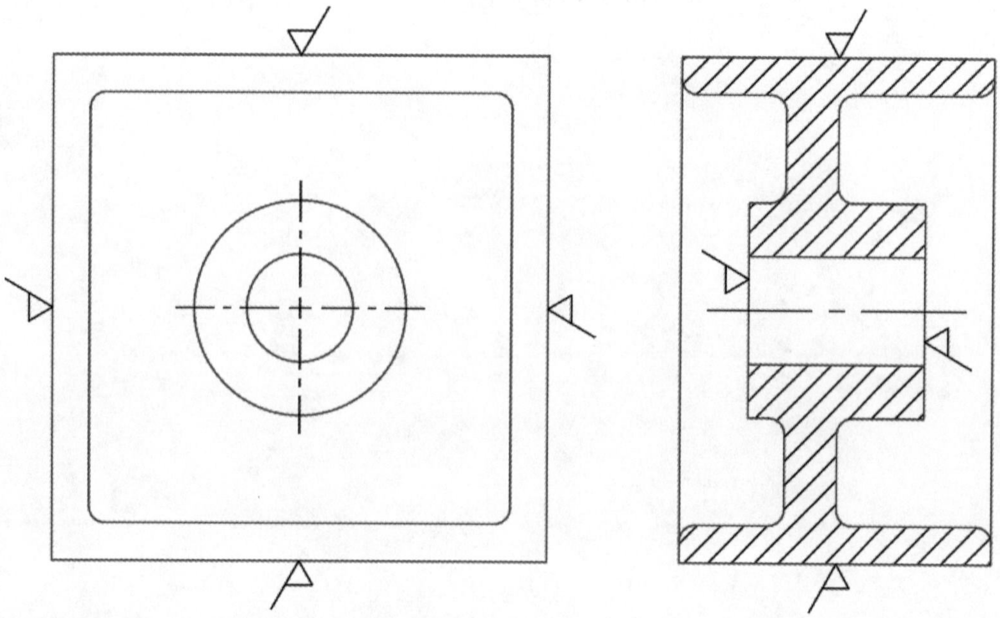

6) **Save** and **Print** the machined drawing.

NOTES:

ADVANCED DRAWINGS IN AUTOCAD PROBLEMS

P17-1) Create an orthographic projection of the following object. Draw an auxiliary view that shows the angled surface's true shape. Use partial views where appropriate. Dimensions given in inches.

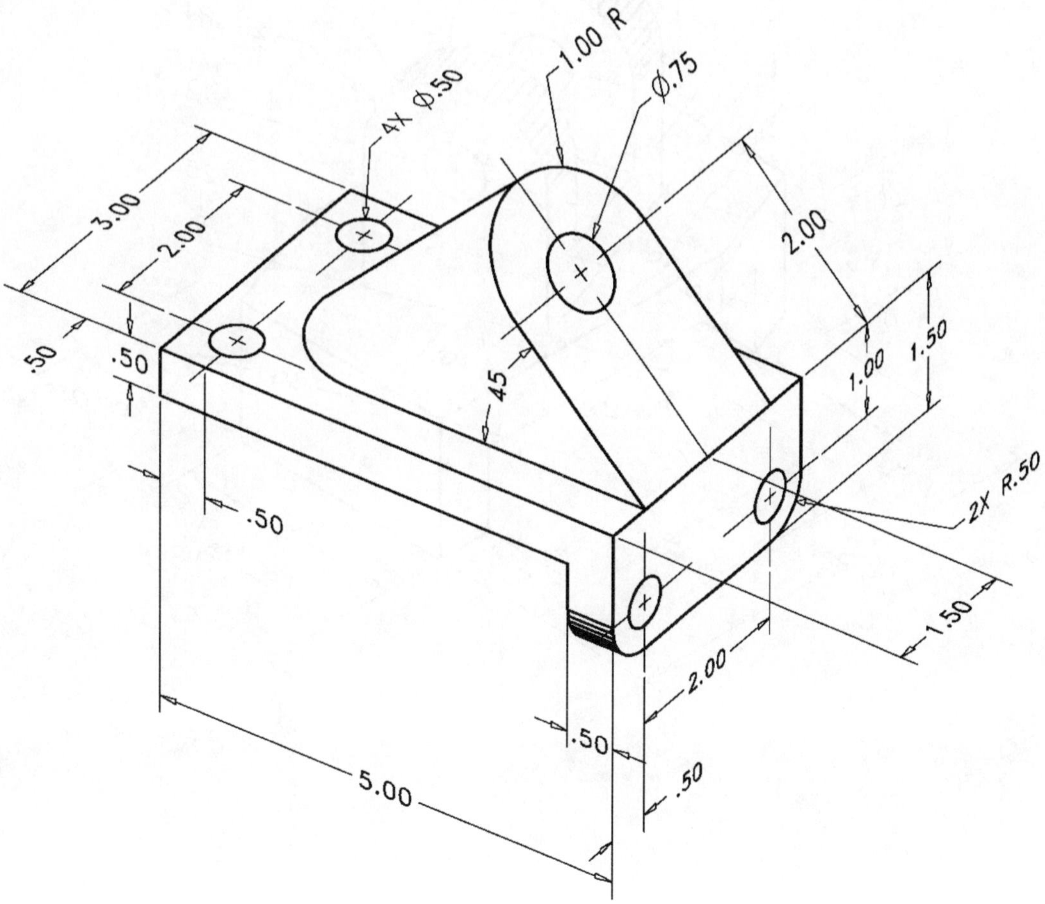

P17-2) Create an orthographic projection of the following object. Draw an auxiliary view that shows the angled surface's true shape. Use partial views where appropriate. Dimensions given in millimeters.

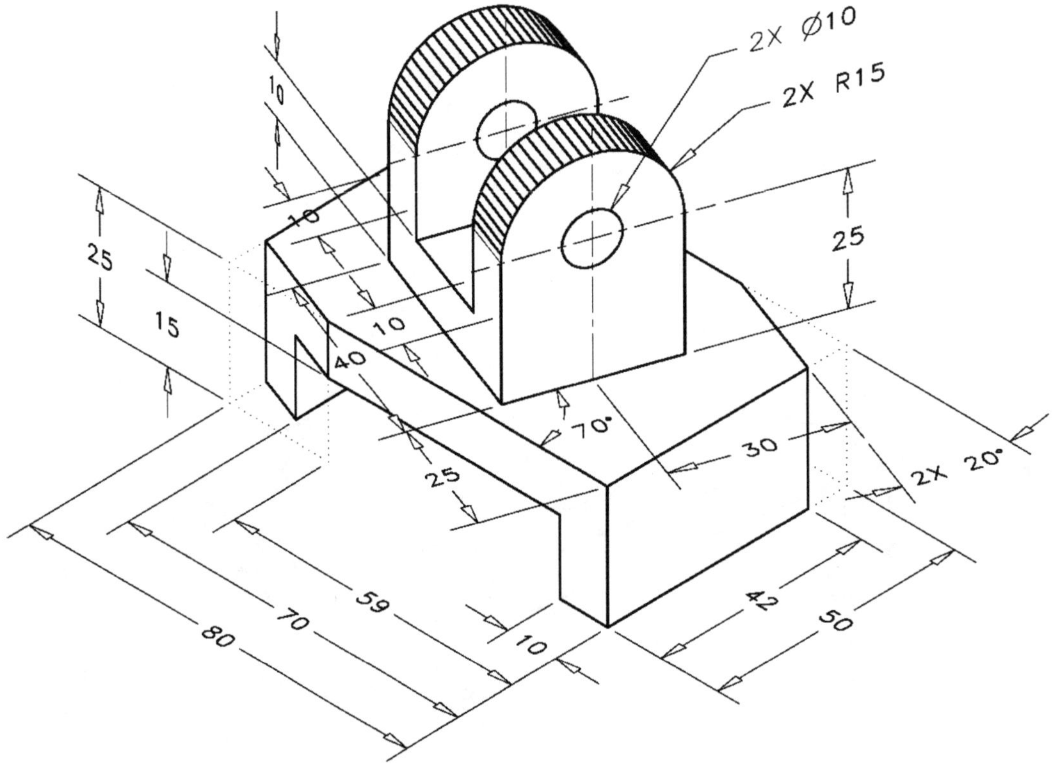

P17-3) Create an orthographic projection of the following object. Draw two auxiliary views that show the angled feature's true shape. Use partial views where appropriate. Dimensions given in millimeters.

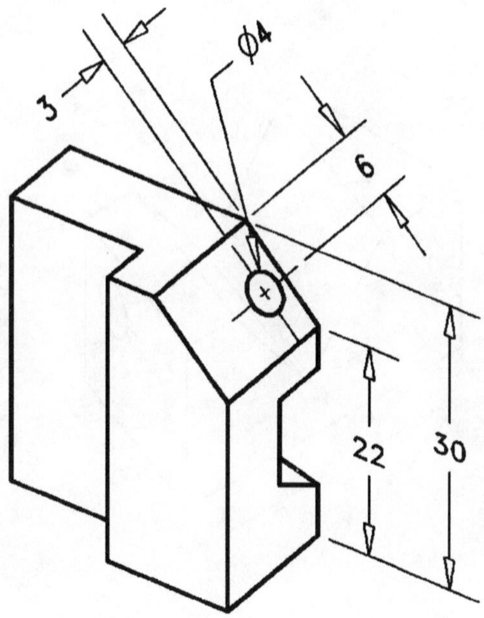

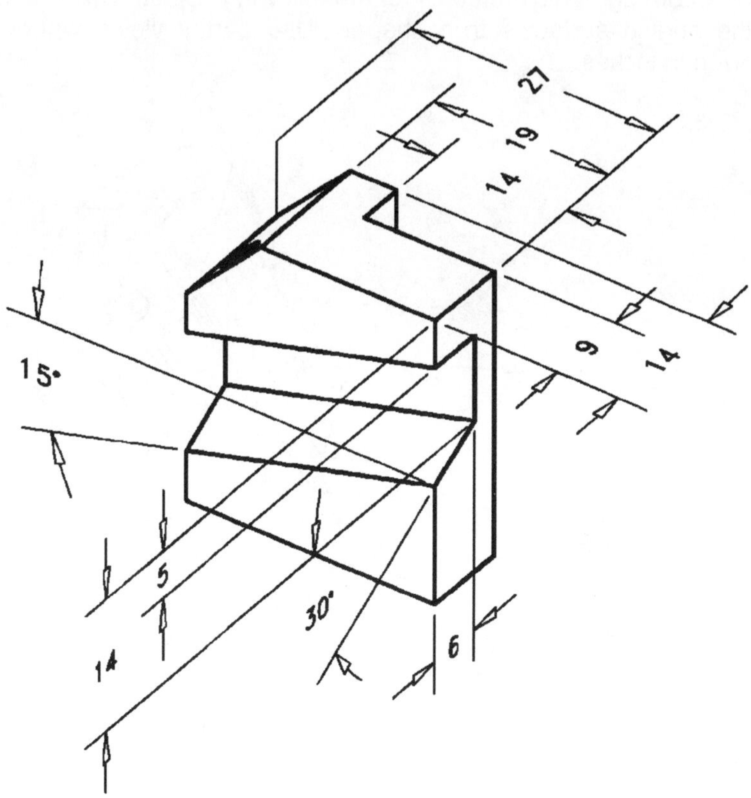

P17-4) Create an orthographic projection of the following object. Draw an auxiliary view that shows the angled feature's true shape. Use partial views where appropriate. Dimensions given in millimeters.

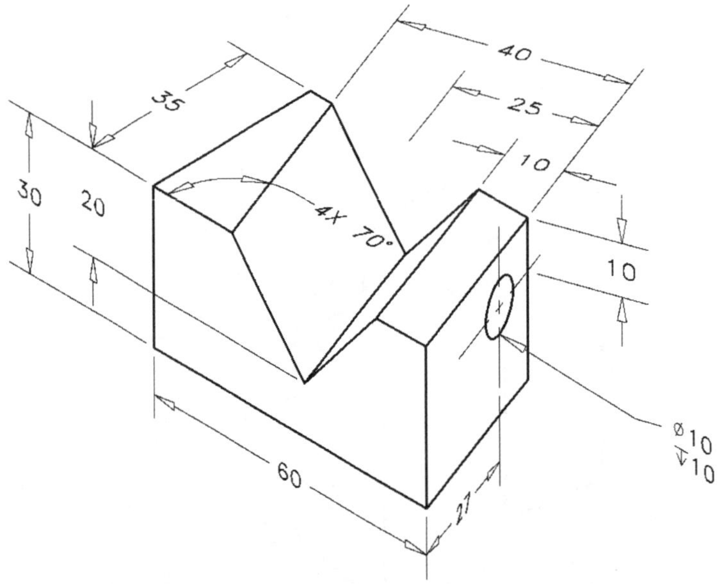

P17-5) Create an orthographic projection of the following object. Draw an auxiliary view that shows the angled surface's true shape. Use partial views where appropriate. Dimensions given in inches.

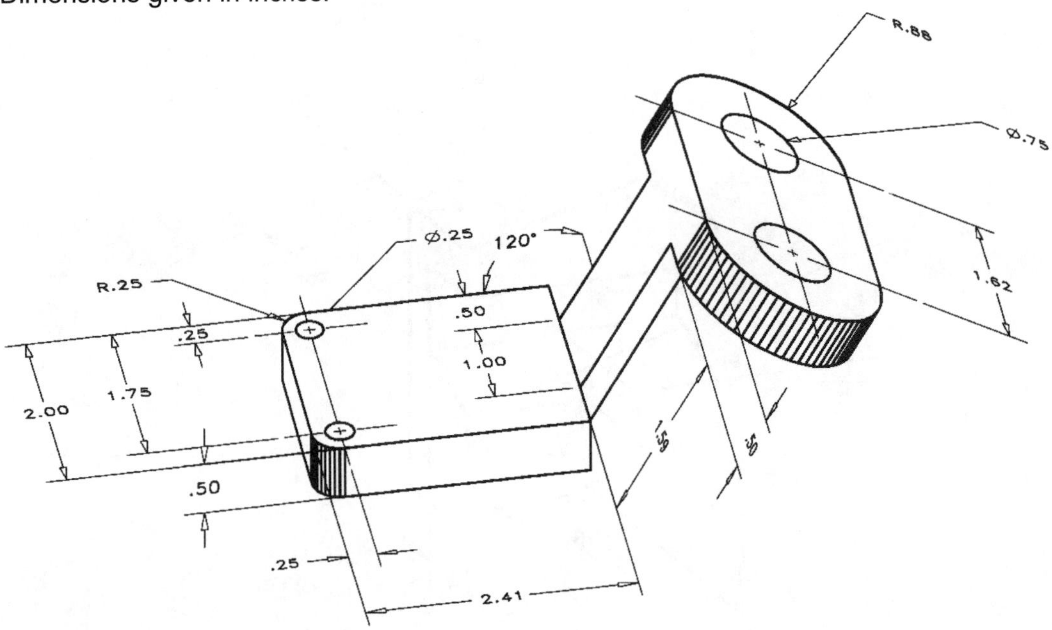

P17-6) Create an orthographic projection of the following object. Draw an auxiliary view that shows the angled surface's true shape. Use partial views where appropriate. Dimensions given in inches.

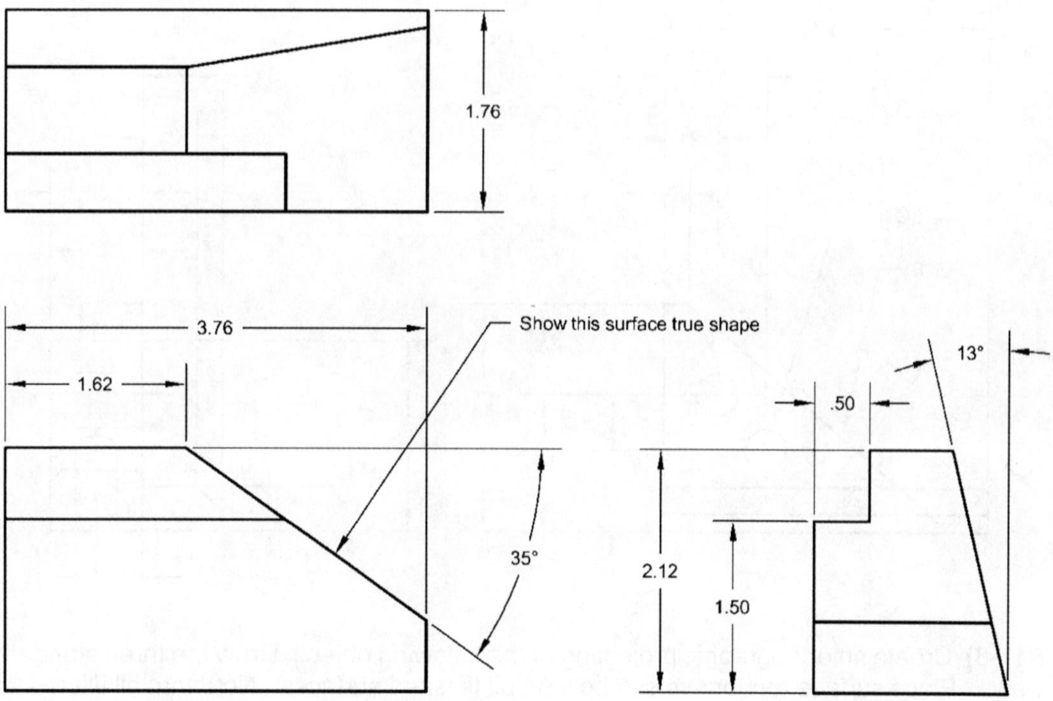

P17-7) Create an orthographic projection of the following object. Draw an auxiliary view that shows the angled surface's true shape. Use partial views where appropriate. Dimensions given in millimeters.

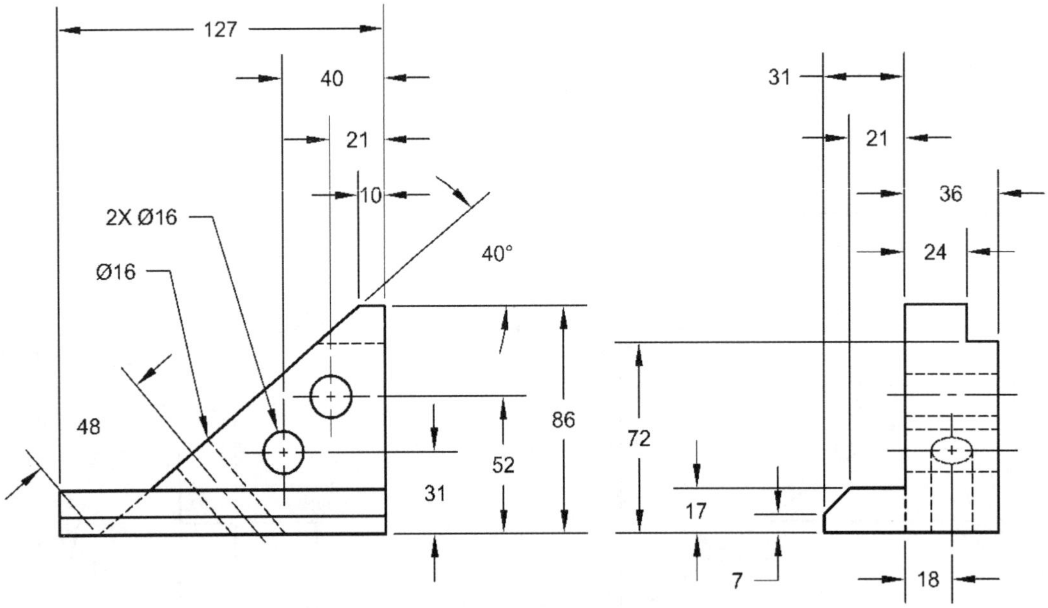

P17-8) Create an orthographic projection of the following object. Draw the three standard views. Place surface roughness symbols on all finished surfaces. Note that all fillets and rounds are R3 unless otherwise specified. Dimensions given in millimeters.

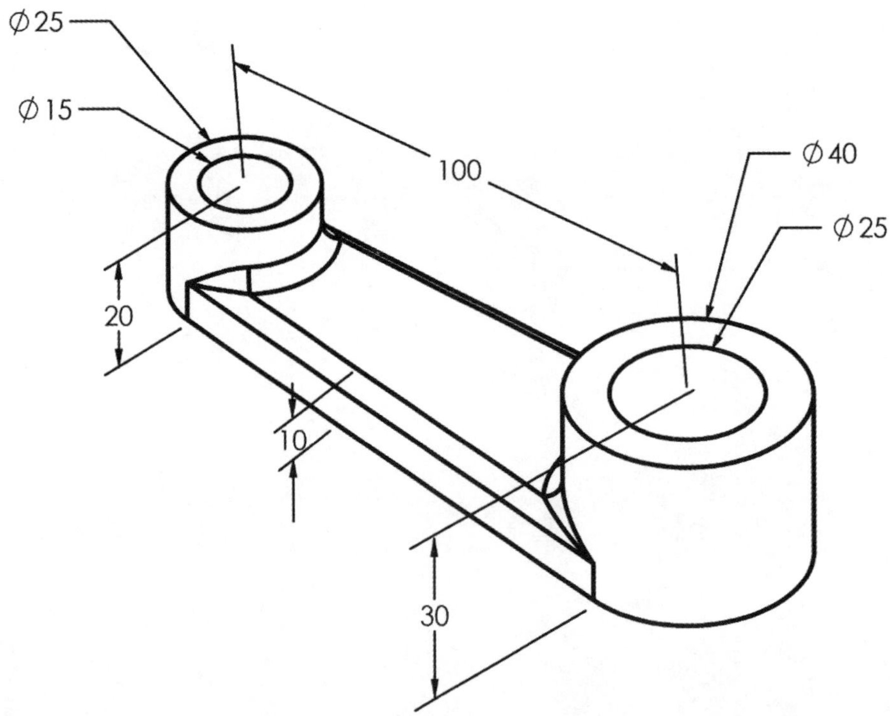

P17-9) Create an orthographic projection of the following object. Draw the three standard views. Place surface roughness symbols on all finished surfaces. Dimensions given in millimeters.

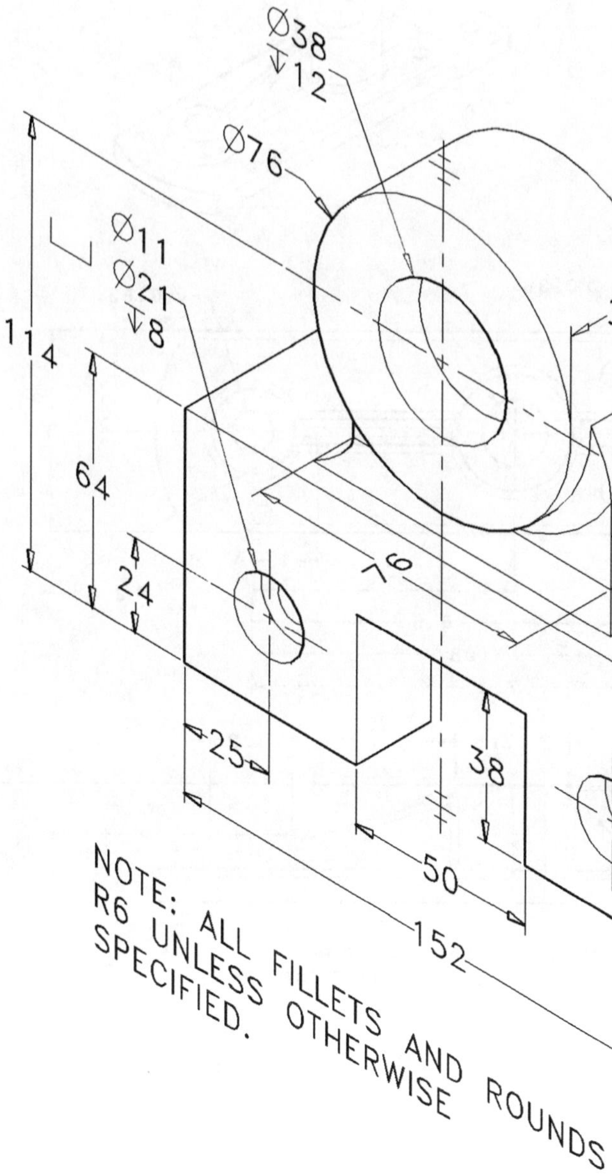

P17-10) Create an orthographic projection of the following object. Draw the three standard views. Place surface roughness symbols on all finished surfaces. Dimensions given in inches.

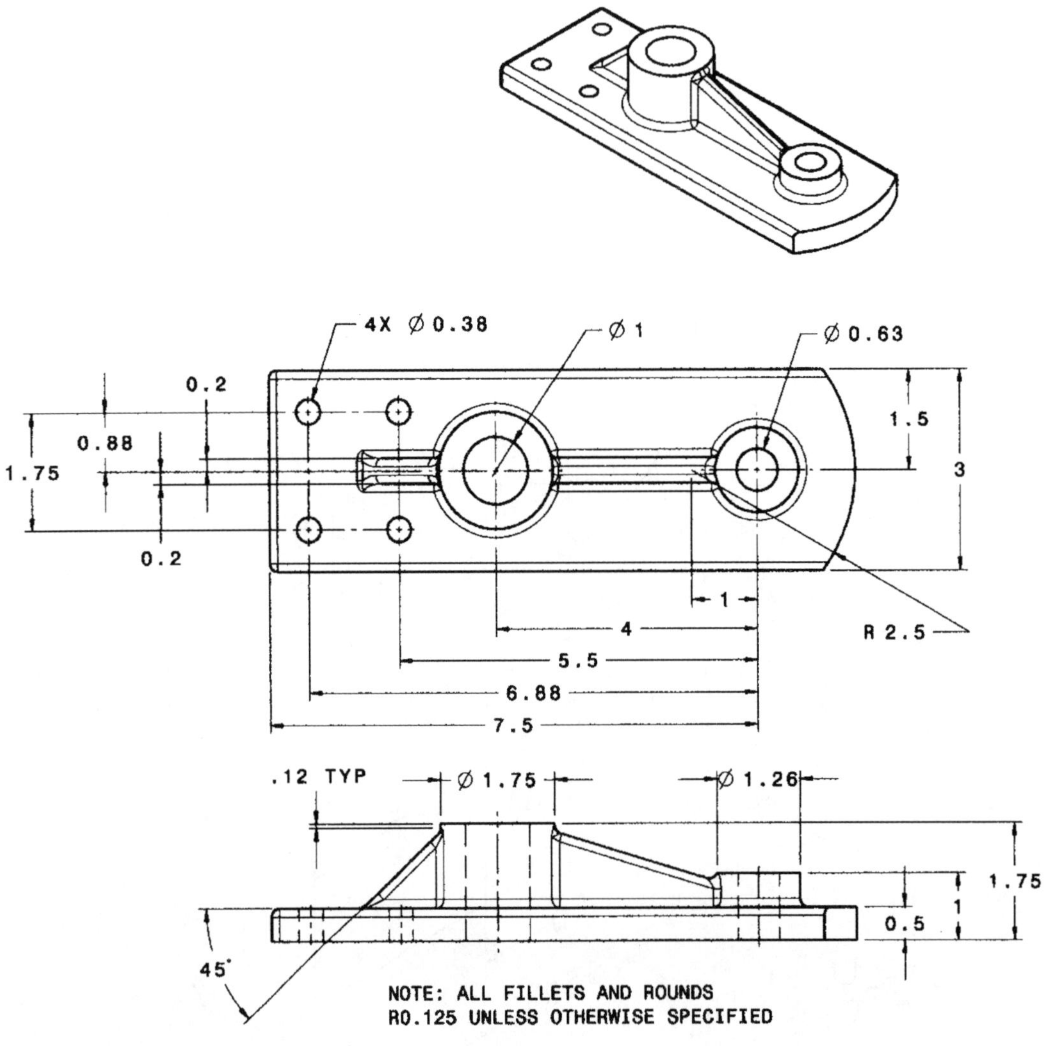

P17-11) Create an orthographic projection of the following object. Draw the three standard views. Place surface roughness symbols on all finished surfaces. Dimensions given in millimeters.

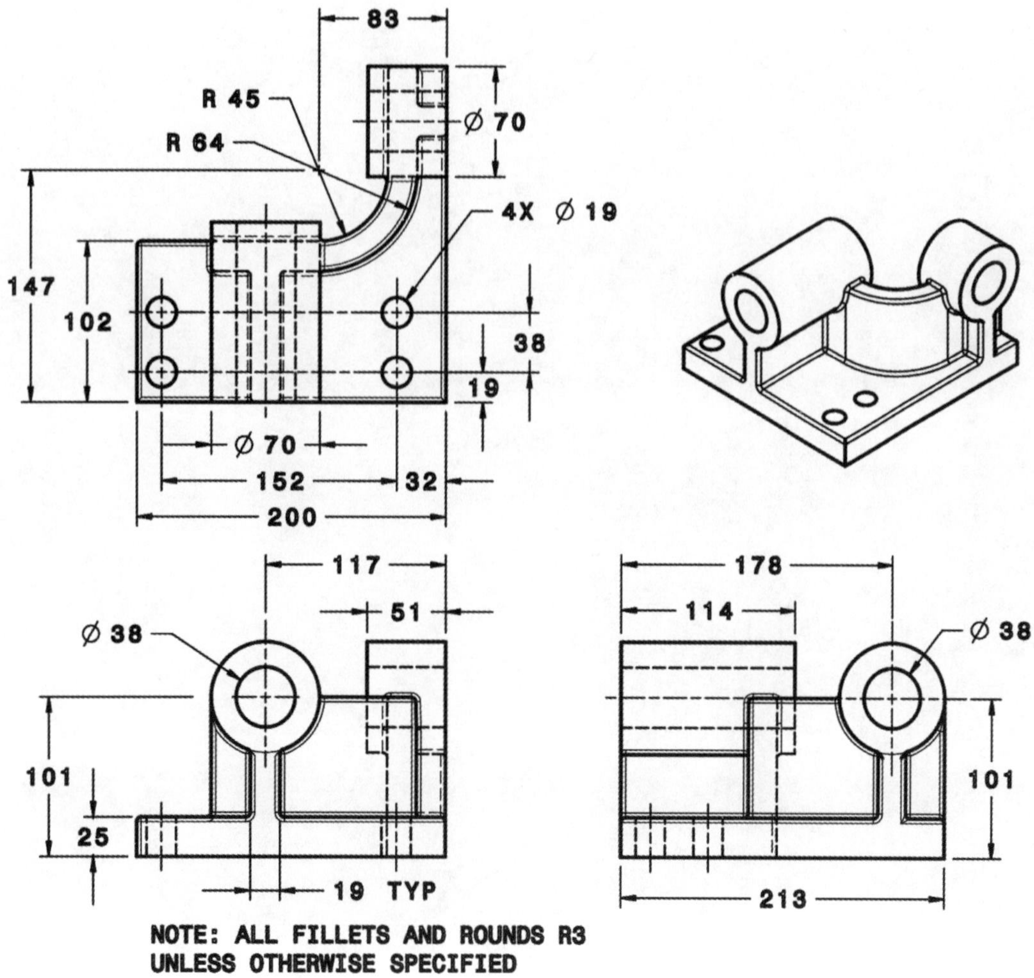

NOTES:

CHAPTER 18

READING TOLERANCES

CHAPTER OUTLINE

CHAPTER SUMMARY

In this chapter you will learn about tolerancing and how important this technique is to mass production. Tolerancing enables an engineer to design interchangeable or replacement parts. If a feature's size is toleranced, it is allowed to vary within a range of values or limits. It is no longer controlled by a single size. By the end of this chapter, you will be able to recognize the different types of tolerances and understand what they mean.

18.1) TOLERANCING AND INTERCHANGEABILITY

Tolerancing is dimensioning for interchangeability. An interchangeable part is a part that possesses functional and physical characteristics equivalent in performance to another part for which it is intended to replace. Features of an interchangeable part will have dimensions that are not a single value but a range of values that the part must fall within.

Tolerancing and interchangeability are an essential part of mass production. **Tolerances are necessary because it is impossible to manufacture parts without some variation.** A key component of mass production is the ability to buy replacement parts that are interchangeable or can substitute for the part being replaced.

Interchangeability is achieved by imposing tolerances or limits on a dimension. **A tolerance is the total amount of dimensional variation permitted.** In other words, it is the difference between the maximum and minimum size of the feature. Tolerancing enables similar parts to be near enough alike so that any one of them will fit properly into the assembly. For example, you would like to replace your mountain bike's seat post with a seat post that contains a shock absorber. You expect that all seat posts designed for mountain bikes will be interchangeable.

18.2) TOLERANCE TYPES

Tolerancing on an engineering drawing may be describing two very different types of dimensional variation. The type of tolerancing that will be discussed in this chapter may be referred to as *standard tolerancing* or *x-y coordinate tolerancing*. This type of tolerancing is used to control position and size. The other type of tolerancing is called *geometric dimensioning and tolerancing* (i.e., GD&T). This type of tolerancing controls things such as form (i.e., feature shape), location, and position. Geometric dimensioning and tolerancing is beyond the scope of this book.

Toleranced dimensions are presented using three general methods. The methods presented in this chapter include *limit* dimensions, *plus-minus* tolerances, and *page* or *block* tolerances.

- <u>Limit Dimensions:</u> **Limits are the maximum and minimum size** that a part can obtain and still function properly. For example, the diameter of a shaft may vary between ∅.999 inch and ∅1.001 inches. On a drawing, you would see this dimension specified as the *limit tolerance* shown in Figure 18.2-1.
- <u>Plus-Minus Tolerances:</u> **Plus-minus tolerances give a basic size and the variation** that can occur around that basic size. On a drawing, a *plus-minus tolerance* dimension would look like that shown in Figure 18.2-1.

- Page or Block Tolerances: **A block tolerance is a general note that applies to all dimensions that are not covered by some other tolerancing type.** The format of a block tolerance is shown in Figure 18.2-1. Block tolerances are located in the tolerance block to the left of the title block and above the projection block.

$\varnothing^{1.001}_{.999}$ or $\varnothing .999 - 1.001$

Limit tolerance

$10.0^{+0.1}_{-0.2}$

Plus-minus tolerance

UNLESS OTHERWISE SPECIFIED
DIM ARE IN INCHES
TOL ON ANGLE ±.XX°
2 PL ±.XX 3 PL ±.XXX
INTERPRET DIM AND TOL PER
ASME Y14.5 - XXXX

Block tolerance

Figure 18.2-1: Tolerance methods

18.3) SHAFT-HOLE ASSEMBLY

In the intervening sections, a simple shaft and hole assembly will be used to illustrate different concepts and definitions. Figure 18.3-1 shows a shaft that is designed to fit into a hole. Both the shaft and the hole are allowed to vary between a maximum and minimum diameter.

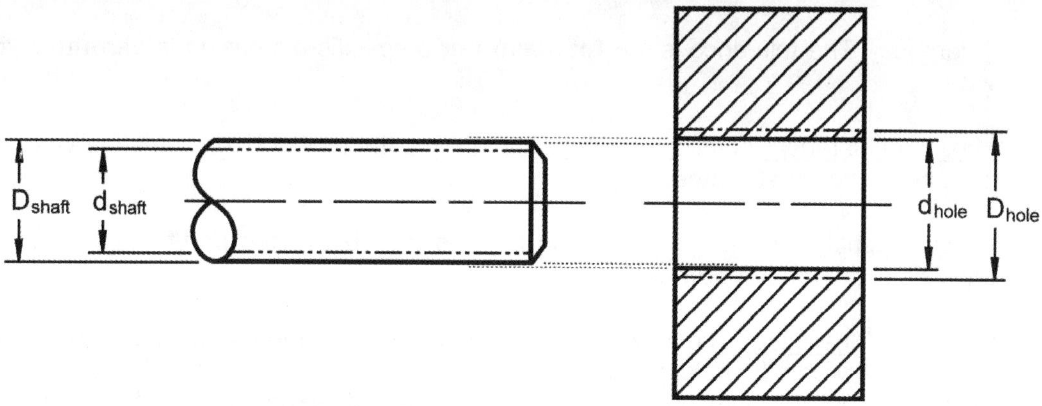

Figure 18.3-1: Shaft and hole assembly.

18.4) INCH TOLERANCES

Consider a simple shaft and hole assembly, like that shown in Figure 18.4-1. Both the diameter of the shaft and hole are allowed to vary between a maximum and minimum value. Picture this assembly when reading the following definitions relating to tolerancing in inches.

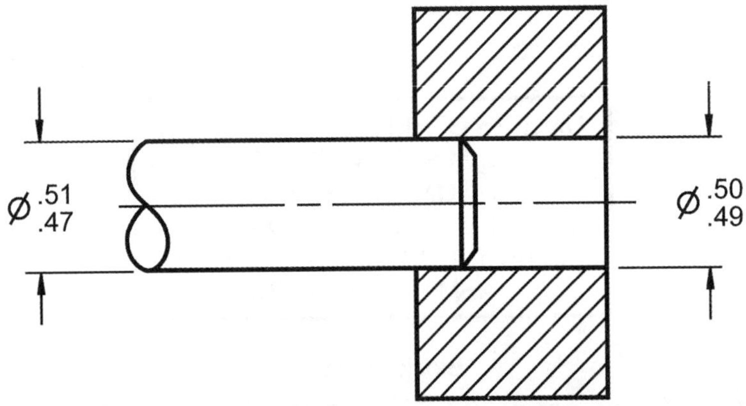

Figure 18.4-1: Toleranced shaft and hole pair (English).

- <u>Limits:</u> The limits are the **maximum and minimum size** that the feature is allowed to be.
- <u>Basic Size:</u> The basic size is the size from which the limits are calculated. It is **common for both the hole and the shaft** and is usually the value of the closest fraction.
- <u>Tolerance:</u> The tolerance is the **total amount** a specific dimension is **permitted to vary**.
- <u>Maximum Material Condition (MMC):</u> The MMC is the size of the part/feature when it consists of the **most material**.
- <u>Least Material Condition (LMC):</u> The LMC is the size of the part/feature when it consists of the **least material**.
- <u>Maximum Clearance:</u> The maximum clearance is the maximum amount of space that can exist between the hole and the shaft. Don't let the word clearance fool you. The maximum clearance may be positive (a space) or negative (no space). The maximum clearance is calculated by using the following equation:

$$\text{Max. Clearance} = LMC_{hole} - LMC_{shaft}$$

- Minimum Clearance (Allowance): The minimum clearance is the minimum amount of space that can exist between the hole and the shaft. Don't let the word clearance fool you. The minimum clearance may be positive (a space) or negative (no space). The minimum clearance is calculated by using the following equation:

$$\text{Min. Clearance} = MMC_{hole} - MMC_{shaft}$$

Try Exercise 18.4-1

Exercise 18.4-1: Inch tolerance definitions

Referring to Figure 18.4-1, fill in the following table.

	Shaft	Hole
Limits		
Basic Size		
Tolerance		
MMC		
LMC		
Max. Clearance		
Min. Clearance (Allowance)		

18.4.1) Types of fits

Within the set of inch tolerances, there are four major types of fits. Within each fit there are several degrees or classes. The type of fit and class that was chosen depends on the function of the design. The major categories of fits are *clearance*, *interference*, *transition*, and *line*. Table 18.4-1 lists and defines each of the four types of fits.

Type of Fit	Definition	When it exists
Clearance Fit	The internal member (shaft) fits into the external member (hole) and always leaves a space or clearance between the parts.	Min. Clear > 0
Interference Fit	The internal member is larger than the external member such that there is always an actual interference of metal.	Max. Clear $\leq$ 0
Transition Fit	The fit might result in either a clearance or interference fit condition.	Min. Clear < 0 Max. Clear > 0
Line Fit	The limits of size are specified such that a clearance or surface contact may result.	Min. Clear = 0 Max. Clear >0

Table 18.4-1: Types of fits.

Try Exercise 18.4-2 and 18.4-3

Exercise 18.4-2: Types of fits

From everyday life, list some examples of clearance and interference fits.

Fit	Examples
Clearance	
Interference	

Exercise 18.4-3: Determining fit type

Determine the basic size and type of fit given the limits for the shaft and hole.

Shaft Limits	Hole Limits	Basic Size	Type of Fit
1.498 - 1.500	1.503 – 1.505		
.751 - .755	.747 - .750		
.373 - .378	.371 - .375		
.247 - .250	.250 - .255		

18.5) METRIC TOLERANCES

Consider a simple shaft and hole assembly, like that shown in Figure 18.5-1, when reading the following definitions relating to tolerancing in millimeters. Both the diameter of the shaft and hole are allowed to vary between a maximum and minimum value. These dimensions are shown in Figure 18.5-1.

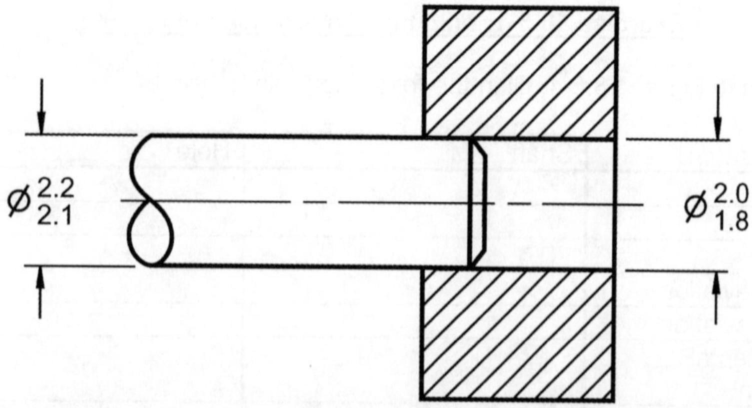

Figure 18.5-1: Toleranced shaft and hole pair (metric).

- Limits: The limits are the **maximum and minimum size** that the feature is allowed to be.

- Basic Size: The basic size is the **size from which the limits are calculated**.

- Tolerance: The tolerance is the **total amount** a dimension is **permitted to vary**.

- Upper deviation: The upper deviation is the **difference between the basic size and the permitted maximum size** of the feature.

  UD = | basic size – max size |

- Lower deviation: The lower deviation is the **difference between the basic size and the minimum permitted size** of the feature.

  LD = | basic size – min size |

- Fundamental deviation: The fundamental deviation is the **closest deviation to the basic size**. To determine the fundamental deviation, compare the upper deviation and the lower deviation. The fundamental deviation is the smaller of the two.

Try Exercise 18.5-1 and 18.5-2

Exercise 18.5-1: Millimeter tolerance definitions

Referring to Figure 18.5-1, fill in the following table.

	Shaft	Hole
Limits		
Basic Size		
Tolerance		
Upper deviation		
Lower deviation		
Fundamental deviation		
Type of fit		

Exercise 18.5-2: Determining fit type

Determine the basic size and type of fit given the limits for the shaft and hole.

Shaft Limits	Hole Limits	Basic Size	Type of Fit
4.855 – 4.930	5.000 – 5.075		
12.001 – 12.012	12.000 – 12.018		
6.023 – 6.031	6.000 – 6.012		
19.979 – 20.000	20.020 – 20.053		

READING TOLERANCES QUESTIONS – SET 1

Name: ______________________________ Date: _____________

Q18-1) Interchangeable parts need to be ____________. Fill in the blank.

Q18-2) The ____________ is the difference between the maximum and minimum size of the feature. Fill in the blank.

Q18-3) Circle the three different tolerance types that you may find on a drawing.

a) Block
b) Plus-minus
c) Varying
d) Limit
e) Design

Q18-4) The basic size is usually a decimal number that can be converted into a common fraction. (True, False)

Q18-5) The maximum and minimum size of a feature is called the ___________. Fill in the blank.

Q18-6) The ___________ deviation is the difference between the basic size and the maximum size of the feature.

READING TOLERANCES QUESTIONS – SET 2

Name: ______________________________ Date: ______________

Q18-7) Is it possible to machine a part to an exact size? (yes, no)

Q18-8) A tolerance is the maximum amount a part is allowed to ________. Fill in the blank.

Q18-9) A fit that always leaves space between the mating parts.

a) clearance
b) interference
c) transition
d) line

Q18-10) A fit that sometimes leaves a space between the mating parts.

a) clearance
b) interference
c) transition

Q18-11) The fit that never leaves a space between the mating parts.

a) clearance
b) interference
c) transition
d) line

Q18-12) If a shaft has a diameter of ∅9.9 – ∅10.0. What is its maximum material condition?

Q18-13) If a hole has a diameter of ∅9.9 – ∅10.0. What is its maximum material condition?

Q18-14) The fundamental deviation is determined by looking at the upper and lower deviations and picking the ____________ one.

a) Smaller
b) Larger

READING TOLERANCES PROBLEMS

Name: ______________________________ Date: ______________

P18-1) Fill in the given table for the following shaft and hole limits.

	(a)	(b)	(c)	(d)	(e)	(f)	(g)	(h)
Shaft Limits	.9975 .9963	4.7494 4.7487	.494 .487	5.0005 4.9995	1.2513 1.2507	.1256 .1254	2.5072 2.5060	8.9980 8.9878
Hole Limits	1.002 1.000	4.751 4.750	.507 .500	5.0016 5.0000	1.251 1.250	.1253 .1250	2.5018 2.5000	9.0018 9.0000

	Shaft	**Hole**
Limits		
Basic Size		
Tolerance		
MMC		
LMC		
Max. Clearance		
Min. Clearance (Allowance)		
Type of Fit (Select one)	Clearance, Transition, Interference, Line	

	Shaft	**Hole**
Limits		
Basic Size		
Tolerance		
MMC		
LMC		
Max. Clearance		
Min. Clearance (Allowance)		
Type of Fit (Select one)	Clearance, Transition, Interference, Line	

	Shaft	**Hole**
Limits		
Basic Size		
Tolerance		
MMC		
LMC		
Max. Clearance		
Min. Clearance (Allowance)		
Type of Fit (Select one)	Clearance, Transition, Interference, Line	

P18-2) Fill in the given table for the following shaft and hole limits.

	(a)	(b)	(c)	(d)	(e)	(f)	(g)	(h)
Shaft Limits	5.970 5.940	79.990 79.971	16.029 16.018	25.061 25.048	120.000 119.780	2.000 1.994	30.000 29.987	8.000 7.991
Hole Limits	6.030 6.000	80.030 80.000	16.018 16.000	25.021 25.000	120.400 120.180	2.012 2.002	30.006 29.985	7.978 7.963

	Shaft	**Hole**
Limits		
Basic size		
Tolerance		
Upper Deviation		
Lower Deviation		
Fundamental Deviation		
Fit (Select one)	Clearance, Transition, Interference	

	Shaft	**Hole**
Limits		
Basic size		
Tolerance		
Upper Deviation		
Lower Deviation		
Fundamental Deviation		
Fit (Select one)	Clearance, Transition, Interference	

	Shaft	**Hole**
Limits		
Basic size		
Tolerance		
Upper Deviation		
Lower Deviation		
Fundamental Deviation		
Fit (Select one)	Clearance, Transition, Interference	

SP18-1) Fill in the given table for the following shaft and hole limits. The answers to this problem are given on the *Independent Learning Content.*

	Shaft	Hole
Limits	1.2518-1.2524	1.2500-1.2510
Basic Size		
Tolerance		
MMC		
LMC		
Max. Clearance		
Min. Clearance (Allowance)		
Type of Fit		

SP18-2) Fill in the given table for the following shaft and hole limits. The answers to this problem are given on the *Independent Learning Content.*

	Shaft	Hole
Limits	1.994-2.000	1.990-2.000
Basic size		
Tolerance		
Upper Deviation		
Lower Deviation		
Fundamental Deviation		
Fit		

NOTES:

CHAPTER 19

CREATING TOLERANCES

CHAPTER OUTLINE

CHAPTER SUMMARY

In this chapter you will learn how to apply various types of tolerances. No part can be made to an exact size; therefore, tolerancing enables an engineer to design interchangeable or replacement parts. By the end of this chapter, you will be able to apply tolerances to a basic dimension and calculate a feature's limits.

19.1) WHY TOLERANCING?

No part or feature can be manufactured to an exact size. There is always some variation. Tolerancing gives a designer the means to specify dimensions with whatever degree of accuracy that is required for the design to work properly. Tolerances should be chosen so that they are not unnecessarily accurate or excessively inaccurate. **Choosing the correct tolerance for a particular application depends on the design intent (i.e., the end use) of the part, cost, how it is manufactured, and experience.**

19.2) TOLERANCING STANDARDS

Standards are needed to establish dimensional limits for parts that are to be interchangeable. Standards make it possible for parts to be manufactured at different times and in different places with the assurance that they will meet assembly requirements. The two most common standards agencies are the American National Standards Institute (ANSI) and the International Standards Organization (ISO). The ANSI standards are now being compiled and distributed by the American Society of Mechanical Engineers (ASME). The information contained in this chapter is based on the following standards: ASME Y14.5 - 2018, USAS B4.1 – 1967 (R2004), and ANSI B4.2 – 1978 (R2004).

19.3) CHOOSING A TOLERANCE TYPE

Toleranced dimensions may be presented using three general methods. The methods presented in this chapter include *limit* dimensions, *plus-minus* tolerances, and *page* or *block* tolerances.

- <u>Limit Dimensions:</u> Limits are the maximum and minimum size that a part can obtain and still function properly. On a drawing, you would see this dimension specified as the *limit tolerance* shown in Figure 19.3-1. Notice that the upper limit is placed above the lower limit in the stacked version. When both limits are placed on one line, the lower limit precedes the upper limit. Limit dimensions provide the blueprint reader with the limits of **allowable variation without any calculation**. It eliminates potential calculation mistakes.
- <u>Plus-Minus Tolerances:</u> Plus-minus tolerances give a basic size and the variation that can occur around that basic size. On a drawing, a *plus-minus tolerance* dimension would look like that shown in Figure 19.3-1. When the positive and negative variations are the same, it is referred to as an equal bilateral tolerance. When they are not the same, the specification is called an unequal bilateral and when one of the variances is zero, the tolerance is unilateral. The type of tolerance chosen depends on the direction in which variation is most detrimental. Plus-minus tolerances are convenient because a **design may be initially drawn and dimensioned using basic sizes**. As the design progresses, tolerances may be added.

- Page or Block Tolerances: A block tolerance is a general note that applies to all dimensions that are not covered by some other tolerancing type. The format of a block tolerance is shown in Figure 19.3-1. Block tolerances are placed in the tolerance block to the left of the title block and above the projection block. Block tolerances are used for two reasons. First, they act as a default tolerance for any dimensions that may have been overlooked when tolerances were assigned. Second, they are often used to **quickly tolerance non-critical dimensions**.

$\varnothing^{1.001}_{.999}$ or $\varnothing$.999 - 1.001

Limit tolerance

$10.0^{+0.1}_{-0.2}$

Plus-minus tolerance

UNLESS OTHERWISE SPECIFIED
DIM ARE IN INCHES
TOL ON ANGLE ±.XX°
2 PL ±.XX 3 PL ±.XXX
INTERPRET DIM AND TOL PER
ASME Y14.5 - XXXX

Block tolerance

Figure 19.3-1: Tolerance methods

19.4) INCH TOLERANCES

In the previous chapter, we learned about definitions associated with inch tolerances. To refresh your memory, try the following exercise.

Try Exercise 19.4-1

19.4.1) ANSI standard limits and fits

The following fit types and classes are in accordance with the USAS B4.1-1967 (R2004) standard.

- Running or Sliding Clearance Fits (RC)

Running and sliding clearance fits are intended to provide running performance with suitable lubrication. The classes are categorized from RC1 to RC8. The smaller the number indicates a closer or smaller tolerance. Table 19.4-1 lists the different classes of running and sliding clearance fits and their design uses.

- Locational Fits (LC, LT, LN)

Locational fits are intended to determine only the location of the mating parts. They are divided into three groups: clearance fits (LC), transition fits (LT), and interference fits (LN). Table 19.4-2 lists the different classes of locational fits and their design uses.

- FN: Force Fits:

Force fits provide a constant bore pressure throughout the range of sizes. The classes are categorized from FN1 to FN5. The higher the number, the more interference there will be. Table 19.4-3 lists the different classes of force fits and their design uses.

Exercise 19.4-1: Inch tolerance definitions

Match the term with its corresponding definition.

Term	Definition
Limits	The size from which the limits are calculated.
Basic size	There is never a space between the two mating features.
Tolerance	There is always a space between the two mating features.
MMC	$LMC_{hole} - LMC_{shaft}$
LMC	The maximum and minimum size that the part is allowed to be.
Maximum Clearance	The size of the part when it consists of the least material.
Minimum Clearance	The total amount a specific dimension is permitted to vary.
Clearance fit	There is sometimes a space between the two mating features.
Interference fit	The size of the part when it consists of the most material.
Transition fit	$MMC_{hole} - MMC_{shaft}$

Class of Fit	Description	Design use
RC9 -RC8	Loose running fit	Used with material such as cold rolled shafting and tubing made to commercial tolerances.
RC7	Free running fit	Used where accuracy is not essential, or where large temperature variations occur.
RC6 -RC5	Medium running fit	Used on accurate machinery with higher surface speeds where accurate location and minimum play is desired.
RC4	Close running fit	Used on accurate machinery with moderate surface speeds where accurate location and minimum play is desired.
RC3	Precision running fit	This is the closest fit, which can be expected to run freely. Intended for slow speeds. Not suitable for appreciable temperature changes.
RC2	Sliding fit	Used for accurate location. Parts will move and turn easily but are not intended to run freely. Parts may seize with small temperature changes.
RC1	Close Sliding fit	Used for accurate location of parts that must be assembled without perceptible play.

Table 19.4-1: Running and sliding clearance fit classes.

Class of Fit	Description	Design use
LC	Locational clearance fit	Intended for parts that are normally stationary, but which can be freely assembled or disassembled. They run from snug fits (parts requiring accuracy of location), through the medium clearance fits (parts where freedom of assembly is important). The classes are categorized from LC1 being the tightest fit to LC11 being the loosest.
LT	Locational transition fit	Used where accuracy of location is important, but a small amount of clearance or interference is permissible. The classes are categorized from LT1 to LT6.
LN	Locational interference fit	Used where accuracy of location is of prime importance, and for parts requiring rigidity and alignment with no special requirements for bore pressure. The classes are categorized from LN1 to LN3.

Table 19.4-2: Locational fit classes.

Class of Fit	Description	Design use
FN1	Light drive fit	This fit produces a light assembly pressure and a more or less permanent assembly.
FN2	Medium drive fit	Suitable for ordinary steel parts or for shrink fits on light sections. About the tightest fit that can be used with high-grade cast iron.
FN3	Heavy drive fit	Suitable for heavier steel parts or for shrink fit in medium sections.
FN4 - FN5	Force fit	Suitable for parts that can be heavily stressed, or for shrink fits where the heavy pressing forces required are impractical.

Table 19.4-3: Force fit classes.

19.4.2) Calculating limits

Figure 19.4-1 shows an excerpt of the RC fits table found in Appendix A. The following example will illustrate how to calculate limits using this table. Imagine that you have a ¼ inch nominal diameter shaft. You want to design a journal bearing to fit on the shaft that will be able to run freely. You choose an RC7 fit and want to calculate the limits of the shaft and the inner diameter of the bearing. The first step is to find the nominal size range. Figure 19.4-1 highlights the row in which ¼ inch falls within. Then find the fit column that you want. In this case, RC7. Figure 19.4-1 highlights the fit column. The row and column intersection contains the plus and minus values that we apply to the basic size. The only trick here is that these values are given in thousands of an inch. For example, if we want to calculate the limits of the hole, we take 0.2500 and add 0.0014 to it and subtract 0 from it giving us the limits ∅0.2500 – ∅0.2514. Finding the limits for the shaft is similar, we subtract 0.0025 and 0.0016 giving us the limits ∅0.2475 – ∅0.2484.

Nominal Size Range Inches		Class RC5		Class RC6		Class RC7		Class RC8		Class RC9	
		Standard Limits		Standard Limits		Standard Limits		Standard Limits		Standard Limits	
Over	To	Hole	Shaft	Hole	Shaft	Hole	Shaft	Hole	Shaft	Hole	Shaft
0	– 0.12	+0.6 0	-0.6 -1 .0	+1.0 0	-0.6 -1.2	+1.0 0	-1.0 -1.6	+1.6 0	-2.5 -3.5	+2.5 0	-4.0 -5.6
0.12	– 0.24	+0.7 0	-0.8 -1.3	+1.2 0	-0.8 -1.5	+1.2 0	-1.2 -1.9	+1.8 0	-2.8 -4.0	+3.0 0	-4.5 -6.0
0.24	– 0.40	+0.9 0	-1.0 -1.6	+1.4 0	-1.0 -1.9	+1.4 0	-1.6 -2.5	+2.2 0	-3.0 -4.4	+3.5 0	-5.0 -7.2
0.40	– 0.71	+1.0 0	-1.2 -1.9	+1.6 0	-1.2 -2.2	+1.6 0	-2.0 -3.0	+2.8 0	-3.5 -5.1	+4.0 0	-6.0 -8.8
0.71	– 1.19	+1.2 0	-1.6 -2.4	+2.0 0	-1.6 -2.8	+2.0 0	-2.5 -3.7	+3.5 0	-4.5 -6.5	+5.0 0	-7.0 -10.5

Figure 19.4-1: Running and Sliding Clearence fits

Try Exercise 19.4-2

Exercise 19.4-2: Limits and fits

Given a basic size of .50 inches and a fit of RC8, calculate the limits for both the hole and the shaft. Use the ANSI limits and fit tables given in Appendix A.

Shaft:

Hole:

19.5) METRIC TOLERANCES

In the previous chapter, we learned about definitions associated with metric tolerances. To refresh your memory, try the following exercise.

Try Exercise 19.5-1

Exercise 19.5-1: Metric tolerance definitions

Match the term with its corresponding definition.

Term	Definition
Basic size	The size from which the limits are calculated.
Tolerance	The difference between the basic size and the minimum permitted size of the part.
Upper Deviation	The closest deviation to the basic size.
Lower Deviation	The total amount a specific dimension is permitted to vary.
Fundamental Deviation	The difference between the basic size and the maximum permitted size of the part.

19.5.1) ANSI standard limits and fits (Metric)

The following fit types are in accordance with the ANSI B4.2 – 1978 (R2004) standard. Available metric fits and their descriptions are summarized in Table 19.5-1.

19.5.2) Tolerance designation and tolerance zone

Metric fits are specified using the fundamental deviation (represented by a letter) and the international tolerance grade (represented by a number). In the fit designation, a capitalized letter refers to the hole's fundamental deviation and a lower-case letter refers to the shaft. Table 19.5-1 lists the possible metric fit designation. Note the letter/number combinations.

The tolerance zone is a region in which the limits of the part can exist and still pass inspection. The **tolerance zone is controlled by the fundamental deviation (represented by a letter) and the international tolerance grade (represented by a number).** The **fundamental deviation establishes the position of the tolerance zone,** and the **international tolerance grade controls its size.**

The fundamental deviation is the closest deviation to the basic size. The international tolerance grade or IT# is a number that describes how big or small the tolerance zone is. **A smaller number provides a smaller and more accurate tolerance.** The size of the tolerance zone varies according to the basic size and provides the same relative level of accuracy within a given grade.

To better understand the tolerance zone let's look at the example of a shaft and hole assembly shown in Figure 19.5-2. Both the shaft and hole size are defined by a minimum diameter and a maximum diameter. These limits create the tolerance zone. The shaded area in Figure 19.5-2 indicates the tolerance zone. The tolerance zone has both a size and a position. The size of the tolerance zone is controlled by the IT#, as shown in Figure 19.5-3. You can see that as the IT# decreases, the size of the tolerance zone decreases. The tolerance zone position is controlled by the fundamental deviation as shown in Figure 19.5-4. You can see that different fundamental deviation designations results in the tolerance zone being outside, inside or straddling the basic size.

Try Exercise 19.5-2

FIT SYMBOL			
Hole Basis	**Shaft Basis**	**Fit**	**Description**
H11/c11	C11/h11	Loose running fit	For wide commercial tolerances or allowances.
H9/d9	D9/h9	Free running fit	Good for large temperature variations, high running speeds, or heavy journal pressures.
H8/f7	F8/h7	Close running fit	For accurate location at moderate speeds and journal pressures.
H7/g6	G7/h6	Sliding fit	Not intended to run freely, but to move and turn freely and locate accurately.
H7/h6	H7/h6	Locational clearance fit	For locating stationary parts but can be freely assembled and disassembled.
H7/k6 and H7/n6	K7/h6 and N7/h6	Locational transition fit	For accurate location.
H7/p6	P7/h6	Locational interference fit	For parts requiring rigidity where accuracy of location is important, but without special bore pressure requirements.
H7/s6	S7/h6	Medium drive fit	For ordinary steel parts or shrink fits on light sections, the tightest fit usable with cast iron.
H7/u6	U7/h6	Force fit	Suitable for parts that can be highly stressed.

Table 19.5-1: Metric standard fits.

Exercise 19.5-2: Metric fit designation

Fill in the appropriate name for the fit component.

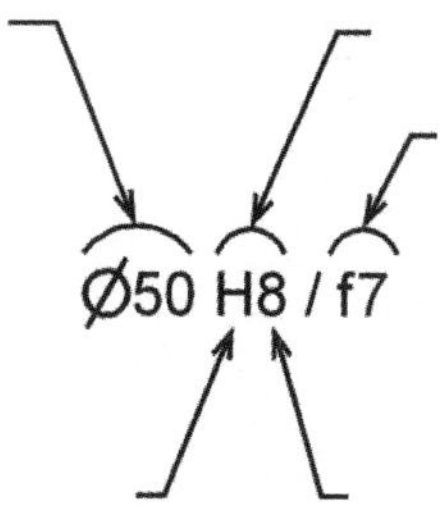

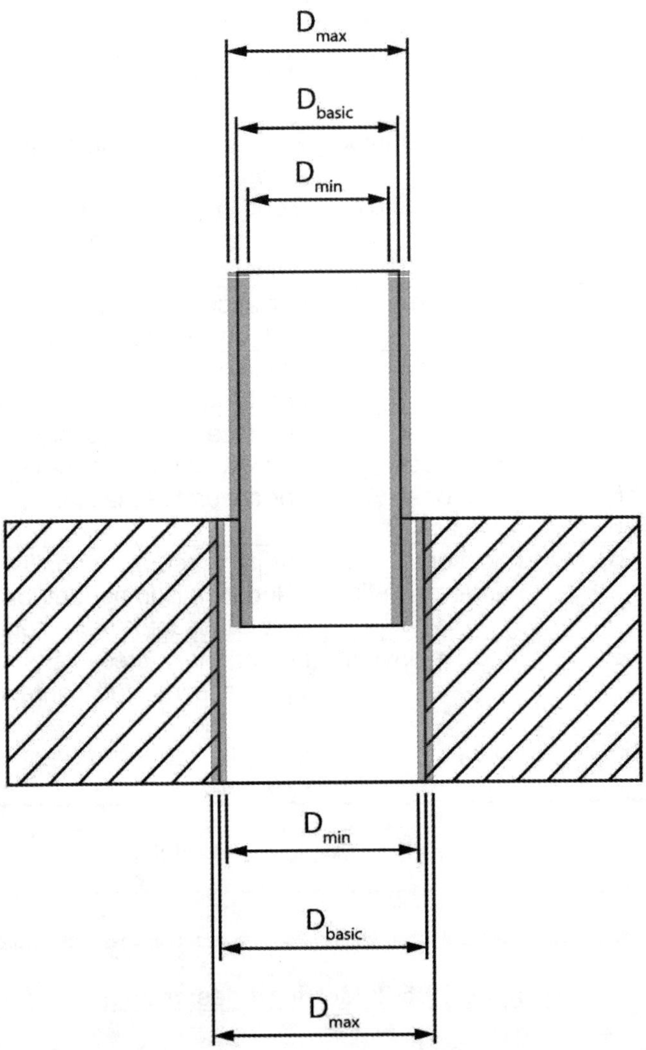

Figure 19.5-2: Shaft and hole assembly

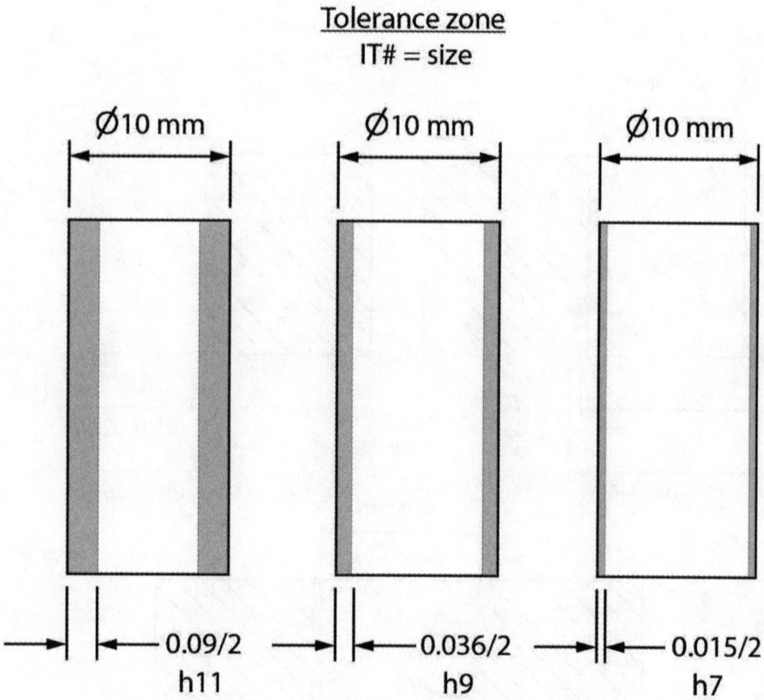

Figure 19.5-3: IT# controls tolerance zone size

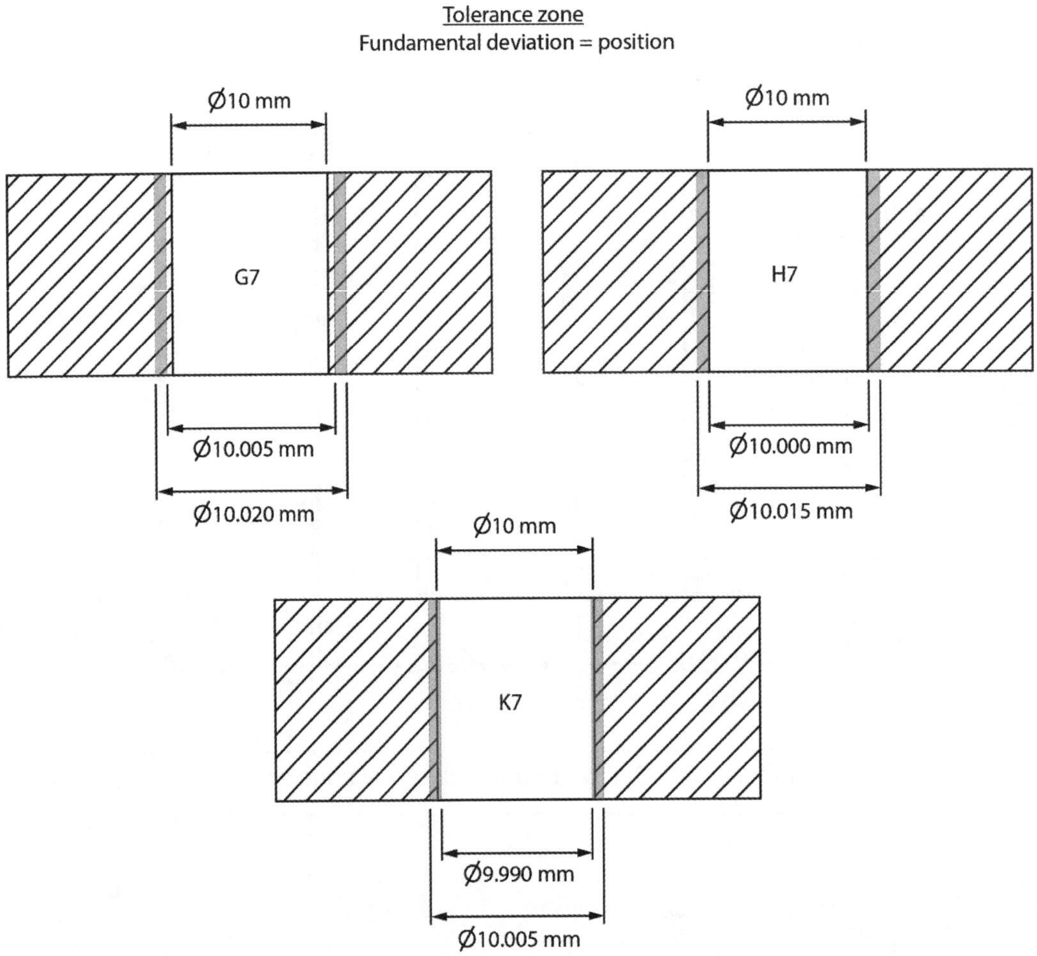

Figure 19.5-4: Fundamental deviation controls tolerance zone position

19.5.3) Basic hole and basic shaft systems

Notice that Table 19.5-1 gives two different tolerance designations for each type of fit. Metric limits and fits are divided into two different systems: the basic hole system and the basic shaft system. Each system has its own designation.

- Basic hole system: The basic hole system is used when you want the **basic size** to be **attached to the hole dimension**. For example, if a standard drill, reamer, broach, or another standard tool is used to produce a hole, you would want to use the hole system. In this system, the minimum hole diameter is taken as the basic size.
- Basic shaft system: The basic shaft system is used when you want the **basic size** to be **attached to the shaft dimension**. For example, you would use the shaft system if you need to tolerance a hole based on the size of a purchased standard drill rod. In this system, the maximum shaft diameter is taken as the basic size.

19.5.4) Calculating limits

Figure 19.5-5a and 19.5-5b show excerpts of the metric fit tables found in Appendix A. The following example will illustrate how to find limits using these tables. Let's say you have a shaft-hole assembly, with a basic size of ∅2 mm, that needs to slide but not necessarily run freely. You may want to choose a sliding fit. If we are modifying the shaft to fit the hole, we would choose the hole basis H7/g6 fit (see Figure 19.5-5a). The diameters for the hole and shaft are ∅2.000 – ∅ 2.010 and ∅1.992 – ∅1.998, respectively. If we are modifying the hole to fit the shaft, we would choose the shaft basis H7/g6 fit (see Figure 19.5-5b). The diameters for the hole and shaft are ∅2.002 – ∅ 2.012 and ∅1.994 – ∅2.000, respectively.

A.2.1) Hole basis clearance fits

Preferred Hole Basis Clearance Fits. Dimensions in mm.

Basic Size	Loose Running		Free Running		Close Running		Sliding		Locational Clearance	
	Hole H11	Shaft c11	Hole H9	Shaft d9	Hole H8	Shaft f7	Hole H7	Shaft g6	Hole H7	Shaft h6
1 max min	1.060 1.000	0.940 0.880	1.025 1.000	0.980 0.955	1.014 1.000	0.994 0.984	1.010 1.000	0.998 0.992	1.010 1.000	1.000 0.994
1.2 max min	1.260 1.200	1.140 1.080	1.225 1.200	1.180 1.155	1.214 1.200	1.194 1.184	1.210 1.200	1.198 1.192	1.210 1.200	1.200 1.194
1.6 max min	1.660 1.600	1.540 1.480	1.625 1.600	1.580 1.555	1.614 1.600	1.594 1.584	1.610 1.600	1.598 1.592	1.610 1.600	1.600 1.594
2 max min	2.060 2.000	1.940 1.880	2.025 2.000	1.980 1.955	2.014 2.000	1.994 1.984	2.010 2.000	1.998 1.992	2.010 2.000	2.000 1.994

Figure 19.5-5a: Metric fits table, hole basis

A.2.3) Shaft basis clearance fits

Preferred Shaft Basis Clearance Fits. Dimensions in mm.

Basic Size	Loose Running		Free Running		Close Running		Sliding		Locational Clearance	
	Hole C11	Shaft h11	Hole D9	Shaft h9	Hole F8	Shaft h7	Hole G7	Shaft h6	Hole H7	Shaft h6
1 max min	1.120 1.060	1.000 0.940	1.045 1.020	1.000 0.975	1.020 1.006	1.000 0.990	1.012 1.002	1.000 0.994	1.010 1.000	1.000 0.994
1.2 max min	1.320 1.260	1.200 1.140	1.245 1.220	1.200 1.175	1.220 1.206	1.200 1.190	1.212 1.202	1.200 1.194	1.210 1.200	1.200 1.194
1.6 max min	1.720 1.660	1.600 1.540	1.645 1.620	1.600 1.575	1.620 1.606	1.600 1.590	1.612 1.602	1.600 1.594	1.610 1.600	1.600 1.594
2 max min	2.120 2.060	2.000 1.940	2.045 2.020	2.000 1.975	2.020 2.006	2.000 1.990	2.012 2.002	2.000 1.994	2.010 2.000	2.000 1.994

Figure 19.5-5b: Metric fits table, shaft basis

Try Exercise 19.5-3

<u>Exercise 19.5-3: Metric limits and fits.</u>

Find the limits, tolerance, type of fit, and type of system for a ∅30 H11/c11 fit. Use the tolerance tables given in Appendix A.

	Shaft	Hole
Limits		
Tolerance		
System		
Fit		

Find the limits, tolerance, type of fit, and type of system for a ∅30 P7/h6 fit.

	Shaft	Hole
Limits		
Tolerance		
System		
Fit		

19.6) SELECTING TOLERANCES

Tolerances will govern the method of manufacturing. **When tolerances are reduced, the cost of manufacturing rises very rapidly.** Therefore, specify as generous a tolerance as possible without interfering with the function of the part.

Choosing the most appropriate tolerance depends on many factors. The tolerance choice depends on design intent, cost, and how the part will be manufactured. Choosing a tolerance that will allow the part to function properly is the most important. Things to consider are length of engagement, bearing load, speed, lubrication, temperature, humidity, and material. Experience also plays a significant role.

Table 19.6-1 may be used as a general guide for determining the machining processes that will under normal conditions produce work within the tolerance grades indicated. As the tolerance grade number decreases, the tolerance becomes smaller. Tolerance grades versus actual tolerances may be found in any Machinery's Handbook.

	IT Grades							
Machining Operation	4	5	6	7	8	9	10	11
Lapping & Honing	■	■						
Cylindrical Grinding		■	■	■				
Surface Grinding		■	■	■	■			
Diamond Turning		■	■	■				
Diamond Boring		■	■	■				
Broaching		■	■	■	■			
Reaming			■	■	■	■	■	
Turning				■	■	■	■	■
Boring					■	■	■	■
Milling							■	■
Planing & Shaping							■	■
Drilling							■	■
Punching							■	■
Die Casting								■

Table 19.6-1: Relation of machining processes to international tolerance grades.

19.7) TOLERANCE ACCUMULATION

The tolerance between two features of a part depends on the number of controlling dimensions. Distance can be controlled by a single dimension or multiple dimensions. The maximum variation between two features is equal to the sum of the tolerances placed on the controlling dimensions. **As the number of controlling dimensions increases, the tolerance accumulation increases**. Remember, even if the dimension does not have a stated tolerance, it has an implied tolerance.

Try Exercise 19.7-1

Exercise 19.7-1: Tolerance accumulation

What is the tolerance accumulation for the distance between surface A and B for the three different dimensioning methods?

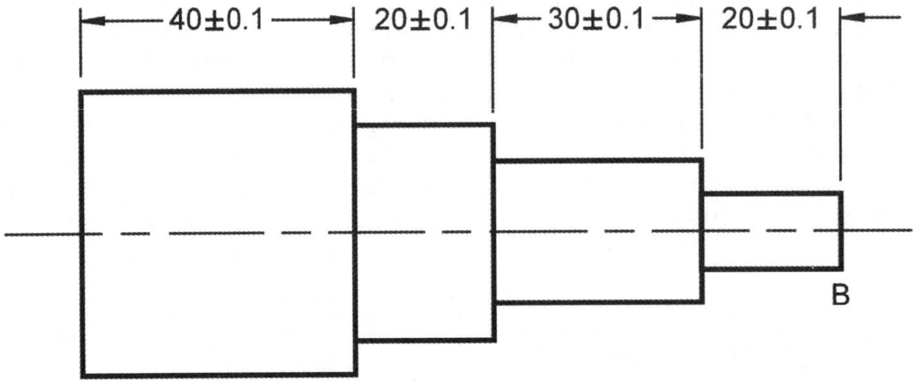

Tolerance accumulation between surface A and B =

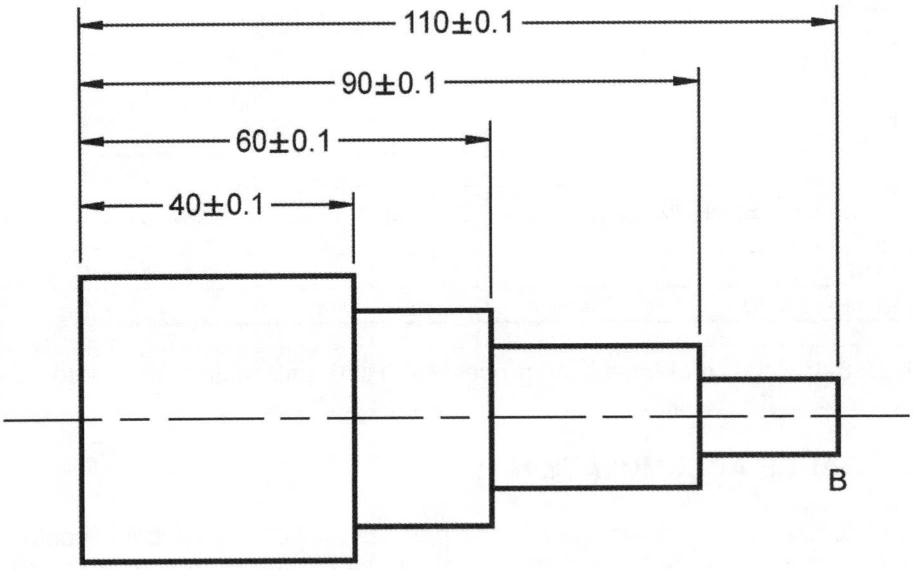

Tolerance accumulation between surface A and B =

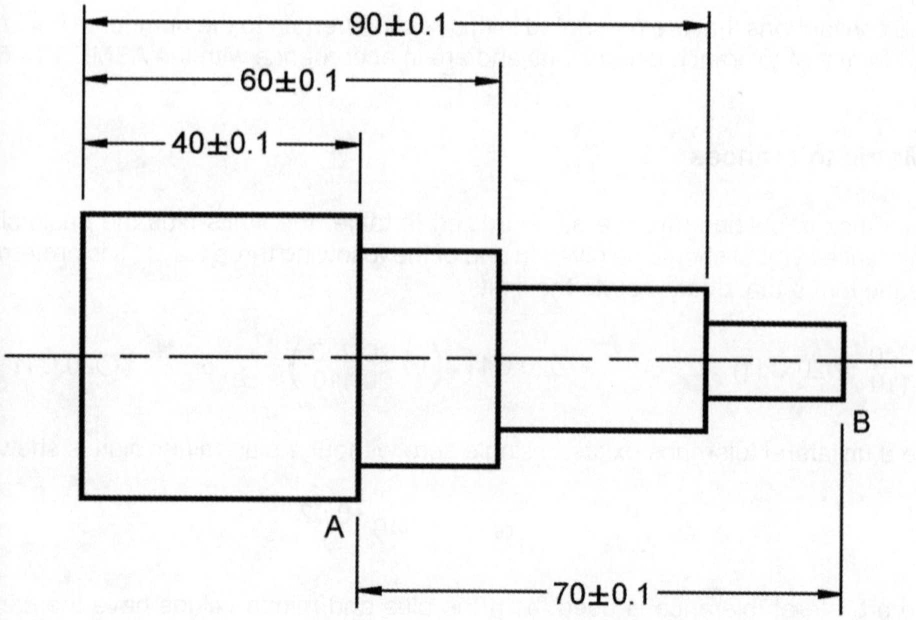

Tolerance accumulation between surface A and B =

If the accuracy of the distance between surface A and B is important, which dimensioning method should be used?

19.8) FORMATTING TOLERANCES

The conventions that are presented in this section pertain to the number of decimal places and format of tolerance dimensions and are in accordance with the ASME Y14.5M standard.

19.8.1) Metric tolerances

- If a tolerance is obtained from a standardized fit table, the limits plus the basic size and tolerance symbol should be given in one of the following three ways. It is preferred to use the forms that directly state the limits.

$$\varnothing\begin{matrix}20.240\\20.110\end{matrix}\ (\varnothing 20\ \mathrm{C11}) \quad \text{or} \quad \varnothing 20\ \mathrm{C11}\ \left(\varnothing\begin{matrix}20.240\\20.110\end{matrix}\right) \quad \text{or} \quad \varnothing 20\ \mathrm{C11}$$

- Where a unilateral tolerance exists, a single zero without a plus-minus sign is shown.

$$40\,^{0}_{-0.02} \quad \text{or} \quad 40\,^{+0.02}_{0}$$

- Where a bilateral tolerance is used, both the plus and minus values have the same number of decimal places, using zeros where necessary.

$$10\,^{+0.25}_{-0.10} \quad \text{not} \quad 10\,^{+0.25}_{-0.1}$$ (crossed out)

- If limit dimensions are used, both values should have the same number of decimal places, using zeros where necessary.

$$\begin{matrix}15.45\\15.00\end{matrix} \quad \text{not} \quad \begin{matrix}15.45\\15\end{matrix}$$ (crossed out)

- Basic dimensions are considered absolute. When used with a tolerance, the number of decimal places in the basic dimension does not have to match the number of decimal places in the tolerance.

45 ± 0.15 not ~~45.00 ± 0.15~~

19.8.2) Inch tolerances

- For unilateral and bilateral tolerances, the basic dimension and the plus and minus values should be expressed with the same number of decimal places.

$.500^{+.000}_{-.002}$ not ~~$.500^{0}_{-.002}$~~

$.500^{+.001}_{-.002}$ not ~~$.50^{+.001}_{-.002}$~~

- If limit dimensions are used, both values should have the same number of decimal places, using zeros where necessary.

$\begin{array}{c}.252\\.250\end{array}$ not ~~$\begin{array}{c}.252\\.25\end{array}$~~

- When basic dimensions are used, the number of decimal places should match the number of decimal places in the tolerance.

2.000 ± 0.015 not ~~2.0 ± 0.015~~

19.8.3) <u>Angular tolerances</u>

- Where angle dimensions are used, both the angle and the plus and minus values have the same number of decimal places.

$30.0^\circ\pm.2^\circ$ not ~~$30^\circ\pm.2^\circ$~~

NOTES:

19.9) APPLYING WHAT WE HAVE LEARNED

Exercise 19.9-1: Milling Jack assembly tolerances

Name: ______________________________ Date: ______________

Consider the *Milling Jack* assembly shown. Notice that there are many parts that fit into or around other parts. Each of these parts are toleranced to ensure proper fit and function.

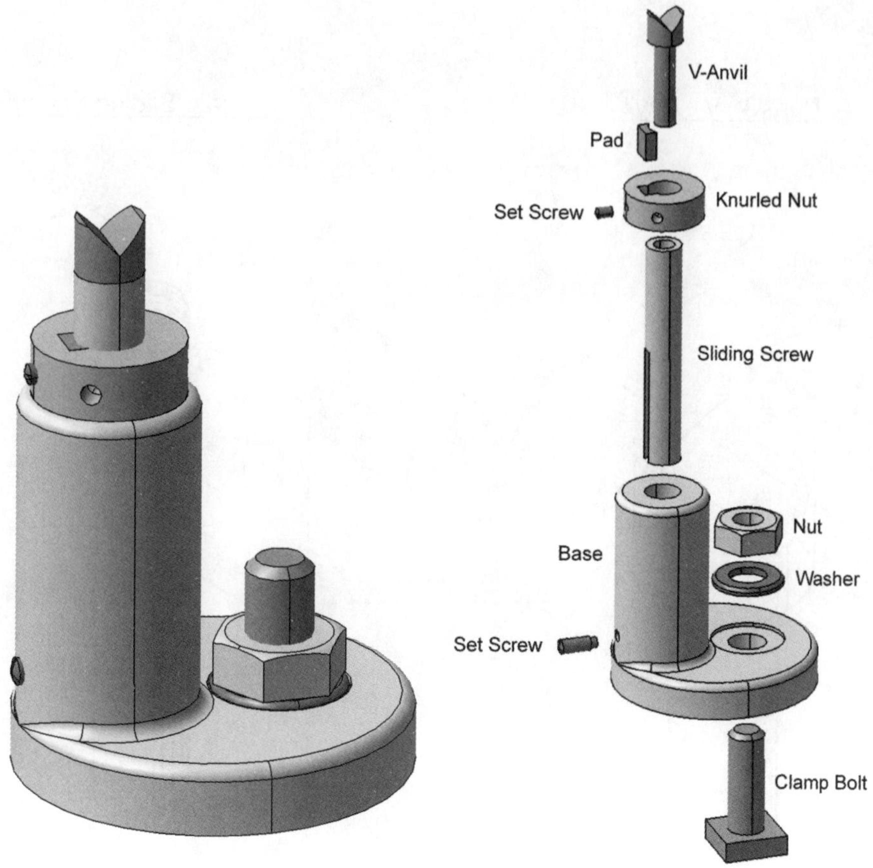

Exercise 19.9-1 Cont.: Milling Jack assembly tolerances

The *V-Anvil* fits (shaft) into the *Sliding Screw* (hole) with a RC4 fit. The basic size is .375 (3/8). Determine the limits for both parts.

- V – Anvil limits: ______________________________
- Sliding Screw limits: ___________________________

Part#3: V - Anvil

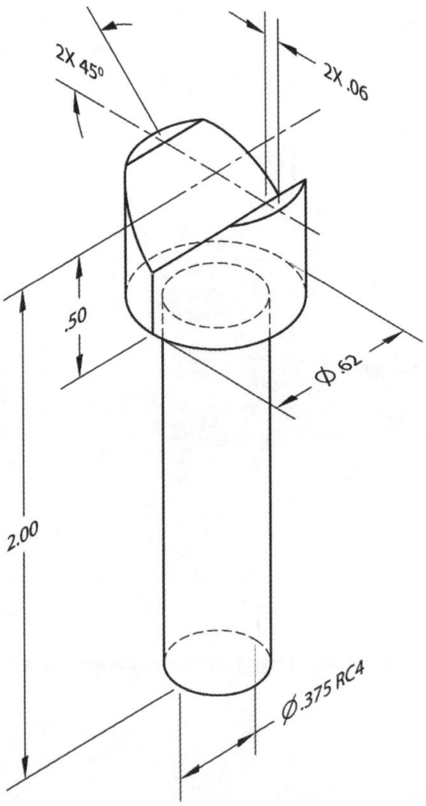

Part#2: Sliding Screw

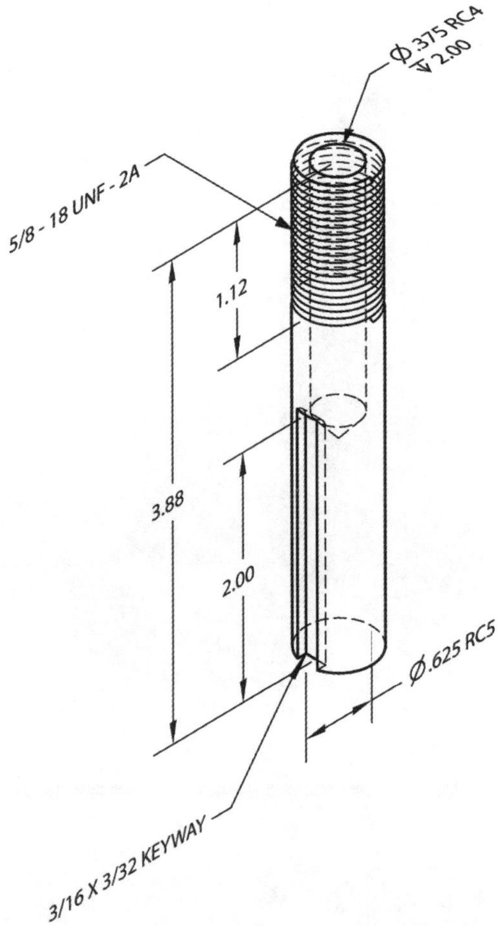

Exercise 19.9-1 Cont.: Milling Jack assembly tolerances

Name: ______________________________ Date: ______________

The *Sliding Screw* (shaft) fits into the *Base* (hole) with a RC5 fit. The basic size is .625 (5/8). Determine the limits for both parts.

- Sliding Screw limits: ________________________
- Base limits: ________________________

Part#1: Base

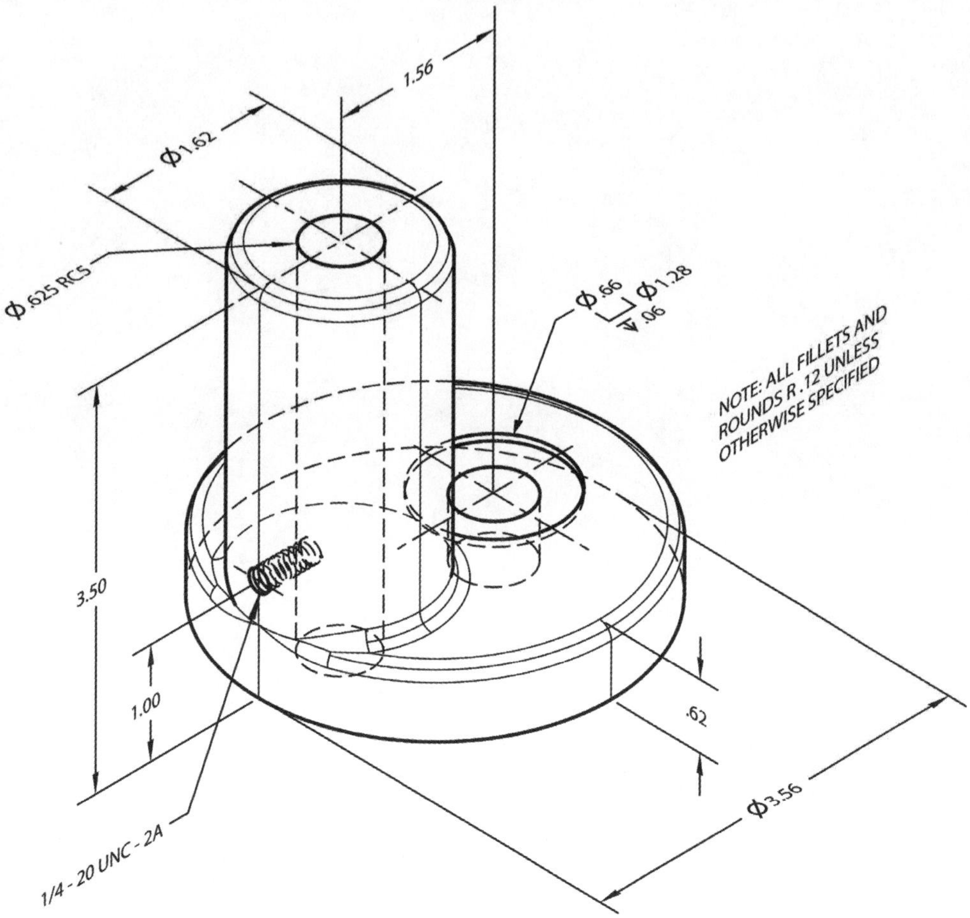

NOTES:

Exercise 19.9-2: Drill jig tolerances

Name: ______________________________ Date: ______________

Circle the explicitly toleranced dimensions and determine their limits.

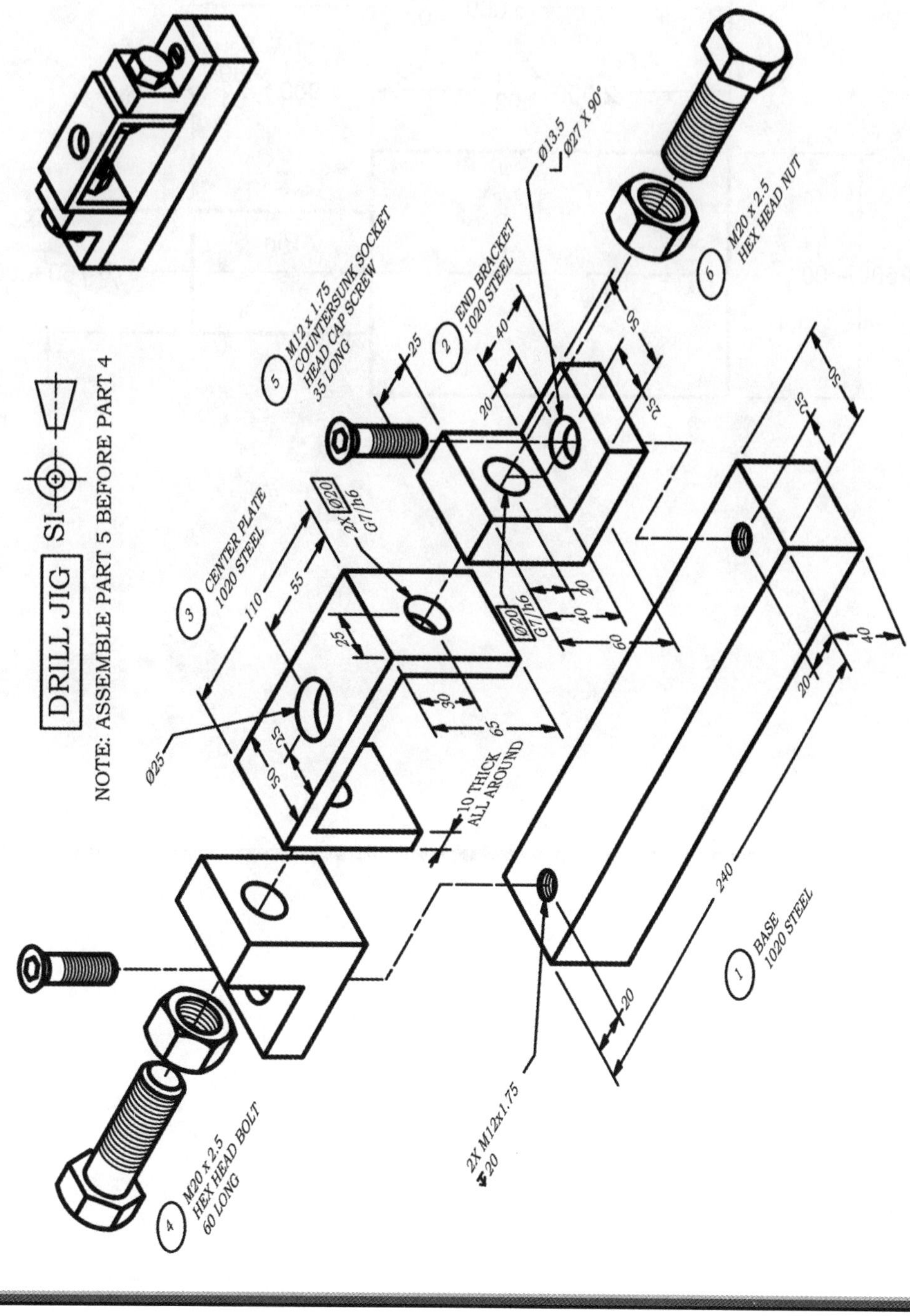

Exercise 19.9-3: Over dimensioning

Assuming that the diameter dimensions are correct, explain why this object is dimensioned incorrectly.

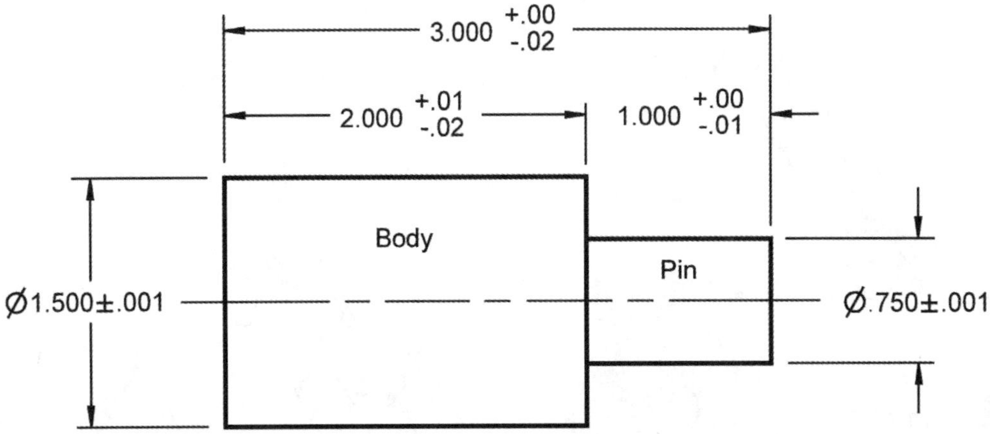

CREATING TOLERANCES QUESTIONS – SET 1

Name: ______________________________ Date: _____________

Tolerancing

Q19-1) This type of dimension has the advantage of providing the print reader with the allowable variation without any calculation.

a) limit dimension
b) block tolerance
c) plus minus dimension
d) basic dimension

Q19-2) This type of tolerancing is convenient because a design may be initially drawn and dimensioned using basic sizes.

a) limit dimension
b) block tolerance
c) plus minus dimension
d) basic dimension

Q19-3) This type of tolerancing type applies a tolerance to all dimensions not covered by some other tolerance type.

a) limit dimension
b) block tolerance
c) plus minus dimension
d) basic dimension

Inch tolerances

Q19-4) What does the fit designation RC stand for?

Q19-5) What does the fit designation LT stand for?

Q19-6) What does the fit designation FN stand for?

Metric tolerances

Q19-7) When designating a metric fit, what does the letter represent?

a) fundamental deviation
b) international tolerance grade
c) tolerance zone
d) upper deviation

Q19-8) When designating a metric fit, what does the number represent?

a) fundamental deviation
b) international tolerance grade
c) tolerance zone
d) upper deviation

Q19-9) What are the two systems used in the metric tolerance tables?

Selecting tolerances

Q19-10) Will tightening a tolerance increase or decrease the cost of manufacturing?

Tolerance Accumulation

Q19-11) As the number of controlling dimensions increases, the tolerance accumulation decreases. (True, False)

CREATING TOLERANCES QUESTIONS – SET 2

Name: ______________________________ Date: ______________

Tolerancing

Q19-12) Can a part/feature be machined to an exact size? (yes, no)

Q19-13) When specifying a limit dimension, the (lower, upper) limit goes first.

Q19-14) When specifying a limit dimension, the (lower, upper) limit goes on top.

Inch tolerances

Q19-15) The type of fit that provides running performance with suitable lubrication. (Choose all that apply)

a) RC
b) LC
c) LT
d) LN
e) FN

Q19-16) The type of fit that is intended only to locate mating parts. (Choose all that apply)

a) RC
b) LC
c) LT
d) LN
e) FN

Q19-17) The type of fit that provides constant bore pressure. (Choose all that apply)

a) RC
b) LC
c) LT
d) LN
e) FN

Metric tolerances

Q19-18) When specifying the tolerance zone, does a capital letter represent the fit for the hole or the shaft?

Q19-19) Given the fit designation H11/c11, would the hypothetical fit H9/c9 be looser or tighter?

Q19-20) The fundamental deviation controls the position of the tolerance zone relative to the basic size. (True, False)

Q19-21) What does the fit designation H11/c11 stand for?

Q19-22) What does the fit designation P7/h6 stand for?

Q19-23) This type of clearance fit is good for large temperature variations. (Choose all that apply.)

a) H11/c11
b) H9/d9
c) H8/f7
d) H7/g6
e) C11/h11
f) D9/h9
g) F8/h7
h) G7/h6

Q19-24) This type of locational fit is good for assemblies that need to be freely assembled and disassembled. (Choose all that apply.)

a) H7/h6
b) H7/k6
c) K7/h6
d) H7/p6
e) P7/h6

Selecting tolerances

Q19-25) What are some of the factors that influence tolerance choice? (Circle all that apply.)

a) cost
b) manufacturing capability
c) design intent
d) material

NOTES:

CREATING TOLERANCES PROBLEMS

Name: ______________________________ Date: ______________

P19-1) Find the limits of the shaft and hole for the following basic size – fit combinations. Note that the problem is asking for the limits and not just the tolerances from the table.

	(a)	(b)	(c)	(d)	(e)	(f)	(g)
Basic Size	.25	.5	.75	1	1.375	2	2.125
Fit 1	RC3	RC5	RC1	RC9	RC7	RC4	RC6
Fit 2	LC2	LC7	LC11	LC6	LC1	LC9	LC4
Fit 3	LT1	LT2	LT3	LT4	LT5	LT6	LT3
Fit 4	LN2	LN1	FN1	FN5	LN3	FN4	FN2

	Shaft	Hole
Basic Size		
Limits		

	Shaft	Hole
Basic Size		
Limits		

	Shaft	Hole
Basic Size		
Limits		

	Shaft	Hole
Basic Size		
Limits		

	Shaft	Hole
Basic Size		
Limits		

	Shaft	Hole
Basic Size		
Limits		

	Shaft	Hole
Basic Size		
Limits		

	Shaft	Hole
Basic Size		
Limits		

Name: ______________________________ Date: _______________

P19-2) Find the limits of the shaft and hole for the following basic size – fit combinations.

	(a)	(b)	(c)	(d)	(e)	(f)	(g)
Basic Size	5	10	12	16	20	25	30
Fit 1	H11/c11	H7/k6	H7/p6	H7/u6	H8/f7	H7/n6	H7/s6
Fit 2	U7/h6	N7/h6	G7/h6	C11/h11	S7/h6	H7/h6	K7/h6

	Shaft	**Hole**
Basic Size		
Limits		

	Shaft	**Hole**
Basic Size		
Limits		

	Shaft	**Hole**
Basic Size		
Limits		

	Shaft	**Hole**
Basic Size		
Limits		

	Shaft	**Hole**
Basic Size		
Limits		

	Shaft	**Hole**
Basic Size		
Limits		

	Shaft	**Hole**
Basic Size		
Limits		

	Shaft	**Hole**
Basic Size		
Limits		

P19-3) Draw the following object including dimensions. Apply a H7/g6 Sliding clearance fit to the ∅20 hole and shaft. Apply a U7/h6 force fit to the ∅10 hole and shaft. Insert your title block and print.

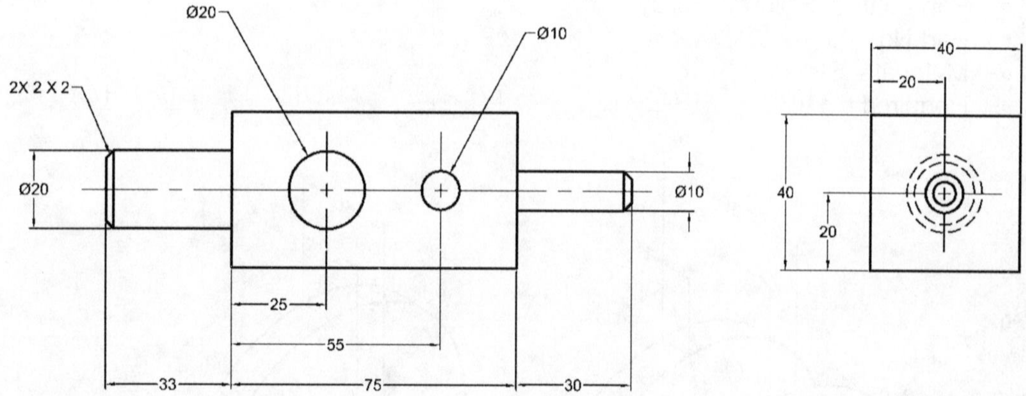

P19-4) Draw and dimension the *Drive Pulley* using proper dimensioning techniques. This *Drive Pulley* is part of the *Pulley Assembly* given in the Assembly chapter problem section. Notice that the dimensioned isometric drawing does not always use the correct symbols or dimensioning techniques.

- Part name = Drive Pulley
- Part No. = 2
- Material = Steel
- Required = 1

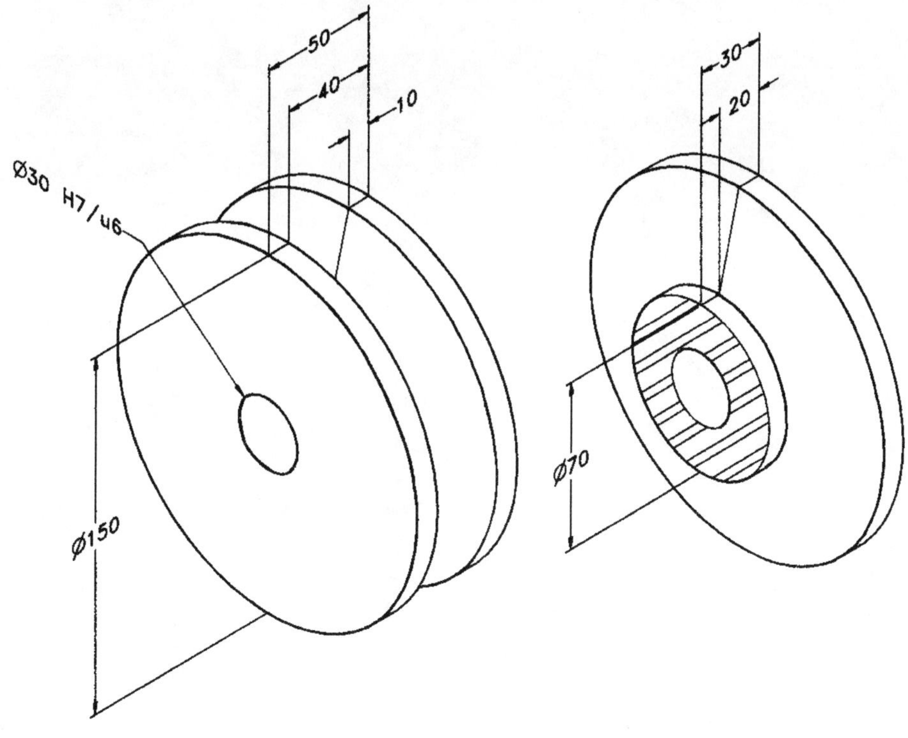

P19-5) Draw and dimension the *Follower Pulley* using proper dimensioning techniques. This *Follower Pulley* is part of the *Pulley Assembly* given in the Assembly chapter problem section. Notice that the dimensioned isometric drawing does not always use the correct symbols or dimensioning techniques.

- Part name = Follower Pulley
- Part No. = 3
- Material = Steel
- Required = 1

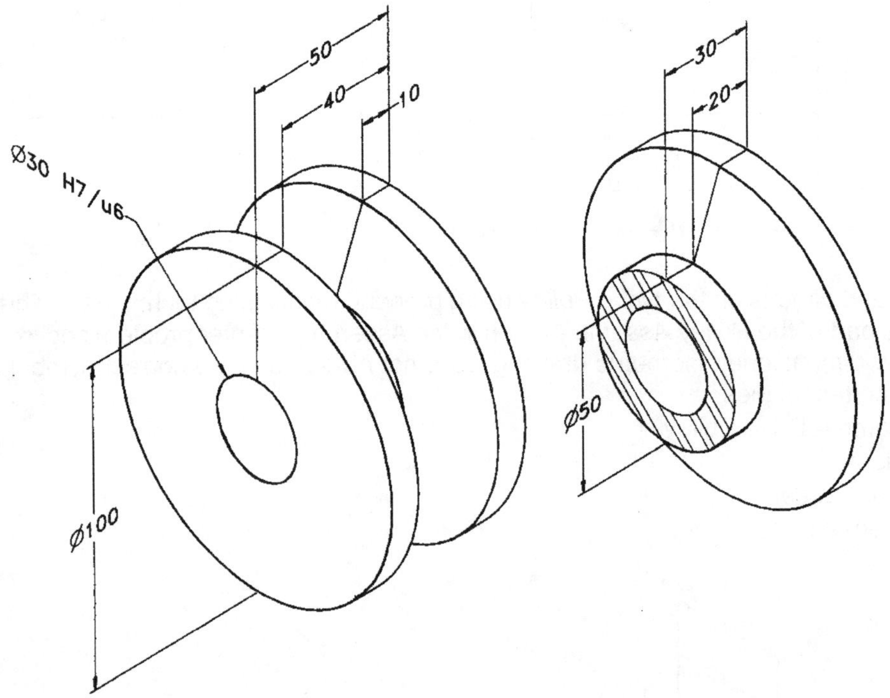

P19-6) Draw and dimension the *Shaft* using proper dimensioning techniques. This *Shaft* is part of the *Pulley Assembly* given in the Assembly chapter problem section. Notice that the dimensioned isometric drawing does not always use the correct symbols or dimensioning techniques.

- Part name = Shaft
- Part No. = 4
- Material = Hardened Steel
- Required = 1

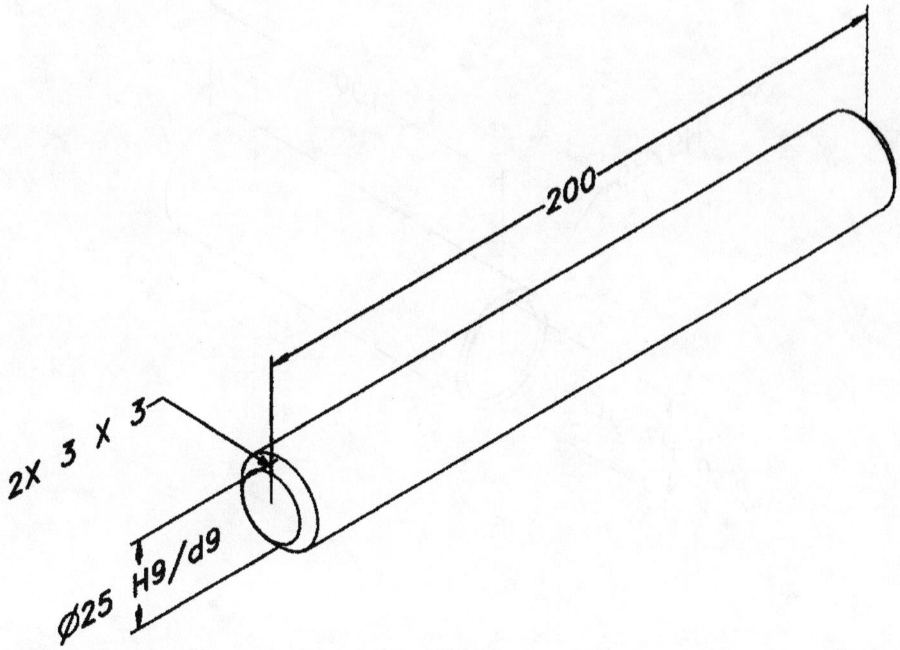

P19-7) Draw and dimension the *Bushing* using proper dimensioning techniques. This *Bushing* is part of the *Pulley Assembly* given in the Assembly chapter problem section. Notice that the dimensioned isometric drawing does not always use the correct symbols or dimensioning techniques.

- Part name = Bushing
- Part No. = 5
- Material = Brass
- Required = 1

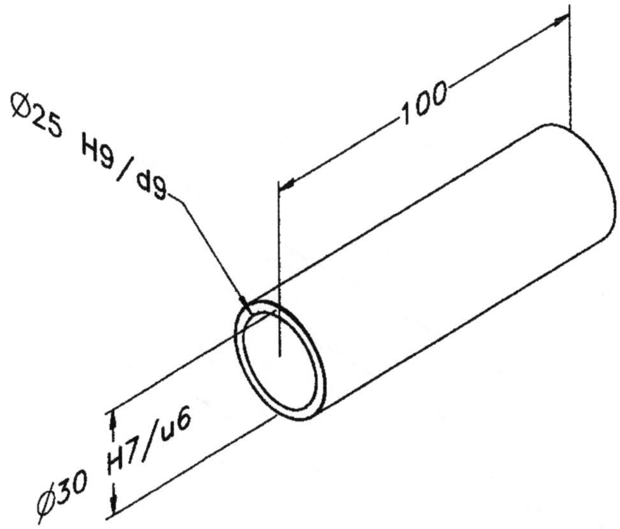

P19-8) Draw and dimension the *V-Anvil* using proper dimensioning techniques. This *V-Anvil* is part of the *Milling Jack* given in the Assembly chapter problem section. Notice that the dimensioned isometric drawing does not always use the correct symbols or dimensioning techniques.

- Part name = V-Anvil
- Part No. = 3
- Material = SAE 1045 – Heat Treat
- Required = 1

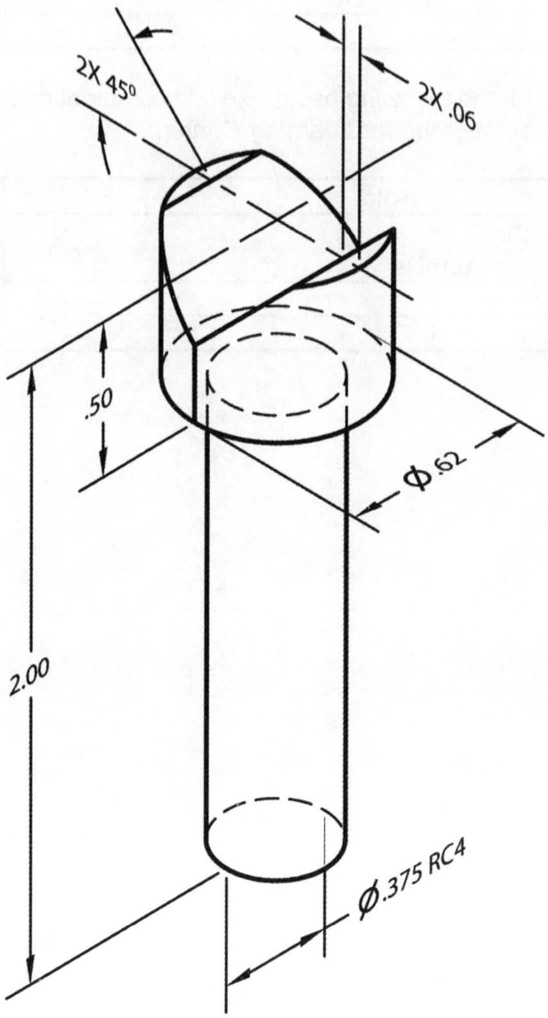

SP19-1) Find the limits of the shaft and hole for the following basic size – fit combinations. The answers to this problem are given on the *Independent Learning Content*.

	Shaft	**Hole**
Basic Size	.625	
Fits	**Limits**	
RC9		
LC2		
LT3		
FN1		

SP19-2) Find the limits of the shaft and hole for the following basic size – fit combinations. The answers to this problem are given on the *Independent Learning Content*.

	Shaft	**Hole**
Basic Size	8	
Fits	**Limits**	
H7/k6		
S7/h6		

CHAPTER 20

TOLERANCING IN AUTOCAD®

CHAPTER OUTLINE

CHAPTER SUMMARY

In this chapter you will learn how to apply tolerances to existing dimensions. The tolerance parameters may be set in the Tolerancing tab of the Dimension Styles Manager window. By the end of this chapter, you will be able to create toleranced dimensions using the limit and plus-minus tolerance forms.

20.1) INTRODUCTION

AutoCAD® gives you the ability to add toleranced dimensions to a detailed drawing. You can specify the tolerance form (limit or plus-minus) in the *Dimension Styles Manager* window.

There are three different procedures for adding toleranced dimensions to your drawing. The method you choose depends on the degree of forethought and the number of toleranced dimensions required.

1) You can change an existing dimension to a toleranced dimension using the **Override** button in the *Dimension Styles Manager* window and the **Dimension Update** command. This method is used if you only have a few toleranced dimensions and each dimension has different plus and minus tolerance values.
2) You can add new toleranced dimensions using the **Override** button in the *Dimension Styles Manager* window. This method is used if you have a number of toleranced dimensions.
3) You can add toleranced dimensions by creating and using a *Tolerance* dimension style. This is most useful if you have many toleranced dimensions that have the same plus and minus tolerance values.

20.2) TOLERANCE PARAMETERS

The parameters used to control the values and look of your toleranced dimensions are set in the *Tolerance* tab of the *Dimension Styles Manager* window. To enter the *Dimension Styles Manager* window use the command **DDIM**, **DIMSTYLE** or it can be accessed through the *Dimensions* panel.

Setting tolerance parameters

1) Command: **dimstyle** or *Dimensions* panel: 
2) *Dimension Styles Manager* window: ***Override...*** (Select ***New...*** if you want to create a *Tolerance* dimension style.)
3) *Override Current Style: ASME* window – *Tolerance* tab - *Tolerance format* area:
   a) *Method* field: Select the tolerance form.
      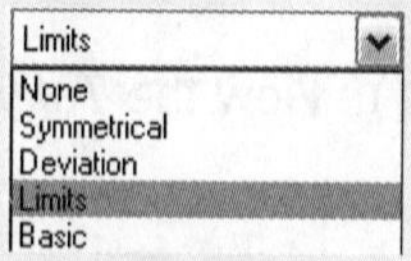

      - None = No tolerance
      - Symmetric = A plus-minus tolerance that is symmetric.
      - Deviation = A plus-minus tolerance.
      - Limits = A limit tolerance
      - Basic = Places a box around the dimension indicating a basic (non-toleranced) dimension.
   b) *Precision* field: Select the number of decimal places that your dimension will have.
   c) *Upper value* field: Enter the value that will be added to the basic or nominal size.
   d) *Lower value* field: Enter the value that will be subtracted from the basic or nominal size. (Note: If a negative number is placed in this box, the value will be added to the basic size.)
   e) *Vertical position field:* Select the position of the dimension symbols such as ∅ and R.
   f) ***OK***
4) *Dimension Styles Manager* window: ***Close***
5) Newly created dimensions will have the override properties. To change an existing dimension, use the *update* icon  located in the *Dimensions* panel.

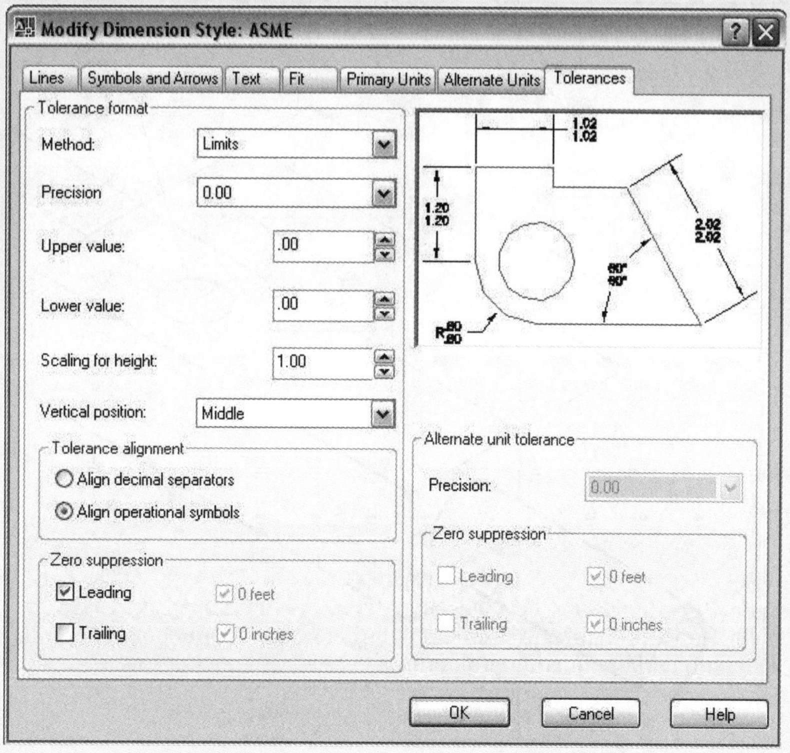

20.3) TOLERANCING TUTORIAL

The objective of this tutorial is to familiarize the user with the different tolerance settings and how to apply them.

20.3.1) Drawing the object

1) View the *Tolerancing* video and read sections 20.1) and 20.2).

2) 

set-inch.dwt. Your default dimension style should be the ASME style which was created in a chapter Exercise in the Dimensioning in AutoCAD chapter.

3) 

Tolerancing Tut.dwg.

4) Set your **LIMITS** to ***22*** x ***17***, **Zoom All**, and draw the necessary views and dimension the object as shown. Verify that your dimensions are annotative. Hover your mouse over a dimension. If the annotative symbol appears , they are annotative.

> **NOTE:** Don't worry if your dimensions are small. They are annotative and will be larger than they appear when you print your drawing.

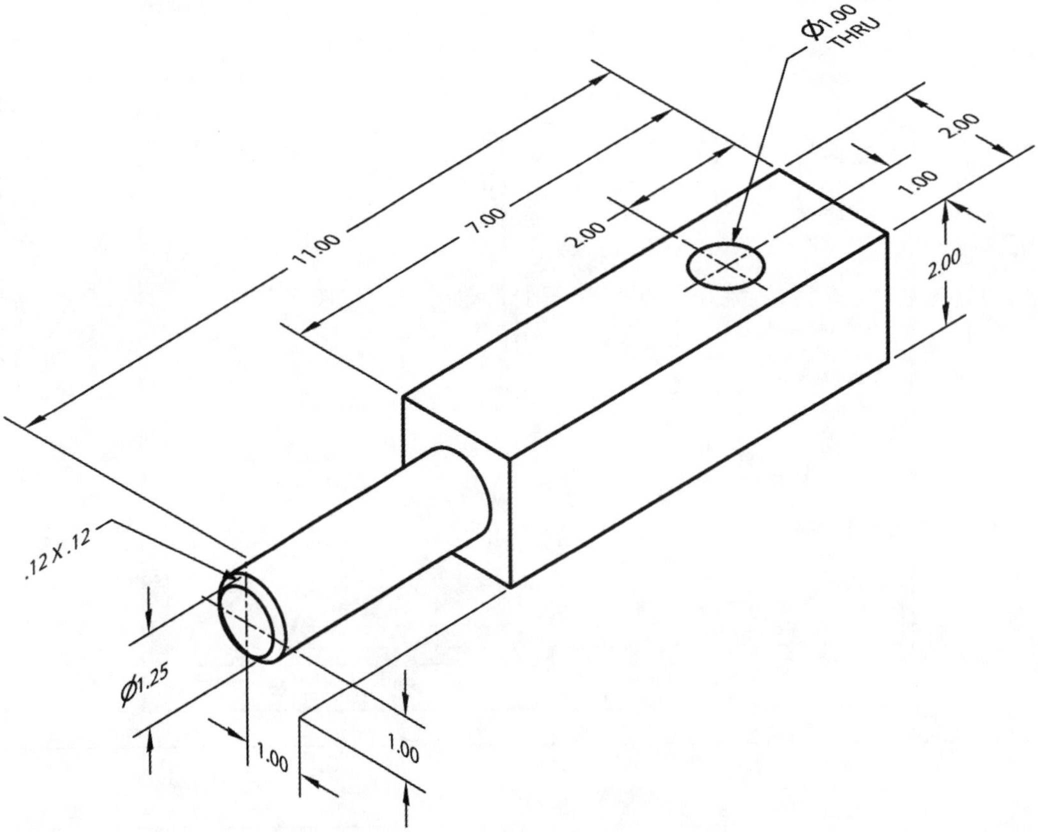

20.3.2) Tolerancing

Your detailed drawing should look something like the figure shown. There may be slight differences in the dimension placement. Your dimensions will look smaller when viewed in *Model* space. When working on an individual dimension, you may want to zoom in to get a better view.

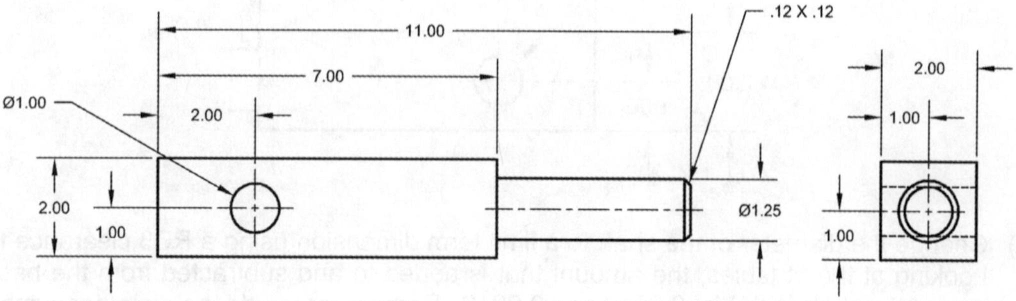

1) Change the dimension of the hole to a limit form dimension using a locational clearance fit of LC6. Looking at the fit tables, the amount that is added and subtracted to the basic size of the hole (1.00) is +0.002 and 0.

   a) Command: **dimstyle** or *Dimensions* panel:
   b) *Dimension Styles Manager* window: ***Override...***
   c) *Override Current Style: ASME* window – *Tolerance* tab – *Tolerance format* area:
      i. *Method* field: ***Limits***
      ii. *Precision* field: ***0.000***
      iii. *Upper value* field: **0.002**
      iv. *Lower value* field: **0**
      v. *Vertical position* field: ***Middle***
      vi. ***OK***
   d) *Dimension Styles Manager* window: ***Close***

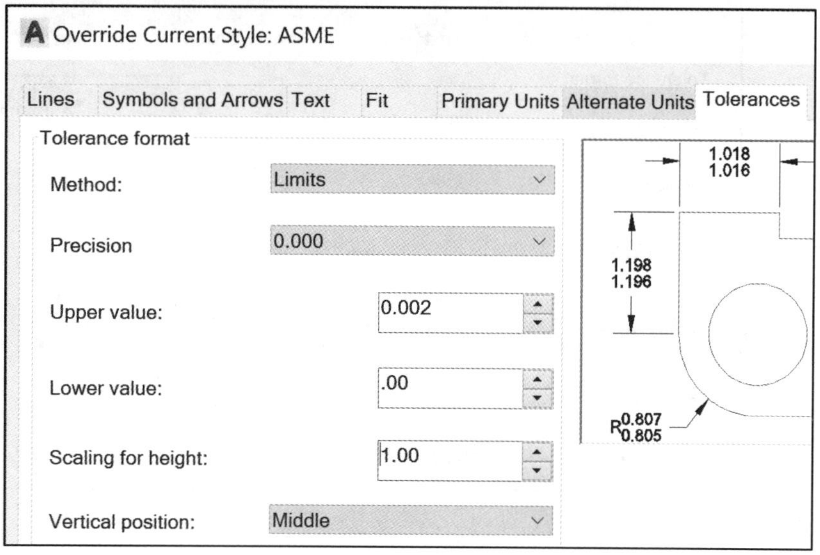

e) *Dimensions* panel:

f) `Select objects:` Select the ∅1.00 dimension of the hole.

g) `Select objects:` **Enter**

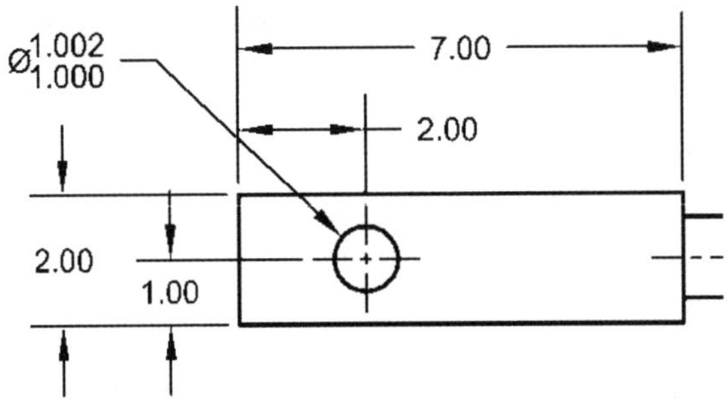

2) Change the diameter of the shaft to a limit form dimension using a RC3 clearance fit. Looking at the fit tables, the amount that is added to and subtracted from the basic size of the shaft (1.25) is -0.0010 and 0.0016. Remember to add the diameter symbol if you have not done so already. Don't worry; your dimensions will look much smaller.

a) Command: **dimstyle** or *Dimensions* panel:

b) *Dimension Styles Manager* window: ***Override...***

c) *Override Current Style: ASME* window – *Tolerance* tab – *Tolerance format* area:

   i. *Method* field: ***Limits***

   ii. *Precision* field: ***0.0000***

   iii. *Upper value* field: **0.0016**

   iv. *Lower value* field: **0.001**

   v. *Vertical position* field: ***Middle***

   vi. ***OK***

d) *Dimension Styles Manager* window: ***Close***

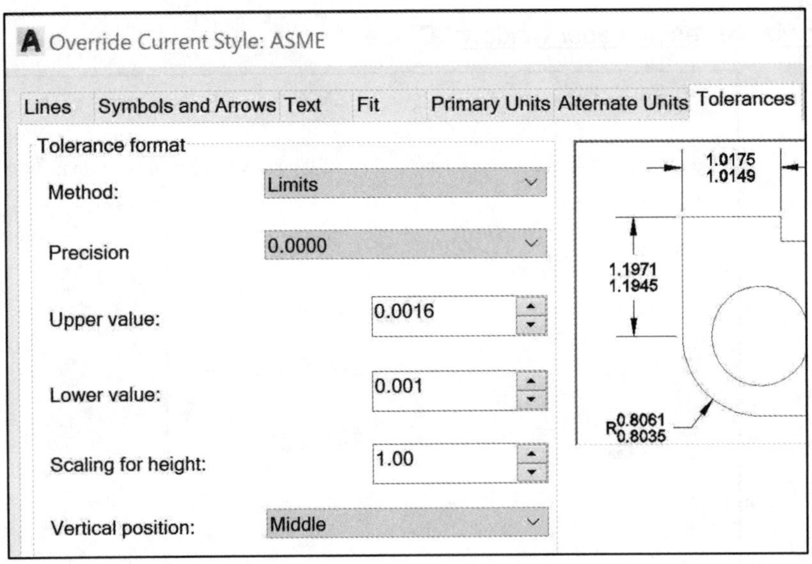

e) *Dimensions* panel: 

f) `Select objects:` Select the ∅1.25 dimension of the hole.

g) `Select objects:` **`Enter`**

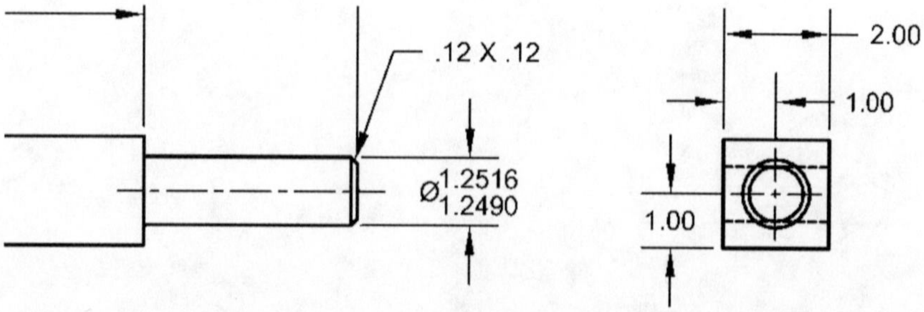

3) In a similar fashion, apply a ±0.001 ***symmetric*** tolerance to the dimensions that locate the shaft and a +0.0005 and -0.001 ***deviation*** tolerance to the 2.00 hole location dimension. The basic size and tolerance values should have the same number of decimal places and the leading zero on the tolerance values should be suppressed.

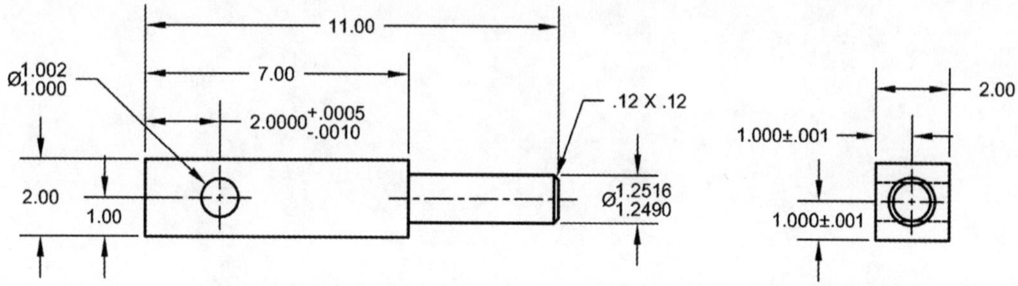

4) Save your drawing, enter ***Layout*** space, **insert** your title block and ***print*** your drawing using a 1:3 scale. By default, there is no 1:3 scale. You will have to add a custom scale and then add that scale support to your annotative objects.

NOTES:

TOLERANCING IN AUTOCAD QUESTIONS

Name: ______________________________ Date: ____________

Q20-1) This dimension was created using the ... tolerancing method. 10.0 ± 0.1

a) symmetrical
b) deviation
c) limit
d) basic

Q20-2) This dimension was created using the ... tolerancing method. $10.0^{+0.1}_{-0.2}$

a) symmetrical
b) deviation
c) limit
d) basic

Q20-3) This dimension was created using the ... tolerancing method. $\varnothing^{1.001}_{.999}$

a) symmetrical
b) deviation
c) limit
d) basic

Q20-4) If -0.001 is typed into the lower value field, then 0.001 will be ... to/from the basic size.

a) added
b) subtracted
c) multiplied
d) divided

Q20-5) This option allows you to change the settings of your current dimension style and apply those changes.

a) new
b) modify
c) override
d) create

Q20-6) This option allows you to change the settings of your current dimension style and apply those changes without corrupting the original style.

a) new
b) modify
c) override
d) create

NOTES:

TOLERANCING IN AUTOCAD PROBLEMS

P20-1) Draw the following object including dimensions. Apply a H7/g6 Sliding clearance fit to the ∅20 hole and shaft. Apply a U7/h6 force fit to the ∅10 hole and shaft. Insert your title block and print.

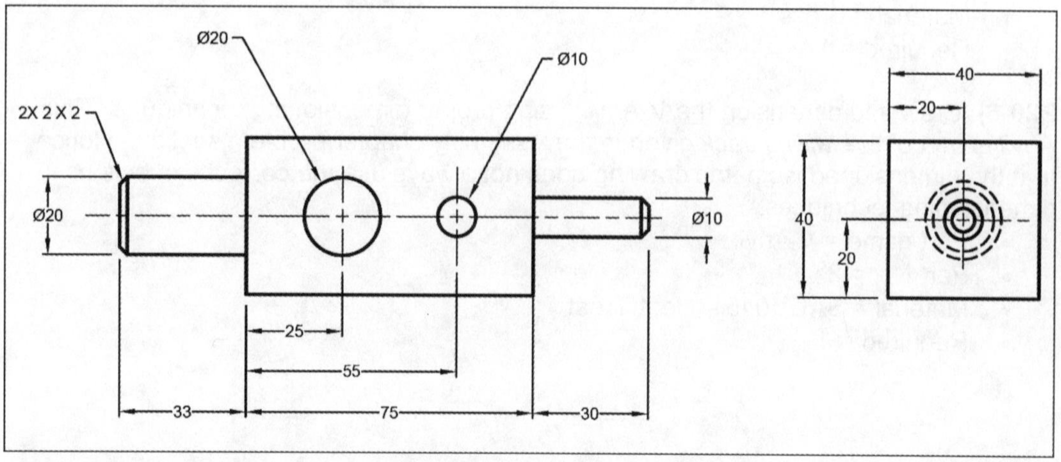

P20-2) Draw and dimension the *Drive Pulley* using proper dimensioning techniques. This *Drive Pulley* is part of the *Pulley Assembly* given in the Assembly chapter problem section. Notice that the dimensioned isometric drawing does not always use the correct symbols or dimensioning techniques.

- Part name = Drive Pulley
- Part No. = 2
- Material = Steel
- Required = 1

P20-3) Draw and dimension the *Follower Pulley* using proper dimensioning techniques. This *Follower Pulley* is part of the *Pulley Assembly* given in the Assembly chapter problem section. Notice that the dimensioned isometric drawing does not always use the correct symbols or dimensioning techniques.

- Part name = Follower Pulley
- Part No. = 3
- Material = Steel
- Required = 1

P20-4) Draw and dimension the *Shaft* using proper dimensioning techniques. This *Shaft* is part of the *Pulley Assembly* given in the Assembly chapter problem section. Notice that the dimensioned isometric drawing does not always use the correct symbols or dimensioning techniques.

- Part name = Shaft
- Part No. = 4
- Material = Hardened Steel
- Required = 1

P20-5) Draw and dimension the *Bushing* using proper dimensioning techniques. This *Bushing* is part of the *Pulley Assembly* given in the Assembly chapter problem section. Notice that the dimensioned isometric drawing does not always use the correct symbols or dimensioning techniques.

- Part name = Bushing
- Part No. = 5
- Material = Brass
- Required = 1

P20-6) Draw and dimension the *V-Anvil* using proper dimensioning techniques. This *V-Anvil* is part of the *Milling Jack* given in the Assembly chapter problem section. Notice that the dimensioned isometric drawing does not always use the correct symbols or dimensioning techniques.

- Part name = V-Anvil
- Part No. = 3
- Material = SAE 1045 – Heat Treat
- Required = 1

CHAPTER 21

READING THREADS AND FASTENERS

CHAPTER OUTLINE

CHAPTER SUMMARY

In this chapter you will learn about fasteners. Fasteners give us the means to assemble parts and to later disassemble them if necessary. Most fasteners have threads; therefore, it is important to understand thread notation when learning about fasteners. By the end of this chapter, you will be able to recognize thread symbols and interpret a thread note. You will also be introduced to the standard parts sheet. This sheet contains information about purchased items.

21.1) FASTENERS

Fasteners include items such as bolts, nuts, set screws, washers, keys, and pins, just to name a few. Fasteners are not a permanent means of assembly, such as welding or adhesives. They are used in the assembly of machines that, in the future, may need to be taken apart and serviced. The most common type of fastener is the screw. There are many types of screws and many types of screw threads or thread forms.

Fasteners and threaded features are specified on engineering drawings. If the fastener is to be machined, a detailed drawing is produced. If, however, the fastener is purchased, specifications are given to allow the fastener to be ordered correctly. All fasteners that are going to be purchased are specified on a standard parts sheet. Information about the type, size and quantity (among other information) is given on the standard parts sheet. Most of this chapter will focus on how to recognize threads and interpret the thread note.

It is important that you understand how to identify threads on a print. To save time and computer memory, threads are usually not drawn to look realistic. A thread symbol is used. The different thread symbols used and how to read thread notes will be described in this chapter.

21.2) SCREW THREAD DEFINITIONS

Fill in *Exercise 21.2-1* as you read through these definitions.

- Screw Thread: A screw thread is a ridge of uniform section in the form of a helix (see Figure 21.2-1).
- External Thread: External threads are on the outside of a member. A chamfer on the end of the screw thread makes it easier to engage the nut.
- Internal Thread: Internal threads are on the inside of a member. A chamfer on the entrance of the threaded hole makes it easier to receive the screw.
- Major DIA (D): The major diameter is the largest diameter for both internal and external threads. Sometimes referred to as the nominal or basic size.
- Minor DIA (d): The minor diameter is the smallest diameter.
- Pitch DIA (d_P): Consider a line that cuts across the threads such that the distance on the line that cuts the thread space equals the distance of the line that cuts the actual thread. The pitch diameter is the location of this line.
- Crest: The crest is the top surface of the thread.
- Root: The root is the bottom surface of the thread.
- Side: The side is the surface between the crest and root.

- Depth of thread: The depth of thread is the perpendicular distance between the crest and the root and is equal to (D-d)/2.
- Pitch (P): The pitch is the distance from a point on one thread to the corresponding point on the next thread. The pitch is given in inches per thread or millimeters per thread.
- Angle of Thread (A): The angle of thread is the angle between the sides of the threads.
- Screw Axis: The screw axis is the longitudinal centerline.
- Lead: The lead is the distance a screw thread advances axially in one turn.
- Right-Handed Thread: Right-handed threads advance when turned clockwise (CW). Threads are assumed RH unless specified otherwise.
- Left-Handed Thread: Left-handed threads advance when turned counterclockwise (CCW).

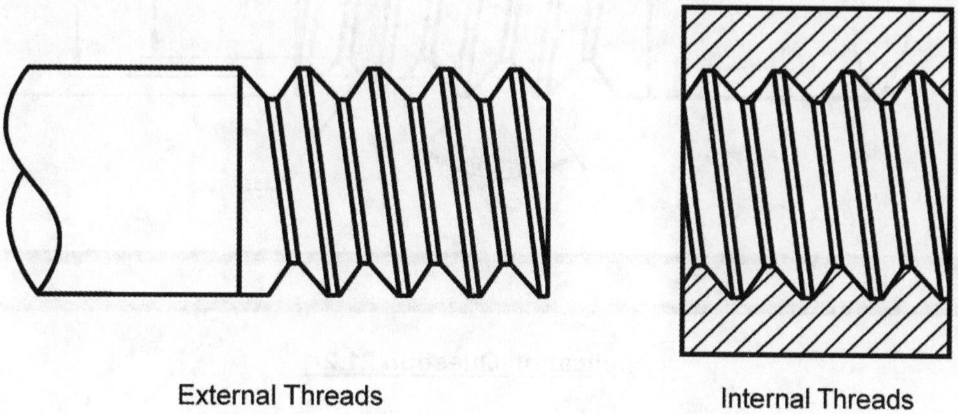

Figure 21.2-1: External and internal threads.

Exercise 21.2-1: Screw thread features

Identify the screw thread features using the preceding definitions as a guide.

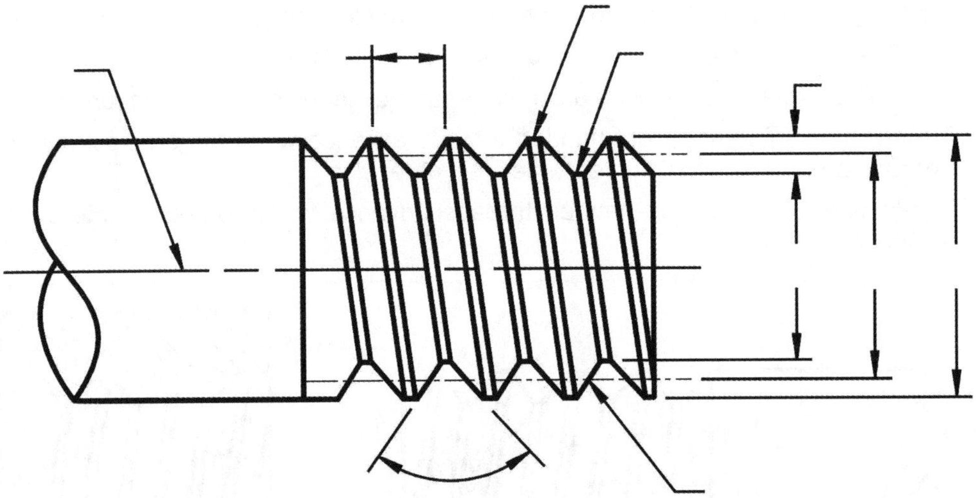

Application Question 21.2-1

Name an example of a left-handed thread.

21.3) RECOGNIZING SCREW THREADS

There are three methods of representing screw threads on a drawing: ***detailed, schematic,*** and ***simplified.***

21.3.1) Detailed representation

A detailed representation is a close approximation of the appearance of an actual screw thread (see Figure 21.2-1).

21.3.2) Schematic representation

The schematic representation is nearly as effective as the detailed representation. Staggered lines are used to represent the thread roots and crests (see Figure 21.3-1)

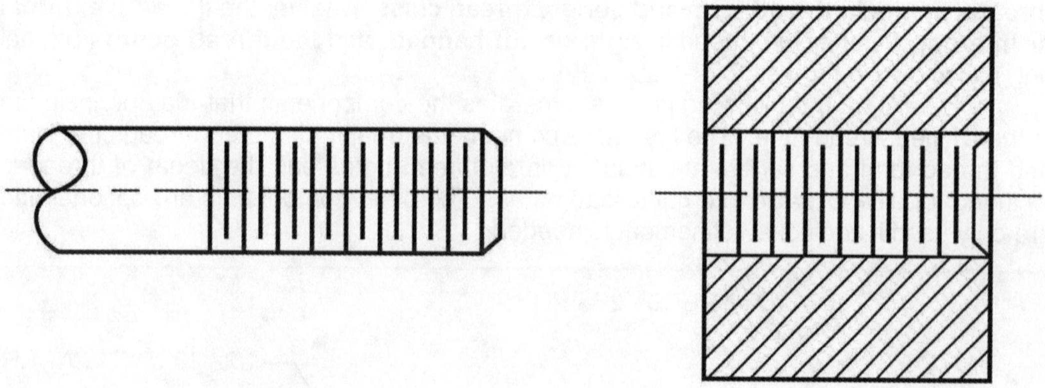

External Threads | Internal Threads

Figure 21.3-1: Schematic representation of threads.

21.3.3) Simplified representation

In the simplified representation, the screw threads are drawn using visible and hidden lines to represent the major and minor diameters (See Figure 21.4-2). This method is the most widely used because of its simplicity. However, it is important that you recognize the simplified representation of a thread as threads. Many times, this symbol can be confused for a hollow tube.

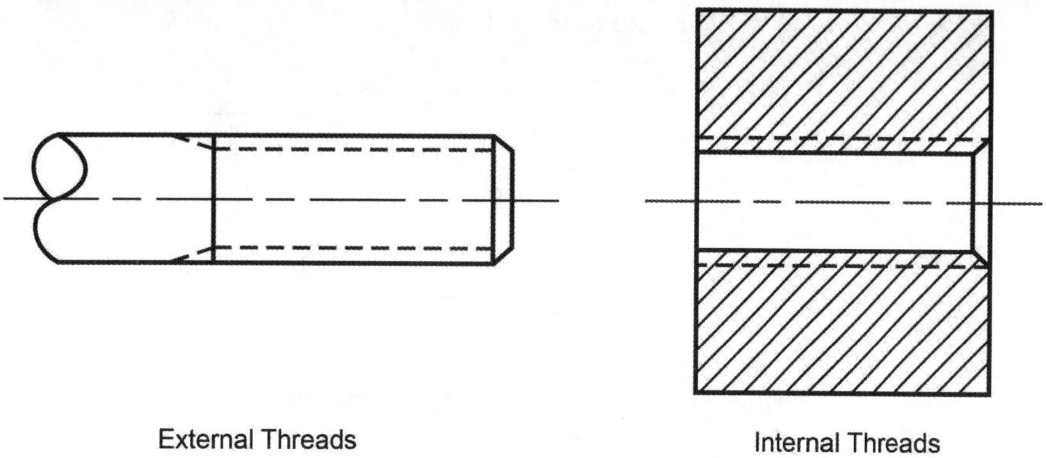

External Threads | Internal Threads

Figure 21.3-2: Simplified representation of threads.

21.4) UNIFIED THREAD NOTE

Threads need to be identified with a note that specifies the thread form and size among other things. Each type of thread (Unified, Metric, ACME, etc...) has its own way of being identified. Unified threads are identified in a thread note by their **major diameter, threads per inch, thread form and series, thread class**, whether the thread is **external or internal**, whether the thread is **right or left handed**, and the **thread depth** (internal only) as shown in Figures 21.4-1 and 21.4-2.

The list on the following page enumerates the components that may be included in the Unified thread note. The first three components (major diameter, threads per inch, and thread form and series) are included in all thread notes and the depth of thread is included for all applicable internal thread notes. The other components are optional and are only used if additional refinement is needed.

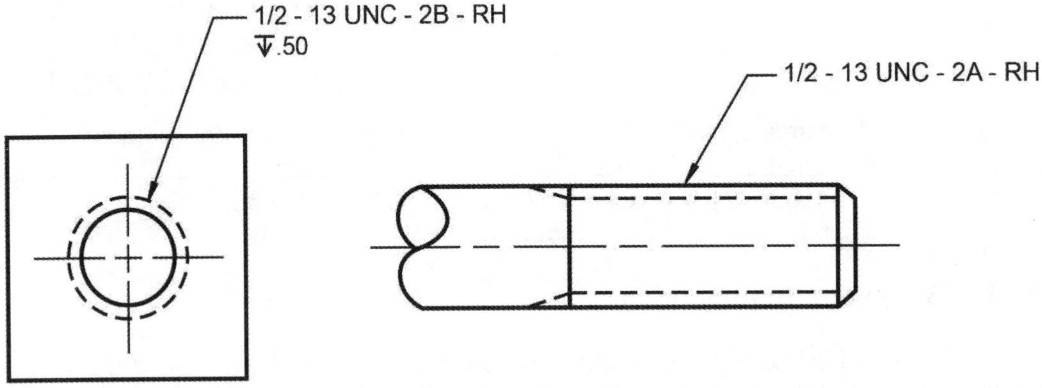

Figure 21.4-1: Examples of Unified thread notes

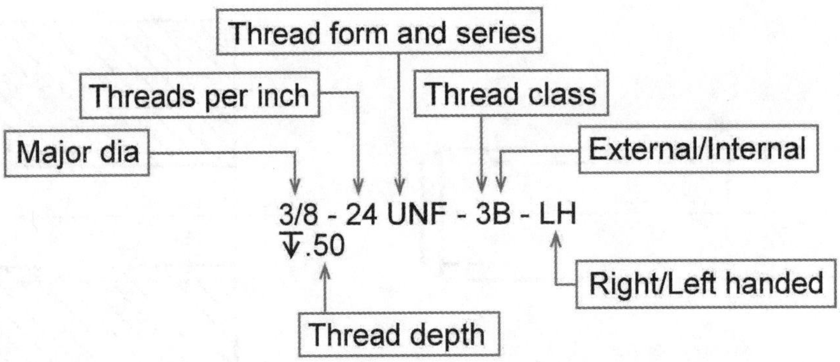

Figure 21.4-2: Unified thread note components

Unified thread note components

1. Major Diameter: The major diameter is the largest diameter for both internal and external threads.
2. Threads per Inch: The number of threads per inch is equal to one over the pitch.
3. Thread Form and Series: The thread form is the shape of the thread cut (Unified) and the thread series is the number of threads per inch for a particular diameter (coarse, fine, extra fine).
   - UNC: UNC stands for *Unified National coarse*. Coarse threads are the most commonly used thread.
   - UNF: UNF stands for *Unified National fine*. Fine threads are used when high degree of tightness is required.
   - UNEF: UNEF stands for *Unified National extra fine*. Extra fine threads are used when the length of engagement is limited (e.g., sheet metal).
4. Thread Class: The thread class indicates the closeness of fit between the two mating threaded parts. There are three thread classes. A thread class of "1" indicates a generous tolerance and used when rapid assembly and disassembly is required. A thread class of "2" is a normal production fit. This fit is assumed if none is stated. A thread class of "3" is used when high accuracy is required.
5. External or Internal Threads: An "A" (external threads) or "B" (internal threads) is placed next to the thread class to indicate whether the threads are external or internal.
6. Right-handed or left-handed thread: Right-handed threads are indicated by the symbol "RH" and left-handed threads are indicated by the symbol "LH." Right-handed threads are assumed if none is stated.
7. Depth of thread: The thread depth is given at the end of the thread note and indicates the thread depth for internal threads. The stated depth is the depth of complete threads. There may be some incomplete threads at the end that are present due to how the threads are manufactured.

Try Exercise 21.4-1

Exercise 21.4-1: Unified National thread note components

Identify the different components of the following Unified National thread note.

1/4 – 20 UNC – 2A – RH

1/4	
20	
UNC	
2	
A	
RH	

21.5) METRIC THREAD NOTE

Metric threads are identified, in a thread note, by "**M**" for Metric thread form, the **major diameter** followed by a lower case "**x**", **pitch, tolerance class**, whether the thread is **right or left-handed**, and **thread depth** (internal only) as shown in Figures 21.5-1, 21.5-2 and 21.5-3.

The list of components that may be included in a Metric thread note is given on the following page. The first three components (Metric form, major diameter, and pitch) are included in all thread notes and the depth of thread is included for all applicable internal thread notes. The other components are optional and are only used if additional refinement is needed.

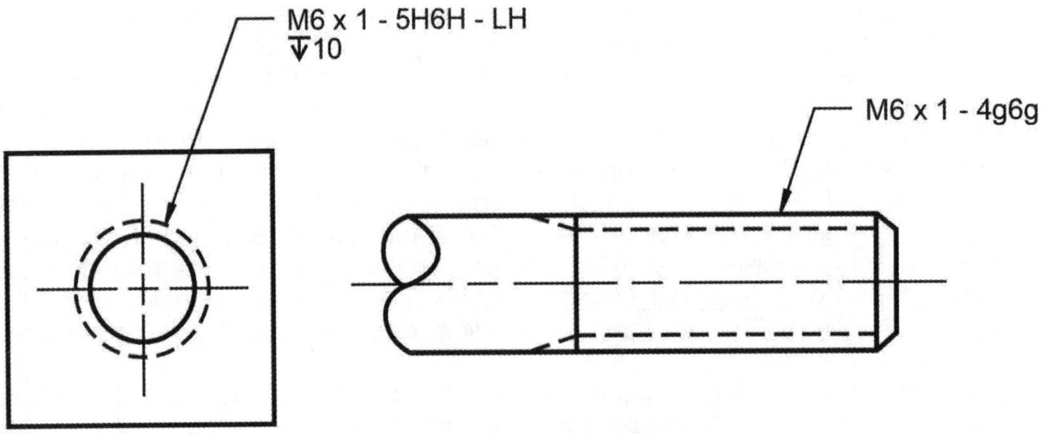

Figure 21.5-1: Examples of Metric thread notes

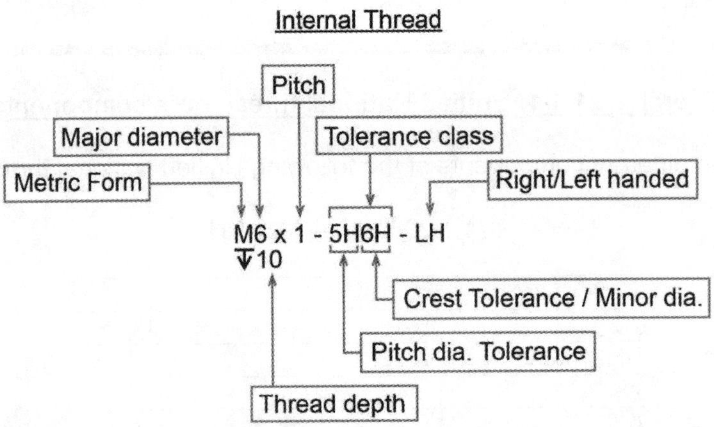

Figure 21.5-2: Metric thread note example for internal threads

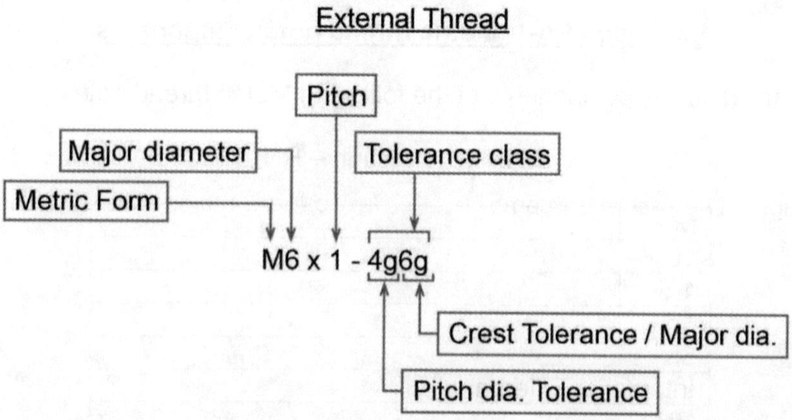

Figure 21.5-3: Metric thread note example for internal threads

Metric thread note components

1. Metric Form: Placing an "M" before the major diameter indicates the Metric thread form.
2. Major Diameter: This major diameter is the largest diameter for both internal and external.
3. Pitch: The pitch is given in millimeters per thread.
4. Tolerance Class: The tolerance class describes the looseness or tightness of fit between the internal and external threads. The tolerance class contains both a **tolerance grade** given by a number and **tolerance position** given by a letter. In a thread note, the pitch diameter tolerance is stated first followed by the crest diameter tolerance if it is different. The crest diameter tolerance is the tolerance on the major diameter for an external thread and the tolerance on the minor diameter for an internal thread. Two classes of Metric thread fits are generally recognized. For general purpose, the fit "6H/6g" is used. This fit is assumed if none is stated. For a closer fit, "6H/5g6g" is used.
   - Tolerance Grade: The tolerance grade is indicated by a number. The smaller the number the tighter the fit. The number "5" indicates good commercial practice. The number "6" is for general purpose threads and is equivalent to the thread class "2" used for Unified National threads.
   - Tolerance Position: The tolerance position specifies the amount of allowance and is indicated by a letter. Upper case letters are used for internal threads and lower-case letters for external threads. The letter "e" is used for large allowances, "g" and "G" are used for small allowances, and "h" and "H" are used for no allowance.
5. Right-handed or left-handed thread: Right-handed threads are indicated by the symbol "RH" and left handed threads are indicated by the symbol "LH." Right-handed threads are assumed if none is stated.
6. Depth of thread: The thread depth is given at the end of the thread note and indicates the thread depth for internal threads, not the tap drill depth.

Try Exercise 21.5-1

Exercise 21.5-1: Metric thread note components

Identify the different components of the following Metric thread notes.

M10 x 1.5 – 4h6h – RH

M	
10	
1.5	
4h	
6h	
Internal or External	
RH	

21.6) STANDARD PARTS

Standard parts include any part that can be bought off the shelf. **Standard parts are not drawn.** This could include bolts, nuts, washers, keys, etc. Purchasing information is specified on a standard parts sheet attached to the back of a working drawing package. Figure 21.6-1 shows an example of a standard parts sheet which lists four different items. Some of the components of the standard parts sheet will become clearer after learning about assembly drawings.

21.6.1) General fastener specifications

The information that is usually specified on a standard parts sheet for a general fastener is listed below.

1. Thread specification (only if the fastener contains threads)
2. Head/point style or shape and name of the fastener
3. Fastener length or size
4. Fastener series
5. Material
6. Special requirements (e.g., coatings, finishes, specifications to meet)
7. QTY REQ'D (i.e., number required)

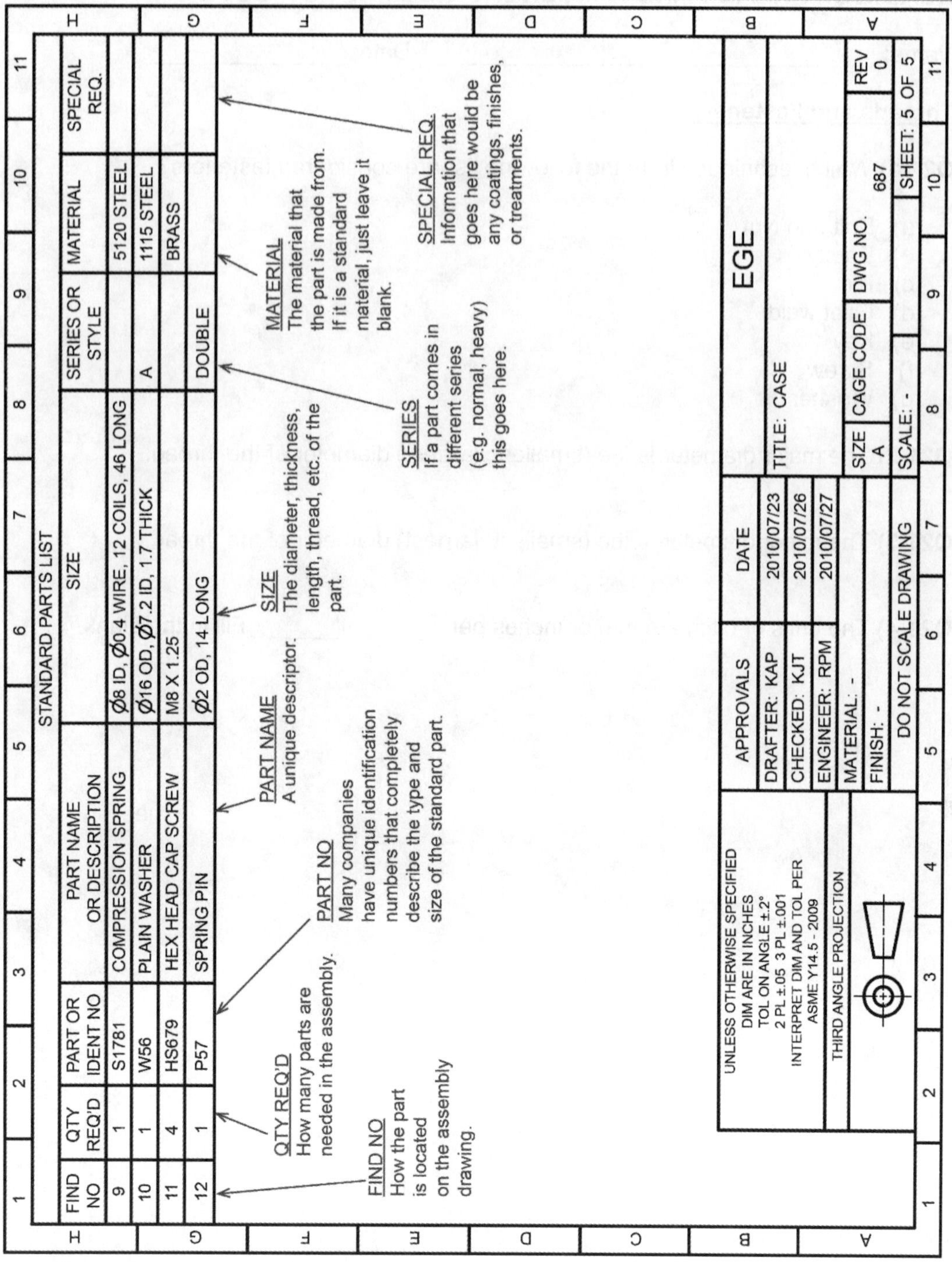

Figure 21.6-1: Standard parts sheet.

READING THREADS AND FASTENERS QUESTIONS – SET 1

Name: ______________________________ Date: ______________

Threads and Fasteners

Q21-1) Which techniques from the following list are considered fasteners?

a) Bolt and Nut
b) Epoxy
c) Pin
d) Fillet weld
e) Key
f) Screw
g) Washer

Q21-2) The major diameter is the (smallest, largest) diameter of the thread.

Q21-3) The minor diameter is the (smallest, largest) diameter of the thread.

Q21-4) The units of pitch are mm or inches per ____________. Fill in the blank.

Q21-5) Label the following thread representations as *Detailed*, *Schematic*, or *Simplified*.

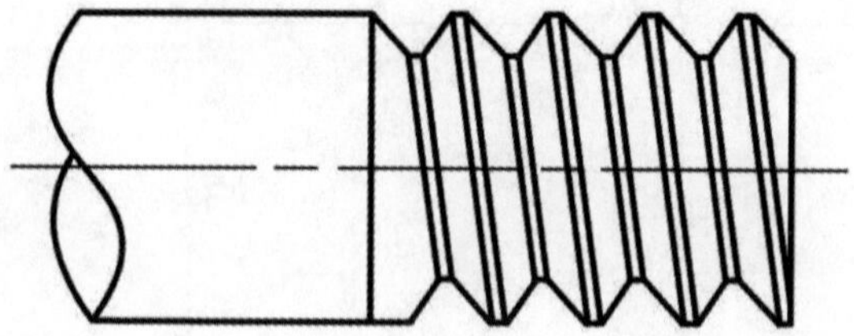

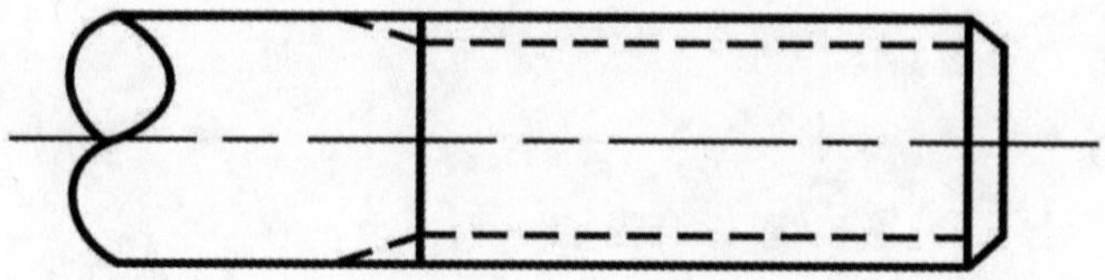

Q21-6) M5 x 0.8. M stands for ______________________? Fill in the blank.

Q21-7) Of the two listed threads, circle the one that is the fine thread.

1/4 – 20 1/4 - 28

Q21-8) Of the two listed threads, circle the one that is the fine thread.

M20 x 2.5 M20 x 1.5

Q21-9) What are the two most common thread forms (i.e., types)?

READING THREADS AND FASTENERS QUESTIONS – SET 2

Name: ________________________________ Date: _______________

Unified national threads

Q21-10) 1/4 - 20 UNC. What is 20?

a) Major diameter
b) Pitch
c) One over the pitch
d) Thread form
e) Thread series

Q21-11) 1/2 - 13 UNC. What is UN?

a) Major diameter
b) Pitch
c) One over the pitch
d) Thread form
e) Thread series

Q21-12) 3/8 - 24 UNF. What is F?

a) Major diameter
b) Pitch
c) One over the pitch
d) Thread form
e) Thread series

Q21-13) 5/8 - 24 UNEF – 2A - RH. What is 2?

a) Right handed threads
b) Left handed threads
c) Thread series
d) Thread class
e) External threads
f) Internal threads

Q21-14) 1 - 8 UNC – 3B - RH. What is B?

a) Right handed threads
b) Left handed threads
c) Thread series
d) Thread class
e) External threads
f) Internal threads

Q21-15) 1/2 - 20 UNF – 2B - LH. What is LH?

a) Right handed threads
b) Left handed threads
c) Thread series
d) Thread class
e) External threads
f) Internal threads

Q21-16) #10 - 24 UNC. What is #10?

a) Major diameter
b) Pitch
c) One over the pitch
d) Thread form
e) Thread series

Metric threads

Q21-17) M4 x 0.7. What is 4?

a) Major diameter
b) Pitch
c) One over the pitch
d) Thread form
e) Thread series
f) Tolerance class

Q21-18) M12 x 1.25. What is 1.25?

a) Major diameter
b) Pitch
c) One over the pitch
d) Thread form
e) Thread series
f) Tolerance class

Q21-19) M6 x 1 – 4h6h – RH. What is 4h6h?

a) Major diameter
b) Pitch
c) One over the pitch
d) Thread form
e) Thread series
f) Tolerance class

NOTES:

READING THREADS AND FASTENERS PROBLEMS

Name: ______________________________ Date: ______________

P21-1) The figure shown is an assembly drawing of a Tool Post. Each distinct part is identified by a number. The Tool Post has 7 distinct threaded parts. Circle the number of each part that contains a threaded feature. For example, part 9 is circled because it represents a set screw.

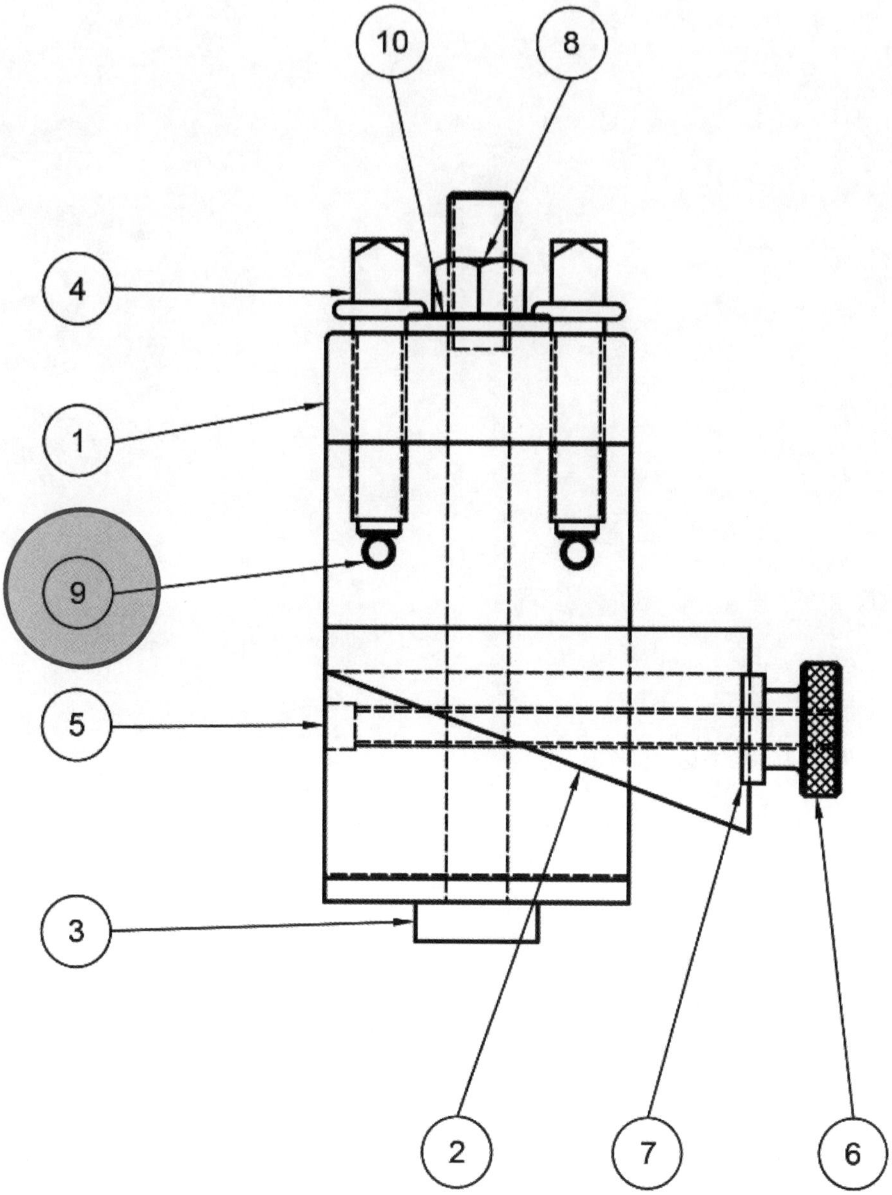

NOTES:

CHAPTER 22

CREATING THREADS AND FASTENERS

CHAPTER OUTLINE

CHAPTER SUMMARY

In this chapter you will learn how to draw and note fastener information. Most fasteners have threads; therefore, it is important to understand thread notation. By the end of this chapter, you will be able to draw and correctly annotate threads on an orthographic projection. You will also be able to calculate an appropriate bolt or screw clearance hole and generate a standard parts sheet.

22.1) FASTENERS REVIEW

In the previous chapter we learned about the different features on a helical screw and three different ways to represent screw threads on a drawing. Let's refresh our memories by doing the following exercises.

Try Exercise 22.1-1 and 22.1-2

Exercise 22.1-1

Dimension the following features on the given screw thread. Indicate on both the external and internal thread.

- Major diameter
- Minor diameter
- Pitch

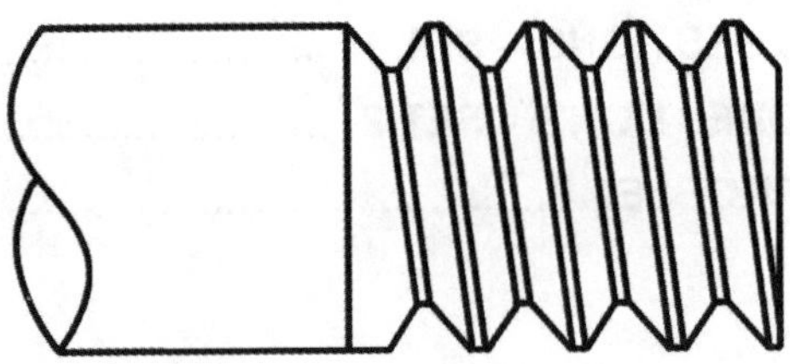

External Threads

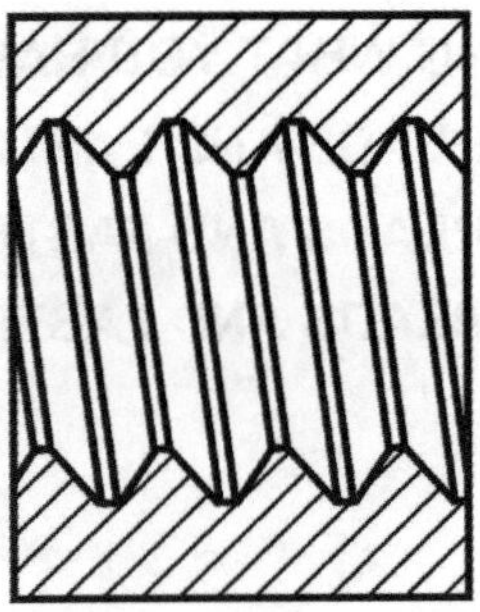

Internal Threads

Exercise 22.1-2

- Identify which type of thread symbol is being used.

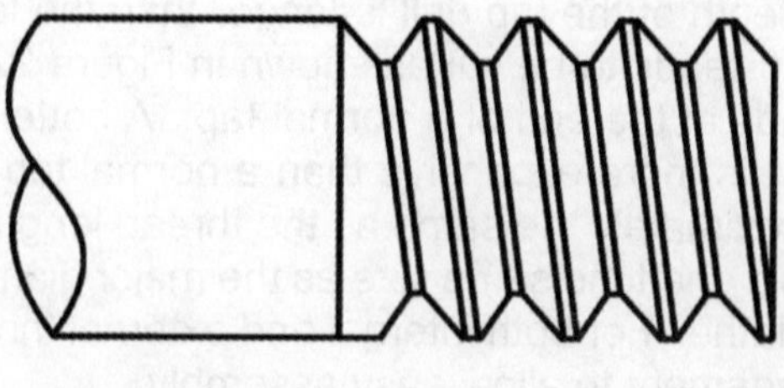

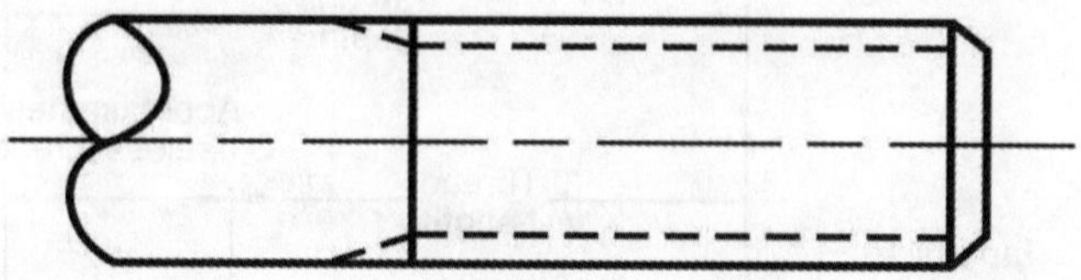

22.2) MANUFACTURING SCREW THREADS

Before proceeding with a description of how to draw screw threads, it is helpful to understand the manufacturing processes used to produce threads.

To cut internal threads, a tap drill hole is drilled first and then the threads are cut using a tap. The tap drill hole is a little bigger than the minor diameter of the mating external thread to allow engagement. The depth of the tap drill is longer than the length of the threads to allow the proper amount of threads to be cut as shown in Figure 22.2-1. There are approximately three useless threads at the end of a normal tap. A bottom tap has useful threads all the way to the end but is more expensive than a normal tap. If a bottom tap is used, the tap drill depth is approximately the same as the thread length.

To cut external threads, you start with a shaft the same size as the major diameter. Then, the threads are cut using a die or on a lathe. For both internal and external threads, a chamfer is usually cut at the points of engagement to allow easy assembly.

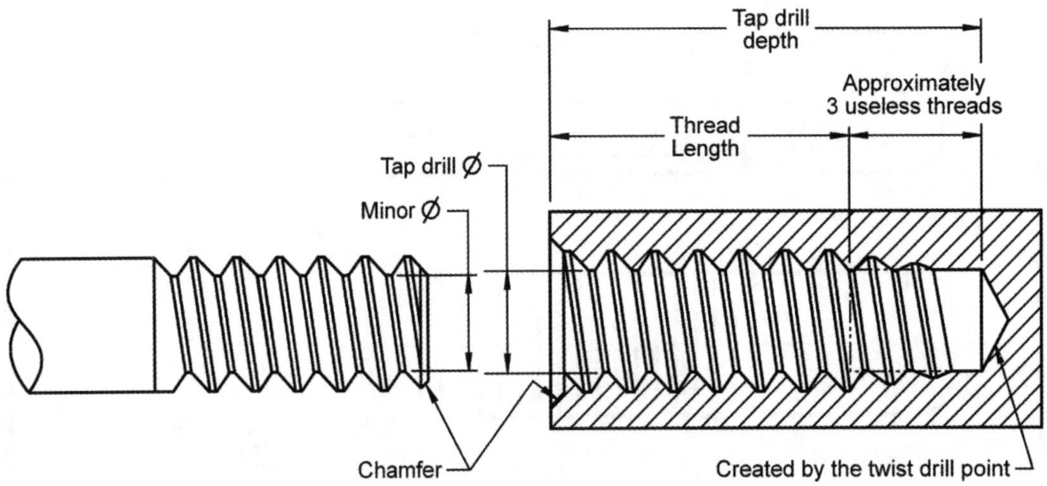

Figure 22.2-1: Manufacturing screw threads.

22.3) DRAWING SCREW THREADS

There are three methods of representing screw threads on a drawing: ***detailed, schematic,*** **and** ***simplified.*** The screw thread representations and standards presented in this chapter are in accordance with the ASME Y14.6-2001 standard. The physical dimension of a particular thread may be obtained in Appendix B.

22.3.1) Detailed representation

A detailed representation is a close approximation of the appearance of an actual screw thread. The form of the thread is simplified by showing the helix structure with straight lines and the truncated crests and roots as a sharp 'V' similar to that shown in Figure 22.3-1. This method is comparatively difficult, time consuming, and takes up a lot of computer memory.

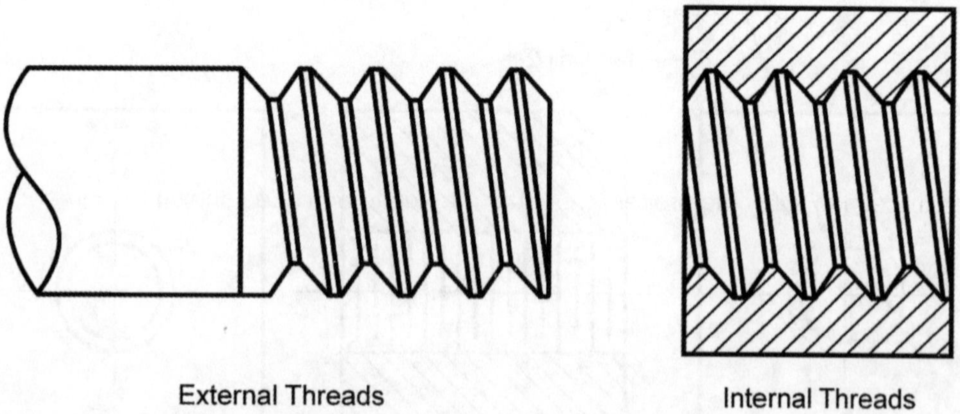

Figure 22.3-1: External and internal threads.

22.3.2) Schematic representation

The schematic representation is nearly as effective as the detailed representation and is much easier to draw. The schematic representation draws staggered lines that represent the thread roots and crests (see Figures 22.3-2 and 22.3-3). This method should not be used for hidden internal threads or sections of external threads.

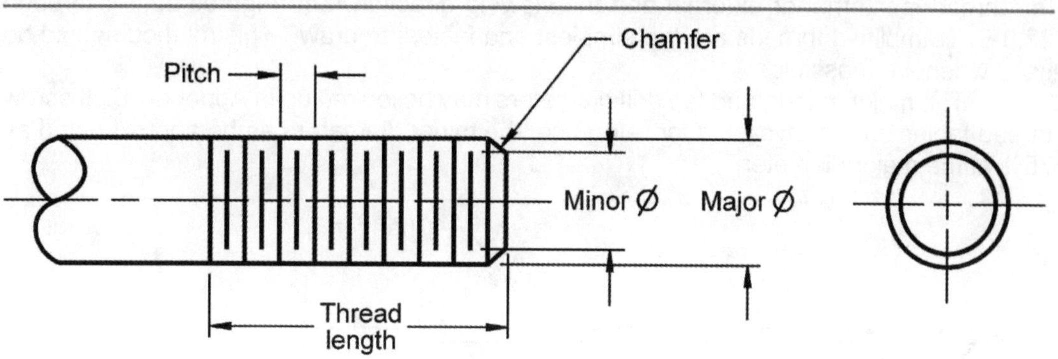

Figure 22.3-2: Schematic representation of external threads.

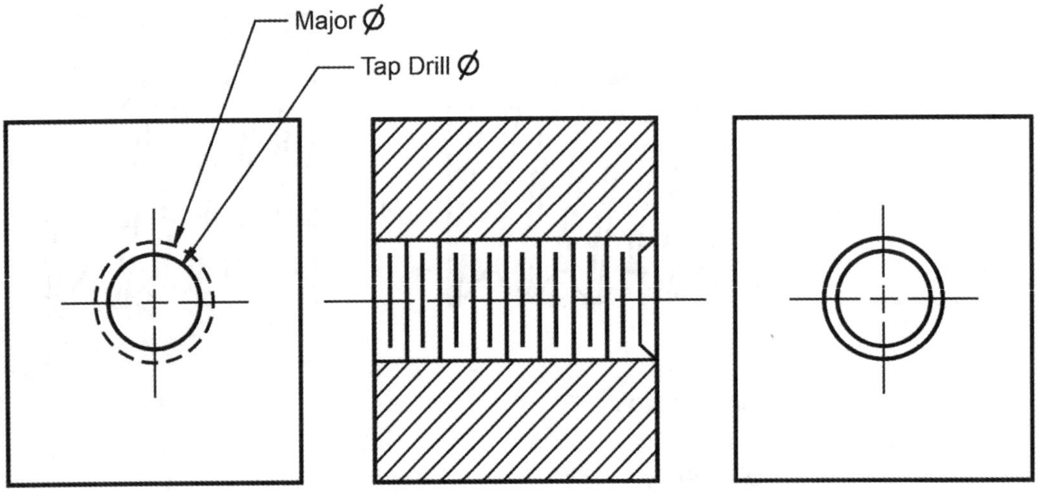

Figure 22.3-3: Schematic representation of internal threads.

22.3.3) Simplified representation

In the simplified representation, the screw threads are drawn using visible and hidden lines to represent the major and minor diameters. Line choice depends on whether the thread is internal or external and the viewing direction (see Figures 22.3-4 through 22.3-6). Simplified threads are the simplest and fastest to draw. This method should be used whenever possible.

The major, minor, and tap drill diameters may be looked up in Appendix B. If screw thread tables are not available for reference, the minor diameter can be approximated as 75% of the major diameter.

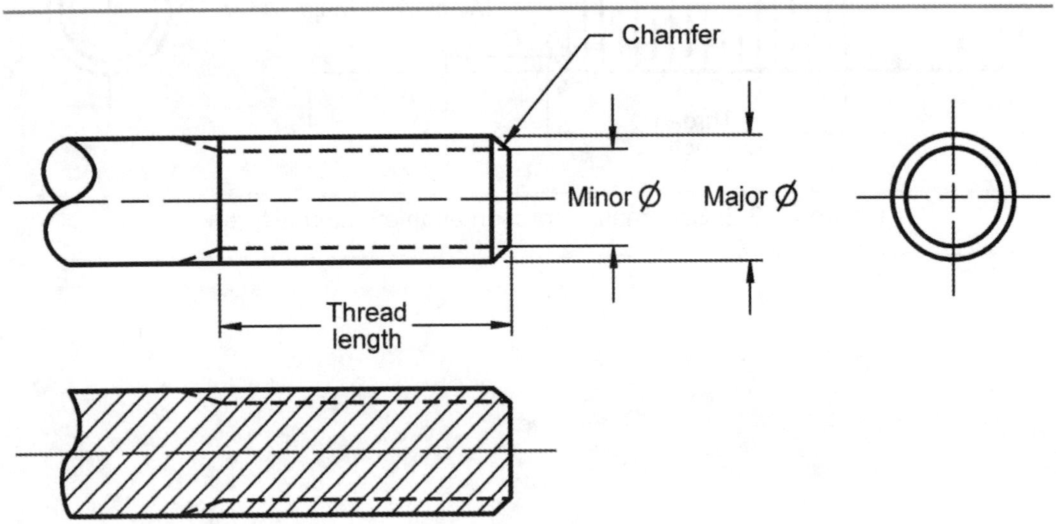

Figure 22.3-4: Simplified representation of external threads.

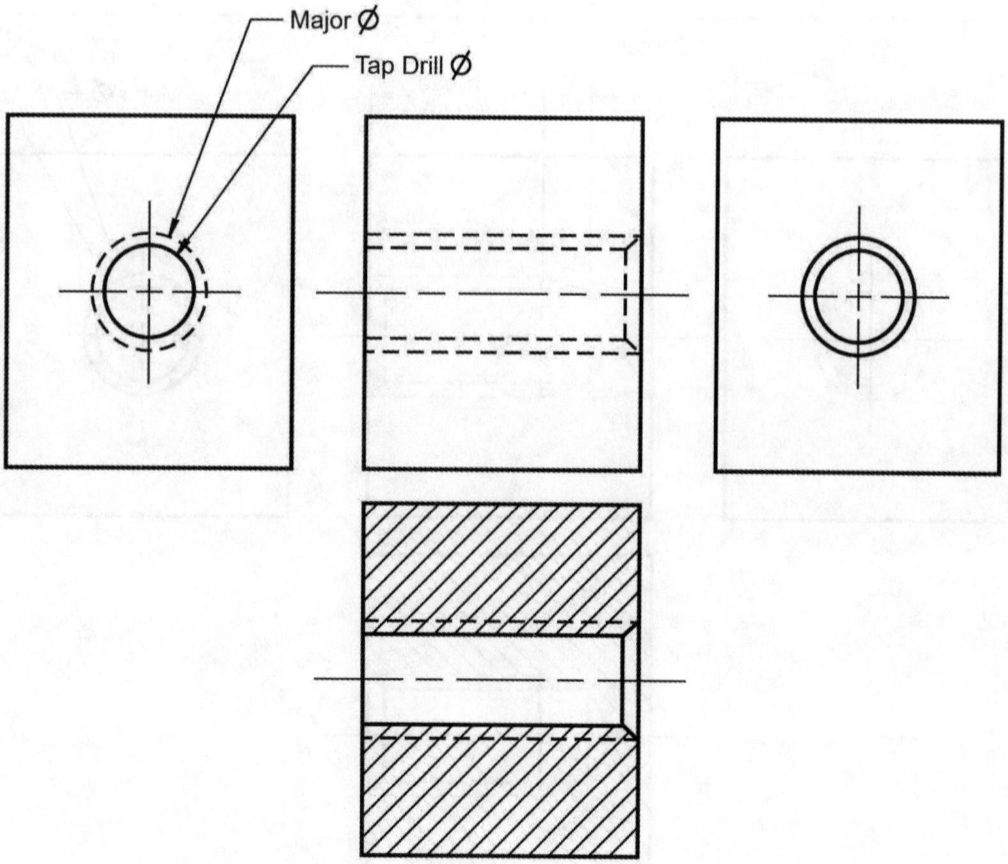

Figure 22.3-5: Simplified representation of internal threads.

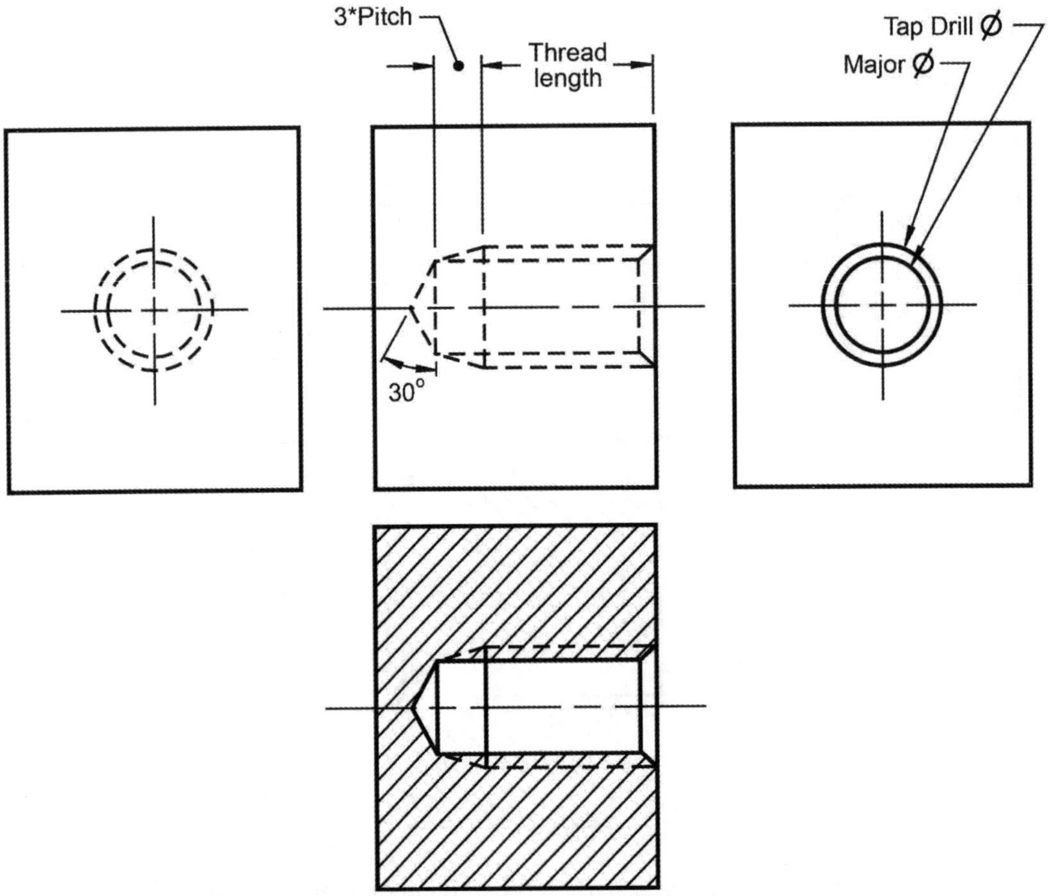

Figure 22.3-6: Simplified representation of internal threads cut on a blind hole.

22.4) CREATING UNIFIED THREAD NOTES

In the previous chapter, we learned how to read a unified thread note. Let's refresh our memories by completing the following exercise.

Try Exercise 22.4-1

Exercise 22.4-1: Unified National thread note components

Identify the different components of the thread notes given.

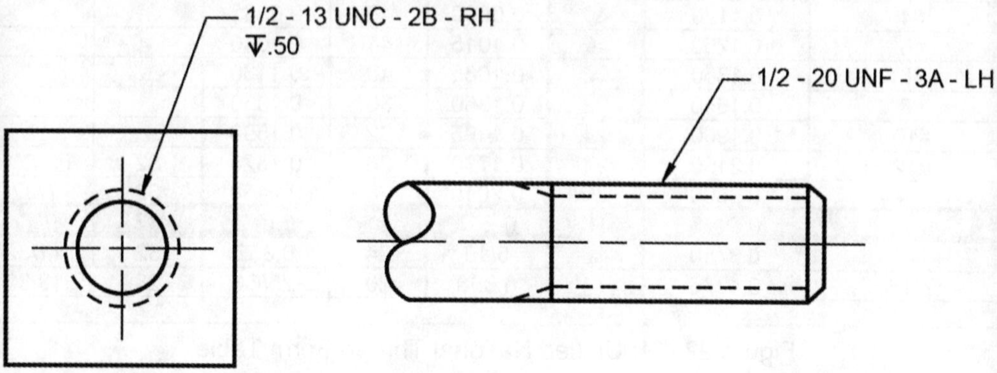

Thread note component	Description
1/2	
13 and 20	
UN	
C and F	
2 and 3	
A and B	
RH and LH	

22.4.1) Unified thread tables

Standard screw thread tables are available in order to look up the major diameter, threads per inch, tap drill size, and minor diameter for a particular thread. These thread tables are given in the ASME B1.1-2024 standard and are restated in Appendix B. Figure 22.4-1 shows an excerpt from these tables. Notice, in the Nominal Size column, that numbers are used for all threads that are less than 1/4 of an inch. This table can be used to create a thread note. For example, let's say we have a 5/16-inch coarse thread, and we want to create a thread note. First, locate the 5/16-inch row and then locate the *Threads per inch* under the *Coarse UNC* column. Where the row and column intersect is the threads per inch for this screw thread. The thread note would be 5/16 – 18 UNC. This table also indicates the equation used for calculating the minor diameter for an external thread and the tap drill diameter for internal threads.

B.1) UNIFIED NATIONAL THREAD FORM

(External Threads) Approximate Minor diameter = $D - 1.0825P$ P = Pitch

Nominal Size, in.	Basic Major Diameter (*D*)	Coarse UNC		Fine UNF		Extra Fine UNEF	
		Thds. Per in.	Tap Drill Dia.	Thds. Per in.	Tap Drill Dia.	Thds. Per in.	Tap Drill Dia.
#0	0.060	...	...	80	3/64	...	...
#1	0.0730	64	0.0595	72	0.0595	...	...
#2	0.0860	56	0.0700	64	0.0700	...	...
#3	0.0990	48	0.0785	56	0.0820	...	...
#4	0.1120	40	0.0890	48	0.0935	...	...
#5	0.1250	40	0.1015	44	0.1040	...	...
#6	0.1380	32	0.1065	40	0.1130	...	...
#8	0.1640	32	0.1360	36	0.1360	...	...
#10	0.1900	24	0.1495	32	0.1590	...	...
#12	0.2160	24	0.1770	28	0.1820	32	0.1850
1/4	0.2500	20	0.2010	28	0.2130	32	7/32
5/16	0.3125	18	0.257	24	0.272	32	9/32
3/8	0.3750	16	5/16	24	0.332	32	11/32
7/16	0.4375	14	0.368	20	25/64	28	13/32

Figure 22.4-1: Unified National Thread Form Table

Try Exercise 22.4-2

Exercise 22.4-2: Unified National thread note

Write the thread note for a #10 fine thread.

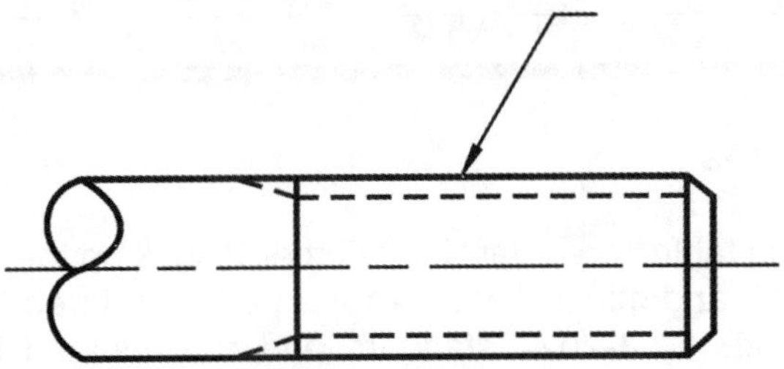

What are the major and minor diameters in inches?

- Major
- Minor

22.5) METRIC THREADS

In the previous chapter, we learned how to read a Metric thread note. Let's refresh our memories by completing the following exercise.

Try Exercise 22.5-1

Exercise 22.5-1: Unified National thread note

Identify the different components of the thread notes given.

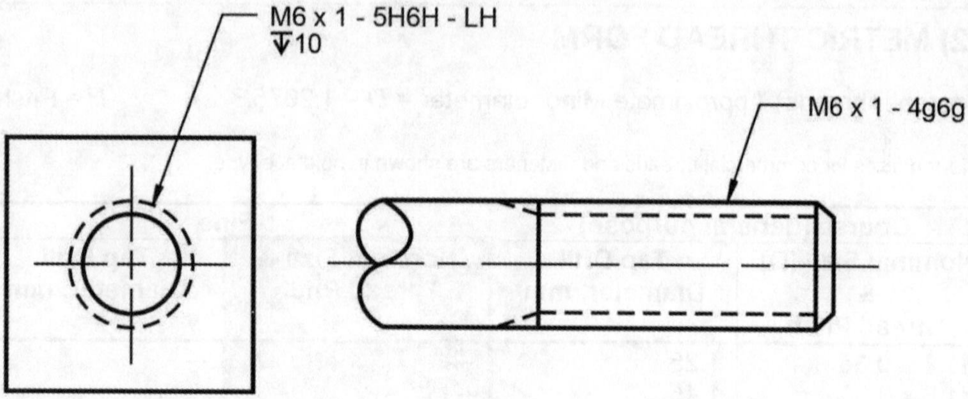

Thread note component	Description
M	
6	
1	
5H6H and 4g6g	
LH	
Is the external thread LH or RH	
10	

22.5.1) Metric thread tables

Standard screw thread tables are available in order to look up the major diameter, threads per inch, tap drill size, and minor diameter for a particular thread. These thread tables are given in the ASME B1.13M-2005 (R2020) standard and are given in Appendix B. Figure 22.5-1 shows an excerpt from these tables. This table can be used to create a thread note. For example, let's say we have a 30 mm fine thread, and we want to create a thread note. First, locate the 30 mm row and then locate the *Threads pitch* under the *Fine* column. Where the row and column intersect is the pitch for this screw thread. The thread note would be M30 x 2. This table also indicates the equation used for calculating the minor diameter for an external thread and the tap drill diameter for internal threads.

B.2) METRIC THREAD FORM

(External Threads) Approximate Minor diameter = $D - 1.2075P$ P = Pitch

Preferred sizes for commercial threads and fasteners are shown in boldface type.

Coarse (general purpose)		Fine	
Nominal Size (D) & Thread Pitch	**Tap Drill Diameter, mm**	**Nominal Size & Thread Pitch**	**Tap Drill Diameter, mm**
M1.6 x 0.35	1.25	---	---
M1.8 x 0.35	1.45	---	---
M2 x 0.4	1.6	---	---
M2.2 x 0.45	1.75	---	---
M2.5 x 0.45	2.05	---	---
M20 x 2.5	17.5	**M20 x 1.5**	18.5
M22 x 2.5[b]	19.5	**M22 x 1.5**	20.5
M24 x 3	21.0	**M24 x 2**	22.0
M27 x 3[b]	24.0	**M27 x 2**	25.0
M30 x 3.5	26.5	**M30 x 2**	28.0
M33 x 3.5	29.5	M33 x 2	31.0
M36 x 4	32.0	**M36 x 2**	33.0
M39 x 4	35.0	M39 x 2	36.0

Figure 22.5-1: Metric Thread Form Table

Try Exercise 22.5-2

Exercise 22.5-2: Metric thread tables

For a ∅16 internal Metric thread, what are the two available pitches and the required tap drill diameter and the corresponding minor diameter for the mating external thread?

Pitch	Tap drill size	Minor DIA

Which has the finer thread?

The finer thread is M16 x (   )

Write the thread note for a 16 mm diameter coarse thread.

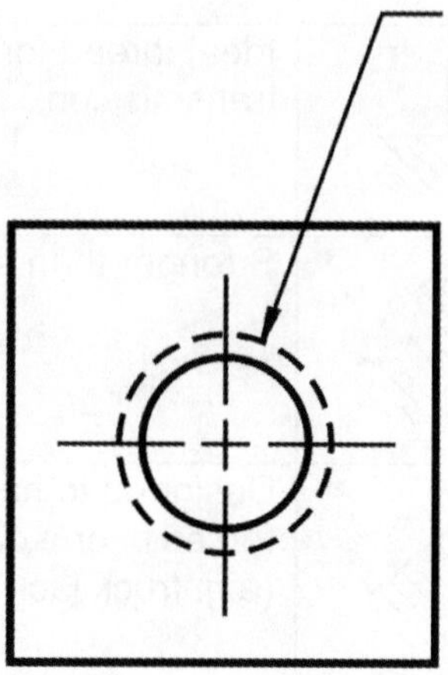

22.6) TYPES OF THREAD

There are many different types of threads or thread forms available. The thread form is the shape of the thread. The choice of thread form used for a particular application depends on length of engagement and load among other factors. ***Unified* and *Metric* threads are the most widely used thread forms.** Table 22.6-1 describes just a few of the different thread forms available and their uses.

Thread Name	Figure	Uses
Unified screw thread		General use.
Metric screw thread		General use.
Square	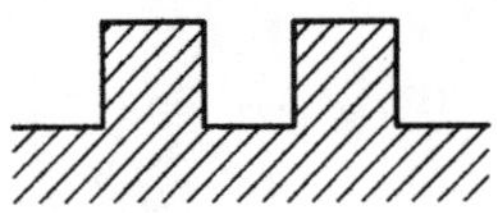	Ideal thread for power transmission.
ACME	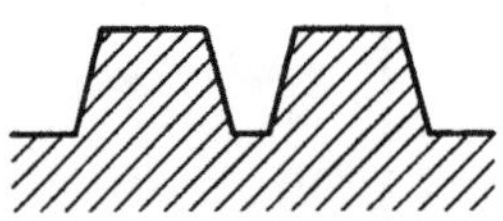	Stronger than square thread.
Buttress	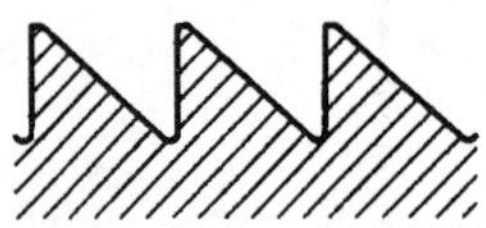	Designed to handle heavy forces in one direction (e.g. truck jack).

Table 22.6-1: Screw thread examples

22.7) DRAWING BOLTS

Figure 22.7-1 illustrates how to draw bolts. The variable D represents the major or nominal diameter of the bolt. Nuts are drawn in a similar fashion.

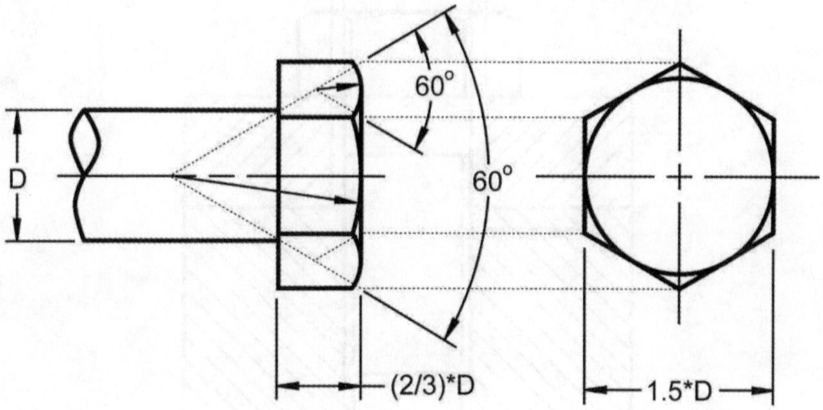

Figure 22.7-1: Drawing bolts.

22.8) BOLT AND SCREW CLEARANCES

Bolts and screws attach one material with a clearance hole to another material with a threaded hole. The size of the clearance hole depends on the major diameter of the fastener and the type of fit that is required for the assembly to function properly. Clearance holes can be designed to have a *normal*, *close* or *loose* fit. Table 22.8-1 gives the normal fit clearances which are illustrated in Figure 22.8-1. For detailed information on clearances for bolts and screws, refer to the ASME B18.2.8-1999 standard also given in Appendix B.

Sometimes bolt or screw heads need to be flush with the surface. This can be achieved by using either a counterbore or countersink depending on the fastener's head shape. Counterbores are holes that are designed to recess bolt or screw heads below the surface of a part as shown in Figure 22.8-2. Countersinks are angled holes that are designed to recess screws with angled heads as shown in Figure 22.8-3. Appendix B gives the clearance hole diameters illustrated in Figure 22.8-2 and 22.8-3. If screw clearance tables are not available, typically CH = H + 1/16 (1.5 mm) and C1 = D1 + 1/8 (3 mm).

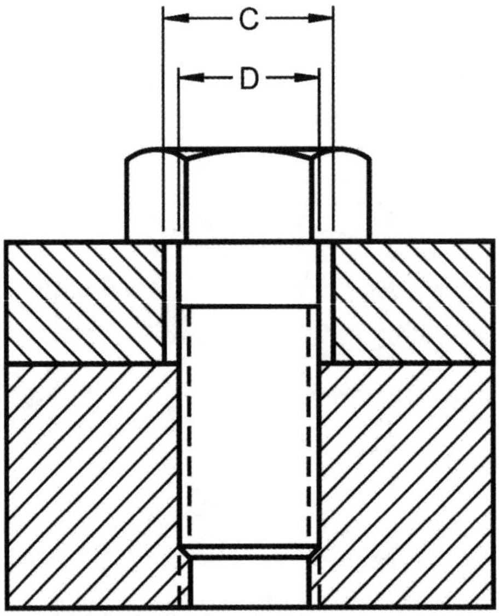

Figure 22.8-1: Bolt clearance.

Inch clearances	
Nominal screw size (D)	Clearance hole (C)
#0 - #4	D + 1/64
#5 – 7/16	D + 1/32
1/2 – 7/8	D + 1/16
1	D + 3/32
1 1/8, 1 1/4	D + 3/32
1 3/8, 1 1/2	D + 1/8

Metric clearances	
Nominal screw size (D)	Clearance hole (C)
M1.6	D + 0.2
M2, M2.5	D + 0.4
M4, M5	D + 0.5
M6	D + 0.6
M8, M10	D + 1
M12 – M16	D + 1.5
M20, M24	D + 2
M30 – M42	D + 3
M48	D + 4
M56 – M90	D + 6
M100	D + 7

Table 22.8-1: Bolt and screw normal fit clearance holes.

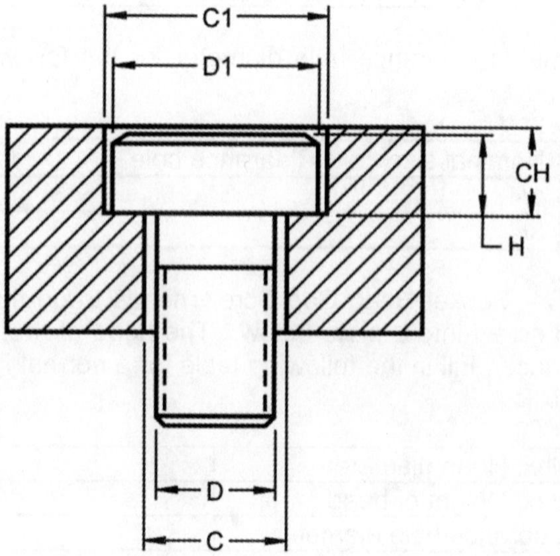

Figure 22.8-2: Counterbore clearances.

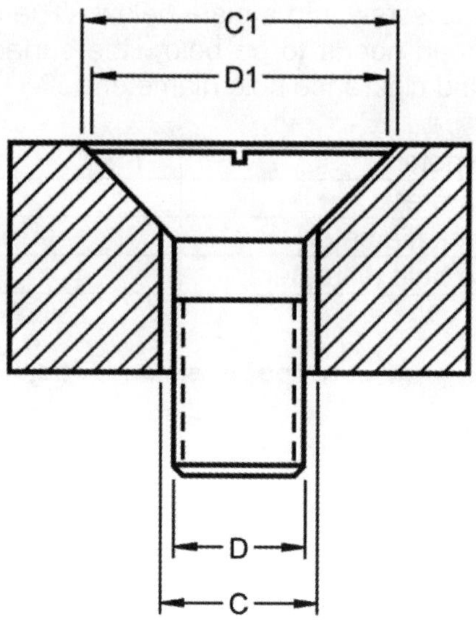

Figure 22.8-3: Countersink clearances.

Try Exercise 22.8-1

Exercise 22.8-1: Fastener tables and clearance holes

What is the normal fit clearance hole diameter for the following nominal bolt sizes?

Nominal size	Clearance hole
1/4	
3/4	

A 5/16 - 18 UNC – Socket Head Cap Screw needs to go through a piece of metal in order to screw into a plate below. The head of the screw should be flush with the surface. Fill in the following table for a normal fit clearance hole. Refer to Appendix B.

Max. Head diameter	
Max. Height of head	
Clearance hole diameter	
Counterbore diameter	
Counterbore depth	

An M8 x 1.25 Flat Countersunk Head Metric Cap Screw needs to go through a piece of metal in order to screw into a plate below. The clearance hole needs to be close, and the head needs to go below the surface. What should the countersink diameter and clearance hole diameter be?

Major diameter	
Head diameter	
Countersink diameter	
Clearance hole diameter	

22.9) STANDARD PARTS

Standard parts include any part that can be bought off the shelf. **Standard parts do not need to be drawn.** Purchasing information is specified on a standard parts sheet attached to the back of a working drawing package. Keep in mind that the format of the standard parts sheet may change depending on a company's policies. The type of information given may depend on how a company identifies regularly used fasteners. If fasteners are completely identified by a part or identification number, it may not be necessary to create a standard parts sheet at all. This part information may be given in the parts list on the assembly drawing. How to create an assembly drawing and parts list will be discussed in an upcoming chapter. Some of the components of the standard parts sheet will become clearer after learning about assembly drawings.

Try Exercise 22.9-1

Exercise 22.9-1: Standard Parts Sheet

A standard parts sheet is shown with some missing headers. Fill in the appropriate header label.

STANDARD PARTS LIST

FIND NO							SPECIAL REQ.
9	1	S1781	COMPRESSION SPRING	Ø8 ID, Ø0.4 WIRE, 12 COILS, 46 LONG		5120 STEEL	
10	1	W56	PLAIN WASHER	Ø16 OD, Ø7.2 ID, 1.7 THICK	A	1115 STEEL	
11	4	HS679	HEX HEAD CAP SCREW	M8 X 1.25		BRASS	
12	1	P57	SPRING PIN	Ø2 OD, 14 LONG	DOUBLE		

UNLESS OTHERWISE SPECIFIED
DIM ARE IN INCHES
TOL ON ANGLE ±.2°
2 PL ±.05 3 PL ±.001
INTERPRET DIM AND TOL PER
ASME Y14.5 - 2009

THIRD ANGLE PROJECTION

APPROVALS	DATE
DRAFTER: KAP	2010/07/23
CHECKED: KJT	2010/07/26
ENGINEER: RPM	2010/07/27

MATERIAL: -
FINISH: -
DO NOT SCALE DRAWING

EGE
TITLE: CASE
SIZE A | CAGE CODE | DWG NO. 687 | REV 0
SCALE: - | SHEET: 5 OF 5

NOTES:

22.10) APPLYING WHAT YOU HAVE LEARNED

Exercise 22.10-1: Milling Jack assembly fasteners

Name: ______________________________ Date: ____________

Consider the *Milling Jack* assembly shown. Notice that there are many parts that fasten to other parts.

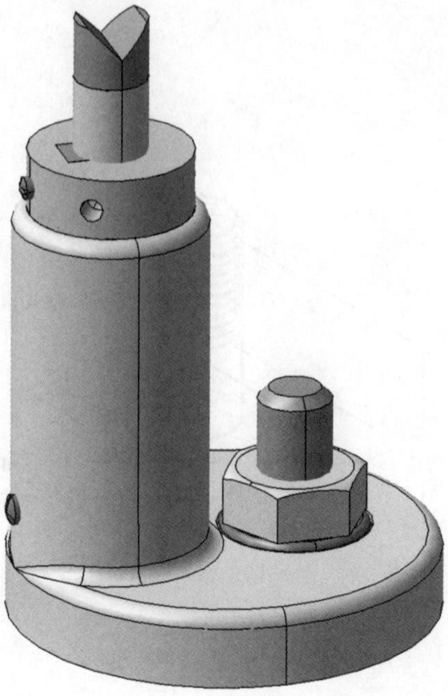

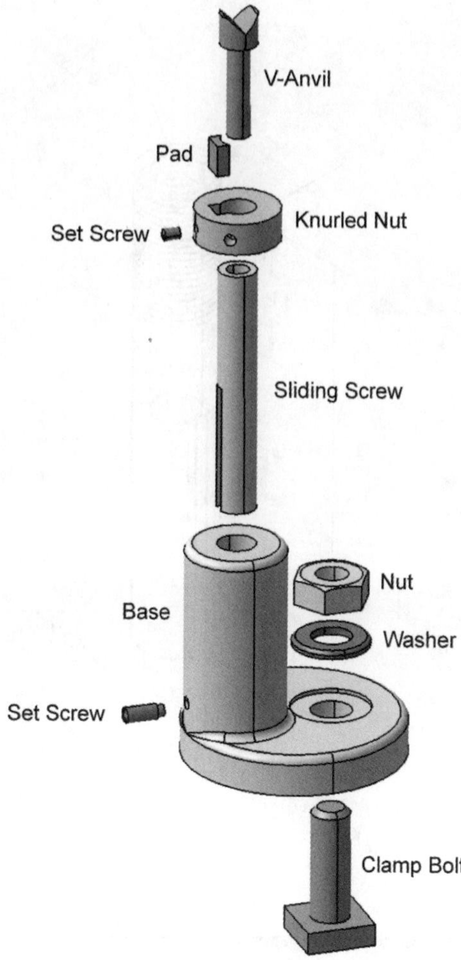

Exercise 22.10-1 Cont.: Milling Jack assembly fasteners

The *Sliding Screw* and *Clamp Bolt* have 5/8 inch thread cut into their bodies. The *Sliding Screw* has a fine thread and the *Clamp Bolt* has a coarse thread. Write the thread note that would appear on the print for both parts.

Thread Note (Sliding Screw): ________________________________

Thread Note (Clamp Bolt): ________________________________

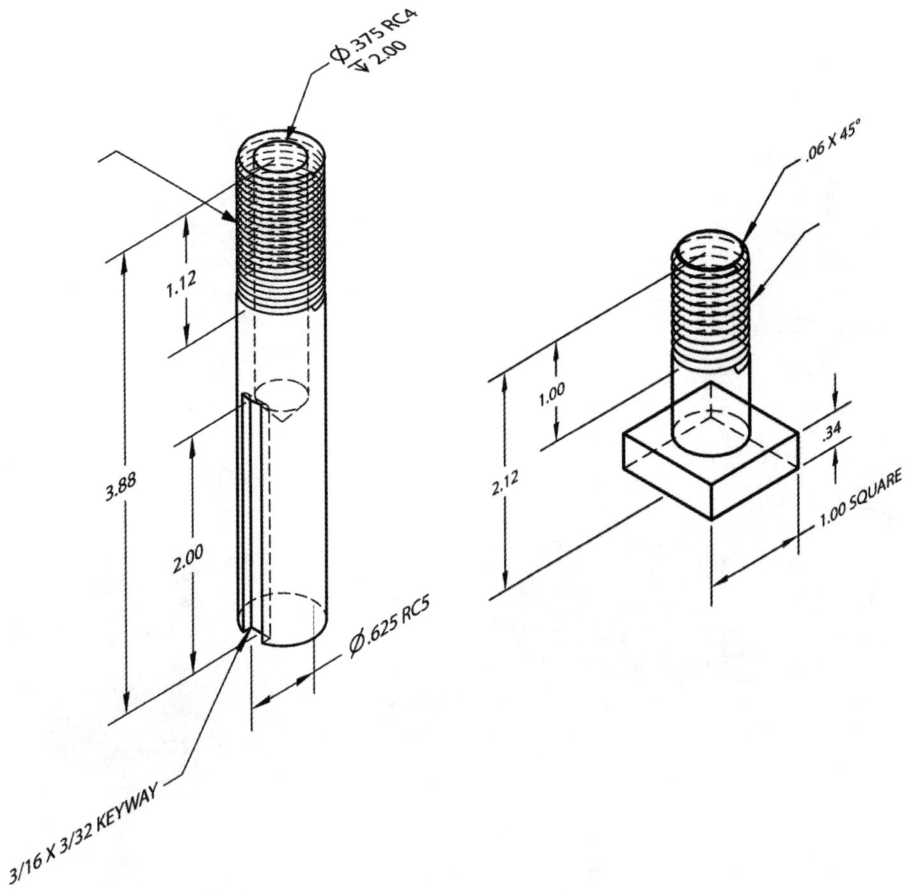

Exercise 22.10-1 Cont.: Milling Jack assembly fasteners

Name: ______________________________ Date: ______________

The *Base* has a 1/4-inch coarse thread drilled and tapped into its body. Write the thread note that would appear on the print. What is the tap drill size?

Thread Note: ______________________________

Tap Drill Size: ______________________________

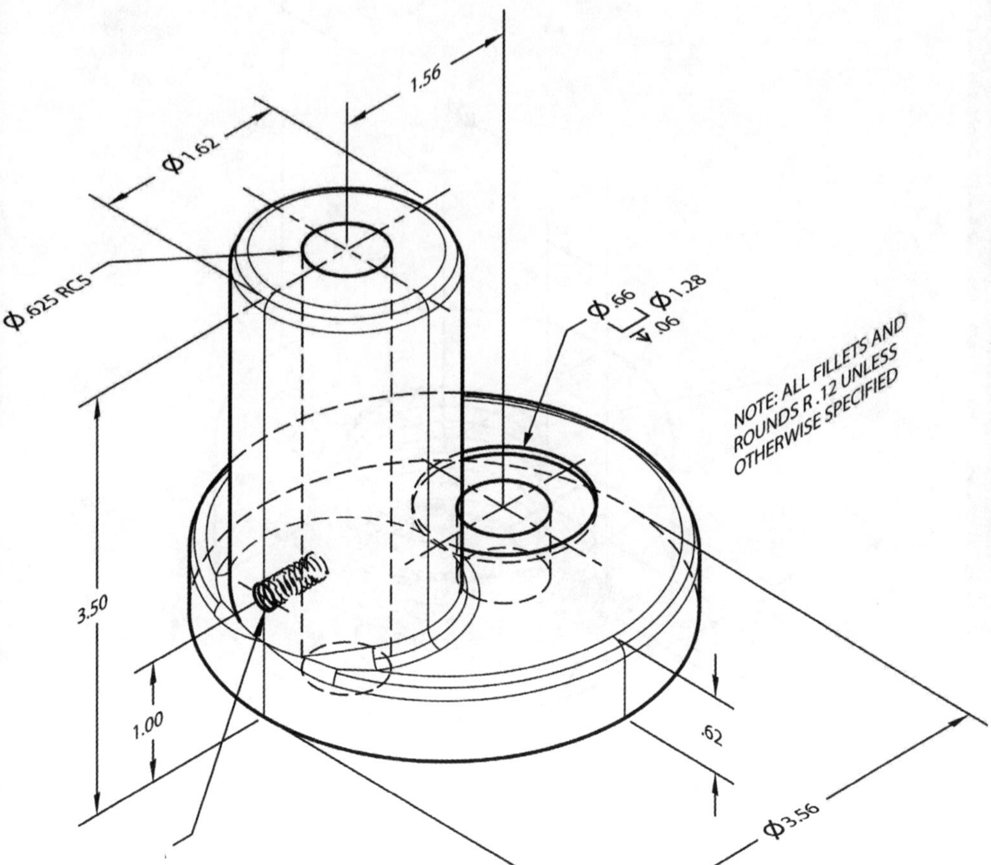

Exercise 22.10-1 Cont.: Milling Jack assembly fasteners

The *Knurled Nut* has a 0.190-inch major diameter coarse thread drilled and tapped into its body. Write the thread note that would appear on the print. What is the tap drill size?

Thread Note: ______________________________

Tap Drill Size: _____________________________

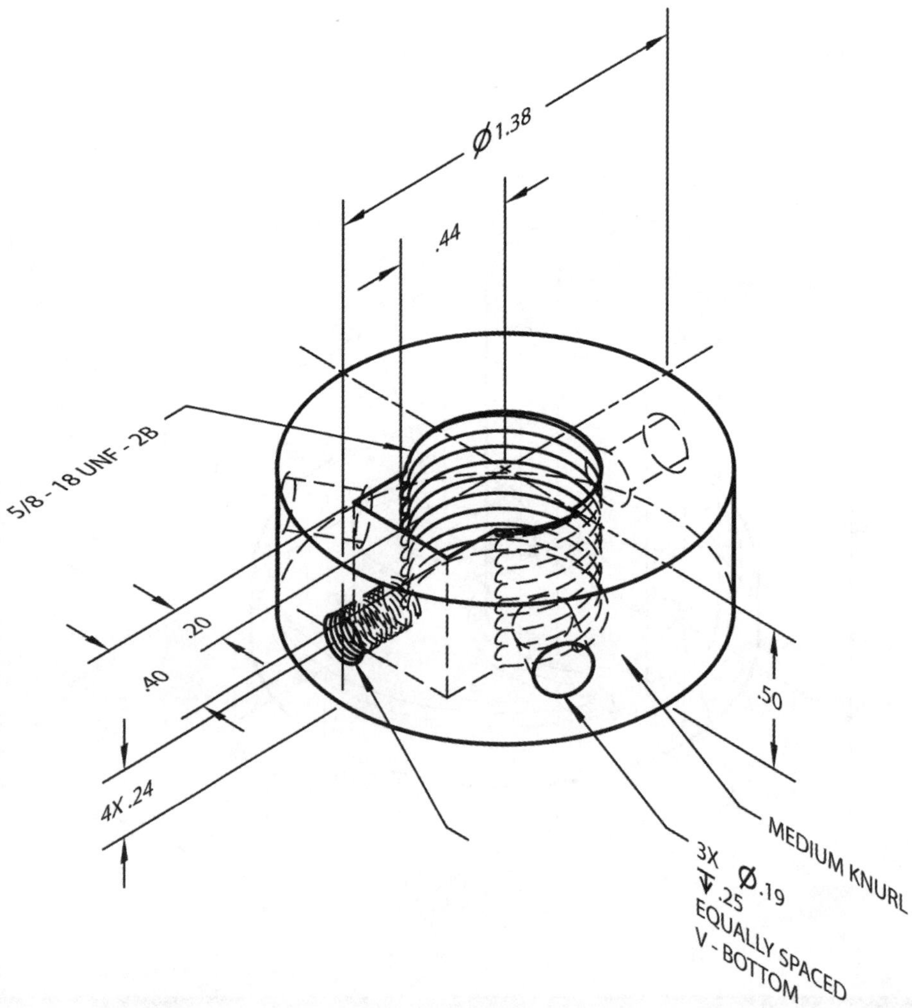

Exercise 22.10-2: Drill jig fasteners

Determine the normal fit clearance hole and countersink dimension for the M12 x 1.75 countersunk socket head cap screw.

Clearance hole: ______________________

Countersink diameter and angle: ____________________

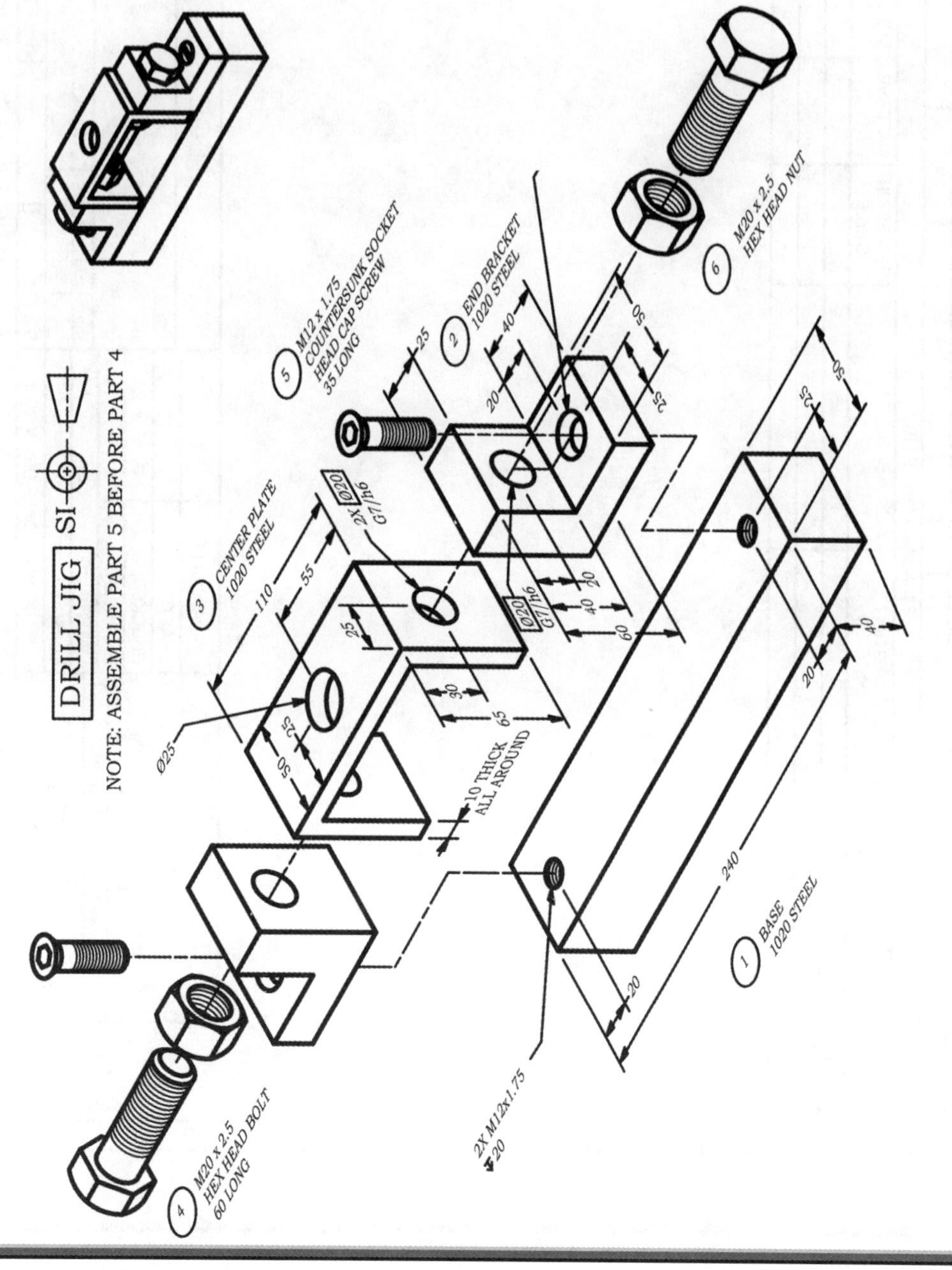

Exercise 22.10-2 Cont.: Drill jig fasteners

Create a standard parts sheet for the *Drill jig*.

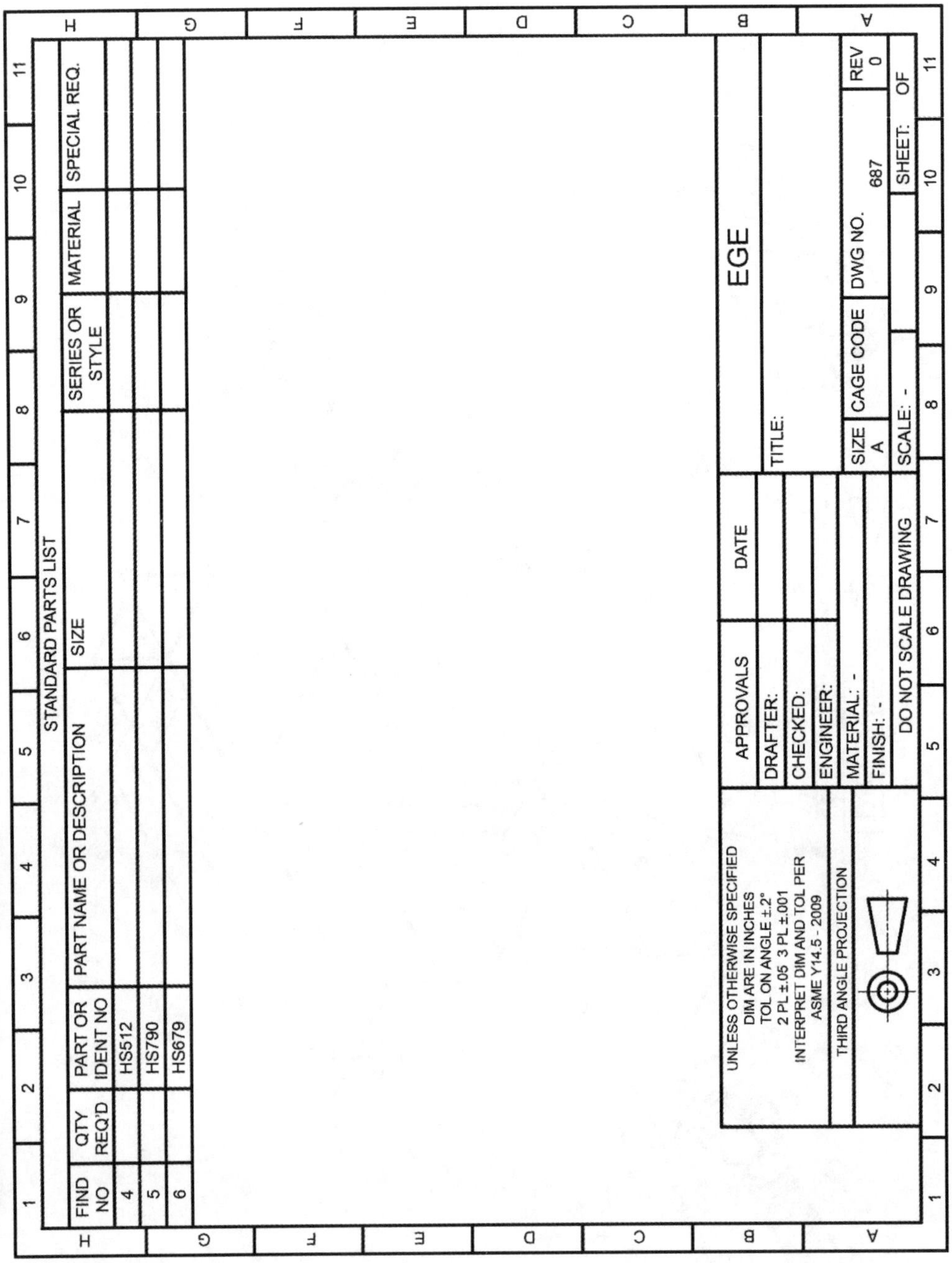

CREATING THREADS AND FASTENERS QUESTIONS – SET 1

Name: ______________________________ Date: ______________

Threads Manufacturing

Q22-1) External threads may be cut using a (die, tap).

Q22-2) Internal threads may be cut using a (die, tap).

Q22-3) How much longer is the tap drill depth than the thread depth when using a taper tap?

a) 1 times the pitch
b) 2 times the pitch
c) 3 times the pitch
d) 4 times the pitch

Thread Form and Notes

Q22-4) How would you determine the correct drill size to prepare a hole for tapping an M5 x 0.8 thread?

Q22-5) An M6 screw will always have the same thread pitch regardless of manufacturer. (True, False)

Q22-7) Why is it important to match the thread class (e.g., 2A with 2B) when selecting a bolt and nut?

Bolt and screw clearances

Q22-8) A bolt or screw clearance hole diameter depends on what factors? (Circle all that apply.)

a) major diameter
b) minor diameter
c) fit
d) thread depth

Standard parts sheet

Q22-9) A standard parts sheet contains drawings of all purchased parts. (True, False)

CREATING THREADS AND FASTENERS QUESTIONS – SET 2

Name: ________________________________ Date: ______________

Threads Representation

Q22-10) The schematic thread symbol draws lines at every crest and _________. Fill in the blank.

Q22-11) The simplified thread symbol uses a _______ line to represent the minor diameter on external threads.

a) visible
b) hidden
c) center
d) phantom

Q22-12) A tap drill is used when manufacturing (external, internal) threads.

Q22-13) A taper tap has useful threads along its entire length. (True, False)

Q22-14) The tap drill diameter is closest in size to the _______ diameter.

a) major
b) minor
c) pitch

Thread Form and Notes

Q22-15) What dimension type is used to apply a thread note?

Q22-16) When would you use a coarse thread (e.g., M8 x 1.25) versus a fine thread (e.g., M8 x 1.0)?

Q22-17) Which part of the thread note determines whether the thread is external or internal?

Standard parts sheet

Q22-18) A standard parts sheet contains enough information about the standard parts so that they may be ....

a) manufactured
b) drawn
c) purchased
d) modeled

CREATING THREADS AND FASTENERS PROBLEMS

Name: ______________________________ Date: ____________

P22-1) Write the thread notes for the following external threads. Also, what are the minor diameter and the pitch? Thread class = 2.

	(a)	(b)	(c)	(d)	(e)	(f)	(g)
Major ∅	1/4	7/8	3/4	1/2	1	3/8	5/16
Series	Fine	Coarse	Fine	Coarse	Fine	Extra Fine	Coarse

Thread Note	
Minor diameter	
Pitch	

Thread Note	
Minor diameter	
Pitch	

Thread Note	
Minor diameter	
Pitch	

P22-2) Write the thread notes for the following internal threads. Also, what are the tap drill size and/or diameter and the pitch? Thread class = 3.

	(a)	(b)	(c)	(d)	(e)	(f)	(g)
Major ∅	7/16	1/4	5/8	1 1/4	3/8	1/2	1
Series	Fine	Coarse	Fine	Coarse	Fine	Extra Fine	Coarse

Thread Note	
Tap drill size and/or diameter	
Pitch	

Thread Note	
Tap drill size and/or diameter	
Pitch	

Thread Note	
Tap drill size and/or diameter	
Pitch	

P22-3) Write the thread notes for the following threads. Also, what is the major diameter in inches?

	(a)	(b)	(c)	(d)	(e)	(f)	(g)
Major ∅	#0	#2	#4	#5	#6	#8	#10
Series	Fine	Coarse	Fine	Coarse	Fine	Fine	Coarse

Thread note	
Major diameter	

Thread note	
Major diameter	

Thread note	
Major diameter	

Name: ________________________________ Date: ______________

P22-4) Write the thread notes for the following external threads. Also, what are the minor diameter and the number of threads per mm?

	(a)	(b)	(c)	(d)	(e)	(f)	(g)
Major ∅	M3	M4	M8	M10	M12	M20	M24
Series	Coarse	Coarse	Fine	Coarse	Fine	Fine	Coarse

Thread Note	
Minor diameter	
# of threads per mm	

Thread Note	
Minor diameter	
# of threads per mm	

Thread Note	
Minor diameter	
# of threads per mm	

P22-5) Write the thread notes for the following internal threads. Also, what are the tap drill size and/or diameter and the number of threads per mm?

	(a)	(b)	(c)	(d)	(e)	(f)	(g)
Major ∅	M1.6	M5	M6	M12	M18	M22	M27
Series	Coarse	Coarse	Coarse	Coarse	Fine	Fine	Coarse

Thread Note	
Tap drill size and/or diameter	
# of threads per mm	

Thread Note	
Tap drill size and/or diameter	
# of threads per mm	

Thread Note	
Tap drill size and/or diameter	
# of threads per mm	

Name: ________________________________ Date: ______________

P22-6) Fill in the given table for a hex head bolt with the following major diameters.

	(a)	(b)	(c)	(d)	(e)	(f)	(g)	(h)
Major ∅	1/4	5/16	1/2	7/8	1	9/16	3/8	7/16

Major diameter	
Width across flats	
Max. width across corners	
Head height	
Normal clearance hole	

Major diameter	
Width across flats	
Max. width across corners	
Head height	
Normal clearance hole	

Major diameter	
Width across flats	
Max. width across corners	
Head height	
Normal clearance hole	

P22-7) Fill in the given table for a hexagon (socket) head cap screw with the following major diameters.

	(a)	(b)	(c)	(d)	(e)	(f)	(g)	(h)
Major ∅	1/4	5/16	1/2	#8	#5	9/16	3/8	#10

Major diameter	
Max. head diameter	
Max. head height	
Normal clearance hole	
Counterbore diameter	
Counterbore depth	

Major diameter	
Max. head diameter	
Max. head height	
Normal clearance hole	
Counterbore diameter	
Counterbore depth	

P22-8) Fill in the given table for a slotted flat countersunk head cap screw with the following major diameters.

	(a)	(b)	(c)	(d)	(e)	(f)	(g)	(h)
Major ∅	1/4	5/16	3/8	7/16	1/2	9/16	5/8	3/4

Major diameter	
Max. head diameter	
Max. head height	
Normal clearance hole	
Countersink diameter	
Countersink angle	

Major diameter	
Max. head diameter	
Max. head height	
Normal clearance hole	
Countersink diameter	
Countersink angle	

Name: ________________________________ Date: ______________

P22-9) Fill in the given table for a hex head bolt with the following major diameters.

	(a)	(b)	(c)	(d)	(e)	(f)	(g)	(h)
Major ∅	M5	M12	M20	M30	M36	M48	M14	M24

Major diameter	
Max. width across flats	
Max. width across corners	
Max. head height	
Thread length for a screw that is shorter than 125 mm	
Normal clearance hole	

Major diameter	
Max. width across flats	
Max. width across corners	
Max. head height	
Thread length for a screw that is shorter than 125 mm	
Normal clearance hole	

P22-10) Fill in the given table for a socket head cap screw with the following major diameters.

	(a)	(b)	(c)	(d)	(e)	(f)	(g)	(h)
Major ∅	M1.6	M2.5	M4	M6	M12	M16	M24	M42

Major diameter	
Max. head diameter	
Max. head height	
Normal clearance hole	
Counterbore diameter	
Counterbore depth	

Major diameter	
Max. head diameter	
Max. head height	
Normal clearance hole	
Counterbore diameter	
Counterbore depth	

Name: ______________________________ Date: ______________

P22-11) Fill in the given table for a flat countersunk head cap screw with the following major diameters.

	(a)	(b)	(c)	(d)	(e)	(f)	(g)	(h)
Major ∅	M16	M3	M12	M5	M6	M8	M10	M4

Major diameter	
Head diameter	
Head height	
Normal clearance hole	
Countersink diameter	
Countersink angle	

Major diameter	
Head diameter	
Head height	
Normal clearance hole	
Countersink diameter	
Countersink angle	

NOTES:

P22-12) Draw and dimension the *Knurled Nut* using proper dimensioning techniques. This *Knurled Nut* is part of the *Milling Jack* given in the *Assemblies* chapter problem section. Notice that the dimensioned isometric drawing does not always use the correct symbols or dimensioning techniques.

- Part name = Knurled Nut
- Part No. = 4
- Material = SAE 1045 – Heat Treat
- Required = 1

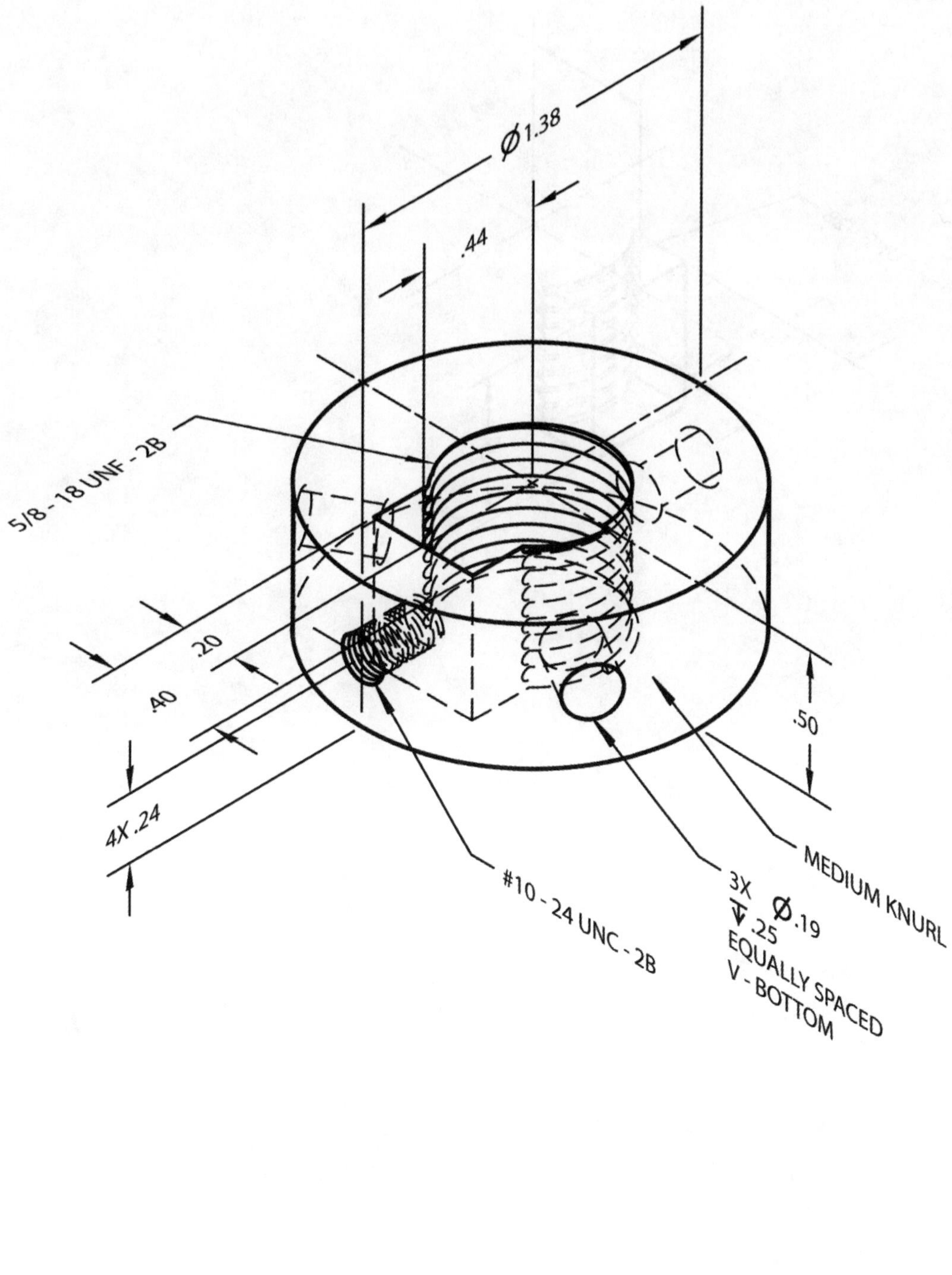

P22-13) Draw and dimension the *Pad* using proper dimensioning techniques. This *Pad* is part of the *Milling Jack* given in the *Assemblies* chapter problem section. Notice that the dimensioned isometric drawing does not always use the correct symbols or dimensioning techniques.

- Part name = Pad
- Part No. = 5
- Material = Phosphor Bronze - FAO
- Required = 1

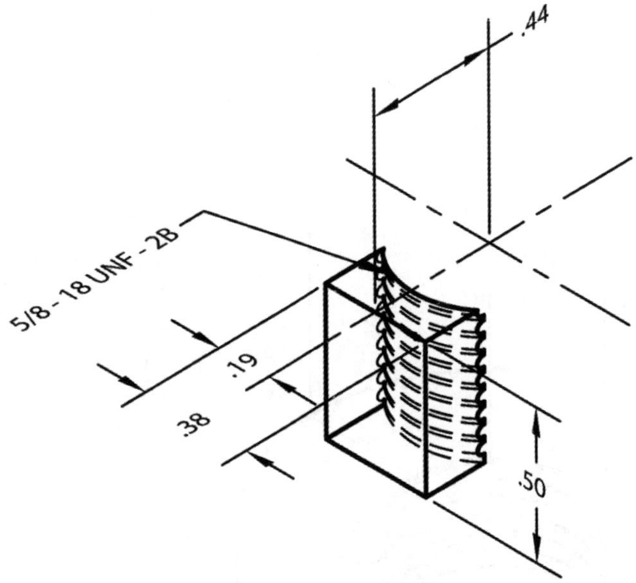

P22-14) Draw and dimension the *Clamp Bolt* using proper dimensioning techniques. This *Clamp Bolt* is part of the *Milling Jack* given in the *Assemblies* chapter problem section. Notice that the dimensioned isometric drawing does not always use the correct symbols or dimensioning techniques.

- Part name = Clamp Bolt
- Part No. = 6
- Material = SAE 1020 – Case Hardened
- Required = 1

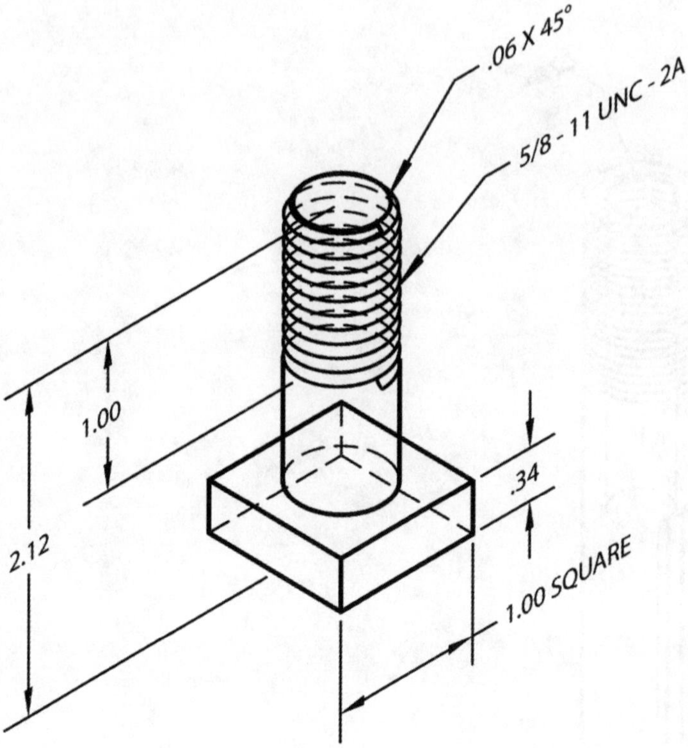

P22-15) Draw and dimension the *Sliding Screw* using proper dimensioning techniques. This *Sliding Screw* is part of the *Milling Jack* given in the *Assemblies* chapter problem section. Notice that the dimensioned isometric drawing does not always use the correct symbols or dimensioning techniques.

- Part name = Sliding Screw
- Part No. = 2
- Material = SAE 1045 – Heat Treat
- Required = 1

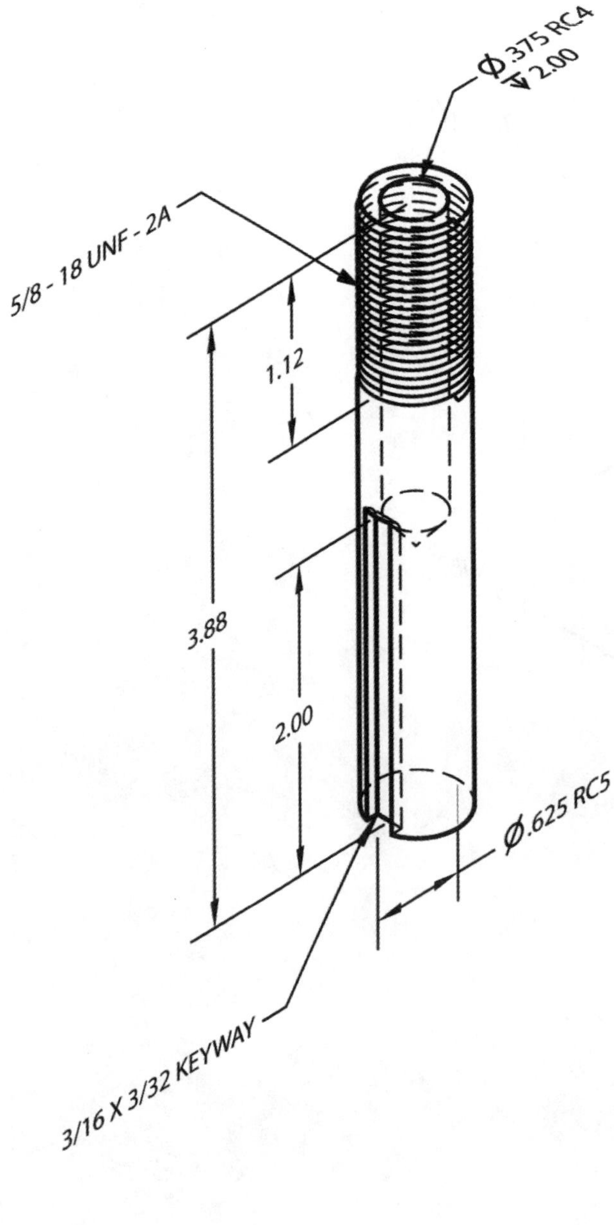

SP22-1) Write the thread notes for the following external threads. Also, what are the minor diameter and the pitch? Thread class = 2. The answer to this problem is given on the *Independent Learning Content*.

Major ∅	7/16
Series	Coarse
Thread Note	
Minor diameter	
Pitch	

SP22-2) Write the thread notes for the following internal threads. Also, what are the tap drill size and/or diameter and the pitch? Thread class = 3. The answer to this problem is given on the *Independent Learning Content*.

Major ∅	9/16
Series	Fine
Thread Note	
Tap drill size and/or diameter	
Pitch	

SP22-3) Write the thread notes for the following threads. Also, what is the major diameter in inches? The answer to this problem is given on the *Independent Learning Content*.

Major ∅	#3
Series	Coarse
Thread note	
Major diameter	

SP22-4) Write the thread notes for the following external threads. Also, what are the minor diameter and the number of threads per mm? The answer to this problem is given on the *Independent Learning Content*.

Major ∅	M33
Series	Fine
Thread Note	
Minor diameter	
# of threads per mm	

SP22-5) Write the thread notes for the following internal threads. Also, what are the tap drill size and/or diameter and the number of threads per mm? The answer to this problem is given on the *Independent Learning Content*.

Major ∅	M24
Series	Coarse
Thread Note	
Tap drill size and/or diameter	
# of threads per mm	

SP22-6) Fill in the given table for a hex head bolt with the following major diameters. The answer to this problem is given on the *Independent Learning Content*.

Major ∅	3/4
Width across flats	
Max. width across corners	
Head height	
Normal clearance hole	

SP22-7) Fill in the given table for a hexagon (socket) head cap screw with the following major diameters. The answer to this problem is given on the *Independent Learning Content*.

Major ∅	7/8
Max. head diameter	
Max. head height	
Normal clearance hole	
Counterbore diameter	
Counterbore depth	

SP22-8) Fill in the given table for a slotted flat countersunk head cap screw with the following major diameters. The answer to this problem is given on the *Independent Learning Content*.

Major ∅	1
Max. head diameter	
Max. head height	
Normal clearance hole	
Countersink diameter	
Countersink angle	

SP22-9) Fill in the given table for a hex head bolt with the following major diameters. The answer to this problem is given on the *Independent Learning Content*.

Major ∅	M8
Max. width across flats	
Max. width across corners	
Max. head height	
Thread length for a screw that is shorter than 125 mm	
Normal clearance hole	

SP22-10) Fill in the given table for a socket head cap screw with the following major diameters. The answer to this problem is given on the *Independent Learning Content*.

Major ∅	M14
Max. head diameter	
Max. head height	
Normal clearance hole	
Counterbore diameter	
Counterbore depth	

SP22-11) Fill in the given table for a flat countersunk head cap screw with the following major diameters. The answer to this problem is given on the *Independent Learning Content*.

Major ∅	M20
Head diameter	
Head height	
Normal clearance hole	
Countersink diameter	
Countersink angle	

NOTES:

CHAPTER 23

DRAWING THREADS IN AUTOCAD®

CHAPTER OUTLINE

CHAPTER SUMMARY

In this chapter you will learn how to represent threads using the simplified thread symbol. You will also be taken through a procedure that will enable you to draw realistic looking hexagonal nuts and bolts. By the end of this chapter, you will be able to represent threads on a drawing and identify them using a thread note.

23.1) INTRODUCTION

There are three ways to represent threads on a drawing. The detailed representation of a thread is visually very striking, but time consuming to draw. The schematic representation is nearly as effective at indicating a thread, but it does require the use of arrays and other techniques that make it more time consuming to draw than the simplified representation. The simplified representation of a thread is very simple and easy to draw. It doesn't look much like a thread. However, after you become accustomed to looking at simplified threads on a drawing, you will begin to see real threads. The simplified representation consists of nothing more than straight visible and hidden lines.

Bolts and nuts are usually specified on a standard parts sheet and do not require a detailed drawing. However, they do need to be drawn and included as part of an assembly drawing. AutoCAD® has a limited selection of predefined nuts and bolts available in the *Mechanical Tool* palette. If your nut or bolt is among one of the predefined shapes, then it is easiest to use it. You will probably have to EXPLODE and modify the bolt or nut block to fit your purposes. However, it is more likely that you will have to draw your own nut, bolt or screw. After it is drawn, you can then add it to the *Tool* palette and reuse it from there.

23.2) EXTERNAL THREADS TUTORIAL

Upon completion of this tutorial you will be able to draw and identify external threads using the simplified thread representation. You will be drawing the shaft shown below. This shaft has a different thread at each end.

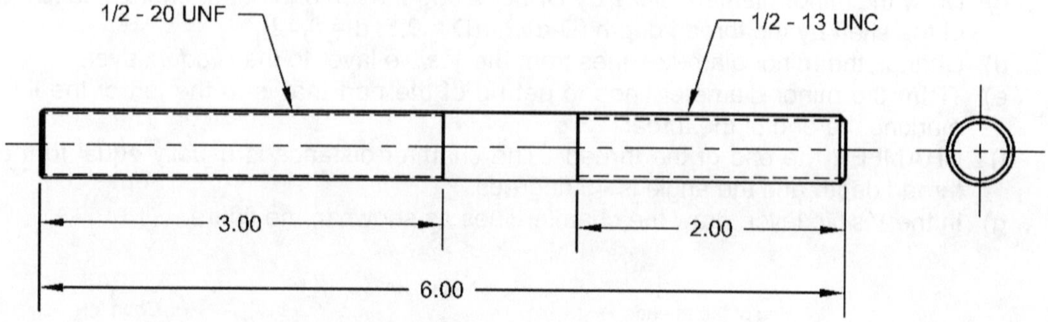

23.2.1) Drawing external Unified National threads

1) Read section 23.1).

2)  ***set-inch.dwt*** and  **External Threads Tut.dwg.**

3) In your ***Visible*** layer, draw the front and side views of a cylindrical shaft that has a diameter of **0.50** inch and a length of **6** inches.

4) In your ***Center*** layer, add the appropriate centerlines.

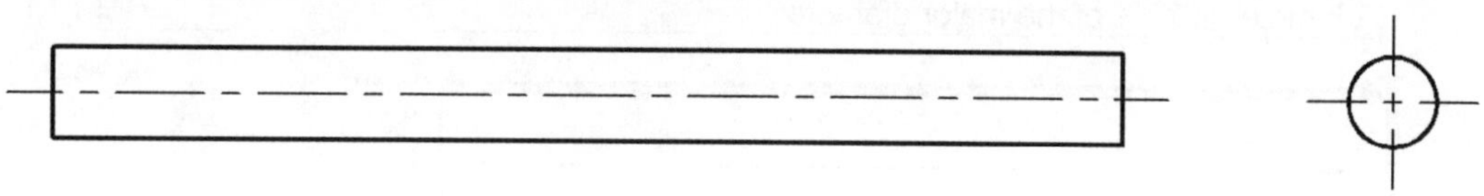

5) Draw a 1/2 - 13 UNC – 2 LONG thread on the right end of the shaft.
   a) Draw a vertical line 2 inches from the right end of the shaft to mark the end of the threads. (A fast way to do this is to OFFSET the right vertical line by 2 inches. If you used a RECTANGLE to draw the shaft, you will need to EXPLODE it before you can OFFSET the end.)
   b) Using the formula given in Appendix B, the minor diameter is calculated to be 0.42.
   c) Draw the minor diameter lines by **OFFSET**ting the top and bottom horizontal lines of the shaft by the thread depth (D-d)/2. (D = 0.5, d = 0.42).
   d) Change the minor diameter lines from the *Visible* layer to the *Hidden* layer.
   e) **TRim** the minor diameter lines to get rid of the part that is to the left of the line marking the end of the thread.
   f) **CHAMFER** the end of the thread. The chamfer distance is usually equal to the thread depth and the angle is 45 degrees.
   g) In the *Visible* layer, draw the chamfer lines as shown in the figure.

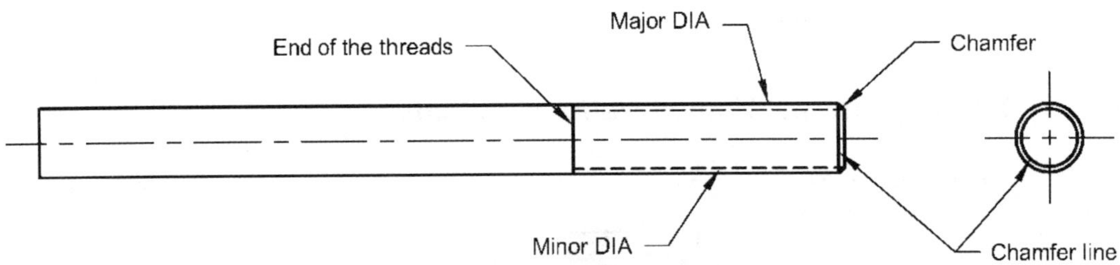

6) Use a similar procedure as above to draw a 1/2 - 20 UNF – 3 LONG thread on the left end of the shaft. Calculate the following…
   a) Minor dia =
   b) Thread depth =

> **Note:** The hidden lines representing the minor diameter are very close to the visible lines. This may be a case where you would want to draw the minor diameter at 75% of the major diameter.

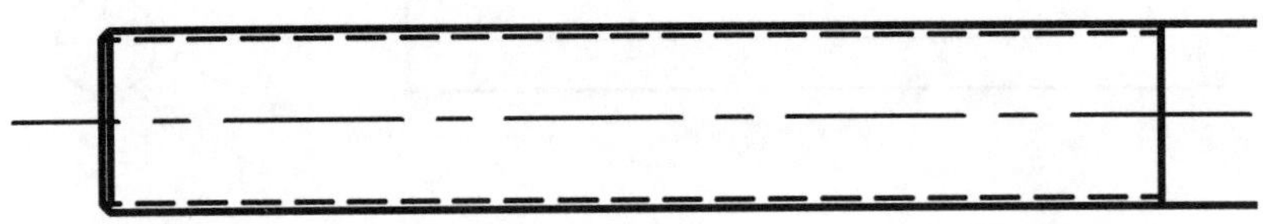

7) In your dimension layer, dimension the shaft as shown. Use an **MLEADER** and the **NEARest** *OSNAP* to create the thread notes.

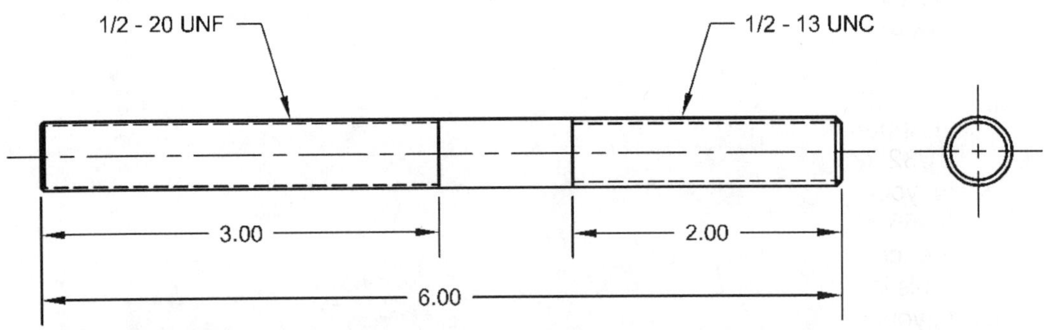

8) Insert your title block, ***save*** your drawing and ***print*** at a ***1:1*** scale.

23.3) INTERNAL THREADS TUTORIAL

Upon completion of this tutorial you will be able to draw internal threads using the simplified thread representation. You will be drawing the internal thread shown.

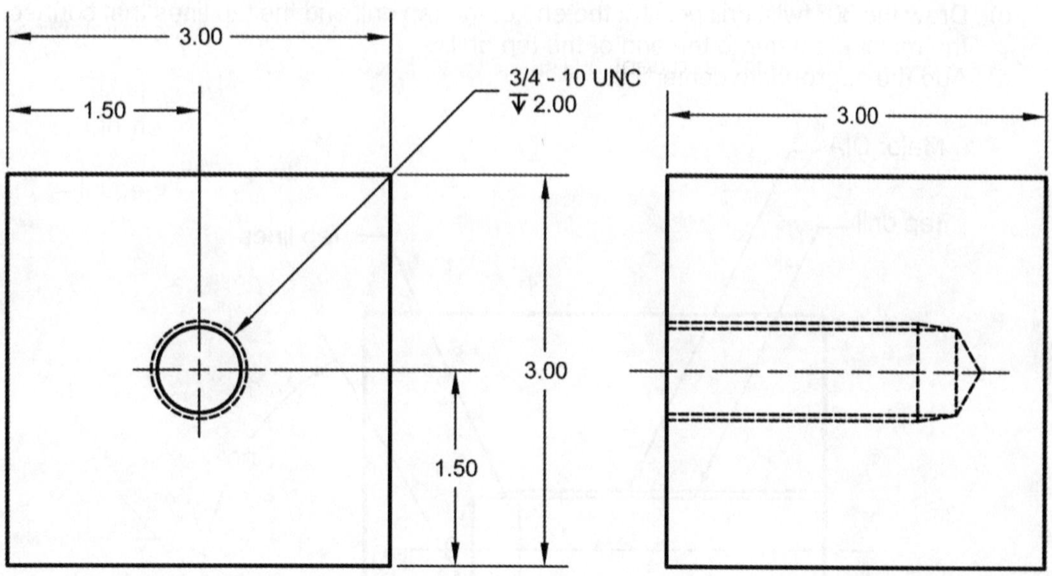

23.3.1) Drawing Unified National internal threads

1) 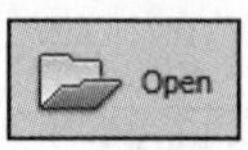

set-inch.dwt and 

Internal Threads Tut.dwg.

2) In your ***Visible*** layer, draw the boundaries of the front and right side views. Both will be 3 inches square.

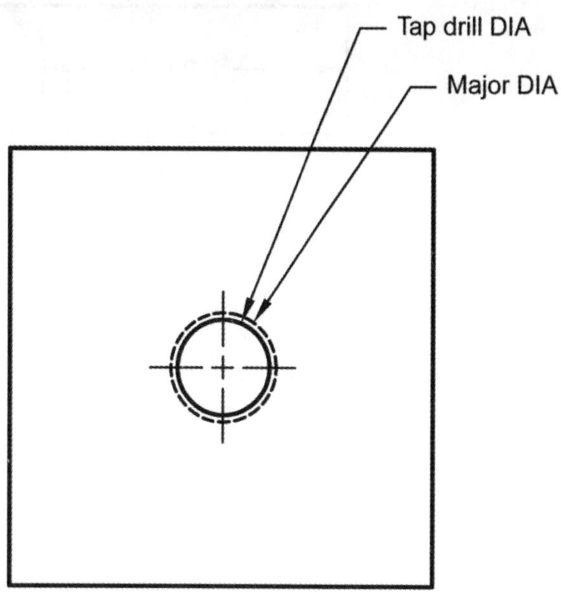

3) Draw the circular view of a 3/4 - 10 UNC internal thread in the center of the cube.
   a) In your ***Hidden*** layer, draw a 3/4 inch diameter circle in the center of the front view. (This is your major diameter.)
   b) Look up the tap drill diameter in Appendix B. It should be 21/32 inch.
   c) In your ***Visible*** layer draw a 0.6562 inch diameter circle in the center of the front view. (This is your tap drill diameter.)
   d) In your ***Center*** layer add the appropriate centerlines.

4) Draw the 3/4 - 10 UNC – ↧2.00 internal threads in the right side view.
   a) In your ***Hidden*** layer, draw the rectangular view of the major diameter at a depth of 2 inches.
   b) Draw the rectangular view of the tap drill at a depth equal to the thread depth plus three times the pitch (2 + 3P = 2+ 3(1/10) = 2.3).
   c) Draw the 30° twist drill point at the end of the tap drill and the tap lines that connect the major diameter to the end of the tap drill.
   d) Add the appropriate centerline.

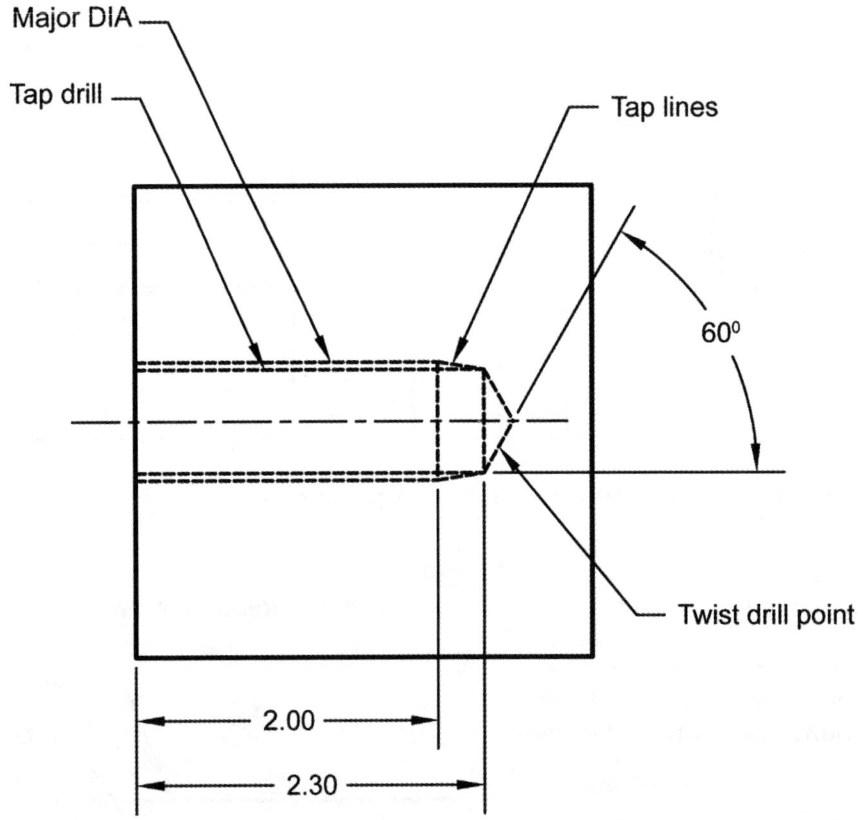

5) In your dimension layer, dimension the drawing. Dimension the internal thread as shown. Use the ***Diameter*** 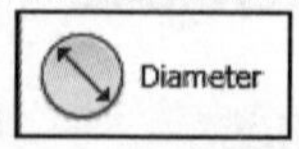

command and edit (**DDEDIT**) the dimension text to create the thread note. If AutoCAD prompts you, disable the automatic fraction stacking. (NOTE: The depth symbol is a small 'x' in the GDT font.)

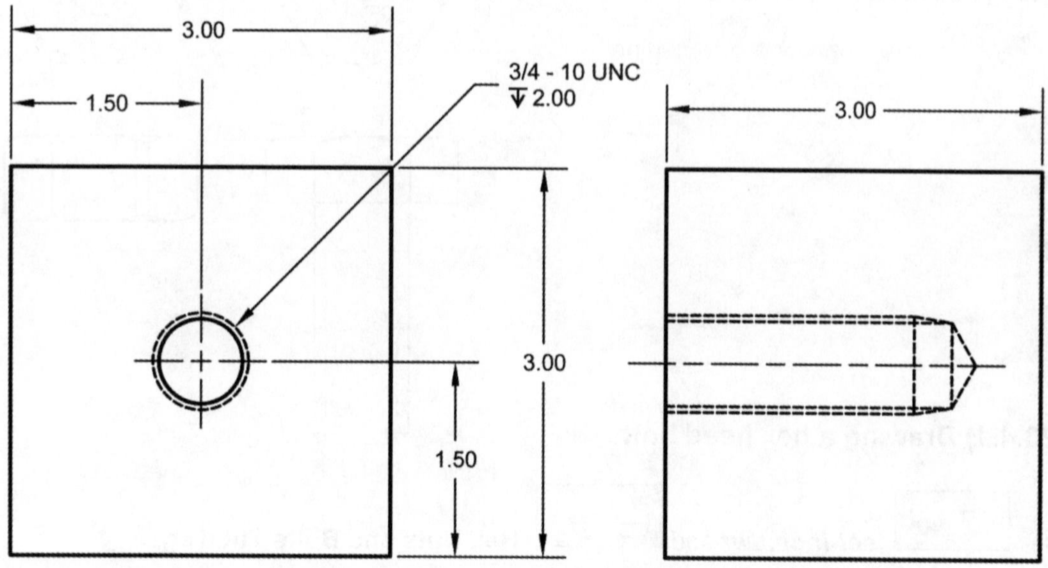

6) Insert your title block, ***save*** your drawing and ***print*** at an appropriate scale.

23.4) HEX NUTS AND BOLTS TUTORIAL

The purpose of this tutorial is to illustrate the procedure used to draw hexagonal nuts and bolts. We will be drawing the 1/4 - UNC hexagonal nut and bolt shown.

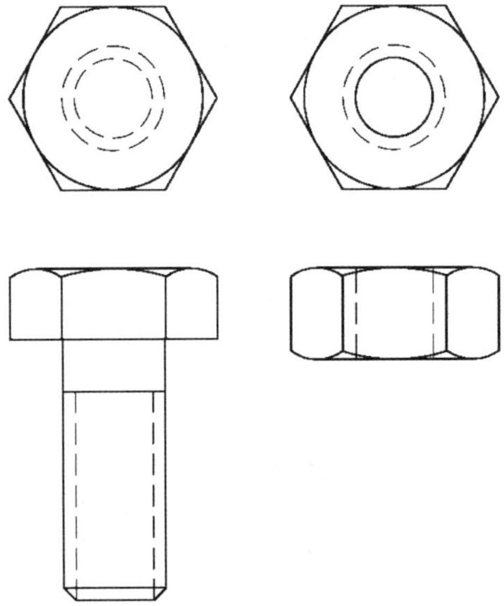

23.4.1) Drawing a hex head bolt

1) 

set-inch.dwt and 

Hex Nuts and Bolts Tut.dwg.

2) From Appendix B look up the bolt dimensions that we will need:
   - *D* = Major diameter = 0.25
   - *H* = Head height = 0.17
   - *F* = Width across the flats = 0.44

3) In the ***Visible*** layer draw a **Circle** that has a diameter equal to *F*.

4) Draw a hexagon (**POLYGON**) that is circumscribed about the circle.

5) In the ***Construction*** layer, draw vertical construction lines (**XLine**) off of every corner of the hexagon.

6) Using the construction lines as a guide, draw a box that is *H* high in the ***Visible*** layer.

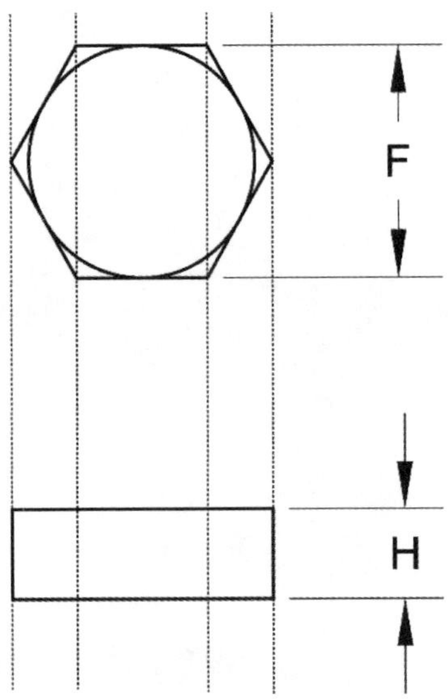

7) In the ***Construction*** layer, draw **Lines** at a 60 degree angle off of the top 4 intersections of the bolt head (see figure).

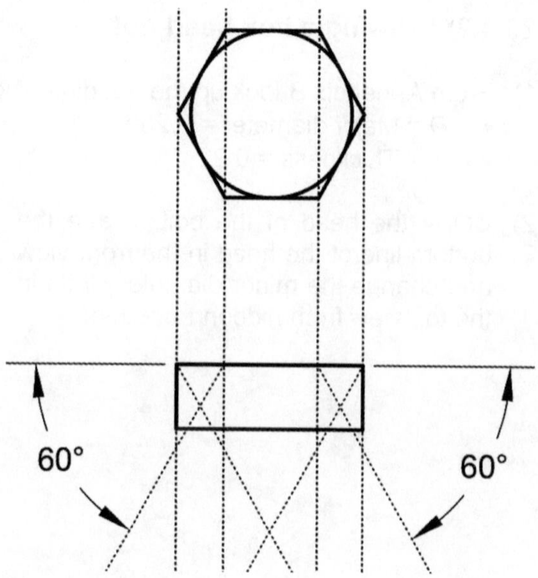

8) In the Visible layer draw three **Circles** that have the centers indicated and are tangent to the top surface of the bolt.

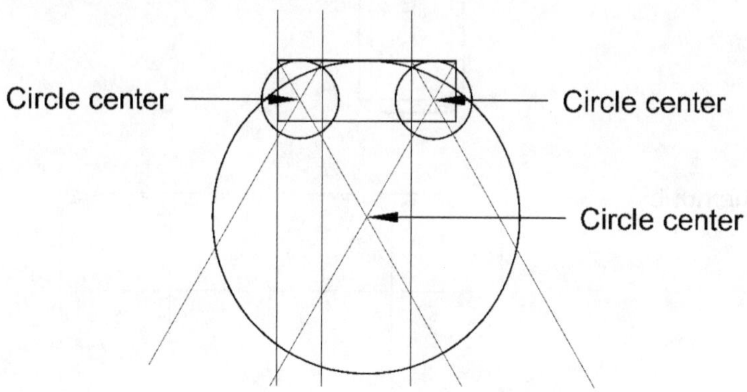

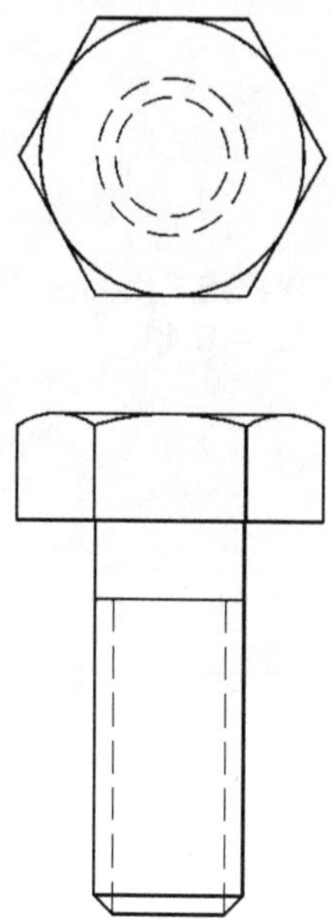

9) Finish the bolt by **TRim**ming the circles and lines in the bolt head as shown, add a bolt body of length 5/8 inches and a thread length of 1/2 inch. Then add the major and minor diameter circles in the hexagonal view.

23.4.2) Drawing a hex head nut

1) From Appendix B look up the nut dimensions that we will need:
   - *D* = Major diameter = 0.25
   - *H* = Thickness = 0.22

2) **COpy** the head of the bolt, **Erase** the bottom line of the head in the front view and change the minor diameter circle in the top view from hidden to visible.

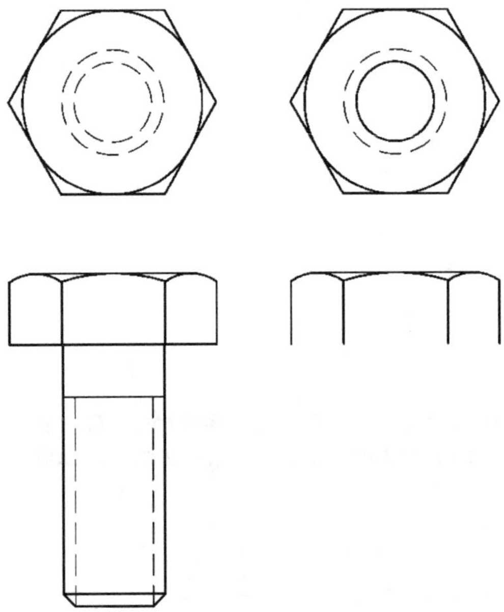

3) **OFFSET** the top line of the nut by *H*/2 = 0.11.

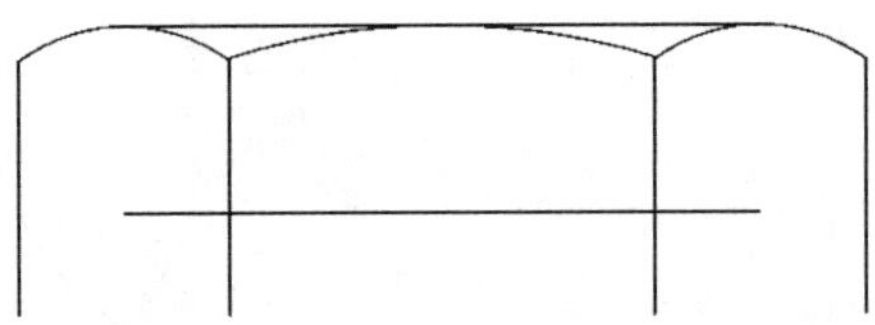

4) **MIrror** the nut using the offset line as the mirror line.

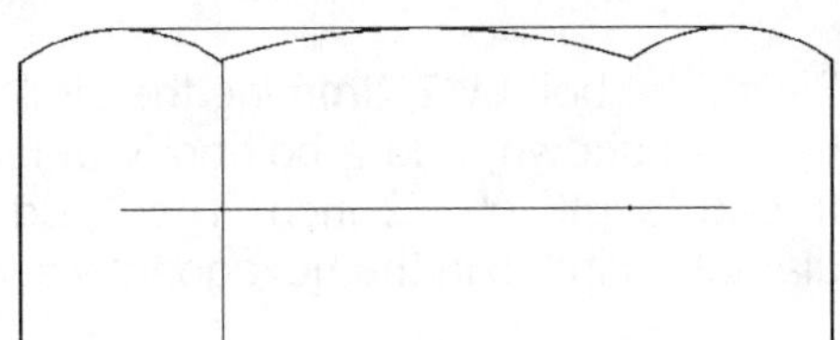

5) **Erase** the mirror line and add the threads.

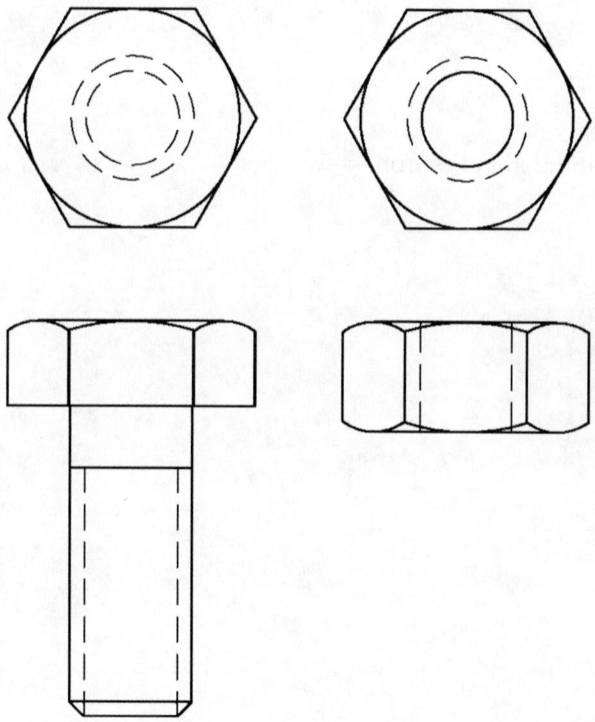

6) Insert your title block, ***save*** your drawing and ***print*** at an appropriate scale.

NOTES:

DRAWING THREADS IN AUTOCAD PROBLEMS

P23-1) Draw and dimension the *Knurled Nut* using proper dimensioning techniques. This *Knurled Nut* is part of the *Milling Jack* given in the *Drawing Assemblies in AutoCAD®* chapter problem section. Notice that the dimensioned isometric drawing does not always use the correct symbols or dimensioning techniques.

- Part name = Knurled Nut
- Part No. = 4
- Material = SAE 1045 – Heat Treat
- Required = 1

P23-2) Draw and dimension the *Pad* using proper dimensioning techniques. This *Pad* is part of the *Milling Jack* given in the *Drawing Assemblies in AutoCAD®* chapter problem section. Notice that the dimensioned isometric drawing does not always use the correct symbols or dimensioning techniques.

- Part name = Pad
- Part No. = 5
- Material = Phosphor Bronze - FAO
- Required = 1

P23-3) Draw and dimension the *Clamp Bolt* using proper dimensioning techniques. This *Clamp Bolt* is part of the *Milling Jack* given in the *Drawing Assemblies in AutoCAD®* chapter problem section. Notice that the dimensioned isometric drawing does not always use the correct symbols or dimensioning techniques.

- Part name = Clamp Bolt
- Part No. = 6
- Material = SAE 1020 – Case Hardened
- Required = 1

P23-4) Draw and dimension the *Sliding Screw* using proper dimensioning techniques. This *Sliding Screw* is part of the *Milling Jack* given in the *Drawing Assemblies in AutoCAD®* chapter problem section. Notice that the dimensioned isometric drawing does not always use the correct symbols or dimensioning techniques.

- Part name = Sliding Screw
- Part No. = 2
- Material = SAE 1045 – Heat Treat
- Required = 1

NOTES:

CHAPTER 24

READING ASSEMBLY DRAWINGS

CHAPTER OUTLINE

CHAPTER SUMMARY

In this chapter you will learn how to read an assembly drawing. An assembly drawing is a drawing of an entire machine with each part located and identified. After each part of a machine is manufactured, the assembly drawing shows us how to put these parts together. The assembly drawing together with all the detailed part drawings and the standard parts sheet is called a working drawing package. A working drawing package contains all the information necessary to manufacture and put together a machine or system. By the end of this chapter, you will be able to understand the components of a working drawing package.

An assembly drawing is a drawing of an entire machine or system with all of its components located and identified.

24.1) DEFINITIONS

- Detail Drawing: A detail drawing is a drawing of an **individual part**, which includes an orthographic projection with dimensions. One detail/part per sheet.

- Assembly Drawing: **An assembly consists of a number of parts that are joined together to perform a specific function** (e.g., a bicycle). The assembly may be disassembled without destroying any part of the assembly. An assembly drawing shows the assembled machine or structure with all of the parts in their functional position.

- Subassembly Drawing: A subassembly is two or more parts that form a portion of an assembly (e.g., the drive train of a bicycle). A subassembly drawing shows only **one unit of a larger machine**.

- Working Drawing Package: A typical working drawing package includes an assembly drawing, detailed drawings, and a standard parts sheet. **The drawing package contains the specifications that will enable the design to be manufactured.**

24.1.1) Drawing order

Drawings included in a working drawing package are presented in the following order. **Find numbers are usually assigned based on the size or importance of the part.**

1) Assembly drawing (first sheet)
2) Part Assigned to Find Number 1
3) Part Assigned to Find Number 2
4) ....
5) Standard parts sheet (last sheet)

24.2) COMPONENTS OF AN ASSEMBLY DRAWING

Figure 24.2-1 illustrates the components of an assembly drawing.

24.2.1) Assembly drawing views

Assembly drawings may contain one or more of the standard views (i.e., Front, top, right-side, left-side, bottom, rear). It may also include specialized views such as section views or auxiliary views.

24.2.2) Part identification

A part is located and identified by using a circle or balloon containing a *find number* and a leader line that points to the corresponding part. A balloon containing a *find number* is placed adjacent to the part. A leader line, starting at the balloon, points to the part to which it refers.

24.2.3) Parts list / bill of material (bom)

The parts list is an itemized table of the parts that make up the assembled machine. The important columns of the table are the following.

- Find number: The find number helps you find the part within the assembly. This number is assigned based on size and importance of the part and indicated in the parts list. Then the find number is placed in a balloon and points to the part that it corresponds to.
- Part number: The part number, if different from the find number is usually a catalog part number or a combination of the find number and the drawing number.
- Nomenclature or description: The name or description of the part.
- Number of parts required (QTY REQ'D): The number of that part used in the assembly.
- Part material: The material in which the part is made of.

24.3) SECTION VIEWS

Since assemblies often have parts fitting into or overlapping other parts, section views are often used. **Section lines in adjacent parts in the assembly are drawn in opposing directions.** Figure 24.2-1 shows the use of a section view. Notice the section lines of the two parts are in opposing directions.

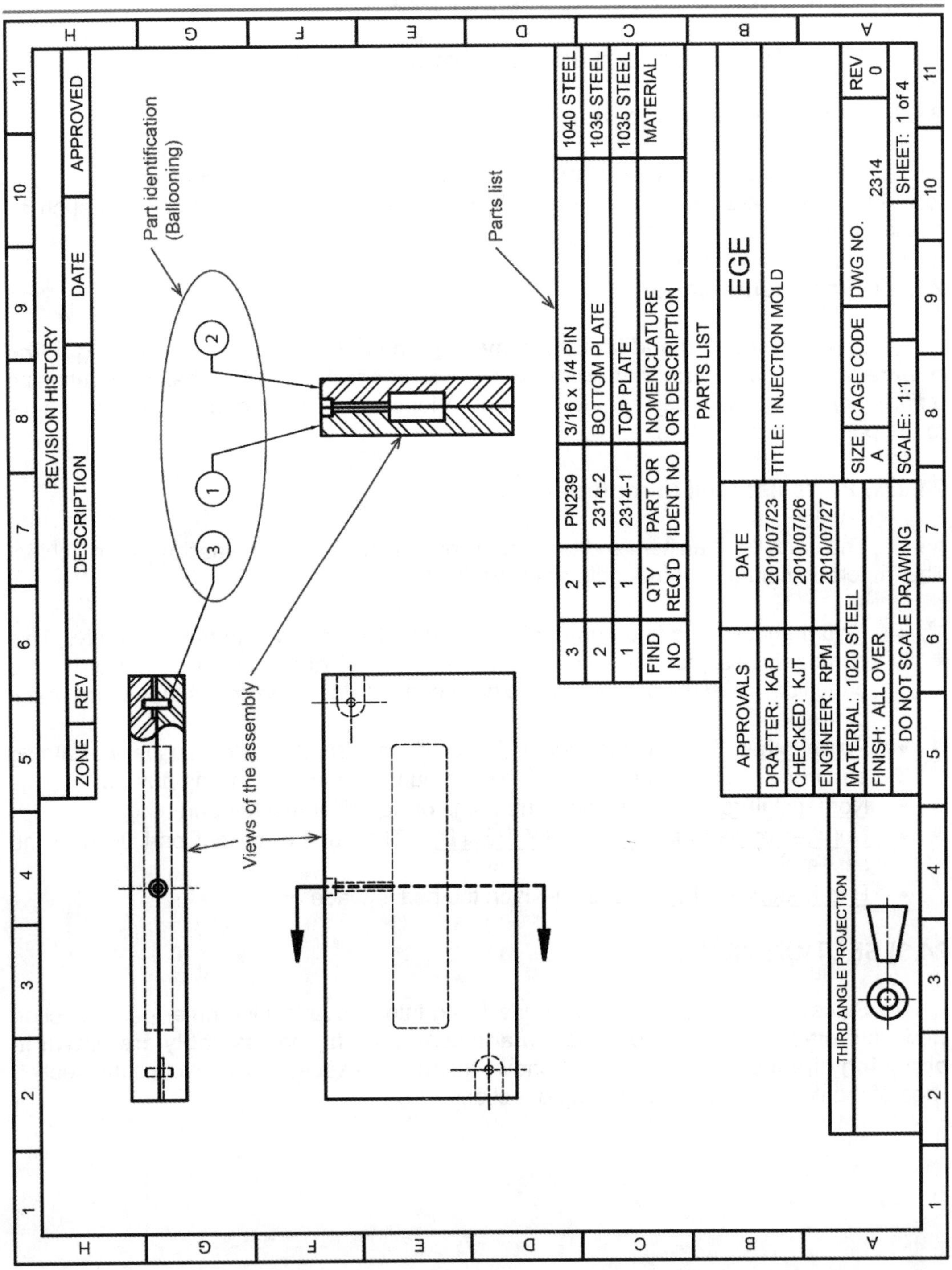

Figure 24.2-1: Components of an assembly drawing.

24.4) APPLYING WHAT WE HAVE LEARNED

Exercise 24.4-1: Reading assembly drawings

Name: ______________________________ Date: ____________

Answer the following questions about the assembly drawing shown on the next page.

a) What is the name of the assembly/device?

b) How many sheets are there in the working drawing package?

c) Which part would you expect to be on SHEET 2?

d) What is the name of part number 5687 - 2?

e) What is the find number of the ADJUSTING SCREW?

f) What type of material is the CAP made of?

g) What is the inner diameter of the 3/8 PLAIN WASHER?

h) On the assembly, circle the WEDGE.

i) On the assembly, circle the SET SCREW.

Exercise 24.4-1 Cont.: Reading assembly drawings

FIND NO	QTY REQ'D	PART OR IDENT NO	PART NAME	DESCRIPTION	MATERIAL
1	1	5687 - 1	CAP		CAST IRON
2	1	5687 - 2	WEDGE		A2 TOOL STEEL
3	1	5687 - 3	ADJUSTING SCREW	3/8 - 16 UNC	1020 STEEL
4	1	42PA98	3/8 - 16 UNC HEX BOLT	LENGTH = 2, THD LENGTH = 1	GRADE 5 STEEL, ZINC PLATED
5	1	22UF89	3/8 PLAIN WASHER	OD = 0.375, ID = 5/32, THICK = 0.031	STAINLESS STEEL
6	1	5TCD0	3/8-16 UNC SET SCREW	LENGTH = 0.75, DOG POINT	ALLOY STEEL

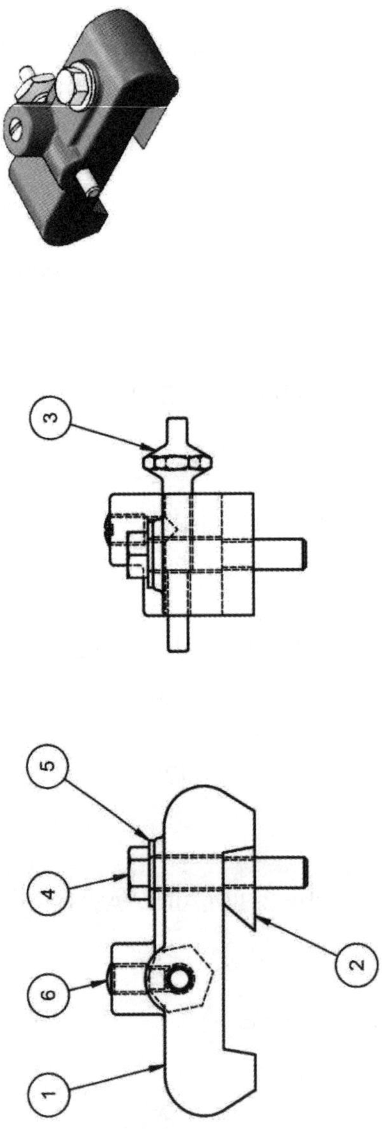

REVISION HISTORY

ZONE	REV	DESCRIPTION	DATE	APPROVED

UNLESS OTHERWISE SPECIFIED
DIM ARE IN INCHES
TOL ON ANGLE ±2°
2 PL ±.05 3 PL ±.001
INTERPRET DIM AND TOL PER
ASME Y14.5 - 2009

THIRD ANGLE PROJECTION

APPROVALS	DATE
DRAFTER: KAP	2022/07/23
CHECKED: KJT	2022/07/26
ENGINEER: RPM	2022/07/27
MATERIAL: -	
FINISH: -	

EGE

TITLE: CLAMP STOP

SIZE	CAGE CODE	DWG NO.	REV
A		5687	0

DO NOT SCALE DRAWING — SCALE: 1:2 — SHEET: 1 of 5

READING ASSEMBLY DRAWINGS QUESTIONS – SET1

Name: ______________________________ Date: _____________

Q24-1) The purpose of an assembly drawing is to show how the individual parts _________ _____________. Fill in the blank.

Q24-2) This is a place where you can get a quick overall view of all the parts that comprise an assembly and how many of each are required in the assembly. (Circle all that apply.)

a) parts list
b) table of contents
c) standard parts sheet
d) bill of materials

Q24-3) Parts are located in an assembly drawing using …. (Choose all that apply)

a) Balloons
b) Find numbers
c) Leader line
d) Part numbers

Q24-4) What is a BOM?

NOTES:

READING ASSEMBLY DRAWINGS QUESTIONS – SET2

Name: ______________________________ Date: ______________

Q24-5) The first sheet in a working drawing package is the .... drawing.

a) part#1
b) the last part
c) assembly drawing
d) standard parts sheet

Q24-6) The last sheet in a working drawing package is the .... drawing.

a) part#1
b) the last part
c) assembly drawing
d) standard parts sheet

Q24-7) Section lines are drawn in opposing directions when there are ....

a) adjacent parts
b) small parts
c) non-sectioned parts
d) moving parts

Q24-8) Which of the following are columns in a parts list? (Choose all that apply)

a) Find Number
b) Quantity required
c) Part material
d) Description of the part

NOTES:

READING ASSEMBLY DRAWING PROBLEMS

Name: ________________________________ Date: ______________

P24-1) Answer the following questions about the assembly drawing shown.

a) What is the name of the assembly?

b) How many sheets are there in the working drawing package?

c) What is the name of part number 303200 - 4?

d) What is the find number of the BOLT?

e) What type of material is the WEDGE made of?

f) How many SET SCREWS are used in the assembly?

g) On the assembly, circle the ADJUSTING NUT.

h) On the assembly, circle the HEX NUT.

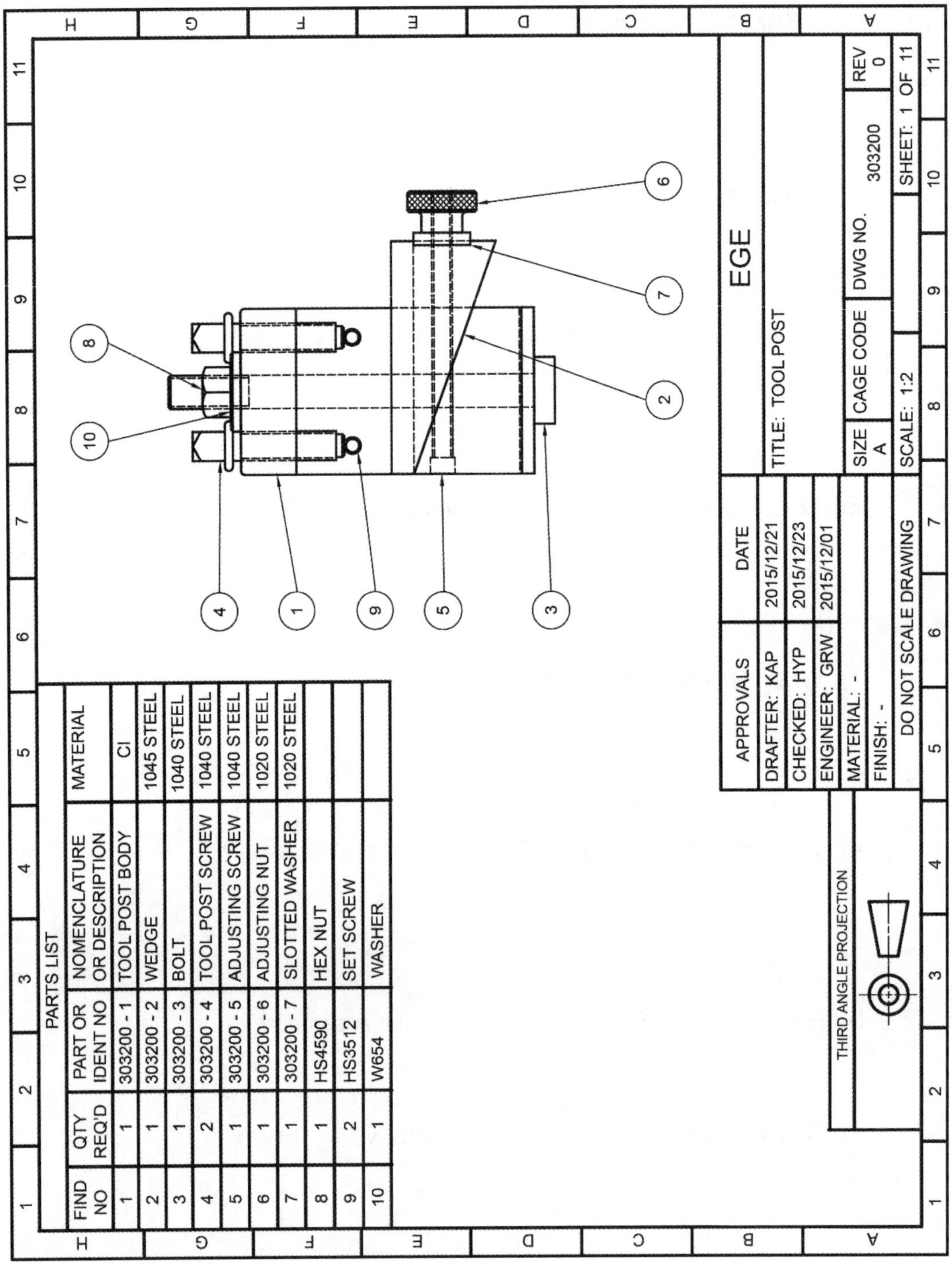

PARTS LIST

FIND NO	QTY REQ'D	PART OR IDENT NO	NOMENCLATURE OR DESCRIPTION	MATERIAL
1	1	303200 - 1	TOOL POST BODY	CI
2	1	303200 - 2	WEDGE	1045 STEEL
3	1	303200 - 3	BOLT	1040 STEEL
4	2	303200 - 4	TOOL POST SCREW	1040 STEEL
5	1	303200 - 5	ADJUSTING SCREW	1040 STEEL
6	1	303200 - 6	ADJUSTING NUT	1020 STEEL
7	1	303200 - 7	SLOTTED WASHER	1020 STEEL
8	1	HS4590	HEX NUT	
9	2	HS3512	SET SCREW	
10	1	W654	WASHER	

CHAPTER 25

CREATING ASSEMBLY DRAWINGS

CHAPTER OUTLINE

CHAPTER SUMMARY

In this chapter you will learn how to create an assembly drawing. This includes properly identifying each part in the assembly, creating a parts list, and properly ordering the sheets in a working drawing package. By the end of this chapter, you will be able to determine which type of views are needed in an assembly drawing and how to identify each part.

25.1) ASSEMBLY DRAWING REVIEW

An assembly drawing is a drawing of an entire machine or system with all of its components located and identified. The assembly drawing along with the detailed drawings and the standard parts sheet are combined into a working drawing package. Drawings included in a working drawing package are presented in the following order.

1) Assembly drawing (first sheet)
2) Part Assigned to Find Number 1
3) Part Assigned to Find Number 2
4) ....
5) Standard parts sheet (last sheet)

25.2) SELECTING APPROPRIATE VIEWS

When deciding which view or views to include in your assembly drawing you should keep in mind the purpose of an assembly drawing. **The purpose of an assembly drawing is to show how the parts fit together** and to suggest the function of the entire unit. Its purpose is not to describe the shapes of the individual parts. Sometimes only one view is needed and sometimes it is necessary to draw all three principal views. Given the complexity of the assembly, it may be necessary to include additional advanced views such as section views, partial views, and auxiliary views.

25.3) COMPONENTS INCLUDED ON AN ASSEMBLY DRAWING

25.3.1) Part identification

A part is located and identified by using a circle or balloon containing a *find number* and a leader line that points to the corresponding part. Balloons identifying different parts are placed in orderly **horizontal or vertical rows**. The leader lines are never allowed to cross and adjacent leader lines should be as parallel to each other as possible as shown in Figure 25.3-1.

25.3.2) Parts list / bill of materials (BOM)

The parts list is an itemized list of the parts that make up the assembled machine. A parts list may contain, but is not limited to, the following.

- Find number: The *find number* links the *parts list* description of the part to the balloon locating the part on the assembly drawing.
- Part number: A *part number* is an identifier of a particular part design. It is common practice, but not a requirement, to start the part number with the drawing

number followed by a dash and then a unique number identifying the part. This unique number usually matches the find number. Standard parts usually do not contain the drawing number because they are used across designs not just in a particular design.

- Nomenclature or description: The part name or description.
- Number of parts required (QTY REQ'D): The number of that part used in the assembly.
- Part material: The material the part is made of.
- Stock size: The pre-machined size of the part.
- Cage code: A cage code is a five position code that identifies companies doing or wishing to do business with the Federal Government.
- Part weight: The weight of the finished part.

Parts lists are arranged in order of their find number. **Find numbers are usually assigned based on the size or importance of the part.** The parts list is placed either in the upper left corner of the drawing, with part number 1 at the top, or lower right corner of the drawing, with part number 1 at the bottom (see Figures 25.3-2).

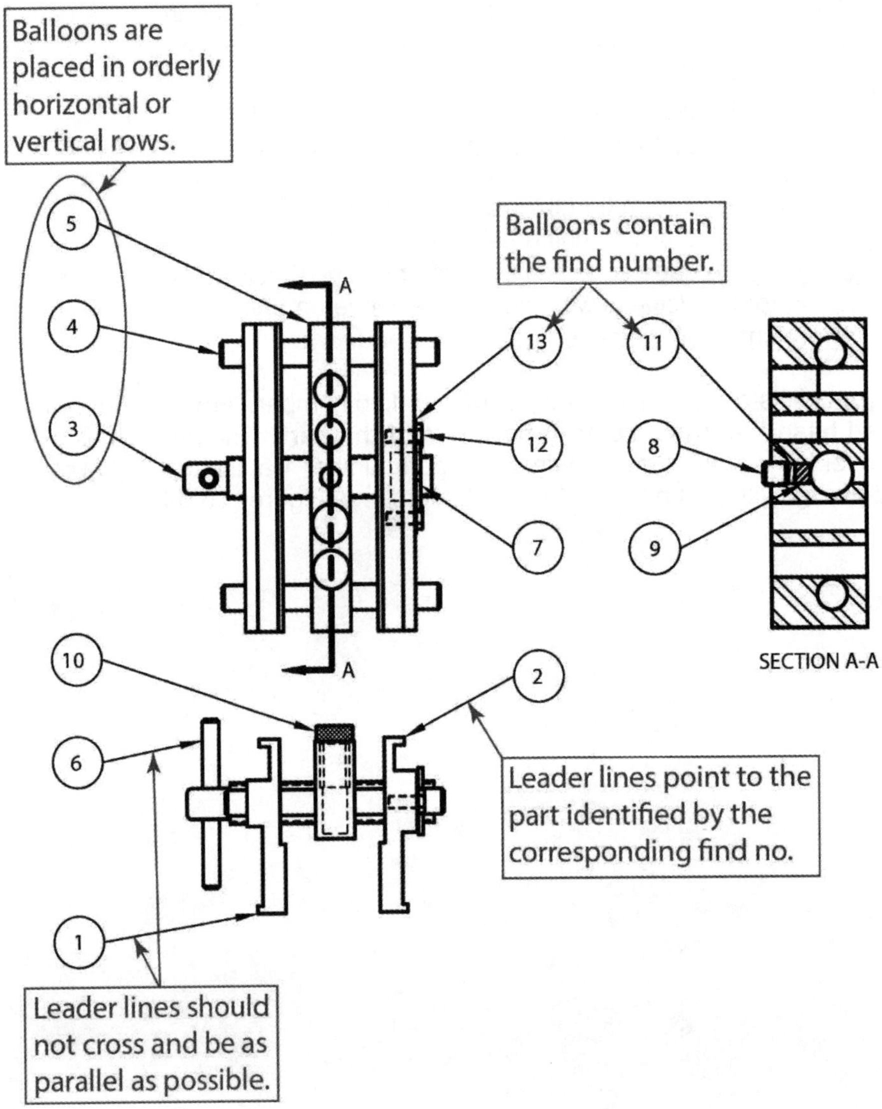

Figure 25.3-1: Part identification

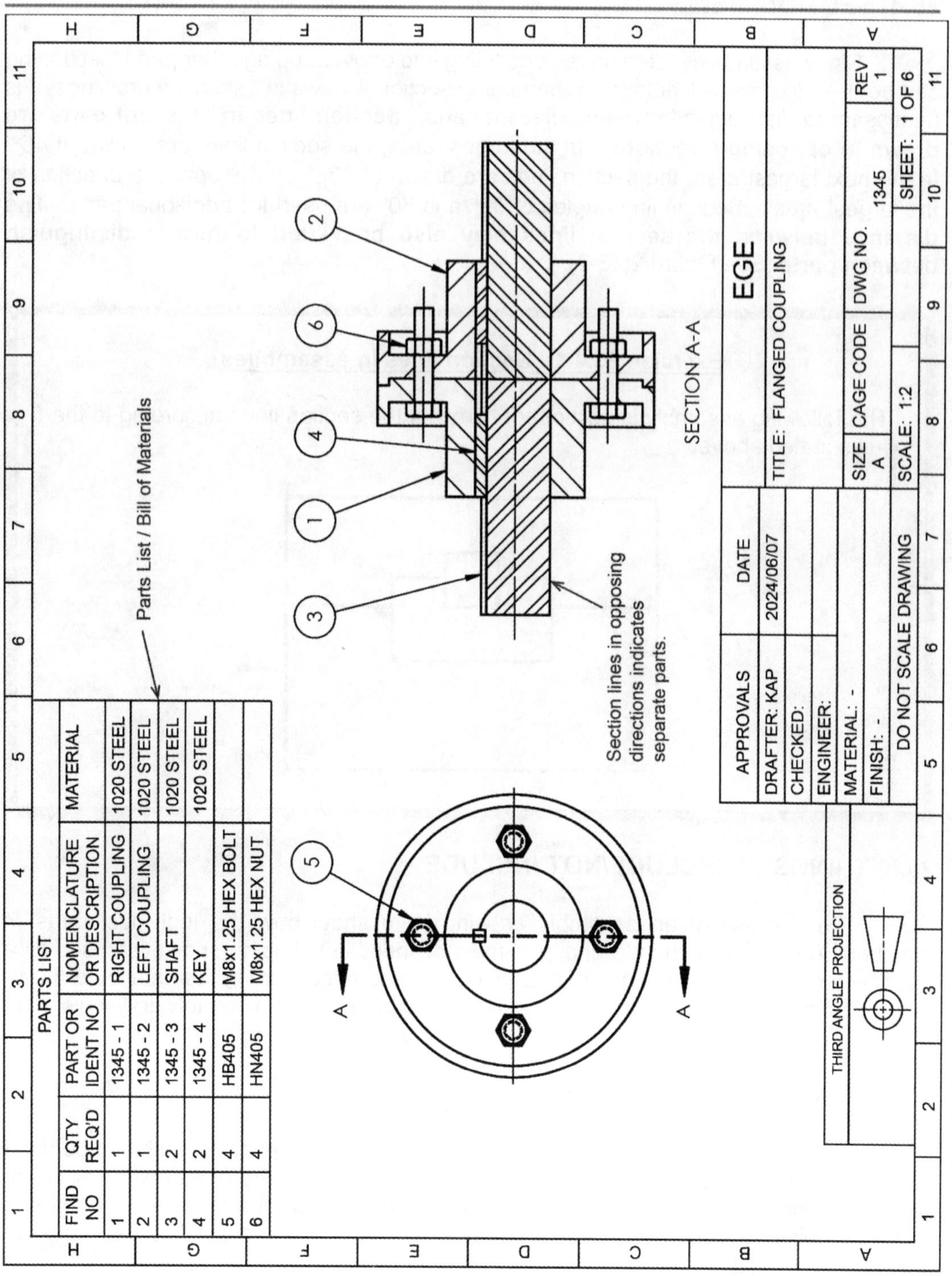

Figure 25.3-2: Parts list

25.4) SECTION VIEWS

Since assemblies often have parts fitting into or overlapping other parts, sectioning can be used to great advantage. When using sectional views in assembly drawings, it is necessary to distinguish between adjacent parts. **Section lines in adjacent parts are drawn in opposing directions.** In the largest area, the section lines are drawn at 45°. In the next largest area, the section lines are drawn at 135° (in the opposite direction of the largest area). Section line angles of 30° and 60° are used for additional parts. **The distance between the section lines may also be varied to further distinguish between parts** (See Figure 25.3-2).

Exercise 25.4-1: Section lines in assemblies

The following assembly is sectioned. Draw in the section lines according to the rules stated above.

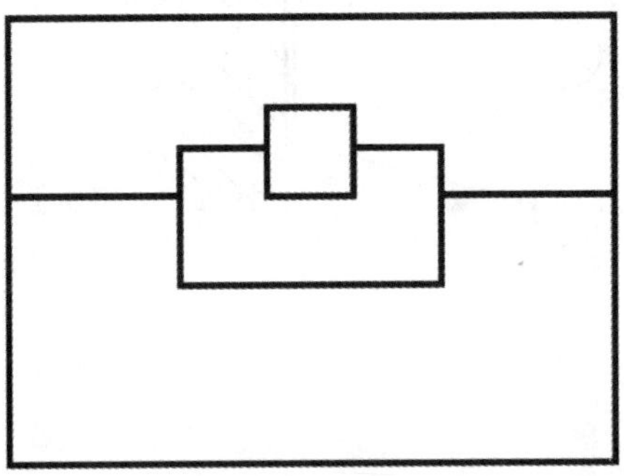

25.5) THINGS TO INCLUDE/NOT INCLUDE

The purpose of an assembly drawing is to show how the individual parts fit together. Therefore, each individual part must be identified. It is not, however, used as a manufacturing print. Some lines that are included and necessary in the detailed drawing may be left off the assembly drawing to enhance clearness. The assembly drawing should not look overly cluttered.

25.5.1) Hidden and center lines

Hidden and center lines are often not needed. However, they should be used wherever necessary for clearness. It is left to the judgment of the drafter whether or not to include hidden lines. A good practice is to include all hidden and center lines at first and then delete or hide the lines that impair clearness. When a section view is used, hidden lines should not be used in the sectional view.

25.5.2) Dimensions

As a rule, dimensions are not given on assembly drawings. If dimensions are given, they are limited to some function of the object as a whole.

25.6) APPLYING WHAT WE HAVE LEARNED

Exercise 25.6-1: Working drawing package

Consider the *Clamp* shown. On the following pages, there are full descriptions on each part and sheets of an incomplete working drawing package. Follow the directions and complete the drawing sheets. Note that the drawing number is 31578.

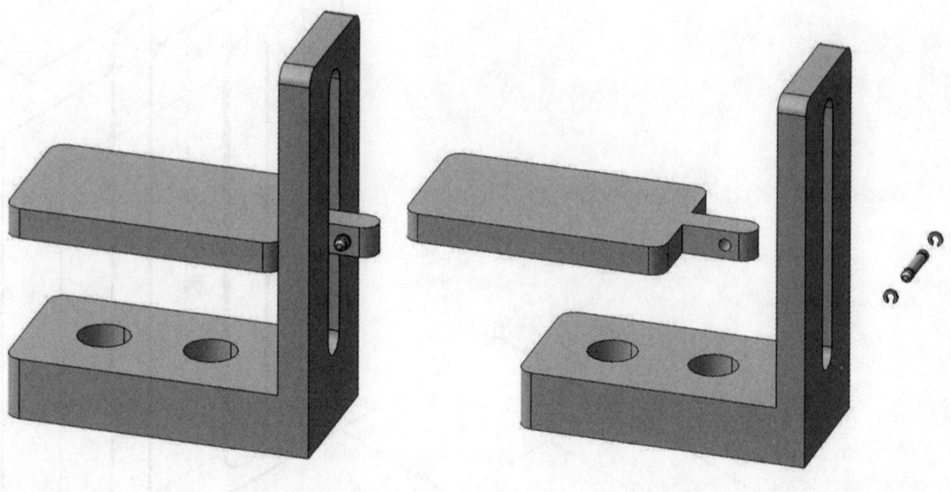

Exercise 25.6-2: Working drawing package

Part 1: The *Base* is made of steel.

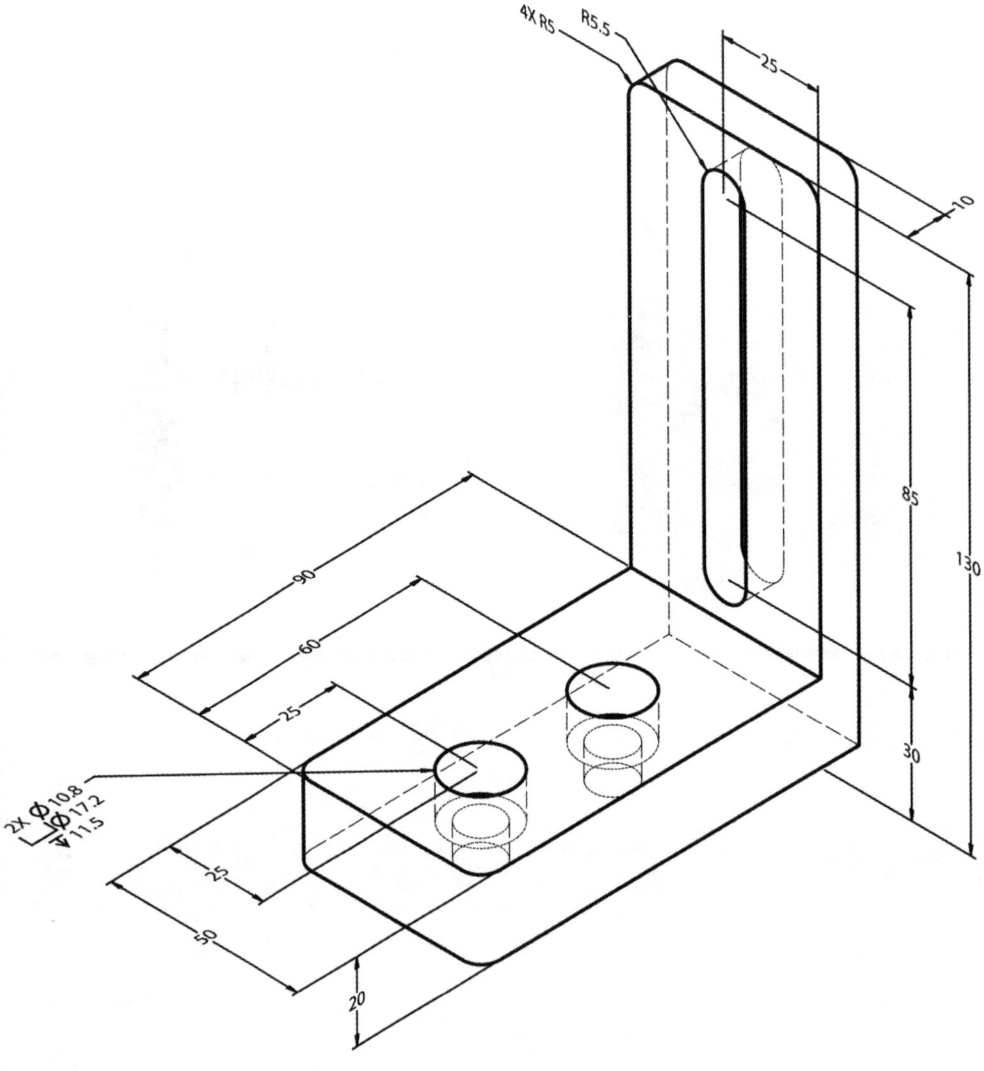

Exercise 25.6-2: Working drawing package

Part 2: The *Weight Plate* is made of steel.

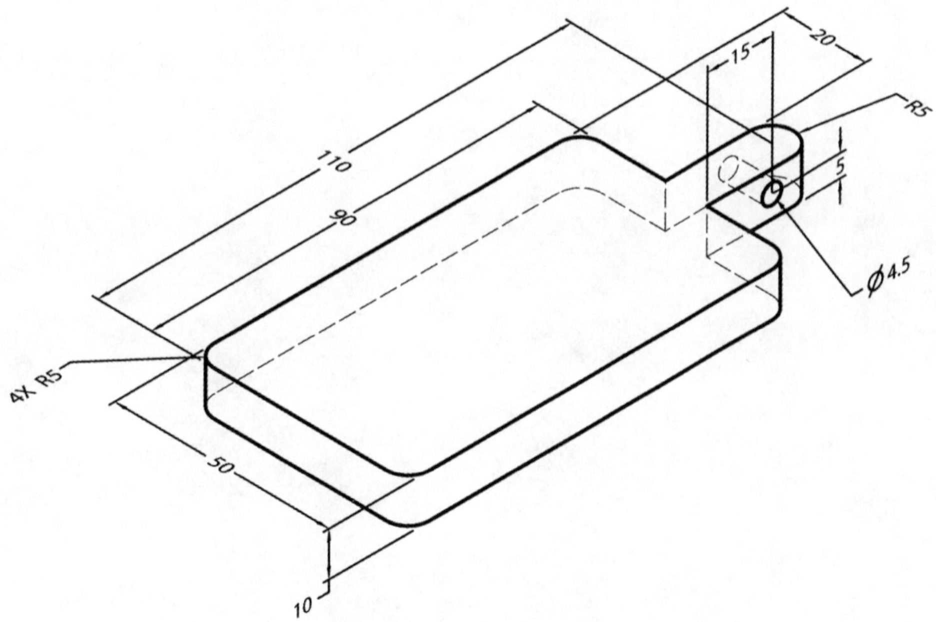

Part 3: The *Pin* is made of hardened steel.

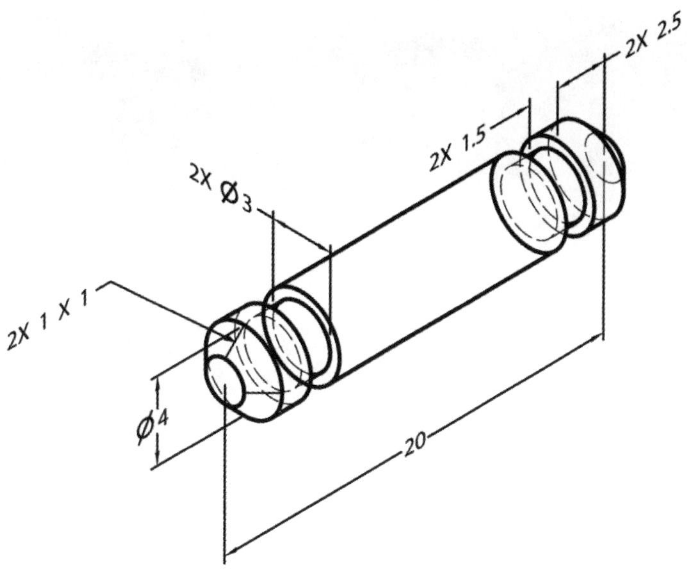

Part 4: The *Snap Ring* has an inner diameter of 3 mm, an outer diameter of 5 mm, and a thickness of 1 mm. The snap ring part number is SR67.

NOTES:

Name: ______________________________ Date: ____________

Balloon the assembly and fill in the parts list and title block.

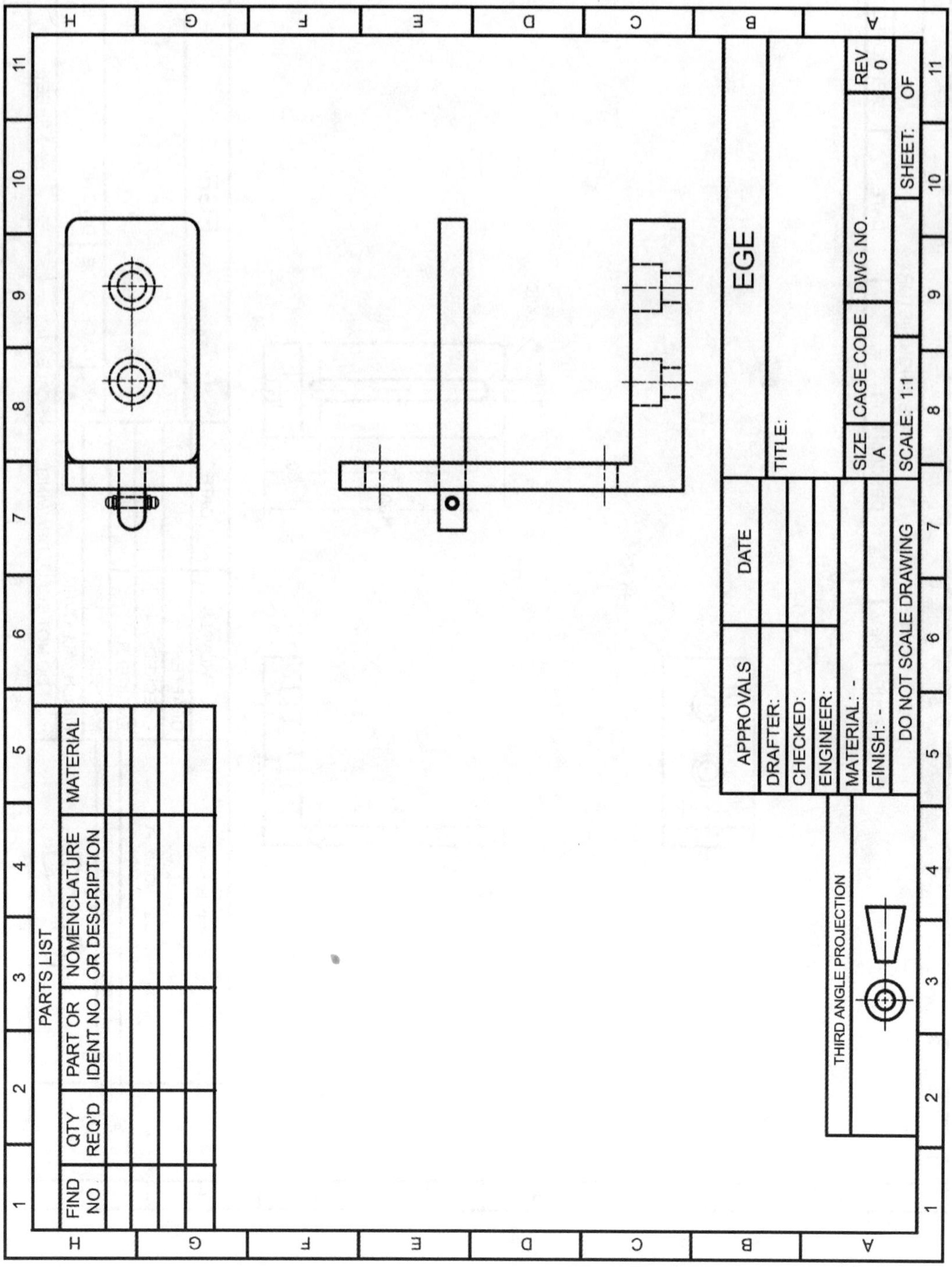

Fill in the title block and add the 7 missing dimensions.

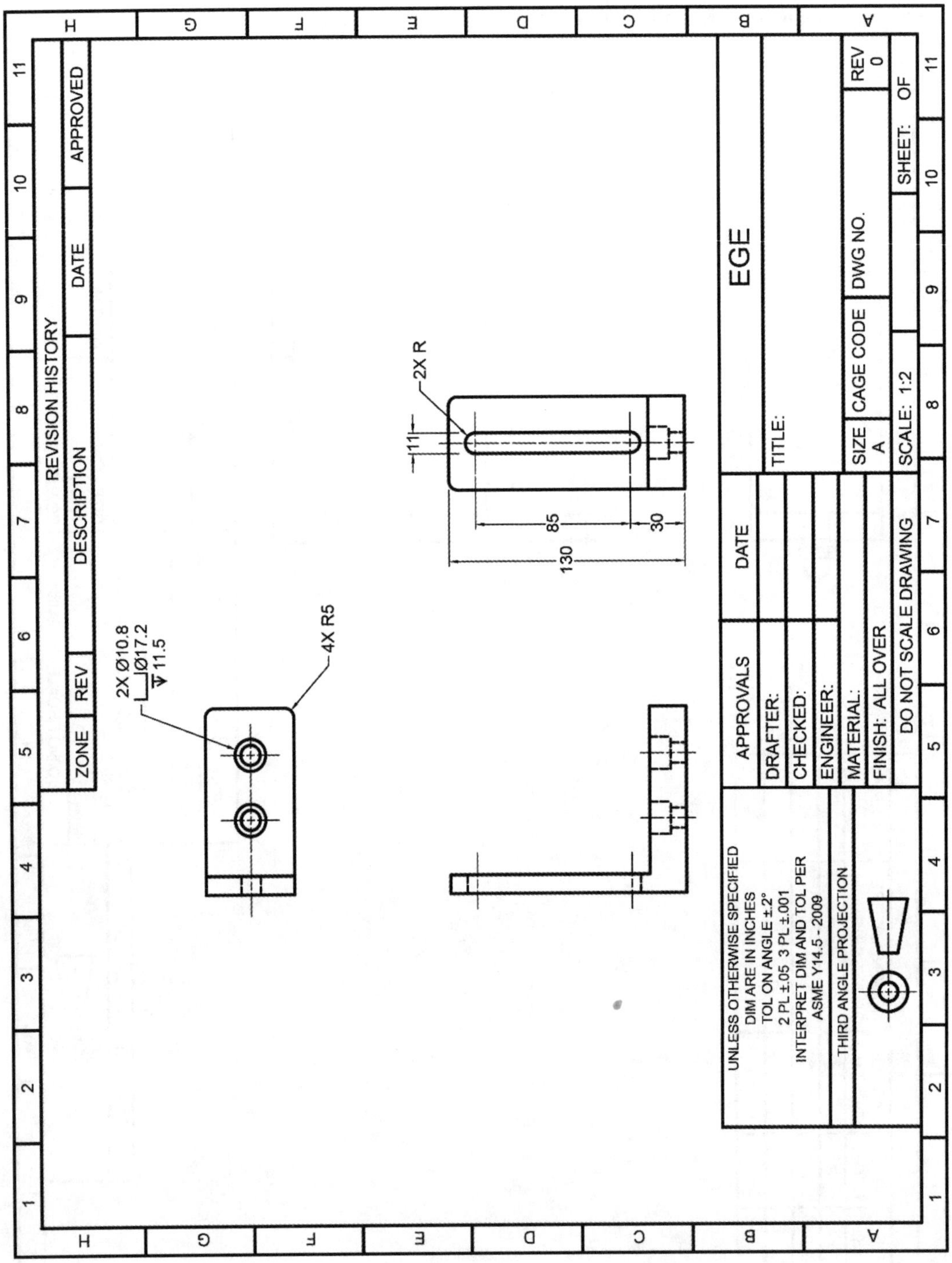

Name: ______________________________ Date: ____________

Fill in the title block and add the 3 missing dimensions.

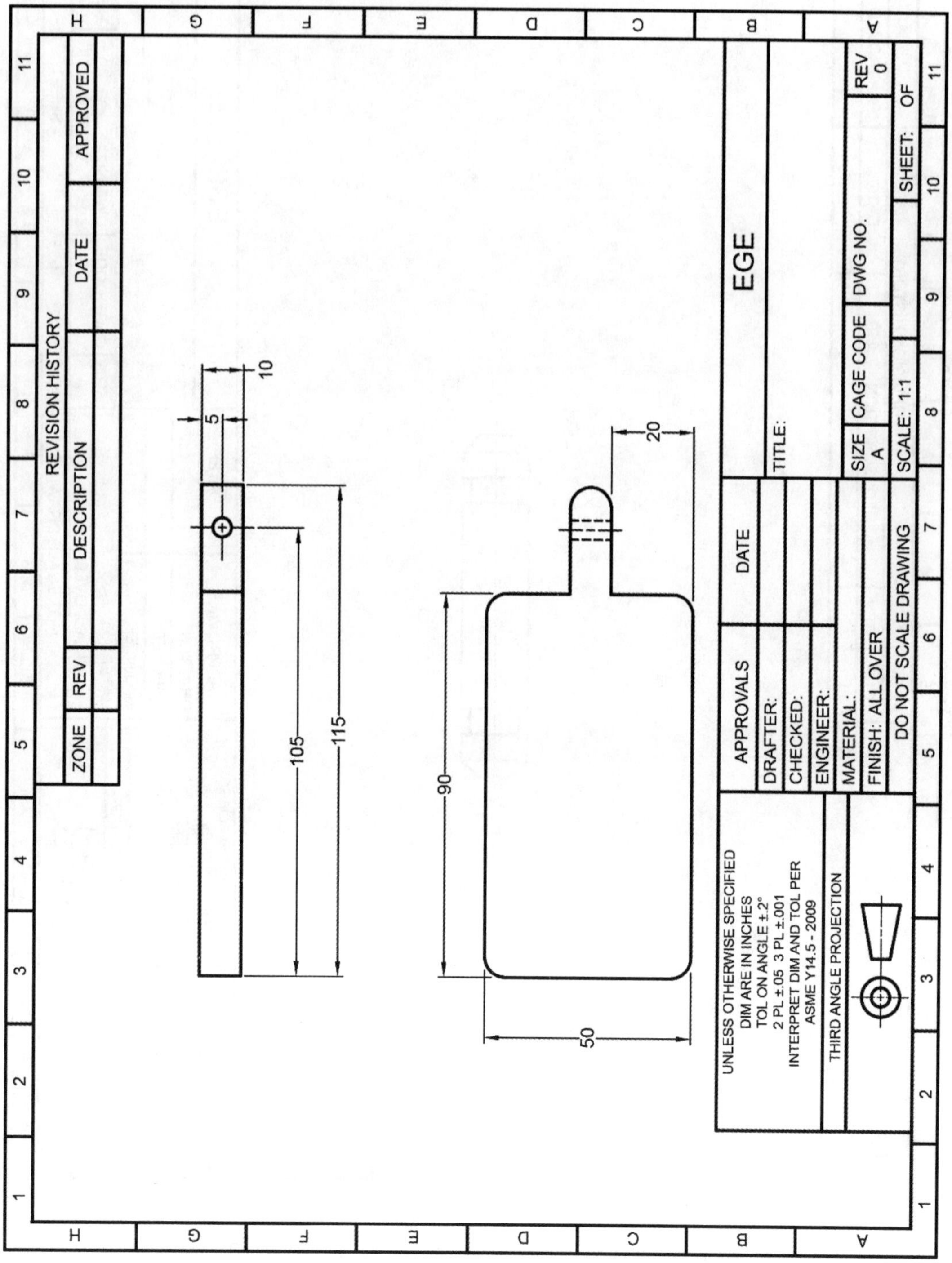

Dimension the *Pin* and fill in the title block.

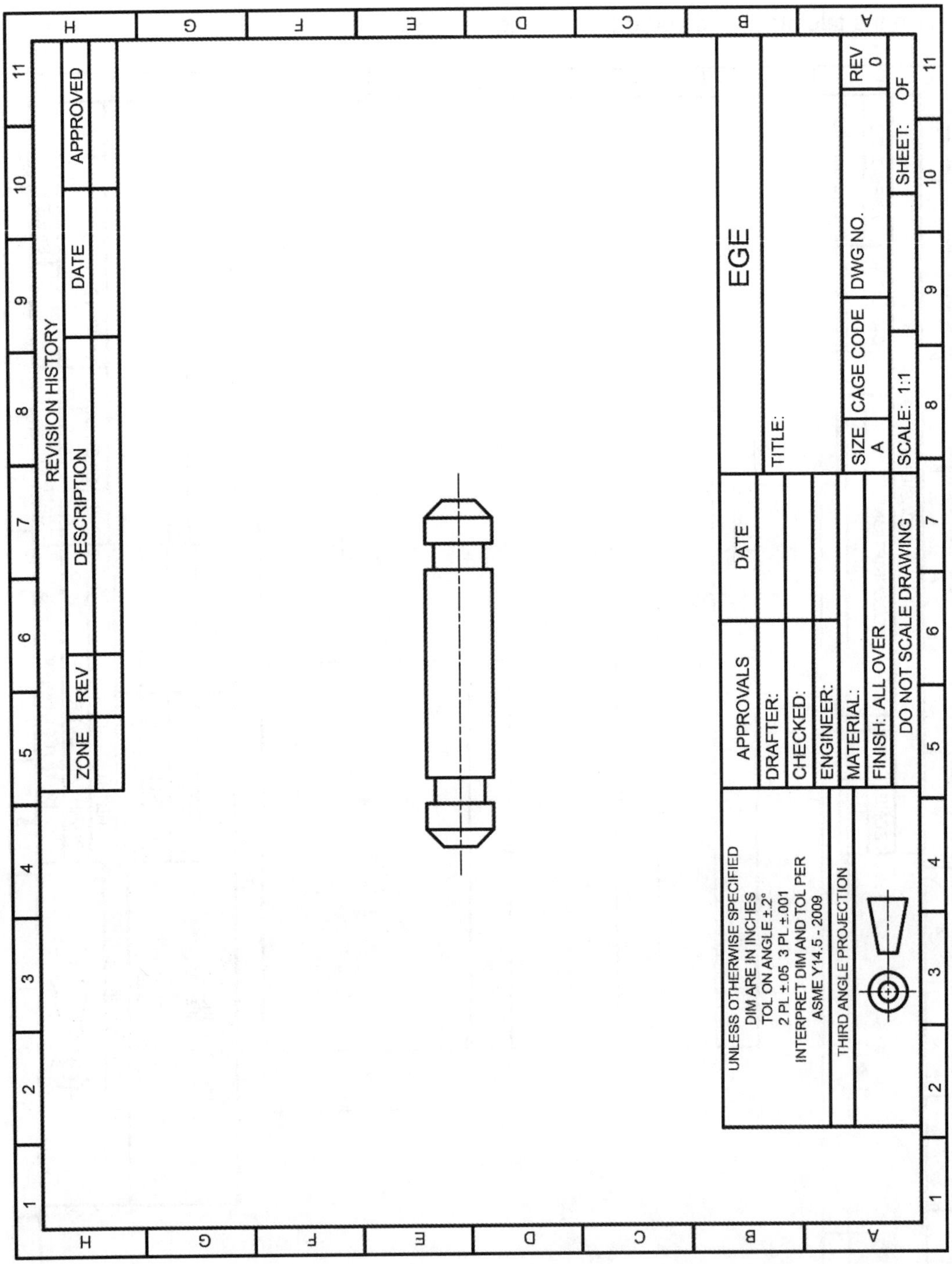

Name: ______________________________________ Date: ______________

Create a standard parts sheet.

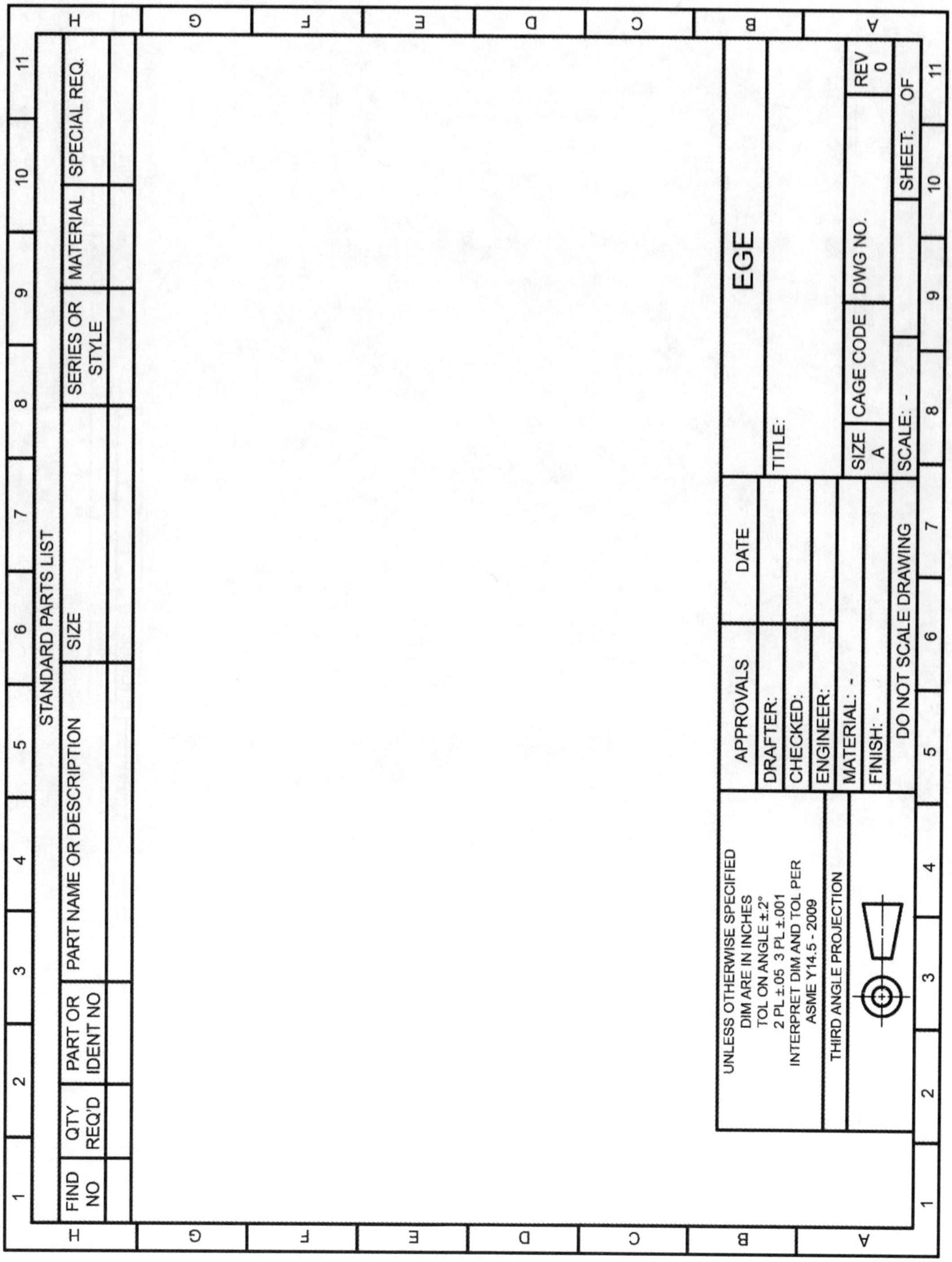

NOTES:

CREATING ASSEMBLY DRAWINGS QUESTIONS

Name: ______________________________ Date: ______________

Q25-1) What is always included on a detailed drawing but rarely included on an assembly drawing?

a) section lines
b) hidden lines
c) center lines
d) dimensions

Q25-2) Criteria that are used to assign part/find numbers. (Circle all that apply.)

a) size
b) shape
c) importance
d) color

NOTES:

CREATING ASSEMBLY DRAWING PROBLEMS

P25-1) Consider the *Trolley* assembly shown. Sheets of an incomplete working drawing package are given in the following pages. Complete the working drawing package.

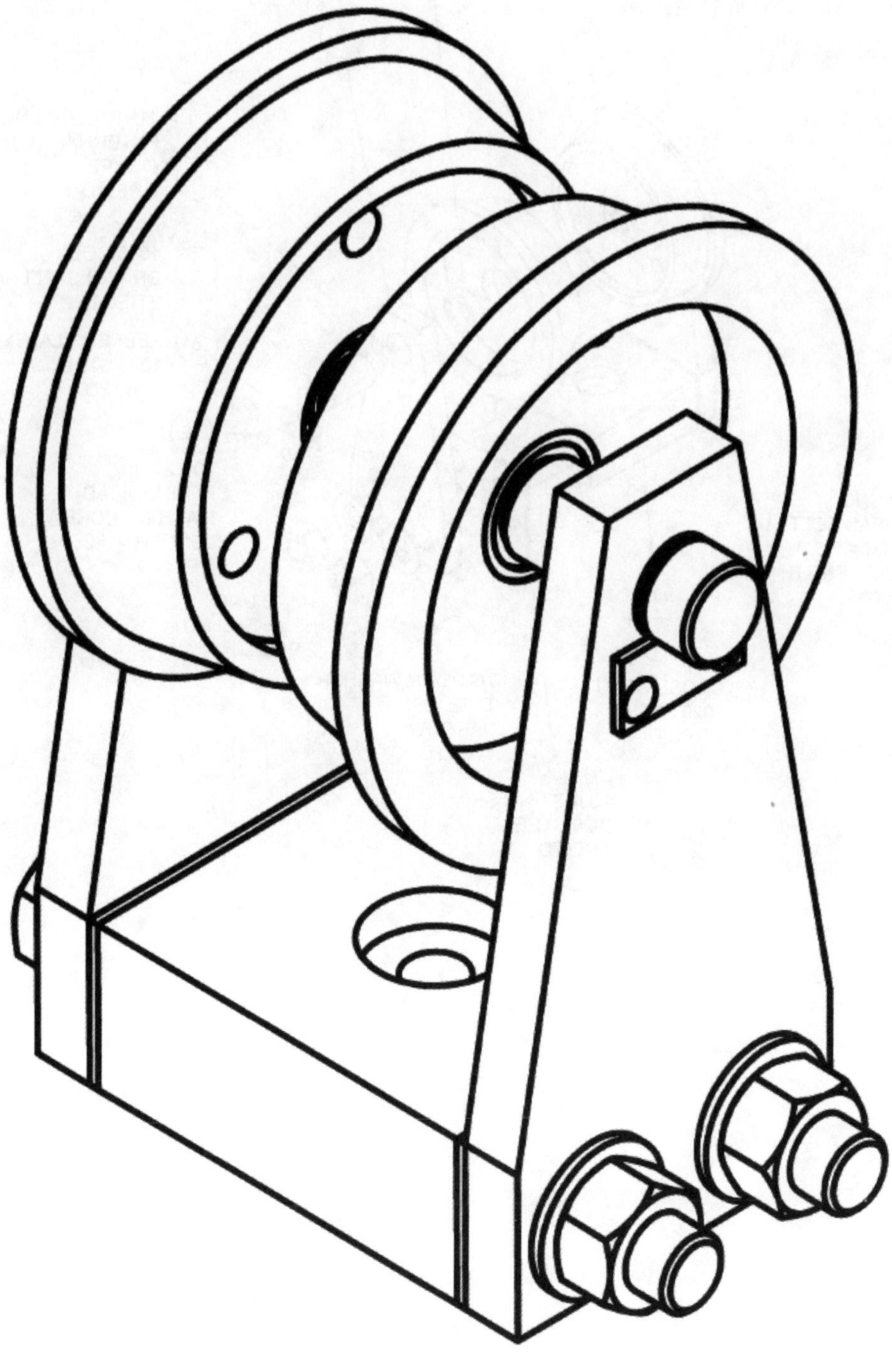

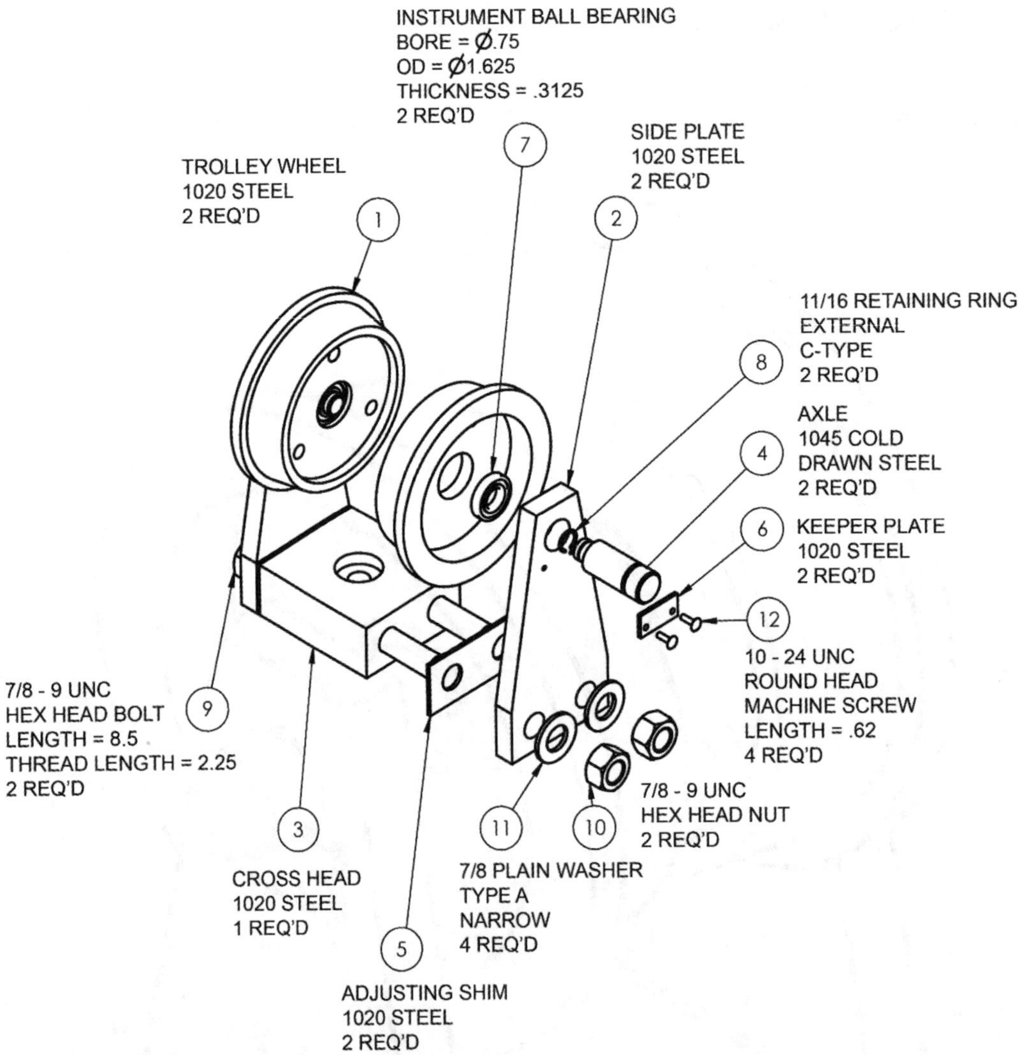
INSTRUMENT BALL BEARING
BORE = Ø.75
OD = Ø1.625
THICKNESS = .3125
2 REQ'D
7
SIDE PLATE
1020 STEEL
2 REQ'D
TROLLEY WHEEL
1020 STEEL
2 REQ'D
1
2
11/16 RETAINING RING
EXTERNAL
C-TYPE
2 REQ'D
8
AXLE
1045 COLD
DRAWN STEEL
2 REQ'D
4
6
KEEPER PLATE
1020 STEEL
2 REQ'D
12
10 - 24 UNC
ROUND HEAD
MACHINE SCREW
LENGTH = .62
4 REQ'D
7/8 - 9 UNC
HEX HEAD BOLT
LENGTH = 8.5
THREAD LENGTH = 2.25
2 REQ'D
9
7/8 - 9 UNC
HEX HEAD NUT
2 REQ'D
3
11
10
CROSS HEAD
1020 STEEL
1 REQ'D
7/8 PLAIN WASHER
TYPE A
NARROW
4 REQ'D
5
ADJUSTING SHIM
1020 STEEL
2 REQ'D

Name: ______________________________ Date: ______________

Fill in the find numbers in the appropriate balloons and complete the part list and title block information.

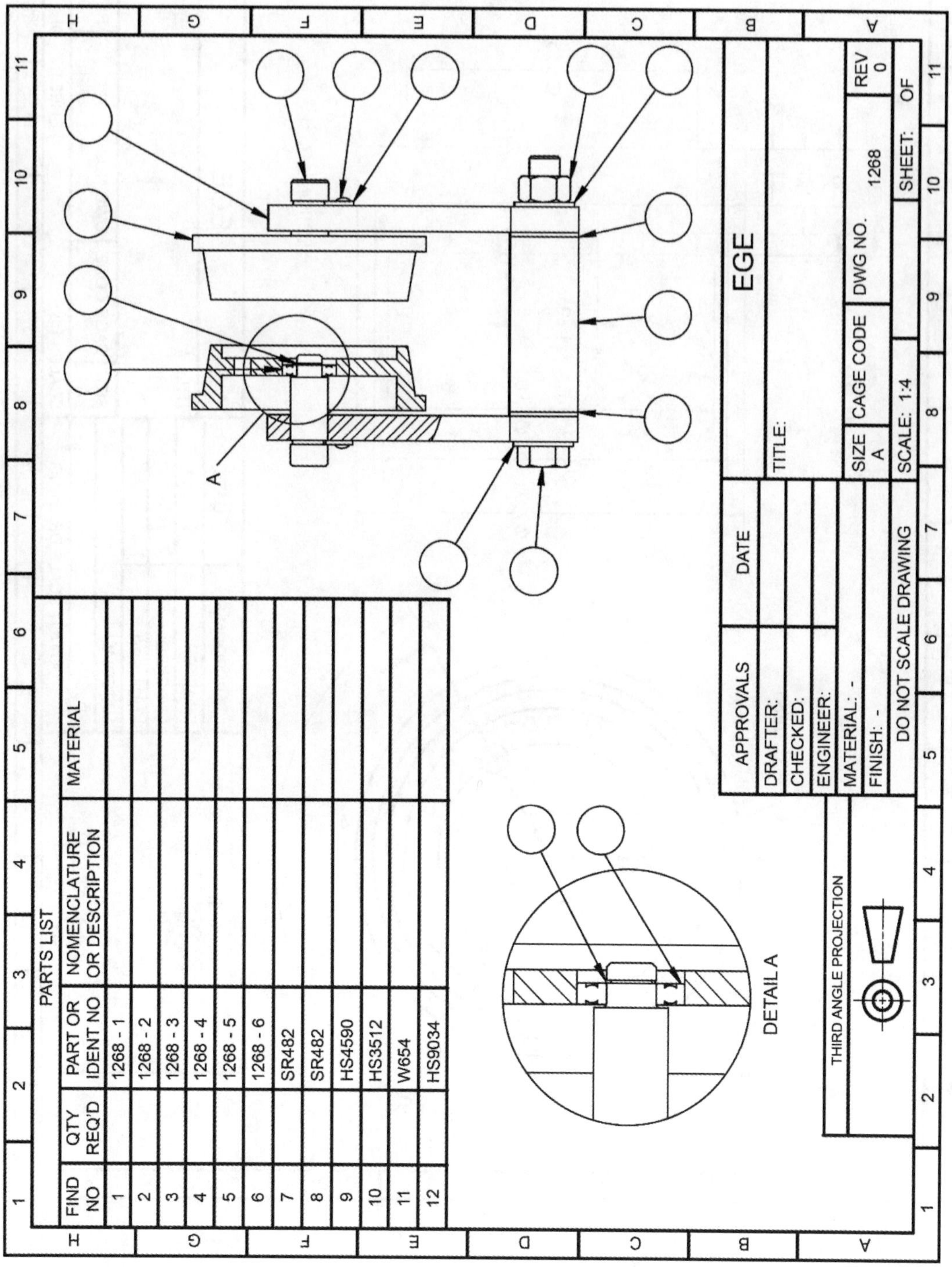

Name: ______________________________ Date: ______________

Draw the missing section view and complete the title block information.

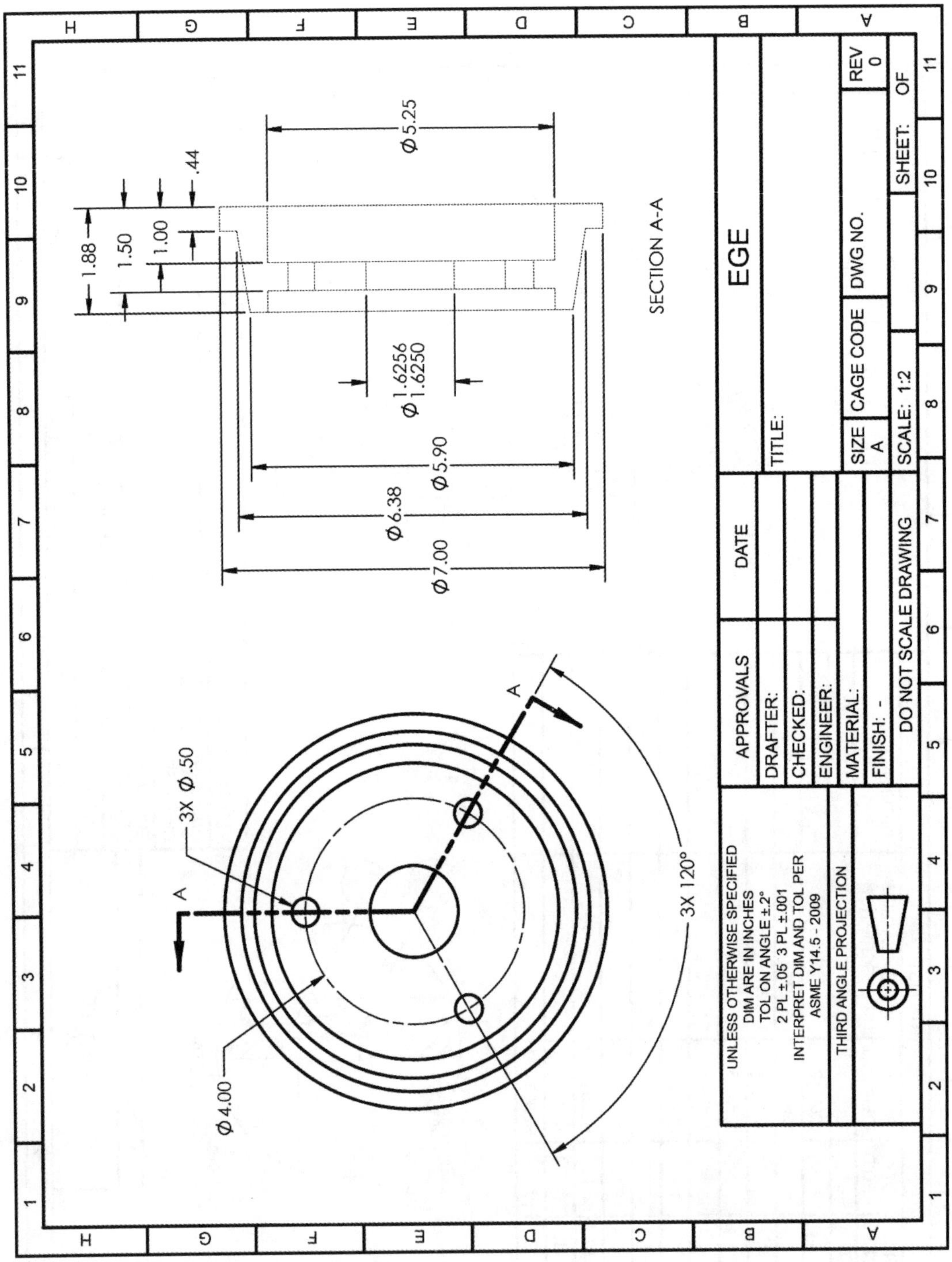

Name: ____ Date: __________________

Complete the title block information.

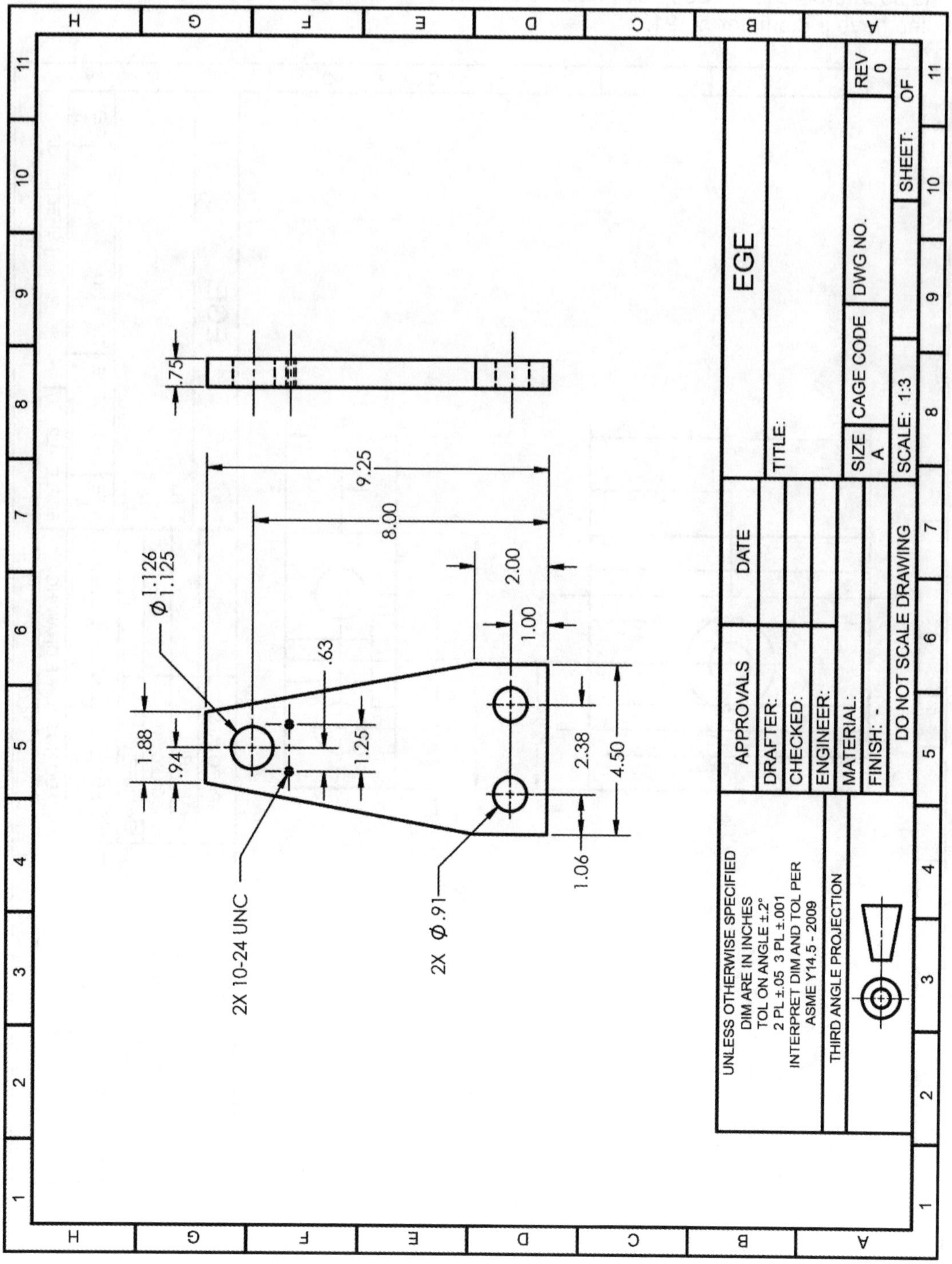

Name: ______________________________ Date: ______________

Fill in the counterbore and hole dimensions, and complete the title block information. The counterbore is .44 deep and has a diameter of 1.62. The drill diameter is .75. The holes have a diameter of .91.

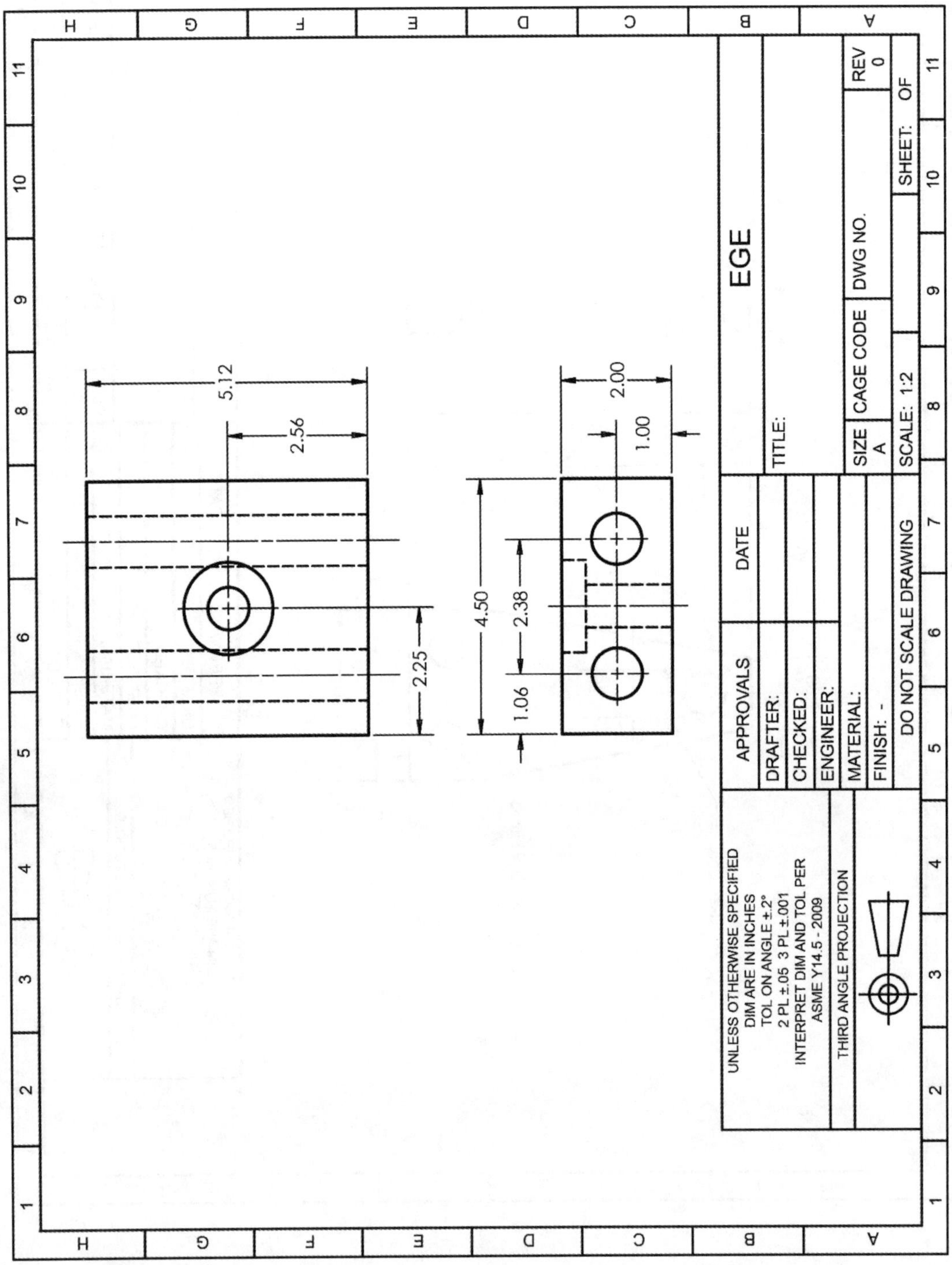

Name: ______________________________ Date: ______________

Complete the title block information.

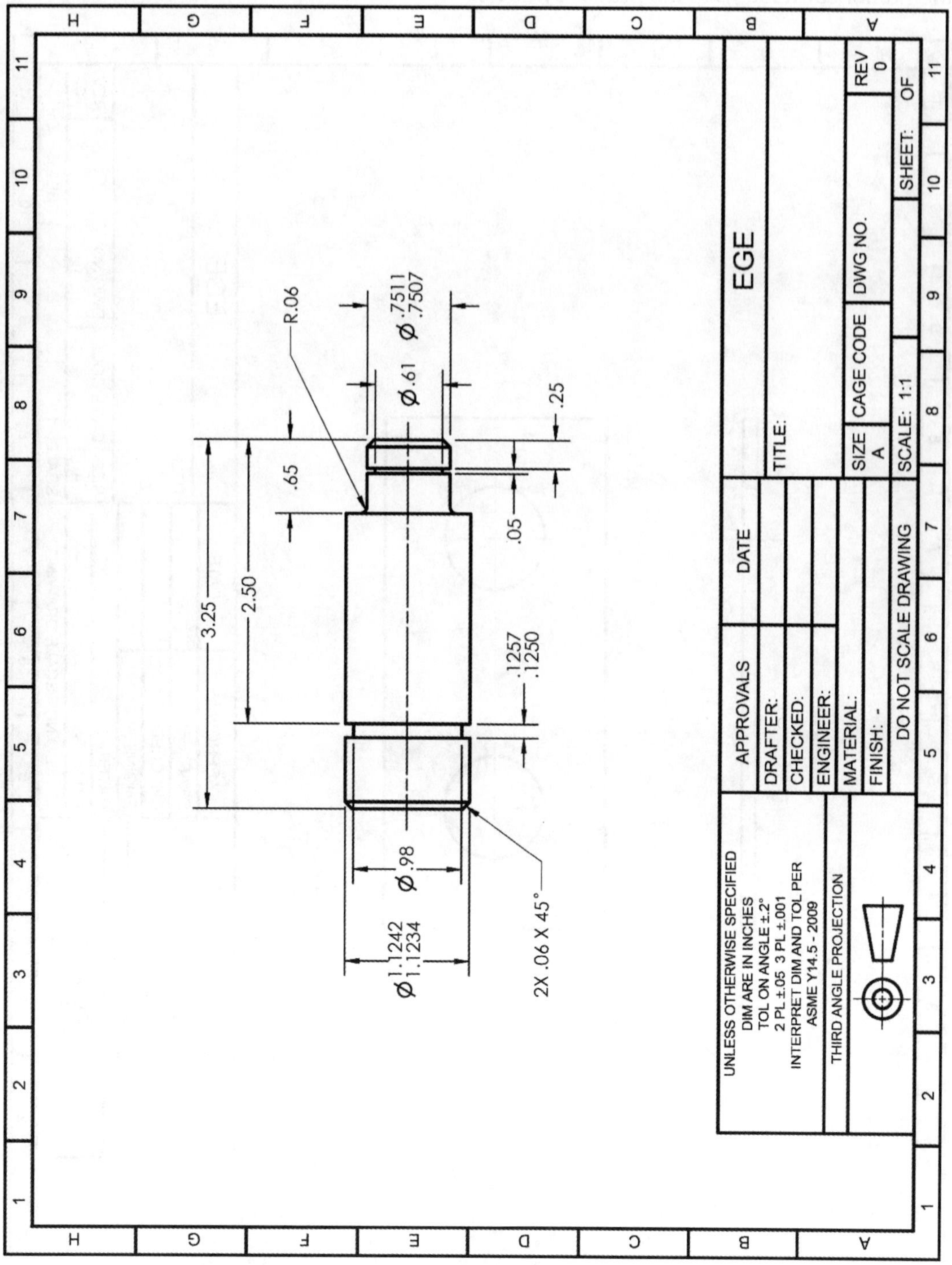

Name: ______________________________ Date: ____________

Dimension the part, and fill in the title block. When dimensioning the part, use an 'n' for the numerical value. Use the proper symbols.

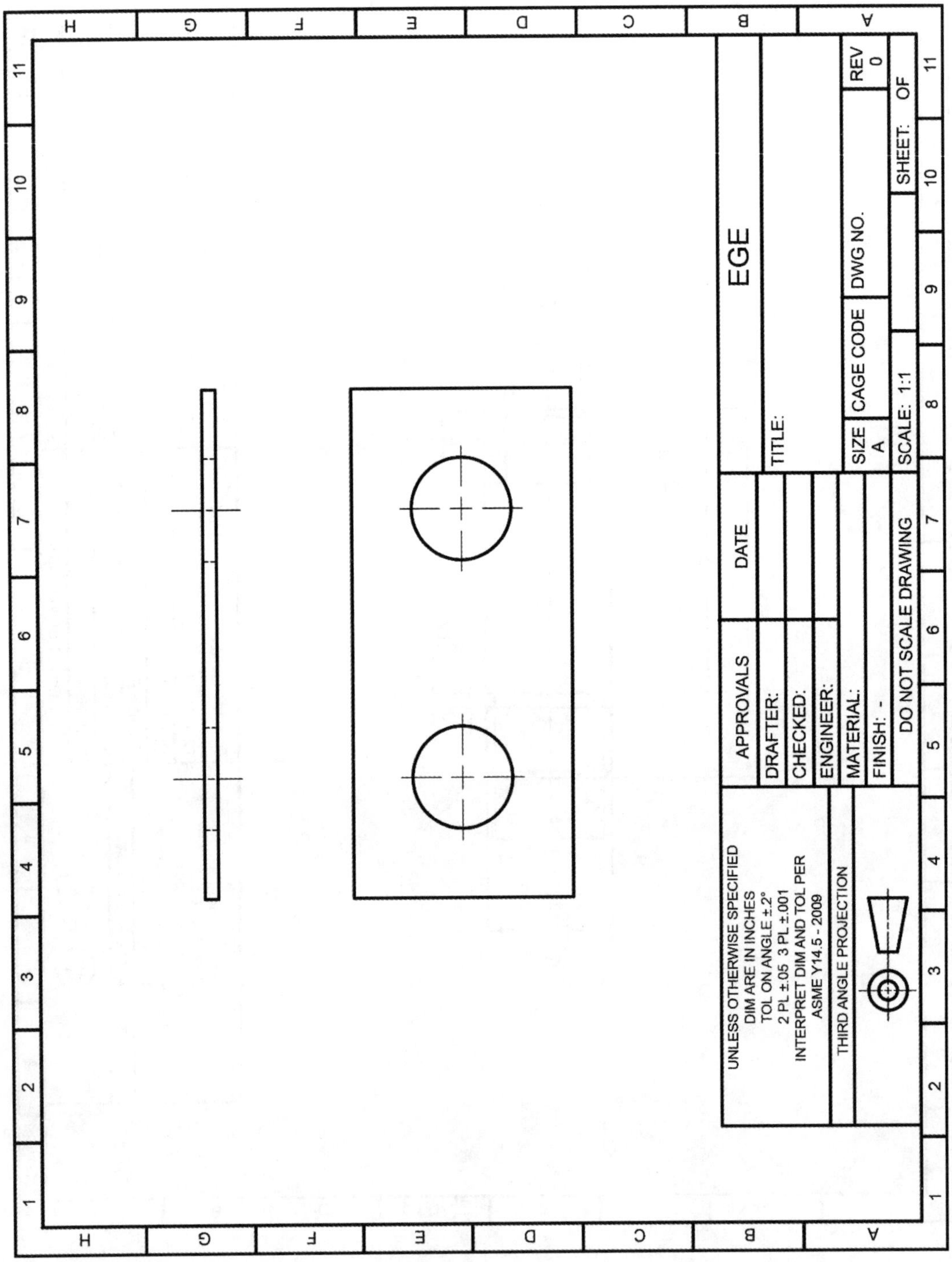

Name: ______________________ Date: ____________

Complete the title block.

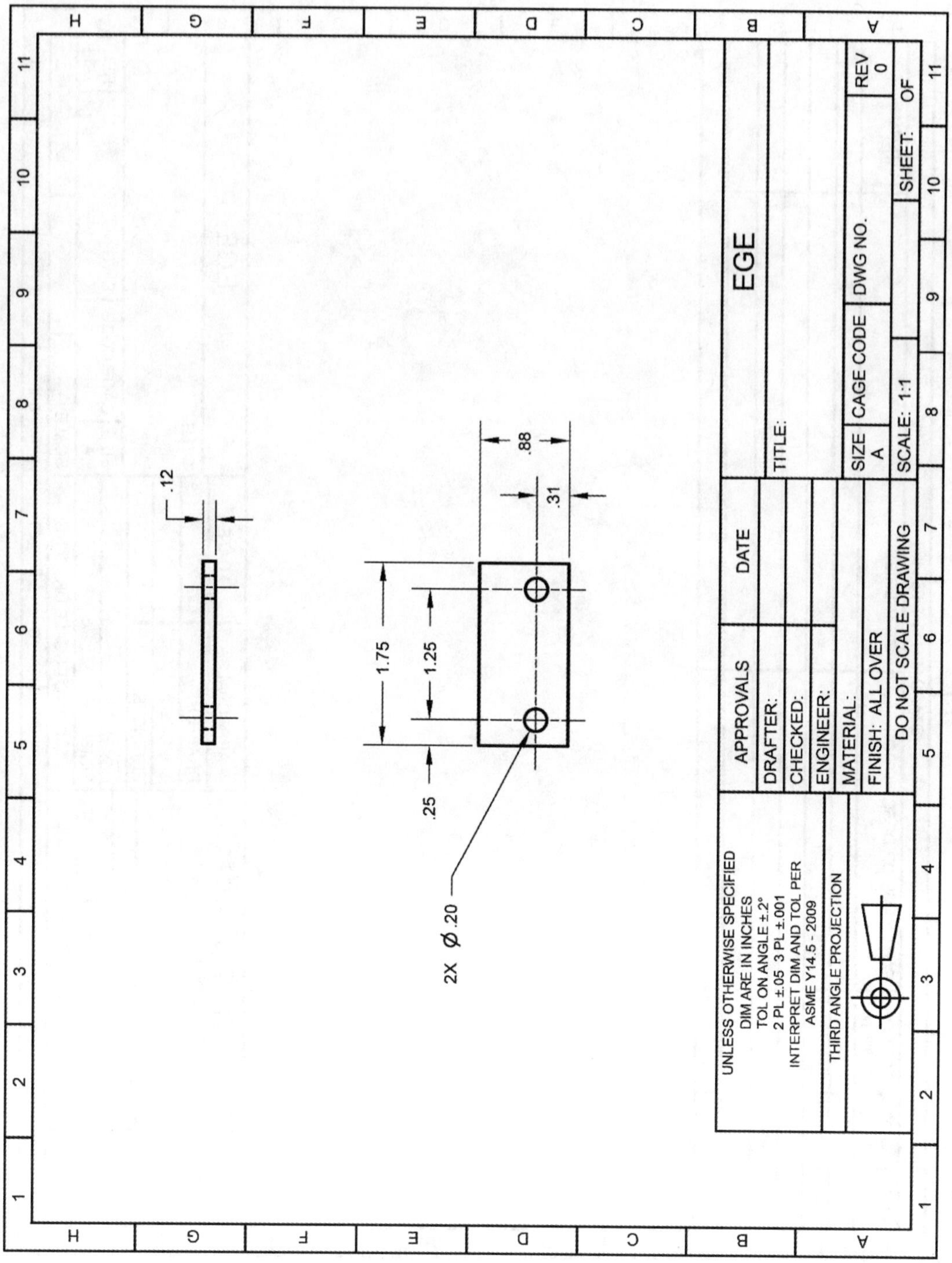

Name: ______________________________ Date: ____________

Complete the information on the standard (stock) parts and fill in the title block.

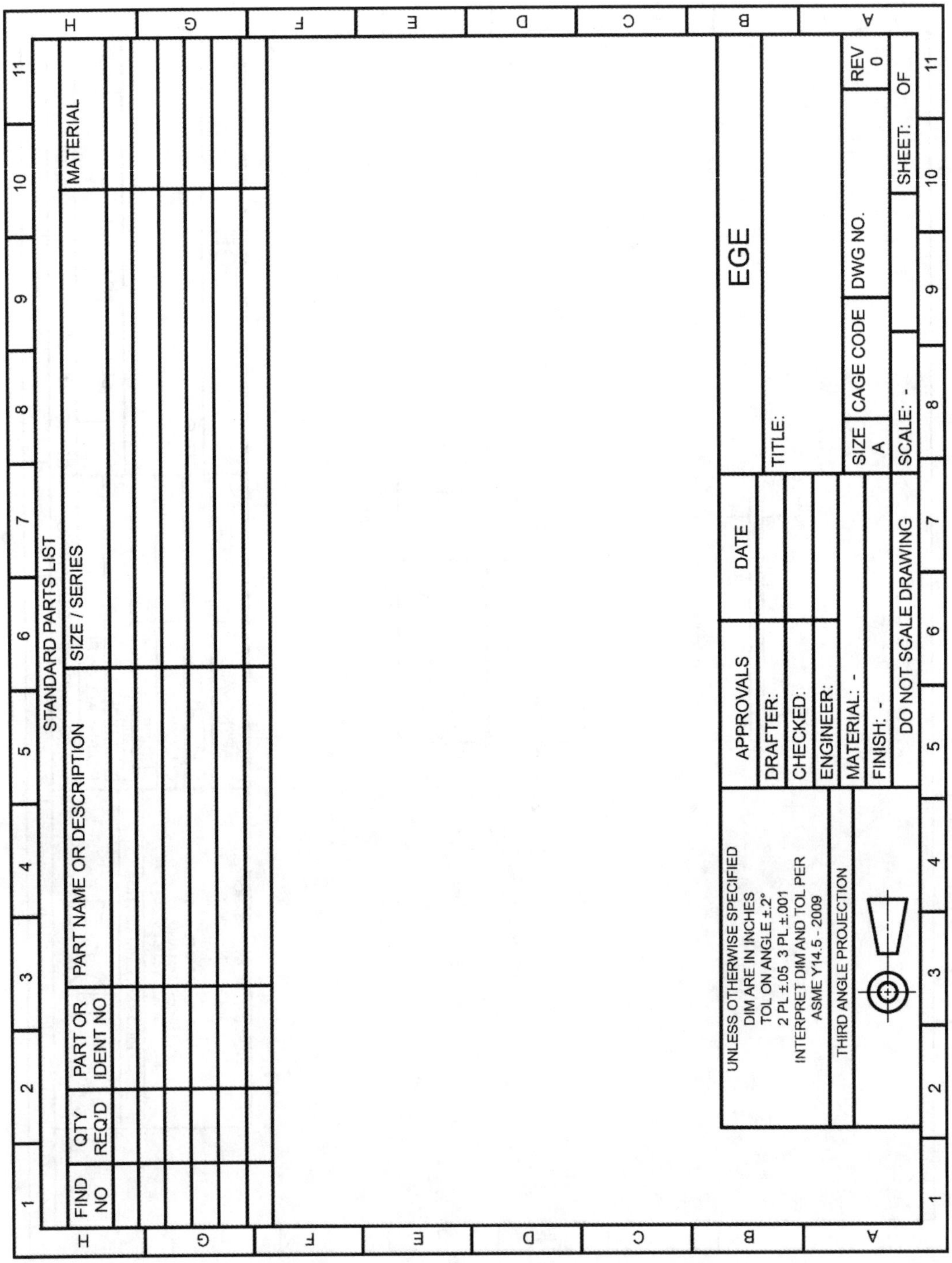

P25-2) Consider the *Drill Jig* assembly shown. Sheets of an incomplete working drawing package are given in the following pages. Follow the directions and complete the sheets. The *Drill Jig* dimensions are shown in the exploded assembly shown on the next page.

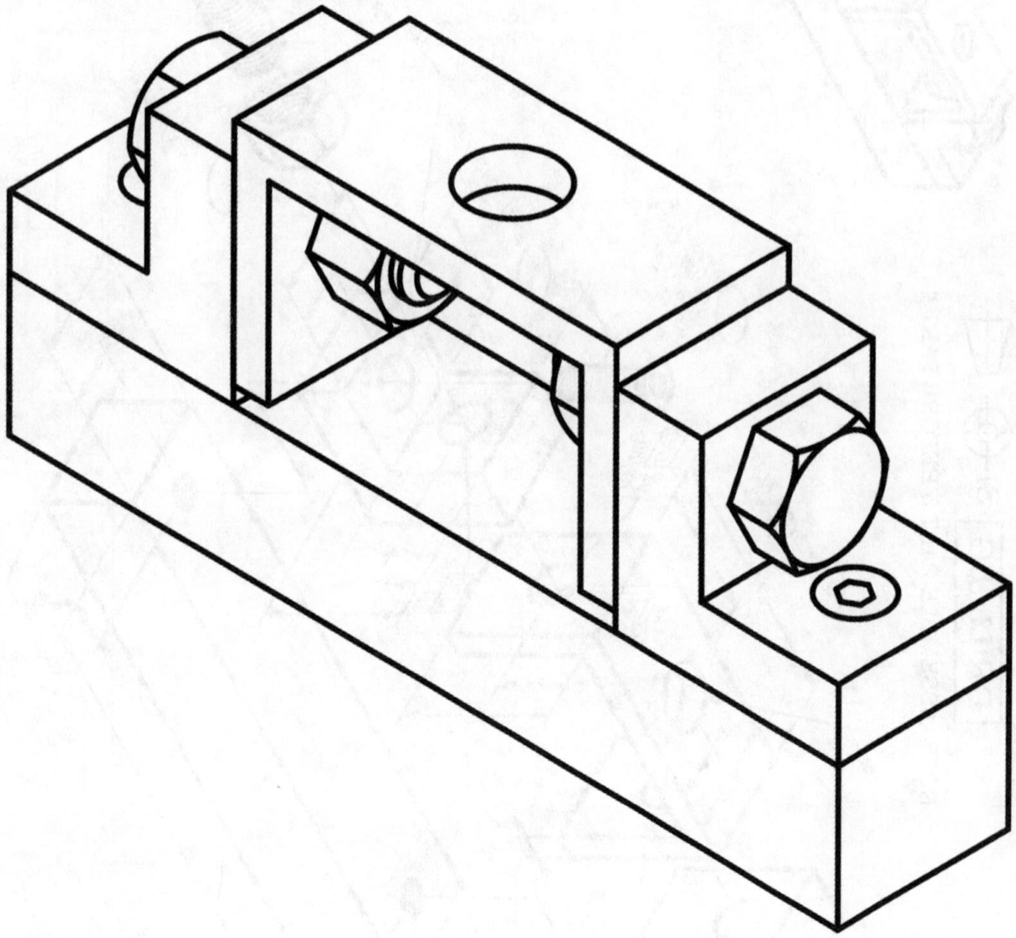

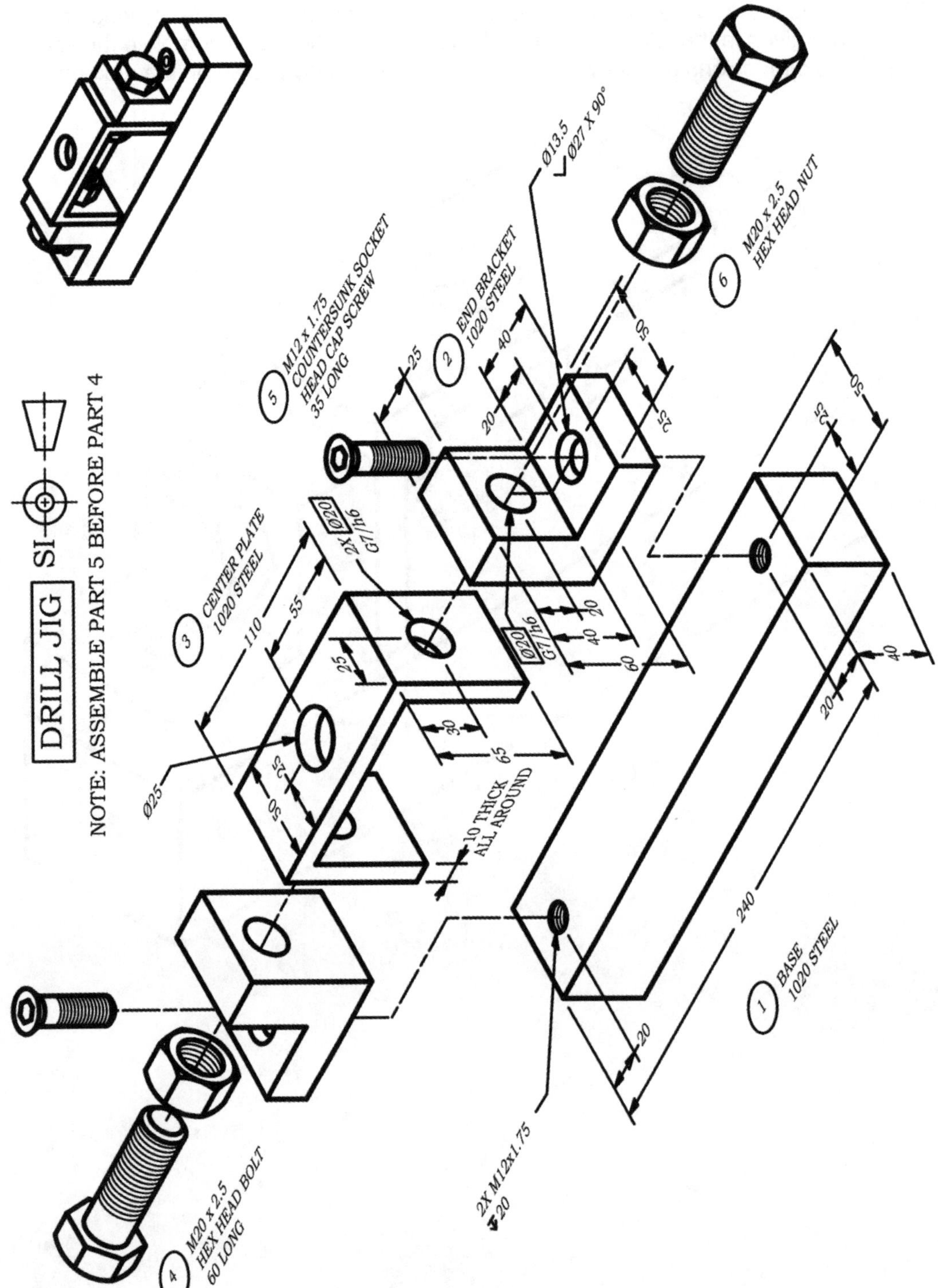
DRILL JIG
SI
NOTE: ASSEMBLE PART 5 BEFORE PART 4
1 BASE 1020 STEEL
2 END BRACKET 1020 STEEL
3 CENTER PLATE 1020 STEEL
4 M20 x 2.5 HEX HEAD BOLT 60 LONG
5 M12 x 1.75 COUNTERSUNK SOCKET HEAD CAP SCREW 35 LONG
6 M20 x 2.5 HEX HEAD NUT
2X M12x1.75 ↧20
Ø13.5 ⌵Ø27 X 90°
10 THICK ALL AROUND
2X Ø20 G7/h6
Ø20 G7/h6
Ø25

Name: ______________________________ Date: _____________

Complete the section view by adding the appropriate section lines. Then, fill in the find numbers in the correct balloon, fill in the parts list, and fill in the title block.

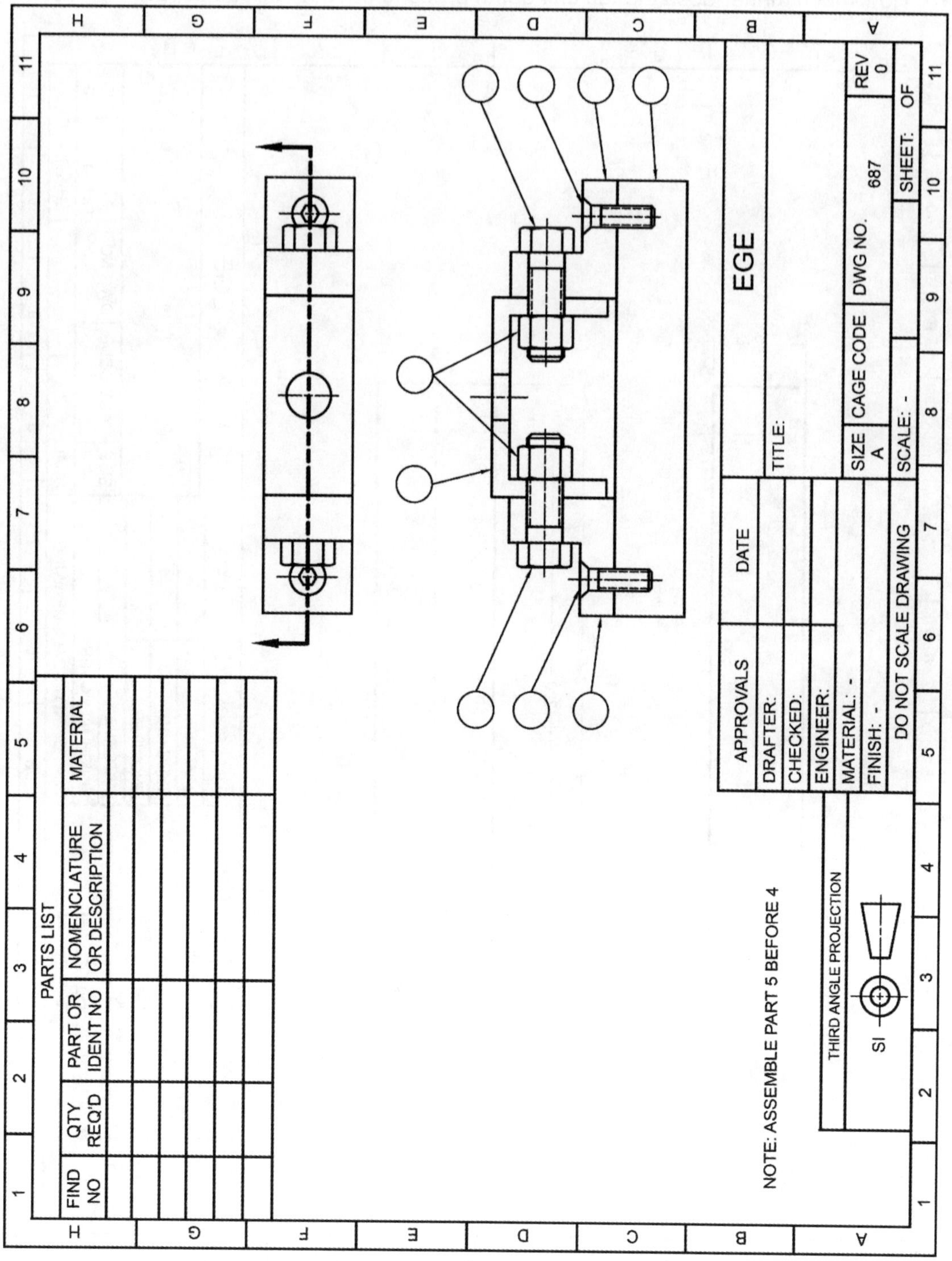

Draw and dimension the threaded features of the BASE, fill in the title block, and answer the following questions.

- What is the tap drill size for the M12x1.75 thread? Tap drill diameter = __________
- How much further does the tap drill depth proceed past the thread depth?

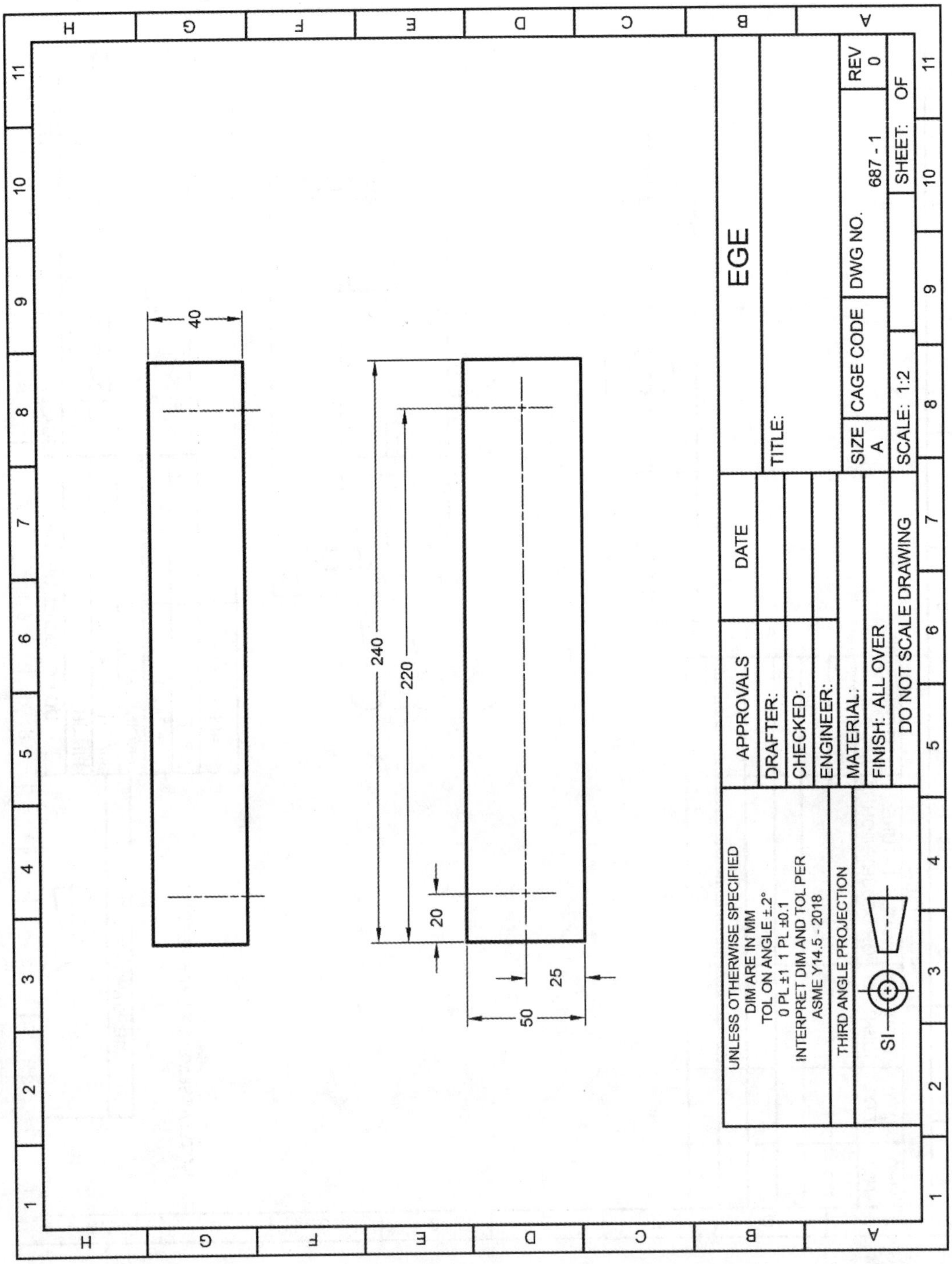

Dimension the END BRACKET and fill in the title block.

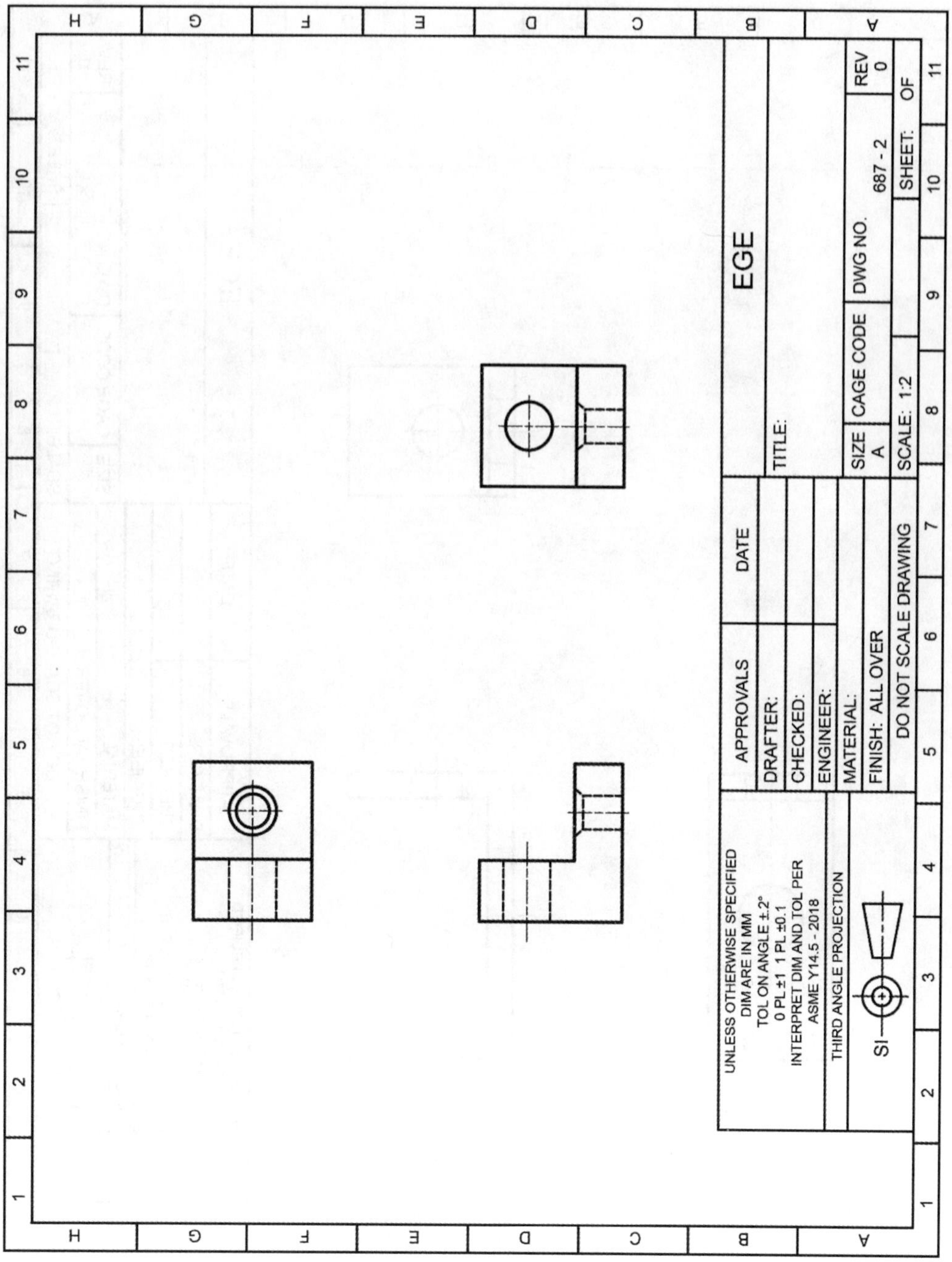

Dimension the CENTER PLATE, and fill in the title block.

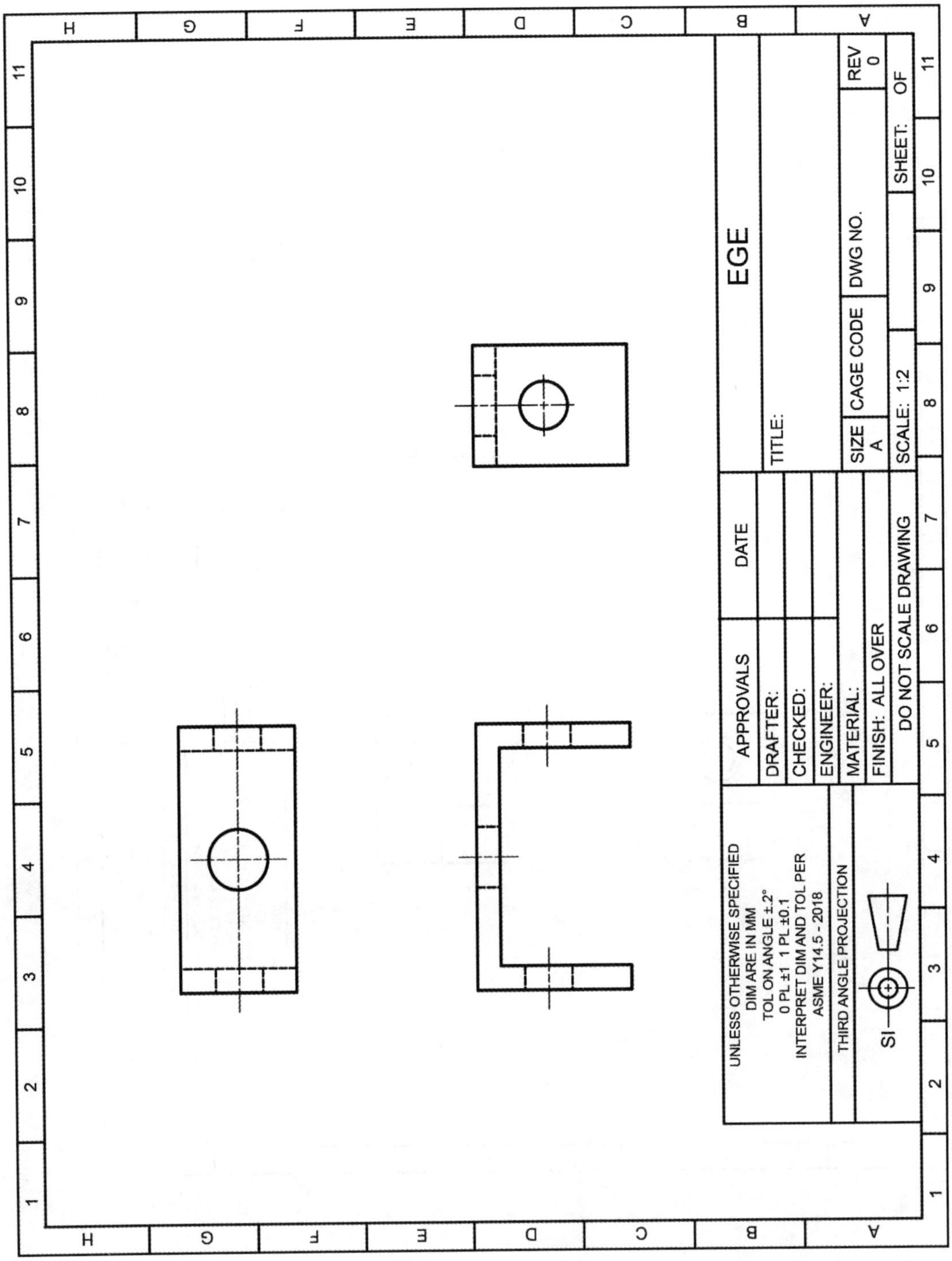

Create a standard parts sheet and fill in the title block.

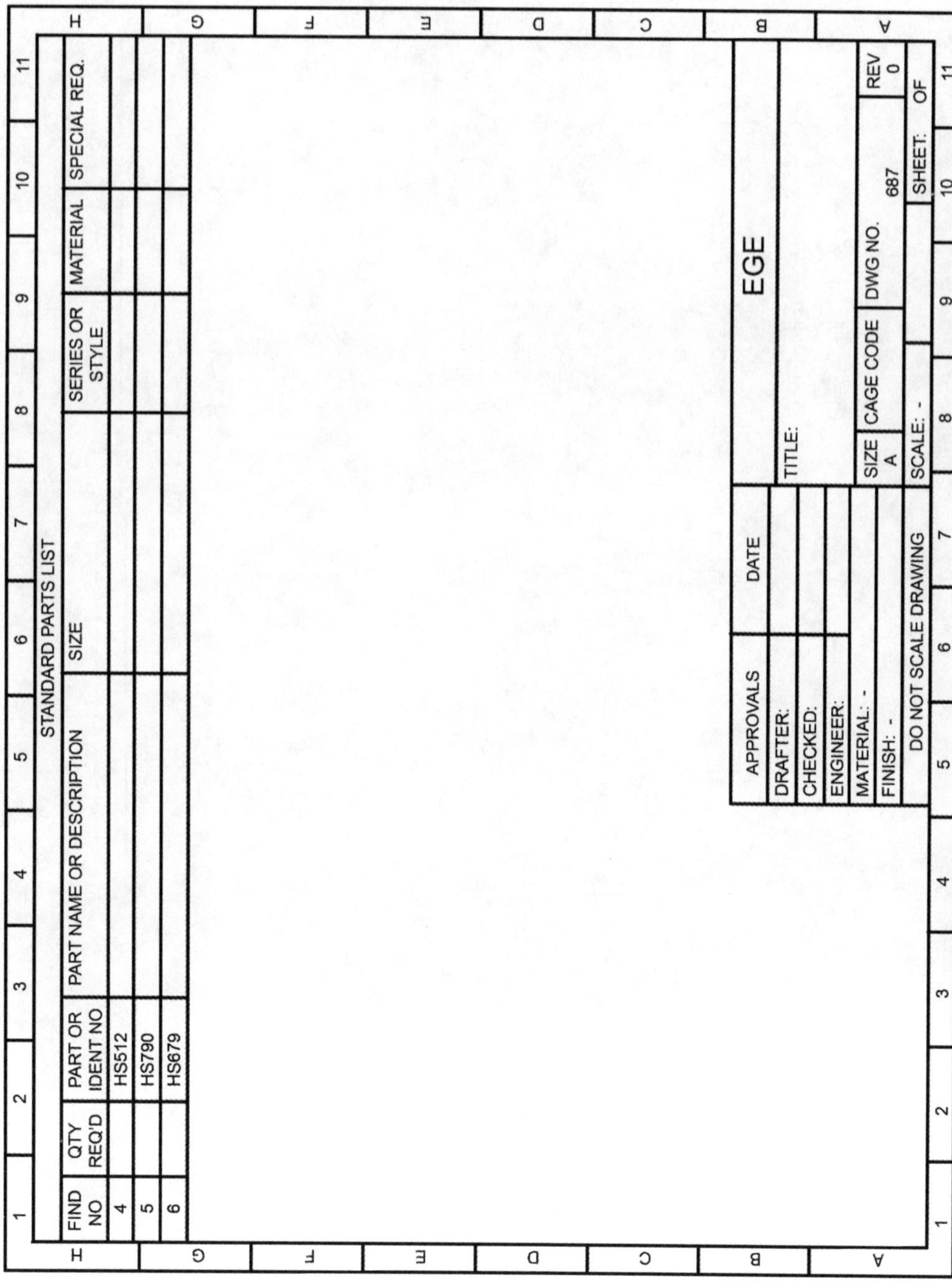

NOTES:

P25-3) Create a working drawing package for the following *Pulley Assembly*. The working drawing package should contain an assembly drawing, details of all the parts, and a standard parts sheet. Notice that some of the dimensioned isometric drawings are not dimensioned using proper dimensioning techniques. When drawing the detailed drawings use proper symbols and dimensioning techniques.

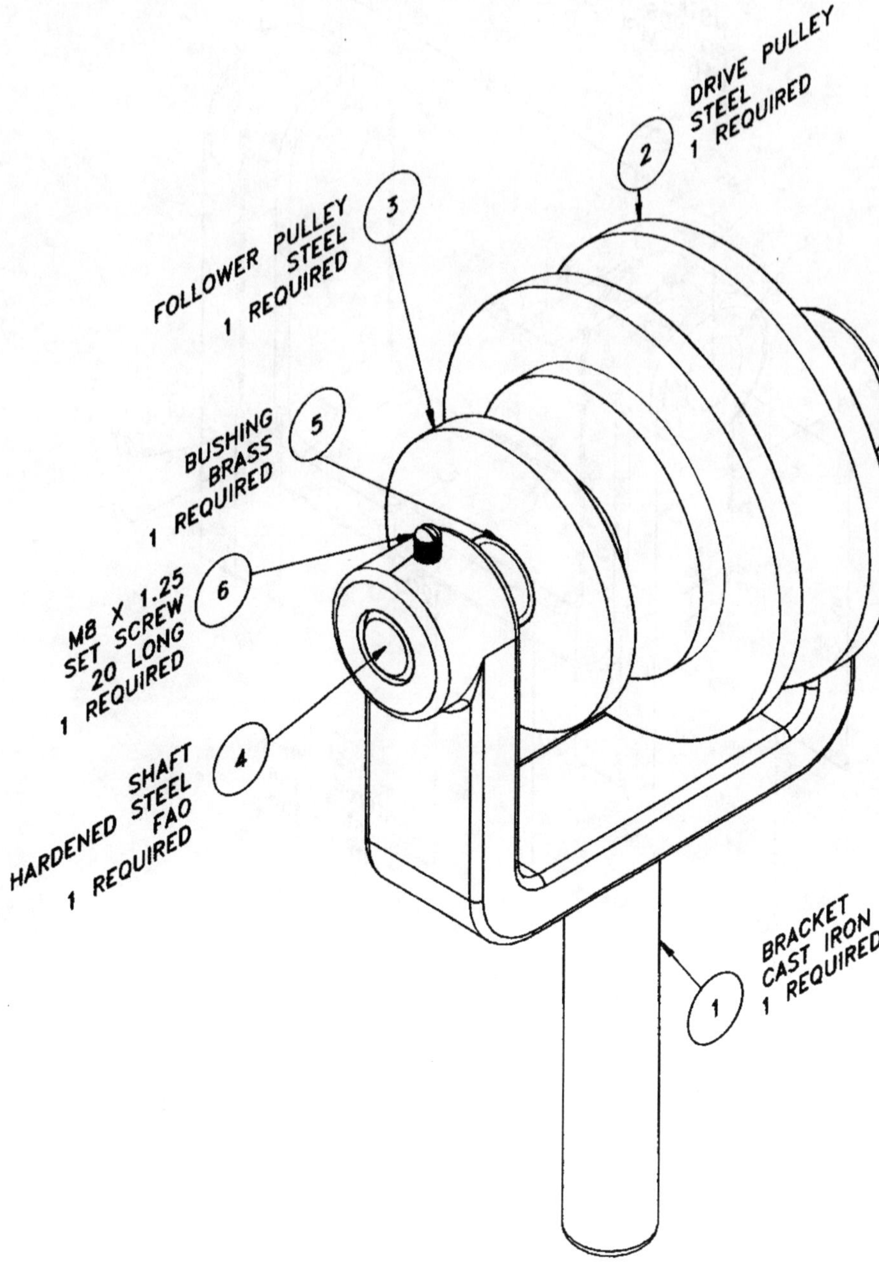

Bracket

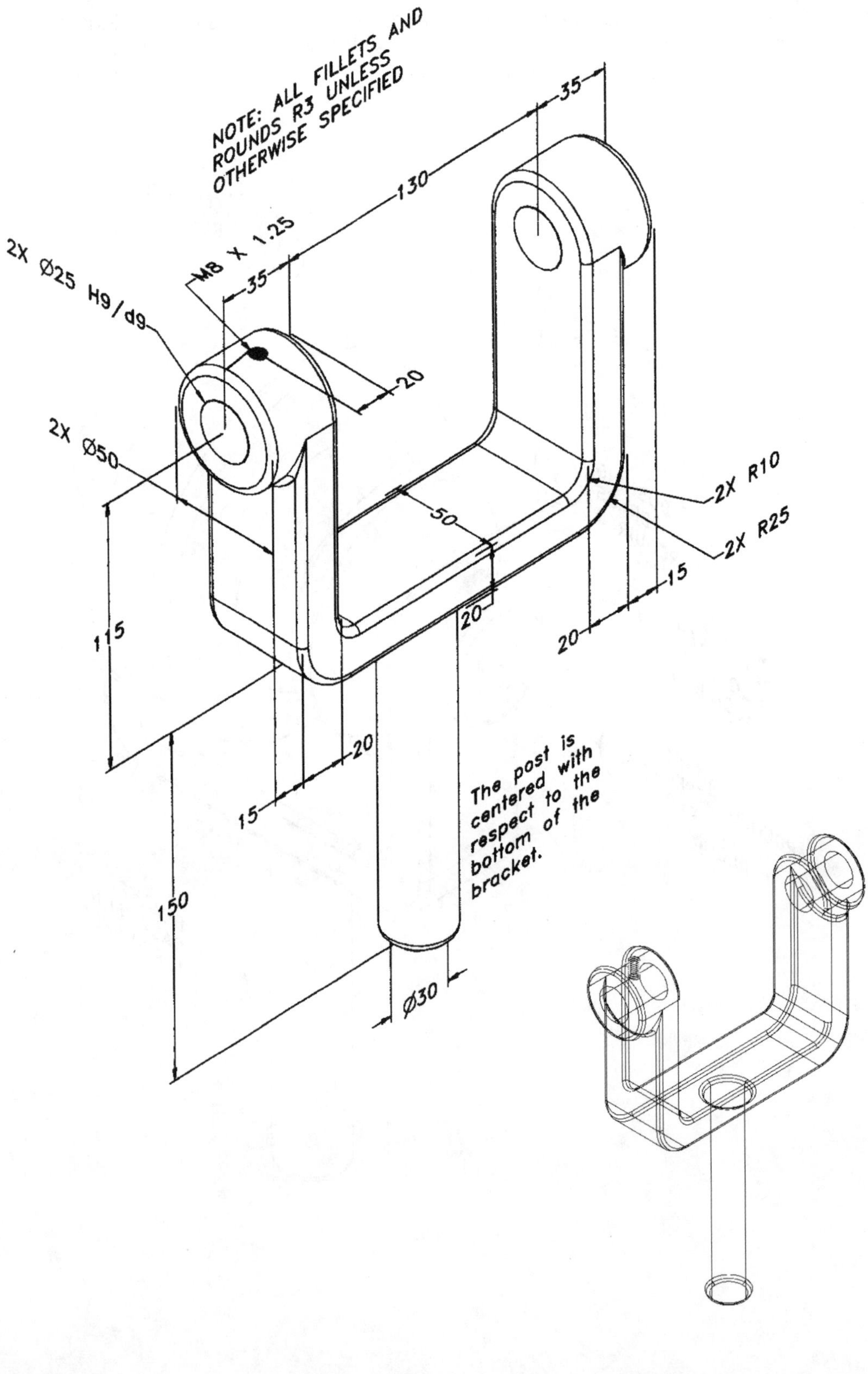
NOTE: ALL FILLETS AND
ROUNDS R3 UNLESS
OTHERWISE SPECIFIED
35
130
M8 X 1.25
35
2X Ø25 H9/d9
20
2X Ø50
50
2X R10
2X R25
15
20
20
115
20
15
The post is
centered with
respect to the
bottom of the
bracket.
150
Ø30

Drive Pulley

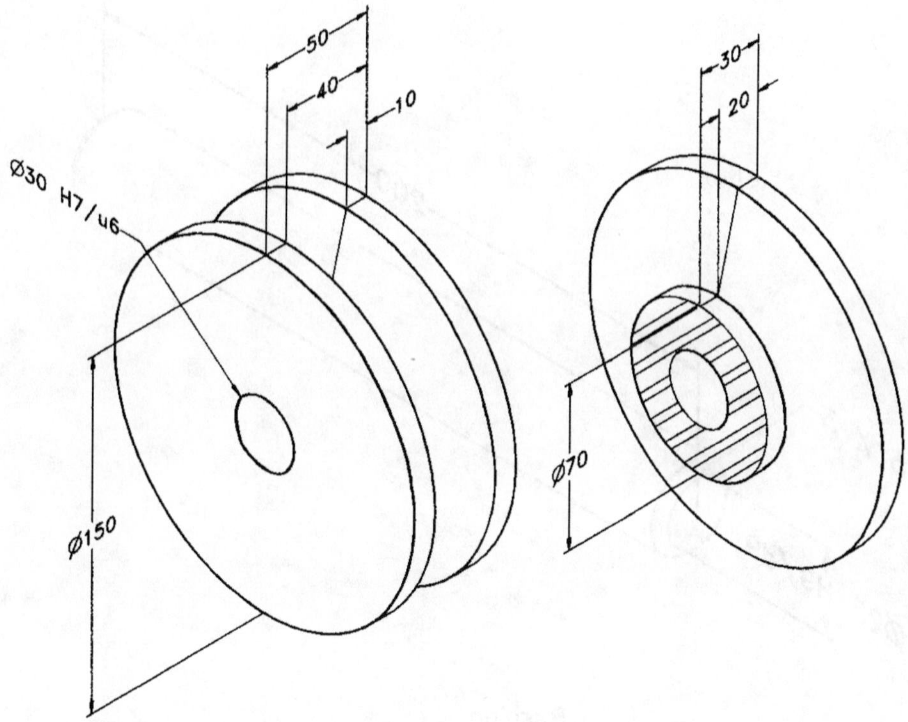

Follower Pulley

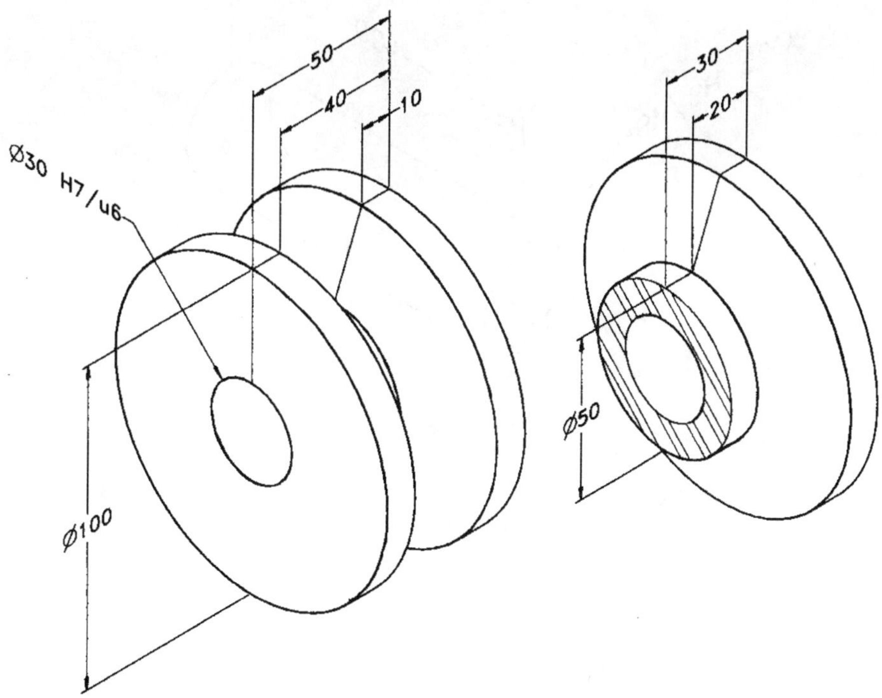

Shaft

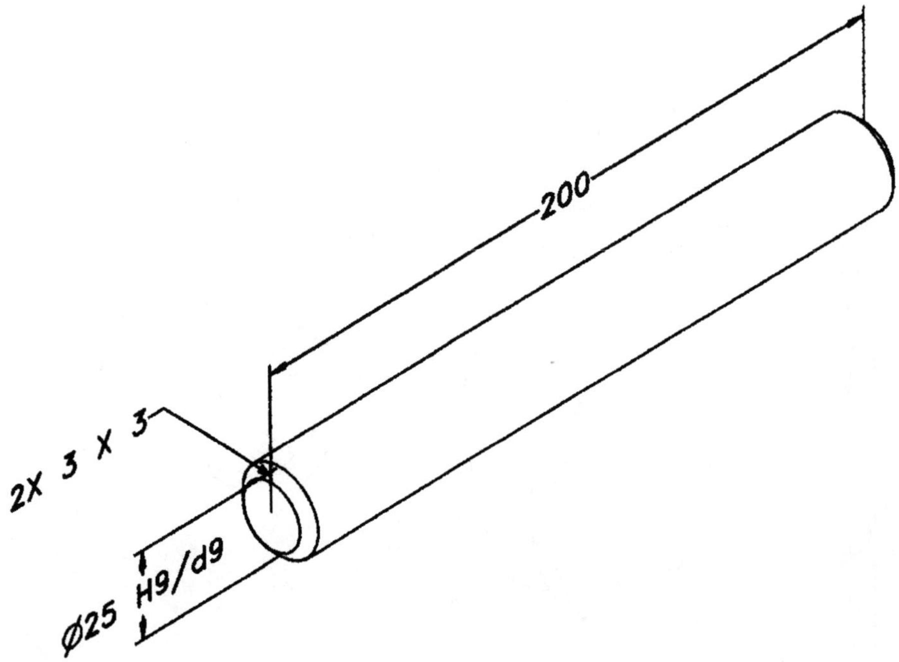

Bushing

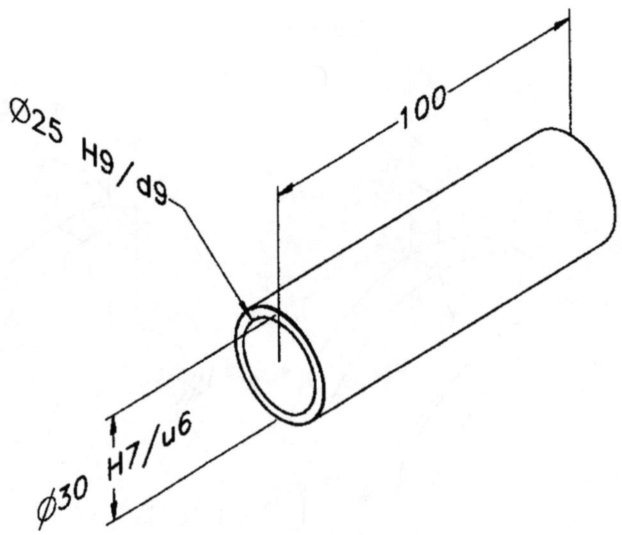

P25-4) Create a working drawing package for the following *Milling Jack*. The working drawing package should contain an assembly drawing, details of all the parts, and a standard parts sheet. Notice that some of the dimensioned isometric drawings are not dimensioned using proper dimensioning techniques. When drawing the detailed drawings use proper symbols and dimensioning techniques.

Milling Jack

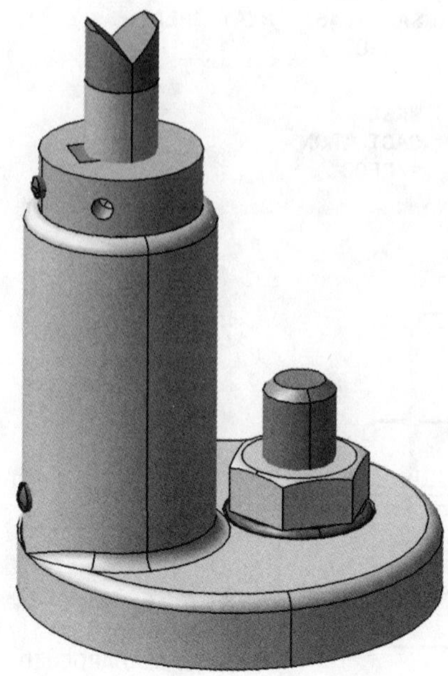

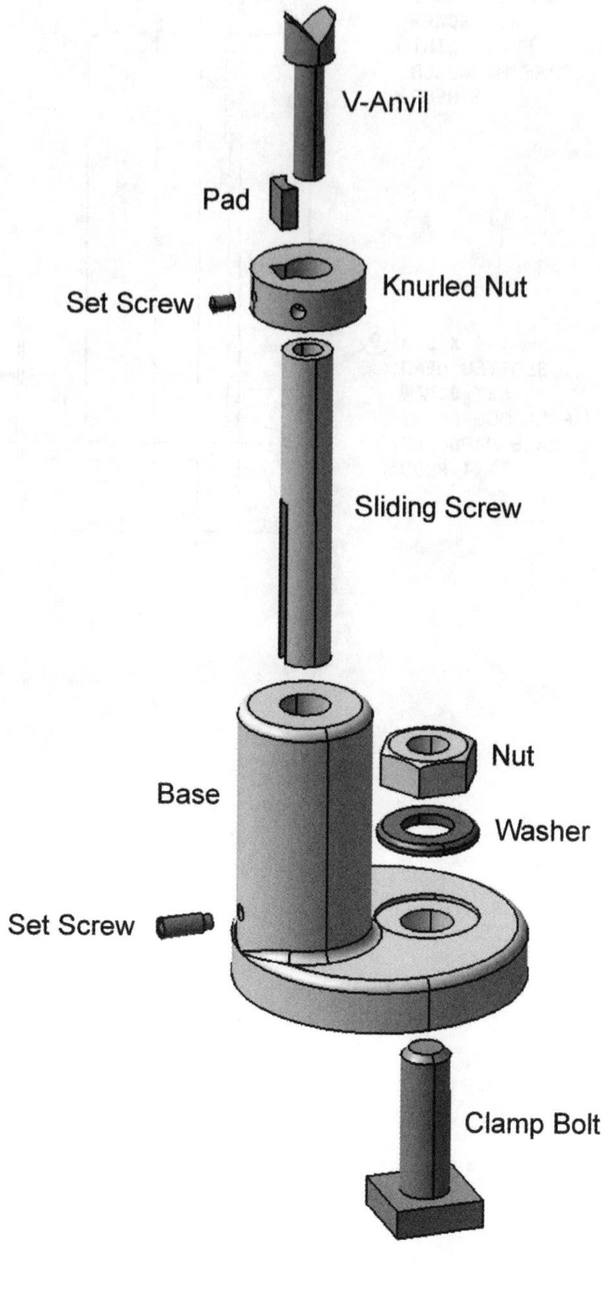

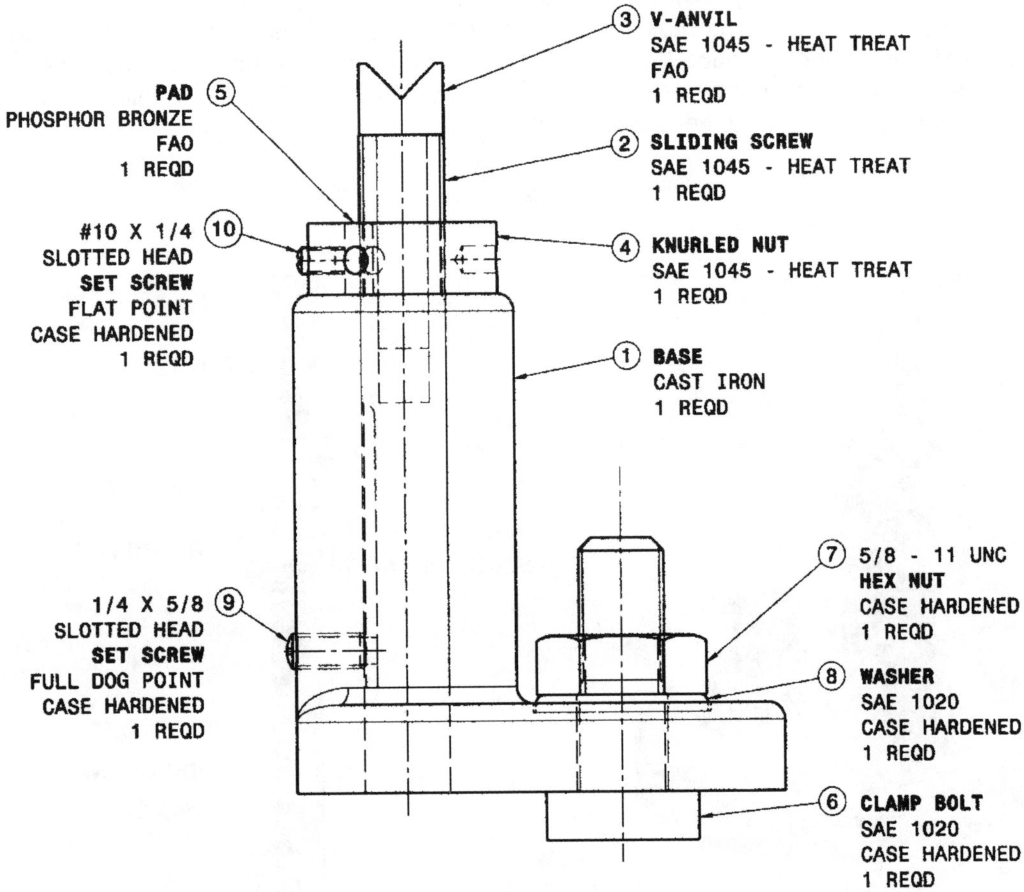

③ V-ANVIL
SAE 1045 - HEAT TREAT
FAO
1 REQD
PAD ⑤
PHOSPHOR BRONZE
FAO
1 REQD
② SLIDING SCREW
SAE 1045 - HEAT TREAT
1 REQD
#10 X 1/4 ⑩
SLOTTED HEAD
SET SCREW
FLAT POINT
CASE HARDENED
1 REQD
④ KNURLED NUT
SAE 1045 - HEAT TREAT
1 REQD
① BASE
CAST IRON
1 REQD
⑦ 5/8 - 11 UNC
HEX NUT
CASE HARDENED
1 REQD
1/4 X 5/8 ⑨
SLOTTED HEAD
SET SCREW
FULL DOG POINT
CASE HARDENED
1 REQD
⑧ WASHER
SAE 1020
CASE HARDENED
1 REQD
⑥ CLAMP BOLT
SAE 1020
CASE HARDENED
1 REQD

Base

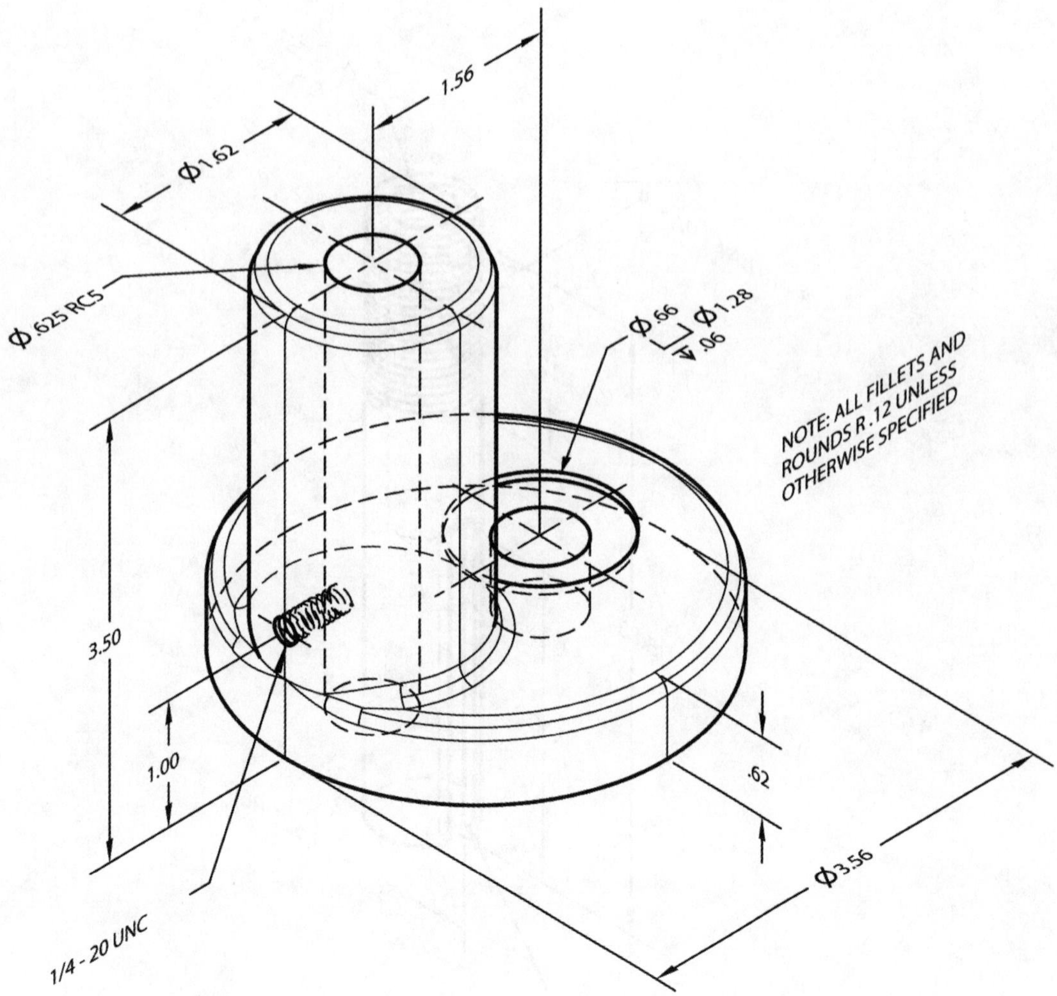
1.56
Φ1.62
Φ.625 RC5
Φ.66 ⌴ Φ1.28 ↧ .06
NOTE: ALL FILLETS AND ROUNDS R.12 UNLESS OTHERWISE SPECIFIED
3.50
1.00
.62
Φ3.56
1/4 - 20 UNC

Sliding Screw

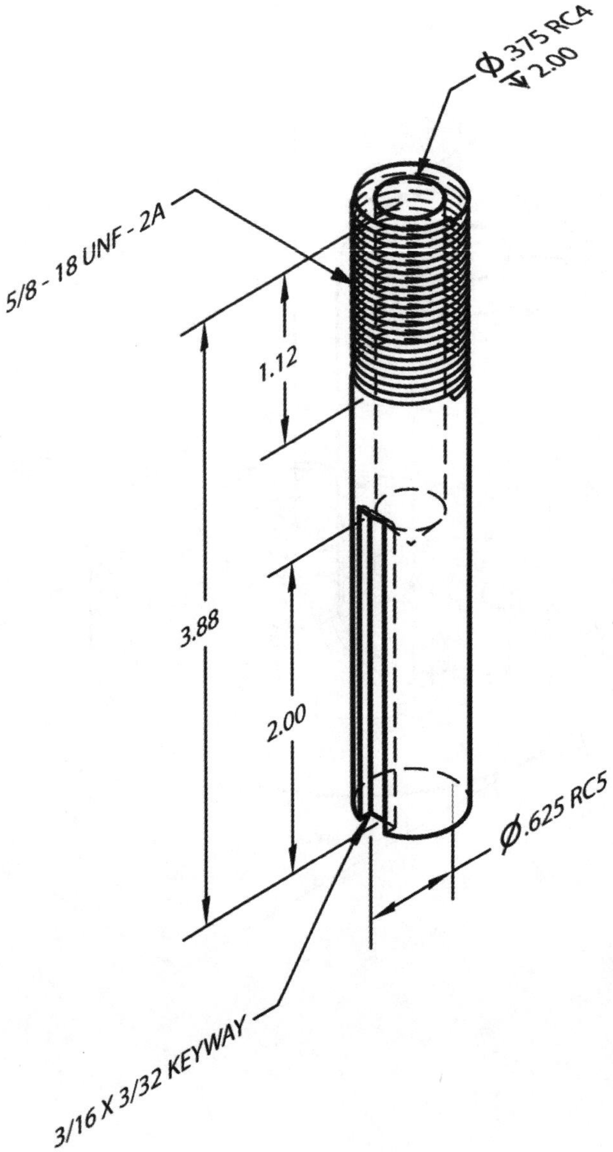

V-Anvil

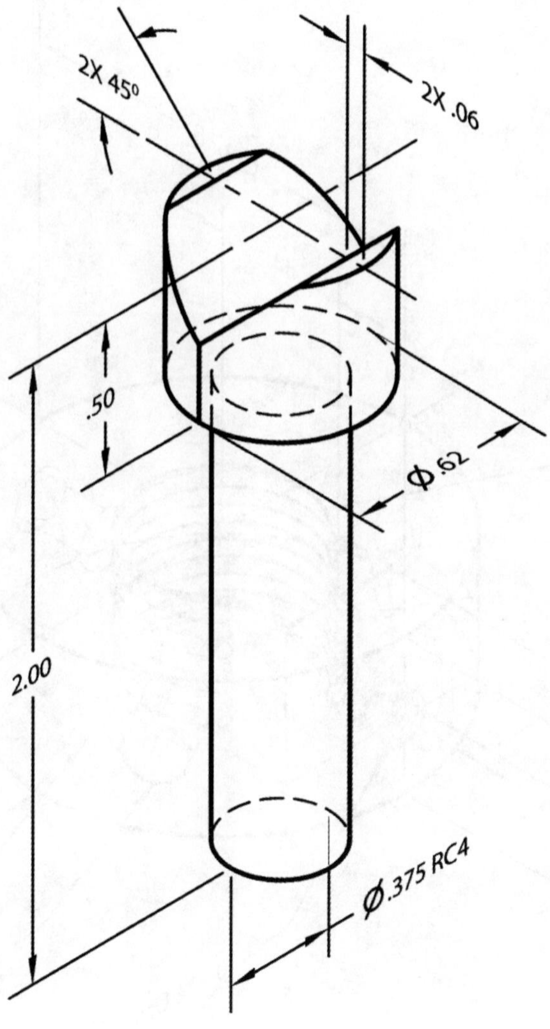

Knurled Nut

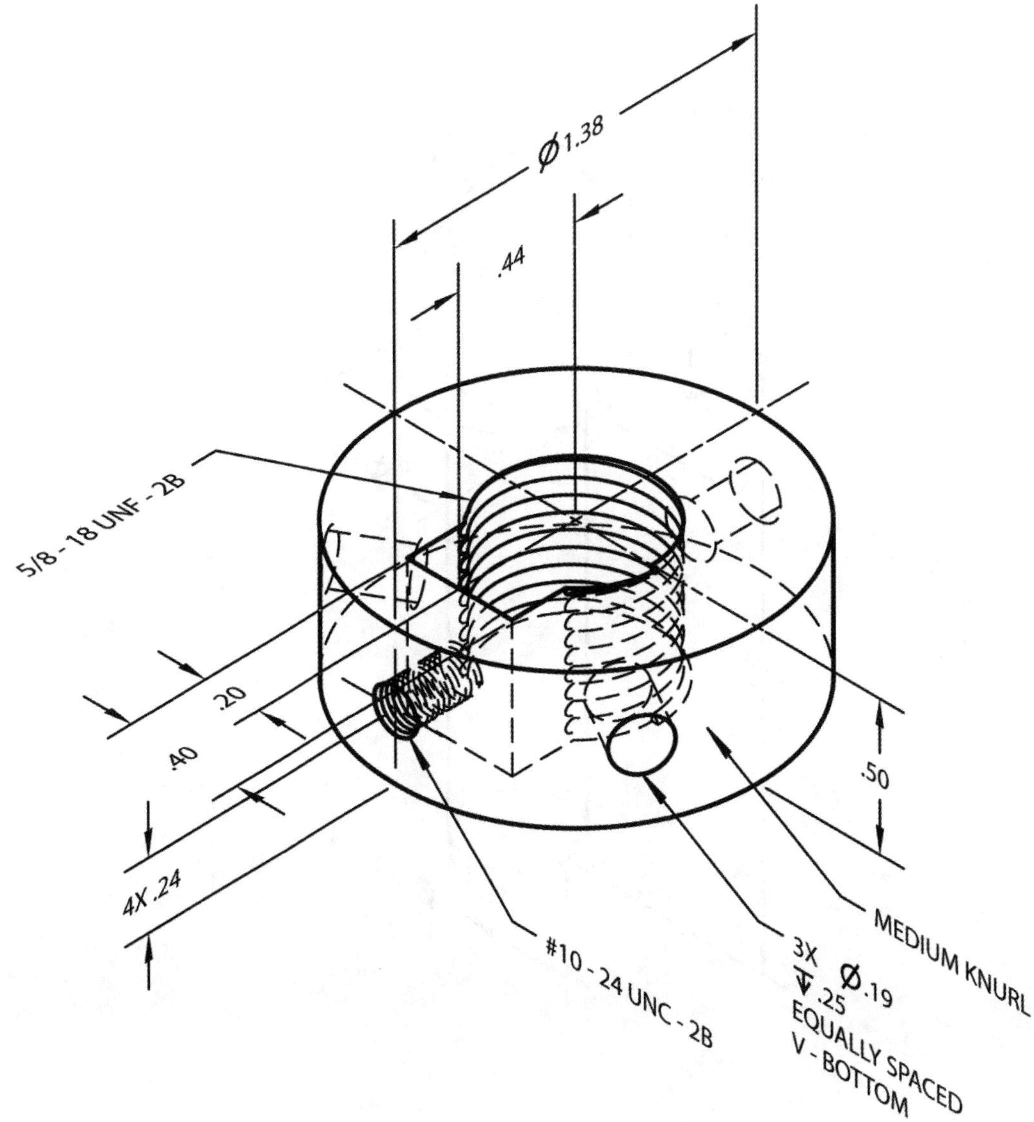
Ø1.38
.44
5/8 - 18 UNF - 2B
.20
.40
4X .24
.50
MEDIUM KNURL
#10 - 24 UNC - 2B
3X Ø.19
↧.25
EQUALLY SPACED
V - BOTTOM

Pad

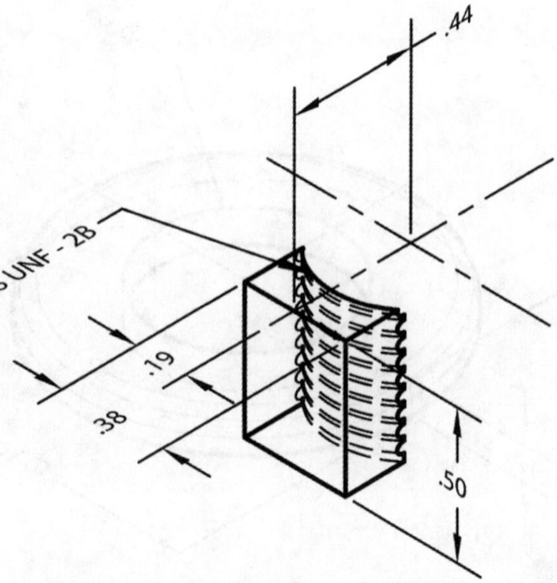

Clamp Bolt

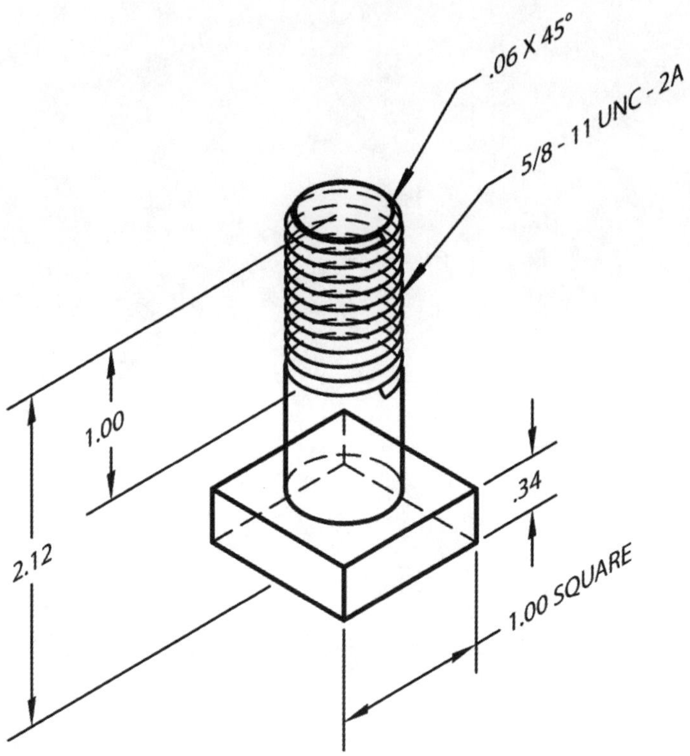

Washer

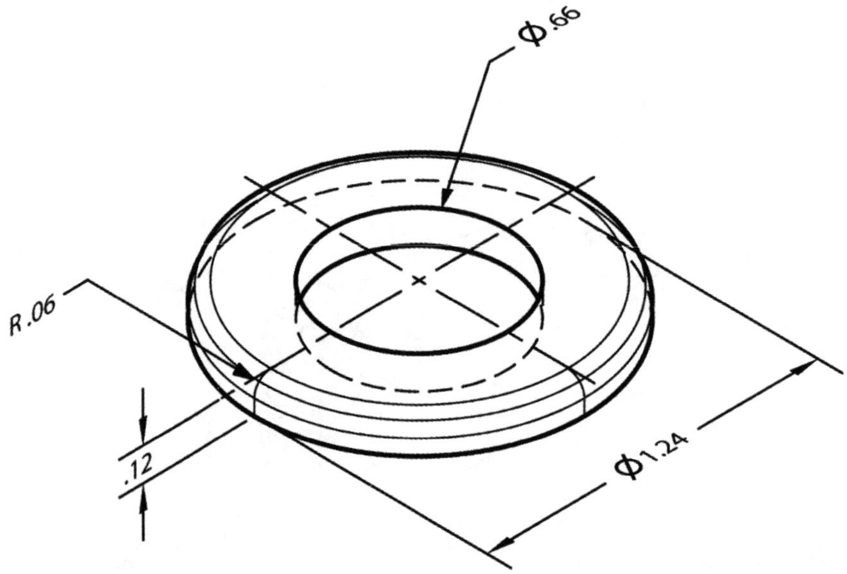

SP25-1) Create a working drawing package for the following *Linear Bearing*. The working drawing package should contain an assembly drawing, details of all the parts, and a standard parts sheet. Notice that some of the dimensioned isometric drawings are not dimensioned using proper dimensioning techniques. When drawing the detailed drawings use proper symbols and dimensioning techniques. The answer to this problem is given on the *Independent Learning Content*.

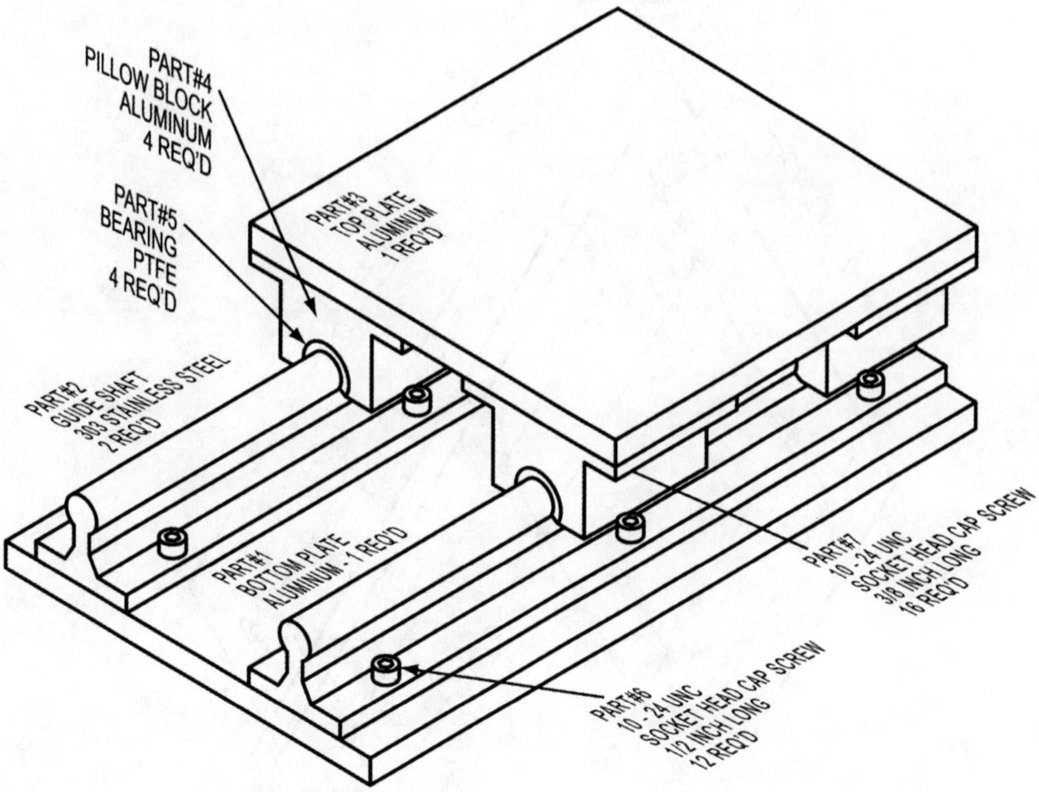

Part#1: Bottom Plate If you are just studying the basics and have not covered threads and fasteners, replace the 12X 10 – 24 UNC dimension with a 12x ∅.19 dimension.

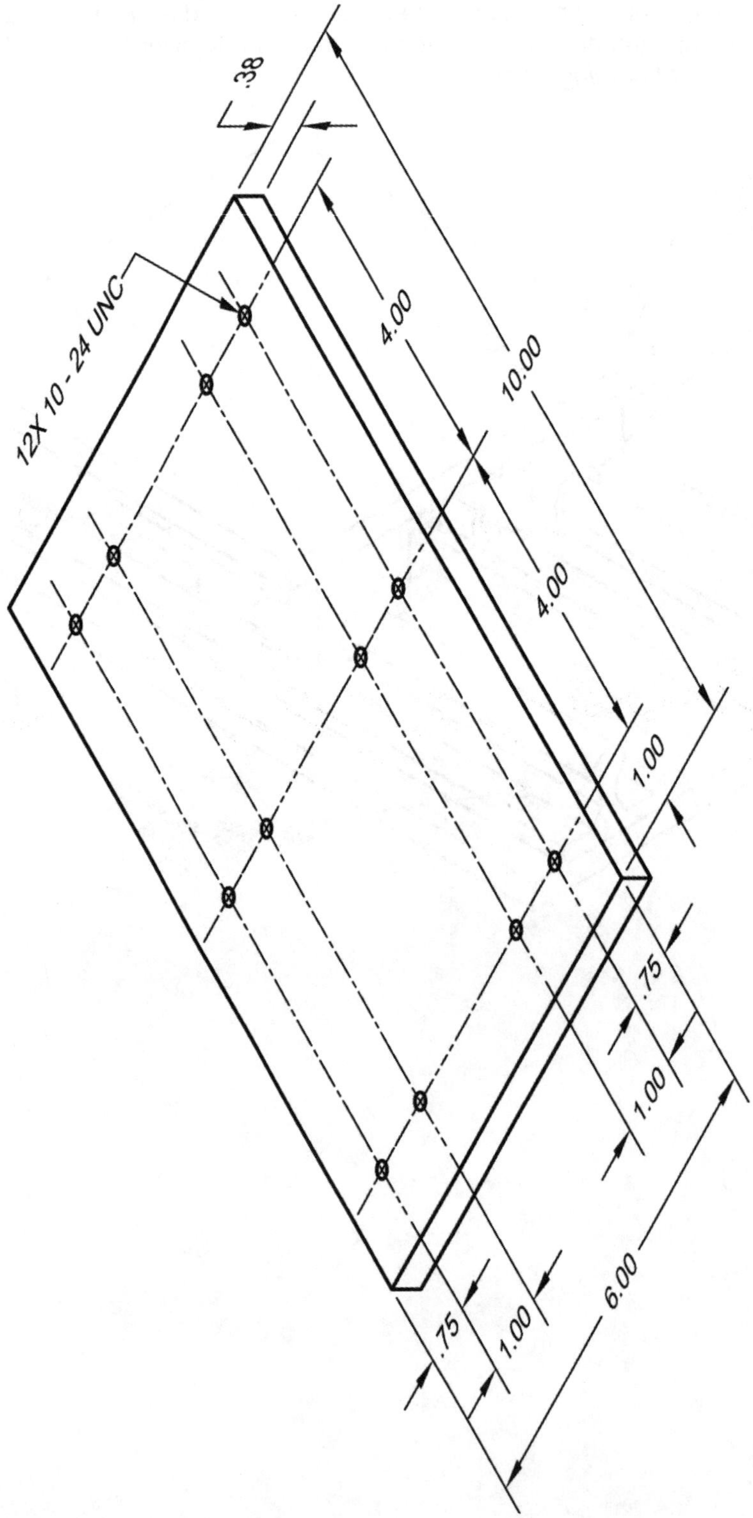

<u>Part#2: Guide Shaft</u> If you are just studying the basics and have not covered tolerancing, ignore the RC4 tolerance. NOTE TO DRAFTER: This part is symmetric and all fillets are R.12.

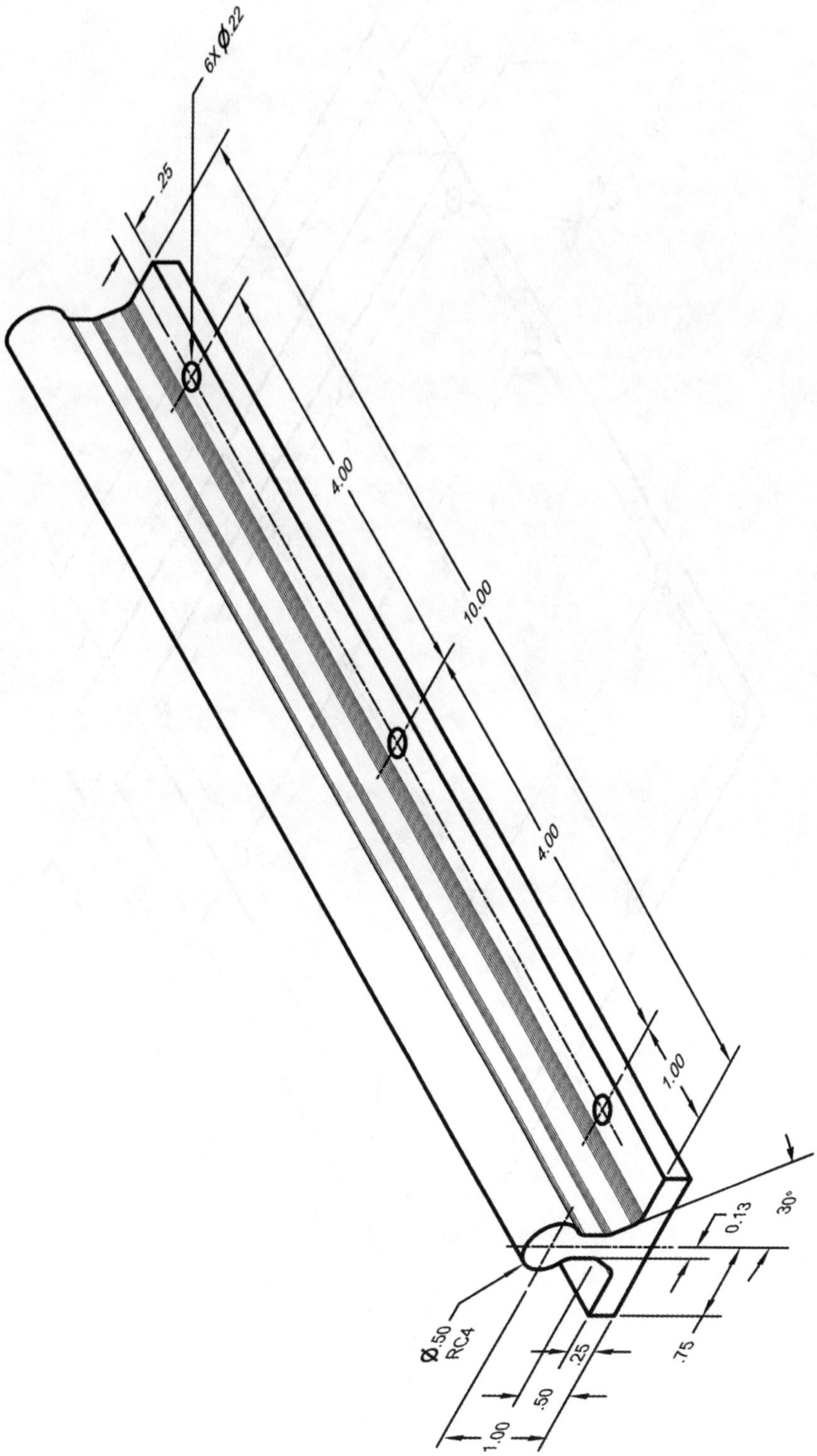

Part#3: Top Plate If you are just studying the basics and have not covered threads and fasteners, replace the 16X 10 – 24 UNC dimension with a 16x ∅.19 dimension.

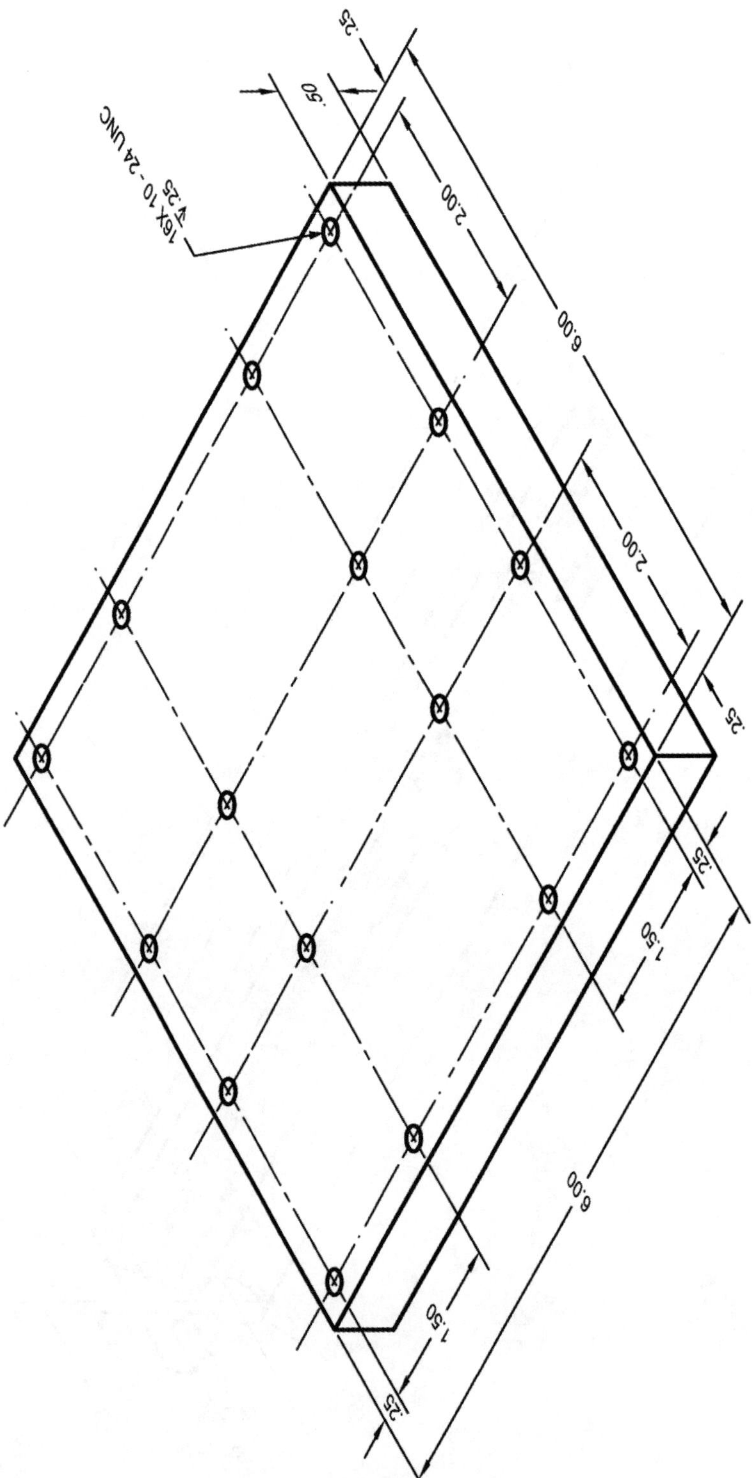

Part#4: Pillow Block If you are just studying the basics and have not covered tolerancing, ignore the FN1 tolerance.

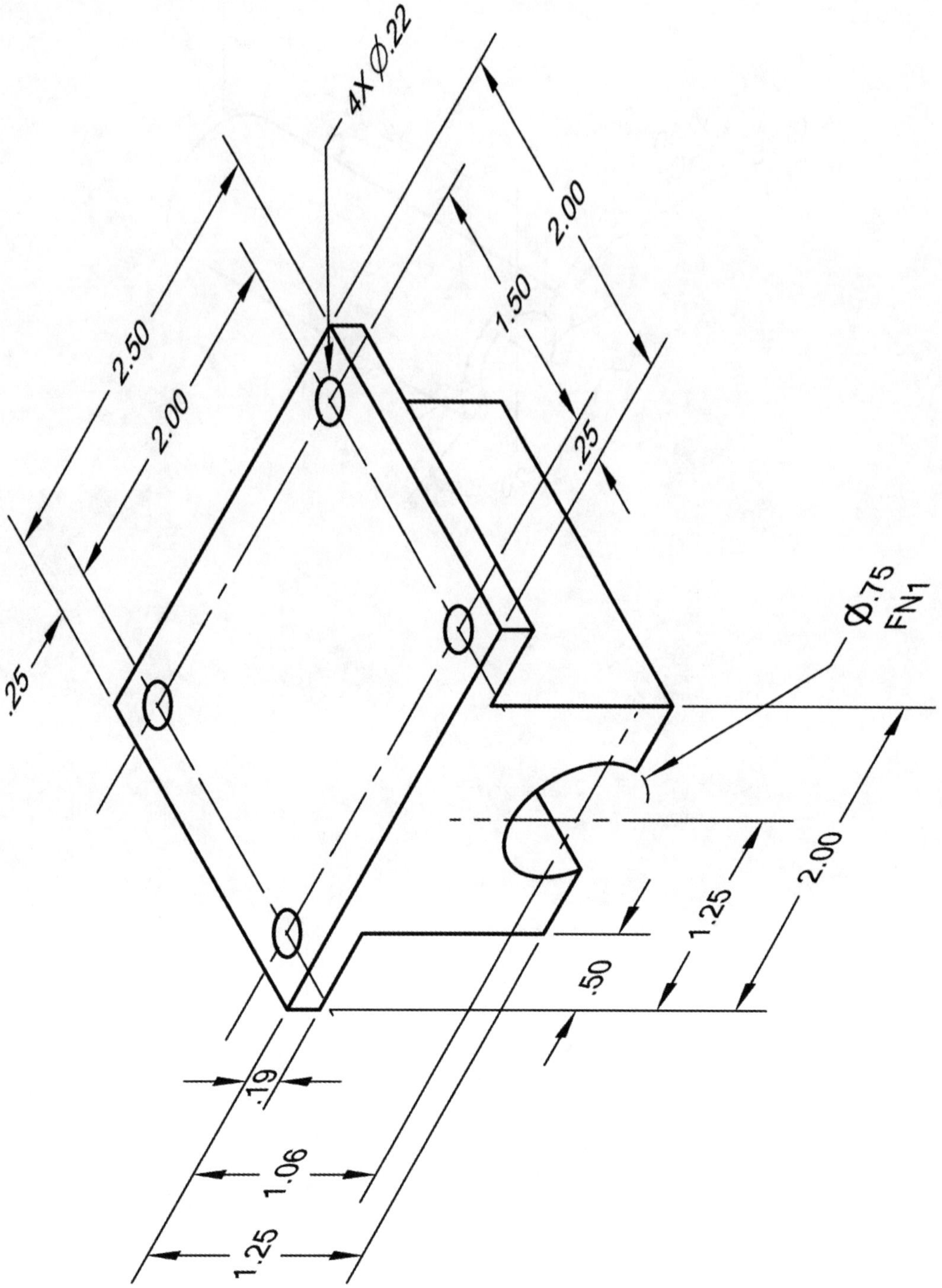

Part#5: Bearing If you are just studying the basics and have not covered tolerancing, ignore the RC4 and FN1 tolerances.

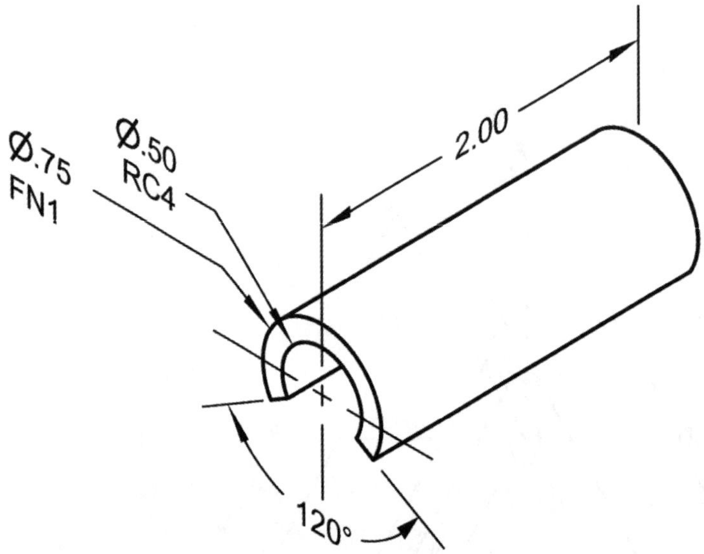

CHAPTER 26

CREATING ASSEMBLY DRAWINGS IN AUTOCAD®

CHAPTER OUTLINE

CHAPTER SUMMARY

In this chapter you will learn how to use individual part views to construct an assembly drawing. You will also learn how to balloon an assembly and make a parts list. By the end of this chapter, you will be able to construct a complete and fully annotated assembly drawing.

26.1) INTRODUCTION

The assembly drawing, included as part of a working drawing package, is usually created after all the detailed part drawings are completed. Conceptual or design idea assembly drawings are drawn at the beginning stages of the design process to test out an idea. However, these types of assembly drawings are not usually included as part of a working drawing package.

An assembly drawing is relatively easy to create if all the detailed part drawings are complete. Selected views of each part are copied and pasted into an assembly drawing file. Once all parts are combined into one file, an assembly may be created using various MODIFY commands. Some lines may have to be changed from visible to hidden or vice versa and some may need to be deleted. The only new parts that may need to be drawn are standard parts that were not detailed. And, the ballooning process has been greatly simplified with the advent of multileaders.

26.2) ASSEMBLY TUTORIAL

In this tutorial we will use previously drawn details to create a complete assembly drawing of the following *Drill Jig*. Assembly of the details will be accomplished using functionally related features and modify commands such as MOVE, MIRROR, COPY, etc...

IMPORTANT! Throughout the tutorial you will be instructed to choose points that relate to geometric locations on an object. Select them with an *OSNAP*.

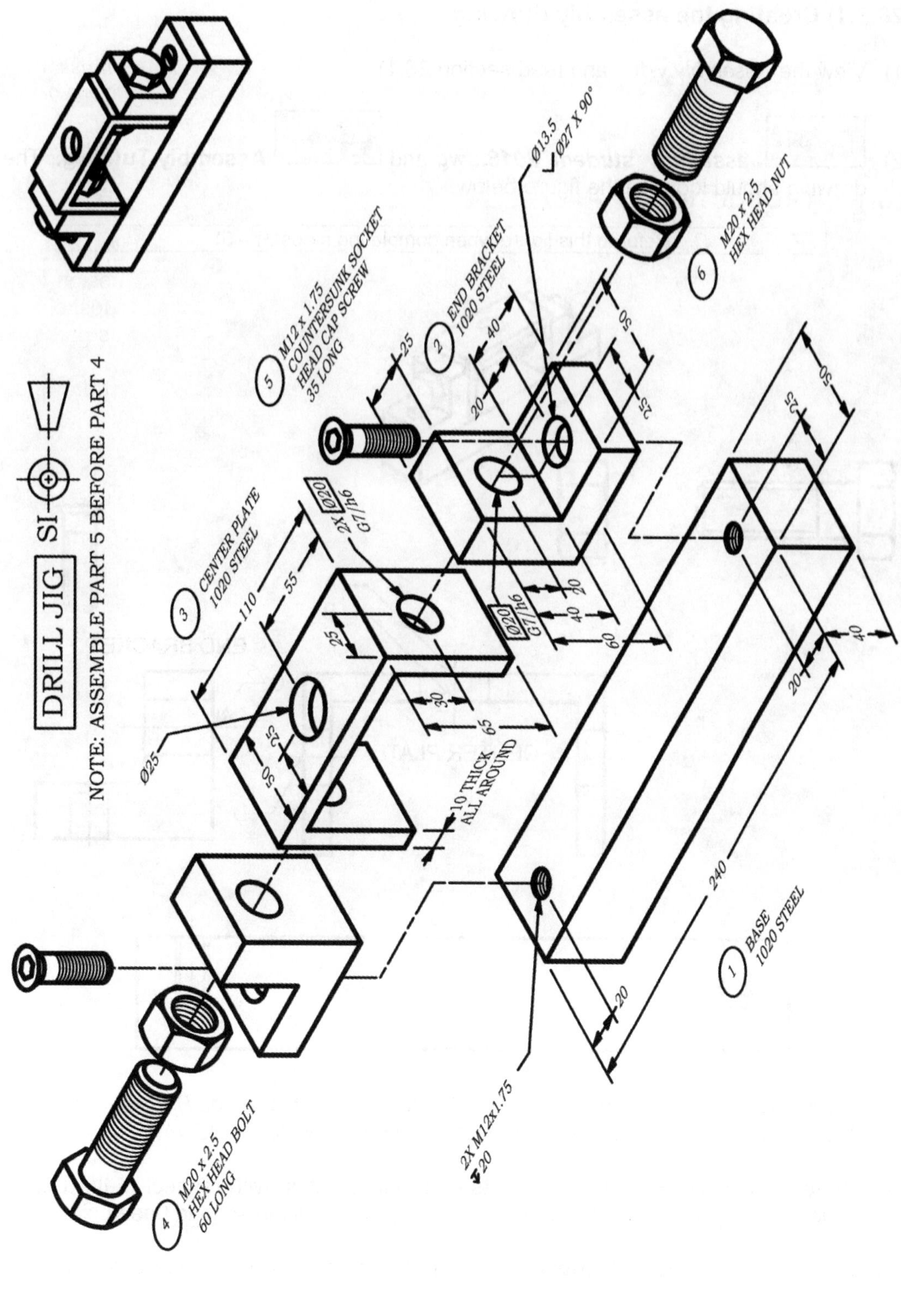
DRILL JIG
SI
NOTE: ASSEMBLE PART 5 BEFORE PART 4
1 BASE 1020 STEEL
2 END BRACKET 1020 STEEL
3 CENTER PLATE 1020 STEEL
4 M20 x 2.5 HEX HEAD BOLT 60 LONG
5 M12 x 1.75 COUNTERSUNK SOCKET HEAD CAP SCREW 35 LONG
6 M20 x 2.5 HEX HEAD NUT
Ø13.5
⌴Ø27 X 90°
2X Ø20 G7/h6
Ø20 G7/h6
Ø25
10 THICK ALL AROUND
2X M12x1.75
↧20
240
110
55
65
60
50
40
30
25
20

26.2.1) Creating the assembly drawing

1) View the *Assembly* video and read section 26.1).

2) 

assembly_student_2018.dwg and 

Assembly Tut.dwg. The drawing should look like the figure below.

Refer to this figure when completing steps 3) – 5)

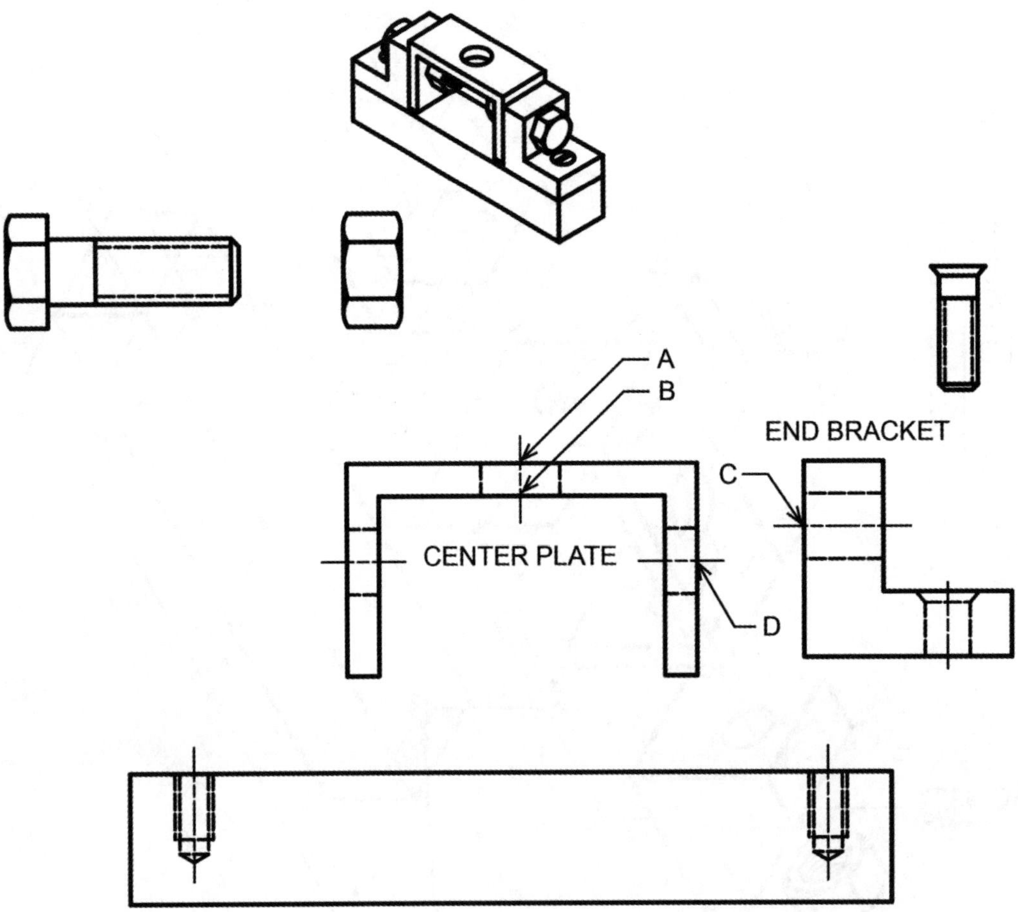

3) **MIrror** the *End Bracket* on the right side to create the left side *End Bracket*. Use point A and B to create the mirror line. Select these points using an *OSNAP*.

4) **Move** the original *End Bracket* into its functional position with respect to the *Center Plate*. Use point C as the first base point and point D as the second base point.

5) Use a similar procedure to **Move** the *End Bracket* copy into its functional position.

Refer to this figure when completing steps 6) – 12)

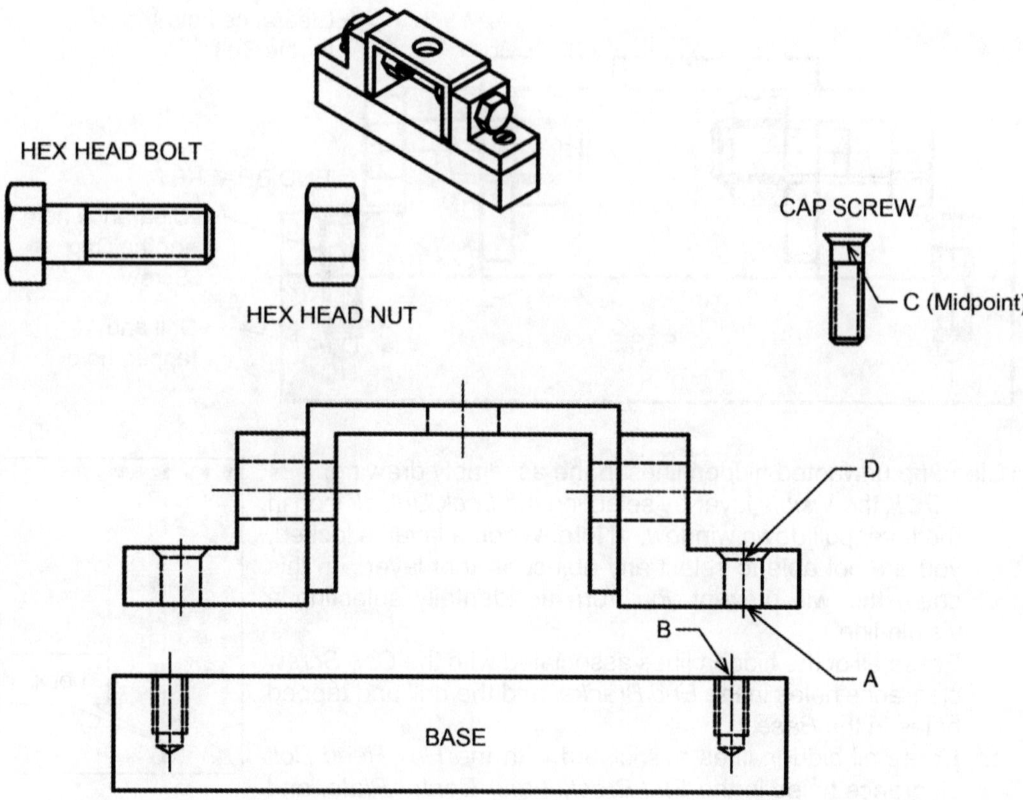

6) **Move** the *End Bracket/Center Plate* assembly to their functional placement relative to the *Base*. Use point A as the first base point and B as the second base point.

7) Make a **COpy** of the *Cap Screw.*

8) **Move** the original *Cap Screw* into its functional position. Use point C as the first base point. You will have to **Zoom** in to locate point C. Use point D as the second base point.

9) Use a similar procedure to **Move** the *Cap Screw* copy.

10) On your own, **MIrror** the *Hex Head Bolt* and *Nut.*

11) Using similar procedures, as described above, **Move** the *Hex Head Bolts* and *Hex Head Nuts* into their functional positions. (See figure below.)

12) 

Refer to this figure when completing step 13)

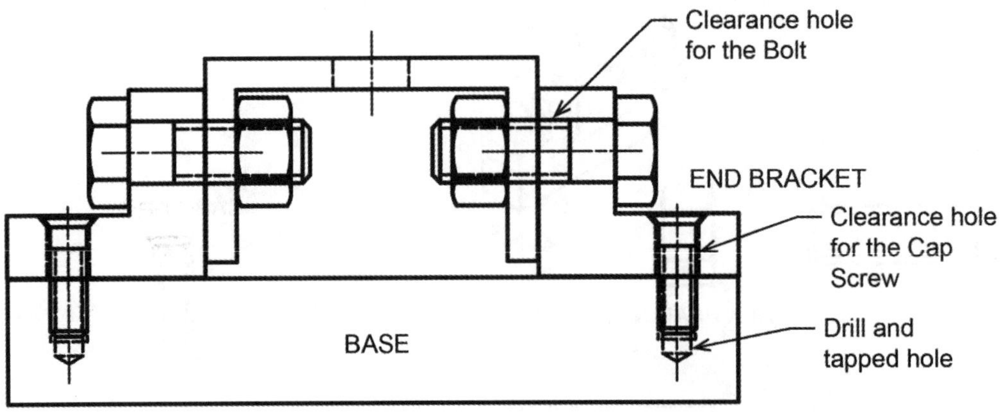

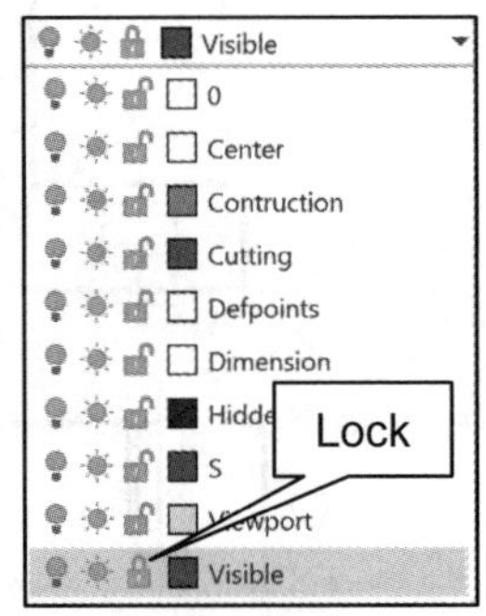

13) Clean up unwanted hidden lines in the assembly drawing.

a. ***LOCK*** the *Visible* layer by selecting the *Lock/Unlock* icon in the layer pull down window. (Note: When a layer is locked, you are not able to select any object on that layer. In this case, this will prevent you from accidentally selecting a visible line.)

b. **Erase** all of the hidden lines associated with the *Cap Screw* clearance holes in the *End Bracket* and the drill and tapped holes in the *Base*.

c. **Erase** all hidden lines associated with the *Hex Head Bolt* clearance holes in the *End Bracket* and *Center Plate,* and the hidden lines associated with the drill and tapped hole in the *Base*. (Note: If you are having difficulty selecting the hidden lines, use a crossing window by clicking and dragging up and to the left.)

d. ***UNLOCK*** the *Visible* layer.

Refer to this figure when completing step 14)

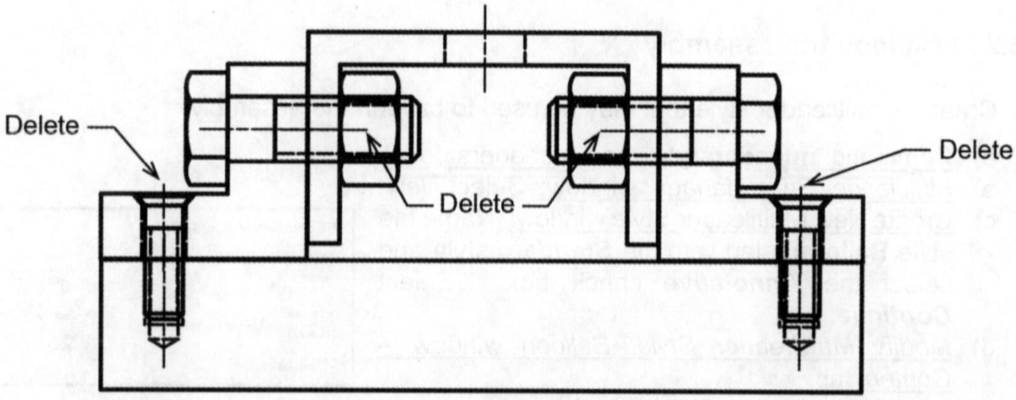

14) **Erase** duplicate centerlines and adjust the length of the remaining centerlines.
   a. **Erase** the four centerlines labeled in the above figure.
   b. Adjust the length of the remaining centerlines using grip boxes and *Polar Tracking*.

Refer to this figure when completing steps 15) – 18)

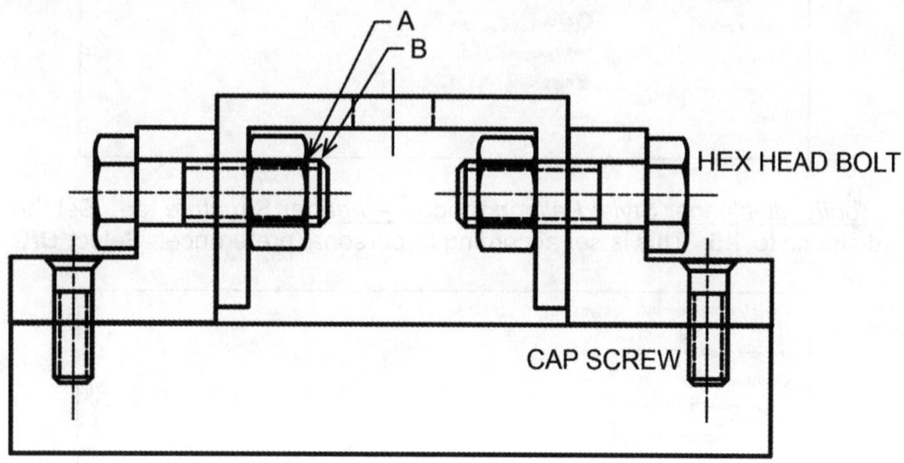

15) Change all visible lines in the *Cap Screws* to hidden lines. Select all visible lines in both *Cap Screws*. Don't worry if hidden lines also get selected. In the *Layer* pull down window select the *Hidden* layer. Hit **Esc** to get rid of the grip boxes. (Hint: Create a selection window by clicking and dragging down and to the right. This will select only things completely inside the window.)

16) On your own, change the visible lines of the *Hex Head Bolts* that run inside the *End Brackets* and *Center Plate* to hidden lines. (Note: You will end up changing a portion of some visible lines to hidden that should remain visible. We will fix that later.)

17) Deselect all by hitting the **Esc** key and change your current layer to ***Visible***.

18) Draw a visible line from point A to point B (see above figure). Draw a similar visible line on the bottom portion of the bolt and on the other bolt.

26.2.2) Balloon the assembly

1) Create a multileader style that may be used to balloon the assembly.
   a) Command: **mleaderstyle** or Leaders panel: 
   b) *Multileader Style Manager* window: Select ***New...***
   c) Create New Multileader Style window: Name the style **Balloon**, start with the ***Standard*** style and select the ***Annotative*** check box. Select ***Continue***.
   d) *Modify* ***Multileader*** *Style: Balloon* window – *Content* tab:
      i. *Multileader type* field: ***Block***
      ii. *Source block* field: ***Circle***

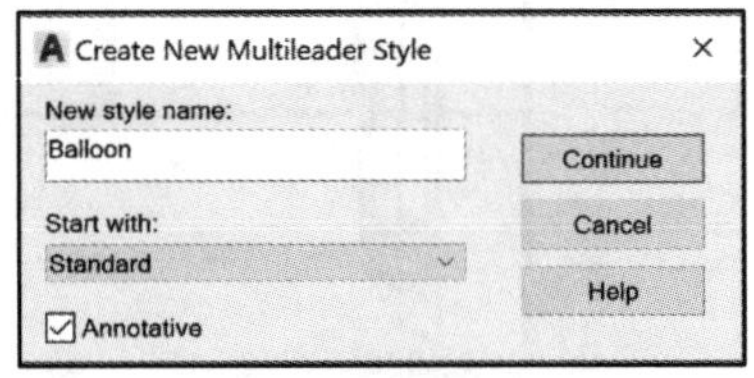

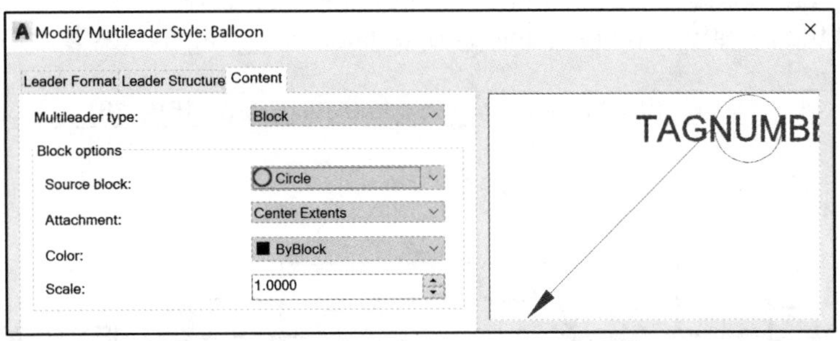

   e) *Modify Multileader Style: Balloon* window – *Leader Structure* tab: Set the landing distance to **1.5**. This is set according to personal preference. Select ***OK***.

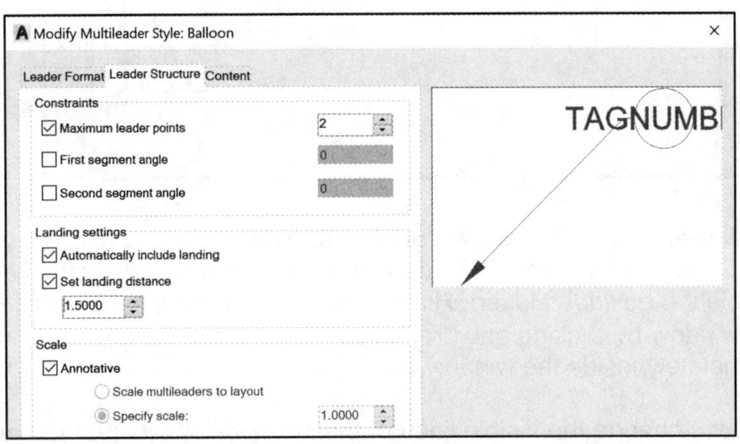

   f) *Multileader Style Manager* window: Select the ***Balloon*** multileader style and then ***Set Current*** and then select ***Close***.

Refer to this figure when completing steps 2) & 3)

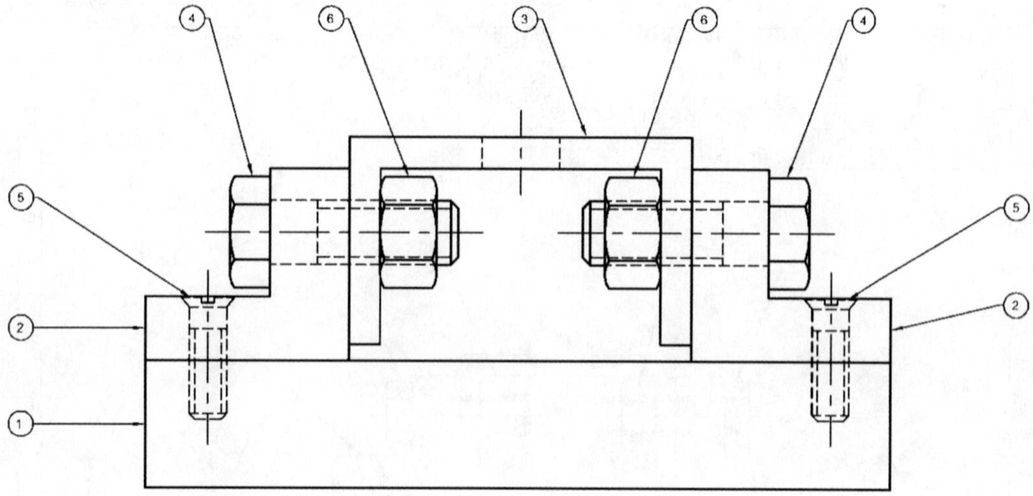

2) Draw the balloons and part numbers.
   a) Set your current layer to be the ***Dimension*** layer.
   b) Use the *Balloon* multileader at a 1:1 annotative scale to balloon the assembly. Your balloons and part numbers will look small, but remember they are annotative; therefore, they will print out at the correct size. Don't worry if your balloons are not perfectly horizontal or vertical. We will fix that in the next step.

3) Align the balloons.

   a) Command: **mleaderalign** or *Leaders* panel: 
   b) `Select multileaders:` Select the balloons containing the part numbers 1, 2, and 5 on the left side. **`Enter`**
   c) `Select multileader to align to or [Options]:` Select the balloon that you wish to align the other two with.
   d) `Specify direction:` Select a 90 degree polar tracking line.
   e) Repeat for the other two sets of balloons.
   f) If you don't like the position of your balloons, you may move them using grip boxes and then reapply the MLEADERALIGN command.

4) Add a 1:2 scale support Add/Delete Scales to all the balloons.

Refer to this figure when completing steps 5) – 8)

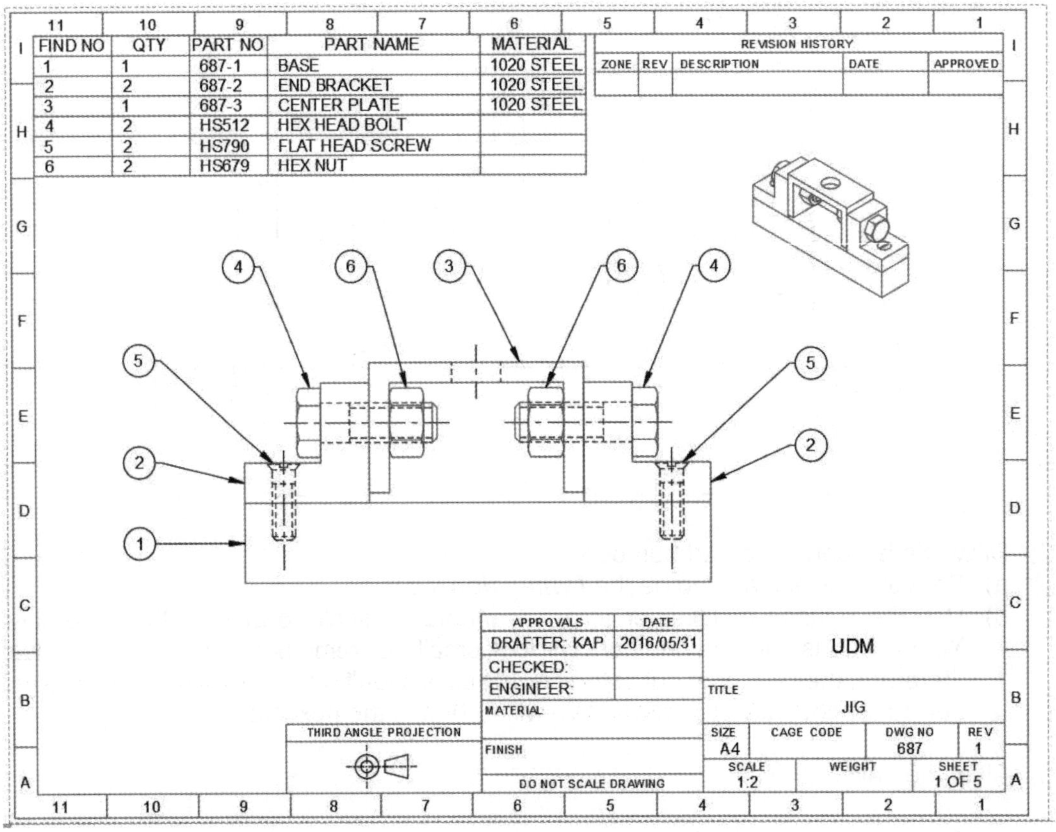

5) Enter paper space on ***Layout1***.

6) Enter the ***Page Setup*** and prepare your metric drawing to be printed on an ***A4*** sheet of paper. Make sure that you choose a printer. The printer will define the printable area (i.e. the dotted line). If you don't know the printer type, choose that you will be printing to PDF.

7) **Insert** your metric title block and **Scale** as necessary.

8) Click on the viewport border, change it to the ***Viewport*** layer, expand it to beyond the size of the title block.

9) Double click inside your viewport border and set the viewport scale to ***1:2***. Notice that the multileaders adjust their size to match the viewport scale.

10) **Move/Pan** your drawing components so that they fit within your title block.

26.2.3) Create a parts list

Refer to this figure when completing steps 1) – 4)

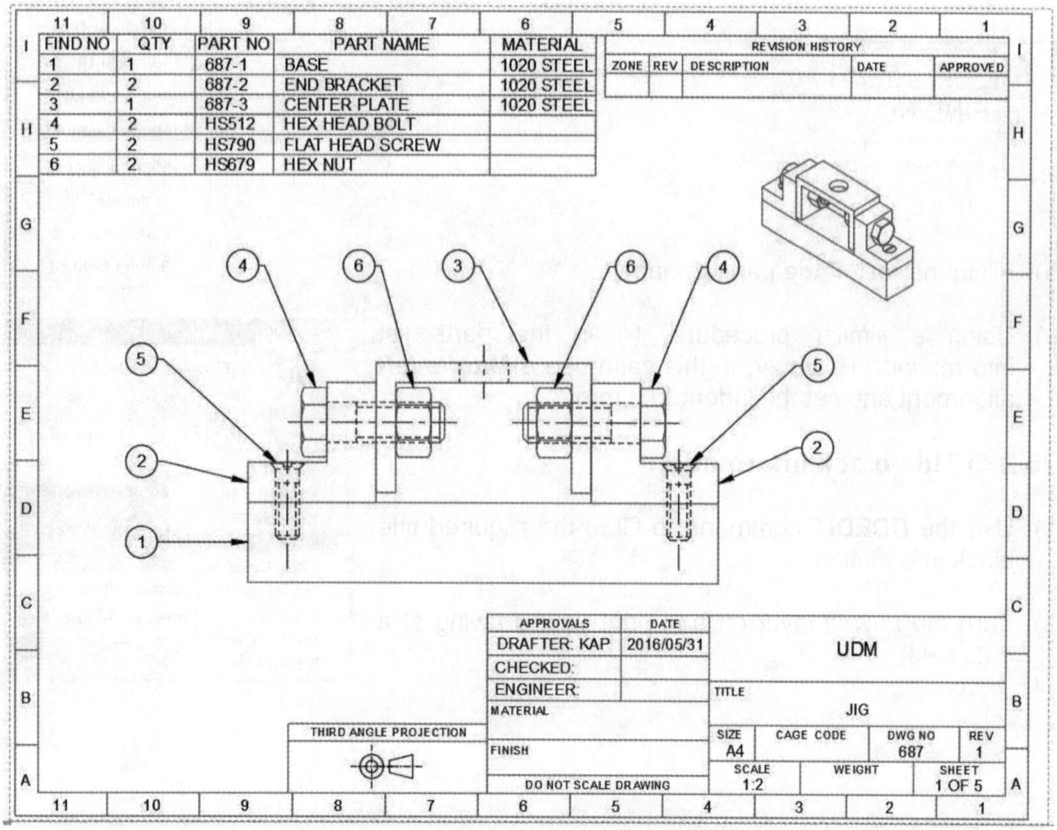

1) In paper space, create the horizontal lines of the parts list.
   a) **EXPLODE** your title block.
   b) **OFFSET** the top inside horizontal line of the title block 7 times by **5** mm using the **Multiple** option.

2) Create the vertical lines of the parts list. **OFFSET** the left inside vertical line of the title block border by **20**, **40**, **60**, **115**, and **142** mm.

3) **TRim** the unwanted lines.

4) In your ***Dimension*** layer, use **MText** to fill in the parts list. Draw an enclosing box that covers the entire extents of the parts list compartment that you are entering text into. Use the ***Middle Center*** alignment.

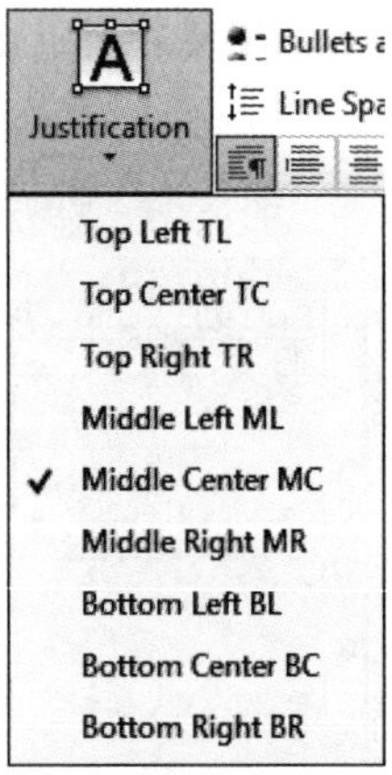

5) Fill in the rest of the parts list labels.

6) Using a similar procedure, fill in the parts list information. However, in this case use a ***Middle-left*** alignment and set the indent to 3 mm.

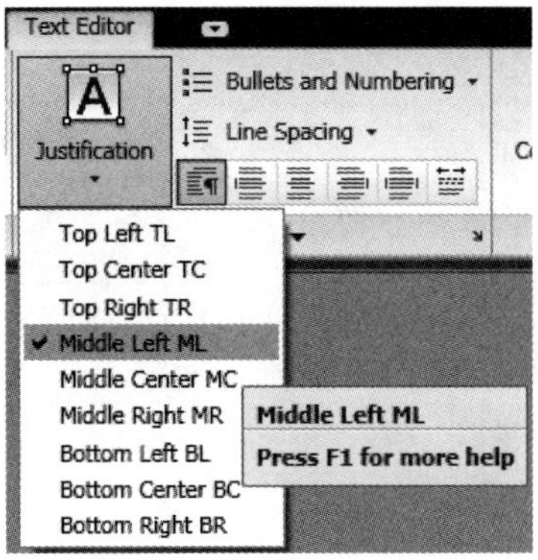

26.2.4) Title block information

1) Use the **DDEDIT** command to fill in the required title block information.

2) Turn the *Layout* layer off and print your drawing at a 1:2 scale.

ASSEMBLY DRAWINGS IN AUTOCAD PROBLEMS

P26-1) Create a working drawing package for the following *Pulley Assembly*. The working drawing package should contain an assembly drawing, details of all the parts, and a standard parts sheet. Notice that some of the dimensioned isometric drawings are not dimensioned using proper dimensioning techniques. When drawing the detailed drawings use proper symbols and dimensioning techniques.

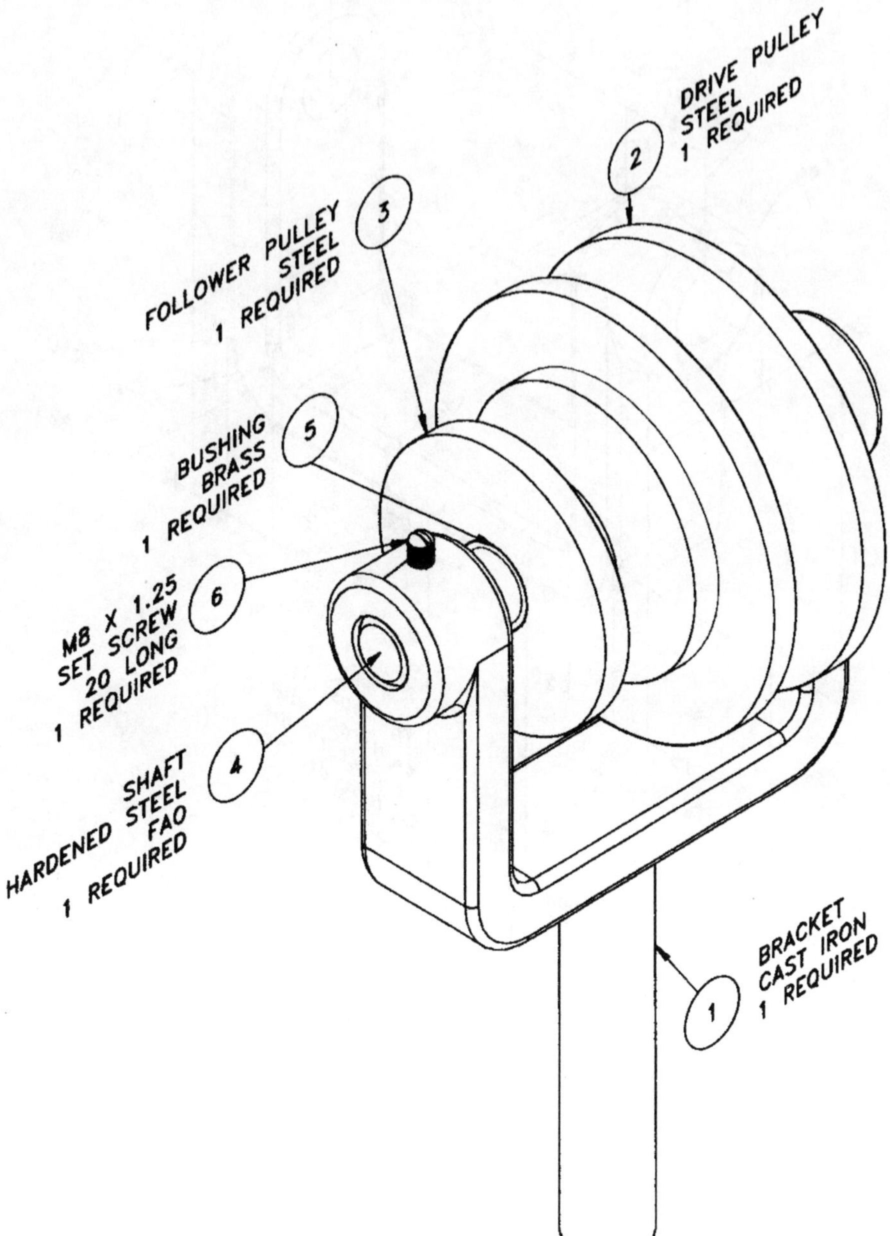

Bracket

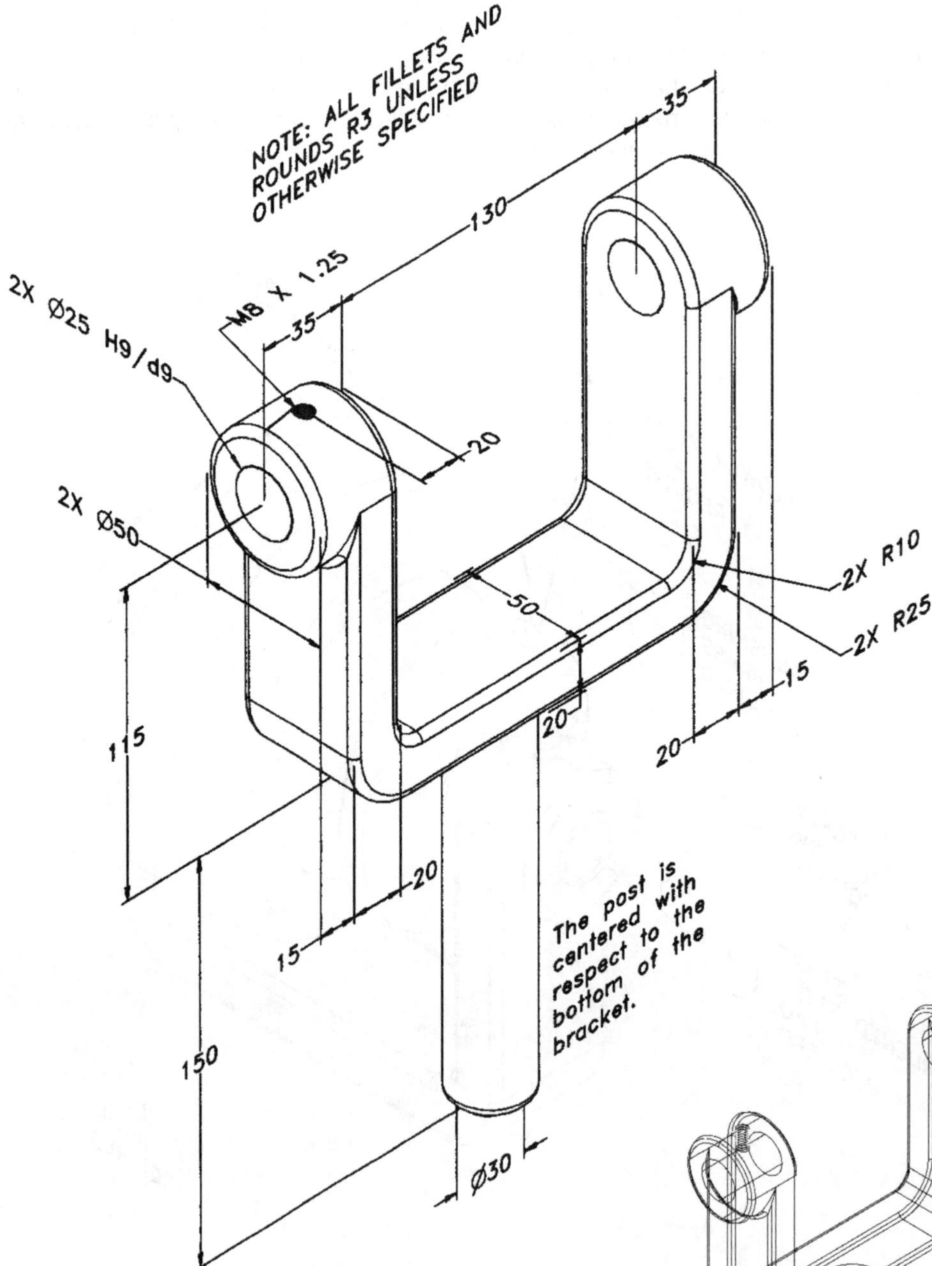
NOTE: ALL FILLETS AND ROUNDS R3 UNLESS OTHERWISE SPECIFIED
35
130
M8 X 1.25
35
2X Ø25 H9/d9
20
2X Ø50
50
2X R10
2X R25
15
20
20
115
20
15
150
The post is centered with respect to the bottom of the bracket.
Ø30

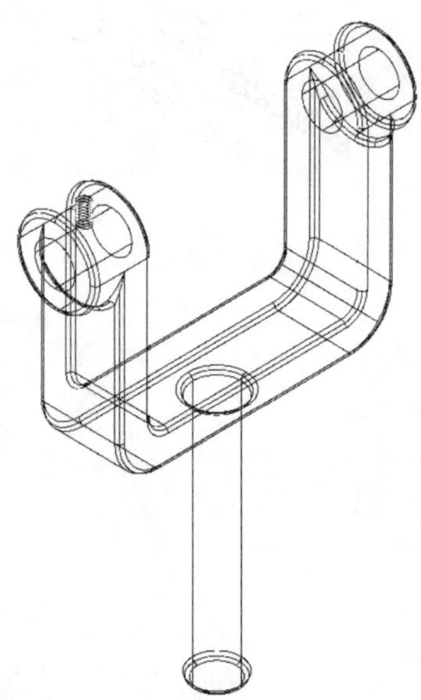

Drive Pulley

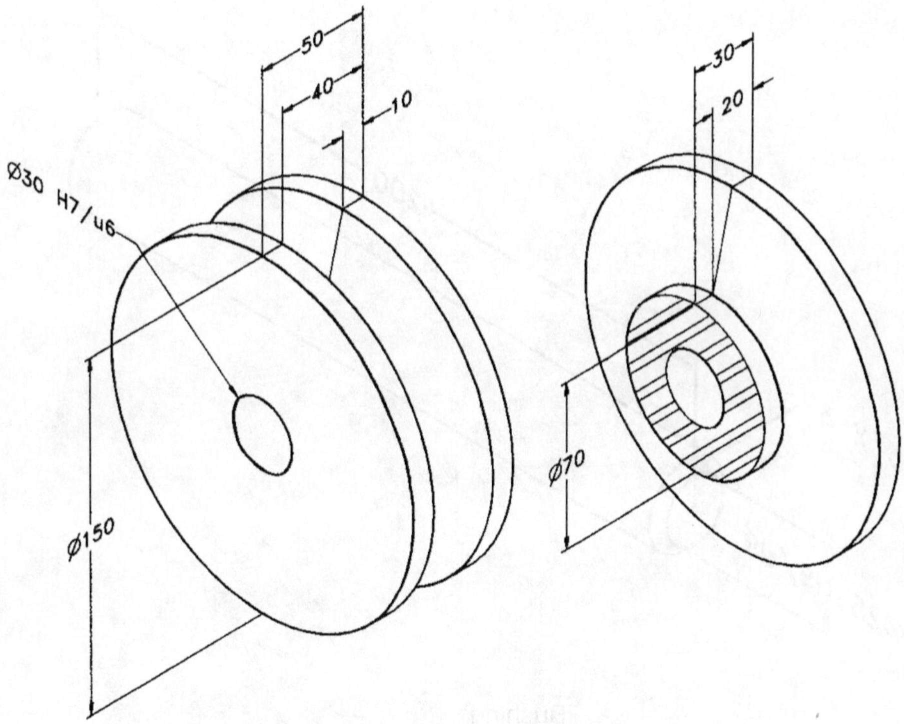

Follower Pulley

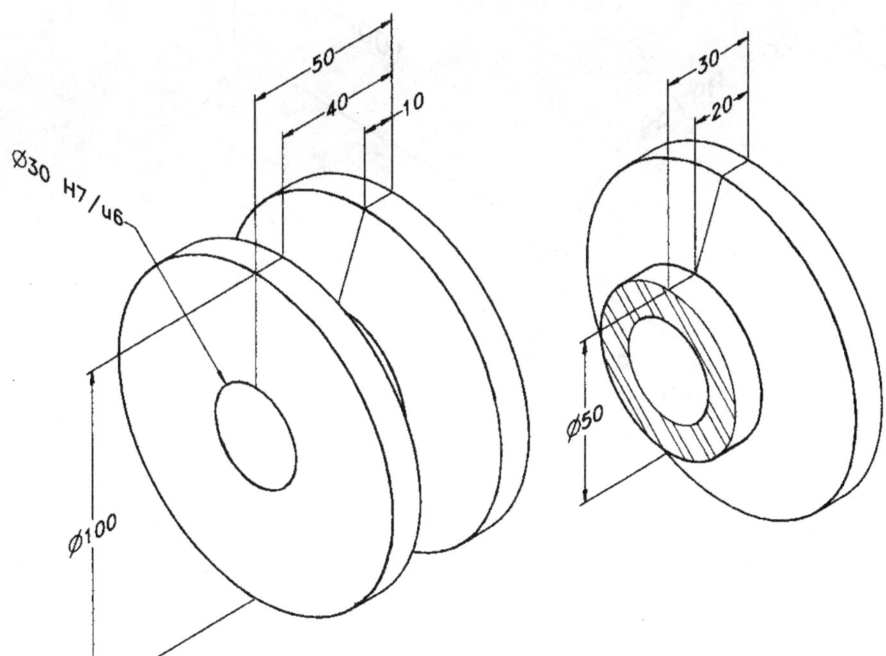

Shaft

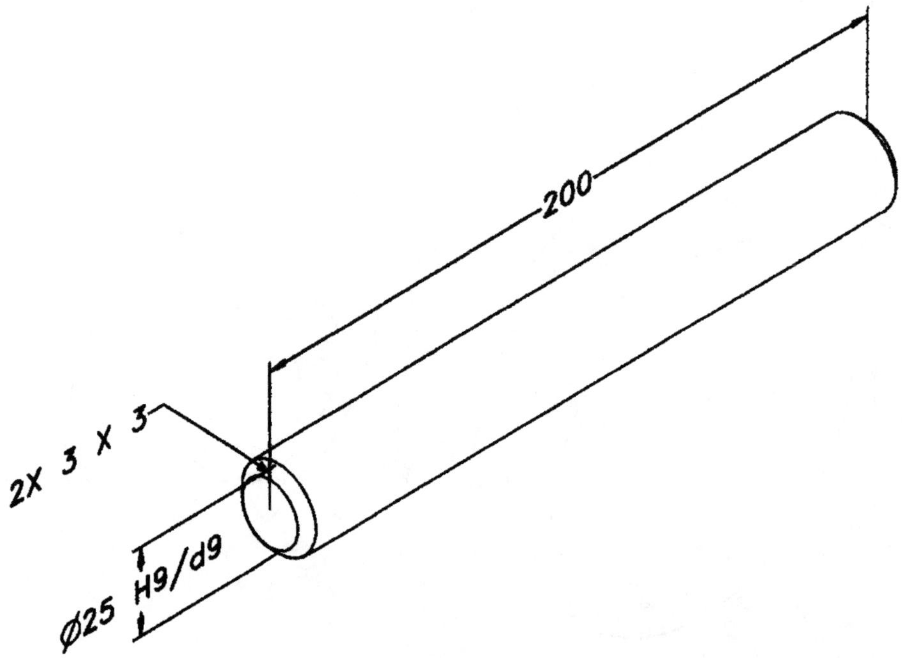

Bushing

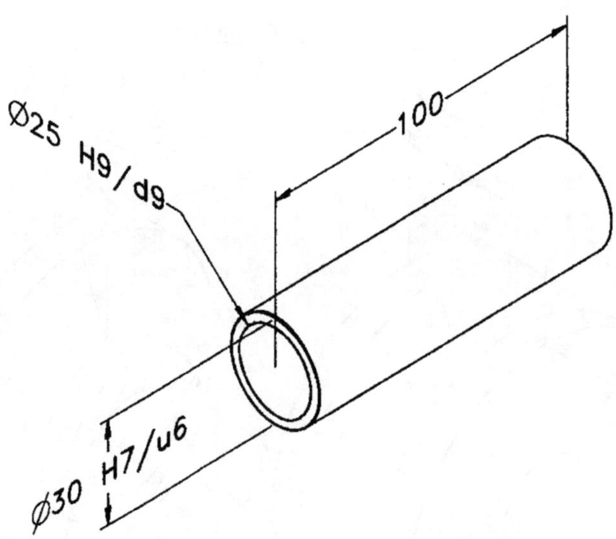

P26-2) Create a working drawing package for the following *Milling Jack*. The working drawing package should contain an assembly drawing, details of all the parts, and a standard parts sheet. Notice that some of the dimensioned isometric drawings are not dimensioned using proper dimensioning techniques. When drawing the detailed drawings use proper symbols and dimensioning techniques.

Milling Jack

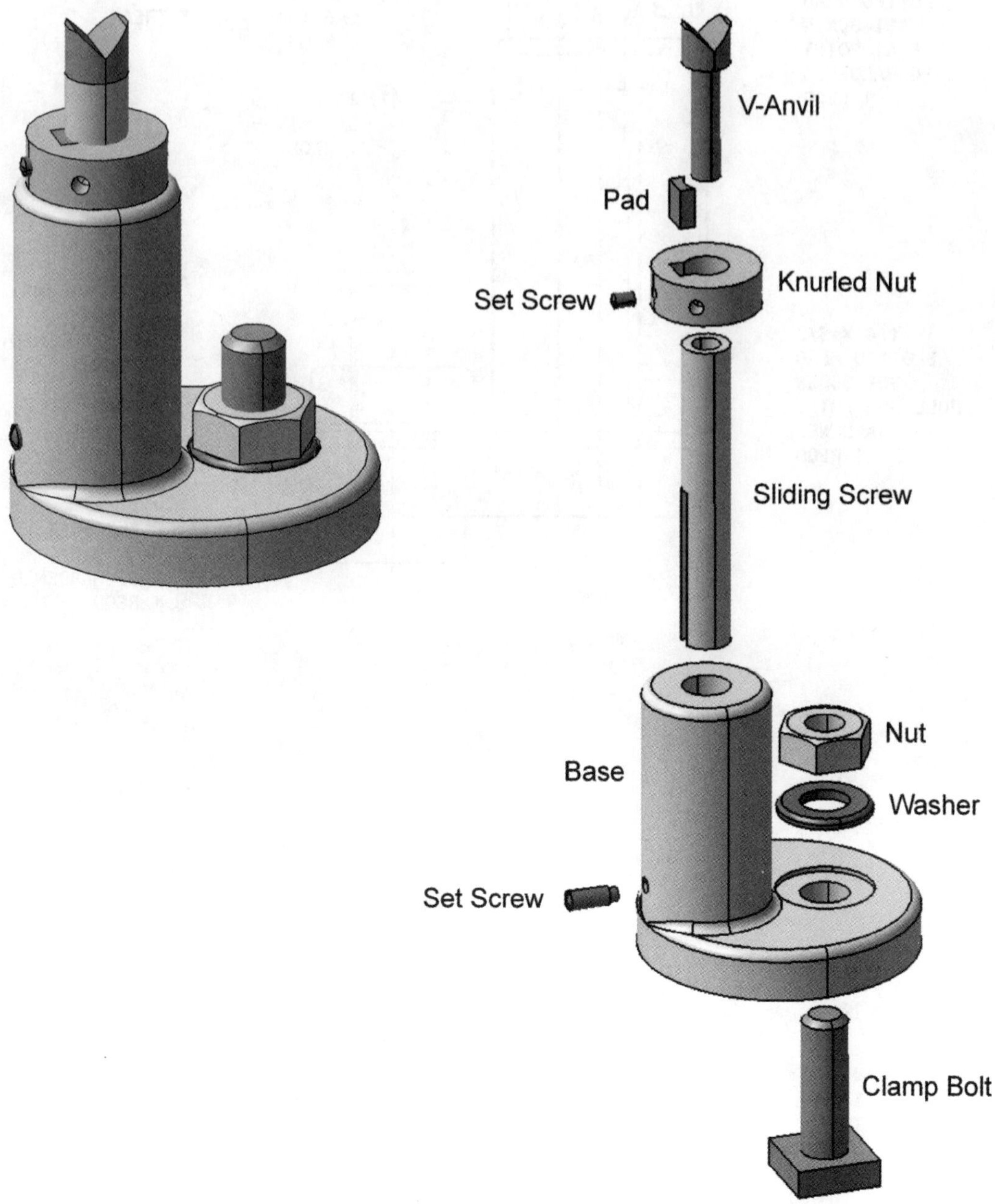

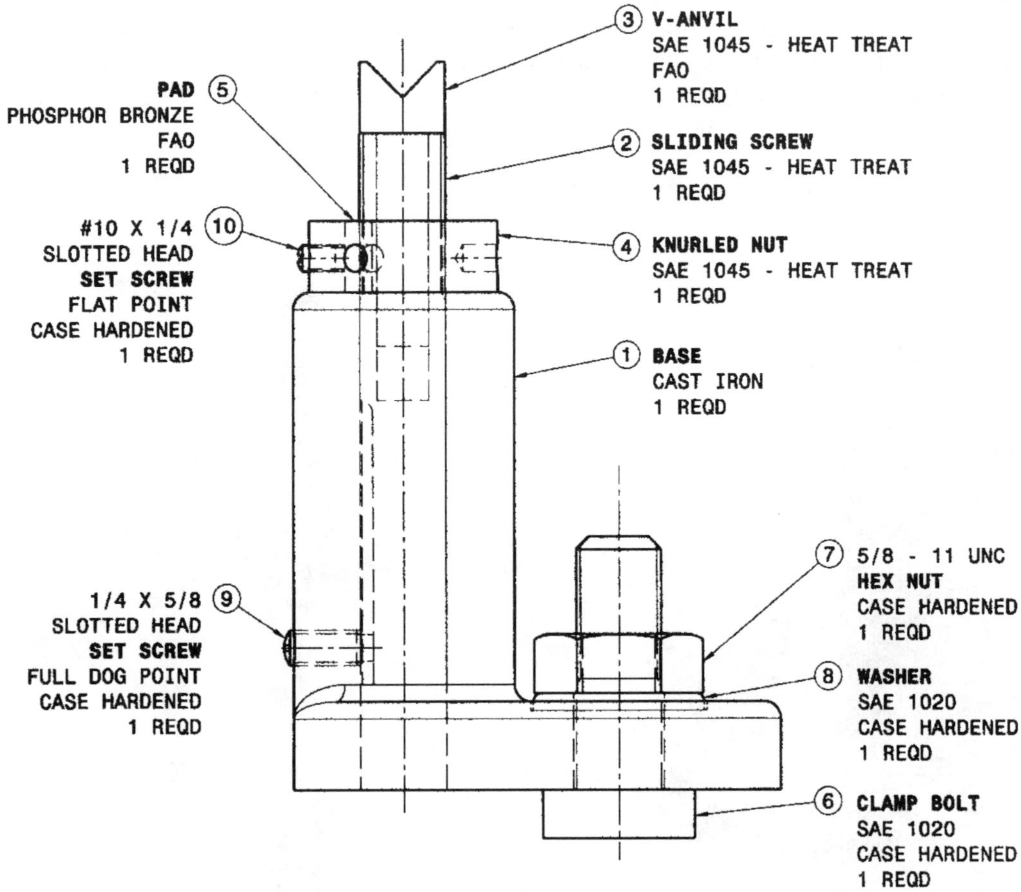
3 V-ANVIL
SAE 1045 - HEAT TREAT
FAO
1 REQD
PAD 5
PHOSPHOR BRONZE
FAO
1 REQD
2 SLIDING SCREW
SAE 1045 - HEAT TREAT
1 REQD
#10 X 1/4 10
SLOTTED HEAD
SET SCREW
FLAT POINT
CASE HARDENED
1 REQD
4 KNURLED NUT
SAE 1045 - HEAT TREAT
1 REQD
1 BASE
CAST IRON
1 REQD
7 5/8 - 11 UNC
HEX NUT
CASE HARDENED
1 REQD
1/4 X 5/8 9
SLOTTED HEAD
SET SCREW
FULL DOG POINT
CASE HARDENED
1 REQD
8 WASHER
SAE 1020
CASE HARDENED
1 REQD
6 CLAMP BOLT
SAE 1020
CASE HARDENED
1 REQD

Base

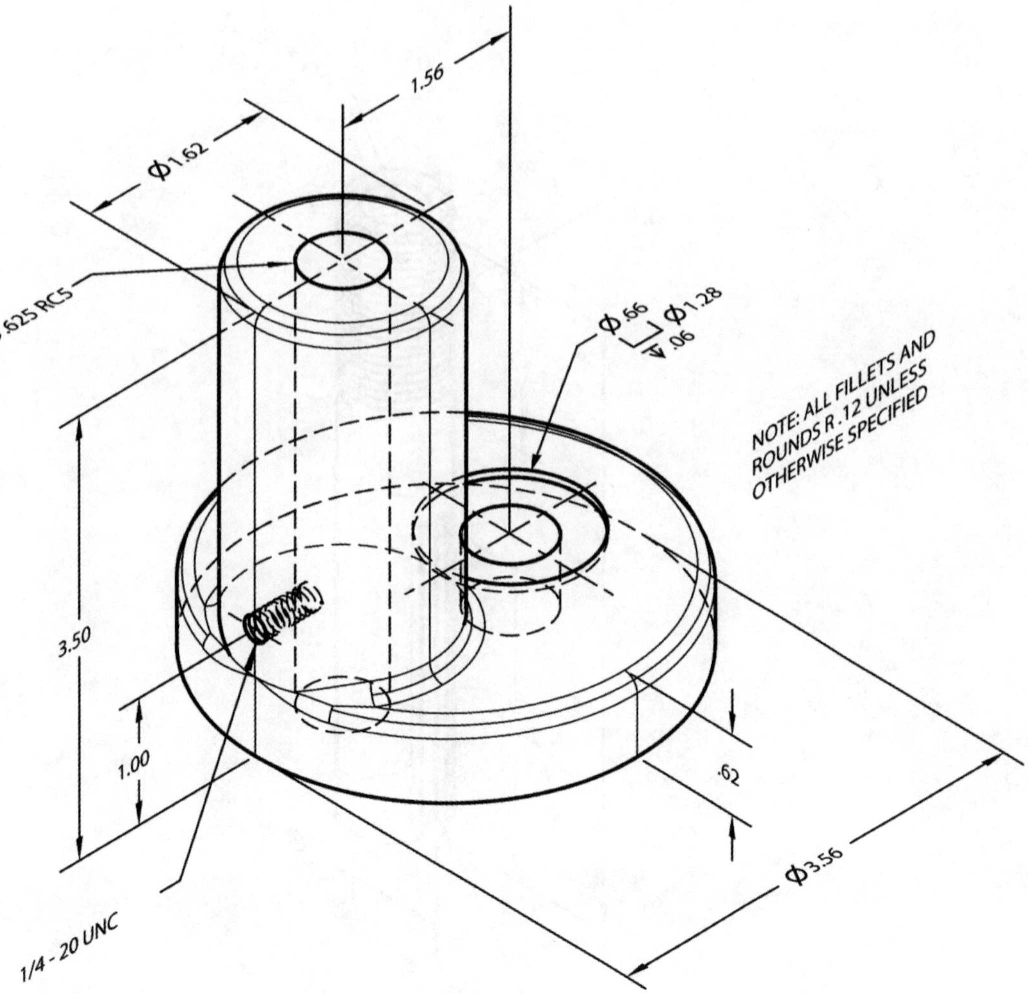
1.56
Φ1.62
Φ.625 RC5
Φ.66 Φ1.28
⌴ .06
NOTE: ALL FILLETS AND
ROUNDS R.12 UNLESS
OTHERWISE SPECIFIED
3.50
1.00
.62
Φ3.56
1/4 - 20 UNC

Sliding Screw

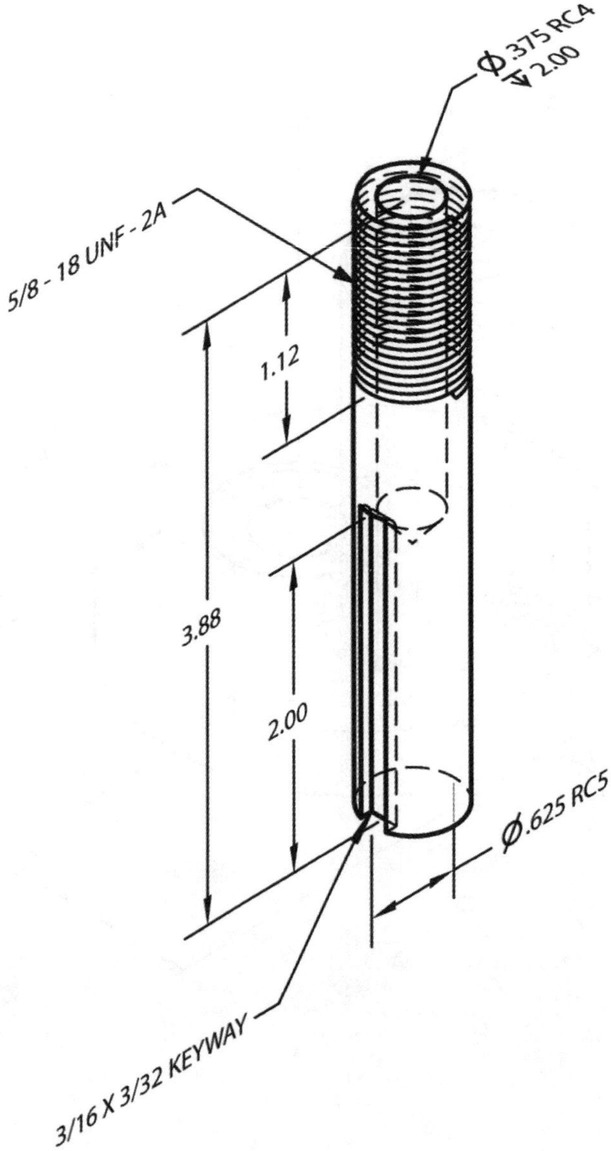

V-Anvil

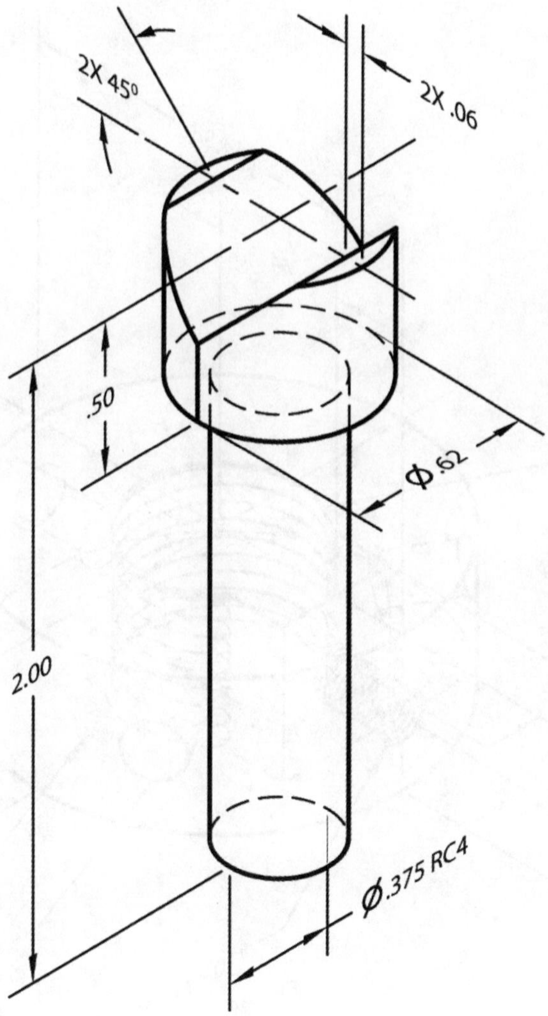

Knurled Nut

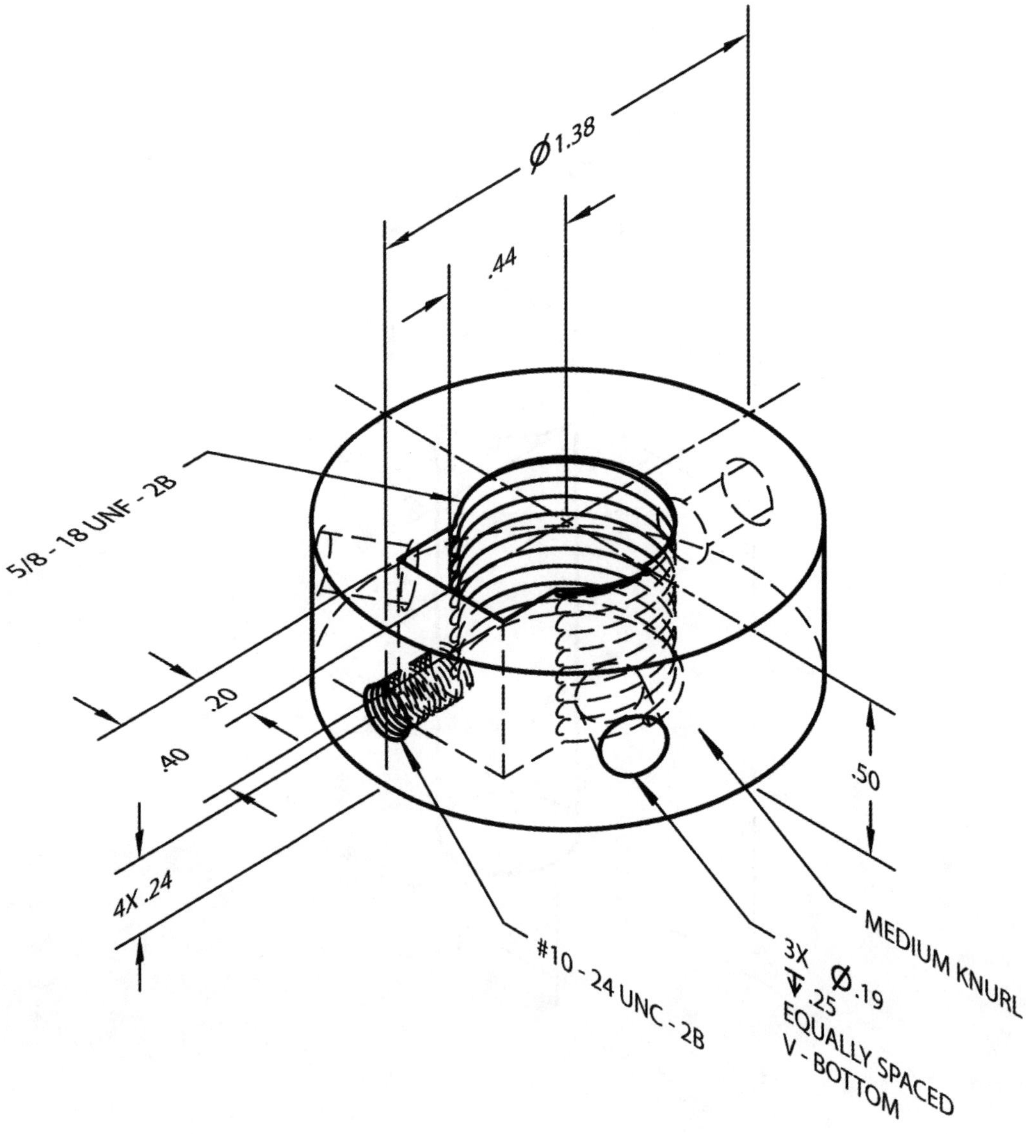
Ø1.38
.44
5/8 - 18 UNF - 2B
.20
.40
4X .24
.50
#10 - 24 UNC - 2B
3X Ø.19
↧.25
EQUALLY SPACED
V - BOTTOM
MEDIUM KNURL

Pad

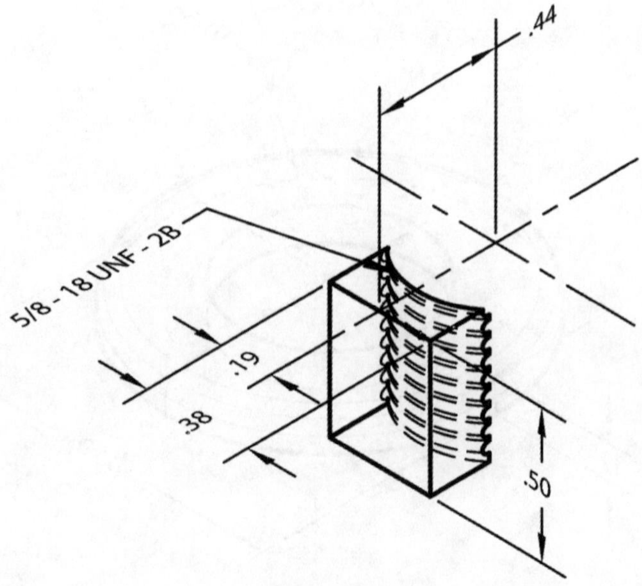

Clamp Bolt

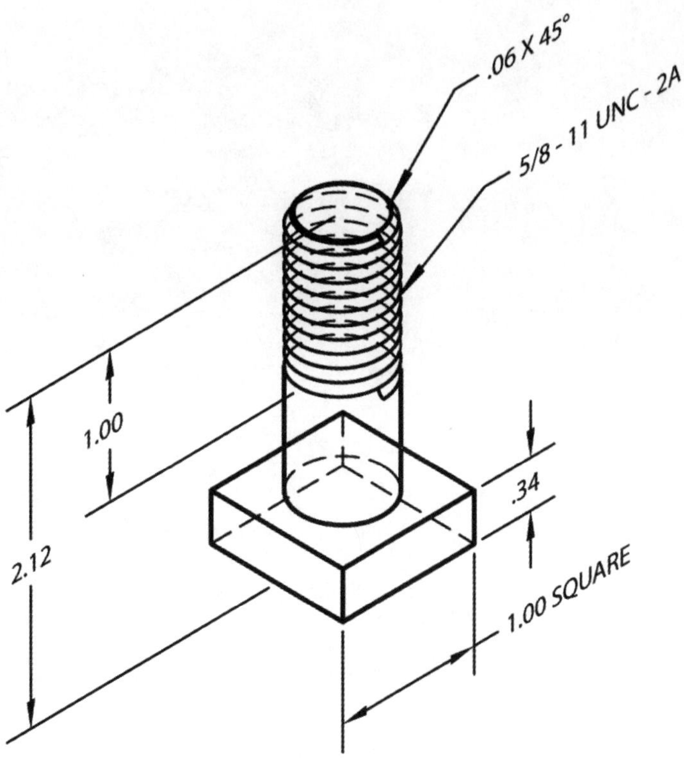

Washer

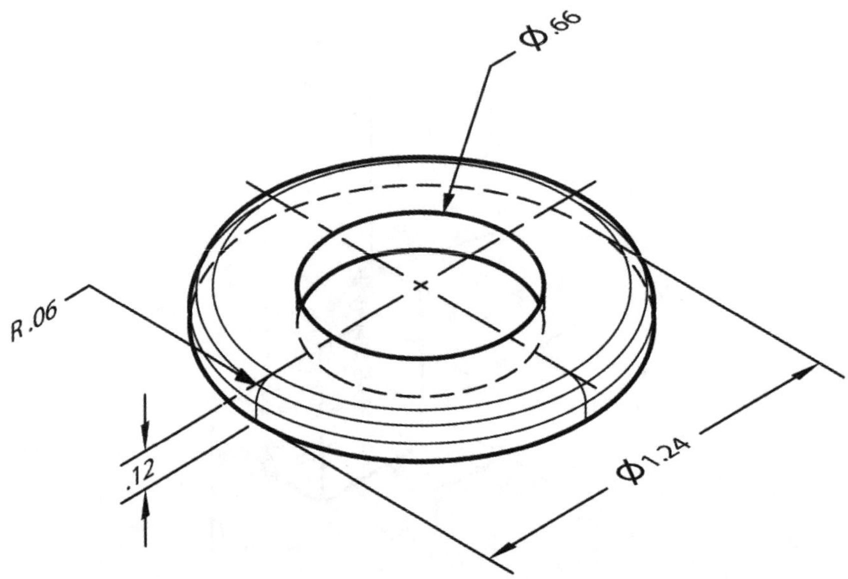

SP26-1) Create a working drawing package for the following *Linear Bearing*. The working drawing package should contain an assembly drawing, details of all the parts, and a standard parts sheet. Notice that some of the dimensioned isometric drawings are not dimensioned using proper dimensioning techniques. When drawing the detailed drawings use proper symbols and dimensioning techniques. The answer to this problem is given on the *Independent Learning Content*.

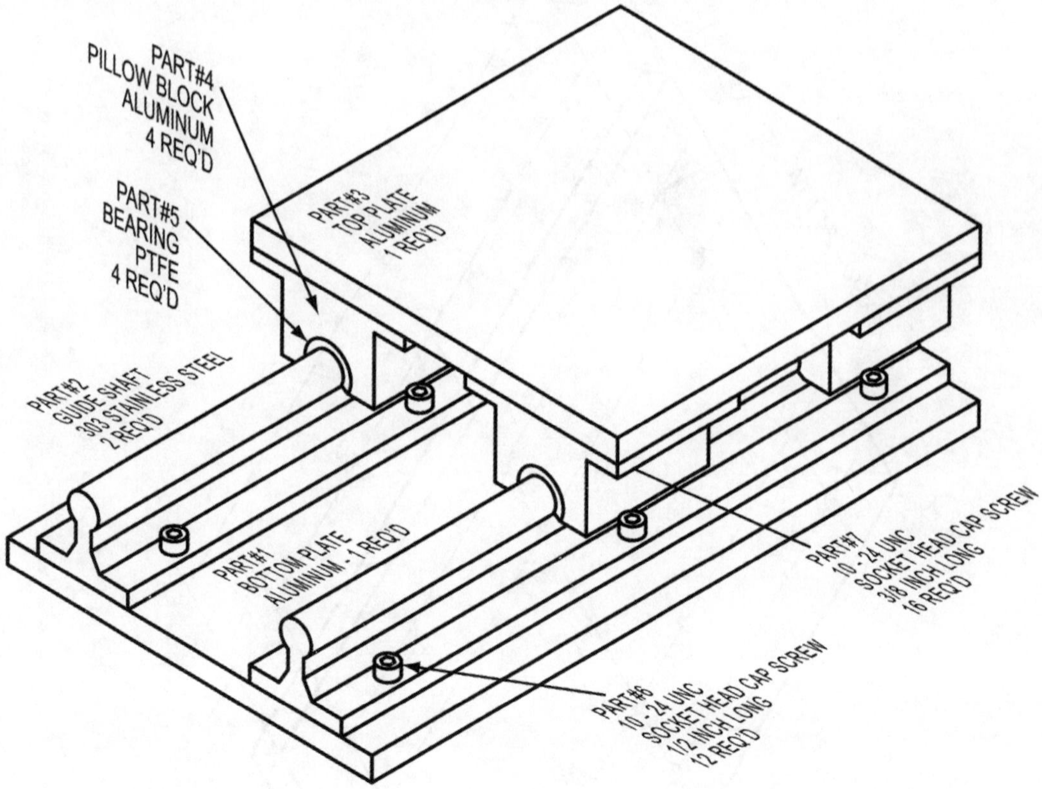

Part#1: Bottom Plate If you are just studying the basics and have not covered threads and fasteners, replace the 12X 10 – 24 UNC dimension with a 12x ∅.19 dimension.

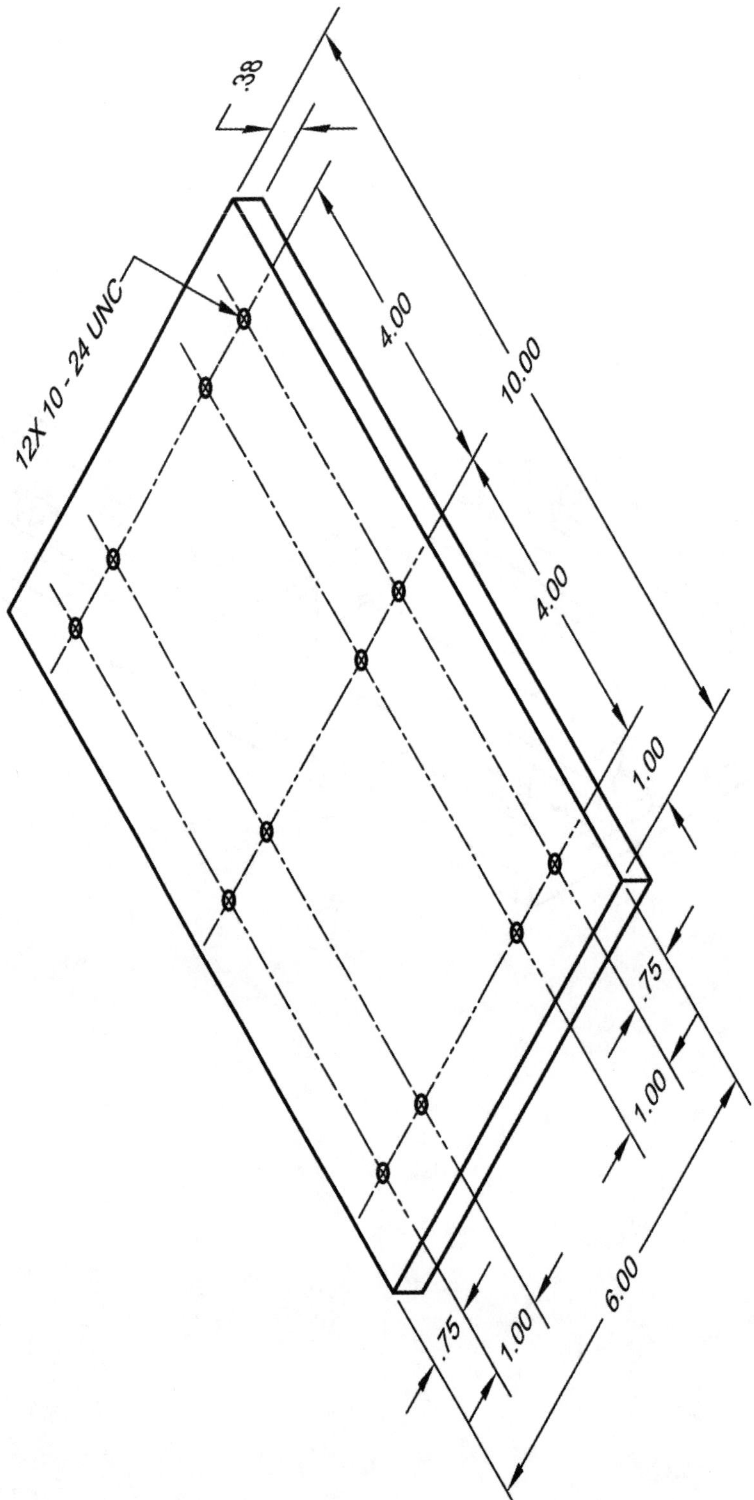

Part#2: Guide Shaft If you are just studying the basics and have not covered tolerancing, ignore the RC4 tolerance. NOTE TO DRAFTER: This part is symmetric and all fillets are R.12.

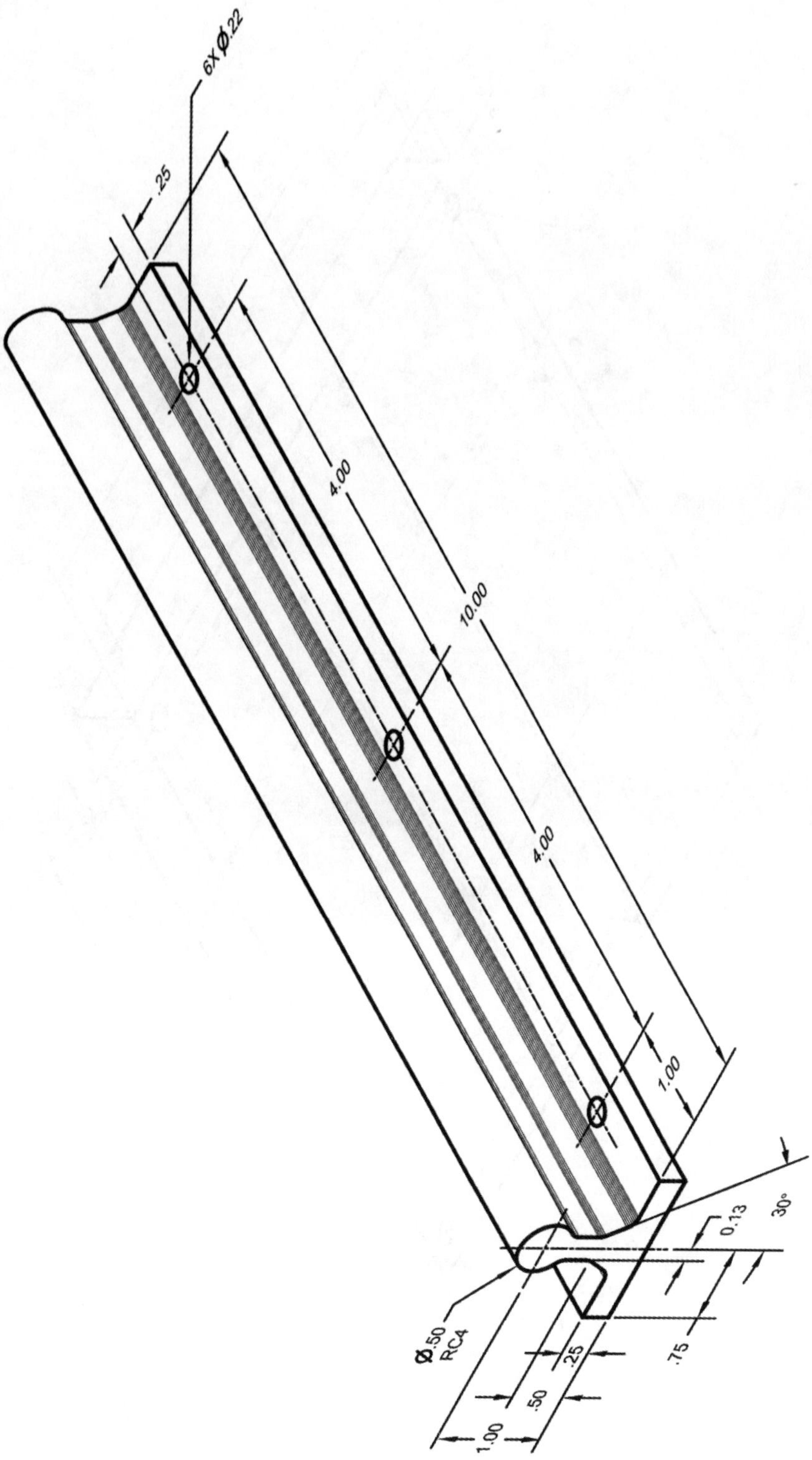

Part#3: Top Plate If you are just studying the basics and have not covered threads and fasteners, replace the 16X 10 – 24 UNC dimension with a 16x ∅.19 dimension.

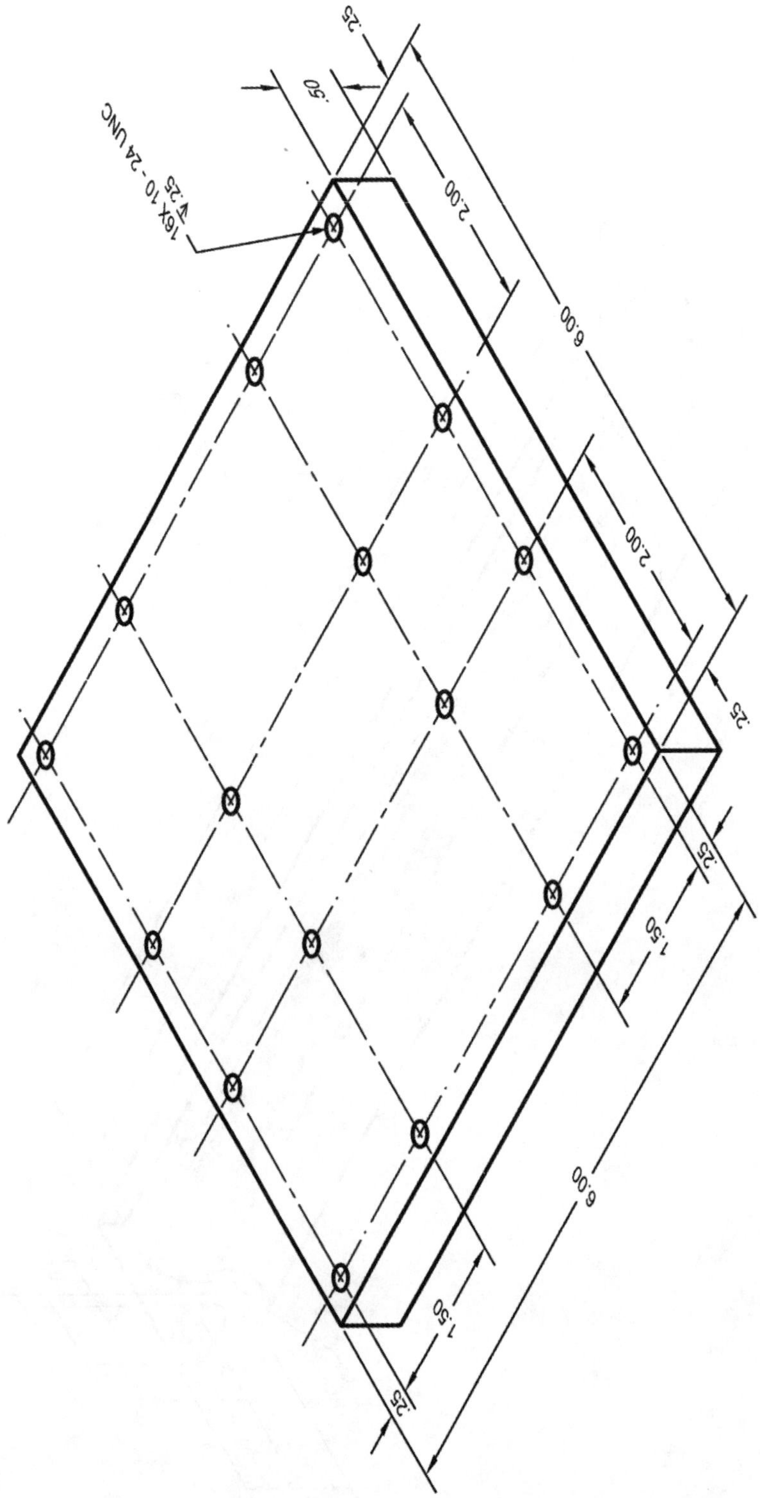

Part#4: Pillow Block If you are just studying the basics and have not covered tolerancing, ignore the FN1 tolerance.

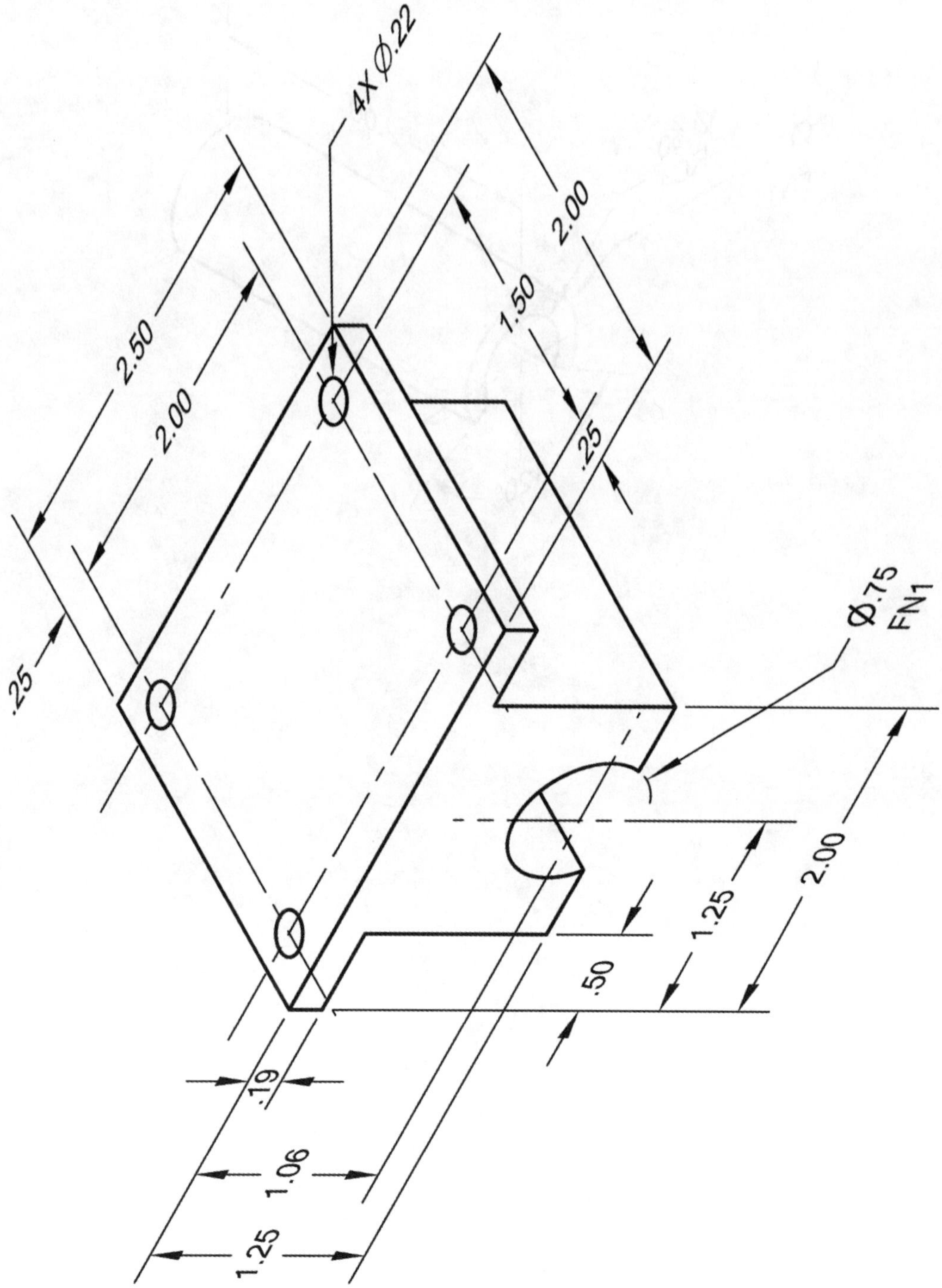

Part#5: Bearing If you are just studying the basics and have not covered tolerancing, ignore the RC4 and FN1 tolerances.

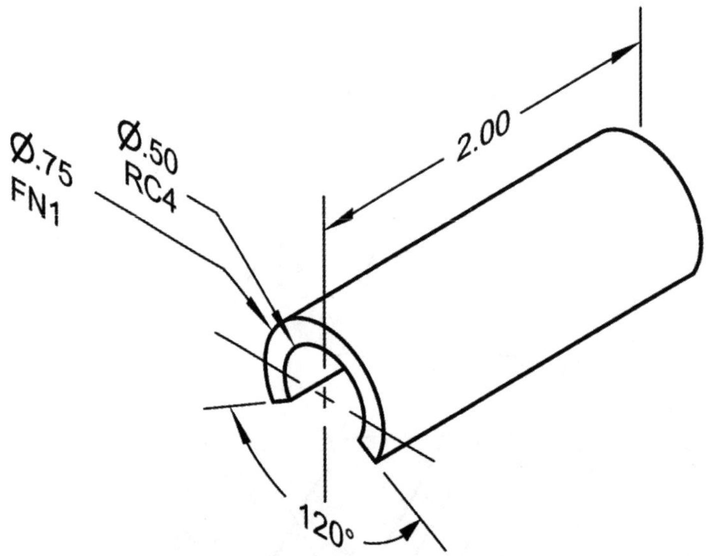

APPENDIX A: LIMITS AND FITS

APPENDIX OUTLINE

A.1) LIMITS AND FITS (INCH)

A.1.1) Running or sliding clearance fits

Basic hole system. Limits are in thousandths of an inch.
Limits for hole and shaft are applied algebraically to the basic size to obtain the limits of size for the parts.

Nominal Size Range Inches		Class RC1 Standard Limits		Class RC2 Standard Limits		Class RC3 Standard Limits		Class RC4 Standard Limits	
Over	To	Hole	Shaft	Hole	Shaft	Hole	Shaft	Hole	Shaft
0	– 0.12	+0.2 0	-0.1 -0.25	+0.25 0	-0.1 -0.3	+0.4 0	-0.3 -0.55	+0.6 0	-0.3 -0.7
0.12	– 0.24	+0.2 0	-0.15 -0.3	+0.3 0	-0.15 -0.35	+0.5 0	-0.4 -0.7	+0.7 0	-0.4 -0.9
0.24	– 0.40	+0.25 0	-0.2 -0.35	+0.4 0	-0.2 -0.45	+0.6 0	-0.5 -0.9	+0.9 0	-0.5 -1.1
0.40	– 0.71	+0.3 0	-0.25 -0.45	+0.4 0	-0.25 -0.55	+0.7 0	-0.6 -1.0	+1.0 0	-0.6 -1.3
0.71	– 1.19	+0.4 0	-0.3 -0.55	+0.5 0	-0.3 -0.7	+0.8 0	-0.8 -1.3	+1.2 0	-0.8 -1.6
1.19	– 1.97	+0.4 0	-0.4 -0.7	+0.6 0	-0.4 -0.8	+1.0 0	-1.0 -1.6	+1.6 0	-1.0 -2.0
1.97	– 3.15	+0.5 0	-0.4 -0.7	+0.7 0	-0.4 -0.9	+1.2 0	-1.2 -1.9	+1.8 0	-1.2 -2.4
3.15	– 4.73	+0.6 0	-0.5 -0.9	+0.9 0	-0.5 -1.1	+1.4 0	-1.4 -2.3	+2.2 0	-1.4 -2.8
4.73	– 7.09	+0.7 0	-0.6 -1.1	+1.0 0	-0.6 -1.3	+1.6 0	-1.6 -2.6	+2.5 0	-1.6 -3.2
7.09	– 9.85	+0.8 0	-0.6 -1.2	+1.2 0	-0.6 -1.4	+1.8 0	-2.0 -3.2	+2.8 0	-2.0 -3.8
9.85	– 12.41	+0.9 0	-0.8 -1.4	+1.2 0	-0.7 -1.6	+2.0 0	-2.5 -3.7	+3.0 0	-2.2 -4.2
12.41	– 15.75	+1.0 0	-1.0 -1.7	+1.4 0	-0.7 -1.7	+2.2 0	-3.0 -4.4	+3.5 0	-2.5 -4.7
15.75	– 19.69	+1.0 0	-1.2 -2.0	+1.6 0	-0.8 -1.8	+2.5 0	-4.0 -5.6	+4.0 0	-2.8 -5.3

Nominal Size Range Inches		Class RC5		Class RC6		Class RC7		Class RC8		Class RC9	
		Standard Limits		Standard Limits		Standard Limits		Standard Limits		Standard Limits	
Over	To	Hole	Shaft	Hole	Shaft	Hole	Shaft	Hole	Shaft	Hole	Shaft
0	– 0.12	+0.6 0	-0.6 -1.0	+1.0 0	-0.6 -1.2	+1.0 0	-1.0 -1.6	+1.6 0	-2.5 -3.5	+2.5 0	-4.0 -5.6
0.12	– 0.24	+0.7 0	-0.8 -1.3	+1.2 0	-0.8 -1.5	+1.2 0	-1.2 -1.9	+1.8 0	-2.8 -4.0	+3.0 0	-4.5 -6.0
0.24	– 0.40	+0.9 0	-1.0 -1.6	+1.4 0	-1.0 -1.9	+1.4 0	-1.6 -2.5	+2.2 0	-3.0 -4.4	+3.5 0	-5.0 -7.2
0.40	– 0.71	+1.0 0	-1.2 -1.9	+1.6 0	-1.2 -2.2	+1.6 0	-2.0 -3.0	+2.8 0	-3.5 -5.1	+4.0 0	-6.0 -8.8
0.71	– 1.19	+1.2 0	-1.6 -2.4	+2.0 0	-1.6 -2.8	+2.0 0	-2.5 -3.7	+3.5 0	-4.5 -6.5	+5.0 0	-7.0 -10.5
1.19	– 1.97	+1.6 0	-2.0 -3.0	+2.5 0	-2.0 -3.6	+2.5 0	-3.0 -4.6	+4.0 0	-5.0 -7.5	+6.0 0	-8.0 12.0
1.97	– 3.15	+1.8 0	-2.5 -3.7	+3.0 0	-2.5 -4.3	+3.0 0	-4.0 -5.8	+4.5 0	-6.0 -9.0	+7.0 0	-9.0 -13.5
3.15	– 4.73	+2.2 0	-3.0 -4.4	+3.5 0	-3.0 -5.2	+3.5 0	-5.0 -7.2	+5.0 0	-7.0 -10.5	+9.0 0	-10.0 -15.0
4.73	– 7.09	+2.5 0	-3.5 -5.1	+4.0 0	-3.5 -6.0	+4.0 0	-6.0 -8.5	+6.0 0	-8.0 -12.0	+10.0 0	-12.0 -18.0
7.09	– 9.85	+2.8 0	-4.0 -5.8	+4.5 0	-4.0 -6.8	+4.5 0	-7.0 -9.8	+7.0 0	-10.0 -14.5	+12.0 0	-15.0 -22.0
9.85	– 12.41	+3.0 0	-5.0 -7.0	+5.0 0	-5.0 -8.0	+5.0 0	-8.0 -11.0	+8.0 0	-12.0 -17.0	+12.0 0	-18.0 -26.0
12.41	– 15.75	+3.5 0	-6.0 -8.2	+6.0 0	-6.0 -9.5	+6.0 0	-10.0 -13.5	+9.0 0	-14.0 -20.0	+14.0 0	-22.0 -31.0
15.75	– 19.69	+4.0 0	-8.0 -10.5	+6.0 0	-8.0 -12.0	+6.0 0	-12.0 -16.0	+10.0 0	-16.0 -22.0	+16.0 0	-25.0 -35.0

USAS/ASME B4.1 – 1967 (R2004) Standard. For larger diameters, see the standard. ASME/ANSI B18.3.5M – 1986 (R2002) Standard. Reprinted from the standard listed by permission of the American Society of Mechanical Engineers.

A.1.2) Locational clearance fits

Basic hole system. Limits are in thousandths of an inch.
Limits for hole and shaft are applied algebraically to the basic size to obtain the limits of size for the parts.

Nominal Size Range Inches		Class LC1 Standard Limits		Class LC2 Standard Limits		Class LC3 Standard Limits		Class LC4 Standard Limits	
Over	To	Hole	Shaft	Hole	Shaft	Hole	Shaft	Hole	Shaft
0	– 0.12	+0.25	0	+0.4	0	+0.6	0	+1.6	0
		0	-0.2	0	-0.25	0	-0.4	0	-1.0
0.12	– 0.24	+0.3	0	+0.5	0	+0.7	0	+1.8	0
		0	-0.2	0	-0.3	0	-0.5	0	-1.2
0.24	– 0.40	+0.4	0	+0.6	0	+0.9	0	+2.2	0
		0	-0.25	0	-0.4	0	-0.6	0	-1.4
0.40	– 0.71	+0.4	0	+0.7	0	+1.0	0	+2.8	0
		0	-0.3	0	-0.4	0	-0.7	0	-1.6
0.71	– 1.19	+0.5	0	+0.8	0	+1.2	0	+3.5	0
		0	-0.4	0	-0.5	0	-0.8	0	-2.0
1.19	– 1.97	+0.6	0	+1.0	0	+1.6	0	+4.0	0
		0	-0.4	0	-0.6	0	-1.0	0	-2.5
1.97	– 3.15	+0.7	0	+1.2	0	+1.8	0	+4.5	0
		0	-0.5	0	-0.7	0	-1.2	0	-3.0
3.15	– 4.73	+0.9	0	+1.4	0	+2.2	0	+5.0	0
		0	-0.6	0	-0.9	0	-1.4	0	-3.5
4.73	– 7.09	+1.0	0	+1.6	0	+2.5	0	+6.0	0
		0	-0.7	0	-1.0	0	-1.6	0	-4.0
7.09	– 9.85	+1.2	0	+1.8	0	+2.8	0	+7.0	0
		0	-0.8	0	-1.2	0	-1.8	0	-4.5
9.85	– 12.41	+1.2	0	+2.0	0	+3.0	0	+8.0	0
		0	-0.9	0	-1.2	0	-2.0	0	-5.0
12.41	– 15.75	+1.4	0	+2.2	0	+3.5	0	+9.0	0
		0	-1.0	0	-1.4	0	-2.2	0	-6.0
15.75	– 19.69	+1.6	0	+2.5	0	+4.0	0	+10.0	0
		0	-1.0	0	-1.6	0	-2.5	0	-6.0

Nominal Size Range Inches		Class LC5 Standard Limits		Class LC6 Standard Limits		Class LC7 Standard Limits		Class LC8 Standard Limits	
Over	To	Hole	Shaft	Hole	Shaft	Hole	Shaft	Hole	Shaft
0	– 0.12	+0.4	-0.1	+1.0	-0.3	+1.6	-0.6	+1.6	-1.0
		0	-0.35	0	-0.9	0	-1.6	0	-2.0
0.12	– 0.24	+0.5	-0.15	+1.2	-0.4	+1.8	-0.8	+1.8	-1.2
		0	-0.45	0	-1.1	0	-2.0	0	-2.4
0.24	– 0.40	+0.6	-0.2	+1.4	-0.5	+2.2	-1.0	+2.2	-1.6
		0	-0.6	0	-1.4	0	-2.4	0	-3.0
0.40	– 0.71	+0.7	-0.25	+1.6	-0.6	+2.8	-1.2	+2.8	-2.0
		0	-0.65	0	-1.6	0	-2.8	0	-3.6
0.71	– 1.19	+0.8	-0.3	+2.0	-0.8	+3.5	-1.6	+3.5	-2.5
		0	-0.8	0	-2.0	0	-3.6	0	-4.5
1.19	– 1.97	+1.0	-0.4	+2.5	-1.0	+4.0	-2.0	+4.0	-3.0
		0	-1.0	0	-2.6	0	-4.5	0	-5.5
1.97	– 3.15	+1.2	-0.4	+3.0	-1.2	+4.5	-2.5	+4.5	-4.0
		0	-1.1	0	-3.0	0	-5.5	0	-7.0
3.15	– 4.73	+1.4	-0.5	+3.5	-1.4	+5.0	-3.0	+5.0	-5.0
		0	-1.4	0	-3.6	0	-6.5	0	-8.5
4.73	– 7.09	+1.6	-0.6	+4.0	-1.6	+6.0	-3.5	+6.0	-6.0
		0	-1.6	0	-4.1	0	-7.5	0	-10.0
7.09	– 9.85	+1.8	-0.6	+4.5	-2.0	+7.0	-4.0	+7.0	-7.0
		0	-1.8	0	-4.8	0	-8.5	0	-11.5
9.85	– 12.41	+2.0	-0.7	+5.0	-2.2	+8.0	-4.5	+8.0	-7.0
		0	-1.9	0	-5.2	0	-9.5	0	-12.0
12.41	– 15.75	+2.2	-0.7	+6.0	-2.5	+9.0	-5.0	+9.0	-8.0
		0	-2.1	0	-6.0	0	-11.0	0	-14.0
15.75	– 19.69	+2.5	-0.8	+6.0	-2.8	+10.0	-5.0	+10.0	-9.0
		0	-2.4	0	-6.8	0	-11.0	0	-15.0

Nominal Size Range Inches		Class LC9 Standard Limits		Class LC10 Standard Limits		Class LC11 Standard Limits	
Over	To	Hole	Shaft	Hole	Shaft	Hole	Shaft
0	– 0.12	+2.5 0	-2.5 -4.1	+4.0 0	-4.0 -8.0	+6.0 0	-5.0 -11.0
0.12	– 0.24	+3.0 0	-2.8 -4.6	+5.0 0	-4.5 -9.5	+7.0 0	-6.0 -13.0
0.24	– 0.40	+3.5 0	-3.0 -5.2	+6.0 0	-5.0 -11.0	+9.0 0	-7.0 -16.0
0.40	– 0.71	+4.0 0	-3.5 -6.3	+7.0 0	-6.0 -13.0	+10.0 0	-8.0 -18.0
0.71	– 1.19	+5.0 0	-4.5 -8.0	+8.0 0	-7.0 -15.0	+12.0 0	-10.0 -22.0
1.19	– 1.97	+6.0 0	-5.0 -9.0	+10.0 0	-8.0 -18.0	+16.0 0	-12.0 -28.0
1.97	– 3.15	+7.0 0	-6.0 -10.5	+12.0 0	-10.0 -22.0	+18.0 0	-14.0 -32.0
3.15	– 4.73	+9.0 0	-7.0 -12.0	+14.0 0	-11.0 -25.0	+22.0 0	-16.0 -38.0
4.73	– 7.09	+10.0 0	-8.0 -14.0	+16.0 0	-12.0 -28.0	+25.0 0	-18.0 -43.0
7.09	– 9.85	+12.0 0	-10.0 -17.0	+18.0 0	-16.0 -34.0	+28.0 0	-22.0 -50.0
9.85	– 12.41	+12.0 0	-12.0 -20.0	+20.0 0	-20.0 -40.0	+30.0 0	-28.0 -58.0
12.41	– 15.75	+14.0 0	-14.0 -23.0	+22.0 0	-22.0 -44.0	+35.0 0	-30.0 -65.0
15.75	– 19.69	+16.0 0	-16.0 -26.0	+25.0 0	-25.0 -50.0	+40.0 0	-35.0 -75.0

USAS/ASME B4.1 – 1967 (R2004) Standard. For larger diameters, see the standard. ASME/ANSI B18.3.5M – 1986 (R2002) Standard.

A.1.3) Locational transition fits

Basic hole system. Limits are in thousandths of an inch.
Limits for hole and shaft are applied algebraically to the basic size to obtain the limits of size for the parts.

Nominal Size Range Inches		Class LT1 Standard Limits		Class LT2 Standard Limits		Class LT3 Standard Limits	
Over	To	Hole	Shaft	Hole	Shaft	Hole	Shaft
0	– 0.12	+0.4	+0.10	+0.6	+0.2		
		0	-0.10	0	-0.2		
0.12	– 0.24	+0.5	+0.15	+0.7	+0.25		
		0	-0.15	0	-0.25		
0.24	– 0.40	+0.6	+0.2	+0.9	+0.3	+0.6	+0.5
		0	-0.2	0	-0.3	0	+0.1
0.40	– 0.71	+0.7	+0.2	+1.0	+0.35	+0.7	+0.5
		0	-0.2	0	-0.35	0	+0.1
0.71	– 1.19	+0.8	+0.25	+1.2	+0.4	+0.8	+0.6
		0	-0.25	0	-0.4	0	+0.1
1.19	– 1.97	+1.0	+0.3	+1.6	+0.5	+1.0	+0.7
		0	-0.3	0	-0.5	0	+0.1
1.97	– 3.15	+1.2	+0.3	+1.8	+0.6	+1.2	+0.8
		0	-0.3	0	-0.6	0	+0.1
3.15	– 4.73	+1.4	+0.4	+2.2	+0.7	+1.4	+1.0
		0	-0.4	0	-0.7	0	+0.1
4.73	– 7.09	+1.6	+0.5	+2.5	+0.8	+1.6	+1.1
		0	-0.5	0	-0.8	0	+0.1
7.09	– 9.85	+1.8	+0.6	+2.8	+0.9	+1.8	+1.4
		0	-0.6	0	-0.9	0	+0.2
9.85	– 12.41	+2.0	+0.6	+3.0	+1.0	+2.0	+1.4
		0	-0.6	0	-1.0	0	+0.2
12.41	– 15.75	+2.2	+0.7	+3.5	+1.0	+2.2	+1.6
		0	-0.7	0	-1.0	0	+0.2

Nominal Size Range Inches		Class LT4 Standard Limits		Class LT5 Standard Limits		Class LT6 Standard Limits	
Over	To	Hole	Shaft	Hole	Shaft	Hole	Shaft
0	– 0.12			+0.4	+0.5	+0.4	-0.65
				0	+0.25	0	+0.25
0.12	– 0.24			+0.5	+0.6	+0.5	+0.8
				0	+0.3	0	+0.3
0.24	– 0.40	+0.9	+0.7	+0.6	+0.8	+0.6	+1.0
		0	+0.1	0	+0.4	0	+0.4
0.40	– 0.71	+1.0	+0.8	+0.7	+0.9	+0.7	+1.2
		0	+0.1	0	+0.5	0	+0.5
0.71	– 1.19	+1.2	+0.9	+0.8	+1.1	+0.8	+1.4
		0	+0.1	0	+0.6	0	+0.6
1.19	– 1.97	+1.6	+1.1	+1.0	+1.3	+1.0	+1.7
		0	+0.1	0	+0.7	0	+0.7
1.97	– 3.15	+1.8	+1.3	+1.2	+1.5	+1.2	+2.0
		0	+0.1	0	+0.8	0	+0.8
3.15	– 4.73	+2.2	+1.5	+1.4	+1.9	+1.4	+2.4
		0	+0.1	0	+1.0	0	+1.0
4.73	– 7.09	+2.5	+1.7	+1.6	+2.2	+1.6	+2.8
		0	+0.1	0	+1.2	0	+1.2
7.09	– 9.85	+2.8	+2.0	+1.8	+2.6	+1.8	+3.2
		0	+0.2	0	+1.4	0	+1.4
9.85	– 12.41	+3.0	+2.2	+2.0	+2.6	+2.0	+3.4
		0	+0.2	0	+1.4	0	+1.4
12.41	– 15.75	+3.5	+2.4	+2.2	+3.0	+2.2	+3.8
		0	+0.2	0	+1.6	0	+1.6

USAS/ASME B4.1 – 1967 (R2004) Standard. For larger diameters, see the standard. ASME/ANSI B18.3.5M – 1986 (R2002) Standard. Reprinted from the standard listed by permission of the American Society of Mechanical Engineers.

A.1.4) Locational interference fits

Basic hole system. Limits are in thousandths of an inch.
Limits for hole and shaft are applied algebraically to the basic size to obtain the limits of size for the parts.

Nominal Size Range Inches		Class LN1 Standard Limits		Class LN2 Standard Limits		Class LN3 Standard Limits	
Over	To	Hole	Shaft	Hole	Shaft	Hole	Shaft
0	– 0.12	+0.25 0	+0.45 +0.25	+0.4 0	+0.65 +0.4	+0.4 0	+0.75 +0.5
0.12	– 0.24	+0.3 0	+0.5 +0.3	+0.5 0	+0.8 +0.5	+0.5 0	+0.9 +0.6
0.24	– 0.40	+0.4 0	+0.65 +0.4	+0.6 0	+1.0 +0.6	+0.6 0	+1.2 +0.8
0.40	– 0.71	+0.4 0	+0.8 +0.4	+0.7 0	+1.1 +0.7	+0.7 0	+1.4 +1.0
0.71	– 1.19	+0.5 0	+1.0 +0.5	+0.8 0	+1.3 +0.8	+0.8 0	+1.7 +1.2
1.19	– 1.97	+0.6 0	+1.1 +0.6	+1.0 0	+1.6 +1.0	+1.0 0	+2.0 +1.4
1.97	– 3.15	+0.7 0	+1.3 +0.8	+1.2 0	+2.1 +1.4	+1.2 0	+2.3 +1.6
3.15	– 4.73	+0.9 0	+1.6 +1.0	+1.4 0	+2.5 +1.6	+1.4 0	+2.9 +2.0
4.73	– 7.09	+1.0 0	+1.9 +1.2	+1.6 0	+2.8 +1.8	+1.6 0	+3.5 +2.5
7.09	– 9.85	+1.2 0	+2.2 +1.4	+1.8 0	+3.2 +2.0	+1.8 0	+4.2 +3.0
9.85	– 12.41	+1.2 0	+2.3 +1.4	+2.0 0	+3.4 +2.2	+2.0 0	+4.7 +3.5
12.41	– 15.75	+1.4 0	+2.6 +1.6	+2.2 0	+3.9 +2.5	+2.2 0	+5.9 +4.5
15.75	– 19.69	+1.6 0	+2.8 +1.8	+2.5 0	+4.4 +2.8	+2.5 0	+6.6 +5.0

USAS/ASME B4.1 – 1967 (R2004) Standard. For larger diameters, see the standard. ASME/ANSI B18.3.5M – 1986 (R2002) Standard.

A.1.5) Force and shrink fits

Basic hole system. Limits are in thousandths of an inch.
Limits for hole and shaft are applied algebraically to the basic size to obtain the limits of size for the parts.

Nominal Size Range Inches		Class FN1		Class FN2		Class FN3		Class FN4		Class FN5	
		Standard Limits		Standard Limits		Standard Limits		Standard Limits		Standard Limits	
Over	To	Hole	Shaft	Hole	Shaft	Hole	Shaft	Hole	Shaft	Hole	Shaft
0	– 0.12	+0.25 0	+0.5 +0.3	+0.4 0	+0.85 +0.6			+0.4 0	+0.95 +0.7	+0.6 0	+1.3 +0.9
0.12	– 0.24	+0.3 0	+0.6 +0.4	+0.5 0	+1.0 +0.7			+0.5 0	+1.2 +0.9	+0.7 0	+1.7 +1.2
0.24	– 0.40	+0.4 0	+0.75 +0.5	+0.6 0	+1.4 +1.0			+0.6 0	+1.6 +1.2	+0.9 0	+2.0 +1.4
0.40	– 0.56	+0.4 0	+0.8 +0.5	+0.7 0	+1.6 +1.2			+0.7 0	+1.8 +1.4	+1.0 0	+2.3 +1.6
0.56	– 0.71	+0.4 0	+0.9 +0.6	+0.7 0	+1.6 +1.2			+0.7 0	+1.8 +1.4	+1.0 0	+2.5 +1.8
0.71	– 0.95	+0.5 0	+1.1 +0.7	+0.8 0	+1.9 +1.4			+0.8 0	+2.1 +1.6	+1.2 0	+3.0 +2.2
0.95	– 1.19	+0.5 0	+1.2 +0.8	+0.8 0	+1.9 +1.4	+0.8 0	+2.1 +1.6	+0.8 0	+2.3 +1.8	+1.2 0	+3.3 +2.5
1.19	– 1.58	+0.6 0	+1.3 +0.9	+1.0 0	+2.4 +1.8	+1.0 0	+2.6 +2.0	+1.0 0	+3.1 +2.5	+1.6 0	+4.0 +3.0
1.58	– 1.97	+0.6 0	+1.4 +1.0	+1.0 0	+2.4 +1.8	+1.0 0	+2.8 +2.2	+1.0 0	+3.4 +2.8	+1.6 0	+5.0 +4.0
1.97	– 2.56	+0.7 0	+1.8 +1.3	+1.2 0	+2.7 +2.0	+1.2 0	+3.2 +2.5	+1.2 0	+4.2 +3.5	+1.8 0	+6.2 +5.0
2.56	– 3.15	+0.7 0	+1.9 +1.4	+1.2 0	+2.9 +2.2	+1.2 0	+3.7 +3.0	+1.2 0	+4.7 +4.0	+1.8 0	+7.2 +6.0
3.15	– 3.94	+0.9 0	+2.4 +1.8	+1.4 0	+3.7 +2.8	+1.4 0	+4.4 +3.5	+1.4 0	+5.9 +5.0	+2.2 0	+8.4 +7.0
3.94	– 4.73	+0.9 0	+2.6 +2.0	+1.4 0	+3.9 +3.0	+1.4 0	+4.9 +4.0	+1.4 0	+6.9 +6.0	+2.2 0	+9.4 +8.0
4.73	–5.52	+1.0 0	+2.9 +2.2	+1.6 0	+4.5 +3.5	+1.6 0	+6.0 +5.0	+1.6 0	+8.0 +7.0	+2.5 0	+11.6 +10.0
5.52	–6.30	+1.0 0	+3.2 +2.5	+1.6 0	+5.0 +4.0	+1.6 0	+6.0 +5.0	+1.6 0	+8.0 +7.0	+2.5 0	+13.6 +12.0
6.30	–7.09	+1.0 0	+3.5 +2.8	+1.6 0	+5.5 +4.5	+1.6 0	+7.0 +6.0	+1.6 0	+9.0 +8.0	+2.5 0	+13.6 +12.0
7.09	–7.88	+1.2 0	+3.8 +3.0	+1.8 0	+6.2 +5.0	+1.8 0	+8.2 +7.0	+1.8 0	+10.2 +9.0	+2.8 0	+15.8 +14.0
7.88	–8.86	+1.2 0	+4.3 +3.5	+1.8 0	+6.2 +5.0	+1.8 0	+8.2 +7.0	+1.8 0	+11.2 +10.0	+2.8 0	+17.8 +16.0
8.86	–9.86	+1.2 0	+4.3 +3.5	+1.8 0	+7.2 +6.0	+1.8 0	+9.2 +8.0	+1.8 0	+13.2 +12.0	+2.8 0	+17.8 +16.0
9.85	–11.03	+1.2 0	+4.9 +4.0	+2.0 0	+7.2 +6.0	+2.0 0	+10.2 +9.0	+2.0 0	+13.2 +12.0	+3.0 0	+20.0 +18.0

USAS/ASME B4.1 – 1967 (R2004) Standard. For larger diameters, see the standard. ASME/ANSI B18.3.5M – 1986 (R2002) Standard.

A.2) METRIC LIMITS AND FITS

A.2.1) Hole basis clearance fits

Preferred Hole Basis Clearance Fits. Dimensions in mm.

Basic Size	Loose Running		Free Running		Close Running		Sliding		Locational Clearance	
	Hole H11	Shaft c11	Hole H9	Shaft d9	Hole H8	Shaft f7	Hole H7	Shaft g6	Hole H7	Shaft h6
1 max	1.060	0.940	1.025	0.980	1.014	0.994	1.010	0.998	1.010	1.000
min	1.000	0.880	1.000	0.955	1.000	0.984	1.000	0.992	1.000	0.994
1.2 max	1.260	1.140	1.225	1.180	1.214	1.194	1.210	1.198	1.210	1.200
min	1.200	1.080	1.200	1.155	1.200	1.184	1.200	1.192	1.200	1.194
1.6 max	1.660	1.540	1.625	1.580	1.614	1.594	1.610	1.598	1.610	1.600
min	1.600	1.480	1.600	1.555	1.600	1.584	1.600	1.592	1.600	1.594
2 max	2.060	1.940	2.025	1.980	2.014	1.994	2.010	1.998	2.010	2.000
min	2.000	1.880	2.000	1.955	2.000	1.984	2.000	1.992	2.000	1.994
2.5 max	2.560	2.440	2.525	2.480	2.514	2.494	2.510	2.498	2.510	2.500
min	2.500	2.380	2.500	2.455	2.500	2.484	2.500	2.492	2.500	2.494
3 max	3.060	2.940	3.025	2.980	3.014	2.994	3.010	2.998	3.010	3.000
min	3.000	2.880	3.000	2.955	3.000	2.984	3.000	2.992	3.000	2.994
4 max	4.075	3.930	4.030	3.970	4.018	3.990	4.012	3.996	4.012	4.000
min	4.000	3.855	4.000	3.940	4.000	3.978	4.000	3.988	4.000	3.992
5 max	5.075	4.930	5.030	4.970	5.018	4.990	5.012	4.996	5.012	5.000
min	5.000	4.855	5.000	4.940	5.000	4.978	5.000	4.988	5.000	4.992
6 max	6.075	5.930	6.030	5.970	6.018	5.990	6.012	5.996	6.012	6.000
min	6.000	5.855	6.000	5.940	6.000	5.978	6.000	5.988	6.000	5.992
8 max	8.090	7.920	8.036	7.960	8.022	7.987	8.015	7.995	8.015	8.000
min	8.000	7.830	8.000	7.924	8.000	7.972	8.000	7.986	8.000	7.991
10 max	10.090	9.920	10.036	9.960	10.022	9.987	10.015	9.995	10.015	10.000
min	10.000	9.830	10.000	9.924	10.000	9.972	10.000	9.986	10.000	9.991
12 max	12.110	11.905	12.043	11.950	12.027	11.984	12.018	11.994	12.018	12.000
min	12.000	11.795	12.000	11.907	12.000	11.966	12.000	11.983	12.000	11.989
16 max	16.110	15.905	16.043	15.950	16.027	15.984	16.018	15.994	16.018	16.000
min	16.000	15.795	16.000	15.907	16.000	15.966	16.000	15.983	16.000	15.989
20 max	20.130	19.890	20.052	19.935	20.033	19.980	20.021	19.993	20.021	20.000
min	20.000	19.760	20.000	19.883	20.000	19.959	20.000	19.980	20.000	19.987
25 max	25.130	24.890	25.052	24.935	25.033	24.980	25.021	24.993	25.021	25.000
min	25.000	24.760	25.000	24.883	25.000	24.959	25.000	24.980	25.000	24.987
30 max	30.130	29.890	30.052	29.935	30.033	29.980	30.021	29.993	30.021	30.000
min	30.000	29.760	30.000	29.883	30.000	29.959	30.000	29.980	30.000	29.987

ANSI B4.2 – 1978 (R2004) Standard. ASME/ANSI B18.3.5M – 1986 (R2002) Standard. Reprinted from the standard listed by permission of the American Society of Mechanical Engineers.

A.2.2) Hole basis transition and interference fits

Preferred Hole Basis Clearance Fits. Dimensions in mm.

Basic Size	Locational Transition		Locational Transition		Locational Interference		Medium Drive		Force	
	Hole H7	Shaft k6	Hole H7	Shaft n6	Hole H7	Shaft p6	Hole H7	Shaft s6	Hole H7	Shaft u6
1 max	1.010	1.006	1.010	1.010	1.010	1.012	1.010	1.020	1.010	1.024
min	1.000	1.000	1.000	1.004	1.000	1.006	1.000	1.014	1.000	1.018
1.2 max	1.210	1.206	1.210	1.210	1.210	1.212	1.210	1.220	1.210	1.224
min	1.200	1.200	1.200	1.204	1.200	1.206	1.200	1.214	1.200	1.218
1.6 max	1.610	1.606	1.610	1.610	1.610	1.612	1.610	1.620	1.610	1.624
min	1.600	1.600	1.600	1.604	1.600	1.606	1.600	1.614	1.600	1.618
2 max	2.010	2.006	2.010	2.020	2.010	2.012	2.010	2.020	2.010	2.024
min	2.000	2.000	2.000	2.004	2.000	2.006	2.000	1.014	2.000	2.018
2.5 max	2.510	2.506	2.510	2.510	2.510	2.512	2.510	2.520	2.510	2.524
min	2.500	2.500	2.500	2.504	2.500	2.506	2.500	2.514	2.500	2.518
3 max	3.010	3.006	3.010	3.010	3.010	3.012	3.010	3.020	3.010	3.024
min	3.000	3.000	3.000	3.004	3.000	3.006	3.000	3.014	3.000	3.018
4 max	4.012	4.009	4.012	4.016	4.012	4.020	4.012	4.027	4.012	4.031
min	4.000	4.001	4.000	4.008	4.000	4.012	4.000	4.019	4.000	4.023
5 max	5.012	5.009	5.012	5.016	5.012	5.020	5.012	5.027	5.012	5.031
min	5.000	5.001	5.000	5.008	5.000	5.012	5.000	5.019	5.000	5.023
6 max	6.012	6.009	6.012	6.016	6.012	6.020	6.012	6.027	6.012	6.031
min	6.000	6.001	6.000	6.008	6.000	6.012	6.000	6.019	6.000	6.023
8 max	8.015	8.010	8.015	8.019	8.015	8.024	8.015	8.032	8.015	8.037
min	8.000	8.001	8.000	8.010	8.000	8.015	8.000	8.023	8.000	8.028
10 max	10.015	10.010	10.015	10.019	10.015	10.024	10.015	10.032	10.015	10.037
min	10.000	10.001	10.000	10.010	10.000	10.015	10.000	10.023	10.000	10.028
12 max	12.018	12.012	12.018	12.023	12.018	12.029	12.018	12.039	12.018	12.044
min	12.000	12.001	12.000	12.012	12.000	12.018	12.000	12.028	12.000	12.033
16 max	16.018	16.012	16.018	16.023	16.018	16.029	16.018	16.039	16.018	16.044
min	16.000	16.001	16.000	16.012	16.000	16.018	16.000	16.028	16.000	16.033
20 max	20.021	20.015	20.021	20.028	20.021	20.035	20.021	20.048	20.021	20.054
min	20.000	20.002	20.000	20.015	20.000	20.022	20.000	20.035	20.000	20.041
25 max	25.021	25.015	25.021	25.028	25.021	25.035	25.021	25.048	25.021	25.061
min	25.000	25.002	25.000	25.015	25.000	25.022	25.000	25.035	25.000	25.048
30 max	30.021	30.015	30.021	30.028	30.021	30.035	30.021	30.048	30.021	30.061
min	30.000	30.002	30.000	30.015	30.000	30.022	30.000	30.035	30.000	30.048

ANSI B4.2 – 1978 (R2004) Standard. ASME/ANSI B18.3.5M – 1986 (R2002) Standard. Reprinted from the standard listed by permission of the American Society of Mechanical Engineers.

A.2.3) Shaft basis clearance fits

Preferred Shaft Basis Clearance Fits. Dimensions in mm.

Basic Size	Loose Running		Free Running		Close Running		Sliding		Locational Clearance	
	Hole C11	Shaft h11	Hole D9	Shaft h9	Hole F8	Shaft h7	Hole G7	Shaft h6	Hole H7	Shaft h6
1 max	1.120	1.000	1.045	1.000	1.020	1.000	1.012	1.000	1.010	1.000
min	1.060	0.940	1.020	0.975	1.006	0.990	1.002	0.994	1.000	0.994
1.2 max	1.320	1.200	1.245	1.200	1.220	1.200	1.212	1.200	1.210	1.200
min	1.260	1.140	1.220	1.175	1.206	1.190	1.202	1.194	1.200	1.194
1.6 max	1.720	1.600	1.645	1.600	1.620	1.600	1.612	1.600	1.610	1.600
min	1.660	1.540	1.620	1.575	1.606	1.590	1.602	1.594	1.600	1.594
2 max	2.120	2.000	2.045	2.000	2.020	2.000	2.012	2.000	2.010	2.000
min	2.060	1.940	2.020	1.975	2.006	1.990	2.002	1.994	2.000	1.994
2.5 max	2.620	2.500	2.545	2.500	2.520	2.500	2.512	2.500	2.510	2.500
min	2.560	2.440	2.520	2.475	2.506	2.490	2.502	2.494	2.500	2.494
3 max	3.120	3.000	3.045	3.000	3.020	3.000	3.012	3.000	3.010	3.000
min	3.060	2.940	3.020	2.975	3.006	2.990	3.002	2.994	3.000	2.994
4 max	4.145	4.000	4.060	4.000	4.028	4.000	4.016	4.000	4.012	4.000
min	4.070	3.925	4.030	3.970	4.010	3.988	4.004	3.992	4.000	3.992
5 max	5.145	5.000	5.060	5.000	5.028	5.000	5.016	5.000	5.012	5.000
min	5.070	4.925	5.030	4.970	5.010	4.988	5.004	4.992	5.000	4.992
6 max	6.145	6.000	6.060	6.000	6.028	6.000	6.016	6.000	6.012	6.000
min	6.070	5.925	6.030	5.970	6.010	5.988	6.004	5.992	6.000	5.992
8 max	8.170	8.000	8.076	8.000	8.035	8.000	8.020	8.000	8.015	8.000
min	8.080	7.910	8.040	7.964	8.013	7.985	8.005	7.991	8.000	7.991
10 max	10.170	10.000	10.076	10.000	10.035	10.000	10.020	10.000	10.015	10.000
min	10.080	9.910	10.040	9.964	10.013	9.985	10.005	9.991	10.000	9.991
12 max	12.205	12.000	12.093	12.000	12.043	12.000	12.024	12.000	12.018	12.000
min	12.095	11.890	12.050	11.957	12.016	11.982	12.006	11.989	12.000	11.989
16 max	16.205	16.000	16.093	16.000	16.043	16.000	16.024	16.000	16.018	16.000
min	16.095	15.890	16.050	15.957	16.016	15.982	16.006	15.989	16.000	15.989
20 max	20.240	20.000	20.117	20.000	20.053	20.000	20.028	20.000	20.021	20.000
min	20.110	19.870	20.065	19.948	20.020	19.979	20.007	19.987	20.000	19.987
25 max	25.240	25.000	25.117	25.000	25.053	25.000	25.028	25.000	25.021	25.000
min	25.110	24.870	25.065	24.948	25.020	24.979	25.007	24.987	25.000	24.987
30 max	30.240	30.000	30.117	30.000	30.053	30.000	30.028	30.000	30.021	30.000
min	30.110	29.870	30.065	29.948	30.020	29.979	30.007	29.987	30.000	29.987

ANSI B4.2 – 1978 (R2004) Standard. ASME/ANSI B18.3.5M – 1986 (R2002) Standard. Reprinted from the standard listed by permission of the American Society of Mechanical Engineers.

A.2.4) Shaft basis transition and interference fits

Preferred Shaft Basis Transition and Interference Fits. Dimensions in mm.

Basic Size	Locational Transition		Locational Transition		Locational Interference		Medium Drive		Force	
	Hole K7	Shaft h6	Hole N7	Shaft h6	Hole P7	Shaft h6	Hole S7	Shaft h6	Hole U7	Shaft h6
1 max	1.000	1.000	0.996	1.000	0.994	1.000	0.986	1.000	0.982	1.000
min	0.990	0.994	0.986	0.994	0.984	0.994	0.976	0.994	0.972	0.994
1.2 max	1.200	1.200	1.196	1.200	1.194	1.200	1.186	1.200	1.182	1.200
min	1.190	1.194	1.186	1.194	1.184	1.194	1.176	1.194	1.172	1.194
1.6 max	1.600	1.600	1.596	1.600	1.594	1.600	1.586	1.600	1.582	1.600
min	1.590	1.594	1.586	1.594	1.584	1.594	1.576	1.594	1.572	1.594
2 max	2.000	2.000	1.996	2.000	1.994	2.000	1.986	2.000	1.982	2.000
min	1.990	1.994	1.986	1.994	1.984	1.994	1.976	1.994	1.972	1.994
2.5 max	2.500	2.500	2.496	2.500	2.494	2.500	2.486	2.500	2.482	2.500
min	2.490	2.494	2.486	2.494	2.484	2.494	2.476	2.494	2.472	2.494
3 max	3.000	3.000	2.996	3.000	2.994	3.000	2.986	3.000	2.982	3.000
min	2.990	2.994	2.986	2.994	2.984	2.994	2.976	2.994	2.972	2.994
4 max	4.003	4.000	3.996	4.000	3.992	4.000	3.985	4.000	3.981	4.000
min	3.991	5.992	3.984	5.992	3.980	5.992	3.973	5.992	3.969	5.992
5 max	5.003	5.000	4.996	5.000	4.992	5.000	4.985	5.000	4.981	5.000
min	4.991	4.992	4.984	4.992	4.980	4.992	4.973	4.992	4.969	4.992
6 max	6.003	6.000	5.996	6.000	5.992	6.000	5.985	6.000	5.981	6.000
min	5.991	5.992	5.984	5.992	5.980	5.992	5.973	5.992	5.969	5.992
8 max	8.005	8.000	7.996	8.000	7.991	8.000	7.983	8.000	7.978	8.000
min	7.990	7.991	7.981	7.991	7.976	7.991	7.968	7.991	7.963	7.991
10 max	10.005	10.000	9.996	10.000	9.991	10.000	9.983	10.000	9.978	10.000
min	9.990	9.991	9.981	9.991	9.976	9.991	9.968	9.991	9.963	9.991
12 max	12.006	12.000	11.995	12.000	11.989	12.000	11.979	12.000	11.974	12.000
min	11.988	11.989	11.977	11.989	11.971	11.989	11.961	11.989	11.956	11.989
16 max	16.006	16.000	15.995	16.000	15.989	16.000	15.979	16.000	15.974	16.000
min	15.988	15.989	15.977	15.989	15.971	15.989	15.961	15.989	15.956	15.989
20 max	20.006	20.000	19.993	20.000	19.986	20.000	19.973	20.000	19.967	20.000
min	19.985	19.987	19.972	19.987	19.965	19.987	19.952	19.987	19.946	19.987
25 max	25.006	25.000	24.993	25.000	24.986	25.000	24.973	25.000	24.960	25.000
min	24.985	24.987	24.972	24.987	24.965	24.987	24.952	24.987	24.939	24.987
30 max	30.006	30.000	29.993	30.000	29.986	30.000	29.973	30.000	29.960	30.000
min	29.985	29.987	29.972	29.987	29.965	29.987	29.952	29.987	29.939	29.987

ANSI B4.2 – 1978 (R2004) Standard. ASME/ANSI B18.3.5M – 1986 (R2002) Standard. Reprinted from the standard listed by permission of the American Society of Mechanical Engineers.

APPENDIX B: THREADS AND FASTENERS

APPENDIX OUTLINE

B.1) UNIFIED NATIONAL THREAD FORM

(External Threads) Approximate Minor diameter = $D - 1.0825P$ P = Pitch

Nominal Size, in.	Basic Major Diameter (*D*)	Coarse UNC		Fine UNF		Extra Fine UNEF	
		Thds. Per in.	Tap Drill Dia.	Thds. Per in.	Tap Drill Dia.	Thds. Per in.	Tap Drill Dia.
#0	0.060	...	...	80	3/64	...	...
#1	0.0730	64	0.0595	72	0.0595	...	...
#2	0.0860	56	0.0700	64	0.0700	...	...
#3	0.0990	48	0.0785	56	0.0820	...	...
#4	0.1120	40	0.0890	48	0.0935	...	...
#5	0.1250	40	0.1015	44	0.1040	...	...
#6	0.1380	32	0.1065	40	0.1130	...	...
#8	0.1640	32	0.1360	36	0.1360	...	...
#10	0.1900	24	0.1495	32	0.1590	...	...
#12	0.2160	24	0.1770	28	0.1820	32	0.1850
1/4	0.2500	20	0.2010	28	0.2130	32	7/32
5/16	0.3125	18	0.257	24	0.272	32	9/32
3/8	0.3750	16	5/16	24	0.332	32	11/32
7/16	0.4375	14	0.368	20	25/64	28	13/32
1/2	0.5000	13	27/64	20	29/64	28	15/32
9/16	0.5625	12	31/64	18	33/64	24	33/64
5/8	0.6250	11	17/32	18	37/64	24	37/64
11/16	0.675	...	...	...	...	24	41/64
3/4	0.7500	10	21/32	16	11/16	20	45/64
13/16	0.8125	...	...	...	...	20	49/64
7/8	0.8750	9	49/64	14	13/16	20	53/64
15/16	0.9375	...	...	...	...	20	57/64
1	1.0000	8	7/8	12	59/64	20	61/64
1 1/8	1.1250	7	63/64	12	1 3/64	18	1 5/64
1 1/4	1.2500	7	1 7/64	12	1 11/64	18	1 3/16
1 3/8	1.3750	6	1 7/32	12	1 19/64	18	1 5/16
1 1/2	1.5000	6	1 11/32	12	1 27/64	18	1 7/16
1 5/8	1.6250	...	...	...	...	18	1 9/16
1 3/4	1.7500	5	1 9/16	...	...	...	...
1 7/8	1.8750	...	...	...	...	...	...
2	2.0000	4 1/2	1 25/32	...	...	...	...
2 1/4	2.2500	4 1/2	2 1/32	...	...	...	...
2 1/2	2.5000	4	2 1/4	...	...	...	...
2 3/4	2.7500	4	2 1/2	...	...	...	...

ASME B1.1 – 2003 Standard. Reprinted from the standard listed by permission of the American Society of Mechanical Engineers.

B.2) METRIC THREAD FORM

(External Threads) Approximate Minor diameter = $D - 1.2075P$ P = Pitch

Preferred sizes for commercial threads and fasteners are shown in boldface type.

Coarse (general purpose)		Fine	
Nominal Size (D) & Thread Pitch	**Tap Drill Diameter, mm**	**Nominal Size & Thread Pitch**	**Tap Drill Diameter, mm**
M1.6 x 0.35	1.25	---	---
M1.8 x 0.35	1.45	---	---
M2 x 0.4	1.6	---	---
M2.2 x 0.45	1.75	---	---
M2.5 x 0.45	2.05	---	---
M3 x 0.5	2.5	---	---
M3.5 x 0.6	2.9	---	---
M4 x 0.7	3.3	---	---
M4.5 x 0.75	3.75	---	---
M5 x 0.8	4.2	---	---
M6 x 1	5.0	---	---
M7 x 1	6.0	---	---
M8 x 1.25	6.8	**M8 x 1**	7.0
M9 x 1.25	7.75	---	---
M10 x 1.5	8.5	**M10 x 1.25**	8.75
M11 x 1.5	9.50	---	---
M12 x 1.75	10.30	**M12 x 1.25**	10.5
M14 x 2	12.00	**M14 x 1.5**	12.5
M16 x 2	14.00	**M16 x 1.5**	14.5
M18 x 2.5	15.50	**M18 x 1.5**	16.5
M20 x 2.5	17.5	**M20 x 1.5**	18.5
M22 x 2.5[b]	19.5	**M22 x 1.5**	20.5
M24 x 3	21.0	**M24 x 2**	22.0
M27 x 3[b]	24.0	**M27 x 2**	25.0
M30 x 3.5	26.5	**M30 x 2**	28.0
M33 x 3.5	29.5	M33 x 2	31.0
M36 x 4	32.0	**M36 x 2**	33.0
M39 x 4	35.0	M39 x 2	36.0
M42 x 4.5	37.5	**M42 x 2**	39.0
M45 x 4.5	40.5	M45 x 1.5	42.0
M48 x 5	43.0	**M48 x 2**	45.0
M52 x 5	47.0	M52 x 2	49.0
M56 x 5.5	50.5	**M56 x 2**	52.0
M60 x 5.5	54.5	M60 x 1.5	56.0
M64 x 6	58.0	**M64 x 2**	60.0
M68 x 6	62.0	M68 x 2	64.0
M72 x 6	66.0	**M72 x 2**	68.0
M80 x 6	74.0	**M80 x 2**	76.0
M90 x 6	84.0	**M90 x 2**	86.0
M100 x 6	94.0	**M100 x 2**	96.0

[b]Only for high strength structural steel fasteners

ASME B1.13M – 2001 Standard. Reprinted from the standard listed by permission of the American Society of Mechanical Engineers.

B.3) FASTENERS (INCH SERIES)

CAUTION! All fastener dimensions have a tolerance. Therefore, each dimension has a maximum and minimum value. Only one size for each dimension is given in this appendix. That is all that is necessary to complete the problems given in the "Threads and Fasteners" chapter. For both values, please refer to the standards noted.

B.3.1) Dimensions of hex bolts and heavy hex bolts

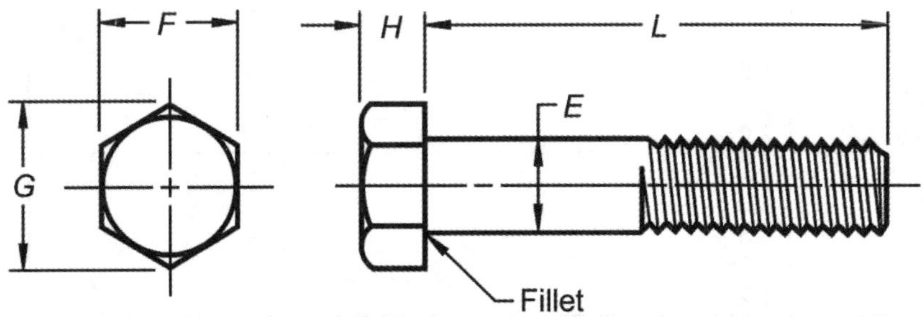

Regular Hex Head Bolts

<table>
<tr><th>Size
(D)</th><th>Head Height
Basic*</th><th>Width Across Flats
Basic
Adjust to sixteenths</th><th>Width Across
Corners
Max.</th></tr>
<tr><td>1/4</td><td>$H = 0.625\,D + 0.016$</td><td>$F = 1.500\,D + 0.062$</td><td rowspan="6">Max. $G = 1.1547\,F$</td></tr>
<tr><td>5/16 – 7/16</td><td>$H = 0.625\,D + 0.016$</td><td rowspan="5">$F = 1.500\,D$</td></tr>
<tr><td>1/2 – 7/8</td><td>$H = 0.625\,D + 0.031$</td></tr>
<tr><td>1 – 1 7/8</td><td>$H = 0.625\,D + 0.062$</td></tr>
<tr><td>2 – 3 3/4</td><td>$H = 0.625\,D + 0.125$</td></tr>
<tr><td>4</td><td>$H = 0.625\,D + 0.188$</td></tr>
</table>

Heavy Hex Head Bolts

Size (*D*)	Head Height Basic*	Width Across Flats Basic Adjust to sixteenths	Width Across Corners Max.
1/2 - 3	Same as for regular hex head bolts.	$F = 1.500\,D + 0.125$	Max. $G = 1.1547\,F$

* Size to 1 in. adjusted to sixty-fourths. 1 1/8 through 2 1/2 in. sizes adjusted upward to thirty-seconds. 2 3/4 thru 4 in. sizes adjusted upward to sixteenths.

B.3.2) Dimensions of hex nuts and hex jam nuts

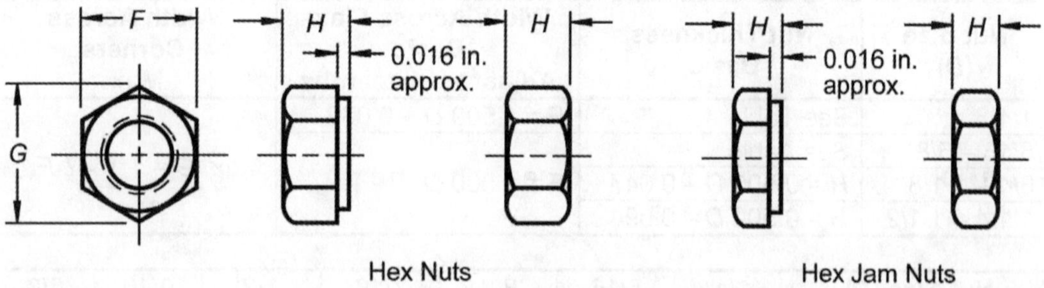

Hex Nuts

Nut Size (*D*)	Nut Thickness Basic*	Width Across Flats Basic Adjust to sixteenths	Width Across Corners Max.
1/4	*H* = 0.875 *D*	*F* = 1.500 *D* + 0.062	Max. *G* = 1.1547 *F*
5/16 – 5/8	*H* = 0.875 *D*	*F* = 1.500 *D*	
3/4 – 1 1/8	*H* = 0.875 *D* – 0.016		
1 1/4 – 1 1/2	*H* = 0.875 *D* – 0.031		

Hex Thick Nuts

Nut Size (*D*)	Width Across Flats Basic Adjust to sixteenths	Width Across Corners Max.	Nut Thickness Basic
1/4	*F* = 1.500 *D* + 0.062	Max. *G* = 1.1547 *F*	See Table
5/16 – 5/8	*F* = 1.500 *D*		
3/4 – 1 1/2	*F* = 1.500 *D*		

Nut Size (*D*)	1/4	5/16	3/8	7/16	1/2	9/16	5/8
Nut Thickness Basic	9/32	21/64	13/32	29/64	9/16	39/64	23/32

Nut Size (*D*)	3/4	7/8	1	1 1/8	1 1/4	1 3/8	1 1/2
Nut Thickness Basic	13/16	29/32	1	1 5/32	1 1/4	1 3/8	1 1/2

Hex Jam Nut

Nut Size (*D*)	Nut Thickness Basic*	Width Across Flats Basic Adjust to sixteenths	Width Across Corners Max.
1/4	See Table	$F = 1.500\ D + 0.062$	Max. $G = 1.1547\ F$
5/16 – 5/8	See Table	$F = 1.500\ D$	
3/4 – 1 1/8	$H = 0.500\ D - 0.047$		
1 1/4 – 1 1/2	$H = 0.500\ D - 0.094$		

Nut Size (*D*)	1/4	5/16	3/8	7/16	1/2	9/16	5/8
Nut Thickness Basic	5/32	3/16	7/32	1/4	5/16	5/16	3/8

B.3.3) Dimensions of hexagon and spline socket head cap screws

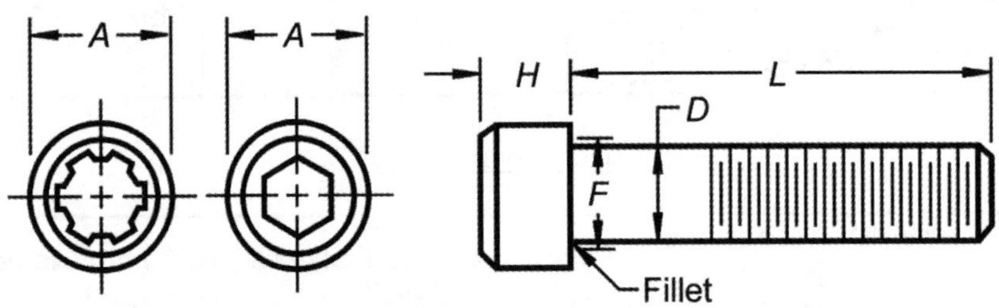

Screw Size (*D*)	Head Diameter	Head Height
#0 - #10	See Table	Max. $H = D$
1/4 - 4	Max. $A = 1.50\ D$	

Screw Size (*D*)	#0	#1	#2	#3	#4
Max. Head Diameter (*A*)	0.096	0.118	0.140	0.161	0.183

Screw Size (*D*)	#5	#6	#8	#10
Max. Head Diameter (*A*)	0.205	0.226	0.270	0.312

B.3.4) Drill and counterbore sizes for socket head cap screws

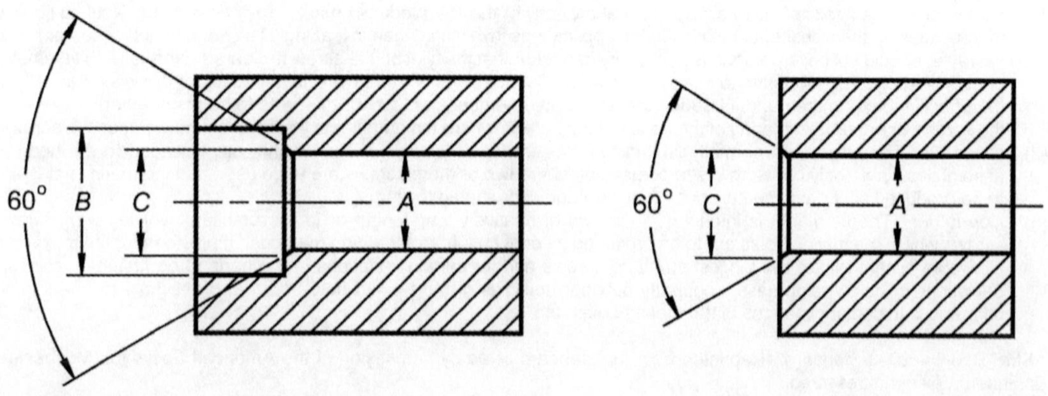

Nominal Size of Screw (*D*)	Nominal Drill Size (*A*)		Counterbore Diameter (*B*)	Countersink (*C*)
	Close Fit	Normal Fit		
#0 (0.0600)	(#51) 0.067	(#49) 0.073	1/8	0.074
#1 (0.0730)	(#46) 0.081	(#43) 0.089	5/32	0.087
#2 (0.0860)	3/32	(#36) 0.106	3/16	0.102
#3 (0.0990)	(#36) 0.106	(#31) 0.120	7/32	0.115
#4 (0.1120)	1/8	(#29) 0.136	7/32	0.130
#5 (0.1250)	9/64	(#23) 0.154	1/4	0.145
#6 (0.1380)	(#23) 0.154	(#18) 0.170	9/32	0.158
#8 (0.1640)	(#15) 0.180	(#10) 0.194	5/16	0.188
#10 (0.1900)	(#5) 0.206	(#2) 0.221	3/8	0.218
1/4	17/64	9/32	7/16	0.278
5/16	21/64	11/32	17/32	0.346
3/8	25/64	13/32	5/8	0.415
7/16	29/64	15/32	23/32	0.483
1/2	33/64	17/32	13/16	0.552
5/8	41/64	21/32	1	0.689
3/4	49/64	25/32	1 3/16	0.828
7/8	57/64	29/32	1 3/8	0.963
1	1 1/64	1 1/32	1 5/8	1.100
1 1/4	1 9/32	1 5/16	2	1.370
1 1/2	1 17/32	1 9/16	2 3/8	1.640
1 3/4	1 25/32	1 13/16	2 3/4	1.910
2	2 1/32	2 1/16	3 1/8	2.180

Notes on next page.

Notes:
(1) *Countersink.* It is considered good practice to countersink or break the edges of holes that are smaller than F (max.) in parts having a hardness which approaches, equals, or exceeds the screw hardness. If such holes are not countersunk, the heads of screws may not seat properly or the sharp edges on holes may deform the fillets on screws thereby making them susceptible to fatigue in applications involving dynamic loading. The countersink or corner relief, however, should not be larger than is necessary to ensure that the fillet on the screw is cleared. Normally, the diameter of countersink does not heave to exceed F (max.). Countersinks or corner reliefs in excess of this diameter reduce the effective bearing area and introduce the possibility of embedment where the parts to be fastened are softer than the screws or brinelling or flaring of the heads of the screws where the parts to be fastened are harder than the screws.
(2) *Close Fit.* The close fit is normally limited to holes for those lengths of screws that are threaded to the head in assemblies where only one screw is to be used or where two or more screws are to be used and the mating holes are to be produced either at assembly or by matched and coordinated tooling.
(3) *Normal Fit.* The normal fit is intended for screws of relatively long length or for assemblies involving two or more screws where the mating holes are to be produced by conventional tolerancing methods. It provides for the maximum allowable eccentricity of the longest standard screws and for certain variations in the parts to be fastened, such as deviations in hole straightness, angularity between the axis of the tapped hole and that of the hole for the shank, differences in center distances of the mating holes, etc.

B.3.5) Dimensions of hexagon and spline socket flat countersunk head cap screws

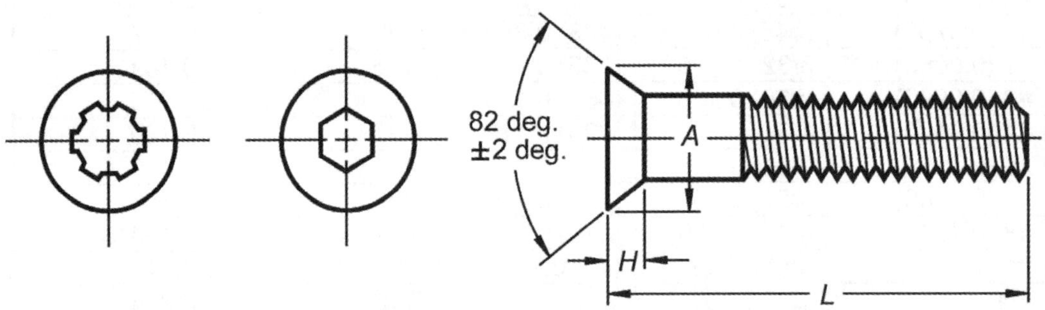

Screw Size (*D*)	Head Diameter (*A*) Theor. Sharp	Max. Head Height (*H*)
#0 - #3	See Table	Max. *H* = 0.5 (Max. *A* – *D*) * cot (41°)
#4 – 3/8	Max. *A* = 2 *D* + 0.031	
7/16	Max. *A* = 2 *D* – 0.031	
1/2 – 1 1/2	Max. *A* = 2 *D* – 0.062	

Screw Size (*D*)	Head Diameter (*A*) Theor. Sharp
#0	0.138
#2	0.168
#3	0.197
#4	0.226

B.3.6) Dimensions of slotted flat countersunk head cap screws

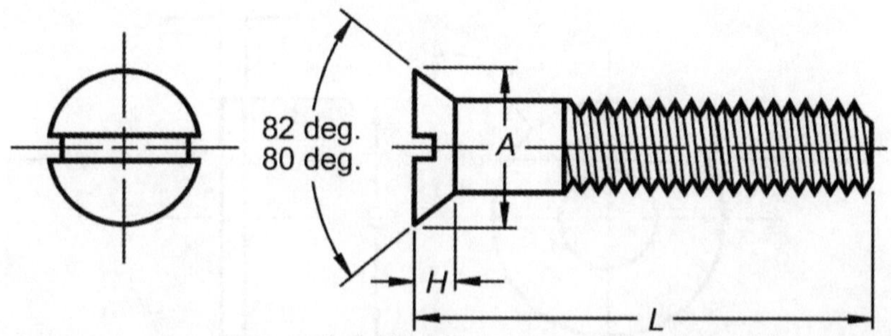

Screw Size (*D*)	Head Diameter (*A*) Thero. Sharp	Head Height (*H*)
1/4 through 3/8	Max. *A* = 2.000 *D*	Max. *H* = 0.596 *D*
7/16	Max. *A* = 2.000 *D* – 0.063	Max. *H* = 0.596 *D* – 0.0375
1/2 through 1	Max. *A* = 2.000 *D* – 0.125	Max. *H* = 0.596 *D* – 0.075
1 1/8 through 1 1/2	Max. *A* = 2.000 *D* – 0.188	Max. *H* = 0.596 *D* – 0.112

ASME B18.6.2 – 1998 Standard. Reprinted from the standard listed by permission of the American Society of Mechanical Engineers.

B.3.7) Dimensions of slotted round head cap screws

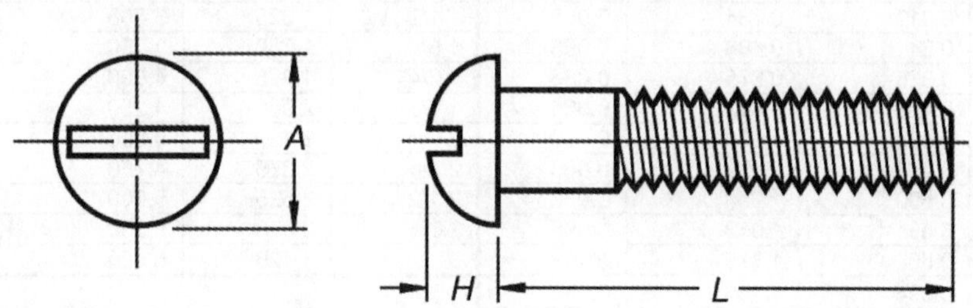

Screw Size (*D*)	Head Diameter (*A*) Thero. Sharp	Head Height (*H*)
1/4 and 5/16	Max. *A* = 2.000 *D* – 0.063	Max. *H* = 0.875 *D* – 0.028
3/8 and 7/16	Max. *A* = 2.000 *D* – 0.125	Max. *H* = 0.875 *D* – 0.055
1/2 and 9/16	Max. *A* = 2.000 *D* – 0.1875	Max. *H* = 0.875 *D* – 0.083
5/8 and 3/4	Max. *A* = 2.000 *D* – 0.250	Max. *H* = 0.875 *D* – 0.110

ASME B18.6.2 – 1998 Standard. Reprinted from the standard listed by permission of the American Society of Mechanical Engineers.

B.3.8) Dimensions of preferred sizes of type A plain washers

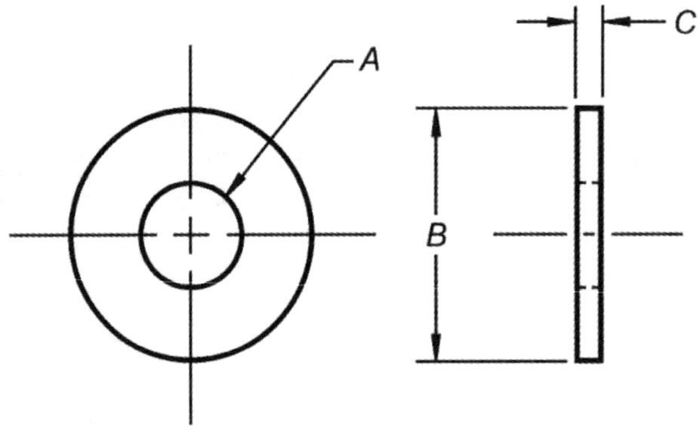

Nominal Washer Size*	Inside Diameter (*A*) Basic	Outside Diameter (*B*) Basic	Thickness (*C*)	Nominal Washer Size*	Inside Diameter (*A*) Basic	Outside Diameter (*B*) Basic	Thickness (*C*)
	0.078	0.188	0.020	1 N	1.062	2.000	0.134
	0.094	0.250	0.020	1 W	1.062	2.500	0.165
	0.125	0.312	0.032	1 1/8 N	1.250	2.250	0.134
#6 (0.138)	0.156	0.375	0.049	1 1/8 W	1.250	2.750	0.165
#8 (0.164)	0.188	0.438	0.049	1 1/4 N	1.375	2.500	0.165
#10 (0.190)	0.219	0.500	0.049	1 1/4 W	1.375	3.000	0.165
3/16	0.250	0.562	0.049	1 3/8 N	1.500	2.750	0.165
#12 (0.216)	0.250	0.562	0.065	1 3/8 W	1.500	3.250	0.180
1/4 N	0.281	0.625	0.065	1 1/2 N	1.625	3.000	0.165
1/4 W	0.312	0.734	0.065	1 1/2 W	1.625	3.500	0.180
5/16 N	0.344	0.688	0.065	1 5/8	1.750	3.750	0.180
5/16 W	0.375	0.875	0.083	1 3/4	1.875	4.000	0.180
3/8 N	0.406	0.812	0.065	1 7/8	2.000	4.250	0.180
3/8 W	0.438	1.000	0.083	2	2.125	4.500	0.180
7/16 N	0.469	0.922	0.065	2 1/4	2.375	4.750	0.220
7/16 W	0.500	1.250	0.083	2 1/2	2.625	5.000	0.238
1/2 N	0.531	1.062	0.095	2 3/4	2.875	5.250	0.259
1/2 W	0.562	1.375	0.109	3	3.125	5.500	0.284
9/16 N	0.594	1.156	0.095				
9/16 W	0.625	1.469	0.109				
5/8 N	0.656	1.312	0.095				
5/8 W	0.688	1.750	0.134				
3/4 N	0.812	1.469	0.134				
3/4 W	0.812	2.000	0.148				
7/8 N	0.938	1.750	0.134				
7/8 W	0.938	2.250	0.165				

* Nominal washer sizes are intended for use with comparable nominal screw or bolt sizes.

ANSI B18.22.1 – 1965 (R2003) Standard. Reprinted from the standard listed by permission of the American Society of Mechanical Engineers.

B.3.9) Dimensions of regular helical spring-lock washers

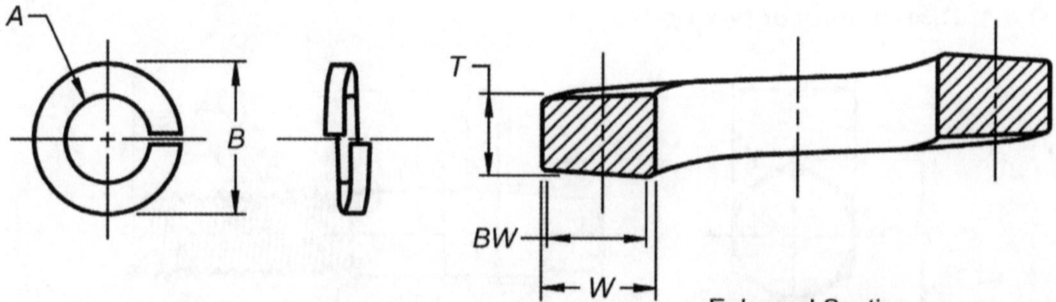

Nominal Washer Size	Min. Inside Diameter (A)	Max. Outside Diameter (B)	Mean Section Thickness (T)	Min. Section Width (W)	Min. Bearing Width (BW)
#2 (0.086)	0.088	0.172	0.020	0.035	0.024
#3 (0.099)	0.101	0.195	0.025	0.040	0.028
#4 (0.112)	0.114	0.209	0.025	0.040	0.028
#5 (0.125)	0.127	0.236	0.031	0.047	0.033
#6 (.0138)	0.141	0.250	0.031	0.047	0.033
#8 (0.164)	0.167	0.293	0.040	0.055	0.038
#10 (0.190)	0.193	0.334	0.047	0.062	0.043
#12 (0.216)	0.220	0.377	0.056	0.070	0.049
1/4	0.252	0.487	0.062	0.109	0.076
5/16	0.314	0.583	0.078	0.125	0.087
3/8	0.377	0.680	0.094	0.141	0.099
7/16	0.440	0.776	0.109	0.156	0.109
1/2	0.502	0.869	0.125	0.171	0.120
9/16	0.564	0.965	0.141	0.188	0.132
5/8	0.628	1.073	0.156	0.203	0.142
11/16	0.691	1.170	0.172	0.219	0.153
3/4	0.753	1.265	0.188	0.234	0.164
13/16	0.816	1.363	0.203	0.250	0.175
7/8	0.787	1.459	0.219	0.266	0.186
15/16	0.941	1.556	0.234	0.281	0.197
1	1.003	1.656	0.250	0.297	0.208
1 1/16	1.066	1.751	0.266	0.312	0.218
1 1/8	1.129	1.847	0.281	0.328	0.230
1 3/16	1.192	1.943	0.297	0.344	0.241
1 1/4	1.254	2.036	0.312	0.359	0.251
1 5/16	1.317	2.133	0.328	0.375	0.262
1 3/8	1.379	2.219	0.344	0.391	0.274
1 7/16	1.442	2.324	0.359	0.406	0.284
1 1/2	1.504	2.419	0.375	0.422	0.295
1 5/8	1.633	2.553	0.389	0.424	0.297
1 3/4	1.758	2.679	0.389	0.424	0.297
1 7/8	1.883	2.811	0.422	0.427	0.299
2	2.008	2.936	0.422	0.427	0.299
2 1/4	2.262	3.221	0.440	0.442	0.309
2 1/2	2.512	3.471	0.440	0.422	0.309
2 3/4	2.762	3.824	0.458	0.491	0.344
3	3.012	4.074	0.458	0.491	0.344

ASME B18.21.1 – 1999 Standard. Reprinted from the standard listed by permission of the American Society of Mechanical Engineers.

B.4) METRIC FASTENERS

B.4.1) Dimensions of hex bolts

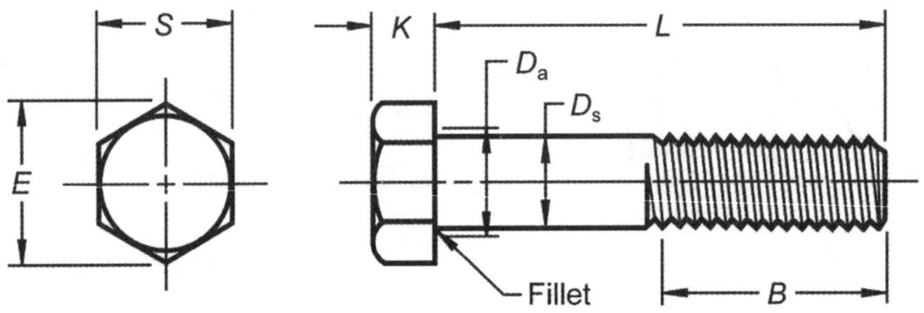

D	D_s	S	E	K	D_a	Thread Length (B)		
Nominal Bolt Diameter and Thread Pitch	**Max. Body Diameter**	**Max. Width Across Flats**	**Max. Width Across Corners**	**Max. Head Height**	**Fillet Transition Diameter**	**Bolt Lengths ≤ 125**	**Bolt Lengths > 125 and ≤ 200**	**Bolt Lengths > 200**
M5 x 0.8	5.48	8.00	9.24	3.88	5.7	16	22	35
M6 x 1	6.19	10.00	11.55	4.38	6.8	18	24	37
M8 x 1.25	8.58	13.00	15.01	5.68	9.2	22	28	41
M10 x 1.5	10.58	16.00	18.48	6.85	11.2	26	32	45
M12 x 1.75	12.70	18.00	20.78	7.95	13.7	30	36	49
M14 x 2	14.70	21.00	24.25	9.25	15.7	34	40	53
M16 x 2	16.70	24.00	27.71	10.75	17.7	38	44	57
M20 x 2.5	20.84	30.00	34.64	13.40	22.4	46	52	65
M24 x 3	24.84	36.00	41.57	15.90	26.4	54	60	73
M30 x 3.5	30.84	46.00	53.12	19.75	33.4	66	72	85
M36 x 4	37.00	55.00	63.51	23.55	39.4	78	84	97
M42 x 4.5	43.00	65.00	75.06	27.05	45.4	90	96	109
M48 x 5	49.00	75.00	86.60	31.07	52.0	102	108	121
M56 x 5.5	57.00	85.00	98.15	36.20	62.0		124	137
M64 x 6	65.52	95.00	109.70	41.32	70.0		140	153
M72 x 6	73.84	105.00	121.24	46.45	78.0		156	169
M80 x 6	82.16	115.00	132.79	51.58	86.0		172	185
M90 x 6	92.48	130.00	150.11	57.74	96.0		192	205
M100 x 6	102.80	145.00	167.43	63.90	107.0		212	225

ASME/ANSI B18.3.5M – 1986 (R2002) Standard. Reprinted from the standard listed by permission of the American Society of Mechanical Engineers.

B.4.2) Dimensions of hex nuts, style 1

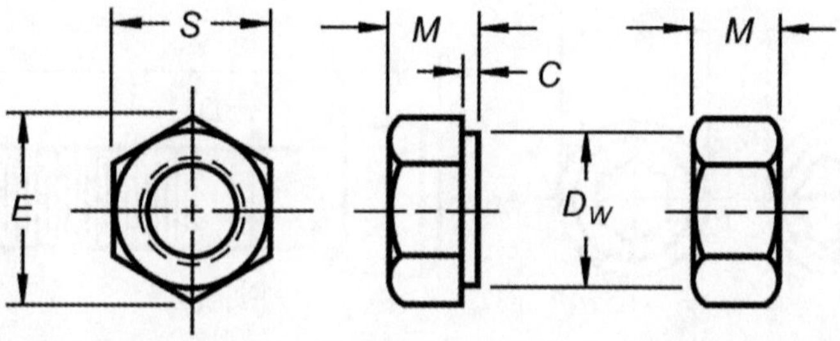

D Nominal Bolt Diameter and Thread Pitch	S Max. Width Across Flats	E Max. Width Across Corners	M Max. Thickness	D_W Min. Bearing Face Diameter	C Max. Washer Face Thickness
M1.6 x 0.35	3.20	3.70	1.30	2.3	
M2 x 0.4	4.00	4.62	1.60	3.1	
M2.5 x 0.45	5.00	5.77	2.00	4.1	
M3 x 0.5	5.50	6.35	2.40	4.6	
M3.5 x 0.6	6.00	6.93	2.80	5.1	
M4 x 0.7	7.00	8.08	3.20	6.0	
M5 x 0.8	8.00	9.24	4.70	7.0	
M6 x 1	10.00	11.55	5.20	8.9	
M8 x 1.25	13.00	15.01	6.80	11.6	
M10 x 1.5	15.00	17.32	9.10	13.6	
M10 x 1.5	16.00	18.45	8.40	14.6	
M12 x 1.75	18.00	20.78	10.80	16.6	
M14 x 2	21.00	24.25	12.80	19.4	
M16 x 2	24.00	27.71	14.80	22.4	
M20 x 2.5	30.00	34.64	18.00	27.9	0.8
M24 x 3	36.00	41.57	21.50	32.5	0.8
M30 x 3.5	46.00	53.12	25.60	42.5	0.8
M36 x 4	55.00	63.51	31.00	50.8	0.8

B.4.3) Dimensions of metric socket head cap screws

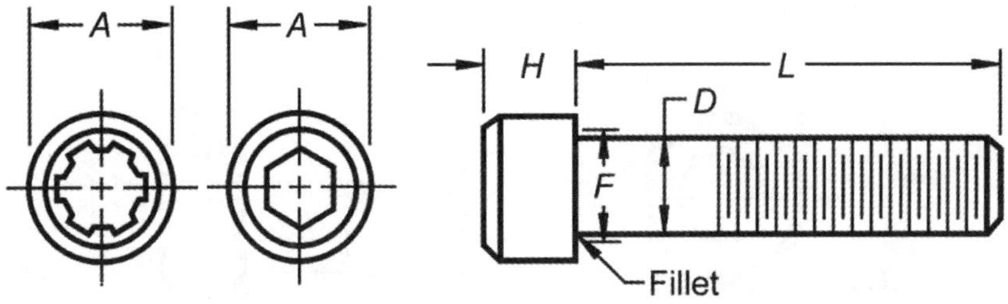

Dimensions in mm

Screw Size (*D*)	Head Diameter (*A*)	Head Height (*H*)
1.6 through 2.5	See Table	Max. *H* = *D*
3 through 8	Max. *A* = 1.5 *D* + 1	
> 10	Max. *A* = 1.5 *D*	

Screw Size (*D*)	1.6	2	2.5
Max. Head Diameter (*A*)	3.00	3.80	4.50

B.4.4) Drill and counterbore sizes for socket head cap screws

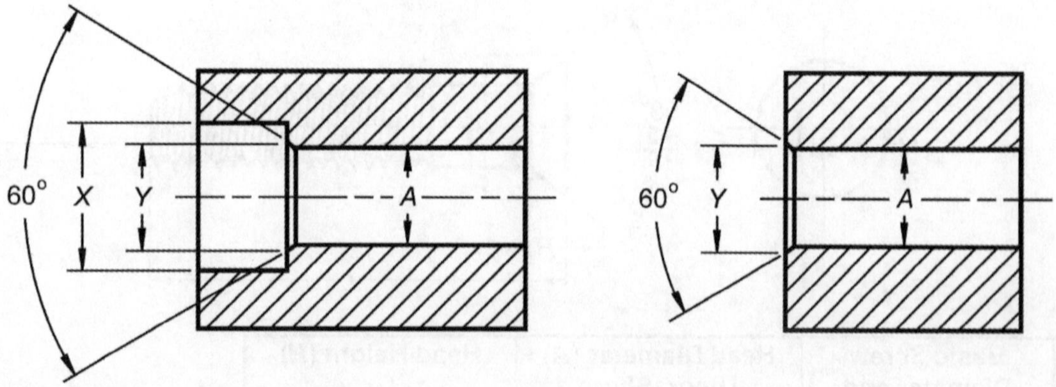

Nominal Size or Basic Screw Diameter	*A* Nominal Drill Size		*X* Counterbore Diameter	*Y* Countersink Diameter
	Close Fit	Normal Fit		
M1.6	1.80	1.95	3.50	2.0
M2	2.20	2.40	4.40	2.6
M2.5	2.70	3.00	5.40	3.1
M3	3.40	3.70	6.50	3.6
M4	4.40	4.80	8.25	4.7
M5	5.40	5.80	9.75	5.7
M6	6.40	6.80	11.25	6.8
M8	8.40	8.80	14.25	9.2
M10	10.50	10.80	17.25	11.2
M12	12.50	12.80	19.25	14.2
M14	14.50	14.75	22.25	16.2
M16	16.50	16.75	25.50	18.2
M20	20.50	20.75	31.50	22.4
M24	24.50	24.75	37.50	26.4
M30	30.75	31.75	47.50	33.4
M36	37.00	37.50	56.50	39.4
M42	43.00	44.00	66.00	45.6
M48	49.00	50.00	75.00	52.6

ASME/ANSI B18.3.1M – 1986 (R2002) Standard. Reprinted from the standard listed by permission of the American Society of Mechanical Engineers.

B.4.5) Dimensions of metric countersunk socket head cap screws

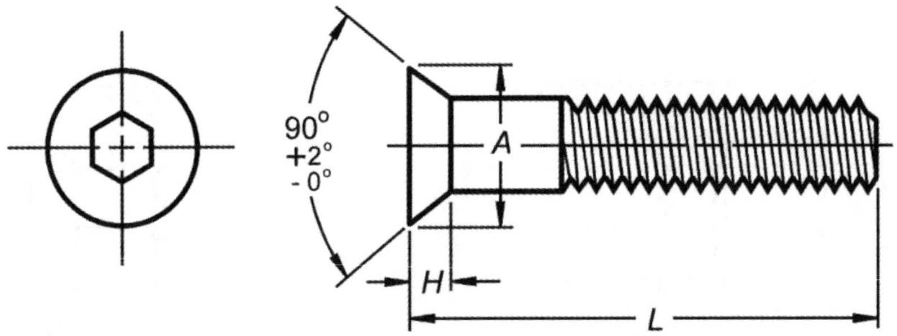

Basic Screw Diameter and Thread Pitch	Head Diameter (*A*) Theor. Sharp	Head Height (*H*)
M3 x 0.5	6.72	1.86
M4 x 0.7	8.96	2.48
M5 x 0.8	11.20	3.10
M6 x 1	13.44	3.72
M8 x 1.25	17.92	4.96
M10 x 1.5	22.40	6.20
M12 x 1.75	26.88	7.44
M14 x 2	30.24	8.12
M16 x 2	33.60	8.80
M20 x 2.5	40.32	10.16

ASME/ANSI B18.3.5M – 1986 (R2002) Standard. Reprinted from the standard listed by permission of the American Society of Mechanical Engineers.

B.4.6) Drill and countersink sizes for flat countersunk head cap screws

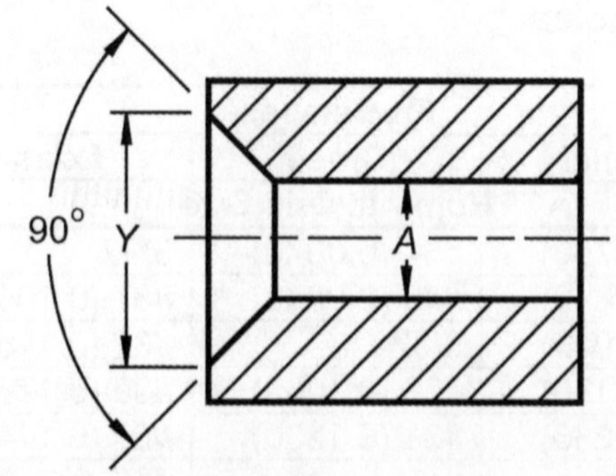

D Nominal Screw Size	*A* Nominal Hole Diameter	*Y* Min. Countersink Diameter
M3	3.5	6.72
M4	4.6	8.96
M5	6.0	11.20
M6	7.0	13.44
M8	9.0	17.92
M10	11.5	22.40
M12	13.5	26.88
M14	16.0	30.24
M16	18.0	33.60
M20	22.4	40.32

ASME/ANSI B18.3.5M – 1986 (R2002) Standard. Reprinted from the standard listed by permission of the American Society of Mechanical Engineers.

B.5) BOLT AND SCREW CLEARANCE HOLES

B.5.1) Inch clearance holes

Nominal Screw Size	Fit Classes		
	Normal	Close	Loose
	Nominal Drill Size		
#0 (0.06)	#48 (0.0760)	#51 (0.0670)	3/32
#1 (0.073)	#43 (0.0890)	#46 (0.0810)	#37 (0.1040)
#2 (0.086)	#38 (0.1015)	3/32	#32 (0.1160)
#3 (0.099)	#32 (0.1160)	#36 (0.1065)	#30 (0.1285)
#4 (0.112)	#30 (0.1285)	#31 (0.1200)	#27 (0.1440)
#5 (0.125)	5/32	9/64	11/64
#6 (0.138)	#18 (0.1695)	#23 (0.1540)	#13 (0.1850)
#8 (0.164)	#9 (0.1960)	#15 (0.1800)	#3 (0.2130)
#10 (0.190)	#2 (0.2210)	#5 (0.2055)	B (0.238)
1/4	9/32	17/64	19/64
5/16	11/32	21/64	23/64
3/8	13/32	25/64	27/64
7/16	15/32	29/64	31/64
1/2	9/16	17/32	39/64
5/8	11/16	21/32	47/64
3/4	13/16	25/32	29/32
7/8	15/16	29/32	1 1/32
1	1 3/32	1 1/32	1 5/32
1 1/8	1 7/32	1 5/32	1 5/16
1 1/4	1 11/32	1 9/32	1 7/16
1 3/8	1 1/2	1 7/16	1 39/64
1 1/2	1 5/8	1 9/16	1 47/64

B.5.2) Metric clearance holes

Nominal Screw Size	Fit Classes		
	Normal	Close	Loose
	Nominal Drill Size		
M1.6	1.8	1.7	2
M2	2.4	2.2	2.6
M2.5	2.9	2.7	3.1
M3	3.4	3.2	3.6
M4	4.5	4.3	4.8
M5	5.5	5.3	5.8
M6	6.6	6.4	7
M8	9	8.4	10
M10	11	10.5	12
M12	13.5	13	14.5
M14	15.5	15	16.5
M16	17.5	17	18.5
M20	22	21	24
M24	26	25	28
M30	33	31	35
M36	39	37	42
M42	45	43	48
M48	52	50	56
M56	62	58	66
M64	70	66	74
M72	78	74	82
M80	86	82	91
M90	96	93	101
M100	107	104	112

NOTES:

APPENDIX C: REFERENCES

[1] "3D Master Drive Accuracy into your Business", Brochure distributed by Dassault Systemes
[2] ASME Y14.1-2020: Drawing Sheet Size and Format
[3] ASME Y14.100-2017 Engineering Drawing Practices
[4] ASMEY14.24-2020 Types and Applications of Engineering Drawings
[5] ASME Y14.2-2014 (R2020): Line Conventions and Lettering
[6] ASME Y14.3-2012: Orthographic and Pictorial Views
[7] ASME Y14.5M – 2018: Dimensioning and Tolerancing Standard
[8] ASME Y14.8-2022: Castings, Forgings, and Molded Parts
[9] Machinery's Handbook 26th Ed., Industrial Press
[10] USAS/ASME B4.1 – 1967 (R2004): Preferred Limits and Fits for Cylindrical Parts
[11] ANSI B4.2 – 1978 (R2004): Preferred Metric Limits and Fits
[12] ASME Y14.6 – 2001: Screw Thread Representation
[13] ASME B1.1 – 2024: Unified Inch Screw Threads (UN, UNR, and UNJ Thread Form)
[14] ASME B1.13M – 2005 (R2020): Metric Screw Threads: M Profile
[15] ASME B18.2.8 – 1999: Clearance Holes for Bolts, Screws, and Studs
[16] ASME B18.2.1 – 2012 (R2021): Square and Hex Bolts and Screws (Inch Series)
[17] ASME/ANSI B18.2.2 – 2022: Square and Hex Nuts (Inch Series)
[18] ANSI B18.2.3.5M – 1979 (R2001): Metric Hex Bolts
[19] ASME B18.3 – 2012: Socket Cap, Shoulder, and Set Screws, Hex and Spline Keys (Inch Series)
[20] ASME/ANSI B18.3.1M – 1986 (R2002): Socket Head Cap Screws (Metric Series)
[21] ASME/ANSI B18.3.5M – 1986 (R2002): Hexagon Socket Flat Countersunk Head Cap Screws (Metric Series)
[22] ASME 18.6.2 – 2020: Square Head Set Screws, and Slotted Headless Set Screws (Inch Series)
[23] ASME B18.21.1 – 2009 (R2016): Washers: Helical Spring-Lock, Tooth Lock, and Plain Washers (Inch Series)

NOTES: